The Blackwell Encyclopedia of Sociology

Volume III

D–E

Edited by

George Ritzer

Blackwell
Publishing

© 2007 by Blackwell Publishing Ltd

BLACKWELL PUBLISHING
350 Main Street, Malden, MA 02148-5020, USA
9600 Garsington Road, Oxford OX4 2DQ, UK
550 Swanston Street, Carlton, Victoria 3053, Australia

First published 2007 by Blackwell Publishing Ltd

1   2007

Library of Congress Cataloging-in-Publication Data

Blackwell encyclopedia of sociology, the / edited by George Ritzer.
   p. cm.
Includes bibliographical references and index.
ISBN 1-4051-2433-4 (hardback : alk. paper) 1. Sociology—Encyclopedias. I. Ritzer, George.

HM425.B53 2007
301.03—dc22

                                        2006004167

ISBN-13: 978-1-4051-2433-1 (hardback : alk. paper)

A catalogue record for this title is available from the British Library.

Set in 9.5/11pt Ehrhardt
by Spi Publisher Services, Pondicherry, India
Printed in Singapore
by COS Printers Pte Ltd

The publisher's policy is to use permanent paper from mills that operate a sustainable forestry policy, and which has been manufactured from pulp processed using acid-free and elementary chlorine-free practices. Furthermore, the publisher ensures that the text paper and cover board used have met acceptable environmental accreditation standards.

For further information on
Blackwell Publishing, visit our website:
www.blackwellpublishing.com

Contents

daily life pollution

Koichi Hasegawa

Daily life pollution refers to the type of environmental contamination caused by the everyday life activities of ordinary citizens and consumers. In contrast with main pollution caused by industrial production processes, daily life pollution includes detergent pollution in rivers, lakes, or the ocean caused by washing clothes and landfill and incineration pollution caused by excess household garbage. Although the individual impact each citizen has on the environment is negligible, cumulatively their behavior can create severe environmental and social problems.

The cumulative effect of about 70 million households (in the US) or about 40 million households (in Japan) resembles the old proverb, "Many drops make a flood." "The ecological footprint" data of each country show the respective ecological impact per capita. In many countries the ecological impact exceeds the available biologically productive area of the country (Chambers et al. 2001), clearly showing this agglomeration effect for one environment. Theoretically, the "tragedy of the commons" by Hardin (1968) and subsequent studies of the "social dilemma" neatly model this mechanism. The social dilemma is defined as a dilemma or conflict between collectively and individually rational action, where the action required for achieving the collectively best outcome or goal is in conflict with the action required for achieving the individually best outcome (Yamagishi 1995).

For instance, a well-organized garbage collection system that separates various kinds of garbage can reduce the whole amount of daily garbage and the whole amount of the related municipal expenditure (collective best outcome). However, citizens may feel that separating their garbage takes too much attention and too many minutes. To save time, some of them may violate the rules by merging organic waste and non-organic waste (individual "best outcome"). Every citizen has a similar temptation. As a result, the separated garbage collection system may not work as planned. The malfunctioning of the separated collection system discourages other citizens from obeying the regulations, finally causing the collection system to disappear. Garbage may flood the streets and parks and citizens must pay more tax to collect it (collective worst outcome). Thus, the ordinary citizen can easily be both the perpetrator and the victim of this vicious cycle of pollution.

Spiked tire pollution is another good example. Spiked tires have metal studs embedded to prevent cars from slipping on icy roads. They are highly effective, and unlike chains do not require any effort to put on or take off. In the 1970s they rapidly came into wide use, especially in snowy northern Japan. But when used on dry roads, they tear up the road surface and create dust. Thus in the late 1970s and early 1980s, spiked tires brought serious air pollution in major cities such as Sendai and Sapporo. In Sendai, a broad movement to encourage voluntary restraint in the use of spiked tires developed, including cooperation between public authorities, the mass media, residents' groups, and the local lawyers' association. In 1985, Miyagi prefecture including Sendai as its prefectural capital first enacted restrictive ordinances at the prefectural level. Similar ordinances were subsequently enacted by Sapporo and other prefectures. This led to nationwide legislation in 1990 that prohibited the use of spiked tires altogether. In other cases, public administration officials have taken the lead, working with residents' groups to sometimes promote or sometimes discourage the use of certain products, such as the movement that started in 1975 around Lake Biwa to abstain from using phosphorous synthetic detergents and instead use soap powder.

In these cases, the possibility of resolving the issue through the use of alternative technologies or alternative products was high, and the concerned industries were not antagonistic to these movements. From a relatively early stage the industries endeavored to develop and market alternative products (e.g., studless tires, four-wheel-drive vehicles, and non-phosphorous synthetic detergents). In situations where the perpetrators are also the victims and the movement is not facing a powerful adversary, it is relatively easy to reach a social consensus (although not necessarily an adequate solution – for example, the introduction of non-phosphorous detergents did not entirely resolve the problem of detergent pollution, merely the issue of phosphorous pollution). This relatively uncontested consensus-making process makes it easier for politicians and public officials to take the initiative.

In many cases of daily life pollution, the effects appear directly and visibly for ordinary citizens in a relatively limited geographical range. But daily life pollution, such as in driving automobiles, also contributes to much more widespread problems as global warming. In its basic logic, the issue of global warming closely resembles the "tragedy of the commons" or social dilemma process of local daily life pollution. But in the global warming case, the effect goes to the global level and pushes the most severe effects of the degradation on to future generations. In addition, the consensus-building process has to occur among sovereign states, not local groups, making it more difficult.

Although ordinary citizens and general consumers are responsible for daily life pollution, this does not discharge producers, industries, and administrators of their responsibilities. Especially in mass consumption society, big industries strongly influence the market and consumers through advertising, stimulating customers' needs or desires as a "dependent effect" (Galbraith 1958). In the purchasing decisions of ordinary citizens, the image or package stimulated by advertising can become more important than the utility value of the goods.

The case of spiked tires shows that appropriate regulation can work effectively to solve the problems of daily life pollution. It may be the only way to overcome the "social dilemma." That means the government is responsible for solving this kind of problem. The government should prohibit the use of harmful commodities by legislative policy or administrative regulation. European countries first prohibited the use of spiked tires in the late 1970s because they tore up and damaged roads. Tire producers, car industries, legislators, and government administrators in other regions could have prevented spiked tire pollution in their own countries by paying attention to these foreign examples. On this point they were responsible.

Daily life pollution varies by domestic class structure, ethnic and racial differences, and global differences in wealth and poverty. These factors create serious gaps in consumption levels producing daily life pollution as well as in exposure to the resulting hazards. For instance, environmental racism can lead to the placement of waste disposal facilities near minority communities (Bullard 1994). At all levels, from community to the globe, richer people and countries consume more and produce more ecological damage than poorer or minority people. When we think of solutions to daily life pollution that involve reducing consumption, we have to remember that the poor of the world often do not yet have enough to meet basic needs. Given these disparities, wealthy people and nations have to take the initiative to adopt more eco-friendly consumption patterns that reduce daily life pollution while meeting needs. These new consumption models will then diffuse to the poorer populations.

SEE ALSO: Environment and Urbanization; High-Speed Transportation Pollution; Life Environmentalism; Local Residents' Movements; Pollution Zones, Linear and Planar

REFERENCES AND SUGGESTED READINGS

Bullard, R. D. (1994) *Dumping in Dixie: Race, Class, and Environmental Quality*, 2nd edn. Westview, Boulder, CO.

Chambers, N., Simmons, C., & Wackernage, M. (2001) *Sharing Nature's Interest: Ecological Footprints as an Indicator of Sustainability*. Earthscan, London.

Galbraith, J. K. (1958) *The Affluent Society*. Cambridge University Press, Cambridge.

Hardin, G. (1968) Tragedy of Commons. *Science* 162: 1243–8.

Yamagishi, T. (1995) Social Dilemmas. In: Cook, K., Fine, G., & House, J. (Eds.), *Sociological Perspectives on Social Psychology*. Allyn & Bacon, Boston, pp. 311–35.

dangerousness

Christian Debuyst

The term dangerousness is a neologism, invented in the context of the Italian positivist school of criminology and especially attributed to Garofalo, who, in the framework of his biopsychological approach to the criminal, considered taking into account the essential element of *temebilità*, or the constant and active perversity of the criminal and the extent to which one is afraid of him based on this characteristic (Garofalo 1905; see also Kinberg 1959: 44–5). Garafalo replaced this older term with the concept of *periculosità*, which means dangerousness, and reformulated its definition: the capacity of an individual to adapt, or to resist adapting, to social demands. In this definition the American criminologist F. A. Allen (1960) perceived the fundamental objective of Garafalo: the elimination from society of those who, because of a moral abnormality, are not capable of making social adjustments.

Another meaning of the concept of dangerousness is found in the definitions of the terms dangerous populations and dangerous mental state. The former term appeared first in European and Latin American discourses of the eighteenth century and concerned subjects whose style of living was considered dangerous: vagabonds, beggars, etc. The term dangerous classes appeared in discourses of the nineteenth century and referred to the poor and the working classes. Also falling into the category of those from whom society must be protected were persons with mental deficiencies, who

(especially around the year 1920) were considered to be incapable of resisting their genetically inscribed impulses. Sexual deviants have historically been viewed in a similar way and portrayed as sick people to be imprisoned and sometimes as psychopaths, from whom it is also important to protect society. A similar concept of dangerousness is used nowadays in the US in connection with recidivists and the so-called "three strikes and you're out" laws, under which criminals who have been convicted of three felonies are sentenced to life terms in prison.

The Italian positivist school found its starting point in Darwin's theory of evolution. According to the positivists, some individuals by nature cannot adapt to the complex demands of society. In this context, and in opposition to the views of the classical school of criminology, crime is not defined in legal terms, but as an expression of personality which results in a direct threat to society. Whereas the classical school defended the notion of free decision-making, the positivist school emphasized the biological, psychological, and social determinism of human actions. From the perspective of the classical school, it follows that punishment would be effective as a deterrent to criminal acts, whereas from the positivists' point of view punishment should be replaced by scientific treatment as a better way of protecting society.

One reason for the development of the positivist perspective, especially in Western Europe, was rising crime rates which could not be efficiently handled by penal policy based on the classical model. In the same manner, other scientific approaches to dealing with crime were developed when the International Union of Penal Law was founded in 1889 and integrated into its program the idea of "social defense." For the US, the situation seems to have been different; under pressure from the media and from what Becker (1997) called "moral entrepreneurs," certain categories of persons (recidivists, psychopaths, sexual delinquents) and specific scandalized events gave rise to a single and concentrated change in legislation.

The first problem concerning the application of the concept of dangerousness is that of diagnostics and prognosis. Such critiques have always accompanied the ideas of the Italian posi-tivists. However, there have been some efforts to systematize the concept. In 1935, for instance, Kinberg introduced the differentiated view of dangerousness as "habitual" and caused by "temporal circumstances" (see also Megargee 1969). Clinical diagnostics done by psychiatrists seem mostly to overestimate the dangerousness of individuals, and the use of prediction tables as a basis of decision (at least between 1925 and 1960) always produced a great volume of falsely positive and falsely negative results. As a conse-quence of this, decisions about dangerousness are mostly based on the type and nature of offenses committed in the past.

Another critique is aimed at the theoretical basis of dangerousness, especially the concept of "criminal personality." Social-psychological theory and empirical research emphasize that behavior is always a product of situational con-ditions and more stable factors of personality. Other critiques apply a more sociopolitical per-spective by emphasizing that giving too much significance to personality leaves aside more important aspects of social problems which the actors are confronted with. The same can be said of the types of offenses commonly taken into consideration when talking about danger-ousness; these notions always leave aside other offenses that can arguably cause more harm to society, like white-collar crime, political crime, or delinquency connected to drug trafficking. These critiques underscore the fact that the concept of dangerousness is marked by differ-ences in ideology (Debuyst & Tulkens 1981).

Many psychologists and sociologists have criticized the notion of determinism, but in two different directions. On the one hand, it is argued that the notion of determinism denies the idea of personal responsibility, which is the basis of both penal law and the classical school of criminology. On the other hand, there are some critiques that enlarge the concept of responsibility to include the idea of society and social reactions, emphasizing that violent offenses and individuals in society who are called dangerous reflect conditions of social exclusion in which acts of violence can seem to be a rational reaction (Crawford 2002).

SEE ALSO: Crime; Crime, Biosocial Theories of; Crime, Psychological Theories of; Criminal Justice System; Criminology; Deviance, Positi-vist Theories of; Deviance, Theories of; Mental Disorder; Social Pathology; Violence

REFERENCES AND SUGGESTED READINGS

Allen, F. A. (1960) Raffaele Garofalo. In: Mannheim, H. (Ed.), *Pioneers in Criminology*. Stevens & Sons, London.

Becker, H. S. (1997) *Outsiders : Studies in the Sociol-ogy of Deviance*. Free Press, New York.

Crawford, A. (2002) La Réforme de la justice en Angleterre et aux Pays de Galles. *Déviance et Société* 3.

Debuyst, C. & Tulkens, F. (Eds.) (1981) Dangerosité et Justice pénale, Ambiguïté d'une pratique. Coll. Déviance et Société, Masson, Paris, Médecine et Hygiène, Geneva.

Garofalo, R. (1905 [1885]) *La Criminologie*. Paris.

Kinberg, O. (1959 [1935]) *Les Problèmes fondamen-taux de la criminologie*. Cujas, Paris.

Megargee, E. (1969) A Critical Review of Theories of Violence. In: *Crimes of Violence: Staff Report Sub-mitted to the National Commission on the Causes and Prevention of Violence*, Vol. 13, pp. 1037–115. Washington, DC.

Davis, Kingsley (1908–97)

Donald J. Hernandez

Kingsley Davis, one of the most influential and eminent sociologists of the twentieth century, made major contributions to sociology, anthro-pology, and demography. A pioneer of socio-logical theory as it emerged during the 1930s and 1940s, he published prominent papers on the social and normative foundations of legit-imate and illicit sexual behavior, marriage and divorce in contemporary societies, intermar-riage in caste societies, and the place of children in the family and the broader social structure. Concerned with issues central to the struc-ture and functioning of society, and therefore ideologically, morally, and emotionally charged, Davis's analyses were illuminating, but often perforce subject to extensive debate and controversy, sometimes the focus of challenge from conservatives and other times confounding liberals.

A grandnephew of Confederate President Jefferson Davis, and born in Tuxedo, Texas on August 20, 1908, Kingsley Davis earned a BA in English in 1930 from the University of Texas, where he edited the campus literary magazine, and where he continued with graduate study in philosophy, economics, and sociology, earning an MA in philosophy in 1932. He then enrolled at Harvard University, studying with Talcott Parsons, Pitrim Sorokin, W. Lloyd Warner, and Carle Zimmerman, and he taught at Smith College from 1934 to 1936. Davis also was central in the prominent discussion group led by Talcott Parsons, who was then writing *The Structure of Social Action* (published in 1937). After receiving his PhD in 1936 with a dissertation titled "A Structural Analysis of Kinship," Davis taught at Clark University (1936–7) and then Pennsylvania State University (1937–44), while also pursuing studies in statistics, mathematics, and demography as a Social Science Research Council postdoctoral fellow at the University of Chicago with Samuel Stouffer and at the US Census Bureau.

Beyond his contributions to family sociology during the 1940s, Davis published (with Wilbert Moore in 1945) the most systematic and fully developed functional theory of social stratification, explaining the inequality found across social positions in all societies as the necessary consequence of their diverse positive contributions to the survival of the larger social system. Fierce debate followed as some critics took the theory to be an attack on the value position that equality is a virtue. They chafed against the idea that social inequality is necessary for a society to survive, and argued that the theory ignored the potentially dysfunctional effects of too much inequality, overstated the amount of social mobility occurring in actual societies, and did not address the issue of social conflict. Thus, opponents highlighted limits of the theory, effectively widening its scope, but the original underlying paradigm for analyzing relationships that link social positions, their incumbents, and social institutions has remained central to sociology. Important subsequent contributions advancing theoretical

sociology were his lucid synthesis in *Human Society* (1949) of fundamental sociological concepts and principles using ethnographic data, and his controversial presidential address to the American Sociological Association (1959) arguing that sociological analysis cannot be distinguished from functional analysis.

Davis's seminal theoretical and empirical contributions to social demography began in the 1930s, with a provocative article on "Reproductive Institutions and the Pressure for Population." Moving to Princeton University (1942–8), where he founded the department of sociology and anthropology, he wrote an extremely influential article, "The World Demographic Transition," in 1945, as well as his first empirical research on cities, *Urbanization in Latin America* (with Ana Casis in 1946). Davis's prominence as a demographer grew at Columbia University (1949–55) with the publication of *The Population of India and Pakistan* (1951), which stands as the classic work on the topic for 1880–1940, but also an exemplar of social demography for how to analyze and interpret the fertility, mortality, migration, family, education, and religion of a nation, and with his penetrating critique (1955) of Malthus's work as a scientific theory of fertility.

At the University of California at Berkeley (1955–77), Davis continued to lead the theoretical development of social demography, first by conceiving (with Judith Blake, his wife) the analytic framework for studying intermediate variables through which social structure can affect fertility (1956). His subsequent presidential address to the Population Association of America in 1963, "The Theory of Response and Change in Modern Demographic History," offered an integrated understanding of the central role that individual motivations for social and economic success played in the multiphasic response of populations in all developed countries, not only in reducing fertility in response to declining mortality, but also by changing marital behaviors, and fostering migration out of agriculture and beyond national borders.

With characteristic incisiveness, Davis ignited a long-running controversy with the publication of a logical, theoretical, and empirical critique in *Science* (1967) of family planning programs as a policy for reducing rapid population growth in third world countries. The article argued that a policy of simply making contraception available to women will not be successful because fertility will decline substantially only if there are fundamental changes in features of social organization that determine the motivation to bear children. The article was lauded by conservatives and berated by liberals, despite the explicitly stated corollary, and essentially feminist argument, that achieving the goal of sharply reduced fertility would better be achieved by policies making educational, occupational, and income opportunities for women equal to those of men. Davis continued to contribute to understanding changes in the family, economy, and women's roles at the University of Southern California (1977–92), most notably in "Wives and Work: The Sex Role Revolution and its Consequences" (1984).

Davis's early interest in cities and urbanization also was abiding. Prominent among his contributions were "The Origin and Growth of Urbanization in the World" (1955), "Colonial Expansion and Urban Diffusion in the Americas" (1960), "World Urbanization 1950–1970" (V. 1, 1969; V. 2, 1972), *Cities: Their Origin, Growth, and Human Impact* (1973), and "Asia's Cities: Problems and Options" (1975). In the final years of his career at the Hoover Institution (from 1981 until his death on February 27, 1997), Davis organized conferences and edited books addressing causes, consequences, and policies for below-replacement fertility in industrial societies (1987) and the connections linking resources, environment, and population change (1991).

Davis's creativity and the breadth of his influence in academia, in the Washington policy community, and the discourse of the general public are reflected in the terms *demographic transition*, *population explosion*, and *zero population growth* which he coined, and in the honor bestowed upon him as the first sociologist to be elected to the US National Academy of Sciences. As one of the giants among twentieth-century social scientists, Kingsley Davis's legacy to scholarly and public discourse will endure for generations to come.

SEE ALSO: Demographic Transition Theory; Economic Development; Family Planning, Abortion, and Reproductive Health; Fertility and Public Policy; Function; Industrial Revolution; Malthus, Thomas Robert; Stratification and Inequality, Theories of; Structural Functional Theory; Urbanization

REFERENCES AND SUGGESTED READINGS

Davis, K. (1949) *Human Society*. Macmillan, New York.

Davis, K. (1963) The Theory of Change and Response in Modern Demographic History. *Population Index* 29(4): 345–66.

Davis, K. (1974) The Migration of Human Populations. *Scientific American* 231.

Heer, D. M. (2003) Davis, Kingsley. In: Demeny, P. & McNicoll, G. (Eds.), *Encyclopedia of Population*. Macmillan Reference, New York.

Heer, D. M. (2004) *Kingsley Davis: A Biography and Selections from his Writings*. Transaction, London.

Peterson, W. (1979) Davis, Kingsley. In: Sills, D. L. (Ed.), *International Encyclopedia of the Social Sciences*. Free Press, New York.

death and dying

Deborah Carr

Sociology of death and dying is the study of the ways that values, beliefs, behavior, and institutional arrangements concerning death are structured by social environments and contexts. Although death is a universal human experience, societal responses to death vary according to cultural attitudes toward death, as well as contextual factors including the primary causes of death, and normative age at which death occurs.

Conceptualizations of and practices surrounding death in the United States have come full circle over the past two centuries. In the eighteenth century, death was public and visible. Death tended to occur at a relatively young age, at home, and due to infectious diseases that could not be "cured." The loss of a loved one was expressed by dramatic displays of grief among survivors, and elaborate efforts to memorialize the deceased (Ariès 1981). Throughout the late nineteenth and most of the twentieth centuries, death became "invisible" (Ariès 1981) and "bureaucratized" (Blauner 1966). Physicians and hospitals assumed control over dying, death and mourning became private, the handling of dead bodies and funeral rites were transferred from private homes to funeral parlors, and people were encouraged to deny death and believe in medical technologies (Blauner 1966). Treating dying persons in isolation was believed to help smooth the transition beyond death; reducing the social status of those who were about to die would minimize disruption of ongoing social and economic relationships.

The epidemiology of death also changed dramatically (Omran 1971). In the nineteenth and early twentieth centuries deaths occurred primarily due to infectious diseases, which were not stratified by social class or gender. Men and women, rich and poor, were equally likely to become ill and die, and death often occurred relatively quickly after the initial onset of symptoms. Death during the latter half of the twentieth and early twenty-first centuries, in contrast, occurs overwhelmingly due to chronic diseases, including cancer and heart disease. These diseases tend to strike older rather than younger adults, men more so than women, and persons with fewer rather than richer economic resources. Death typically occurs at the end of a long, often debilitating, and painful illness where the dying patients' final days are spent in a hospital or nursing home, and where life-sustaining technologies are used.

In the late twentieth and early twenty-first centuries, death is again becoming visible and managed by the dying and their families. Patients' and care providers' recognition that dying is often a socially isolated, physician-controlled experience has triggered a number of political and social movements with the explicit goal of placing control of the dying process in the hands of patients and their families. The Patient Self-Determination Act, passed by Congress in 1990, requires all government-funded health providers to give patients the opportunity to complete an advance directive (or living will) when they are admitted to a hospital. The hospice movement, which began in the United States in the early 1970s to promote palliative care at the end of life, also has grown in popularity. Hospice care, whether in hospital or at home, provides an alternative to the medical, scientific model of dying. Pain management, open communication among family, patient, and care providers, and a peaceful accepted death are core goals.

As the context of death and dying has changed, research foci also have shifted. In the 1950s and early 1960s, research and theory were guided by the assumption that the United States was a death-denying society (Gorer 1955). Influential works included an examination of the problems associated with transferring death and funeral rites from private homes to professional funeral homes, and explorations of the ways that health care providers, dying patients, and their family members mutually ignore and shield one another from their knowledge that the patient is dying (Glaser & Straus 1965).

In the late 1960s and 1970s, the "death awareness" movement guided research and theory. Key scholarly works of this era offered important advancements in conceptualizing the dying process. Barney Glaser and Anselm Straus (1968) proposed that dying tends to follow one of three trajectories: lingering, expected quick, and unexpected quick. The latter was considered most distressing for both health care providers and surviving family members. Elizabeth Kubler-Ross (1969) delineated the emotional and cognitive stages that dying persons pass through, before reaching the final stage of "acceptance." The interdisciplinary field of death studies and the two leading scholarly journals of death and dying also were launched in the 1970s: *Omega: The Journal of Death and Dying* debuted in 1970, while *Death Studies* has been published since 1977.

In the late twentieth and early twenty-first centuries, research on death and dying has flourished (for an excellent and comprehensive compendium, see Bryant 2003). Scholarly and public concern about death reflects two broad social patterns. First, increasingly large numbers of older adults are living longer than ever before, with most suffering from at least one chronic and terminal disease at the end of life. Second, technological innovations to extend life, including life-support systems, organ transplants, and advances in cancer treatment, extend the life span, but also raise important questions about the meaning of life and death.

Despite dramatic growth in death-related research, the claim by William Faunce and Robert Fulton (1958) that the sociology of death is "a neglected area" remains at least partially true. The development of broad and unifying theoretical perspectives on the sociology of death and dying has not occurred alongside the explosion of empirical work (Marshall 1980; George 2002). Rather, subdisciplines of sociology have each claimed distinct – and seldom overlapping – topics of study pertaining to death and dying.

For example, demographers study the timing and social patterning of mortality. Social gerontologists investigate a broad array of issues pertaining to death, dying, and end of life, but their analyses focus nearly exclusively on persons age 65 and older. Sociologists of culture examine the ways that death is depicted in humor, art, literature, and other forms of media, cross-cultural differences in death rites and rituals, and public discourses about controversial issues related to death and dying, including euthanasia and the death penalty. Medical sociologists investigate interactions between patients, family members, and their physicians at the end of life, as well as ethical, social, and financial issues pertaining to life-extending technologies and practices. Sociologists of law focus on legal definitions of death, and the implications and problems created by such definitions for heroic medical efforts, transplantation, inheritance, and insurance. Sociologists of religion focus on rites and rituals at the end of life, the impact of religion and spirituality on beliefs about life and death, and changes in religious attitudes and practices as individuals manage their own dying process and the deaths of family members. Sociologists of deviance investigate deaths that violate traditional norms, such as murder and suicide, as well as reactions to death that are considered deviant, such as anniversary suicides.

Despite the absence of an overarching theoretical framework, one broad theme that underlies much current research is the importance of personal control and agency, among both dying persons and their survivors. Two specific lines of inquiry which have developed over the past ten years are personal control over practical aspects of the dying process, and active

"meaning-making" among the dying and bereaved.

Mounting research explores how dying persons and their families make decisions about the type, site, and duration of care they want to receive at the end of life. Sociologists' key contributions have included identifying the cognitive, emotional, and structural factors that may enable or prevent individuals from receiving the type of care they hope to receive. Recent research reveals that patients and their family members seldom have sufficient information about their illness trajectory and future life span so that they can make informed decisions. Nicholas Christakis (1999) argues persuasively that physicians are extremely poor at prognosis, or projecting how much longer a dying patient has to live, and they often convey an unrealistically optimistic picture of their patient's future.

A second area of inquiry that has attracted renewed scholarly attention is meaning-making among both the dying and their loved ones following loss. This concept was first set forth in *Death and Identity*, where Fulton (1965) argued that "preserving rather than losing ... personal identity" was a critical aspect of the dying process. Victor Marshall (1980) proposed that heightened awareness of one's impending death triggers increased self-reflection, reminiscence, and the conscious construction of a coherent personal history. More recently, Edwin Schneidman (1995) proposed that dying persons actively construct a "post-self" or a lasting image of the self that will persist after their death.

The ways that bereaved survivors actively find meaning in death was articulated early on by Herman Feifel (1977: 9), who observed that the mourning period following loss provides a time for the bereaved to "redefine and integrate oneself into life." Current research explores the ways that active meaning-making among the newly bereaved helps to reestablish predictability and one's sense of security. Other goals for the bereaved include personal growth, an adaptive broadening of philosophical perspectives, and an increased appreciation of other interpersonal relations.

Scholars of death and dying face several important methodological challenges. First, bereavement research focuses nearly exclusively on the loss of a spouse, children, and parents; few studies investigate personal responses to the deaths of friends, siblings, or unmarried romantic partners, including gay and lesbian partners. A further limitation is that studies vary widely in their operationalization of "dying." Common measures include one's current illness diagnosis, combinations of diagnoses, symptom expression, and functional capacity (see George 2002 for a review). Although rich conceptual models of dying trajectories have been developed, formal operationalizations need further refinement. Finally, although most conceptual models of the dying process and bereavement are dynamic, such as the stage theory of dying (Kubler-Ross 1969), most empirical studies still rely on single point-in-time evaluations that retrospectively recall the dying and bereavement process.

In the future, the research agenda may focus increasingly on positive aspects of dying, including psychological resilience in the face of loss, and the characteristics of and pathways to a "good death." Important research goals include pinpointing modifiable factors of social contexts and relationships that may help ensure a smooth transition to death and bereavement. Early theories of loss proposed that persons who were not depressed following the loss of a loved one were "pathological." Researchers now are documenting that the non-depressed bereaved may experience "resilience" rather than pathological "absent grief" (Bonanno 2004).

Research on the "good death" also is accumulating. A good death is characterized as one where medical treatments minimize avoidable pain and match patients' and family members' preferences. A "good death" also encompasses important social, psychological, and philosophical elements, such as accepting one's impending death and not feeling like a burden to loved ones. However, as norms for the "good death" are solidified, a fruitful line of inquiry may be the consequences for bereaved family members and health care providers when a death occurs under conditions that fail to meet the widely accepted ideal. Failure to achieve the "good death" may reflect enduring social and structural obstacles. For example, family member (or caregiver) involvement is essential to a patient's participation in hospice; few studies have explored the extent to which unmarried or childless people rely on hospice. Such inquiries may further reveal the ways that the experience of death reflects persistent social inequalities.

SEE ALSO: Aging, Sociology of; Disease, Social Causation; Euthanasia; Gender, Health, and Mortality; Healthy Life Expectancy; Medicine, Sociology of; Mortality: Transitions and Measures; Social Epidemiology; Suicide; Widowhood

REFERENCES AND SUGGESTED READINGS

Ariès, P. (1981) *The Hour of Our Death*. Trans. H. Weaver. Alfred A. Knopf, New York.

Blauner, R. (1966) Death and Social Structure. *Psychiatry* 29: 378–94.

Bonanno, G. A. (2004) Loss, Trauma, and Human Resilience: Have We Underestimated the Human Capacity to Thrive After Extremely Aversive Events?" *American Psychologist* 59: 20–8.

Bryant, C. D. (Ed.) (2003) *Handbook of Death and Dying*. Sage, Thousand Oaks, CA.

Christakis, N. A. (1999) *Death Foretold: Prophecy and Prognosis in Medical Care*. University of Chicago Press, Chicago.

Faunce, W. A. & Fulton, R. L. (1958) The Sociology of Death: A Neglected Area in Sociological Research. *Social Forces* 36: 205–9.

Feifel, H. (Ed.) (1977) *New Meanings of Death*. McGraw-Hill, New York.

Feifel, H. (1990) Psychology and Death: Meaningful Rediscovery. *American Psychologist* 45: 537–43.

Fulton, R. (1965) *Death and Identity*. Wiley, New York.

George, L. K. (2002) Research Design in End-of-Life Research: State of the Science. *Gerontologist* 42 (special issue): 86–98.

Glaser, B. G. & Straus, A. L. (1965) *Awareness of Dying*. Aldine, New York.

Glaser, B. G. & Straus, A. L. (1968) *Time for Dying*. Aldine, Chicago.

Gorer, G. (1955) *Death, Grief, and Mourning*. Doubleday, Garden City, NY.

Kubler-Ross, E. (1969) *On Death and Dying*. Macmillan, New York.

Marshall, V. (1980) *Last Chapters: A Sociology of Aging and Dying*. Brooks/Cole, Monterey, CA.

Omran, A. R. (1971) The Epidemiologic Transition: A Theory of the Epidemiology of Population Change. *Milbank Memorial Fund Quarterly* 29: 509–38.

Schneidman, E. (1995) *Voices of Death*. Kodansha International, New York.

death penalty as a social problem

Evi Girling

The death penalty (also known as capital punishment) is the sentencing of offenders to death after conviction following due process of law. The practice of the death penalty has undergone two key transformations in modern times. The first one is an unremitting restriction on the kinds of crimes and categories of offender on whom the death penalty could be applied, leading to its eventual abolition in the majority of jurisdictions. The second shift is its transformation from brutal public displays of excess (famously depicted by Foucault in *Discipline and Punish*, 1977) to private, detached, and medicalized executions where pain and the body is elided, where execution is rendered a non-event. Within the sociology of punishment these shifts have been mostly explained either by the cultural dynamic of the privatization of disturbing events or by the transformation in technologies of power from punishment as a public and violent spectacle inflicting pain on the body to the emergence of disciplinary power and the surveillance of the soul.

The death penalty can be traced to antiquity from the Lex Talionis of the Code of Hamurabi (1750 BCE) to the laws of Draco in ancient Greece (seventh century BCE) and its prescription by Roman Law (fifth century BCE). It also has established provenance in some of the world's major religions, such as Christianity, Judaism, and Islam, all of which have at times provided justification or condoned the practice. Its widespread use during the middle ages was defended during the Renaissance and Reformation by many Enlightenment thinkers such as Hobbes, Locke, and Rousseau. It was however during this same period that the first seeds of at least partial abolitionism began to emerge. The Italian criminologist Cesare Beccaria in his work *Dei Delitte, et delle Penne* (1764) argued for the abolition of the death penalty and became influential in the development of the modern abolitionist movement. Abolitionism grew in the nineteenth century through the work of the jurists Jeremy Bentham and Samuel Rommilly.

By the end of the 1920s several European countries had eradicated the death penalty for peacetime offenses. This momentum was reversed with the rise of authoritarian regimes and the reinstatement and expansion of the practice in jurisdictions such as Italy and Germany.

The end of World War II proved a turning point in the development of international sensibilities and legal instruments to regulate punishment by death. A number of international and regional treaties that restricted or provided for the abolition of the death penalty were put in place. The transformation has been at its most dramatic in Europe, where from the 1960s onwards increasing numbers of states abolished the use of the death penalty. In 1986 Protocol No. 6 to the European Convention of Human Rights came into force, abolishing the death penalty in peacetime. Since 1998 a condition for entry to the European Union has been the abolition of the death penalty. Beyond Europe the Universal Declaration of Human Rights (1948) recognized each person's right to life and states that "No one shall be subjected to torture or to cruel, inhuman, or degrading treatment or punishment." Opponents of the death penalty argue that the death penalty violates these rights both at the point of execution and in the length, conditions, and experience of prisoners in death row. Article 6 of the International Covenant on Civil and Political Rights (1989) proclaims the right to life, but precognizes capital punishment as a permissible exception. It also sets out procedural safeguards for its application and significantly prohibits the execution of juveniles and pregnant women. The Second Optional Protocol to the International Covenant on Civil and Political Rights (1989) provides for the total abolition of the death penalty, but allows states to retain the death penalty for the most serious crimes if they make a reservation to that effect at the time of ratifying or acceding to the protocol. The International Criminal Court (1998) excluded the death penalty from the punishments which it is authorized to impose. A similar stance has been taken by the International Criminal Tribunal for the Former Yugoslavia (1993) and the International Criminal Tribunal for Rwanda (1994).

Yet the abolitionist movement cannot claim global success. According to Amnesty

International, by 2005 121 countries had abolished the death penalty either in law or in practice, 86 countries had abolished the death penalty for all crimes, 11 had retained the death penalty only for exceptional crimes, and 24 countries retain the death penalty in law but have not carried out executions for the last 10 years. According to the best estimates during 2004, at least 3,797 people were executed in 25 countries and at least 7,395 people were sentenced to death in 64 countries. A small number of countries are responsible for the vast majority of executions: 97 percent of all known executions took place in China, Iran, Vietnam, and the US (Amnesty International 2005). Within this group the People's Republic of China is estimated to have carried out 3,400 (9 out of 10 executions).

Support and opposition to the death penalty rest on the fine balancing between philosophical questions about its justice or morality and pragmatic questions about its usefulness, its possible discriminatory or capricious distribution among the guilty, and the inherent risk of executing the innocent.

Arguments in support of the death penalty usually evoke the principle of retribution or the principle of deterrence. Arguments against the death penalty challenge retribution and construct the death penalty as an extreme form of torture that violates the sanctity of life in particular and human rights in general. The deterrent justification is the one most often deployed by retentionist states and rests on the extent to which the death penalty stops other offenders from committing the same offense, thus saving innocent lives. Supporters of capital punishment argue that it has a deterrent effect on potentially violent offenders, especially where the threat of imprisonment is not a sufficient restraint, for example those already serving life imprisonment. Studies in the 1970s and 1980s (e.g., Ehrlich 1975) showed support for the deterrent effect of execution. Such studies have been subject to extensive methodological criticism and other studies using similar data refuted the deterrent effect of executions. Bowers and Pierce (1980) have found that rather than a deterrent effect, executions appear to contribute to an increase in the number of homicides. There is at the moment no conclusive and undisputed evidence that executing

offenders is more effective deterrence than life imprisonment.

In jurisdictions which take into account mitigating and aggravating factors in sentencing to death, capital punishment is only inflicted in a relatively small proportion of those legally eligible, raising questions of possible arbitrariness and discrimination. One of the most striking disparities is in the geographical distribution of capital sentences and executions both within and across individual states. In the 1970s the US Supreme Court suspended the use of the death penalty (*Furman* v. *Georgia* 1972), accepting the argument that the death penalty was applied in an arbitrary and capricious manner and that members of racial minorities were unfairly treated. After that decision many states introduced new laws structuring the use of discretion at the sentencing stage and the death penalty was reinstated in 1976 after the decision in *Gregg* v. *Georgia* (1976). Subsequent attempts to present to the Supreme Court social scientific evidence of discrimination in the application of the death penalty have failed. In *McCleskey* v. *Kemp* (1987) the Supreme Court agreed that evidence of discrimination in death penalty cases in general was disturbing, but it held that discretion was essential to the criminal justice process and the standard of proof for its abuse must be set high and the petitioner had to prove discriminatory intent in their particular case. This is a fine balancing between individualization and equality. Since the 1990s numerous studies have sought to establish whether the death penalty is applied in a discriminatory way according to race, sex, and wealth. For example, a study by Paternoster and Brame (2003) in Maryland found that discrimination permeates every stage of case handling in capital cases, echoing similar findings by researchers in other US states. One of the most consistent findings of such studies has been that offenders who kill white victims, especially if the offender is black, are significantly and substantially more likely to be charged with a capital crime than if both the victim and defendant are black.

In 1997 the American Bar Association responded to a growing concern about the reliability of the death penalty and the risk of executing innocent people by calling for a national moratorium on all executions, in part to "minimize the risk that innocent persons may be executed." In a study of every death penalty appeal from 1973 through 1995 it was found that of all the thousands of cases that had completed the appeals process, 68 percent were found to contain errors serious enough for a retrial or a new sentencing trial. The study highlighted the need to maintain what has been termed super due process in capital cases safeguarding the appeal process, which had come under attack in the 1990s for its cost and the delay. In the beginning of the twenty-first century a series of miscarriages of justice led to a moratorium on executions in Illinois and many states have enacted legislation to allow evidence from DNA testing to be considered after the normal appeals in capital cases have concluded.

It could be argued that the risks of error, arbitrariness, and discrimination are endemic in even the most sophisticated legislation and for all kinds of sanctions. Capital punishment is not in that respect a special case, yet the risk of mistake in capital cases is often used to challenge the legitimacy of this sanction. Zimring (2003) argues that this may be because the punishment is irreversible, because its application is incompatible with substantial error, and because unlike imprisonment the usefulness of executions can be more readily challenged.

SEE ALSO: Abolitionism; Capital Punishment; Deterrence Theory; Discrimination; Elias, Norbert; Foucault, Michel; Human Rights; Race and the Criminal Justice System

REFERENCES AND SUGGESTED READINGS

Bedau, H. A. (2004) *Killing as Punishment: Reflections on the Death Penalty in America*. Northeastern University Press, Boston.

Bowers, W. J. & Pierce, G. L. (1980) Deterrence or Brutalization: What is the Effect of Executions? *Crime and Delinquency* 26: 453–84.

Ehrlich, I. (1975) The Deterrent Effect of Capital Punishment – A Question of Life and Death. *American Economic Review* 65(2): 397–417.

Gattrell, V. A. C. (1994) *The Hanging Tree: Execution and the English People, 1779–1868*. Oxford University Press, Oxford.

Hodgkinson, P. & Schabas, W. (2003) *Capital Punishment: Strategies for Abolition*. Cambridge University Press, Cambridge.

Hood, R. (2002) *The Death Penalty: A Worldwide Perspective*. Oxford University Press, Oxford.

Kaufman-Osborne, T. (2002) *From Noose to Needle: Capital Punishment and the Late Liberal State*. University of Michigan Press, Ann Arbor.

Paternoster, R. & Brame, R. (2003) *An Empirical Analysis of Maryland's Death Sentencing System with Respect to the Influence of Race and Legal Jurisdiction (The Maryland Report)*. University of Maryland, College Park.

Sarat, A. (2001) *When the State Kills: Capital Punishment and the American Condition*. Princeton University Press, Princeton.

Schabas, W. A. (2003) *The Abolition of the Death Penalty in International Law*. Cambridge University Press, Cambridge.

Zimring, F. E. (2003) *The Contradictions of American Capital Punishment*. Oxford University Press, New York.

death of the sociology of deviance?

Erich Goode

Over the past decade or so, the claim that the sociology of deviance is "dead" has become increasingly vocal. Colin Sumner (1994), advocating an outspoken leftist agenda, dates the field's "death" to 1975. Unfortunately for his argument, he offers aphorisms, plays on words, and polemical assertions about the field's role in the political economy, but no empirical evidence to test his proposition.

Miller et al. (2001) demonstrate that works in the sociology of deviance published in the 1990s cite criminologists more often than recognized deviance specialists; and among the most frequently cited works of recognized deviance figures, only two were published after 1975. These findings, they argue, offer an "empirical test" of the "declining influence of scholarship in the sociology of deviance" (p. 43). In spite of the possible methodological limitations of the authors' measurements, the tests of Miller et al. do suggest the field's declining theoretical vitality, although they do not support Sumner's "death" claim.

Hendershott (2002) agrees with Sumner that the sociology of deviance is "dead." She argues that "few sociologists want to teach" courses on deviance, that the subject is "being eliminated" from sociology's curriculum. The field of deviance studies "died," she claims, because of its relativistic stance; increasingly, she asserts, Americans are rejecting the field's neutral, amoral, relativistic cloak because it justifies immoral behaviors that deserve to be stigmatized and vilified. It is time, she says, to return to "common sense" and "natural law." In short, it is time to redefine deviance as behavior that is inherently, intrinsically, and objectively bad, wrong, harmful, disruptive, and subversive, rather than a mere social construction, as the sociologists of deviance have claimed. Her agenda, she says, is to engage in "remoralizing" America.

In a balanced argument, Joel Best (2004) traces the "trajectory" of sociological studies of deviance from the late 1950s into the 1990s. He argues that the field "has come to occupy an insecure, even precarious, place in sociology." His conclusion is that the sociology of deviance "no longer plays as prominent a role in sociology's thinking as it once did." This is documented by a decline in the citation count of articles using the word "deviance" published in sociology's three most prominent journals between the 1970s and the 1990s. As Best points out, the field of deviance may not be dead, "but neither does it seem to be thriving."

Goode (2003) found that just under two thirds (16) of the sociology departments in the 25 leading US institutions of higher learning offer a deviance course. Enrollment figures for deviance courses in the 17 departments examined were found to be as robust today as they were in the 1970s. In short, Hendershott's charges – not endorsed by Best – that no one wants to teach the course, and that it is being eliminated from sociology's curriculum, are contradicted by the available evidence. While Best (2004) dismisses the notion that undergraduate enrollments and textbook sales indicate the field's continued intellectual vitality, Goode (1997) disagrees by demonstrating that the major deviance textbooks generate a substantial number of citations from the field as a whole. This, according to Goode, indicates their continued intellectual utility. A tabulation of the more than 1,700 scholarly articles located by the Social Science Citation Index (1957–2004) that bore "deviance" or "deviant" in their titles indicates that the 1980s was the field's peak year for scholarly productivity, and that the 1990s was more productive than the 1970s; expressed as a yearly average, the 2000s (2000–3) were only slightly less productive than the 1990s. Hence, the field's scholarly productivity seems to be as strong as it was during a decade (the 1970s) its critics claim was its peak productive era.

Not one of these claims or tests compares deviance with any other subfield of sociology; it is possible that other subfields are no different from deviance in this respect. Indeed, evidence indicates that the field of sociology, taken as a whole, is less conceptually and theoretically innovative than it was in the past. Still, nearly all indicators point to the fact that the productivity, conceptual and theoretical creativity, and influence of the sociology of deviance have declined somewhat since the 1980s. It is possible that the field's split from criminology is responsible for this decline. However, to adequately test the hypothesis, the productivity and vitality of other fields – and sociology generally – would have to be compared with deviance to determine whether the latter is exceptional in this respect. By no measure, however, can the sociology of deviance be said to be "dead." Evidence suggests that the charge is empirically false and, in all likelihood, politically motivated, energized, on both the political left and right, by a dread of the field's foundational assumption: social and cultural relativism.

SEE ALSO: Deviance; Deviance, Absolutist Definitions of; Deviance, Theories of; Sociocultural Relativism

REFERENCES AND SUGGESTED READINGS

Best, J. (2004) *Deviance: Career of a Concept.* Wadsworth, Belmont, CA.
Goode, E. (1997) Some Thoughts on Textbooks in the Sociology of Deviance. *Newsletter of the Crime, Law, and Deviance Division of the American Sociological Association* (Spring): 1–4.
Goode, E. (2003) The MacGuffin That Refuses to Die: An Investigation into the Condition of the Sociology of Deviance. *Deviant Behavior* 24: 507–33.

Hendershott, A. (2002) *The Politics of Deviance.* Encounter Books, San Francisco.

Miller, J. M., Wright, R. A., & Dannels, D. (2001) Is Deviance "Dead?" The Decline of a Sociological Research Specialization. *American Sociologist* 32: 43–59.

Sumner, C. (1994) *The Sociology of Deviance: An Obituary.* Open University Press, Milton Keynes.

Debord, Guy (1931–94)

David Redmon

The *Situationist Internationale* extended French avant-garde social movements by identifying how the spectacle replaced the commodity as the dominating mode of social life. Guy Debord was perhaps the foremost thinker in this group of French intellectuals who were influenced by Dadaism, Surrealism, and the sociologist Henri Lefebvre. Debord was not an academic, yet citations of his works are included in numerous sociological texts. Debord never graduated from college, barely graduated high school, and lived the majority of his life as a drifter who roamed to and from different urban locations. He eventually settled down in a rural village where he committed suicide by shooting himself in the heart at the age of 62 (Merrifield 2005).

Debord is most famous for his polemic "Society of the Spectacle" – a montage of theoretical writings which analyzed the transformation from a society organized around production to one organized around the consumption of "an immense accumulation of spectacles." According to Best and Kellner (1997: 81), Debord sought to update the Marxian emphasis on class struggle and factory work with a project focused on the transformation of the city and liberating subjectivity from the hegemonic integration of media and consumer culture which manufactures a spectacular society. Spectacular society, Debord explained, was an apparatus of fabricated social relations in which institutions socialized people through relationships with images; it is a reified world where consumers and producers are alienated from each other and can only experience their social world through the accumulation of spectacles. Debord (1994) writes: "The spectacle is the moment when the commodity has attained the total occupation of social life. The relation to the commodity is not only visible, but one no longer sees anything but it: the world one sees is its world." All that remains from the spectacle are representations of life.

In spectacular society represented life is reduced to a hegemonic network of consumer gadgets, leisure is reduced to shopping, and the logo or brand becomes the dominating category of status and prestige for people. The apparatus of surface appearances effectively controls people precisely because they unite into a coherent glossy image that renders the rational techniques that manufactured them invisible; all that remains is the desire to possess the signifier of the sign. Therefore, the spectacle does not socially control its subjects by force, but through the pacification of creativity and the consensus of collective desire. The spectacle extends its subtle forms of normalization and domination by constituting the desires of subjects to conform to the glossy images in magazines, advertisements, commercials, and movies. "The spectacle," Debord notes, "is the moment when the commodity has attained the total occupation of social life" (Thesis 42). The spectacle is a chain of images that flattens and reduces landscapes into a vacuum of TGI Fridays, Applebees, GAP, Abercrombie and Finch, glistening billboards, and Starbucks located next to fast-food restaurants and chain hotels.

Debord is adamant in pointing out, however, that spectacular society is socially constructed by an apparatus of modern men and women: advertisers, city council planners, international financial institutions, corporations, special economic zones, architects, fashion designers, and so on. Therefore, he claims, it is imperative to understand that the spectacle is vulnerable to disruption and eventual eradication. The concept he applies to this possible transformation is *détournement.* Détournement is a conceptual and physical tactic employed by opponents of the spectacle who desire to alter, destroy, and replace it with a more humane alternative, one that advances creativity and the ability to fully participate in the creation of their everyday lives. Examples of détournement include squatting in abandoned spaces; resignifying or inverting the intended meaning of advertisements through graffiti or street art; reclaiming streets, parks, or abandoned gardens so that the public can participate in them through actions such as growing organic food, playing with children, creating music, or participating in games, chess, soccer, or carnivals. Pleasure, passion, and organic relationships based on difference and self-creativity are the values upon which the Situationists attempted to transform everyday life.

These intentional revolts were meant to influence everyday people to create their own détournement actions. May 1968 provided the defining moment of Situationism in that the historical rupture could not be attributed directly to a crisis in the economy. Perhaps the most controversial organization that emerged in Paris out of May 1968, and influenced by the Situationists, was the Angry Brigade. The Angry Brigade was a marginal yet influential organization of anonymous activists who set off more than 20 bombings. None of the bombs, however, were designed to kill or maim anyone (and no one was ever killed or maimed). Instead, their bombing targets were identified for their symbolic value. Consider one statement from their communiqué: "Life is so boring, there's nothing to do except spend all our wages on the latest skirt or shirt. Brothers and sisters, what are your real desires?"

Contemporary examples of détournement include international social movements against global capitalism and neoliberalism: Critical Mass and Reclaim the Streets. The twentieth-century birth of these contemporary movements is marked by the 1989 uprisings in Venezuela against the International Monetary Fund. The mainstream media visualized them on January 1, 1994, when the Zapatistas rose up against neoliberalism and for humanity. They erupted in Seattle, WA against the World Trade Organization on November 30, 1999 – exactly 5 years after Debord's suicide. Appropriately, masked anarchists were invited to join local activists and citizens to damage the spectacle. Targets included the spectacular images that Debord sought to eradicate, the pillars of the global spectacle themselves: McDonald's, Starbucks, Niketown, and banks were all vandalized, windows were smashed, and graffiti was painted, "Fuck the WTO," "Stop sweatshops," and perhaps most famously, "We are winning!"

Individuals who employ Black Bloc tactics are made up of decentralized affinity groups who employ a diversity of tactics in reclaiming streets, desires, and autonomy. In regard to the destruction of corporate property in Seattle during the World Trade Organization meetings, for example, groups who employed "Black Bloc tactics" circulated a communiqué influenced by the writings of Debord. In true Debordian style, these groups explained that they "took on an offensive role regarding the conscious destruction of capitalist private property. Here, affinity groups within the Bloc would facilitate the smashing of windows, spray painting of revolutionary messages and trashing of police and/or military vehicles. Of course, all such activity was clearly directed against capitalist targets … In short, the demonstration here begins to assume its own identity free of the social spectacle of the commodified-consumer culture, and begins to move in a more fluid, self-defining manner" (Green Mountain Anarchist Collective). The Black Bloc papers go on to provide a comprehensive critique of the "society of the spectacle" and the international financial institutions through a critical analysis in which Debord is quoted in several passages.

SEE ALSO: Anarchism; Capitalism; Consumption, Mass Consumption and Consumer Culture; Consumption, Spectacles of; Lefebvre, Henri; Media and Consumer Culture; Situationists

REFERENCES AND SUGGESTED READINGS

Best, S. & Kellner, D. (1997) *The Postmodern Turn.* Guilford Press, New York.

Debord, G. (1994 [1967]) *The Society of the Spectacle.* Zone Books, New York.

Merriefield, A. (2005) *Guy Debord.* Reaktion Books, Chicago.

decision-making

Lois A. Vitt

Decision-making is the process by which individuals and groups identify, combine, and integrate information in order to choose one of several possible courses of action. In social psychology, research traditions involve the cognition, affect, and behavior that drive both *individual* decision-making (including attitudes, beliefs, values, and actions) and *group* decision-making (including group formation, group preference, performance and influence, social decision schemes, straw poll, social comparison, and groupthink).

Although some social psychologists have taken up decision-making as a focused research interest, social psychology generally is seen as informing the emerging interdisciplinary areas of the decision sciences. As a topic area within social psychology, decision-making is not guided by a single theoretical framework that researchers use to organize and guide their work. Rather, a number of theories in which decision-making is either explicit or implicit can be found within symbolic interactionism, exchange theory, rational choice, cognitive consistency theories, and other research on attitudes, beliefs, values, and behaviors. Dissonance theory, for instance, is a comprehensive framework that describes cognition and behavior before, during, and after people make decisions. It is based upon the general proposition that inconsistent cognitions arouse an unpleasant subjective state, which leads to behaviors designed to reduce dissonance and achieve consistency, a satisfactory subject state. People feel discomfort in virtually all unresolved decision situations – the more important the decision, the greater the dissonance.

Historically, the heading of "judgment and decision research" is broad and work has been conducted over many years using differing methods within and across disciplines. Since the 1940s and 1950s, such research generally has followed two lines of inquiry. One group of researchers set out to learn how people decide on a particular course of action. How do people choose what to do next? Are their decisions rational? If not, by what processes do they make choices? A second group of researchers was motivated by people's perceptions. Do people integrate conflicting thoughts and ideas, arrive at an understanding of the situation they are facing, and then make a judgment? Does their judgment improve with experience? How does human judgment compare with actuarial prediction?

From the first set of inquiries a formal modeling approach evolved, which has most commonly been used in economics and organization management. It typically compares the cost or utility of alternatives, characterizes choice as the maximization of value, and assumes that rational, self-interested persons make the correct, most efficient choice on the basis of available information. Rational decision-making involves sufficiently reducing uncertainty so as to allow a reasonable choice to be made from among alternatives. This classical approach has contributed illuminating tools of thought and substance to the social sciences, but it also has been seen as both too strong and too weak: too strong because it sets impractical – if not impossible – standards and too weak because it fails to capture the subtleties of human concerns (Bacharach 1994). Sharir and his colleagues (1997), for example, have argued that rational models do not deal with significant aspects of actual deliberations, which are essentially subjective and can be experienced, and appear to others, as vague.

Evidence is accumulating in economics, particularly behavioral economics, and organization management that decision-making requires persons, individually or in groups, to expend cognitive effort, and more often than not, feeling effort as well when identifying alternatives and choosing among them. Choice is a motivational condition that arouses both cognition and emotion and affects decision-making behavior. Argyris (2001) argues that in order to be effective in group decision-making, it is necessary to understand interpersonal factors during the decision process itself. According to Hayashi (2001), effective decision-making involves having the ability to intuit, or "trust your gut."

A second set of inquiries involving judgment can be found in the scholarship on history, politics, and the law, where quantitative modeling and cost analysis can be difficult or implausible to apply. Using a reason-based approach to decision-making, this perspective identifies reasons and arguments that influence decisions and explains choice in terms of the balance of for and against alternatives. One school within this perspective sees judgments and decisions reached by groups through sets of relatively simple rules known as "social decision schemes."

Rules within social decision schemes relate the initial distribution of members' views or preferences to the group's final decisions. A *majority-wins* rule suggests that a group will decide according to whatever position is initially supported by most of its members. Other social decision schemes involve the familiar *two-thirds majority* rule in use by some juries and other decision-making groups, and an alternative known as a *first-shift* rule, in which groups tend to adopt a decision consistent with the direction of the first shift in opinion shown by any members. In contrast, a fourth alternative is the *truth-wins* rule, which indicates that a decision will be reached by members' recognition of the "correctness" of a solution. The results of many studies indicate that these straightforward social decision schemes underlie, and are successful in predicting (up to 80 percent of), even complex group decisions.

Although some scholars have contributed to both choice and judgment areas of decision research, controversy over which approach is superior and efforts to integrate the two are still ongoing. For instance, one review of some 20 studies found that intuitive ("clinical") judgments are less accurate than a simple statistical combination of the same information available to the judge (Goldstein & Hogarth 1997). A third historical or meta-approach called deciding how to decide is used to compare and explain the selection of one decision strategy over another, depending upon the conditions involved.

Recent developments in the field of judgment and decision-making include the emergence of a formal interdisciplinary field of decision science, which seeks to understand and improve judgment and decision-making of individuals, groups, and organizations. Theories that provide the core for decision science draw on insights from a diverse set of disciplines, including social psychology as well as cognitive psychology, economics, statistics, neurology, and philosophy. Applications of decision-making research are being used to improve decision capabilities of fields as diverse as medicine, military science, law, organization management, and consumer finance.

At one end of the field, judgment and decision researchers now include higher-order thought processes, thus blurring the line between decision research and cognitive psychology. Researchers cite and conduct studies that involve memory, mood, and motivation, learning and language, attention and attitude, reasoning and representation, problem solving and perception, expertise and explanatory coherence. At the other end of the field, researchers are conducting intensive study of the social aspects of decision-making, thereby blurring lines between parts of social psychology, sociology, economics, political science, and anthropology. These areas of judgment and decision research are moving forward rapidly. However, another discipline exists that has long incorporated an understanding of the subjective nature of decision-making – the field of market research that supports commercial advertising and consumer decision-making.

Among the tools of market researchers are concepts originally developed by social psychologists and sociologists. Some market researchers, for instance, hold that human values inform the processes of preference, choice, and purchase decisions. Targeted efforts often are designed to tap into what is known about consumer values in order to sell them products and services. The idea that individuals or groups of individuals prefer and choose among what they value most is not new to social psychology. Although discussions about values and how values function at personal levels have occurred over centuries and can be found in all fields of the social sciences (and in law, the physical sciences, education, philosophy, and religion), it was social psychologist Milton Rokeach who may be best known for his work on the nature of human values and value systems. Rokeach argued that values drove decisions and although difficult to accomplish, changes in human values have the power to change even entrenched behaviors.

Other behavioral and social scientists (and philosophers) have used the term values to refer to ideals in the world toward which people are oriented and to what is regarded as personally desirable. Individuals hold beliefs and attitudes about the way things are, make judgments about the way things should be, make tradeoffs among choices, then choose and take action according to what they value. Although the study of human values in sociology has more or less languished (perhaps for want of better measurement tools), in

Value-Focused Thinking decision researcher Ralph Keeney (1996) argues that values drive the best decisions of both individuals and businesses. New theoretical frameworks are being introduced into the values and decision-making research literature in order to reenergize thinking in that research area, and also to present explanations of consumers' financial and health care decision-making behaviors (e.g., Vitt 2004).

Decision-making based on values alone, however, is not without controversy. Not much is known, for example, about the links between consumers' stated values and their sometimes inconsistent decision behavior. A better understanding of values awaits further research in social psychology and the decision sciences. How and why these inconsistencies operate in health care, purchase behaviors, savings and investment behaviors, and environmental choices could improve understanding of both individual and group judgment and decision-making in these and other areas in society.

In addition to links to human values in decision-making, connections have been made to the attitude literature, exchange theory, literature on the self, role and identity, and many other social psychological conceptualizations. Meanings elaborated in decision-making also have importance beyond the task of rendering decisions. Decision-making and the activities that surround it have symbolic significance as well. Decision-makers develop and communicate meaning not only about decisions, but also about what is happening in the world and why. They define morally important issues, create understandings, and impact events, actions, policies, and even cultures. They allocate resources that define who is powerful, who is smart, who is prosperous, and who is virtuous. Thus, the process of judgment and decision-making affects individual, organizational, and societal esteem and standing. It helps to create and sustain a social order of relationships, trust and distrust. It builds bridges to disciplines of study, both basic and applied.

The reality is that individual and group decisions result in outcomes as significant as life and death, war and peace, prosperity and impoverishment, social justice, foreign relations and the domestic policies of nations. Organizations can succeed or fail as a consequence of the decision-making skills, mindsets, and practices of managers. The theories and research of social psychologists have contributed to the vast decision sciences and will undoubtedly continue to fit into and work within this growing network, helping to improve knowledge about judgment and decision-making by individuals and groups.

SEE ALSO: Attitudes and Behavior; Cognitive Dissonance Theory (Festinger); Identity Theory; Rational Choice Theories; Role; Symbolic Interaction; Values

REFERENCES AND SUGGESTED READINGS

Argyris, C. (2001) Interpersonal Barriers to Decision-Making. In: *Harvard Business Review on Decision-Making*. Harvard Business School, Cambridge, MA.
Bacharach, M. (1994) Decision Theory. In: Outhwaite, W. & Bottomore, T. (Eds.), *Twentieth-Century Social Thought*. Blackwell, Oxford.
Goldstein, W. M. & Hogarth, R. M. (1997) Judgment and Decision Research: Some Historical Context. In: Goldstein, W. M. & Hogarth, R. M. (Eds.), *Research on Judgment and Decision-Making: Currents, Connections, and Controversies*. Cambridge University Press, Cambridge.
Hayashi, A. M. (2001) When to Trust Your Gut. In: *Harvard Business Review on Decision-Making*. Harvard Business School, Cambridge, MA.
Keeney, R. L. (1996) *Value-Focused Thinking: A Path to Creative Decisionmaking*. Harvard University Press, Cambridge, MA.
Rokeach, M. (1979) *Understanding Human Values: Individual and Societal*. Free Press, New York.
Sharir, E., Simonson, I., & Tversky, A. (1997) Reason-Based Choice. In: Goldstein, W. M. & Hogarth, R. M. (Eds.), *Research on Judgment and Decision-Making: Currents, Connections, and Controversies*. Cambridge University Press, Cambridge.
Vitt, L. (2004) Consumers' Financial Decisions and the Psychology of Values. *Journal of Financial Service Professionals* 58, 6 (November).

decolonization

Julian Go

Decolonization typically refers to a shift in a society's political status from colony to autonomous state or independent nation. It can also refer to a shift from colonial status to full incorporation into the dominant polity such that it is no longer subordinate to the latter. While decolonization has occurred in many different places and times, typical usage of the term in the modern period refers to the decolonization by western colonial powers of dependencies in Asia, Africa, or the Americas. It is strongly associated with the fall of modern empires and the spread of nationalism and the nation-state around the world. Decolonization has also been used to refer to a cultural or psychological process that may or may not correlate with formal political decolonization.

The first major period of decolonization in the modern era occurred in the late eighteenth and early nineteenth centuries. In this period, colonies of England, France, Portugal, and Spain emerged as independent nations. The period began with the revolution of Britain's continental colonies and the formation of the United States and the emergence of independent Haiti, formerly the French colony of Saint Domingue. Thereafter, in the early nineteenth century, colonies of Spain and Portugal in Latin America obtained independence in the wake of the occupation of Spain by Napoleon in 1808. The second major era of decolonization occurred in the mid-twentieth century. This period saw a far-reaching, global spread of decolonization. Most colonies in the Indian subcontinent, the Pacific, Southeast Asia, Africa, the Caribbean, and the Middle East obtained independence. The process began after World War I but was accelerated after World War II. From 1945 to 1981, approximately 105 new nations emerged as a direct or indirect result of decolonization. Most of these nations then joined the United Nations, such that the number of members in the United Nations expanded from 56 members to 156 in this period.

The two periods of decolonization differ in several respects, in part due to the character of the colonies involved. In the first period, decolonization was led by revolts among creoles and settlers who sought independence from their former mother country. In the second period, decolonization was led by indigenous groups rather than settlers or creoles. Furthermore, decolonization in the Americas during the late eighteenth and nineteenth centuries was localized in the western hemisphere. By contrast, decolonization in the second period was global in scope, covering nearly all colonies. While a handful of countries remained dependencies of western powers after World War II, decolonization in this period is typically associated with the end of the western empires and the concomitant diffusion of the nation-state ideal around the globe. Finally, decolonization in the first period was typically initiated by anti-colonial revolutions. In North America, Central and South America, and Haiti, independence was won through war (the exception is the independence of Brazil from Portugal). In contrast, decolonization in the twentieth century most often occurred without violence. Except for Algeria, Angola, Indonesia, and Vietnam, colonies won their independence after initial signs of discontent were expressed and as imperial powers decided to let them become independent.

There is little consensus on the causes of decolonization, but several classes of causation can be discerned. One includes factors internal to the colony, such as the emergence of nationalism among local populations and associated resistance to the metropolitan power. A second includes the relative capacity or willingness on the part of metropolitan powers. The third includes larger systemic factors in the global system of international politics, which might in turn shape the metropolitan powers' willingness to decolonize. Some theories suggest, for example, that when an imperial state is "hegemonic" in the world system, it prefers global free trade and therefore becomes more supportive of decolonization. A related factor is global political culture. After World War II, for example, colonial empires began to lose legitimacy and the ideal of the nation-state became most pronounced, in part because the United States lent support to anti-colonial sentiment.

The results of decolonization in the twentieth century have been complex. While decolonization was heralded by national elites as the first step toward modernization and economic growth, modeled after the development of their former imperial rulers, these developmental dreams proved difficult to realize even in the absence of direct political control by outside rulers. The effects of colonialism upon local socioeconomic structures were difficult to cast off and neocolonialism or relations of dependency continued with western powers. Many decolonized countries saw an influx of foreign capital that, as some studies argued, slowed if not impeded economic growth. They also became subject to the policies of global institutions such as the World Bank or International Monetary Fund. Political legacies were also strong, as postcolonial nations created governments often modeled after the government of their former ruler. The global diffusion of western political forms such as constitutions can partly be attributed to decolonization.

One of the most significant consequences of decolonization, however, is the emergence of the nation-state as the dominant form for organizing societies and the related realization of the modern interstate system around the world. After decolonization in the twentieth century, empires have become illegitimate in the eyes of the international community, and few territories have become recolonized. Decolonization has meant that empire, a major form for organizing peoples for centuries, has ended. Whether this legacy of decolonization will persist, or whether a new era of empires will emerge, remains to be seen.

SEE ALSO: Colonialism (Neocolonialism); Dependency and World-Systems Theories; Manifest Destiny; Methods, Postcolonial; Nation-State

REFERENCES AND SUGGESTED READINGS

Betts, R. (2004) *Decolonization*. Routledge, New York.

Boswell, T. (1989) Colonial Empires and the Capitalist World-Economy: A Time Series Analysis of Colonization, 1640–1960. *American Sociological Review* 54: 180–96.

Cardoso, F. & Faletto, E. (1979) *Dependency and Development in Latin America*. University of California Press, Berkeley.

Fieldhouse, D. (1966) *The Colonial Empires*. Dell, New York.

McMichael, P. (2004) *Development and Social Change: A Global Perspective*. Pine Forge Press, Colorado.

Strang, D. (1990) From Dependency to Sovereignty: An Event History Analysis of Decolonization. *American Sociological Review* 55: 846–60.

deconstruction

George Pavlich

At first blush, placing a term like deconstruction in a sociology encyclopedia seems entirely incongruous. The word *encyclopedia* derives from the Greek prefix *en* (in) and *kúklos* with *paideíā*, connoting education (Ayto 1990: 201). Together, the implication is this: encyclopedias encircle education by gathering general, but definitive, discussions on particular topics between the covers of one reference work. This activity undoubtedly runs contrary to the spirit of deconstructive practices that expressly involve undoing language where it gathers itself into closed circles – especially when it purports to reflect the necessary, essential, absolute, or fixed. By contrast, the prospect of reinventing encyclopedic traditions from within is certainly not counter to deconstructive thought. Without clinging to the *en-*, one could, for instance, allude to the deconstructive potential of generally circling around educative meaning horizons.

Associated with the French writer Jacques Derrida, deconstruction appears alongside several neologisms he initially created to read, yet reach beyond, the Platonic auspices of western metaphysics. Key among those auspices are oppositions that distinguish between appearance and reality, matter and form, temporal manifestation and essential principle (Derrida 1976, 1979, 1981). As well, metaphysical writing privileges logical arguments (*logocentrism*), formulating them as the center and marginalizing all other aspects of the text (Derrida 1982). So, the real, formal, and essential is assumed to be apodictic; logic within language faithfully represents, names, or classifies what is already there. Heidegger, who cast himself as among the first post-metaphysical thinkers, sought to undo such thinking, appealing at times to nostalgic strategies of remembrance that recall "authentic" forms of Being ignored by metaphysical languages. Although markedly influenced by Heidegger's work, Derrida offers a rather different, non-nostalgic tack.

His now-famous adage suggests that language may be approached as constitutive in its own right, without assuming the external existence of its referents: "*There is nothing outside the text*" (Derrida 1976: 158; emphasis in original). Contextually sanctioned arrangements of words compose not only the entities enunciated through language (e.g., subjects, objects, things, transcendental ideas), but also the very concept of existence. Consequently, metaphysics' primordial suppositions about being as that which is present, or indeed its emphasis on such oppositions as appearance–reality, are the products of language usage in given locales. For Derrida, anything said to exist or deemed present always achieves that status by virtue of specific iterations of language use. For instance, Being is enunciated as presence because of the way signs are locally deployed in relation to one another, and its meaning emerges from particular patterns of deferral. Consider another example. If asked "what does the word airplane mean?" a language user must respond by deferring to other words, signs with which that word is internally related in a given context – "it is a machine that flies," "it is not a ground vehicle," and so on. Dictionaries and encyclopedias also provide good examples of the ways meaning arises through deferral. Derrida (1976, 1981) famously explored this "play of differences" and coined the term *différance* (which in French can connote both "to differ" and "to defer") to indicate how meaning, presence, and referents are generated by deferment to other signs. Such deferrals are not inconsequential; they literally shape both identities and how these live.

Moreover, language systems are governed by historically situated rules and conventions whose authority is premised on absence, rupture, aporia, and paradox. Patterns of *différance* are therefore never stable, necessary, fixed, or closed; they always can be – by virtue of their contingent, aporetic structure – disrupted, dispersed, opened, and dissociated to make way for new deferral patterns, meaning horizons, and existences. Disruptions to language formations have potentially vast consequences for the everyday meanings subjects use to encompass being at any given point in history. If that reflects Derrida's direct relevance to ethical questions of how to be with others, it also suggests how deconstructing given

organizations of *différance* is ultimately about incipient ways of existing.

But what precisely is deconstruction? Although this question is not unproblematic in context, one might say that deconstruction has to do with opening up given linguistic arrangements to the mostly silent, background suppositions and aporias that enable their particular patterns of deferral. Its opening gambit, "guardrail," is to read a classic text closely (never abandoning it or rejecting it out of hand), surveying especially what it eclipses, ignores, rejects, expels, dismisses, marginalizes, renders supplemental, excludes, and eliminates. Deconstruction pores over these delegitimated elements of a text to make room for alternate interpretations that open up a reading to what is completely unforeseeable from the vantage of its meaning horizons. Through such openings, deconstruction seeks to reorganize a given language use by realigning conventional oppositions, creating space for unexpected linguistic possibilities and being. Like the host, perhaps, it offers an unconditional welcome to the arrival of what is strange, unfamiliar, and other (Derrida 1997b, 1999, 2001; Derrida & Dufourmantelle 2000).

From here, the waters get muddy for those in search of singular definitions that expect one to decide definitively about deconstruction. The very question "what is …?" poses a unique problem: while it appears to open discussion, the *is* commits respondents to the existence of the very thing placed in question. Yet, as Derrida (1995, 1997) repeatedly indicates, deconstruction is not a finite being (a presence) that can be defined universally, once and for all. Indeed, formulating an essential, fixed definition of deconstruction would replicate the very "metaphysics of presence" that he challenges. Instead, a different approach to language is required, and one that immediately faces a definitional intricacy: the word "deconstruction" cannot be defined once and for all, with any fixed unity, because any meaning or feature attributed to it is always, in its turn, deconstructable (see Derrida 1988: 4).

Several further things may be said about deconstructive analysis. Each such analysis is, as noted in the above quotation, subject to further deconstruction – the process is unending and without final decision. There is never a point at which deconstruction ends, for every emergent meaning horizon is traced through deconstructible grammars. Moreover, attempts at deconstruction do not approximate a sustained method, methodology, procedure, or unified strategy. Rather, their emergence is as diverse as the contexts in which they are located, and in each case a close familiarity with the analyzed text is required. Its contingent path is, however, never determined or predictable. As Derrida insists: "Deconstruction is not a method or some tool that you apply to something from the outside. Deconstruction is something which happens and which happens inside" (Derrida 1997a: 9). It is not an intentional act that produces predictable results – it emerges by happening, if at all. And that happening is pleasurable, structurally desirable, and playful. Derrida (in Kearney 1984: 126) even suggests that deconstructing a text entails revealing how it "functions as desire," how the quest to render present, to secure a stable plenitude, is always deferred. The reader engages this "desire of language" through his or her own desire to appropriate in the text an absence, or something that is other to the self who reads.

In addition, since deconstruction is always located as somewhat of a "double gesture" that both reads and exceeds given texts, it never breaks fully with the past: "I do not believe in decisive ruptures, in an unequivocal 'epistemological break,' as it is called today. Breaks are always, and fatally, reinscribed in an old cloth that must continually, interminably be undone" (Derrida 1981: 24).

So, deconstruction takes place, or not as the case may be, through particular instances where attempts are made to open (dissociate) given arrangements of language to other possible arrangements. It attends closely to the unspoken elements that enable the central, or privileged, theses of a given meaning formation; it transpires by working with the lowly, unstable, contingent, and aporetic foundations upon which any open system of *différance* resides.

While the emphasis on language may appear to render deconstruction particularly well suited to literary and philosophical discourses, its effects have reverberated through many discourses, including socio-legal studies, women's studies, cultural studies, anthropology, religious studies, politics, criminology, and so on. Within the context of sociology, specifically, deconstruction's ethical pursuit of how to be with others is directly pertinent. But it also strikes a potentially rich chord in several other ways.

First, to the extent that deconstruction privileges dissociation over "gathering," opening over closure, it dovetails with inaugurating strands of sociological thought that viewed social formations as contingent, changeable, and amenable to historically situated openings. In later muses on the idea of deconstruction, Derrida (1997a: 13) tells us his focus has always been on "heterogeneity" and "dissociation" rather than practices that privilege "gathering" and unified formulations of concepts like "community" or even "society." He senses in such unities potentially dangerous closures that direct responsibility from members and fail to recognize basic ethical commitments to excluded others, the absences which render possible intimations of identity. Deconstruction is a way to keep open such unities and to prevent them from closing themselves off as necessary, inevitable, or the like.

If this concern with contingent, heterogeneous openings echoes elements of sociology, deconstruction assuredly does not endorse the latter's Eurocentric visions of social progress, or any quests to engineer absolute social or communal formations (see Pavlich 2001). At most, its call is to keep associative patterns interminably open, to spring into play precisely where discourses try to sign themselves off as necessary, unavoidable, unquestionably just, and so on.

Second, Derrida explicitly engages with seemingly canonical sociological texts, including his discussions of Rousseau and Marx (Derrida 1976, 1994, 2002b). His *Specters of Marx* recovers the significance of Marx by reading key texts deconstructively, making place for the idea that – despite talk to the contrary – we continue to be heirs to diverse Marxist legacies. Marx's multiple intellectual ghosts still haunt our times. One of these, often portrayed as his chief bequest, addresses the essential ontology (laws, processes, effects) of capitalist societies. Yet Derrida argues that this somewhat anachronistic ontology is not Marx's most enduring legacy. The memory of Marx also continues to surface, for example, in the personal suffering, exploitation, and inequalities that persist on a global scale. Derrida deconstructively quarries the margins of texts like Marx and Engels's *Communist Manifesto*, or *The German Ideology*, to disclose still other specters. He surfaces with Marx's emphasis on radical, historically placed self-critique that opens up to what is to come, and which strives for what cannot be known from within present possibilities. While Derrida (1994: 89) may worry about Marx's ontological formulations, he tells us he is not prepared to relinquish the critical, probing "spirit" of Marxism; but even more than this, he remains committed to the promise of emancipation and even to the "messianic" pledge to deliver new ways of being, new events that usher in new collective associations. Marx's legacy here is to have alluded to the experience of a "messianic affirmation," without a messianism, that welcomes unconditionally the promise of existence beyond current social relations.

Finally, much of sociological thinking has been undertaken in the name of various conceptions of social justice; similarly, Derrida (2002a: 243) insists that deconstruction is a language of justice, and even more forcefully proclaims that it *is* justice. For him, justice appears as a promise, beyond law, and is itself incalculable, infinite, and undeconstructable. This is not to say that deconstruction pursues the *telos* of a known justice; rather, he asserts that justice is radically unknowable, infinite, undetermined, and incalculable. Yet for all that, we are required to calculate justice, and we do so through finite calculations that find expression in law. He therefore locates deconstruction in the "interval" between law (which is deconstructible) and justice (which is not). By relentlessly opening the law (rule, grammar), refusing to allow any finite calculation to close itself off as necessary, deconstruction perpetually opens up to a limitless promise of justice that is always to come, that never fully arrives. And it is precisely in the name of that promise that both deconstruction and sociology, commendably, proceed.

SEE ALSO: Derrida, Jacques; Poststructuralism; Postmodern Social Theory; Postmodernism

REFERENCES AND SUGGESTED READINGS

Ayto, J. (1990) *Dictionary of Word Origins*. Bloomsbury, London.

Derrida, J. (1976) *Of Grammatology*. Johns Hopkins University Press, Baltimore.

Derrida, J. (1979) *Writing and Difference*. Routledge & Kegan Paul, London.

Derrida, J. (1981) *Positions*. Athlone Press, London.

Derrida, J. (1982) *Margins of Philosophy*. Harvester Press, Brighton.

Derrida, J. (1988) Letter to a Japanese Friend. In: Wood, D. & Bernasconi, R. (Eds.), *Derrida and Difference*. Northwestern University Press. Evanston.

Derrida, J. (1994) *Spectres of Marx: The State of the Debt, the Work of Mourning and the New International*. Routledge, London.

Derrida, J. (1995) *Points ... Interviews, 1974–1994*. Stanford University Press, Stanford.

Derrida, J. (1997a) The Villanova Roundtable. In: Caputo, J. D. (Ed.), *Deconstruction in a Nutshell: A Conversation with Jacques Derrida*. Fordham University Press, New York, pp. 3–28.

Derrida, J. (1997b) *Adieu to Emmanuel Levinas*. Stanford University Press, Stanford.

Derrida, J. (1998) *Monolingualism of the Other or the Prosthesis of Origin*. Stanford University Press, Stanford.

Derrida, J. (1999) Marx and Sons. In: Sprinker, M. (Ed.), *Ghostly Demarcations: A Symposium on Jacques Derrida's Spectres of Marx*. Verso, New York, pp. 213–69.

Derrida, J. (2001) *On Cosmopolitanism and Forgiveness*. Routledge, London.

Derrida, J. (2002a) Force of Law: The "Mystical Foundation of Authority." In: Anidjar, G. (Ed.), *Acts of Religion*. Routledge, London, pp. 228–98.

Derrida, J. (2002b) *Marx and Sons*. Presses universitaires de France, Paris.

Derrida, J. & Dufourmantelle, A. (2000) *Of Hospitality*. Stanford University Press, Stanford.

Kearney, R. (Ed.) (1984) *Dialogues With Contemporary Philosophers: The Phenomenological Heritage*. Manchester University Press, Manchester.

Pavlich, G. (2001) Sociological Promises: Departures, or Negotiating Dissociation. In: Derrida, J., Simmons, L., & Worth, H. (Eds.), *Derrida Downunder*. Dunmore Press, Palmerston North, NZ, pp. 216–32.

deference

Paul T. Munroe

Deference refers to the granting of influence, esteem, or simply the "right of way" from one person to another person, persons, or impersonal entities. When one defers, the interest is in the other with whom one is interacting. Deference is a necessary element of a status relation, and deference often characterizes a large portion of the interaction among close personal friends, intimates, and family members.

Deference is a pivotal concept in the status characteristics and expectation states research program initiated by Berger, Cohen, and Zelditch in the mid-1960s. Groups of people who are working collectively toward the best solution to a task behave in ways that, if viewed externally, look very much like a hierarchy. Some people talk more than others, are listened to more, and are more influential than others. However, viewed from within the group, people are often unaware of the inequality. Group members can be remarkably satisfied with their interactions and not unhappy about the inequality at all. Deference is a key factor here. People look to the group members whom they think have the best ideas and defer to them.

The trouble with this process is that often the reason for deferring has to do with status characteristics like age, sex, or race rather than actual ability. So the relations are often unfair and inefficient, regardless of the group members' sense of ease within the group process.

Deference is the most frequent dependent variable measure in status characteristics research. The standardized experiment compares the proportion of times a subject chooses to stay with their own choice or to defer to a partner's choice. The higher the status of the other person relative to oneself, the more likely one is to defer to that person.

For Kemper (2000), deference is what distinguishes status from power relations in interaction. In status relations, lower-status persons defer to the higher-status person(s). In power or coercive relations, the low-power actor responds to the high-power actor because they

have to do so. Scheff (1988) argues that conformity is prevalent in much of interaction, leading to a state of normative control, because people defer to the norms and expectations of others to avoid the feeling of shame.

Goffman's "interaction rituals" often involve deference behaviors. Interactions among those who are familiar or wish to be so are made smooth and disruptions are minimized by a pattern of each person offering deference to the other. This comes in the form of interest in the point of view of the other, looking at the other while listening, nodding, "back-channeling" (saying "mm-hmm," "ah yes," and so on), and overt statements of agreement. All these examples of deference facilitate interaction.

Deference can only be shown by people, individually or in groups, but the *object* of the deference can be another person, an object, idea, or imagined entity. One can show deference to another person, the law, God, or symbols such as the flag of one's country. Behavioral examples include removing one's hat in a courtroom, kneeling before an altar, or observing a moment of silence in memory of some person or event. Deference, viewed in these terms, is the key process that leads to social solidarity.

SEE ALSO: Expectation States Theory; Norms; Power, Theories of; Social Influence; Status

REFERENCES AND SUGGESTED READINGS

Berger, J., Cohen, B. P., & Zelditch, M., Jr. (1972) Status Characteristics and Social Interaction. *American Sociological Review* 37(3): 241–55.

Goffman, E. (1959) *The Presentation of Self in Everyday Life*. Anchor Books, New York.

Kemper, T. D. (2000) Social Models in the Explanation of Emotions. In: Lewis, M. & Haviland-Jones, J. M. (Eds.), *Handbook of Emotions*, 2nd edn. Guilford Press, New York, pp. 45–58.

Scheff, T. J. (1988) Shame and Conformity, the Deference-Emotion System. *American Sociological Review* 53(3): 395–406.

Webster, M., Jr. & Foschi, M. (1988) Overview of Status Generalization. In: Webster, M., Jr. & Foschi, M. (Eds.), *Status Generalization: New Theory and Research*. Stanford University Press, Stanford, pp. 1–20.

definition of the situation

J. I. (Hans) Bakker

The term "definition of the situation" has come to signify the "Thomas theorem," the idea expressed by W. I. Thomas as follows: "If men define situations as real, they are real in their consequences" (Thomas & Thomas 1928: 571–2). That is, when the phrase is used, it usually carries with it the connotation of the whole theorem. However, the phrase "definition of the situation" predates Thomas's famous theorem. The more general conceptualization seems to be closely related to the concept of norms and culture. The interpretation of collective norms is important for all social action. It is only in certain situations where the agent chooses to redefine the norms. Park and Burgess (1921: 763–9) cite a Carnegie study (1919) where the term is used to discuss the topic of assimilation to American society, especially in terms of "Americanization": "common participation in common activities implies a common 'definition of the situation.' In fact, every single act, and eventually all moral life, is dependent upon the definition of the situation. A definition of the situation precedes and limits any possible action, and a redefinition of the situation changes the character of the action." Clearly the theorem, as it is often interpreted, applies more to the "redefinition" of a situation than to the norms defined by the collectivity. There is confusion concerning the history of the idea. Park worked with Thomas on the Americanization Studies series sponsored by Carnegie, but Thomas's name did not appear as the lead author of the book they wrote with Herbert Miller until 30 years later (Thomas et al. 1951 [1921]). Hence, the first clear and contemporaneously recognized use by Thomas of the phrase can be said to be chapter 2 of *The Unadjusted Girl* (Thomas 1923: 41–69): "Preliminary to any self-determined act of behavior there is always a stage of examination and deliberation which we may call the *definition of the situation*. And actually not only concrete acts are dependent on the definition of the situation, but gradually a whole life policy and the personality of the individual himself would follow from a series of such definitions." He cites examples from the ethical code of the Russian *mir* as instances of the definition of the situation "by the community as a whole," which indicates that it is not just individuals who do the defining. Merton (1995) examines the publishing history of the concept in detail and argues that the "Thomas theorem" was first articulated in Thomas and Thomas (1928: 571–2) but that Dorothy Swain Thomas apparently had relatively little to do with the theoretical idea since she mainly contributed to the statistical argument. Maines (2001: 244–6) argues that Thomas's "definition of the situation" has been falsely perceived by many sociologists as "subjectivistic" in contrast to Merton's (1948) notion of "self-fulfilling prophecies" as pertaining to objective social structures. To bolster that claim, Maines cites Thomas (1937: 8–9), where Thomas discusses "definitions" giving rise to "patterns." But the later usage seems to be scarcely distinguishable from cultural norms and values. Merton's self-fulfilling prophecy focuses on the false definition of the situation which evokes behavior that then makes the original false belief seem true, as in a teacher believing a student has a low IQ and therefore not helping that student learn. In that way, the self-fulfilling prophecy is a subset of the definition of the situation, not the other way around, as is often held. The Thomas theorem is frequently viewed as specific to symbolic interactionism and irrelevant to other research paradigms, but it can also be interpreted as a contribution to general sociology. Thomas clearly did not mean that all human choice is limited to social constructions that may lack objectivity; there is an "obdurate" reality and many definitions are real due to group pressures as manifested, for example, in gossip. The beliefs of members of a collectivity can create a positive feedback loop (e.g., Black is Beautiful). The "Protestant ethic" may be a definition of the situation that put social action on a new track. A more refined statement of the Thomas theorem might be: if human beings, individually or collectively, define a situation or set of situations as real, such social constructs can sometimes be real in their consequences, for better or for worse. However, that statement would not have the same punch. The extent to which "situation" is limited to small groups and communities rather than nation-states remains problematic.

Is a situation the same as a frame? But Thomas's contribution is valuable as a reminder that there are indeed times when the objective consequences of holding a false belief can be very real and yet not be exactly equivalent to a self-fulfilling prophecy. Moreover, his ideas are not restricted to symbolic interaction or even just interpretive approaches to interaction generally; his sociological and anthropological "social psychological" interest in cognition and motivation overlaps with other approaches in disciplines such as cognitive neuroscience, psychology, and psychoanalysis (e.g., Langman 1998).

SEE ALSO: Agency (and Intention); Community; Culture; Frame; Merton, Robert K.; Norms; Self-Fulfilling Prophecy; Thomas, W. I.

REFERENCES AND SUGGESTED READINGS

Carnegie Corporation (1919) Memorandum on Americanization. Division of Immigrant Heritages, New York. Extract in Park & Burgess (1921: 763–9).
Langman, L. (1998) Identity, Hegemony, and Social Reproduction. *Current Perspectives in Social Theory* 18: 185–226.
Maines, D. R. (2001) *The Faultline of Consciousness: A View of Interactionism in Sociology*. Aldine de Gruyter, New York.
Merton, R. K. (1948) The Self-Fulfilling Prophecy. *Antioch Review* 8: 193–210.
Merton, R. K. (1995) The Thomas Theorem and the Matthew Effect. *Social Forces* 74(2): 379–424.
Park, R. E. & Burgess, E. W. (Eds. and Comp.) (1921) *Introduction to the Science of Sociology*. University of Chicago Press, Chicago.
Stehr, N. & Meja, V. (Eds.) (2005 [1984]) *Society and Knowledge: Contemporary Perspectives in the Sociology of Knowledge and Science*, 2nd rev. edn. Transaction Publishers, New Brunswick, NJ.
Thomas, W. I. (1923) *The Unadjusted Girl, with Cases and Standpoint for Behavior Analysis*. Criminal Science Monograph No. 4. Little, Brown, Boston.
Thomas, W. I. (1937) *Primitive Behavior: An Introduction to the Social Sciences*. McGraw-Hill, New York.
Thomas, W. I. & Thomas, D. S. (1928) *The Child in America: Behavior Problems and Programs*. Alfred A. Knopf, New York.
Thomas, W. I., Park, R. E., & Miller, H. A. (1951 [1921]) *Old World Traits Transplanted*. Harper & Brothers, New York. [This is a volume in the Americanization Studies series, Allen T. Burns, director. Thomas's name did not appear as lead author until 1951 due to a "scandal" in 1918.]

deindustrialization

Nicole Flynn

Deindustrialization is a general term used to describe the shift in production from manufacturing to services beginning in the United States in the mid- to late 1960s. Although the transformation of the economy in terms of output is primary, the collateral changes are nearly impossible to separate. Changes in skills required for work and changes in the location of work stemming from the shift in output are often included as part of the concept of deindustrialization. Deindustrialization, or more optimistically industrial restructuring, is an expected development of advanced capitalism and a globalized economy. The implications of it, for both workers and industry, are debated by social scientists and economists.

The expansion and investment of capital, combined with wartime needs, drove the development of the manufacturing sector. As early as the Civil War, when manufacturing provided a more robust economy for the North than the agrarian South, the building of goods was recognized as providing both jobs for workers and goods for market. Cities developed around centers of manufacturing, and the spatial concentration of capital, both human and financial, created diverse and thriving communities. Chicago and New York are early examples of manufacturing cities, along with Philadelphia, Detroit, and Pittsburgh.

Following World War II, the population of the United States expanded and shifted, notably with the growth of the middle class. With this expansion, the demand for goods and services increased. Technology developed that made automation possible and increased both the effectiveness of manufacturing and the potential of the service sector. Expanding service sector industries included health and health care, education, social services, personal services, and more recently financial, insurance, and real estate services, and hospitality/tourism. The increased demand for goods was accompanied by a push for cheaper production, which was made possible through automation, lower rents or land costs, and less expensive labor. The increased demand for services occurred during a time of increases in educational attainment, increases in female labor force participation, and increases in civil rights.

Both land and labor were cheaper in more rural areas, so initially deindustrialization meant a move from traditional manufacturing centers in the Northeast and Midwest, also known as the Frostbelt, to the South or the Sunbelt. Geographically, land was also cheaper outside cities, so when manufacturing plants relocated, they did so in more rural areas. Because of urban growth and residential patterns, less skilled workers were generally concentrated in the older areas of cities and towns. More affluent families and skilled labor lived in the suburban fringe. In former manufacturing cities, when service industries did expand and enter into urban areas, they brought jobs that required skills urban residents lacked. Lower-skilled services and the remaining manufacturing jobs relocated or developed in the suburbs. The result is often referred to as "spatial-skills mismatch" (Kain 1968; Kasarda 1995).

The decline in unionization is also a consideration in deindustrialization. As labor became less powerful and capital more concentrated, there was less potential for resistance when manufacturing reduced jobs or relocated. Traditional blue-collar jobs, with high levels of unionization, were slowly disappearing. The diverse service sector, dominated by white-collar and pink-collar jobs, has yet to develop strong union representation.

As manufacturing left for cheaper markets, the service sector expanded. Production of services had advantages not available to goods-producing industries. First, horizontal space was less important. Skyscrapers provided an effective way for industry to grow in space without having to purchase large tracts of expensive land. Office buildings rose in the air, and large cities became centers of financial and legal services, information processing, and hospitality/tourism.

Demand for skilled labor in the service sector was very different from traditional manufacturing jobs. While most management manufacturing jobs did not require extensive formal schooling, service sector expansion increased the demand for more highly educated labor and workers skilled in specific areas such as medicine, the law, and technology. It also provided a share of lower-skilled and lower-paid positions that were often supervised by the more educated workers.

The expansion of the service sector and the bifurcation of skills and rewards associated with employment in these industries contributed to a shift in the class structure. Many blue-collar jobs that paid living wages were relocated and the remaining options for workers with less education were lower-skilled and lower-paid service positions. The expansion of higher-skilled services also ensured employment for the increasing number of college graduates and persons with professional and postgraduate training. A related outcome was increases in low wage earners and an expanding upper-wage class, with fewer workers earning middle-income wages. This shift has implications for class, race, and gender inequality.

In general, white men and women are more likely to benefit from these industrial changes than other race and ethnic groups. Workers with more access to higher education were initially best served by deindustrialization. As the service sector expanded, more women, especially white women, also entered and completed college and professional schooling. Their rise in educational levels, later age at first marriage and childbearing, and increasing presence in the labor force all coincided with the increasing availability of jobs in areas that were long accustomed to hiring women. Black women, a group with a long history of labor force participation and increasing levels of education, also stood to benefit from expansion of educational opportunities. Black men and immigrants with less education, a group that relied on low-skilled manufacturing jobs, were most disadvantaged. The decline in unions that occurred with deindustrialization was an important factor explaining the wage gap between black and white men.

Recent research critically examines globalization as it shapes the context of deindustrialization. The ability to communicate and move both capital and people around the world makes possible an economy situated in a global labor market. World-systems theory describes the interdependencies of advanced capitalist countries, developing nations, and countries rich in either labor, raw materials, or both. Goods-producing industries dependent on unskilled labor search the rest of the world for cheaper locations for labor and land. Increasingly, less skilled service jobs are also relocated to countries with a surplus of inexpensive workers. Policy that encourages multinational corporations through tax benefits and exemptions further stimulates this movement of capital outflow and inflow of foreign investment.

Some researchers argue that deindustrialization is merely a feature of advanced capitalist economies, and that eventually the expansion of services will increase the standard of living for all persons in these post-industrial countries. Post-industrialists, as they are sometimes called, link any increases in inequality with the transition process or with qualities of the population, not the labor market. Others view the shift as a more permanent imbalance in the economy, one that will eventually not only increase inequality but also result in reductions in competitiveness and a decline in quality of output. The work of Bluestone, Harrison, Wilson, and others points toward a permanent change in the class structure, into one more reminiscent of pre-industrialization characterized by a large class of poor workers and a class of wealthy persons, with little variation in between. The long-term consequences of deindustrialization are still being debated. However, the transition of the United States economy from manufacturing to service production is a major transformation that clearly affects relationships between groups and shifts the structure of social institutions.

SEE ALSO: Braverman, Harry; Capitalism; Dual Labor Markets; Economic Development; Economic Sociology: Neoclassical Economic Perspective; Economy (Sociological Approach); Global Economy; Markets; Occupations; Post-Industrial Society; Women, Economy and

REFERENCES AND SUGGESTED READINGS

Alderson, A. S. (1997) Globalization and Deindustrialization: Direct Investment and the Decline of Manufacturing Employment in 17 OECD Nations. *Journal of World-Systems Research* 3(1): 1–34.

Bell, D. (1973) *The Coming of Post-Industrial Society.* Basic Books, New York.

Bluestone, B. & Harrison, B. (1982) *The Deindustrialization of America: Plant Closings, Community Abandonment, and the Dismantling of Basic Industry.* Basic Books, New York.

Chevan, A. & Stokes, R. (2000) Growth in Family Income Inequality, 1970–1990: Industrial Restructuring and Demographic Change. *Demography* 37(3): 365–80.

Harrison, B. & Bluestone, B. (1988) *The Great U-Turn: Corporate Restructuring and the Polarizing of America.* Basic Books, New York.

Kain, J. (1968) Housing Segregation, Negro Employment, and Metropolitan Decentralization. *Quarterly Journal of Economics* 26: 110–30.

Kasarda, J. (1995) Urban Industrial Transition and the Underclass. *Annals of the American Academy of Political and Social Science* 501: 26–47.

McCall, L. (2001) *Complex Inequality: Gender, Race, and Class in the New Economy.* Routledge, New York.

Morris, M. & Western, B. (1999) Inequality and Earnings at the Close of the Twentieth Century. *Annual Review of Sociology* 25: 623–57.

Wilson, W. J. (1996) *When Work Disappears: The World of the New Urban Poor.* Random House, New York.

deinstitutionalization

Raymond M. Weinstein

In 1955 there were 559,000 patients in public mental hospitals in the United States, the highest there had ever been. At that time, patients were largely committed involuntarily and had long hospital stays. For more than a century, the number of patients at state institutions, historically the primary facilities for the treatment of psychiatric disorders, had been rising steadily. By 1980, however, this number had declined to just over 132,000, despite the fact that the national population grew considerably.

In 2003, fewer than 53,000 remained. The 93 percent drop in the resident census of state hospitals was accompanied by the growth of outpatient clinics and community mental health centers as primary care facilities, the sharp reduction in patients' average length of hospitalization, and the shift to policies emphasizing more voluntary admissions.

These statistics, however, did not reflect a precipitous reduction in the number of seriously mentally ill persons. What took place, especially from 1965 to 1980, was a *transfer* of patients from state institutions to a range of institutional settings such as nursing homes, board-and-care facilities, halfway houses, and community treatment centers. This massive and unprecedented patient relocation from hospital to community, termed "deinstitutionalization" by both social scientists and the mass media, was supported by certain ideologies and political actions. Deinstitutionalization was the most important social movement in the second half of the twentieth century, one that affected the lives of millions of mental patients, their families, community residents, and health-care workers.

Changes in the locus of patient care were part of a psychiatric revolution that swept the country. A number of forces extant in society have been identified as causes. First, the introduction of psychotropic drugs in the mid-1950s – remarkable in their ability to attenuate flagrant symptoms and reduce the frequency of psychotic episodes – permitted psychiatrists to treat patients in the community rather than simply institutionalize them for indefinite periods of time. Second, the growth of new forms of psychotherapy in the 1960s (dealing with alcoholism, drug addiction, developmental disorders, and sexual dysfunctions) greatly expanded the definition of mental illness and its treatment on an outpatient basis. A third force for change was the new legislation in 1963 that provided funds for the construction and operation of non-hospital patient care facilities. The idea of community-based care of the mentally ill was not new, but the decades-old vision was not realized until John F. Kennedy (president of the United States 1961–3) made a historic initiative and there was strong political support for it. Fourth, the deinstitutionalization movement was hastened by the call for

patients' rights from both inside and outside the mental health professions. A series of court decisions in the late 1960s and 1970s affirmed a patient's right to refuse treatment and to due process in commitment proceedings. Finally, the rising cost of inpatient care to state governments in the 1970s and 1980s coupled with increased federal support for community care was a powerful incentive for states to shift their financial burden to Washington. The payment structure and matched funding allowances of Medicare and Medicaid, as well as the expansion of federal welfare disability programs, encouraged the transfer of elderly and poor chronically ill patients from state-supported hospitals to privately run nursing homes.

The process of deinstitutionalization involved two other goals aside from the release of hospital patients. It likewise entailed the use of alternative facilities to treat those with first-time psychiatric disorders. Before the policy and practice of deinstitutionalization, these persons would have simply been placed in mental hospitals without any clear treatment plans or discharge dates. In addition, an important objective, arguably the most difficult of the three to achieve, was the development of community-based mental health and social support services to maintain a non-hospital patient population.

Deinstitutionalization had a distinctive social philosophy. In the post-World War II period, the idea that state hospitals were inhumane warehouses and anti-therapeutic environments for the mentally ill was featured prominently in the mass media as well as in scientific literature. Former patients wrote personal accounts about the negative effects of institutionalization. Journalists, at times playing the role of pseudopatient, published scathing exposés. Social scientists, via participant observation, researched large mental hospitals and documented the widespread patient abuse, staff incompetence, deplorable living conditions, and poor treatment. The post-war era was also dominated by optimism that positive action could change social conditions. The Civil Rights Movement of the 1950s and 1960s encouraged the notion that hospitalized patients were a disenfranchised class and doors should be opened for them as well. The deinstitutionalization movement, characterized by a strong conviction that community-based care was more cost effective than institutional treatment, wedded social reformers and fiscal conservatives.

Important political actions hastened the process of deinstitutionalization. In 1963, under the provision of what is now called Supplemental Security Income, the mentally ill living in the community became eligible for federal financial assistance. This enabled patients who otherwise would be in state hospitals to stay at home, in board-and-care facilities, or in apartment hotels. Entrepreneurs, not always skilled in the management of psychiatric disorders, converted old houses and buildings into residential facilities for former patients. The passage of the Community Mental Health Centers Act the same year provided large-scale funding for community-based programs to treat released hospital patients and those with first-time psychiatric disorders. Both pieces of legislation and their amendments provided much of the financial underpinning for deinstitutionalization. Later changes in state commitment laws tightened the criteria for admission and retention and also furthered the shift from hospital to community treatment. Lastly, a 1975 landmark Supreme Court case, which ruled that non-dangerous patients who were not receiving treatment should be released if they could survive outside the mental hospital, accelerated the move toward community care.

The era of deinstitutionalization succeeded in gaining the release of a substantial proportion of hospitalized patients and in significantly reducing psychiatric admissions. However, the development of a full array of community-based mental health and social services sufficient to maintain a non-hospital patient population is the one goal that has not been realized. Various problems related to service delivery account for this. To begin with, achieving continuity of care for chronic patients outside of hospitals was inherently problematic. Treatment programs often focused on patients' immediate needs with little or no attention given to future requirements. In the early years, many proponents of deinstitutionalization believed chronicity would be abated once the negative effects of institutional living were removed. Second, the treatment needs of the mentally ill living in the community could not always be met. Before deinstitutionalization,

most hospital patients stayed for long periods of time, the rest of their lives in many cases, and there was little variation in the treatments afforded them. Today, the non-hospital population is fragmented; patients have varying degrees of chronicity, some are shuttled in and out of hospitals, many mentally disturbed are in jail, others become homeless. Few communities have been able to service the treatment needs of patients who varied greatly in diagnosis, symptomatology, functional level, and family support.

A third problem of service delivery was the difficulty of providing comprehensive care. In the hospital, psychiatric, medical, social, rehabilitative, and vocational services were offered within a single physical setting. In the community, the locus and authority for such human services were typically divided among different public and private agencies that seldom achieved effective coordination. Fourth, the most disturbed persons in the community were frequently least likely to receive psychiatric treatment. Deinstitutionalization clearly intended that the new mental health programs would serve those most severely ill. However, many agencies, both intentionally and unintentionally, selected patients for treatment who were less disturbed or disabled. Persons least likely to secure psychiatric services on their own were left to do just that. Finally, community-based care was lacking in effective measures of program outcome. Mental health administrators and clinicians seldom had reliable information concerning patient populations to be served and the effectiveness of treatments actually delivered. The statistical analysis used for program evaluation was more often than not irrelevant for the disjointed system of care that prevailed in most communities.

Aside from the problems related to service delivery, an important question is *why* community-based care or aftercare programs failed to meet the objectives of deinstitutionalization. One important reason pertains to public attitudes toward the mentally ill. Research has consistently shown that most people do not want to associate with former mental patients or the mentally ill and that these negative attitudes have changed little over the years. Opportunities for discharged patients to find satisfactory employment and housing in the community are thus limited by the public's prejudices. Deinstitutionalization occurred as a result of ideological, political, and legal forces in society, not public pressure to reintegrate former patients into communities. The public has been more willing to accept deinstitutionalization as a means of social control than treatment or rehabilitation. Former patients in nursing homes, jails, or halfway houses and board-and-care facilities in marginal neighborhoods are tolerated more than next door or at work.

A second explanation for the failure of aftercare programs deals with organizational processes within the mental health system. Sociologists have discovered that human service organizations are confronted with operational problems and compromising choices related to the establishment of priorities, acquisition of resources, adjustment of expectations, development of interorganizational networks, and rationalization of activities. Thus, state mental hospitals, which faced reduced resources in the era of deinstitutionalization, gave priority to inpatient care rather than discharge planning, and became more concerned with the number of patients discharged than their later quality of life in the community. Community mental health centers, in order to control costs and justify their effectiveness, chose to devote more of their resources to the non-chronically ill and to enroll only the best patients for their vocational rehabilitation and substance abuse programs. Chronic patients were mainly treated with medications, their need for more comprehensive services ignored. Public and private social service agencies saw the chronically ill as outside the scope of their mission and refused to treat them. The lack of continuity of care between hospitals and community agencies reflected the role adaptations professional staff workers made adjusting idealistic goals to realistic accomplishments.

The inadequacy of community-based care for the mentally ill is likewise explained through a political economy perspective. Mental patients, especially those with long-term disabilities, are part of the so-called underclass in American society, a growing army of unemployed persons, unskilled laborers, drug addicts, alcoholics, welfare recipients, illegal aliens, poorly educated racial minorities, and other incompetent or disreputable groups. Members of the underclass lack sufficient power or resources to change social conditions that affect their lives. Thus, mental patients in hospitals, nursing homes, jails, on the streets, or in community halfway houses and board-and-care homes are unlikely to effectively organize and lobby the government for changes in the mental health laws or policies. Mental patients were decidedly *not* involved in the deinstitutionalization movement that sought to help them. Community housing for the mentally ill flourished only when there was an economic incentive to provide such services to this downtrodden group.

Despite its problems and failures, deinstitutionalization has been an integral part of mental health policy in the United States for almost half a century. Its ideology of concern for the well-being of mental patients combined with the pragmatism of its promise of cost savings have probably sustained the movement over the years, often in the face of harsh criticism. Today, even with the experience of some notable program deficiencies, it is still widely assumed that community-based care for the mentally ill is intrinsically more humane and more therapeutic than hospital treatment. Support for deinstitutionalization, however, has not resulted in corresponding increases in public monies for community mental health programs. Economy-minded state officials have been willing to close state hospitals but are less willing to put the money saved into community programs for the patients they released. Advocates of deinstitutionalization have argued that dumping patients into neighborhoods ill prepared to deal with their needs does not constitute community treatment, and that the movement has not had a fair chance to demonstrate its merits since adequate public funding and program planning were lacking from the start.

The early history of deinstitutionalization offered promise to patients with chronic disorders: freedom from the sometimes inhumane conditions of public mental hospitals, reintegration with family and friends, management of their illness in community facilities. There was also hope that the new treatment programs would cure existing disorders in less chronic patients and prevent the occurrence of future illnesses among those who experience first-time psychiatric episodes. Caregivers and service providers, however, often did not distinguish between those with severe or lifelong conditions and those with less serious or intermittent disorders. Service programs during the early years were mainly designed for the latter group whose needs could be met with brief therapy and crisis interventions. The deinstitutionalization that took place failed to attend to the needs of the most severely ill and efforts at prevention failed to reduce the incidence of the most serious mental disorders. The very patients whom the movement was supposed to help, those forced out of state and county hospitals, fell through the cracks of the inadequate community service system.

In the 1980s and 1990s, one of the most important unintended consequences of deinstitutionalization was the dramatic increase in the homeless population. Inexpensive housing in large cities was unavailable and many discharged mental patients simply had no place to go and ended up living on the streets, in alleyways, or in subway caverns with other homeless people. Unable to make decisions for themselves or follow a consistent program of treatment, these novice outpatients suffered badly from a well-meaning but poorly implemented social policy. Some discharged patients no doubt benefited from community care, but others found themselves bereft of adequate food, clothing, shelter, medical care, and psychiatric treatment, the very necessities and services formerly provided to them by the hospital. As early as 1984, the American Psychiatric Association proclaimed that deinstitutionalization was a failure and a major social tragedy.

By the close of the twentieth century, more than 90 percent of the state psychiatric hospital beds that existed in 1960 were eliminated. Thanks to lawsuits by civil liberties attorneys, it is now virtually impossible to treat severely mentally ill individuals involuntarily in the hospital or the community until they commit some overt criminal act. Increasingly, state mental health officials have been abdicating their responsibility to care for disturbed persons, preferring instead to hand them over to for-profit health maintenance organizations (HMOs), who in turn eschew paying the $400 a month per patient it would take for the newest antipsychotic medications. The outcome has been predictable: a significant rise in criminal homicide. Deinstitutionalization has turned deadly, as approximately 1,000 homicides are committed each year nationwide by untreated mentally disturbed persons.

In recent years, the philosophical bases of deinstitutionalization have been reassessed. It is now generally recognized that the initial ideology of reform for hospitalized mental patients and conviction that substantial cost savings could be realized with community-based treatment were misguided. Although it is unlikely that states will ever go back to a system of care based almost totally on hospital treatment, it is apparent that state hospitals continue to perform important functions for society. Such institutions serve as backup facilities for patients who cannot be treated effectively in outpatient clinics or nursing homes. Because of their size, hospitals are able to offer specialized services unavailable in community-based programs. Decades of experience with deinstitutionalization have demonstrated that it is just as costly to provide effective and comprehensive care to mental patients with long-term disabilities in the community as in state hospitals, equally as dear for that care to be provided by public institutions as by contracts with private facilities or practitioners. Current advocates of the policy stress that humane concern for the mentally ill, not presupposed cost advantages, should motivate society in its allocation of per capita treatment expenditures.

Deinstitutionalization never realized its promise or potential because it was largely a political rather than a clinical solution to the problem of chronic mental illness. Research has shown that the lives of patients can be improved by transferring them from large institutional settings to various neighborhood residences, provided that appropriate treatment and service programs are available to them in the community. The question is whether twenty-first-century politicians will be willing to commit the necessary financial resources to clinics and outpatient facilities their twentieth-century counterparts did not.

SEE ALSO: Health Care Delivery Systems; Health Maintenance Organization; Homelessness; Hospitals; Managed Care; Mental Disorder; Social Movements; Social Services; Social Support

REFERENCES AND SUGGESTED READINGS

Bachrach, L. L. (1978) A Conceptual Approach to Deinstitutionalization. *Hospital and Community Psychiatry* 29: 573–8.

Bachrach, L. L. (1989) Deinstitutionalization: A Semantic Analysis. *Journal of Social Issues* 45: 161–71.

Bachrach, L. L. (1996) Deinstitutionalization: Promises, Problems, and Prospects. In: Knudsen, H. C. & Thornicroft, G. (Eds.), *Mental Health Service Evaluation*. Cambridge University Press, Cambridge, pp. 3–18.

Bachrach, L. L. & Lamb, H. R. (1989) Public Psychiatry in an Era of Deinstitutionalization. In: Beels, C. C. & Bachrach, L. L. (Eds.), *Survival Strategies for Public Psychiatry*. New Directions for Mental Health Services, 42. Jossey-Bass, San Francisco, pp. 9–25.

Cockerham, W. C. (2003) *Sociology of Mental Disorder*. Prentice-Hall, Upper Saddle River, NJ, pp. 295–302.

Mechanic, D. (1999) *Mental Health and Social Policy*. Allyn & Bacon, Boston, pp. 176–9.

Ozarin, L. D. & Sharfstein, S. S. (1978) The Aftermath of Deinstitutionalization: Problems and Solutions. *Psychiatric Quarterly* 50: 128–32.

Talbott, J. A. (1979) Deinstitutionalization: Avoiding the Disasters of the Past. *Hospital and Community Psychiatry* 30: 621–4.

Torrey, E. F. & Zdanowicz, M. (1998) Why Deinstitutionalization Turned Deadly. *Wall Street Journal*, August 4, p. A18.

Torrey, E. F. & Zdanowicz, M. (1999) Deinstitutionalization Hasn't Worked. *Washington Post*, July 9, p. A29.

Wegner, E. L. (1990) Deinstitutionalization and Community-Based Care for the Chronic Mentally Ill. In: Greenley, J. R. (Ed.), *Research in Community and Mental Health*, vol. 6. JAI Press, Greenwich, CT, pp. 295–324.

Deleuze, Gilles (1925–95)

Sam Binkley

Gilles Deleuze was a significant twentieth-century philosopher whose critiques of essentialism and rationalism made important contributions to theories of postmodernity and poststructuralism. The philosophical standpoint he elaborated was one which emphasized the immanent possibilities for change manifested in things themselves. Bodies, objects, ideas, and social formations all possessed potentials for difference and deviation inherent in themselves. This view contradicted that of his chief philosophical interlocutor, Hegel (and all those upholding a Hegelian dialectical tradition), in which change was viewed as the result of external encounters or "negations" imposed from without. Deleuze's philosophical project followed that of Nietzsche in emphasizing the affirmative property of things, and linking the agent with the act itself, denying traditional philosophical concepts of causality, will, and intention. Indeed, his philosophical oeuvre is defined by interrogations of the philosophical canon ranging from Plato to Nietzsche, Spinoza, Bergson, and Hume for conceptions of the world that emphasized such immanent properties of becoming and change.

These themes were developed and applied more broadly to a range of political and social arenas through books co-authored with his longtime writing partner Félix Guattari. Most notably it was through a two-part investigation of the contemporary social, cultural, and psychological nexus he termed "capitalism and schizophrenia" that Deleuzian conceptions of immanent difference were thematized and exported to other fields (Deleuze & Guattari 1977, 1987). Here Deleuze developed an identifiable nomenclature and rhetorical style whose influence extended to fields such as sociology, cultural studies, media studies, and throughout the humanities and social sciences more broadly.

Defined by Michel Foucault in the book's opening pages as an introduction to anti-fascism (not the fascism of the political state but the fascism of the mind which we as members of capitalist societies carry within us), *Anti-Oedipus* (Deleuze & Guattari 1977) provides a critique of capitalist political economy that weds post-Freudian psychoanalysis with Deleuze's thesis on the generative capacity of things. It offers an overview of desire not as a reactive (as dictated by the law of Oedipal desire) but as an active and productive capacity, capable of affirming new differences and investing new objects. Deleuze and Guattari discuss capitalism's success in denying desire its creative and affirmative quality through its incorporation into flows and chains of production governed by abstract systems (money), divorced entirely from the contexts and bodies in which they are generated. Against these limitations the book prescribes different flows of desire and production whose pattern escapes the Oedipalizing effects of capital through non-linear and schizoid lines of flight: heading off in multiple directions, refusing to remain the same, escaping capture by slipping between dominant categories which threaten to consign desire to specific territories and purposes. *Thousand Plateaus* (Deleuze & Guattari 1987) continues this interrogation, adding the phrase that has become the most widely associated with Deleuze's contribution: the *rhizome*, a root or branch that twists, knots, splits, and grows in unpredictable, non-linear directions (like a ginger root, as opposed to the linear structure of a carrot), serving as a metaphor for paths of desire, for modes of production, and movements of populations.

While his turgid and eccentric philosophic prose has drawn criticism from many sociological readers, Deleuzian thought has been influential in several areas, including postmodern social theory, where non-linear, non-teleological processes are considered as alternatives to modernization narratives of progress, social differentiation, and change (Delanda 1997). They have also been significant in theories of globalization, virtuality and the Internet, and in alternative conceptions of resistance to those provided by traditional Marxism (Hardt & Negri 2000).

SEE ALSO: Guattari, Félix; Postmodernism; Poststructuralism

REFERENCES AND SUGGESTED READINGS

Delanda, M. (1997) *A Thousand Years of Non-Linear History*. Zone Books, New York.

Deleuze, G. & Guattari, F. (1977) *Anti-Oedipus: Capitalism and Schizophrenia*. Trans. R. Hurley. Viking, New York.

Deleuze, G. & Guattari, F. (1987) *Thousand Plateaus: Capitalism and Schizophrenia*. Trans. B. Massumi. University of Minnesota Press, Minneapolis.

Hardt, M. & Negri, A. (2000) *Empire*. Harvard University Press, Cambridge, MA.

Massumi, B. (1992) *A User's Guide to Capitalism and Schizophrenia: Deviations from Deleuze and Guattari*. MIT Press, Cambridge, MA.

democracy

Stephen K. Sanderson

It is only within the past two centuries – and mostly within the past century – that genuinely democratic governments have flourished. What is democracy? Rueschemeyer et al. (1992) identify four main characteristics of the most fully developed democracies:

- Parliamentary or congressional bodies with a power base independent of presidents or prime ministers.
- The regular, free, and fair election of government officials, with the entire adult population having the right to vote.
- Responsibility of other divisions of government to the parliament or legislature.
- Individual rights and freedoms pertaining to the entire population and their general honoring.

It is important to distinguish between *formal* democracies, in which the formal apparatus of democracy exists but democratic principles are usually not upheld in practice, and *substantive* democracies, which have not only the formal machinery of democratic government, but generally consistently implement this machinery. Another important distinction is that between *restricted* democracies, or those in which the right to vote is limited to certain segments of the adult population (such as men, property owners, or whites), and *unrestricted* democracies, or those in which the entire adult population has the right to vote.

Democracy is not an all-or-none process, but rather a matter of degree. The modern democracies of North America and Western Europe are today unrestricted and substantive democracies, but all started out as restricted and, to some extent, formal democracies. The earliest modern democracies developed in the most developed societies of Western Europe and the settler colonies that hived off from Great Britain. The US was the first democracy, established in 1776. It was followed in order by Norway (1815), France (1815), Belgium (1831), the UK (1832), Germany (1848), Switzerland (1848), the Netherlands (1849), Denmark (1849), Italy (1861), Sweden (1866), and Japan (1889) (Flora 1983). Democracy has taken much longer to come to the less-developed world, much of which is still today under the control of highly autocratic and often brutally repressive regimes. However, a major new wave of democratization swept through many third world countries beginning in the 1980s (Markoff 1996; Schaeffer 1997; Kurzman 1998; Green 1999; Doorenspleet 2000). Most third world democracies, however, are still not full substantive democracies, and it may be several more decades before that is achieved.

It has long been noted that democratic government and economic development are closely linked. In an early study, Lipset (1959) used a small sample of countries and found a strong relationship between a country's level of democratization and its levels of wealth, industrialization, education, and urbanization. Later, Cutright (1963), studying 77 countries, found high positive correlations between an index of democracy and indexes of levels of communication, urbanization, and education, and a high negative correlation between democracy and the percentage of the labor force working in agriculture.

Bollen and Jackman (1985), using a sample of 100 countries, looked at the effects of the level of economic development along with several other independent variables: the degree of ethnolinguistic pluralism, percentage of the population that was Protestant, British colonial experience, and a New Nation effect (independence obtained between 1958 and 1962). Regression results showed that all five independent variables explained 58 percent of the variance in the level of democracy, but that economic development alone explained 46 percent.

Lipset et al. (1993), using a large cross-national sample, looked at the effects of several independent variables on the level of democratization: per capita GNP, British versus French colonization, political mobilization (the annual sum of protests, riots, and strikes), regime coerciveness (the ratio of military expenditure to GNP), and trade dependence (the ratio of total trade to GNP). Results showed that economic development was clearly the best predictor.

Diamond (1992) found that economic development was closely related to democracy, whether measured by per capita GNP or by the World Bank's Human Development Index (an unweighted average of literacy, life expectancy, and per capita GNP). The HDI was a somewhat better predictor. Of 17 countries at the highest level of the HDI, all 17 had governments that Diamond classified as liberal democracies. Of 11 countries at the lowest level of the HDI, all 11 had what Diamond called closed state hegemonic regimes. Diamond also reported the results of earlier regression analyses conducted with Lipset and Seong. These showed that the most powerful predictive variable was the Physical Quality of Life Index, a composite of infant mortality, life expectancy at age 1, and adult literacy.

Why should greater economic development be closely associated with democracy? At least three lines of thinking can be discerned. Marxian scholars (e.g., Szymanski 1978) have argued that democracy has been promoted by rising capitalist classes because it is the form of government most suited to their economic interests. Capitalists want, above all else, freedom of economic action, and democracy is an ideal system for promoting such freedom. The problem with this argument, however, is that the historical evidence shows that capitalists have actually been quite hostile to democracy in the form of mass suffrage because they have feared the consequences of giving the working class the vote (Rueschemeyer et al. 1992). Capitalists have generally favored *parliamentary* government, especially because they or their representatives have constituted the most prominent members of parliaments. But parliamentary government alone is a far cry from true democracy.

A second line of thinking, endorsed by such thinkers as Lipset and Diamond, is a type of modernization theory. Education and literacy promote beliefs in the importance of democratic norms. An ideology of "secular reformist gradualism," highly favorable to the development of democracy, emerges, largely as the result of higher living standards. As lower social strata become better off and better educated, they are less likely to be receptive to extremist ideologies. Economic development leads to the formation of a sizable middle class, much of which tends to work to moderate political conflict.

A third strand of thought emphasizes the resource balance between political elites and the rest of the population. Bollen (1983) notes that economic development creates a more educated and literate population that can gain access to the mass media of communication, thus allowing for increasing understanding of the political processes of their society. This increased understanding tends to generate greater demands for political representation. By the same token, a workforce that is better educated can become better organized and mobilized. In Bollen's mind the key issue is the general population's acquisition of resources that can be used to pressure political elites to accede to their demands for democracy. Tilly (2000, 2004) has taken a similar view.

In an exceptionally detailed cross-national study of democracy using 172 countries and covering the entire period from 1850 to the early 1990s, Vanhanen (1997) based his analysis on the kind of balance of resources argument discussed above. Vanhanen argues that democracy emerges when the large mass of the population acquires resources it can use to force autocratic states to open themselves up to mass suffrage and political rights. Vanhanen identifies six types of resources that contribute to democratization: size of the nonagricultural population, size of the urban population, the degree to which farms are owned by independent families, the literacy rate, the enrollment rate in higher education, and the deconcentration of nonagricultural economic resources. Vanhanen measured all of these variables for most decades between 1850 and the early 1990s, combined them into a comprehensive supervariable called the Index of Power Resources, and then correlated this index with an index of democracy. The average correlation of the Index of Power Resources

with the level of democracy for three different years (1991, 1992, and 1993) was r = .786. Correlations for earlier years were not as strong, but were still very high. Vanhanen assumed that the correlation is causal in the sense that the acquisition of power resources preceded and brought about changes in the level of democracy.

Vanhanen stopped with simple correlations, failing to control for any other variables. He also assumed that all of the six subvariables within his Index of Power Resources were of equal significance in producing democracy. Sanderson (2004) reanalyzed Vanhanen's data by looking at his six subcomponents separately. He consistently found that the best predictor of the level of democratization was the literacy rate, with the deconcentration of nonagricultural resources an important secondary predictor. Size of the nonagricultural population and size of the urban population turned out to be essentially unpredictive.

These last findings seem to contradict the conclusions of the best comparative-historical (nonquantitative) study of democracy ever undertaken, that of Rueschemeyer et al. (1992). They found that the factor most critical to democracy was the level of industrialization and thus the size of the working class, which became an organized political force that struggled to establish democratic institutions, especially the right to vote. Democracy developed earliest and most fully in those societies with the largest working classes and latest and least in those societies with the smallest working classes. In these latter societies the landlord class was still powerful and the peasantry politically weak. Landlords were vehemently opposed to democracy because the key to their economic success was labor-repressive agriculture, which democracy would obviously undermine. However, with industrialization, the role of the landlord class in society declined and the role of industrialists and workers increased, thus removing a major barrier to democratization. In the third world today, landlords still play a major economic role in many societies, which is perhaps the main reason that democracy has advanced only little in many of these societies.

Sanderson (2004) suggests that his findings are, in fact, not incompatible with those of

Rueschemeyer et al. (1992). Indeed, they are complementary; it is just that the latter authors have omitted a crucial variable. Industrialization and working-class formation were crucial to democracy, Sanderson argues, but workers have to be made politically aware and ready to engage in political action. Literacy – itself largely a product of the development of mass primary education – provided the key. Literate workers could read newspapers and political pamphlets and could communicate with each other about what they read. This seemed to be critical to the working class's struggle for political incorporation.

In the most recent cross-national study of democracy, which spanned the entire period between 1800 and 1999, Wejnert (2005) compared the relative roles of internal social and economic development and diffusionary effects coming from other societies. Regression results showed that diffusionary effects, especially the location of a country within a world region packed with democratic countries and the degree of participation of a country in economic and political networks containing largely democratic countries, were much greater than internal developmental forces. However, it is not clear what to make of these findings, since Wejnert's study is one of the first to take diffusionary effects into account and her findings have not yet been replicated. Moreover, her finding that literacy was unrelated to democracy is extremely curious in light of Sanderson's (2004) finding that it was the most important predictor of democratization.

What is clear is that democracy has historically been closely tied to economic development and that it has been steadily expanding on a global scale. Whether democracy is promoted more by a country's internal economic and social development or by its connections to other democratic countries (or some combination of the two), it seems reasonable to predict that democratization will be a continuing, if not continuous, trend.

SEE ALSO: Citizenship; Democracy and Organizations; Global Justice as a Social Movement; Globalization and Global Justice; Human Rights; Social Movements, Participatory Democracy in; Welfare Regimes

REFERENCES AND SUGGESTED READINGS

Bollen, K. A. (1983) World-System Position, Dependency, and Democracy: The Cross-National Evidence. *American Sociological Review* 48: 468–79.

Bollen, K. A. & Jackman, R. W. (1985) Economic and Noneconomic Determinants of Political Democracy in the 1960s. *Research in Political Sociology* 1: 27–48.

Cutright, P. (1963) National Political Development: Measurement and Analysis. *American Sociological Review* 28: 253–64.

Diamond, L. (1992) Economic Development and Democracy Reconsidered. In: Marks, G. & Diamond, L. (Eds.), *Reexamining Democracy: Essays in Honor of Seymour Martin Lipset*. Sage, Newbury Park, CA, pp. 93–139.

Doorenspleet, R. (2000) Reassessing the Three Waves of Democratization. *World Politics* 52: 384–406.

Flora, P. (1983) *State, Economy, and Society in Western Europe, 1815–1975*, Vol. 1. Campus Verlag, Frankfurt.

Green, D. M. (1999) Liberal Moments and Democracy's Durability: Comparing Global Outbreaks of Democracy – 1918, 1945, 1989. *Studies in Comparative International Development* 34: 83–120.

Kurzman, C. (1998) Waves of Democratization. *Studies in Comparative International Development* 33: 42–64.

Lipset, S. M. (1959) Some Social Requisites of Democracy: Economic Development and Political Legitimacy. *American Political Science Review* 53: 69–105.

Lipset, S. M., Seong, K.-R., & Torres, J. C. (1993) A Comparative Analysis of the Social Requisites of Democracy. *International Social Science Journal* 136: 155–75.

Markoff, J. (1996) *Waves of Democracy: Social Movements and Political Change*. Pine Forge Press, Thousand Oaks, CA.

Rueschemeyer, D., Stephens, E. H., & Stephens, J. D. (1992) *Capitalist Development and Democracy*. University of Chicago Press, Chicago.

Sanderson, S. K. (2004) World Democratization, 1850–2000: A Cross-National Test of Modernization and Power Resource Theories. Paper presented at the annual meeting of the American Sociological Association, San Francisco, August.

Schaeffer, R. K. (1997) *Power to the People: Democratization Around the World*. Westview Press, Boulder.

Szymanski, A. (1978) *The Capitalist State and the Politics of Class*. Winthrop, Cambridge, MA.

Tilly, C. (2000) Processes and Mechanisms of Democratization. *Sociological Theory* 18: 1–16.

Tilly, C. (2004) *Contention and Democracy in Europe, 1650–2000.* Cambridge University Press, New York.

Vanhanen, T. (1997) *Prospects of Democracy: A Study of 172 Countries.* Routledge, London.

Vanhanen, T. (2003) *Democratization: A Comparative Analysis of 170 Countries.* Routledge, London.

Wejnert, B. (2005) Diffusion, Development, and Democracy, 1800–1999. *American Sociological Review* 70: 53–81.

democracy and organizations

David Courpasson

Still a controversial issue, the idea that the "civilian" world might be becoming more democratic is juxtaposed with an opposite trend with respect to the organizational world. As Rousseau and Rivero, among others, put it: "Although we are increasingly likely to be governed by democratic political systems, our workplaces are seldom democratic" (2003: 116). The increasingly dominant corporate power (Bernstein 2000), the persistence and refurbishment of hierarchy and bureaucratic systems (Courpasson & Reed 2004), the endless reproduction of corporate elite (Ocasio 1994; Courpasson 2004; Davis et al. 2003) are all trends highlighting the fact that the post-bureaucratic dream of decentralized power and of people's participation in the political decisions within organizations might be gone.

The supposedly post-September 11 shift in the global power balance does not explain by itself the apparently legitimate use of strong central powers in the political structures of most western countries. In other words, the emergence of a "culture" of threat and terror is not exclusively the product of late modern patterns of civilization or of tragic and unprecedented events. Likewise, in the business world, the concentration of power is an old phenomenon (see, for instance, in Ocasio 1994) which is not exclusively related to the threatening and hectic movements of markets and the dynamics of capitalism. The wavering balance between democratic and oligarchic

tendencies is one of the most ancient political features of societies.

Addressing the complex issue of democracy in the context of organizations requires us to go beyond these partial accounts in order to make the connection between organizational models and the functioning of contemporary democratic societies. There are important questions relating to the elective affinities between the meaning of democracy and its diverse facets, and government as a complex and intermingled set of values and mechanisms.

THE MEANING AND MEANINGS OF DEMOCRACY

There are scores of available and relatively acceptable definitions of the concept of democracy. So numerous are they that the concept itself is in danger of becoming one of the most popular "buzzwords" of organization studies. As a means of clarifying this conceptual "hodgepodge," we suggest adopting a twofold approach to understanding democracy: a political version and a competitive version.

Usually, democracy is defined as both a form of rule (the sovereignty of the people) and a symbolic framework within which this rule is exercised (such as individual liberty) (Mouffe 2000). This pertains to the well-known duality within studies on democracy: the *liberal tradition*, according to which what counts is the rule of law and the respect of individual freedom encompassed in democratic regimes, and the *democratic tradition*, which privileges the notion of equality and the identity between governors and the governed. These traditions, when confronted, unveil the unassailable tension between liberty and equality. Dahl reminds us that for Tocqueville, the major phenomenon threatening democracy is that equality will crush liberty, that political equality is likely to destroy liberty, "because equality facilitates majority despotism, it threatens liberty" (1985: 9).

Therefore, the *political* definition of democracy leads to envisaging democratic politics not as the search for an unreachable consensus, but as an "agonistic confrontation" (Mouffe 2000: 9), necessitating the creation of a pluralistic body of actors. According to Mouffe, the main question of democratic politics "becomes then not how to eliminate power, but how to constitute forms of power which are compatible with democratic values" (2000: 22). In short, the political perspective on democracy argues that democracy is not the absence of domination and the mere diffusion of social powers in the (organizational) body, but the genuine attempt to establish institutions which can limit and eventually contest domination. Dahl (1971) proposes to analyze the concrete forms of democracy through the notion of "polyarchy." Polyarchy is an approximation of democracy, where a permanent activity of institutional design and "engineering" (Poggi 1972) helps contestation to take roots within the social body.

The political perspective of democracy also implies that equality is not automatically taken for granted. It cannot exist without inequality, without exclusion. As Mouffe puts it, democratic equality "requires the political moment of discrimination between 'us' and 'them'" (2000: 44). Obviously, this view of democracy rejects the idea of "deliberative democracy" which can be found extensively in the organizational literature, especially under the auspices of the "managerial revolution" or of "post-bureaucratic" management. The underlying argument of this latter perspective is that politics is identified with the exchange of arguments "among reasonable persons guided by the principle of impartiality" (Mouffe 2000: 86), which obliterates the possibility of legitimate struggles and debates between "adversaries."

For the *competitive* approach to democracy, a key characteristic of democratic regimes is the existence of a permissible opposition. This regards public contestation and political contestation (Dahl 1971: 4) as natural features of the system. Democracy is therefore a competitive regime. Ultimately, Dahl and the whole Tocquevillean tradition of which he is a part conceptualize democracy as being constituted by at least two dimensions: public contestation and the right to participate, i.e. the "inclusiveness" of the political regime. In that perspective, Dahl (1971: 8) defines polyarchy as a "highly inclusive" and an "extensively open to public contestation" regime, the closest to concrete expressions of democracy.

The contribution of the competitive explanation is to clearly separate the generation of democratic regimes at the national level with the circumstances of the organizational level. As Dahl (1971: 13) puts it, "while polyarchies may be competitive at the national level, a great many of the subnational organizations, particularly private associations, are hegemonic or oligarchic."

Wilde (1978) completes this definition by adding a more "procedural" nuance to the competitive aspect of bureaucracies. Democracies are, according to him, largely defined by "those rules that allow (though they do not necessarily bring about) genuine competition for authoritative political roles. No effective political office should be excluded from such competition, nor should opposition be suppressed by force" (p. 29). The corollary of this view is that organizations could be considered as democracies insofar as they develop "infra-democratic" systems (p. 33), i.e., structural ingredients (comprising the distribution of power, specific political institutions, and social structure) which render democracy practically possible. But they are also "experiential" systems, characterized by the commitment of people to these very rules of competition and consent. We are clearly close to the seminal view of Montesquièu, when in *The Spirit of the Laws* he defines a political regime through the expectations and perceptions of individuals toward the governors, and through the degree to which power is concentrated.

Behind the scenes of the competitive framework lurks the notion of equality. This derives from Tocqueville's analyses on the tendency of equality to contribute to the degenerative process of democracy: "In democracies, not only are servants equal among themselves; one can say that they are in a way the equals of their masters" (2000: 549). This is the result of the credible potential for anybody (including the servant) to become a master himself. Democracy as competition is therefore connected to a vision of the temporary character of social hierarchies. But simultaneously, it requires from governors to invest constantly in the social fabric of their legitimation. As Tocqueville puts it, "servants are not sure that they should not be the masters and they are disposed to consider whoever commands them as the unjust usurper of their right" (p. 553).

Tocqueville's concerns go to the heart of the debate between bureaucratic and post-bureaucratic models. The design of the latter model aims explicitly to shatter the bureaucratic image of the unassailable bureaucratic hierarchy (Heckscher 1994). But once again, Tocqueville's reminder is timely: this type of hierarchical relationship, generating rivalries and endless struggles, necessitates the design of a constraining administration stipulating to each "what he is, what he can do, or what he should do" (Tocqueville 2000: 553). A rejuvenated bureaucracy, freshly legitimized by the requirement to "close the debates," arises from the very functioning and core values of democracy.

At the same time, both the political and competitive definitions of democracy offer another alternative. By saying that, we put forward the idea that organizations could be theorized as fundamentally antagonistic places, where a plurality of values and interests is never solved through a rational consensus (a notion dear to liberal democratic theories of management; see, e.g., Osborne & Gaebler 1992), nor through a pure domination or hegemony. It might be thought of as a complex and hybrid oligarchy, permanently producing acts of power and constituting itself as a political community through these very acts of power. A complex oligarchy is a political order of organizations based on certain forms of precarious and contestable dominations, always vulnerable and striving relentlessly to solidify themselves. It is precisely because of this precariousness that organizations can be seen partly as (very imperfect) democracies, "competitive oligarchies" to take Dahl's expression.

THE DEMOCRATIC PROBLEM: OLIGARCHIC DRIFT AND THE PRODUCTION OF INTERMEDIATE BODIES

At least since Tocqueville, we know democracy faces two major problems. First, the development of despotic/oligarchic trends spawned by the "circular" nature of democracy. Second, the consecutive necessity for democratic regimes to develop an institutional design likely to keep government from transmogrifying into despotism.

No principle, no procedural requirements, nor "absolute rights can prevent tyranny from emerging" (Dahl 1985: 18). In other words, any governing body, majority or minority, may use democratic processes to destroy democracy itself. Democratic regimes are prone to self-destruction (Linz & Stepan 1978). As Poggi (1972: 49) puts it, despotism is a degeneration of the inertial tendencies of democracy and not an intentional and implicit goal of a governing elite. To Tocqueville, oligarchy reproduces itself through the processes of democratization, what Poggi calls the circularity of democracy. As individual concerns are increasingly "privatized," the leaders must take powerful decisions in order to move away from despotic tendencies. In other words, oligarchs sustain their power by developing democratic principles and peculiar intermediate groups of political actors. But it is the central power which determines and delineates the type of groups, their prerogative and who, within these groups, is likely to reach the "inner circles" (Useem 1984).

According to Tocqueville, the very dynamics of equality might turn democracy into a new species of tyranny, a "breeding ground for mass-despotism" (in Dahl 1985: 31). The Tocquevillean perspective outlines three major dangers to which democracies are prone: the atomization of societies into isolated individuals; the emergence of authoritarian regimes; and the support by people of these centralized forms of administration. Democratic collapse arises from the sometimes amazingly overwhelming public support toward authoritarian regimes. Moreover, the ascent of dictatorial forms of government stems often more from the persistence of inequalities than from an excess of equality, fragmenting the citizenry into hostile camps and enhancing confidence for a dictatorship (Dahl 1985).

Mild despotism emerges therefore from two parallel mechanisms. First, the illusions generated by the consensual vision of deliberative governments. In other words, consensus might be the very expression of hegemony and "the crystallization of [asymmetric] power relations" (Mouffe 2000: 49). The reconciliatory move observable in the post-bureaucratic school of thought (Heckscher 1994), by insisting on the necessary initialization of debates, on the importance of speech acts (Benhabib 1996: 9), on symmetry, equality, and consensus, obliterates the fact that democratic politics in organizations is mostly about the negotiation of paradoxes and the articulation of precarious solutions to these paradoxes (Mouffe 1999). Consensus is necessary but it must be accompanied by dissent, otherwise hegemonic regimes are likely to appear. This possible drift is also due to the fact that the very competitive essence of democracy implies a high degree of insecurity for those in governing positions. As Lipset et al. (1956: 10) put it, "the more truly democratic the governing system, the greater the insecurity." In other words, what Poggi (1972) terms "status insecurity" supposes that organizations need to be combined with oligarchic modes of selection. Oligarchic principles provide arguments to justify discrepancies between individuals, the "us and them" principle in Mouffe's terms. For Tocqueville, any mass of equals and atomized individuals needs an oligarchy to avoid being permanently threatened by anarchy. Under a tutelary oligarchy, people feel the obligation to cooperate, at least because they share similar concerns, fears, and weaknesses. Dresher (1968: 6–7) adds his voice by arguing that democracies should be defined as limited egalitarian ideologies. Thisx presupposes certain inequalities and authority–obedience relationships as "necessary inequalities within general equality." Dresher, using the Tocquevillean framework, insists upon the influence of the emergence of a "politically disinterested individualism" arising from a democratic appeal to "material interests"; as a consequence, the danger of drifting toward despotic regimes comes not mostly from the "tyranny of the majority" but from the "apathy of the masses" (p. 42).

In sum, any concrete democratic structure must define whether the central government should be arbitrary or moderate, i.e., does it "oppose or allow the existence of nongovernmental centers of power" (Poggi 1972: 41). This leads us to our second point: the production of intermediate political bodies.

As Rousseau and Rivero (2003: 119) suggest, it might seem easier to promote democratic practices in organizations than in broader social bodies; consensus regarding tasks and purposes, socialization capacities, educational systems, and the focus on work provide cultural "cornerstones" in most organizations, whatever their size. Through recent corporate post-bureaucratic upheavals, new forces sustaining democratic values and practices have appeared. These include the decentralization of organizing and information, the transformation of certain bases of power distribution, the broadening of the array of stakeholders, and the concomitant awareness of broader interdependencies and mutual impact of acts of power in "network organizations." But democracy has also to struggle with the persistence of hierarchy. The egalitarian aspects of democracy are hampered by the overwhelming competition among individuals, and with the contradictory effects of mobility on the organizational cohesiveness necessary to collective decision-making and deliberative systems (Dahl 1985; Rousseau & Rivero 2003).

From these contradictory forces arises the absolute necessity for organizations to invent certain forms of "institutional engineering" (Poggi 1972) likely to tip the balance in the democratic direction. The idea is to counter the effects of the emergence of a "consumerist view of politics" (p. 45), which is the major threat to democracy as it facilitates the political monopoly of a specific oligarchy. Institutional engineering implies the creation of intermediate groups that prevent the displacement of social ties by more transitory relationships. For Tocqueville, intermediate groupings aim to create local powers that act as a counterbalance to the political concentration at the top of organizations and societies. They also aim to intensify individual commitments and enhance the construction of strong, efficient, and reliable internal elites. This institutional differentiation in the political system rests upon a "constitutional design" creating a distinction between a relatively small set of stable laws and an extensive set of peripheral laws subject to contestation, modification, or abolition. What rules are to become steady is a crucial issue for democracies to perpetuate. It implies that going further into the distinction between governmental and administrative issues, the former will affect the interests of the organization as a whole, the latter will affect primarily locally individuals.

The interest for organizations in installing local intermediate powers is especially important in times of economic deprivation which affect large numbers of people. In the context of societies, we know that under difficult conditions, individuals can be subject to

the seductive appeals of politically cynical leaders, without the will to take a hand in governmental affairs (Poggi 1972). For bitterness,
feelings of insecurity or injustice, they could
renounce any ambition and commitment, or
withdraw exclusively into the private sphere,
which could shatter social ties and make the
social body collapse. Intermediate bodies are
also a means for leaders to shed light on the
benefits and interests of the collective body in
times when individuals could prefer to neglect
shared values and common political and cultural frames to step into the chilling dynamics
of despotism. In the context of organizations,
the political indifference or apathy, and the
resulting focus on self-fulfillment that one can
observe (which is largely a result of the threatening and competitive "spirit" of contemporary liberal organizations; see Courpasson 2005),
could lead to this type of dynamic: brushing off
the ethical side of leaders' legitimacies, people
could prefer to depend politically on strong and
efficient centers of power, distributing the
fruits of economic success, whatever the means
used. The possibility of a political professionalization of leadership, foreshadowed a long time
ago by Michels, might therefore doom the political aspirations of the forthcoming generation
of workers and executives. Tocqueville's prophesy would then prove to be right. The urgent
necessity of establishing strong intermediate
(professional) powers could prevent organizations from becoming slowly and unobtrusively
apolitical entities where the democratic idea
would be restricted to the upbeat discourses
of utopian thinkers and scholars.

CORPORATE ELITE PRODUCTION AND THE DYNAMICS OF DEMOCRACY

We have adopted a political framework to make
sense of the dynamics of organizational regimes:
the structures of power, the organization of coercion, the formation of coalitions and the production of political elites provide, in this
perspective, the most relevant guides to the
explanation of these dynamics (Tilly 1973: 447).
  More particularly, understanding the emergence and production of a political regime supposes to focus on "the incumbents and their
actions, their formulation of the agenda for the
regime, their way of defining problems and

their capacity to solve them, the ability of the
pro-regime forces to maintain sufficient cohesion to govern" (Linz & Stepan 1978: 40). We
suggest now that this has important implications for understanding the stability of political
structures of organizations. Such factors are
likely to inform both the definitions of democracy and the accounts regarding the evolution
of democratic regimes toward oligarchy.
  As Lipset et al. (1956) remind us, the insecurity of leadership status is one of the cornerstones of democracies. However, a broad range
of literature suggests firmly that contemporary
corporate elites are perpetuating themselves
relatively smoothly. This poses an interesting
counterfactual for the supposed "circulation of
power" or "circulation of control" put forward by
some authors (Ocasio 1994; Ocasio & Kim 1999).
  Two major phenomena might help account
for the apparently seamless reproduction of
corporate elites. First, the social fabric of a
"class-wide" principle (Useem 1984), according to which a certain number of mechanisms,
especially interlocking directorates (Mizruchi
1996), facilitate the production of both cohesiveness among elite members and educational
ingredients helping the selection and the socialization of coopted individuals, according to the
well-known "small world" phenomenon (Davis
et al. 2003). In that view, a corporate elite can
be represented as a powerful network of powerful individuals sustaining strategies of "power
entrenchment" through the very management
of the interlocks and friendship ties (Ingram &
Roberts 2000). Second, the permanence of an
"upper-class" principle (Useem 1984), according to which the major ingredient of elite stability is its embeddedness in a specific social
milieu of established wealthy families, "sharing
a distinct culture, occupying a common social
status, and unified through intermarriage and
common experience in exclusive settings"
(p. 13). At the corporate level, the power of
social closeness and similarity has been pin-
pointed as a strong determinant of CEO succession and appointment (Westphal & Zajac
1995). Other studies have suggested that intra-
organizational mechanisms were also likely to
produce endogenously an elite body through
selective education and socializing mechanisms,
as well as through the production of specific
internal professions (Courpasson 2004).

If we follow Allen (1974), we could easily argue that the conjunction of these external and internal mechanisms is downright anti-democratic, as it generates an "increasingly pervasive and integrated structure of elite cooptation among major corporations" (p. 404), restraining per se the quality of the competition and the principle of elite insecurity which has been put forward as the pillar of democratic regimes.

We have argued that the relationship between democracy and organizations is extremely ambivalent. A certain number of contemporary forces are clearly promoting democracy in the workplace. Others are clearly hampering any possibility of implementing true participation, contestation, and inclusiveness within organizations. When related to democracy, organizations appear more and more as regimes, i.e., "political forms ordering symbolically and structurally a set of social relations" (Mouffe 2000), organizing human coexistence and managing inequality between people and their relations of subordination. In organizations, "the stability of any democracy depends not on imposing a single unitary loyalty and viewpoint but on maintaining conflicting loyalties and viewpoints in a state of tension" (Crossman 1956). According to this general political definition of organizations, three major lines of inquiry may be suggested to better understand the relationship between democracy and the organizational world.

First, the study of the paradoxical roles played by contemporary oligarchies in the shaping of future organizations should be developed. Under a theory of political pluralism, it becomes urgent to understand that, in contemporary organizations, democracy and oligarchy are not necessarily opposite models. Oligarchy can become the very ferment of the production of a fragmentation of the complex social body. This can enable people not only to be related to the larger organization, but also to be affiliated with or loyal to subgroups within the organization (Lipset et al. 1956: 15), and therefore, to keep a close hand on their own fates and decisions. Contemporary processes such as the (re)emergence of professions and collegial forms in organizations (Lazega 2000) suggest undoubtedly that organizations could be politically shaped in a "polycratic" fashion, to take Weber's expression.

Second the study of democracy in/for organizations cannot neglect the determination of political regimes by the specific profiles of business leaders. For instance, does the development of global corporations serve to develop a "global corporate elite"? In contrast, do the stiff competition and the uncertainties deriving from the growing multiplicity of stakeholders necessitate the generation of a more "parochial elite" deeply committed to the interests of individual companies but not fulfilling the political dimensions of the "managerial class"? At any rate, studying leadership as a profession, as some seminal studies have shown (Selznick 1957), more than as a practice could help scholars to better understand the very reasons why, maybe, key stakeholders do not consider developing democracy is in their interest.

Third, it is obviously crucial for organizational scholars to keep on studying the dynamics of authority within organizations, especially to understand why, while most people consider organizations have too much power over their members, very few think the latter should exercise more power in the workplace (Rousseau & Rivero 2003: 130). In other words, is democracy "thin" or "weak" because of a shared vision of legitimate authority within organizations? If yes, business leaders would have achieved a political tour de force. If not, we should give more attention to why the apparent zone of indifference (Barnard 1938) might be larger than ever in the contemporary workplace.

Other issues are of great importance, such as the link between the rise of the knowledge economy and the increasingly differential treatment of knowledge workers. The greater individual employability of these workers requires a rethinking of assumptions of the latent power asymmetry between firms and employees, and to what extent this dynamic has the capacity to enhance democratic practices or whether it forecloses any possibility of the development of a durable commitment of workers in the political affairs of the organizations for whom they work and in which they live.

CONCLUSION

We have argued that the current political dynamics of organizations and of surrounding societies bear the seeds of mild despotic regimes, as Tocqueville predicted two centuries ago. At the same time, we have suggested that the incumbent economic leaders cannot brush aside the effects of recent corporate scandals in the engineering of the power structures of organizations. Moreover, recent investigations suggest that some deeply rooted patterns of corporate elite production could have been shattered for at least two decades (Cappelli & Hamori 2004).

Without envisaging that democratic organizations could miraculously emerge out of the shadows of corporate scandals, we think the quest for accountability and responsibility could be one of the political touchstones of organizations of the twenty-first century. The constitution of a notion of *political performance* (Eckstein 1969) applied to organizations could help to find a new equilibrium for the excessive dominance of economic variables in the contemporary notion of survival. A politically efficient government is not necessarily the most democratic, but that which is capable of sharing out what is produced by a collective endeavor.

Organization studies on democracy are influenced by the post-war optimism about the durability of democracies, once established. They are mostly grappling with the eternal question of why organizations are not democratic. We think organizational scholars should leave this question to jump to two complementary questions: (1) How far is democracy necessary to the functioning of organizations? (2) What are the contemporary concrete hybrids which are shaping the political structures of tomorrow's organizations? It is by understanding the complexity and fragility of these political hybrids that organizational scholars will be able to help future business elites to avoid some mistakes of the past.

SEE ALSO: Alliances; Culture, Organizations and; Democracy; Industrial Relations; Organizations

REFERENCES AND SUGGESTED READINGS

Allen, P. (1974) The Structure of Interorganizational Elite Cooptation: Interlocking Corporate Directorates. *American Sociological Review* 39: 393–406.

Barnard, C. (1938) *The Functions of the Executive.* Harvard University Press, Cambridge, MA.

Benhabib, S. (1996) *Democracy and Difference: Changing Boundaries of the Political.* Princeton University Press, Princeton.

Bernstein, A. (2000) Too Much Corporate Power? *Business Week,* September 11: 144–58.

Cappelli, P. & Hamori, M. (2004) The Path to the Top: Changes in the Attributes and Careers of Corporate Executives, 1980–2001. *Working Paper 10507,* National Bureau of Economic Research, Cambridge, MA.

Courpasson, D. (2004) Contested Oligarchies. *Organization Science* Winter Conference, Steamboat Springs, CO, February.

Courpasson, D. (2005) *Soft Constraint: Liberal Organizations and Domination.* Copenhagen Business School Press, Copenhagen.

Courpasson, D. & Reed, M. I. (2004) Introduction: Bureaucracy in the Age of Enterprise. *Organization* 11(1): 5–12.

Crossman, R. H. S. (1956) On Political Neuroses. *Encounter* 2: 66.

Dahl, R. A. (1971) *Polyarchy: Participation and Opposition.* Yale University Press, New Haven.

Dahl, R. A. (1985) *A Preface to Economic Democracy.* University of California Press, Berkeley.

Davis, G. F., Yoo, M., & Baker, W. E. (2003) The Small World of the American Corporate Elite, 1982–2001. *Strategic Organization* 1(3): 301–26.

Dresher, S. (1968) *Dilemmas of Democracy: Tocqueville and Modernization.* University of Pittsburgh Press, Pittsburgh.

Eckstein, H. (1969) Authority Relations and Governmental Performance: A Theoretical Framework. *Comparative Political Studies:* 269–325.

Heckscher, C. (1994) Defining the Post-Bureaucratic Type. In: Heckscher, C. & Donnellon, A. (Eds.), *The Post-Bureaucratic Organization: New Perspectives on Organizational Change.* Sage, London.

Ingram, P. & Roberts, P. W. (2000) Friendships Among Competitors in the Sydney Hotel Industry. *American Journal of Sociology* 106(2): 387–423.

Lazega, E. (2000) *The Collegial Phenomenon.* Oxford University Press, Oxford.

Linz, J. J. & Stepan, A. (Eds.) (1978) *The Breakdown of Democratic Regimes: Crisis, Breakdown, and Reequilibration.* Johns Hopkins University Press, Baltimore.

Lipset, S. M., Trow, M. A., & Coleman, J. S. (1956) *Union Democracy: The Internal Politics of the International Typographical Union.* Free Press, Glencoe, IL.

Michels, R. (1915) *Political Parties: A Sociological Study of the Oligarchical Tendencies of Modern Democracy.* Hearst's International Library, New York.

Mizruchi, M. S. (1996) What Do Interlocks Do? An Analysis, Critique, and Reassessment of Research on Interlocking Directorates. *Annual Review of Sociology* 22: 271–98.

Mouffe, C. (Ed.) (1999) *The Challenge of Carl Schmitt*. Verso, London.

Mouffe, C. (2000) *The Democratic Paradox*. Verso, London.

Ocasio, W. (1994) Political Dynamics and the Circulation of Power: CEO Succession in US Industrial Corporations, 1960–1990. *Administrative Science Quarterly* 39: 285–312.

Ocasio, W. & Kim, H. (1999) The Circulation of Corporate Control: Selection of Functional Backgrounds of New CEOs in Large US Manufacturing Firms, 1981–1992. *Administrative Science Quarterly* 44: 532–62.

Osborne, D. & Gaebler, T. (1992) *Reinventing Government*. Addison Wesley, Reading, MA.

Poggi, G. (1972) *Images of Society: Essays on the Sociological Theories of Tocqueville, Marx, and Durkheim*. Stanford University Press, Stanford.

Rousseau, D. M. & Rivero, A. (2003) Democracy, a Way of Organizing in a Knowledge Economy. *Journal of Management Inquiry* 12(2): 115–34.

Selznick, P. (1957) *Leadership in Administration*. Row, Peterson, Evanston, IL.

Tilly, C. (1973) Does Modernization Breed Revolution? *Comparative Politics* 5(3): 424–47.

Tocqueville, A. de (2000) *Democracy in America*. Trans. H. C. Mansfield & D. Winthrop. University of Chicago Press, Chicago.

Useem, M. (1984) *The Inner Circle*. Oxford University Press, New York.

Westphal, J. D. & Zajac, E. J. (1995) Who Shall Govern? CEO/Board Power, Demographic Similarity, and New Director Selection. *Administrative Science Quarterly* 40: 60–83.

Wilde, A. W. (1978) Conversations Among Gentlemen: Oligarchical Democracy in Columbia. In: Linz, J. J. & Stepan, A. (Eds.), *The Breakdown of Democratic Regimes: Crisis, Breakdown, and Reequilibration*. Johns Hopkins University Press, Baltimore.

demographic data: censuses, registers, surveys

Mark Mather

Population censuses, registers, and surveys are the primary sources of demographic data, including information about the size, composition, and characteristics of a population or population subgroups. A census is an enumeration of all households in a well-defined territory at a given point in time. Population registers are systems of continuous registration, maintained by certain countries, to keep demographic records of individuals. Surveys are used to collect detailed data on a particular subject from a sample or subset of the population. All three sources of data – censuses, registers, and surveys – are often used to monitor changes in population size and composition.

CENSUSES

For hundreds of years, censuses have been used to collect demographic, social, and economic information about individuals and households. The first modern census was conducted in Quebec in 1666, but there are much earlier references to census taking in the Bible and in early civilizations in China, Egypt, India, and Rome. The first US census was conducted in 1790, followed by the United Kingdom and France in 1801.

After World War II, the United Nations encouraged all countries to conduct national censuses, and today, more than 90 percent of the world's population is covered by a census enumeration. Recent censuses conducted in China and India – arguably the most ambitious censuses ever taken – together counted more than 2 billion people. The rich data from population censuses are used not only to monitor demographic changes within countries, but also to keep track of global changes in the size and characteristics of the world's population. In the United States, data from the decennial census are used to apportion Congressional seats in the US House of Representatives, draw new boundaries for legislative districts, and allocate billions of dollars in federal funds to states and local areas. Census data are also widely used by researchers, business groups, and local planners, who use them to monitor population trends, the demand for goods and services, and social and economic inequalities between groups.

Conducting a high-quality, nationwide census is a complex and expensive process – depending on the size, geographical distribution, and level of cooperation of the population – and often requires years of planning. Census administrators need to develop an address list, prepare detailed maps, prepare for advertising or outreach efforts, develop questionnaires (often in multiple languages), conduct tests of questionnaire items, and recruit and train census enumerators. Once the demographic data have been collected, the census staff need to analyze the data and prepare data products and reports for public use.

Census data can be collected through mail-out questionnaires, by telephone, or through personal interviews. In the US census, which is conducted every 10 years, a questionnaire is mailed to every household in the United States. Census enumerators follow up with households that do not return their forms by telephone or with personal interviews. In the United States and in many other countries, census response rates have declined in recent decades because of growing concerns about privacy and confidentiality. The Netherlands has not conducted a national census since 1971 because of growing concerns among Dutch citizens about privacy and rights violations. Today, the Netherlands relies on a combination of surveys and administrative registers (see "Registers," below) to collect demographic data.

No census is wholly accurate. One source of error relates to the difficulty in counting every household and resident in a population. Residents who fear the government or outsiders, speak non-native languages, or live in mobile or complex households are the most likely to be missed in a census. In the United States, past censuses have also overlooked a disproportionate share of children and minorities, resulting in an undercount of those groups. In developing countries, census counts tend to be less accurate for populations with low levels of literacy and poor transportation networks. Other errors in census data can result from respondents' inability or unwillingness to provide correct information or errors made in data collection or processing. In a few countries, census figures have been manipulated to bolster the numbers of a specific ethnic group or region.

In order to test the accuracy of census results, the US Census Bureau conducted special post-enumeration surveys (see "Surveys," below) after the 1990 and 2000 Censuses. Census population counts were compared with independent estimates from these surveys for different geographical areas and for subgroups of the population. Census counts were also compared with 2000 population estimates derived through analyses of birth, death, and migration records. These comparisons have been useful in evaluating census undercounts, particularly for minority groups.

Census questionnaires are typically completed by the household head or "reference" person and may include questions about age, gender, marital status, place of birth, relationship, educational level, occupation, religion, race/ethnicity, or other demographic characteristics. Information is collected for each member of the household. There are two methods used to conduct a census: in a "de facto" enumeration, people are counted at their actual place of residence at the time the census is conducted. In a "de jure" enumeration, residents are assigned to their "usual place of residence." The United Kingdom counts people using the de facto method, while Canada, Mexico, and the United States use a de jure approach.

REGISTERS

Countries with national population registers keep records of individuals from the time of birth (or immigration) to death (or emigration) and update the record over time with life events. In general, population registers are used to record four basic demographic events: births, deaths, marriages, and migration. However, registers vary in the type of demographic data that are collected and how those data are used. The earliest registration systems were maintained by parishes and date back to the 1300s. National population registers were first established in Europe during the fourteenth and fifteenth centuries. Today, the most complete population registers can be found in Denmark, Finland, Japan, the Netherlands, Norway, and Sweden. What distinguishes these countries from most others is that they collect and store information about demographic events in a central government office, instead of using separate systems of birth, death, and marriage registration.

Bryan (2004) notes that these "universal" registers are less common than "partial" registers that are set up for specific administrative purposes. For example, several US agencies, including the Social Security Administration, the Department of Homeland Security, and the Internal Revenue Service, maintain large administrative data files that can be considered partial registers.

Population registers are most often used for government administrative purposes, but can also be used to monitor changes in a country's population size and composition, keep track of trends in fertility and mortality, or select random samples of individuals from the population. Data from pre-industrial registers in Europe have been used for historical demographic research on family structure, fertility, and mortality. Population registers can also be used as a substitute to conducting a national census. The main advantage of a national register is timeliness; demographic events are recorded on a continuous basis, rather than once every 5 or 10 years.

Population registers are expensive to maintain, however, and require a high level of cooperation in order to produce high-quality data. Universal registers are probably not feasible in a country like the United States, where there is growing public concern about invasion of privacy and protecting confidentiality.

VITAL REGISTRATION SYSTEMS

Like population registers, vital registration systems collect data on a continuous basis, but are generally limited to information about births, deaths, marriages, and divorces. Data on vital events are drawn from birth certificates and other forms that are completed at the time the events occur. Most developed countries have fairly complete vital registration systems, while developing countries are more likely to rely on surveys to collect the information. Along with basic statistics about the number of vital events that occur in a given month or year, vital registration systems often collect more detailed information on age, racial and ethnic composition, marital status, and other characteristics.

In the United States, the National Center for Health Statistics (NCHS) compiles and disseminates information about vital events based on data received from state health departments.

NCHS data are often used in combination with census or survey data to produce demographic rates and ratios (e.g., fertility and mortality rates) and to monitor national, state, and local demographic trends.

SURVEYS

Unlike censuses and registers, which enumerate the entire population, a survey is conducted for a sample or subset of the population. Surveys are generally used to collect detailed information about a specific topic, such as labor force participation, health, economic status, religious affiliation, or life course events. Surveys can also be used as a primary or supplemental source of demographic data in countries without a regular, high-quality national census, population register, or vital registration system. While most census data are collected by the government, surveys are collected by a variety of governmental and private organizations.

The quality of survey data is dependent on many of the same factors that affect census data quality – response rates, respondents' knowledge and level of cooperation, and errors made in data collection or processing – but survey data quality is also linked to the size and design of the sample. Surveys are often administered using a "probability" or random sample of the population, so that findings can be generalized to the population as a whole. Data based on a probability sample are subject to "sampling error," which indicates the extent to which sample estimates might differ from actual population characteristics.

Modern surveys were first introduced in the Gallup Poll in the 1930s, and were focused on measuring public opinion. The US Current Population Survey (CPS) dates back to the mid-1940s and was the first survey to collect detailed social, demographic, and economic information about the US population. In the 1950s and 1960s many countries conducted "knowledge, attitudes, and practice" (KAP) surveys to measure contraceptive use. The World Fertility Survey (WFS) revolutionized demographic analysis during the 1970s and 1980s with detailed surveys of women's fertility and contraceptive use in over 60 countries.

Today, the Demographic and Health Survey (DHS), modeled after the WFS, asks detailed questions about fertility, family planning, infant mortality, and maternal and child health.

Surveys are generally divided into two types: cross-sectional and longitudinal. Cross-sectional surveys, like the CPS and DHS surveys, collect information from a cross-section of the population at a given point in time. Cross-sectional surveys provide a snapshot of the population and are best for descriptive analyses, while longitudinal surveys ask questions of people at two points in time and are more suitable for measuring causal relationships between variables.

Worldwide, one of the largest surveys is the US decennial census "long form." While the census "short form" is mailed to every household in the United States, the long form questionnaire is mailed to approximately one out of every six households – about 5 million households nationwide. The long form includes detailed questions about social and economic characteristics of the population, while the census short form includes only a subset of questions on age, gender, race, ethnicity, and household tenure.

The United States is conducting a new survey called the American Community Survey (ACS), designed to replace the census long form in 2010. Instead of having to wait 10 years for long form data, the ACS will provide demographic estimates for the American population each year. The ACS is the first US survey to provide continuous data on social, economic, and demographic characteristics for states and local areas.

SEE ALSO: Age, Period, and Cohort Effects; Demographic Techniques: Population Projections and Estimates; Demography: Historical; Descriptive Statistics; Fertility: Transitions and Measures; Mortality: Transitions and Measures; Random Sample; Survey Research

REFERENCES AND SUGGESTED READINGS

Bryan, T. (2004) Basic Sources of Statistics. In: Siegal, J. S. & Swanson, D. A. (Eds.), *The Methods and Materials of Demography*. Elsevier Academic Press, San Diego, pp. 9–41.

Edmonston, B. & Schultze, C. (Eds.) (1995) *Modernizing the US Census*. National Academy Press, Washington, DC.

Hollingsworth, T. H. (1969) *Historical Demography*. Cornell University Press, Ithaca, NY.

McFalls, J. A. (2003) Population: A Lively Introduction, 4th edn. *Population Bulletin* 58, no. 4.

Pollard, A. H., Yusef, F., & Pollard, G. N. (1990) *Demographic Techniques*, 3rd edn. Pergamon Press, Elmsford, NY.

Siegal, J. S. (2002) *Applied Demography*. Academic Press, San Diego.

Weeks, J. R. (2005) *Population: An Introduction to Concepts and Issues*, 9th edn. Wadsworth/Thomson Learning, Belmont, CA.

demographic techniques: decomposition and standardization

Prithwis Das Gupta

Demographers are often interested in comparing rates (e.g., birth rates, mortality rates) in populations cross-nationally and/or over time. Interpreting difference between rates requires an understanding of the various factors that comprise that rate. Crude birth rates, for example, depend not just on the fertility of women of childbearing age, but also the proportion of the population that consists of such women. In such cases, in which the overall rate of a phenomenon for a population depends on a number of factors, a detailed comparison of two such rates from two different populations can be made in two distinctly different but closely related ways. One way is to see how the overall rates would change if one of the factors varied as it did in the two populations, while the other factors were kept at the same levels. The rates obtained in this way are called the standardized rates with respect to the unchanged factors, and the process is called *standardization*. The other way of comparing the two overall rates is to break the difference between these two rates into additive components constituting the effects of the factors involved. The effects of the factors obtained in this way are called the decomposed effects and the process is called *decomposition*. These two processes of standardization and decomposition are closely linked because, if they are developed correctly, the difference between the two standardized rates from the two populations corresponding to the only factor that has changed should be equal to the effect of the same factor in the decomposition process. Authors who have contributed to this subject include Kitagawa (1955), Cho and Retherford (1973), Das Gupta (1978, 1991, 1993), and Kim and Strobino (1984)

AN EXAMPLE: THE RATE AS THE PRODUCT OF TWO FACTORS

This example illustrates the use of standardization and decomposition by examining the respective roles that two factors play in constituting a rate. The Crude Birth Rate (CBR) is defined as the number of live births per 1,000 members of the population. In 1981, Austria had a CBR of 12.512 and Chile had a CBR of 32.845. The difference between the two rates is a substantial 20.333.

However, the CBR can also be calculated by multiplying the General Fertility Rate (GFR: the number of births per 1,000 women aged 15–49), which is represented by α in this example, by the proportion of women aged 15–49 in the total population, represented by β, so that:

$$CBR = \alpha\beta.$$

In 1981, Austria had a GFR (α) of 51.767 and the proportion of women aged 15–49 in the population (β) was .24170. For Chile, the numbers were $\alpha = 84.905$ and $\beta = .38684$.

The CBRs for Austria and Chile can be standardized on the β factor (i.e., the proportion of the population that is made up of women aged 15–49). This is done by multiplying the average of the two countries' βs by the respective α. The β-standardized rates for Austria and Chile are:

β-standardized CBR (Austria)

$= .5 * (\beta(\text{Chile}) + \beta(\text{Austria})) * \alpha(\text{Austria})$

$= .5 * (.38684 + .24170) * 51.767$

$= 16.269$

β-standardized CBR (Chile)

$= .5 * (\beta(\text{Chile}) + \beta(\text{Austria})) * \alpha(\text{Chile})$

$= .5 * (.38684 + .24170) * 84.905$

$= 26.684$

The α-effect – the amount of the difference between CBRs that is attributable to differences in GFRs – is the difference between the two β-standardized CBRs: $26.684 - 16.269 = 10.415$.

Similarly, the α-standardized rates for Austria and Chile are, respectively,

α-standardized CBR (Austria)

$= .5 * (\alpha \,(\text{Chile}) + \alpha \,(\text{Austria})) * \beta \,(\text{Austria})$

$= 16.517$

α-standardized CBR (Chile)

$= .5 * (\alpha \,(\text{Chile}) + \alpha \,(\text{Austria})) * \beta \,(\text{Austria})$

$= 26.435$

The $\beta - \text{effect} = 26.435 - 16.157 = 9.918$

The α-effect (10.415) is 51.2 percent of the total difference in CBRs (20.333), and the β-effect (9.918) is 48.8 percent of the total. These standardized rates demonstrate that 51.2 percent of the difference between the CBRs of Austria and Chile for 1981 can be attributed to the difference in their general fertility rates and the remaining 48.8 percent can be attributed to the difference in their proportions of women aged 15–49 in the total population. Although Austria and Chile had quite different crude birth rates in 1981, standardizing the rates shows that almost half of this difference is due to the different age structures in the two countries.

This technique can similarly be extended to the *product* of three or more factors (Das Gupta 1991, 1993).

OTHER FORMS OF RATES

Standardization and decomposition can also be used to analyze rates that are *functions of two factors*. For example, the General Fertility Rate (GFR) per woman aged 15–44 can be thought of as a function of two factors, viz., the number of births per married woman aged 15–44 (α) and the ratio of single to married women in the age group 15–44 (β). In this case, the GFR can be written not as a simple multiplication of two factors, but as a function

$$\text{GFR} = \alpha/(1 + \beta)$$

of the two factors. Still, the technique is similar to that used for standardized rates that are the product of two factors; for example, β-standardized GFR is computed by averaging two GFRs using the same α and different βs. This technique can be extended to functions of more than two factors (Das Gupta 1991, 1993).

In many situations, a factor may be represented by several numbers. For example, in a crude birth rate, seven age-specific fertility rates together may be considered one factor (α) and seven numbers of women in the age groups as proportions of the total population the other factor (β). Such factors may be called *vector-factors* (as opposed to scalar-factors). Standardization and decomposition techniques can be applied to vector-factors. For example, β-standardized crude birth rate is computed by the sum of the products of all the age-specific fertility rates and the average proportions of the population in that age range for the two populations.

Most of the papers on standardization and decomposition published so far perform standardization and decomposition techniques on *cross-classified data* involving one or more factors. Unlike the situations in the preceding examples, the decomposition in this case involves the effect of the differences in the cell-specific rates, called the rate-effect, in addition to the effects of the factors. This might be done to compare subgroups of the population. For example, standardizing the age structure of two groups of women – those with one child and those with four or more – allows a more meaningful comparison of expressed future fertility preferences. When this is done as a one-factor cross-classified case with a single factor effect and rate effect, it is very similar to the case of two vector-factors. However, the treatment of cross-classified data with two or more factors is very different, and is discussed in Das Gupta (1991, 1993).

CONCLUSION

The four broad categories of decomposition – product of two or more factors, function of two or more factors, function of two or more vector-factors, and rates from cross-classified data – should cover virtually all cases of decomposition of the difference between two rates for any number of factors. In the absence of general methods of decomposition to be used under various circumstances, social scientists have devised in the past their own ad hoc methods to handle their respective problems. Although their approaches have produced meaningful results, sometimes they have been less than satisfactory in terms of mathematical rigor and elegance.

The problem of decomposition is different from the problem of regression analysis. In the decomposition problem with cross-classified data, the rate effect may not always decrease (it may even increase) with the addition of a new factor, whereas in the regression analysis the addition of each independent variable to the equation increasingly explains the variation in the dependent variable. For example, it is very likely that, in a regression analysis, poverty status would be explained significantly by race, but that the difference in the race composition in two years would not be an important factor in explaining the difference in the poverty rates in those years.

The decomposition problem can also be handled using statistical modeling approaches such as log-linear analysis and the purging method involving errors (Clogg & Eliason 1988; Liao 1989) instead of the above mathematical approaches of solving unknowns from algebraic equations. The modeling approach is handicapped by the fact that it is often too complicated to be of any practical use even for data involving only two factors. Also, this approach leads to several widely different sets of results depending on the type of purging used and it is not clear how to justify choosing one set over all others.

Unlike the statistical modeling approach, the method presented decomposes the difference between two rates into additive main effects and does not involve any interaction effects. This elegance is achieved not by ignoring the parts in the total difference that other models might label interactions, but by fully accounting for the total difference in terms of main effects, and thereby distributing the so-called interactions among the main effects. This distribution does not change the conclusions about the relative importance of the factors, it only simplifies the picture.

The effects of factors do not necessarily imply any causal relationships. They simply indicate the nature of the association of the factors with the phenomenon being measured. There might be some hidden forces behind the factors that are actually responsible for the numbers we allocate to different factors as effects, but identifying those forces is beyond the scope of the decomposition analysis.

When there are more than two populations to be compared, the decompositions can be carried out more than once by taking two populations at a time. However, this procedure may lead to internally inconsistent results. For example, the effects of the factor α in the comparison of populations 1 and 2, and of populations 2 and 3, may not add up to the α-effect when populations 1 and 3 are compared. A unique way of achieving consistency in the effects based on the multiple populations being compared, without bringing in an exogenous population as standard, is provided in Das Gupta (1991, 1993).

SEE ALSO: Demographic Techniques: Population Projections and Estimates; Demographic Techniques: Population Pyramids and Age-Sex Structure; Fertility: Transitions and Measures; Mortality: Transitions and Measures

REFERENCES AND SUGGESTED READINGS

Cho, L. J. & Retherford, R. D. (1973) Comparative Analysis of Recent Fertility Trends in East Asia. *Proceedings of IUSSP International Population Conference* 2: 163–81.

Clogg, C. C. & Eliason, S. R. (1988) A Flexible Procedure for Adjusting Rates and Proportions, Including Statistical Methods for Group Comparisons. *American Sociological Review* 53: 267–83.

Das Gupta, P. (1978) A General Method of Decomposing a Difference Between Two Rates Into Several Components. *Demography* 15: 99–112.

Das Gupta, P. (1991) Decomposition of the Difference Between Two Rates and Its Consistency When More Than Two Populations Are Involved. *Mathematical Population Studies* 3: 105–25.

Das Gupta, P. (1993) *Standardization and Decomposition of Rates: A User's Manual*. US Bureau of the Census, Current Population Reports, Series P23–186, Washington, DC.

Kim, Y. J. & Strobino, D. M. (1984) Decomposition of the Difference Between Two Rates with Hierarchical Factors. *Demography* 21: 361–72.

Kitagawa, E. M. (1955) Components of a Difference Between Two Rates. *Journal of the American Statistical Association* 50: 1168–94.

Liao, T. F. (1989) A Flexible Approach for the Decomposition of Rate Differences. *Demography* 26: 717–26.

demographic techniques: event history methods

Steven Martin

Event history analysis is a term used in sociology for numerous statistical methods that use information about *whether* and *when* an individual experiences an event. Almost any social phenomenon can be thought of as an event that happens to an individual, whether that individual is (for example) a woman having a third child, a city experiencing a race riot, or a state legislature passing women's suffrage. It is not surprising, then, that as computer software has made event history techniques easier to use since the 1980s, researchers have found many imaginative applications for these techniques.

Sociologists use the term event history analysis to describe models for duration data, but similar models are used in other disciplines with different names and slightly different terminologies. For example, models for duration data are called survival analysis by health scientists, duration analysis by economists, and failure-time analysis by engineers. Many of the original and ongoing developments in duration modeling come from the health sciences, and some of the terms used in event history analysis (such as *risk* and *hazard*) reflect this heritage.

EVENT HISTORY DATA

Event history data generally require three pieces of information. These are *whether* an individual experienced an event, *when* an individual who experienced an event experienced that event, and *when* the last valid observation came for an individual who was "censored" – that is, for an individual who had not yet experienced the event when the last observation was made.

Data for event history analysis can be collected and assembled in a variety of ways. In survey research, event history data are usually obtained by asking respondents to remember when events occurred in their lives. Traditionally, such retrospective data come from standard lists of survey questions. Examples would be: "Have you ever been married?" and "What year did your first marriage begin?" Increasingly, however, survey researchers have found that respondents do better at recalling long past events or difficult-to-remember events using *event history calendars* that allow the respondents to map several timelines at once (cf. Belli et al. 2001). For example, a welfare history calendar could include timelines for landmark events, residence changes, changes in family structure, employment changes, and use of entitlement programs. The increased use of event history calendars in survey research is one indication of the growing range of social questions being addressed through event history analysis.

AN EVENT HISTORY MODEL

Once the event history data have been organized, there are a number of event history models to analyze the results in a familiar regression-style framework. Commonly used models include proportional hazard models for continuous-time data. In such models, the outcome variable is the *hazard* or *rate* of the event of interest. The hazard is defined as the conditional probability that an event occurs in a given time interval (given that it has not already occurred), divided by the length of the time interval. An example would be a rate (or "hazard") of .03 per month hazard of returning to welfare for single mothers who have just left welfare.

For continuous time data, the conditional probability of an event in a given time interval is $P(t, t + \Delta t)$, where t is the start of a time interval and $t + \Delta t$ is the end of the time interval. The time interval Δt is defined to be vanishingly small, and the hazard function takes the following form:

$$h(t) = \lim_{\Delta t = 0} \frac{P(t, t + \Delta t)}{\Delta t}$$

Besides $h(t)$, other commonly used symbols for the hazard function include $r(t)$ and $\lambda(t)$.

The general form of the proportional hazard model is as follows:

$$h(t) = \exp(\gamma(t) + \beta_1 x_1 + K + \beta_k x_k),$$

where $\gamma(t)$ is some function that describes how the rate of the event changes over time (the "*duration dependence*"), x_i are a set of explanatory variables, and β_i are a set of coefficients to describe how the explanatory variables predict differences in the hazard rate.

A proportional hazard model differs from a standard regression model in three notable respects. The first difference is that the coefficients are all exponentiated, so the explanatory variables are defined to have multiplicative rather than additive effects on the hazard. Second is the inclusion of $\gamma(t)$ to allow the hazard to vary as a function of time. The notion that the hazard is a function of time forces the researcher (usually) to choose a functional form for the duration dependence based on theoretical criteria or simple observed patterns. The duration dependency also forces the researcher to define a starting time t_0. In many hazard models t_0 is implicitly obvious, but in other hazard models t_0 can be quite arbitrary. The last notable difference between a standard regression model and a proportional hazard model is the lack of an error term in a proportional hazard model; hazard models are estimated by maximum likelihood procedures rather than least squares procedures.

Continuous-time event history models bear a strong resemblance to logistic regression models, which examine *whether* an individual experiences an event. Because a hazard model adds information on *when* events occur, the explicit time dimension makes it possible to determine the order of changes in explanatory variables and changes in the outcome variable. Establishing the time order of events is critical to building causal interpretations from observed social patterns. Another advantage of hazard models is the full use they make of the available data. Event history models allow one to distinguish between two events that happened at different durations. A final advantage of event history models over traditional logistic regression models is that event history models enable the researcher to draw some information from individuals who could only be observed for part of the time they were at risk of the event ("censored" cases).

Event history models also have unique weaknesses. One is the problem of unmeasured heterogeneity. Any control variables left out of an event history model will distort the baseline duration function $\gamma(t)$ and bias the coefficients for the key explanatory variables to some extent. Many researchers have developed complex estimation procedures to correct for problems of unmeasured heterogeneity, but the statistical fixes themselves often rest on tenuous assumptions. For a description of problems of unmeasured heterogeneity see Vaupel and Yashin (1985). Another problem is that of non-proportional hazards. The proportional hazard model assumes that covariates have the same effect on the outcome variable across all possible durations of exposure, and this is simply not the case for many social phenomena. The problem of non-proportional hazards can be remedied fairly easily by interacting the covariate of interest with the duration function.

AN EXAMPLE

One example of an application of event history analysis comes from demography. The subsequent fertility of teen mothers has been a topic of social interest due to concerns that early births may lead to rapid repeat births, a particular social concern when the teen mothers are not married. One can test for such a difference using data from the June 1995 Current Population Survey (CPS), with a sample of 2,952 US women born in the years 1965 to 1970. Standard life-table procedures indicate that 23.5 percent of teen mothers in the sample had a second birth within 24 months of the first birth, compared to only 19 percent of mothers with a first birth at age 20 or older. An application of a proportional

hazard model can show whether this difference is statistically significant, and whether this difference is evident at all birth intervals or only at short birth intervals.

A popular variant of the proportional hazard model is the Cox regression model, in which the duration function $\gamma(t)$ is not estimated directly (Cox 1972). The Cox model implicitly controls for duration since the first birth, with rates of second births very low immediately after a first birth, rising rapidly to a peak rate at about 3 years postpartum, and declining thereafter. In Cox regression models, the researcher need not specify a baseline duration function. The model controls for race and ethnicity, and includes a dichotomous variable that identifies women with a teen first birth. Finally, to identify possible non-proportional effects of time, a series of interactions between a teen first birth and duration since first birth are also added in Model 2.

Results using the Stata statistical package are shown in Table 1. The first model shows coefficients for age at first birth, averaged across all durations since the first birth, plus controls for race/ethnicity. In the first model, the coefficient for a teen first birth is small (.08) and not statistically significant. This coefficient shows the *overall* effect of a teen first birth on the rate of a subsequent birth, but the effect may not be even (or proportional) across time (or duration) since the first birth. For non-proportional results, look to the second model. The "main effect" of a teen first birth is essentially zero (.00); this coefficient refers to the comparison durations of the third to sixth years postpartum. However, there is a statistically significant *non-proportional interaction* effect in the second year postpartum, indicating that the monthly hazard of a subsequent birth increases by a factor of $\exp(.28) = 1.32$ times in the second year after a first birth. This means that teen mothers' second birth rates are much higher in the second year postpartum than we would expect from teen mothers' second birth rates at longer durations. Note also the marginally statistically significant *negative interaction* for teen mothers in the seventh and later years postpartum, perhaps indicating very low second birth rates at long durations.

From this analysis one can infer that the overall rate of second births is similar for teen and

Table 1   Coefficients from Cox regression models predicting the monthly hazard of a second birth

Variable	Model 1: Proportional effect of age at first birth	Model 2: Non-proportional effects of age at first birth
Age at first birth		
19 or younger	.08 (.05)	.00 (.07)
20 or older (comparison group)	–	–
Age at first birth* duration since first birth		
19 or younger*1st year postpartum		−.11 (.27)
19 or younger*2nd year postpartum		.28** (.10)
19 or younger*3rd–6th years postpartum (comparison duration)		–
19 or younger*7th and later years postpartum		−.47* (.23)
Race/Ethnicity		
Hispanic	.15* (.07)	.14* (.07)
Non-Hispanic black	.04 (.07)	.03 (.07)
Non-Hispanic white (comparison group)	–	–
Other non-Hispanic	.30** (.11)	.30** (.11)

Source: June 1995 Current Population Survey (CPS).

Standard errors are in parentheses. *P*-values are shown by stars. ** $p < .01$ * $p < .05$

non-teen mothers, but the exact timing of those second births might be much sooner for teen mothers than non-teen mothers. Hence, the techniques of event history modeling provide some justification to social concerns about closely spaced second births among teen mothers.

OTHER EVENT HISTORY MODELS

There is a large and growing number of variants on event history models. The Cox proportional hazard model represents only one type of proportional hazard model; there are many other proportional hazard models that explicitly define the duration dependency $\gamma(t)$. Furthermore, the expanded use of event history models has led to increased use of models for repeated events, events with more than one possible outcome, and events with more than one possible origin. Such complicated event patterns often arise in analyses of political events (Box-Steffensmeier & Zorn 2002) and life course studies (Wu 2003).

There are also types of event history models that are not based on the hazard function.

Whereas proportional hazard models use as an outcome the hazard of an event, *accelerated failure time* models use as an outcome the expected time to the event. A set of methods called *discrete time* methods are useful when event times are measured in large units such as years. The issue of long time intervals in event history data is important because commonly used surveys increasingly suppress information about the month and day of events to protect the privacy of survey respondents.

To learn more about the variety of event history models and their uses, the reader should refer to specialized texts on the subject. Useful treatments for social scientists can be found in Yamaguchi (1991) and Blossfeld and Rohwer (2002), and a more general treatment can be found in Kalbfleisch and Prentice (2002). Many readily available software packages have modules for estimating basic to moderately complicated event history models, including the Cox regression model. Allison (1995) describes in detail various techniques for event history analysis in SAS. Other popular programs include SPSS, Stata, and S-Plus. Researchers have also developed a number of statistical packages for estimation of non-standard event history models of various sorts, including CTM (Yi et al. 1987), TDA (Blossfeld et al. 1989), and aML (Lillard & Panis 2000). As event history analysis continues to develop and evolve, researchers will no doubt continue to write new programs and expand the capabilities of the existing programs.

SEE ALSO: Demographic Data: Censuses, Registers, Surveys; Demographic Techniques: Life-Table Methods; Fertility: Transitions and Measures; Life Course Perspective

REFERENCES AND SUGGESTED READINGS

Allison, P. D. (1995) *Survival Analysis Using the SAS System: A Practical Guide*. SAS Institute, Cary, NC.

Belli, R. F., Shay, W. L., & Stafford, F. P. (2001) Event History Calendars and Question List Surveys. *Public Opinion Quarterly* 65: 45–74.

Blossfeld, H. & Rohwer, G. (2002) *Techniques of Event History Modeling: New Approaches to Causal Analysis*. Lawrence Erlbaum, Mahwah, NJ.

Blossfeld, H., Hammerle, A., & Mayer, K. U. (1989) *Event History Analysis*. Lawrence Erlbaum, Hillsdale, NJ.

Box-Steffensmeier, J. M. & Zorn, C. (2002) Duration Models for Repeated Events. *Journal of Politics* 64(4): 1069–94.

Cox, D. R. (1972) Regression Models and Life Tables (with discussion). *Journal of the Royal Statistical Society* B34(2): 187–220.

Kalbfleisch, J. D. & Prentice, R. L. (2002) *The Statistical Analysis of Failure Time Data*, 2nd edn. Wiley, New York.

Lillard, L. & Panis, C. J. (2000) *aML Multiprocess Multilevel Statistical Software, Release 1.0*. EconWare, Los Angeles.

Vaupel, J. W. & Yashin, A. (1985) Heterogeneity's Ruses: Some Surprising Effects of Selection on Population Dynamics. *American Statistician* 39(3): 176–85.

Wu, L. (2003) Event History Models for Life Course Analysis. In: Mortimer, J. & Shanahan, M. (Eds.), *Handbook of the Life Course*. Kluwer Academic/Plenum, New York, pp. 477–502.

Yamaguchi, K. (1991) *Event History Analysis*. Sage, Newbury Park.

Yi, K., Honoré, B., & Walker, J. (1987) CTM: A Program for the Estimation and Testing of Continuous Time Multi-State Multi-Spell Models. NORC/ERC and University of Chicago.

demographic techniques: life-table methods

Robert Schoen

A life table describes the survival of a hypothetical group of persons from birth, through successive ages, to the death of the last member. In doing so, it shows the implications of a set of mortality rates for the probability of surviving from one age to another, and provides useful summary measures such as the expectation of life at birth. Beyond its wide use in studies of mortality, the life table has been used in analyses of marriage, divorce, contraceptive use, and many other topics where it is valuable to examine how rates of decrement reduce the number of persons in a closed group.

The life table dates back to the seventeenth century. In 1662, John Graunt advanced the first, rather crude, table based on English experience. In 1694, Edmund Halley (of comet fame) constructed a life table for Breslau (now Wroclaw, Poland), adding actuarial functions to facilitate the calculation of life annuities. Life tables are now available for nearly all countries, and are routinely produced by government statistical offices, insurance companies, and academic demographers. Life tables describe the mortality experience of a population, facilitate population projections, and are central to calculating the costs of life insurance and life annuities.

Mortality (death) rates are the basis of most life tables. Demographers typically use death rates of the form

$$M(x, n) = D(x, n)/P(x, n) \qquad (1)$$

where age-specific death rate $M(x, n)$ reflects mortality between ages x and $x + n$ (or more precisely from exact age x to the instant before the attainment of exact age $x + n$), $D(x, n)$ gives the number of deaths in the population between the ages of x and $x + n$, and $P(x, n)$ is the number of persons in the population between the ages of x and $x + n$. Rates in the form of equation (1) are known as occurrence-exposure rates, because they relate the number of deaths (occurrences) to the number of persons at risk of dying (i.e., the exposed population). Death rates are generally calculated separately by sex, as male and female mortality patterns differ. Complete life tables show age in single years up to some high age (100 or over), but most life tables are "abridged," and show ages 0, 1, and every fifth year from 5 to at least 85. Age 1 is shown because mortality at age 0 is very different from mortality at ages 1 to 5. Given contemporary survivorship, many recent abridged life tables go to age 90 (or higher).

To start the life table, a "radix" value is chosen to establish the size of the life-table cohort, where that cohort is the hypothetical group of persons, closed to migration, whose survivorship is described by the table. Denoting the number of persons in the life-table cohort who survive to exact age x by $l(x)$, the radix value, represented by $l(0)$, is generally set at 100,000. Essentially that radix indicates that the data are considered reliable to about five significant digits. Life tables based on small datasets sometimes start with a radix of 1,000, while insurance company life tables, based on extensive and detailed data, have used radix values of 10,000,000.

The central problem in life-table construction is to transform death rates into probabilities of dying, and thus generate the number of survivors to each age in the table. Let us define $d(x, n)$ as the number of deaths in the life-table cohort between the ages of x and $x + n$. Because the life-table cohort is a closed group, we have

$$l(x + n) = l(x) - d(x, n) \quad (2)$$

or that the number surviving to exact age $x + n$ is the number surviving to exact age x less the number of deaths between those ages. Using equation (2), we can write the probability of dying between ages x and $x + n$, $q(x, n)$, as:

$$q(x, n) = d(x, n)/l(x) \quad (3)$$

In terms of life-table functions, the death rate in equation (1) can be written:

$$M(x, n) = d(x, n)/L(x, n) \quad (4)$$

where $L(x, n)$ is the number of person-years lived by the life-table cohort between the ages

of x and $x + n$. (A person-year is one year lived by one person.) Finding death probabilities from rates is thus equivalent to finding the number of person-years lived in an interval in terms of the number of survivors to different exact ages.

Many ways of transforming rates to probabilities have been used in life-table construction. One simple approach is to assume that the survivorship function, $l(x)$, is linear between ages x and $x + n$. That yields the solution:

$$q(x, n) = n\,M(x, n)/[1 + (n/2)\,M(x, n)] \quad (5)$$

A second approach is to assume that the survivorship function is exponential within each age interval. In that case,

$$q(x, n) = 1 - e^{-n\,M(x, n)} \quad (6)$$

While the linear assumption in equation (5) is usually accurate for 5-year age intervals in a mortality-only life table, the exponential assumption in equation (6) is not. However, the frequently used Reed–Merrell modification, that is:

$$q(x, 5) = 1 - \exp[-5\,M(x, 5) - \{M(x, 5)\}^2] \quad (7)$$

generally yields an acceptably accurate abridged life table.

Two other life-table functions are commonly encountered. $T(x)$ is the total number of person-years lived above exact age x, and is thus the sum of the L values from age x through the highest age in the table. The life expectancy at age x, $e(x)$, is given by:

$$e(x) = T(x)/l(x) \quad (8)$$

The average number of years a person age x will live is the total number of years lived above age x by the life-table cohort divided by the number of persons in the cohort who survive to age x.

Given a method for relating rates and probabilities, survivorship $[l(x)]$ values can be found for all ages from equations (2) and (3), and person-year $[L(x, n)]$ values can be found from equation (4). The $T(x)$ and $e(x)$ values follow

Table 1 Abridged life table: US females, 1996

Age interval	Proportion dying	Of 100,000 born alive		Stationary population		Average remaining lifetime
Period of life between two exact ages stated in years	Proportion of persons alive at beginning of age interval dying during interval	Number living at beginning of age interval	Number dying during age interval	In the age interval	In this and all subsequent age intervals	Average number of years of life remaining at beginning of age interval
(1)	*(2)*	*(3)*	*(4)*	*(5)*	*(6)*	*(7)*
x to x + n	q(x, n)	l(x)	d(x, n)	L(x, n)	T(x)	e(x)
0–1............	0.00659	100,000	659	99,435	7,907,507	79.1
1–5............	0.00135	99,341	134	397,043	7,808,072	78.6
5–10..........	0.00083	99,207	82	495,812	7,411,029	74.7
10–15.........	0.00093	99,125	92	495,426	6,915,217	69.8
15–20.........	0.00220	99,033	218	494,654	6,419,791	64.8
20–25.........	0.00242	98,815	239	493,488	5,925,137	60.0
25–30.........	0.00311	98,576	307	492,128	5,431,649	55.1
30–35.........	0.00430	98,269	423	490,336	4,939,521	50.3
35–40.........	0.00608	97,846	595	487,848	4,449,185	45.5
40–45.........	0.00858	97,251	834	484,325	3,961,337	40.7
45–50.........	0.01269	96,417	1,224	479,247	3,477,012	36.1
50–55.........	0.02036	95,193	1,938	471,421	2,997,765	31.5
55–60........	0.03150	93,255	2,938	459,363	2,526,344	27.1
60–65.........	0.05068	90,317	4,577	440,808	2,066,981	22.9
65–70.........	0.07484	85,740	6,417	413,497	1,626,173	19.0
70–75.........	0.11607	79,323	9,207	374,780	1,212,676	15.3
75–80.........	0.17495	70,116	12,267	321,360	837,896	12.0
80–85.........	0.27721	57,849	16,036	250,275	516,536	8.9
85 and over...	1.00000	41,813	41,813	266,261	266,261	6.4

Source: Adapted from US National Center for Health Statistics (1998).

from the L(x, n) and from equation (8). Special procedures are needed at ages under 5 and to close out the table. Readers interested in making a life table are referred to the discussions in Preston et al. (2001) and Schoen (1988).

Table 1 shows a life table for US females, 1996. It is a period life table, in that it is based on rates observed during a single year (or period). Cohort life tables, which follow the experience of actual birth cohorts, have been calculated, but are much less common because they require data over a long time interval. The M(x) column is not shown in the table, but the age-specific life-table death rates can readily be found using equation (4).

As is commonly the case, there are 100,000 persons in the life-table cohort. Life expectancy at birth is 79.1 years. Since 659 persons die at age 0, the probability of dying before attaining age 1 is .00659. Some 90,317 persons survive to attain age 60 where, on average, they will live another 22.9 years. At age 85, only 41,813 persons remain alive. Their probability of dying is 1, but on average they will live another 6.4 years.

The mortality patterns shown in the table are rather typical of contemporary low-mortality populations. Japanese females, the population that currently has the lowest known mortality, have an expectation of life at birth approaching 85 years, and some select subpopulations have been found with even longer life expectancies. Longevity in low-mortality populations has been steadily increasing in recent years, and no limiting life expectancy is in sight.

The life table can be seen as a population model that goes beyond the experience of a single birth cohort. Consider a long series of birth cohorts, each of l(0) births uniformly distributed over the year, exposed to an unchanging regime of age-specific death rates. After 120 or so years, a stationary population will result, one that is constant in both size and age composition. Each year there are l(0) deaths in the stationary population, d(x, n) of them between the ages of x and x + n. There are l(x) persons attaining every age x, L(x, n) person-years lived between ages x and x + n and, at any time, L(x, n) persons between the ages of x and x + n. The L(x, n) function thus has two distinct interpretations: the number of person-years lived by each cohort between the ages of x and x + n, and the number of persons in that segment of the stationary population. The total number of persons in the stationary population is T(0), and its crude death rate is always l(0)/T(0) or 1/e(0). Each year, behavior in the stationary population reproduces the lifetime experience of one life-table birth cohort.

The basic life-table model has been generalized in a number of ways. The table need not follow a birth cohort – any closed group will do. For example, numerous analyses have been done examining attrition in a marriage cohort, where time is represented by duration of marriage rather than age.

A common extension is to recognize more than one cause of exit (or decrement) from the life-table cohort. Multiple causes of death are probably the most common example. However, studies have also been made of birth cohorts subject to the risks of mortality and first marriage, marriage cohorts subject to mortality and divorce, and many other subjects. Multiple causes of decrement are easily recognized. The total life-table decrement function, d(x, n), is simply apportioned to the different causes in the same proportion as observed decrements. A cause-of-death life table can reflect the probability of ever dying from a specified cause.

A further extension is the "cause eliminated" or "associated single decrement" life table. This model considers the hypothetical question of what survivorship would be if a particular cause of decrement were eliminated. The simplest way to calculate such tables is to assume that age–cause-specific *rates* (not probabilities) of decrements remain unchanged, though caution is in order because hypothetical rather than actual behavior is being described. Age-specific probabilities of death for the remaining cause(s) always increase, because the population at risk of decrement to those causes must increase. The most common application is to cause-of-death life tables, where one can estimate the addition to life expectancy that would follow the elimination of a particular cause of death. The model is also useful in a number of other instances, for example to eliminate the possibly distorting effects of mortality from nuptiality-mortality double decrement life tables.

An important generalization recognizes more than one living state in the life-table model, and follows persons as they move between model states. Such multistate or increment–decrement life tables have been applied to numerous situations, especially studies of marriage, divorce, and remarriage; migration between geographical regions; changes in parity (i.e., a woman's number of live births); health status; and labor force status. Numerous useful summary measures can be found from such models. For example, a marital status life table recognizing the four living states of "Never Married," "Presently Married," "Widowed," and "Divorced" can yield the probability of ever marrying, the proportion of life lived married, the probability a marriage will end in divorce, and the average duration of a marriage.

Multistate life tables can be constructed from a set of age-specific rates of decrement using techniques analogous to those used for the basic life table, though multiple equations (or matrices) are needed. Conceptually, multistate models introduce important new distinctions. In calculating probabilities, one must be clear whether the starting population consists of all persons of a given age or just persons in a specific state at that age. The same is true with respect to life expectancies. The number of years a man age 60 can expect to live widowed depends substantially on his marital status at age 60.

It is commonplace – and analytically useful – to talk about measures such as life expectancy that do not refer to actual people but to the experience of a life-table cohort. The life-table model remains a basic tool in demography because it shows the cumulative implications of a set of behavioral rates, and thus summarizes long-term (and possibly complex) behavior.

SEE ALSO: Demographic Data: Censuses, Registers, Surveys; Demographic Techniques: Population Projections and Estimates; Gender, Health, and Mortality; Healthy Life Expectancy; Infant, Child, and Maternal Health and Mortality; Mortality: Transitions and Measures; Race/Ethnicity, Health, and Mortality; Socioeconomic Status, Health, and Mortality

REFERENCES AND SUGGESTED
READINGS

Preston, S. H., Heuveline, P., & Guillot, M. (2001) *Demography: Measuring and Modeling Population Processes*. Blackwell, Oxford.
Schoen, R. (1988) *Modeling Multigroup Populations*. Plenum, New York.
US National Center for Health Statistics (1998) United States Abridged Life Tables, 1966. *National Vital Statistics Reports* 47(13), Hyattsville, MD.

demographic techniques: population projections and estimates

John F. Long

Population projections and estimates constitute a core focus of demographic techniques. Both activities calculate the size and often the demographic characteristics of a given population in the absence of complete data such as might be available from a population census. Population projections and estimates play an important role in analysis of societal trends and in planning and policy decisions.

Population projections and estimates are sometimes distinguished from each other by the statement that population estimates refer to current or past dates while population projections refer to future dates. A better distinction would be based on the time period of the input data relative to the output data. Population projections take the data on trends in population size and/or in the components of population change (births, deaths, and migration) and use mathematical models to extrapolate these trends into a time period not covered by the data. Usually, but not always, projections are done for some point in the future that is not only beyond the last date of the input data but also beyond the date that the projection is actually prepared.

Population estimates relate to a past time period for which population counts are not available (such as the years after the most recent population census). In contrast to population projections, population estimates take advantage of actual measurements of indicator variables related to population size or to the components of population change.

COMPONENT-BASED PROJECTIONS

Population projections use a wide variety of methods, but the methods that are most commonly used take advantage of knowledge of the ways populations change. These methods, known as component methods, use information on the size and demographic characteristics of the beginning population (often measured by a census) and then add measures, extrapolations, or assumptions about the components of population change – births, deaths, and migration. In the most general form, the component method reduces to a basic accounting equation for population change.

$$P_{i,t} = P_{i,0} + (B_i - D_i + I_i - O_i) \qquad (1)$$

where $P_{i,t}$ = population of area i at time t, $P_{i,0}$ = population in area i at beginning of period, B_i = births in area i since beginning of period, D_i = deaths in area i since beginning of period, I_i = inmigration to area i, and O_i = outmigration from area i during the period.

If we add to this basic formulation information about the size of the population in each age group and the age-specific probabilities of giving birth, dying, or moving, the resulting methodology is known as the cohort-component method. This method is the basis for many population projections since it has the advantage of using data on a known population age composition from the last decennial census to determine the future momentum of the population. For instance, populations with younger age structures are more likely to have higher growth rates due to a larger number of births and fewer deaths, while populations with an older beginning population will show the opposite trends.

The art in population projections comes from the choices made to predict the changes in the age-specific birth, death, and migration rates. Many methods have been used ranging from holding previous rates constant, building in a time trend either from simple extrapolation or time-series models, setting ultimate assumptions and interpolating to get to those results, or predicting future change with multivariate models. Each of the components of population change requires decisions about a number of issues as future rates are constructed.

Fertility rates have varied markedly over time, with a long-term decline occasionally interrupted by major deviations like the post-World War II baby boom in North America and many European countries. More recently, the rapid decline of fertility toward replacement or below in the developing world and the dramatic fall of fertility to well below replacement levels in much of Europe has made forecasting fertility much more difficult. Early uses of birth expectations data to forecast the short-term future of fertility behavior achieved mixed success as many women's actual experiences failed to match their initial expectations. Time-series analysis of the distribution of age-specific fertility rates, sometimes taking into account the number of children already born to a woman (parity), has proved useful where there is a well-behaved change in fertility patterns. Often, the approach has been to use expert judgment to assume an ultimate level of fertility – often related to the level of fertility needed to replace the population (roughly 2.1 children per woman). The assumption of this replacement-level fertility level has been highly debated and there seems to be no agreement that future fertility for a given society needs to be near replacement.

Future trends in death rates have gone through similar discussions. Fortunately, the basic mechanics of population projections are closely related to the construction of a life table and age-specific mortality rates can be cumulated into life expectancies. The difficulty here is assessing medical and public health improvements that offer the possibility of substantially improved life expectancies and estimating the speed at which progress to those higher life expectancies can be made. There is no agreement as to whether there is an ultimate limit to the life span and hence to the improvement in life expectancies. As with fertility, not all changes are monotonic and declines in life expectancies have been noted in several countries over specific periods of time (e.g., in Russia since the disintegration of the Soviet Union). Typically, time-series and extrapolation models set ultimate assumptions based on levels reached by other societies that are further along in achieving higher life expectancies.

Dealing with migration brings its own set of problems. Unlike births or deaths, migration can be in two directions. Moreover, the probability models based on current population of an area that work for births and deaths might work for outmigration but the population at risk of inmigrating is not the current population of an area. For these reasons migration is often handled as exogenous to the system with assumptions made about the level rather than the rate of inmigration. Alternatively, migration can be handled in a multistate model where the populations of various areas are projected jointly and the outmigration flows from one area become the inmigration flows for other areas. Again, one has the problem of projecting future rates and often the origin-destination rates are held constant and the major dynamic in migration flows become the shifting size of the populations of origin.

COMPONENT-BASED ESTIMATES

Although population estimates can be produced based only on trends in the growth of the population as a whole, the more sophisticated methods use component-based techniques similar to those used for population projections. However, rather than developing methods to forecast these components into the future, the task of population estimation methods is to measure the size of each component since the last census or – lacking a direct measure – to find an indicator that can be used to model the level of that component. An indicator variable can be any measured characteristic that varies regularly with the component being estimated.

Direct measurement is possible for some of the components of population change. Births and deaths are often well measured by a vital statistics registration system. International migration is something of a mixed picture, with administrative data measuring most of the legal immigration into the country but often providing little or no information on emigration or illegal immigration. Unmeasured migration across international borders requires the use of assumptions about the quantity and characteristics of the population flows missed and is a major cause of estimation error.

The other major aspect of migration, domestic or internal migration between subareas of a country, is the focus of much effort in population estimation procedures. There is seldom a direct measure of internal migration, so it must be estimated using an indicator variable based on an alternative data source devised for another purpose. One method for estimating the internal migration rate uses administrative data that provide addresses for individuals at two different points in time (usually a year apart). Such data provide approximate information on inmigration, outmigration, and even area-to-area flows. While there are several potential sources of these administrative data – changes in postal addresses, drivers' license records, tax returns, and health insurance information – the problem is to find a source that provides representative coverage and consistency in reporting and tabulation.

The US Census Bureau uses an administrative records method that compares tax returns from the Internal Revenue Service (IRS) for changes in filing addresses between two consecutive annual tax filings. In the estimation process, tax returns from one year are matched with those from previous years by matching Social Security numbers of the filers. For persons with a new address, the new mailing address is coded to state, place, and county. If the state, place, or county is different from the previous year, the filer and all exemptions are classified as migrants. These data are then used to construct net migration rates for each county

and place as an input to the population estimation formula. An estimate of the rate of net migration is calculated by dividing the net flow of exemptions (the tax filer plus his or her dependents) moving into the area by the number of exemptions filed in the area.

$$\mu_i = \frac{\sum_j (T_{ji} - T_{ij})}{T_{i.}} \tag{2}$$

where $T_{i,j}$ = flow of tax exemptions from area i to j and $T_{i.}$ = total number of matched tax exemptions living in area i at the beginning of the period. This net migration rate (μ_i) is then multiplied by the initial population to get the estimated net internal migration for the period.

A critical assumption in this method is that the population not covered by the administrative dataset moves similarly to the population covered or that the uncovered population is too small to affect the results markedly. Since this assumption is especially inappropriate for the population over 65 and for certain military and institutionalized populations, those populations are handled separately. Other potential problems include the difficulty of coding addresses to geography, changes in administrative coverage over time, and the elimination of administrative data sources as governmental programs change. Despite these limitations, the population estimates made using this indicator model have repeatedly proven better than extrapolations of trends in these components based on data from previous time periods.

MODELING UNCERTAINTY IN PROJECTIONS AND ESTIMATES

Population projections and estimates have substantial uncertainty due to the approximations to reality made in specifying a model and in the unexpected events that inevitably arise as we go further into the future. Unlike sampling theory, there is no set model or series of models that can be used to determine future forecast error. One approach often used is to develop several different series of population projections that might represent reasonable high and low future levels of each component and create a set of alternative assumptions based on each assumed level. More recently, there has been increased interest in a more formalized procedure for producing sto-chastic forecasts. These forecasts begin not with a single trajectory for the rates of each compo-nent of change but with a distribution of future fertility levels based on statistical time-series analysis of past trends. These distributions are then used to develop simulations of future growth paths in which each year's value for each of the age-specific rates is randomly selected from the distribution and the resulting forecast trajectory is calculated. This process is repeated for a large number of simulations giving a resulting distribution of forecast values of each component and for each age for all years of the projection period. Population estimates also have a substantial level of uncertainty, although probably not as much as projections, given the shorter time frame and the fact that they are based on actual measures.

SEE ALSO: Demographic Data: Censuses, Registers, Surveys; Demographic Techniques: Life-Table Methods; Demographic Techniques: Population Pyramids and Age/Sex Structure

REFERENCES AND SUGGESTED
READINGS

Bryan, T. (2004) Population Estimates. In: Siegal, J. S. & Swanson, D. A. (Eds.), *The Methods and Materials of Demography*. Elsevier Academic Press, San Diego.
George, M. V., Smith, S. K., Swanson, D. A., & Tayman, J. (2004) Population Projections. In: Sie-gal, J. S. & Swanson, D. A. (Eds.), *The Methods and Materials of Demography*. Elsevier Academic Press, San Diego.
Statistics Canada (1987) *Population Estimation Meth-ods, Canada*. Statistics Canada, Ottawa.

demographic techniques: population pyramids and age/sex structure

Joan R. Kahn

Age and sex are among the most fundamental demographic characteristics of individuals. Viewed in the aggregate, age/sex composition forms the basic structure of human popula-tions. It tells us the relative numbers of young and old as well as the balance of men and women at different ages. By characterizing the "raw materials" of human populations, the age/sex structure indicates the numbers of people "at risk" or "available" to engage in a wide range of behaviors that vary by age (e.g., going to school, getting a job, committing a crime, getting mar-ried, starting a family, buying a home, getting divorced, retiring, getting sick and dying). By itself, it does not tell us who will engage in any of these behaviors, yet it does help determine overall patterns and trends.

Population aging is one of the most univer-sal demographic trends characterizing early twenty-first-century populations. The age of a population simply refers to the relative num-bers of people in different age groups. Popula-tions around the world vary from being quite youthful (e.g., Uganda, where 51 percent of the population is under age 15 as of 2004), to being much older on average (e.g., Germany, where only 15 percent of the population is under age 15). The trend toward increasingly older popu-lations is directly linked to declines in both fertility and mortality. With fewer births, the proportion of children declines, thereby raising the proportions at older ages; similarly, declines in adult mortality imply greater longevity and hence a larger proportion surviving to older ages. Trends in population aging are most evi-dent in the more industrialized countries of Europe, North America, and Japan, where the percentage of population over age 65 is pro-jected to surpass 20 percent by 2030. However, a great many less developed countries can also anticipate rapid population aging in the near future as a result of their recent steep declines in both fertility and mortality.

As can be seen from the demographic causes of population aging, the age structure is dynamic and can change as a result of shifting demographic patterns. It is also a major deter-minant of the demographic patterns themselves. Because vital events do not occur equally to people of all ages and both sexes, the numbers of births, deaths, and moves also depend on the numbers of men and women at different ages (i.e., the age/sex structure). For example, if population size and fertility rates are held constant, a more youthful population (with relatively large numbers of people in the child-bearing ages) will produce more births than an older one. Thus, very young populations have built-in potential for rapid population growth even after fertility rates start to decline. This phenomenon is often referred to as "population momentum." Conversely, an older population will have relatively more deaths and disabled persons than a younger population of similar size. Hence, understanding the age/sex structure of a population is vital to explaining social trends and planning for the future.

The most common measure of the sex composition of a population is the sex ratio, which is simply the ratio of males to females (multiplied by 100). In a few countries, such as India, government agencies calculate the sex ratio as the number of females for every 100 males. It is often assumed that populations are fairly balanced between men and women, but in most countries women outnumber men overall, though not necessarily at all ages. The sex ratio often declines with age because of progressively higher male than female mortality rates at older ages. In the US, for example, the overall sex ratio is about 95 males for every 100 females; however, at birth, there are about 105 males for every 100 females, and by ages 85 and over, there are only about 40 males for every 100 females.

Of course, not all countries follow this pattern; in places characterized by high levels of gender inequality and higher female than male mortality (e.g., India, Afghanistan), it is not unusual to find an excess of males at every age. High sex ratios may also reflect underreporting of females, as with the large number of "missing daughters" in China, who are thought to have been given up for adoption and not reported as live births (Tien et al. 1992, cited in Rowland 2003). Similarly, the growing popularity and availability of sex-selective abortion in countries with strong preferences for sons has driven up the sex ratio in countries such as India and China.

DEPENDENCY RATIOS

The dependency ratio is a summary measure of the age structure and is typically defined as the ratio of economically inactive to economically active persons. Since the economically inactive tend to be the young and the old, the dependency ratio is simply measured as the ratio of age groups (i.e., (Children + Elderly) / Working Ages). The precise ages used depends on the population being studied as well as the availability of data broken down by specific ages. In the US for example, the dependency ratio is often measured as the ratio of "persons under age 15 and over age 65" to "persons of ages 15–64." While it is recognized that many persons over age 15 are not yet economically active, and many persons over age 65 are still economically active, the dependency ratio approximates the number of inactive persons whom each active person must support. Given the different needs of children and elders, it is often useful to look separately at the child dependency ratio (Children / Working Ages) and the aged dependency ratio (Elderly / Working Ages).

Data on age/sex structure are typically presented graphically in the form of an age pyramid, also known as a population pyramid. The pyramid can be thought of as two histograms placed on their sides and facing back to back, showing the age distributions for males on the left and females on the right. The vertical axis is age, coded in single years, or in 5-year age categories, with the youngest at the bottom. Each bar of the pyramid shows either the number or proportion of the population who are males or females in a given age group. The size of each bar reflects past patterns of fertility, mortality, and migration. For example, the number of people in age group X reflects the survivors of the births that occurred X years earlier, plus or minus the migrants from the same birth cohort who entered or departed the population during the intervening years.

Since each bar is determined by past demographic patterns, it follows that the overall shape of the pyramid does as well. Rapidly growing populations, in which births far exceed deaths, are typically characterized by a wide base and a classic "pyramid-like" shape (i.e., each new cohort is larger than the previous one). In contrast, a population which is neither growing nor declining has a more rectangular shape whereby each new cohort entering at the bottom is roughly the same size as the preceding cohort. A population which is declining due to an excess of deaths over births would have an age pyramid which is narrower at the base than at older ages.

In addition to reflecting population growth patterns, the shape of an age pyramid can also serve as a kind of historical record of past events that may have affected fertility, mortality, or migration. For example, one of the most obvious demographic consequences of war is the large numbers of deaths to young adult males. However, there are also brief declines in the numbers of births, either because spouses are separated or because couples choose to postpone getting pregnant until the war is over. In either case, the demographic impact would be unusually narrow bars in the pyramid representing small cohorts of males in their twenties and also newborns of either sex. As these cohorts grow older, their narrow size remains with them as they move up the pyramid.

After wars end, there is often a surge in births as couples reunite and attempt to make up for lost time. The post-World War II baby boom is perhaps the defining demographic event for the United States in the second half of the twentieth century. The surge in births between 1946 and 1964 (the cohorts aged 35–55 in 2000) was unprecedented and unexpected, especially given the low fertility of American women prior to World War II. Every US age pyramid after 1960 shows the progression of the unusually large baby boom cohorts (and the smaller baby bust cohorts which followed in the 1970s) as they move through the life course. The visual impact of an age pyramid showing the baby boomers approaching retirement ages starting in the year 2010 helped to stimulate the policy debate on the future of Social Security and Medicare.

SEE ALSO: Age, Period, and Cohort Effects; Demographic Techniques: Decomposition and Standardization; Demographic Techniques: Life-Table Methods; Demographic Techniques: Population Projections and Estimates; Fertility: Transitions and Measures

REFERENCES AND SUGGESTED READINGS

Hinde, A. (1998) *Demographic Methods*. Arnold, London.

Newell, C. (1988) *Methods and Models in Demography*. Guilford Press, New York.
Rowland, D. T. (2003) *Demographic Methods and Concepts*. Oxford University Press, Oxford.

demographic techniques: time use

Sara Raley

Time is a scarce, some would say increasingly scarce, resource. However, unlike other resources, time is equally distributed because everyone faces the same 24-hour constraint as they make decisions about how to allocate their limited time to various and often competing commitments. Despite its apparent equality, time allocation is a major indicator of social differentiation and stratification. For example, people with high levels of human capital may be better able to afford to trade paid work time for leisure time as well as purchase time-saving goods and services (such as prepared meals and house cleaning) than people with lower levels of human capital.

Further, the choices people make about their time use has important implications for their health, financial security, and general life satisfaction. In addition to people's personal preferences, myriad norms (and even laws) govern how people should use their time – how much time is appropriate to spend at work, how much time is needed to care for family, and even how much time one should spend brushing one's teeth each night. Thus, at the social level, people's time use patterns reflect how societies value categories such as work, family, and leisure.

MEASUREMENT

There are three primary ways to measure people's time use: (1) asking respondents to indicate on questionnaires how much time they spend in various activities; (2) observing people in their daily routines; and (3) prompting respondents to recount their day in a time diary. Of these three methods, the time diary has become the preferred methodology because of its accuracy relative to estimates based on questionnaires and cost-effectiveness relative to observational methods.

Estimating weekly hours spent in certain activities is difficult because people do not spend their time in clearly delineated time frames. A person may go to the office at 9 a.m. and return at 5 p.m., but it does not necessarily mean she worked an 8-hour day. She may have taken a 1-hour lunch break, left the office for an hour and a half for a doctor's appointment, and spent 30 minutes in the afternoon talking on the phone with a child. Once home, the respondent may engage in a series of activities simultaneously (e.g., put in two loads of laundry, start cooking dinner, and answer a work-related telephone call), making it extremely difficult to add up the exact minutes of the day spent in each activity. Further, there are some activities, like childcare, that are deemed more socially desirable than others, like television viewing. Thus, when asked about their time use, people may be more inclined to overestimate their time with their children and underestimate time spent watching television.

One way of getting around the biases inherent in people's estimates of their time use is to follow them around and keep track of their activities for them. This is likely to produce more accurate measures of time use, is a method often used by anthropologists, but is extremely costly. The high cost associated with this methodology means that only a few cases can be observed, making it difficult to draw representative samples and make practical comparisons between groups. People may also be reluctant to have researchers follow them around, particularly when they engage in behaviors requiring privacy like changing clothes and engaging in sexual activity.

Time diary methodology gets around some of these issues by asking respondents to provide an account of one or more of their days, or even a week. Because respondents are constrained to a 24-hour period in each day and must recount their activities sequentially (i.e., in the order they occurred throughout the day), it is more difficult to exaggerate time expenditures. It is less mentally taxing than responding to survey questions that ask respondents to quickly add up time in various activities. Respondents go

through their day's activities, which prompts them to remember things more precisely than if they are asked to sum all time spent in a single activity, like market work, in a day. Time diaries also capture the complexity of time use. They indicate multitasking, or when people engage in more than one activity simultaneously, as well as the location and people present for each reported activity. At the same time, diaries are not perfect measures of time use as people may be reluctant to report socially deviant or embarrassing behaviors.

HISTORY OF TIME USE DATA COLLECTION

Although the history of time diary methodology extends back to the mid-1920s, the most comprehensive and well-known time diary study is the 1965 Multinational Comparative Time-Budget Research Project. In this study, 2,000 respondents from each of 12 different countries completed single-day diaries. The sampling procedure, diary format, and data collection procedures of this landmark study set the standard for several subsequent international time diary collections. In addition, several of the countries in the original 1965 collection replicated their studies in later years. The Harmonized European Time Use Study was developed between 1996 and 1998 and captured time use data on 20 countries. To date, time diary studies have been administered in over 60 countries spanning North America, South America, Europe, Australia, Africa, and Asia.

In the US, a series of cross-sectional time diary studies based out of the Universities of Michigan and Maryland have been conducted at roughly 10-year intervals since the 1960s. Whereas most of these studies focus on the time use of adult men and women, smaller-scale studies of adolescents and children were administered in the 1980s and 1990s. In 1997, the Panel Study of Income Dynamics (PSID) survey added time diaries for 3,000 children aged 3 to 12 as part of the Child Development Supplement (CDS). These children were followed up and asked to complete another diary in 2003, making this one of the few longitudinal diary collections. The study is particularly innovative not only because it is longitudinal, but also because the time diary data in the CDS can be linked to the respondent's detailed income histories in the PSID.

Time diary methodology has become so popular that in January 2003, the Bureau of Labor Statistics launched the American Time Use Survey, which is now the largest time use survey ever conducted in the world. This nationally representative data collection makes it possible to make more detailed comparisons of time use across groups by such indicators as age, race, employment status, gender, and income.

TRENDS IN WORK AND LEISURE TIME

The time-harried American trying to squeeze in time for market work, household labor, exercise, a healthy diet, family, sleep, and, of course, leisure is a common image in the popular media. Particularly in light of technological advances like beepers, pagers, cell phones, email, and instant messaging, it seems that everyone is on the go. In the context of this fast-paced lifestyle, changes in work and leisure time are of central concern, with the prevailing viewpoint being that work time has increased greatly and leisure time is on the decline.

This perspective was underscored and popularized by Juliet Schor, author of the *Overworked American: The Unexpected Decline of Leisure* and *The Overspent American: Upscaling, Downshifting, and the New Consumer*, who argues the nature of work and consumption have changed so dramatically in the US that people are working longer hours than ever before so they can earn enough money to buy and accumulate large numbers of consumer durables. Relying heavily on government survey data as well as newspaper articles, she made the astonishing assertion that between 1979 and 1987, working hours increased by the equivalent of a month, or 163 hours, a year. Her arguments were echoed by Arlie Hochschild (1997), who claims the increased commitment to market work has moved society to an age where work has become home and home has become work.

In stark contrast to those who argue work hours are rapidly encroaching on quality leisure time are scholars like John Robinson and Geoffrey Godbey (1999), whose analysis of time diary data on Americans' time since the mid-1960s argues that leisure time, if anything, increased in recent decades. Their estimates showed gains in free-time activities (all those outside of market work, non-market work, and childcare) amounted to an additional month and a half of *vacation* between 1965 and 1985. Others also pointed out that the average workweek has changed little over the last few decades (Rones et al. 1997). Hence, the dramatic decline in leisure may be more a perception than a reality.

Both sides bring to bear convincing evidence on this issue, so it seems impossible that *both* work and leisure time could be simultaneously increasing. Jacobs and Gerson (2001) suggest, however, that even though the two sides *seem* thoroughly at odds, they may not necessarily be mutually exclusive trends. First, if the unit of analysis is shifted from individuals to families, where the once normative male breadwinner, female homemaker household has been replaced by dual-earner and single-parent families, it becomes clear that the combined working hours of families have skyrocketed. With the increase in women, particularly married mothers, in the labor force, far fewer families have a member available to focus exclusively on non-market work. Second, changes in the distribution in the population might make averages across the population seem misleading. For example, the universe of people who are of working age has shifted. People are entering the workforce later in their lives because of increased educational attainment and exiting the labor market earlier as retirement ages decline. Thus, it is possible that people may be working more when they are in the prime working ages, but working less over the life course as a whole.

FUTURE DIRECTIONS: SUBJECTIVE FEELINGS ABOUT TIME

Time use data capture the objective measures of people's time use: what they are doing, where they are doing it, who is accompanying them, and how long they are engaging in their various activities. However, the sense of pressure and anxiety associated with daily activities is not a major component of most time diary collections. Who feels responsibility for the family caretaking and the added stress that comes along with this responsibility is not captured by time use data. Further, the extent to which people enjoy the activities they engage in regularly is not measured in most time use studies. For example, some people enjoy spending 40 hours a week at work while others may find 40 hours of market work stressful. Hence, the field is moving to incorporate methodologies that evaluate the subjective as well as the objective dimensions of time use.

In experiential sampling studies, or "beeper" studies, respondents are randomly "beeped" and asked to report not only what they are doing, but how they feel about their selected activity. A major strength of this approach is that it provides a broad set of information about how daily life is experienced by capturing both the quantity and quality of time use. Further, it avoids the problems associated with the intrusive observer, which is particularly useful for interviewing self-conscious adolescents reluctant to be followed by an outside observer. Like the diary method, it also avoids the pitfalls of recall bias because respondents report their feelings as they experience them. Procedures of this kind were used as far back as the 1940s, but did not gain popularity among researchers until the 1980s when the term "experiential sampling method" was coined.

Since that time, several projects utilizing this methodology have been conducted, focusing primarily on adolescents, children, and families. These studies shed light on how adolescents and families organize their time, what activities they find the most enjoyable, what activities they find the most stressful, and how adolescents and their parents experience their interactions. Future studies can be used to better understand how men, women, and children experience time expenditures differently as well as how families collectively experience phenomena like work–family conflict. This is particularly significant in light of rising concern popularized by Juliet Schor that the time-pressed nature of modern society is increasingly putting people's physical and mental health at risk.

SEE ALSO: Demographic Techniques: Event History Methods; Gender, Work, and Family; Time

REFERENCES AND SUGGESTED READINGS

Bianchi, S. M., Robinson, J. P., & Milkie, M. A. (2006) *Changing Rhythms of American Family Life.* Russell Sage, New York.

Hochschild, A. R. (1989) *The Second Shift.* Avon Books, New York.

Hochschild, A. R. (1997) *The Time Bind: When Work Becomes Home and Home Becomes Work.* Metropolitan Books, New York.

Jacobs, J. A. & Gerson, K. (2001) Overworked Individuals or Overworked Families? Explaining Trends in Work, Leisure, and Family Time. *Work and Occupations* 21(4): 40–63.

Larson, R. & Richards, M. (1994) *Divergent Realities: The Emotional Lives of Mothers, Fathers, and Adolescents.* Basic Books, New York.

Robinson, J. & Godbey, G. (1999) *Time for Life*, 2nd edn. Penn State Press, State College, PA.

Rones, P., Gardner, J., & Ilg, R. (1997) Trends in Hours of Work Since the Mid-1970s. *Monthly Labor Review* 120: 3–14.

demographic transition theory

John R. Weeks

Although it dominated demographic thinking in the latter half of the twentieth century, demographic transition theory actually began as only a description of the demographic changes that had taken place over time in the advanced nations. In particular, it described the transition from high birth and death rates to low birth and death rates, with an interstitial spurt in growth rates leading to a larger population at the end of the transition than there had been at the start. The idea emerged in 1929, when Warren Thompson gathered data from "certain countries" for the period 1908–27 and showed that the countries fell into three main groups, according to their patterns of population growth: (1) Northern and Western Europe and the United States had gone from high rates of natural increase to very low rates of natural increase, and were on the verge of depopulating at that time; (2) Italy, Spain, and the "Slavic" peoples of Central Europe showed some evidence of a decline in both birth rates and death rates but it seemed likely that the birth rates would remain higher than the death rates for some time to come; and (3) the rest of the world, where there was little evidence of control over either births or deaths. The populations of these latter countries, comprising about 75 percent of the world's population at the time, were living at subsistence levels and would likely increase in size if economic conditions improved enough for death rates to decline a bit.

In 1945, following the end of World War II, there was a growing concern about population growth. Frank Notestein (1945) picked up the threads of Thompson's thesis and provided labels for the three types of growth patterns. Notestein labeled the first "incipient decline," the second "transitional growth," and the third "high growth potential." By reversing Thompson's order, one could describe the transition from high birth and death rates to a transitional drop in death rates followed by a drop in birth rates, and finally to a stage where both are low. That same year, Kingsley Davis (1945) edited a volume of the *Annals of the American Academy of Political and Social Sciences* titled *World Population in Transition*, and in the lead article (titled "The World Demographic Transition") he noted that the world's population had been analogous for a long time to a powder fuse burning slowly toward the charge, but now it was about to reach that charge and explode. The term population explosion, alluded to by Davis, refers to the phase that Notestein called transitional growth. Thus in 1945 was born the term *demographic transition*.

At this point in the 1940s, the demographic transition was merely a picture of demographic change, not a theory, but each new country studied fit into the picture, and it seemed as though some new universal law of population growth – an evolutionary scheme – was being developed. Between the mid-1940s and the late 1960s rapid population growth became a worldwide concern, and demographers devoted a great deal of time to the demographic transition perspective. Explanations were developed for why and how countries pass through the transition. These explanations tended to be derived from the modernization theory, which is based on the idea that in premodern times human

society was generally governed by "tradition," and that the massive economic changes wrought by industrialization forced societies to alter traditional institutions. In traditional societies fertility and mortality rates are high, whereas in modern societies the birth and death rates are low. Spanning these two extremes is the demographic transition. In the process, behavior has changed and the world has been permanently transformed. It is a macro-level theory that sees human actors as being buffeted by changing social institutions. Thus, individuals did not deliberately lower their risk of death to precipitate the modern decline in mortality. Rather, society-wide increases in income and improved public health infrastructure brought about this change. Similarly, people did not just decide to move from the farm to town to take a job in a factory. Economic changes took place that created those higher-wage urban jobs while eliminating many agricultural jobs. These same economic forces improved transportation and communication and made it possible for individuals to migrate in previously unheard-of numbers.

Modernization theory provided the vehicle that allowed the demographic transition to move from a mere description of events to a demographic perspective. In its initial formulations this perspective was expressed by sentiments such as "take care of the people and population will take care of itself" or "development is the best contraceptive" (Teitelbaum 1975). The theory drew on the available data for most countries that had gone through the transition. Death rates declined as the standard of living improved, and birth rates almost always declined a few decades later, eventually dropping to low levels, although rarely as low as the death rate. It was argued that the decline in the birth rate typically lagged behind the decline in the death rate because it takes time for a population to adjust to the fact that mortality really is lower, and because the social and economic institutions that favored high fertility require time to adjust to new norms of lower fertility that are more consistent with the lower levels of mortality. Since most people value the prolongation of life, it is not hard to lower mortality, but the reduction of fertility is contrary to the established norms of societies that have required high birth rates to keep pace with high death rates. Such norms are not easily changed, even in the face of poverty.

Birth rates eventually declined, it was argued, as the importance of family life was diminished by industrial and urban life, thus weakening the pressure for large families. Large families are presumed to have been desired because they provided parents with a built-in labor pool, and because children provided old-age security for parents. The same economic development that lowered mortality is theorized to transform a society into an urban industrial state in which compulsory education lowers the value of children by removing them from the labor force, and people come to realize that lower infant mortality means that fewer children need to be born to achieve a certain number of surviving children. Finally, as a consequence of the many alterations in social institutions, people feel less pressure to have children and the idea of consciously controlling fertility begins to take hold.

Over time it has become obvious that the demographic transition is too complex to be explained by simple reference to the modernization theory. One of the most important social scientific endeavors to cast doubt on the classic explanation was the European Fertility Project, directed by Ansley Coale at Princeton University. In the 1960s, researchers at Princeton began looking at changes over time in marriage and fertility patterns in various European provinces. They quickly discovered that cultural factors such as language and religion were important predictors of fertility patterns, even when controlling for economic variables. Economic development emerges, then, as a sufficient cause of fertility decline, though not a necessary one. For example, many provinces of Europe experienced a rapid drop in the birth rate even though they were not very urban, infant mortality rates were high, and a low percentage of the population was in industrial occupations. The data suggest that one of the more common similarities in those areas that have undergone fertility declines is the rapid spread of secularization, which often spreads quickly, being diffused through social networks as people imitate the behavior of others to whom they look for clues to proper and appropriate conduct.

The work of the European Fertility Project focused on explaining regional differences in fertility declines. This was a very important theoretical development, but not a comprehensive one because it only partially dealt with a central issue of the demographic transition theory: How (and under what conditions) can a mortality decline lead to a fertility decline? To answer that question, Kingsley Davis (1963) asked what happens to individuals when mortality declines. The answer, which came to be known as the *theory of demographic change and response*, is that more children survive through adulthood, putting greater pressure on family resources, and people have to reorganize their lives in an attempt to relieve that pressure; that is, people respond to the demographic change. But Davis argued that their response will be in terms of personal goals, not national goals. It rarely matters what a government wants. If individual members of a society do not stand to gain by behaving in a particular way, they probably will not behave that way. Davis believed that the response that individuals make to the population pressure created by more members joining their ranks is determined by the means available to them. A first response, non-demographic in nature, is to try to increase resources by working harder. If that is not sufficient or there are no such opportunities, then migration of some family members (typically, unmarried sons or daughters) is the easiest demographic response. But what will be the response of that second generation, the children who now have survived when previously they would not have, and who have thus put the pressure on resources? Davis argued that if there is in fact a chance for social or economic improvement, then people will try to take advantage of those opportunities by avoiding the large families that caused problems for their parents. Davis suggested that the most powerful motive for family limitation is not fear of poverty or avoidance of pain; rather, it is the prospect of rising prosperity that will most often motivate people to find the means to limit the number of children they have.

A shortcoming of all of the explanations of the demographic transition has been that they have focused largely on the causes of the mortality and fertility declines, without paying close attention to the other changes that are predictably put into motion as the rate of natural increase changes in a society. Interaction between population change and societal change is, in fact, at the heart of the realization that the demographic transition is really a whole set of transitions, rather than simply being one big transition. These transitions include the mortality (also known as the epidemiological) transition, the fertility transition, the age transition, the migration transition, the urban transition, and the family and household transition.

Usually (although not always), the first transition to occur is the mortality transition – the shift from deaths at younger ages due to communicable disease to deaths at older ages due to degenerative diseases. This process is brought about by changes in society that improve the health of people and thus their ability to resist disease, and by scientific advances that prevent premature death. However, death rates do not decline evenly by age; rather, it is the very youngest and the very oldest – but especially the youngest – whose lives are most likely to be saved by improved life expectancy. Thus, the initial impact of the mortality transition is to increase the number of young people who are alive, ballooning the bottom end of the age structure in a manner that looks just like an increase in the birth rate. This typically sets all the other transitions in motion.

The fertility transition is the shift from natural (and high) to controlled (and low) fertility, typically in a delayed response to the mortality transition. Although it can begin without a decline in mortality (as happened in France), in nearly all places in the world it is the decline in mortality, leading to greater survival of children, that eventually motivates people to think about limiting the number of children they are having. Throughout most of human history the average woman had two children who survived to adulthood. The decline in mortality, however, obviously increases that number and thereby threatens the very foundation of the household economy. At the community or societal level, the increasing number of young people creates multiple pressures to change, often leading to peer pressure to conform to new standards of behavior, including the deliberate control of reproduction. Another extremely important change that occurs in the context of mortality transition is that the scope of life expands for women as they, too, live longer. They are increasingly empowered to delay

childbearing and to have fewer children because they begin to realize that most of their children will survive to adulthood and they themselves will survive beyond the reproductive ages, beyond their children's arrival into adulthood. This new demographic freedom offers the promise of vastly greater opportunities than ever before in human history to do something with their lives besides bearing and raising children. This realization may be a genuine tipping point in the fertility transition, leading to an almost irreversible decline.

The predictable changes in the age structure (the age transition) brought about by the mortality and fertility transitions produce social and economic reactions as societies adjust to constantly changing age distributions. The age transition is the "master" transition in that the changing number of people at each age that occurs with the decline in mortality and then the decline in fertility presents the most obvious demographic pressure for social change. When both mortality and fertility are high, the age structure is quite young, but the decline in mortality makes it even younger by disproportionately increasing the number of young people. Then, as fertility declines, the youngest ages are obviously again affected first, since births occur only at age 0, so a fertility decline shows up first as simply fewer young children than before. However, as the bulge of young people born prior to the fertility decline pushes into the older ages while fertility begins to decline, the age structure moves into a stage that can be very beneficial to economic development in a society – a large fraction of the population is composed of young adults of working age who are having fewer children as dependents at the same time that the older population has not yet increased in size enough to create problems of dependency in old age. This phase in the age transition is often associated with a golden age of advancement in the standard of living. That golden age can be transitory, however, if a society has not planned for the next phase of the age transition, when the older population begins to increase more rapidly than the younger population. The baby bulge created by the initial declines in mortality reaches old age at a time when fertility has likely declined, and so the age structure has a much greater number and a higher fraction of older people than ever before. We are only now learning how societies will respond to this challenge of an increasingly older population.

The rapid growth of the population occasioned by the pattern of mortality declining sooner and more rapidly than fertility almost always leads to overpopulation of rural areas, producing the migration transition, especially toward urban areas, which in turn creates the urban transition. In rural areas, where most of the population lived for most of human history, the growth in the number of young people will lead to an oversupply of young people looking for jobs, which will encourage people to go elsewhere in search of economic opportunity, producing an inevitable flow of migrants out of rapidly growing rural areas.

With all good agricultural land being accounted for, migrants from the countryside in the world today have no place to go but to cities, and cities have historically tended to flourish by absorbing labor from rural areas. A majority of humans now live in cities, and the fraction is steadily increasing. The urban transition thus begins with migration from rural to urban areas, but then becomes the urban "evolution" as most humans wind up being born, living, and dying in cities. The complexity of human existence is played out in the cities, leading us to expect a constant dynamism of urban places for most of the rest of human history. Because urban places are historically associated with lower levels of fertility than rural areas, as the world's population becomes increasingly urban we can anticipate that this will be a major factor in bringing and keeping fertility levels down all over the world.

The family and household transition is occasioned by the massive structural changes that accompany longer life, lower fertility, an older age structure, and urban instead of rural residence – all of which are part and parcel of the demographic transition. These changes occurred first in Europe, leading van de Kaa (1987) to talk about the "second demographic transition." A demographic centerpiece of this change in the richer countries has been a fall in fertility to below-replacement levels, but van de Kaa suggested that the change was less about just not having babies than it was about the personal freedom to do what one wanted, especially among women. So, rather than grow up, marry, and have children, this transition is associated with a postponement of marriage, a rise in single living, cohabitation, and prolonged residence in the parental household. There has also been an increasing lack of permanence in family relationships, leading to higher divorce rates and instability in cohabiting relationships. Furthermore, when families do reconstitute, it is increasingly likely that it will involve cohabitation rather than remarriage. It is reasonable to think, however, that this transition in family and household structure is not so much a second transition as it is another set of transitions within the broader framework of the demographic transition. The family and household transition is influenced by all of the previously mentioned transitions. The mortality transition is pivotal because it gives women (and men, too, of course) the dramatically greater number of years to live in general, and more specifically the greater number of years that do not need to be devoted to children. Low mortality reduces the pressure for a woman to marry early and start bearing children while she is young enough for her body to handle that stress. Furthermore, when mortality was high, marriages had a high probability of ending in widowhood when one of the partners was still reasonably young, and families routinely were reconstituted as widows and widowers remarried. But low mortality leads to a much longer time that married couples will be alive together before one partner dies, and this alone is related to part of the increase in divorce rates.

The age transition plays a role at the societal level as well, because over time the increasingly similar number of people at all ages – as opposed to a majority of people being very young – means that any society is bound to be composed of a greater array of family and household arrangements. Diversity in families and households is also encouraged by migration (which breaks up and reconstitutes families) and by the urban transition, especially since urban places tend to be more tolerant of diversity than are smaller rural communities.

SEE ALSO: Davis, Kingsley; Demographic Techniques: Population Pyramids and Age/ Sex Structure; Family Demography; Fertility: Low; Fertility: Transitions and Measures; Healthy Life Expectancy; Malthus, Thomas

Robert; Migration: Internal; Modernization; Mortality: Transitions and Measures; Second Demographic Transition; Urban–Rural Population Movements

REFERENCES AND SUGGESTED READINGS

Coale, A. (1973) The Demographic Transition. In: IUSSP (Ed.), *International Population Conference*, vol. 1. IUSSP, Liège, Belgium, pp. 53–72.

Davis, K. (1945) The World Demographic Transition. *Annals of the American Academy of Political and Social Science* 237: 1–11.

Davis, K. (1963) The Theory of Change and Response in Modern Demographic History. *Population Index* 29: 345–66.

Demeny, P. (1968) Early Fertility Decline in Austria-Hungary: A Lesson in Demographic Transition. *Daedalus* 97: 502–22.

Easterlin, R. (1978) The Economics and Sociology of Fertility: A Synthesis. In: Tilly, C. (Ed.), *Historical Studies of Changing Fertility*. Princeton University Press, Princeton.

Lesthaeghe, R. J. (1998) On Theory Development: Applications to the Study of Family Formation. *Population and Development Review* 24: 1–14.

Notestein, F. W. (1945) Population: The Long View. In: Schultz, T. W. (Ed.), *Food for the World*. University of Chicago Press, Chicago.

Teitelbaum, M. (1975) Relevance of Demographic Transition for Developing Countries. *Science* 188: 420–5.

Thompson, W. (1929) Population. *American Journal of Sociology* 34: 959–75.

van de Kaa, D. J. (1987) Europe's Second Demographic Transition. *Population Bulletin* 42.

Weeks, J. R. (2005) *Population: An Introduction to Concepts and Issues*, 9th edn. Wadsworth/Thomson Learning, Belmont, CA.

demography

Vanessa R. Wight

Demography is the scientific study of human population. The discipline uses empirical investigation to analyze populations and its processes. This includes the study of fertility, mortality, and migration and how these factors change over time and affect population size, growth, structure, and composition.

The field of demography typically has been thought of in terms of two strands of scholarship. *Formal demography* focuses on the conceptualization and measurement of population processes. This area within the field emphasizes the methods by which to measure fertility, mortality, and migration, how these processes operate across different populations and within the same population over time, and mathematical modeling for estimating population growth and structure. Yet demography is also interested in the relationship between demographic behavior and the larger social context. Thus *social demography* not only measures and quantifies population processes, but it also seeks to understand more broadly the context within which demographic behavior takes place, how this context influences demographic patterns, and the relationship between this behavior and subsequent social, economic, and biological processes. Hence, family and labor force patterns that are related to key demographic events, such as union formation and dissolution, household transitions and living arrangements, intergenerational relationships and exchanges, and employment status, become important objects of consideration.

Finally, demography has long been interested in the effect of demographic processes on the natural environment. It is perhaps here where demography gained its popularity. Concern over runaway population growth or "population explosion" and subsequent increases in the level of consumption of scarce resources has historically fueled doomsday reports of the expiration of human society. However, despite the general indictment that population growth is one of the main culprits of environmental degradation, others would argue that it is the bedrock of technological innovation, economic expansion, and efficient markets – all of which are, for the most part, considered beneficial to social welfare.

POPULATION CHANGE AND DEMOGRAPHIC PROCESSES

Populations change under a limited number of conditions (Hinde 1998). That is, the change observed in any given population over a period of time (e.g., from time t to $t + 1$) is a function of the difference in the number of births ($B_{(t)}$) and deaths ($D_{(t)}$) experienced by a population plus the difference in the number of people moving in to ($IM_{(t)}$) and out of ($OM_{(t)}$) the population. Thus, population change over time can be expressed in the following *basic demographic equation*:

$$P_{(t+1)} = P_{(t)} + B_{(t)} - D_{(t)} + IM_{(t)} - OM_{(t)}$$

The main demographic processes that account for population change are *fertility*, *mortality*, and *migration*. Fertility refers to actual reproduction (e.g., number of births), which is substantively different from fecundity or the capacity of an individual to bear children. Fertility can be measured by estimating a crude birth rate (CBR), which is the number of births per 1,000 people in the population. However, this rate includes people who cannot bear children, such as men, girls, and older women. Therefore, using a crude birth rate can result in an underestimation of fertility at a particular point in time. Thus, age-specific fertility rates (ASFR) and the total fertility rate (TFR) are generally used to estimate fertility behavior. The ASFR is the number of births to women of a specific age per 1,000 women who are that age. The TFR is estimated using a life table, which is a method widely used by demographers to calculate variation in such vital events as births and deaths, as well as migration. Life-table estimates are derived by subjecting a birth cohort to a set of fixed age-specific rates. It is a mathematical exercise that allows demographers to make inferences about future demographic behavior in a given population (e.g., the probability that a childless woman at age 30 will have a child by age 35 or the number of years a child born in 2000 can expect to live). The total fertility rate, thus, is a measure of completed fertility and represents the average total number of births a woman can expect to have provided the age-specific fertility rates remain constant over her reproductive lifespan. It is derived by summing the age-specific fertility rates. The various fertility rates can be expressed as:

$$CBR = \frac{\# \text{ of births}}{Total\ Pop} \times 1,000$$

$$ASFR = \frac{\# \text{ of births } W_i}{Total\ W_i} \times 1,000$$

$$TFR = \sum ASFR$$

Mortality is the study of deaths within a population. Like fertility, the extent of mortality can be estimated using a crude death rate (i.e., the number of deaths per 1,000 people in a given population at a particular point in time). However, because the risk of death can vary by age, demographers typically use age-specific death rates to estimate mortality. As discussed above, age-specific rates provide the number of events, in this case deaths, to people of an exact age or age group per 1,000 people who are of the exact age or age group. A commonly used age-specific death rate among demographers is the infant mortality rate (IMR). The IMR is an estimate of the number of deaths to children less than 1 year old per 1,000 live births at a particular point in time. It is expressed as:

$$IMR = \frac{\begin{array}{c} \# \text{ of deaths to children} \\ \text{under age 1 in a given year} \end{array}}{\# \text{ of live births in the given year}} \times 1,000$$

Life expectancy is also commonly used to assess the degree of mortality within a particular population. Like the total fertility rate, life expectancy is estimated using a life table and the measure represents the average number of years, typically measured at birth, that a person can be expected to live, assuming that the rate of mortality at each age remains fixed.

Demographers who study *migration* focus on the movement of people. The effect of migration on societies (both senders and receivers) can be positive or negative. On the positive side, migration can act as a safety valve, alleviating social and economic pressures associated with overpopulation. People can also benefit from remittances received from family members who have migrated. Furthermore, migration can help some countries meet labor shortages that may be the result of declines in fertility. However, out-migration can also lead to labor shortages. Furthermore, some of the loss in labor can be among the most highly skilled (i.e., a brain drain). The challenges to studying migration are tremendous and most of this is related to the paucity of data available on the global movement of people. Thus, migration is typically estimated using an intercensal component method. That is, if the size of the population at two points in time is known, as well as the number of births and deaths occurring during this time period, then the amount of net migration can be estimated as the residual. Thus,

if $P_{(t+1)} = P_{(t)} + B_{(t)} - D_{(t)} + IM_{(t)} - OM_{(t)}$;

then Net Migration $(IM_{(t)} - OM_{(t)}) =$

$P_{(t+1)} - P_{(t)} - B_{(t)} - D_{(t)}$

SOURCES OF DEMOGRAPHIC INFORMATION

In order to analyze a particular population, it is necessary to measure the number of people currently alive, the number of births and deaths, and how many people move in and out of the population. One source of basic demographic information is a population count or census. Population counts provide demographers with the number of people in a given area, such as the world, nation, or state, at a given period of time. Another source of demographic information is a vital register. The registration of vital events documents processes that most closely come to bear on population change, such as births, deaths, migration, marriages, and divorce. Sample surveys are another source of demographic information. They are good sources of data for two primary reasons. First, most surveys offer additional information beyond the enumeration of people and vital events that can be helpful in assessing the relationship between demographic behavior and broader social and economic change. Second, sample surveys can provide demographic information for estimating fertility, mortality, and migration in places where census counts or vital registration systems are poor or nonexistent. The Demographic and Health Surveys (DHS) are a good example of this. Originally known as the World Fertility Survey (WFS) and the Contraceptive Prevalence Surveys (CPS), DHS is a worldwide research project offering data on population, health, and the nutritional status of women and children in developing countries. Over time, the DHS has been adopted and widely used as an important source for estimating demographic rates of change.

DEMOGRAPHIC PERSPECTIVES: THEORIES OF POPULATION CHANGE

The study of human population size and growth has captured the popular imagination of societies for centuries (see Weeks 2004 for discussion). The field of demography has enjoyed a long history of exchange and debate over the theories that seek to explain the causes of population change, the conditions under which vital events such as mortality and fertility change, and the consequences of these changes for society.

The Malthusian Perspective

Perhaps one of the most influential arguments on the dangers of population growth, and certainly one of the longest standing, is that proposed by Thomas Malthus. In his *Essay on the Principle of Population* (1798), Malthus argued that "population, when unchecked, increases in a geometrical ratio. Subsistence increases only in an arithmetical ratio" (p. 4). According to Malthus, the world was expected to expand at a rate that could not be supported by the environment – population growth was projected to outstrip the earth's resources.

Continued growth on a global scale over the last two centuries without a complete depletion of the earth's resources has led some critics to suggest that Malthus's theory of population growth may have been flawed. Demographic evidence today indicates that the world has not experienced the geometric growth rate in the population that he originally proposed. Furthermore, global society has managed to make progress in producing food at a tempo far above that projected by Malthus (Weeks 2004). This is evidenced by the presence today of large agricultural conglomerates whose aim is to develop technology-based food production enabling people to better process food crops as well as renewable sources of fuel – something Malthus did not foresee. In short, Malthus assumed that food would continue to be produced in the same manner in which it was produced in his lifetime. He did not consider humans' capacity for innovation as a protective agent against dangers of rampant population growth.

Despite the shortcomings of his perspective, we still see evidence today of the Malthusian tension between population growth and resources. In 1968, Paul Ehrlich garnered popular support and critical attention with his book *The Population Bomb*. Characterized by some as a modern version of Thomas Malthus, Ehrlich predicted widespread famine and economic devastation as the result of overpopulation. However, unlike Malthus, Ehrlich also emphasized increasing environmental degradation. According to Ehrlich, food security could not be sustained indefinitely. Ultimately, unchecked population growth would outstrip the nutritional carrying capacity or "the maximum number of people that can be provided with adequate diets at any given time without undermining the planet's capacity to support people in the future" (Ehrlich et al. 1993). Ehrlich's solution, like Malthus's, was to limit population growth by moral restraint or, if this failed, by contraceptive use.

Classic Demographic Transition Theory

More than a century after Malthus the field of demography was the proving ground for yet another theory of population growth – that of the theory of demographic transition. The first formulation of the theory was a description of demographic processes that evolved into a typology of a group of countries that by today's standards would be considered developed (Thompson 1929). Additional expansion on the themes originally advanced by Thompson launched the inculcation of the demographic transition theory – a broad framework that has been a predominant influence on demographers and their preoccupation with the determinants of population change (Kirk 1996; Weeks 2004). The theory argued that societies typically moved through three stages of growth patterns. First, societies were characterized by levels of high mortality and high fertility and exhibited either stable or low rates of population growth. Under this demographic regime, high levels of mortality were instrumental in promoting high levels of fertility. As economic organization in pretransitional societies was largely structured around the family, the survival of it was essential to the long-term functioning of society (Coale 1973). Thus high levels of fertility were necessary to balance high rates of mortality.

During the second stage, mortality declined as the standard of living improved. Declines in fertility typically lagged behind declines in mortality and this was thought to be the case because fertility behavior was largely determined by social norms and values that supported higher levels of fertility in the presence of high levels of mortality. It also took people time to recognize that more children were living longer and that the need to hoard them for insurance against old age was no longer necessary. In short, it took a while for norms and values to recalibrate to a level more consistent with low mortality.

The third stage of the transition was marked by declines in fertility. Industrialization and urbanization were thought to change parents' conscious calculus about having children. For example, the value of children changed as education requirements removed children from families' labor supply. Decreases in infant mortality meant that fewer births were necessary in order to achieve a desired family size. Hence, fertility declines were the result of an increasing economic advantage to limiting family size (Coale 1973; Kirk 1996; Weeks 2004).

Reformulations of the Demographic Transition Theory

The subtle assumption of demographic transition theory was that economic development created the necessary preconditions for declines in mortality and subsequent declines in fertility. Findings from the European Fertility Project organized by Ansley Coale in 1963 challenged this theory. Reexamination of fertility and mortality declines in approximately 600 administrative divisions in Europe revealed a high level of regional variation in *when* fertility declined. As Coale (1973) stated, "the demographic transition correctly … predicted that mortality would decline before fertility … In neither instance does it specify … the circumstances under which the decline of fertility begins." In short, the demographic transition theory could not reliably identify a threshold at which fertility declined. The evidence suggested that economic development was important. However, given variation across regions in the timing of fertility declines, critics argued that economic development was not enough.

Thus began a series of reformulations aimed at explaining the conditions under which fertility fell in the wake of declines in mortality. The somewhat ethnocentric nature of theory, in that it was postulated entirely by and about people in developed countries, and its economic determinism spawned a series of reformulations in which cultural and social context were thought to moderate the economic factors that influence fertility.

For example, some critics argued that despite the increasing importance of material conditions in explaining fertility decline, ideational components that give meaning to the various costs and benefits of children are also important. In other words, the examination of fertility behavior should consider both the decision-making process (the cost-benefit framework) and the context within which fertility decisions are made (Lesthaeghe 1983; Lesthaeghe & Surkyn 1988). Similarly, Caldwell (1976) argued that what mattered was what people thought about children – both the economic and social value placed on having them.

Central to Caldwell's restatement of the demographic transition theory was the idea that fertility would not decline until the flow of wealth, which had typically been from children to parents, was reversed. In the process of modernization, large family networks collapsed and were replaced by smaller families that were both economically and emotionally independent and self-sufficient. In the midst of familial and emotional nucleation, wealth flows from children to parents changed direction. As a result, ideas and attitudes about children changed. The economic value of children declined as they became the financial beneficiaries of family life – thereby increasing the cost to parents of having them. Therefore fertility declined as families decreased their family size to adjust to change in wealth flows. Yet, Caldwell argued the economically rational behavior

influencing fertility decisions was determined by non-economic factors, such as social and cultural conditions that exist in societies. It is these conditions that influence the social value of children and prevent fertility in societies from falling below replacement level, even when this may be at odds with the economic benefits of remaining childfree (van de Kaa 1996).

In a further elaboration, and in response to demography's failure to foresee the high levels of fertility resulting in the baby boom birth cohort of the 1950s and early 1960s, Robert Easterlin argued that economic well-being was an important factor in explaining fertility declines (Easterlin 1978; Weeks 2004). Specifically, Easterlin argued that the standard of living experienced as children becomes the foundation or "yardstick" by which current economic well-being as adults is measured. Therefore, if individuals are able to achieve a level of economic well-being similar to their parents', they will marry earlier and exhibit higher birth rates. If, however, economic prospects appear bleak and adults perceive it to be more difficult to achieve a standard of living similar to what they experienced as a child, they may delay marriage and childbearing.

According to Easterlin (1978), how the age structure of a population interacts with the economy influences the degree to which adults face economic prosperity. Thus, if the number and proportion of people entering working age are small in the presence of a burgeoning economy, their labor will most likely be in high demand and well compensated. If this compensation can afford individuals a lifestyle similar to what they experienced as children, this will exert an upward pressure on fertility. People will feel comfortable assuming the increased financial burden of having children. If, however, there is a glut in the number of young adults entering the labor force, regardless of the state of the economy, their overabundance will increase the competition for jobs and lower wage rates. This makes it more difficult for individuals to achieve the standard of living comparable to that of their parents at the same age and will thus exert a downward pressure on fertility. In short, people will be reluctant to have children, or at least a large number of them (Easterlin 1978; Weeks 2004).

The Second Demographic Transition

Many of the aforementioned theories on population change were preoccupied with either high fertility or the transition from high to low fertility. Recent trends, however, suggest that we are witnessing a deceleration in population growth on a global scale and most of this is due to widespread declines in fertility rates. So while the level of fertility still remains high in some areas of the world, the average number of children born to women has declined, resulting in a reduction in the overall rate of growth (see below). This has led many in the field to shift their focus from an overwhelming concern about high fertility to a concern about low fertility. Some have argued that these demographic changes since the 1960s warrant the label "second demographic transition" (Lesthaeghe 1995). Like the first, this transition was also described in three stages. The first stage, which took place between 1955 and 1970, was characterized by an acceleration in divorce rates, the end of the baby boom, and an increase in the age of marriage. During the second stage, around 1975–80, cohabitation and childbearing outside of marriage increased. In the third stage, which marks the mid-1980s and onwards, divorce rates flattened, remarriage was largely replaced with cohabitation, and delays in fertility characteristic at younger ages were recouped after age 30 (Lesthaeghe 1995). However, unlike the first, the motivations for the second demographic transition were notably different. While fertility declines in the first transition were linked to economic development and changes in the value of children with an increased focus on child quality, the second demographic transition was inspired by an increase in secularization or rising individualism and an increased focus on the quality of adult relationships. In short, fertility behavior, such as low or below replacement fertility, under the new demographic regime is linked to delays in marriage and increases in contraception and the motivation of this shift in behavior is thought to be more a function of increasing individual autonomy, a move toward gender symmetry, and a greater focus on the relationship between adult partners than had previously been the case.

Developed and Developing Countries Compared

Many of the theories originally aimed at explaining changes in fertility focused largely on developed countries. The fertility behavior and demographic transitions of developing countries, however, differed somewhat from their developed counterparts. While the timing of the transition from high to lower fertility was compatible with theories of economic development, the pace of transition was much faster than what had been observed in other countries, suggesting that other factors related to fertility behavior were at play (Watkins 1987). Some demographers argued that the importance of institutional change, such as the control and distribution over family planning funds and methods, as well as of ideational change was missing from theories seeking to explain fertility behavior. For example, diffusion such as the exchange of ideas about family size and family-limiting practices was thought to be an important and powerful solvent of traditional fertility behavior – explaining the pace with which developing countries moved through the transition (Watkins 2000). Others went further to argue that *what* was being diffused was important. That is, the diffusion of westernized family values, which typically accompanied modernization, was thought to be one of the most important social exports to developing countries (Caldwell 1976). With its emphasis on smaller, emotionally nucleated families and increased attention and expenditures on children, the export and diffusion of westernized social values, according to Caldwell, eclipsed the role of economic modernization in explaining fertility change.

POPULATION PROFILE IN THE BEGINNING OF THE TWENTY-FIRST CENTURY

Apart from the ebbs and flows in fertility and the theories that seek to explain population change, the profile of the world's population today is marked by a deceleration in growth. In 2002, the annual average growth rate of the world's population was approximately 1.2

percent, compared to 2.2 percent approximately 40 years before (US Census Bureau 2004). Considering the long history of fertility decline and the theories attempting to explain it, a decreasing growth rate may not be much of a surprise. Indeed, most of the deceleration in population growth can be traced to fertility decline. In 2002, women globally were averaging about one-half more of a child than necessary to maintain levels of population replacement. In response to relatively high, albeit declining, global fertility combined with moderate levels of mortality, the largest share of the world's population are the very young under age 15. The distribution of women and men is approximately equal. China with a population of approximately 1.3 billion, India with 1.0 billion, and the United States with 298 million hold the top three spots as the most populous countries. However, in 2002 developing countries constituted the remainder of the top ten ranking (US Census Bureau 2004).

In 2002, the overall life expectancy at birth was 63.8 years. That is, assuming that the rate of mortality remained constant across each age group, a person born in 2002 was expected to survive an average of 63.8 years. There is considerable variation in life expectancy across countries. European and North American countries had the highest levels of life expectancy – upwards of 70 to 79 years – while Sub-Saharan Africa had the lowest – ranging from approximately 50 years or less. This variation is due, in part, to the HIV/AIDS pandemic which has taken its largest toll on the African continent (US Census Bureau 2004). In 2002, the effect of migration flows on population change was not large. Approximately 3 million people were estimated to cross national boundaries. Mexico was the largest sender of people, followed by China and Tanzania. The top three receivers were the United States, followed by Afghanistan and Canada (US Census Bureau 2004).

It is important to note that the onset of HIV/AIDS has important implications for the study of demography, particularly demographic trends in developing countries that face the highest rates of infection and disease. The full demographic impact of the disease has yet to be realized. However, the nature of the disease, such as how it is transmitted (i.e., by horizontal transmission from partner to partner or by vertical transmission from mother to child), as well as where mortality is concentrated in the population, can already be observed in the declines in life expectancy, declines in the growth rate, and the distortions in the age structure among the hardest-hit regions of the world.

SEE ALSO: Age, Period, and Cohort Effects; Demographic Techniques: Decomposition and Standardization; Demographic Techniques: Event History Methods; Demographic Techniques: Life-Table Methods; Demographic Techniques: Population Projections and Estimates; Demographic Techniques: Population Pyramids and Age/Sex Structure; Demographic Techniques: Time Use; Demographic Transition Theory; Demography: Historical; Fertility: Transitions and Measures; Malthus, Thomas Robert; Migration: Internal; Migration: International; Migration: Undocumented/Illegal; Mortality: Transitions and Measures; Population and the Environment; Second Demographic Transition

REFERENCES AND SUGGESTED READINGS

Caldwell, J. C. (1976) Toward a Restatement of Demographic Transition Theory. *Population and Development Review* 2(3/4): 321–66.

Coale, A. J. (1973) The Demographic Transition. Paper presented at the Proceedings of the IUSSP International Population Conference, Liège.

Easterlin, R. (1978) What Will 1984 Be Like? Socioeconomic Implications of Recent Twists in Age Structure. *Demography* 15(4): 397–432.

Ehrlich, P. R. (1968) *The Population Bomb*. Ballantine, New York.

Ehrlich, P. R., Ehrlich, A. H., & Daily, G. C. (1993) Food Security, Population, and Environment. *Population and Development Review* 19(1): 1–32.

Hinde, A. (1998) *Demographic Methods*. Arnold, London.

Kirk, D. (1996) Demographic Transition Theory. *Population Studies* 50(3): 361–87.

Lesthaeghe, R. (1983) A Century of Demographic and Cultural Change in Western Europe: An Exploration of Underlying Dimensions. *Population and Development Review* 9(3): 411–35.

Lesthaeghe, R. (1995) The Second Demographic Transition in Western Countries: An Interpretation. In: Mason, K. & Jensen, A. (Eds.), *Gender and Family Change in Industrialized Countries*. Clarendon Press, Oxford.

Lesthaeghe, R. & Surkyn, J. (1988) Cultural Dynamics and Economic Theories of Fertility Change. *Population and Development Review* 14(1): 1–45.

Malthus, T. (1798) *An Essay on the Principle of Population*. J. Johnson, in St. Paul's Church-Yard, London.

Thompson, W. (1929) Population. *American Journal of Sociology* 34: 959–75.

United Nations (published since 1948) *Demographic Yearbook*. Department of Economic and Social Affairs, New York.

United Nations World Population Prospects: The 2004 Revision Population Database. Online. esa. un.org/unpp/.

US Census Bureau (2004) *Global Population Profile: 2002*. Government Printing Office, Washington, DC.

US Census Bureau, International Database (IDB) www.census.gov/ipc/www/idbnew.html.

van de Kaa, D. J. (1996) Anchored Narratives: The Story and Findings of Half a Century of Research into the Determinants of Fertility. *Population Studies* 50(3): 389–432.

Watkins, S. C. (1987) The Fertility Transition: Europe and Third World Compared. *Sociological Forum* 2(4): 645–73.

Watkins, S. C. (2000) Local and Foreign Models of Reproduction in Nyanza Province, Kenya. *Population and Development Review* 26(4): 725–59.

Weeks, J. R. (2004) *Population: An Introduction to Concepts and Issues*, 3rd edn. Wadsworth, Belmont, CA.

demography: historical

Etienne van de Walle

The history of population has long been of interest to historians and demographers. Historical writings were used to estimate the population of the Roman Empire, of China, and of the world over time. Local historians used monthly numbers of burials and baptisms in parish records to ascertain the effect of epidemics or food crises. Starting in the mid-1950s, the work of the French demographer Louis Henry is generally credited for initiating a new discipline, historical demography, based this time not only on the careful accounting of

vital events at the aggregate level, but also on the nominal linking of records. This became an essential tool of historians, and the appellation "historical demography" is often reserved for that auxiliary branch of history that deals with the quantitative aspects of past populations, whereas "demographic history" deals with more substantive aspects.

Adopting a more inclusive definition, historical demography is the discipline that studies the structure and the evolution of populations of the past for which written sources exist, and the determinants and consequences of population trends over time, both at the individual and at the aggregate level. This definition is broad enough to encompass literary sources or historical accounts (e.g., on the history of contraception), or medical or epidemiological evidence (e.g., on the history of disease). "The past" as used in the definition will depend on the situation and the use of the data; historical demography commonly uses sources in ways for which these sources were not meant at the time they were collected (as in the nominal use of census records) or applies new techniques to old data sets (as in regression analysis of population registers).

The field has focused heavily on methodological procedures meant to avoid the biases inherent in the data. The geographical coverage of its sources is spotty and they privilege certain individuals (e.g., the more stable and rural families) and typically only part of their life (e.g., the time they were observed in village records). Moreover, the quantitative data include a limited number of variables. Qualitative data derived from contemporary accounts or from literary, medical, and judicial sources are normative in nature, may reflect a written tradition rather than actual behavior, and are socially biased toward the upper classes; they provide insight, but must be used critically.

Louis Henry (1970) perfected the method of family reconstitution, which consists in linking all the information concerning individual couples and their children found in the registers kept by local church or civil authorities. The technique was applied to parish records of villages, and served first to investigate the fertility of individual married couples in eighteenth-century rural France. Other researchers have followed his lead to study parish records in various European countries, most notably England, and in Canada. Similar techniques can be used with already reconstituted families, as accessible through genealogies or population registers. Such registers that provide information on both the population and its vital events have existed in Sweden since 1750, and in several European countries during the nineteenth century. Akira Hayami (1979) initiated the study of the Japanese population registers of the Tokugawa era (the religious faith investigation registers); population registers and genealogies from Taiwan and mainland China have also yielded information on non-western populations.

Henry's initial interest was the decomposition of the biology of fertility. He was searching past records for examples of "natural fertility," i.e., the marital fertility that would prevail in the absence of family limitation. The family reconstitution method proved useful to investigate additional characteristics of the demography of the old regime, such as infant and child mortality. The focus here was microdemographic. Henry also laid down a plan to study a representative sample of rural French parishes using non-nominal counts of vital events, to study such topics as their seasonality, illegitimacy, marriage patterns (age at marriage, permanent celibacy, widowhood), and even literacy (ability to sign a marriage certificate). He also pioneered the technique of population reconstruction, the macrodemographic analysis of parish records over time to establish the age and sex distribution of a population as well as its fertility, nuptiality, and mortality trends.

Historical demography was widely accepted by historians because the study of common village people fitted well in the "serial" history of the Annales School (as opposed to "evential" history that focused on major events and figures). It contributed to an understanding of underlying structures and trends over the long term. The demographic system of past societies became the trunk on which other studies of the socioeconomic structure could be grafted. The methodology was extended to larger units, e.g., cities, regions, whole countries, where social differences between individuals and groups were more marked than in rural parishes. It was applied to large samples where the results could be extrapolated to rural France (Séguy

2001), England (Wrigley & Schofield 1981), Germany (Knodel 1988), Canada (Charbonneau et al. 1993), and the pioneer trail to Utah (Bean et al. 1990).

Parallel developments in historical demography involved the use of censuses, either alone or in combination with vital registration. At the aggregate level, they are used to compute long series of fertility and mortality indices to shed light on major demographic changes at the secular level. The European fertility project (Coale & Watkins 1986) produced standardized measures of fertility and nuptiality for a comparative study of the demographic transition in Europe. At the individual level, nominal listings of inhabitants are used to investigate household structure in the past (Laslett & Wall 1972). In the United States, the study of historical censuses has been facilitated by the systematic conservation of census lists. The interest in microdata from censuses stems in part from the new availability of computers facilitating the manipulation of large stores of data and from the development of analytical methods that did not exist at the time the information was collected. These include information on the occupational and ethnic composition of the population and on infant and child mortality (Watkins 1994) at the time of a particular census. Equally important in the eyes of social historians is the creation of historical series of comparable structural data where the evolution of social phenomena can be followed though time.

From a sociologist's point of view, historical demography provides insights into individual behavior and the complex social life of communities. Data from the past have served as a store of comparative materials on which hypotheses on human behavior can be tested and models of demographic evolution can be derived and applied to populations of the developing world with inadequate statistics. Theories about the demographic past have been regrouped in a series of general explanatory frameworks or models, which remain controversial and serve as battlefields for dissenting researchers. The most important of these models relate to fertility, mortality and health, and marriage and household formation. The long-term study of fertility change is subsumed in the model of the fertility transition. Fertility transition is interpreted as a change from natural fertility to deliberate control of childbearing. In natural fertility regimes, the duration of birth intervals within marriage is the result of involuntary behavior determined by social norms (e.g., on abstinence or breastfeeding), by health, and by environmental variables. After the fertility transition, the deliberate action of the spouses to limit their births is a function of their desire for children. The model posits that there is a clear divide between demographic regimes where couples had no precise reproductive targets, and regimes where they attempted to stop childbearing upon reaching certain parity and to replace deceased children. This fundamental change in behavior has been variously explained as an adaptation to socioeconomic change or as the result of the diffusion of new ideas, norms, and techniques (e.g., birth control).

The dominant model accounting for the decline of mortality in the western world has received the name of epidemiologic transition. Historical demography produced estimates of steadily declining mortality from the middle of the eighteenth century onward (Schofield et al. 1991). The decline reflects the progressive transition from a stage dominated by food crises and infectious diseases to a situation where most people die in old age from chronic diseases. The main explanations of the change have ranged from exogenous (the effect of climatic or epidemiological factors, and later the diffusion of medical knowledge) to endogenous causes (the high mortality resulting from population pressure and low standards of living giving way, under the influence of economic development, to better nutrition and a better control of the environment).

A third important model relates to nuptiality and household formation. John Hajnal (1965) pointed out the singularity of the Western European pattern of marriage characterized by a late age at onset and extensive celibacy. He associated it with a pattern of household formation where men had to defer marriage until they could establish sufficient livelihood to support a family. The study of household structure in European census lists confirmed that the conjugal family unit had long constituted the basic residential pattern. Extended family households appear to have been rare in Western Europe for several centuries, whereas they dominate in

many other contexts. If economic circumstances allow or prevent the contracting of marriages and the establishment of households, a feedback mechanism will link fertility population increase to economic growth. British historians have demonstrated the effectiveness of nuptiality as a long-term regulator of population growth, and have adopted a Malthusian paradigm.

From its beginnings in the study of the fertility and mortality of individuals, historical demography has evolved toward the consideration of demographic systems and their dynamics in the historical context of specific economy and societies. In the process, it has grown increasingly comparative. The opening up of new data sources with historical depth in Japan and China has allowed a comparative approach that has often challenged the generalizations derived from the study of western countries (Bengtsson et al. 2004). It has been argued, for example, that the Chinese demographic system was more preoccupied than the European one with lineage perpetuation, and resorted more to adoption and to infanticide to attain that goal (Lee & Wang 1999). An attraction of historical demography is the opportunity it provides to analyze other data sets, other cultures, and other social and epidemiological contexts.

SEE ALSO: Age, Period, and Cohort Effects; Annales School; Demographic Data: Censuses, Registers, Surveys; Demographic Techniques: Decomposition and Standardization; Demographic Techniques: Event History Methods; Demographic Techniques: Life-Table Methods; Demographic Techniques: Population Projections and Estimates; Demographic Techniques: Population Pyramids and Age/Sex Structure; Demographic Techniques: Time Use; Demographic Transition Theory; Fertility: Transitions and Measures; Mortality: Transitions and Measures; Second Demographic Transition

REFERENCES AND SUGGESTED READINGS

Bean, L. L., Mineau, G. P., & Anderton, D. L. (1990) *Fertility Change on the American Frontier: Adaptation and Innovation.* University of California Press, Berkeley.

Bengtsson, T., Campbell, C., Lee, J. Z. et al. (2004) *Life under Pressure: Mortality and Living Standards in Europe and Asia, 1700–1900*. MIT Press, Cambridge MA.

Charbonneau, H. et al. (1993) *The First French Canadians: Pioneers in the St. Lawrence Valley*. University of Delaware Press, Newark.

Coale, A. J. & Watkins, S. C. (Eds.) (1986) *The Decline of Fertility in Europe*. Princeton University Press, Princeton.

Hajnal, J. (1965) European Marriage Patterns in Perspective. In: Glass, D. V. & Eversley, D. E. C. (Eds.), *Population in History*. Edward Arnold, London, pp. 101–43.

Hayami, A. (1979) Thank You Francisco Xavier: An Essay in the Use of Micro-Data for Historical Demography of Tokugawa Japan. *Keio Economic Studies* 6 (1–2): 65–81.

Henry, L. (1970) *Manuel de démographie historique* (*Manual of Historical Demography*), 2nd edn. Droz, Geneva.

Knodel, J. E. (1988) *Demographic Behavior in the Past: A Study of Fourteen German Village Populations in the Eighteenth and Nineteenth Centuries*. Cambridge University Press, Cambridge.

Laslett, P. & Wall, R. (Eds.) (1972) *Household and Family in Past Time*. Cambridge University Press, Cambridge.

Lee, J. Z. & Wang, F. (1999) *One Quarter of Humanity: Malthusian Mythology and Chinese Realities*. Harvard University Press, Cambridge, MA.

Schofield, R., Reher, D., & Bideau, A. (1991) *The Decline of Mortality in Europe*. Clarendon Press, Oxford.

Séguy, I. (Ed.) (2001) *La Population de la France de 1670 à 1829. L'Enquête Louis Henry et ses données*. INED, Paris.

Watkins, S. C. (Ed.) (1994) *After Ellis Island: Newcomers and Natives in the 1910 Census*. Russell Sage Foundation, New York.

Wrigley, E. A. & Schofield, R. S. (1981) *The Population History of England, 1541–1871*. Cambridge University Press, Cambridge.

denationalization

Saskia Sassen

Denationalization is an emerging category for analysis that aims at capturing a specific set of components in today's major global transformations for which the typical terms in use – globalization, postnationalism, and transnationalism – are inadequate. These three terms all point to locations for change that lie outside the nation-state. The effort behind developing a fourth category – denationalization – arises out of an as yet small but growing body of research showing that critical components of today's major transformations actually take place inside the nation-state. The actual processes that constitute the transformation in this case have the effect of denationalizing what has historically been constructed as national. These processes are partial, often highly specialized and obscure. Further, they frequently continue to be coded, represented, and experienced in the vocabulary of the national, and hence can remain unrecognized and undetected. Thus this new category for analysis opens up a vast research and theorization agenda connected to global trends but focused on the nation-state. Sociology is particularly well situated to develop this agenda because its theories, methods, and data sets have to a large extent been shaped by the fact of nation-states. But while this new agenda can use and benefit from sociology's existing resources, it will require new interpretive instruments and framings.

The ongoing development of categories for analysis is today shaped in good part by the fact of cross-border processes such as economic, political, and cultural globalization and the resulting theoretical and methodological challenges they pose. Such challenges arise out of the fact that the global – whether an institution, a process, a discursive practice, or an imaginary – simultaneously transcends the exclusive framing of national states yet partly inhabits national territories and institutions. Seen this way, globalization is more than the common notion of growing interdependence of the world generally and the formation of global institutions. It also includes subnational locations.

When the term globalization is used, it tends to cover the presence and further formation of explicitly global institutions and processes, such as the World Trade Organization, global financial markets, the new cosmopolitanism, and the War Crimes Tribunals. The practices and organizational forms through which these dynamics operate constitute what is typically thought of as global. Although they are partly enacted at the national scale, they are to a very large extent novel and self-evident global formations.

But there are processes that do not necessarily scale at the global level as such, yet are part of large global changes. These processes take place deep inside territories and institutional domains that have largely been constructed in national terms in much, though by no means all, of the world. Although localized in national, indeed, subnational settings, these processes are part of globalization in that they involve transboundary networks and entities connecting multiple local or "national" processes and actors. Among these are included, for instance, cross-border networks of activists engaged in specific localized struggles with an explicit or implicit global agenda, as is the case with many human rights and environmental organizations; particular aspects of the work of states, e.g., certain monetary and fiscal policies being implemented in a growing number of countries, often with enormous pressure from the IMF and the US, because they are critical to the constitution of global financial markets; the fact that national courts are now using international instruments – whether human rights, international environmental standards, or WTO regulations – to address issues where before they would have used national instruments. It also includes more elusive emergent conditions, such as forms of politics and imaginaries which are focused on localized issues and struggles, yet are part of global lateral networks containing other similar issues and struggles, with all participants increasingly aware of this and connecting around their shared local issues; these can be thought of as non-cosmopolitan forms of globality.

But if the global partly inhabits the national, it becomes evident that globalization in its many different forms directly engages two key assumptions in the social sciences generally, and in sociology in particular. The first is the explicit or implicit assumption about the nation-state as the container of social process. The other is the implied correspondence of national territory with the national, i.e., if a process or condition is located in a national institution or in national territory, it must be national. Both assumptions describe conditions that have held, though never fully, throughout

much of the history of the modern state, especially since World War I, and to some extent continue to do so. What is different today is that these conditions are now partly but actively being unbundled. Different also is the scope of this unbundling.

Conceiving of globalization not simply in terms of interdependence and global institutions but also as inhabiting the national opens up a vast field for study that remains largely unaddressed within the globalization and related scholarships. The assumptions about the nation-state as container of social process continue to work well for many of the subjects studied in the social sciences, and have indeed allowed social scientists to develop powerful methods of analysis and the requisite data sets. Further, these same assumptions are typically also present in much of the scholarship on globalization, transnationalism, and postnationalism, from where come definitions of globalization as growing interdependence and the global as exogenous to the national. But these assumptions are not helpful in elucidating questions about how today's global, transnational, and postnational processes and formations are constituted partly inside the national, and are not merely exogenous forces that "attack" the national.

Theories based on the assumption that the nation-state is a closed unit, that the state has exclusive authority over its territory, and hence that what takes place inside the nation-state is national cannot fully accommodate the series of instances that the category "denationalization" seeks to capture. We might formulate this effort as follows. We need to recognize that the fact that a process or entity is located within the territory of a sovereign state does not necessarily mean it is a national process or entity; it might be a localization of the global. While most such entities and processes are likely to be national, there is a growing need for empirical research to establish this for what is in turn a growing range of localizations of the global. Much of what we continue to code as national today may well be precisely such a localization – whether endogenous to the national or an insertion from the outside.

Developing the theoretical and empirical specifications that allow us to accommodate such conditions is a difficult and collective effort.

However, some of the empirical knowledge on subnational processes and conditions – especially in sociology, anthropology, and political science – can be of use, as can the methods used to produce such knowledge. Including the national allows us to use many of the existing research techniques and data sets in sociology developed with national and subnational settings in mind. But we will still need to use and develop new conceptual frameworks for interpreting findings – frameworks that do not assume the national is a closed system and one that excludes the global. Surveys of factories that are part of global commodity chains, in-depth interviews that decipher individual imaginaries about globality, and ethnographies of national financial centers all focus on national settings and thereby expand the analytic terrain for understanding global processes. Denationalization is an analytic category that provides a potentially much-encompassing conceptual architecture for this type of work.

Using (and developing) the category denationalization for studying these processes means mapping an analytic terrain for the study of globalization that moves inside the national. It includes but also moves beyond understandings of globalization that focus on growing interdependence and self-evident global institutions. Thus part of the research work entails detecting the presence of globalizing dynamics in thick social environments which mix national and non-national elements. Structurations of the global inside the national produce a partial, typically highly specialized, and specific denationalization of particular components of the national.

If we conceive of it narrowly, the research literature on denationalization is still small but growing rapidly. In the 1980s, Zorn did some initial work on the subject, and in the 1990s Sassen (1996) began a serious effort to develop the term into a category for analysis. The work of Gereffi and Korzeniewicz (1994) contains critical elements for this effort. There have been other efforts, notably Bosniak (2000), but a careful reading shows that denationalization is there used as equivalent to postnationalism. Closer to the mark is the type of analysis found in Rubenstein and Adler (2000), Koh (1997), and Jacobson and Ruffer (2006). Ulrich Beck (e.g., 2006) has for years developed a critique of

methodological nationalism that is a key ingredient for an elaboration of the category denationalization. The most developed treatment, and perhaps the book that introduces the category formally, is Sassen (2006). This book also examines a large body of contemporary work in all the social sciences (e.g., on global cities, on translocal households, on the incorporation of human rights norms in national law, on the reorientation of state policy toward global agendas) that has done a type of research we might see as fitting but has done so without knowingly developing this particular category for analysis, and hence would not be right to cite here. The most developed of these bodies of scholarship is that on global cities (e.g., Taylor 2004). In the last few years we have seen a significant increase in the number and kinds of studies wherein the critical organizing variable is the subnational constitution of global processes. This research ranges from studies focused on markets for global trading that have only one location, such as the Gold Fix in London, to particular types of ghettos that are becoming part of cross-border networks of ghettos, often through cultural practices, most notably rapping. Multi-scalar analytics are one framing that is critical in this effort, especially as a heuristic (Jones 1998).

SEE ALSO: Global Economy; Global Justice as a Social Movement; Global Politics; Globalization; Globalization and Global Justice; Postnationalism; Transnationalism

REFERENCES AND SUGGESTED READINGS

Beck, U. (2006) *Cosmopolitan Vision*. Polity Press, Cambridge.

Bosniak, L. (2000) Citizenship Denationalized. In: "Symposium: The State of Citizenship." *Indiana Journal of Global Legal Studies* 7(2): 447–510.

Gereffi, G. & Korzeniewicz, M. (1994) *Commodity Chains and Global Capitalism*. Greenwood Press, Westport, CT.

Jacobson, D. & Ruffer, G. B. (2006) Courts Across Borders: The Implications of Judicial Agency for Human Rights and Democracy. In: Giugni, M. (Ed.), *Dialogues on Migration Policies*. Lexington Books, Lexington, MA.

Jones, K. T. (1998) Scale as Epistemology. *Political Geography* 17(1): 25–8.

Koh, H. H. (1997) How Is International Human Rights Law Enforced? *Indiana Law Journal* 74: 1379.

Rubenstein, K. & Adler, D. (2000) International Citizenship: The Future of Nationality in a Globalized World. *Indiana Journal of Global Legal Studies* 7(2): 519–48.

Sassen, S. (1996) *Losing Control? Sovereignty in an Age of Globalization*. Columbia University Press, New York.

Sassen, S. (2006) *Territory, Authority, Rights: From Medieval to Global Assemblages*. Princeton University Press, Princeton.

Taylor, P. J. (2004) *World City Network: A Global Urban Analysis*. Routledge, New York.

denomination

William H. Swatos, Jr.

The term denomination was innovated in the late seventeenth century by those groups of Christians in England who dissented from the established Church of England, but considered themselves loyal to the British state and recognized the monarch as having rights with respect to the Church of England. In 1702, specifically, Presbyterian, Baptist, and Congregationalist clergy formed "the body of the Dissenting Ministers of the Three Denominations in and about the City of London." The term was introduced to counter the pejorative term sect, which in popular usage carried a sense not only of deviant or undesirable practices, but also, as sectaries, implied political radicalism. *Denomination* is now used in pluralist societies for those forms of organized religious expression that generally support the established social order and are mutually tolerant of each other's practices.

TYPOLOGY

The term denominationalism was significantly introduced into the literature of the sociology of religion by H. Richard Niebuhr in his book *The Social Sources of Denominationalism* (1929). The central thesis of this work is that new religious organizations ("sects") begin among the socially "disinherited" within a population, but in the US, as these groups attain to higher social status, their religious expressions become more "respectable" or socially accepted; thus, there is a movement across generations from sectarian to denominational religious life – or else the sectarian group dies out. This strongly evolutionary view of religious innovation and organizational development has been considerably modified today. A particularly important contribution to the study of denominationalism was David Martin's seminal article "The Denomination" (1962), wherein he argued for a reconsideration of this structural form as a historically and culturally specific type of religious organization, rather than as a stage on a quasi-evolutionary continuum.

A standard current definition of the denomination has been provided by Wilson (1959: 4–5), who writes that the denomination is "a voluntary association" that "accepts adherents without imposition of traditional prerequisites of entry," such as belonging to a particular ethnic or national group, or sectarian testimonies of spiritual regeneration. "Breadth and tolerance are emphasized ... Its self-conception is unclear and its doctrinal position unstressed ... One movement among many ... it accepts the standards and values of the prevailing culture ... Individual commitment is not very intense; the denomination accepts the values of the secular society and the state."

Furthermore, and most significantly, individuals in a denomination coalesce around a notably open view of their religious purpose. The elusive goal of a denomination's members is to build and maintain a particular identity as believers without losing sight of all that, at the roots, unites religious groups and their purposes in a free society.

The association between religious denominationalism and sociocultural pluralism is crucial to its organizational success. In pluralism one may belong to any denomination or none at all. Religion is pigeonholed and privatized. It is a voluntary activity undertaken or dismissed at the discretion of the individual. The denomination is thus marked most significantly by this voluntarism of support coupled to mutual respect and forbearance of all other competing religious groups. It is indeed this quality of *competition* that is the unique hallmark of the pluralistic religious situation; acceptance of the "free market" of religious ideas is the critical operating principle of denominationalism as an ideology. Denominations are the organizational forms that dominant religious traditions assume in a pluralistic culture. The distinction between monopolistic and pluralistic societies in typological differentiation between the church and the denomination appears particularly in Swatos's (1979, 1981) church–sect model.

Although denominationalism is now characteristic of virtually all western societies, it reaches its quintessential expression in the US; that is, American denominationalism has been the model for religious pluralism throughout the world. (Andrew Greeley, for example, titled a text on American religious life *The Denominational Society*, 1972.) The particular effect this had on American religiosocial development up to the 1950s is chronicled in Will Herberg's benchmark volume *Protestant–Catholic–Jew* (1955). Although, strictly speaking, denominationalism is a Protestant dynamic, it has become fully accepted in principle by all major religious groups in the US; in fact, one could say that the denominationalizing process represents the *Americanizing* of a religious tradition, which is at the same time and in the same measure a *relativizing* process. Religious groups that too strongly resist this process are likely eventually to face run-ins with the legal system. Since the 1940s, social scientists have been particularly interested in the relationship between denomination and both social stratification and sociopolitical variables; the term *class church* was first applied as an equivalent to denomination by J. Milton Yinger in the 1940s.

Although some religious groups have made specific efforts to eschew the term as a label, denomination nevertheless has been the most neutral and general term used to identify religious organizations in the US. Denominationalism is an institutional pattern that both governs relations among religious groups and organizes contact between them and the wider community. Such common phrases in sociological research as organized religion and religious affiliation anticipate denominationalism as the dominant religious expression in society. Religious belief and action "work together" with the sociocultural system to develop a legitimation system as a result of mutual interdependence.

Denominationalism is a structure that allowed Americans to resolve religious differences peacefully. A concomitant result was to create a context for both a deemphasis on and eventual discrediting of theology as a source for authoritative knowledge in American civil society.

DENOMINATIONS TODAY

Since the 1980s, and particularly with the publication of Robert Wuthnow's *The Restructuring of American Religion* in 1988, there has been considerable debate within the sociology of religion over the current significance of denominationalism in American society. This debate was presaged by a distinction drawn by the church historian Martin Marty in *Righteous Empire* (1970) between two "parties" in American religion. According to Wuthnow's elaboration of this view, each denomination is now divided between the two parties (roughly, liberals and conservatives) on critical sociopolitical issues, reflecting in turn the relative rise in importance of "the state" as a sociocultural actor since the 1940s, whereas prior to that time the state's field was largely limited to the political–economic sphere. The ecclesiastical "party" with which people identify as a part of their cultural lifestyle hence is more important to both their spiritual and their moral lives than is a particular denominational label, according to this theory.

This realignment involves two related changes in the structure of American religion. First, official denominationalism, even that of the broadest sort analyzed by Herberg, appears to some analysts to be waning. They claim less and less distinctive information is conveyed by denominational labels, while more and more these organizations have been reaping distrust and alienation from members. Second, in their place hosts of movements with narrower objectives have emerged, ordinarily ones that cluster loosely around items from either conservative or liberal political agendas.

Attention has thus turned away from interdenominational ecumenical activity, for example, not because the churches themselves deem it to be unimportant, but because there is no need to negotiate peace among noncombatants. "The primary axis defining religious and cultural pluralism in American life has shifted. The important divisions are no longer ecclesiastical but rather 'cosmological'" (Hunter 1988: 22). They no longer revolve around specific doctrinal issues or styles of religious practice and organization, but rather around fundamental assumptions about values, purpose, truth, freedom, and collective identity. (Thus the most heated controversies swirl around such issues as abortion and sexual orientation rather than whether people kneel or stand or sit to receive Holy Communion or have or have not been confirmed by a bishop in apostolic succession. The growth of "nondenominational" and "parachurch" organizations is seen as part of this process.)

Others argue that this view is historically shortsighted and needs modification. Swatos, for example, uses the local–cosmopolitan distinction elaborated specifically in the sociology of religion by Wade Clark Roof to argue that denominationalism in the context of American voluntarism is preeminently a *local* dynamic, providing people "place" in a specific setting, and that this dynamic operates as much as it ever did to the extent that cosmopolitan elaborations (e.g., denominational agency structures) can be discounted from analyses. Cosmopolitan denominational bureaucracies are not, according to this thesis, the crucial social dynamic of the typology, but a specific, transitory development. In addition, intradenominational debates have created more internally consistent denominational worldviews – conservatives now dominate the Southern Baptists, while liberals have won the day among Episcopalians and the United Church of Christ. James Davidson and colleagues have also shown that the various denominations continue to remain significantly disproportionately represented among elites in the US across the twentieth century, with corrections required only to accommodate specific immigration effects. Reform Jews, for example, are now also significantly over-represented among elites, along with Episcopalians, Unitarians, and Presbyterians; Roman Catholics have achieved approximate parity with their share of the general population. On the other hand, conservative Protestants generally remain significantly under-represented among American elites, which may explain their attempts to

achieve greater political visibility, hence to influence both economic and cultural policies.

An often overlooked historical dimension of American denominationalism is the role women played in maintaining the life of the different denominations and in the social ranking system that they may have implied – again, particularly at the local level. The decline of membership in some mainline denominations (e.g., Methodists, Presbyterians, Episcopalians, Congregationalists [United Church of Christ]) is at least partially due to the increased presence of women in the workforce, which has resulted in a corresponding absence of women to undertake volunteer activities. Women in these denominations are also more likely to be in the professional classes and thus to have job responsibilities that do not end with the workday. Denominations that have declined in membership directly correspond to those that have most endorsed gender equality, while those that have gained membership are more gender differentiated. They also tend to attract membership from the working stratum, where even women working outside the home are, relatively speaking, more likely to be able to devote more of their discretionary time to church activities and are less likely to experience role redefinition in the home.

Regardless of which side of the debate on the significance of denominationalism is ultimately vindicated, both perspectives emphasize the crucial role of the congregation as the place where religious ideology and the lived experience of the people who wear a particular denominational label meet. This points to a crucial dialectic in American religiosity between organization and action: denominationalism is not now nor has it ever been realized except through the life of specific local units or congregations.

CONGREGATIONALISM

Used in three interconnected senses, the term congregationalism emphasizes the role of lay persons (or the laity, as contrasted to ordained, set-apart clergy) within a religious organization. While congregationalism is especially important to understanding religion in the US, it is characteristic of denominationalism globally. Congregational religiosity may be contrasted to both historic state-church monopolies and to shrine or pilgrimage religion where a group of resident devotees maintains a shrine to which the public comes either for festivals or for specific clientelistic needs (funerals, weddings, healing services, fortune telling, etc.). Religious congregations in the US form the largest and most significant community group that weaves through American society, but at the same time their diversity on crucial sociopolitical, socioeconomic, and sociomoral issues diffuses their potential impact on the larger society, as outsiders tend to see these cleavages in central values as diluting confidence in the authority of the stance of any specific group.

One sense of the term is to refer to a specific denomination of Christians, once called the Congregational Church – since a 1950s merger with the Evangelical and Reformed Church now formally titled the United Church of Christ (UCC). This body is the inheritor of the established church of New England formed through a Pilgrim–Puritan alliance in the early seventeenth century, shortly after immigration from England. In England today, historically Congregational churches are now part of the United Reformed Church; in Canada, most Congregational churches merged into the United Church of Canada in the 1920s; one group of Congregational churches in the US that did not join the UCC merger is now known as Congregational Christian Churches. New England Congregationalism spawned a number of offshoots, including Unitarianism and virtually all Baptist churches.

The name Congregational Church is taken from the fact that this denomination vests authority in the local congregation; that is, it has a congregational polity, or organizational structure. Other forms of polity are presbyterian, where authority is vested in the regional clergy associations, and episcopal, where authority is vested in a singular regional head, known in Christian traditions as a bishop. These forms of polity historically have named the major streams of American Protestant Christianity. (The United Methodist Church, for example, was originally named the Methodist Episcopal Church, contrasting it with the Protestant Episcopal Church, now known simply as the Episcopal Church in the US, the Anglican Church in most

of the rest of the world.) Both the presbyterian and episcopal forms in actual practice in the US, however, are modified significantly by congregationalism. In strict usage, however, the core principle of congregationalism is that the local congregation *is* the church; that is, no other earthly institution can claim religious authority over the corporate worship of believers. It hires ("calls") its own minister (and can fire him or her as well). It also decides acceptable forms of doctrinal profession, worship style, and so on, and decides on what forms of "fellowship" it will accept with other churches – for example, whether it will allow members who belong to a different congregation to receive various sacramental ministrations, particularly Holy Communion, and the terms on which it will allow individuals who have belonged to some other congregation to join its congregation. The congregation also normally corporately owns the property on which any facilities it uses are located (e.g., the worship building, education facilities, and offices).

As a form of polity, congregationalism descends from the Jewish synagogue tradition (synagogue is a Greek word for "gathering together"), where in Orthodox practice a synagogue is created whenever 10 men gather together for prayer. In its modern usage, however, congregationalism has come to symbolize a greater principle – namely, the religious *voluntarism* of denominationalism. The upshot of modern western political ideology is that religion is an entirely voluntary activity: one may not only go to whatever church one chooses, but one may also go or stay home whenever one chooses, and one does not have to go to or join any church at all. Furthermore, the church is largely seen as serving the needs of its congregation, rather than the reverse. The greater the extent to which, as in the US, support for the church is on an entirely voluntary basis as well, rather than through some tax scheme, the role of the congregation is correspondingly increasingly magnified. In this sense all churches in the US and other nations which lack either an explicit or covert system of government subsidization are congregationalist in a radical way: unless a church has been extremely well endowed by prior generations, if the congregation leaves, the church must be closed. This is very different, for example, from some Scandinavian countries, where state support ensures that a regular program of activities will go on, even though only a tiny percentage of the population attends church. By the same token, persons from these traditions may find offensive the practice of passing and offering (collection) plate or basket during worship – perhaps the one common worship experience that cuts across virtually all religious traditions in the US.

Steeped deeply in the Pilgrim myth and Puritan culture, the worldview of the Protestant ethic, the voluntaristic principle that is inherent in congregationalism colors all religion in the US, not simply the Congregational Church or even Protestantism or even Judeo-Christianity. Buddhist, Islamic, Roman Catholic, and national Orthodox groups in the US all must adjust to aspects of this organizational norm in order to survive. Similarly, the missionary activity of European Protestants throughout much of the Southern hemisphere and Far East has made congregationalism normative at least as far as Christian congregations are concerned. There was also a Catholic version of congregationalism in the US (called trusteeism) in the early years of the American experiment, but it was officially discontinued in the nineteenth century. Several recent studies of American Catholics, however, have emphasized continued popular attachment to a local parish as distinct from a hierarchical structure. Indeed, although the observation is most often credited to G. K. Chesterton, more than one commentator has remarked that in America even the Catholics are Protestants!

Americans can and do worship as well as vote with their feet and their pocketbooks. A degree of accommodation to this aspect of the "American way of life" is structured into virtually all corporate religious practice. By the same token, Americans are more likely to see "religion," whether they value it positively or negatively, as a congregational activity ("belonging to a church," or sometimes "organized religion"), and in recent usage to distinguish this from personal religiosity by referring to the latter as spirituality. Denominationalism, expressed through congregational religious life, provides definition for a sociocultural space in societies as they create institutional subsystems that attempt to differentiate public and private worlds. In historically monarchical societies religious and political lines were certainly blurred and possibly obliterated. To hold a religious opinion contrary to the official church was to be disloyal to state and society. The move toward a measure of separation between worlds of public obedience and private opinion began in the British Isles, but was almost immediately exported to the American colonies, where it grew far more rapidly and produced more abundantly.

GLOBALIZATION

From both American and British missionaries the public/private distinction lying behind denominationalism was widely exported and has become internationally recognized as a normative principle for political–religious relations and articulations of religious freedom. At the same time, however, specific denominational traditions in Anglo-America have at times had to face up to global realities in ways they did not necessarily expect. While on the one hand denominations in the mother countries gradually came to support an end to "colonialism" both in practice and in the ideology that lay behind it, they often were surprised that the doctrinal seeds they sewed would bloom as profusely as they have. For example, the largest number of Anglicans now reside in sub-Saharan Africa, and from a number of those countries they are being taken to task by their co-religionists for what are perceived by those whom they evangelized as betrayals of the basic tenets of the Christian faith, particularly with respect to human sexuality. This is also true for the southern cone of South America and parts of Asia. A similar situation exists among African Methodists. Some denominations of specifically American origin, such as the Church of Jesus Christ of Latter-day Saints (Mormons) and Seventh-day Adventists, have also globalized so successfully that their majority constituencies lie outside the US. In short, the denominational principle has been exported as a political solution but not necessarily as an ecclesiastical value of compromise to a set of standards that is not characteristic of the indigenous population's appropriation of the moral values of Christianity.

In Europe, by contrast, the denominational principle has been appropriated in terms of a gradual disestablishment of specific religious expressions, but not necessarily of state support. Thus, it remains the case that "denominational" churches that have had historical state church ties remain largely the province of small numbers of attendees, with clergy salaries and building maintenance underwritten from state or parastate agencies. Potentially the most interesting cases for the future of denominationalism are in the countries of the former Soviet Union, where religious monopolies (primarily either Orthodox Christian or Islamic) vie with challenges from religious groups of primarily western denominational origin (e.g., Baptists and Pentecostals, and to a lesser extent New Religious Movements). In Greece as well, the issue of European Union pluralism versus historic Orthodox primacy has arisen, primarily in respect to the inclusion of "religion" on passports and identity cards in contravention of EU standards, but also with regard to the treatment of adherents to such "marginal" denominations as Jehovah's Witnesses.

SEE ALSO: Church; Globalization, Religion and; Protestantism; Religion; Religion, Sociology of

REFERENCES AND SUGGESTED READINGS

Barrett, D. B. & Kurian, G. T. (Eds.) (2000) *World Christian Encyclopedia*. Oxford University Press, Oxford.

Davidson, J. (1995). Persistence and Change in the Protestant Establishment, 1930–1992. *Social Forces* 74: 157–75.

Hunter, J. (1988) American Protestantism: Sorting Out the Present, Looking Toward the Future. In: Neuhaus, R. (Ed.), *The Believable Futures of American Protestantism*. Eerdmans, Grand Rapids, MI, pp. 18–48.

Martin, D. (1962) The Denomination. *British Journal of Sociology* 13: 1–14.

Mead, S. (1954) Denominationalism: The Shape of Protestantism in America. *Church History* 23: 291–320.

Mead, S. (1956) From Coercion to Persuasion: Another Look at the Rise of Religious Liberty and the Emergence of Denominationalism. *Church History* 25: 317–37.

Roof, W. (1972) The Local–Cosmopolitan Orientation and Traditional Religious Commitment. *Sociological Analysis* 33: 1–15.

Stark, R. (2005) *The Rise of Mormonism*. Columbia University Press, New York.

Swatos, W. (1979) *Into Denominationalism: The Anglican Metamorphosis*. Society for the Scientific Study of Religion, Storrs, CT.

Swatos, W. (1981) Beyond Denominationalism? Community and Culture in American Religion. *Journal for the Scientific Study of Religion* 20: 217–27.

Swatos, W. (1994) Western Hemisphere Protestantism in Global Perspective. In: Cipriani, R. (Ed.), *Religions sans Frontières?* Presidenza del Consiglio dei Ministri, Rome, pp. 180–96.

Wilson, B. (1959) An Analysis of Sect Development. *American Sociological Review* 24: 3–15.

Yinger, J. (1946) *Religion and the Struggle for Power*. Duke University Press, Durham, NC.

department store

Wendy A. Wiedenhoft

Department stores by definition offer a large variety of merchandise organized into specialty departments under one roof. The first department stores were unique not simply because of the variety of goods they offered, but also because their policies were "consumercentric." Department stores instituted fixed prices – often advertised in newspapers – so consumers would not have to engage in the time-consuming practice of haggling over the cost of the goods that they purchased. Catering to the whims of consumers, department stores established the "no questions asked" policy of merchandise exchanges and refunds, money-back guarantees on purchased products, and free delivery. The first department stores offered cooking and knitting classes; some became "Saturday bankers," cashing checks when banks were closed. Other consumercentric policies included personal attention by sales clerks and clothing alterations. These policies engendered consumer loyalty and trust, as did the participation by department store owners in local civic life (Rosenberg 1985; Leach 1993).

Aristide Boucicaut opened the first department store, Bon Marché, in Paris in 1852. It did not take long for retail merchants in the United States to institutionalize the department store as a fixture of the urban landscape. Alexander Turney Stewart has been credited with opening the first department store in New York City in 1862. Named the Cast Iron Palace, it contained 19 departments from silks to toys. Other cast iron department stores were established near Stewart's store on lower Broadway between 8th and 23rd, popularly known as "Ladies' Mile," including Lord & Taylor, Siegel-Cooper, Stern Brothers, LeBoutellier, James McCreery, and Simpson-Crawford. John Wanamaker, the "Merchant Prince," opened the Grand Depot in Philadelphia in 1876. It became the largest single-floor department store in the world with 129 concentric counters surrounding a central ballroom of female fashions. Marshall Field built the largest department store in the world on State Street in Chicago when he added a 20-story men's store in 1917 across the street from his existing 12-story structure erected in 1907. Macy's department store soon took over this title when it came to occupy an entire city block and stand 30 stories tall in 1924.

THE DEMOCRATIZATION OF DESIRE

Department stores created a "dream world" (Williams 1982) for consumers with extravagant displays and spectacular atriums that encouraged them to browse and fantasize about current and future purchases and identities. However, these dream worlds would have been impossible without technological and organizational advances in mass production and consumption and business management (Leach 1993). The sensational array of goods displayed at department stores depended upon the mass production of consumer goods, especially ready-to-wear clothing. Reliable distribution methods were necessary to continually stock merchandise. This was particularly important because many of the first department stores sold food products. Elevators and escalators were installed to provide comfort and convenience as well as to methodically navigate consumers through different departments. Pneumatic tube systems were used

to efficiently handle the high volume of cash transactions until credit. Installment payment plans were established to tempt consumers to immediately gratify their desires. Thus, a hidden, formally rationalized system supported the enchanting façade of the department store (Ritzer 2005).

Although department stores catered to an overwhelmingly bourgeois consumer base, they did not close their doors to working-class consumers who wanted a glimpse of luxury. Members of all classes were encouraged to spend hours walking through these vast emporiums, wandering from department to department, fantasizing about the novel array of consumer goods on display – all without having to spend any money at all. Marshall Field even tried to tempt consumers from the city sidewalk, installing spectacular window displays to create desire. According to Leach (1993: 63), glass was used by department stores to democratize desire while "dedemocratizing access to goods." Displaying goods under the protection of glass allowed all consumers to gaze at luxurious products, even if they could not physically touch them or financially afford them. While department stores may have democratized consumer desire by inviting all individuals to enter their dream worlds, most stores were privy to the fact that working-class consumers could not afford many of the goods they offered. To solve this dilemma some department stores created bargain basements with marked-down goods and cheap imitations of products for sale on the upper levels (Leach 1993).

A PRIVILEGED SPACE FOR WOMEN

One may question the democratic nature of this desire because it was primarily directed at one group: women (Reekie 1993). Although men certainly consumed goods, they were viewed as too rational to be tempted into buying something they did not really need. Store managers did not think that most men had the time to waste spending hours wandering through a variety of departments; conventional wisdom held that most men would be uncomfortable walking through women's departments. Women, on the other hand, were stereotypically viewed as not only having the time to shop, but also possessing an irrationality that could be managed through created desire. The department store became the female public sphere, replacing, in the words of Émile Zola, the church. According to Zola, the department store "marches to the religion of the cash desk, of beauty, of coquetry, and fashion. [Women] go there to pass the hours as they used to go to church" (cited in Miller 1981: 19). Like the church, the department store was a place where middle-class women could legitimately be alone in the city. Their access to this part of the public sphere was a consequence of their domestic duty to take care of the private sphere. While women could fantasize about the latest fashions, much of their shopping revolved around purchasing items for their households.

Women, however, were not just shopping at the department store but were also working as sales clerks within them. Furthermore, men were not entirely absent from this female public sphere as they owned and managed most department stores (Benson 1986). Thus, a sexual division of labor and a class division of shopping existed as a concrete reality in these dream worlds. Young, unmarried female sales clerks were overworked and underpaid, yet they were still expected to look and act professional. Female shoppers were not ignorant of this exploitation. During the Progressive era middle- and upper-class female shoppers formed a consumers' league to help ameliorate the working conditions of female sales clerks in New York City, publishing a "white list" of department stores that treated their female sales clerks fairly. Interestingly, the success of securing shorter working days for sales clerks came at the expense of working-class women, who did not have the leisure to shop during what became regular department store hours.

THE DEPARTMENT STORE AND THE SHOPPING MALL

The rise of the enclosed, suburban shopping mall in the post-war era marked both the success and the eventual downfall of the traditional department store. The original grand emporiums remained in the city center, but when department stores began creating national chains they lost much of their distinctiveness. Mall developers courted the large department stores to anchor their shopping centers. Most mall developers provided either low or no rent from department stores because they knew that they brought in prized foot traffic. Early shopping malls mimicked a "dumb bell" architectural model with department stores as the anchors to force consumers to walk through the interior of the mall and hopefully be tempted to shop at smaller, specialty shops. However, smaller specialty shops began to rob the department store of its actual departments. Consumers could now shop at Victoria's Secret for lingerie or Footlocker for athletic apparel instead of searching for these departments at Macy's or Bloomingdale's.

No longer rooted in a local city culture, chain department stores became increasingly rationalized or "McDonaldized" (Ritzer 2004). The physical architecture of the stores lost their enchantment. The homogeneous products they offered for sale did little to distinguish one department store chain from another. Prices remained low, but at the expense of personal service. Mergers have been one of the primary causes of this disenchantment. Mergers, of course, are not a recent development. The first significant department store mergers occurred in the 1920s, culminating in the creation of Federated Department Stores in 1929. In 2005 Federated Department Stores spent $11 billion to acquire May Department Stores Company. This mega-merger of about 950 department stores has resulted in many May department stores, such as Lazarus, Rich's, Hecht's, and Kaufman's, being renamed Federated's most popular chain, Macy's.

THE DEATH OF THE DEPARTMENT STORE?

In recent years the department store has been in a state of decline with the rise of "big box" stores, such as Home Depot, Office Max, and Petsmart. Big box stores are free-standing spaces that specialize in selling large quantities of a distinct category of merchandise at low prices. Dubbed "category killers" (Spector 2005), big box stores seek to monopolize the market of a specific category at the expense of both local retail stores and department stores. Essentially, big box stores have taken the "departments" out of the department store. Charles Lazarus, the founder of Toys R Us, institutionalized the modern big box store. Department stores dominated the market for toys until this category killer was established. Department stores have steadily decreased their number of departments since the birth of the big box stores, including home furnishings, home goods, and electronics.

The initial success of big box stores was built upon discount prices, convenience, and self-service. Unlike the department store, big box stores did not seek customer loyalty or offer personal services. Instead, they sought to attract the bargain hunter who was willing to sacrifice the dream-world quality of the department store for low prices. Indeed, the mentality of these consumers rests upon the notion that self-service in a warehouse-like setting keeps prices low. Over the years big box stores have gone through a transformation from low-maintenance warehouses to lifestyle centers. Interestingly, they have come to incorporate many of the elements that once made department stores so enchanting to consumers. Some provide resting areas, cafés, day-care facilities, and lavish displays; customer service is improving at many of them. Many big box stores have attempted to enchant their disenchanted spaces through implosion (Ritzer 2005). Although most of these stores are popular because they appear differentiated, many implode distinct categories or departments under one roof. For example, Barnes and Noble is not simply a book store, it is also a music store, a video store, a gift store, and a coffee shop.

Big box stores have not been the only competition that the traditional department store has faced. Discount department stores, like Wal-Mart and Target, have also taken over their share of the retail market. The creation of the "festival marketplace" (Hannigan 1998) has also hurt department stores. These open-air, Main Street-style marketplaces combine eating, entertainment, and shopping. Unlike the enclosed shopping mall, most do not need, or want, department stores as anchors. While the festival marketplace began in the city, many are opening in the suburbs and threatening the vitality of the enclosed shopping mall. Enclosed shopping mall owners are trying to compete with the festival marketplaces by courting big box stores, like Old Navy, Target, and Costco, to become new anchors and by creating open-air wings. In order to survive, some department stores have begun to imitate big box stores, building free-standing stores and abandoning the traditional anchor spaces they used to occupy in the shopping mall. The question remains, however, whether the department store can be sustained in an artificial space independent of either the city or the shopping mall.

SEE ALSO: Arcades; Consumption, Cathedrals of; Consumption, Landscapes of; Consumption, Urban/City as Consumerspace; Gender, Consumption and; McDonaldization; Shopping; Shopping Malls

REFERENCES AND SUGGESTED READINGS

Benson, S. P. (1986) *Counter Culture: Saleswomen, Managers, and Customers in American Department Stores, 1890–1940*. University of Illinois Press, Champaign, IL.

Hannigan, J. (1998) *Fantasy City*. Routledge, New York.

Lancaster, B. (1995) *The Department Store: A Social History*. Leicester University Press, London.

Leach, W. (1993) *Land of Desire: Merchants, Power, and the Rise of a New American Culture*. Pantheon Books, New York.

Miller, M. (1981) *The Bon Marché: Bourgeois Culture and the Department Store, 1869–1920*. Princeton University Press, Princeton.

Reekie, G. (1993) *Temptations: Sex, Selling, and the Department Store*. Allen & Unwin, St. Leonards, Australia.

Ritzer, G. (2004) *The McDonaldization of Society*. Pine Forge Press, Thousand Oaks, CA.

Ritzer, G. (2005) *Enchanting a Disenchanted World: Revolutionizing the Means of Consumption*. Pine Forge Press, Thousand Oaks, CA.

Rosenberg, M. (1985) A Sad Heart at the Department Store. *American Scholar* 54 (Spring).

Spector, R. (2005) *Category Killers: The Retail Revolution and Its Impact on Consumer Culture*. Harvard Business School Press, Boston.

Williams, R. (1982) *Dream Worlds: Mass Consumption in Late Nineteenth-Century France*. University of California Press, Berkeley.

dependency and world-systems theories

Christopher Chase-Dunn

Dependency approaches emerged out of Latin America in the 1960s in reaction to modernization theories of development. *Dependentistas* attributed the difficulties of development in the global South to the legacies of the long history of colonialism as well as contemporary international power relations. This approach suggested that international inequalities were socially structured and that hierarchy is a central feature of the global system of societies.

The world-systems perspective is a strategy for explaining social change that focuses on whole intersocietal systems rather than single societies. The main insight is that important interaction networks (trade, information flows, alliances, and fighting) have woven polities and cultures together since the beginning of human social evolution. Explanations of social change need to take intersocietal systems (world-systems) as the units that evolve. However, intersocietal interaction networks were rather small when transportation was mainly a matter of hiking with a pack. Globalization, in the sense of the expansion and intensification of larger interaction networks, has been increasing for millennia, albeit unevenly and in waves.

The intellectual history of world-systems theory has roots in classical sociology, Marxian political economy, and the thinking of the *dependentistas*. But in explicit form the world-systems perspective emerged only in the 1970s when Samir Amin, André Gunder Frank, and Immanuel Wallerstein began to formulate the concepts and to narrate the analytic history of the modern world-system.

The idea of the *whole system* ought to mean that all the human interaction networks, small and large, from the household to global trade, constitute the world-system. It is not just a matter of "international relations" or global-scale institutions such as the World Bank. Rather, at the present time, the world-system is all the people of the earth and all their cultural, economic, and political institutions and the interactions and connections among them. The world-systems perspective looks at human institutions over long periods of time and employs the spatial scales that are required for comprehending these whole interaction systems.

The modern world-system can be understood structurally as a stratification system composed of economically, culturally, and militarily dominant core societies (themselves in competition with one another), and dependent peripheral and semiperipheral regions. Some dependent regions have been successful in improving their positions in the larger core/periphery hierarchy, while most have simply maintained their peripheral and semiperipheral positions. This structural perspective on world history allows us to analyze the cyclical features of social change and the long-term patterns of development in historical and comparative perspective. We can see the development of the modern world-system as driven primarily by capitalist accumulation and geopolitics in which businesses and states compete with one another for power and wealth. Competition among states and capitals is conditioned by the dynamics of struggle among classes and by the resistance of peripheral and semiperipheral peoples to domination and exploitation from the core. In the modern world-system, the semiperiphery is composed of large and powerful countries in the third world (e.g., Mexico, India, Brazil, China) as well as smaller countries that have intermediate levels of economic development (e.g., the newly industrializing countries of East Asia). It is not possible to understand the history of social change without taking into account both the strategies and technologies of the winners, and the strategies and forms of struggle of those who have resisted domination and exploitation.

It is also difficult to understand why and where innovative social change emerges without a conceptualization of the world-system as a whole. New organizational forms that transform institutions and that lead to upward mobility most often emerge from societies in semiperipheral locations. Thus all the countries that became dominant core states in the modern system had formerly been semiperipheral (the Dutch, the British, and the United States). This is a continuation of a long-term pattern of social evolution that Chase-Dunn and Hall

(1997) have called "semiperipheral development." Semiperipheral marcher states and semiperipheral capitalist city-states had acted as the main agents of empire formation and commercialization for millennia. This phenomenon arguably also includes organizational innovations in contemporary semiperipheral countries (e.g., Mexico, India, South Korea, Brazil) that may transform the now-global system.

This approach requires that we think structurally. We must be able to abstract from the particularities of the game of musical chairs that constitutes uneven development in the system to see the structural continuities. The core/periphery hierarchy remains, though some countries have moved up or down. The interstate system remains, though the internationalization of capital has further constrained the abilities of states to structure national economies. States have always been subjected to larger geopolitical and economic forces in the world-system, and as is still the case, some have been more successful at exploiting opportunities and protecting themselves from liabilities than others.

In this perspective many of the phenomena that have been called "globalization" correspond to recently expanded international trade, financial flows, and foreign investment by transnational corporations and banks. Much of the globalization discourse assumes that until recently there were separate national societies and economies, and that these have now been superseded by an expansion of international integration driven by information and transportation technologies. Rather than a wholly unique and new phenomenon, globalization is primarily international economic integration, and as such it is a feature of the world-system that has been oscillating as well as increasing for centuries. Recent research comparing the nineteenth and twentieth centuries has shown that trade globalization is both a cycle and a trend.

The Great Chartered Companies of the seventeenth century were already playing an important role in shaping the development of world regions. Certainly, the transnational corporations of the present are much more important players, but the point is that "foreign investment" is not an institution that only became important since 1970 (nor since World War II). Arrighi (1994) has shown that finance capital has been a central component of the commanding heights of the world-system since the fourteenth century. The current floods and ebbs of world money are typical of the late phase of very long "systemic cycles of accumulation."

Most world-systems scholars contend that leaving out the core/periphery dimension or treating the periphery as inert are grave mistakes, not only for reasons of completeness, but also because the ability of core capitalists and their states to exploit peripheral resources and labor has been a major factor in deciding the winners of the competition among core contenders. And the resistance to exploitation and domination mounted by peripheral peoples has played a powerful role in shaping the historical development of world orders. Thus world history cannot be properly understood without attention to the core/periphery hierarchy.

McMichael (2000) has studied the "globalization project" – the abandoning of Keynesian models of national development and a new (or renewed) emphasis on deregulation and opening national commodity and financial markets to foreign trade and investment. This approach focuses on the political and ideological aspects of the recent wave of international integration. The term many prefer for this turn in global discourse is "neoliberalism," but it has also been called "Reaganism/Thatcherism" and the "Washington Consensus." The worldwide decline of the political left predated the revolutions of 1989 and the demise of the Soviet Union, but it was certainly also accelerated by these events. The structural basis of the rise of the globalization project is the new level of integration reached by the global capitalist class. The internationalization of capital has long been an important part of the trend toward economic globalization, and there have been many claims to represent the general interests of business before. Indeed, every modern dominant state has made this claim. But the real integration of the interests of capitalists all over the world has very likely reached a level greater than at the peak of the nineteenth-century wave of globalization.

This is the part of the theory of a global stage of capitalism that must be taken most seriously, though it can certainly be overdone. The world-system has now reached a point at which the old interstate system based on separate national capitalist classes exists simultaneously with new institutions representing the global interests of capital, and both are powerful forces. In this light each country can be seen to have an important ruling class faction that is allied with the transnational capitalist class. The big question is whether or not this new level of transnational integration will be strong enough to prevent competition among states for world hegemony from turning into warfare, as it has always done in the past, during a period in which a dominant state (now the United States) is declining.

The insight that capitalist globalization has occurred in waves, and that these waves of integration are followed by periods of globalization backlash, has important implications for the future. Capitalist globalization increased both intranational and international inequalities in the nineteenth century and it has done the same thing in the late twentieth century (O'Rourke & Williamson 2000). Those countries and groups that are left out of the "beautiful époque" either mobilize to challenge the status of the powerful or they retreat into self-reliance, or both.

Globalization protests emerged in the non-core with the anti-IMF riots of the 1980s. The several transnational social movements that participated in the 1999 protest in Seattle brought globalization protest to the attention of observers in the core, and this resistance to capitalist globalization has continued and grown despite the setback that occurred in response to the terrorist attacks on New York and Washington in 2001.

There is an apparent tension between, on the one hand, those who advocate deglobalization and delinking from the global capitalist economy and the building of stronger, more cooperative and self-reliant social relations in the periphery and semiperiphery and, on the other hand, those who seek to mobilize support for new, or reformed, institutions of democratic global governance. Self-reliance by itself, though an understandable reaction to exploitation, is not likely to solve the problems of humanity in the long run. The great challenge of the twenty-first century will be the building of a democratic and collectively rational global commonwealth. World-systems theory can be an important contributor to this effort.

SEE ALSO: Capitalism; Colonialism (Neocolonialism); Development: Political Economy; Empire; Global Economy; Global Justice as a Social Movement; Global Politics; International Gender Division of Labor; Kondratieff Cycles; Revolutions; Transnational Movements; World Conflict

REFERENCES AND SUGGESTED READINGS

Amin, S. (1997) *Capitalism in the Age of Globalization*. Zed Press, London.

Arrighi, G. (1994) *The Long Twentieth Century*. Verso, London.

Cardoso, F. H. & Faletto, E. (1979) *Dependency and Development in Latin America*. University of California Press, Berkeley.

Chase-Dunn, C. (1998) *Global Formation*. Rowman & Littlefield, Lanham, MD.

Chase-Dunn, C. & Hall, T. D. (1997) *Rise and Demise: Comparing World-Systems*. Westview, Boulder, CO.

McMichael, P. (2000) *Development and Social Change: A Global Perspective*. Pine Forge Press, Thousand Oaks, CA.

O'Rourke, K. H. & Williamson, J. G. (2000) *Globalization and History*. MIT Press, Cambridge, MA.

Shannon, T. R. (1996) *An Introduction to the World-Systems Perspective*. Westview, Boulder, CO.

Wallerstein, I. (2000) *The Essential Wallerstein*. New Press, New York.

Derrida, Jacques (1930–2005)

Michael Lipscomb

Jacques Derrida was an Algerian-born philosopher remembered for his development of deconstruction, an approach to thinking that seeks carefully to analyze signifying objects in terms of the differences that are constitutive of those objects. Typically, this deconstructive approach proceeds through a close analysis of the ambivalent and marginal terms that help secure the bounded understanding of a text, concept, or phenomenon, but which cannot be reduced to a final, stable meaning intended by the author or by orthodox interpretation.

Derrida's writing has been attacked for both its difficulty and its supposedly nihilistic implications. Regarding the first charge, his work certainly reflects the density and complexity of the philosophical tradition from which it emerges, but there are numerous places in his later work and his published interviews that offer fairly straightforward summaries of his thinking. Regarding the second charge, Derrida worked hard to counter the common conception that deconstruction entails a kind of textual free play that inevitably leads to a moral and intellectual relativism. In fact, his work represents a scrupulous commitment to the practice of carefully reading any text (written or otherwise), which, above all, respects the probity of the text under consideration. Thus, though his work offers a general strategy for thinking about conditions of knowledge and representation, the power of that approach is derived from its attentiveness to how those conditions are manifested in specific contexts. Throughout his long and prolific career, Derrida brought this practice of close reading to bear on examinations of an impressive variety of subjects, ranging across considerations of major figures in the western philosophical canon (e.g., Plato, Kant, Hegel, Husserl, Heidegger, Nietzsche, and Freud), literary productions (including the works of Ponge, Genet, Joyce, and Mallarmé), and a wide array of social and political themes (education, internationalism, telecommunications, political economy, and the death penalty, to offer a partial list).

Throughout the breadth of this output, and despite repeated criticisms to the contrary, Derrida's efforts were not aimed against the possibility of coherent interpretations; instead, he sought to show how the possible coherence of any interpretation, the very possibility of communicative meaning, is derived within a specific semantic code and is thus premised upon the possibility of repeating that code, its "iterability." In the temporal and spatial movement of a repetition, there is always the possibility of slippage, and thus the recurring possibility of the new and the unforeseen, the possibility that any text might be grafted into new contexts that would begin to reshape its meaning. For Derrida, this iterative inevitability suggests a certain continuity and stability, but it also points to the inherently open-ended status of any text, phenomenon, or representation. On the one hand, Derrida decidedly does not seek to reduce all phenomena to a literary text; rather, his famous declaration that "there is nothing outside of the text" (Derrida 1974) points to the ways in which texts are unendingly opened by the very terms that mark the bounded field of meaning that makes any immediate understanding possible. On the other hand, Derrida's thinking does not seek to destroy the conceptual traditions from which it emerges (they are, in fact, its very condition of possibility); rather, it seeks to solicit them in a way that denaturalizes that which might otherwise seem natural and already decided.

Derrida's approach to reading, therefore, has both epistemological and ethical implications, linking an insistence on careful descriptive work with an always present normative orientation. Descriptively, this line of thinking has helped complicate working concepts within a broad range of intellectual disciplines, opening those concepts to an ongoing reconsideration and thus stressing a kind of scientific and intellectual practice that remains open to new perspectives and events. To take but one example, Derrida's work has provided tools for productively troubling liberal, Marxist, structuralist, feminist, and psychoanalytic understandings of the "human subject" and its relation to its social environment. Normatively, Derrida's general approach emphasizes a respect for the "other" that comes from outside of our previously consecrated and currently present understandings, resisting the tendency to reduce that which is different to the interpretive grids that we have inherited. Deconstruction, then, carries an ethical imperative that productively complicates our other-regarding orientations, and it is in this sense that Derrida would insist that deconstruction is always, in the very movement of its critical posture, an affirmative gesture that is capable of saying "yes" to that which is yet to come.

SEE ALSO: Deconstruction; Foucault, Michel; Postmodern Feminism; Postmodernism; Poststructuralism; Semiotics

REFERENCES AND SUGGESTED READINGS

Derrida, J. (1974) *Of Grammatology*. Trans. G. C. Spivak. Johns Hopkins University Press, Baltimore.

Derrida, J. (1978) *Writing and Difference*. Trans. A. Bass. University of Chicago Press, Chicago.

Derrida, J. (1988) *Limited Inc*. Trans. S. Weber & J. Mehlman. Northwestern University Press, Evanston.

Derrida, J. (1994) *Spectres of Marx: The State of the Debt, the Work of Mourning, and the New International*. Trans. P. Kamuf. Routledge, New York.

Derrida, J. (1995) *Points . . .: Interviews, 1974–1994*. Stanford University Press, Stanford.

Derrida, J. (1997) *Deconstruction in a Nutshell: A Conversation with Jacques Derrida*. Fordham University Press, New York.

Bennington, G. & Derrida, J. (1993) *Jacques Derrida*. Trans. G. Bennington. University of Chicago Press, Chicago.

descriptive statistics

Karen Lahm

Descriptive statistics, also known as univariate statistics, are most often used to describe the distribution of a variable or variables in a sample. A distribution of a variable can be thought of as all of the individual scores or categories of a variable contained in a sample or population. For example, if the variable being measured in a sample of 100 people is age, then the distribution for the age variable would be all of the 100 separate ages of the people contained in the sample.

The most common examples of descriptive statistics are the mean, median, mode, range, standard deviation, and variance. It is important to note that one can obtain descriptive statistics for a sample or a population. However, in the population these values would be referred to as parameters, not statistics. So, when the term descriptive statistics is used to describe a variable or variables, the researcher is referring to a sample, not a population.

When taken together, the mode, median, and mean are most often referred to as measures of central tendency. They are used to describe the center of a distribution of a variable. The mode is the most frequently occurring category or score in the distribution of a variable. For example, if one had a sample of eight test scores – 80, 50, 72, 65, 80, 80, 99, and 90 – then the mode would be the score of 80 because it is the score that is repeated most often. Even though the mode is considered a measure of central tendency, the mode is not the exact center of the distribution. It is just the most frequently reported score or category.

The exact center of a distribution of a variable is the median. Half of the sample lies above the value of the median and half lies below. The median can also be described as a value or category that lies at the 50 percentile of the distribution. Using a sample of five test scores – 50, 60, 70, 80, and 90 – in order to obtain the median one would first have to order the scores from lowest to highest. Using the formula for the median $[(n + 1)/2]$ with n being sample size of five, the formula would give us the placeholder of the median. Thus, in this example, the placeholder of the median is the third score and that is 70. Thus, two scores lie above 70 and two below. No matter how many scores are in a distribution, or the values of those scores, the median is always the exact center score.

The final measure of central tendency is the mean. The mean is simply the average score in the distribution of a variable. Adding up all of the observed scores of a variable in a sample and then dividing that summed value by the sample size (n) will result in the mean of that variable. Thus, if one had five scores in a sample – 60, 75, 82, 88, and 90 – one would add up those five scores and divide by five to get the mean (395/5 = 79).

The mean acts like a teeter-totter by balancing all of the values of the scores in the distribution of a variable. As a result, the mean may not be, and usually is not, the exact center of a distribution. One reason for this is because the mean is highly affected by extreme scores (i.e., outliers) in a sample of scores. Extreme scores can be either very high or low scores when compared to the other scores in the distribution. For example, if one had a sample of seven test scores – 15, 65, 70, 72, 85, 90, 96 – the outlier in this case may be the 15. Moreover, because the score of 15 is so low, the mean is actually pulled toward it, thus deflating the actual center score. This gives an inaccurate picture of the real center of the distribution of scores. So, when one has a sample containing outliers, it is often called a skewed distribution. Extreme caution should be used when examining the mean in a skewed distribution because it is often not the best representation of the center of that distribution. Rather, the median should be used as the best measure of central tendency for any skewed distributions.

Three other very important descriptive statistics are the range, variance, and standard deviation. These descriptive statistics are often called measures of dispersion because they typically describe the variation of the observed scores of a variable around the mean. The range is simply the difference between the lowest (i.e., minimum) and highest score (i.e., maximum) in the distribution.

The variance is the average squared difference of scores from the mean. Since the variance is measured in squared units (e.g., years squared, dollars squared, etc.) it is commonly not discussed as much as other measures of dispersion. A more frequently examined measure of dispersion is the standard deviation. Mathematically, the standard deviation is found by taking the square root of the variance. Thus, standard deviation can be interpreted as the average difference of scores from the mean.

Some samples have a wide variety of scores (i.e., heterogeneous samples) and some have observed scores that are very similar or close to one another (i.e., homogeneous samples). For example, if a sample of 100 people were all the same age then the measures of dispersion would both be zero because there is no variation in the ages of the sample respondents. Moreover, heterogeneous samples (i.e., having a wide variety of scores) would have high values for the variance and standard deviation, while homogeneous samples (i.e., very little variation in the scores) would have lower values for the variance and standard deviation. There is no commonly accepted value indicating a high or low measure of dispersion because variables can be represented in a wide array of units. For example, a standard deviation of six can represent a high measure of dispersion for a variable, such as number of children. However, that same

standard deviation of six can also actually be a very small measure of dispersion for a variable such as income.

SEE ALSO: Measures of Centrality; Outliers; Statistics; Variance

REFERENCES AND SUGGESTED READINGS

Bulmer, M. (1979) *Principles of Statistics*. Dover, New York.
Donnelly, R. A. (2004) *Complete Idiot's Guide to Statistics*. Alpha, New York.
Healey, J. (2004) *Statistics: A Tool for the Behavioral Sciences*. Wadsworth, New York.
Larson, R. & Farber, E. (2005) *Elementary Statistics: Picturing the World*, 3rd edn. Prentice-Hall, Englewood Cliffs, NJ.
Triola, M. (2003) *Elementary Statistics*, 9th edn. Addison Wesley, Boston.

deterrence theory

Mark Stafford and Gini Deibert

Deterrence theory can be traced to such early utilitarians as Cesare Beccaria and Jeremy Bentham (Johnson & Wolfe 2003). The underlying idea is that people will commit crimes to the extent they are more pleasurable than painful. Certain, severe, and swift legal punishments increase the pain for crimes and, thereby, can deter people from committing them.

Neither Beccaria nor Bentham systematically defined *deterrence*. However, Gibbs's (1975) definition is conventional: deterrence is the omission or curtailment of a crime from fear of legal punishment. The terms "omission" and "curtailment" identify two possibilities: (1) people may refrain entirely from committing a crime from fear of legal punishment, or (2) they may only curtail or restrict their commission of it (e.g., a motorist may speed only occasionally in the belief that repetitive speeding eventually will result in a fine).

No single version of deterrence theory is accepted universally. However, any version is likely to include something like this proposition:

Proposition 1: The greater the certainty, severity, and celerity of legal punishment for a type of crime, the less the rate of that crime.

Certainty refers to the likelihood (e.g., probability) of legal punishment; severity refers to the punishment's magnitude; and celerity refers to its swiftness. A high certainty of legal punishment has been considered a more effective deterrent than either high severity or high celerity, and consequently it has been the principal variable in deterrence theory and research (Gibbs 1975; Nagin 1998).

There are two ways to consider legal punishments. The first is to consider them as *objectively given*. For example, for a particular time and place, the objective certainty of imprisonment for a type of crime could be estimated by taking the number of persons imprisoned for that crime, divided by the number of such crimes; and the objective severity of imprisonment for the crime could be estimated by the average number of years in prison people actually served for it. The second way to consider legal punishments is *perceptually*. For example, people could be asked about their perceptions of the certainty and severity of imprisonment for a type of crime. The distinction between objective and perceived punishments is reflected in these three deterrence propositions:

Proposition 2: The greater the objective certainty, severity, and celerity of legal punishment for a type of crime (OP), the less the rate of that crime (CR).

Proposition 3: The greater the objective certainty, severity, and celerity of legal punishment for a type of crime (OP), the greater the perceived certainty, severity, and celerity of legal punishment for that crime (PP).

Proposition 4: The greater the perceived certainty, severity, and celerity of legal punishment for a type of crime (PP), the less the rate of that crime (CR).

Or, combining and expressing the three propositions diagrammatically:

$$OP >\!\!-\!\!> PP <\!\!-\!\!< CR$$

where $>\!\!-\!\!>$ denotes a positive relation and $<\!\!-\!\!<$ denotes a negative relation.

Prior to 1980, most deterrence research focused on Proposition 2. For example, Gibbs (1968) found a negative association among US states between the objective certainty and severity of imprisonment for homicide and the homicide rate.

Both Beccaria and Bentham posited a positive relationship between objective and perceived legal punishments, which is stated as Proposition 3, and policymakers agree in expecting to increase people's perceptions of punishment by increasing the levels of objective punishments (e.g., by increasing the objective certainty of arrest for crimes). Despite that expectation, most of the relevant findings have been contrary to it. For example, Erickson and Gibbs (1978) found only a moderately strong positive association among 10 types of crimes between the objective and perceived certainty of arrest. Moreover, they found no support for a central implication of Propositions 2–4 "that the objective certainty of punishment is related to crime rates *through* the perception of punishment" (p. 263).

Doubts about the relationship between objective and perceived legal punishments have led deterrence researchers more recently to focus on Proposition 4 that perceived punishments (e.g., perceptions of the certainty of punishment) for a type of crime are negatively related to the rate of that crime (Nagin 1998). That focus is justified because Proposition 4 comes closer than the others in capturing the element of fear that is integral to the definition of deterrence (see above). Scores of studies over the past several decades have found that "perceptions of ... [the certainty of] punishment have negative, deterrent-like associations with ...offending" (Nagin 1998: 13). This is not the case with the perceptions of the severity of punishment, "but when individual assessments of the cost of ... sanctions are taken into account ... significant negative associations ... emerge" (ibid.).

Many "non-deterrence" variables are related to rates of crime, which makes deterrence theory more complex than the foregoing propositions suggest. For example, while crime rates are related to perceived punishments (Proposition 4), they also are related to threats of *extralegal* punishments, such as stigma, divorce, and loss of job. Extralegal punishments are relevant for deterrence theory in at least three ways. First, legal and extralegal punishments may have independent effects on crime rates. Second, legal punishments may prevent people from committing crimes *through* their effects on extralegal punishments (e.g., people may refrain from crime for fear of job loss if arrested). Finally, legal and extralegal punishments may have interactive effects on crime rates (e.g., people may be deterred by fear of legal punishment *only if* they believe they will suffer an extralegal punishment, such as divorce).

SEE ALSO: Beccaria, Cesare; Crime; Criminal Justice System; Crime, Psychological Theories of

REFERENCES AND SUGGESTED READINGS

Erickson, M. L. & Gibbs, J. P. (1978) Objective and Perceptual Properties of Legal Punishment and the Deterrence Doctrine. *Social Problems* 25: 253–64.

Gibbs, J. P. (1968) Crime, Punishment, and Deterrence. *Social Science Quarterly* 48: 515–30.

Gibbs, J. P. (1975) *Crime, Punishment, and Deterrence.* Elsevier, New York.

Johnson, H. A. & Wolfe, N. T. (2003) *History of Criminal Justice.* Anderson, Cincinnati.

Nagin, D. S. (1998) Criminal Deterrence Research at the Outset of the Twenty-First Century. In: Tonry, M. (Ed.), *Crime and Justice: A Review of Research.* University of Chicago Press, Chicago, pp. 1–42.

development: political economy

Manuela Boatca

The emergence of the idea of development in western culture is closely linked to the evolutionary worldview that began to gain ground in Europe in the eighteenth century and has as such also been constitutive for sociology as a discipline. Like evolution, development has taken on a variety of meanings, the common denominator of which can be seen in the idea of continuous, orderly social change usually proceeding in several, clearly demarcated stages and entailing an improvement of living conditions. However, as will be shown in the following, while most evolutionary theories implicitly are theories of development, the reverse does not apply.

In contrast to the relative social stability and the deterministic outlook characteristic of previous centuries, such major political upheavals of the eighteenth and nineteenth centuries as the French Revolution, the American Revolutionary War, and the South American Wars of Independence, along with the rise in social mobility that accompanied the spread of industrialization, gradually imposed the notion that social and political change, rather than being exceptional, was the norm. Modern society, and with it western civilization, were increasingly seen as the product of progress in which such constant change had resulted. Viewed in turn as static, undifferentiated, and lacking in complexity, traditional societies were relegated to an earlier stage in the course of human development. The theological explanation according to which the "savages" and "barbarians" of the non-European world had hitherto been considered less than human was consequently replaced by a historicist interpretation that perceived them as (merely) less developed. An evolutionary perspective postulating the unidirectionality and inherent progressiveness of human history thus became central to both western sociology and anthropology, as disciplines whose institutionalization in the nineteenth century was intimately linked to the European project of civilizing the world. Their task therefore consisted of identifying the different stages of development and the corresponding laws of social evolution through which each society must pass in order to reach the western standard of civilization. Classical political economy, best illustrated within sociology by Marx's theory of historical materialism, concurred in this view by conceiving of modes of production as chronologically structured and nationally determined. In this classical understanding, development thus represented the outcome of an immanent historical process to be traversed by individual social organisms on their way to maturity – the equivalent of modern society.

Massive criticism directed at evolutionism in the first half of the twentieth century, ultimately leading to its temporary discrediting as an academic endeavor, prevented a resumption of the issue of development until the post-war era. During the 1950s, development again became central to both social scientific concerns and policymaking. The bipolar geopolitical structure characterizing the aftermath of World War II, as well as the simultaneous process of decolonization of European empires in Asia, Africa, and Latin America that resulted in the emergence of an array of new nation-states in the so-called third world, accordingly led to a competition for potential economic and political spheres of influence between the US and the Soviet Union. In response to the need to discredit the communist model as a viable alternative for the new nations, the multidisciplinary US modernization school identified the problem of third world countries in their traditionalism and viewed the solution to it in modernization, understood as a stage-by-stage replication of the economic development of Western Europe and North America. Drawing on evolutionary as well as functionalist assumptions, modernization theory saw societies as becoming increasingly similar in the course of a slowly operating process of social change considered unidirectional, progressive, and irreversible. It thus revived basic premises of nineteenth-century evolutionary theory, such as the stage theory of development and the clear-cut distinction between traditional and modern societies. At the same time, it replaced the notion of development as a byproduct of an immanent historical process with one of development strategy, deliberately triggered and controlled by political actors with the help of state-led policies. In *The Stages of Economic Growth*, one of the most widely debated works of the modernization school, W. W. Rostow (1960) identified the lack of productive investment as the main problem of third world societies and was among the first to suggest that the obvious solution was to provide US aid to these countries – understood in terms of capital, technology, and expertise. It can thus be said that the models brought forth by the modernization school were neither evolutionary nor

functionalist large-scale *theories of social change*, *theories of development* of limited spatial and temporal scope. They were born out of an attempt to solve the issue of development of particular regions of the world with respect to other particular regions at a specific moment in history – although researchers often extrapolated both across time periods and geographical locations. In this modern variant, development therefore became coterminous with planned economic growth and political modernization, to be implemented with the help of development agencies and foreign aid projects especially created for the purpose.

Rejecting both the main theoretical assumptions and the policy implications of the modernization school with respect to development, the largely neo-Marxist dependency theory focused instead on underdevelopment (and is therefore sometimes referred to as underdevelopment theory). Arising in Latin America in the early 1960s in reaction to the failure of the United Nations' economic program to promote development, and the modernization school's inability to explain the ensuing economic stagnation in the region, the dependency school claimed that modernization was an ideology used in order to justify the US's intervention in third world affairs. In the wake of Lenin's and J. A. Hobson's theories of "imperialism," dependency theorists characterized modern capitalism as a center–periphery (i.e., asymmetrical) relationship between the developed, industrialized West and the underdeveloped, agricultural third world. Rejecting the theoretical division between "traditional" and "modern" society, which modernization policies were meant to bridge, dependency theorists claimed that the modern world's center–periphery structure mirrored an underlying international division of labor, established during the European colonial expansion and still maintained in the present through mechanisms of economic domination. In this view, the economies of the colonized regions had been reorganized so as to meet the needs of the colonizer countries, and ended up producing raw materials that served the latter's interests. Hence, in sharp contrast to modernization theory, the dependency school did not view underdevelopment as a "stage" previous to development, but as a distinct historical process that industrialized economies have not experienced. For dependency theorists, therefore, just as center and periphery are relational notions, existing only simultaneously, development and underdevelopment are only different aspects of the same phenomenon, not different stages in an evolutionary continuum. Moreover, in their view, underdevelopment is not the natural condition the modernization school liked to presuppose, but an artifact created by the long history of colonial domination in third world countries, and as such a process of "development of underdevelopment" (Frank 1967). Accordingly, studying individual societies, as modernization theories did, meant leaving all exogenous factors of change out of the analysis and thus could not lead to a valid explanation of social change. Since the development of the US and Western Europe had been based on the underdevelopment of the third world, foreign aid policies could only result in the latter falling further and further behind. Consequently, dependency theorists saw the only concrete solution to the termination of dependency situations in third world countries in severing the ties with the core and choosing a socialist path of autonomous development, on the model of China and Cuba. In response to mounting criticism pointing out the economic success of other former colonies such as South Korea or Taiwan, a modified version of the theory later combined the notions of dependency and development into "associated-dependent development" (Cardoso 1973). This approach postulated that the industrial capital invested by multinational corporations in peripheral countries could induce some amount of development and as such constituted a viable alternative for the states that did not want to take the chance of a socialist revolution.

World-systems analysis expanded on the basis of the criticism that the dependency school had directed at the methodology of modernization studies. It claimed that the developmentalist view of social change which modernization theorists shared had a flawed logic. In a world-economy such as the one represented by the current capitalist world-system, it was the world-system as a whole, and not individual societies, that should constitute the basic unit of analysis. Reifying political-cultural units (i.e., states) into autonomously evolving entities, as most theories of social change commonly did, led to ahistorical models of social transformation, as in the "traditional" vs. "modern" distinction. For world-systems analysis, as for dependency theory, underdevelopment was not an earlier stage in the transition to development, but the necessary result of the international division of labor underlying the capitalist world-economy. Although the world-systems model advanced by Immanuel Wallerstein included an additional structural position, the semiperiphery, as well as a historical account of the evolution of the entire structural hierarchy since the sixteenth century, upward mobility within the capitalist division of labor (e.g., a semiperiphery's rise to core status) was not considered development (since it was achieved at the expense of other regions), but merely successful expropriation of world surplus. While the dependency school, unlike world-systems analysis, did not advance a general evolutionary theory, but one of social change in the periphery, both approaches retained a notion of development in which progress was represented by the – however uncertain – transition to (world) socialism.

The long-term result of the neo-Marxist critiques of the notion of development espoused by modernization theories was growing skepticism toward classical development theory, as well as added attention being devoted to the issue of underdevelopment both by scholars and policymakers. By the end of the twentieth century, development as a theme of academic research was largely considered outdated and treatment of the political and economic factors affecting macrostructural social change increasingly occurred within the more neutral, but less specifically defined, theoretical framework of globalization. In conceptual terms, this translated into a shift in the process of development from nationally to globally managed economic growth (McMichael 2005). Especially after the demise of communism in Eastern Europe and the end of the Cold War, global tendencies toward a withering away of the state as an agent of development on the one hand and toward a strengthening of the self-regulating global market on the other were accompanied on the political level by the advance of neoliberalism and a corresponding trend toward privatization and anti-statism. At the same time, the language of globalization, whether in terms of the liberalization of market economies, democratization, or transition from the second to the first world, revealed the same teleological understanding of world history on which nineteenth-century evolutionary models were premised, while adhering to a similar progressivistic logic as the one inherent in the successive western models of "development" represented by Christianization, the civilizing mission, or modernization (Mignolo 2000). Questioning the extent to which the evolutionist outlook central to the self-definition of the modern world is complicitous with a model of global economic growth responsible for excluding the great majority of the world's population from the development process while depleting the world's natural resources has, therefore, raised more than once the issue of available alternatives and their respective scope. The answers have, on the one hand, often entailed the search for alternative developments – whether an "ethnodevelopment" focusing on indigenous peoples and ethnic minorities, a "sustainable development" targeting the preservation of resources, or a feminist development economics centered on gender-sensitive development policies. However, dissatisfaction with the inherent limitations of the development paradigm as such has on the other hand prompted increasing demands for alternatives *to* development (Escobar 1995) that would fundamentally question the principle of economic growth and the model of modernity that has been based on it.

SEE ALSO: Decolonization; Dependency and World-Systems Theories; Developmental State; Modernization; Political Economy; Political Sociology; Social Change

REFERENCES AND SUGGESTED READINGS

Cardoso, F. H. (1973) Associated-Dependent Development: Theoretical and Practical Implications. In: Stephen, A. (Ed.), *Authoritarian Brazil*. Yale University Press, New Haven, pp. 142–76.

Escobar, A. (1995) *Encountering Development: The Making and Unmaking of the Third World*. Princeton University Press, Princeton.

Frank, A. G. (1967) *Capitalism and Underdevelopment in Latin America: Historical Studies of Chile and Brazil*. Monthly Review Press, New York.

McMichael, P. (2005) *Development and Social Change: A Global Perspective*. Pine Forge Press, Thousand Oaks, CA.

Mignolo, W. (2000) *Local Histories/Global Designs: Coloniality, Subaltern Knowledge, and Border Thinking*. Princeton University Press, Princeton.

Rostow, W. W. (1960) *The Stages of Economic Growth: A Non-Communist Manifesto*. Cambridge University Press, Cambridge.

So, A. Y. (1990) *Social Change and Development: Modernization, Dependency and World-System Theories*. Sage, Newbury Park.

Wallerstein, I. (1979) *The Capitalist World-Economy: Essays*. Cambridge University Press, Cambridge.

developmental stages

Cynthia Schellenbach

The developmental stage approach refers to the socially or developmentally defined, age-related sequence of stages individuals experience from birth through death. The assumption underlying the stage theories is that each stage represents a qualitatively unique period of development, indicating that the type of development is completely different and not reducible to earlier forms. That is, the developmental process occurs in an invariant sequence. The stage theory assumes that development is cumulative in nature and that development is based on each preceding step. It is expected that development proceeds toward increasingly complex levels of functioning. From a traditional viewpoint, the process of development proceeds in an irreversible sequence. Theoretically, one cannot return to an earlier form of development. The sequence of development is universal in nature. Development proceeds toward predictable end-states. These end-states may be influenced by maturational factors or environmental factors.

FREUD

Psychoanalytic theory was based on the contention that personality develops from a series of qualitatively different stages of development from infancy through adolescence. The mental structures consist of the id, ego, and the super-ego. The id is the force that seeks pleasure and self-satisfaction at any cost, and is the primary force of energy during the infancy stage. The ego functions as a mediator between the urgent needs of the id and the constraints of the real world. The superego is the psychic mechanism by which the individual begins to internalize standards for right and wrong. The psychic stages of personality development include the oral stage (0–1), the anal stage (ages 2–3), infantile-genital (ages 3–4), latency (age 4 to puberty), and the mature genital stage (mid-teens to adulthood). The oral stage is the time at which energy is derived from oral satisfaction (as in the hunger–feeding–satisfaction beha-vioral sequence). The anal period focuses psy-chic energy on the child's emergent abilities to retain bowel control, or to feel satisfaction with the ability to retain a valued part of the self. The latency period finds the child emphasizing same-sex relationships in an attempt to quell the disturbing thoughts and feelings of sexual-ity that emerged during the previous stage. The final stage emphasizes the mature emotional resolution of sexuality.

The contributions of the theory focus on the developmental approach, an emphasis on maturational processes, and an illustration that personality is sequential and cumulative. The theory is limited in that the concepts were never verified in empirical research, that the stages of personality development were narrowly con-ceptualized (to the exclusion of other domains of development), and that the role of culture and society was not emphasized sufficiently.

ERIKSON

Erikson developed a theory that emphasized a predetermined plan for healthy personality development. Erikson believed that several lim-itations needed to be addressed in Freud's the-ory. First, Freud emphasized that the steps in personality development were predetermined but failed to acknowledge any influence of the cultural environment on the individual. Sec-ond, Freud believed that little development occurred following puberty. Third, Freud

overemphasized sexuality to the exclusion of other domains of development that may influ-ence personality development.

Erikson developed a theory of psychosocial development that emphasized the simultaneous process of psychological change (inward) and social change (outward) that occurs during the process of personality development. He also suggested that developmental change occurs throughout the lifespan. Erikson posited devel-opmental turning points at designated times of enhanced vulnerability and the potential for positive development at eight times during the lifespan. Each developmental stage highlights a specific crisis, which will strengthen personality when mastered but will leave a weakness if the crisis is not mastered successfully. For exam-ple, stage one underscores the conflict of trust versus mistrust in which the primary objective is to provide a sense of predictability for the infant from birth through age 1. The toddler stage from age 1 through 3 highlights the crisis of autonomy (or the development of will) ver-sus a sense of doubt or shame about one's abilities. During the preschool years of 3 to 5, children begin to take on increasing responsi-bility and initiative versus internalizing a sense of guilt. During the early elementary school years, children master skills and knowledge based on their personal sense of industry versus feeling inferior to peers.

The building block of the theory is the per-iod of adolescence, when the young person develops a sense of identity based on how they see themselves and how society views them as individuals. Early adulthood highlights a devel-opmental turning point that focuses on a sense of intimacy with another, but not at the expense of personal isolation. Adulthood, with responsibilities toward children, work roles, and society, focuses on generativity versus stag-nation. The older years of adulthood are years when adults turn inward and internalize a sense of integrity or despair depending on the level of personal reward or satisfaction with past decisions and lives.

Erikson was the first to elaborate in detail the psychological change that extends into adult-hood and old age. He also sharpened the use of techniques such as psychohistory as well as the use of sociological and anthropological techniques to enhance the importance of the social environment in shaping personality development. Critiques suggest that elements of each crisis may exist at other age levels, not exclusively at the time of ascendance, as Erikson implies.

KOHLBERG

Kohlberg conceptualized moral development as a series of six qualitatively different stages of development. Each stage represents a specific mode of moral reasoning, ending with the highest and most complex level of moral development. The endpoint is a preservation of justice for the rights of individuals. The content of the values is not relevant to the type of reasoning within each stage. The progress of an individual is indicated by a gradual shift from an externally controlled sense of morality to an internally controlled sense of morality through the process of internalization.

Kohlberg suggests that there are three levels of moral reasoning: the preconventional level, the conventional level, and the postconventional level. Each level consists of two sublevels of reasoning. For example, at the preconventional stage, decision-making is controlled by external rules (usually from parents). In stage one, the child's definition of good and bad is based totally on obedience to authority. In stage two, moral behavior is based on doing what is best because others will reward the behavior.

At the conventional level of reasoning, the individual defines moral behavior as conforming to the rules of the external society and maintaining order based on a set of external laws. In stage three, the person is motivated to gain the approval of others who are significant, and the motivation is now internal. In stage four, the individual typically believes that the social order should be maintained in order to support the legitimate rights and expectations of others.

The postconventional stage is the time at which moral decisions are governed by internal, shared principles. At this point, moral behavior is completely internalized. At stage five, moral behavior is defined in terms of contract, as opposed to the needs of the individual. Stage six is the morality of the principles of conscience, although individuals at this stage

are respectful of the authority of mutual respect and trust. The highest level of internalized authority, or the greatest good for the largest number, dictates behavior. Judgments of moral behavior at this stage may or may not be consistent with the laws of the country or the state.

Several critiques have been leveled at Kohlberg's theory as a result of more recent research. For example, although much research does support the notion of invariant sequence, recent evidence indicates that many adults (especially those who do not receive higher education) show no advancement in moral reasoning over time. Moreover, there is no clear evidence that stage six always follows stage five. Another criticism suggests that there is no evidence to suggest that moral reasoning will necessarily be transferred to behavior. Finally, many researchers suggest that Kohlberg's theory is based primarily on moral reasoning, or cognitive processing, with little attention to the influence of other variables such as gender or context. In fact, while Kohlberg's theory is based on the justice perspective, or a perspective that focuses on the rights of the individual, other theorists such as Carol Gilligan suggest an alternative care perspective. Gilligan suggests that the care perspective is a moral perspective that views individuals in light of connectedness with others. Moral decisions are based on the balance of justice and concern for others. Many females, as well as some males, make moral decisions based on the impact of their decision on the relationship rather than on the precise rights of the individual. In other words, males and females may utilize different strategies for moral decision-making, as influenced by gender and culture.

FAMILY LIFE CYCLE

Carter and McGoldrick propose an alternative view of the stages in the life course. These researchers shift the unit of analysis from the individual to the family, tracing the developmental stages of the family from its inception to its dissolution. For example, the first stage involves leaving home and becoming a single adult, or launching from the family of origin. The launching period is complete when a young adult separates from the family of origin and becomes fully independent. The mate selection and marriage stage is second, in which two individuals from separate families of origin join to form a new system. The third stage in the family life cycle is becoming a parent with children, and taking on the role of parent in addition to the roles of spouse and worker. The next stage is the family with adolescents, in which parents embark on the lengthy process (10–15 years) of supporting their children through the process of achieving independence. The fifth stage of the family life cycle involves completion of the process of launching children, caring for aging parents, and adapting to changes in mid-life. The last stage of the family life cycle is the family in later life. The challenges in this stage involve taking on the role of grandparenting and either entering the retirement phase or making a change in career.

Although the family life cycle is recognized as a considerable contribution to sociology as a research paradigm, it is important to recognize that the framework is limited to cultures in which marriage precedes childbearing, and one in which marriages continue until the death of one partner. Demographic data indicate that there are many diverse family units other than married couples. Moreover, a large proportion of marriages will end by divorce before the last child is successfully launched into the world. With the addition of remarriage following divorce, new family life cycles must be recognized.

SEE ALSO: Aging and the Life Course, Theories of; Aging, Sociology of; Freud, Sigmund; Life Course; Life Course and Family; Psychoanalysis; Socialization

REFERENCES AND SUGGESTED READINGS

Erikson, E. (1968) *Identity: Youth and Crisis*. Norton, New York.
Freud, S. (1964) *The Standard Edition of the Complete Psychological Works of Sigmund Freud*. Hogarth, London.
Gilligan, C. (1982) *In a Different Voice*. Harvard University Press, Cambridge, MA.
Kohlberg, L. (1969) Stage and Sequence: The Cognitive-Developmental Approach. In: Lickona, T. (Ed.), *Moral Development and Behavior*. Holt, Rinehart, & Winston, New York.

developmental state

Brad Williams

The developmental state is one that strongly influences the direction and pace of economic development by directly intervening in the development process, rather than simply relying on market forces to allocate economic resources (Beeson 2003). American scholar Chalmers Johnson is widely credited with coining the term in his seminal work *MITI and the Japanese Miracle: The Growth of Industrial Policy, 1925–1975* (1982), although the notion of state intervention in the market to ensure growth was not necessarily new. Johnson's book subsequently triggered a boom in studies of the state's role in the economy.

Like many observers in the 1960s and 1970s, Johnson was puzzled by Japan's post-war economic miracle. His response was to highlight the important role of a plan-rational capitalist developmental state, which combined private ownership and state guidance, as the key to Japan's remarkable industrial transformation and growth. By doing so, Johnson created a third category of state classification that transcended the traditional liberal (free market)–Stalinist (command economy) dichotomy. In Asia, this pattern of state intervention in the market was initially and successfully emulated by Japan's former colonies South Korea and Taiwan, and then later with mixed success by the countries of Southeast Asia, as well as China. The economic success of the East Asian states, rightly or wrongly, led many observers to perceive the developmental state "as a causal argument linking interventionism with rapid economic growth" (Woo-Cumings 1999) throughout the world. The East Asian development experience challenged the arguments of dependency and world-systems theorists – influential at the time – who were skeptical about the ability of the peripheral regions of an interconnected global economy to escape exploitation by the advanced industrialized states of Western Europe and North America. The developmental state thesis emerged during a period in which Japan, in particular, achieved rising trade surpluses with the US. In a manifestation of Orientalist thinking, scholars from the so-called "revisionist" school saw this as the result of the mysterious Other's unfair adoption of a deviant form of capitalism that threatened not only established western economic thinking, but also its way of life.

The developmental state can also be located within the contexts of late developments and the influences of social mobilization and economic nationalism (Woo-Cumings 1999). Modern Japanese history has been characterized by the determined attempt to catch up with the West – first, following the stagnation of the isolationist Tokugawa period, and then after the destruction resulting from its disastrous wartime defeat. The Japanese state devised a system of political economy that would enable it to achieve this task and survive in a western-dominated world. Nationalism emerged from the war and imperialism and was an important component of the East Asian development experience, serving as an ideological mobilizing force behind the sacrifices the populace were forced to endure in pursuit of reconstruction and growth objectives.

There is a divergence of views regarding the factors contributing to the developmental state's success, which can be broadly linked to the agency–structure debate within the social sciences. Some observers are critical of the inward orientation of Johnson's model, believing it overlooks important structural factors such as the superpower conflict. Johnson downplays (but does not dismiss) the influence of the Cold War, arguing that Japan would have grown anyway. However, it is difficult to deny that Japan benefited enormously from the US security guarantee, which allowed it to concentrate on economic growth without being burdened by excessive defense outlays, and unfettered access to the vast consumer market of its superpower patron facilitated by its status as a bulwark against communist expansion in East Asia.

At the heart of the developmental state and the key institution of social mobilization was the economic bureaucracy. In Japan this was the Ministry of International Trade and Industry, or MITI (now METI) – the analytical focus of Johnson's study – and its institutional equivalents in South Korea and Taiwan, the Economic Planning Board and Council for Economic Planning, respectively. In true Weberian fashion, the economic bureaucracy that administered the developmental state was extremely professional, meritocratic, and rational. In the case of Japan, elite state bureaucrats were recruited from the top ranks of the best law schools in the country and entry into this world of prestige and power was limited to those who passed legally binding and highly competitive national examinations (Johnson 1995). For Johnson, the locus of state power in Japan was found in elite economic bureaucrats who formulated industrial policy, identified the means for implementing it, and ensured highly regulated competition in designated strategic sectors.

This is not to say that the state completely dominated society. The developmental state's relationship to society has been described variously as "embedded" (Evans), "governed interdependence" (Weiss), and "dependent development" (Gold). State and society, in the form of big business (in Japan the *zaibatsu* and its post-war successor the *keiretsu*, and in Korea the *chaebol*), are in a mutually beneficial relationship, with the state providing, inter alia, access to low-cost finance, as well as markets and business helping to achieve the state's development goals. According to Woo-Cumings (1999), the developmental state is diachronic: the cooperative relationship between the bureaucracy and business had been learned and perfected over time through a process of institutional adaptation that meets the demands of the time.

While instrumental in achieving rapid growth, the close relationship between the bureaucracy and big business in South Korea and Japan, in particular, also has a negative aspect manifested as severe structural corruption. Here, the money made available by the state for business often found its way into the pockets of politicians from the ruling government parties. The bureaucracies' role in these illicit flows, used to protect vested interests, suggested a significant deviance from Weberian ideals.

In addition to protecting vested interests, the East Asian developmental state was often undemocratic and authoritarian. While there was no inevitable causal link between authoritarianism and developmentalism, Johnson did acknowledge that authoritarian states could be successful in mobilizing people to work and sacrifice for developmental goals. There existed what Woo-Cumings referred to as an "elective affinity" between these two components. Many western observers sought culturalist explanations for the developmental state's ability to mobilize the populace, or its legitimacy, highlighting the importance of Asian political acquiescence and the notion of "Asian values" with their accordant emphasis on community before the individual. The truth is its legitimacy rested on both violent and non-violent foundations.

The 1997 Asian financial crisis represented a watershed for the developmental state. The collapse of several of Asia's economies and the international community's intervention to help the ailing region led to claims that the developmental state was inefficient, obsolete, and unable to cope with the forces of globalization. Laudatory labels such as "Asian miracle" were replaced by more pejorative expressions such as "booty capitalism" and "crony capitalism" in western analyses of East Asian political economy.

While many observers were quick to point out the obsolescence of the developmental state in East Asia, others surveying events a few years beyond the economic malaise of the late 1990s instead saw resilience, which derived from its adaptive qualities. Articles by Pekkanen, Peng, and Wong featuring in a special issue of the *Journal of East Asian Studies* devoted to the developmental state highlight the various ways in which the Japanese and South Korean variants have adapted in order to cope with emerging demands in public policymaking, social welfare reform, post-industrial structuring, and state–society–global relations. Wong (2004) notes that the East Asian developmental state is currently undergoing an empirical and theoretical transformation, having moved beyond its initial narrow objective of rapid economic growth. The future of the developmental state model to a large extent depends on this continued ability to adapt, and especially whether government and business are prepared to eschew the corrupt and collusive practices of the past, provide greater accountability and transparency, and address new social demands in the face of a declining capacity to exercise power and authority.

SEE ALSO: Bureaucracy and Public Sector Governmentality; Capitalism; Corruption; Democracy; Dependency and World-Systems Theories; Development: Political Economy; Legitimacy; Nationalism; Orientalism; Structure and Agency

REFERENCES AND SUGGESTED
READINGS

Beeson, M. (2003) The Rise and Fall (?) of the Developmental State: The Vicissitudes and Implications of East Asian Interventionism. Online. eprint.uq.edu/archive/00000603/01/mb-ds-03.pdf. Accessed December 7, 2004.
Evans, P. (1995) *Embedded Autonomy: States and Industrial Transformation.* Princeton University Press, Princeton.
Gold, T. (1981) *Dependent Development in Taiwan.* Harvard University Press, Cambridge, MA.
Johnson, C. (1982) *MITI and the Japanese Miracle: The Growth of Industrial Policy, 1925–1975.* Stanford University Press, Stanford.
Johnson, C. (1995) *Japan, Who Governs? The Rise of the Developmental State.* W. W. Norton, New York.
Pekkanen, R. (2004) After the Developmental State: Civil Society in Japan. *Journal of East Asian Studies* 4(3): 363–89.
Peng, I. (2004) Postindustrial Pressures, Political Regime Shifts, and Social Policy Reform in Japan and South Korea. *Journal of East Asian Studies* 4(3): 389–427.
Weiss, L. & Hobson, J. (1995) *State and Economic Development: A Comparative Historical Analysis.* Polity Press, Cambridge.
Wong, J. (2004) The Adaptive Developmental State in East Asia. *Journal of East Asian Studies* 4(3): 345–63.
Woo-Cumings, M. (1999) Introduction: Chalmers Johnson and the Politics of Nationalism and Development. In: Woo-Cumings, M. (Ed.), *The Developmental State.* Cornell University Press, Ithaca, NY, pp. 1–31.

deviance

Erich Goode

To the majority of sociologists, deviance is defined as the violation of a social norm which is likely to result in censure or punishment for the violator. Behind this seemingly simple and clear-cut definition, however, lurks a swarming host of controversies. A perusal of course curricula verifies that most sociologists who teach a course on deviance divide the field into two distinctly different perspectives: constructionist approaches and explanatory theories. The constructionist approach sees deviance as "subjectively problematic," that is, "in the eye of the beholder," and takes as its primary task an understanding of how judgments of deviance are put together, and with what consequences. Explanatory theories regard deviance as "objectively given," that is, a syndrome-like entity with more or less clear-cut, identifiable properties whose causal etiology can be explicated by the social scientist. Each perspective has its own mission, agenda, enterprise, and methodology. And though these two approaches define deviance in superficially similar ways, their definitions point to sharply divergent universes of meaning. The enterprises in which these perspectives are engaged are in fact linked only by the objectively similar nature of their subject matter; conceptually and theoretically, they are worlds apart.

CONSTRUCTIONISM

The majority of sociologists of deviance are constructionists; that is, they argue that their mission is to understand how deviance is created or defined subjectivistically and culturally. They argue that what is important about deviance is the dynamics and consequences of its social construction rather than its objectivistic or essentialistic reality or its causal origin. Sometimes referred to as the western or the Chicago/California School (Ben-Yehuda 1985: 3–4; Petrunik 1980), the proponents of constructionism tend to adopt symbolic interactionism as their theoretical inspiration, use participant observation as their principal methodology, and typically focus on "soft" or low-consensus deviance – that is, acts that may or may not be crimes, but if they are, stand a low likelihood of arrest and incarceration, behavior that tends to be punished predominantly through the mechanism of informal social control. Constructionism seeks to shift the focus of deviance researchers away from the objective nature and causes of deviant behavior per se

to the processes by which phenomena and persons "come to be defined as deviant by others" (Kitsuse 1964).

The term deviance is used principally by sociologists rather than the lay public; to the extent that laypeople use the term, its meaning differs markedly from that used by the sociologists. To the constructionist, the concept is defined or *constituted* by particular reactions from observers or "audiences," real or potential, *inferred* as a result of what persons *do* or *say* when they discuss or discover something they regard as reprehensible. In other words, it is a "definition in use." According to this definition, deviance is implicit in all social interaction; one does not have to name it to see it in action. And the reactions that constitute deviance are universal, transhistorical, and transcultural; they are found everywhere humans congregate. The phenomena – the behavior, beliefs, or conditions – that have generated this reaction differ from one time and place to another, but identification and condemnation of the norm violator is a fixture in all societies and social groupings throughout history. Hence, the fact that laypeople do not use the term deviance says nothing about its sociological purchase. The fact is deviance is a fundamental sociological process, as essential to human existence as identity, social structure, status, and culture. All human collectivities establish and enforce norms; in all collectivities these norms are violated; as a consequence, the enforcement of norms ("social control") constitutes the life-blood of all social life.

The constructionist approach defines deviance (or "social deviance") as a normative violation that is regarded among specified collectivities as reprehensible and, if made public, is likely to elicit negative reactions against the violator (such as censure, condemnation, punishment, scorn, stigma, and social isolation) from members of such collectivities. These collectivities are referred to as "audiences." The issue of audiences addresses the question, "Deviance to whom?" The "to whom?" question indicates that definitions of what constitutes a normative violation vary from one collectivity to another. Audiences need not literally witness the violation in question; they may be told about it or they may be potential audiences whose reactions may be inferred from their ongoing talk, that is, stated beliefs and attitudes. An even more radically constructionist definition of deviance is the *strict* constructionist or ethnomethodological definition, which argues that deviance *does not exist* in the absence of literal, concrete labeling or condemnation (Pollner 1974). No condemnation, no deviance. By the lights of this definition, "secret deviance" is an oxymoron, a contradiction in terms. Many sociologists believe that such a definition would paralyze the study of deviance, since the overwhelming majority of behavior, beliefs, and conditions that *would* generate disapproval in most collectivities are never detected or sanctioned. Moreover, it excludes behavior, beliefs, and conditions that the person enacting, holding, or possessing them *knows* would discredit him or her in the eyes of others, but are kept secret from them (Goffman 1963: 41). Very few sociologists adopt the "strict" constructionist or "hard" reactivist definition of deviance, hence it is not discussed here.

As indicated above, to the constructionist, persons violate norms not only by engaging in certain acts but also by holding unacceptable attitudes or beliefs and possessing undesirable characteristics; attitudes, behavior, and characteristics constitute the "ABCs" of deviance (Adler & Adler 2003: 8). In addition, in certain collectivities, the presence of a "tribal" outsider, that is, one who possesses what is considered in those circles an "unacceptable" or "inappropriate" racial, national background, or religious membership, will elicit hostile or other negative reactions (Goffman 1963: 4). Constructionist sociologists also study false accusations of deviance, since that generates condemnation, a defining element in their definition of deviance (Becker 1963: 20). The fact that the person who elicits negative reactions is not "at fault" or "to blame" is irrelevant to a sociological definition of deviance. The fact is, people can be, and are, punished for entirely involuntary – or nonexistent – normative violations over which they had no control or choice.

To the constructionist, "deviance" refers to the negative reactions, actual or potential, that are likely to follow the discovery of an act, belief, or trait that is regarded as reprehensible *in* a particular collectivity or *to* a particular audience. (That collectivity can include, but is not

coterminous with, the entire society.) A given person becomes *a* deviant to the extent that he or she is stigmatized within or by the members of a given collectivity or audience. In Becker's well-known formulation: "*social groups create deviance by making the rules whose infraction constitutes deviance*, and by applying those rules to particular people and labeling them as outsiders." According to this definition, then, the deviance of a person, that is, whether he or she can be regarded as *a* deviant "is *not* [solely] a quality of the act the person commits, but rather a consequence of the application by others of rules and sanctions to an 'offender.' The deviant is one to whom that label has successfully been applied" (Becker 1963: 9).

Constructionists emphasize that the two defining building blocks of deviance mentioned above – the violation of a norm and the negative reactions to the normative violation – do not necessarily occur together, as Becker (1963: 19–22) has pointed out. In fact, the punishment or condemnation of the norm violator is influenced by contingencies, one of which is *who* engages in the violation. The ancillary characteristics of the rule violator can influence whether and to what extent others react negatively to the infraction; these include, among others, age, race, sex, socioeconomic status, and – perhaps most important – degree of intimacy between the violator and the person evaluating the supposed infraction. In addition, if there is a victim, just *who* is victimized by the act may determine whether and to what extent the actor is punished or condemned. Moreover, to repeat, false accusations represent a case in which someone did not violate a norm but attracts censure anyway. To the constructionist, an accusation of deviance that is successfully lodged against an innocent party represents a case of sociological deviance, whether baseless or justified. Here we have an instance of a deviant *person* who did not engage in deviant *behavior*. Whether or not such accusations are successful, the literal facticity of the charge is only one of the many reasons why it succeeds or fails.

It is axiomatic to the constructionist that deviance is a social convention, "relative" to time and place, and that an act, belief, or trait that is non-normative in one collectivity or setting may be normative in another. Even more fundamental, independent of the issue of normative valuation, the constructionist position argues that the very *categories* that constitute what is defined as deviant are constructed variously in different societies, indeed even within different collectivities in the same society. The same partners who are regarded as incestuous in society A are acceptable, even mandatory, marital partners in society B (Ford & Beach 1951), hence the very definition or conceptualization of what constitutes "incest" is a social construct, not an objective reality. In ritual contexts, same-sex intercourse among the Sambia is not regarded as "homosexuality" at all, although it would be so regarded nearly everywhere else (Herdt 1987). In most quarters in the western world, the use of one mind-altering substance (alcohol) is not conceptualized as "drug use," but the use of another such substance (marijuana) is so regarded. Hence, to the constructionist, behavior and other phenomena that are outwardly and objectively "the same" are not sociologically the same; conceptually, they may belong to entirely different categories or universes of meaning. In short, social and cultural relativism, both in terms of conceptualizing categories of phenomena and in evaluating representatives of these categories, is the foundation-stone of the constructionist approach to deviance.

Constructionists divide into more "radical" and more "moderate" camps. For the radical constructionists, the issue of the cause or "etiology" of deviance or its constituent components is entirely irrelevant, even illusory. Seeking the cause or causes of deviance and its constituent elements is a fool's errand, most in this camp would say. If deviance is socially created, there is no objective or essential common thread independent of the label that ties it all together – in effect, there is no "there there" – and hence, any attempt to explain its causality is by its very nature futile. In contrast, the moderate constructionists argue that seeking an explanation for deviance is secondary to and to some degree separate from their mission; phenomena labeled "deviant" may or may not share an objective common thread, but their etiology is not the deviance specialist's central mission. Interestingly, however, some sociologists who study the social construction of deviance also examine the etiological impact of one or more legal or social constructions on the commission of deviant behavior. For instance, some conflict theorists (who are mainly interested in the role of power and social class in the construction of the law) are also interested in how power and class influence behavioral violations of the law (Messerschmidt 1993); some labeling theorists, who typically look at the social construction of deviance labeling, argue that labeling may influence further, and more serious, deviant behavior (Scheff 1966).

Constructionists distinguish between "societal" deviance, which is the violation of the norms of the society at large, and "situational" deviance, which is the violation of the norms that apply within a particular context (Plummer 1979: 97–9). Hence, widespread agreement on the legitimacy of the norms in the society is not necessary to define situational deviance – although it is to define *societal* deviance – since the concept is always relative to specific contexts. In other words, a particular *audience* defines deviance; something is deviant *to* a particular audience *in* a particular context. If tattooing is normative among Hell's Angels, it is not deviant *to them*; if it is non-normative among fundamentalist Christians and Orthodox Jews, it *is* deviant to them. The fact that tattooing is or is not deviant in the society at large is irrelevant to the issue of its normativity *within specified social circles*. Hence, "deviance" does not exist as an abstraction; it takes on relevance only within specified collectivities and in specified social contexts. Of course, *one* of these collectivities may be the society at large, which is how "societal" deviance is defined.

To the advocates of the constructionist approach, *social control* is the core of any sociological understanding of deviance. Social control is defined as any and all efforts to ensure conformity to a norm. Humans are irrepressible; all of us have a tendency to violate some of the norms. To engage in normative violations is tempting both because they more surely than conformity secure for us what we value, and because many of the things we have been told we cannot have are intrinsically rewarding (Gottfredson & Hirschi 1990). Hence, efforts to ensure conformity to the norms may be found in all collectivities, both historically and trans-societally. These include positive efforts such as rewards, and negative efforts such as punishment; formal efforts such as arrest, and informal efforts such as an insult or a slap in the face; and internal efforts, through the process of socialization, as well as external ones, such as censuring someone for engaging in a non-normative act. Hence, while the state plays a major role in social control, it is only one of a wide range of agents dedicated to ensuring conformity. The many faces of social control represent the flip side of deviance; social control is an effort to deal with and suppress normative violations, as well as encourage by rewarding normative conformity. And it is the many efforts of social control that *define* and *constitute* deviance.

Nearly all constructionist definitions of deviance and social control include the component of power. Collectivities that control more of society's resources tend to have relatively more power to influence deviance-defining social institutions, including the law and its enforcement. Members of relatively low-status collectivities are more likely to find their behavior, beliefs, and traits defined and reacted to as deviant than those who have higher status and more power. Collectivities that have more power tend to have more influence on, in addition to the law, the content of the media as well as the educational, religious, and political institutions, all of which, in turn, influence definitions of right and wrong and hence what is considered deviant. Power over subordinate collectivities does not, however, ensure their conformity or agreement among members of those collectivities that dominant definitions of right and wrong are just or righteous. As we saw, humans are rebellious and irrepressible; smaller, non-mainstream collectivities everywhere construct their own rules of right and wrong, independent of those of the most powerful strata of society. In all societies, the dominant institutions, regardless of how hegemonic they may seem, are incapable of intruding into each and every aspect of the lives of all human collectivities and groups within their scope. Still, power is a factor in the social construction of norms – and hence, in defining what is deviant. This is especially the case for "societal" deviance. It is often the case that the powerless are subject to the norms of the powerful, whereas it is rarer that the powerful are subject to the norms of the powerless. This is more likely to be true, however, of formal definitions of crime than of informal definitions of deviance.

EXPLANATORY THEORIES OF DEVIANCE

The second approach to deviance encompasses explanatory theories. Explanations of deviance attempt to account for *why* non-normative behavior occurs. (Some explanatory formulations turn the equation around and ask why *normative* – but for them, the logic is the same.) Their driving question is: "Why do they do it?" (or, alternatively, "Why *don't* they do it?"). Explanatory theories always take crime or deviance as the dependent variable and the explanatory factor they focus on as the independent or causal variable. Not all explanatory theories seek explanations of deviance in general; in fact, most attempt to explain one or more of its constituent components, such as mental disorder, drug abuse or addiction, crime, juvenile delinquency, white-collar crime, embezzlement, burglary, motor vehicle theft, and so on. For the most part, adopting an explanatory paradigm entails examining deviance through the natural science model, an approach that is commonly referred to as positivism or, sometimes, methodological (as opposed to substantive) positivism (Hirschi & Gottfredson 1994). Positivism is characterized by *empiricism*, that is, reliance on the data of the five senses; *abstraction*, that is, the tendency to generalize beyond specific cases; the tendency to seek *cause-and-effect explanations* of phenomena in the material world; and, most important for our purposes, essentialism or *objectivism*. The last of these is the tendency to regard phenomena as pregiven entities, those that are internally consistent, containing one or more "common threads" that may be found more or less everywhere, or at the very least within a given society. For instance, the explanatory approach is comfortable referring to and studying the "epidemiology" of deviance (Crews 2001) – that is, the distribution of "deviance" in the population – whereas constructionists are likely to reject the very basis of such an enterprise. Explanation *presupposes* objectivism, since explanations are predicated on the existence of one or more common threads shared by the phenomena being explained. In other words, to the approach that seeks explanations, deviance and its constituent components are a specific *type of action* – in medical terms, a "syndrome" – and not *merely* a convention or a social construction. And *because* it is a type of action, possessing internal coherence, it is the mission of the sociologist to account for it – that is, render a causal explanation of its origin. (Gottfredson and Hirschi (1990: 49) discuss the contradiction between substantive positivism's acceptance of the legalistic definition of crime and their adoption of the natural science model, which presupposes objectivism.) Sociologists who seek explanations for deviance usually study behavior (or psychic conditions that presumably cause behavior), only very rarely beliefs, and practically never physical traits. They take for granted, assume, or hold in abeyance the social construction of definitions of deviance. For them, social control is interesting only insofar as it influences or causes deviant and criminal behavior, which is what they aim to explain in the first place (Hirschi 1969; Gottfredson & Hirschi 1990).

Although most do not articulate it in this fashion, many explanatory theorists would argue that societies tend to criminalize or penalize actions that are most harmful and disruptive both on a micro and a macro level, that is, both interpersonally and with respect to the viability of the society as a whole. For example, Gottfredson and Hirschi (1990: 15) define crime as "force or fraud in pursuit of self-interest." Rejecting the central tenet of constructionism, sociologists who seek explanations argue that it is incorrect to argue that "deviance" is relative to time and place. Though explanatory theorists would admit that while many customs and conventions do indeed vary the world over and throughout history, certain behavioral syndromes have identifiable, universal properties. For instance, even though mental disorder and illness, crime and delinquency, and alcoholism may be *thought of*, and persons characterized by them *dealt with*, differently in different societies, nonetheless, each has a common thread and hence a common etiology (Nettler 1974). Clearly – as with the constructionists – explanatory theorists may be divided into more "radical" and more "moderate" camps. The radical explanatory theorist argues that deviant categories are universal everywhere and for all times, and hence a universal explanation of deviance can

be devised (Gottfredson and Hirschi 1990). The moderate explanatory theorist says that deviance is shaped by the societies in which it occurs, and hence explanations of deviance and its components may apply only within each society. But both camps look for cause-and-effect explanations of behavioral syndromes that share one or more common, internally consistent components or elements.

For instance, practitioners of one explanatory theory, "self-control" theory, adopt a "non-relativistic position on the causes of crime." This is the case, they say, because their theory does not regard deviance, crime, and delinquency as the products of unique cultures, peoples, settings, historical periods, or even variable legal definitions. Instead, self-control theory assumes that the causes of crime are the same everywhere and at all times. In short, they argue, the mission of the sociologist of deviance, crime, and delinquency is to explain these phenomena, and in order to accomplish this mission it is necessary to conceptualize them essentialistically and objectivistically, that is, as possessing common, universal elements or components. Gottfredson and Hirschi (1990), two major advocates of this theory, use the term deviance throughout their theoretical discussion of crime. Crime, they argue, "is only part of a much larger set of deviant acts" (p. xvi). And they insist that a common explanation can be found for the constituent elements of crime and deviance, such as violence, white-collar crime, reckless behavior, illicit, impulsive sex, and drug abuse.

To repeat, all explanatory theorists are aware that definitions of right and wrong are relative from one society to another; all criminologists that seek explanations for crime are aware that laws criminalizing certain acts vary the world over. But accounting for that variation, they would say, is not the sociologist's mission. Moreover, they would argue, in spite of this variation, there are common threads running through the most fundamental of society's norms and laws. Societies outlaw certain actions for a reason, and that is because the acts societies outlaw tear at the social fabric. Even if sociologists were to confine their analysis to a single society, the same logic applies: certain behaviors demand an explanation because of their internal consistency, and one *aspect* of that consistency, many argue, is the harm and disruption these behaviors cause to the social order. Explaining phenomena bearing an internal consistency, a common thread, underlies *all* efforts to explain or account for crime, delinquency, violence, mental disorder, drug abuse, alcoholism, suicide, and prostitution. Such behaviors (or psychic conditions) demand an explanation because they are "different" from law abiding or "normal" behaviors and conditions. And the *way* they are different, many explanatory theorists argue, is that these behaviors are disordered, pathological, harmful, and/or exploitative. This approach is even less concerned about the fact that the lay public may not use such terms, or, when they do, mean different things by them from what the social scientist intends. To the scientifically inclined theorist, it is what the scientist says that counts, not the lay public.

In the most radical of explanatory arguments, the term deviant refers to a person with one or more specific, essentialistic or indwelling conditions that *manifest themselves* in specific actions. Certain people enact seriously deviant and criminal behavior, behavior that harms and exploits others and tears at the fabric of the society, because they are "different" from the rest of us. For instance, in one formulation, the overlap between the social deviant and persons characterized by the psychiatric terms "psychopath," "sociopath," and "antisocial personality disorder" is considerable (DeLisi 2003). Even in less radical formulations, criminals and deviants are persons primed to act in a certain fashion because they are certain *kinds of persons*. Other factors *in addition to* their characteristics may influence their deviant behavior, but with this approach individual characteristics are crucial.

Most *sociological* theories that attempt to account for the enactment of deviant behavior argue that the essentialistic, indwelling factors that cause (or inhibit) crime are to be found in actors' environments, not in their individual traits or preconditions. These factors include the degree of social disorganization in the neighborhood in which people live; anomie, or society's cultural and social malintegration; bonding with conventional others; and differential association with others who espouse positive definitions of normative violations. Here, the explanatory factor producing a particular

and "different" kind of behavior is shifted from specific *kinds of persons* to specific *kinds of social arrangements* and the actor's place in them.

Opportunity theories, including routine activity theory, dispense altogether with explaining the propensity or tendency of individuals to engage in deviant or criminal acts, as well as the sociocultural environments that may influence actors to commit deviant and criminal acts, and focus entirely on the *situation* or *context* within which certain types of acts are likely to take place. Crime is committed to the extent that a motivated offender is in juxtaposition with a suitable target in the absence of a capable guardian (Cohen & Felson 1979). In this sense, then, the factor determining the criminal act is the context or situation – the opportunity to commit the crime. What accounts for the untoward behavior – in this perspective, nearly always crime, and usually economic crime – is neither a particular kind of person nor a particular kind of social arrangement, but particular kinds of opportunities, those that maximize potential rewards and minimize cost, of which punishment is a major component.

Most forms of crime that explanatory theorists study may be referred to as "hard," serious, or *high consensus* deviance. Positivistic sociologists who see their mission as explaining or accounting for the origins of crime tend to be criminologists. All sociologists of deviance discuss and refer to the work of criminologists, but very few criminologists identify any longer with the field of the sociology of deviance. (This is less true of the UK than the US. For instance, in *Understanding Deviance*, 2003, Downes and Rock make little distinction between "deviance" and "crime.") Criminologists typically study deviance only by implication, that is, conceptually and theoretically, but not as members of an intellectual community. As an identifiable field, the explanatory study of crime is separate and distinct from the field that is referred to as the sociology of deviance – and has been for more than a generation. Much the same can be said of sociologists who attempt to explain the etiology of the behavioral components of deviance, such as mental disorder, drug abuse, and alcoholism: they are sociologists of behavior that is regarded as deviant, but most do not adopt a "deviance" perspective, and few belong to the intellectual community of the sociology of deviance. This intellectual split between these two camps – the constructionist and the explanatory theorists – as well as the departure of criminologists from the field of the sociology of deviance, have resulted in a smaller, less influential, and possibly less theoretically innovative school of deviance studies. The long-term impact of this split has yet to be determined.

SEE ALSO: Conflict Theory; Deviance, Constructionist Perspectives; Deviance, Crime and; Deviance, Explanatory Theories of; Deviance, Theories of; Identity, Deviant; Labeling; Labeling Theory; Social Control; Sociocultural Relativism; Symbolic Interaction

REFERENCES AND SUGGESTED READINGS

Adler, P. A. & Adler, P. (2003) *Constructions of Deviance: Social Power, Context, and Interaction*, 4th edn. Wadsworth, Belmont, CA.

Becker, H. S. (1963) *Outsiders: Studies in the Sociology of Deviance*. Free Press, New York.

Ben-Yehuda, N. (1985) *Deviance and Moral Boundaries*. University of Chicago Press, Chicago.

Cohen, L. E. & Felson, M. (1979) Social Change and Crime Rate Trends: A Routine Activity Approach. *American Sociological Review* 44: 588–608.

Crews, G. A. (2001) Epidemiology of Deviance. In: Bryant, C. D. (Ed.), *Encyclopedia of Criminology and Deviant Behavior*, Vol. 1. Sage, Thousand Oaks, CA, pp. 142–7.

DeLisi, M. (2003) Self-Control Pathology: The Elephant in the Living Room. In: Britt, C. L. & Gottfredson, M. R. (Eds.), *Control Theories of Crime and Delinquency*. Transaction Publishers, New Brunswick, NJ, pp. 21–38.

Ford, C. S. & Beach, F. A. (1951) *Patterns of Sexual Behavior*. Harper & Row, New York.

Goffman, E. (1963) *Stigma: Notes on the Management of a Spoiled Identity*. Prentice-Hall/Spectrum, Englewood Cliffs, NJ.

Gottfredson, M. R. & Hirschi, T. (1990) *A General Theory of Crime*. Stanford University Press, Stanford.

Gottfredson, M. R. & Hirschi, T. (2002) Self-Control and Opportunity. In: Britt, C. L. & Gottfredson, M. R. (Eds.), *Control Theories of Crime and Delinquency*. Transaction Publishers, New Brunswick, NJ, pp. 5–19.

Herdt, G. (1987) *The Sambia: Ritual and Gender in New Guinea*. Holt, Rinehart, & Winston, New York.

Hirschi, T. (1969) *Causes of Delinquency*. University of California Press, Berkeley.

Hirschi, T. & Gottfredson, M. R. (1994) Substantive Positivism and the Idea of Crime. In: Hirschi, T. & Gottfredson, M. R. (Eds.), *The Generality of Deviance*. Transaction Publishers, New Brunswick, NJ, pp. 253–69.

Kitsuse, J. I. (1964) Societal Reaction to Deviant Behavior: Problems of Theory and Method. In: Becker, H. S. (Ed.), *The Other Side: Perspectives on Deviance*. Free Press, New York, pp. 87–102.

Messerschmidt, J. W. (1993) *Masculinities and Crime: Critique and Reconceptualization of Theory*. Rowman & Littlefield, Lanham, MD.

Nettler, G. (1974) On Telling Who's Crazy. *American Sociological Review* 39: 893–4.

Petrunik, M. (1980) The Rise and Fall of "Labeling Theory": The Construction and Deconstruction of a Strawman. *Canadian Journal of Sociology* 5: 213–33.

Plummer, K. (1979) Misunderstanding Labelling Perspectives. In: Downes, D. & Rock, P. (Eds.), *Deviant Interpetations*. Martin Robinson, London, pp. 17–29.

Pollner, M. (1974) Sociological and Commonsense Models of the Labeling Process. In: Turner, R. (Ed.), *Ethnomethodology: Selected Readings*. Penguin, Baltimore, pp. 27–40.

Rubington, E. & Weinberg, M. S. (2004) *Deviance: The Interactionist Perspective*. Allyn & Bacon, Boston.

Scheff, T. J. (1966) *Being Mentally Ill: A Sociological Theory*. Aldine, Chicago.

deviance, absolutist definitions of

Craig B. Little

Absolutist definitions of deviance distinguish conformity from nonconformity by reference to an invariant moral standard. Some external agent such as a religious, philosophical, scientific, or international authority may establish the moral standard. From an absolutist perspective, a given activity, like homosexual behavior, might be considered deviant because the majority in a society claim it violates a religious dictate or even because it appears to affront a declared conception of the natural order.

The sociologically relevant aspect of an absolutist position is that it places the basis for moral judgment on a behavior or practice beyond the social and cultural context of the society or social situation in which the behavior or practice takes place. Therefore, the definitional standard for proclaiming an activity deviant has nothing to do with the norms of the particular society or culture in which the activity occurs. Absolutist definitions of deviance assume that a given activity, according to the particular higher authority, is deviant for all time in all places.

In general, deviant behavior theorists and researchers do not subscribe to absolutist definitions of deviance. Rather, they more typically hold to definitional approaches that are normative or reactivist. The normative approach defines deviance according to the expressed or implied standards of the particular group in which the activity takes place. Thus, a behavior will be considered deviant if it violates the social group's formal rules (often articulated as laws) or typical norms and practices (customs, mores, rules of etiquette, and the like). According to the reactivist perspective, deviance need not even entail norm violation; it states that an activity or a condition, such as being physically handicapped, can be defined as deviant merely if the audience viewing it reacts negatively to it.

The divine expression of absolutist definitions of deviance is often associated with religious fundamentalism, where scripture is taken as the relevant external authority. From a philosophical perspective, Plato and Hegel both erected moral systems that defined deviance in relation to absolute standards. Many eighteenth- and nineteenth-century Europeans believed the world's cultures could be arrayed along an evolutionary continuum, with the cultural norms and practices of the West representing the highest stage of development. Thus, when Europeans made contact with non-western cultures, the invaders frequently attempted to discourage or eradicate what they interpreted as these peoples' "backward," deviant activities, such as wearing immodest clothing or engaging in promiscuous sexual activity. Conquest itself was often justified in the name of imposing the absolute standards of Christianity on native peoples. By the nineteenth century, the social Darwinism of Herbert Spencer provided a "scientific" rationale for the alleged absolute superiority of European cultural and behavior norms.

Sociological opposition to absolutist definitions of deviance finds its roots in early twentieth-century cultural anthropology. Attacking nineteenth-century absolutist and ethnocentric judgments concerning non-western cultural practices, Franz Boas and his students, including Ruth Benedict, Melville Herskovits, and Margaret Mead, formulated the anthropological perspective of cultural relativism, stating that any society's customs and practices can only be understood and assessed in reference to the particular culture itself. For the strong relativist, there are no absolute standards for defining deviance, only culturally specific ones.

During most of the twentieth century, relativism was the dominant perspective of cultural anthropologists and sociological students of deviant behavior. In both disciplines, relativism entails an empathetic methodological approach in which the observer attempts to understand any given behavior or practice relative to the normative standards of the culture, or even subculture, in which it takes place. In recent years, however, relativism has been challenged by those who insist on the need for universalist standards of human conduct. The most commonly cited referent for the assertion of such standards is the 1948 United Nations Universal Declaration of Human Rights. Those opposed to a relativist standpoint argue that a practice like female genital mutilation, though culturally prescribed in a number of African societies, must be declared deviant and condemned because it violates one or more articles of the UN Declaration, taken to be the absolute definitional standard.

Any definition of deviance must confront the question: deviant according to what or whose standard? In a world rife with international contact and conflict, sociologists (and other social scientists) are likely to be debating the merits of alternative definitions of deviance – especially absolutist versus relativist approaches – well into the future.

SEE ALSO: Cultural Relativism; Deviance; Deviance, Explanatory Theories of; Deviance, Normative Definitions of; Deviance, Reactivist Definitions of; Deviance, Theories of

REFERENCES AND SUGGESTED READINGS

Benedict, R. (1961) *Patterns of Culture.* Houghton Mifflin, Boston.

Boas, F. (1938) *The Mind of Primitive Man*, rev. edn. Macmillan, New York.

Clinard, M. B. & Meier, R. F. (2004) *Sociology of Deviant Behavior*, 12th edn. Wadsworth/Thompson, Belmont, CA.

Goode, E. (2000) *Deviant Behavior*, 6th edn. Prentice-Hall, Upper Saddle River, NJ.

Herskovits, M. J. (1972) *Cultural Relativism: Perspectives on Cultural Pluralism.* Random House, New York.

Tittle, C. R. & Paternoster, R. (2000) *Social Deviance and Crime: An Organizational and Theoretical Approach.* Roxbury, Los Angeles.

deviance, academic

John W. Heeren

If we consider deviance as a breach of expectations, then any organization or occupation is likely to provide distinct opportunities for legal and/or ethical violations. College and university faculty members are professionals employed within the occupational context of higher education. Thus, the opportunities for deviance available to them derive from their roles in professional disciplines and in the occupational setting of the university. While some professors are more involved in teaching or governance at their home campus, others are more focused on research or other activities of nationwide professional associations. Both these "local" and "cosmopolitan" roles can produce deviant behavior.

Two dimensions of activities are helpful in delineating the nature of academic deviance (Heeren & Shichor 1993). First, one can distinguish between professional and occupational forms of deviance. The first of these refers to breaches of the ethics associated with professions, while the second points to the kind of normal crimes that people may commit in their usual line of work. This second dimension also has to do with deviance vis-à-vis property or persons. Though there is some overlap in these categories, they do permit the differentiation of four basic classes of academic deviance (see Fig. 1).

Occupational deviance among academics shares many features in common with deviance in other occupations. Just as white-collar workers or laborers pilfer property belonging to the organization which employs them, so also may professors. It seems that the more universities become entrepreneurial in obtaining outside funding, the more these kinds of opportunities will be available and exploited by faculty members. An academic example of misappropriation of resources occurred in 1995 when doctors working at a fertility clinic affiliated with the University of California at Irvine gave the eggs of some women/patients to others without the donors' knowledge or permission (Dodge & Geis 2003). Occupational deviance with interpersonal implications would include such behavior as sexual harassment of students, staff, or colleagues and exploitation of human participants in research.

Professional deviance reflects the distinctive features of university and disciplinary organizations, especially their reward and opportunity structures, constitutive roles, and systems of social control. Because academics are rarely strongly motivated to pursue a professional career for reasons of money or power, the attractions of occupational deviance found in material gain and personal domination seem less central to their efforts. However, professional deviance, centering on issues of intellectual capital, is inherently closer to the career goals of faculty. Hence, when such misbehavior is likened to property offenses, it takes the form of misappropriating intellectual property. Two well-known and serious forms of this type of deviance are plagiarism and the fabrication or misrepresentation of research findings. These offenses are essentially acts of theft and fraud.

Where professional deviance is interpersonal, it entails evaluations of the work of others in the academic roles of scholar, teacher, and colleague. Such evaluations are evident in refereeing journal articles and grant proposals, grading student work, and evaluating faculty colleagues who are candidates for promotion or tenure. Deviance in these contexts involves breaches of the expected impartiality. For example, a reviewer may recognize the author of a

		Norms Violated	
		Occupational	*Professional*
Focus of Deviation	*Property*	Theft or misuse of resources	Plagiarism or falsification of data
	Interpersonal	Sexual harassment or exploitation	Biased evaluation as referee for grants, jobs, articles, etc.

Figure 1 Dimensions and examples of academic deviance.

manuscript and slant the review positively or negatively accordingly. Because of the ambiguity of evaluation criteria and the meager accountability of the review process, the biased offender is not likely to be caught. Peer reviews for tenure and promotion and letters of recommendation provide similar opportunities for partiality in evaluation.

The teaching situation also allows biased evaluation to occur, as in the overvaluing of student work in light of the student's physical attractiveness, litigious attitude, or importance to the university's athletic program. According to the norms of universalism, none of these particularistic criteria should enter into the assessment of student performance. A more general overvaluation of students is the widely reported practice of grade inflation (Arnold 2004). Among the reasons suggested for this trend are attracting or retaining students where budgets are enrollment-driven or improving student evaluations of a faculty member coming up for promotion. Whatever its sources, this grade inflation is deviant in that standards are lowered for ulterior reasons.

Though academic social control is similar to other forms of professional social control, in key ways it is also very different. Much of the evaluation of peers and students is protected by layers of confidentiality, anonymity, collegiality, and claims of academic freedom. Consequently, professors are granted considerable trust in carrying out these responsibilities. At the same time, scholarly work has a collective side which can operate to ensure that, prior to publication, academic work is ethically and competently done. One aspect of this is the existence of Institutional and Human Subjects Review Boards, which aim to prevent exploitation before the launching of a research project. In addition, prior to publication, most articles will be scrutinized through the peer review process. After publication, this skepticism is continued through the critical response of peers to weaknesses and gaps in the finished work. Contrary to other work settings where open criticism of peers is regarded as a breach of personal loyalty, academics are more likely to prize and reward that kind of "whistle-blowing." Finally, in most cases, the immediate professional rewards of academic success and recognition are relatively minor. Instead, the most important rewards are associated with more lengthy and distinguished contributions to scholarship. A single instance of plagiarism or falsifying results is not likely to provide significant reward. If a discovery is so spectacular as to provide immediate recognition, it would be the subject of careful scholarly scrutiny and would increase the chances of having the offense discovered.

Some occupational offenses, such as sexual harassment, have been thoroughly researched (e.g., Elgart & Schanfield 1991). However, the extensive professional trust granted professors, along with the confidentiality and anonymity of much of their work, has made it difficult to do much systematic research on most forms of academic deviance. What is known is often anecdotal and, even when thoroughly studied, findings are simply qualitative case studies of "scandals." Whereas journalists have uncovered violations such as the extensive "ghost-writing" of medical journal articles (Barnett 2003), our understanding of academic deviance would be significantly enhanced if disciplinary organizations would undertake more methodical investigations.

SEE ALSO: Colleges and Universities; Crime, White-Collar; Medical Malpractice; Peer Review and Quality Control in Science

REFERENCES AND SUGGESTED READINGS

Arnold, R. A. (2004) Way that Grades are Set is a Mark Against Professors. *Los Angeles Times*, April 22.

Barnett, A. (2003) Revealed: How Drug Firms "Hoodwink" Medical Journals. *Guardian*, December 6.

Dodge, M. & Geis, G. (2003) *Stealing Dreams: A Fertility Clinic Scandal*. Northeastern University Press, Boston.

Elgart, L. D. & Schanfield, L. (1991) Sexual Harassment of Students. *Thought and Action* 7: 21–42.

Heeren, J. W. & Shichor, D. (1993) Faculty Malfeasance: Understanding Academic Deviance. *Sociological Inquiry* 63: 49–63.

Kennedy, D. (1997) *Academic Duty*. Harvard University Press, Cambridge, MA.

Kohn, A. (1997) *False Prophets*, rev. edn. Barnes & Noble, New York.

deviance, constructionist perspectives

Stuart Henry

Constructionist perspectives are ways of viewing reality as a human cognitive or social production. The extent to which reality is seen as having an independent existence outside the human mind or social processes distinguishes different versions of constructionist theory, as does whether the construction occurs individually or socially. Individual or personal constructionism refers to how humans make cognitive meaning of their experiences of their environment. Social constructionism is about how people interactively make sense of their world by defining it and categorizing it, by representing it through language, symbols, maps, etc., and by acting toward the representations as though they were real.

Constructionists see deviance as the consequence of humans attempting to create a moral order by defining and classifying some behaviors, appearance, or statuses as normal, ethical, and acceptable, and creating rules that ban, censure, and/or sanction violators of normality.

Deviance is taken to be a variation from social norms that is perceived as different, judged as significant, and negatively evaluated as threatening. Social action or reaction by authorities or control agencies toward those so designated can result in a labeling effect or "self-fulfilling prophesy" that amplifies the original deviant behavior or appearance, entrenches the incumbent in a deviant role, produces additional deviance as a result of attempting to maintain secrecy, and ultimately results in an identity transformation which, if not reversed, may produce "career deviance" as the rule violator becomes engulfed in attempts to cope with the associated stigma that comes with his or her transformed social identity. Social constructionist perspectives toward deviance have tended to focus on the practices of authoritative agents in creating moral panics through claims about the perceived threat posed by the activities of various types of deviance, real or imagined, and less on those who engage in such behavior.

SOCIAL AND INTELLECTUAL ROOTS

It is significant that much of the groundwork for the constructionist perspective on deviance emerged during the mid-1960s, at a time when significant elements of western society were challenging past traditions of social order, and embracing a social, sexual, and personal freedom. The Vietnam-era protests against imperial state militarism, combined with political developments in civil rights and women's movements, created a social climate that was resonant with intellectual analyses that showed how social processes could be oppressive, and how taken-for-granted institutional forces could be transformed. Social constructionism offered a theoretical basis for personal and social empowerment and promised liberation from the preordered world. As psychologist Henderikus Stam (2001: 294) notes, "the emergence of social constructionism also coincides with the coming of age of a generation of scholars whose academic tutelage was colored by a political activism and the rapid growth of the post-war universities followed by their recent and equally dramatic restructuring as branch plants of the corporate world." In sociology, social constructionism was part of a critique of positivism and structuralism, represented on the conservative side by Parsonian and Mertonian functionalism that dominated the discipline during the 1950s, and on the radical side by Marxist conflict theory. Constructionism, initially through interactionism using interpretive rather than positivist methods, represented a third way of theorizing about the social world and one that brought human agency, meaning, and social process into the analysis.

While constructionism in general is rooted in the philosophy of Kant and Nietzsche, and has been traced back to eleventh-century realist-nominalist debates between Abelard and Anselm through the fourteenth-century nominalist ideas of William Ockham (Ockham's razor), constructionist theory in deviance is intellectually rooted in five strands of the twentieth-century hermeneutic (interpretive) tradition. The first of these is phenomenological sociology, beginning with Alfred Schütz's *Phenomenology of the Social World* (1932, 1967) and manifest in the work of Peter Berger and Thomas Luckmann's *The Social Construction of Reality* (1966) and branching into Harold Garfinkel's *Ethnomethodology* (1967). Second is symbolic interactionist theory, particularly Charles Horton Cooley's *Human Nature and the Social Order* (1902) and George Herbert Mead's *Mind, Self, and Society* (1934), that came to fruition in Herbert Blumer's *Symbolic Interactionism* (1969) and was evident in Charles Lemert's ideas on primary and secondary deviance, Howard Becker's *Outsiders* (1963), and Erving Goffman's *Stigma* (1963). A third strand of twentieth-century intellectual thought that underlies constructionism is social problems theory in the tradition of Spector and Kitsuse's *Constructing Social Problems* (1977, 1987), and reflected in Joel Best's *Images of Issues* d Norman Ben-Yehuda's *Moral Panics* (1994). Fourth is the poststructuralism of Anthony Giddens's structuration theory in his *Constitution of Society* (1984) and its integration with late Foucauldian postmodernism and Schützian sociological phenomenology in Henry and Milovanovic's *Constitutive Criminology* (1996). Finally, the fifth twentieth-century influence stems from psychology and psychotherapy, originating in George Kelly's *Personal Construct Theory* (1955), through Kenneth Gergen's

narratives of the relational self in *Saturated Self* (1991) and *Realities and Relationships* (1994), Rom Harré's realist social constructionism, to the more recent postmodernist-influenced narrative therapies, and meaning-making for psychotherapists in Hugh Rosen and Kevin Kuehlewein's *Constructing Realities* (1996).

More broadly, constructionism has become a transcendent social theory, appearing not only in sociology and psychology but also in feminism, queer theory, the history and philosophy of science, narrative philosophy, literary theory, and everything from housing studies to duck shooting. As Stam (2001) has noted, not only has social constructionism permeated many fields of study, it has also broken out into popular culture.

Since its inception, constructionist theory has itself been differentiated into different approaches. One distinction is that made by Gergen in *Realities and Relationships* between the psychological version rooted in Kelly's personal construct theory, which concerns itself with how individuals cognitively construct their world, making sense of their own experiences of their environment, and the other rooted in the sociological interactionist-phenomenological tradition of the shared construction of meaning, shaped by situational and social context, culture, and history. It is this second social constructionist approach that has been adopted by those examining deviance.

Social Construction of Reality

Social theorist Alfred Schütz was concerned with how humans, in their everyday lives, create a social world that seems real to them, and how they act toward that world, taking for granted its reality. He explored the way humans, based on their past biographical experience, develop ideal-typical constructions that serve as working models or representations of the world, which contain recipe knowledge designed to allow them to achieve projected goals and objectives. These constructions or "typifications" are shared intersubjectively and can result in multiple realities.

Building on the work of Schütz, Berger and Luckmann described a series of interconnected social processes through which humans create institutionalized social phenomena that are seen as having an independent existence outside of the people who created them. In this process humans lose sight of their own authorship of the world, "reifying" it into an apparent objective reality that then acts back on its producers. Thus, like Schütz, Berger and Luckmann revealed the dialectical relationship between social phenomena, experienced as typifications (taken-for-granted patterns of behavior and social types) that appear to exist independently and objectively, while simultaneously being created from humans' meaningful subjective experiences. Berger and Luckmann saw typifications stemming from three linked processes: externalization, objectification, and internalization.

Externalization occurs when humans interact and communicate their experiences with others. Through communication humans construct categories to define the events they experience. Over time these social groupings, categories, and shared concepts become objectified by becoming institutionalized, formalized, and codified. Through this process the experiences, now categories, are made to appear independent of the people who created them and who develop recipe knowledge about them and about how to routinely act in relation to them. Through related processes, humans provide justifications and explanations for the existence of such institutionalized typifications that serve to legitimate their independent existence. Finally, this knowledge is communicated back to other members of society who internalize it and take it for granted as part of their knowledge of social reality. The overall effect of these three ongoing processes is reification: humans lose sight of what they author or create and thereby lose sight of their ability to change the apparent objective reality that stands before them.

Core Elements of Social Constructionism

Scholars who have adopted social constructionist perspectives more or less subscribe to the following core elements. First, social constructionists argue that knowledge or truth about the social world should not be uncritically accepted as real or self-evident; its taken-for-grantedness

as a reality should be questioned. Thus, social constructionism takes a relativist epistemology rather than a realist one. Second, while communities of people may seem to agree on their understanding of certain phenomena or events as "the same," this should not be seen as evidence that there is an underlying reality, nor even that what they accept as the same is identical. Third, the use of terms to label and classify social phenomena need not reflect an underlying real object. Fourth, commonsensical assumptions and expert knowledge are historically and culturally bound to time and place. Fifth, neither commonsense nor expert knowledge has a privileged claim to reveal the truth. Sixth, all knowledge is a result of social processes based on interaction and shared (intersubjective) meaning that is subject to negotiation by the participants involved. Seventh, the social construction of meaning is an ongoing production, gaining significance from the specific occasions of its use or displayed through its performance. Eighth, scholars who study the social process of knowledge production are themselves subject to the same critique as all knowledge production, and as such their claims are no more privileged than others. Ninth, knowledge production is a political process, subject to being shaped by concentrations of interests with a view to producing social effects; in other words, knowledge is intertwined with power and social action. Tenth, knowledge and meaning are not fixed but multiple and variable, and therefore changeable through reconstructing the language and altering the discursive processes that generate it.

Varieties of Social Constructionist Theory

Differences in social constructionist theory (recognizing that making such distinctions is itself to engage in social construction) are based on epistemology – how far its advocates reject realism and how reflexive is the perspective in subjecting its own analysis to a constructionist critique. (This same distinction also applies in the individualist version of constructionism.) Two contrasting approaches in social constructionist theory serve to illustrate their differences. In the most extreme version, developed in relation to the study of the history of science, and referred to by Paul Gross and Norman

Levitt in *Higher Superstition* (1994) as "strong social constructionism," everything is seen as socially constructed. "Reality" is the product of specialized interpretive communities and can only be interpreted and verified in relation to agreed assumptions made by the community that created the assumptions; in other words, it is self-referential. Versions of strong constructionism, also called "strict," "extreme," or "radical," take the view that there is no way to objectively verify the existence of reality, and that all we are doing is observing the world from different communities and making "truth claims" about constructions of that world. Instead of engaging in "claims making," scholars such as Ibarra and Kitsuse (1993) argue that we should be studying the language of truth claims.

In contrast, those taking a "minimalist," "moderate," or "contextual" view of constructionism believe that some underlying reality exists, we can know what it is, and that by selecting from and classifying this basic reality, humans build social constructions having different appearances, depending upon the social and cultural context. The task of analysis, according to Best (1993), is to locate social constructions in real cultural-structural contexts, avoid being exclusively reflexive, and to focus on the substance of issues, evaluating false claims, and even creating new claims. The view of the contextual constructionist is that we need to examine the generation and sustenance of social phenomena; describe how they are defined, defended, and reacted to, with a view to making changes for the better. Those taking this more moderate contextual position thus afford themselves the basis of making judgments about which approach is better able to discern the nature of the construction process, how far it distorts any underlying reality, the extent of the "discrepancies" between objective reality and subjective experience, how realities can appear to exist and be sustained, and how changes may be made in the process to produce less harmful constructions. Unlike the strict constructionist who claims that positivism (a belief in reality) and constructionism are contradictory, the moderate or contextual constructionists argue that positivism and constructionism are separate, independent, and complementary.

While this distinction is important for allowing contextualists to use empirical evidence to support their claims that others are making fallacious claims (thus privileging their method of claims making), some commentators have argued that there is neither one constructionism nor many but a cluster of core themes (as identified above) engaged in differently depending on the authors' aims and intent. In other words, social constructionism is itself seen as a politically framed claims-making process.

CONSTRUCTING DEVIANCE

From the constructionist perspective, deviant behavior is a joint human enterprise between actors and audiences. Deviance is created by human agents making distinctions, perceiving differences, engaging in behaviors, interpreting their effects, and passing judgments about the desirability or unacceptability of the behaviors or people identified as deviant, as though they possessed object-like qualities. In considering deviant behavior, constructionists identify five aspects of the deviancy construction process: (1) why and how rules are made; (2) how people interpret rules and act in ways that others perceive as deviant; (3) how behavior taken as deviant comes to represent an actor's identity; (4) how people reject, avoid, resist, manage, or accept the deviant labels conferred upon them by others; and (5) how human actors develop new lives, either incorporating or transcending that which others label them as being.

While some social constructionist approaches to deviance have considered each of these as part of the process of creating deviance (Pfuhl & Henry 1993; Adler & Adler 1997), most constructionist work focuses on the first – the use of authoritative positions in society to create what British criminologist Stanley Cohen defined as "moral panics" around the perceived fear of certain designated behaviors, whether or not these behaviors exist, and whether or not persons actually engage in them. Classic historical examples include the sixteenth-century European witch-hunts and the twentieth-century anti-Semitism by the Nazis against those of Jewish religion or identity.

Moral Panics

According to Erich Goode and Norman Ben-Yehuda (1994), moral panics are societal reactions to perceived threats that are characterized by several features. First is their volatility, seen in their sudden appearance and rapid spread among large sections of the population via mass media, followed by a rapid decline in further instances of the problem. Second is the growth of experts who are claimed authorities in discerning cases of the feared behavior. Third, there is an increased identification of cases of the behavior that build into a "wave." Fourth, hostility and persecution are directed toward the accused, seen now as enemies of society. Fifth, measurement is made of society's concern through attitude surveys. Sixth, consensus is established about the seriousness of the threat. Seventh, there is a disproportionate fear of the threat relative to evidence of actual harm. Eighth, a backlash occurs against the persecution. Finally, there is an exposure of the flaws in identifying the problem. An excellent illustration is found in Jeffrey Victor's study of satanic ritualistic child abuse in his book *Satanic Panic* (1993). This explores the moral panic over the claimed existence of secret international organizations and/or family clans who abuse their own children or kidnap runaway youth, exposing them to ritual torture and sexual abuse, in order to brainwash them into the ideology of Satan worship. The members of such satanic cults are said to be immune from the law because Satanists have infiltrated society's institutions and protect them. Victor explored the process of accusations and claims made by adult psychotherapy patients, therapists, social workers, police officers, and the clergy. Thus constructionist perspectives on deviance tend to examine the agencies involved in the claims-making process that produces the panic, rather than those designated as deviant or their behavior.

Goode and Ben-Yehuda (1994) explain the production of moral panics, and thereby the social construction of deviance, by one of three models – grassroots, elite domination, or interest group conflict – that are similar to those used by sociologists to explain law creation. The grassroots model suggests that displaced anxiety from societal stress among a population results in a spontaneous moral panic that scapegoats new categories of deviants. Here control agencies reflect opinion rather than create it. The elite domination model holds those in positions of power, whether government, industry, or religious leaders, responsible for promoting moral panic as a diversion from problems whose solution would undermine their own positions of power. The interest group conflict model sees the creation of moral panics as the outcome of moral entrepreneurs seeking to gain greater influence over society by defining its moral domain, which in turn brings reaction from other interest groups vying for their own prominence.

Victor (1998) has pointed out that moral panics claiming crime or deviance need not be based in reality but in imaginary deviants whose existence gains credibility in the eyes of the public when authorities, and those who claim expert knowledge, particularly science or medicine, legitimize the accusations that may begin as contemporary or urban legends. In such panics, actual people need not even be identified, but a category of behavior may be created, vilified, and demonized, without any real people being accused. Indeed, the behavior that the supposed perpetrators practice need not even have taken place for a moral panic to ensue. Research shows that moral panics are particularly likely to occur when bureaucratic interest, such as competing agencies, are vying for jurisdiction of authority, when methods of detection result in errors, and as Victor says, when there is a symbolic resonance with a perceived threat identified in a prevailing demonology – which serves as a master cognitive frame that organizes problems, gives meaning to them, explains them, and offers solutions.

In addition to explaining how moral panics occur, social constructionists examine the process of claims making.

The Politics of Claims Making

Social constructionists of deviance and social problems share a concern to examine how interest groups, moral entrepreneurs, and social movements create claims rather than examine the behavior of those about whom claims are made. Claims making not only occurs in particular historical moments but also involves a process of, first, assembling and diagnosing claims about behavior or conditions seen as morally problematic. Second, it involves presenting these claims as legitimate to significant audiences, not least the news media. Third, a key task in framing a moral problem involves the prognosis of how to address the problem to bring about a desired outcome by defining strategies, tactics, and policy. Fourth, claims making involves contesting counterclaims and mobilizing the support of key groups.

CRITICISMS AND EVALUATION

Perhaps not surprisingly, critics both from outside and from within constructionism have challenged one another's epistemological position by taking either a pro- or anti-realist position. Pro-realists accuse constructionists of being nihilistic and unscientific; anti-realists ridicule any attempt at science as just another truth claim using scientific ideology to claim legitimacy for its own political ends. For example, Woolgar and Pawluch (1985) accuse moderate or contextual social constructionists of "ontological gerrymandering." They argue that claiming to be able to observe and document the variability in claims about a condition assumes the objectivity (i.e., reality) of the condition, without reflexively subjecting their own analysis to the same questioning. This, they argue, is theoretically inconsistent, if not contradictory. Instead, Woolgar and Pawluch suggest the development of forms of discourse about the social world that transcend the objectivist/relativist debate. For their part, contextual constructionists reject Woolgar and Pawluch's critique, arguing that it, and the attempts by Ibarra and Kitsuse to return to a "strict" anti-realist reading of the original statement, lead to dead-end, "armchair" sociology (Best 1993: 138). Best says that it is an illusion to believe that focusing on language avoids the problem of assuming reality because language is embedded in society: "An analyst who ignores the social embeddedness of claims-makers' rhetoric takes that embeddedness for granted; this is another form of ontological gerrymandering" (Best 1993: 141).

More broadly, pure or strict social constructionism has been criticized for implying that problems of crime and deviance are merely fabrications, which is protested by those suffering their consequences, even though constructionists argue that there are often real consequences of acting toward constructions as though they are real. The point of constructionism, and here there are parallels with postmodernism, is that revealing how what is taken to be real can be deconstructed enables the possibility of its being reconstructed differently through replacement discourse. Social problems, deviance and crime, subject to a deconstructionist analysis, can be reframed in ways that enable their reproduction to be slowed and even reversed, such that they become differently and less harmfully constituted (Henry & Milovanovic 1996). The question, indeed, the challenge for constructionists is how to demonstrate the value of this kind of analysis in bringing about changes in objective conditions, while maintaining that these conditions are only as real as we allow them to be. The value of social constructionism is that it seeks not only to understand the way humans constitute their world and are constituted by it, but also to use that knowledge to help them transform it into a more comfortable place.

SEE ALSO: Accounts, Deviant; Blumer, Herbert George; Bourdieu, Pierre; Constructionism; Derrida, Jacques; Doing Gender; Essentialism and Constructionism; Foucault, Michel; Frame; Framing and Social Movements; Goffman, Erving; Identity, Deviant; Labeling Theory; Lacan, Jacques; Mead, George Herbert; Moral Panics; Narrative; Postmodernism; Schütz, Alfred; Status Construction Theory; Symbolic Interaction

REFERENCES AND SUGGESTED READINGS

Adler, P. A. & Adler, P. (Eds.) (1997) *Constructions of Deviance: Power, Context, and Interaction.* Wadsworth, Belmont, CA.

Best, J. (1993) But Seriously Folks: The Limitations of the Strict Constructionist Interpretation of Social Problems. In: Miller, G. & Holstein, J. A. (Eds.), *Reconsidering Social Constructionism.* Aldine de Gruyter, New York, pp. 129–47.

Gergen, K. (1999) *An Invitation to Social Construction*. Sage, London.

Goode, E. & Ben-Yehuda, N. (1994) *Moral Panics: The Social Construction of Deviance*. Blackwell, Oxford.

Henry, S. & Milovanovic, D. (1996) *Constitutive Criminology: Beyond Postmodernism*. Sage, London.

Hoyt, M. F. (1994) *Constructive Therapies*. Guilford Press, New York.

Ibarra, P. I. & Kitsuse, J. I. (1993) Vernacular Constituents of Moral Discourse: An Interactionist Proposal for the Study of Social Problems. In: Miller, G. & Holstein, J. A. (Eds.), *Reconsidering Social Constructionism*. Aldine de Gruyter, New York, pp. 25–58.

Miller, G. & Holstein, J. A. (Eds.) (1993) *Reconsidering Social Constructionism*. Aldine de Gruyter, New York.

Pfuhl, E. H. & Henry, S. (1993) *The Deviance Process*, 3rd edn. Aldine de Gruyter, New York.

Rosen, H. & Kuehlwein, K. T. (Eds.) (1996) *Constructing Realities: Meaning-Making Perspectives for Psychotherapists*. Jossey-Bass, San Francisco.

Stam, H. (2001) Introduction: Social Construction and its Critics. *Theory and Psychology* 11(3): 291–6.

Victor, J. S. (1998) Moral Panics and the Social Construction of Deviant Behavior: Theory and Application to the Case of Ritual Child Abuse. *Sociological Perspectives* 41(3): 541–65.

Woolgar, S. & Pawluch, D. (1985) Ontological Gerrymandering. *Social Problems* 32: 214–27.

deviance, crime and

Erich Goode and Alex Thio

The study of deviance is sometimes confused with criminology, or the study of crime. Sociologists define deviance as the violation of a norm which is likely to generate a negative reaction, such as censure, condemnation, punishment, hostility, or stigma. Stigmatized persons are socially disvalued and discredited by those who accept conventional norms. Norms apply to behavior (the way one acts), physical characteristics (the way one looks), beliefs (what one believes) – indeed, to any dimension along which people can and do evaluate one another. And norms are relevant to specific contexts, whether to the society at large or to specific groups, social circles, or units within the society. Hence, a particular action may be condemned in one society but not another, one community but not another, one group but not another. Indeed, what is deviant in one collectivity may be regarded as praiseworthy in another. Sociologists always ask the question, "Deviant to *whom?*" Without reference to a specific collectivity, or *audience*, the concept of deviance is meaningless. Hence, deviance is by its very nature *relativistic*, not only with respect to cross-cultural comparisons, but also when comparing one collectivity in the same society with another.

All contemporary nation-states have developed a set of formally spelled-out statutes enacted by a legislature, court precedent, or decree; in earlier times, a monarch decreed formal rules, or laws, and even spelled out the punishments for their violation. A violation of one or more such statutes is referred to as a crime. Sociologists define crime as a violation of a *formal* norm, that is, as spelled out in the criminal law. The criminal law calls for a state-mandated punishment, ranging from a fine, through imprisonment, to execution. In principle, *universality* is one condition of the criminal law: all citizens in the same society or nation-state are subject to the same laws. A crime in one collectivity or region of the country is a crime in another. This is the central idea behind "common law," the innovation instituted by King Henry II (r. 1154–89), who sought to unify the many disparate customs, traditions, norms, rules, and laws in the many English shires throughout the kingdom through a system of case law or "judge-made" law, law rendered in court that acquired precedent everywhere. Common law thus came to be a legal norm that applied throughout the kingdom, a law that everyone had "in common." Hence, the first and most fundamental difference between deviance and crime is that deviance is *micro*-relativistic, that is, it is variable from one group to another in the same society, whereas crime is *macro*-relativistic, that is, in principle, it is non-relativistic within a given society and varies only from one society or nation-state to another. Indeed, some observers argue that the criminal law is not even variable across societies (Newman 1976; Gottfredson & Hirschi 1990).

The difference between deviance and crime can be captured in a definition-in-use, that is, by comparing what sociologists of deviance and criminologists study. A comparison of the articles published in the flagship journal of the sociology of deviance, *Deviant Behavior*, with those that appear in criminology's most prominent journal, *Criminology*, verifies that, though the subject matter of these fields is similar, it overlaps very imperfectly. A perusal of the chapters in the introductory textbooks of these two fields, again, conveys how different is the subject matter of the sociology of deviance and criminology. Even more significantly, the two fields differ strikingly with respect to their conceptual and theoretical approaches.

One complicating factor is that the difference between the two fields is sharper in the United States, where the sociology of deviance and criminology are more clearly demarcated, than in the United Kingdom, where they overlap much more heavily. In addition, criminology is a huge field while the sociology of deviance is tiny. In 2002, the circulation of *Deviant Behavior* was 632; that of *Criminology* was 4,181. There are roughly 100 textbooks in criminology and criminal justice; there are at most 10 or 12 in-print texts and "text readers" in deviance. Introductory criminology enrolls perhaps a quarter of a million students, not including criminal justice; deviance, fewer than 100,000. In criminology and criminal justice programs, typically, a range of courses is offered beyond the introductory level; in deviance, typically, there are none (Goode 2002). This means, willy-nilly, that the field of deviance studies inevitably borrows heavily from criminology, while the reverse is rarely true. As a result, the two fields cannot always be neatly and cleanly distinguished. And lastly, to make matters even more complicated, a number of prominent sociologists of deviance are also criminologists (Cullen 1983; Tittle 1995; Akers 1998).

There are distinct differences between the two fields, however. First as to subject matter. As we saw, a crime is the violation of a specific type of formal norm – the criminal law – which calls for a state-sanctioned punishment, typically imprisonment. Any act that is likely to result in arrest, conviction, and punishment of the perpetrator is by definition a crime. In contrast, deviance is not *necessarily* criminal. Many actions are deviant without being criminal, that is, they are condemned or punished entirely informally, interpersonally: nude dancing, binge drinking, joining a religious cult, and becoming emotionally disturbed at work. Hence, a great deal of behavior is deviant but not a crime.

However, the question of whether all criminal acts are by definition deviant is controversial. Many sociologists define deviance as the violation of *any and all* norms; hence, they consider crime *as a subtype* of deviance, since such violations encompass both formal and informal norms (Clinard & Meier 2004: 130–3). According to this definition, all crime is deviance but not all deviance is crime. In contrast, other sociologists refer to the violation of a *formal* norm as a crime and the violation of an *informal* Quinney 1965; Robertson & Taylor 1973). According to this definition, no deviance is crime and no crime is deviance.

One problem with the definition that sees crime as the violation of a formal norm and deviance as the violation of an informal norm is that many criminal acts violate informal norms as well, that is, in addition to generating arrest, they are *also* interpersonally stigmatizing and discrediting. Being known in the community as a criminal, especially as an ex-convict, is regarded by most audiences as deviant. Illicit drug use and sale are clearly criminal, but they are also regarded as a form of deviance.

Hence, the subject matter of deviance and crime, although distinct, overlaps heavily. But the topics of study of the two fields differ substantially. Most criminologists consider the study of the Federal Bureau of Investigation's Index crimes – that is, murder, rape, robbery, aggravated assault, burglary, motor vehicle theft, and larceny-theft – as the foundational core of criminology. Indeed, chapters on these criminal acts constitute most of the chapters on types of crimes in criminology textbooks. These are "high-consensus" crimes, that is, acts for which there is widespread public agreement that they *should be* illegal. In addition, some criminologists study white-collar crime, for which consensus is lower, but are nonetheless very rarely studied by sociologists of deviance. And lastly, criminologists investigate the criminal justice system – the police, the courts, and jails and prisons.

In contrast, again, with respect to subject matter, sociologists of deviance *tend to* study what are referred to, in criminology, as "public order" or "vice" crimes (prostitution, homosexuality, drug use, and gambling), which are lower-consensus crimes and have a lower likelihood of resulting in arrest; and they study acts which are not criminal at all. But the Index crimes are much less likely to attract the attention of deviance specialists. In addition, while criminologists study *only* behavior, sociologists of deviance study anything and everything that generates condemnation, punishment, and stigma – including physical characteristics and beliefs, both of which can be regarded as deviant. Both physical characteristics ("abominations of the body") and beliefs ("treacherous and rigid beliefs") are included in Goffman's types of stigma (1963: 4), as are "tribal stigma of race, nation, and religion," which are extremely rarely studied as a form of deviance but, in principle and by definition, could be.

In addition to their subject matter, conceptually and theoretically, the sociology of deviance and criminology differ as well. Insofar as sociologists of deviance do examine high-consensus crimes such as rape, white-collar crime, or any of criminology's classic topics, they look at them through a very different lens. Most criminologists are positivists; they regard crime as a phenomenon whose epidemiology, or distribution in the population, and etiology, or causes, can be studied quantitatively. They tend to study crime by means of survey methods or the use of official police records, such as the FBI's *Uniform Crime Reports*. In contrast, most sociologists of deviance are symbolic interactionists and constructionists, and take as their primary subject matter the social organization of the condemnation of particular beliefs, physical characteristics, or forms of behavior, as well as the impact of said condemnation on the identity, social interaction, and career of persons subject to said condemnation. For instance, a popular topic among sociologists of deviance is the "stigma neutralization" of criminal behaviors, such as rape (Scully & Marolla 1984), child molestation (McCaghy 1967, 1968), stealing drugs (Dabney 1995),

and shoplifting (Cromwell & Thurman 2003). Clearly, the concept of stigma neutralization is also applicable to deviant but not criminal acts, such as student cheating (McCabe 1995) and topless dancing (Thompson et al. 2003), as well as (with varying degrees of success) to physical characteristics such as obesity (Gimlin 2002: 110–40). This distinction between criminologists and deviance specialists is far from clear cut, however; some deviance specialists, a minority, still test etiological models, while some criminologists conduct research on deviant identities and the social construction of crime and criminals.

Since the 1960s, criminology has evolved into a profession as well as a field of study. Dozens, perhaps hundreds, of academic programs in criminology and criminal justice have been established during the past two decades; they are regarded as a stepping-stone to a career outside of academia. Many criminology and criminal justice departments were formed after breaking away from sociology departments; today, non-sociologists form a substantial minority of criminologists, and a majority of criminal justice specialists. Unlike the sociology of deviance, criminology is a distinctly policy-oriented discipline. Perhaps the most important distinction between the study of deviance and the study of crime is that the majority of criminologists – and even more emphatically, criminal justice specialists – adopt a "correctional" view, conceiving of their research as a means of combating the problem of crime, whereas very few deviance specialists view their work in this fashion. In fact, a substantial proportion of sociologists of deviance harbor a certain *appreciation* for their subject matter and the people they study (Matza 1969: 24ff.), a fact likely to generate stigma and condemnation for the field as well as its practitioners (Hendershott 2002).

SEE ALSO: Anomie; Crime; Crime, Social Learning Theory of; Criminal Justice System; Criminology; Death of the Sociology of Deviance?; Deviance; Deviance, Absolutist Definitions of; Deviance, Explanatory Theories of; Deviance, Theories of; Deviance Processing Agencies; Labeling; Labeling Theory; Moral Panics; Organizational Deviance; Public Order Crime; Social Control; Social Disorganization

Theory; Stigma; Strain Theories; Subcultures, Deviant; Transcarceration

REFERENCES AND SUGGESTED READINGS

Akers, R. L. (1998) *Social Learning and Social Structure: A General Theory of Crime and Deviance*. Northeastern University Press, Boston.

Clinard, M. B. & Meier, R. F. (2004) *Sociology of Deviant Behavior*, 12th edn. Wadsworth, Belmont, CA.

Cromwell, P. & Thurman, Q. (2003) The Devil Made Me Do It: Use of Neutralizations by Shoplifters. *Deviant Behavior* 24 (November/December): 535–50.

Cullen, F. T. (1983) *Rethinking Crime and Deviance Theory: The Emergence of a Structuring Tradition*. Rowman & Allanheld, Totowa, NJ.

Dabney, D. (1995) Neutralization and Deviance in the Workplace: Theft of Supplies and Medicines by Hospital Nurses. *Deviant Behavior* 16(3): 313–31.

Gimlin, D. L. (2002) *Body Work: Beauty and Self-Image in American Culture*. University of California Press, Berkeley.

Goffman, E. (1963) *Stigma: Notes on the Management of Spoiled Identity*. Prentice-Hall/Spectrum, Englewood Cliffs, NJ.

Goode, E. (2002) Does the Death of the Sociology of Deviance Claim Make Sense? *American Sociologist* 33 (Fall): 116–28.

Gottfredson, M. R. & Hirschi, T. (1990) *A General Theory of Crime*. Stanford University Press, Stanford, CA.

Hendershott, A. (2002) *The Politics of Deviance*. Encounter Books, San Francisco.

McCabe, D. L. (1995) The Influence of Situational Ethics on Cheating Among College Students. *Sociological Inquiry* 63(3): 362–74.

McCaghy, C. H. (1967) Child Molesters: A Study of Their Careers as Deviants. In: Clinard, M. B. & Quinney, R. (Eds.), *Criminal Behavior Systems: A Typology*. Holt, Rinehart, & Winston, New York, pp. 75–88.

McCaghy, C. H. (1968) Drinking and Deviance Disavowal: The Case of Child Molesters. *Social Problems* 16 (Summer): 43–9.

Matza, D. (1969) *Becoming Deviant*. Prentice-Hall, Englewood Cliffs, NJ.

Newman, G. (1976) *Comparative Deviance: Perception and Law in Six Cultures*. Elsevier, New York.

Quinney, R. (1965) Is Criminal Behavior Deviant Behavior? *British Journal of Criminal Behavior* 5 (April): 132–42.

Robertson, R. & Taylor, L. (1973) *Deviance, Crime, and Socio-Legal Control*. Martin Robertson, London.

Scully, D. & Marolla, J. (1984) Convicted Rapists' Vocabulary of Motive: Excuses and Justifications. *Social Problems* 31 (June): 530–44.

Thio, A. (2006) *Deviant Behavior*, 8th edn. Allyn & Bacon, Boston.

Thompson, W. E., Harred, J. L., & Burks, B. E. (2003) Managing the Stigma of Topless Dancing. *Deviant Behavior* 24 (November/December): 551–70.

Tittle, C. R. (1995) *Control Balance: Toward a General Theory of Deviance*. Westview Press, Boulder, CO.

deviance, criminalization of

Daniel Hillyard

Imputations of deviance occur whenever there is stigmatization, condemnation, segregation, retribution, or rehabilitation. Criminalization refers to the process of applying the criminal law to certain behaviors. Criminalization reinforces the dominant standards in a society through threatened criminal penalties, criminal prosecution, and punishment. Not all deviant behaviors are criminal. Many scholars study the processes through which, and conditions under which, the criminal sanction is applied to particular deviance categories.

To change the status of a deviant category to a crime requires collective action. Thus studies of the criminalization of deviance reveal the links between deviance, political action, and social change. The dominant approaches to studying criminalization are the deviance and social control viewpoint, which asks whether criminalization is a neutral process or if it serves the interests of the powerful, and the social problems viewpoint, which looks at the social meanings, or collective definitions of crime.

In his highly regarded book *The Politics of Deviance*, Edwin M. Schur offers a definitive statement about the social processes of characterizing behaviors and conditions as deviant: "When people engage in organized political activity on deviance issues they are, in fact, intentionally trying to ensure that a particular balance of power will tip in their favor." On this account, the criminalization of deviance involves not only groups who wield the power to impose or extend deviance definitions and see to it that others who deviate from favored moral stances are subjected to state-administered punishment, but also a process of stigmatization that implies social standing or acceptability for these groups. Three propositions can be derived from these observations. First, what is officially designated as deviant is often a political decision. Second, official rules are tied to interest groups and power. Third, the criminalization of deviance is a form of social control.

Jenness (2004) presents an authoritative review and evaluation of criminalization scholarship. Organizing this massive literature both chronologically and thematically, she examines three lines of inquiry. The first is classic work examining criminal laws that emerge in response to demographic changes that upset the balance between powerful interest groups and those they control. Classic work demonstrates the roles of both instrumental and symbolic politics in deviance defining and the emergence of criminal law. The second, contemporary line of inquiry "unpacks" the relative influences of organizational, social movement, and state-related factors involved in efforts to criminalize deviance. The focus is less on changes in structural conditions than on the specific strategies for producing criminal law. The third, more recent line of inquiry looks to connect local criminal law formation politics with broader processes of institutionalization, globalization, and modernization. This line of inquiry asks whether deviantization and criminalization at the local level (i.e., county, region, state, country, etc.) intersect with some larger social, political, or cultural system. For each of these three lines of inquiry, Jenness (2004) details the factors which influence the criminalization of deviance.

FACTORS INFLUENCING THE CRIMINALIZATION OF DEVIANCE

Generally, there are two approaches to examining the content of a specific criminal law. The first approach entails merely deciphering what specific acts are criminal. The second approach, by contrast, ensues from conceptualizing law as a field of critical inquiry. To demonstrate the distinction, consider the Texas sodomy statute struck down by the US Supreme Court in the summer of 2003: "A person commits an offense if he engages in deviate sexual intercourse with another individual of the same sex." Employing the first approach, lawyers, judges, and law students examine the definition of "deviate sexual intercourse" and find that it includes "any contact between any part of the genitals of one person and the mouth or anus of another person." Typically, that ends the analysis. But to those who follow the second approach, the content of the anti-sodomy law is not simply the definition of homosexual conduct, but the social processes by which criminal status has been assigned to sex acts between individuals of the same sex, and the reasons for it. The second approach thus expands the examination of law to the social context of the issue in question, and hence its political dimension. This is the approach taken by criminologists, sociolegal scholars, and others who concern themselves with the criminalization of deviance.

Demographic Changes, Social Control, and Criminalization

The criminalization literature is packed with empirically grounded case studies which indicate that the construction of deviant categories and outlawing of ensuing behaviors can be linked to changes in the size, density, or distribution of human populations. There are two accounts of this relationship. The first focuses on changes in economic relations between status groups. The second focuses on the struggle between these groups to secure deference through the control of symbols, including the law.

The classic example of the materialist account (pertaining to the economic institutions of society) is William Chambliss's 1964 study of the English creation of vagrancy laws. When the bubonic plague spread into northern Europe in the fourteenth century, it decimated the labor force, causing wages to rise beyond what landowners were willing to pay. As landowners sought to keep wages low, laborers sought to migrate, in search of better pay. In response, landowners invented vagrancy laws to force workers to remain and work cheaply. Chambliss interpreted these events as evidence that the criminalization of deviance is often a reaction to demographic changes which upset the balance of power that inheres in economic relationships. Supporting this claim, Chambliss observed that later in history, vagrancy laws were expanded to cover loitering, associating with reputed criminals, prostitution, and drunkenness, during periods when demographic changes made cheap labor more readily available. Following in this vein, even homelessness, Jenness (2004) observes, has been criminalized in the United States – in response to gentrification and redevelopment in principal cities.

The second approach to studying demographic changes and the criminalization of deviance focuses less on the material basis for social control than on the role of symbolic politics. Here the classic study is Joseph Gusfield's 1963 analysis of the 18th Amendment, which made it a crime in the United States to manufacture, sell, transport, import, or export intoxicating liquors. Here again the analysis begins with a population shift, namely the mass influx of Europeans to major US cities in the 1800s. The swelling numbers of Catholic immigrants challenged the traditional dominance and prestige of Protestantism in American life, the response to which was defining the distribution and sale of alcoholic beverages as criminal. In Gusfield's view, although law enforcement played a role in Prohibition, the criminalization of liquor was more symbolic, for it "established the victory of Protestant over Catholic, rural over urban, tradition over modernity, [and] the middle class over both the lower and upper strata" (Gusfield 1963: 7).

While Chambliss and Gusfield each highlight the role of changing populations in the criminalization of deviance, they emphasize different means of social control. The example of vagrancy laws focuses on instrumental legislation, which attempts to control the actual behavior of those classified as deviant. The example of the 18th Amendment, on the other hand, focuses on the symbolic nature of criminalization, which for Gusfield does not depend on law enforcement for its effect (Jenness 2004).

Hundreds of case studies in the criminalization literature demonstrate the emergence of both instrumental and symbolic criminal law. Typical to these studies are populations perceived as threatening and "in need of control" by those in a position to bring about legal change.

Of course, not all demands to criminalize deviant behaviors and conditions are successful – many are ignored; others are overshadowed by new demands. Contemporary research seeks to discover and model how legal change is stimulated, defined, and institutionalized.

Organizational, Social Movement, and State-Related Factors Involved in Criminalization

In 1971, Herbert Blumer called for reconceptualizing social problems as "products of a process of collective definition" rather than "objective conditions and social arrangements" (Blumer 1971: 298). Although undertaken more than 20 years earlier, Edwin Sutherland's groundbreaking and now classic study of the origins and diffusion of sexual psychopath laws illustrates Blumer's point.

Sexual psychopath laws called for taking criminals who were diagnosed as sexual psychopaths and confining them indefinitely. Sutherland depicted these laws as "futile" – noting first that they were rarely enforced, and second that there was no discernible difference between trends in rates of sex crimes among states with them and neighboring states without them. He argued that state legislatures hastened to adopt sexual psychopath laws not because they were effective, but in response to public hysteria, media hype, the institutionalization of erroneous claims about the nature and threat of sex crimes, and the influence of experts on the legal process.

Specifically, Sutherland observed, once a few serious sex crimes had been committed in quick succession, the stories were picked up by press associations and spread by news outlets across the country. Two to four spectacular sex crimes in a few weeks were enough to evoke the phrase "sex crime wave." The public hysteria which ensued led to the creation of committees to study the problem. Psychiatrists played an important part on many of these committees, and they made up the primary interest group backing sexual psychopath laws. Most psychiatrists favored the view that criminals should be treated as patients, and frequently their opinions went unquestioned by state lawmakers. These views included what Sutherland believed to be erroneous claims about the prevalence of serious sex crimes, as well as their etiology, diagnosis, and curability. These events corresponded with a social movement to treat criminals rather than punish them. The result was a diffusion of laws that Sutherland feared "may injure the society more than do the sex crimes which [they are] designed to correct" (Sutherland 1950: 142).

Sutherland's study, and many others since, demonstrate Blumer's observation that more significant than the objective conditions of a putative (i.e., reputed) social problem are the definitional activities of social actors who perceive and judge them as offensive and undesirable. Sutherland's study also demonstrated the significance of the tactics, power, and motivations of those who seek to influence the law.

Jenness (2004) summarizes a second line of contemporary research that builds upon efforts to identify the political conditions and processes necessary for social actors to effect criminalization. An example is her research with Kendal Broad detailing the activities of grassroots activists to criminalize violence against gays and lesbians. These activities included documenting and publicizing anti-gay and anti-lesbian violence, providing victim assistance and crisis intervention programs, and launching educational campaigns. By these means, a sector of the larger gay and lesbian movement succeeded in getting people to notice violence against gays and lesbians, and to recognize it as a social problem in need of a political response. These and other actions gained the attention of the media and further facilitated the institutionalization of calls for legal reform. And as the movement gained legitimacy, activists succeeded in framing the response to bias-motivated violence, and in drafting actual legislation.

Research in this vein also demonstrates how efforts to criminalize deviance are affected by timing and the presence or absence of organizational support. Lowney and Best (1995), for example, characterize the early failure and later success of efforts to criminalize what became known as "stalking." They report that although

there had been past attempts, no state legislature passed a law making stalking a crime until "star-stalking" became an issue of concern for the Screen Actors Guild and that caught the interest of the general public. Similarly, not until the issue became part of the larger response to domestic violence did anti-stalking laws become widespread. Thus, success and failure were related to whether claims were supported by significant organizational resources and whether they resonated with larger cultural concerns (Jenness 2004).

Significant factors in criminalizing deviance also include professional groups and networks, as well as the state (Jenness 2004). For example, Wolfson's (2001) study of the increasing social and legal control of tobacco use demonstrates how activists have been able to build upon the preexisting work of public health organizations, such as the American Lung Association and the American Cancer Society, and how the fight against big tobacco has spread on account of activities of people working within state, local, and federal agencies such as the Office of the Surgeon General and the National Cancer Institute.

METHODOLOGICAL ISSUES, CURRENT EMPHASES, FUTURE DIRECTIONS

The study of when and how deviant behaviors and statuses become defined as criminal has expanded in many directions since Sutherland wrote in 1950. The literature now reflects the work of criminologists, sociologists, political scientists, and sociolegal scholars. Areas of inquiry include demographic, organizational, political, structural, and institutional conditions. Theoretical accounts of criminalization have moved away from traditional consensus and conflict models and toward integrative models which point to multiple factors, including individual activists, interest groups, the media, and organized social movements; the tactics, power, and motivations of these social forces, entities, and actors; and the political opportunities and structural conditions that make the criminalization of deviance possible. Contemporary work includes more sophisticated analyses of combinations of these factors, as well as how they operate across time. And very recent work is beginning to examine criminalization as a social process operating across geopolitical units. Thus empirical and theoretical accounts of the criminalization of deviance have progressed from the now classic studies of the relationship between demographic changes, social control, and criminalization to contemporary scholarship identifying and detailing the organizational, social movement, and state-related factors which structure and mediate this relationship, and most recently to the larger processes of institutionalization, globalization, and modernization from which criminalization may arguably derive (Jenness 2004).

Methods for studying criminalization have progressed as well. Assessments of the field (e.g., Hagan 1980; McGarrell & Castellano 1993) argued that research on the emergence of criminal law suffered from a tendency to unconsciously vacillate between description and explanation, to focus on historically grounded case studies rather than general processes of criminalization, to substitute moral prejudgments for empirical inquiry, and to bog down in the stale debate between consensus and conflict theories. In response to these critiques, scholars began to inject other areas of sociological inquiry, to examine multiple case studies, and to create general models of the criminal law formation process. In a recent evaluation of this work, Jenness (2004) stresses that only recently have researchers begun seeking to understand processes of criminalization across diverse geopolitical units. One example is empirical research on innovation and diffusion in state hate crime laws (Grattet et al. 1998), which the authors argue is "affected by a state's internal political culture and traditions as well as by its location within the larger interstate system" (Grattet et al. 1998: 286).

Most recently, scholars have begun to address the impact of globalization on the origins of criminal law. Two hypotheses dominate this research. The first postulates that when local factors are paramount, there will be significant variation and tailoring of national laws. Support for this hypothesis is contained in the finding that distinctions between sexual harassment policies in France and the United States are due to particularities in the opportunities and constraints that activists and lawmakers

faced in their respective contexts. By sharp contrast, research on prohibitions against female genital cutting (Boyle 2002) shows that despite local opposition and widespread practice, international pressure has succeeded in getting countries to pass such laws. This finding supports the hypothesis that when factors external to nation-state polities are paramount, there will be little variation between national laws. More subtly, however, Boyle's second finding that local context plays a role in the content, timing, and implementation of newly adopted anti-female genital cutting laws and policies suggests that there is support for a third hypothesis: that both local context and particularities and global norms and system pressures matter (Jenness 2004).

Jenness (2004) suggests a variety of future directions for research, theory, and methodology. These include comparing the origins and making of criminal law to other forms of social control, elucidating the distinctions, if any exist, between instrumental and symbolic law, and examining how processes of decriminalization compare to processes of criminalization. Analyses of these processes may be expanded to include the influences of organizational fields and institutional logics, preexisting policy domains, and the workings of culture. These goals may be accomplished by linking research on the criminalization of deviance to the policy studies literature – particularly studies of the development of policy domains, the social processes involved in the generation of policy, and the influences of these processes on implementation.

SEE ALSO: Crime; Criminology; Deviance; Deviance, Crime and; Law, Criminal; Social Control; Sutherland, Edwin H.

REFERENCES AND SUGGESTED READINGS

Blumer, H. (1971) Social Problems as Collective Behavior. *Social Problems* 18: 298–306.

Boyle, E. H. (2002) *Female Genital Cutting: Cultural Conflict in the Global Economy*. Johns Hopkins University Press, Baltimore.

Chambliss, W. J. (1964) A Sociological Analysis of the Law of Vagrancy. *Social Problems* 12: 67–77.

Grattet, R., Jenness, V., & Curry, T. (1998) The Homogenization and Differentiation of Hate Crime Law in the United States, 1978–1995: Innovation and Diffusion in the Criminalization of Bigotry. *American Sociological Review* 63: 286–307.

Gusfield, J. (1963) *Symbolic Crusade: Status Politics and the American Temperance Movement.* University of Illinois Press, Urbana.

Hagan, J. (1980) The Legislation of Crime and Delinquency: A Review of Theory, Method, and Research. *Law and Society Review* 14: 603–28.

Jenness, V. (2004) Explaining Criminalization: From Demography and Status to Globalization and Modernization. *Annual Review of Sociology* 30: 147–71.

Lowney, K. S. & Best, J. (1995) Stalking Strangers and Lovers: Changing Media Typifications of a New Crime Problem. In: Best, J. (Ed.), *Images of Issues: Typifying Contemporary Social Problems*, 2nd edn. Aldine de Gruyter, Hawthorne, NY.

McGarrell, E. & Castellano, T. C. (1993) Social Structure, Crime and Politics: A Conflict Model of Criminal Law Formation. In: Chambliss, W. J. & Zatz, M. S. (Eds.), *Making Law: The State, the Law, and Structural Contradictions*. Indiana University Press, Bloomington, pp. 347–78.

Sabatier, P. A. (1999) *Theories of the Policy Formation Process*. Westview, Boulder, CO.

Schneider, J. (1985) Social Problems Theory: The Constructionist View. *Annual Review of Sociology* 11: 209–29.

Schur, E. M. (1980) *The Politics of Deviance: Stigma Contests and the Uses of Power*. Prentice-Hall, Englewood Cliffs, NJ.

Spector, M. & Kitsuse, J. I. (1973) Social Problems: A Reformulation. *Social Problems* 20: 145–59.

Sutherland, E. H. (1950) The Diffusion of Sexual Psychopath Laws. *American Journal of Sociology* 56: 142–8.

Wolfson, M. (2001) *The Fight Against Big Tobacco: The Movement, the State, and the Public's Health.* Aldine de Gruyter, New York.

deviance, explanatory theories of

Erich Goode

Sociologists define deviance as the violation of a norm that, if discovered, would typically result in punishment, scorn, or stigmatization of the offender. The normative violation can include acts, beliefs, and traits or characteristics, and it can be a violation of both formal norms (laws) and informal norms (folkways and mores). This definition opens two radically different though complementary missions or lines of inquiry: those that attempt to explain the causes of normative violations, and those that explore the dynamics underlying the social construction, accompaniments, and consequences of the norms, including laws, and their enforcement. Criminologists and sociologists who attempt to explain deviance and crime nearly always study non-normative *behavior*, while constructionists look at the full gamut of normative violations – behavior, beliefs, and physical characteristics.

Not all deviance is criminal, that is, is a violation of society's laws. Many actions that are likely to be punished informally are not against the law and entail no risk of arrest. Nonetheless, all the explanatory sociological theories that are discussed in deviance textbooks were originally formulated to account for both deviance and crime, and they play a prominent role in the field of criminology. During the past two decades or so, practitioners in the fields of criminology and the sociology of deviance have gone their separate ways. Today, criminology is mainly an empirical and explanatory field, while the sociology of deviance has become a field concerned mainly with detailed studies of deviant scenes, the social construction of deviance and conventionality, and the interaction between respectables and persons with discredited or deviant identities, as well as among deviant persons themselves. Hence, increasingly, theories that were originally devised to explain deviant behavior generally now apply more specifically to the field of criminology than to the field of the sociology of deviance.

EXPLANATORY THEORIES OF DEVIANCE AND CRIME

A theory is an explanation or cause-and-effect account of a general phenomenon. The epistemological foundation of the explanatory mission is usually referred to as *positivism* (or "methodological positivism") and is made up of the following assumptions: *objectivism* (that is, phenomena take on a reality independent of their social construction); *empiricism* (we can know the world through our five senses); and *determinism* (the phenomena of the material world, including the social world, are linked together in a cause-and-effect fashion). The goal of all explanatory theories is to explain or account for as wide a range of phenomena as possible. Hence, an explanation accounting for embezzlement in general is superior to an explanation only accounting for the illegal appropriation of money by bank tellers living in small cities; and an explanation for crime in general is superior to one accounting only for embezzlement specifically (Hirschi & Gottfredson 1994: 263).

Objectivism refers to the fact that any attempt to account for the occurrence of deviance and crime is predicated on the view that the violation of social and legal norms constitutes an objectively real, pregiven entity that contains a common thread that demands an explanation. If deviance, including crime, and its constituent elements did not contain a common thread – that is, if it were a social construction and nothing else – then no explanation attempting to account for it would be possible. *Empiricism* typically refers to the fact that the violations of social norms can be investigated by means of highly sophisticated, quantitative social research methodologies, such as surveys, which stress reliability and validity. And *determinism* refers to the fact that the central question in explanatory research is: "Why do they do it?" (Or, contrarily, "Why *don't* they do it?") In the field of the sociology of deviance and crime, theorists assume that they can discover law-like generalizations that account for normative violations. All explanatory theories of deviance and crime – whether they focus on the individual, the individual in a particular context or social structure, or the social structure itself – address their research to the same basic question. In all of them, the *dependent* variable is the normative violation, and the *independent* variable is the factor their theory posits as the causal factor.

The Positive School. The earliest attempt to explain criminal behavior objectively, empirically, and in a materialistic cause-and-effect fashion was undertaken by a school of criminologists who are referred to as positivists, of whom Adolphe Quetelet (1796–1874) was perhaps the first. Positivism broke with a much earlier, more legalistic tradition that ignored the characteristics of the offender. The most well known of the early positivists were the proponents of what came to be referred to as "the Positive School," associated with the work of Italian physician Cesare Lombroso (1835–1909), author of *L'Uomo Delinquente* (1876, and subsequent editions). The Positive School was characterized by the following postulates. First, that legalistic investigations into the nature of crime be set aside for a scientific study of the characteristics of the criminal. This postulate led to accepting the criminal law as a given, and its violation as a crime. Second, that the criminal engaged in violations of the law as a result of forces that were beyond his awareness and understanding. This postulate was based on the assumption that the criminal lacked a free will. And third, the early criminological positivists attributed the cause of criminal behavior principally to a biological factor: one or more physical defects (or "atavisms") in the human organism. Atavisms were thought to be ape-like "throwbacks," primitive characteristics that appear in some modern humans. They included a small brain, a sloping forehead, a large jaw, and a stooped posture. These defects, the theory argued, induce some people to commit crime.

Lombroso's theory was a "kinds of people" explanation that looked no further than the individual, specifically, the biological characteristics of offenders. Over time, however, Lombroso modified his explanation; with each new edition of his book, he attributed a decreasing impact of biological factors and an increasing role to social and structural factors. Lombroso's influence on the study of crime is immense. His focus on biological factors fell out of favor during the 1920s, when psychological behaviorism came into vogue, but made a comeback during the 1960s, and remains an emphasis among a few criminological circles to this day. However, his insistence that criminal behavior be studied objectively and scientifically is the foundational assumption of explanatory criminology. In spite of his emphasis on biological factors as a cause of criminal behavior, Lombroso is regarded as the "father" of scientific criminology.

CONTEMPORARY EXPLANATORY THEORIES OF DEVIANCE AND CRIME: AN INTRODUCTION

For the most part, explanatory theorists of deviance and crime take the social construction of the norms and the laws for granted; they do not regard an explanation of the content of norms and laws or their enforcement as their mission. Indeed, how laws and norms come into being and what their consequences are for the violators is not an issue for the explanatory theorist. And, while agreeing that all behavior, including deviance, is caused, contemporary sociological explanatory theories of deviance and crime do not universally share the Positive School's assumption about the norm violator's lack of free will. All agree that potential norm violators make choices, but they do so within constrained circumstances.

The most influential contemporary sociological explanatory theories (or theories devised by sociologists) of deviant behavior include: social disorganization theory; anomie theory; learning theory and the theory of differential association; social control theory; self-control theory; and routine activity theory. In addition, several of the most prominent constructionist theories – labeling theory, conflict theory, including Marxism and feminism – harbor a "minor" explanatory mode.

Social disorganization theory. During the 1920s, the sociology faculty and graduate students at the University of Chicago developed a perspective toward deviance, crime, and delinquency that has come to be called the "Chicago School," or social disorganization theory. Using the city of Chicago as their laboratory, these researchers took as their explanatory or independent variable the instability of entire neighborhoods and communities. Regardless of their individual characteristics, people who live in such communities are more likely to engage in illegal and non-normative behaviors than persons residing in more stable communities. What makes for unstable or disorganized communities is that they are characterized by low rents, which means that residents who live in them invest little financially or emotionally in their community of residence, and tend to be socially and geographically mobile. Hence, the residents of unstable communities tend not to monitor or sanction the behavior of wrongdoing in their midst. As a result, residents can commit infractions of the law and the social norms without consequence, and tend to do so with greater frequency than in communities in which co-residents monitor and sanction one another's behavior. In socially disorganized communities, street crime, drug abuse, alcoholism, prostitution, juvenile delinquency, and mental disorder are common; a high proportion of law-abiding residents tend to move out as soon as they can, contributing to further crime, deviance, delinquency, and social disorganization. By the 1940s, the Chicago School had become regarded as obsolete (in the 1960s, a school of deviance research came to be dubbed the "neo-Chicagoans," but they had a very different orientation). However, by the late 1980s, social disorganization theory experienced a rebirth of interest, and is now a major perspective in the study of crime, delinquency, and social problems (Stark 1987; Skogan 1990; Bursik & Grasmick 1993).

Anomie theory. Émile Durkheim's book *Suicide* was the inspiration for anomie theory. Durkheim regarded anomie as a disturbance in the traditional social order which caused one form of deviant behavior in particular – suicide. In 1938, Robert K. Merton refashioned the concept of anomie as a disjunction or "malintegration" between a society's culture, that is, what members learn to value, what they are motivated to want and seek – material success – and its social and economic structure, which places limits on some of its members' ability to succeed. This disjunction places strain on members of the society who fail to achieve what they have been taught to want and strive for, which, in turn, results in deviant "modes of adaptation," or behavioral consequences of this failure to achieve.

In the mode of adaptation Merton referred to as "innovation," people retain the cultural goal of success but seek to achieve it in an unconventional, illegitimate, or deviant manner. Examples include pimping, drug dealing, and engaging in white-collar crime. "Ritualism," another deviant mode of adaptation, results from abandoning or scaling down success goals but compulsively following to the letter the norms and routines of proper behavior. A petty bureaucrat who insists that all regulations be adhered to in every detail but has forgotten what the rules are for exemplifies this mode of adaptation. "Retreatism" represents the failure to achieve society's success goals in the conventional manner and giving up on those goals as well as giving up on any and all manner of achieving them. The ritualist is a "double failure" who has adapted by withdrawing from society's rat race in every way; examples include alcoholics, drug addicts, psychotics, and the homeless. And the last of Merton's modes of adaptation is "rebellion," the attempt to deal with the malintegration of society's culture and social and economic structure by overthrowing its culturally defined goals (material success) and any and all legitimate means to achieve those goals and replacing them with an alternative social, political, and economic structure. Clearly, the revolutionary fits here.

Merton's anomie theory argued something quite different from all prior theories of deviance and crime: that the conventional norms and the institutionalized social structure exerted pressures on actors in a social structure to violate the norms and the laws. Ironically, it was conventionality that produced deviance. While Durkheim argued that deviance resulted from a *too-weak* hold of society's norms, Merton asserted the opposite – that anomie was a consequence of a *too-strong* hold of the norms, that is, resulted from actors *following* society's norms. Merton's theory presupposes that it is deviance (not conformity) that is intellectually problematic, that is, that demands an explanation, that actors need to be motivated to commit infractions of the norms and the laws. It is also based on a high degree of consensus regarding the legitimacy of the norms and the laws. The theory is not concerned with how the laws or norms come to be devised nor how they come to be enforced. Indeed, the laws and norms are taken for granted. In addition, the theory does not explain how, once a person feels strain, he or she comes to devise one or another deviant adaptation. Anomie theory was a, perhaps the, dominant explanation of deviance and crime in the 1950s and the early-to-mid-1960s – indeed, the article that spawned the theory, "Social Structure and Anomie" (Merton 1938), is the most often cited article written by a sociologist ever written – but by the late 1960s

it fell out of favor and in some quarters was considered "disconfirmed." Like social disorganization, however, anomie theory made a comeback and is currently one of the more influential theories in the field (Messner & Rosenfeld 1997).

Differential association theory. In the third edition of his criminology textbook, Edwin Sutherland (1939) spelled out the theory of differential association. It has become one of a small number of important perspectives in the field. The first and most fundamental proposition of Sutherland's theory is that criminal behavior – and, by extension, deviant behavior as well – is learned. Hardly anyone stumbles upon or dreams up ways of violating the law. This must be passed on from one person to another in a genuine, more or less straightforward, learning process. The norms or values – or, in Sutherland's terminology, the *definitions* – favorable to committing crime must be learned in face-to-face interaction between and among people who are close or intimate with one another. Criminal knowledge, skills, sentiments, values, traditions, and motives are all passed down as a result of interpersonal – not impersonal – means. And the earlier in one's life this process takes place, as well as the more intense the relationship one has with one's interacting parties, the more influential it is. Sutherland's theory argued that people who eventually embark on engaging in criminal acts *differentially associate* with persons who endorse violations of the law. A person becomes criminal or delinquent because of an excess of definitions favorable to the violation of the law over definitions unfavorable to the violation of the law. The key to this process is the *ratio* of definitions favorable to the violation of the law to those that are unfavorable. When favorable definitions exceed unfavorable ones, an individual will turn to crime. Notice that Sutherland insisted that persons must *learn* and *be motivated to* commit crime; it is not simply something that someone would do naturally, spontaneously, or in the absence of social conditioning. Both crime and conformity to the legal code need explaining, Sutherland argued. There is no such thing as an asocial or culturally bereft social actor: we do what we have learned is good to do, and that includes both crime and law-abiding behavior. Learning to violate the law is no different from learning to speak English or eat with a fork or brush one's teeth. What is different for the criminal is that he or she has associated, and continues to associate, with persons who have promulgated the positive value of committing crime. Sutherland's theory has remained popular in criminology and the study of juvenile delinquency and deviant behavior; it has spawned a host of theoretical offspring, including the theory of "culture transmission" (Miller 1958), or the view that lower-class culture is criminogenic, and the social learning school of crime and deviance (Akers 1998), which incorporates principles of operant conditioning into the theory of differential association.

Social control theory. Control theorists turn the traditional question – "Why do they do it?" – around and ask, "Why *don't* they do it?" Deviance, they argue, is not intellectually problematic. If left to our own devices, most of us would deviate from the rules of society and cheat, lie, steal, get drunk or high, and engage in all manner of sexually gratifying behavior. This approach takes the allure of deviance, crime, and delinquency for granted. What needs to be explained, they say, is conventional, law-abiding behavior. Why don't we all violate the law and society's norms? What causes deviant behavior, control theorists argue, is the *absence* of the social control that ensures conformity to the rules. Conformists do not engage in deviant, criminal, or delinquent acts because of their strong bonds with or ties to conventional others, conventional institutions, their adherence to conventional beliefs, and involvement in conventional activities (Hirschi 1969). To the extent that persons have a stake in conformity – jobs, an education, a house, a relationship, a family – they will tend to conform to the norms of the society and not risk losing that stake. To the extent that persons lack that stake in conformity, they are more willing to violate the law, since they have "nothing to lose."

Self-control theory. In 1990, a book was published that proclaimed itself "a general theory of crime" (Gottfredson & Hirschi 1990). The authors define crime as "force or fraud in pursuit of self-interest" and argue that their explanation applies to any and all forms of crime, including white-collar and corporate crime,

drug use, street crime, or the forms of crime traditionally studied by criminologists, as well as acts that may not be technically illegal, such as illicit or risky sex, the abuse of alcohol, and smoking. Like social control theory, self-control theory argues that what needs to be explained is not violations of the law but conformity to the law. Crime does not need to be learned or motivated, Gottfredson and Hirschi argue. It is what anyone would do in the absence of controls. What causes violations of the law? True to its name, self-control theory argues that a lack of self control is the cause of crime, and what causes a lack of self-control is inadequate, inconsistent, and ineffective parenting or caregiving. Parents who fail to monitor or control the wrongdoing of their children produce offspring who lack self-control and engage in criminal, deviant, delinquent, and high-risk behavior. All of these behaviors have one thing in common: they are impulsive, intended to seize short-term gratification without concern for long-run risk to the actor or harm to the victim. Criminal and other high-risk behavior is especially attractive to people who lack self-control because these people "tend to lack diligence, tenacity, or persistence in a course of action," and such acts provide immediate and easy or simple gratification of desires, are "exciting, risky, or thrilling," provide "few or meager long-term benefits," require "little skill or planning," and often result in "pain or discomfort for the victim" (p. 89).

Their "general theory of crime," Gottfredson and Hirschi argue, both is consistent with the facts of criminal behavior and contradicts nearly all competing theories of crime. The authors are not modest about the reach of their theory; they say they intend to explain "all crime, at all times" (p. 117). Indeed, they say, their theory also explains many other forms of deviant behavior that are not criminal, including alcohol abuse, risky sex, and being accident-prone. Nor are they modest about their theory's devastating implications for the other explanations of crime, specifically, anomie and learning theory, as well as the explanatory component of labeling, conflict, and feminist theories. The only other explanations of deviance and crime that are compatible with self-control theory, Gottfredson and Hirschi argue, are social disorganization theory (since, in failing to exercise social control, the community, like the criminal's parents, fails to monitor or control wrongdoing) and routine activity theory (since that perspective focuses on criminal opportunity, not the criminal offender). Self-control theory is based on the idea that the appeal of crime does not have to be learned or motivated. Deviants do not learn the value of engaging in deviance or crime. One does not learn to engage in crime because no learning is required. Criminal acts are simple, commonsensical, concrete, and result in immediate gratification. What causes criminal behavior is not the presence of something but the absence of something, that is, self-control. Crime is in fact *asocial* rather than social in nature. In this sense, then, self-control theory is a non-sociological theory of crime. Though criminal opportunities may be sociologically structured, criminality, or the propensity to commit criminal acts, is a sociological factor only by virtue of its absence of social influence.

Routine activity theory. Routine activity theory is a contemporary version of the perspective put forth by the late eighteenth-century utilitarians such as Jeremy Bentham (1748–1832) and Cesare Beccaria (1738–94), who argued for the importance of free will and the individual's rational calculation of pleasure and pain. Routine activity theory has purchase only among criminologists; typically, it is not discussed by sociologists of deviance. It focuses on crime rather than deviance, and most often monetary crimes rather than crimes of violence. A type of opportunity and rational choice theory, routine activity theory argues that crime takes place when there is a conjunction of a *motivated offender*, a *suitable target*, and *the lack of a capable guardian* (Cohen & Felson 1979). Since the theory is not an explanation of *criminality*, that is, the *tendency* or propensity to commit crime, but a theory of *crime*, or the likelihood of the commission of criminal acts, the "motivated offender" is assumed rather than explained. Routine activity theory argues that it is the opportunity to commit crime that is the key explanatory variable rather than the presence or absence of criminally inclined individuals. There will always be enough motivated offenders eager to capitalize on a criminal opportunity; what varies systematically is

social-structural opportunities that increase the likelihood of offending. Hence, nighttime minimizes the presence of capable guardians and, hence, maximizes the likelihood of criminal behavior. An increase in the number of women working after 1945 removed persons (capable guardians) from domiciles and, hence, increased the likelihood of household burglaries. The rise in affluence increased the existence of movable goods in post-World War II America, increasing the number of suitable targets, and thus increased rates of theft. The increase in ATMs led to increases in ATM-related crime. In each case, the relevant variables are the suitable targets and the absence (or presence) of capable guardians – not the number of motivated offenders. The theory also focuses on the issue of victimization: the likelihood of being victimized by a predatory crime is directly proportional to the likelihood of being physically in juxtaposition with routine offenders, for instance, often being present, at night, outside the home, interacting with members of categories of the population more likely than the average to engage in criminal behavior – young, unmarried, relatively poor, especially minority, males. Routine activity theory is based on the assumption that people are more or less rational and act out of a free will, minimizing cost (or risk, that is, the likelihood of apprehension) and maximizing reward. It argues that crime is not a unique form of behavior, distinctly different from law-abiding behavior, but follows the principles of all behavior, criminal or law-abiding. The costs of crime are somewhat different from those of obeying the law, but the same principles apply: people are motivated to minimize cost and maximize reward. In this sense, then, routine activity theory challenges the basic assumption of the Positive School, which argued that criminals lacked a free will and acted without understanding what they are doing.

Constructionist theory's explanatory mode. The perspective in the sociology of deviance that is referred to as "labeling theory" arose in the 1960s as a reaction against the dominant positivistic study of normative violations. Labeling theory's principal focus was mainly on how conceptions of wrongdoing are developed, how rules are enforced, and what the consequences of being labeled as a deviant are. In other words, its approach was mainly in the constructionist vein. However, a "minor" mode of labeling theory argued that being stigmatized as a wrongdoer – being labeled as a "deviant" – often has the ironic consequence of solidifying a deviant identity and entrenching patterns of deviant behavior. In other words, one aspect of this approach is causal or positivistic in its orientation: *labeling causes deviance*.

In a like vein, conflict theory is focused mainly on inequality in power as the primary determinant of the social construction of the criminal law and its enforcement – an entirely constructionist endeavor. Nonetheless, conflict theorists also examine inequality as a major *cause* of criminal behavior. Members of the lower class are more likely to commit common street crimes, this perspective argues, because in a society based on social class their options for success and social mobility are extremely limited. In contrast, corporate crime – the ability of executives to commit and, usually, get away with crimes that are vastly more lucrative than street crimes – is a manifestation of the immense power wielded by the corporate elite. "What is the cause of crime?" conflict theorists ask. Their answer: inequality. Similarly, Marxists argue that capitalism is the primary cause of crime in capitalist society.

And feminists, who usually focus on how norms and laws tend to reinforce patriarchal institutions, also argue that the cause of crimes against women is patriarchy. In tracing abusive, criminal behavior such as rape, sexual harassment, wife battering, and the molestation of children to male privilege, feminists adopt an explanatory approach to the study of criminal behavior. "What causes crimes against women?" they ask. Their answer: patriarchy.

CONCLUSION

The coin of the sociological study of deviance has two halves – the explanatory and the constructionist. The explanatory half accounts for the causes of deviant behavior as one or more pregiven entities, behavioral syndromes with a coherent common thread whose etiology demands to be studied, located, and explicated. Even the constructionist half harbors a "minor" positivist mode. The explanatory

approach is the dominant perspective in criminology, while, today, most researchers who identify themselves as sociologists of deviance tend to adopt a more constructionist orientation. These missions are radically different. Although an explanation of deviant behavior and the social construction of deviance are not contradictory, to a major extent their respective practitioners are separate. These two camps no longer form a single coherent intellectual community whose members refer to and make extensive use of one another's work.

SEE ALSO: Anomie; Beccaria, Cesare; Criminology; Deviance; Deviance, Constructionist Perspectives; Deviance, Normative Definitions of; Deviance, Positivist Theories of; Deviance, Theories of; Lombroso, Cesare; Merton, Robert K.; Positivism; Social Control; Social Disorganization Theory; Sutherland, Edwin H.; Theory

REFERENCES AND SUGGESTED READINGS

Akers, R. L. (1998) *Social Learning and Social Structure: A General Theory of Crime and Deviance*. Northwestern University Press, Boston.

Bursik, R. J., Jr. & Grasmick, H. G. (1993) *Neighborhoods and Crime: The Dimensions of Effective Community Control*. Lexington Books, New York.

Cohen, L. E. & Felson, M. (1979) Social Change and Crime Rate Trends: A Routine Activity Approach. *American Sociological Review* 44: 588–608.

Gottfredson, M. R. & Hirschi, T. (1990) *A General Theory of Crime*. Stanford University Press, Stanford.

Hirschi, T. (1969) *Causes of Delinquency*. University of California Press, Berkeley.

Hirschi, T. & Gottfredson, M. R. (1994) Substantive Positivism and the Idea of Crime. In: Hirschi, T. & Gottfredson, M. R. (Eds.), *The Generality of Deviance*. Transaction, New Brunswick, NJ, pp. 253–69.

Merton, R. K. (1938) Social Structure and Anomie. *American Sociological Review* 3: 672–82.

Messner, S. F. & Rosenfeld, R. (1997) *Crime and the American Dream*, 2nd edn. Wadsworth, Belmont, CA.

Miller, W. B. (1958) Lower Class Culture as a Generating Milieu of Gang Delinquency. *Journal of Social Issues* 14: 5–19.

Skogan, W. G. (1990) *Disorder and Decline: Crime and the Spiral of Decay in American Neighborhoods*. Free Press, New York.

Stark, R. (1987) Deviant Places: A Theory of the Ecology of Crime. *Criminology* 25: 893–909.

Sutherland, E. H. (1939) *Principles of Criminology*, 3rd edn. Lippencott, Philadelphia.

deviance, the media and

David L. Altheide

The mass media feature deviance as entertainment. It is as though deviance has become part of our popular culture and everyday lives. There are many reports about prostitution, pornography, gay rights – including marriage and having families – legalizing drugs such as marijuana, gang-member initiation rites, and polygamy. Mass media reports about deviance and crime comprise a large portion of television and popular culture entertainment (Winick 1978). Most media messages rely on audience stereotypes about "weird behavior" and simply play back many of the moral messages in order to attract even larger audiences. Audiences learn to play with deviance by, on the one hand, sharing in stereotypes, being repulsed by certain conduct, and cheering on authorities who seek to eliminate deviance, while, on the other hand, celebrating deviance for its innovations and resistance to convention, and in many instances emulating deviant lifestyles. However, the mass media coverage of deviance, especially crime, has changed over the last 40 years.

Deviance and the mass media are closely joined as audiences and social control agencies (e.g., police departments) rely on, as well as promote, social meanings via the mass media. Deviance does not refer to some objective behavior, but is rather a concept that reflects socially constructed moral meanings attached to certain behavior (e.g., crime, suicide, mental illness, prostitution) that may run counter to the moral meanings of some groups (Pfuhl & Henry 1993: 33). Crime, a special segment of deviance, refers to behavior that violates the law and is therefore illegal. The mass media do not simply inform audiences about deviant behavior; rather, the mass media increasingly help shape definitions and perceptions about deviance and social order. The relationship between what is deviant and what is illegal is somewhat complex since most of what certain audiences regard as deviant is not illegal; by the same token, however, some illegal behavior is not deviant, e.g., parental spanking and physical punishment of their own children. Moreover, widespread drug use, particularly of marijuana, is quite common even though it is illegal.

The mass media refer to information technologies that permit broadcasting and communication to a large audience. Traditionally, these media have included print (e.g., books, newspapers, magazines, billboards) and electronic media (e.g., cinema, radio, television) and, more recently, various computer communication formats, particularly the Internet. They also include personal communication devices (e.g., CD players, game players, music players – iPods), as well as pagers and cell telephones, especially when the latter are used for broadcasting messages to subscribers of paging and telephone services. The mass media are significant for our lives because they are both form and content of cultural categories and experience. As form, the mass media provide the criteria, shape, rhythm, and style of an expanding array of activities, many of which are outside of the communication process. As content, the new ideas, fashions, vocabularies, and a myriad of types of information (e.g., politics) are acquired through the mass media. Moreover, the advent of new media technologies also opens up new possibilities for deviance and crime (e.g., Internet fraud, identity theft, the use of digital camera-phones for taking pictures surreptitiously of people in locker rooms).

The mass media and deviance illustrate a perspective about how perceptions of social reality are socially constructed. The key aspect is the way in which symbols become meaningful and familiar to people, who define situations as one thing rather than something else (Spector & Kitsuse 1977). From this perspective, social power is the ability to define situations. The mass media are important for defining situations and making them familiar to audiences. Numerous studies of deviance have documented the life cycle or career of public definitions of certain acts as deviant, e.g., illegal drugs (Becker 1973), alcohol (Gusfield 1986), child abuse (Johnson 1978, 1995), and missing children (Fritz & Altheide 1987).

Contemporary life cannot be understood without acknowledging the role of various communication media in the temporal and spatial organization and coordination of everyday life. The important work of Harold Innis (Innis & Innis 1972) and Marshall McLuhan (McLuhan & Fiore 1967) not only directed attention to the contribution of the technology of media for any message, but further argued that it is the technology that is most important in altering information and social relationships. However, it has remained for others to examine their thesis and incorporate the surviving corpus within an awareness of culture and especially popular culture, commonly associated with mass production, including mass media programming and other information (Couch 1984; Couch et al. 1996). These media are important in understanding deviance for two reasons. First, the mass media have altered public perceptions about deviance, social problems, and especially crime by stressing the most violent attacks as typical of criminal behavior. Presentations about law enforcement and police behavior have influenced public views about the nature and effectiveness of criminal justice. Second, the deviance process is also affected by the mass media. This process involves how some behavior comes to be regarded as deviant, on the one hand, and how behavior that was once regarded as deviant becomes more acceptable, on the other hand.

A key aspect of mass media influence on deviance is due to the entertainment orientation of popular culture. As suggested by Snow's (1983) analysis of media culture, the entertainment format emphasizes: (1) an absence of the ordinary; (2) the openness of an adventure, outside the boundaries of routine behavior; (3) audience members' willingness to suspend disbelief. In addition, while the exact outcome may be in doubt, there is a clear and unambiguous point at which a scenario will be resolved. Packaging such emphases within formats that are visual, brief, action-oriented, and dramatic produces an exciting and familiar tempo to audiences. Moreover, as audiences spend more time with these formats, the logic of advertising, entertainment, and popular culture becomes taken for granted as a normal form

of communication. For example, research suggests that corporate media seek to harvest audiences by promoting fear as entertainment throughout popular culture and news (Furedi 1997; Glassner 1999; Altheide 2002). Moreover, such emphasis cultivates audiences to support political campaigns and domestic policies on crime and control as well as foreign interventions.

Crime, as one aspect of deviance, illustrates some of these points. Crime news is so pervasive that most people believe that crime is constantly increasing and that our lives are increasingly in danger from wild, drug-crazed criminals who, seemingly, choose victims at random; in other words, criminal assaults can happen to anybody, at anytime.

Criminals and victims are not the only parties featured in crime news. The police and SWAT teams also star in nightly news reports that typically feature a reporter talking with a police spokesperson about a crime that has occurred, against a backdrop of flashing red lights illuminating yellow police tape. The scenario is repeatedly played out in other television reality shows, interview programs, and numerous action movies featuring super sleuths, who solve crimes by acting as maverick investigators, often outside the boundaries of law enforcement organizations. The reality programs present scenarios and language that most viewers have heard, seen, or read about, so the tough dramatic action that is being presented seems quite plausible, especially when no-nonsense crime fighters get physically abusive with "perps," browbeat reluctant witnesses who do not want to get involved, and demean judges, defense attorneys, and the criminal justice bureaucracy for "technical details" (e.g., procedures) and the rights of the accused (Fishman & Cavender 1998).

The development of television was largely built on celebrating the protectors of "normal, decent" life and people. Ranging from the western marshals, who wore white hats and enforced the law against nineteenth-century desperadoes, to twenty-first-century superheroes and sleuths battling crime and deviance, there has been a structural role relationship between the appearance, style, and behavior of law enforcement and the relentless battle against deviance and disorder. Surette (1998) suggests that the metaphor of sheep and wolves is appropriate, with the sheep (citizens) being protected from predatory wolves (criminals – and deviants) by sheepdogs (police and law enforcement). Perhaps the prime example of the development of this entertaining genre of television was the show *Dragnet*, produced by and starring Jack Webb. *Dragnet*'s depiction of the Los Angeles Police Department illustrates the relationship between entertainment and reality, and had tremendous influence on the planning, financing, recruitment, and perception of the LAPD, as well as deviance and social problems (Shaw 1992).

Television and other popular culture materials about crime do not cover all aspects of the criminal justice system (Surette 1998). Little attention is paid to corrections and prisons, on the one hand, while court and adjudication procedures receive scant attention, on the other. Indeed, except for the occasional nasty remark about the "leniency" of the courts, American audiences receive little information about how the courts actually operate. It is not surprising that opinion polls reveal that the majority of the American public agrees with President Reagan's attorney general, Edwin Meese III: "You don't have many suspects who are innocent of a crime. That's contradictory. If a person is innocent of a crime, then he is not a suspect" (*US News and World Report*, October 14, 1985).

It is apparent that the mass media contribute to definitions and images about deviance and deviant actors. When there were fewer media outlets, such as in the 1950s, during the early days of television, social problems such as alcoholism, illegal drug use, prostitution, and some criminal behavior, but usually not white-collar crime, were presented very simplistically as social pathology due to moral failings of weak and evil individuals. For example, the movie *Reefer Madness* presented stereotypical images of drug users and the consequences of drug use, and is now a cult film that audiences, including law enforcement officers, now regard as absurd. However, police officials were very important news sources or claims makers about illegal drugs and their personal and social consequences. While police remain important spokespersons for news reporters, the spread of the mass media has opened up greater channels

of communication, and therefore greater opportunities for minority group members as well as individuals and organizations involved in activities that are regarded as deviant and undesirable. Numerous organizations that focus on the promotion or the control of deviant activities are claims makers that rely on mass communication to promote their issues.

The entertainment-oriented mass media, especially local television newscasts, tend to be interested in presenting enticing reports about deviance. However, this interest also provides an opportunity for organized spokespersons associated with deviant behavior to express themselves and offer counterclaims about their activities, their meanings, and, quite often, their humanity. For example, stereotypical images of drug users were challenged by persons supporting ballot propositions to legalize medical marijuana; elderly women pleading for public approval to use this drug to alleviate their dying husbands' pain appear to have been quite successful in shifting public opinion to support the passage of medical marijuana legislation in several states.

One of the major contributions of the mass media to the study of deviance and crime is familiarizing audiences with very rare behavior and scenarios. For example, sex-change operations are quite rare, but individuals who have had them are featured on numerous cable channels, and increasingly the Internet as well (e.g., Jerry Springer, Oprah). As audience members, we become more familiar with the stories, scenarios, problems, and rationale for undergoing these rare treatments and surgeries. We can converse about them with friends and co-workers, we can develop opinions, and even speculate on what we would do if we wanted to change, or if a son or daughter was faced with certain urges.

In sum, the mass media and deviant behavior are closely linked. Deviance, after all, is not a characteristic of the behavior per se, but rather is a result of human beings interpreting some act as deviant and undesirable. The mass media can contribute to this definition either by presenting very limiting stereotypical propaganda, or by providing more information to audiences. This entails turning to numerous claims makers, who can present accounts and experiences that may strike a responsive chord. In the final analysis, then, the future of varieties of behavior defined as deviant will continue to be linked to the mass media.

SEE ALSO: Crime; Deviance, Crime and; Deviance, Explanatory Theories of; Deviance, Theories of; Drug Use; Mass Culture and Mass Society; Media; Popular Culture; Social Change; Social Control; Symbolic Interaction

REFERENCES AND SUGGESTED READINGS

Altheide, D. L. (2002) *Creating Fear: News and the Construction of Crisis*. Aldine de Gruyter, Hawthorne, NY.

Becker, H. S. (1973) *Outsiders: Studies in the Sociology of Deviance*. Free Press, New York.

Best, J. & Horiuchi, J. (1985) The Razor Blade in the Apple: The Social Construction of Urban Legends. *Social Problems* 35: 488–99.

Couch, C. J. (1984) *Constructing Civilizations*. JAI Press, Greenwich, CT.

Couch, C. J., Maines, D. R., & Chen, S.-L. (1996) *Information Technologies and Social Orders*. Aldine de Gruyter, New York.

Fishman, M. & Cavender, G. (1998) *Entertaining Crime: Television Reality Programs*. Aldine de Gruyter, New York.

Fritz, N. & Altheide, D. L. (1987) The Mass Media and the Social Construction of the Missing Children Problem. *Sociological Quarterly* 28: 473–92.

Furedi, F. (1997) *Culture of Fear: Risk-Taking and the Morality of Low Expectation*. Cassell, London.

Glassner, B. (1999) *The Culture of Fear: Why Americans are Afraid of the Wrong Things*. Basic Books, New York.

Gusfield, J. R. (1986) *Symbolic Crusade: Status Politics and the American Temperance Movement*. University of Illinois Press, Urbana.

Innis, H. A. & Innis, M. Q. (1972) *Empire and Communications*. University of Toronto Press, Toronto.

Johnson, J. M. (1978) *Doing Field Research*. Free Press, New York.

Johnson, J. M. (1995) Horror Stories and the Construction of Child Abuse. In: Best, J. (Ed.), *Images of Issues*. Aldine de Gruyter, Hawthorne, NY, pp. 17–31.

McLuhan, M. & Fiore, Q. (1967) *The Medium is the Massage*. Bantam Books, New York.

Pfuhl, E. H. & Henry, S. (1993) *The Deviance Process*. Aldine de Gruyter, New York.

Shaw, D. (1992) Onetime Allies: Press and LAPD. For Most of LA's Early, Violent History, Its

Police and News and Entertainment Media Were Intertwined From the Chief's Office to the Cop on the Street. *Los Angeles Times*, May 24: A1.

Snow, R. P. (1983) *Creating Media Culture*. Sage, Beverly Hills, CA.

Spector, M. & Kitsuse, J. I. (1977) *Constructing Social Problems*. Benjamin Cummings, Menlo Park, CA.

Surette, R. (1998) *Media, Crime, and Criminal Justice: Images and Realities*. Wadsworth, Belmont, CA.

Winick, C. (1978) *Deviance and Mass Media*. Sage, Beverly Hills, CA.

deviance, medicalization of

P. J. McGann and Peter Conrad

Medicalization is the process whereby previously non-medical aspects of life come to be seen in medical terms, usually as disorders or illnesses. A wide range of phenomena has been *medicalized*, including normal life events (birth, death), biological processes (aging, menstruation), common human problems (learning and sexual difficulties), and forms of deviance. The medicalization of deviance thus refers to the process whereby non-normative or morally condemned appearance (obesity, unattractiveness, shortness), belief (mental disorder, racism), and conduct (drinking, gambling, sexual practices) come under medical jurisdiction. The tendency to see badness – whether immoral, sinful, or criminal – as illness is part of a broader historical trend from overtly punitive to ostensibly more humanitarian responses to deviance. Within this trend most scholars agree that medicalization has been on the increase. They disagree, though, as to why, to what degree, and with what consequences this is the case. It is clear, however, that medicalization processes are caught up in and complicate struggles to define and respond to deviance. Constructing deviance as illness confers a moral status different from crime or sin. As such, medicalization has implications for social control, power, knowledge, authority, and personal liberty.

Deviance has been medicalized when it is defined in medical terms, described using medical language, or a medical framework has been adopted to understand deviance. Due to the centrality of definition in medicalization, most studies are presented in a social constructionist genre. Work on medicalization has been conducted in sociology, history, psychology, psychiatry, medicine, education, anthropology, social work, and sexology. Across these disciplines, most scholars bypass the question of whether a form of deviance is "really" a medical disorder or disease in favor of analyses of how things become medicalized.

Medicalization is a collective and political achievement that requires moral entrepreneurs who champion a medical framing of a problem. Individuals, groups, and institutions have various stakes in questions over the applicability, desirability, extent, and consequences of the medical frame. Advocacy and self-help groups, social movements, clinicians, lay people, even deviants themselves have been players in medicalization dramas. Sometimes physicians support medicalization, as in premenstrual syndrome (PMS) and transsexualism. In others they actively resist it, as when medical identification of domestic violence was first introduced. Early scholarship noted the possibility of medical imperialism or colonization in cases of medicalization, typically because it serves physicians' material, strategic, or symbolic interests. The "discovery" of child abuse, for example, has been analyzed as enhancing the prestige and legitimacy of pediatric radiologists.

Constituencies outside medicine have also been advocates for medicalization. With autoimmune deficiency syndrome (AIDS) and posttraumatic stress disorder (PTSD), social movement and advocacy group pressure increased medicalization through patient–physician collaboration. Hyperactivity disorder illustrates how the prior existence of a medical treatment (Ritalin) helped consolidate a nascent medical understanding of deviant childhood behavior as illness. Recent use of human growth hormone to treat "shortness" in children with normally functioning pituitary glands illustrates how difficult it is to disentangle therapeutic, cultural, and economic interests. The Human Growth Foundation (HGF), the primary supporter for the use of synthetic human growth hormone in children, grounded its advocacy in the difficulties that shorter than average children and adults face. However, pharmaceutical companies, e.g., Genentech, provided most of HGF's funding.

New evidence suggests that the engines driving medicalization are changing. The role of physicians in the expansion and contraction of medicalization has been declining. The Food and Drug Administration Modernization Act of 1997 allows pharmaceutical companies to advertise directly to US patients/consumers, perhaps facilitating an increased demand for medical intervention. Newly aware of disorders and treatments alike, potential patients now increasingly self-diagnose then approach doctors, oftentimes asking for drugs by name. Thus men concerned about meeting rising standards of heterosexual potency "ask [their] physicians if Viagra is right for" them; shy people may request Paxil; those burdened with sadness seek relief with Wellbutrin. The shift to managed care is another factor in changing medicalization dynamics. Managed care organizations are now central to deciding what kinds of problems will be covered by health insurance. Whether this development inhibits rather than increases medicalization is a question for more politically and economically attuned constructionist analyses.

Because medicalization is a process, different phenomena reveal different *levels* of medicalization. At the *conceptual* level, medical vocabulary or a medical model organizes the problem; neither actual medical treatment nor doctors need be involved. The construction of deviant drinking as alcoholism is the exemplar here. Alcoholics Anonymous uses a medical model of understanding but eschews medical intervention. At the *institutional* level, organizations adopt a medical response and the medical model predominates, although medical professionals may or may not be directly involved. With gambling addictions and eating disorders, for example, physicians legitimate the treatment organization's approach but are not necessarily involved in direct care. In contrast, at the *interactional* level, physicians tend to be directly involved either through diagnosis or through the provision of treatment as part of the doctor–patient relationship. For example, patients may come to their physicians with vague life problems, and be prescribed psychoactive drugs without any particular medical diagnosis.

The *degree* a problem is medicalized can vary from minimal (sexual addiction), to partial (obesity), through nearly complete (mental illness). Such differences in the degree of medicalization mean that competing definitions of a form of deviance may exist. Remnants of previous understandings further complicate the definitional struggle; is compulsive shopping an illness or immature failure to inhibit desire? In addition, a medical definition may be salient in one context but not another. PMS, for example, is widely understood to be a medical disorder. But whether an individual woman experiences her menstruation as illness is another matter. Similarly, behavior that many people think of as run-of-the-mill sissiness or tomboyism is medicalized in *Diagnostic and Statistical Manual of Mental Disorders, Fourth Edition* (DSM-IV) as gender identity disorder. This dormant medical frame can be mobilized if the child's behavior or appearance comes to the attention of persons familiar with the diagnostic category; in such an instance, the "normal" tomboy or sissy is reframed as pathological.

With levels and degrees we see that medicalization is not an either/or phenomenon. Nor is medicalization a one-way process. Just as deviance may become medical, the medical framing of deviance may be undone (in part or in full). As medical meaning is diluted or replaced, medical terminology and intervention are deemed inappropriate. Masturbation is the classic example of near total *demedicalization*; in the nineteenth century, masturbation was medicalized as "onanism," a disease in itself, as well as a gateway perversion that rendered those of weak constitutions more susceptible to other forms of sexual deviation. Another example is the removal of homosexuality from the third edition of the American Psychiatric Association's *Diagnostic and Statistical Manual of Mental Disorders* (DSM-III). But whereas earlier medical framing of masturbation now seems absurd to many, the reclassification of homosexuality illustrates *contested* demedicalization. Despite the 1973 decision by the American Psychiatric Association to remove homosexuality from the roster of mental disorders, a small but vocal psychiatric minority provides reparative or conversion therapy, and a portion of the public still views homosexuality as deviance (but not necessarily as illness). Homosexuality thus also illustrates that demedicalization does not automatically mean a form of deviance has or will become conventional, only that the official medical framing has ended. Medicalization may also be contested between institutions with different jurisdictions. Deviant drinking and illicit drug use, for example, may be seen as medical, criminal, or both, setting the stage not only for "turf" battles, but also for vastly different deviant careers depending on how and by whom an individual's drinking or drugging is interpreted and responded to.

The consequences of medicalization may be positive or negative – oftentimes both. As noted, the therapeutic ethos of medicine changes the moral status of both deviance and deviant. Extension of the sick role to the deviant diminishes stigma and culpability, both of which may increase the likelihood that a pedophile, batterer, or addict for example might seek treatment. Medical explanations for inchoate or diffuse difficulties can provide coherence to symptoms, validate and legitimate troubles, and support their self-management. In addition, medical recognition may facilitate insurance coverage of medical treatment, thereby transforming potential deviants into disease victims seen worthy of care and compassion. Chronic fatigue syndrome, PMS, post-partum depression, and PTSD illustrate these positive effects. Moreover, as with child abuse, medicalization may increase the visibility of a form of deviance, which in turn may help transform a seemingly isolated individual trouble into a socially recognized public issue.

Despite these benefits, many analysts are wary of medicalization and its potential negative consequences. The sick role, for example, may provide a "medical excuse" for deviance; certainly, it diminishes individual responsibility. As the medical model becomes more attuned to physiological and genetic "causes" of behavior, blame shifts from the person to the body, further displacing responsibility. Medicalization allows for the use of powerful forms of social control, such as psychoactive drugs or surgical procedures. But the guise of medical-scientific neutrality and/or a therapeutic modality means medicalization may be an insidious expansion of social control. Tendencies to individualize and depoliticize social problems are also linked to medicalization. Both obscure insight that deviance may be a reflection of or adaptation to the social organization of a situation; focus on the individual symptoms of gender identity disorder or battery, for example, deflects attention from the heteronormative gender order, gender inequality, and patriarchal values. Medicalization also enlarges medical jurisdiction. Medical expertise may then be privileged at the expense of lay or competing views. Some transsexuals, for example, decline – or cannot afford – surgical intervention for "gender dysphoria." Others exhibit less than stereotypically conventional expressions of gender and/or refuse to pass as nontranssexuals. Because such people do not fit the prevailing medical framing of transsexualism, they may be subject to ridicule, censure, or denial of service by medical gatekeepers.

Medicalization appears to be on the increase, but how much depends in part on what is measured. One approach looks at the growing number of people diagnosed. Another considers the increasing number of diagnostic categories. In addition to the proliferation of categories, medicalization increases through expansion of extant categories. That is, diagnostic categories themselves may be stretched, encompassing more behavior within their bounds over time. Psychiatric categories, especially the functional disorders, seem especially prone to such expansion. The emergence of adult attention deficit hyperactivity disorder (ADHD), the extension of the uses of PTSD, and the widespread use of psychoactive medications like Prozac for unspecified psychological discomfort are examples of this.

The movement to medicalization has also normalized medical intervention in some forms of deviance, such as plastic surgery for unattractiveness, aging, and obesity. This proliferation of medical fixes may create an imperative to submit to medicalization such that failure to use medical enhancements or treatments itself becomes a form of deviance. Thus refusal to take antidepressants for unhappiness, or failure to surgically reconstruct racialized facial features, may be seen as deviant in some circles.

The turn toward genetic understandings of personality and social behavior also has implications for medicalization processes. But geneticization is not the same as medicalization, although interpretation is the key to both. Discovery of a genetic component of homosexuality, for example, may fuel medicalization if medical technology (genetic screening, abortion, genetic therapy) is used to decrease the homosexual "defect." In this case, a genetic link may catalyze a *remedicalization* of homosexuality. Alternatively, a genetic cause may be viewed as evidence of the naturalness of homosexuality, perhaps facilitating further demedicalization.

Finally, genetics suggests that a further shift in medicalization processes may be under way, from external control of deviant bodies and behaviors toward manipulation of internal processes. Whether such *biomedicalization* is a change in medicalization strategy or a new beast altogether is an open question. Some argue that medicalization is a modernist phenomenon concerned with imposing and maintaining bodily homogeneity. In contrast, biomedicalization's transformation of bodily processes produces customized bodies and identities, a dynamic characterized as postmodern. Either way, medicalization and biomedicalization processes coexist. Both are implicated in and are facilitating new patterns of physician–patient/consumer collaboration. And both are part of the trend toward increased levels of self-surveillance in the pursuit of new norms of health and bodily perfection.

SEE ALSO: Deviance, Constructionist Perspectives; Medical Sociology and Genetics; Mental Disorder; Moral Entrepreneur; Sick Role; Social Control

REFERENCES AND SUGGESTED READINGS

Clarke, A., Mamo, L., Fishman, J. R., Shim, J., & Fosket, J. R. (2003) Biomedicalization: Technoscientific Transformations of Health, Illness, and US Biomedicine. *American Sociological Review* 68: 161–94.

Conrad, P. (1992) Medicalization and Social Control. *Annual Review of Sociology* 19: 209–32.

Conrad, P. & Potter, D. (2000) From Hyperactive Children to ADHD Adults: Observations on the Expansion of Medical Categories. *Social Problems* 47: 559–82.

Conrad, P. & Schneider, J. (1992) *Deviance and Medicalization: From Badness to Sickness*. Temple University Press, Philadelphia.

Horwitz, A. (2002) *Creating Mental Illness*. University of Chicago Press, Chicago.

Kutchins, H. & Kirk, S. (1997) *Making Us Crazy*. Free Press, New York.

Pfohl, S. (1977) The Discovery of Child Abuse. *Social Problems* 24: 310–23.

Riessman, C. K. (1983) Women and Medicalization: A New Perspective. *Social Policy* (Summer): 3–18.

Zola, I. K. (1972) Medicine as an Institution of Social Control. *Sociological Review* 20: 487–50.

deviance, moral boundaries and

Pat Lauderdale

Through a variety of social mechanisms, most human diversity is categorized as normal variation and a varying fraction as deviance. This area of research asks how the moral boundaries of these categories are drawn, i.e., normal versus deviant, and what determines the placement of specific actors and acts within the categories (Lauderdale 1976; Ben-Yehuda 1985). The sociologist, therefore, can examine how certain actions are defined as deviant from specific social reactions and the creation of moral boundaries that separate the varying definitions of normal from deviant ones. The creation of the boundaries and the placement of individuals as either normal or deviant are viewed as basic processes of social definition that often are found to be outcomes of political variables.

Extending the seminal work of Émile Durkheim, this line of research is contrary to the conventional view of deviance as social pathology that must be normalized or eradicated. Durkheim suggested the relevance of the relationship between political power and deviance in his analysis of sanctioning, in which he posited that increases in the consolidation of power in society will lead to proportional increases in the repressive sanctioning of people who are defined as the most deviant (i.e., criminal). Deviance is studied as a normal phenomenon, which under certain conditions can play a part in facilitating social change. Socrates in his time, for example, was seen as a serious deviant under the law of Athens. His offense, however, was his independent thought and his call to his students to think as independently as possible. Now, Socrates is viewed as having acted for a higher moral good, not only for his country but also for all people. Under the Fugitive Slave Laws of the 1850s, aiding and abetting escaped slaves was a crime. With the passage of the 14th Amendment less than a decade later, however, slavery itself was the crime. In 1800, the organization of a labor union was defined as a crime (conspiracy in restraint of trade), yet by 1940 labor unions were legal, and many employers were even required by law to engage in collective bargaining (Lauderdale 2003). Definitions of deviance not only presage actions that come to be accepted later but also reveal that some actions continue to be unacceptable.

A basic question, thus, concerns how the boundary between normal and deviant, or good and bad, is constructed, maintained, or changed. In his watershed book entitled *Wayward Puritans* (1966), Kai Erikson attempted to answer part of this question. His book focuses on a variety of central issues in politics and power, and who and what might account for the shift in the boundary between normal and deviant. His analysis of specific cases of deviance amplification or creation by the Puritans is critical because the Puritans encountered diversity and reacted to it as deviance. The people who were designated as deviants, i.e., the religious dissenters, the Quakers, and the witches, were caught in a set of larger crises. For example, the designation of Anne Hutchinson, a religious dissenter, as a deviant resulted more from the power struggle among the male religious leaders than any of her actions. Erikson (1966: 68) presents the conditions under which the boundary might shift, for example, by "a realignment of power within the group," or threats from outside the group. Moreover, the redefinition of many Japanese Americans from normal to deviant (often including imprisonment in "relocation" camps) following the invasion of Pearl Harbor suggests similar conditions and processes. During times of crises such as "terrorist" attacks or war, external threats and realignments of power continue to be key concepts in this area of study.

Such changing social conditions also are particularly useful when we extend the ideas by also focusing upon an emerging group or larger forces in society, and the emergence of "modern" society. Mies notes in her research on the terrorizing of midwives as witches that the terror was directly related to changes in society and the state, including medical professionalization, the increasing view of medicine as a "natural science," and the legitimation of science. Witch-hunters used torture chambers as the "laboratories where the texture, the anatomy, the resistance of the human body – mainly the female body – was studied." Mies suggests that modern medicine and hegemony in this area were established on the base of "millions of crushed, maimed, torn, disfigured and finally burnt, female bodies" (1986: 83).

At more specific levels of analysis, researchers have examined how the moral boundaries have changed via the actions of moral entrepreneurs, social movements, organizations, the state, and global institutions (Goode & Ben-Yehuda 1994; Oliverio 1998; Lauderdale 2003). Moral entrepreneurs, for example, initiate public discourses on particular issues trying to persuade the public and the state of their view of the truth. Joseph McCarthy, a classic example, who was a senator from Wisconsin, called for the purge of suspected communists in the 1950s. Initially, he was lauded as a great leader as he helped shift the moral boundaries, but evidence later revealed that many of the suspects were simply exercising their freedom of speech or were misidentified. The sociological literature on the changes in status, i.e., from normal to deviant or vice versa, of moral entrepreneurs such as McCarthy can be extended to examine other entrepreneurs working on various crusades or projects. Such entrepreneurs include people such as Ralph Nader (his early work on consumer protection), Leonard Peltier (his concerns with American Indian issues), Bobby Seals (his actions on racialization and freedom), and Mother Teresa (her projects on charity and love).

Social movement research has included people protesting in numerous arenas, such as the diverse movements against the North American Free Trade Agreement and the World Trade Organization, where protestors demand free access to water, air, and public space. Other movements are those such as MADD (Mothers Against Drunk Driving), the anti-abortion a.k.a. pro-life movement, the pro-gun or anti-gun movement, anti-pornography groups, and the anti-smoking movement. Researchers also are exploring the factors that lead to the transformation of a social movement into a social organization, which is important because most social movements do not reach institutional levels.

Research on the role of social organizations in creating, maintaining, or transforming moral boundaries recently has concentrated narrowly on the media. This research agenda can be extended by examining organizational forces that influence the media. In addition, the historical overview of scholars such as Annamarie Oliverio (1998) suggests the importance of unraveling the deep connections between expanding organizations, law, trials, the state, and globalization.

SEE ALSO: Deviance; Durkheim, Émile; Power, Theories of; Social Movements; State

REFERENCES AND SUGGESTED READINGS

Ben-Yehuda, N. (1985) *Deviance and Moral Boundaries.* University of Chicago Press, Chicago.

Ben-Yehuda, N. (2001) *Betrayals and Treason: Violations of Trust and Loyalty.* Westview Press, Boulder, CO.

Durkheim, E. (1973 [1899]) Two Laws of Penal Evolution. Trans. T. Anthony Jones and A. Scull. *Economy and Society* 2: 285–308.

Durkheim, E. (1982 [1893]) *Rules of the Sociological Method.* Free Press, New York.

Erikson, K. T. (1966) *Wayward Puritans: A Study in the Sociology of Deviance.* Wiley, New York.

Farrell, R. A. & Case, C. (1995) *The Black Book and the Mob: The Untold Story of the Control of Nevada's Casinos.* University of Wisconsin Press, Madison.

Goode, E. & Ben-Yehuda, N. (1994) *Moral Panics: The Social Construction of Deviance.* Blackwell, Cambridge, MA.

Gusfield, J. R. (1963) *Symbolic Crusade: Status Politics and the American Temperance Movement*. University of Illinois Press, Urbana.

Inverarity, J., Lauderdale, P., & Feld, B. (1983) *Law and Society*. Little, Brown, Boston.

Lauderdale, P. (1976) Deviance and Moral Boundaries. *American Sociological Review* 41: 660–76.

Lauderdale, P. (2003) *A Political Analysis of Deviance*, new edn. De Sitter Publications, Willowdale, Canada.

Lauderdale, P., Smith-Cunnien, P., Parker, J., & Inverarity, J. (1984) External Threat and the Definition of Deviance. *Journal of Personality and Social Psychology* 46: 1058–70.

McAdam, D. & Su, Y. (2002) The Political Impact of the War at Home: Antiwar Protests and Congressional Voting, 1965–1973. *American Sociological Review* 67: 696–721.

Mies, M. (1986) *Patriarchy and Accumulation on a World Scale: Women in the International Division of Labor*. Palgrave MacMillan, New York.

Mills, C. W. (1942) The Professional Ideology of Social Pathologists. *American Journal of Sociology* 49: 165–80.

Oliverio, A. (1998) *The State of Terror*. SUNY Press, New York.

deviance, normative definitions of

Robert F. Meier

Sociologists tend to define deviance in one of two ways: by the negative reactions an act, the expression of a belief, or a physical characteristic generates, or by the violation of the norms or the rules that prevail in a given society or group. Reactivist definitions come in two varieties: the "hard" or strict reactivist definition, which defines deviance as acts, beliefs, or conditions that have already attracted a negative reaction from one or more audiences, and the "soft" or moderate definition, which defines deviance as behavior, beliefs, or conditions that are likely to generate negative reactions from audiences. In contrast, the normative definition identifies deviance as a violation of a norm held in certain social circles or by a majority of the members of the society at large. A norm is a standard about "what human beings should or should not think, say, or do under given circumstances" (Blake & Kingsley 1964). Put another way, a norm is a social expectation concerning thought or behavior in particular situations. Violations of norms tend to draw reactions or sanctions from their social audiences. These sanctions generate the pressure that most people feel to conform to social norms. However, even if the actor, the believer, or the possessor is not detected or chastised for a normative violation, the non-normative act, belief, or trait is deviant nonetheless. To the normative definition, what defines something as deviance is a formal violation of the rules.

Norms evaluate conduct; recognizing that some acts (including beliefs and the expression of beliefs) ought or ought not to occur, either in specific situations (e.g., no smoking in public elevators) or at any time or place (e.g., no armed robbery, ever). The use of proper etiquette reflects deliberate decisions to adhere to norms of respect and consideration for others (Post 2003). The norms that comprise etiquette are also situational, but are more likely to be codified than norms in many social situations.

The conception of norms as expectations highlights regularities of behavior based on habit or traditional customs. People expect a child, for example, to act a certain way in church, another way on the playground. This raises another dimension of norms: they are situationally bound. Running and yelling of children is appropriate for the playground, but not in church. Laughing is expected behavior in a comedy club, but not at a funeral.

Norms are not necessarily clear-cut rules; instead, they are social properties. They are shared group evaluations or guidelines, and many of them are learned implicitly in the more general process of socialization. Rules come from one or more authorities which formulate them individually and impose them on members of a particular society. This authority could be the state, which reserves the right to exercise coercive force over the citizenry, or a monarch or a despot. Norms are an absolutely essential component of the social order.

No one has attempted to count norms because the number is quite large, depending on the group. There is an enormous number of possible situations in which norms regulate behavior. There is, for example, a norm that guides people's behavior in elevators: one is expected to face the door. Sometimes the rationale for norms is vague. In this example, everyone facing the same direction avoids invading someone else's "personal space," the distance between two strangers that feels most comfortable. This distance varies from culture to culture. Italians are comfortable with less distance between them than are Americans.

People risk being labeled as a deviant by audiences when they express unacceptable beliefs (such as worshiping devils), violate behavioral norms (such as engaging in proscribed sexual acts), or possessing certain physical traits widely regarded as undesirable, which include physical handicaps (being confined to a wheelchair) and violations of appearance norms (e.g., obesity) (Clinard & Meier 2004). However, even if audiences do not witness or learn about the normative violation, it is deviant nonetheless. In other words, to the normative definition, "secret" deviance is not a contradiction in terms; it exists, and is an important variety of deviance. In fact, it is possible that most normative violations remain a secret and never generate negative reactions of any kind from disapproving audiences. The normative definition is based on a certain measure of predictability that normative violations are likely to attract negative reactions, even if they are never observed. The fact that in a particular context or instance, a given observed act, expressed belief, or physical characteristic did not generate negative sanctions for the actor, believer, or possessor is beside the point. The normative sociologist does not have to wait until condemnation takes place to know that something is deviant. It is the violation of what the norms of a society or group say about proper and improper behavior, beliefs, and characteristics that defines them as deviant. For instance, we know in advance that it is a violation of society's norms to walk down the street, nude (Gibbs 1972), and hence, that that act is deviant. In contrast, the "strict" reactivist definition denies the predictability that negative sanctions follow normative violations, and denies the existence of "secret" deviance, arguing that the concept is an oxymoron (Pollner 1974). Most sociologists of deviance adopt some version of a normative definition of the concept, arguing that the strict normative definition makes it

impossible to study most normative violations as deviance, hence, fatally restricting the sociologist's domain of investigation.

SEE ALSO: Deviance; Deviance, Reactivist Definitions of; Norms; Positive Deviance; Social Control

REFERENCES AND SUGGESTED READINGS

Becker, H. S. (1963) *Outsiders: Studies in the Sociology of Deviance*. Free Press, New York.
Blake, J. & Kingsley, D. (1964) Norms, Values, and Sanctions. In: Faris, R. E. L. (Ed.), *Handbook of Modern Sociology*. Rand McNally, Chicago.
Clinard, M. & Meier, R. F. (2004) *Sociology of Deviant Behavior*, 12th edn. Wadsworth, Belmont, CA.
Gibbs, J. P. (1972) Issues in Defining Deviant Behavior. In: Scott, R. A. & Douglas, J. D. (Eds.), *Theoretical Perspectives on Deviance*. Basic Books, New York, pp. 39–68.
Pollner, M. (1974) Sociological and Common-Sense Models of the Labeling Process. In: Turner, R. (Ed.), *Ethnomethodology: Selected Readings*. Penguin, Baltimore, pp. 27–40.
Post, P. (2003) *Essential Manners for Men*. Harper Resource, New York.

deviance, positivist theories of

Robert F. Meier

Sociologists define deviance as the violation of a norm that, if discovered, typically results in punishment, scorn, or stigmatization of the offender. The normative violation can include acts, beliefs, and traits or characteristics. This definition opens two radically different though complementary missions or lines of inquiry: those that attempt to explain the causes and consequences of normative violations, and those that explore the dynamics underlying the social construction, accompaniments, and consequences of the norms, including laws and their enforcement. Sociologists of deviance – including criminologists – who adopt the first of these missions are usually referred to as "positivists"; those who adopt the second are called "constructionists." Positivistic sociologists of deviance and crime nearly always study non-normative behavior, while constructionists look at the full gamut of normative violations – behavior, beliefs, and physical characteristics.

In the social sciences, positivism is usually defined as the natural science approach to social life. This means that the methods by which scientists study the world of biology, chemistry, and physics can be applied – taking their different subject matter into account, of course – to the social, anthropological, economic, psychological, political, and even religious worlds. The positivist approach is made up of the following assumptions: objectivism (i.e., phenomena take on a reality independent of their social construction); empiricism (we can know the world through our five senses); and determinism (the phenomena of the material world, including the social world, are linked together in a cause-and-effect fashion).

Objectivism refers to the fact that the positivist approach to deviance would argue that the violation of social and legal norms constitutes an objectively real, pre-given entity that contains a common thread that demands an explanation. If deviance, including crime, and its constituent elements did not contain a common thread – that is, if it were a social label and nothing else – then no explanation attempting to account for it would be possible. *Empiricism* typically refers to the fact that the violations of social norms can be investigated by means of highly sophisticated, quantitative social research methodologies, such as surveys, which stress reliability and validity. *Determinism* refers to the fact that the central question in positivist research is: "Why do they do it?" In the field of the sociology of deviance and crime, positivists assume that they can discover law-like generalizations that account for normative violations. Positivistic approaches are not confined to sociology, of course; the factor attempting to explain crime has included biological, psychological, and sociological variables. All positivist theories of deviance – whether they focus on the individual, the individual in a particular context or social structure, or the social structure itself – address their research to the same basic question. In all of them, the *dependent*

variable is the normative violation, and the *independent* variable is the factor their theory addresses.

THE EARLY POSITIVISTS

The first positivists of deviance and crime belonged to a group of social statisticians who studied the social, physical, and environmental conditions associated with normative and legal violations, the most well known of whom was Adolphe Quetelet (1796–1874). Quetelet identified the existence of law-like regularities in officially recorded criminal behavior, suggesting to him that crime was subject to causal laws that could be revealed through an approach and a research methodology similar to those of the natural sciences. By implying that crime is a product of society, Quetelet opened the possibility of a sociological analysis of crime.

The early years of the positivist approach to deviance and crime are most closely associated with the Positive School founded by Italian physician Cesare Lombroso (1835–1909). The Positive School was an attempt to apply the methods of studying the physical world to the world of crime. Advocates of the Positive School believed that violations of the law could be accounted for by natural causes rather than by free will. In this sense, the Positive School was a rejection of the free will hedonism of the Classical School, associated with the writings of Cesare Beccaria (1738–94), Jeremy Bentham (1748–1832), and Adam Smith (1723–90). The approach of the Positive School was far more radically positivistic than that adopted by Quetelet, in that it identified the cause of criminal behavior principally as a biological factor: one or more physical defects (or "atavisms") in the human organism. Atavisms are ape-like "throwbacks," primitive characteristics that appear in some modern humans. They included a small brain, a sloping forehead, a large jaw, and a stooped posture. These defects, the theory argued, induce some people to commit crime. Lombroso's early focus on biological factors has led some observers to dub his approach as the "born criminals" theory. Unlike Quetelet's theory, which was structural and sociological, Lombroso's was a "kinds of people" explanation that looked no further than the individual characteristics of offenders. Over time, however, Lombroso modified his explanation; with each new edition of his book, *The Criminal Man*, he attributed a decreasing impact of biological factors and an increasing role for social factors. Lombroso's influence on the study of crime is immense, both in his insistence that criminal behavior be studied objectively and scientifically and in his focus on biological factors, an emphasis that remains in certain quarters of the field of criminology to this day. Lombroso argued that engaging in criminal behavior was the result of forces that diminish the role of free will or rational choice – again, a hallmark of contemporary positivistic approach to deviance and crime.

All positivists *assume but do not investigate* the social construction of the norms and the laws. Indeed, how laws and norms come into being and what their consequences are for the violators is not an issue for the positivist, who assumes that answers to the "Why do they do it?" question would be the same regardless of how they emerged and operate. In other words, the relativity of the social norms and the law is irrelevant; the same cause-and-effect mechanisms would produce more or less the same pattern of normative and legal violations, regardless of what society or historical time period we are discussing. Positivists are interested in the cause or causes of deviant and criminal behavior under any and all normative and legal circumstances.

POSITIVIST THEORIES OF CRIME AND DEVIANCE

Positivist theories of crime and deviance run the gamut from genetic and biochemical through psychological to sociological. The *sociological* theories that attempt to explain or account for normative or legal violations include: social disorganization theory; anomie theory; learning theory; social control theory; and self-control theory. In addition, several of the most prominent constructionist theories harbor a "minor" or positivistic mode: labeling theory; control theory, including Marxism; and feminism.

Social disorganization theory. During the 1920s, the sociology faculty and graduate students at the University of Chicago developed a perspective toward deviance, crime, and delinquency that has come to be called the Chicago School, or social disorganization theory. Using the city of Chicago as their laboratory, these researchers took as their explanatory variable the instability of entire neighborhoods and communities. Regardless of their individual characteristics, people who live in such communities are more likely to engage in illegal and non-normative behaviors than persons residing in more stable communities. What makes for unstable or disorganized communities is that rents are inexpensive, the populations who live in them invest little financially or emotionally in living there, and they tend to be socially and geographically mobile. Hence, they tend not to monitor or sanction the behavior of wrongdoing in their midst. As a result, residents can commit infractions of the law and the social norms without consequence, and tend to do so with greater frequency than in communities in which their co-residents monitor and sanction their behavior. In such communities, street crime, drug abuse, alcoholism, prostitution, juvenile delinquency, and mental disorder are common; law-abiding residents tend to move as soon as they can, contributing to further crime, deviance, delinquency, and social disorganization. By the 1940s, the Chicago School had become regarded as obsolete (in the 1960s, a school of deviance research came to be dubbed the "neo-Chicagoans," but they had a very different orientation). But by the late 1980s, social disorganization theory experienced a rebirth of interest, and is now a major perspective in the study of crime, delinquency, and social problems.

Anomie theory. Closely associated with the early work of Robert Merton (1968), the anomie perspective was a structural theory of crime and delinquency. Modern societies, Merton reasoned, especially the United States, offered their residents substantial opportunities. But while status goals, like materialism and wealth, are stressed, access to these goals is limited. Important status goals remain inaccessible to many groups, including the poor, the lower class, and certain racial and ethnic groups who suffer discrimination, such as blacks and Chicanos. Anomie develops as a result of an acute disjuncture between culturally valued goals and the legitimate means through which society allows certain groups to achieve those goals. So, while everyone learns to aspire to the "American Dream" of financial success, in reality the social structure can provide legitimate opportunities to only a few, leaving others frustrated in their search for success. As a result, some will turn to alternative means by which to reach their success goals. These will be mainly lower-class minority males in urban areas whom the system fails to benefit. Anomie theory continues to be popular, as do variations of anomie theory that provide more detail about both societal pressure to succeed and adapting to those pressures.

Learning theory. There are a number of learning theories of deviance, but one of the most respected is criminologist Edwin Sutherland's (1947) theory of differential association. Crime and other forms of deviance are the result not of biological or psychological defect but of learning criminal norms. Sutherland, like other learning theorists, believed that the most powerful learning takes place in small, intimate groups among people who know one another well, such as close friends. These groups are very important because the members have high credibility with one another. During social interaction, people can teach other people many things, including techniques and rationale for committing crimes. Sutherland called the content of most of this learning "definitions favorable to violation of law." In other words, the content of the learning was a justification or motivation to commit a crime. Such definitions can, of course, be reinforced over time. There are other kinds of learning theories which identify the psychological processes involved in the learning, but all learning theories are consistent on a central point: crime is neither inherited nor inevitable. Rather, it is acquired from others in a process of communication and interaction.

Social control theory. Social control theory, or more conventionally just control theory, asserts that deviance is not so much learned or the result of societal pressure as it is simply not controlled (Hirschi 1969). Popularized in the late 1960s, control theory stresses not things that push people to crime (like criminal motivation) but things that keep a person restrained and in conformity. Control theorists believe that crime results when a person is not restrained or controlled by society. The control of particular interest in control theory is the individual's bond with society. The closer the bond, the less likely that person will commit a deviant act. There are several elements of the bond, including attachment, commitment, involvement, and belief. The more a person is attached to his or her group, the more that person is committed to the group and its goals, the more time the person spends in the group, and the more the person believes in the norms of the group, the less likely will that person deviate from the group's norms. Control theory generated a good deal of research and was a leading positivist theory in the 1970s and 1980s.

Self-control theory. Self-control theory, developed by Michael Gottfredson and Travis Hirschi (1990), is a theory with both learning and control elements. Self-control theory posits that through the general socialization process, some people fail to develop self-control over their behavior. They are therefore more likely to engage in risky acts, including crime, drugs, alcohol, and other behavior that overlooks or neglects the long-term consequences of continuing to engage in that behavior.

Constructionist theory's positivistic mode. The perspective in the sociology of deviance that is referred to as "labeling theory" arose in the 1960s as a reaction against the dominant positivistic study of normative violations (Lemert 1951; Becker 1973). Labeling theory's principal focus was on how conceptions of wrongdoing are developed, how rules are enforced, and what the consequences of being labeled as a deviant are. In other words, its approach was mainly in the constructionist vein. However, a "minor" mode of labeling theory argued that being stigmatized as a wrongdoer – a "deviant" – often has the ironic consequence of solidifying a deviant identity and entrenching patterns of deviant behavior. In other words, one aspect of this approach is causal or positivistic in its orientation: *labeling causes deviance.*

In a like vein, conflict theory is focused mainly on inequality in power as the primary determinant of the criminal law and its enforcement – an entirely constructionist endeavor. Nonetheless, conflict theorists also examine inequality as a major *cause* of criminal behavior. Members of the lower class are more likely to commit common street crimes, this perspective argues, because in a society based on social class, their options for success and social mobility are extremely limited. In contrast, corporate crime – the ability of executives to commit and, usually, get away with crimes that are vastly more lucrative than street crimes – is a manifestation of the immense power wielded by the corporate elite. "What is the cause of crime?" conflict theorists ask. Their answer: inequality. Similarly, Marxists argue that capitalism is the primary cause of crime in capitalist society.

Feminists, who usually focus on how norms and laws tend to reinforce patriarchal institutions, also argue that the cause of crimes against women is patriarchy. In tracing abusive, criminal behavior such as rape, sexual harassment, wife battering, and the molestation of children to male privilege, some feminists adopt a positivist approach to the study of criminal behavior.

The coin of the sociological study of deviance has two halves – the positivist and the constructionist. The positivist half examines the causes of deviant behavior as one or more pre-given entities, behavioral syndromes with a coherent common thread whose etiology demands to be studied, located, and explicated. Even the constructionist half harbors a "minor" positivist mode. Positivism is the dominant approach in criminology, while today most researchers who identify themselves as sociologists of deviance tend to adopt a more constructionist orientation. Although positivism and constructionism are not contradictory, to a major extent, their respective practitioners are to some degree separate; they no longer form an intellectual community who refer to one another's work.

SEE ALSO: Anomie; Beccaria, Cesare; Conflict Theory; Criminology; Deviance, Constructionist Perspectives; Deviance, Crime and; Empiricism; Feminist Criminology; Labeling Theory; Lombroso, Cesare; Objectivity; Self-Control Theory; Social Control; Social Disorganization Theory; Sutherland, Edwin H.

REFERENCES AND SUGGESTED READINGS

Beccaria, C. (1963 [1764]) *On Crimes and Punishments*. Trans. H. Paolucci. Bobbs-Merrill, Indianapolis.
Becker, H. S. (1973) *Outsiders: Studies in the Sociology of Deviance*, enlarged edn. Free Press, New York.
Gottfredson, M. & Hirschi, T. (1990) *A General Theory of Crime*. Stanford University Press, Palo Alto.
Hirschi, T. (1969) *Causes of Delinquency*. University of California Press, Berkeley.
Lemert, E. M. (1951) *Social Pathology*. McGraw-Hill, New York.
Lombroso-Ferrero, G. (1972 [1911]) *Criminal Man: According to the Classification of Cesare Lombroso*. Patterson Smith, Montclair, NJ.
Merton, R. K. (1968) *Social Theory and Social Structure*. Free Press, New York.
Sutherland, E. H. (1947) *Criminology*, 4th edn. Lippincott, Philadelphia.

deviance processing agencies

George S. Rigakos

Deviance processing agencies refers to a wide gamut of institutions and agencies both public and private involved in the identification, vetting, and dispensation of populations considered at risk, dangerous, or that presumably require monitoring and surveillance to mitigate potential harms. Deviance processing agencies have been considered in a more comprehensive manner since the 1960s and 1970s and constitute a central focus of inquiry for social theorists interested in governmentality risk and social control. During anti-war student protests and the radicalization of academia in the 1960s and 1970s, sociologists and criminologists employed critical approaches often born out of a Marxian orientation (e.g., Spitzer 1975) to critically analyze developments in police practices, punitive legal measures, and inhumane prison conditions. They offered explanations of repressive state practices (Cooper et al. 1975) against dissidents and socially constructed deviants within the context of managing crises of capitalist legitimacy, the symbolic importance of the labeling process, and the inherently biased function of legal norms (Quinney 1974). By the 1980s, a rather substantial body of scholarly work tied to an evolving critical criminology movement analyzed and deconstructed the practices of criminal justice agencies, particularly in the context of rising crime rates, mass imprisonment, and punitive neoconservative crime control policies (Lowman et al. 1987).

While interest in a critical analysis of state agencies was piqued by the unrest of the 1960s and 1970s, perhaps the best-known deconstruction of the internal classification practices of a deviance processing agency is Goffman's (1961) ethnographic analysis of the asylum. His approach exposed how both initial classification and subsequent personal bias and discretion on the part of institutional workers reinforced the interpretation of seemingly innocuous behaviors as constitutive of a pre-diagnosed mental malady. Thus, central to an understanding of how deviance processing agencies operate is to come to terms with the logics by which such organizations identify deviancy in the first place and how this vetting process accomplishes institutional objectives. Another focal concern, of course, is how these targeted populations are managed (or treated).

Reflecting general political and meta-theoretical changes in academic climate, contemporary analyses of deviance processing agencies have moved away from Marxian interpretations. The most influential work in this area is now by Foucault (1977), whom some later analysts have read as both a rejection of Marxist functionalist interpretations and as an impetus for the decentering of the state in sociological explanations. The utility of Foucauldian notions such as panoptics, governmentality, and surveillance has significantly altered the lexicon of analysis in this area (Garland 1997). This shift in thinking is comprised of two main attributes. First, a realization that a significant proportion of deviance processing is accomplished by state, quasi-state, and private institutions or organizations outside the context of the criminal justice system. Contemporary analysts have, for example, turned their attention towards state welfare agencies, private policing, and the profound disciplinary powers of insurance companies. Second, that

in the historical development of the science of "knowing" populations an important qualitative shift has occurred with the mass availability and distribution of computers after World War II. Sociologists have offered both substantive empirical examinations and general theoretical explanations for this profound transformation. A central element of this conversion is the institutional reliance on statistical *deviation* from a prescribed norm as actually constituting *deviance*. Thus, increasingly, private agencies such as insurance companies rely on actuarial grids to assess risky populations that in the eyes of such institutional needs constitutes deviance – a potential harm to the corporation.

Of course, such techniques are also widespread in the criminal justice system, including important decision-making on likelihood to reoffend, the classification of prisoners within levels of custodial security, and even the designation of dangerous offenders based on indicators such as the psychopathy checklist. In other words, deviance processing has become multifarious and ubiquitous as we consistently come into contact with institutional requirements that we provide identification and that our credentials (ranging from criminal history to credit standing) become known. This routine provision of personal data is alternately considered part of a system of dataveillance, the move to a superpanopticon (Poster 1990), and even the ushering in of a new risk society. Indeed, risk and probability thus become unavoidable components of the deviance processing system acting as not only methodological solutions but also the problems (i.e., a bottomless barrel of risks) (Beck 1992).

Some of the critiques of these schools of thought have to do with the perceived "newness" of such surveillance practices for deviance processing and to what extent the purpose and function of such processing is qualitatively different from the targeted populations previously identified under Marxian formulations; the extent to which these processes are largely an expansion of Weberian-identified tendencies toward rationalization and bureaucratization; and a conceptual slippage between deviance, social control, risk, and regulation. Each of these three issues has significant theoretical implications for our understanding of not only deviance processing but also, by implication, political and social theory and historiography (Rigakos & Hadden 2001).

SEE ALSO: Courts; Criminal Justice System; Deviance, Criminalization of; Governmentality and Control; Risk, Risk Society, Risk Behavior, and Social Problems; Social Control; Surveillance

REFERENCES AND SUGGESTED READINGS

Beck, U. (1992) *Risk Society: Towards a New Modernity*. Sage, London.

Cooper, L., Currie, E., Frappier, J., Platt, T., Ryan, B., Schauffler, R., Scruggs, J., & Trujillo, L. (Eds.), (1975) *The Iron Fist and the Velvet Glove*. Center for Research on Criminal Justice, Berkeley.

Foucault, M. (1977) *Discipline and Punish*. Vintage Books, New York.

Garland, D. (1997) "Governmentality" and the Problem of Crime: Foucault, Criminology, Sociology. *Theoretical Criminology: An International Journal* 1 (2): 173–214.

Goffman, E. (1961) *Asylums: Essays on the Social Situations of Mental Patients and Other Inmates*. Anchor, New York.

Lowman, J., Menzies, R. J., & Palys, T. (1987) Introduction. In: *Transcarceration: Essays in the Sociology of Social Control*. Gower, Aldershot, pp. 1–10.

Poster, M. (1990) *The Mode of Information*. University of Chicago Press, Chicago.

Quinney, R. (1974) *A Critical Philosophy of Legal Order*. Little Brown, Boston.

Rigakos, G. S. & Hadden, R. W. (2001) Crime, Capitalism and the Risk Society: Towards the Same Olde Modernity? *Theoretical Criminology* 5 (1): 61–84.

Spitzer, S. (1975) Toward a Marxian Theory of Deviance. *Social Problems* 22 (5): 638–51.

deviance, reactivist definitions of

Henry N. Pontell

The sociology of deviance entails two major perspectives, both of which emphasize the relative nature of the phenomenon. The normative perspective, which most sociologists adhere to, views deviance as being located in customs and rules; deviance is the formal violation of one or more norms. The reactivist perspective, which has been associated with the labeling theory of deviance, takes a more radical approach to the relative nature of deviance, and views the existence and characteristics of deviance in how real behaviors, beliefs, or conditions are actually judged by relevant audiences (Goode 2001). Labeling theory has been marked by controversy since it arrived on the sociological scene in the 1960s. Two of its major proponents (Kitsuse 1972; Becker 1973) do not consider it a theory at all, and reject the term labeling, in characterizing what they view as the interactionist perspective. This term derives from the sociological perspective of symbolic interactionism, which sees all acts emanating from meanings that persons attach to social phenomena, with these meanings growing and changing through a continual interpretive process involving interactions with others (Blumer 1969). In a major review of labeling theory, Goode (1975) concludes that it "isn't a theory at all," and further relates that it might not even be a "general perspective," but rather a way of considering specific aspects of deviance through the application of symbolic interactionism.

The reactivist perspective is commonly traced to the writings of historian Frank Tannenbaum (1938), who highlighted the nature of community reactions to juvenile delinquency as the "dramatization of evil," whereby the social definition of the behavior was attached instead to the people who behaved that way, making them more prone to take on a deviant (evil) role. A little over a decade later, sociologist Edwin M. Lemert (1951) greatly expanded upon this general idea, including broader conceptualizations that related symbolic interactionism to the study of deviance. His classic distinction between primary deviance (related to the original causes of deviant behavior, which he termed "polygenetic," or due to a wide range of causes) and secondary deviance (related to the effective causes, after labeling took place, and a person formed a deviant identity), and his insistence that reactions form the essential quality of the social reality of deviance, formed the basis for the reactivist definition of deviance.

"Strict" reactivists (Kitsuse 1962) claim that in order for deviance to exist, the act, condition, or belief must first be heard about or witnessed, and second, must be met with concrete social disapproval, condemnation, or punishment. If these conditions are not satisfied, according to strict reactivists, deviance does not socially exist. If acts, beliefs, or conditions are known about and not reacted to as deviant, or if they remain hidden, makes no difference to strict reactivists. Real responses by audiences to concrete phenomena are what matter, and not the act, belief, or condition. Strict reactivists deny that audiences react to phenomena "in the abstract," that is, as *classes* of acts, beliefs, or conditions (Gibbs 1972). It is the real-life expression of some disapproval or condemnation to a specific act that defines deviance, according to strict reactivists.

Although Lemert's work was among the most influential in what became known as the labeling perspective, it is quite clear that he was not a "strict" reactivist. In his landmark work *Social Pathology* (1951), he acknowledges deviant acts that are "clandestine," have "low visibility," and "escape the public eye." That is, deviant forms can exist without actual reactions of audiences. What he does draw major intellectual attention to, however, is that socially visible deviations can attract a wide range of expressions and attitudes from a conforming majority. This entails an important dynamic process between *doing* deviance (for whatever reasons) and *becoming* a deviant (forming a deviant identity) that comprises the heart of the reactivist definition of deviance and the labeling perspective. He wrote that "older sociology ... tended to rest heavily upon the idea that deviance leads to social control. I have come to believe that the reverse idea, i.e., social control leads to deviance, is equally tenable and the potentially richer premise for studying deviance in modern society"(Lemert 1967: v).

While both Lemert and Tannenbaum highlighted the ironic consequences of condemning deviance, in that this could produce further rule-breaking behavior, Lemert (1951) noted that sometimes a reduction or elimination of the behavior in question resulted as well; an idea that fell by the wayside as later labeling proponents, in an effort to distinguish their new perspective from older ones, emphasized the notion that negative reactions lead to further deviance.

Goode (2001: 27–8) notes three major criticisms of strict reactivism. "First, it ignores secret behavior or conditions that would be reacted to as deviance, were they known to the community." Gibbs (1972) and Polsky (1969), among others, claim that strict reactivism is self-defeating, as it poses a theoretical dilemma that concerns the notion of "secret deviance," or phenomena that would be condemned if they were viewed by the community or other relevant audience. Secret deviance does not exist according to the strict reactivist; it is a contradiction in terms. This dilemma makes it impossible to research behavior and conditions that have not been reacted to or punished as deviance. A professional thief, white-collar criminal, terrorist, or drug dealer who had not been reacted to would not be a legitimate subject for the study of deviance according to a strict reactivist perspective. "Second, the strict reactivist definition ignores secret behavior and conditions that would be reacted to as deviant, even where the actor or possessor knows that it would be condemned by the community at large" (Goode 2001). Strict reactivism ignores the views of persons who would be considered deviant by others. Such persons know they are different, usually disagree that they are worthy of condemnation, and have beliefs about how they would be treated upon discovery by others. These "secret deviants" are different than conformists, even though they exist among them. Denying this through strict reactivism denies a good part of the social reality of deviance. "Third, the strict reactivist definition denies the possibility that there is predictability in the reactive process" (Goode 2001). Strict reactivism assumes that researchers cannot predict in advance what real acts or conditions will be responded to negatively. A more reasonable assumption would be that there is a general association between types of acts and types of reactions (Gibbs 1972), a position that is taken by "moderate" reactivists, who acknowledge and incorporate the normative aspects of deviance into their analyses.

The utility of a moderate reactivist definition of deviance is demonstrated in the seminal work of symbolic interactionist Erving Goffman

(1963) on the concept of stigma. Goffman distinguishes between discredited and discreditable individuals. The former have already been negatively labeled. The latter are in danger of being discredited if information about them becomes known. These "potential" deviants would stand a high probability of being condemned and stigmatized if their true status were revealed. By relating the fact that a person who holds such discrediting information is sociologically different from one who does not, Goffman shows that actual labeling by audiences is but one aspect of defining deviance, and not the sole criterion for making such a determination (Goode 2001).

Others theorists, most notably Howard Becker (1963, 1973) and Kai Erikson (1962, 1966) – the latter of whose work can also be placed within the functionalist school of thought – can be considered moderate reactivists. Unlike strict reactivists, they do not view deviance as simply residing in a concrete negative reaction to an actual behavior. Rather, moderate reactivists believe that the labeling process is crucial to understanding deviance as a social phenomenon and cannot be ignored scientifically. Their approach centers on the problems inherent in the origins and consequences of labeling, which behaviors are condemned at different times and in different places, selectivity issues, the role and consequences of stigmatization, and the differences between known and secret deviants. In other words, the "soft" or moderate reactivist argues that *categories* of deviance exist, even if *specific* actors, believers, and possessors of non-normative characteristics have not been *concretely* punished or labeled.

A critical defining variable used by both strict and moderate reactivists is the audience involved in the labeling process. Audiences vary from single individuals (even the perpetrators themselves), to small groups, intimates, communities, official agents of social control, societies, or all humanity (Schur 1971). The question that separates strict and moderate reactivists is whether or not audiences always have to directly respond to deviant acts in order for these acts to be considered deviant. Moderate reactivists (which include most labeling proponents) would assert that audiences do not always have to witness an act for it to be deviant. In many common instances the

reaction can be predicted. This also means that acts are not deviant in some absolute sense, but only as so judged by real or potential audiences.

Labeling proponents, whether they are strict or moderate reactivists, have been referred to as "neo-Chicagoans" (Matza 1969) in that – unlike the Chicago School, which focused on social disorganization as a cause of deviance – they do not consider the etiology of deviant behavior other than that which may further emanate from the labeling process. However, labeling researchers follow in the Chicago tradition of applying anthropological ethnography to the study of deviance, including an up-close examination of the deviant's world, as well as the audiences who label them.

SEE ALSO: Deviance; Deviance, Absolutist Definitions of; Deviant Beliefs/Cognitive Deviance; Deviance; Normative Definitions of; Lemert, Edwin; Symbolic Interaction

REFERENCES AND SUGGESTED READINGS

Becker, H. S. (1963) *Outsiders: Studies in the Sociology of Deviance*. Free Press, New York.

Becker, H. S. (1973) Labeling Theory Reconsidered. In: *Outsiders: Perspectives on Deviance*, expanded edn. Free Press, New York, pp. 177–212.

Blumer, H. (1969) *Symbolic Interactionism: Perspective and Method*. Prentice-Hall, Englewood Cliffs, NJ.

Erikson, K. T. (1962) Notes on the Sociology of Deviance. *Social Problems* 9 (Spring): 307–14.

Erikson, K. T. (1966) *Wayward Puritans: A Study in the Sociology of Deviance*. John Wiley, New York.

Gibbs, J. P. (1972) Issues in Defining Deviance. In: Scott, R. A. & Douglas, J. D. (Eds.), *Theoretical Perspectives on Deviance*. Basic Books, New York, pp. 39–68.

Goffman, E. (1963) *Stigma: Notes on the Management of Spoiled Identity*. Prentice-Hall/Spectrum, Englewood Cliffs, NJ.

Goode, E. (1975) On Behalf of Labeling Theory. *Social Problems* 22 (June): 570–83.

Goode, E. (2001) *Deviant Behavior*, 6th edn. Prentice-Hall, Upper Saddle River, NJ.

Kitsuse, J. (1962) Societal Reaction to Deviant Behavior: Problems of Theory and Method. *Social Problems* 9 (Winter): 247–56.

Kitsuse, J. (1972) Deviance, Deviant Behavior, and Deviants: Some Conceptual Problems. In: Filstead, W. J. (Ed.), *An Introduction to Deviance: Readings in the Process of Making Deviants.* Markham, Chicago, pp. 233–43.

Lemert, E. M. (1951) *Social Pathology: A Systematic Approach to the Study of Sociopathic Behavior.* McGraw-Hill, New York.

Lemert, E. M. (1967) *Human Deviance, Social Problems, and Social Control.* Prentice-Hall, Englewood Cliffs, NJ.

Matza, D. (1969) *Becoming Deviant.* Prentice-Hall, Englewood Cliffs, NJ.

Polsky, N. (1969) *Hustlers, Beats, and Others.* Doubleday-Anchor, Garden City, NY.

Schur, E. M. (1971) *Labeling Deviant Behavior: Its Sociological Implications.* Harper & Row, New York.

Tannenbaum, F. (1938) *Crime and the Community.* Ginn, New York.

deviance, research methods

Scott Grills

It is in part through their methodologies that sociological studies of deviance are distinguished from other disciplinary interests (e.g., philosophical, legal) in troublesome or otherwise offensive aspects of human group life. Questions of method are fundamentally questions related to our theories of knowing: how we claim to know what we know, how we go about the work of supporting our knowledge claims, and how we construct the intersubjective realities we share. The process of doing research involves a critical assessment of our theories of the social world in light of the empirical world that we are claiming to represent.

Sociology is a discipline that is marked by internal controversies about the preferred ways to conceptualize the social world and to study it. Unlike many of the traditional disciplines within the natural sciences, sociology is not dominated by one theoretical tradition, but is best understood as a discipline that is home to multiple paradigms. Of the various understandings of deviance that are to be found in the extended literature, this author's commitments are best contextualized relative to interactionist understandings of deviance. Deviance is understood therein as a negative quality that is attributed to any social act or social object by some audience. From these perspectives, deviance is not a quality of any thought, act, or object, but rather is a quality that is attributed by an audience. Understanding deviance as a social construction firmly distances these sociological interests from those of the moralists. By so doing the work and commitment of moral entrepreneurs (e.g., rule creators, promoters of definitions of social problems, those promoting particular campaigns and crusades) is distinguished from those whose interests are more fully grounded in the sociological traditions of empirical inquiry, conceptual development, and theoretically attentive analysis. The sociological life is of course also a form of commitment – a commitment to research practice, to theorizing, and to empirically grounded and referential research. This is not a value-free enterprise, but is one that reflects a commitment to understanding the social world. As such, a sociological interest in deviance is meaningfully distinct from the agenda of the moral entrepreneur, whose position ultimately shares more with other promoters of definitions of good and evil than it does with the sociological method or the sociological imagination.

Additionally, an understanding of deviance that is attentive to the moral attributions of some audience thereby clearly distinguishes "deviance" from "difference." While any aspect of social life may be attributed with negative definitions, simple statistical difference is never enough to establish some aspect of social life as deviant. Therefore, a sociological understanding of deviant behavior is necessarily attentive to the moral dramas that accompany the social production of deviance. As such, an air of disrespectability accompanies the work of deviance scholars.

As Prus and Grills (2003) have argued, the study of deviance is marked by the deviant mystique. That is, what people think of as deviant may be defined simultaneously as offensive, immoral or otherwise troubling, and intriguing, fascinating, and alluring. The interest that the inquirer and various audiences may bring to the study of deviance in no way absolves the researcher from the best practices that accompany good research. In fact, the reverse is the case. In the context of studies that may see researchers experience stigma arising from their chosen areas of study, the requirement to sustain committed and articulated research practices for the problem at hand remains rather crucial. Students of deviance and deviant behavior face the professional imperative to resist the deviant mystique in order to bring the same rigorous commitment to this inquiry as is to be expected of the sociological tradition more generally. The methodological practice that sociologists bring to the studies of deviance are not, in their most fundamental forms, distinct. However, the real-life obstacles to understanding deviance – research in settings that may be marked by disrespectability, participants who define themselves at risk, the problems of the distinction between the discredited and the discreditable, formal control and institutionalization, and subcultural dynamics – establish deviance research as particularly challenging professionally and personally.

The challenges that accompany the empirical study of deviant behavior are many and each strategy that researchers may employ brings with it a mixture of insight and blindness. Where some aspects of social life are highlighted, others are necessarily lost to the gaze of the researcher. While some have argued for multiple methods as a proposed solution to this problem (e.g., survey research and participant observation and experimental design as component parts of a single project), others are less than convinced that methodological eclecticism is a reasonable position for the theorist to adopt. The methods we employ reflect the interests of the researcher and are not in any way neutral, accompanied as they are with their own theories of knowing and assumptions about the fundamental qualities of human group life. For example, if one's intention is to collect data amenable to statistical analysis and one's analytical modeling is linear, then some very specific assumptions about population, sample, and the causation of human action are necessarily incorporated into one's analysis. Where the researcher is willing to argue for and defend these assumptions this is non-problematic relative to the diversity that is found within the discipline. However, should the same research simultaneously "triangulate"

by adopting methods which make divergent and contradictory assumptions about human group life and human action, one might reasonably ask upon which rock they are standing, for the contradictions in such a circumstance are irresolvable. Quite apart from the specific methodological practices that are utilized to engage the empirical world, it is essential that students of deviant behavior attend to the relative congruence of the methodological and theoretical positions adopted in the study of deviant behavior.

At the risk of doing harm to the wonderful diversity which is to be found in the sociological study of deviant behavior, the distinction made by Rubington and Weinberg (1996) between those theorists of deviance who take deviance to be objectively given and those who understand deviance to be subjectively problematic remains a useful one. Prus and Grills (2003) argue that there is (or ought to be) a reciprocity between the methodological positions of theorists and where they place their work relative to this rather rough-edged typology. Ultimately, it is the questions we ask that define our interests, reveal our theoretical commitments, and position us as inquirers. Given the various theoretical positions that scholars bring to the study of deviance, some methods are more appropriate for the questions that accompany their interests than others.

QUANTITATIVE RESEARCH
METHODS: COUNTING DEVIANCE

For some researchers, questions pertaining to "offense" rates are particularly salient to their work. What proportion of the population is gay or lesbian? What is the age of first sexual intercourse and how has this changed over time? How do homicide rates vary between the cities of Seattle and Vancouver? Questions of this order are most appropriately addressed through quantitative measures. C. Wright Mills's grand question for the sociological imagination, "What are the major issues for publics and the key troubles of private individuals in our time?" requires an attentiveness to the characteristics of a given society and its historical social structures (Mills 1959: 11–22). The ability to frame deviance relative to unemployment, changing religiosity, perceived quality of life, changing gender roles, and societal change rests, in part, on being able to secure reliable and valid data that appropriately pertain to the population under study.

Official data may be particularly helpful for those who are interested in learning more about the formal regulation of deviance – the quantity of targets who have come to the attention of control agents, the demographic characteristics of targets, treatments and punishments applied by control agents, official assessment of treatment program successes, and regional variations manifested in preceding indicators.

In the US the Uniform Crime Reports represent the most fully articulated source of official data of the Federal Bureau of Investigation index of crimes. As Grove et al. (1985) argue, these data reflect a valid measure of offenses that the public and the police jointly consider to be crimes that are a threat to order and community. Since 1961 Canada has also established a uniform crime reporting system. Official statistics pertaining to deviant behavior are collected and publicly disseminated by Statistics Canada and the Canadian Centre for Justice Statistics.

These data include relatively complete and thorough accountings of those who are incarcerated, as well as related recidivism rates. Of course, this aspect of the criminal justice system is but a small part of the production of deviance. A limited range of behavior considered deviant is represented in data collected by the state or state-related agencies. As researchers move further from the corrections system, official data become less and less convincing. For example, at the risk of stating the obvious, data on convicted bank robbers is limited to those whose level of relative effectiveness as a bank robber or abilities to engage the justice system were inadequate to avoid conviction. Likewise, the system of plea bargaining produces a context where researchers would be naïve at best to assume the crime for which a conviction is registered is, in fact, the offense which brought the deviant actor to the attention of the criminal justice system.

Official quantitative data is necessarily socially constructed, as targets determine the appropriateness of informing agents of control, as policing and like agencies manage caseloads, as pleas are bargained and judicial systems make determinations. The officially derived quantitative data that are employed to test theories, evaluate the efficacy of programs, and establish funding priorities reflect this constructive process.

Respondent-Derived Quantitative Data

For students of deviant behavior, official data may be useful, but they are also inherently limited. The range of behavior considered deviant by some audience is more wide-ranging and encompassing than behavior that is defined by the official crime reports. Additionally, those who are publicly and officially identified as having engaged in this or that deviant behavior are a subset of those who participate in such deviant activities. For example, those identified by control agents will include those who are wrongly accused and exclude those who participate in the deviant activity yet have not or will not come to the attention of control agents (Becker 1963). Official statistics are not measures of deviant behavior as much as measures of the formal control of deviance.

Researchers who are interested in describing and theorizing about deviance more generally have made a concerted effort to move beyond official data sources to self-report surveys. Self-report surveys allow researchers to resist the systemic bias in official data and to study aspects of deviance that are excluded from official data.

Short and Nye's (1958) seminal work has established the relative analytical value of asking those involved in deviant behavior to report on their own activities. Self-report studies tend to suggest the following: that the rate of offense is higher than that attended to by official agencies, that offenses committed by those of lower classes are more likely to come to police attention than those committed by those with greater financial resources, and, importantly, that much informal (and some would argue less serious) deviance is excluded from the public gaze.

While respondents' ability/willingness to self-disclose will vary relative to perceived risk-levels and the extent to which respondents attend to and recall deviant involvements, self-report surveys also continue to be challenged by the extent to which respondents are willing and able to accurately portray or disclose their involvements. For example, a 2004 Canadian Community Health Survey conducted by Statistics Canada (n = 83,729; 2003 data) found that 1.7 percent of Canadians self-identified as gay, lesbian, and bisexual. This rate of participation in homosexual and bisexual activities tends to be lower than the 5–10 percent participation rate suggested by advocacy groups or by those extrapolating from behaviorally based studies.

At the risk of being trite, self-report surveys only tell researchers what respondents are willing to reveal to them. As the above example illustrates, there may be a rather important disjunction between what people say they do and what they do. While self-report surveys may be shown to be internally consistent (e.g., Hindelang et al. 1981) they are far removed from the accomplishment of everyday life. As Couch (1995) has argued, for a discipline that claims to attend to the social, sociology has historically been exceptionally reliant on the individual as the primary unit of analysis. Survey research perpetuates this concern, as it is inherently individualizing. As it is often derived from one person's responses to a series of prescribed questions, it thereby establishes the individual as the primary unit of analysis.

ETHNOGRAPHIC RESEARCH TRADITION: PARTICIPANT OBSERVATION AND CASE STUDIES

Ethnographic research refers to the various research practices that scholars may use to study and represent the way of life of a group of people. The extended ethnographic tradition is grounded in the research practices of observation, participant observation, and in-depth interviewing. While ethnographers may draw on a variety of other research strategies to support their work (e.g., unobtrusive measures, visual records, diaries, auto-ethnography, textual analysis, content analysis), field-based research is as central to this tradition as is the survey to more quantitatively oriented research. Given the nature of fieldwork, researchers are less likely to present their data quantitatively or to use the language of the natural sciences in their analysis. Readers are cautioned against assuming, however, that this work is any less empirically grounded or any less appropriate for developing meaningful theories of deviant behavior. In fact, field research may be the only means by which empirically grounded knowledge of aspects of deviance can be achieved.

Given that deviant subcultures may be marked by illegal activity, secrecy, purposive misdirection, and skepticism, and may sustain an amplified suspicion awareness context, investigative field research (Douglas 1976) may be the only way to develop a scientific understanding of deviant subcultures. This argument is eloquently made by Adler (1985) in the context of her membership role with drug dealers and smugglers. She clearly demonstrates that the only way to get close enough to the activities of upper-level drug dealers was to take up a membership role (in this specific case, a peripheral role) within the subculture. This general point is also most certainly true of the most complete study we have on outlaw motorcycle gangs (Wolf 1991). Wolf's participation in the Rebels offers a clarity of understanding of the social organization of the group, the marginality of its members, and accompanying gender roles that would simply be unavailable to the non-member.

Membership status is not a prerequisite for the development of ethnographic understandings of deviant behavior. The case study is an example of a research posture that is not predicated on membership status. Case studies are a research strategy that may be employed to develop a rich understanding of a subculture, a person's life, an organization, or a community. The case study model is marked by the depth of data collected and is often derived from participant observation, in-depth interviews, and the personal involvement of the researcher(s) in the field site for an extended period of time. While most certainly not exclusive to sociology (for example, field-derived case studies have been employed by biologists to better understand primate behavior), foundational work employing the case study model marked the development of the Chicago School in the 1920s, 1930s, and 1940s. Early work such as Anderson's *The Hobo* (1923), Cressey's *The Taxi-Dance Hall* (1932), Shaw's *The Jack-Roller* (1930), and Thomas's *The Unadjusted*

Girl (1923) served to place deviance in a community context. It was framed in the context of the city and the tension between urban and rural life, of differing life chances, and life as it was lived.

The case study approach is particularly appropriate where researchers are interested in understanding the creation of local cultures and the social construction of multiple realities. An interest in the lives and perspectives of slum dwellers, the homeless, and juvenile delinquents is an important move away from the moral certainty that had accompanied the work of earlier social pathologists, who tended to view deviance as indicative of sick persons or sick societies or perhaps both. While case studies attempt to be "true" to the lived experiences of the people whose lives inform the research, the contributions to the sociological study of deviance extend well beyond the "thick description" (Geertz 1973). The import to sociological theory of the case study is significant. For example, our collective understanding of the social construction of gender and the management of disrespectability owes much to Garfinkel's (1967) ability to move beyond the particular to the general, while grounding his account in the lived experiences of Agnes, an "intersexed" person.

IN SUM

Maines (2001: 225) suggests our theoretical commitments and our methodological inclinations are "not because any of them make a priori sense, but because we like these things and are reasonably good at them." There is wisdom in this deceptively simple claim. Research methodologies are in part skills based. The quantitative skills required for inferential modeling are not for everyone; neither is the commitment required to sustain a meaningful field presence in the context of a deviant subculture. Likewise, our theoretical commitments are an extension of the perspectives we bring to our work and our life. In many respects, a variety of sociological theories distil human group life into a conceptual heuristic that is unknown to experience. As Cooley (1922) taught many years ago, the distinction between individual and society may be analytically

useful, but pragmatically it is much less so. Likewise, we do a significant violence to our research on deviance if we adopt a simple structural determinism that views social interaction as a neutral medium through which social factors merely pass, or if we become so enamored with "lived experience" that participants become isolated from their histories, their institutions, and the circumstances of their lives that are not of their own choosing.

The study of deviant behavior is in part a pragmatic exercise. The sociological study of deviance requires that researchers attend to a phenomenon that is situationally defined by some audience, a population that is rarely known, participants who may be reluctant to more openly associate with discreditable identities, careers of involvement that vary rather markedly over time, and the reality that deviance occurs within a community context that extends well beyond practitioners and their confederates. As Grills (1998) has argued, the work of doing research is productively understood as problem-solving activity. The more that one is interested in how people come to view the world as they do, how relationships are created and sustained, how activities are accomplished, how people come to be involved in various subcultural affiliations, and how identities are managed, embraced, or resisted, the more it is imperative that researchers focus on naturally occurring events rather than self-reported data or laboratory experiments. Likewise, the more one is attentive to issues of measuring the incidence of deviant behavior, attempting to measure the effectiveness of control agents or self-report data based upon random sampling techniques, the more one's research demands rigorous survey-based quantitative analysis.

At the close of his essay entitled "The Methodological Position of Symbolic Interactionism," Herbert Blumer (1969: 60) writes: "Respect the nature of the empirical world and organize a methodological stance to reflect that respect." This is exceptionally fine advice for the student of deviant behavior, for to do so resists the deviant mystique and brings the same intellectual standards to the study of deviance as is to be demanded of other research endeavors. The study of deviance is marked by disrespectability – the disrespectability of topic, of spoiled identities, of subculture, and the contagion that may be experienced by the scholar. Quite apart from the specific methodological positions that researchers may adopt, respecting the nature of deviance as a social phenomenon requires that we fully attend to deviance in a community context.

SEE ALSO: Criminology: Research Methods; Descriptive Statistics; Deviance, Theories of; Ethnography; Measuring Crime; Methods, Case Study; Observation, Participant and Non-Participant

REFERENCES AND SUGGESTED READINGS

Adler, P. (1985) *Wheeling and Dealing*. Columbia University Press, New York.

Anderson, N. (1923) *The Hobo*. University of Chicago Press, Chicago.

Becker, H. (1963) *Outsiders: Studies in the Sociology of Deviance*. Free Press, New York.

Blumer, H. (1969) *Symbolic Interaction*. Prentice-Hall, Englewood Cliffs, NJ.

Cooley, C. H. ((1922 [1902]) *Human Nature and the Social Order*. Shocken, New York.

Couch, C. (1995) Oh What Webs Those Phantoms Spin. *Symbolic Interaction* 18: 229–45.

Cressey, P. (1932) *The Taxi-Dance Hall*. University of Chicago Press, Chicago.

Denzin, N. (Ed.) (1978) *Sociological Methods: A Sourcebook*, 2nd edn. McGraw-Hill, New York.

Douglas, J. (1976) *Investigative Social Research*. Sage, Beverly Hills, CA.

Garfinkel, H. (1967) *Studies in Ethnomethodology*. Prentice-Hall, Englewood Cliffs, NJ.

Geertz, C. (1973) *The Interpretation of Cultures*. Basic Books, New York.

Grills, S. (Ed.) (1998) *Doing Ethnographic Research: Fieldwork Settings*. Sage, Newbury Park, CA.

Grove, W. R., Hughes, M., & Geerken, M. (1985) Are Uniform Crime Reports a Valid Indicator of Index Crimes? An Affirmative Answer With Minor Qualifications. *Criminology* 23: 452–501.

Hindelang, M. J., Hirchi, T., & Weis, J. G. (1981) *Measuring Delinquency*. Sage, Beverly Hills, CA.

Maines, D. (2001) *The Faultline of Consciousness*. Aldine de Gruyter, New York.

Mills, C. W. (1959) *The Sociological Imagination*. Oxford University Press, Oxford.

Prus, R. & Grills, S. (2003) *Engaging the Deviant Mystique: Involvements, Realities, and Regulatory Endeavors*. Praeger, Westport, CT.

Rubington, E. & Weinberg, M. S. (Eds.) (1996) *Deviance: The Interactionist Perspective*, 6th edn. Allyn & Bacon, Toronto.

Shaw, C. (1930) *The Jack-Roller*. University of Chicago Press, Chicago.

Short, J. & Nye, F. (1958) Extent of Unrecorded Juvenile Delinquency: Tentative Conclusions. *Journal of Criminal Law, Criminology, and Police Science* 49: 296–302.

Statistics Canada (2004) Canadian Community Health Survey. *The Daily*. Online. www.statcan.ca/Daily/English/040615/d040615b.htm.

Thomas, W. I. (1923) *The Unadjusted Girl*. Little, Brown, Boston.

Webb, E. J., Campbell, D. T., Schwartz, R. D., & Sechrest, L. (1966) *Unobtrusive Measures: Nonreactive Research in the Social Sciences*. Rand McNally, Chicago.

Wolf, D. (1991) *The Rebels*. University of Toronto Press, Toronto.

deviance, sport and

Timothy Jon Curry

Sports may be defined as physical contests that are competitive, fair, and guided by rules, organization, and/or tradition. The roots of sport are ancient, and probably stem from hunting. Although modern sports have more symbolic quests than the choice cuts of meat available to the successful prehistoric hunter, the thrill of the chase is much the same (Carroll 2000). The rules and traditions of sport may or may not be codified, but they ensure that the ritualistic aspects of sport are respected. And the ritualistic aspects of sport, the before and after ceremonies and events, the coin-toss that ensures a fair beginning, the awarding of trophies and medals, and so on, are every bit as important as the game itself.

Deviance refers to behavior that goes against widely accepted traditions, norms, values, ideology, rules, and laws of society, and that draws mild to severe sanctions. Deviance in sport has existed across time and space and throughout the world, and whether or not someone commits a deviant act depends upon the time and place and who does the judging. Determining what deviance is, in other words, is a social process. The behavior itself is not enough; there must also be a reaction to it. For instance, when Art Modell moved his Cleveland Browns football team from Cleveland to Baltimore in 1995, he broke no criminal law. But his actions precipitated violent outbursts on the part of Cleveland fans, who believed he went against accepted norms that bind professional sports teams to the cities that support them.

Deviance in sport includes a wide assortment of behavior. Many types of people are involved, and the perpetrators of deviance in sport cut across gender, race, and class lines. An abbreviated list of transgressors includes owners of professional teams, athletes, coaches, sport agents, fans, professional gamblers, pharmacists, educational institutions, corporations that promote sport, cities, states, and international organizations that govern sport. In contemporary society, deviance in sport is seen as newsworthy, and newspapers and television news channels routinely feature stories of deviant sports figures. Misdeeds that occur at educational institutions affiliated with religious organizations have special fascination. When a basketball player at Baylor University was shot and killed apparently by a teammate in 2003, newspapers were anxious to report every detail of the incident partly because it took place at the world's largest Baptist University.

Previous generations of reporters and writers thought of sport as a character-building exercise, and they were reluctant to report on the misdeeds of sport heroes (Dinan 1998). As a result of the attention given to deviance in sport by media today, it seems that it is more prevalent than a generation ago, but this is more than likely due to the coverage given to the topic rather than the actual rate of deviant acts committed. Even so, empirical research has failed to support the idea that sport participation builds character. If anything, the longer one participates in sport, the more likely it is that moral constraints such as fair play and honesty give way to the desire to win (see Miracle & Rees 1994).

CLASSIC TOPICS

Some of the classic topics studied by those interested in deviance and sport are cheating,

drug abuse, gambling, and violence (particularly among athletes or between athletes and fans). These are classic or standard topics because they concern the fundamental social conditions defining sport. Any activity that destroys or vastly alters the physical challenges of sport or the fair competition between opponents poses a threat to the basic premises of sport, and a serious threat to its continuation. For instance, consider the following examples.

Cheating – the intentional violation of rules and norms for one's advantage – has long been associated with sport. The National Collegiate Athletic Association (NCAA) estimated that 14 percent of member schools engaged in serious cheating in the 1970s, an estimate that seemed too low at the time according to Curry and Jiobu (1984). Today, without good data, it is impossible to tell whether the figure is the same or much higher or lower, but cheating is still an important concern for the NCAA and its member institutions. Cheating can take many forms, and is especially serious when it involves coaches and others responsible for the integrity of the sports program. When Georgia Tech coach George O'Leary successfully applied for the head coach position at Notre Dame, he falsified information on his résumé by claiming to have acquired a master's degree (which he never earned) and to have lettered at a college where he never played. When this was discovered, he was immediately fired from Notre Dame. As sociologist Stan Eitzen (2003) notes, coaches who cheat on their résumés can hardly qualify as role models for their athletes.

Drug abuse – particularly *additive* drugs that are meant to stimulate the body beyond normal capabilities – are not a recent discovery. Anabolic steroids were first marketed in 1958 under the name of Dianabol and they proved to be effective when combined with exercise to produce gains in muscle mass. Sport historian Allen Guttman (1988: 165) notes that this effectiveness has been a "curse" because steroids can cause serious negative side-effects to the body. Even so, athletes continue to use them, and the records they set through the help of additive drugs only encourage others to violate rules. Even the most talented professional athletes, who seemingly could get along without using banned substances, use them. In 2004, the names of some of the most respected and highest-paid professional baseball players were linked to the use of steroids during testimony to a US federal grand jury investigating possible steroid distribution by the Bay Area Laboratory Cooperative in California.

Gambling – particularly gambling that involves athletes or others in a position to alter the outcome of a contest – has long been associated with sport. Perhaps the most famous incident of sports gambling is the Black Sox Scandal (Curry & Jiobu 1984). In 1919 the Cincinnati Reds upset the Chicago White Sox – soon to be called "Black Sox" – to win the World Series. Rumors of a fix circulated, and a year later eight players who were on the White Sox World Series team were indicted and charged with complicity in a conspiracy with gamblers to throw the game. Two of the players confessed. The Commissioner of Baseball at the time was Judge Kenesaw Mountain Landis; he strove to make an example of the players by banning them for life, even though the accused players were later found innocent in a court of law. In spite of the harsh penalties, gambling continues to be a problem in baseball, most recently with controversy over Pete Rose, an accomplished player whose admittance to the Baseball Hall of Fame seemed assured until it was discovered he bet on baseball games in 1985, 1986, and 1987 while manager of the Cincinnati Reds. Other sports, including collegiate and professional football and basketball, have had serious problems with gambling; so have boxing and horseracing. The problem stems from the great popularity of gambling in society. Billions of dollars are waged on sports events by millions of respectable people. The Internet has increased opportunities for gambling on all types of sports. Athletes are tempted to gamble, partly because they enjoy competition and winning and see gambling as another challenge. According to some sociologists, the sheer volume of dollars involved in betting on sport attracts people who will look for ways to fix a sporting event despite the harsh penalties invoked if they are caught.

Violence – defined as the use of excessive physical force intended to cause mental or physical pain to another person – has long been associated with sport. Particularly alarming is when excessive violence is used as part of the strategy of competition. In 1905 President Theodore Roosevelt became so concerned about violence in college football he spearheaded a move to clean up the excessive violence through rule changes and modifications to equipment. Such formations as the "flying wedge" were eliminated, and players were required to wear more protective gear. Even so, football remains a violent game, and some players take advantage of the rules to injure or maim their opponents. Coaches frequently overlook borderline violence, and applaud brutal body contact. Sport sociologist Jay Coakley (2004) believes that acceptance of excessive physical force can be looked at as deviant *overconformity* to the norms of sport. Both male and female athletes are so focused on maintaining their identities as athletes and so caught up in the emotions and physicality of sport that they fail to consider the consequences of unquestioned normative conformity. Serious injury and shortened careers can result.

THEORY

There is no single theoretical approach that dominates research in deviance, and sport sociologists employ a number of theories drawn from mainstream sociology and criminology. Two of the most popular are differential association and strain theory. Differential association is based on the work of Edwin Sutherland, who emphasized that people learn conformity or deviance from the people with whom they associate. In the case of young athletes, teammates might prove to be especially important, since peers typically have strong influences on young people. Sutherland noted that like behavior in general, deviant behavior is learned through interaction with others, especially in small, intimate groups. Such learning of deviant behavior consists of acquiring techniques, motives, drives, and attitudes. An individual learns "definitions" (mindsets or attitudes) that are favorable or unfavorable to prevailing norms, and becomes deviant when he or she learns to accept more unfavorable definitions than favorable definitions. The frequency, length, and intensity of a person's associations determine the impact of associations on the person. Infrequent contacts of limited duration will have less impact than frequent, intense contact (Sutherland & Cressey 1978: 80–3). To illustrate, Curry (2000) studied the interactions of a group of athletes in an elite sport program who engaged in bar fights and inappropriate sexual behavior. He found that the athletes knew that this behavior would be considered deviant by others, but that the prevailing norms among their teammates encouraged an occasional visit to what they called the "dark side."

Strain or anomie theory is less concerned with the interaction among team members, and more concerned with the structure of opportunity in society. According to Robert Merton, who first constructed the theory, structural strain develops when the culturally prescribed goals of the social system cannot be achieved through socially approved means. The strain may produce deviance, and Merton outlined five typical social responses or adaptations to such a situation.

Conformity, the only non-deviant response, is the first adaptation. A *conformist* accepts the conventional goals of society and the conventional means to obtain them. For example, an athlete who desires to win an Olympic gold medal will spend many years practicing and improving his or her skills until able to perform and succeed at the highest levels. In contrast, an *innovator* accepts the goals, but rejects the socially approved means and thus opts for deviance to attain the goals. In the case of Olympic athletes who use banned substances such as steroids, they are still trying to win medals, but are doing so through innovative practices with performance-enhancing drugs (Lüschen 2001).

Other athletes may decide to continue to go through the motions of competing for an Olympic medal, yet abandon the goal of actually winning one. They realize that the competition is too difficult and so become *ritualists*. Merton also recognized *retreatism* and *rebellion* as reactions to strain. The retreatist rejects both the means and the goals of society. In the case of sports, the competitive athlete who gives up the sport entirely has retreated from the scene rather than try to compete to win. The rebel, on the other hand, rejects the goals and means of society but replaces them with new goals and means. Athletes who rebel against the Olympic Games might substitute other games that allow for a greater chance of success. For instance,

Tom Waddell began the Gay Games competition in 1988, to provide a more accepting environment for homosexuals. The Gay Games have been held periodically ever since, and in 2002 included over 11,000 athletes competing in over 30 events.

The major strength of Merton's approach is that it places the origins of deviance in the broader social setting. To the extent that those who control sport, particularly elite sport, narrowly define what constitutes success, they encourage deviance. In other words, many gifted athletes feel they must cheat in order to win because the opportunities for success are so limited (see Leonard 1998: 139–72).

While these classic topics and theoretical approaches have long dominated research on deviance in sport, several new topics and theories are emerging. For instance, persons closely associated with sport may become involved in sexual harassment and sexual assault cases, homophobia and attacks on gay men, hazing in high school and collegiate sport, celebratory violence, eating disorders, excessive drinking, and many other deviant activities. Sport sociologists researching these topics face the difficult methodological problem of tracing the influence sport participation may have had in creating social conditions that encourage such deviance, while at the same time recognizing that these deviant activities are engaged in by others outside of sport.

Masculinity issues in the study of crime and deviance have come to the forefront, and sport sociologists are becoming aware of how boys and men strive through risky behavior, including deviance, to establish masculinity (Messner & Sabo 1994). Off-the-field violence toward women is increasingly understood through the dynamics of gender (Benedict 1997, 1998). Pressures on young men and women athletes to perform at the highest levels may result in psychological disorders that lead to numerous problem behaviors.

In addition, corporate or organizational deviance in sport is now recognized as a serious problem (Coakley 2004). Since corporations control vast resources, they are able to influence the media and create symbolic representation of sport that makes it difficult for the public to recognize their actions as deviant. For instance, sport sociologist Helen Lenskyj

(2000) notes that those in charge of the International Olympic Committee have been very eager to control the image of the Olympic Games. The Olympic "industry," as she calls it, has until recently been able to disguise much of its deviance as the occasional misbehavior of certain individuals rather than part of its corporate culture. She argues that inside the Olympic industry, bribery and scandals involving high-ranking political figures are common.

As sport sociologists research more of the corporate and organizational cultures that govern professional and big-time amateur sport, the more the topic of deviance and sport moves away from the individual athlete and coach. This is all to the good, because many of the forces perpetuating deviance in sport lie outside the individual. In the future, a better understanding of deviance and sport may be generated through analysis of the close ties between corporations, the media, and consumer culture (Blackshaw & Crabbe 2004). Researchers have come to understand that the image of the athlete as a superior being is only an image; elite sport is not conducive to the development of moral behavior. But such images can be used to sell vast amounts of consumer goods. This does not mean that the idea of physical tests or challenges and fair competition is itself flawed. Humans have long enjoyed physical challenges, and the idea of fair competition, while more recent, has broad appeal. As in other spheres of human endeavor, the devil is in the details.

SEE ALSO: Anomie; Drugs/Substance Use in Sport; Football Hooliganism; Gambling and Sport; Health and Sport; Sexuality and Sport; Socialization and Sport; Sport, College; Sport and Social Resistance; Sport and the State; Strain Theories; Violence Among Athletes; Violence Among Fans

REFERENCES AND SUGGESTED READINGS

Benedict, J. R. (1997) *Public Heroes, Private Felons: Athletes and Crimes against Women.* Northeastern University Press, Boston.
Benedict, J. R. (1998) *Athletes and Acquaintance Rape.* Sage, Thousand Oaks, CA.
Blackshaw, T. & Crabbe, T. (2004) *New Perspectives on Sport and Deviance.* Routledge, London.
Carroll, D. M. (2000) *An Interdisciplinary Study of Sport as Symbolic Hunt: A Theory of the Origin and Nature of Sport Based on Paleolithic Hunting.* Edwin Mellen Press, Lewiston, NY.
Coakley, J. (2004) *Sports in Society: Issues and Controversies.* McGraw-Hill, Boston.
Curry, T. J. (2000) Booze and Bar Fights: A Journey to the Dark Side of College Athletics. In: McKay, J., Messner, M. A., & Sabo, D. (Eds.), *Masculinities, Gender Relations, and Sport.* Sage, Newbury Park, CA, pp. 162–75.
Curry, T. J. & Jiobu, R. M. (1984) *Sports: A Social Perspective.* Prentice-Hall, Englewood Cliffs, NJ.
Dinan, J. (1998) *Sports in the Pulp Magazines.* McFarland, Jefferson, NC.
Eitzen, D. S. (2003) *Fair and Foul: Beyond the Myths and Paradoxes of Sport,* 2nd edn. Rowman & Littlefield, New York.
Guttman, A. (1988) *A Whole New Ball Game: An Interpretation of American Sports.* University of North Carolina Press, Chapel Hill.
Lenskyj, H. J. (2000) *Inside the Olympic Industry: Power, Politics, and Activism.* State University of New York Press, Albany, NY.
Leonard, W. M., II. (1998) *A Sociological Perspective of Sport.* Allyn & Bacon, Boston.
Lüschen, G. (2001) Doping in Sport as Deviant Behavior. In: Coakley, J. & Dunning, E. (Eds.), *Handbook of Sport Studies.* Sage, London, pp. 461–76.
Merton, R. K. (1938). Social Structure and Anomie. *American Sociological Review* 3: 672–82.
Messner, M. & Sabo, D. (1994) *Sex, Violence, and Power in Sport.* Crossing Press, Freedom, CA.
Miracle, A. W. & Rees, C. R. (1994) *Lessons of the Locker Room: The Myths of School Sports.* Prometheus Books, Amherst, NY.
Sutherland, E. & Cressey, D. (1978) *Principles of Criminology.* Lippencott, Chicago.

deviance, theories of

Paul Rock and David Downes

"Deviance" and its companion words, deviant and deviation, have their roots in Latin and point to a straying from the *via*, road or path. Some of its variants have a long history: the thirteenth-century *Romance of the Rose*, for example, talks of "deviant" in the sense of being out of the way; "deviation" appeared in publications in the sixteenth century; and Durkheim powerfully foreshadowed its sociological usage in *Les Règles de la méthode sociologique* (1895), where he took deviance (which he did not name as such but rather awkwardly referred to as crimes against religion, ceremony, etiquette, tradition, "and so on") to be the pivotal concept for what turned out to be his founding theory of functional analysis. (Durkheim contrasted his own approach with a more limited notion of crime he somewhat misleadingly attributed to Garofalo's *La Criminologie*, 1890.) But "deviance" itself is a neologism with multiple meanings. The *Oxford English Dictionary* traces its first appearance in English to a piece written in 1944 by the psychologist Gregory Bateson, who presented it as a corollary of "standardization" (and see Bateson 1972). The English sociologist Walter Sprott employed it ten years later to refer to departures from culturally expected rules of conduct (Sprott 1954). And the most celebrated, if not the most elusive, description was offered nine years later still in 1963 by Howard Becker. In a passage that avoided exact definition, but which would have the greatest impact, he insisted on the social character of deviance: deviance, he said, "is *not* a quality of the act the person commits, but rather a consequence of the application by others of rules and sanctions to an 'offender.' The deviant is one to whom that label has been successfully applied; deviant behavior is behavior that people so label" (Becker 1963: 9).

That etymology is important because "deviance" is a latecomer which does not appear to be part of the currency of everyday speech. It was imported into the sociology of the English-speaking world in the early 1960s by a number of its sponsors precisely because it did not seem to be freighted with the unwelcome or extraneous meanings that its predecessors, such as social disorganization (Faris 1955), social pathology (Wootton 1959), sociopathic behavior, and social problems, were thought to have acquired. Neither was it marred by what many of its proponents saw as the abstracted empiricism, "correctionalism" (Matza 1969), excessive positivism, and atheoretical leanings of the criminology of the time One may see the transition marked in the titles of academic works of the period. Edwin Lemert, for

instance, published *Social Pathology* in 1951 but, in 1967, he titled a collection of essays *Human Deviance, Social Problems, and Social Control*. On the very cusp of change in 1961, and listing three variations simultaneously, was Robert Merton and Robert Nisbet's *Contemporary Social Problems: An Introduction to the Sociology of Deviant Behaviour and Social Disorganization*.

"Deviance" had for a while the semblance of a moderately neutral term which implied no adverse or unnecessary social, political, or moral judgment. (That confidence was probably short-lived. If the 1953 edition of *Roget's Thesaurus* did not contain the term, the 2002 *Collins Thesaurus* gives among its synonyms "perverted," "sick," "twisted," "bent," "abnormal," "queer," "warped," "perverse," "wayward," "kinky," "devious," "freaky," and "aberrant.") But, because it was in effect thought to be a new term of art, a term that was employed principally to distinguish it from its discredited antecedents rather than being an accepted definition in its own right, it rendered itself open to multiple interpretations that encapsulated the larger systems of theorizing that framed it. It was used by the self-taught social statistician and criminologist Leslie Wilkins (1964) to mean a statistically uncommon event with peculiar social consequences. Wilkins made much of the alleged correspondence between the outlying location on a normal statistical distribution curve of certain forms of conduct and the social position of the person or group exhibiting them. Almost all people lie, Wilkins said, but there are a few, furthest from the mean, who are pathological in the high or low frequency of their lying and they are deviants. Those who were the furthest were somehow held structurally to be the most remote from the commonality of people in a society. The idea was misconceived (after all, much deviance, like traffic infractions or sexual misconduct, is commonplace), but it did engender some interesting ideas about how feedback loops could distort information as it traveled over large social distances, affected people's reactions to populations at the extremes, and so amplified deviant conduct (see Young 1971) and led to what were called moral panics (Cohen 1972). It also raised the prospect of studying the saintly as deviants, although it was an invitation accepted almost alone by Cohen (1966) inside criminology, but with greater alacrity by the sociologists of new religious movements outside (Barker 1984).

Deviance could be represented by the functionalist Talcott Parsons (1951) as the temporary or longer-lasting failure of individual or group adjustment in social systems undergoing change. It could be said by other functionalists to play the unintended role of acting as an illicit support to conventional institutions – prostitution supporting monogamy by providing an emotionally sanitized outlet for otherwise dangerous sexual liaisons, or the taint of an illegitimate birth preserving primogeniture. It could, by extension, present the dialectical contrasts by which the respectable, normal, and conventional would be recognized and strengthened. And there were those who argued in their turn that deviance is manufactured precisely to support the moral order (Erikson 1966), deviance and morality being symbolically interdependent twins. In structuralist anthropology and sociology it could be a property of classification systems where the deviant was a worrying anomalous phenomenon that did not fit neatly into existing categories, and so posed a threat to the project of collective sense-making and social order (Scott 1972). Deviance was there both symbolic matter out of place and, potentially, new matter coming into being, an experiment with the new and a foretaste of future existential styles (Scott and Lyman 1970). It could mirror the symbolic workings of systems of social stratification, where some symmetry may be expected between authority, wealth, and moral esteem, and where deviants are typically to be found among the lowest and least-valued strata (Duster 1970) or, indeed, outcast altogether (see Heymowski 1969). It could thereby refract the capacity of some effectively to assign others to a devalued social status, although such assignments could be, and were, frequently challenged (Haug & Sussman 1969). And it was that link with signifying processes that was perhaps most strongly to promote its elective affinity with the ideas of symbolic interactionism, phenomenology, and ethnomethodology. The ensuing bundle of ideas was probably the most distinctive theory of deviance of all. What came to be called labeling theory (to the distaste of Edwin Lemert and

Howard Becker, its progenitors), methodically explored the symbolic work undertaken when attempts are made to affix the deviant "label" to some person or group of persons, event, process, or phenomenon, encouraging power, "signification" (Matza 1969), and moral passages to become central topics.

Deviance was held in those theories to be an attribute bestowed on behavior and people by a defining audience. John Kitsuse (1968: 19), for instance, declared that he proposed "to shift the focus of theory and research from the forms of deviant behavior to processes by which persons come to be defined as deviant by others." And Kai Erikson (1964: 11) proposed that analysis should turn away from the actor and towards the audience of behavior because it is the audience that will ultimately determine significance. Vital to that conception was the distinction mapped by Edwin Lemert (1951) between "primary" and "secondary" deviation, the first a possibly uneventful instance of the abounding violation of rules which escape public notice, the second, consequent upon public response, which required the rule-breaker not only to react to his or her own behavior, but also to others' reactions to that behavior. Secondary deviation was a social phenomenon shaped by social processes. The idea invited consideration of the symbolic adjustments that might have to be made to others' responses, and of the reorganization of identity that could well have less to do with the "innate" character of the violator or violation and more to do with the assumptions, stereotypes, and stigmas that were incorporated in public judgment and imposed in practical action.

In that formulation, deviance was held to be the object of defining procedures that are themselves contingent on audience, time, place, power, and occasion. What is deviant in one setting will not be so in another, what is deviant for one may not be so for another, and it is not always easy to cast in absolute or categorical terms the rules by which it may be identified. To the contrary: it was a precept of many of those who studied deviance that the phenomenon resisted neat or absolute definition. Bittner (1963), for example, argued that there is such an infinite regression of rules for judging when and where rules should be applied that it becomes quite impossible to establish absolute categories. It followed that deviance was thought often to be marked by experiential confusion, contradiction, and absurdity, prompting David Matza (1969) to suggest that deviance ineluctably coexists with ambiguity and "shifting standards."

Subjectively problematic, multiform, contested, and uncertain, deviance had major attractions for the phenomenological sociologist. Often involving extended exchanges between definers and defined, it invited an examination of existential processes that unfolded not only in interaction between a putative deviant and those who ascribed his or her identity, but also reflexively within the deviant himself or herself as the moral meanings of acts and selves were tested and explored (Becker 1963). Deviance was characteristically presented not as a stable or fixed state but as an emergent *process* of becoming, a moral career (Goffman 1959), that might at times be more or less orderly but which also lacked certain or necessary outcomes.

As a site of contestation, where meanings were problematic and people were marginal, deviance was also especially appealing to those who sought to use the methods of participant observation to achieve an anthropological distance from the world of the taken for granted and commonplace. By looking at and through deviance, they argued, by adopting perspective through incongruity, they might see the familiar as new and strange and so discover what might otherwise have escaped attention (Hughes 1958). Many of the deviant worlds which have thus been analyzed were amenable to ethnographic inquiry, and they tended to overlap or adjoin the sociologist's own.

It must be emphasized that the term deviance is at once theoretically denotative and connotative. It points, on the one hand, to thinking about an ill-assorted range of behavior with fuzzy boundaries and indeterminate definition, including homosexuals, the blind, the mad, stutterers, alcoholics, strippers, nudists, drug users, thieves, convicts, robbers, prostitutes, delinquents, and those whom Gouldner (1962) rather disparagingly dismissed as the inhabitants of "the world of hip ... drug addicts, jazz musicians ... drifters, grifters and skidders." It attends to the way in which the meaning of deviance is contingent on a

politics of power and authority. Where control becomes a variable, it has been argued, crime is but one of a number of possible outcomes. Control might just as readily lead to conduct being informally regulated, mitigated or condoned, or treated as a matter for medical, psychiatric, religious, or political intervention (Gusfield 1968).

Theories of deviance were thus potentially wider by far in their reach than criminology and they made the criminal law, criminalization, and the facts of crime newly and interestingly problematic. Indeed, Lemert (1967) and Ditton (1979) came to propose that attention should shift away from deviant acts and people towards the phenomena of control. And where control was the variable, rule-making, policing (Reiss 1971), and regulation (Hawkins 1984) came newly into view, no longer to be taken for granted as the backdrop of criminology, but occupying center stage.

It was but a step to study what came to be known as crimes of the powerful. Presaged by Sutherland (1949) (himself rooted in symbolic interactionism), it looked at how crime and control were bound up in a politics of naming, shaming, accounting, and enforcement (Geis & Jesilow 1993). Those matters, involving the trading of critical definitions of the situation, were also to be at the heart of labeling theory. Much was to be made of how people portrayed their motives and actions to themselves and others, how their deviance and conformity were eased by the narratives that could be so told, and how those narratives might be challenged, corroborated, and negotiated as deviant careers unfolded (Mills 1940; Sykes & Matza 1957; Maruna 2001).

But theories of deviance were also importantly connotative. Institutionally anchored in the British National Deviancy Symposium and in the American Society for the Study of Social Problems and its journal *Social Problems*, they advertised for many that there had been a conceptual, indeed, for some, political, break with past work whose errors and omissions were sometimes caricatured for dramatic effect. They stood for the treatment of deviance as a social process to be described, not as a thing apart, but in the stock language of sociological analysis, and of interactionist sociology in particular.

By and large the new theories succeeded in their object. Criminology is more fully sociological than before. It is now more responsive to the argument that deviant phenomena are emergent, political, negotiated, contingent, and meaningful. And it is has moved on. Theories of deviance are still being advanced, and the ethnographic mapping of deviance is still vigorous (Duneier 1992, 2001), but they no longer hold sway as in the past. They had their period of flowering – perhaps something of a false dawn – in which crime, mental illness, sexual deviance, political deviance, and the like were to be analyzed afresh and in a way that transcended the limitations of criminology. Theirs was the era indicated by the dates of the publications cited in this entry and by three generations of encyclopedias: *The Encyclopedia of the Social Sciences*, published in 1931 (Seligman), made no mention of deviance or deviation; *The International Encyclopedia of the Social Sciences*, published in 1968 (Sills), had an extensive treatment of deviant behavior and deviance; and the *The International Encyclopedia of the Social and Behavioral Sciences*, published in 2001 (Smelser & Baltes), had none. It is now criminology that people again practice, but it is a criminology that has absorbed theories of deviance (and many other, more recent theories) in its passage (Lea & Young 1984).

SEE ALSO: Criminology; Death of the Sociology of Deviance?; Deviance; Deviance, Constructionist Perspectives; Deviance, Explanatory Theories of; Deviance, Normative Definitions of; Deviance, Positivist Theories of; Deviance, Reactivist Definitions of; Deviance, Research Methods; Deviant Beliefs/Cognitive Deviance; Deviant Careers; Symbolic Interaction

REFERENCES AND SUGGESTED READINGS

Barker, E. (1984) *The Making of a Moonie*. Blackwell, Oxford.

Bateson, G. (1972) *Steps to an Ecology of Mind*. Ballantine, New York.

Becker, H. (1963) *Outsiders*. Free Press, New York.

Bittner, E. (1963) Radicalism and the Organization of Radical Movements. *American Sociological Review* 28.

Cohen, A. (1966) *Deviance and Control*. Prentice-Hall, Englewood Cliffs, NJ.

Cohen, S. (1972) *Folk Devils and Moral Panics*. MacGibbon & Kee, London.

Collins, P. & Hands, P. (2002) *Collins Thesaurus*. Harper Collins, Glasgow.

Ditton, J. (1979) *Controlology: Beyond the New Criminology*. Macmillan, London.

Duneier, M. (1992) *Slim's Table*. University of Chicago Press, Chicago.

Duneier, M. (2001) *Sidewalk*. Farrar, Straus, & Giroux, New York.

Durkheim, E. (1895) *Les Règles de la méthode sociologique*. Ancienne Librairie Germer Baillière, Paris.

Duster, T. (1970) *The Legislation of Morality*. Free Press, New York.

Erikson, K. (1964) Notes on the Sociology of Deviance. In: Becker, H. (Ed.), *The Other Side*. Free Press, New York.

Erikson, K. (1966) *Wayward Puritans*. Wiley, New York.

Faris, R. (1955) *Social Disorganization*. Ronald, New York.

Garofalo, B. (1890) *La Criminologie*, 2nd edn. Ancienne Librairie Germer Baillière, Paris.

Geis, G. & Jesilow, P. (1993) *White Collar Crime*. Sage, Newbury Park, CA.

Goffman, E. (1959) The Moral Career of the Mental Patient. *Psychiatry* 22: 2.

Gouldner, A. (1962) Anti-Minotaur: The Myth of a Value-Free Sociology. *Social Problems* 10.

Gusfield, J. (1968) Moral Passage. *Social Problems* 15: 2.

Haug, M. & Sussman, M. (1969) Professional Autonomy and the Revolt of the Client. *Social Problems* 17: 2.

Hawkins, K. (1984) *Environment and Regulation: Regulation and the Social Definition of Pollution*. Clarendon Press, Oxford.

Heymowski, A. (1969) *Swedish Travellers and their Ancestry*. Acta Universitatis Upsaliensis, Uppsala.

Hughes, E. (1958) *Men and their Work*. Free Press, Glencoe, IL.

Kitsuse, J. (1968) Societal Reaction to Deviant Behavior. In: Rubington, E. & Weinberg, M. (Eds.), *Deviance: The Interactionist Perspective*. Macmillan, New York.

Lea, J. & Young, J. (1984) *What is to be Done about Law and Order?* Penguin, London.

Lemert, E. (1951) *Social Pathology: A Systematic Approach to the Theory of Sociopathic Behavior*. McGraw-Hill, New York.

Lemert, E. (1967) *Human Deviance, Social Problems, and Social Control*. Prentice-Hall, Englewood Cliffs, NJ.

Maruna, S. (2001) *Making Good: How Ex-Convicts Reform and Rebuild Their Lives*. American Psychological Association, Washington, DC.

Matza, D. (1969) *Becoming Deviant*. Prentice-Hall, Englewood Cliffs, NJ.

Merton, R. & Nisbet, R. (1961) *Contemporary Social Problems: An Introduction to the Sociology of Deviant Behaviour and Social Disorganization*. Hart-Davis, London.

Mills, C. Wright (1940) Situated Actions and Vocabularies of Motive. *American Sociological Review* 5: 4.

Parsons, T. (1951) *The Social System*. Free Press, New York.

Reiss, A. (1971) *The Police and the Public*. Yale University Press, New Haven.

Roget, P. (1953) *Roget's Thesaurus*. Penguin, London.

Scott, M. & Lyman, S. (1970) *The Revolt of the Students*. Merrill, Columbus.

Scott, R. (1972) A Proposed Framework for Analyzing Deviance as a Property of Social Order. In: Scott, R. & Douglas, J. (Eds.), *Theoretical Perspectives on Deviance*. Basic Books, New York.

Seligman, E. (Ed.) (1931) *The Encyclopedia of the Social Sciences*. Macmillan, New York.

Sills, D. (Ed.) (1968) *The International Encyclopedia of the Social Sciences*. Crowell Collier & Macmillan, New York.

Smelser, N. & Baltes, P. (Eds.) (2001) *The International Encyclopedia of the Social and Behavioral Sciences*. Elsevier, Amsterdam.

Sprott, W. (1954) *Science and Social Action*. Watts, London.

Sutherland, E. (1949) *White Collar Crime*. Holt, Rinehart, & Winston, New York.

Sykes, G. & Matza, D. (1957) Techniques of Neutralization. *American Sociological Review* 22.

Waddington, P. (1994) *Liberty and Order*. UCL Press, London.

Wilkins, L. (1964) *Social Deviance*. Tavistock, London.

Wootton, B. (1959) *Social Science and Social Pathology*. Allen & Unwin, London.

Young, J. (1971) *The Drugtakers*. MacGibbon & Kee, London.

deviant beliefs/cognitive deviance

Robin D. Perrin

Sociological discussions of deviance typically focus on non-normative *behaviors*. Cognitive deviance, on the other hand, refers to deviant *beliefs*. The study of cognitive deviance "reveals that social rules apply not only to how one behaves but also to how and what one thinks" (Douglas & Waksler 1982: 366). Beliefs are deviant if they fall outside the norms of acceptability and are deemed wrong, irrational, eccentric, or dangerous in a given society or by the members of a particular collectivity within a given society. Deviant beliefs are important to study because they reveal basic social processes and affirm the belief structure on which the culture of a society is built. In addition, the study of deviant beliefs is important because deviance is often the first step toward social change. Today's deviant idea may well be tomorrow's norm.

History is filled with fascinating examples of attempts to control or eliminate beliefs that threaten those in power. During the Inquisition, for example, real and imagined beliefs were severely sanctioned. In the United States in the 1950s, people who supposedly held communist beliefs were ostracized, fired from jobs, and sometimes imprisoned. An examination of most of the world's major religions reveals that early followers were despised and sometimes killed for their beliefs.

Goode (2000) maintains that deviant beliefs are not always, or necessarily, minority beliefs. In fact, many widespread beliefs are rejected by society's dominant social institutions. He suggests that paranormal beliefs – those that science regards as contrary to the laws of nature – are deviant despite the fact that many are widely endorsed. Belief in the validity of such phenomena as extrasensory perception, astrology, lucky numbers, ghosts, and UFOs is deviant, he maintains, because it is derided in the educational system, the dominant media, and the medical profession. That is to say, the most powerful representatives of society's dominant institutions regard these beliefs as deviant. Yet, the deviant status of a given belief is only secured when the person who holds that belief is ostracized and stigmatized. The person who has a lucky number is not stigmatized, despite the fact that his view is seen as empirically indefensible by the scientific mainstream. Ultimately, therefore, it is the powerful and stigmatizing reaction of others – mainstream culture, people in power, interest groups – that determines the deviate status of a belief.

To define a belief as deviant is not necessarily to suggest that it is wrong or misguided. Its empirical, objective, or scientific erroneousness is a separate issue. Nearly all scientists regard paranormal beliefs as scientifically wrong, but what makes these beliefs deviant is the negative reaction they evoke from the scientific community, not the presumed wrongness of the beliefs themselves. The non-judgmental approach of the sociologist is especially evident in matters of religious faith. Beliefs that challenge religious norms will likely be ridiculed by the religious mainstream, which may label the competing religion a "cult." The sociologist, however, uses the term "cult" without prejudice. "Cult" merely distinguishes "new" religion from more established churches and sects. A cult is a deviant religion not because it is evil, but because it violates the norms of conventional religion, and because others react negatively to it. It is worth noting that all religions, including culturally acceptable religions like Christianity, began as deviant/cult movements (Stark & Bainbridge 1985).

One of the most fascinating areas within cognitive deviance is studies which focus on the process by which presumably erroneous beliefs come to be accepted by many people. This area of research fits into the larger sociological literature on collective behavior (e.g., panics, rumors, moral crusades, social movements) and the social construction of social problems (see Spector & Kitsuse 1977). For example, during the 1980s and 1990s many people, including prominent clergy and mental health professionals, came to believe that a large and active satanic cult had infiltrated the highest level of government and business. The satanists allegedly committed many heinous crimes, including the sexual exploitation of women and children, and human sacrifices. The beliefs persisted despite the fact that law enforcement personnel charged with the task of investigating the crimes routinely dismissed the claims. The "satanism scare" is a fascinating example of how widespread belief in a threat can persist even in the absence of evidence that the threat is real (Victor 1993).

Sociologists maintain that beliefs are formed in interaction with others – they are *socially constructed* (Berger & Luckmann 1966). Even commonly accepted "facts" are socially produced. Most people accept that the earth is round, but they did not reach this conclusion all by themselves. The social constructionist perspective is especially relevant in the production of cognitive deviance, which often focuses on supernatural or otherworldly beliefs that must be accepted as a matter of faith. People can be convinced to believe in something they cannot see if those around them are convinced that the claims are true. The commitment of others provides for us, in the words of Peter Berger, a "plausibility structure." Others will help convince us that the unbelievable is believable. We will be drawn to the convictions, commitment, sacrifice, and enthusiasm of others.

The study of deviant beliefs reveals to the sociologist the socially constructed nature of reality. What members of the society, or of specific social collectivities, take to be real and true has momentous consequences for the nature of the society. Beliefs that challenge these collective understandings may be reacted to negatively, and the punishment of alternate beliefs constitutes a major segment of the apparatus of social control. Since the costs can be significant, deviant beliefs are difficult to maintain. Occasionally, the fringe may become the mainstream, blasphemy the inspiration, or the nutcase the prophet. Yet more commonly they remain fringe and lunatic. Most deviant beliefs, in fact, come and go with hardly a notice.

SEE ALSO: Deviance, Absolutist Definitions of; Deviance, Constructionist Perspectives; Deviance, Reactivist Definitions of; Deviance, Theories of; Moral Entrepreneur; New Religious Movements; Religious Cults

REFERENCES AND SUGGESTED READINGS

Berger, P. L. & Luckmann, T. (1966) *The Social Construction of Reality: A Treatise in the Sociology of Knowledge*. Doubleday, Garden City, NY.

Douglas, J. D. & Waksler, F. C. (1982) *The Sociology of Deviance: An Introduction*. Little, Brown, Boston.

Goode, E. (2000) *Paranormal Beliefs: A Sociological Introduction*. Waveland Press, Prospect Heights, IL.

Spector, M. & Kitsuse, J. I. (1977) *Constructing Social Problems.* Benjamin Cummings, Menlo Park, CA.

Stark, R. & Bainbridge, W. S. (1985) *The Future of Religion.* University of California Press, Berkeley.

Victor, J. S. (1993) *Satanic Panic: The Creation of a Contemporary Legend.* Open Court, Chicago.

deviant careers

Axel Groenemeyer

The concept of career has its origin in the sociology of professions, where it has been used since the 1950s with different meanings. Corresponding to everyday meaning, career refers to certain occupations and professions of high status and stable upward mobility. In this context career means a highly institutionalized social and cultural pattern of social positions in an orderly sequence or a system of sequences of positions with growing prestige and earnings within a bureaucratic organization. This definition was first applied in functionalist perspectives and was linked to the question of the social function of this patterned organization of professions for the integration of modern societies (Wilensky 1960).

Besides this narrow meaning, career refers also to a structure of an occupational biography in general, as the sequence of occupations in the life of an individual or a group of individuals. In this meaning career is not linked to professions or to vertical mobility within an organization, but indicates any pattern of occupational change or – even more generally – individual movement through a sequence of roles and status, which does not necessarily have to be institutionalized or prescribed by a system of rules. This definition refers to questions on the social conditions and processes for changes of occupations, roles, and positions within the life course. Whether and how these patterns of mobility are in fact institutionalized are empirical questions. The research on life course development has shown that the idea of a standardized career pattern with institutionalized upward mobility always only concerned a minority of individuals. In high modern societies life courses and career mobility are increasingly destandardized and individualized. As a consequence, in life course research the concept of career has lost meaning (Marshall et al. 2001) and very often is replaced by the concepts of trajectory or status passage (Heinz 1991).

In a third meaning career refers to processes of individual adaptations and socialization within roles and positions of an occupational biography. In this context career is defined as a series of adjustments made to institutions, formal organizations, and informal social relationships involved in the occupation. This definition partly is used also in research on social conditions of positional changes, but normally is linked to analyses of individual developments of social and personal identities that take place in the context of occupational mobility as individual adaptation to the organization and culture of an occupation (Strauss 1971). In this perspective career development has to be analyzed within an action frame of reference, and changes of positions are the result or the consequence of individual developments and decisions.

The metaphor of career thus in general stands for the link between social structures, biographical development, and individual action within the life course: "development as action in context" (Silbereisen et al. 1986). Career refers to the social structure of the individual's movement through defined social positions, to the individual's movement through these positions; it can also focus on the intersection of individual biography and social structures.

The common frame of the career concept is the construction of a related sequence of stages and positions that have to be passed through one after the other. Preceding stages and positions constitute specific preconditions for succeeding stages or positions. In this sense the sequences of a career form an inherent causal connection, but changes of positions as turning points or transitions between stages have to be explained by specific social conditions and processes. The career concept also allows analysis of individual changes of positions and roles as a process of active individual adaptations of orientations, competencies, and perspectives that take place before "turning points" in the life course, as well as processes of socialization that are the consequence of taking a new position or status.

At the same time, careers also constitute a pattern of providing meaning; they are constructed in prospect and accounted for in retrospect. The construction of a structured and coherent career provides meaning and sense, not only for institutions that guide and control individual biographies, but also for the individuals themselves (Collin & Young 2000).

Individual developments in deviant behavior normally do not follow institutionalized or organized sequences. Nevertheless, in a retrospective view there can be constructed typical patterns and sequences of development, organized around the deviant behavior itself, by patterns of problematic social conditions seen as causes of the deviant behavior, or by a sequence of consecutive institutions that have reacted to the deviant behavior (Cicourel 1969). Also in this context the assumption of a continuity and coherence of the individual biography constitutes the guiding idea of constructing a career pattern.

Another meaning of the career concept is emphasized when specific forms of deviant behavior are interpreted as a profession to earn one's living. In fact, some types of deviant behavior could be described as occupation, like some forms of organized larceny, fraud, or economic crime, but also prostitution and drug dealing, where different social positions or a status hierarchy and processes of learning and role adaptations could be analyzed in analogy with positions in respectable occupations (Letkemann 1973).

The sociology of deviance first adopted a perspective of career implicitly within analyses of deviant biographies in the context of the Chicago School of sociology (Shaw 1931; Sutherland 1937) and in the perspective of the theory of differential association (Sutherland and Cressey 1939). Also, the multifactor approach of Eleanor and Sheldon Gluck used the concept of career, but only to order variables in a temporal sequence. Synonymous with the career concept, very often the term natural history has been employed.

It was the development of the labeling approach that promoted the concept of deviant career in the 1960s. As a critique of etiological theories of deviant behavior with emphasis on personality defects, the labeling approach demands explicit analyses of the dynamic processes by which the labels of deviant behavior are constructed, applied to specific persons, and adopted by them. Classical works from this perspective include Becker's analyses of the learning processes of "Becoming a Marihuana Smoker" (1953), Erving Goffman's (1961) description of individual adaptations and processes of identity development in the context of the total institution, Scheff's (1966) theory of psychic disorders, Suchman's (1965) work on patient careers, and the analyses of drug careers by Rubington (1967). Since then the notion of deviant career has spread into everyday meaning in different connections, such as drug career, criminal careers, illness career, and poverty career.

The biographies of drug addicts very often have a typical sequence of drug use that can be reconstructed as a sequence from soft to hard drug or patterns of increasing usage. The typical sequences are constructed as a drug career and laid the groundwork for ideological versions of the stepping-stone hypothesis: the assumption of a quasi-naturally progressing involvement into drug addiction that ends in the total misery of addiction. Empirical research has shown that this hypothesis cannot find justification without taking into consideration the social and institutionalized reaction, as well as the social context of drug use, marked by stigmatization and criminalization. In a sociological career perspective the use of drugs could increase the statistical probability of using other drugs, which also means that most of the persons involved in the use do not go on to other drugs. The transition between different stages of drug use is marked by specific biographical and social conditions, so that the causes for starting smoking or drinking alcohol are quite different from those of smoking marijuana, which are different from taking hard drugs (Kandel 1980).

But in fact the use of the career concept in this context always is only a very rough simplification. Biographical research on drug use has shown that drug careers only very seldom follow a linear sequence. They are always marked by interruptions, by processes of reintegration into respectable social contexts, and subcultural integration. This also holds for processes for giving up drug addiction, for processes of reintegration and maturing out of the drug-using context (Biernacki 1986), and also for the effectiveness of intervention and treatment (Groenemeyer 1990). In this approach, the career perspective has to be integrated into a larger analysis of deviant life courses and biographies, marked by status passages, turning points, and transitions.

The idea of criminal careers refers either to crime as work or occupation (Letkemann 1973), to the consequences of interventions of social control (Cicourel 1969), or to the causes and consequences of crime and criminal offenses in the life course (Sampson & Laub 1993; Farrington 1994).

One starting point for the rediscovery of the careers metaphor in criminology has been the development of self-report studies in the 1960s and 1970s, which showed that criminal offenses are quite common behaviors for certain age groups, but for most offenders this behavior must be interpreted as transitory and occurs only once or very seldom. In this perspective a concept of criminal careers does not make much sense when it is defined analogously to that of the drug career as a sequence of different offenses. In the Philadelphia birth cohort study, Wolfgang et al. (1972) came to the conclusion that about 70 percent of all serious offenses are committed by about 6 percent of offenders. With this result they identified a small group of "career criminals," variously characterized as dangerous, habitual, or chronic offenders, who commit serious offenses with high frequency over extended periods of time (Blumstein et al. 1986). In this context criminal careers are defined as the longitudinal sequence of offenses committed by an individual offender (Farrington 1994). This construction of the career criminal gave way to extended research activities on patterns of individual offending and constituted the scientific base for the development of "three strikes and you're out" policies in the US.

Whereas in this perspective the differentiation between offenders is the starting point, other perspectives using the career metaphor start from the multifactor approach of Glueck and Glueck (1943) in searching for specific conditions in the development of crime. The results of this branch of empirical research are extremely varied (Farrington et al. 1986; Loeber & LeBlanc 1990). In this context the career concept is only used to give the choice of factors and variables a temporal order from birth (and even before) to adulthood, without much claim to developing theoretical generalizations.

SEE ALSO: Crime; Deviance; Drugs, Drug Abuse, and Drug Policy; Drugs and the Law; Labeling; Labeling Theory; Professions; Work, Sociology of

REFERENCES AND SUGGESTED READINGS

Becker, H. S. (1953) Becoming a Marihuana User. *American Journal of Sociology* 59(2): 235–42.

Biernacki, P. (1986) *Pathways from Heroin Addiction: Recovery Without Treatment*. Temple University Press, Philadelphia.

Blumstein, A., Cohen, J., Roth, J. A., & Visher, C. A. (Eds.) (1986) *Criminal Careers and "Career Criminals,"* 2 vols. National Academy Press, Washington, DC.

Cicourel, A. V. (1969) *The Social Construction of Juvenile Justice*. Wiley, New York.

Collin, A. & Young, R. A. (Eds.) (2000) *The Future of Career*. Cambridge University Press, Cambridge.

Farrington, D. P. (1994) Human Development and Criminal Careers. In: Maguire, M., Morgan, R., & Reiner, R. (Eds.), *The Oxford Handbook of Criminology*. Clarendon Press, Oxford, pp. 511–84.

Farrington, D. P., Ohlin, L. E., & Wilson, J. Q. (1986) *Understanding and Controlling Crime: Toward a New Research Strategy*. Springer, New York.

Glueck, S. & Glueck, E. (1943) *Criminal Careers in Retrospect*. Commonwealth Fund, New York.

Goffman, E. (1961) *Asylums*. Doubleday, New York.

Groenemeyer, A. (1990) *Drogenkarriere und Sozialpolitik. Entwicklungsbedingungen der Drogenabhängigkeit und Möglichkeiten der Intervention durch stationäre Behandlung*. Centaurus, Pfaffenweiler.

Heinz, W. R. (Eds.) (1991) *Theoretical Advances in Life Course Research*, Vol. 1. Deutscher Studien, Weinheim.

Kandel, D. B. (1980) Drug and Drinking Behavior Among Youth. *Annual Review of Sociology* 6: 235–85.

Letkemann, P. (1973) *Crime as Work*. Englewood Cliffs, NJ, Prentice-Hall.

Loeber, R. & LeBlanc, M. (1990) Toward a Developmental Criminology. In: Tonry, M. and Morris, N. (Eds.), *Crime and Justice: An Annual Review of Research*, Vol. 12. University of Chicago Press, Chicago, pp. 375–73.

Marshall, V. W., Heinz, W. R., Krüger, H., & Verma, A. (Eds.) (2001) *Restructuring Work and the Life Course*. University of Toronto Press, Toronto.

Rubington, E. (1967) Drug Addiction as a Deviant Career. *International Journal of Addictions* 2(1): 3–20.

Sampson, R. J. & Laub, J. H. (1993) *Crime in the Making: Pathways and Turning Points Through Life*. Harvard University Press, Cambridge, MA.

Scheff, T. J. (1966) *Being Mentally Ill: A Sociological Theory*. University of Chicago Press, Chicago.

Shaw, C. R. (1931) *The Natural History of a Delinquent Career*. University of Chicago Press, Chicago.

Silbereisen, R. K., Eyferth, K., & Rudinger, G. (Eds.) (1986) *Development as Action in Context: Problem Behavior and Normal Youth Development*. Springer, Berlin.

Strauss, A. L. (1971) *Professions, Work and Careers*. Sociology Press, San Francisco.

Suchman, E. A. (1965) Stages of Illness and Medical Care. *Journal of Health and Human Behavior* 6(3): 114–28.

Sutherland, E. H. (1937) *The Professional Thief*. University of Chicago Press, Chicago.

Sutherland, E. H. & Cressey, D. R. (1939) *Principles of Criminology*. Lippincott, Chicago.

Wilensky, H. L. (1960) Work, Careers, and Social Integration. *International Social Science Journal* 12 (fall): 543–60.

Wolfgang, M. E., Figlio, R. M., & Sellin, T. (1972) *Delinquency in a Birth Cohort*. University of Chicago Press, Chicago.

Dewey, John (1859–1952)

Mark D. Jacobs

John Dewey, perhaps the most prominent US public philosopher in the first half of the twentieth century, has cast a large shadow over many fields of sociology: social psychology, urban sociology, the sociology of education, the sociology of culture, political sociology, and public sphere theory, among others. Above all, he helped infuse much of American sociology with a spirit of pragmatism. In addition to his seminal contributions to the study of method and of ethics, his sociological works focus on the active nature of education, democracy as community, and art and experience – and their interrelations. His students and colleagues – George Herbert Mead, W. I. Thomas, Robert Park, and Jane Addams – helped spread his influence almost immediately over sociological research and practice; it is not accidental that the three universities to which he devoted the bulk of his faculty career – Michigan, Chicago, and Columbia – all nurtured elite departments of sociology, and that the New School for Social Research, which he helped found, has continually sharpened the critical-normative edge of sociology.

Dewey led a team at Chicago in elaborating and systematizing the insights of William James, among other pragmatists, to produce what James himself recognized as the first "school" of American philosophy. Pragmatism is an approach to philosophy that dispenses with metaphysical assumptions and hierarchies, relying instead on practical experimentation – seeing what works – to arrive at provisional assessments of truth. The focus is on ameliorating problems that arise in experience. Reality is seen as uncertain – probabilistic and contingent. Meanings are relational and emergent, conditioned by particular contexts; moral judgments rest on evaluations of consequences. The method is reflexive, involving the exercise of cooperative and deliberative intelligence to choose among projected alternative paths of social action, while making value and other assumptions as explicit as possible, and continually adjusting plans to incorporate the lessons of experience. Reflexivity extends to the method itself: there is continual inquiry into the very process of inquiry, as well as into the very meanings of the core ideas.

Pragmatism dissolves metaphysical dualisms between subjects and objects, nature and culture, facts and values, the knower and the known, means and ends, self and society. Dewey himself preferred the label "instrumentalism" to "pragmatism," although by instrumentalism he meant the very opposite of adherence to instrumental reason, since he considered ends and values themselves to require constant reevaluation.

It is impossible even to summarize the range of Dewey's scholarly interests, which encompassed all branches of philosophy, including psychological philosophy. But perhaps his overarching *sociological* research problem involves the simultaneous strengthening of individualism and community. The interrelations of his core sociological concepts describe an arc from micro-analysis to macrostructure. *Habits* are not personal properties, but rather interpersonal adaptations to *institutional* arrangements, which are therefore amenable to improvement through the exercise of *deliberative intelligence* exercised by *communities*. The most important such institution is the school, which is therefore optimally organized as a community of active doers (students and teachers alike), integrated as fully as possible into the larger community. *Democracy* (an ideal far from realized in the US) is the process of participation in communities of deliberation. In addressing social problems, the *public* must rely on communities of social scientists for alternative policy formulations, continually evaluated (as the public is perfectly capable of doing) according to their consequences. A public exists as a community of shared interest, containing all those whose lives are touched by the consequences of conjoint action. Reconstructing communities and institutions is necessary to endow practical activity with the expressive quality of aesthetic experience, making normal life processes into living works of art.

Dewey's pragmatic methods and conceptions shaped in fundamental ways not only the Chicago School of Sociology, but the Second, postwar, Chicago School as well. Dewey's influence is explicit, for example, in Becker's (1992) classic argument that the very meaning of art is the cooperative product of art worlds. It is equally evident in the "logic of systemic analysis" and the core concept of "social control" that guides Morris Janowitz's magisterial survey of *The Last Half-Century* (1978), as well as Janowitz's prescription for *Institution-Building in Urban Education* (1969). But Dewey's influence reaches far beyond Chicago; for example, to Philip Selznick's masterly analysis of the naturalistic ethics, moral persons, moral institutions, and moral communities that make up *The Moral Commonwealth* (1992), and to Jürgen Habermas's *Theory of Communicative Action* (1984).

SEE ALSO: Addams, Jane; Art Worlds; Chicago School; Chicago School: Social Change; Critical Theory/Frankfurt School; Democracy; James, William; Mead, George Herbert; Pragmatism; Public Realm; Schools, Public; Self; Social Movements, Participatory Democracy in; Symbolic Interaction

REFERENCES AND SUGGESTED READINGS

Becker, H. (1992) *Art Worlds*. University of California Press, Berkeley.

Dewey, J. (1969–72) *The Early Works of John Dewey, 1882–1898*, 5 vols. Ed. J. A. Boydston. Southern Illinois University Press, Carbondale.

Dewey, J. (1976–83) *The Middle Works of John Dewey, 1899–1924*, 15 vols. Ed. J. A. Boydston. Southern Illinois University Press, Carbondale.

Dewey, J. (1981–90) *The Late Works of John Dewey, 1925–1953*, 17 vols. Ed. J. A. Boydston. Southern Illinois University Press, Carbondale.

Habermas, J. (1984) *The Theory of Communicative Action*, 2 vols. Trans. T. McCarthy. Beacon Press, Boston.

Janowitz, M. (1969) *Institution-Building in Urban Education*. University of Chicago Press, Chicago.

Janowitz, M. (1978) *The Last Half-Century*. University of Chicago Press, Chicago.

Selznick, P. (1992) *The Moral Commonwealth*. University of California Press, Berkeley.

dialectic

Kevin B. Anderson and Peter Hudis

While its roots go back to the Socratic dialogues, dialectics as social theory begins with G. W. F. Hegel, and extends through Karl Marx to today. With Hegel, the dialectic takes the form of a double negation. Ideas or social forms face negativity from within. If the process deepens, the old idea or form is overthrown. However, such a first or bare negation remains a "formless abstraction" unless it develops some determinateness or specificity (Hegel 1969: 113). This requires going beyond "the first negation as negation in general," to "the second negation, the negation of the negation," which is "concrete, absolute negativity" (p. 116). This absolute negativity creates a new idea or social form in place of the old. Then the process may resume, with negation growing again within what has been newly created. Some have erroneously described this process as one of thesis-antithesis-synthesis, an expression Hegel himself never used (Pinkard 2000).

As against such formulaic notions, Hegel's dialectic is deeply rooted in historical and social development, especially the period of the Enlightenment and the French Revolution. These form the backdrop to all of his major works. As against the earlier Socratic dialectic, conflict and dialogue take place between real social forces, as well as between ideas. In the *Phenomenology of Mind* (1807), Hegel traces the development of consciousness and knowledge, from the ancient world to his own time. Successive forms of consciousness are negations of previous ones. For example, in the much-discussed dialectic of the master and the slave (literally, lordship and bondage), slaves in the Greco-Roman world acquire a more developed form of self-consciousness than their masters. This is because they have experienced "absolute negativity," as their personal world has been shattered through the wrenching experience of slavery. This form of consciousness, he writes, has had "that experience melted into its every fiber," leading to a negation of the self (Hegel 1967: 237). But the fact that the slave performs physical labor, while the master enjoys a life of leisure, points in the direction of a second or absolute negation: "Thus precisely in labor where there seemed to be merely some outsider's mind and ideas involved, the bondsman becomes aware, through this rediscovery of himself by himself, of having and being 'a mind of his own'" (p. 239). This leads in turn to a new form of consciousness, Stoicism, which Hegel portrays as an advance. Alluding to the fact that several prominent Stoics were manumitted slaves, however, Hegel also stresses the limitations placed upon human consciousness by a historical period he characterizes as "a time of universal fear and bondage" (p. 245).

Hegel develops a number of other dialectical categories, including identity, difference, and contradiction. He writes that although identity between two forms also includes of necessity some sort of difference, difference also has to involve some identity, a common set of terms or a framework through which they can express that difference. This could include a common language, for example. The impasse is overcome in a third stage, that of contradiction. Expanding the notion of contradiction from the sphere of ideas to that of social life, Hegel concludes that "everything is inherently contradictory" and that "contradiction is the root of all movement and all vitality" (Hegel 1969: 439).

Hegel's negations and contradictions create ground for a radical form of subjectivity, and he enjoins us to grasp reality "not as substance but as subject as well" (Hegel 1967: 80). He sees a drive for freedom as the overarching theme of human history, although this involves contradiction, even sometimes retrogression. As humanity strives for the universal, for an absolute liberation, internal barriers to its realization repeatedly manifest themselves. Prominent among these are abstract universals, which lack particularity or concreteness. The French Revolution, especially its Jacobin phase, was marked by universals of "pure abstraction," which "lacked a filling and a content," thus lapsing into the "sheer horror of the negative that has nothing positive in it" (p. 608). However, Hegel's system ends not here, but with a series of absolutes in which freedom is concretized, ultimately as the idea "engenders and enjoys itself as absolute mind" (Hegel 1971: 315).

Marx attacks the conservative side of Hegel's social and political philosophy, for example in his 1843 critique of the anti-democratic *Philosophy of Right*. At the same time, Marx takes over the dialectic. In his "Critique of the Hegelian Dialectic" in the unpublished *1844 Manuscripts*, he characterizes Hegel's "outstanding achievement" as "the dialectic of negativity as the moving and creative principle" (Marx, in Fromm 1961: 176). At the same time, Marx distances himself from some aspects of Hegel's idealism: "For Hegel, human life ... is equivalent to self-consciousness" (p. 179). Nonetheless, many core principles of Hegel's dialectic – negation of the negation, contradiction, the concrete universal, etc. – are retained in the Marxian dialectic. Nor is idealism rejected *in toto*. A year later, in the "Theses on Feuerbach," Marx writes that many forms of materialism lack the subjective element, are too contemplative: "Hence, in contradistinction to materialism, the active side was set forth abstractly by idealism" (MECW 5: 3).

With Marx, the notion of contradiction migrates to the sphere of political economy, where social change is driven by class struggle, as he and Engels maintain in *The Communist Manifesto* (1848). Change also occurs when, due to social development, "the material productive forces of society come into contradiction with the existing production relationships," as he wrote in the preface to the *Critique of Political Economy* in 1859 (Marx, in Fromm 1961: 218). Eight years later, in volume 1 of *Capital*, Marx confirms his debt to Hegel by writing of "the Hegelian 'contradiction,' which is the source of all dialectics" (Marx 1976: 744).

In the closing pages of *Capital* Marx uses the Hegelian negation of the negation to frame a discussion of the possible demise of capitalism. In the section on "primitive accumulation" he describes the expropriation of the English peasantry during the agricultural revolution as "the first negation of private property," as the peasants lose their land. Driven into the cities, they become the working class. Capitalism eventually "begets its own negation," however, the revolt of the working class, a class that it has called into existence. "This," Marx concludes, "is the negation of the negation" (pp. 929–30). Elsewhere, for example in the 1873 preface to a new edition of *Capital*, he criticizes "the mystificatory side of the Hegelian dialectic," and writes: "It must be inverted, in order to discover the rational kernel within the mystificatory shell." Nonetheless, he avows himself "a pupil of that mighty thinker" (pp. 102–3). In a letter to Engels of January 16, 1858, Marx expresses the intention to publish an essay on what was "rational" in Hegel's dialectic, this after he reviewed Hegel's *Logic* while in the process of writing the *Grundrisse* (MECW 40: 249). He never did so.

In his *Ludwig Feuerbach and the End of Classical German Philosophy* (1886), Engels develops two schema, which are embraced to this day by more orthodox currents within Marxism. First, Engels writes that Hegel's "system" is conservative, while his "dialectical method" was revolutionary. Second, he divides all of philosophy into "two great camps," idealism and materialism, with the latter the progressive and revolutionary one (MECW 26: 363, 366). It was in this spirit that Georgi Plekhanov coined the term "dialectical materialism" five years later. Engels also enunciated three "laws" of dialectics: (1) transformation of quantity into quality, (2) interpenetration of opposites, and (3) negation of the negation.

Until the publication of the *1844 Manuscripts* in German in 1932 (a Russian edition appeared in 1927), Marx's concept of dialectic and its relation to that of Hegel was obscured. Some Marxists delved directly into Hegel, however. In his 1914–15 *Notebooks* on Hegel's *Logic*, Lenin returns directly to Hegel's writings, modifying some aspects of the dominant form of dialectical materialism. Concerning the Hegelian notion of consciousness, he writes: "cognition not only reflects the objective world, but creates it" (LCW 38: 212). Lenin also expresses reservations about Engels and Plekhanov, attempting to go beyond the rigid divide between idealism and materialism by attacking not only abstract idealism, but also "vulgar materialism" (LCW 38: 114). He kept these reflections on the dialectic mostly private, however, allowing the very "vulgar materialism" he had critiqued to reign relatively unchallenged in the Soviet Union.

In his *History and Class Consciousness* (1923), Georg Lukács independently recovers the Hegelian dialectic for Marxism. He accuses Engels of confusing "the scientific experiment" with "praxis in the dialectical, philosophical sense" (Lukács 1971: 132). Moreover, he attacks Engels for neglecting the element of subjectivity in his three laws of dialectic: "But he does not even mention the most vital interaction, namely the dialectical relation between subject and object in the historical process." The mere recourse to "fluid" concepts does not solve this problem, Lukács holds (p. 3). He also develops a concept of concrete totality, which allows a move from the factory – "in concentrated form the whole of capitalist society" (p. 90) – to the concept of fetishism or reification. The first to point to commodity fetishism as the core of Marx's critique of capital, Lukács also extended reification from the factory to the entire human condition under capitalism – to the white-collar worker, or the scientist, for example. In doing so, he incorporated Weber's theory of rationalization. Later, Lucien Goldmann (1969) discussed Lukács in relation to sociological methodology.

Frankfurt School member Herbert Marcuse's *Reason and Revolution* (1941) was the first major study of dialectics that appeared after the publication of Marx's *1844 Manuscripts*. Marcuse again places negativity at the center of dialectical thought: "Hegel's philosophy is indeed what the subsequent reaction termed it, a negative philosophy. It is originally motivated by the conviction that the given facts that appear to common sense as the positive index of truth are in reality the negation of truth, so that truth can only be established by their destruction" (Marcuse 1941: 27). Commonsense reason also traps consciousness in the particular and the empirical, blocking it from grasping the universal, and therefore the possibilities for radical change. With dialectical reason, in contrast, "possibility belongs to the very character of reality" (p. 150). In this sense, universals such as human emancipation are actually part of social reality, whereas oppressive social forms are in an ultimate sense unreal and false. Theodor Adorno, also of the Frankfurt School, parts company with Hegel on absolute negativity, taking issue with the concept of totality as well. Adorno, who seeks to expunge the affirmative character from dialectics, goes so far as to link absolute negativity to the Holocaust, this in his *Negative Dialectics* (1966).

Dialectic also marks some of the major treatments of race and colonialism, whether in W. E. B. Du Bois's notion of "double consciousness" in *Souls of Black Folk* (1903), or in Frantz Fanon's dialectic of colonialism and resistance in *Wretched of the Earth* (1961). C. L. R. James in his *Notes on Dialectics* (1948) and especially Raya Dunayevskaya developed a concept of dialectic that eschews abstract universals, elaborating a multiple concept of subjectivity that includes not only the traditional working class, but also blacks, women, and youth. Writing later on as a Marxist humanist, Dunayevskaya makes absolute negativity her point of departure, arguing in *Philosophy and Revolution* (1973) that Hegel's absolutes are not closures, but imbued with absolute negativity. She holds that dialectical thought, if concretized, can impact radical social movements,

helping to give them form and direction: "Philosophy and revolution will then liberate the innate talents of men and women who will become whole" (p. 292). Hegel's dialectic also allows oppositional movements to navigate periods of retrogression as well as progressive ones: "Far from expressing a sequence of never-ending progression, the Hegelian dialectic lets retrogression appear as translucent as progression" (Dunayevskaya 2002: 332).

Strong challenges to dialectics have come from scientific positivism, and more recently from poststructuralism. Among others, poststructuralists attack the dialectic as too affirmative, counterposing a Nietzschean notion of absolute difference. These critics have also argued that Hegel's universals swallow up particularity and difference in grand totalities or narratives. Nonetheless, dialectical thought persists, especially through the traditions of Marxism and critical theory.

SEE ALSO: Adorno, Theodor W.; Critical Theory/Frankfurt School; Dialectical Materialism; Engels, Friedrich; Hegel, G. W. F.; Horkheimer, Max; Lukács, Georg; Marcuse, Herbert; Marx, Karl

REFERENCES AND SUGGESTED READINGS

Dunayevskaya, R. (1973) *Philosophy and Revolution*. Delacorte, New York.

Dunayevskaya, R. (2002) *The Power of Negativity*. Ed. P. Hudis & K. B. Anderson.

Fromm, E. (1961) *Marx's Concept of Man*. Ungar, New York.

Goldmann, L. (1969) *The Human Sciences and Philosophy*. Jonathan Cape, London.

Hegel, G. W. F. (1967) *Phenomenology of Mind*. Harper, New York.

Hegel, G. W. F. (1969) *Science of Logic*. Allen & Unwin, London.

Hegel, G. W. F. (1971) *Philosophy of Mind*. Oxford University Press, New York.

Lenin, V. I. [LCW] *Philosophical Notebooks*. In: *Collected Works*, Vol. 38. Progress Publishers, Moscow.

Lukács, G. (1971) *History and Class Consciousness*. MIT Press, Cambridge, MA.

Marcuse, H. (1941) *Reason and Revolution*. Oxford University Press, New York.

Marx, K. (1976) *Capital*, Vol. 1. Penguin, New York.

Marx, K. & Engels, F. [MECW] (1975–2004) *Collected Works*, 50 vols. International Publishers, New York.

Ollman, B. (1993) *Dialectical Investigations*. Routledge, New York.

Pinkard, T. (2000) *Hegel: A Biography*. Cambridge University Press, New York.

dialectical materialism

Rob Beamish

The term "dialectical materialism" first appeared in Joseph Dietzgen's 1887 essay "Excursions of a Socialist into the Domain of Epistemology," but only became a central concept within Marxism following George Plekhanov's 1891 essay commemorating the sixtieth anniversary of Hegel's death and his ensuing efforts to establish a monist view of history. Dialectical materialism became the dominant philosophy of Marxism during the Second International (1889–1917) and the official, formulaic philosophy of communist parties controlled by the USSR during Joseph Stalin's dictatorship (1929–53).

As the official philosophy of Soviet communism, dialectical materialism brought together a simplistic notion of Hegel's dialectical method – one that presented change as the result of the internal struggle of opposites in which a thesis gives way to its antithesis and is then followed by a higher synthesis of the original opposites – with Marx and Engels's materialism to constitute a single, allegedly coherent science that applied to all material, biological, historical, social, and political phenomena. Its supporters claimed that it represented the extension and culmination of "historical materialism" – a term Engels used to designate a formalized philosophy of history based on Marx's 1859 sketch of his "materialist conception of history." All change, according to dialectical materialists, resulted from the thesis–antithesis–synthesis dialectic inherent in historical, social, even natural phenomena.

Marx himself never used the terms historical or dialectical materialism and, despite a few expressions of interest, never wrote a comprehensive philosophical or methodological statement. On the contrary, Marx resisted attempts to convert his materialist conception into a substantive theory of history or totalizing philosophy, although in reading *Anti-Dühring* and not rejecting the extension of dialectics to nature he gave Engels's ideas tacit support. Marx's own materialism was limited to the labor process and the material conditions of production. As the social relations of production developed, Marx argued, they became, at a certain stage, fetters to the material forces of production, creating the conditions for revolutionary change. In grasping such events, Marx noted, one had to distinguish between the transformation of the material conditions of production and the ideological forms through which people became aware of the conflict and engaged in struggles for change. This guideline focused on the key factors involved in historical change but it was not a rigid or comprehensive theory of history. Marx's own historical writings demonstrate his appreciation for nuance and detail rather than slavish conformity to a restrictive rubric.

From 1875 until his death, Engels sought to bring greater coherence to his and Marx's work by developing a philosophy which incorporated Hegel's dialectics into an eighteenth-century-inspired materialism. This thrust, contrary to Engels's and Marx's original conception that conscious human action, directed against particular social relations, created social change, began to reduce history to one aspect of a general, material, natural evolution, in which social history and nature were subject to the same laws. Engels sought to extend his dialectical conception of nature – itself a questionable theory – to the study of historical development in all branches of science.

Socialism Utopian and Scientific popularized Engels's claim that one could unify socialist history, idealist philosophy, and mechanistic materialism into a "scientific socialism." Plekhanov and Lenin gave added intellectual and political credence to the Engelsian-inspired materialist philosophy and by 1938 Stalin, the General Secretary of the Communist Party of the Soviet Union (CPSU), affirmed that dialectical materialism was the sole and correct philosophy of Marxism-Leninism. Maintaining that all material phenomena constitute an interconnected whole, the explanations for all historical change were based on "diamat's" three laws: the transformation of quantity into quality (small quantitative changes lead to abrupt "leaps" of qualitative transformation), the unity of opposites (all phenomena are comprised of opposites which internally "struggle" with each other), and the negation of the negation (in the "struggle of opposites," one negates the other but it is later negated, leading to a higher, more developed unity). The crude triad of thesis–antithesis–synthesis was diamat's dialectical conception. As the philosophy of Marxism, dialectical materialism encompassed all aspects of thought, events, and the material world.

Diamat's major significance was political rather than philosophical or scientific. By maintaining that nature and the material world were primary and thought was derivative, the Marxism of the CPSU rejected human reason and consciousness as key factors in social change and focused exclusively on the dialectics of material reality. Because one could only provide after the fact reconstructions of events through diamat's three laws, the powerful CPSU became the official interpreter of social events and the guide to further social change.

The critique of dialectical materialism began with Karl Korsch's *Marxism and Philosophy* and Georg Lukács's *History and Class Consciousness*. Written independently, both rejected the reduction of history to a materialist dialectic, emphasized the importance of consciousness in history, and stimulated ensuing western Marxists to focus on questions of epistemology, method, and a renewed understanding of Marx's critique of Hegel. Korsch and Lukács's focus on the active, mediated engagement of humankind with the natural world through labor was buttressed by the 1932 publication of Marx's 1844 manuscripts, which, along with the *Grundrisse*, undermined diamat as a credible legacy to Marx's materialist conception of history.

SEE ALSO: Base and Superstructure; Communism; Dialectic; Economic Determinism; Engels, Friedrich; Marx, Karl; Marxism and Sociology

REFERENCES AND SUGGESTED READINGS

Central Committee of the Communist Party of the Soviet Union (Eds.) (1939) *History of the Communist Party of the Soviet Union (Bolsheviks): Short Course*. Foreign Languages Publishing House, Moscow.

Engels, F. (1935 [1880]) *Socialism Utopian and Scientific*. Trans.. E. Aveling. International Publishers, New York.

Engels, F. (1959 [1878]) *Anti-Dühring Herr Eugen Dühring's Revolution in Science*. Lawrence & Wishart, London.

Lenin, V. I. (1927 [1908]) *Materialism and Empirio-Criticism*. Trans.. D. Kvitko. International Publishers, New York.

Steger, M. & Carver, T. (Eds.) (1999) *Engels After Marx*. Pennsylvania State University Press, University Park.

Wetter, G. (1958) *Dialectical Materialism: A Historical and Systematic Survey of Philosophy in the Soviet Union*. Trans. P. Heath. Routledge & Kegan Paul, London.

diaspora

Larissa Remennick

The term "diaspora" originates from the Greek "dia" (over) and "speiro" (to sow). The Greeks understood diaspora as migration and colonization of new lands. In modern parlance the term diaspora usually refers to ethnic groups whose sizable parts have lived outside their country of origin for at least several generations, while maintaining some ties (even if purely symbolic or sentimental) to the historic homeland. The "classic" diasporas in terms of the ancient history of dispersion are Jewish, Armenian, and Greek; the more modern (and also more numerous) diasporas include the African ("Black American") diaspora resulting from the forced migration of slaves to the Americas, and Irish, Italian, Polish, Chinese, and Indian diasporas resulting from voluntary migrations.

Today the word diaspora is applied to a broad range of migrant populations whose current or historic uprooting was politically or economically motivated, including political refugees, voluntary migrants, guest workers, expatriates, stable ethnic minorities, and other dispersed groups. Modern political and social thinkers (Sheffer 1986; Safran 1991; Cohen 1997) put forward several criteria for defining ethnic communities as diasporas: a history of dispersal (often forced or motivated by harsh living conditions), myths and memories of a homeland, alienation in the host country, a desire for eventual return (which can be ambivalent, eschatological, or utopian), ongoing support of the homeland, and a collective identity (often including common linguistic and cultural practices). Thus, the German diaspora embraces many generations of *Aussiedler* in Eastern Europe and the former Soviet Union (now making a mass return to a reunified Germany); the Turkish/Kurdish diasporas include at least two generations of guest workers in Germany; and the Filipino diaspora embraces two generations of women and men working in medical and personal services across the western world. New diasporas may appear on the global map as a result of seminal geopolitical events, such as the founding of the State of Israel in 1948, with the following War of Independence and the dispersion of thousands of Palestinian Arabs across the Middle East and western countries. Another recent example of diasporization of a seemingly monolith ethnic entity is an estimated 25 million Russians and other Slavs remaining in the former Soviet successor states as a result of the collapse of the unitary USSR. Another result of the post-communist transition is the emigration of about 1.7 million former Soviet Jews who resettled in Israel and in the West (mainly the US, Canada, and Germany), enlarging and invigorating the existing multi-ethnic global diaspora of Russian speakers (Remennick 2002).

Some communities that used to have strong diasporic consciousness during the initial two or three generations upon resettlement later assimilated in the receiving societies and lost active ties with their homelands – the examples include Irish and Italian immigrants in North America and Australia. Other diasporas continued to exist for centuries without actual homelands (e.g., 1,500 years of living in *galut* – dispersion – in the case of the Jews), or even without a tangible concept of a homeland, like Gypsies, also known as Roma people, scattered across Europe and Asia. Indeed, the term diaspora has acquired metaphoric implications and is used as a generic description of displaced people who feel, maintain, invent, or revive a connection with a prior home, real or imagined (Safran 1991). Robin Cohen (1997) has proposed another typology of diasporas in relation to the circumstances of their formation, social contexts, mythologies, and grounds for solidarity. These include: victim diasporas (e.g., refugees from war-stricken regions), labor and imperial diasporas (Russians and other Slavs in the former Soviet Union), trade diasporas, cultural diasporas (e.g., today's secular Jews living outside Israel), and global-deterritorialized diasporas such as the Roma.

In the late twentieth and early twenty-first centuries, the closely entwined processes of mass migration, globalization, and ethnic revival led to a fortification and thriving of transnational diasporas, i.e., global communities with common ethnic origins whose economic, political, and social networks cross the borders of nation-states. Diaspora discourse reflects a sense of being part of an ongoing transnational network and includes dispersed people who retain a sense of their uniqueness and an interest in their ancestral homeland. From a sociological standpoint, a diaspora is a social construct founded on group identity, common history, cultural practices, narratives, and dreams, i.e., it includes many virtual elements that nevertheless play a central role in its sustainability. The diasporic mindset is characterized by a sense of living in one place while simultaneously belonging to another, or even to many others, as many contemporary diasporas have multiple centers (e.g., the Russian Jewish diaspora stretching between Israel, North America, and Europe). As a result of the cross-fertilization of different traditions, diasporic minorities often develop cultural hybrids between home and host styles of clothing, eating, socializing, and so on that often entail the invention and use of hybrid languages and new vocabularies (e.g., Turkish German, Israeli Russian).

The maintenance of close ties between diasporic centers has been strongly reinforced by new communication and transportation technologies that compress time and space (Castells 1996). Electronic media including television channels transmitted via cable and satellite across diasporic communities, Internet, and email make the contemporary world increasingly interconnected. Relatively cheap phone calls and air travel make homeland and other branches of the ethnic diaspora easily accessible. Altogether, these vehicles of globalization have dramatically increased the amount and intensity of contacts between co-ethnics scattered across the globe. Many members of diasporic communities (expatriates) hold dual citizenship, vote in elections (and sometimes sponsor political parties or activist groups) in both the home and host countries, and participate in their economic life via entrepreneurial activities, sending remittances to families, and so on (Portes et al. 1999).

It can be argued that the majority of today's immigrants display some elements of diasporic consciousness and lifestyle. These are often seen as a challenge to the dominance of the existing nation-states, especially if immigrants show a reluctance to assimilate into the mainstream and exhibit signs of cultural separatism. Nationalism and nativist sentiments of the hegemonic majority can lead to social and political exclusion of minority groups that are often seen as a threat to national unity and security. The issue of dual or multiple loyalties of diasporic immigrants is often heralded by the conservative and right-wing political forces in order to limit their access to citizenship and political participation, and thus to reaffirm their marginal status (e.g., Turkish and Kurdish guest workers in Germany). Anti-immigrant tendencies have been further stimulated by the recent upsurge in international terrorism and the ensuing fears of the western nations that feel under attack and in an enhanced need for self-defense. Despite this backlash, contemporary global diasporas continue to question the binary mode of identity and loyalty to one nation-state and make hyphenated or multitiered identities more common and gradually more acceptable.

SEE ALSO: Assimilation; Ethnic Enclaves; Ethnic Groups; Ethnicity; Ethnonationalism; Globalization, Culture and; Middleman Minorities; Migration: International; Refugees; Transnationalism

REFERENCES AND SUGGESTED READINGS

Castells, M. (1996) *The Rise of the Network Society*. Blackwell, Oxford.

Cohen, R. (1997) *Global Diasporas: An Introduction*. University College of London Press, London.

Portes, A., Guarnizo, L., & Landolt, P. (1999) The Study of Transnationalism: Pitfalls and Promise of an Emerging Research Field. *Ethnic and Racial Studies* 22(2): 217–37.

Remennick, L. (2002) Transnational Community in the Making: Russian Jewish Immigrants of the 1990s in Israel. *Journal of Ethnic and Migration Studies* 28(3): 515–30.

Safran, W. (1991) Diasporas in Modern Societies: Myths of Homeland and Return. *Diaspora: A Journal of Transnational Studies* 1(1): 83–99.

Sheffer, G. (Ed.) (1986) *Modern Diasporas in International Politics*. Croom Helm, London and Sydney.

Shuval, J. T. (2001) Diaspora Migration: Definitional Ambiguities and a Theoretical Paradigm. *International Migration* 38(5): 41–57.

difference

Hasmita Ramji

The concept of difference seeks to recognize social diversity. Its growing profile is underpinned by a refiguration of the discourses of "multi," "commonality," and "universalism" in a variety of arenas and forms. Spurred by the postmodern turn, difference has been a key way to problematize universal categories such as "women" and "men." An analysis of gender, race, and other categories of difference points to the multilayered and fractured construction of collective and individual identities. The current interest in difference has in part been because of a belief that as a concept it can illuminate social diversity, but also in part because of its importance in recent recognition claims. Debates here have highlighted the relational underpinnings of diversity. What has attracted attention is "what are significant markers of difference in society" and "how are they made so"? The creation of difference on the basis of race, gender, or class at social, economic, and political levels is crucial, not as individual characteristics but insofar as they are primary organizing principles of a society which locates and positions groups within opportunity structures. They can unlock how social inequality is created.

The key importance of difference in social existence was highlighted by the deconstructionism of Derrida. Derrida's starting point was his rejection of a common model of knowledge and language, according to which understanding something requires acquaintance with its meaning – ideally a kind of acquaintance in which this meaning is directly present to consciousness. For him, this model involved the "myth of presence," the supposition that we gain our best understanding of something when it – and it alone – is present to consciousness. He argued that understanding something requires a grasp of the ways in which it relates to other things, and a capacity to recognize it on other occasions and in different contexts – which can never be exhaustively predicted. He coined the term "differance" (*différance* in French, combining the meanings of difference and deferral) in 1968 in response to structuralist theories of language (such as Saussure's structuralist linguistics) to characterize these aspects of understanding, and proposed that differance is the phenomenon lying at the heart of language and thought, at work in all meaningful activities in a necessarily elusive and provisional way.

The deconstructionist account of difference argues that opposites are already united; they depend on each other integrally; thus, there is no black without white, etc. Reality is fragmented and saturated with difference, and language is a key way of understanding this fragmentation. Derrida quotes Saussure, who wrote: "in language there are only differences. Even more important: a difference generally implies positive terms between which the difference is set up; but in language there are only differences without positive terms." Derrida reemphasizes the point that meaning is not in the signifier itself, but that it only exists in a network, in relation to other things. *Différance* comes before being. This throws the idea of "origin," of true original meaning, into radical question. With the idea of origin in question, Derrida pushes further than Saussure did to claim that there is no absolute identity, nothing that "is itself" by virtue of its being. This can be related to the current debate in multicultural societies about difference.

The key issue, for many, is not about "difference" per se, but about the question of who defines difference, how different categories of previously conceived universal categories (e.g., women) are represented within the discourses of "difference," and whether "difference" differentiates laterally or hierarchically. How does difference designate the "other"? Who defines difference? What are the presumed norms from which a group is marked as being different? What is the nature of attributions that are claimed as characterizing a group as different? How are boundaries of difference constituted, maintained, or dissipated? How is difference interiorized in the landscapes of the psyche? How are various groups represented in different discourses of difference? Questions such as these raise a more general problematic about difference as an analytical category. Brah (1996) suggests four ways in which difference may be conceptualized: difference as experience, difference as social relations, difference as subjectivity, and difference as identity.

The concept of difference, then, refers to the variety of ways in which specific discourses of difference are constituted, contested, reproduced, or resignified. Some constructions of difference, such as racism, posit fixed and immutable boundaries between groups signified as inherently different. Other constructions may present difference as relational, contingent, and variable. In other words, difference is not always a marker of hierarchy and oppression. Therefore, it is a contextually contingent question whether difference pans out as inequity, exploitation, and oppression or as egalitarianism, diversity, and democractic forms of political agency. Sandra Harding expresses the shift best in her claim that "there are no gender relations per se, but only gender relations that are constructed by and between classes, races, and cultures" (in Zinn & Dill 1999: 104).

Charles Taylor's (1994) seminal essay discusses difference as a need for (individual) recognition. Increasing cultural diversity and the emergence of multiculturalism leads to potentially contradictory discourses on two levels. On the one hand, the politics of universalism means emphasizing the equal dignity of individuals through the equalization of rights and entitlements. On the other hand, the modern notion of identity has given rise to a politics of difference, based on recognition of the unique identity of individuals or groups, and their distinctness from everyone else. The politics of universalism require norms of non-discrimination which are blind to difference, while the politics of difference require special rights and treatment for certain groups.

The contradictory implications of the recognition of difference that Taylor's work highlights are apparent in recent feminist debates. Many feminists now contend that difference occupies a central stage as the project of women's studies today. If difference has helped revitalize academic feminisms, it has also "upset the apple cart" and introduced new conflicts into feminist studies. For example, in a widely discussed essay, Jane Rowland Martin argues that the current preoccupation with difference is leading feminism into dangerous traps. She fears that it is giving privileged status to a predetermined set of analytical categories (race, ethnicity, and class): "we affirm the existence of nothing but difference" (in Zinn & Dill 1999: 104). Despite the much-heralded diversity trend within feminist studies, difference is often reduced to mere pluralism: a "live and let live" approach where principles of relativism generate a long list of diversities which begin with gender, class, and race and continue through a range of social structural as well as personal characteristics.

However, despite seeing the pitfalls in some strands of the difference project, it is still the case that it has prised open discursive closures which asserted the primacy of, say, class or gender over all other axes of differentiation, and it has interrogated the constructions of such privileged signifiers as unified autonomous cores. The political subject of black feminism, for example, decenters the unitary, masculinist subject of Eurocentric discourse, as well as masculinist rendering of "black" as a political color, while seriously disrupting any notion of "woman" as a unitary category.

Conceptualizing the postmodern category of difference, then, remains paramount. Breaking down the barriers of artificial (socially constructed) difference enables the cultural politics of genuine difference based on achieving the principles of justice, freedom, and equality for students occupying varying historical locations

to commence. Giroux organized his understanding of the concept of difference into the categories of conservative, liberal, and radical (Miron 1999). There is a clear relevance to contemporary multicultural politics in western societies. As Giroux observes, conservative ideological forces such as the New Right have invoked the notion of difference to justify social relations of racism, male dominance, and classism. Invoking the supposed natural laws of science and culture, New Right groups have justified these unequal power relations by equating the category of difference with the idea of deviance.

SEE ALSO: Deconstruction; Derrida, Jacques; Postmodern Social Theory; Postmodernism

REFERENCES AND SUGGESTED READINGS

Brah, A (1996) *Cartographies of Diaspora*. Routledge, London.
Derrida, J. (1976) *Of Grammatology*. Johns Hopkins University Press, Baltimore.
Derrida, J. (1979) *Writing and Difference*. Routledge & Kegan Paul, London.
Miron, F. L (1999) Postmodernism and the Politics of Racialized Identities. In: Torres, R. D., Miron, L. F., & Inda, J. X (Eds.), *Race, Identity, and Citizenship: A Reader*. Blackwell, Oxford, pp. 79–100.
Taylor, C. (1994) The Politics of Recognition. In: Gutmann, A. (Ed.), *Multiculturalism: Examining the Politics of Recognition*. Princeton University Press, Princeton, pp. 25–74.
Zinn, M. B. & Dill, B. T. (1999) Theorizing Difference from Multiracial Feminism. In: Torres, R. D., Miron, L. F., & Inda, J. X (Eds.), *Race, Identity, and Citizenship: A Reader*. Blackwell, Oxford, pp. 103–11.

differential treatment of children by sex

Erin Trapp and Jane Menken

In nearly all populations, in the absence of special circumstances, the numbers of males and females are approximately equal; female advantage in life expectancy balances the slightly higher birth rate of boys. Cultural practices such as infanticide, differential feeding, and provision of health care by sex have, in some populations in the past, led to an unequal ratio of boys to girls and higher mortality and morbidity for girls compared to boys. The last two decades of the twentieth century have, however, seen a rapid convergence in the treatment of children by sex, particularly in the developed world. Despite improvements in the treatment of girls and women, inequalities still exist, most notably in developing countries in Asia and Africa.

FUNDAMENTAL CAUSES AND SOCIAL CONTEXT

In the developed world, waning parental preference for sons has led to a corresponding decline in differential treatment of children by sex. In the past, sex preferences were thought to be the result of the differing value of children of each sex in many cultures, gender roles enforced by traditionally patriarchal societies, and the desire of both parents to have a child whose sex matches their own. The decline in sex preference is thought to be the result of increased gender equality and broad attitudinal shifts across economic and socioeconomic lines. Further, in industrialized countries, children are seen less as an economic asset, but rather an economic burden due to educational and maintenance costs associated with extended adolescence. Therefore, sex preference is a value only the very well-off can afford.

Evidence of a decline in differential treatment of children by sex also is abundant in many parts of the developing world, but disparities remain. In parts of Asia, previously observed advantages in male life expectancy have disappeared, and more girls now have access to education. Sex preferences in traditionally patrilocal societies were thought to be immutably embedded in cultural, religious, and behavioral norms. Change has occurred, but only in the context of some combination of fertility decline, female empowerment, and/or economic development, which are necessary, if not sufficient, conditions for improvement in the status of women and girls. Additionally,

since high rates of fertility permit sex preferences to be satisfied easily, fertility transition also corresponds with declining sex preference.

In populations in which male life expectancy exceeds that of females, the differential usually is attributed to cultural practices that lead to discrimination against girls and women and to the low social standing of mothers and their lack of power within the household. Maternal education and well-being generally are found to lead to more equal treatment of children, affecting their mortality and morbidity as well as life chances. The higher standing of these mothers in the household is believed to be responsible for these changes. However, some research finds that maternal education has a negligible effect on standing in the household. Further, while mortality rates have equalized in many countries, girls still may experience higher rates of morbidity, including malnutrition, wasting, and/or stunting.

These changes illustrate a shift in our understanding of differential treatment of children, and point to resource-dependent causes of differential treatment of family members, including household economies, the cost and efficacy of fertility control, education, and family planning.

MAJOR DIMENSIONS OF REMAINING DISPARITIES IN DEVELOPING COUNTRIES

The existence and effects of differential treatment of children by sex in developing countries can be illustrated in three major areas: mortality, health, and education. Although mortality (expressed in higher than expected ratios of boys to girls, higher mortality rates for girls, and/or a male life expectancy advantage) is the most obvious outcome of differential treatment, human capital effects such as poor health and less education provide evidence of disparities in treatment short of death.

Higher rates of mortality in girls than boys or higher than expected sex ratios favoring males, the clearest demonstration of the preference for sons, are found in some countries in Africa and Asia (most notably China, discussed below). Little documentation of excess female mortality exists outside of these regions.

Further, discerning female disadvantage from mortality data can be difficult because biological factors favor girls, so that female disadvantage may actually be more severe than is immediately apparent.

In the 1970s and 1980s, the median sex ratio of infant mortality in 82 countries in Latin America, Asia, and Africa averaged 118 male deaths to 100 female deaths; the median ratio was much lower in countries in Northern Africa (111), Western Asia (111), and South-Central Asia (108), suggesting regional concentrations of female disadvantage. Significant female disadvantage, particularly in infant mortality, also is reported in the Middle Eastern Crescent. Factors such as low income, lack of maternal education, inadequate health care use, and large family size are associated with higher mortality risks in South Asia and affect all children. However, girls' excess mortality risks transcend socioeconomic status, and more recent studies continue to find selective neglect of girls based on certain sex and birth-order combinations. For example, those with an older surviving sister may fare less well than those without a sister. Research evaluating programs aimed at reducing child mortality has found that improved maternal education serves to decrease child mortality as well as to equalize child mortality by sex, but sex differentials still exist.

These differentials in mortality are troubling, but fail to capture the human capital consequences of female disadvantage adequately. According to the United Nations (1998), child health disparities, like mortality disparities, by sex are most evident in South-Central Asia, and girls in Northern and Western Africa also experience poorer health than boys due to disparate treatment. Girls in three countries in South-Central Asia (Bangladesh, northern India, and Pakistan) also are far less likely to receive necessary immunizations than boys, although differential rates of immunization are small in other parts of the world and do not favor either sex. Studies of morbidity typically use malnutrition, wasting, and/or stunting to pinpoint the existence and mechanisms of differential treatment. In Bangladesh, nutritional and educational differences that were previously reported have narrowed after two decades of fertility decline. In India family

composition rather than sex leads to poorer health; both boys and girls with two or more surviving siblings of the same sex are worse off in terms of severe stunting and incomplete immunization. By contrast, evidence exists of better nourishment among girls than boys in six African countries. Although trends are not the same everywhere, the status and treatment of girls is improving in Asia and Africa, but significant room for improvement still exists.

The well-known benefits of education in developing countries include declining fertility, improved child mortality and morbidity rates, improved health and status of women, and more educational attainment for subsequent generations. Yet educational opportunities remain limited, and female enrollment in primary school is significantly lower than male enrollment in 39 out of 40 developing countries in one study, which leads to higher mortality risks for girls than boys in these countries. Education differences persist at nearly all levels of socioeconomic status. Adherence to traditional gender roles in many countries contributes to unequal rates of education, with girls benefiting less from educational opportunities in Ghana, for example, and at higher risk of dropping out of school. In Thailand, the belief prevails that schooling is more important for boys than for girls. Thus, while family planning and economic development programs have improved girls' educational prospects in the developing world and their education has increased, traditional attitudes and resource limitations continue to limit opportunities for formal schooling.

AN IN-BETWEEN CASE: CHINA

China often is thought of as an "in-between" case, straddling the developed and developing worlds. As such, the treatment of children in China provides a stark example of the changes in the treatment of children by sex over time. Cultural preferences for sons led to high rates of female infanticide as late as the 1950s, a practice that waned with the establishment of the People's Republic of China, and a strong government that enacted policies aimed at modifying this and other cultural norms. However, the interruption in excess female mortality during this period was brief due to famines experienced during the Great Leap Forward, and high rates of "missing" girls have persisted since the establishment of the one-child policy in 1979. In this later period, sex-selective abortion and adopting-out of females are thought to be the means used to create the unequal ratio of boys and girls. The Chinese government modified the one-child policy in rural areas in the late 1990s, allowing families with a first-born daughter to pay "social compensation fees" in order to have an additional child, partially in response to this demographic imbalance. Yet China still is experiencing a deficit of marriageable girls, which could in turn affect the norms favoring boys and actually increase the value of daughters, lead to practices such as infant betrothal and bride buying, and create a large glut of unmarried men (already underway).

CURRENT EMPHASES, METHODOLOGICAL ISSUES, PROBLEMS, AND FUTURE DIRECTIONS

It is important to note that a high ratio of boys to girls exists in Korea, illustrating the potential for cultural practices to persist even absent government policies like those in China. Therefore, the need to study the differential treatment of children by sex – a complex and expensive process – persists. In particular, data concerning household allocation of resources that illustrate intra-household access to nutrition, education, health care, and other resources are time consuming and labor intensive to collect. Proxy measures such as weight- and height-for-age and weight-for-height (body mass index) are useful for measuring child treatment, absent direct observation, but have their own limitations. Low weight-for-age is considered an indicator of recent morbidity or poor nutrition, while low height-for-age is used as a marker of long-term or chronic malnutrition. Yet the lack of an international, developing world-based set of standards by which to judge the health of children is particularly troubling. Although the World Health Organization has endorsed a nutritional standard for developing countries that classifies a child as malnourished if weight-for-age is more than two

standard deviations below the median in the standard population from the US, researchers recognize that a standard based on US children may be inappropriate in developing world contexts, particularly given the growing problem of obesity in American children. Further, the biologically different rates at which children of both sexes develop confounds our understanding of their treatment in the home.

Increasingly, we recognize the interdependence of resource and cultural theories of child preference and treatment. Resource-dependent explanations in the past suggested that parents would only value daughters for the economic benefit they bring to the household. Yet if this were the case, the dividends accruing from increased budgets or smaller family sizes would merely be used to more aggressively discriminate against daughters. Conversely, declining sex preferences can be expected to occur only if the status of women and their relative importance to their parents increases. Improvements in female nutrition, education, and status provide potentially powerful insight into this hypothesis. They suggest that family planning, microcredit, and other programs aimed at women's empowerment have a direct effect on incentives to invest in daughters. It is also possible, however, that declining gender inequality in child outcomes reflects not just the role of programs in subsidizing and encouraging investment in daughters, but an increasing awareness of an emerging equalization of sons' and daughters' roles in providing support in old age.

Given the success in changing cultural practices that favor boys, development programs that aim to improve the status of girls have taken many shapes. In South Asia, girls' education has increased, in part through government scholarship programs aimed at girls. Microcredit programs such as those run by Grameen Bank and BRAC in Bangladesh focus specifically on empowering women to participate in market and monetary activities. Employment of women outside the home has become acceptable and opportunities for their employment now exist, especially in the cities.

Unequal treatment of children by sex continues, with particularly egregious examples of female disadvantage found in developing countries in Africa and South Asia. There is room for optimism, however, as differential valuation and treatment of children by sex is largely disappearing in developed countries. Further, traditional cultural practices in developing countries that favor sons appear to be subject to economic forces and resource development, and programs aimed at family planning, educating women, and providing health care to families appear to reduce differentials by sex in mortality, morbidity, and education.

SEE ALSO: Family Demography; Family Structure and Child Outcomes; Fertility and Public Policy; Gender Bias; Gender, Health, and Mortality; Inequality/Stratification, Gender; Infant, Child, and Maternal Health and Mortality; Socialization, Gender

REFERENCES AND SELECTED READINGS

Coale, A. J. & Banister, J. (1994) Five Decades of Missing Females in China. *Demography* 31: 459.
Das Gupta, M., Jiang, Z., Xie, Z., Li, B., Chung, W., & Bae, H. O. (2003) Why is Son Preference So Persistent in East and South Asia? A Cross-Country Study of China, India, and the Republic of Korea. *Journal of Development Studies* 40: 153–87.
Hill, K. & Upchurch, D. M. (1995) Gender Differences in Child Health: Evidence from the Demographic Health Surveys. *Population and Development Review* 21: 127.
Knodel, J., Havanon, N., & Sittitrai, W. (1990) Family Size and the Education of Children in the Context of Rapid Fertility Decline. *Population and Development Review* 16: 31.
Pollard, M. S. & Morgan, S. P. (2002) Emerging Parental Gender Indifference? Sex Composition of Children and the Third Birth. *American Sociological Review* 67: 600.
United, Nations (1998) *Too Young to Die: Genes or Gender?* United Nations, New York.

digital

Luke Goode

To understand the significance of the term "digital," we must place it alongside its "other" – the term "analogue." The technical distinction between these terms is relatively straightforward. Each signifies a different method by which data are captured, transported, processed, distributed, and represented, that is, the means by which they are *mediated*. Whilst analogue media "encode" data using "traces" – such as light burnt on to chemical film stock, or grooves cut into vinyl records – whose patterns have a physical connection to the source data, digital media translate source data into strings of binary computer code lacking that physical connection. Like the written word, digital code is an "arbitrary" signifier. Unlike the written word, however, it is a system comprising just two "symbols" (the "on" and "off" states of an electrical current), making it unreadable by human beings (it first has to be translated back into analogue forms such as light or sound waves) and robust enough to encode many different types of data simultaneously, including words, images, and sounds.

A commonly held assumption is that whilst we may still be in a transition phase, the future will be wholly digital. This is problematic on both technological and cultural grounds. Technologically, mediation is never *purely* digital: when "Cypher" in *The Matrix* (1999) performs the unthinkable feat of reading raw digital code – green cascades of zeros and ones – even he is separated from the data by two layers of representation: light waves represent a numeric system which, in turn, constitutes a cultural representation of the underlying molecular activity occurring within the machine. Culturally, moreover, the digitization of the mediascape constitutes a process that contributes to a range of complex tensions and conflicts, rather than a gestalt switch pitting "old" against "new." Digitization reconfigures some very old social and cultural issues. These include: access and democracy; authorship and intellectual property; and the social status of competing cultural forms. Other controversies linked with digitization may be more recent but also have pre-digital genealogies. These include: the globalization of media; the significance of "interactivity"; and the ascendancy of "network" and "decentered" models of social agency within sociological discourse. Digitization, then, is best understood as a tension-charged process which spans and provides a stage for various social controversies. As such, we can avoid the twin pitfalls of *technological determinism*, which treats technological change as an independent cause of broader social changes, and *technological voluntarism*, which overlooks the role technology plays in shaping various choices faced by human societies by assuming that the significance of technology lies only in the uses to which human actors choose to put it.

CHARACTERISTICS OF DIGITAL MEDIA

It can be argued that computers have always functioned as communications media. From their inception, they have both enabled *and* shaped (i.e., mediated) various forms of communication between *humans* (as in computer-generated data used in scientific discourse), and between *machines* (as in early military "cybernetics" research on computer-guided missiles), as well as between humans *and* machines (as in early artificial intelligence experiments or chess-playing computers). But the term "digital media" is usually associated with a cluster of more recent developments: the rise of the PC, multimedia applications, video games, and the popularization of the Internet, to name a few. These developments collectively brought the computer into the purview of everyday popular culture. And, as computers became conduits for images and sounds (and for "entertainment"), and not merely alphanumeric data, they became "media machines." As digital technology was becoming more "mediatized," extant media were becoming more digitized. Media industries began to explore new outreach opportunities, including the Internet and proprietary digital broadcasting and telecommunications networks.

Discussions of digital media have revolved especially around two keywords: "interactivity" and "convergence." In the analogue era, interactivity was limited by various factors. Production and transmission facilities were costly. In the case of broadcast technologies, spectrum was scarce and had to be carefully managed. (Concerns about the power of radio and television as a propaganda tool were also drivers for political regulation of access to the airwaves.) In the digital age, the situation is radically changed. Streams of digital code can be transmitted in close proximity without causing the interference that would occur with analogue data. They can also be compressed to eliminate redundant data. As such, digitization dramatically increases data flow capacity through channels such as copper telephone wires, radio waves, and fiber-optic cables. In principle, the traditional "mass media" imbalance between "transmitters" and "receivers" could be radically reduced (a hope that predates the digital era as in the Brechtian vision of democratic radio and, later, public access television experiments). In reality, most digital broadcasting and broadband Internet networks are structured asymmetrically with greater "download" than "upload" capacity, countering this potential "democratizing" effect.

The singular term "interactivity" is problematic because it conflates diverse possibilities (Manovich 2000), including: forms of conversation, e.g., in chat rooms, via mobile phones or email; distributed or "networked" cultural production, e.g., collaborative "net art"; menu-based interactivity and "bespoke" media, e.g., selecting the camera angle for an action replay during televised sport; multilinear navigation that has users determining a sequence of events or data, e.g., video games or hypertext literature; and experiments in reality TV and game shows where audiences can influence the narrative through remote controls or cell phones.

It is important to note that various forms of "interactivity" predate digitization. These include talk radio, TV channel "zapping," and letters to the editor. Digitization has greatly expanded the scope for interactive practices *and* stimulated an unprecedented level of cultural fascination with "two-way" media. John Durham Peters (1999) suggests that contemporary fascination with the interactive potentials of digital media reflects a largely unquestioned tendency in western culture (with ancient, Socratic roots), to treat one-way communication as intrinsically inferior to conversation and dialogue.

Convergence is another digital keyword. The fact that all digital technology speaks the universal language of binary code has stimulated debate about the opportunities and dangers of media convergence. Digital data are, in principle, able to traverse and integrate different sites and devices (such as PCs, handheld computers, mobile phones, digital cameras), whereas different media remained largely discrete in the analogue era. Certainly, there is an unprecedented degree of connectivity between media and communications devices (interacting with TV shows via mobile phones, for example). This is a source of concern for some analysts, conjuring up images of a seamless, seductive, and commercialized web of information and entertainment that leaves little room for independent thought or engagement with the "real world." For others, it is a cause for optimism, promising not only convenience but also better communication flows: being able to switch between a television news report and a "primary source" it cites (such as a government document) may make us better informed, critical, and discerning citizens.

In reality, the "universal language" of digital code has been, and looks set to remain, beset by technological, cultural, and economic obstacles. Technologically, devices are actually programmed using various "higher-level" languages rather than binary code. Unless protocols are developed carefully and cooperatively, large-scale convergence remains a pipe dream. Corporations often prefer proprietary rather than common standards, in the hope of exerting greater control over markets and future innovations. Culturally, there are still question marks over the value of convergence. Despite unprecedented cross-media connectivity, the genres, conventions, locations, and discourses of various media are still characterized by a remarkable degree of separation: common technical standards will not necessarily lead to a melting pot of the diverse media forms that have emerged in the modern era.

A significant tension within digital discourse exists between visions dominated by "hi-fidelity," on the one hand, and "multiplication," on the other. In the first vision, the radical increase in data capacity afforded by the digitization of media networks is understood primarily as the basis for technically improved "signals": typically, these visions are populated by high-definition and wide-screen television sets, home-theater systems with pristine 3D audio, stunning cinematic realism in video games, virtual reality environments, CGI (computer-generated imagery) animations, and digital special effects. The second vision emphasizes instead the enlarged scope for multiplication and differentiation of media texts: here, the focus tends to be on the dense communication flows of the Internet, digital compression formats such as MP3 audio, the multiplication of channels, interactive services, and customization facilities in digital television, and the proliferation of mobile and increasingly miniaturized media devices including Internet-capable mobile phones and wireless handheld computers.

DIGITAL POLITICAL ECONOMY

A significant amount of sociological research and discourse has emerged as a reaction against the optimistic prognoses for the digital age offered by libertarian commentators in the early to mid-1990s. Influential analysts such as Nicholas Negroponte of the MIT Media Lab and his colleagues at *Wired* magazine, alongside various politicians from both the right and center-left, argued that digital technology heralded a new economy in which entrepreneurial individuals would triumph over large corporations. The Internet would become an arena of vigorous economic competition, where overheads would be slashed and great advantages would accrue to small electronic "cottage industries" that were sufficiently flexible to adapt quickly to changing market conditions. "Middlemen" such as advertisers and retailers would be swept aside as companies would interact directly with customers through "smart" systems able to automate and personalize transactions. In this account, the "cyberspace" economy would also make geography irrelevant, meaning that developing countries would be able to compete on a level playing field.

Since these optimistic forecasts, we have witnessed the infamous "dot.com" crash of the late 1990s. Financial markets finally lost confidence in the new economy as e-commerce enterprises, propped up by "venture capital," struggled to turn a profit. From the beginning, however, a strong vein of skeptical discourse challenged the claims of the optimistic libertarians. For example, research has highlighted the large vested interests that control the gateways to digital networks such as the Internet, and the rise of "electronic sweatshops" in the developing world whereby corporations outsource database management, technical support, and other aspects of digital industry to low-wage economies. Dan Schiller's (1999) neo-Marxist analysis of "digital capitalism" argues that networks such as the World Wide Web, digital broadcasting, and mobile telecommunications lend themselves to hyperlinked webs of mass consumption, advertising, and marketing, favoring corporate synergies and vested interests rather than independent or small-scale producers. Much attention has also been directed toward the global "digital divide," where unequal access to digital technology is patterned by class and gender, but also by factors such as age, language, culture, and geography. In order to participate in digital networks, both specific and transferable skills have to be acquired by older generations, whilst they are increasingly "second nature" for younger people socialized within technology-rich environments. In terms of language and culture, American English is a virtual lingua franca in globalized digital environments; and in terms of geography, even affluent rural populations often have poorer access to digital networks than their urban counterparts.

With the libertarian discourse losing much of its potency, sociological discourses on digital political economy have begun to shift in emphasis, supplementing macro analysis of ownership, control, and the corporatization of digital networks with closer attention to particular sites of tension and contestation. In particular, issues of intellectual property and "digital rights management" have a major currency. The "open source" movement promotes the development and distribution of non-copyright software "source code." Although the movement is characterized by some internal tensions, for the most part it is motivated by something other than simple antipathy toward large corporations such as Microsoft. The movement is also imbued with ideals that can be traced back to the 1960s and 1970s "hacker" counterculture. Here, digital networks are considered to be a matter of public, and not merely private, interest. Society as a whole stands to benefit from new technology, in this account, and technologies develop most efficiently when anybody with the requisite expertise can contribute to their development. Interestingly, echoes of the early hacker counterculture also resonate in the libertarian discourse mentioned above. *Wired* magazine, for example, has frequently promoted the values of "netizenship" and digital democracy, celebrating the potential role of digital networks as spaces for political debate, polling, and voting. Libertarian groups campaigning against government regulation and censorship of the Internet have drawn heavily on hacker idealism which argues that information must be "set free."

By comparison with the open source movement, the development of file-sharing networks in which copyrighted music, movies, and other media are freely circulated does not readily lend itself to analysis as a "movement." Instrumental motives, guilty pleasures, and anti-corporate values can all play their part in these complex, anonymous, and contradictory spaces. Another fertile area for analysis is the emergence of flexible digital copyright arrangements, such as the "Creative Commons" license, which, unlike the "all rights reserved" arrangements favored by large corporations, allows for compromise between authorial rights and the impulse, prevalent within digital culture, to treat borrowing, sampling, and remixing as an integral aspect of creativity.

Opportunities and constraints in digital creative industries constitute another important aspect of political economy. On the one hand, digitization has made many areas of cultural production more capital intensive, to the detriment of small-scale and independent producers. Special effects budgets have tended to spiral upwards, for example, as sophisticated illusions and visual spectacles become increasingly de rigueur for popular films, television shows, and music videos. Some smaller-scale digital ventures and creative industries in smaller countries have, though, benefited from the outsourcing of digital graphics and special effects by Hollywood studios and other large media corporations. On the other hand, "second-tier" desktop technologies have tended to advance rapidly in terms of sophistication and to decline rapidly in cost. Technical capabilities in music, film, animation, and publishing that were only recently the sole preserve of the few are becoming much more widely accessible. To generalize, the paradox of digitization is that it has opened the way for burgeoning sites of diverse, creative, and increasingly sophisticated independent cultural production, but opportunities for making a living by it or getting mainstream distribution are fewer and further between.

DIGITAL CREATIVITY

Although "digital culture" is generally associated with novel and rapidly changing practices, we are already witnessing the emergence and consolidation of various digital "disciplines," each demanding specific skills and approaches, and each giving rise to particular styles, conventions, and genres. Some of the key disciplines include: digital imaging; digital video; animation; 3D graphic design; digital music and sound design; web and interface design. But despite the emergence of these distinct disciplines, many "digital creatives" (and employers) attach great importance to flexible and cross-disciplinary skills.

Digital creative and aesthetic tactics are too diverse to summarize here. But we can at least point to some recurring themes that are best understood as a series of tensions rather than a coherent set of principles. The first of these is the tension between immersion and self-referentialism. Whilst digital special effects and 3D animation are often geared toward the creation of believable, "hyperreal" fantasy worlds, into which audiences, players, and users can become immersed, temporarily suspending their awareness of their artificiality, many digital cultural forms (such as dance and hip-hop music, and various styles of graphic design) actively emphasize their technological provenance through the appearance of phenomena such as dissonant juxtapositions, "noise" (e.g., deliberately "pixellated" images or warped sounds), or computer-related tropes (computer-related noises or icons, for example). Some digital forms, such as computer games, that switch between sequences of "cinematic realism" and complex "interface" shots featuring level indicators, maps, and so forth combine both perspectives. The importance of the "interface" is, itself, a strong theme in digital culture. The way we interact with digital texts (with a mouse and cursor, for example) can become so culturally familiar as to recede from view. But alongside the desire to create self-effacing and naturalistic interfaces, digital culture is also characterized by frequent experiments with novel types of interface designed to be interesting and stimulating in their own right, rather than simply a conduit for "content." Examples include the still young discipline of DVD interface design, which often brings elements of gaming into the experience of filmic consumption, many computer games themselves, and experimental website interfaces.

A related tension within visual digital culture revolves around the status of two different elements of creativity: the "pixel" and the "vector." A digital imaging tradition has emerged that places great store by compositing (merging multiple images in technically proficient, though frequently surrealistic, fashion), texture (shading, shadows, and grain), depth (building images out of multiple "layers"), blending (seamless as opposed to harsh juxtaposition), and visual "noise" (blurs, graininess, and washed-out colors, for example). In other words, there is a strong "painterly" tradition in digital imaging. This tradition is caught between the desire to showcase the visual feats of digital technology and the desire to erase its cold, machinic characteristics in favor of something more organic (something mirrored in hip-hop and other pop music forms, where scratches, hisses, and so forth are used to add depth or "authenticity"). But a very different tradition has also emerged, based on mathematical "vectors" rather than pixels. "Vector" images are comprised of lines and flat color fills, whereas "bitmap" images, such as digital photographs and complex textures, represent matrices of discrete pixels that each have their own hue, saturation, and brightness values. Because vector images contain fewer data and are scalable (they can be enlarged indefinitely without deteriorating in quality), they lend themselves to more efficient distribution over digital networks such as the Internet and to "repurposing," that is, they can easily be transferred between different sites, from large billboards to miniature handheld devices. The vector tradition is populated by many different styles including a minimalist and geometric modernism, and brash, cartoonish styles evoking a range of aesthetic influences including pop art, trash culture South Park style, "Japanimation," and Nintendo. Experiments in combining the vector and bitmap traditions continue to grow.

Linearity is another important site of tension within digital aesthetics. Early fascination with hypertext literature where readers construct their own pathways through texts, with cyclical loops in digital video and dance music, and with split screen or "windowed" video and computer screens, contributed to a sense that digitization heralded the ascendancy of a non-linear and spatial (as opposed to temporal) media culture. The emergence of devices such as MP3 players or hard-disk digital video recorders, which allow for previously linear forms to break down in favor of more archival, random access structures, gives even more credence to this view. This is complicated, however, by the growing popularity of time-based digital forms, including filmic sequences in computer games, "Flash" animation on the World Wide Web, and the online phenomenon of "blogging." At most, we can say that digital culture is increasingly "multilinear," rather than "non-linear."

As well as calling into question the concept of beginnings, middles, and ends, digital texts often call into question the idea of the center, traditionally premised on the figure of the "author," "auteur," or "artist" as "originator." Whilst hypertexts have been heralded as exemplars of the poststructuralist "death of the author" thesis, many digital texts appear to take this theme even further in two senses: firstly, the prevalence of "sampling," modifying and remixing, within audiovisual culture, where very basic digital tools allow for the multiplication of pristine and malleable copies of "original" texts, has aroused debates not only around ethics and copyright, but also around the value of originality in the digital age; secondly, digital texts that are designed to be reworked over and over by multiple "authors," such as collaborative "net art" projects, call into question the stability of the text and the notion of origins, authors, and centers. But despite these postmodern characteristics, digital media such as desktop video production suites, "virtual" music studios, and blogging tools multiply the opportunities and sites for individuals to become "authors," "artists," and "auteurs" and, if anything, modern dreams of

authorship and publicity are being nourished rather than diminished in the digital age.

SEE ALSO: Author/Auteur; Hyperreality; Internet; McLuhan, Marshall; Media; Media and Globalization; Multimedia; Poststructuralism; Semiotics; Simulation and Virtuality; Technological Determinism; Technological Innovation; Technology, Science, and Culture; Text/Hypertext

REFERENCES AND SUGGESTED READINGS

Bolter, J. D. & Grusin, R. (1999) *Remediation: Understanding New Media*. MIT Press, Cambridge, MA.

Cubitt, S. (1998) *Digital Aesthetics*. Sage, London.

Lessig, L. (2004) *Free Culture: How Big Media Uses Technology and the Law to Lock Down Culture and Control Creativity*. Penguin Press, New York.

Manovich, L. (2000) *The Language of New Media*. MIT Press, Cambridge, MA.

Negroponte, N. (1996) *Being Digital*. Coronet, London.

Peters, J. D. (1999) *Speaking into the Air: A History of the Idea of Communication*. University of Chicago Press, Chicago.

Schiller, D. (1999) *Digital Capitalism: Networking the Global Market System*. MIT Press, Cambridge, MA.

direct action

Kelly Moore

Direct action is a method and a theory of stopping objectionable practices or creating more favorable conditions using immediately available means to obstruct another agent or organization from performing some objectionable practice. It is direct in the sense that users seek an immediate remedy for perceived ills, as opposed to indirect tactics such as electing representatives who promise to provide remedy at some later date. Direct action is usually undertaken by individuals and groups for three reasons: the group believes that the urgency of the problem requires immediate intervention; they believe that any other form of action is unlikely to solve the problem; they do not have rights to affect targets in any other way. Examples of direct action include vigils, blockades, wildcat strikes, demonstrations, the occupation of buildings and other spaces, the destruction of property, street parties and theater, encampments, and symbolic illegal activities, such as cutting one piece of wire from a fence surrounding a military base to protest war.

The use of strategies to invoke an immediate response to an injustice is not new. For thousands of years people have drawn attention to problems using immediate means, such as "rough music," refusal to work, and attacks on property. The use of the term direct action did not emerge until the late nineteenth century during labor struggles and revolutionary activity in Western Europe, Russia, and the US.

There are two main political theories that have advocated and justified the use of direct action. The first is anarchism. Anarchism is a political philosophy that first emerged during the Enlightenment. It rejects the moral legitimacy and utility of the state, and advocates instead the organization of individuals into self-governing groups and federations. It was not until the nineteenth century that writers such as Proudhon, Bakunin, Kropotkin, and Goodwin began fully to develop anarchism as a viable means of governing. In the 1870s Bakunin, a Russian-born writer and active participate in the labor movement, first articulated the link between direct action and the achievement of an anarchist political system (Crowder 1991).

The second political theory of direct action is based on the ideas and practices of the Indian political leader, Mohandas K. Gandhi. In the early twentieth century he began to develop a new form of direct action. His method, called Satyagraha or "the way of truth," greatly influenced many other users of direct action in the twentieth and twenty-first centuries. Satyagraha was inspired by the writings of Tolstoy and Ruskin, and by Gandhi's Hindu religious beliefs. The core principle of Satyagraha was the appeal to the moral goodness of opponents through the acceptance of the consequences of refusing to participate in unjust systems (Diwakar 1949). Users of Satyagraha were required to make sacrifices, such as fasting, and be prepared and willing to accept the consequences of their actions, including incarceration or violence. Between 1906 and 1913 Gandhi worked for equal rights for Indians in South Africa using Satyagraha. Thousands of people went to jail for refusing to pay an annual tax levied on former indentured servants, among whom were Indians, and for refusing to carry identification papers that the government required of Indians. He later used this method to help unite Indians and help them gain independence from Great Britain in 1947.

Gandhi's methods inspired religiously based peace and civil rights activists in the US during the 1940s, 1950s, and 1960s. Men who refused to fight in World War II for religious or other moral reasons were given conscientious objector status and assigned to work camps. Some of the members of the camps refused to engage in menial or degrading labor because they believed that they should be able to contribute to ending the war in more significant ways. Many were jailed as a result of their refusal to cooperate with camp authorities. At the end of the war some of those who were jailed and other religiously based peace activists used Satyagraha methods. Among them were the Moscow–San Francisco Peace March in 1961, sailing a boat into nuclear testing zones in the South Pacific, and refusal to cooperate with government-mandated civil defense drills. Martin Luther King, Jr., the leader of the civil rights group Southern Christian Leadership Conference, used methods based on Satyagraha in a series of campaigns to end segregation in the Southern United States between 1954 and 1965. These methods included the use of sit-ins, Freedom Rides, and mass arrest. In the 1960s and 1970s people involved in ending the war in Vietnam also used Gandhi's methods, but evolved them into more confrontational forms such as destroying draft cards and the occupation of buildings.

The use of direct action took a more carnival-like and celebratory form when it was used by anti-Vietnam War activists and members of the counterculture in the late 1960s. Taking inspiration from the Bohemian art community in San Francisco, groups such as the Diggers, Yippies, and the San Francisco Mime Troupe used direct action that embodied principles of freedom, playfulness, and joy. Distributing free food, engaging in street theater, and mocking traditional culture through new styles of dress and living, as well as parodying conventional life, were hallmarks of these groups.

In the late 1960s and early 1970s the use of violent direct action reemerged as the mass-based political movements of the previous decade dissolved. Small, armed, underground, clandestine groups such as the Weather Underground and the German Red Army Faction used robbery and murder to try to start a revolution. During this same time a practice known as "monkeywrenching" was used by ecological activists in the Southwestern United States. Rejecting the legal strategy of environmentalists that had developed in the 1960s, ecological activists destroyed equipment used for logging and other activities that they believed were used to harm the environment.

In the contemporary period, anarchist-inspired direct action, Satyagraha-based passive resistance and moral witnessing, and celebratory direct action can be found in some of the more distinctive forms of earlier periods, and also in more blended forms. Among the most important recent developments is the use of celebratory activities with other kinds of more confrontational direct action. Global justice groups such as the Direct Action Network and People's Global Action, for example, use festivity as well as more serious demonstrations to draw attention to their claims and to build solidarity among themselves. Two other developments that have attracted attention are the growing use of property destruction and violence, especially among radical environmental and animal rights groups, and the role of the police in suppressing direct action.

The earliest sociological study of the use of direct action tactics is Gamson's (1975) study of the relationship between tactics and organizational characteristics and the likelihood that a group wins concessions from targets. Gamson showed that groups that used violence were likely to win new concessions. Gamson's study treated tactics as a set of rationally chosen practices designed to elicit maximum results from opponents. McAdam (1982) and Morris (1986) are now classic studies of the use of direct action in the Civil Rights Movement that further developed Gamson's perspective. Both writers argued that Southern blacks use

marches, demonstrations, sit-ins, and Freedom Rides to end segregation because blacks had no other means of affecting the political system. In their view, direct action was primarily a rational tactic chosen for its ability to pressure opponents. Piven and Cloward's *Poor People's Movements* (1979) shared with earlier studies a focus on when direct action works. They argued that the poor were more likely to win new benefits when they used disruptive tactics such as mass demonstrations and the illegal occupation of their targets' offices. Unlike Gamson, McAdam, and Morris, Piven and Cloward saw direct action as a result of high levels of frustration rather than rationally chosen strategies.

In the 1980s and 1990s the effectiveness of direct action continued to be a central focus of most sociological studies of the subject. In the 1990s writers began to examine several new questions, including how and why groups choose to use direct action techniques. Earlier research had focused on the strategic uses of direct action. New research began to examine the role of moral motivations and social identities in shaping choices to use direct action. One important area of research has been in religiously based direct action. In a study of direct action in the US between World War II and 1968, James Tracy (1996) shows that some peace activists were motivated to use civil disobedience because their religious beliefs compelled them to do so. The act of civil disobedience itself, not only its formal political practices, was considered a politically important act because it revealed the power of users' beliefs. Other research has found a similar pattern in studies of secular groups' choices about direct action, such as AIDS activists (Epstein 1991), women (Naples & Desai 2002), and anti-nuclear activists (Gamson 1989).

A second important direction of new research on direct action is to explain how the use of specific tactics spreads from one group or place to another. Since the middle of the twentieth century and in the present, activists have used workshops, conferences, and other meetings to teach others how to use specific direct action techniques. They also spread when people who used a tactic in one setting or geographical area make use of it in other settings and areas. There is less evidence that reading about or seeing new tactics, in the absence of face-to-face interaction between users and potential adopters, is a major method of diffusion.

The role of repression, in its direct and indirect forms, on the use of direct action is an important new area of research for students of social movements in general and of direct action in particular (Earl 2003). Repression can drive groups to become involved in clandestine and sometimes violent direct action, but it can also force groups to use more routinized or less dramatic direct action.

Direct action has been studied using a variety of research methods. Earlier studies often used survey techniques. Data on many instances in which direct action was used was collected to examine the factors that contributed to its success or failure. Gamson's study is exemplary of this tradition. This method is currently used to study diffusion processes. In this case, researchers count the number of times an action is used in one place or setting at one point in time, and then measure its presence at later times and other places. Another common method for studying direct action is the use of historical records, such as newspapers, personal correspondence, oral history, police reports, and organizational records, to recreate how and why groups chose to use direct action. Tracy's (1996) study is a good example of this method. More recently, researchers have begun to use field observation to gather information about how new tactics are created, and why and how they are used. In these cases, researchers spend time with social movement groups by participating in their meetings and sometimes engaging in direct action with them. This method has the advantage of providing researchers with richer understanding of what direct action means to users and how they decide to use it, but it is less useful for examining effectiveness.

One of the major new initiatives in the study of direct action is the analysis of terrorism. Terrorism is the collective use of violence, especially against people, to intimidate a group or government into granting political demands. Terrorism is not new. It has been used by political actors for many reasons, and usually targeted heads of states or other leaders. More recently, terrorists have used violence against civilians and bystanders and have killed large groups of people at a time. Terrorists are often conventionally understood to be mentally unbalanced or religious fanatics. Current research on armed, underground, clandestine groups and other users of terror, by contrast, has focused on the conditions under which people become involved in terrorist networks (Zwerman et al. 2000), the role of ideology (including religious ideology), and the failure of governments to respond to the demands of citizens.

SEE ALSO: Civil Rights Movement; Collective Action; New Left; Social Movements, Non-Violent

REFERENCES AND SUGGESTED READINGS

Crowder, G. (1991) *Classical Anarchism: The Political Thought of Godwin, Proudhon, Bakunin, and Kropotkin*. Oxford University Press, New York.

Diwakar, R. R. (1949) *Satyagraha in Action: A Brief Outline of Gandhiji's Satyagraha Campaigns*. Signet Press, Calcutta.

Earl, J. (2003) Tanks, Tear Gas, and Taxes: Toward a Theory of Movement Repression. *Sociological Theory* 21: 44–68.

Epstein, B. (1991) *Political Protest and Cultural Revolution: Nonviolent Direct Action in the 1970s and 1980s*. University of California Press, Berkeley.

Gamson, J. (1989) Silence, Death, and the Invisible Enemy: AIDS Activism and Social Movement "Newness." *Social Problems* 36: 351–67.

Gamson, W. A. (1975) *The Strategy of Social Protest*. Dorsey Press, Homewood, IL.

McAdam, D. (1982) *Political Process and the Development of Black Insurgency, 1930–1970*. University of Chicago Press, Chicago.

Morris, A. (1986) *Origins of the Civil Rights Movement: Black Communities Organizing for Change*. Free Press, New York.

Naples, N. A. and Desai, M. (2002) *Women's Activism and Globalization: Linking Global Struggles and Transnational Politics*. Routledge, New York.

Piven, F. F. & Cloward, R. A. (1979) *Poor People's Movements: How They Succeed, Why They Fail*. Vintage, New York.

Tracy, J. (1996) *Direct Action: Radical Pacifism From the Union Eight to the Chicago Seven*. University of Chicago Press, Chicago.

Zwerman, G., Steinhoff, P. G., & Porta, D. D. (2000) Disappearing Social Movements: Clandestinity in the Cycle of New Left Protest in the US, Japan, Germany, and Italy. *Mobilization* 5: 85–104.

disability as a social problem

Anne Waldschmidt

Common sense takes disability as a simple natural fact, but the sociology of disability emphasizes that disability has to be differentiated from impairment. Not every chronic health condition is acknowledged as disability. There are cultures in which the social fact of disability does not exist (Ingstad & Whyte 1995). Disability as a social problem has evolved as a product of the modern welfare state. With the beginning of modernity and, above all, during the period of industrialization, a line was drawn between "the disabled" and other poor and unemployed people. In the course of the twentieth century disability became a horizontal category of social stratification. Even today the ascription process is ambivalent: it includes rights and benefits as well as discrimination and segregation.

Despite many efforts, an internationally accepted definition of disability does not exist (Albrecht et al. 2001). Nonetheless, on the national level classifications that constitute disability as social fact are in operation. Pedagogical diagnostics defining special educational needs are of great significance for establishing individual positions not only in the school system but also in later life. Medical experts serve as gatekeepers to the rehabilitation system and have great influence on disability categories, while legislation and courts serve as agencies to control disability as social problem.

The World Health Organization (WHO) made special efforts to find a universal disability concept on an international level. In 1980 it published the Classification of Impairments, Disabilities, and Handicaps (ICIDH). It was based on a threefold model: "impairment" denoted a defect or disorder in the medical sense, "disability" meant functional limitations, and "handicap" indicated the individual inability to fulfill normal social roles. More than 20 years later, the WHO (2001) revised this classification scheme. The topical Classification of Functioning, Disability, and Health (ICF) uses a multidimensional approach. Its first part,

"functioning and disability," differentiates between "body functions and structures" and "activities and participation." The second part consists of "contextual factors" and contains "environmental" and "personal" factors. The use of the participation concept as well as the reference to environmental factors are important novelties in contrast to the ICIDH. Additionally, terminology was changed. The term disability now comprises medically defined impairments as well as activity limitations and participation restrictions. The term handicap was completely given up. Despite these innovations disability studies scholars criticize the ICF because the social model of disability was only half-heartedly implemented.

The epidemiology of disability aims at answering these three basic questions: (1) How many people have a disability? (2) How is disability distributed within the population? (3) What are the major causes? However, these questions are not easily answered. The complexity, relativity, and multidimensionality of bodily, mental, and psychological phenomena make it difficult to establish a clear-cut disability definition as a starting point and to agree on operational categories that meet the basic requirements of valid statistics, such as one-dimensionality, exclusiveness, and completeness. With regard to methods, there are different possibilities when counting people with disabilities. First, studies focusing on regions, certain groups, subsystems, institutions or programs can be used as sources for estimating the overall number of a disability population. Second, population studies are undertaken, either as a complete recording of the entire population or as representative random surveys. A third means is to officially register all persons who have been certified as having a disability by an official authority. In disability statistics – the history of which can be traced to the early twentieth century – all three ways have been used. Owing to the great methodological problems of counting disabled people, international statistical findings vary to a great extent. The population quotas range from an estimated disability population of 0.2 percent in Qatar (1986) to 8.1 percent officially registered severely disabled people in Germany (2001) and 19.3 percent of the civilian non-institutionalized North American population counted in the 2000 census. The main disability causes have changed over time. War injury and accidents at the workplace used to be prevalent, but in industrialized countries chronic diseases amount to over 80 percent of all causes nowadays. Congenital anomalies and perinatal conditions add up to only 4–6 percent. In all countries chronic health problems correlate with lower class, manual work, low level of education, low income, female sex, and old age, as well as ethnic background and migration status.

As with all social categories, disability has its own history which is closely linked to the development of the modern welfare state (Albrecht et al. 2001; Waldschmidt 2006). Until the early modern age the treatment of bodily differences and health conditions was characterized by religion and magic as well as exclusion and charity. The seventeenth century became the epoch of confinement (Foucault 1961). After the Thirty Years War, in the age of absolutism and mercantilism, legitimized by Protestant ethics, a system of workhouses was installed all over Europe. Even the great majority of war invalids did not get any pensions. During the sixteenth and seventeenth centuries, in connection with the beginning of modern science, attempts were made to treat people with impairments. In eighteenth-century Paris the first public institutions were founded to educate deaf and blind children. Psychiatry and orthopaedics were new medical disciplines that originated in the age of the Enlightenment.

As a consequence of the working and living conditions in early capitalist society, chronic diseases, impairments, and injuries were widespread in the nineteenth century. Poor health was one of the main causes of deprivation and pauperization. At the end of the century, social insurance systems were established with the consequence that victims of work accidents and invalidity pensioners were entitled to individual social security benefits. A distinction was installed between them and the mass of the poor still relying on private or communal welfare. The nineteenth century was also the period of institutionalization, in which asylums for people with impairments were built at great speed around Europe as well as the US. At the end of the century, against a setting of economic crisis and political restoration, Social Darwinism and degeneration theory gained

influence in public and scientific discourse and former educational institutions gradually changed into nursing and custody homes.

World War I served as a turning point in disability history as impairment suddenly became a mass experience and could no longer be ignored by society and the state. The years after the Great War witnessed the birth of modern rehabilitation policy. The old repressive policy of forcing people into work was now given up in favor of medical therapy, training programs, and legislation that aimed at offering paid employment as a means of social integration. The self-help organizations not only of war invalids but also of the civilian disabled that sprang up at that time were important factors in the beginning of recognition of disability as a social problem. On the other hand, radical Social Darwinist attitudes met with more and more public acceptance, due to the financial crisis of the welfare state. The internationally successful eugenic movement led to sterilization policies in many countries. It is estimated that in Germany up to 400,000 people fell victim to compulsory sterilization during National Socialism. In the second phase of the racial hygiene program of Nazi Germany, roughly 275,000 inmates of psychiatric and nursing institutions were systematically murdered (Schmuhl 1992).

After World War II social policy again focused on the problem of war invalidity. Rehabilitation programs were installed during the 1950s and 1960s, which originally aimed at integrating disabled adults into the labor force. Later, they were extended to other groups of people with disabilities and to additional areas of life, such as early childhood, the family, and leisure time. Since the 1970s, the segregation approach has been substituted with the concepts of deinstitutionalization, normalization, and inclusion as a result of efforts by international social movements of disabled people that put ideas like independent living, participation, and civil rights on the disability agenda. Nowadays it is internationally accepted that disabled people form one of the largest minority groups and are entitled to social support.

Since the 1960s, Goffman's (1963) stigma theory has been dominant in the sociology of disability. This microsociological approach views disability as constituted in social interaction. If a person has a highly visible bodily feature or behaves in a peculiar way and is therefore negatively valued by interaction partners, he or she becomes stigmatized. The stigma will result in social distance, but at the same time interaction rules demand "quasi-normalcy" to be maintained. For this reason, "mixed" social situations are typically characterized by feelings of ambivalence and insecurity about how to act. Stigma theory makes it possible to analyze disability not as an inner personal characteristic, but as a product of social relations (Scott 1969).

The labeling approach plays a role in disability discourse as well. In contrast to stigma theory, it emphasizes social power relations and the influence of social control agencies that define norms and sanction individuals who commit violations of these norms. Accordingly, disability can be examined as deviant behavior in a society based on the norms of bodily fitness, functioning at the workplace, individual capacity to self-care, and beautiful outer appearance. As secondary deviance, disability is the effect of diagnostics and special treatment. As a result, people marked as disabled find themselves permanently marginalized. The labeling approach is useful for understanding the interactions between the life course of the individual and the rehabilitation system.

From the view of structural functionalism founded by Talcott Parsons, the question is posed whether or not a "disability role" exists (Haber & Smith 1971). Disability is distinguished from both deviant behavior as conscious norm violation and illness as temporary, legitimate exemption from normal role obligations. In contrast, disability is regarded as a form of socially accepted adaptive behavior that allows persons not able to permanently fulfill normal roles to obtain legitimate role exemption. They also obtain opportunities to fulfill restricted social obligations. The "disability role" enables social control agencies to register and acknowledge health problems and to regulate them by offering caring and rehabilitative programs to those concerned. Structural functionalism perceives disability as a socially functional role pattern that makes it possible to integrate people into society who would otherwise have been excluded.

Besides these three main theories, poststructuralist discourse theory inspired by Foucault (1961) understands disability as an effect of "power/knowledge." Additionally, one can find neo-Marxist perspectives (Oliver 1996) focusing on socioeconomic conditions. The social theory of Pierre Bourdieu is used to analyze disability as a combination of structure and agency.

SEE ALSO: Body and Society; Bourdieu, Pierre; Chronic Illness and Disability; Deinstitutionalization; Deviance; Disability Sport; Eugenics; Euthanasia; Families and Childhood Disabilities; Feminist Disability Studies; Foucault, Michel; Goffman, Erving; Health and Social Class; Interaction; Labeling Theory; Marxism and Sociology; Sick Role; Social Epidemiology; Social Exclusion; Social Integration and Inclusion; Social Policy, Welfare State; Social Problems, Concept and Perspectives; Sociology in Medicine; Stigma; Structural Functional Theory

REFERENCES AND SUGGESTED READINGS

Albrecht, G. L., Seelman, K. D., & Bury, M. (Eds.) (2001) *Handbook of Disability Studies*. Sage, Thousand Oaks, CA.

Foucault, M. (1961) *Histoire de la Folie à l'âge classique* (History of Madness in the Classical Age). Librairie Plon, Paris.

Goffman, E. (1963) *Stigma: Notes on the Management of Spoiled Identity*. Prentice-Hall, Englewood Cliffs, NJ.

Haber, L. D. & Smith, R. T. (1971) Disability and Deviance: Normative Adaptations of Role Behavior. *American Sociological Review* 36: 87–97.

Ingstad, B. & Whyte, S. R. (Eds.) (1995) *Disability and Culture*. University of California Press, Berkeley.

Oliver, M. (1996) *Understanding Disability: From Theory to Practice*. Macmillan, London.

Schmuhl, H.-W. (1992) *Rassenhygiene, Nationalsozialismus, Euthanasie. Von der Verhütung zur Vernichtung, lebensunwerten Lebens, 1890–1945*, 2nd edn. (Racial Hygiene, National Socialism, Euthanasia: From the Prevention to the Elimination of Lives Unworthy of Life). Vandenhoeck & Ruprecht, Göttingen.

Scott, R. (1969) *The Making of Blind Man: A Study in Adult Socialization*. Russell Sage Foundation, New York.

Waldschmidt, A. (2006) (Körper-)Behinderung ((Physical) Disability). In: Albrecht, G. &

Groenemeyer, A. (Eds.), *Handbuch Soziale Probleme*, 2nd edn. (Handbook Social Problems). Verlag für Sozialwissenschaften, Wiesbaden.

World Health Organization (2001) *International Classification of Functioning, Disability and Health: ICF*. World Health Organization, Geneva.

disability sport

Howard L. Nixon II

Disability sport refers to any form of organized physical competition intended specifically for people with disabilities and contrasts with able-bodied or mainstream sport, which is organized for people without disabilities. The historical lack of mainstream sports opportunities for people with disabilities is one of the important rationales for the development of disability sport. People are considered disabled, e.g., regarding physical mobility, sight, hearing, or mental functioning, when they have biomedical conditions or impairments that limit their ability to use certain skills, carry out certain tasks, or participate in certain activities or roles. Although their overall sports participation rates remain relatively low, people with disabilities have become increasingly involved in the pursuit of sport at various levels over the past few decades.

Disability sport has arisen and grown in popularity in recent decades, as people with disabilities have enhanced their rights, status, and perceptions of opportunity in society. Disabled people were relatively invisible in the United States until the 1970s, when federal law mandated the public education of American children and youths with disabilities in appropriate settings. What was known about people with disabilities was typically based on myth and stigma, but increasing public education, advocacy, and research in recent decades has resulted in a more accurate understanding of people with disabilities.

The scholarly study of social and cultural aspects of disability sport is relatively new. The first comprehensive collection of scholarly work in this area, *Sport and Disabled Athletes*, was edited by Sherrill in 1986, and the first comprehensive text on disability sport, *Disability and Sport*, by DePauw and Gavron, was published in 1995. Two major scholarly journals publishing studies of disability sport have been the *Adapted Physical Activity Quarterly* and *Sociology of Sport Journal*. The Disability in Sport Program of the Center for the Study of Sport in Society at Northeastern University is an important source of education, advocacy, and research concerning disability sport and athletes with disabilities.

Disability and mainstream sport opportunities for people with disabilities may vary along a number of structural dimensions, including inclusiveness of eligibility, the amount of segregation or integration of disabled athletes and able-bodied athletes or of athletes with different types or degrees of disability within a sport, disability adaptation, disability classifications, level of competitive intensity, and whether or not there is direct competition between disabled and able-bodied athletes. Disability sports are divided into different classifications, according to the functional ability or medical or vision status of the participants with disabilities. There are also cases of disability sport divisions within mainstream sports, such as the Boston Marathon, but they are relatively few.

Two prominent examples of disability sport are the Special Olympics and the Paralympics. The controlled competition philosophy of the Special Olympics is to treat everyone as a winner, and the Special Olympics is open to everyone with an intellectual disability who is 8 years old or older. The Special Olympics training and competition program involves over 1 million children and adult athletes from around the world, and it has provided international competitive experiences through its World Games since 1968. The International Paralympic Committee organizes elite sports events for athletes with a number of different types of impairments, including spinal cord injury, amputee, intellectual and visual impairment, cerebral palsy, and other motor impairments. The Paralympics developed from a modest start in 1948 in England, was first staged as an Olympic-style competition in Rome in 1960, and has developed into one of the largest sports competitions in the world, drawing nearly 4,000 athletes with physical, visual, or mental disabilities from 140 countries in 19 events to the 2004 Games in Athens, Greece. The International Paralympic Committee (IPC) and International Olympic

Committee (IOC) signed an agreement in 2001 for their respective Games to appear alongside each other in the future. The 1996 Summer Paralympics were the first such Games to get mass media sponsorship. Paralympic sports range from archery to volleyball and winter sports such as Alpine and Nordic skiing.

Despite groundbreaking legislation, such as the Americans with Disabilities Act of 1990, people with disabilities in the US and other countries continue to face barriers to equal rights and full participation in society. These challenges help explain at least part of the appeal of disability sport to people with disabilities and the value of disability sport in reshaping public attitudes and treatment of people with disabilities. Thus, a major focus of some recent studies of disability sport is the empowerment potential of sport to enable people with disabilities to overcome stereotypes, stigma, prejudice, and discrimination based on conceptions of disability as *in*ability. That is, disability sport is seen as a means of enhancing a sense of social identity, status, and power as well as personal competence or self-efficacy. A shift from a rehabilitative philosophy in physical activity to an emphasis on empowerment in disability sport over the past few decades reflects the increasing seriousness of disabled athletes. Although there have been problems operationalizing the empowerment idea, it has been listed as a priority research topic of the International Paralympic Sport Science Committee.

For many disability sport scholars, sport classification is a central issue. Its main purpose is to classify sports and assign participants in ways that make competition fair, so that the outcome of events depends on factors such as ability, skill, training, and motivation rather than the nature or extent of disability. It is intended to avoid, for example, pitting athletes with amputations against those with cerebral palsy or who are blind in the same event. Official classifiers, who have the responsibility of assessing the functional ability or medical status of athletes and assigning them to particular sports classes or events, are important agents of social control in disability sport, and a study of disability swimming showed that classifiers generally maintained the social order of the sport and kept competition fair.

The dominant theoretical perspective in the sociological study of disability sport, especially regarding sport socialization, has been structural functionalism, although its dominance has been challenged in recent years by various forms of critical and feminist theory and sociocultural discourses on the body. We get a sense of the variety of disability and sport topics addressed by sport sociologists from a 2001 special issue of the *Sociology of Sport Journal* on "the sociology of ability and disability in physical activity." It focused on topics such as women's management of their physical disabilities through sport and physical activity; media representations of disabled sport and athletes; the politics of inclusion in sport of university students with mobility impairments; disability, sport, and the body in China; and stereotypes of gender and disability in elite disability sport.

A number of recent critical media analyses have focused on social marginality, inequality, and bias in print and electronic media coverage of disability sport. Some studies have critically pointed to the common "supercrip" image portraying disabled athletes as heroic within the boundaries of the world of disability, which some disabled athletes have strenuously resisted in an effort to portray themselves as a part of the larger society. Critics of this media image also argue that it implies that people with disabilities are only worthy of respect in society if they have overcome seemingly insurmountable odds to "conquer" their disability. In addition, some have observed a "hierarchy of acceptability" in the mass media that has resulted in more attention for athletes with disabilities who looked more like able-bodied or "normal" athletes or for athletes with disabilities that were acquired rather than congenital or seemed more "correctable." A common finding in this type of research has been less attention to female than male disabled athletes.

With the rapid development of elite disability sport, topics concerning integration and inclusion have been among the most debated about disability sport. Major questions have focused on who should be eligible to compete, against whom, and in what sports. More specifically, some have argued in favor of having able-bodied people participate in certain disability sports, as a means of increasing their sensitivity to the needs of people with disabilities, but others have strenuously opposed such "reverse integration" because they believed it reflected an outdated view of disability sport as rehabilitation rather than competitive sport, would reduce competitive opportunities for people with disabilities, and was at odds with the preferences of disabled athletes, who opposed the inclusion of able-bodied athletes in their sports. A potentially useful concept in this context is appropriate integration, which involves matching the abilities and motivation of participants with the structural parameters of a sport. Today, many disability sport advocates and scholars are focusing attention on the recognition and support from mainstream sport organizers needed to be able to include more disability sport divisions in mainstream sports events, from the interscholastic level to the Olympics. Scholars need to learn more about the kinds of sports opportunities pursued by people with disabilities, how they are socialized into, in, and through sport, and how the nature of their integration or segregation in sport influences how they and others with disabilities are integrated into society.

Various methodological approaches have been used in sociological research on disability sport and athletes with disabilities. Relatively little systematic empirical research has been done on the sociology of disability sport. Most of the published studies have relied on qualitative or interpretive approaches, such as participant observation, semi-structured or unstructured interviews, and content analysis. The number of participants in these studies have been small, with few having over 30 participants. Thus, a number of these studies could be viewed as exploratory.

With the sociological study of disability sport still in its relative infancy, it is not surprising to find a limited amount of empirical research on disability sport, small sample sizes, and few attempts to replicate studies of specific research topics in this area. Future studies of disability sport are likely to rely heavily on critical perspectives and qualitative methods to pursue new ways of looking at disability, the disabled body, and sport, but large-scale surveys, guided by more structural perspectives, are also needed. There is much to learn about the culture, organization, governance, commercialization, and

stratification of disability sport; power relations in and affecting disability sport; disability sport socialization and the social identity, status, and experiences of disabled athletes; the impact of the mass media on disability sport, sports experiences of athletes with disabilities, and perceptions of people with disabilities in general; the integrating influence of sport for people with disabilities; and the relationship of disability sport to mainstream sport and the mainstream of society.

SEE ALSO: Disability as a Social Problem; Feminist Disability Studies; Gender, Sport and; Identity, Sport and; Media and Sport; Olympics; Sport, Alternative; Sport and the Body; Sport and Race; Stigma

REFERENCES AND SUGGESTED READINGS

Brasile, F. M. (1992) Inclusion: A Developmental Perspective. A Rejoinder to "Examining the Concept of Reverse Integration." *Adapted Physical Activity Quarterly* 9(4): 293–304.

DePauw, K. P. (1997) The (In)visibility of DisAbility: Cultural Contexts and "Sporting Bodies." *Quest* 49: 416–30.

DePauw, K. P. & Gavron, S. J. (1995) *Disability and Sport.* Human Kinetics, Champaign, IL.

Duncan, M. C. (2001) The Sociology of Ability and Disability in Physical Activity. *Sociology of Sport Journal* 18(1): 1–4.

Hardin, B. & Hardin, M. (2003) Conformity and Conflict: Wheelchair Athletes Discuss Sport Media. *Adapted Physical Activity Quarterly* 20(3): 246–59.

Nixon, H. L., II. (2000) Sport and Disability. In: Coakley, J. & Dunning, E. (Eds.), *Handbook of Sports Studies.* Sage, London, pp. 422–38.

Pensgaard, A. M. & Sorensen, M. (2002) Empowerment through the Sport Context: A Model to Guide Research for Individuals with Disability. *Adapted Physical Activity Quarterly* 19(1): 48–67.

Sherrill, C. (1999) Disability Sport and Classification Theory: A New Era. *Adapted Physical Activity Quarterly* 16(3): 206–15.

Williams, T. & Kolkka, T. (1998) Socialization into Wheelchair Basketball in the United Kingdom: A Structural Functionalist Perspective. *Adapted Physical Activity Quarterly* 15(4): 357–69.

Wolff, E. A., Fay, T., & Hums, M. A. (2004) Raising the Bar: Inclusion of People with Disabilities in Sport. Presented at the 2004 Disability in Sport

Symposium, April 16, Boston. (See also Disability in Sport Program website, www.sportinsociety. org/disability/.)

Wu, S. K., Williams, T., & Sherrill, C. (2000) Classifiers as Agents of Social Control in Disability Swimming. *Adapted Physical Activity Quarterly* 17(4): 421–36.

disasters

Hilary Silver

Disasters are sudden, unexpected, localized, rare, and acute events that disrupt the environment and social structure, and inflict substantial harm on individuals, groups, and property. They differ from accidents in the greater scale of their individual and collective impacts. Roughly speaking, such catastrophes entail over a hundred deaths in a short period of time.

The sociological study of disasters dates to the late 1940s, when governments sought to comprehend the damage of World War II and started planning for potential nuclear holocaust. First at the National Opinion Research Center (NORC) and later at the Disaster Research Center at Ohio State, sociologists drew upon experience from natural disasters. Over time, disaster scholars borrowed from other subfields in the discipline.

The number of disasters has increased, especially since 1990. Ulrich Beck argues that, unlike modern industrial society based upon the distribution of goods, contemporary risk society is founded upon the distribution of dangers. Science and industry are creating more and deadlier risks with impacts less limited in time and space. These physical risks are situated in social systems that aim to control them. However, many technically risky activities require society to depend upon and trust inaccessible, unaccountable, and unintelligible organizations and institutions. Scientific realism should be tempered with the viewpoints of ordinary citizens who may be affected by oversights in rational systems. This means modernization must become "reflexive." These observations hold for most disasters, regardless of cause. For some purposes, however, sociologists classify disasters by type, often distinguishing between natural and technological disasters. Increasingly,

political disasters have become a third category of study.

Natural disasters are often viewed as "acts of God." Yet numerous studies of the social impacts of floods, earthquakes, tornadoes, hurricanes, wildfires, eruptions, famines, plagues, and pandemics demonstrate the importance of social structure and cultural context in determining the incidence and outcomes of these events. For example, Mike Davis's *Ecology of Fear* (1998) argues that profit-driven, sprawling urban development in Southern California without regard to its fragile ecosystem causes any one natural disaster in the area to set off others. John Barry's *Rising Tide* (1997) similarly finds that engineering ineptitude and greed of planters and bankers helped cause the great Mississippi flood of 1927. Similarly, Eric Klinenberg's "social autopsy" of the 1995 Chicago *Heat Wave* (2003) demonstrates the contributions of selective government preparations, privatized service delivery, and biased coverage of the local media to the death of over 700 people.

Technological disasters are often attributed to human error or worse. Thus, some say, they produce more enduring and debilitating impacts – anger, fear, uncertainty, stress, and distrust – than natural ones. Sociologists have studied explosions, dam breaks, blackouts, oil and toxic spills, fires, genetic mishaps, mad cow disease, Y2K and computer viruses, and accidents at nuclear power plants, chemical plants, and NASA. Such studies refute the usual risk management response based upon "high-reliability theory" which maintains that decentralized authority and built-in redundancy enhance reliability and safety.

Vaughan's study of organizational deviance in *The Challenger Launch Decision* (1996) identifies risk-taking, ignored warnings, and deception trickling down from the top to the bottom of the space agency. In uncertain environments such as agency competition for scarce federal funds, formal organizations like NASA develop technical cultures and bureaucratic and political accountability systems that tolerate mistakes, misconduct, and risk-taking for the sake of ultimate goals. Social constructions of reality unnecessarily produce disastrous accidents.

However, Charles Perrow, in *Normal Accidents* (1999), says social constructionist explanations miss the power structure that devises such risky complex systems in the first place. "Normal accidents" are inevitable in complex (vs. linear) interaction systems with tightly coupled, interdependent components. In such systems, failures multiply and spread in unexpected ways, making rational planning impossible and high-reliability approaches even more damaging. Yet such catastrophes, Perrow points out, are rare because they have no one cause. Disasters require a "negative synergy" of combined conditions, from lack of warning to concentrated population.

Webb (2002) notes that sociologists currently know far less about political disasters – riots, revolutions, and terrorism – than about natural and technological ones. Man-made disasters are not accidental, but deliberate. Terrorist disasters are designed to inflict as much death and damage as possible on symbolic victims. The sheer arbitrariness of their targets diffuses fear among entire populations, thereby magnifying the disastrous effects. After the World Trade Center catastrophe, the study of urban disasters became a growth industry. Savitch (2001) identifies three factors – social breakdown; resource mobilization; and global target-proneness (including international media centrality) – that are responsible for which cities around the world are more vulnerable to terrorist disasters. Nancy Foner's collection *Wounded City* (2005) shows there was also variation in the impact of 9/11 among New York City communities. Vale and Campanella (2005) analyze the recovery of a wide range of cities throughout the world. They identify a dozen "axioms of resilience," including narratives to interpret and remember the disaster and the importance of surviving property.

Whether natural or man-made, disasters have many similar social consequences. The majority of property losses in urban disasters are due to housing damage. Disaster victims disproportionately consist of the aged, the isolated, and the destitute. African Americans and renters are also over-represented.

Disasters tend to have a life cycle, says Drabek (1986), progressing through the stages of preparedness, response, recovery, and mitigation. Most scholarly attention has focused on the second. There are widespread myths that, in an emergency, the population will panic and loot, and first-responders will abandon their posts, requiring a paramilitary, command-and-control structure to impose order. In fact, during the immediate crisis, studies find that people become more cohesive and converge upon the disaster site, offering help. This "therapeutic community" reaction is more typical in the wake of disaster than conflict, or what Freudenberg (1997) calls "corrosive community." Established, expanding, extending, and emergent organizations, Dynes (1970) argues, together provide flexible and diverse responses.

Once disasters recede into the past, the political incentives to prepare for future contingencies diminish. Mitigation usually entails tradeoffs between profit and safety, security and civil liberties. Private insurers may withdraw from communities hit by natural catastrophes, forcing the federal government to become the insurer of last resort. Policy continues to be disaster driven, offering short-term compensation rather than long-term prevention strategies.

During the recovery stage, there is an opportunity for social change, but it may not be seized. In some cases, community corrosion ensues, prolonged by endless litigation, uncertainty about long-term health, organizational competition, and "recreancy" (perceived governmental failure). As Kai Erikson's *Everything in Its Path* (1978), a classic study of the Buffalo Creek flood, concludes, the survivors of disasters suffer from both individual and collective trauma. Disasters disrupt the social bonds, networks of relations, and common patterns of life that would otherwise support people. Thus, sociologists are now studying disaster memorials and the social construction of collective memory. Commemorations cement social bonds after a common tragedy.

SEE ALSO: Dangerousness; Ecological Problems; Organizational Deviance; Organizational Failure; Organizational Learning; Risk, Risk Society, Risk Behavior, and Social Problems; Social Structure of Victims

REFERENCES AND SUGGESTED READINGS

Drabek, T. (1986) *Human System Responses to Disaster: An Inventory of Sociological Findings.* Springer, New York.

Dynes, R. (1970) *Organized Behavior in Disaster.* Heath Lexington, Lexington, MA.

Freudenberg, W. (1997) Contamination, Corrosion, and the Social Order: An Overview. *Current Sociology* 45: 19–39.

Savitch, H. (2001) Does Terror Have an Urban Future? *Urban Studies* 38: 2515–33.

Vale, L. & Campenella, T. (2005) *The Resilient City: How Modern Cities Recover from Disaster.* Oxford University Press, New York.

Webb, G. (2002) Sociology, Disasters, and Terrorism: Understanding Threats of the New Millennium. *Sociological Focus* 35(1): 87–94.

disciplinary society

Susanne Krasmann

Talk about the disciplinary society is frequently linked to the idea of a society of total surveillance and adjustment. However, in his seemingly most popular and at the same time highly complex book *Discipline and Punish*, Foucault (1977) describes the disciplinary society not as a social reality but as a *program* of disciplining individuals. Thus it was the "dream" of the old authoritarian police to establish a society organized along military lines, functioning like the cogs of a machine. This aspiration did indeed have historical configurations: in the "social disciplining" (Gerhard Oestreich) of an administrative and regulatory organization of society, already being instituted in early modern times, aimed at producing obedient individuals; and in an unprecedented process of rationalization of power, provoking Weber to speak of the "iron cage" of bureaucratic rulership in modern societies. Foucault's intention, however, is not to point out historical continuities and general principles shaping society, like "capitalism," "modernity," or "rationalization." Rather, the disciplinary society is the effect of micro mechanisms of power and has itself to be distinguished from a type of power that donated the name: *discipline* does not refer to an institution, but designates a technology of power. It is unacquainted with a ruling center as it unfolds beyond the state. It is a mechanism of power localized amid society: the "productivity of the norm" (Macherey 1991), operating in occidental societies since the seventeenth century. It thus differs from the juridical sovereign power of the *ancien régime* legitimized by the implementation and enforcement of law.

The topic of *Discipline and Punish* is the self-conception of modern societies, referring to ideals like humanity, civilization, and progress. Foucault exemplifies his critique of this self-conception, focusing on the transition to a new practice of confinement. The "birth of the prison" marks the new self-conception of the modern constitutional state dissociating itself from cruel practices such as the exhibition of sovereign power through the spectacle of public punishment. However, modern societies cannot count as better societies, as they are not free from power and repression. They operate with different mechanisms of power. This is the central argument in *Discipline and Punish*. The repeatedly evoked process of humanization turns out to be a shift to a new regime of power, a new economy of power, making the prison appear not only as a practice of confinement, punishment, and treatment, but particularly as a more effective and economically useful practice compared to corporeal punishment.

Two kinds of shift are significant for the transition to the disciplinary society, which Foucault exemplifies in his focus on the figure of the delinquent: the mechanisms of power shift from the body to the "soul" and from law to the norm. The practice of the prison is in no way unphysical, as confinement also is a physically noticeable restriction of freedom. Yet, while the offender in the *ancien régime* is punished conspicuously, in order to restore the king's law, his power, disciplinary power is interested in the individual. Thus, rather than the body of the offender, the "soul" of the delinquent; rather than the real, the possible act; rather than the behavior, the character of the person takes center stage. With the emergence of the prison the delinquent has been born as an individual to know. Psychologists and psychiatrists, and later on social workers, are concerned with the motives and the biography of this person in order to reform his or her personality. The delinquent becomes a category describable in generalized terms, and that allows for subsuming the discrete offender like a species. The prison makes possible the establishment of criminology as a science – and as a practice of surveillance and control.

This is what designates discipline: a regime of knowledge and practices of power crystallizing in prison, but not reducible to this institution. Rather, prison is exemplary for the architectural model of the Panopticon that renders the inmates observable at any time from the tower in the middle of the building. Devised by the English lawyer Jeremy Bentham in the eighteenth century, it stands for the program of producing compliant individuals controlling themselves in a state of permanent visibility. In the disciplinary society this mechanism of normalization prevails in the most varied sectors of society and institutions producing their respective "useful" individuals: school, family, psychiatry, and the military impose similar mechanisms to fabricate pupils, soldiers, and workers, with body and soul suitable for the conditions of production. Thus, discipline is effective precisely in that it is a program, rather than social reality; in that it does not come upon individuals already disciplined. Rather, technologies of education, healing, confinement, and correction have to be employed again and again finally to generate discipline. As a result, social norms are constantly being produced and reproduced, regulating the action and the way of life of individuals, their work, their nutrition, their sexuality, their relationships. In this respect Foucault identifies the regime of the welfare state as a prototype of the disciplinary society. Expertise cultures develop the most varied social fields driven by the idea that society can intentionally be created and controlled.

In a double sense disciplinary power is productive. It appears to reproduce itself independently, and, differently from sovereign power, it does not simply prohibit, impede, force, and repress, but constitutes domains of reality and thereby individuals as objects of control and surveillance. At the same time, disciplinary power in no way abstains from law, but it no longer asserts itself primarily by law, as the sovereign power does. The norm now is a principle that predominates over law. It enables and designates the law in modern societies; it operates like a motor and serves as an indication for the production of laws that regulate the functioning of the social system. Norms do not emerge from a sovereign will, but from social processes. Thus, rather than resulting from contracts or from a legislator, they form part of social

systems that they are at the same time establishing. Norms are inherently relational. They establish social relations by being designated in relation to the demands of an environment and, due to their generality, by implementing an anonymous principle of comparability (Ewald 1990): an individual might mark itself only in difference to others. Subjectivation is impossible without objectification. The individual therefore is an inherently social product, certainly without being determined socially. However, subjectivity cannot be conceived of without social experience, and the notion of an autonomous individual self-determined by free acts of will therefore is invalid. Norms imply forms of judgment and of communication and they display mechanisms of reproduction and differentiation. Serving as a normative measure, they demand comparison, while the empirical comparison creates new standards. Prescriptive normalization, the alignment of the individual according to model-like norms, and descriptive, statistically generated normalization that takes the empirical reality itself as a norm, work together hand in hand.

Disciplinary techniques do not seek to operate through violence. They concentrate on the human body in two ways. External practices on the one hand shape, for example, the body of the soldier in military drill, while normalization power on the other hand operates implicitly. Both forms of power conjoin, with the result that a disciplined attitude is at the same time also a manifestation of moral conduct. Disciplinary power nevertheless does not only act on already existing bodies, but it also constitutes these: the body of the sick person holding certain symptoms; the body of sexual desire inhabited by drives and articulating longings; or the female and the male body familiar with their respective sensitivities. This fabrication of bodies is always due to the access of knowledge-based technologies of power, involving specific notions of the human being (Foucault 1972; Butler 1993).

If Foucault's analysis has been accused of having a problematic normative reservation (for example, by Nancy Fraser, Jürgen Habermas, Axel Honneth, Charles Taylor, and Michael Walzer), it is precisely here that it can be seen how appropriately such critics judged, in the best sense: Foucault scrutinizes the norm itself on how it accomplishes, asserts itself, and produces forms of knowledge, perceptions, and worldviews. The norm does not form the prerequisite but the vanishing point of his critique, focusing on the ways of subjectivation of people and the adjustment of the individual as a part of society. Elaborating a normative foundation would mean to close one's mind to understanding and appreciating that changing regimes might result in forms of domination that only recently have worked as forms of resistance. How power is being composed and how it is functioning have to be found out.

In the disciplinary society, man and his body become the objects of knowledge and of economic utility. In this respect, disciplinary power discovers life as a resource, an embodiment of energy, whose productivity might be increased. The "power over life" initially concentrates on "disciplining the individual body," subsequently also on "regulating the population." One precondition for this is an abstract knowledge of society rendered possible by procedures going back to the cameralistics of the seventeeth century, the establishing sciences of political administration, and the social statistics of the nineteenth century. In view of statistics and probability calculation, disease, crime, and accidents no longer appear as individual pathologies, fate, or chance, but as "social facts" (Durkheim). Understanding their social regularity allows for dealing with them as issues of demographic policy and social hygiene, in order to develop the mechanisms of security accordingly. The delinquent thus appears as a danger to society and fighting crime becomes an issue of *social defense* (Pasquino 1991; Foucault 2004).

Sovereign power only knows the right "to kill and to let live" (killing the offender while not being interested further in the individual), whereas "to make live and to let die" becomes the emblem of a "bio-power" (Foucault 1979), designated as much by the aspiration of fostering life as by the dread of killing publicly. This dread appears nowadays, for example, in discussions about euthanasia and in the practice of capital punishment, technically perfected to make it unspectacular and to avoid pain to the delinquent and render invisible the responsibility of executioners. However, such practices reveal that bio-power is based on discretion

and reaches decisions not only about valuable life to be enhanced, but also about degraded, hostile life to be annihilated. Killing forms a disaccord with a power devoted to the productivity of life. This power does not exclude killing. In the name of bio-power racism not only is a matter of ideological attitude, but also to be rationalized as population policy, for the protection of society.

Foucault implicitly conceived of the disciplinary society as situated within the borders of the (nation-)state. Therefore, the noticeable transformation of the modern state (the neoliberal retreat of the welfare state and the "responsibilization" of individuals for the risks of their existence; the inter- and transnationalization of politics; the armament of the state in the name of home security) cannot be problematized by the categories of *Discipline and Punish*. The disciplinary society, however, embodies precisely the type of power that has not lost its currency: discipline, as a positive technique of power, links domination with morality and freedom with subjection. It operates through the suggestion that it is more prudent to dominate oneself than to be dominated, more virtuous to work of one's own free will than to be forced to work, etc. The self-control that modern societies demand from individuals implies this double sense already in the concept: the control of the self by the self *and* through determination by others (Valverde 1996). More freedom can thus be misleading and sometimes only indicates a *shift*: a policy of economic deregulation, for example, may be accompanied by bureaucratic modes of control; the performance of individuals released from regulated paternalism in order to conceive of themselves as entrepreneurs will still be subjected to permanent evaluation and thus control. The flexibilized individual is faced with a new regime.

The panoptic principle – paradigmatic for the disciplinary society – has diversified in the age of media, automatic techniques of control, and practices of optimization in working life. The disciplinary society, operating with prescriptive norms, dissolves with the contingency of norms oriented on average values and constantly creating variable possibilities; the techniques of (self-) disciplining, however, do not disappear.

SEE ALSO: Crime; Criminal Justice System; Discourse; Foucault, Michel; Governmentality and Control; Neoliberalism; Social Control; Surveillance

REFERENCES AND SUGGESTED READINGS

Bröckling, U., Krasmann, S., & Lemke, T. (Eds.) (2004) *Glossar der Gegenwart*. Suhrkamp, Frankfurt am Main.

Butler, J. (1993) *Bodies that Matter*. Routledge, New York.

Deleuze, G. (1995) Postscript on Control Societies. In: *Negotiations*. Columbia University Press, New York, pp. 177–82.

Ewald, F. (1990) Norms, Discipline and the Law. *Representations* 30: 138–61.

Foucault, M. (1972) Orders of Discourse. *Social Science Information* 10: 7–30.

Foucault, M. (1977) *Discipline and Punish: The Birth of the Prison*. Penguin, London.

Foucault, M. (1979) *The History of Sexuality*, Vol. I. Penguin, London.

Foucault, M. (2004) *Society Must Be Defended: Lectures at the College de France, 1975–76*. Penguin, London.

Macherey, P. (1991) Für eine Naturgeschichte der Normen. In: Ewald, F. & Waldenfels, B. (Eds.), *Spiele der Wahrheit. Michel Foucaults Denken*. Suhrkamp, Frankfurt am Main, pp. 171–204.

Pasquino, P. (1991) Criminology: The Birth of a Special Knowledge. In: Burchell, G., Gordon, C., & Miller, P. (Eds.), *The Foucault Effect: Studies in Governmentality*. Harvester Wheatsheaf, Hemel Hempstead, pp. 105–18.

Valverde, M. (1996) "Despotism" and Ethical Liberal Governance. *Economy and Society* 25: 357–72.

discourse

Martin M. Jacobsen

The primary definition of discourse denotes a method of communication that conforms to particular structural and ethnographic norms and marks a particular social group by providing a means of solidarity for its members and a means of differentiating that group from other groups. It is, perhaps, more accurate and useful to regard this concept in the plural, that is, as *discourses*, thus encompassing its capacity not only for marking boundaries for the group and against other groups (using linguistic borders philosopher Kenneth Burke called "terministic screens," which are essentially the points at which one discourse becomes distinct from another), but also as a method in many disciplines.

Discourses come to be in different ways. One discourse may be chosen by the group to specifically designate its identity and membership (called a discourse community and often requiring a highly specialized lexicon and superstructure, perhaps professional training to gain membership, e.g., sociology). Another discourse also may be imposed or identified by others as a means of stratification or "othering" a group, such as a pidgin language or other "non-standard language variety," leading to the recent pejorative overtones in terms like dialect or vernacular. Yet other discourses develop more natively, determined by cultural, technological, or other factors (such as primary orality or computerese).

A second definition of discourse lies within the field of linguistics and underlies the metatheory discourse analysis, a term brought into use in 1952 through an article of the same name by linguist Zelig Harris. This definition, which to some degree defines and therefore precedes the others, holds that discourse describes extragrammatical linguistic units, variably described as speech acts, speech events, exchanges, utterances, conversations, adjacency pairs, or combinations of these and other language chunks. The basic distinction ascribed to this definition is its extra-sentential status. Thus, to the linguist, discourse is often referred to as the study of language above the sentence. Each of the six methodological approaches to discourse analysis posits its own extra-sentential point of departure; thus, determining a central minimal unit for discourse analysis as a discipline remains problematic.

Interestingly, discourse analysis as an academic discipline provides a well-developed example of the concept of discourse. The major methodological stances of discourse analysis restate sociological, anthropological, linguistic, or other related disciplinary approaches and bring them under the aegis of discourse analysis, which unifies the disparate specialties by reframing them within the terministic screen created by and for discourse analysis. An analysis of how this happens may serve to illustrate the ways in which discourse analysis is a discourse community.

An excellent example of how discourse analysis is a discourse in and of itself rests in the formulation of the discipline by Deborah Schiffrin in her influential 1994 textbook, *Approaches to Discourse*. The book defines and elaborates the terministic screen identifying discourse analysis as a discourse community. Schiffrin characterizes discourse analysis as a metatheory that creates a subdiscipline of linguistics (i.e., a discourse community) by unifying six methodological approaches toward the sociolinguistic uses of language. While these approaches do not always agree on what constitutes a minimal unit, with some of them regarding multiple configurations of linguistic data as valid, they do share a focus on the extra-grammatical structures of language. That is, the vast majority of linguistic data in discourse analysis come in units larger than a sentence. Smaller elements are sometimes analyzed for their use in social behavior, but their grammatical status is usually regarded as secondary to their social function, which means that these units are being studied for extra-grammatical reasons.

Schiffrin further characterizes discourse analysis as comprising two theoretical perspectives: formalist and functionalist. The formalist perspective views discourse in terms of its linguistic structures and sequences; the functionalist perspective views discourse in terms of the way language is used for social reasons. These two perspectives (elaborated in Table 1) extend Noam Chomsky's concepts of grammatical (formalist) and communicative (functionalist) competence, thus placing discourse analysis in the discipline of linguistics. Of course, each paradigm contextualizes the other: functionalism needs structuralist data; formalism, for all its claims to be based on the code alone, ultimately serves extra-formalist purposes. These two paradigms exhibit the foundational approach taken by discourse analysis: they are terms in the terministic screen.

The formalist and functionalist paradigms, then, provide a framework for the six methodological approaches to discourse analysis (see Table 2), defining them based on methodological principles and unifying them under the discipline of linguistics, which is not where most of the approaches originated. Table 2 abstracts the starting points, research questions, minimal units, and major theorist (in parentheses) for those six methodological approaches to discourse analysis.

The model of discourse analysis posited above illustrates the way in which discourse analysis constitutes a discourse. Each of the six methodologies under the metatheoretical banner of discourse analysis belongs to an already extant academic discipline such as philosophy or linguistics and is a discourse in its own right. However, all of the methodologies are brought together by the designation of functionalist or formalist approach, the assignment of a starting point for analysis, the identification of a central research question, and the suggestion of a minimal structural unit.

The description of discourse analysis as a methodology has been accomplished by using the concept as the subject of this illustration.

Table 1   Discourse: formalist/functionalist principles

Formalist	*Functionalist*
"Etic" – analysis based on form	"Emic" – analysis based on meaning
Code-centered	Use-centered
Analyze code first	Analyze use first
Referential function	Social function
Elements/structures are arbitrary and universal	Elements/structures are ethnographically appropriate
All languages equivalent	Languages and varieties not necessarily equivalent
One code	Code diversity
Fundamental concepts taken for granted	Fundamental concepts problematic and to be investigated

Source: Schiffrin (1994: 21).

Table 2 Approaches to discourse analysis

	Starting point	Research question	Minimal unit
Formalist			
Conversation analysis (H. Sacks)	Sequencing/adjacency	Why that next?	Adjacency pair
Variation analysis (W. Labov)	Structural variable	Why that form?	Multiple possibilities
Functionalist			
Speech act theory (J. Austin; J. Searle)	Speaker intention	How to do things with words?	Speech act
Ethnography of communication (D. Hymes)	Speech events/speech acts	How does discourse reflect culture?	Speech event
Interactional sociolinguistics (E. Goffman)	Interpersonal goals	What are they doing?	Interchange
Pragmatics (H. P. Grice)	Grice's maxims/speech acts	What are the cultural norms for speech acts?	Multiple possibilities

Source: Schiffrin (1994).

More important, the description shows discourse analysis to be a method of communication that conforms to particular structural and ethnographic norms and marks a particular social group by providing a means of solidarity for its members and a means of differentiating that group from other groups. Further, while discourse analysis is a discourse, the six methodological perspectives within discourse analysis are themselves separate discourses with their own terministic screens maintaining parallel distinctions as fully realized varieties of discourse analysis, not unlike the distinction accorded to dialects of a language.

Therefore, discourse analysis exhibits characteristics of both definitions of discourse offered here, accounting for every element of those definitions. Clearly, the concept of discourse analysis conforms to the basic definition of discourse by both establishing and following the stylistic and disciplinary norms of the discipline it names. Those adopting the distinction of discourse analyst will situate themselves within the discourse community of discourse analysis, either rejecting or claiming simultaneous membership in a related discourse community. The member of the discourse community of discourse analysis will command the lexicon and training required of a discourse analyst and will recognize the boundaries coincident with the terministic screen that lexicon and training impose, thus adopting the identity of that group.

If the discourse analyst claims additional membership in discourse analysis and another discourse community, say, discursive psychology (which studies language use as social process) or critical discourse analysis (which merges literary, psychological, and other theoretical perspectives with the methods of discourse analysis to challenge political power by challenging the language used to advance it), the discursive psychologist or critical discourse analyst may question the discourse analyst's status as a member of that discourse community by identifying the claimant within the confines of the terministic screen of discourse analysis. In the same way, a discourse analyst may contend that the stances of the discursive psychologist or critical discourse analyst focus on purposes outside the form and function of language above the sentence, therefore excluding them from the discourse community of discourse analysis. Either way, discourse analysis, as defined here, is a discourse.

Current research trends show that discourse is a concept in the social science, natural science, business, engineering, and humanities fields. In addition to the applications of the term detailed here, the term discourse functions as a way of identifying an approach to a subject (as in the case of analyzing a discourse community or terministic screen), a way of identifying the methodology used to extract information (as in the case of therapeutic analysis), or a way of identifying a subject in itself (as in the case of specific extra-grammatical analyses of linguistic phenomena). Further, the number of graduate-level discourse studies programs is growing in English-speaking countries, promising an interest in the subject of discourse now and well into the future. The omnipresence of the term confirms its inherent interdisciplinary and cross-disciplinary value. That said, the term may also be in danger of overuse. Appropriating the term to describe virtually any use of language diminishes its capacity to function as shown above. Interestingly, the very difficulty brought about by overuse of the term discourse is a discourse phenomenon. Thus, an important future project may entail either a firmer definition or redefinition of discourse itself.

SEE ALSO: Conversation; Conversation Analysis; Education; Emic/Etic; Ethnography; Facework; Frame; Globalization; Goffman, Erving; Interaction; Intersubjectivity; Intertextuality; Language; Lifeworld; Mass Culture and Mass Society; Mass Media and Socialization; Media; Media and Globalization; Media Literacy; Metatheory; Orality; Reference Groups; Sacks, Harvey; Semiotics; Social Movements; Sociolinguistics; Stratification, Distinction and; Symbolic Interaction

REFERENCES AND SUGGESTED READINGS

Austin, J. L. (1962) *How To Do Things With Words.* Ed. J. O. Urmson. Clarendon, Oxford.
Brown, G. & Yule, G. (1983) *Discourse Analysis.* Cambridge University Press, Cambridge.
Burke, K. (1966) Terministic Screens. In: *Language as Symbolic Action.* University of California Press, Berkeley, pp. 44–62.
Edwards, D. & Potter, J. (1992) *Discursive Psychology.* Sage, London.
Fairclough, N. (2001) *Language and Power,* 2nd edn. Longman, London.
Garfinkel, H. (1967) *Studies in Ethnomethodology.* Prentice-Hall, Englewood Cliffs, NJ.
Goffman, E. (1974) *Frame Analysis.* Harper & Row, New York.
Grice, H. P. (1975) Logic and Conversation. In: Cole, P. & Morgan, J. (Eds.), *Syntax and Semantics,* Vol. 3. Academic Press, New York, pp. 41–58.
Gumperz, J. (1982) *Discourse Strategies.* Cambridge University Press, Cambridge.
Harris, Z. S. (1952) Discourse Analysis. *Language* 28: 1–30.
Hymes, D. (1974) *Foundations of Sociolinguistics: An Ethnographic Approach.* University of Pennsylvania Press, Philadelphia.
Johnstone, B. (2002) *Discourse Analysis.* Blackwell, Oxford.
Labov, W. (1994) *Principles of Linguistic Change.* Vol. 1: *Internal Factors.* Blackwell, Oxford.
Labov, W. (2000) *Principles of Linguistic Change.* Vol. 2: *Social Factors.* Blackwell, Oxford.
Sacks, H. (1992) *Lectures on Conversation,* 2 vols. Ed. G. Jefferson, with Introductions by E. A. Schegloff. Blackwell, Oxford.
Schegloff, E. A., Jefferson, G., & Sacks, H. (1977) The Preference for Self-Correction in the Organization of Repair in Conversation. *Language* 53(2): 361–82.
Schiffrin, D. (1994) *Approaches to Discourse.* Blackwell, Oxford.
Searle, J. (1969) *Speech Acts: An Essay in the Philosophy of Language.* Cambridge University Press, Cambridge.
Searle, J. (1979) *Expression and Meaning: Studies in the Theory of Speech Acts.* Cambridge University Press, Cambridge.
Tannen, D. (2001) *You Just Don't Understand: Women and Men in Conversation.* Quill, New York.

discrimination

Ian Law

Discrimination refers to the differential, and often unequal, treatment of people who have been either formally or informally grouped into a particular class of persons. There are many forms of discrimination that are specified according to the ways in which particular groups are identified, including race, ethnicity, gender, marital status, class, age, disability, nationality, religion, or language. The United Nations Charter (1954) declared in article 55 that the UN will promote human rights and freedoms for all, "without distinction as to race, sex, language, and religion." Later in 1958, the Universal Declaration of Human Rights added eight further grounds for possible discrimination, which were color, political or other opinion, national or social origin, property, birth, or other status.

Social scientists need to consider all kinds of differential treatment, as this is a general feature of social life. As Banton (1994) notes, for example, the family, the ethnic group, and the state are all based on acts of discrimination. In families, different individuals have differing roles and obligations that require particular types of behavior, for example husband and wife and parent and child. Members of ethnic groups may differentiate in their association with or exclusion of other people depending on the identification of their ethnic origins. States frequently discriminate between citizens and noncitizens in conferring rights and responsibilities. Although discrimination is often an individual action, it is also a social pattern of aggregate behavior. So, structures of inequality may be reproduced over generations through repeated patterns of differential treatment. Here, individuals are denied opportunities and resources for reasons that are not related to their merits, capacities, or behavior but primarily because of their membership of an identifiable group.

Discrimination takes many forms. Marger (2000) identifies a "spectrum of discrimination," which includes wide variations in both its forms and severity. Broadly, three categories of discrimination are identified as comprising this spectrum. Firstly, the most severe acts of discrimination involve mass societal aggression such as the annihilation of native peoples in North America, South Africa, and Australia, the Nazi Holocaust, plantation slavery, or more recent massacres of ethnic groups in Rwanda and Bosnia. Violent racism and domestic violence are two further examples of widespread discriminatory aggression. Secondly, discrimination involves denial of access to societal opportunities and rewards, for example in employment, education, housing, health, and justice. Thirdly, use of derogatory, abusive verbal language that is felt to be offensive (e.g., "Paki," "nigger"), which, together with racist jokes, use of Nazi insignia, and unwitting stereotyping and pejorative phrases, may all constitute lesser forms of discrimination. Dualistic notions of degradation and desire, love and hate, purity and disease, and inferiority and superiority may be involved in discursive strategies through which forms of discrimination are expressed. Explanations for discrimination require complex accounts that are able to embrace micropsychological processes, individual and group experiences, competition and socialization, together with structural power relations and aspects of globalization.

Feminist perspectives on anti-discrimination law have challenged the fundamental assumptions underlying the treatment and analysis of comparators. This position involves a critique of liberal legalism and the invisible construction of white male norms, in law, public policy, and sociology, which provide the benchmarks for assessing the scale of discrimination (Hepple & Szyszczak 1992). Other than using the position of the white majority as a test of differential treatment of minorities, assessment of material position in comparison to indicators of human needs/rights provides an alternative method of sociological analysis (Law 1996).

Poststructuralist and postmodernist directions in contemporary sociological theory have nurtured an increasing focus on the complexity of interactions between different forms of discrimination. The critique of the conceptual inflation of racism, which warns against labeling institutional practices as racist as they may have exclusionary effects on other groups, further supports the building of sociological complexity into the study of how discrimination works. This shift is also apparent in the development of international and national protections and remedies. Here, development of human rights approaches that emphasize particularly freedom from discrimination and respect for the dignity of individuals and their ways of life and personal development seek to build a collective agenda that encompasses the needs and interests of all individuals and groups. The shift toward the creation of general equality commissions in the UK and in Europe and the dismantling of institutions concerned with separate forms of discrimination such as race or disability further exemplifies this process. In future research, focus on the interactions between different structures of discrimination is likely to be key.

The United Nations Third World Conference in Durban 2001 affirmed the paramount importance of implementing the International Convention on the Elimination of Racial Discrimination. It also concluded that the major obstacles to overcoming racial discrimination were lack of political will, weak legislation, and poor implementation of relevant strategies by nation-states. In moving forward, the key role played by non-governmental organizations in campaigning for change and raising awareness of many forms of discrimination was acknowledged.

SEE ALSO: Affirmative Action; Apartheid and Nelson Mandela; Civil Rights Movement; Gender Bias; Homophobia; Race; Race (Racism); Racism, Structural and Institutional; Stereotyping and Stereotypes

REFERENCES AND SUGGESTED READINGS

Banton, M. (1994) *Discrimination*. Open University Press, Buckingham.
Banton, M. (2002) *The International Politics of Race*. Polity Press, Cambridge.
Hepple, B. & Szyszczak, E. M. (Eds.) (1992) *Discrimination: The Limits of Law*. Mansell, London.
Law, I. (1996) *Racism, Ethnicity, and Social Policy*. Harvester Wheatsheaf/Prentice-Hall, Hemel Hempstead.
Marger, M. N. (2000) *Race and Ethnic Relations*. Wadsworth, Stamford, CT.
Poulter, S. (1998) *Ethnicity, Law, and Human Rights*. Clarendon Press, Oxford.

disease, social causation

Joseph T. Young

Social causation of disease is defined as the origin of illness that results from social conditions and social interactions. This definition assumes that human biological factors are not the sole cause of disease. The definition further assumes that social factors such as socioeconomic status (SES), religion, and social networks have an effect on the level and severity of illness and mortality. The idea that social interaction and culture play parts in the causation of disease has been present in social thought since John Gaunt's discussion of the interaction between politics and mortality in 1662.

Social causes of disease can be divided into fundamental causes (Link & Phelan 1995) and proximate (or lifestyle) causes. Proximate causes of illness directly produce illness by affecting biological processes and are individually controlled. For example, diet, smoking, alcohol and drug use, seatbelt use, and exercise behaviors are lifestyle choices that directly affect disease prevalence.

Fundamental causes of disease can be defined as indirect causes of disease that act through specific proximate statuses and behaviors caused by variable access to resources (social capital) that may help people avoid disease, and the negative consequences of disease (Link & Phelan 1995: 81). Social capital is available to an individual through social networks, education, occupation, income and wealth, religious ties, and social power. The amount of social capital available to an individual, as well as other social factors, partially determines the severity and type of diseases the individual is afflicted with and may ultimately be more important as causes of disease than proximate causes (Link & Phelan 1995).

Why is the study of social causation of disease important? The obvious answer is that with adequate linkage between the causes of disease, society is able to achieve remedies for the disease states and reduce the negative effects of these causes of disease on the individual and society as a whole. Understanding causative factors for disease supports disease prevention, potentially improves health, longevity, and quality of life, informs health policy, improves access to care, and increases the level of health knowledge. Major social causes include occupation, income, gender, education, social networks, health care access availability, institutional causes (such as insurance), diet and nutrition, and stress (event related) and psychological factors.

Biological explanations of disease do not fully explain either the prevalence levels or the severity of disease. Disease is thus multicausal in origin and is manifest from multiple causal pathways. We have moved from attempting to eliminate the causal connection between lifestyle, proximate causes, and disease to looking at the reasons that people have such behaviors that negatively impact their health. Those reasons for negative behavior are uniformly social in nature.

Methods used to delineate social causes of disease must, of necessity, be complex because of the complex nature of the topic and the many interactions between levels of inquiry and factors involved. The methods primarily used are quantitative in nature and involve multilevel regression models of various types. General linear models, hierarchical models, and structural equation models are becoming the norms of inquiry, because the data are layered from individual factors to neighborhood factors and social institutions. These interactions require sophisticated models for accurate description, which makes inquiry in the area of study quite intricate.

The difficulty in delineating social causes of disease (hereinafter fundamental causes, because we shall assume that fundamental causes are more important to disease causation) is thus equally methodologically and theoretically complex. The effects of fundamental causes on disease are often indirect, working through more proximate statuses and behaviors, and thus the magnitude of their effect may be difficult to delineate. Methodological problems are compounded by the bidirectional nature of disease causation and the difficulty in defining the social causes. In other words, a single disease may have multiple causes, acting in concert to produce the resultant disorder and its effects. Further, the causes of the disease may interact with the resultant disease to cause further disease. For example, persons who smoke may have sedentary lifestyles, lower educational status, poorer jobs, more stress, and poorer diets because of less income, which may affect the levels of heart, lung, and kidney disease. If one disease state is present, this may lead to other disease states that synergistically affect the overall health of the individual (such as hypertension leading to renal failure, leading to heart disease and stroke). Indirect and direct causes may combine in a complex of causative factors that may be difficult to untangle, both from a methodological and a theoretical standpoint. Further lost in this decidedly social discussion of disease is the obvious effect of genetics and biology that do play some part in disease causation.

The difficulty in measuring social factors (how do we define a social factor and how do we measure it? what is the direction of causation and its level of effect?) may affect the resultant influence of the social factor on disease causation. Factors such as social integration, stress, social support, social capital, and life events must be defined uniformly and systematically in order for meaning to be ascribed to their effects. The measure used to show the effect of social factors on health and disease must be equally precise. For example, mortality as an outcome is relatively precise. We all die, and we all die of something, but that "something" may not be a single disease or have a single cause. If we use cure, or worse yet control, in chronic disease states as a measure of outcome, the standard of what is cure and what is control may vary with the research involved. Standards for outcomes are not present in the literature, in many cases, to guide research.

The old dichotomy of causation, direct and indirect causes, seems to be too imprecise to explain social causation of disease. Direct physical causes of disease occur in a social context. Smoking may have social causes. Direct physical harm from injury occurs in a social milieu (e.g., driving too fast without a seatbelt may be the result of low SES, cultural preference, and excess alcohol use because the stress of life is too much to directly confront). All of these factors comprise a complex interplay of causation grounded in the fundamental causes of disease, which are primarily social in nature. The work of McKeown and associates on public health and smoking, and of Dubos (1959) on environmental factors in health and disease, makes a strong case for multifactorial causation of disease. The effect of nutritional deficits due to poor economic status may affect lifelong immunity and susceptibility to disease. To complicate matters, Barker and associates hypothesized that diseases, thought to be chronic and afflicting the more aged of the population, are perhaps genetically programmed before birth through poor nutrition of the mother, to be later expressed by metabolic pathways (e.g., metabolic syndrome leading to heart, vascular, endocrine, and kidney disease) later in life. Fundamental and social causes of disease may therefore have direct and indirect effects as a result of large, and as yet not fully delineated, social contexts of wealth, power, social capital, and social control, which may partially determine the level and severity of disease in the individual.

The theoretical underpinnings of the social causation of illness are material, cultural, behavioral, psychosocial, sociopolitical, and longitudinal in nature. The common thread of all the theories is that differences in social factors lead to differences in illness levels and the ability to maintain and regain healthy status (Bartley 2004).

The material or socioeconomic status theory (Kitigawa & Hauser 1973; Kawachi & Kennedy 1997) links levels of illness to income. Income determines behaviors, diet, and type of work done, and is linked to housing quality and environmental determinants of illness as well as stress levels and work-related levels of self-identity and worth.

The cultural/behavioral theory states that socialized values and norms determine behavior and social identity, which in turn control health behaviors and levels of disease. A subset of behavioral/cultural theory, psychosocial theory (Wilkinson 1996; Elstad 1998), suggests that social status levels, social networks, and biochemical processes in the body are linked to behavior and thus to levels of illness.

Political economy theory (Lynch 2000) suggests that health and illness differentials are caused by differentials in social power controlled by external political and institutional hierarchies. Finally, life course theory states that events before and after birth affect physical health, the ability to maintain and repair health, and the level of illness through biological and social/behavioral pathways that change with age and the evolution of social institutions. A unified theory of social causation of illness must contain material, socialization and network, longitudinal and biological, stress and psychological, and behavioral/cultural factors. As yet, all the theories ignore the global aspects of illness causation and the interactions between the various aspects of social causation (Young 2004).

The term "social causes of disease" has been supplanted, first by the term social determinants of disease, and now by a field of study termed "social epidemiology," which includes the social determinants of health and disease (Kawachi 2002). This subfield of public health, health sociology, and epidemiology has helped to define social policy related to neighborhood improvement, health services access, and socioeconomic improvements that have decreased disease prevalence and delineated the pathways of social causation of disease.

Future research will depend on the ability of researchers to meet the demands of large, complex longitudinal databases and methodological issues required for adequate analysis of this topic. Certainly, topics extending the idea of the life course perspective will require longitudinal multilevel analysis (Hayward et al. 2000). Other areas of future research should include the relationship of direct causes of disease to social causes and social outcomes; the effects of social causation of disease on the developing world and development (Sen 1987); the development of biomarkers and their reliability in linking health to social variables; and GIS techniques for analysis of area effects. We have only scratched the surface of all the environmental effects on illness and health.

Social epidemiology provides an avenue for formal empirical and theoretical research into the multifactorial causes of disease so that social and medical scientists can work together to improve global health and well-being.

SEE ALSO: Epidemiology; Illness Experience; Social Capital; Social Capital and Health; Social Epidemiology

REFERENCES AND SUGGESTED READINGS

Andersen, R. (1995) Revisiting the Behavioral Model and Access to Medical Care: Does It Matter? *Journal of Health and Social Behavior* 36: 1–10.

Bartley, M. (2004) *Health Inequality*. Polity Press, Cambridge.

Dubos, R. (1959) *Mirage of Health*. Harper & Row, New York.

Elstad, J. (1998) The Psycho-Social Perspective on Social Inequalities in Health. In: Bartley, M., Blane, D., & Davey-Smith, G. (Eds.), *The Sociology of Health Inequalities*. Blackwell, Oxford, pp. 39–58.

Hayward, M., Miles, T., Crimmins, E., & Yang, Y. (2000) The Significance of Socioeconomic Status in Explaining the Racial Gap in Chronic Health Conditions. *American Sociological Review* 65: 910–30.

Kawachi, I. (2002) What is Social Epidemiology? *Social Science and Medicine* 54: 1739–41.

Kawachi, I. & Kennedy, B. (1997) Socioeconomic Determinants of Health, 2. Health and Social Cohesion: Why Care About Income Inequality?. *British Medical Journal* 314: 1037–40.

Kitigawa, E. & Hauser, P. (1973) *Differential Mortality in the United States: A Study in Socioeconomic*

Epidemiology. Harvard University Press, Cambridge, MA.

Link, B. & Phelan, J. (1995) Social Conditions as Fundamental Causes of Disease. *Journal of Health and Social Behavior* 35 (special issue): 80–94.

Lynch, J. (2000) Income Inequality and Health: Expanding the Debate. *Social Science and Medicine* 51: 1001–5.

Macintyre, S., Hunt, K., & Sweeting, H. (1996) Gender Differences in Health: Are Things as Simple as They Seem? *Social Science and Medicine* 42: 617–24.

Pescosolido, B. (1992) Beyond Rational Choice: The Social Dynamics of How People Seek Help. *American Journal of Sociology* 97: 1096–138.

Sen, A. (1987) *The Standard of Living*. Cambridge University Press, Cambridge.

Wilkinson, R. (1996) *Unhealthy Societies: The Afflictions of Inequality*. Routledge, London.

Young, J. (2004) Illness Behaviour: A Selective Review and Synthesis. *Sociology of Health and Illness* 26: 1–31.

Disneyization

Alan Bryman

Disneyization refers to "the process by which *the principles* of the Disney theme parks are coming to dominate more and more sectors of American society as well as the rest of the world" (Bryman 2004: 1). The term was devised by Bryman (2004) to parallel George Ritzer's (2004) notion of McDonaldization and the definition is a deliberate adaptation of that concept. Disneyization does not refer to the spread of theme parks, though that is certainly happening, but to principles that the Disney theme parks exemplify. As such, Disneyization refers to the ways in which modern consumption opportunities in institutions as diverse as hotels, restaurants, shopping malls, and shops are increasingly infused with Disneyization.

In portraying the principles that the Disney theme parks exemplify, four dimensions of Disneyization are distinguished:

1   *Theming*. This refers to the application of a narrative to an institution that is external to that institution. An example is the deployment of a narrative of the cinema or the natural world to a restaurant. Theming can add allure to otherwise commonplace consumption opportunities.

2   *Hybrid consumption*. This is the bringing together of different forms of consumption in a single location or site, such as shops attached to restaurants, amusement park attractions attached to hotels or shopping malls, and fusions of hotels with casinos, as in Las Vegas. The rationale for hybrid consumption is that it keeps consumers at a site for longer and turns it into a destination.

3   *Merchandising*. This term refers to the sale of goods bearing or in the form of company images or logos. It includes such things as tee-shirts, mugs, pens, and other paraphernalia which are used to extract additional revenue from popular images, such as movie and television series tie-ins or company symbols. The idea is to extend people's enjoyment of the underlying image and in the process mining further value from it.

4   *Performative labor*. Workers in consumption environments in service industries are increasingly encouraged to view their labor in ways that suggest a performance, similar to that which occurs in the theater. One of the chief forms of this trend is that service organizations increasingly encourage workers to engage in *emotional labor* (Hochschild 1983). This means that workers are enjoined to display positive emotions through smiling and other external signs.

Bryman (2004) draws a distinction between structural and transferred Disneyization, suggesting that two separate processes may be at work in the spread of Disneyization. The former refers to the essential changes exemplified by the Disney theme parks. Transferred Disneyization refers to the relocation of the principles associated with the Disney theme parks into other spheres, such as shopping malls and restaurants.

The process of Disneyization should be viewed as a platform for rendering goods and particularly services desirable and consequently more likely to be purchased. As such, it is very much a strategy that is at the heart of modern consumerism.

SEE ALSO: Consumption, Cathedrals of; Consumption, Mass Consumption, and Consumer Culture; Emotion Work; Hyperconsumption/Overconsumption; McDonaldization

REFERENCES AND SUGGESTED READINGS

Bryman, A. (2004) *The Disneyization of Society*. Sage, London.

Hochschild, A. (1983) *The Managed Heart*. University of California Press, Berkeley.

Ritzer, G. (2004) *The McDonaldization of Society: Revised New Century Edition*. Pine Forge Press, Thousand Oaks, CA.

Robinson, M. B. (2003) The Mouse Who Ruled the World! How American Criminal Justice Reflects the Themes of Disneyization. *Journal of Criminal Justice and Popular Culture* 10(1): 69–86.

distanciation and disembedding

Christoph Henning

Modern society is based on a functional differentiation of different social systems. Therefore, face-to-face interactions lose their significance in everyday life, as modern media such as money or more recently the Internet step in between. The consequence for individuals is the process of distanciation. It has both a spatial and an emotional side: people who feel a sense of belonging can live far away from each other, and people sharing the same neighborhood may not even talk to one another. Social interdependence is ever more mediated and behavioral patterns often adapt towards a mutual ignorance. The consequence for societal subsystems is that they are increasingly disembedded. They follow their own logic only, without reflecting upon social concerns or society as a whole.

Though these two related processes are but two sides of the same coin of modernization, they have been described in rather different theoretical schools. The term distanciation comes from Nietzsche. It was taken up by authors like Georg Simmel, Helmuth Plessner, and Norbert Elias. The term disembedding was first used by Karl

Polanyi, though the idea was already elaborated a hundred years earlier by Marx. It was taken up by anthropologists and later on by economic sociology (Granoveter & Swedberg 2001) and also by Giddens. Following Polanyi, it is the disembedding of the market in particular that is typical for modern capitalistic society. The economy has become the central process of modern society, yet an economy is more than just the market. It also includes consumption and (most importantly) production. In traditional societies the economy used to be embedded in larger cultural frames. Ethics, politics, and religion had a great influence on economic behavior. In modern society the economy can only process what is inputed into the economic system as *economic* information; that is, as monetary calculation. In Marxian terms, economic thinking was transformed from a logic of use-value to a logic of exchange-value. This logic is blind towards qualitative differences and only cares for quantitative dimensions of how much something costs or pays. The effect on individuals is distanciation: a weakening of social bonds and an increased individuality.

The Marxian interpretation of this process of disembedding and distanciaton was mostly negative: now there are no more limits to growth, even if growth turns out to be ecologically destructive. In other words, the price for disembedding is a much greater social risk. Also, there are no more qualitative criteria for deciding at which point economic progress comes at the price of social instability. Classical sociology stressed the ambivalence of this process, pointing especially to the good sites of this very process. The argument was not capitalism's greater economic efficiency, as used by liberal economists like Hayek and Friedman. The sociological argument was a cultural one. The modern individual can no longer rely on "natural" bonds and ties with neighbors and fellow citizens. Some (e.g., communitarians) judged this as a loss. But at the same time this allows for more freedom. Now that individuals are independent of what neighbours think and do, they are free to do whatever they like. Modern culture is only possible because of this loss. If the economy were not disembedded and individuals could not distance themselves from one another, there would be no culture of individualism, no pluralism, no independent art or a free press.

Simmel and Elias were interested in how modern culture and the modern individuum managed to deal with this distanciation and disembedding. "Distance" here refers to the increased "social space" between different individuals, especially those from different classes, ethnicities, religions, ages, or genders. The concept of social space was further elaborated by Bourdieu. Giddens also followed Simmel's footsteps, claiming that it is especially money as a modern medium that allows for a growing disembedding of social interactions ("the 'lifting out' of forms of life, their recombination across time and space") (Giddens & Pierson 1998: 98). Moneys allows for economic interactions across distances, both in terms of time (via credit) and space (via the banking system).

Recent economic sociology and research on international management have shown that the modern economy is not as distanced and disembedded as Polanyi thought, not even on the market. Even in the heart of economic transactions – be it inside a firm, between firms, or between a firm and its customers – there are many social and cultural bonds that embed economic actions and bring partners closer. The debate on "glocalization" and the cultural turn in many disciplines have shown that this is a fundamental necessity. So, together with growing distanciation and disembedding, one can most likely find counteracting tendencies of reembedding and trust (Giddens 1990).

SEE ALSO: Globalization; Modernity; Money; Risk, Risk Society, Risk Behavior, and Social Problems; Social Embeddedness of Economic Action; Space

REFERENCES AND SUGGESTED READINGS

Bogardus, E. S. (1925) Measuring Social Distance. *Journal of Applied Sociology* 9: 299–308.
Bourdieu, P. (1986) *Distinction: A Social Critique of Judgements of Taste*. Routledge, London.
Elias, N. (2000) *The Civilizing Process: Sociogenetic and Psychogenetic Investigations*. Blackwell, Oxford.
Giddens, A. (1990) *The Consequences of Modernity*. Polity Press, Cambridge.
Giddens, A. & Pierson, C. (1998) *Conversations with Anthony Giddens: Making Sense of Modernity*. Polity Press, Cambridge.
Granovetter, M. & Swedberg, R. (Eds.) (2001) *The Sociology of Economic Life*. Westview Press, Boulder.
Marx, K. (1936 [1867]) *Capital: A Critique of Political Economy*. Modern Library, New York.
Polanyi, K. (1944) *The Great Transformation*. Farrar & Rinehart, New York.
Simmel, G. (1990 [1900]) *Philosophy of Money*. Routledge, New York.
Taylor, C. (1989) *Sources of the Self: The Making of the Modern Identity*. Harvard University Press, Cambridge, MA.

distinction

Douglas B. Holt

Distinction references the social consequences of expressions of taste. When people consume – whether it be popular culture, leisure, fine arts, the home, vacations, or fashion – these actions, among other things, act to express tastes. And tastes are not innocuous. Rather, what and how people consume can act as a social reproduction mechanism. So expressions of taste are acts of distinction to the extent that they signal, and help to reproduce, differences in social class. Distinction can be distinguished from other important class reproduction mechanisms such as educational credentials, the accumulation of financial assets, and membership in clubs and associations.

The term distinction is often used as a synonym for related concepts concerning status display, especially Thorstein Veblen's popular idea of conspicuous consumption. But distinction, as developed by Pierre Bourdieu in his seminal *Distinction: A Social Critique of the Judgment of Taste* (1984), is a more precise term. To understand the nuances of Bourdieu's ideas, we need to compare *Distinction* to prior work. (Bourdieu was more interested in berating Parisian elites than in conversing with related social theory.) The most influential ideas prior to Bourdieu were Simmel's trickle-down theory of fashion and Veblen's theory of the "honorific" consumption of the leisure class.

In Simmel's model, society's elites are in a continual race to distinguish their consumption from their social inferiors, who do their best to

imitate higher status tastes. The constant inflation due to copying creates a very dynamic
fashion system. Simmel proposes what may be
termed a consensus symbol model: what is consumed is irrelevant as long as elites decide
collectively that it will be a class signal. The
anthropologist Lloyd Warner worked with
a similar model in his famous ethnographic
studies of the American social class system.

Veblen, unlike Simmel, is concerned with
claims to distinction that are not necessarily
defined as such by their participants. Much like
Bourdieu, he is a close observer of elite status
signals that have become naturalized as simply
"good taste." But Veblen's model differs from
Bourdieu's in that he defines elites by their
wealth and then looks at how they convert their
wealth into acts of consumption that are not
easily imitated: they spend excessively on "was-
teful" indulgences, they use their wives as stage
props, they define beauty in terms of expense,
and so on.

By comparison, Bourdieu's theory of distinction makes three major contributions. First, he
carefully unpacks and details the independent
contributions of economic capital and what he
terms cultural capital. Economic capital allows
one to express tastes for luxurious and scarce
goods, much like Veblen describes. Cultural
capital is different in that it consists of the
socialized tastes that come from "good breeding": growing up among educated parents and
peers. Cultural elites express tastes that are conceptual, distanced, ironic, and idiosyncratic. So
rather than a unidimensional social class hierarchy, Bourdieu is able to specify carefully how
class fractions are composed (and often clash)
due to differences in their relative amounts of
economic and cultural capital.

Second, he specifies a materialist theory that
explains why different class fractions tend
toward particular tastes. He traces the causal
linkages between social conditions and tastes;
for example, the economic deprivations of the
working class lead to the "taste for necessity."
Rather than a consensus model, with Bourdieu's
theory, one is able to predict the kinds of cultural
products different class fractions will like and the
ways in which they will consume them.

Third, what is most notable about Bourdieu's
book, and least commented upon, is his nuanced

eye for the subtle distinguishing practices that
pervade everyday life. Much like Erving
Goffman, Bourdieu is able to pick apart the
micro details – how one dresses, how one vacations, the way in which one justifies aesthetic
preferences – to reveal their broader sociological
impact.

Bourdieu's research has stimulated a variety
of empirical studies that have sought to test the
relationship between tastes and social reproduction. The results of these studies have been
inconclusive. One of the inherent problems in
such studies is that cultural practices that communicate distinction are often quite subtle.
Many of these practices are not easily captured
by conventional social science constructs, nor
by survey measures, the primary method for
follow-up studies to date.

For this reason, some of the most telling
treatments of distinction have been written by
cultural critics who are acute observers of the
social world around them and are more sensitive to the historical shifts in taste. While less
systematic, books such as Tom Wolfe's *Radical
Chic and Mau-Mauing the Flak Catchers* (1999),
Paul Fussell's *Class: A Guide through the American Status System* (1992), and David Brooks's
*Bobos in Paradise: The New Upper Class and
How They Got There* (2001) capture better than
any sociological study how American elites
signaled distinction in the 1970s, 1980s, and
1990s, respectively. The challenge for future
sociological research is to develop theories
and methods that are sensitive to these
nuances.

Bourdieu's theory has also drawn considerable
criticism, particularly for its overly structural
and economist approach. Certainly, a primary
weakness of Bourdieu's theory is that he posits
a nomothetic model that abstracts away from
historical particulars in order to claim universal
application. There is a fundamental tension
between Bourdieu's universalizing model and
his nuanced description of tastes, many of which
are particular to France. So, rather than "test"
Bourdieu's model in its nomothetic form, the
most fruitful future work will be to treat Bourdieu's framework as a skeleton and then specify
the particular characteristics of distinction across
different societies and historical periods. Mapping these particular formations of distinction

is a massive and important project that has only just begun.

SEE ALSO: Bourdieu, Pierre; Capital: Economic, Cultural, and Social; Cultural Capital; Simmel, Georg; Stratification, Distinction and; Taste, Sociology of; Veblen, Thorstein

REFERENCES AND SUGGESTED READINGS

Bourdieu, P. (1984) *Distinction: A Social Critique of the Judgment of Taste*. Harvard University Press, Cambridge, MA.
Simmel, G. (1971) Fashion. In: Levine, D. (Ed.), *Georg Simmel: On Individuality and Social Forms*. University of Chicago Press, Chicago, pp. 294–323.
Veblen, T. (1979) *The Theory of the Leisure Class*. Penguin, New York.

distributive justice

Guillermina Jasso

Every day, and in all walks of life, the sense of justice is at work. Humans form ideas about what is just; and they make judgments about the justice or injustice of the things they see around them. Both the ideas of justice and the assessments of injustice set in motion a train of individual and social processes, touching virtually every area of the human experience. Thus, in the quest to understand human behavior, understanding the operation of the sense of justice is basic. And justice is central across the subfields of sociology.

This entry summarizes the synthesis of the late twentieth century and the foundation for the coming synthesis of the twenty-first century. The first synthesis looks inward, providing a parsimonious and coherent model for understanding and investigating every aspect of distributive justice. The coming second synthesis looks outward, forging the links between justice and the two other primordial sociobehavioral forces, status and power, and proposing a new unified theory.

JUSTICE ANALYSIS: THE SYNTHESIS OF THE LATE TWENTIETH CENTURY

Justice analysis begins with four central questions (Jasso & Wegener 1997):

1 What do individuals and societies think is just, and why?
2 How do ideas of justice shape determination of actual situations?
3 What is the magnitude of the perceived injustice associated with departures from perfect justice?
4 What are the behavioral and social consequences of perceived injustice?

Justice analysis addresses the four central questions by developing three elements – framework for justice analysis, theoretical justice analysis, and empirical justice analysis (Jasso 2004). Developing the framework entails analyzing each of the four questions, identifying the fundamental ingredients in justice phenomena, and formulating a set of fundamental building blocks – the fundamental actors, quantities, functions, distributions, matrices, and contexts. Theoretical justice analysis focuses on building theories, of both deductive and non-deductive type, each theory addressing one of the central questions and using as a starting premise one of the building blocks provided by the framework. Empirical justice analysis spans testing the implications derived from deductive theories and the propositions suggested by non-deductive theories, and also carrying out measurement of the justice quantities, estimation of the justice relations, and inductive exploration.

The aim is a purity of approach, in which there is a minimum of terms and all terms are related to each other in specified ways.

Framework for Justice Analysis

The first central question – the scientific version of the ancient question, "What is just?" – immediately highlights two fundamental actors, the observer and the rewardee, and one fundamental quantity, the observer's idea of the just reward for the rewardee. Pioneering contributions of the last quarter of the twentieth century include Hatfield's idea that "equity is in the eye of the beholder" (Walster et al. 1976: 4), Brickman's distinction between principles of microjustice and principles of macrojustice, and Berger et al.'s (1972) idea that the just reward is a function of rewardee characteristics. Together these led to (1) the just reward matrix, which collects all the ideas of the just reward for a set of rewardees among a set of observers; (2) the observer-specific just reward function (JRF) and just reward distribution (JRD) and their tight links to the principles of microjustice (now seen to be parameters of the JRF) and the principles of macrojustice (now seen to be parameters of the JRD); and (3) a new approach for pinpointing the effects of observer and social characteristics on the principles of justice (Jasso & Wegener 1997).

The third central question – "What is the magnitude of the injustice associated with departures from perfect justice?" – highlights a new fundamental quantity, the justice evaluation, and a new fundamental function, the justice evaluation function. The justice evaluation is the observer's judgment that a rewardee is justly or unjustly rewarded, and if unjustly rewarded whether underrewarded or overrewarded, and to what degree; it is represented by the full realnumber line, with zero representing the point of perfect justice, negative numbers representing unjust underreward, and positive numbers representing unjust overreward. The justice evaluation function represents the process by which the observer compares the actual reward to the just reward, generating the justice evaluation. The justice evaluation variable has twin roots in Berger et al.'s (1972) theoretical three-category variable and Jasso and Rossi's (1977) empirical nine-category fairness rating, emerging as a fully continuous variable with Jasso's (1978) introduction of the justice evaluation function:

$$justice\ evaluation = \theta \ln \left(\frac{actual\ reward}{just\ reward} \right), \quad (1)$$

abbreviated:

$$J = \theta \ln \left(\frac{A}{C} \right), \quad (2)$$

where J denotes the justice evaluation, A denotes the actual reward, C denotes the just reward, and denotes the signature constant, which governs both framing and expressiveness. The log of the ratio of A to C is the experienced justice evaluation; θ transforms it into expressed J.

The just reward and the justice evaluation may pertain to self (reflexive) or to others (nonreflexive). Both are assembled in the just reward matrix and the justice evaluation matrix.

The justice evaluation function (JEF) has several appealing properties. The first three noticed were: (1) exact mapping from combinations of A and C to J; (2) integration of rival conceptions of J as a ratio and as a difference (Berger et al. 1972); and (3) deficiency aversion, viz., deficiency is felt more keenly than comparable excess (and loss aversion, viz., losses are felt more keenly than gains). These properties were quickly discussed (e.g., Wagner & Berger 1985) and remain the most often cited (Turner 2005). But, as will be seen below, a new theory for which the justice evaluation function served as first postulate was yielding a large number of implications for a wide variety of behavioral domains, and a stronger foundation was needed. In the course of scrutinizing the JEF, two new properties emerged: (4) additivity, such that the effect of A on J is independent of the level of C, and conversely; and (5) scale invariance. Six years later two other desirable properties were noticed: (6) symmetry, such that interchanging A and C changes only the sign of J; and (7) the fact that the log-ratio form of the JEF is the limiting form of the difference between two power functions,

$$\lim_{k \to 0} \frac{A^k - C^k}{k} = \ln \left(\frac{A}{C} \right), \quad (3)$$

which both strengthens integration of the ratio and difference views and also integrates power-function and logarithmic approaches. More recently, an eighth (almost magical) property has come to light, linking the JEF and the Golden Number, $(\sqrt{5} - 1)/2$ (Jasso 2005).

The logarithmic-ratio form is the only functional form which satisfies both scale invariance and additivity.

The JEF connects the two great literatures in the study of justice, the literature on ideas of justice and the literature on reactions to injustice. As well, it generates several useful links, via the justice index (the arithmetic mean of J): (1) a link between justice and two measures of inequality, Atkinson's measure defined as one minus the ratio of the geometric mean to the arithmetic mean and Theil's MLD; (2) a link with ideology, via decomposition of the justice index into the amount of overall injustice due to reality and the amount due to ideology; and (3) a link with poverty and inequality, via another decomposition of the justice index into the amount of overall injustice due to poverty and the amount due to inequality (Jasso 1999).

The JEF is linked to emotions at several crucial junctures. Experienced J releases emotion, variously imagined as an explosion when the logarithm of the A/C ratio is taken or when ln$A$ confronts ln$C$. Next, the signature constant shapes emotion display. Finally, change in J releases a new round of emotion. Further, it is thought that distinct emotions emanate from particular constellations of reflexive and non-reflexive justice evaluations (Turner 2005).

The framework for justice analysis provides a large set of tightly integrated tools for doing theoretical and empirical work. Beyond the foregoing, these include J, for use when the specific type of injustice, underreward or overreward, does not matter, and five context subscripts, for studying the effects of the social milieu, the time period, etc.

Finally, the justice profile – the time series of J – permits assessment of the relative importance in a person's life of goods, bads, groups, self, others, of justice itself, as well as enabling analysis of location, scale, extreme values, dropoffs, etc.

Theoretical Justice Analysis

The JEF has proved fruitful in generating testable implications. The early question, "If we know the distribution of the actual reward, what does the distribution of J look like?" was soon answered, and joined by new questions and new answers (Jasso 1980).

The problem of how to calculate J when rewards are ordinal (for everyone understood that all quantitative characteristics can arouse the sense of justice, not only cardinal things like money but also ordinal things like beauty and intelligence) led to a new rule, "Cardinal rewards are measured in their own units, ordinal things as relative ranks within a group," a rule which would have profound substantive consequences, including the prediction that the most beautiful person in a collectivity experiences less overreward than the wealthiest. The rule for ordinal things also now joined the case in which C arises from a parameter of a distribution (e.g., mean wealth) in securing within justice theory a place for qualitative characteristics, thereby providing yet another instance of the pervasive import of the distinction pioneered by Blau (1974).

The problem of how to represent C led to an identity – with roots in Merton and Rossi's (1950) work on reference groups – in which C is replaced by the product of average A and an idiosyncrasy parameter. Average A was in turn replaced by its constituent factors in the cardinal and ordinal cases, such as the total amount of a cardinal thing and the population size, again leading to profound substantive consequences.

Theoretical derivation is, of course, not automatic, especially if the goal is the "marvelous deductive unfolding" which not only yields a wealth of implications but also reaches novel predictions (Popper 1963: 221, see also pp. 117, 241–8). In this endeavor, mathematics is the power tool, enabling long deductive chains which take the theory "far afield from its original domain" (Danto 1967: 299–300). Purely verbal arguments tend to tether the deduced consequences to overt phenomena in the assumptions, constraining fruitfulness and destroying the possibility of novel predictions. Instantiation, for example, cannot produce novel predictions, for novel predictions are novel precisely because nothing superficially evident in the assumptions could lead to them.

Four main techniques of theoretical derivation have developed, called the micromodel, the macromodel, the mesomodel, and the matrixmodel. They have different starting points (e.g., J, change in J, distribution of J) and use different mathematical approaches.

Examples of testable predictions derived include:

1   A thief's gain from theft is greater when stealing from a fellow group member than from an outsider, and this premium is greater in poor groups than in rich groups.
2   Parents of two or more non-twin children will spend more of their toy budget at an annual gift-giving occasion than at the children's birthday.
3   Blind persons are less at risk of eating disorders than are sighted persons.
4   In a materialistic society, social distance between subgroups always increases with inequality.
5   Veterans of wars fought away from home are more vulnerable to post-traumatic stress disorder than veterans of wars fought on home soil.

As well, justice theory provides interpretation of rare events, such as the invention of mendicant institutions in the thirteenth century and of detective fiction in the nineteenth. And it also suggests the existence of fundamental constants, including a constant governing the switch between valuing cardinal and ordinal goods.

Empirical Justice Analysis

The justice framework and justice theory set in motion a vast array of empirical work – testing derived predictions, testing constructed propositions, and measurement and estimation of justice terms and relations. Testing predictions requires talents in the farflung domains to which the long hand of justice reaches (Turner 2005) and thus brings the synergies of distant ideas and subfields. Measurement and estimation sharpen understanding of the elements in the framework (Jasso & Wegener 1997; Whitmeyer 2004).

In general, measurement and estimation distinguish between justice for self, justice for others, and justice for all. Because, as noted above, A and C are arguments of the JEF, it is convenient to set up a three-equation system, comprised of the JRF, the JEF, and the actual reward function (ARF):

$$
\begin{aligned}
\mathcal{J} &= \theta \ln\left(\frac{A}{C}\right), \\
A &= A(X, Y, \varepsilon) \\
C &= C(X, Q, \varepsilon).
\end{aligned}
\tag{4}
$$

This basic system can be augmented by equations representing determination of the principles of justice (parameters of the JRF and JRD). Specification and estimation of this system yield new insights and new tools, three of which are briefly discussed.

The just reward in the JEF formulas (1), (2), and (4) generates the justice evaluation – it provides the crucial idea of justice against which the actual reward is compared – and hence has come to be called the "true just reward" (Jasso & Wegener 1997). It can be expressed:

$$
C = A \exp(-\mathcal{J}/\theta).
\tag{5}
$$

A challenge is how to estimate it. Of course, respondents can be directly asked what they think is just, as in the International Social Science Project. The possibility remains, however, that the response – called the "disclosed just reward" – differs from the true just reward, incorporating such mechanisms as socialization, response sets, and the like (Jasso & Wegener 1997). Equation (4), together with Rossi's factorial survey method (Jasso & Rossi 1977; Rossi 1979), points the way to a new technique for estimating the true just reward: ask respondents to rate the justice or injustice of the actual rewards randomly attached to a large set of rewardees, estimate the signature constant , and then use equation (5) to estimate C. This procedure yields the estimated true just reward, which substantively is free of disclosure mechanisms and statistically is biased but consistent. A second procedure, proposed by Evans (1989) for estimating the just reward for self and by Jasso and Webster for studying non-reflexive just rewards, obtains ratings for several hypothetical actual rewards for each rewardee. Developments in brain imaging techniques may suggest other approaches for estimating the true just reward.

The multiple-rewards-per-rewardee design has a further appealing property: enabling test for whether the signature constant varies not only by observer but also by rewardee – i.e., enabling test for two new kinds of impartiality in the justice process, framing-impartiality and expressiveness-impartiality.

As a third example, consider the three-equation system in (4). Because J varies only with A and C, the old practice of assessing the "determinants" of J can now be precisely understood and its results correctly interpreted. For example, if J is regressed on schooling, the obtained coefficient equals the actual rate of return to schooling minus the just rate of return to schooling; however, the signs and magnitudes of each rate cannot be identified from the coefficient.

The accumulating empirical record indicates that the judgment that oneself is overrewarded is rare and that societies differ sharply in the proportions who see themselves as underrewarded. In the United States, the independence of mind proposed by Hatfield is dramatic, there being wide variation in the ideas of justice; and college and graduate students view the gender wage gap as unjust. Justice indexes for the formerly socialist countries of Eastern Europe, which in 1991 indicated that inequality was too low, by 1996 indicated that inequality was too high. Finally, initial estimates of impartiality, carried out with US undergraduates, indicate that 70 percent fail the impartiality test, their expressiveness varying across the workers whose earnings they judge.

JUSTICE IN THE UNIFIED THEORY OF SOCIOBEHAVIORAL PROCESSES: THE COMING SYNTHESIS OF THE TWENTY-FIRST CENTURY

Still under the rule of parsimony, the proposed ideas for the new synthesis, to be analyzed and tested, add the spirit of Samuel Smiles: "A place for everything, and everything in its place."

1   Fundamental forces. All observed phenomena are the product of the joint operation of several basic forces (Jasso 2003).
2   Middle-range forces. The basic forces generate middle-range forces, in the spirit of Merton's theories of the middle range.
3   Primordial sociobehavioral outcomes, goods/bads, and groups/subgroups. The middle-range forces produce primordial sociobehavioral outcomes (PSO) from personal quantitative characteristics. Qualitative characteristics provide the groups for calculating relative ranks and distributional parameters and generating subgroup structures.
4   Three rates of change and three PSOs. Because there are three possible rates of change, a useful starting point posits the existence of three middle-range sociobehavioral forces.
5   Justice, status, and power. As Homans believed, justice, status, and power are the three prime candidates for middle-range forces. Justice increases at a decreasing rate, status increases at an increasing rate (Goode 1978; Sørensen 1979). While the rate of change in power processes has not been directly addressed, the reasoning here suggests that power increases at a constant rate.
6   Identity. Each instantaneous combination of a PSO, a quantitative characteristic, and a qualitative characteristic is an identity, consistent with the tenets of identity theory (Stryker & Burke 2000; Tajfel & Turner 1986).
7   Persons. A person is a collection of identities. This classic idea in identity theory is also a generalization of the justice profile to all three PSOs.
8   Personality. Persons can be characterized by the configuration of quantitative characteristics, qualitative characteristics, and PSOs in their identities. Examples include status-obsessed, race-conscious, beauty-fixated. The distinctive configuration constitutes the individual's personality.
9   Groups. A group is a collection of persons. This is a classic idea in identity theory.
10 Culture. Groups can be characterized by the configuration of quantitative characteristics, qualitative characteristics, and PSOs in the identities of their members. Groups, too, may be dominated by one or another element. Examples include materialistic society, status society, jock culture, nerd group. The constellation constitutes the group's culture.

11 Two types of subgroups, preexisting and emergent. Preexisting subgroups arise from the categories of personal qualitative characteristics (e.g., gender-based or race-based subgroups). Emergent subgroups arise from the operation of PSOs (e.g., the overrewarded, the fairly rewarded, and the underrewarded).

12 Theoretical derivation of predictions. The four techniques developed in justice theory – the micromodel, macromodel, mesomodel, and matrixmodel – are used to derive predictions for all three PSOs. Novel predictions include predictions concerning the competition among PSOs and the effects of the relative importance of PSOs in personality and culture. For example, an early prediction is that in a justice group, each person is closer to the neighbor above than to the neighbor below, while in a status group, each person is closer to the neighbor below than to the neighbor above, and in a power group, each person is equally close to the neighbors above and below – a consequence of the distinctive rates of change of the three PSOs.

13 Emotions. Emotion is released by the PSOs and by change in PSO. An early idea is that the valence of the emotion matches the valence of the PSO or the change in PSO. Justice always releases both positive and negative emotions. Status releases only positive emotions, though intensity may be very low. Change in PSO can, of course, be positive or negative.

14 Inequality – form and content. Inequality is distinguished along two dimensions, form and content.

   14.1 Inequality – two types of content. Inequalities of interest include both inequality in quantitative characteristics and inequality in PSOs. A new question immediately arises: is inequality greater in the good or in the PSO, for example, in wealth or in status?

   14.2 Inequality – two types of form. The forms of inequality are inequality between persons and inequality between subgroups. Inequality between persons is typically measured by the dispersion in the distribution of a quantitative characteristic; the Gini coefficient exemplifies this kind of inequality. Inequality between subgroups is typically measured by contrasting the location parameters in the subdistributions of a quantitative characteristic corresponding to two subgroups; examples include the gender gap in earnings and the race gap in wealth. A new question immediately arises: what is the exact relation between the two forms of inequality?

15 Happiness. Happiness is produced by the individual's PSO profile. New questions that can be posed and precisely answered include questions about the effects on happiness of changes in income inequality, changes in valued quantitative and qualitative characteristics, and changes in dominant PSO.

In the coming synthesis, justice will be more deeply understood, its operation contrasted with that of its sibling PSOs. Though only one of three PSOs, justice will be remembered as the first to yield its secrets to exact mathematical expression.

SEE ALSO: Class, Status, and Power; Identity Theory; Income Inequality and Income Mobility; Social Identity Theory; Social Justice, Theories of; Stratification and Inequality, Theories of

REFERENCES AND SUGGESTED READINGS

Berger, J., Zelditch, M., Jr., Anderson, B., & Cohen, B. P. (1972) Structural Aspects of Distributive Justice: A Status-Value Formulation. In: Berger, J., Zelditch, M., Jr., & Anderson, B. (Eds.), *Sociological Theories in Progress*, Vol. 2. Houghton Mifflin, Boston, pp. 119–246.

Blau, P. M. (1974) Presidential Address: Parameters of Social Structure. *American Sociological Review* 39: 615–35.

Danto, A. C. (1967) Philosophy of Science, Problems of. In: Edwards, P. (Ed.), *Encyclopedia of Philosophy*, Vol. 6. Macmillan, New York, pp. 296–300.

Evans, M. D. R. (1989) Distributive Justice: Some New Measures. Presented at the Meeting of the International Sociological Association's Research Committee 28 on Social Stratification and Mobility, Stanford, California, August.

Goode, W. J. (1978) *The Celebration of Heroes: Prestige as a Control System*. University of California Press, Berkeley.

Jasso, G. (1978) On the Justice of Earnings: A New Specification of the Justice Evaluation Function. *American Journal of Sociology* 83: 1398–419.

Jasso, G. (1980) A New Theory of Distributive Justice. *American Sociological Review* 45: 3–32.

Jasso, G. (1999) How Much Injustice Is There in the World? Two New Justice Indexes. *American Sociological Review* 64: 133–68.

Jasso, G. (2003) Basic Research. In: Lewis-Beck, M., Bryman, A., & Liao, T. F. (Eds.), *The Sage Encyclopedia of Social Science Research Methods*, Vol. 1. Sage, Thousand Oaks, CA, pp. 52–3.

Jasso, G. (2004) The Tripartite Structure of Social Science Analysis. *Sociological Theory* 22: 401–31.

Jasso, G. (2005) Theory is the Sociologist's Best Friend. Plenary address presented at the Annual Meeting of the Swedish Sociological Society, Skövde, Sweden, February.

Jasso, G. & Rossi, P. H. (1977) Distributive Justice and Earned Income. *American Sociological Review* 42: 639–51.

Jasso, G. & Wegener, B. (1997) Methods for Empirical Justice Analysis: Part I. Framework, Models, and Quantities. *Social Justice Research* 10: 393–430.

Merton, R. K. & Rossi, A. S. (1950) Contributions to the Theory of Reference Group Behavior. In: Merton, R. K. & Lazarsfeld, P. (Eds.), *Continuities in Social Research: Scope and Method of "The American Soldier."* Free Press, New York, pp. 40–105.

Popper, K. R. (1963) *Conjectures and Refutations: The Growth of Scientific Knowledge*. Basic Books, New York.

Rossi, P. H. (1979) Vignette Analysis: Uncovering the Normative Structure of Complex Judgments. In: Merton, R. K., Coleman, J. S., & Rossi, P. H. (Eds.), *Qualitative and Quantitative Social Research: Papers in Honor of Paul F. Lazarsfeld.* Free Press, New York, pp. 176–86.

Sørensen, A. B. (1979) A Model and a Metric for the Analysis of the Intragenerational Status Attainment Process. *American Journal of Sociology* 85: 361–84.

Stryker, S. & Burke, P. J. (2000) The Past, Present, and Future of an Identity Theory. *Social Psychology Quarterly* 63: 284–97.

Tajfel, H. & Turner, J. C. (1986) The Social Identity Theory of Intergroup Behavior. In: Worchel, S. & Austin, W. G. (Eds.), *The Psychology of Intergroup Relations*. Nelson-Hall, Chicago, pp. 7–24.

Turner, J. (2005) The Desperate Need for Grand Theorizing in Sociology. Presented at the Social Justice Conference, University of Bremen, Germany, March.

Wagner, D. & Berger, J. (1985) Do Sociological Theories Grow? *American Journal of Sociology* 90: 697–728.

Walster, E., Berscheid, E., & Walster, G. W. (1976) New Directions in Equity Research. In: Berkowitz, L. & Walster, E. (Eds.), *Equity Theory: Toward a General Theory of Social Interaction*. Academic Press, New York, pp. 1–42.

Whitmeyer, J. M. (2004) Past and Future Applications of Jasso's Justice Theory. *Sociological Theory* 13: 432–44.

diversity

Gillian Stevens and Heather Downs

In ecology, where the concept is most highly developed, the simplest description of "diversity" is the number of species living in a specific environment: the greater the number of species, the higher the level of diversity. When describing social phenomena, "diversity" generally refers to the distribution of units of analysis (e.g., people, students, families) in a specific social environment (e.g., workplace, classroom, state) along a dimension (e.g., race, social status, political orientation). When measured empirically through one or more of a variety of indexes (such as the index of diversity), the highest levels of diversity occur when the units of analysis (e.g., people) are distributed evenly across the social dimension (e.g., racial categories). However, it is also common for a political ideal to serve as the benchmark for the assessment of levels of diversity. An American work setting may be considered to be appropriately diverse, for example, if the proportions of workers who are African American or Asian are comparable to the proportions of people in the general (or local) population who are African American or Asian. More loosely, some observers consider a setting to be diverse when the proportions of people with a selected characteristic (e.g., membership in a minority group) are relatively high.

Diversity is an important concept along numerous social dimensions, such as ethnicity, race, gender, socioeconomic status, sexuality, age, physical ability, and language repertoires.

Racial and ethnic diversity is a particularly important issue in many societies because race and ethnicity are strongly related to issues of power. Levels of racial and ethnic diversity within a nation as a whole are often used to establish the ideal levels of diversity within a nation's major social institutions, such as its labor force, educational system, and political system. Low levels of diversity within particular social institutions that occur because members of a minority group are underrepresented often lead to studies of gender or racial discrimination including processes of exclusion, and the policies designed to redress these inequalities. Investigating levels of diversity within geographical areas (rather than social institutions) leads to studies of residential segregation. Phenomena such as interreligious marriages or interracial adoption highlight the presumption that the more intimate social domains are expected to be homogeneous, i.e., not diverse, along important dimensions such as race and religion. Studies of the family are increasingly recognizing, however, that these presumptions are too restrictive.

Levels of diversity can change over time through social or demographic processes. For example, levels of ethnic and racial diversity at the national level can change because of migration streams dominated by selected racial or ethnic groups, or by group-specific variation in levels of fertility. Social demographic processes such as racial and ethnic intermarriage or transracial adoption are responsible for introducing diversity within narrower, more intimate spheres such as the family and household.

In smaller settings such as the family, variation in levels of diversity along the lines of age and gender are an underappreciated facet of household and family life cycle stages. Individuals' experiences of age-specific and gender-specific diversity in their immediate households vacillate as they pass through the life cycle stages from childhood to the older ages. For example, people commonly live the first half of their lives in a gender-diverse household but after middle adulthood are increasingly likely to live in households with a higher proportion of women.

Levels of diversity in a specific social setting help determine the number of opportunities for social interaction and the consequent formation of relationships between people of differing characteristics; levels of diversity are also associated with group-specific levels of inequality. For example, high levels of occupational segregation (i.e., low levels of diversity within occupations) help maintain sex-specific and race-specific differentials in income. High (or increases in) levels of racial and ethnic diversity can lead to cultural misunderstandings, or at worst, intergroup conflict. Groups in power may view high levels of diversity as threatening. National immigration policies, such as Australia's "Whites only" policy or the United States' national origins quota system, sought to restrict the entry of selected races to avoid increasing racial diversity in the nation.

In general, though, high levels of diversity along most social dimensions have positive social connotations. Highly diverse settings have numerous opportunities for intergroup interactions and therefore numerous opportunities for the breaking down of misunderstandings and the dissolving of cultural barriers. In racially or ethnically diverse schools, for example, children are more likely to form interracial friendships. Levels of interracial marriage are higher in geographical areas that are racially diverse. The rationale for affirmative action policies in the United States includes the presumptive positive effects of diversity on intergroup relations as well as the issue of equity of opportunity for minority group members. Highly diverse settings, by virtue of including people with a wide variety of characteristics, can also result in a more equitable representation of opinions and sharing of resources.

SEE ALSO: Affirmative Action (Race and Ethnic Quotas); Family Diversity; Interracial Unions; Occupational Segregation; Residential Segregation

REFERENCES AND SUGGESTED READINGS

Allen, K. R. & Demo, D. H. (1995) The Families of Lesbians and Gay Men: A New Frontier in Family Research. *Journal of Marriage and the Family* 57: 111–27.

Blau, P. M., Blum, T. C., & Schwartz, J. E. (1982) Heterogeneity and Intermarriage. *American Sociological Review* 47: 45–62.

Greenberg, J. H. (1956) The Measurement of Linguistic Diversity. *Language* 32: 109–15.

Padavic, I. & Reskin, B. (1994) *Women and Men at Work*. Pine Forge Press, Thousand Oaks, CA.

Rosenblatt, P. C., Karis, T., & Powell, R. R. (1995) *Multiracial Couples: Black and White Voices*. Sage, Thousand Oaks, CA.

division of labor

Michael T. Ryan

The concept of the division of labor is used both by structural functionalists (the students of Durkheim) and conflict theorists (the students of Marx), but the meaning of the concept differs. For Durkheim and his followers, it means the occupational structure, and it also includes a new form of social solidarity, organic solidarity, that integrates the members of industrial societies in contrast to the mechanical solidarity of traditional societies. Durkheim saw this as a weaker, more precarious form of solidarity that was still in the process of development in the early twentieth century. For Marx and his followers, it means a double division of labor, the technical division of labor in the enterprise and in a particular industry that broke down the production process into a sequence of tasks and the social division of labor among enterprises, industries, and social classes that was mediated through commodity exchange in market relations. While the social labor of the enterprise was rationally organized, Marx saw contradictions and class exploitation and domination in the social division of labor.

Despite the chronic warfare of agrarian societies, the social structures of these societies remained relatively stable over hundreds, if not thousands, of years, with most of the changes taking place at the top – a change of regimes. The transition to industrial forms of society involved a lot of dislocations, conflicts, social movements, and chronic technological revolutions that have made this society far more

unstable, with the changes reaching down and disrupting the everyday lives of many members of this society. Durkheim and Marx have some common intellectual roots which have been obscured over time by their interpreters. Both were materialists influenced by German critical philosophy, especially Ludwig Feuerbach. Durkheim has been seen as a conservative theorist whose central focus was on the problem of social order. Marx has been seen as a radical theorist whose central focus was on the problem of social change. As Anthony Giddens points out, this is a simplistic and reductionist interpretation, especially of Durkheim, who was just as concerned as Marx about social change, and while Durkheim saw communists as hopeless utopians, he was a socialist himself, although he saw no possibility for the "withering away of the state." He – like most of the early founders of the discipline of sociology – tried to explain how one form of society was transformed into another form. Durkheim and his school, under the influence of Darwin, were interested in the evolution of societies. So was Marx, who actually sent a letter to Darwin asking him if it was all right with him if he dedicated the first volume of *Capital* to him. Darwin passed on this honor. Yet the violent conflicts, the dislocations, and the social problems that accompanied the early development of industrial societies gave sociology problems to analyze and a reason for being.

Both Durkheim and Marx saw the social order of industrial societies as problematic. Durkheim saw the problems in terms of both the tendency to anomie, or normlessness, and the "forced division of labor." In traditional societies there was a deep consensus over norms, values, and behavioral expectations. This was because members of these societies shared a common religion, performed similar work, and took care of most of their needs in their immediate communities, occasionally trading excess craft products and food with adjoining tribes. These commonalities formed the basis for what Durkheim called mechanical solidarity. However, industrialization created a new form of society where this normative consensus broke down. In the wake of the industrial revolution, urbanization and immigration brought together people with different values and norms, different religions and subcultures. Further, industrial work forced workers to specialize and to take up new occupations and professions. Specialization meant that the members of this new society became dependent upon each other for all of their needs, and now their needs were no longer taken care of in their immediate communities. This division of labor created a new form of solidarity which Durkheim called organic solidarity. But this division of labor produced a form of solidarity that was weaker and more fragile than the mechanical solidarity of traditional societies, hence the structural tendency to anomie. He thought that a new corporate order constituted by professional and occupational organizations would create norms and ethics, a new moral order, which would address this problem. These guild-like organizations would mediate between the level of the state and the level of employers and workers.

The problem with the forced division of labor is that inherited wealth gave a distinct advantage to the children of the capitalist class to take up the most remunerative positions in the division of labor, in many cases regardless of their natural talent. Wealth gave them the money and social capital, or social connections, to go to the best colleges and universities, as well as allowing them to follow their parents into the family business or to launch new enterprises. He thought the abolition of inherited wealth would address this problem and allow those with natural talent to get the education they deserved, so that they could assume appropriate positions in the division of labor regardless of the social locations in which they were born. This would reduce the resentment of talented individuals who would no longer encounter class barriers in their quest for occupational and professional careers; the opportunity structure would be open to those with demonstrable talent, a meritocracy, and it also would mean that the ranks of professionals, managers, and entrepreneurs would be revitalized with new talent and new ideas.

On the other hand, Marx saw most of the problems in this new industrial society as rooted in alienated labor and the exploitation of living labor by "dead labor" (i.e., capital and class relations). One aspect of the problem of alienated

labor is in Marx's analysis of the contradiction between mental and manual labor. The craft laborer in pre-industrial societies produced works that were based on the unity of mental and manual labor and on immediate relations between producers and consumers. The craft worker came up with the idea for a work in relation to the specific demand of a client, planned out the immediate process of production on his own, and managed the creation of this work on his own without taking orders or directions from an entrepreneur or manager. Guilds established fair market prices for the works produced and regulated the relations among apprentices, journeymen, and master craftsmen. Whereas in industrial capitalism when the working class sells its labor power – its only commodity, to the capitalist class – it alienates control of the labor process to the entrepreneur. The unity of mental and manual labor is broken up according to class relations. Mental labor is the prerogative of the capital, or management; they do the thinking and planning. The industrial wage laborer is reduced to manual labor under the direction of capital or management; they do what they are told to do. Work is reduced to indifferent money making. Industrial workers rarely have immediate relations with consumers, the price of the commodity is determined by competitive market relations, and relations between capital and labor were initially unregulated except through class conflict.

As Frederick Winslow Taylor's scientific management theory claims, whenever a worker does any thinking it is bad for the productivity of the organization. Through careful time and motion studies Taylorism reduced work to a series of bit parts that required very little thinking on the part of the worker, although Taylor was simply following the logic of the technical division of labor to its end, deskilling the worker in the process. However, this organization of work creates the possibility for the automation of work, or the "end of work" as we know it, through robots and computers; further, automation requires the return of workers who need to think at work in programming the smart machines as well as getting the machinery back up after the system crashes, thus reestablishing in part the unity of mental and manual labor. Wage workers who know how to use computers potentially have the abilities to work in any industry, breaking the tendency to one-sided development and the deskilling of the worker. This aspect of alienated labor resembles Durkheim's concept of the forced division of labor. There were a number of other ways in which wage workers were alienated. Wage workers were separated from the products and wealth that they produced; while labor was now social and the process of production was socialized, the profits and wealth were privately appropriated by the capitalist class. Capital confronted the workforce as an alien force, and the relation between capital and labor was also a relation of domination and subordination. In competition for jobs, workers were also alienated from each other. Marx also saw in wage labor the alienation of humans from their "species-being" as producers of their material world.

Class exploitation of wage labor by capital is a related problem. The capitalist class takes advantage of the fact that the working class is propertyless and needs to exchange its labor power for a wage that will allow it to reproduce its labor power (and its dependents) in everyday life. Further, the capitalist class takes advantage of the fact that during the labor process the working class creates more value than is returned to it in the form of the wage; the use-value of labor power produces surplus value beyond the exchange-value of labor power and the value of materials and machinery used up in the process. The transformation of value is opaque to the members of the working class in contrast to the transparent process of exploitation and domination in production and property relations based on slavery, caste, or serfdom. In this process the workers transform their labor power, their ability to work, into a commodity which they exchange for wages; they enter the labor process and transform raw materials into finished products and services; the enterprise sells the products, transforming them into money which should have more value than the production costs that went into them if the enterprise is to be successful. This is where profits, capital formation, and luxury consumption for the capitalist class originate.

Marx saw class conflict and a social revolution led by a class-conscious working class, the proletariat, as the agent of societal transformation. The interests of the proletariat were identical to the interests of society as a whole, just as at an earlier stage of social development and class struggle the interests of the capitalist class were identical to the interests of society as a whole in their struggle to overthrow the feudal order. In socialism the working class would regain control over the labor process and the distribution of wealth through some form of self-management; in communism the working class would abolish itself as a class, creating a classless society and the end of the different forms of alienated labor. However, the technical division of labor, the occupational structure, modified by automated technologies, would remain a lasting contribution of the capitalist class to a post-capitalist mode of production and society. But work would no longer define the "species-being" of humans, and we might see a return to *Homo Ludens* in an urban society organized around leisure and play.

SEE ALSO: Consumption; Divisions of Household Labor; Durkheim, Émile; Economy (Sociological Approach); Ethnic and Racial Division of Labor; Marx, Karl; Politics; Social Structure; Solidarity, Mechanical and Organic; Stratification and Inequality, Theories of; Theory

REFERENCES AND SUGGESTED READINGS

Braverman, H. (1974) *Labor and Monopoly Capital.* Monthly Review Press, New York.

Durkheim, E. (1972) *Selected Writings.* Cambridge University Press, New York.

Durkheim, E. (1984) *The Division of Labor in Society.* Free Press, New York.

Giddens, A. (1972), Introduction. In: Durkheim, E., *Selected Writings.* Cambridge University Press, New York.

Lefebvre, H., (1976) *The Survival of Capitalism.* Allison & Busby, London.

Marx, K. (1973) *The Revolutions of 1848.* Penguin, Baltimore.

Marx, K. (1974) *The First International and After.* Vintage, New York.

Marx, K. (1977) *Capital,* Vol. 1, 1st edn. Vintage, New York.

divisions of household labor

Michele Adams

Prior to the Industrial Revolution, economic production was organized around the home, and households were relatively self-sufficient. Households were multifunctional, acting, among other things, as eating establishment, educational institution, factory, and infirmary. Everyone belonging to the household, including family members, servants, and apprentices, did their part in the household's productive labor. The word "housework," first used in 1841 in England and in 1871 in the US, would have made little sense prior to that time, since *all* work was focused in and around the home.

Over the course of the nineteenth century, however, the Industrial Revolution severed the workplace from the place of residence. Coinciding with this process, the ideology of separate spheres emerged, reflecting an increasing tendency for men to seek work in urban factories while women stayed home to look after the family. This ideology defined not only separate spheres, but different personality characteristics and divergent family roles for men and women, as well. In doing so, it naturalized the notion that men, strong and unemotional, should occupy the status of family breadwinner. Conversely, women, frail, pure, and living under the spell of the "cult of true womanhood," should aspire to nothing more profound than being good wives, mothers, and homemakers.

Thus, as men and single women ventured forth to work in the impersonal factories and workplaces of urban centers, married women, particularly those of the middle classes, stayed home to cook, clean, and raise the children. Production and productive activities moved out of these households into the industrializing workplace. Concurrently, the value and status of men's labor went up, while that of women's household labor went down. Previously an integral part of the home-centered production process, middle-class women found themselves with less "productive" work to do. As a result, their energies became more focused on reproductive work, which included making sure that their husbands and children were clean, well-fed, clothed, and nurtured. Although economic necessity continued to force working-class wives and women of color to seek employment outside of the home, the pattern of separate spheres reflected an ideal that most families desired to emulate. Toward the end of the nineteenth century, as households were increasingly motivated to purchase industrially produced necessities, women also became the family household consumption experts. As such, they orchestrated the family's purchase of food, clothing, soap, candles, and other material necessities that they had once helped produce in the home.

In the US, the home economics movement emerged around the turn of the century, at least partly in an attempt to elevate the status of housework. Home economists provided instruction on the "science" of household labor, schooling women in the provision of a scientifically sound and hygienically pure home. As early twentieth-century housewives found themselves at the mercy of these household labor "experts," standards of cleanliness began to rise. Meanwhile, newly developed electricity and indoor plumbing facilities encouraged the invention of household labor-saving devices. Electric refrigerators replaced ice boxes and washing machines replaced wash tubs, scrub boards, and elbow grease. As the public sphere industrialized, so, too, did the household, albeit with certain important differences: in the home, the labor remained unpaid, workplaces were isolated, and the workers were generalists, good at all types of housework. Even with the industrialization of the home, however, the time non-employed women spent doing housework remained stable from the late 1920s through the 1960s, as standards for cleanliness increased, and tasks such as canning and sewing gave way to increased time doing chores like laundry and shopping for prepared food and ready-made clothing.

Before the 1970s few studies examined the division of household labor, since most people accepted as "natural" the separate spheres ideology making women the housework and childrearing experts. As the women's movement gained momentum, however, feminists began pointing out the disproportionate amount of time women spent doing housework, even as they labored alongside men in the paid workforce. Moreover, feminists suggested, the fact that women did the majority of housework disadvantaged them in the workplace. These challenges prompted research examining the household division of labor, its relative distribution, and the relationship of housework contribution to women's status in the paid labor market. In 1965, researchers from the Survey Research Center of the University of Maryland found that women did roughly 92 percent of routine housework, while men did approximately 49 percent of occasional tasks such as lawn care, household repairs, and bill paying.

Changing patterns in the division of housework began to appear in research from the 1970s and 1980s, as women started to reduce their contributions, and men, somewhat less dramatically, began to increase theirs. Reasons for these changes included women's increasing presence in the paid labor market, as well as general trends toward egalitarian attitudes in the home. Nevertheless, even as women assumed more significant roles as family breadwinners, men continued to resist doing housework. By the mid to late 1980s, researchers found that women were still doing approximately three times the amount of routine housework that men were doing. This general pattern continued throughout the 1990s, with men's proportional contribution to routine housework increasing, primarily as the result of the cutbacks made by women. Researchers note that, although the gender gap in family work is reduced when accounting for total hours of paid and unpaid labor, nevertheless, women essentially put in one extra full day of family work per week, a phenomenon that has been referred to as the "second shift" (Hochschild 1989).

Today, in the US and much of the industrialized world, household labor continues to be performed mostly by women, with chores themselves also segregated by gender. Women are still doing the majority of "routine" tasks, including cooking and meal preparation, meal clean-up and dish washing, laundry, house cleaning, and grocery shopping. Men, on the other hand, do the occasional chores such as lawn mowing, household repairs, car maintenance, and, less often, bill paying. Characteristically, routine chores tend to be more repetitive, time consuming, time sensitive, and boring than occasional chores, which are less tedious and can usually be completed when convenient. While studies of household labor tend to separately analyze routine and occasional housework, they often omit childcare or, alternatively, include it as a separate category of family work. Nevertheless, the presence of children also substantially increases the amount of routine housework that needs to be done, so the amount of household labor that women perform tends to go up when children are born. Men, on the other hand, spend more time in paid labor when children arrive, but often reduce their household labor participation. Some studies suggest that when men do more childcare, they may also increase their contributions to housework.

Some researchers see shifts in the division of household labor over the latter part of the twentieth century as dramatic, while others characterize them as relatively modest. For instance, in the US, men's proportionate sharing more than doubled between 1965 and 1985. Nevertheless, the narrowing of the gender gap in housework performance has been driven more by women cutting back their hours than by men augmenting theirs. Moreover, time diary studies have shown that while reductions in women's housework performance continued throughout the 1990s, men's actual housework time has increased little since about 1985, creating what one sociologist has called a "stalled revolution" (Hochschild 1989). Thus, studies continue to show that women do at least two-thirds of the family's routine household labor.

Besides continuing to do the bulk of routine chores, women are still considered to be the household managers. Whether they actually do the chores, delegate the work to other family members, or hire outside help, women are largely responsible for ensuring that the work gets done, as well as establishing the standards by which the completed work is judged. Men, even as they do more, tend to be seen (and to see themselves) as "helpers."

Although the amount of housework performed by unemployed women remained relatively stable over much of the twentieth century, in the US and other industrialized countries, women's participation in the paid labor force increased considerably. In 1890 only 4 percent of married women in the US reported having paid employment outside of the home. By the 1950s that figure jumped to about 22 percent, and by 2002 the labor force participation rate of married women reached 61 percent. Married mothers with children under age 18 made particularly large strides in paid employment, and by 2002, 68 percent worked outside of the home. Importantly, the employment rate of married women with young children under age 6 has more than doubled since 1970 in the US, from 30 percent to 61 percent in 2002. By 2003, women comprised nearly half (47 percent) of the total US labor force. Similarly, the latter part of the twentieth century witnessed a significant increase in female labor force participation in countries such as Canada, Japan, and those of the European Union. Nevertheless, and in spite of the fact that many women worldwide now continue paid employment through their reproductive years, employed mothers report persistent unequal treatment in the workplace.

Although women's earnings remain substantially lower than those of men, the gender gap in wages has decreased in the US to the point that women earn approximately 76 percent of what men earn, based on full-time, year-round work. Thus, with married women sharing more of the family breadwinner duties, it has generally been expected that their husbands would share more of the housework. The absence of men's sustained movement in that direction has been, therefore, a source of some disappointment to advocates of gender equality. Moreover, these paid and unpaid labor patterns appear to extend well beyond the borders of the US.

International trends largely appear to reflect those occurring in the US. Women in most developed countries do the majority of the routine housework, although their contributions are declining while those of their male partners are increasing slightly. Japanese wives, for instance, continue to report doing a large majority of housework. On the other hand, wives in many formerly Soviet countries more often report that their husbands share housework equally than do women in the US. Still, women in most countries devote well over half of their work time to unpaid labor while men devote one-third of their work time or less. The presence of young children increases women's unpaid labor time substantially more than that of men, while, in many countries, women whose education level exceeds that of their husbands do relatively less housework. Moreover, women worldwide are balancing their unpaid family work with increased time spent in the paid labor force, and while men's economic activity rates have decreased in many areas, women's rates have generally increased.

Within the last several decades, the number of family and household types has grown. Studies have begun to examine how housework is shared between cohabitors (both same and opposite sex) and in remarried families. Findings show that in each of these family types, sharing between partners tends to be somewhat more egalitarian than it does between spouses. Children's participation in household labor has also been studied, although much less extensively. Data from one large national survey (the National Survey of Families and Households) showed that, in the late 1980s, all children in the household were doing slightly less than 6 hours total of housework per week. Moreover, children's housework is allocated based on age and sex, with teens delegated more tasks than younger children, and girls allocated more tasks than boys. As teens, in particular, girls are given more of the routine household tasks, while boys are expected to contribute to outdoor chores. In this way, children are socialized into gendered patterns of family work that often replicate those of their parents.

Studies have also started to examine racial and ethnic patterns of household labor sharing. In the US, most research shows that African American men do more housework than either white or Hispanic men, although they still do much less than that done by African American women. Whether Hispanic men do more or less household labor than white men continues to be at issue, although a more consistent finding is that Hispanic women do more housework than either black or white women. Thus, more housework is performed in Hispanic households, although African Americans tend to be more egalitarian in their patterns of sharing. Moreover, when household labor is bought in the marketplace, it tends to be African American or Hispanic women, often undocumented, doing the labor for more well-heeled white women. In this way, gendered ideals about "rightful" domestic workers intersect with race/ethnicity to reproduce patterns of economic disadvantage and privilege.

Studies indicate that the most consistent predictors of men's housework participation are related to women's employment. The more hours wives work outside of the home and, often, the greater their proportional share of family income, the more husbands tend to share in the housework. Gender ideology also has an effect, with women's belief in equal sharing predicting their partner's increased contribution. In some instances, men's egalitarian attitudes predict their increased sharing, although men's attitudes are somewhat less predictive of their own participation. Generally speaking, more highly educated women do less housework and purchase outside domestic help more frequently. On the other hand, men with more education tend to do more housework. Marital status is a consistent predictor, with women doing more housework when they marry, and men doing less. When children arrive, the need for routine household labor increases, and most of the demand is assumed by women. Men tend to increase their hours of employment when children are born, which may have to do with women decreasing their paid employment to care for children.

In spite of the unbalanced division of household labor, most men and women consider their share of housework to be fair. Traditional norms suggesting that men are entitled to women's labor in the home, and correspondingly, that women are obligated to perform it, can lead to this conclusion. Research shows that both men and women perceive housework distribution as fair when women are doing approximately two-thirds of it. Reallocation of household labor, moreover, to create a more balanced division of labor typically does not happen spontaneously, instead requiring focused attention on change. While some may consider household chores to be a way to show love to family members, for the most part neither men nor women consider housework to be fun. Thus, wives may need to confront their husbands in order to get them to do more, thus causing marital conflict to increase. Since traditional norms tend to make women responsible for relationship harmony, wives may avoid "rocking the boat" to increase sharing. Accepting their unbalanced contributions as fair may be preferable for some women to creating disharmony in their marriage.

A number of theoretical perspectives have been proposed to account for the allocation of family labor. Three of the most often cited

perspectives include time availability, relative resources, and gender ideology. Theories invoking time availability imply that the person spending the least time in paid employment will be expected to do the most housework. Because men have historically been more visible in the workforce, working longer hours, women would thus be expected to do the housework. Relative resource theories suggest that the partner with the most resources, including income and education, should be able to avoid large contributions to household labor. Again, drawing on relative resource theory, women's disadvantage in terms of wages and, until recently, educational resources, has created expectations that they would do most of the household labor. Finally, theories implicating traditional notions about separate spheres point to housework as "women's work" and paid labor as "men's work." When spouses subscribe to this conservative gender ideology, it is seen as natural for women and men to do "their jobs," and women are therefore assumed to be the household labor experts. Other theories, such as economic dependency theory and the "new home economics" approach, also attempt to explain the persistence of disproportionate allocation of family work.

Family work includes both paid labor and unpaid household labor. While we are typically aware of the time family members spend in the paid workforce, we are generally less aware of the fact that nearly as much time is spent doing unpaid housework as is spent doing paid labor. We are also less aware of the ties between the two "spheres" and the fact that responsibility for unpaid housework takes away from time (and energy) that could be spent in the paid labor force. Because power accrues with workforce participation, the person responsible for the unpaid household labor is less likely to be empowered, either in the household or when they do participate in paid employment. Moreover, since traditional norms presuppose unpaid housework as women's work, women have been historically disadvantaged by the assumption of these cultural norms as natural and unchangeable.

Nevertheless, family work, both paid and unpaid, is changing. Women today are spending less time doing unpaid domestic labor, either because of constraints surrounding paid labor or diminishing expectations about how much time should be spent doing housework. Nothing suggests that women will spend less time at paid employment in the future. Men, on the other hand, appear to be doing somewhat more housework, particularly when that work is considered as a proportion of total household labor. This may reflect increasingly egalitarian attitudes in the home or it may point to more persistent demands by working wives that their husbands participate more equally at home. Whatever the reason, shifts that have occurred in the division of household labor over the course of the twentieth century are likely to continue into the twenty-first.

SEE ALSO: Gender Ideology and Gender Role Ideology; Gender, Work, and Family; Inequalities in Marriage; Marital Power/Resource Theory; Marital Quality; Women's Empowerment

REFERENCES AND SUGGESTED READINGS

Baxter, J. (1997) Gender Equality and Participation in Housework: A Cross-National Perspective. *Journal of Comparative Family Studies* 28: 220–47.

Bianchi, S. M., Milkie, M. A., Sayer, L. C., & Robinson, J. P. (2000) Is Anyone Doing the Housework? Trends in the Gender Division of Household Labor. *Social Forces* 79: 191–228.

Coltrane, S. (1996) *Family Man: Fatherhood, Housework, and Gender Equity*. Oxford University Press, New York.

Coltrane, S. (2000) Research on Household Labor: Modeling and Measuring the Social Embeddedness of Routine Family Work. *Journal of Marriage and the Family* 62: 1203–33.

Cowan, R. S. (1983) *More Work for Mother*. Basic Books, New York.

Davis, S. N. & Greenstein, T. N. (2004) Cross-National Variations in the Division of Household Labor. *Journal of Marriage and Family* 66: 1260–71.

DeVault, M. L. (1991) *Feeding the Family: The Social Organization of Caring as Gendered Work*. University of Chicago Press, Chicago.

Hochschild, A. R. (1989) *The Second Shift: Working Parents and the Revolution at Home*. Viking, New York.

Robinson, J. P. & Godbey, G. (1997) *Time for Life: The Surprising Ways Americans Use Their Time*, 2nd edn. Pennsylvania State University Press, University Park.

Strasser, S. (1982) *Never Done: A History of American Housework*. Pantheon Books, New York.

United Nations (2000) *The World's Women 2000: Trends and Statistics*. United Nations Publications, New York.

divorce

Stephen J. Bahr, Chao-Chin Lu, and Jonathan H. Westover

Sociologists who study divorce have focused on three major questions. First, some have taken a macro perspective and examined how and why divorce rates have changed over time. In this research, scholars have looked at broad social trends and how they are related to divorce rates. Second, there have been many studies of why individual couples decide to get a divorce. In this research, sociologists have examined the characteristics of individual couples and how they are associated with the risk of divorce. The third major thrust of research has been to explore the consequences of divorce. Major focuses of this research have been on how divorce affects economic well-being, psychological well-being, and physical health.

DIVORCE RATES

A major social trend during the past century has been a global increase in the divorce rate. During the second half of the twentieth century divorce rates increased in most industrialized countries. Divorce rates have been highest in the US, but there have been increases in many other countries as well. In the US the divorce rate was relatively stable between 1950 and 1965, increased dramatically between 1965 and 1980, and decreased slightly between 1980 and 2000. In the US it has been projected that about a half of all marriages will be terminated by divorce, and a half of all children will have spent some time in a single-parent home by the time they reach age 18.

During the past 20 years there has been a gradual decrease in the US divorce rate. Small but consistent yearly decreases in the divorce rate have resulted in a significant reduction in the divorce rate. From 1980 to 2000 the divorce rate per 1,000 married women decreased from 22.6 to 19.0, a decrease of 16.3 percent (US Census Bureau 2004). Recent evidence indicates that this decrease is not due to increased cohabitation or the aging of the population.

Sociologists have observed that the divorce rate is affected by rapid social change and social upheavals such as war and depression. For example, in the US the divorce rate increased after both world wars and during and after the Vietnam War. It decreased during the Great Depression, was relatively stable from 1950 to 1965, and decreased modestly from 1980 to 2000. Some of the social characteristics that appear to have contributed to the increase in the divorce rate are increased individualism, increasing marital expectations, the economic independence of women, and no-fault divorce laws. These are trends that have been occurring globally during the past 50 years.

During the 1960s and 1970s there was social upheaval and change with much emphasis on rights and the questioning of traditional roles, responsibilities, and authority. The civil rights and feminist movements helped stimulate an emphasis on individualism. As a result, in contemporary western culture and across the globe, there has been increased emphasis on individualism, freedom, autonomy, and the pursuit of personal happiness, including individual marital happiness.

As individual happiness has been emphasized, the primary purpose of marriage has become the achievement of individual happiness. If love wanes and one does not achieve the expected happiness in marriage, a logical solution is to dissolve the relationship. In short, one consequence of individualism is a trend toward less commitment to marriage and greater acceptance of divorce, cohabitation, and alternatives to marriage (Waite & Gallagher 2000; Wilson 2002). Recent research illustrates how divorce has become much more common and acceptable during the past 50 years. Compared to the past, young married mothers are much more likely to state that divorce is the best solution to persistent marital problems, and social sanctions against divorce have decreased (Thornton & Young-DeMarco 2001).

Another major social change during the past 50 years has been the increasing economic independence of women. For example, in the US the proportion of bachelor degrees earned by women increased from 35 percent in 1960 to 57 percent in 2002. The percentage of married women employed in the labor force increased from 32 percent in 1960 to 61 percent in 2003. Among married women with children under age six, 60 percent were in the labor force in 2003 compared with only 30 percent in 1970 (US Census Bureau 2004). A woman who is employed may be more likely to leave an unhappy marriage than a woman who is not employed. Similarly, an unhappy man may be more likely to leave if he knows his wife is financially independent (Schoen et al. 2002).

The norms of the broader culture are reflected in the law and as divorce became more common and accepted, no-fault divorce laws were passed. Law is influenced by cultural norms, but it also may help shape cultural norms. The law may teach, reinforce values, and be a model for appropriate behavior. A number of researchers reported that no-fault divorce laws had no effect on the divorce rate. On the other hand, several others found that divorce rates did increase as a result of the passage of no-fault divorce laws. Debate continues over whether or not no-fault divorce laws influenced the divorce rate. In recent research it was estimated that divorce rates would have been 6 percent lower if no-fault laws had not been enacted (Friedberg 1998). Since the increase in divorce rates began before no-fault laws were passed, the passage of no-fault laws appears to have been a reflection of a cultural change already in existence. In addition, however, the findings suggest that no-fault laws had an independent impact which helped shape the cultural acceptance of divorce and increase divorce rates.

DIVORCE RISK FACTORS

Divorce is a complex process influenced by many social and individual characteristics. Factors that have been found to be associated with the risk of divorce include age at marriage, premarital cohabitation, parental divorce, infidelity, alcohol and drug abuse, poor financial management, and domestic violence (Blumel 1992; Amato & Rogers 1997; Sanchez & Gager

2000). However, the nature and strength of risk factors differ across groups. To illustrate, in the US, premarital cohabitation is associated with subsequent marital dissolution among non-Hispanic white women but not among African American or Mexican American women (Phillips & Sweeney 2005).

A major social change during the past century has been the increase in paid labor-force participation of women. There has been debate about the influence of women's employment on the risk of marital dissolution. Schoen et al. (2002) found that women's employment was associated with an increased risk of marital dissolution among unhappily married women but not among happily married women.

There has been considerable study of couple interaction patterns and how they are associated with subsequent divorce. Contrary to expert opinion, Gottman et al. (1998) found that the extent of active listening by couples was not related to subsequent dissolution, nor was the amount of anger expressed. Rather, the risk of divorce was influenced by how couples handled disagreement and anger. Couples who could disagree without contempt or withdrawal were more likely to remain married. The ability to accept the influence of the other, starting discussions softly, and humor were all associated with greater marital stability. On the other hand, contempt, belligerence, and defensiveness were associated with a greater risk of marital dissolution (Gottman et al. 1998; Hetherington 2003).

EFFECTS OF DIVORCE ON ADULTS

Numerous researchers have found that compared with married persons, divorced persons tend to have more economic hardship, higher levels of poverty, lower levels of psychological well-being, less happiness, more health problems, and a greater risk of mortality (Hemström 1996; Amato 2000; Waite & Gallagher, 2000; McManus & DiPrete 2001). Cross-national data have confirmed similar findings in 20 countries across the world (Mastekaasa 1994a; Amato 2000). One of the ongoing questions among social scientists is whether the differences between married and divorced individuals are due to selection or the stress of divorce. The

selection explanation suggests that poorly functioning individuals have a high risk of divorce. Thus, characteristics that existed before the divorce produce the low levels of well-being rather than the divorce itself. If this explanation is correct, then differences between divorced and married persons could be explained by characteristics that existed prior to the divorce. An alternative explanation is that the stress of divorce lowers people's well-being. If this explanation is correct, then divorce would produce significant reductions in well-being net of pre-divorce characteristics. Although selection can account for some of the differences between divorced and non-divorced persons, recent research indicates that divorce appears to have a significant impact on well-being that is not explained by selection (Mastekaasa 1994b; Hemström 1996; Amato 2000; Waite & Gallagher 2000).

Although divorce is a stressful event, its impacts vary greatly according to the circumstances and attitudes of the people involved. Some are stressed by divorce but recover over time, while others are devastated and never recover. Hetherington (2003) observed that the majority of the divorced persons she interviewed were able eventually to build reasonably normal and satisfying lives. She identified six different patterns of adjustment to divorce. At one end of the continuum were the *enhanced* who adjusted well to the divorce. They were successful at work, socially, as parents, and often in remarriages. Ten years after the divorce, 24 percent of the women and 13 percent of the men were in the *enhanced* category.

At the other end of the continuum were the *defeated*, who spiraled downward after divorce and were low in self-esteem, had elevated scores on depression and anti-social behaviors, and often had difficulties with alcoholism or drug abuse. One year after divorce, about one-third of the divorced adults Hetherington studied were in the defeated group. Ten years after the divorce, only 10 percent of her sample remained in the defeated group and they were mired in despair, poverty, and depression.

A key question is what helps adults adjust successfully to divorce. Four key factors have been identified in research: (1) income, (2) a new intimate relationship, (3) age, and (4) social networks (Wang & Amato 2000; Hetherington

2003). First, those with adequate financial resources are more likely to adjust to the divorce. Second, those with a new intimate relationship (dating regularly, cohabiting, or remarried) are better adjusted. Third, divorce adjustment is more difficult for older than younger individuals. In most cases older persons have invested more time in the marriage and may have more difficulty finding another partner. Fourth, social networks provide encouragement, support, and other resources. Hetherington (2003) reported that social networks were important for many in her enhanced group.

FUTURE RESEARCH

There are several questions that need to be addressed in future research. First, there is a need for more extensive study of the process of divorce. When individuals divorce they go through a process in which they change their identity from a married person to a single individual. They make a variety of decisions regarding money, residence, and childrearing. Divorce impacts relations with friends and relatives and it involves processing legal documents. Even though there has been extensive study of the causes and consequences of divorce, there has been relatively little study of the process people go through to obtain a divorce.

Another important area for future research is to study different subcultures and cultures. Relatively little is known about divorce rates and trends in other countries. Related to this is the need to examine how various risk and protective factors operate in different countries.

Finally, it would be useful to study the dissolution of other types of intimate relationships. For example, Avellar and Smock (2005) examined the economic consequences of the dissolution of cohabiting unions. We need to know more about the risk factors, the dissolution process, and the economic and social consequences of the dissolution of cohabiting unions.

SEE ALSO: Children and Divorce; Cohabitation; Family Conflict; Family Demography; Inequalities in Marriage; Infidelity and Marital Affairs; Marital Quality; Marriage

REFERENCES AND SUGGESTED READINGS

Amato, P. R. (2000) The Consequences of Divorce for Adults and Children. *Journal of Marriage and the Family* 62: 1269–87.

Amato, P. R. & Rogers, S. J. (1997) A Longitudinal Study of Marital Problems and Subsequent Divorce. *Journal of Marriage and the Family* 59: 612–24.

Avellar, S. & Smock, P. J. (2005) The Economic Consequences of the Dissolution of Cohabiting Unions. *Journal of Marriage and the Family* 67: 315–27.

Blumel, S. R. (1992) Explaining Marital Success and Failure. In: Bahr, S. J. (Ed.), *Family Research: A Sixty-Year Review, 1930–1990*, Vol. 2. Lexington Books, New York, pp. 1–114.

Friedberg, L. (1998) Did Unilateral Divorce Raise Divorce Rates? Evidence from Panel Data. *American Economic Review* 88: 173–90.

Gottman, J. M., Coan, J., Carrere, S., & Swanson, C. (1998) Predicting Marital Happiness and Stability from Newlywed Interactions. *Journal of Marriage and the Family* 60: 5–22.

Hemström, Ö. (1996) Is Marriage Dissolution Linked to Differences in Mortality Risks for Men and Women? *Journal of Marriage and the Family* 58: 366–78.

Hetherington, E. M. (2003) Intimate Pathways: Changing Patterns in Close Personal Relationships Across Time. *Family Relations* 52: 318–31.

McManus, P. A. & DiPrete, T. A. (2001) Losers and Winners: The Financial Consequences of Separation and Divorce for Men. *American Sociological Review* 66: 246–68.

Mastekaasa, A. (1994a) Marital Status, Distress, and Well-Being: An International Comparison. *Journal of Comparative Family Studies* 25: 183–206.

Mastekaasa, A. (1994b) Psychological Well-Being and Marital Dissolution: Selection Effects? *Journal of Family Issues* 15: 208–88.

Phillips, J. A. & Sweeney, M. M. (2005) Premarital Cohabitation and Marital Disruption Among White, Black, and Mexican American Women. *Journal of Marriage and the Family* 67: 296–314.

Sanchez, L. & Gager, C. T. (2000) Hard Living, Perceived Entitlement to a Great Marriage, and Marital Dissolution. *Journal of Marriage and the Family* 62: 708–22.

Schoen, R., Astone, N. M., Rothert, K., Standish, N. J., & Kim, Y. J. (2002) Women's Employment, Marital Happiness, and Divorce. *Social Forces* 81: 643–62.

Thornton, A. & Young-DeMarco, L. (2001) Four Decades of Trends in Attitudes Toward Family

Issues in the United States: The 1960s through the 1990s. *Journal of Marriage and the Family* 63: 1009–37.

US Census Bureau (2004) *Statistical Abstract of the United States: 2004–2005*. Bernan Press, Washington, DC.

Waite, L. J. & Gallagher, M. (2000) *The Case for Marriage: Why Married People Are Happier, Healthier, and Better Off Financially*. Doubleday, New York.

Wang, H. & Amato, P. R. (2000) Predictors of Divorce Adjustment: Stressors, Resources, and Definitions. *Journal of Marriage and the Family* 62: 655–68.

Wilson, J. Q. (2002) *The Marriage Problem: How Our Culture Has Weakened Families*. HarperCollins, New York.

documentary

Annie Goldson

Documentary has existed as long as film itself. The one-reel actualitiés produced by the Lumière brothers in 1895 and the more complex films that followed these early experiments – for example, *Nanook of the North* (Flaherty 1922) and *The Man with a Movie Camera* (Vertov 1929) – were distinguished by their sense of a "historical real," the depiction of real people and events (Renov 1986). This apparent ability to capture "reality" has continued to distinguish documentary from fiction; indeed, the genre, with its intimate connection to the physical world, appeals because of its truth claims, whether these exist at the level of fact or image. Documentary stimulates what Bill Nichols calls "epistephilia" or a "desire to know," conveying an "informing logic, a persuasive rhetoric, or a moving poetics that promises information and knowledge, insight and awareness" (Nichols 2001: 40). The filmmakers above, however, would hardly have known they were making "documentary" at the time they were in production, as the genre had hardly yet been conceived.

It is difficult to give a comprehensive history of documentary, given the variability and flexibility of the genre. Documentary continuously responds to a changing environment. Technological advances, cultural and political shifts, the production of "break-through" documentary texts, and new market opportunities and pressures all impact on the direction and shape of the genre.

It is John Grierson, founder and leader of the highly influential British Documentary Movement, who is most often credited with coining the term documentary, as well as providing us with the first definition of the genre in the 1930s (Grierson 1966: 13). Describing it as "the creative treatment of actuality," Grierson tended not to dwell on any contradictions implicit within his definition, but the tension between "evidence" and "artifice," as Corner (1996) suggests, has continued to reverberate. Grierson's legacy, as Aitken (1998) suggests, is multi-faceted – the producer wrote copiously on the art of documentary, dreamed of "putting the working class on film," but also linked documentary to the pedagogical purposes of instruction and civic education. His "social issue" documentary, which follows a problem/solution scenario and remains a mainstay of the public broadcasting documentary strands today, established a series of documentary conventions, such as an anonymous narration, interviews that reinforce the "voice" of the documentary, and a rhetorical editing style.

During the interwar period, an influential strand of documentary that fused politically progressive or dissident attitudes, with formal innovation, flourished. This transnational movement included films from the Grierson stable – *Drifters* (1929), *Song of Ceylon* (1934) – as well as European classics such as *Land without Bread* (1933) and *The Spanish Earth* (1937), and American films such as *The Plow that Broke the Plains* (1936) and *The River* (1937). This wave of work was curtailed by the onset of World War II as documentary became harnessed to the war effort and, outside spectacular or poetic texts such as *Triumph of the Will* (Riefensthal 1934) or *Listen to Britain* (Jennings 1942), became predictable in structure and tone.

Ethnographic documentaries, heirs to Flaherty's complex legacy, continued through this period also. These ranged from "travel" films filled with exotic "disappearing savages," to more serious works of some ethnographic worth. Despite the value of some, much ethnographic film retained the "I–You" split of the anthropological gaze, thus replicating the power relationship between colonial powers and colonized peoples. Some films, notably those of Jean Rouch – *Les Maîtres fous* (1955), and *La Chasse au lion à l'arc* (1957–65) – exhibited the strains of failing imperial powers, anticipating more radical anti-colonial documentary practices to come. Rouch was to turn his cameras onto his own tribe (Parisian youth) in his groundbreaking film *Chronique d'un été* (1961), which deployed and defined the techniques of *cinéma vérité*.

Although a number of canonical documentaries – *Blood of the Beasts* (1949), *Night and Fog* (1955), and later *The Sorrow and the Pity* (1971) – continued an earlier more poetic, politicized tradition, the majority of documentaries produced in the immediate post-war period were made by governmental film boards. Documentary was to aid reconstruction and extolled the efforts of governments in creating jobs and developing infrastructures. The films were forced to adhere to set formulae and agendas and, although some filmmakers attempted to push at the boundaries, the documentaries remained largely forgettable.

The experimental edge displayed by documentary since its origins was further eroded by the establishment of television, which became, and remains, the site for most documentary funding and distribution. Television delivered documentary to audiences who in turn delivered advertising revenue back to broadcasters. Hence, documentary was tightly bound into the commercial contract of broadcasting culture, transmuting in the US (again, with some exceptions such as the fly-on-the-wall films of Direct Cinema) to more sensationalist magazine-style programming. Documentary fared a little better in the UK and Commonwealth countries, where a Griersonian notion of public service continued, manifest in such series as *Panorama*.

Today, despite the cultural variations that exist and the volatility of the international broadcast sector, television documentary remains remarkably uniform. Works tend to be gathered into "strands" that run for "seasons." Variations of these strands appear on public and state broadcasting systems, and commercial and the new specialist channels. Current affairs series and investigative programs, as well as nature, history, and science documentaries, remain staples and "national interest" documentary strands mandated with shoring up cultural identity appear on state broadcasting systems. Much of television documentary cited above remains "unauthored," its form and content largely dictated by the genre and timeslot expectations of audiences and network commissioners alike, although again, there are exceptions – "high-end" documentary strands, such as the BBC's *Storyville* or HBO's *Cinemax Reel Life* collect disparate and riskier "independent" documentaries, often produced by "auteurs" into a season.

Television documentary has also had to contend with, and itself has been influenced by, the rapid rise of "reality television" or popular factual programming. There are, by now, sub-genres of popular factual – from the survivor, celebrity, and dating shows, to the observational programs shot in airports or on the police beat. The critical and filmmaking communities remain divided over reality TV. Some argue that it has revived documentary, encouraging broader audiences to be more receptive to non-fiction programming. Others revile reality TV for destroying what they see as documentary's educational and political mandate. Certainly, reality TV is shaped by an economic environment that emphasizes competition, entertainment, and the need to garner ratings, which is remote from the existing traditions of documentary.

Although broadcast television has remained the dominant force in funding and distributing documentary, alternative media movements have continued to coexist. Developing rapidly during the 1960s and 1970s, they drew on the new and relatively inexpensive medium of video. Political, leftist, and agitprop collectives such as Newsreel (US) produced Marxist, radical, and feminist documentaries, while anti-colonial or Third Cinema films, such as the 1968 Argentinian film *La Hora de los Hornos*, were deeply influential in the developed world. Experimental film and video practices that eschewed the commercial and broadcast circuits flourished in metropolitan centers such as New York, Berlin, and London. With the demise of the organized left-wing and Marxist political parties at the end of the Cold War, documentary began to engage with identity-based movements: feminism, AIDS activism, and ethnic liberation movements, as well as environmental struggles and anti-globalization. The rise of digital platforms continues this trend and there is active exploration into "digidocs," often placed within activist and educational websites.

This more political documentary history has influenced a recent phenomenon: the shift of documentary back onto the big screen. If the overt educational and political agendas have faded on broadcast television, they are reemerging in the cinemas. Although not all cinema documentaries are "political," most engage with educational and cultural questions and issues. High-profile works such as *The Thin Blue Line* (Morris 1987) *and Roger and Me* (Moore 1989), and Moore's later films, *Bowling for Columbine* (2002) and *Fahrenheit 9/11* (2004), proved that documentaries can generate not only controversy and critical acclaim but also large profits. A slew of similarly political documentaries have followed, such as *The Corporation* (2003) and *Super Size Me* (2004), alongside softer, unlikely hits such as *Spellbound* (2002) and *Être et avoir* (2002).

Up until the late 1970s, writings on the documentary tended to be insider accounts that underlined the status of the documentary maker as something of a hero/outsider. With some notable exceptions, the wave of critical theory and film studies that emerged around this period had ignored documentary, focusing most attention on Hollywood classical cinema. However, as theory matured, documentary began to be subject to serious investigation. Its closer alignment to "reality" in fact threw "the problem of realism," already thoroughly explored in relationship to dramatic film, into even sharper relief. The problem with recording reality was that it assumes that "there is a real 'out there' in the natural world that can be shown (or that will reveal itself) without the use of linguistic or cinematic signs" (Gaines 1999: 2). This "impossibility" was wedded, in the same theoretical stew, with the Althusserian notion that "reality" is a highly ideological move to begin with. Realist documentary, then, was seen as reinforcing hegemonic belief systems because it appeared to capture "raw truth" while it was really delivering "ideology." As well as dominating the discussion of documentary, these critiques privileged certain styles of documentary – those

more interactive and self-reflexive modes – that are seen to reveal their own "constructedness" and frame.

Documentary theorists took a range of approaches to the genre. Bill Nichols's influential modal analysis, which provided a loose taxonomy, continues to prevail, while Brian Winston (1995) has taken a more historical than structural perspective, exploring the ambiguities and tensions within the Griersonian tradition. Michael Renov's (2004) most recent work traces subjectivity in documentary, a genre historically associated with objectivity. Accompanying the publication of monographs is an increasing number of edited collections on the documentary, some of the most useful emerging out of the "roaming" annual Visible Evidence conference. An increasing number of scholars, too, are breaking with the more canonical focus that has prevailed, engaging more with concepts of reception, audience, and more populist variants of television documentary, such as reality TV, docudrama, and mockumentary (Roscoe & Hight 2000; Hill 2004).

Although they tend to "get on with the job," makers are aware of their role of re-representing "reality." Every step in the production process is mediated by a slew of factors and many ethical and political dilemmas are generated on a daily basis. Documentarians measure up their films, or their films, indeed, are measured up, according to some "truth" or "history" that exists out there. Although couched in different language than that of academic debate, many of the same issues generated by the "problem of realism" are grappled with. The controversy around Michael Moore's "creative" use of timelines, the arguments about the truth or otherwise of reality TV, the rise of the "mockumentary," and the debates around bias, show that the tension between "creative" and "actuality," between "artifice" and "evidence," continues to reverberate in the various documentary communities – makers, audiences, and academics alike.

SEE ALSO: Author/Auteur; Documentary Analysis; Ethnography; Genre; Identity Politics/Relational Politics; Media; Popular Culture Forms (Reality TV); Poststructuralism; Public Broadcasting; Ratings; Realism and Relativism: Truth and Objectivity

REFERENCES AND SUGGESTED READINGS

Aitken, I. (Ed.) (1998) *The Documentary Film Movement: An Anthology*. Edinburgh University Press, Edinburgh.

Corner, J. (1996) *The Art Of Record*. Manchester University Press, Manchester.

Gaines, J. (1999) *Introduction: The Real Returns*. In: Gaines. J. & Renov, M. (Eds.), *Collecting Visible Evidence*. University of Minnesota Press, Minneapolis.

Grierson, J. (1966) *First Principles of Documentary*. In: Hardy, F. (Ed.), *Grierson on Documentary*. University of California Press, Los Angeles.

Hill, A. (2004) *Reality TV: Audiences and Popular Factual Television*. Routledge, New York.

Nichols, B. (2001) *Introduction to Documentary*. Indiana University Press, Bloomington.

Renov, M. (1986) Rethinking Documentary: Towards a Taxonomy of Mediation. *Wide Angle* 8(3–4): 71–7.

Renov, M. (2004) *The Subject of Documentary*. Minnesota University Press, Minneapolis.

Roscoe, J. & Hight, C. (2001) *Faking it: Mock-Documentary and the Subversion of Factuality*. Manchester University Press, Manchester.

Winston, B. (1995) *Claiming the Real: The Documentary Film Revisited*. British Film Institute, London.

documentary analysis

Lindsay Prior

To Max Weber, the written order formed an essential building block of that quintessential form of modern organizational life – bureaucracy. Many later sociologists also noted the importance of documents for structuring and facilitating human interaction. Despite this, documents in sociological studies tend to be somewhat taken for granted and more often than not used as a resource for research rather than as a topic in their own right. Indeed, in the frame of research methods, the use and manipulation of documents is often subsumed under the broader category of "unobtrusive" techniques. This is in strong contrast to the study and use of talk and of speech, which is often linked to tailor-made styles of analysis such as conversation analysis.

There is no obvious way to account for the contrasting fortunes of speech and writing in social scientific research and only a few social scientists have remarked on such differences. Thus, the anthropologist Jack Goody has frequently referred to and illustrated how writing is a rich, yet neglected, field for research studies. In a similar manner, Walter Ong underlined the ways in which the influence of writing – as against "orality" – has been underestimated in western scholarship. Yet the subordinate role of writing to speech is far from deserved. Text and writing are not, of course, coterminous with documentation and not all documents involve written traces. Architectural drawings, photographs, tapestries, scientific images, X-rays, body scans, and various kinds of physical artifacts can all function as documents in a sociological sense. However, a consideration of the written trace will serve as a useful paradigm for this entry.

As already suggested, when documents appear in sociological research they are usually approached in terms of what they contain. That is, the focus is principally on documents as a means of conveying information – as instruments or conduits of communication between, say, a writer and a reader. Documents do, of course, contain information, yet it is also quite clear that each and every document enters into human activity in a dual relation. First, documents enter the social field as a receptacle (of instructions, obligations, contracts, wishes, reports, etc.). Second, they enter the field as agents in their own right. Indeed, as agents, documents have effects long after their human creators are dead and buried (wills and testaments provide a readily available example of such effects). And as agents, documents are always open to manipulation by others: as allies, as resources for further action, as opponents to be destroyed or suppressed (we should not forget that people burn and ban documents as well as read them).

The text (and pictures, plans, and drawings) contained within any specific document can be analyzed using various techniques. These range from simple forms of content analysis to more complicated forms of discourse analysis. The former method, insofar as it focuses on, say, word and phrase counts and numerical measures of textual expression, can offer fundamental insights into what people consider to be significant and insignificant in the world. In this mode it is possible to study how people represent such things as "disease" or "crime," or even "self" and "other" in any given context. More sophisticated approaches to document analysis using strategies derived from the analysis of speech transcripts – such as the deployment of second order coding schemes – can also be applied to the written word. However, the most promising lines of inquiry are probably those developed on the basis of discourse analysis.

Discourse is a complicated concept, and it is not always clear what is meant by discourse analysis even in texts that are devoted to explaining what it might be. The best intellectual starting point for a sociologist, however, is in the work of Michel Foucault, who was essentially interested in the ways in which sets of ideas and concepts in science, medicine, and social science often cohered into determinate ways of seeing the world. More importantly, such "discursive formations," as he called them, were crucially linked to specific forms of social practice. In short, he argued that what is written and said is inextricably locked into what is done. So he assumed an essential connection between documents (and their contents), practical action, and sites of action – all of which express aspects of a discursive formation. With this in mind we can consider three specific moments of documentation in social action. They are, respectively, moments of production, consumption (or use), and circulation.

The production of documents (e.g., statistical and other reports on crime, health, poverty, and the environment) has figured as an object of study in numerous areas of sociology. The standard sociological stance is to use such reports as a resource for further study – as, say, a source of data on crime or health. Following the work of the ethnomethodologists, however, it is quite clear that documents as reports on the world can also be usefully studied as "topic." In the latter frame the key questions revolve around how reports and accounts of the world are actually assembled by social actors. What kinds of conceptual and technical operations become involved in their production and what range of assumptions are deployed so as to achieve the end result of a "report"? In the sociology of health and illness,

for example, studies have focused on the ways in which such things as death certificates for individuals or mortality reports – for towns, cities, regions, and nations – are produced. In the sociology of science, questions have been raised concerning the ways in which scientific findings and papers are produced. Indeed, in numerous studies of scientific controversy it is clear that demonstrating "facts" about the world depends very heavily on documentation – especially the manufacture of visible traces (via graphs, photographs, and tables) of invisible entities.

As to issues concerning the consumption of documents, these often turn on matters of use and function. In this frame, what is important is a study of the manner in which people use written (and non-written) traces to facilitate or to manage features of social organization – whether it be transitory episodes of interaction or the ongoing functioning of a hospital, or a business, or a school. For example, in his renowned study of folders in a suicide prevention clinic, Harold Garfinkel demonstrated how people who drew on such folders often used them for purposes that were not always consonant with the ways in which the files were originally designed. Thus, Garfinkel noted that many items of routine data that should have been contained in the folders (such as the age and occupation of the patient) were frequently missing. In a similar way, reasons for the non-acceptance of patients were missing in 20 percent of the folders, while the names of the staff members in charge of the intake conference were missing in just over 50 percent of cases. Clearly, these were "bad" records, and Garfinkel turned to asking why such incomplete records were, nevertheless, assiduously kept. Some of the reasons for poor record keeping were referred to as normal and natural troubles such as clinic personnel forgetting to enter data. More fundamentally, however, Garfinkel argued that clinic personnel often used the records aware of the possibility that the detail contained within them might be called on at some future stage to demonstrate that patients had always got the treatment they deserved. So clinic folders were, if you like, being constructed in a medico-legal framework such that it could always be shown that the "right" things were done to the "right" person at the "right" time. Such a contractual reading of folder contents explained why it was that basic items of data could be missing from the files on the one hand, while marginal notes and corrections and additions to the folder contents could appear on the other. In short, it accounted for why there were "good" organizational reasons for keeping bad records. Similar reasoning can and has been applied to the use of records in numerous other settings, such as school records, surgical records, and police and welfare agency records. Thus, in medical sociology, there have been numerous studies directed at showing the ways in which patient identities and diagnoses are often shored up through the use of written traces in medical "charts" and patient files.

The creation of identity through documentation is, of course, something that has figured prominently in the history of sociology. Thus, researchers in the so-called Chicago tradition (or school) of sociology gave voice to many human actors through the construction of "life stories." In the latter frame, "delinquents," criminals, and various people seen as outsiders figured largely in such accounts. In parallel mode, anthropologists often sought out autobiographies of those who had played important traditional roles, such as tribal chiefs. These days it is recognized that the work of identity creation and life "storying" is a concern of almost all people in the advanced world. This may be solely through the construction of a curriculum vitae for employment purposes or through a narrative of personal troubles as conveyed to a counselor, or more likely an account at a security check of who one "is" and what one is doing. (Asserting identity is, in the latter case, almost totally dependent on documentation.) Such autobiographical strategies constitute elements of what Foucault had termed "technologies of self" and they form an important cornerstone of everyday life in the modern world.

As for the circulation or exchange of documents – whether these be of good-will cards, Christmas cards, memos, or files – it is possible to see in the trace of exchange the development of social networks and the emergence of identifiable human groupings. For example, studies of citations in scientific papers have been used so as to identify styles of interaction between groups of scientists. Similar work using web-crawlers has been used by sociologists to identify emergent medico-scientific networks in the field of genomics. It is conceivable that a sociological study of email contacts and text messaging contacts among the ordinary public may also serve to demonstrate how the exchange of text and documentation functions both to define and cement social groupings. In a related mode, advocates of what has come to be known as actor-network theory (ANT) highlight the ways in which documents do not simply circulate but how they also often act back and structure their creators or users. In the latter sense some have spoken of the ways in which documents are invariably involved in the *performance* of social organization.

It is evident, then, that documents, and especially written documents, can be taken as a field of research in their own right. In particular, the study of the processes of production and consumption (or use) of written materials is often key to understanding how the social world and the things within it are constructed. Naturally, in the hurly-burly of ordinary everyday activity, issues of production and consumption become entwined, and it is not always easy to distinguish clearly between the one process and the other. Nor should issues of document content be overlooked. Rather, it is the ways in which production, consumption, and content relate to each other that should form the basis of sociological investigation.

SEE ALSO: Actor-Network Theory; Biography; Content Analysis; Discourse; Foucault, Michel; Transcription

REFERENCES AND SUGGESTED READINGS

Foucault, M. (1972) *The Archaeology of Knowledge*. Trans. A. Sheridan. Pantheon, New York.

Garfinkel, H. (1967) *Studies in Ethnomethodology*. Prentice-Hall, Englewood Cliffs, NJ.

Krippendorf, K. (1980) *Content Analysis: An Introduction to Its Methodology*. Sage, Beverly Hills, CA.

Lee, R. M. (2000) *Unobtrusive Methods in Social Research*. Open University Press, Buckingham.

Plummer, K. (2001) *Documents of Life 2: Invitation to a Critical Humanism*. Sage, London.

Prior, L. (2003) *Using Documents in Social Research.*
Sage, Thousand Oaks, CA.

Prior, L. (2004) Doing Things with Documents. In:
Silverman, D. (Ed.), *Qualitative Research: Theory,
Method and Practice*, 2nd edn. Sage, London.

doing gender

Sarah Fenstermaker

Candace West and Don Zimmerman introduced the concept "doing gender" in an article of the same title in 1987. They were the first to articulate an *ethnomethodological* perspective on the creation and affirmation of gender inequality between males and females in western society. The purview of ethnomethodology includes the study of the socially managed accomplishments of all aspects of life that are treated as objective, unchanging, and transsituational. West and Zimmerman's treatment of gender began by making problematic the prevailing cultural perspective: (1) female and male represent naturally defined categories of being that are derived from mutually exclusive (and easily distinguished) reproductive functions, and which result in distinctively different psychological and behavioral proclivities; (2) such divisions are rooted in that biological nature, which makes them both fundamental and enduring; (3) these essential differences between masculine and feminine are adequately reflected in the myriad differences observed between women and men and the social arrangements that solidify around them.

In clear contradiction to these notions, West and Zimmerman asserted that sex is founded on the socially agreed-upon biological criteria for initial assignment to sex category, but that classification typically has little to do with the everyday and commonsense sex categorization engaged in by members of a social group. They argued that it is not a rigid set of criteria that is applied to establish confidence that someone is male *or* female, but a seamless application of an "if–can" test. If someone *can be seen* as a member of an appropriate category, then he or she *should* be categorized accordingly. Following this assertion, West and Zimmerman were obliged to describe the process by which sex

categorization is construed, created, and reaffirmed. They did this through the concept of "doing gender."

This concept challenged the current thinking about gender as an attribute, an individual set of performative displays (largely separate from the ongoing affairs of social life), or a response to vaguely defined role expectations. They completed what Dorothy Smith (2002: x) deemed "a ruthless but invaluable surgery" by distinguishing among sex, sex category, and gender. Under this new formulation, gender could no longer be seen as a social "variable" or individual "characteristic" but as a socially situated accomplishment. West and Zimmerman argued that the implication of such ubiquity is that the design and interpretation of social conduct can at any time be made subject to concerns about sex category. Thus individuals and their behavior – *in virtually any course of action* – can be evaluated in relation to a womanly or manly nature and character. This dynamic, situated rendering of gender points to all aspects of social life – behavioral, emotional, discursive – that mark, note, remind, create, affirm, and reaffirm the social conviction that there is something *essentially* male or female that resides within and justifies sex categorization. The powerful gender *ideals* that abound in popular culture, advertising, and the media certainly serve as resources to guide normative understanding of doing gender, but the actual doing of gender requires much more than a regimented list of "appropriate" behaviors. As West and Zimmerman (1987: 135) explain, "Doing gender consists of managing such occasions so that, whatever the particulars, the outcome is seen and seeable in context as gender appropriate, or, as the case may be, gender inappropriate, that is, *accountable*."

West and Zimmerman maintained that humans might be classified as males or females, but to be treated as competent group members they must learn to feel, behave as if they possessed, and thus *demonstrate*, their essential womanly and manly qualities. By this the authors do not imply necessarily *hyper*masculine ress or deportment, but myriad craftings – according to every conceivable characteristic and expectation of particular settings and situations – that communicate competence as a person *accountably* feminine or masculine.

Moreover, while they allow that it is individuals who "do" gender, "the idiom of accountability [derives] from those institutional arenas in which social relationships are enacted" (Fenstermaker et al. 1991: 294). Categorical attributions like gender (and later, it was argued, race and class) are granted meaning by particular social conditions and are given concrete expression by the specific social and historical context in which they are embedded.

The notion of gender as an accomplishment in response to the ubiquitous dictates of accountability leads away from the notion of static normative ideals, and necessarily focuses attention on gender's *situated, fluid* character. *That* women and men believe themselves to be different by nature is a cultural constant; *how* and *in what ways* those differences are observed, granted social meaning, and rendered consequential varies by the situated particulars of social setting, time, and place. This is not to say that the accomplishment of gender need be confined to interpersonal, so-called "micro"-level interactions. Indeed, this conceptualization does not *narrow* gender's purview only to individuals, but enlarges it to address the myriad dynamics of any social order, at whatever level they operate.

ELABORATIONS

Following the initial formulation in *Gender and Society*, Candace West and Sarah Fenstermaker clarified and extended the concept of "doing gender." Their interest widened to focus on the implications of the concept for explicating practices of inequality and on the application of the concept to empirical work. The subsequent theoretical commentary of West and Fenstermaker focused primarily on the relevance of gender to various forms of interpersonal and institutional inequality and to the extension of the concept to include race and class (see below). They were motivated by an interest in the *social mechanisms* by which the various outcomes of social inequality (e.g., job discrimination, sexual harassment, violence against women, hate crime, differential treatment by gender in school, church, and government) are created and legitimated.

In that spirit, West and Fenstermaker asserted that the accomplishment of gender manifests itself at every level of social arrangement: discursive, interpersonal, organizational, and institutional. West and Fenstermaker argued that as representations of collective action, institutions are subject to gendering in the presentation of their "essential" characters, and are thus assessed (and behave *as if* they are assessable) in relation to gender. We need only look as far as the various recent peregrinations heard on "preserving family values," the United States as a "world cop," or the "immorality" of big corporations like Enron to get a sense of how institutions take on gendered characters that inform expectations of their actions. The broad sweep of the concept poses myriad possibilities for applications to the empirical world, particularly evident in the extension of "doing gender" to the concept of "doing difference."

In their article "Doing Difference" (1995), West and Fenstermaker posed a theoretical problem that took them well beyond their earlier preoccupation with gender. At the time, feminist sociological theory was beginning to pose questions about the categorical "intersectionality" of social life. West and Fenstermaker observed that there was little in the existing literature on gender that provided for an understanding of how race, class, and gender could operate *simultaneously* to shape and ultimately determine the outcomes of inequality. If such "intersections" or "interlocking categories" could go beyond metaphor, what was needed was a conceptual mechanism that illuminated "the relations between individual and institutional practice and among forms of domination" (West & Fenstermaker 1995: 19).

To adapt the argument offered in "Doing Gender," West and Fenstermaker asserted that while the *resulting manifestations* of sexism, class oppression, and racism are certainly different, the mechanism by which such inequalities unfold are the same. That is, "difference" is done (invidious distinctions justified on grounds of race, class, or gender) within individual and institutional domains to produce social inequalities. These practices are influenced by existing social structure, but also serve to reinscribe the rightness of such practices over time.

CRITICAL RESPONSE

The attempt to develop this unitary model of the workings of inequality garnered heated criticism (*Gender and Society* 1995) that captured some of the problematic features of the formulation as well as the ways an ethnomethodological focus on the production of inequality can be misconstrued. First, critics were wary of any formulation that seemed to conflate the distinctive features of class, race, and gender inequality. The implication for some was that this conflation *erased* the very real differences among class, gender, and racial inequalities. Second, critics worried that insofar as the approach rested on analysis of *face-to-face* interactions, it might be ahistorical as well as astructural, and thus neglectful of the workings of power. Finally, critics charged that in its focus on the constructedness of social life, both stable institutional inequality and the possibility of ongoing resistance to it might be missed.

In response, Fenstermaker and West reiterated that by requiring the locus of production of inequality to be *interaction* (broadly defined), one is directed to the center of the creation of raced, classed, and gendered social divisions. However situated, such divisions are hardly ephemeral; indeed, they bear the weight of history, past and ongoing institutional practices, and the day-to-day workings of social structure. Finally, they argue that this is also the way in which social change is made, where resistance has meaning and institutional power can be challenged.

The ethnomethodological insistence on placing interaction at the center of social life was seen by critics as problematic theoretically, but was greeted by empirical researchers as an invitation to productively recast the study of gender, race, and class. Since the 1987 publication of "Doing Gender," scores of empirical studies have demonstrated the empirical usefulness of a concept that directs researchers to the actual production of social life. Studies of the creation of class, race, and gender in high schools (Bettie 2003), the construction of culture and patriarchy among Asian Americans (Pike & Johnson 2002), Dana Britton's (2003) study of prison guards, and Barbara Perry's (2001) study of the construction of hate crime serve as only a few exemplars of the valuable work that begins from an interest in the situated dynamics of inequality.

TOWARD AN INTEGRATED FRAMEWORK

The useful theoretical tensions that now surround the concept "doing gender" speak to the multiple directions of feminist theory in sociology. First, there remains a continued interest in articulating the *simultaneous* management of categorical identities, where for example accountability to gender, race, class, and sexuality are *together* understood as ever available for social evaluation and social consequence. *How* those operate together or vary in individual salience in any given moment of interaction is a question for empirical study. Second are the recent calls to integration where gender is recast as a *social structure* or an *institution*. Here, the accomplishment of gender, race, class, and sexuality is acknowledged to be multidimensional, sometimes interpersonal, and sometimes organizational in character, and consciously builds in the likelihood of social change. It remains to be seen whether such integration can sufficiently direct empirical focus to the actual workings of accountability at all levels of social life. Third, a fruitful area of new study resides in the "destabilization" of social categories (e.g., "trans"-gender, "multi"-racial) that forces a reordering of both categorical definition and expectations surrounding accountability to them.

SEE ALSO: Ethnomethodology; Femininities/Masculinities; Gender Ideology and Gender Role Ideology; Inequality/Stratification, Gender; Intersectionality; Racialized Gender; Sex and Gender; Socialization, Gender

REFERENCES AND SUGGESTED READINGS

Bettie, J. (2003) *Women Without Class: Girls, Race, and Identity.* University of California Press, Berkeley.

Britton, D. (2003) *At Work in the Iron Cage: The Prison as Gendered Organization.* New York University Press, New York.

Fenstermaker Berk, S. (1985) *The Gender Factory: The Apportionment of Work in American Households.* Plenum, New York.

Fenstermaker, S. & West, C. (2002) *Doing Gender, Doing Difference: Inequality, Power, and Institutional Change.* Routledge, New York.

Fenstermaker, S., West, C., & Zimmerman, D. (1991) Gender Inequality: New Conceptual Terrain. In: Blumberg, R. L. (Ed.), *Gender, Family, and Economy: The Triple Overlap.* Sage, London, pp. 289–307.

Gender and Society (1995) Symposium on "Doing Difference" (9, 1). Sage, London, pp. 419–506.

Perry, B. (2001) *In the Name of Hate: Understanding Hate Crime.* Routledge, New York.

Pike, K. & Johnson, D. (2002) Asian American Women and Racialized Femininities. *Gender and Society* 17: 33–53.

Smith, D. (2002) Foreword. In: Fenstermaker, S. & West, C., *Doing Gender, Doing Difference: Inequality, Power, and Institutional Change.* Routledge, New York, pp. ix–xii.

West, C. & Fenstermaker, S. (1993) Power, Inequality, and the Accomplishment of Gender: An Ethnomethodological View. In: England, P. (Ed.), *Theory on Gender: Feminism on Theory.* Walter de Gruyter, New York, pp. 131–58.

West, C. & Fenstermaker, S. (1995) Doing Difference. *Gender and Society* 9(1): 8–37.

West, C. & Zimmerman, D. (1987) Doing Gender. *Gender and Society* 1(2): 125–51.

domestic violence

Dianne Cyr Carmody

Domestic violence is a pattern of coercive behavior designed to exert power and control over a person in an intimate relationship through the use of intimidating, threatening, harmful, or harassing behavior (Dutton 1995). This rather broad definition includes multiple forms of abuse: physical, sexual, and emotional or psychological. There is a lack of agreement about what should be included in the definition of domestic violence. Some argue for a broad definition that includes sexual and emotional harm, like the one above, while others limit their definition to actions that result in physical injury.

The debate over the definition of domestic violence complicates the already difficult problem of measuring the actual incidence of domestic violence. Those who use a broad definition report much higher incidences of domestic violence than those using a narrow definition. In addition, most cases are not reported to police and many victims suffer in silence for years.

In spite of these methodological challenges, research on the incidence, causes, and consequences of domestic violence has progressed in recent decades. This research, much of it conducted in the last 25 years, reveals important patterns and concurrent social problems associated with domestic violence. The victims of domestic violence are primarily female; in 1998, women were victimized at a rate 5 times higher than men (Rennison & Welchans 2000). Women face a higher risk of violent attack from intimates than strangers. Bachman and Saltzman (1995) found that women are up to six times as likely to be assaulted by a partner or ex-partner than by a stranger and they are more likely to suffer an injury when their assailant is an intimate (Bachman & Carmody 1994). Domestic violence is one of the leading causes of injury to women in the US (Tjaden & Thoennes 1998). Research has also revealed important patterns associated with race and ethnicity. African Americans experience the highest rate of domestic violence (Rennison & Welchans 2000). Domestic violence rates also vary by age and economic status, with highest victimization rates among the poor and females between the ages of 16 and 24 years (Rennison & Welchans 2000).

Domestic violence has also been linked to a variety of concurrent social problems. While victims may want to leave an abusive relationship, many remain out of fear or lack of resources or hope for change. Victims' fear is well founded: studies show that victims face the highest risk of serious or lethal injury at the point of separation (Tjaden & Thoennes 1998). In addition, each year, approximately one-third of all female homicide victims are killed by intimates (Bachman & Salzman 1995). While the victims of domestic violence face clear challenges, even those in nonviolent relationships pay some of the costs associated with domestic violence. A recent report from the National Center for Injury Prevention and Control (2003) estimates that domestic violence costs the nation US$5–10 billion annually in medical expenses, police and court costs, shelters, and employee absenteeism. Domestic violence has also been cited as a primary cause of homelessness (United States Conference of Mayors 1999).

While early researchers worked to document the magnitude of the domestic violence problem, more recent studies have focused on prevention and intervention in violent relationships. Some have assessed the impact of mandatory arrest laws (Sherman & Berk 1984; Carmody & Williams 1987; Hirschel & Buzawa 2002) and court-ordered batterer treatment programs (Davis & Taylor 1999; Stephens & Siden 2000). Others have emphasized the link between domestic violence and other types of violence: child abuse (O'Leary 1988), dating violence (Makepeace 1981), sexual assault (Russell 1990), and violence among same-sex couples (Renzetti 1992). With increased understanding of the dynamics and causes of domestic violence, more effective interventions and preventative measures should emerge. The result will benefit us all.

SEE ALSO: Child Abuse; Rape/Sexual Assault as Crime; Sexual Violence and Rape; Violence

REFERENCES AND SUGGESTED READINGS

Bachman, R. & Carmody, D. C. (1994) Fighting Fire with Fire: The Effects of Self-Protective Behavior Utilized by Female Victims of Intimate Versus Stranger Perpetrated Assaults. *Journal of Family Violence* 9(4): 319–31.

Bachman, R. & Saltzman, L. E. (1995) Violence Against Women: Estimates From the Redesigned Survey. In: *Special Report*. US Department of Justice, Office of Justice Programs, Bureau of Justice Statistics, Washington, DC.

Carmody, D. C. & Williams, K. R. (1987) Wife Assault and Perceptions of Sanctions. *Violence and Victims* 2 (Spring): 25–38.

Davis, R. C. & Taylor, B. G. (1999) Does Batterer Treatment Reduce Violence? A Synthesis of the Literature. *Women and Criminal Justice* 10, (2): 69–93.

Dutton, D. G. (1995) *The Domestic Assault of Women*. University of British Columbia Press, Vancouver.

Hirschel, D. & Buzawa, E. (2002) Understanding the Context of Dual Arrest with Directions for Future Research. *Violence Against Women* 8: 1449–73.

Makepeace, J. (1981) Courtship Violence Among College Students. *Family Relations* 30: 383–8.

National Center for Injury Prevention and Control (2003) *Costs of Intimate Partner Violence Against Women in the United States*. Centers for Disease Control and Prevention, Atlanta.

O'Leary, K. D. (1988) Physical Aggression Between Spouses: A Social Learning Perspective. In: Van Hasselt, V. B., Morrison, R. L., Bellack, A. S., & Hersen, M. (Eds.), *Handbook of Family Violence*. Sage, Newbury Park, CA, pp. 7–30.

Rennison, C. M. & Welchans, S. (2000) *Intimate Partner Violence*. NCJ 178247. US Department of Justice, Bureau of Justice Statistics, Washington, DC.

Renzetti, C. M. (1992) *Violent Betrayal: Partner Abuse in Lesbian Relationships*. Sage, Newbury Park, CA.

Russell, D. E. H. (1990) *Rape in Marriage*. Indiana University Press, Bloomington.

Sherman, L. W. & Berk, R. A. (1984) The Specific Deterrent Effects of Arrest for Domestic Assault. *American Sociological Review* 49: 261–72.

Stephens, J. & Siden, P. G. (2000) Victims' Voices: Domestic Assault Victims' Perceptions of Police Demeanor. *Journal of Interpersonal Violence* 15: 534–47.

Tjaden, P. & Thoennes, N. (1998) *Prevalence, Incidence, and Consequences of Violence Against Women: Findings from the National Violence Against Women Survey*. National Institute of Justice, Washington, DC.

United States Conference of Mayors (1999) *A Status Report on Hunger and Homelessness in America's Cities: 1999*, December: 39.

double consciousness

Rutledge M. Dennis

When W. E. B. Du Bois introduced the concept of "double consciousness" in his literary and autobiographical masterpiece, *The Souls of Black Folk* (1903), the idea of doubleness was already a major motif in the literary works of Dostoevsky, Stevenson, Melville, Conrad, Poe, and Goethe. Likewise, the term had been addressed in the psychological and philosophical writings of Nietzsche, Dewey, and James. For both groups, the merger of doubleness and consciousness often suggested an irrational force and the emergence of a dual and split personality entombed in one physical body. The dual and split nature of this consciousness suggested that what was in play was the existence of a "true" and genuine self which could be contrasted to a self which was "false" and inauthentic. Du Bois's use of the term would incorporate many of the psychological and, by reference, sociological assumptions associated with the authors above.

A restatement of the salient features of Du Bois's views on double consciousness permits us to focus on both the origins and consequences of this doubleness; such a restatement will also serve as the basis for a reassessment of the clarity of the concept as explicated by Du Bois. In addition, a reassessment permits us to approach the concept from contemporary sociological perspectives in order to focus on its possible utility in the current era. The core of Du Bois's logic on double consciousness is as follows: (1) it denies an objective consciousness; (2) the "other" becomes the eye through which the world is viewed; (3) it creates an internal warfare between black and white values and norms; (4) ultimately, the black and white selves may merge into a more creative and unique self; and (5) the struggle to appease black and white strivings has greatly handicapped an already distraught and oppressed black population.

In his examination of double consciousness, Du Bois places his thoughts and ideas in a sociological cul-de-sac. For example, his assertion of the absence of "true" self-consciousness assumes that the self-consciousness of blacks emerging from family and community networks, from economic, cultural, and political institutions, and from the dominant society was less than real or true. It was certainly not the consciousness of a free people, but it was a consciousness reflective of their condition and status in the society. For blacks to have had the consciousness of the free, while unfree, would fly in the face of logic and be yet another example of what Marx called false consciousness. That freedom for blacks would have meant another type of consciousness is a foregone conclusion, but the issue raised here addresses the difference between what consciousness would have been in freedom and how the experience of "unfreedom" is a true experience with its own accompanying consciousness, though not the uncomplicated consciousness Du Bois desired.

Du Bois's statement of blacks only seeing themselves "through the revelation of the other world" is simply untrue, and flies in the face of his own empirical research. For example, we now have vivid accounts of blacks during slavery, the Reconstruction, and the beginning of the Jim Crow years. What we see is a picture of a people grounded in the politics of pragmatism and using any and all available resources, strategies, and skills to navigate a system stacked against them. The reality is that they fought against the very idea of "only" seeing themselves "through the revelation of the other." It may seem logical that a people, faced with overwhelming political, military, and cultural power, may have no choice, but that logic is much too simple and does not take into account the highly complex manner in which humans both survive and play a variety of charades and roles in order to retain a positive and normative image of themselves against all odds.

The will to resist negative emotional, psychological, and sociological intrusions from those who wish to destroy one's humanity may be stronger than many believe. But here, one must understand Du Bois's strategy: to alert others, especially those who indirectly oppress, one must paint a picture which captures the horrors of physical, sociological, and psychological oppression and suffering, and these must be sketched in stark and uncompromising ways so that there is no mistaking the awfulness of this existence. Yet there is always the danger of making sufferers cardboard figures devoid of life, fiber, and willfulness, in which they become mere objects, incapable and unwilling to act. The reality of the brutalization of life in slavery and much of the post-slave era is now known through the words and voices of those who shared the horrid experiences. What emerges is a picture of victims who were seeing and defining the "other" who victimized them, while they themselves were simultaneously being victimized and defined by the "other." But the victims were also simultaneously defining themselves and placing a sociological and psychological marker between the "real" self-group and the self-group seen and defined by the other. Thus, the victim–victimizer dance is dialectical and there is a degree of "shadow boxing." Invariably, we must then conclude that the victims are never completely as weak as victimizers assume, nor are the victimizers ever as powerful as they believe themselves to be.

The second problem with the concept of double consciousness as used by Du Bois and as commonly used by others involves an inversion of logic. For example, if there is double consciousness, there must exist a "single" consciousness, and if the double nature of consciousness suggests the intrusion of the white mind and white thoughts and the conflicts resulting from this psychological and sociological invasion of white into black, the single consciousness must conversely connote a separate black thought tied to singular black experiences. Thus, the single consciousness is the black consciousness rooted in the experiences of blacks and their inner world out of which emerges the norms and values, and culture, around which blacks have, according to Ralph Ellison, created a world for themselves "on the horns of the white man's dilemma." The black, single consciousness, therefore, reflects the real and objective life as lived. However, rather than introducing the double consciousness to reflect, as it seems logical to do, how blacks have gained keen insights into whites and their social, cultural, and emotional world, Du Bois stands logic on its head by inverting the double to mean, not an objective view of the white world and how blacks see and define their actual objective condition, but how blacks look at themselves "through the eyes of others." This inversion of logic has kept the focus on a view of blacks as incapable of constructing an objective view of themselves or their world and almost destined to look at themselves and their world through the eyes of their oppressors. Again, there is little evidence to support this view. What makes Du Bois's position of the double more problematic is that, taken to its logical conclusion, it must mean that blacks have placed themselves completely within the consciousness of whites and thus use this white consciousness to assess black life, values, and concerns.

Sociology would be methodologically enriched if it were to "socialize" the term double consciousness and link it analytically and logically to the social. By doing so, we could better understand consciousness as it relates to specific dimensions of social interaction and social relations. In this way, Du Bois's inversion of consciousness, the collective seeing of one group through the eyes of another group, is avoided, placing Du Bois upright, as Marx did to Hegel. Such a new definition of doubleness will not be directed toward how the powerless have accepted the view of themselves as perpetrated by the more powerful. Rather, it will entail a shift which focuses the doubleness more vividly on the dominant powerful community, its institutions and organizations. Perhaps more importantly, such an adjustment in the use of the concept will move us away from one of Du Bois's central themes: a concentration on what powerful groups may think of less powerful groups. What does matter is for powerless groups to have an accurate view of who they are and what must be done as they engage the dominant society, and the need to develop a more accurate and objective critique of the dominant society.

Du Bois's metaphor of the double as "two souls, two thoughts, two unreconciled strivings; two warring ideals in one dark body" has been taken by many to refer to the hopelessness of the task facing blacks. The reality was far different from the picture painted by Du Bois. There was nothing in the black body or mind which mitigated against freedom for itself, hence, Du Bois led us sociologically into a blind alley by explaining the issue primarily as an internal battle, an internal war in which the black body was warring against itself. In reality, the war was external to the black body and stitched into the fabric of the social structure. Metaphorically, we can say that there was one soul occupying the black body, but there was another soul occupying the white body, and that soul was in opposition to the black body and the black soul. But just as the white body lacked two souls, the same can be said for the black body. Could the white soul enter the black body? Did whites have a double consciousness born from oppression and domination? Could the black soul enter the white body? Did Du Bois create a false dichotomy?

As problematic as double consciousness might be, Du Bois, when one reads the social contexts in which the concept is used, situated it in a sociology of black life, though he did not draw the obvious conclusions when he used the term. What must be asserted, however, is the reality that consciousness of whatever type must emerge from the lived experiences of the people. One part of Du Bois's logic is correct: consciousness must originate in the economic and social relations within the society. One of the difficulties of tracing double consciousness is that, like so many examples in Du Bois's sociology, he does not consistently utilize the same terms throughout his empirical and theoretical works. And he does not delineate or even hint at the concept elsewhere in *Souls of Black Folk* outside of chapters 1 and 10. Nor does he use the concept in his subsequent works. This may mean that he really did not consider the concept as a major definer of black life in America. The question must be raised as to the term's sociological relevance, theoretically and methodologically. Was the term merely of metaphorical value to Du Bois, and does it raise more questions than it answers or resolves? Though the concept is widely used today to refer to groups other than blacks – women, homosexuals, and other ethnic and racial groups – we might be faced with the reality that the Du Boisian idea of the double consciousness may best be observed and understood as a legacy developed out of literary works and the legacy of psychology as a discipline which analyzes the internal dynamics of the self. In this manner, the term can be closely allied to the concept of individual and group identity.

SEE ALSO: Acculturation; Class Consciousness; Color Line; Du Bois, W. E. B.; False Consciousness; Majorities; Marginality; Marginalization, Outsiders; Race and Ethnic Consciousness; Socialization; Solidarity

REFERENCES AND SUGGESTED READINGS

Dennis, R. M. (2003) Du Bois and Double Consciousness: Myth or Reality. In: Stone, J. & Dennis, R. M. (Eds.), *Race and Ethnicity: Comparative and Theoretical Approaches*. Blackwell, Malden, MA.

Dennis, R. M. & Henderson, C. (1980) Intellectuals and Double Consciousness. In: Hedgepeth, C., Jr. (Ed.), *Afro-American Perspectives in the Humanities*. Collegate, San Diego, pp. 38–46.

Du Bois, W. E. B. (1961 [1903]) *The Souls of Black Folk*. Fawcett Books, New York.

drag queens and drag kings

Leila J. Rupp and Verta Taylor

Drag queens and drag kings are men, women, and transgendered people who perform femininity, masculinity, or something in between. Drag in various forms can be found in almost all parts of the world, and increasingly a transnational drag culture is evolving. Traditionally, drag queens have been gay men who cross-dress and lip-synch to recorded music in gay or tourist venues, but the world of drag has become much more complicated with the emergence of drag king troupes, ballroom in black and Latino communities in the United States, and the participation of transgender, transsexual, and even heterosexual people in drag performances. Much of the scholarship on drag has focused on the question of how much such performances reify or challenge femininity and masculinity. Drag king troupes, influenced by feminism and queer theory, tend very consciously to deconstruct masculinity and femininity in performances, including by "faux queens" – also called "bio queens" – women who perform femininity or femininity as performed by drag queens. But even traditional drag queens, a variety of scholars have argued, undermine the notion of a polarized gender system by displaying the performative nature of gender.

Not all men who dress as women or women who dress as men identify as drag queens or kings. Other categories include transvestites or cross-dressers, generally straight men who wear women's clothing for erotic reasons; butch lesbians; preoperative transsexuals; and transgendered people who display and embrace a gender identity at odds with their biological sex. Some drag queens and drag kings also identify as transgendered or are in the process of sex-change surgery. Others alter parts of their bodies, as do "tittie queens," drag queens who acquire breasts through either hormones or implants but have no intention of changing their genitals. Ballroom, a cultural phenomenon with origins in New York over 50 years ago and made famous by the film *Paris is Burning*, encompasses a variety of categories: "butch queens" (gay or bisexual men who are masculine, hypermasculine, or effeminate), "femme queens" (male-to-female transsexuals at various stages), "butch queens up in drags" (gay men in drag), "butches" (female-to-male transsexuals, butch lesbians, or any woman dressing as a man), "women," and "men" (straight men).

Drag also encompasses a variety of styles of performance. Esther Newton (1972), in her classic study of US drag in the 1960s, distinguished between "stage impersonators," talented performers who sang in their own voices, and "street impersonators," more marginal drag queens who lip-synched their numbers. "Female impersonators" generally do celebrity impersonation and keep the illusion of being women, in contrast to those who regularly break it by, for example, speaking in their male voices, referring to themselves as men, or discussing their tucked penises. In Germany, this difference is marked by distinct identities: "drag queens" are glamorous female impersonators, while "Tunten," a reclaimed derogatory term for feminine men, are what in the United States would be called street queens or camp queens who dress in trashy and outrageous outfits and perform political theater. A similar distinction can be found in South Africa, where white "drag artists" who adopt a masculine persona offstage contrast with black or colored "common drag queens," effeminate men whose performance extends into everyday life. Ballroom features performances judged by "realness," for example, a gay man dressed as a straight businessman. Kinging involves a wide variety of performances, from impersonation of hypermasculine straight men to campy gay male numbers to enactments of serious political critiques of such issues as rape, hate crimes, and wartime violence.

The term "drag" in the sense of men wearing women's clothing dates back to the mid- or late nineteenth century, when glamorous female impersonators first appeared on stage. But drag also had connections to the subculture of cross-dressing men looking for male sex partners; even before the use of the term "drag" there were subcultures of men – known as "mollies" in England – who used feminine attire and mannerisms to express their same-sex sexual desire. In the 1920s, throughout the major cities of the western world, public drag balls and clubs featuring drag performers attracted mixed crowds. During World War II, in both Canada and the United States, male military personnel staged drag shows to entertain their buddies, although in Canada, as military women increasingly took over female roles, men in drag in theatrical productions aroused suspicion of homosexuality. Despite the conservatism of the post-war era, drag shows survived, in part by catering to straight audiences. In San Francisco, where the tourist industry touted the city's reputation for sexual license, gay men and lesbians mingled with heterosexual tourists at the drag shows at Mona's, "where girls will be boys," and Finocchio's. The Jewel Box Revue, although born in a Miami gay bar in 1939, also aimed at a straight audience. Like the tuxedo-clad Harlem performer Gladys Bentley, Storme DeLaverié, who emceed the Jewel Box Revue, was a predecessor of today's drag kings.

As drag changed in dramatic and less dramatic ways up to the explosion of gay and lesbian activism in the 1970s, two things remained constant: drag both built community among gay and lesbian people and challenged, if more or less politely, the dominant gender-divided and heterosexual order. José Sarria, who performed in drag at the Black Cat in San Francisco and ran for city supervisor in 1961 as part of the struggle against police harassment of the gay bars, formed the Imperial Court System in 1965, arguably the first drag queen movement organization. The Court System (now known as the International Court System, with chapters scattered over the western part of the country) raises money for the gay community (and other charitable purposes) through drag shows, but more importantly provides a "family" and respect for drag queens, the heart of the Court.

Drag as a way of creating family is central to ballroom as well. The ballroom community is organized into houses, family-like structures that sponsor competitive ball events. Each house has a mother (mostly men, but also women or transwomen) and a father who take responsibility for their children. Such familial support is essential for black and Latino youth who have often been rejected by their biological families, communities of origin, and religious institutions, the structures that generally sustain people of color in US society. Likewise, drag king troupes provide a nurturing environment for masculine and transgender women who face hostility and violence in the larger world. Drag king troupes and individual performers come together at an annual conference, the International Drag King Extravaganza, held in Columbus, Ohio, since 1999, where, in addition to attending academic sessions and performances, those interested can learn how to apply facial hair, bind their breasts, "pack" (wear a dildo or in some other way create a penis), and move like men.

If drag historically has created community, it has also always carried the possibility of challenge. Even the tourist shows at Finocchio's or the Jewel Box Revue had a potentially political edge. Comic routines called attention to the illusion of femaleness, and even traditional female impersonation worked to arouse sexual desire in straight male audience members. The role of drag queens in the resistance that followed the 1969 raid on the Stonewall Inn in New York is well known. In the years that followed, groups such as Street Transvestites Action Revolutionaries (founded by Sylvia Rivera, a heroine of Stonewall) and Flaming Faggots, along with men who identified as "radical fairies" and "effeminists," as well as butch women, challenged gender conformity within the movement. But such gender revolutionaries fought an uphill battle with gay liberationists and radical feminists who tended to dismiss drag as politically incorrect. Not until the 1980s, when groups such as the Sisters of Perpetual Indulgence and Church Ladies for Choice took up comic drag in a serious political struggle with the religious right, did transgender presentation again play a more central role in the movement.

Nevertheless, drag queen performances, especially the more "in-your-face" political variety in which there is no pretense at being women and a great deal of direct discussion of gay life, sexuality, and gender-crossing, can be seen as an effective strategy of the gay, lesbian, bisexual, and transgender movement. Drag shows at the 801 Cabaret in Key West, Florida, for example, explicitly challenge audiences composed of heterosexual as well as gay, lesbian, and bisexual people to confront the question of what makes a man a man and what makes a woman a woman, as well as to experience desires outside of their own sexual identities. Drag king performances tend to be very explicitly political, representing an enactment of feminist and queer theory critiques of masculinity, although some numbers are humorous and simply fun.

Drag also involves the performance of and movement across lines of class, race, and ethnicity. Impersonation of middle- and upper-class men by black and Latino working-class youth is part of ballroom events, and in both drag queen and drag king shows, performers sometimes adopt a racial or ethnic identity at odds with the one they normally embrace. Performance studies scholar Jose Muñoz argues that drag performed by people of color has the potential to deconstruct whiteness, and other theorists agree that drag holds the potential to expose the performance of racialized codes of gender.

Drag at the turn of the twenty-first century has taken on a wide variety of forms, but all of them are foreshadowed in drag history. There are talented artists who impersonate female or male icons or create their own personae; there are street queens who live a marginal life; there are professional and amateur drag queens who lip-synch and adopt a range of styles, from female impersonation to campy drag to voguing; there are movement activists who adopt drag for explicitly political purposes; there are mainstream celebrities such as RuPaul and Lady Chablis, who began their careers like other drag queens but became famous. Perhaps nothing illustrates the rags-to-riches possibilities of drag so much as the fortunes of Wigstock, the Labor Day drag festival in New York that began in 1984 with an impromptu performance by tired drag queens leaving a club at the end of the night and grew over the years into an international extravaganza attracting tens of thousands of spectators and official recognition from the city.

The major scholarly critique of drag queens – that they are more gender conservatives than gender revolutionaries, or that they exercise male power in female form – has not extended to drag kings, although there are no doubt some who would see them as aping, as they criticize, traditional masculinity. Some in the gay, lesbian, bisexual, and transgendered communities are critical of both drag queens and drag kings for calling attention to gender transgression and thus undermining the argument that gay people are just like heterosexuals in every way except choice of partners. Gender theorists have been very interested in cross-dressing and transgender performances for what they reveal about the social construction and performativity of gender and sexuality. Recent empirical research on drag queens, drag kings, and ballroom in different national and local contexts is enriching our understanding not only of the complex gender, sexual, racial/ethnic, and class dimensions of drag performances, but also of what they reveal about the fluidity of gender and sexual identity.

SEE ALSO: Doing Gender; Gay and Lesbian Movement; Homosexuality; Sex and Gender; Transgender, Transvestism, and Transsexualism

REFERENCES AND SUGGESTED READINGS

Brubach, H. & O'Brien, M. J. (1999) *Girlfriend: Men, Women, and Drag*. Random House, New York.
Butler, J. (1990) *Gender Trouble: Feminism and the Subversion of Identity*. Routledge, New York.
Garber, M. (1992) *Vested Interests: Cross-Dressing and Cultural Anxiety*. Routledge, New York.
Halberstam, J. (1998) *Female Masculinity*. Duke University Press, Durham, NC.
Newton, E. (1972) *Mother Camp: Female Impersonators in America*. University of Chicago Press, Chicago.
Paulson, D., with Simpson, R. (1996) *An Evening at the Garden of Allah: A Gay Cabaret in Seattle*. Columbia University Press, New York.
Rupp, L. J. & Taylor, V. (2003) *Drag Queens at the 801 Cabaret*. University of Chicago Press, Chicago.
Schacht, S. P., with Underwood, L. (2004) *The Drag Queen Anthology: The Absolutely Fabulous but Flawlessly Customary World of Female Impersonators*. Harrington Park Press, New York.
Senelick, L. (2002) *The Changing Room: Sex, Drag, and Theatre*. Routledge, New York.
Troka, D., LeBesco, K., & Nobel, J. (2003) *The Drag King Anthology*. Harrington Park Press, New York.
Volcano, D. LaGrace Volcano & Halberstam, Judith "Jack" (1999) *The Drag King Book*. Serpent's Tail, London.

dramaturgy

Peter Kirby Manning

A dictionary definition of dramaturgy is "the art of theater, especially the writing of plays." Roget's *Thesaurus* lists it under drama (599.2) and gives the synonyms theatrics, histrionics, acting, play-acting, melodramatics, stagecraft, *mise en scène*, and stage setting. This definition turns attention to the literal process of creating for others a scripted text for its presumed effects. In everyday life the metaphor has its limits and the world is not always a stage, or even dramatic. Most attempts at precise definition of dramaturgy fail because, while it is a powerful metaphor or way of seeing, the concept as employed surfaces differences in emphasis and style.

Dramaturgy points to a family of words associated with the idea of analyzing, or being sensitive to, selective performance to emphasize features of symbolic action, whether they be textual, prose or poetry, or behavior. In social science, dramaturgy is not an actor's perspective or a view with the actor's eyes but a metaperspective that makes sense of action, whether it is carried out by organizations, groups, or actors. Dramaturgy reflects the everyday work of actors, but the perspective does not assume an ironic pose, discount what is done or said, or begin with scientific concepts or theories. As seems apt, dramaturgy assumes neither that we know much more than what we see nor that we understand what lies behind the eyes of actors.

Given this perspective, what does dramaturgy connote about analysis of the social? What is achieved by use of the theatric metaphor and a focus upon how performances are enacted and with what effect(s)? What has an effect must be intelligible to others. In this sense, it requires or assumes feedback and reciprocity from an audience, the process by which claims are validated (verbal or non-verbal, written or electronic). Failure to produce feedback and reciprocity requires repair, apology, recreation.

Kenneth Burke, a leading writer on theater and drama, defines humans (as a logical category) thus: "Man is the symbol-using animal" (Burke 1989: 56). Symbol use is an expression of emotion or sentiment; it could be called a quest for meaning or emotional grounding.

Emotion, it would appear, is what is being symbolized; symbols touch off meaning, response, and emotion or catharsis in an audience. To state that symbols are "used" by "man" means that they are selectively attended to. Of the many symbols present in an encounter, only some will be used or selected to produce a response in others. In situations, parts or elements of action are revealed, given, and given off, but how they might produce a sequence of actions cannot be known fully in advance. Dramaturgy does not honor any particular repertoire of symbols, symbolic actions, conversational moves, or a given poetics of human conduct. However, it is likely that the power and appeal of dramaturgy rest in its applicability to the increasing number of situations in massified society in which strangers must negotiate encounters in the absence of shared values, beliefs, kin, or ethnic ties.

In this context of high modernity, performances rely on trust, evidenced in ongoing sequences of interpretation, what Goffman, following the philosopher Austin, terms the "felicity condition." Social interaction is a communicative dance based on trust and reciprocity. Thus mutuality and duality constitute the "promissory, evidential character" of social life. While trust, or acceptance of forthcoming outcomes, is necessary, it may be violated, new contingencies may arise, and a new line of action may unfold. People perform, respond, perform, respond, and thus they symbolize. It is a false and misleading assumption that trust is absent in modern life; it must be made present more in modern life where strangers have fewer cues to establish it in advance.

Goffman's view is not a full picture of the constraints of social structure. In many respects, the weakness of dramaturgy has been that those who use it casually "overcode" the notion, and apply it widely without qualification, seeing the ordering of life as a kind of bad high school play, or applying it exclusively at the actor's consciousness level rather than explicating the limits of the idea as metaphor to guide careful analysis.

Dramaturgy, or dramatism as Kenneth Burke called it, as a perspective in social science emerged at the University of Chicago. While Burke was an original scholar and an autodidact, other figures in the movement, Goffman, Gusfield, Edelman, and Duncan, were Chicago-trained PhD scholars. They were influenced by the ideas of George Herbert Mead, Herbert Blumer, and Charles Morris, who was himself a student of Mead's. Morris was pioneering and refining an idea related to symbolic interactionism and dramaturgy, semiotics, the science of signs. Burke's earliest works were subtle deconstructions of the singular Marxist materialist portrait of man particularly popular amongst intellectuals in the 1930s. In effect, asserting the partiality of any view of human conduct, Burke also questioned any full organic scheme such as the popular structural functionalism current until the 1970s.

To understand the contours of dramaturgy, one must consider further dramatists. As scholars, they begin with three assumptions. The first is that behavior is a vast, unfolding, deeply complex matter, for the meaning of which we are given cues by others. This is followed by a second assumption: that the human need for order and ordering is fundamental. This assumption suggests that humans are driven to perform for others in some fashion as a condition of sociality. People are civilized, as Durkheim writes, because they are tied to others. The third assumption is that through symbolic action, words, gestures, postures, and facial expressions, we seek to be understood. Symbolic action creates the possibility that sequences producing order will be sustained. While social scientists have seized on interaction as their materials, others have worked on texts, plays, plastic and visual arts, and the sequences of concern need not be face-to-face encounters.

Kenneth Burke and Hugh Dalziel Duncan were critics of written texts. Burke, like William Empson, was an insightful observer of that poignantly ambiguous symbolic action, poetry. Poetry is metaphor in the guise of metonymy. This concern with forms of speech and aesthetics aligns dramaturgy with classic rhetoric (Aristotle in particular), accounts, or vocabularies of motive, as well as any persuasive performance. "Motive" in dramaturgy is a rhetorical form: an account for an action choice when it is questioned. This is how motives are revealed. The underlying and unifying idea is that once tradition and continuity in human relationships are attenuated, meaning must be sought and pointed to again and again rather than assumed. Because complexity of action remains, what is seized upon for analysis, if not in everyday life, is what is *said* about what was done, will be done, or might be done. All renditions of interactions, including responses and interpretations of them, are endlessly partial. This proposition, refined by C. Wright Mills, brings us to the matter of metaphor and other figures of speech, for they provide recipes used to gloss longer sequences and order requests and responses. Strings of words may be extended into stories, allegory, myth, or other narrative genres. All representations are re-representations, and thus are paradoxical, partial, misleading, and open to interpretation and response. Thus, no metaphor, even dramaturgy, can capture the full richness of behavior *mis en scène*.

If we hold these points loosely in mind, several refinements set the scope of dramaturgy. These include the role of the self, of pragmatism, conversational analysis, and the role of the audience. These are critical distinctions, because they account for the tensions between symbolic interactionism, dramaturgy, and ethnomethodology. Dramaturgy does not require a self or selves as central meaning-producing mechanisms. All responses are interpretations, but they need not pass through a master self-like processor. It does not rest upon pragmatism or the social psychology of Mead, Blumer, James, or Peirce. Pragmatism presumes intentions and purposes of some sort which are revealed and refined over the course of interaction. Most attempts to clarify the perspective play on an assumed pragmatism: actors (writers, painters, poets, everyday citizens) seek to convince others (an audience) of what they claim to be by selective presentation of symbols. Life is not captured to be reshown on a VCR or DVD and cannot be rerun, even though it may be understood after the fact. The modern tradition of linguistics, conversation analysis included, posits a range of possible meanings in an interaction, whilst not considering the state of affairs chaotic. Sequential interpretations unfold, but cannot easily be used to reveal intent, purpose, or perspective. Perspective suggests consistency of project that is characteristic over time. Audiences are alert to efforts by others to make claims and to respond. Gusfield's gloss on Burke (Burke 1989: 10) makes the persuasive function of such symbolic action a part of the conflict and reflection inimical to human conduct. Readings

of "conflict" and "order" are done by the theorist, not by those who are embedded in the sense-making. Ethnomethodology and conversation analysis resemble dramaturgy, but differ in the role they attribute to the ordering of conversations according to tacit conventions, and in the degree to which order is problematic. In many ways, dramaturgy opts for a kind of surrealism or search for meaning, while ethnomethodology assumes order prevails.

Dramaturgy burst on the scene soon after the publication of Goffman's reworked, ethnographically based dissertation, *Presentation of Self in Everyday Life* (PSEL 1959). It was first published in 1956 as a research monograph by the University of Edinburgh. Goffman argues very tersely on p. ix: "I shall consider the way in which the individual in ordinary work situations presents himself and his activities, the ways in which he guides and controls the impression they form of him, and the kinds of things he may or may not do while sustaining his performance before them." In this sentence, Goffman states that dramaturgy is about the actor's impression management. His strong connection to dramaturgy in spite of variations in emphases in his career is signaled best by the organizing metaphors he employs, many of them taken from the theater – front and back stage, script, and role. PSEL stimulated both efforts to summarize it and a number of collections.

PSEL has sold well and remains in print after some 40 or so years; it has been very influential on two generations of graduate students. The book is controversial because it renders interaction as a puzzle resolved only in and through interaction, not via a priori concepts such as personality, values, norms, or social systems. Goffman struggled to show how actors display order and ordering conventions in many situations, with an eye always to ways humans adapt, interpret, read off, and make sense of others' behavior. This does not assume life-as-chaos, nor does it require positing people as "puppets" with attributed feelings, aims, goals, and a repertoire of strategies and tactics. It does assume that they act to display for others and to elicit a response. Goffman was associated with dramaturgy, but his work evolved, evading easy understanding or simplification.

The complexity of his ideas, as well as his abiding significance as a scholar, lead many to agonize over his concepts, seeking to fit them to this or that scheme; rendering his work as a cynical dismissal of modern life; attempting to embed his ideas in a sociohistorical context; dismissing them as trivial; seeing them as a paradigm of modern life or an impenetrable enigma. None of these is fully accurate. Tom Burns, an early colleague of Goffman's at Edinburgh, perhaps most accurately dismisses attempts to discover a single consistent theory in Goffman's writing. Philip Manning disagrees, arguing for an emergent puzzle composed of constituent parts.

Scholars have struggled with the basic notions of dramatism with varying success, some shaping it in line as a version of symbolic interaction; performance ethnography that emphasizes the "performative" nature of human action; postmodernism; quasi-organizational theory; of quintessential democratic interactions, and as politics as a grand spectacle arising from the need to dramatize and manage conflicts. The most troubling connections are to structuralism and semiotics, as Goffman cites scholars such as Bakhtin and Russian linguists, and refers to signs in several of his publications. A few salient and useful attempts at exegesis exist.

Criticisms of dramaturgy as theory often come from unsympathetic sources (Brissett & Edgley 1990 summarize these). The point most frequently made, that dramaturgy asserts ontological assumptions about the reality of life-as-theater, is clearly wrong. It is one among many possible perspectives; it is not a perspective on perspectives. A second common criticism is that it is not a theory of the deductive/propositional sort. This perhaps hinges more on a definition of "theory" than on whether dramaturgy qualifies. A third trenchant criticism is the view that the extensive accommodation and impression management of the modern citizen is an indication of normality, not deviance. This modern citizen, sensitive to impressions and their management, seeking to be liked, is an ideologically captured consumer, a shadow of more powerful economic and political forces. Modernity is perhaps more than this, but not less. In this way, Goffman echoes ideas of Robert Musil, Ortega y Gasset, Sartre, and Camus.

SEE ALSO: Chicago School; Conversation Analysis; Ethnomethodology; Everyday Life; Goffman, Erving; Mead, George Herbert; Postmodernism; Self; Semiotics; Symbolic Interaction; Trust

REFERENCES AND SUGGESTED READINGS

Brissett, D. & Edgley, C. (Eds.) (1990) *Life as Theater*, 2nd edn. Aldine de Gruyter, New York.

Burke, K. (1989) *On Symbols and Society*. Ed. with an Introduction by J. Gusfield. University of Chicago Press, Chicago.

Ditton, J. (Ed.) (1980) *The View from Goffman*. St. Martin's Press, New York.

Drew, P. & Wooton, A. (Eds.) (1988) *Erving Goffman: Exploring the Interaction Order*. Northeastern University Press, Boston.

Duncan, H. D. (1962) *Communication and Social Order*. Oxford University Press, New York.

Fine, G. A. & Smith, G. (Eds.) (1998) *Goffman*, 3 vols. Sage, London.

Goffman, E. (1963) *Presentation of Self in Everyday Life*. Doubleday Anchor, Garden City, NY.

Lemert, C. & Branaman, A. (Eds.) (1997) *The Goffman Reader*. Blackwell, Malden, MA.

Manning, P. (1992) *Goffman and Modern Sociology*. Stanford University Press, Stanford.

Riggins, S. H. (Ed.) (1990) *Beyond Goffman: Studies on Communication, Institution, and Social Interaction*. Mouton de Gruyter, New York.

Smith, G. (Ed.) (1999) *Goffman and Social Organization: Studies in a Sociological Legacy*. Routledge, New York.

Trevino, A. J. (2003) *Goffman's Legacy*. Foreword by C. Lemert. Rowman & Littlefield, Lanham, MD.

dropping out of school

Ralph B. McNeal, Jr.

Dropping out of school in a post-industrial society comes with many risks. In the United States, as with most industrialized societies, education is a key factor for predicting social mobility; dropping out clearly undermines one's prospects of moving up the socioeconomic ladder. Dropping out of high school is also accompanied by many other negative outcomes or consequences, including an increased propensity for subsequent criminal behavior, lower occupational and economic prospects, lower lifetime earnings, an increased likelihood of becoming a member of the underclass, lower levels of academic skills, and poorer levels of mental and physical health than non-dropouts.

In addition to the negative consequences for the individual dropout, areas with high concentrations of dropouts also suffer. Areas with higher concentrations of dropouts have decreased tax revenues, increased expenditures for government assistance programs, higher crime rates, and reduced levels of social and political participation. Given all of these negative consequences, what do we know about high school dropouts? Who are they? Why do they fail to complete high school?

Before answering any of these questions, we should first define *dropout*. This is not as easy as it might appear. Oftentimes, attempts to define high school dropouts and actually measuring this status in the many available data sources are at odds. In the purest sense, a high school dropout is *anybody who fails to acquire a high school diploma*. There are two major national studies that are often used to conduct research on high school dropouts, High School & Beyond (1980) and the National Education Longitudinal Study (NELS, 1988). These two databases account for the lion's share of what we know about dropping out of high school during the past two decades, but each data source has its own limitations. In High School & Beyond, dropouts are those students who drop out of school between the tenth and twelfth grades; this clearly misses a large number of dropouts who either leave school prior to the tenth grade (one estimate is that between 10 and 20 percent of dropouts leave school prior to the tenth grade) or those who are still in school in the twelfth grade, but eventually drop out. In NELS:88, high school dropouts are often defined as those who have left school during or after the eighth grade and still have not returned to school or acquired a high school diploma as of two years post the anticipated graduation date (a six-year window). NELS is far more inclusive, but still leaves some students out of the definition because they return to complete their high school diploma outside of the allotted window. Thus, while the abstract definition of a high school dropout is very clear, the actual measurement of who

has, or has not, dropped out is questionable. To help clarify the various statuses, any number of terms have been applied, including "stopouts," "dropouts," "early leavers," and "returnees," just to name a few (Pallas 1986).

To further complicate matters, researchers often define high school dropouts differently than do educators. In some instances, educators actively track students who have left their school and do not include the student as a dropout if he or she enrolls in an alternative education or adult learning program. In other instances, educators do not track the student once he or she has left the school but classify the student as a dropout if that individual withdraws from school and there is no accompanying request to forward the student's academic record to another educational institution. Regardless of how it defines a student who has left school, it is often in the school's best interest to record the lowest possible dropout rate since it is one measure of school quality. Somewhere in the midst of these various operationalizations lies the truth – those students whose educational careers fall short of acquiring a high school diploma.

WHO DROPS OUT AND WHY?

It is not difficult to paint a portrait of the typical high school dropout. There have been a plethora of studies trying to determine who drops out (or does not). Racial and ethnic minority students – in particular blacks and Hispanics – are more likely to drop out than white students. Students of lower academic ability are more likely to drop out than are high-ability students. Lower socioeconomic status (SES) students are more likely to drop out than higher SES students. Being older than one's peers and/or from a single-headed household have also been linked to higher likelihoods of dropping out. Gender prominently factors into the dropout equation; teenage pregnancy is more likely to lead to dropping out for women, whereas acquiring a full-time job has a greater increase on the likelihood of dropping out for men. Beyond demographics, researchers have also examined other individual-level measures including student involvement in extra-curricular activities and adolescent employment. Students who are more involved in extra-curricular activities are less likely to drop out; students who work more than 20 hours a week during the school year have an increased likelihood of dropping out.

Many of these individual-level effects were established by researchers in the 1980s and 1990s using a variety of theoretical models, including the participation-identification model, the social control model, the rational choice model, various integration and process models, and zero-sum models. During the past decade, various elements of social context have also been incorporated into theoretical models, including peer group, family, school, and community factors. In terms of family-based explanations, parents' level of education and/or occupational standing, select aspects of the home environment such as the availability of cultural capital resources, and the relevant social support system (e.g., social capital) have been found to significantly affect a student's likelihood of dropping out. Students with parents or older siblings who are dropouts are at higher risk of dropping out, as are students with uninvolved parents.

More recent research further expands the boundaries of meaningful social context(s) by examining the school's role in producing high school dropouts, as well as the influence of various neighborhood characteristics. Research has consistently found that school size, level of social integration or involvement within the school, resources, and various indicators of school climate all affect whether a student drops out of school. Studies have also shown that spatial/context measures such as higher dropout rates and greater rates of poverty have a disproportionate effect on an individual student's likelihood of dropping out. The majority of studies examining school or community context use some variant of opportunity theory, coupled with the assumption that adolescents are rational actors in the educational decision-making process, to explain dropping out within a multilevel framework.

In summary, research to date has examined an exhaustive number of predictors of dropping out of school at the individual, familial, peer group, school, and community levels. Most of the aforementioned concepts can be thought of as "pushing" or "facilitating" factors. An alternative set of factors can be viewed as "pulling" or "attracting" measures. Previous research established that students often leave school early because they wish to obtain the status of various adult roles, such as mother or worker. These two findings are clearly gender-related. For many young women, pregnancy is a key contributing factor to their decision to drop out of school; scholars contend that the attraction of motherhood draws young women out of school to start families. For many young men, the lure of full-time employment is sufficient for them to prematurely terminate their education; this is especially true in impoverished neighborhoods where full-time jobs are a rare commodity. The so-called "tipping point," the point where school-year employment becomes detrimental to a student's chances of completing high school, seems to be approximately 20 hours a week. What distinguishes both of these effects (pregnancy and employment) from other predictors is the strong possibility of a selection effect. In other words, the research clearly establishes these links, but there is disagreement on the direction of causality. Proponents of adolescent work contend that students who are already disengaged from school choose to work; opponents of adolescent work contend that greater than part-time work draws otherwise engaged students out of school and into the workplace. Similar arguments are made concerning teenage pregnancy. Does the desire to assume adult roles come before or after the student's disengagement from schooling? The truth is, we do not know, because studies have yet to systematically control for the student's adult-role orientation, making it impossible to draw a definitive conclusion.

FUTURE RESEARCH

Given what we know about the consequences of dropping out, and the major predictors, what is yet to be determined concerning high school dropouts? Future research should focus on one of four broad areas: defining and measuring dropout, disentangling early childhood attitudes and behaviors and determining their effect on dropping out, studying dropouts from non-public school settings, and addressing the long-term costs and consequences of dropping out.

As for the first broad need, there are several specific tasks that should be completed. First, there needs to be a clearly articulated and widely agreed-upon method of defining, and perhaps more importantly of measuring, dropout. Most previous research tends to define school dropout in relation to high school, but many students drop out of middle school and are not captured in most studies. Additionally, the category of "dropout" should be more fully refined to recognize that not all dropouts are the same. For example, there are dropouts who fail to acquire any further education, dropouts who return to get their high school diploma, dropouts who earn an equivalency certificate (e.g., GED), and dropouts who continue on to attain college or postgraduate degrees. Future research should strive for better clarity when professing to study "dropouts" and address the subtle, but likely very important, differences across these groups.

The second broad need is to disentangle early childhood attitudes and behaviors, and to determine their effect on dropping out. Some preliminary research has examined how early childhood predictors such as attitudes toward school, exposure to delinquent behaviors, and early childhood parenting practices affect adolescent delinquency and drug use. This is a line of social psychological research that should be applied to dropping out of school since items such as early childhood school readiness, literacy, and elementary school experiences should be critical for understanding dropping out of high school. After all, dropping out often is the final step in a very long and gradual process of disengaging from school.

The third broad area where future research might prove fruitful is the investigation of dropouts from non-public school settings. To date, the lion's share of research has focused on dropouts from public high schools. Research is clearly needed on who drops out of private schools (religious, non-religious, and alternative/charter schools), and why. As with most other educational processes studied during the last 40 or more years, there will surely be differences between public and private schools in this regard. The lack of current research on this matter seems to imply that dropping out of school is only an issue faced by public schools, and this is clearly not the case.

Finally, research should more clearly conceptualize dropping out in a longitudinal framework. Too often research on dropouts looks at predictors approximately two years prior to dropping out and outcomes approximately two to four years after dropping out. Given the importance of educational credentials in a post-industrial society, research should place dropping out of school into the context of the life course perspective and investigate how this act is related to a wider variety of predictors in childhood and outcomes in later life. Such studies should clearly define dropout, including its many subcategories, and investigate the similarities and differences in a variety of outcomes in the later stages of the life course such as life satisfaction, lifetime earnings, and mental and physical health (to name a few).

SEE ALSO: Educational Attainment; Gender, Education and; School Transitions; Schooling and Economic Success; Social Capital and Education; Tracking; Transition from School to Work

REFERENCES AND SUGGESTED READINGS

Pallas, A. (1986) School Dropouts in the United States. In: Stern, J. & Williams, M. (Eds.), *The Condition of Education: Statistical Report*. Government Printing Office, Washington, DC.

drug use

Larry Gaines

Drug addiction and abuse constitute a major social problem that is interlaced throughout our society. Each year it costs billions of dollars in terms of interdiction, prevention, enforcement, treatment, and lost productivity. Moreover, the drug problem exacerbates a number of other social problems including poverty, homelessness, crime, and family discord. Historically, society addressed the drug problem, as well as other social problems, using a generalized, simplistic response. However, if the drug problem is better understood in terms of who is using drugs and what types of drugs are being used, tailored responses can be developed that in the end may be more effective and beneficial.

American society is bombarded constantly by all sorts of messages advocating the use of drugs. Pharmaceutical companies and vendors have inundated society with drug advertising. Few people can open their email accounts without having at least one message that attempts to sell some type of drug. Many of these vendors have their own physicians who can prescribe drugs in absentia. A significant proportion of television advertising is now devoted to prescription drugs, and they all end by urging viewers to ask their physician about some drug that will enhance their lives by making them feel better, look better, or have enhanced sexuality. There are approximately 3 billion prescriptions written annually, and the Center for Disease Control and Prevention (CDC) notes that each year physicians write about 1.5 prescriptions per office visit, demonstrating a substantial amount of medicating in the United States (Cooper et al. 1993; NIDA 2004).

In some quarters of our society, the same pressures exist for using illicit drugs. Young people are enticed to use drugs as a result of cultural norms and expectations. Ample friendship networks exist to deliver club drugs such as Ecstasy, cocaine, and Rohypnol. For many youth, drugs are solidly embedded in the culture, and they desire to be accepted as one of the group. Since alcohol and tobacco consumption is high for young people, it is rather easy for them to slip into using drugs. Research indicates that adolescents who use alcohol and tobacco cigarettes are significantly more likely to use illegal drugs than adolescents who abstain from these legal drugs.

The vast majority of efforts attacking the drug problem are concentrated on illegal drugs, but it must be understood that prescription drugs are just as problematic, although they receive less notoriety. Quantities of prescription drugs are diverted to the street and abused. Nicotine and alcohol are the two most widely used drugs in society, but because of their legal status most people do not see them as such, although this has been moderated somewhat as

government and public groups have attempted to negatively label their use and abuse. Substances that are psychoactive, that is, influence the workings of the mind – and therefore the behavior of organisms that take them – are legally governed in the United States by the Controlled Substance Act of 1970. This Act divides substances into "schedules" according to their medical utility and their potential for abuse. Those substances the federal government regards as having "no medical utility" and a high potential for abuse are Schedule I drugs: it is illegal to possess or sell Schedule I drugs. They include heroin, LSD, marijuana, and Ecstasy. (It must be pointed out that bodies other than the United States government regard a number of Schedule I drugs – marijuana most notably – as having considerable medical utility.)

Many in our society are concerned with America's drug problem. However, America does not have a single drug problem; it has multiple drug problems. Although marijuana is the drug of choice across the social spectrum, different constituencies or groups have a propensity to use or abuse other drugs. Young people tend to abuse marijuana, Ecstasy, and Rohypnol and inhalants. Methamphetamine is predominately a rural drug, while crack cocaine and heroin are associated with inner-city youth and young adults. Middle- and upper-class professionals tend to use powder cocaine at a higher rate relative to other groups. Synthetic narcotics such as Lortab, Dilaudid, and OxyContin are more likely to be abused by middle-aged and older Americans, and a number of prescription drugs are abused by housewives. Although there is overlap in terms of drug consumption, there is a measure of stratification of drug usage within the overall population.

There are different levels of drug usage. Legalistically, the use of any illegal drug or prescription drug in a manner not recommended by the physician is considered abuse, but some people have more problems with drug use than others. Goode (2005) notes that the drug problem cannot be fully understood without considering the amount of drugs that individuals consume. Abdinsky (2004) has developed a continuum of drug use that better illustrates the point. First, there is experimental use where a drug is tried to see what happens. Individuals may experiment with a drug once or a few times and never use the drug again. This is a fairly common occurrence. Second is culturally endorsed use where an individual's culture or peer group has adopted or accepted the use of a drug or set of drugs as normative behavior. When this occurs there is pressure on the deviant non-drug user to conform to the norms of the group. Such pressures are extremely enticing and many youngsters and teens have difficulty resisting. The same can be said of many marginalized neighborhoods where drugs are an everyday part of life. Recreational use is the third category, and this is where drugs are consumed more frequently. Drugs are used increasingly in more social contexts, and the abuser tends to look for opportunities or excuses to consume drugs. Finally, compulsive use is where individuals have developed a physiological or psychological dependence on the drug. Many more life events center around the acquisition and use of drugs as opposed to work or family responsibilities. The Department of Health and Human Services (2003) estimates that there are 22 million Americans classified with substance dependence or abuse, which includes alcohol as well as illicit drugs. This constitutes 9.4 percent of the population aged 12 and older.

Although compulsive drug use begins with experimentation, it is not true that all drug experimenters end up as compulsive drug users. Indeed, many people do not venture beyond the experimentation stage of drug use. For example, the National Survey on Drug Use and Health, which is conducted by the Department of Health and Human Services, provides data on lifetime and past month drug usage. In 2002, 46 percent of the American population aged 12 or older had used an illicit drug in their lifetimes, but only 8.3 percent had used an illicit drug in the past month. While 8.3 percent of the population perhaps showed a pattern of drug usage, about 38 percent of the population appeared to be infrequent drug users or people who were experimenters. Thus, the vast majority of drug users do not become compulsive users.

It is informative to examine drug usage patterns when attempting to understand the amount and patterns of drug consumption in the United States. To this end, there are a variety of surveys that can be enlightening. In 2002, the National Survey on Drug Use and Health survey found that approximately 19.5 million Americans were current drug users. The most widely used drug was marijuana with a use rate of 6.2 percent. There was an estimated 2 million cocaine users with a little over 25 percent being crack cocaine users. This represented less than 1 percent of the population. Cocaine use declined in the early 1990s for youth, but the trend has reversed and in 2002, an estimated 2.7 percent of the population had used cocaine at some point. There were 1.2 million hallucinogen users, and a little over 50 percent of the hallucinogens being abused was Ecstasy. Ecstasy has been driving an increase in hallucinogens for several years. There were 166,000 heroin users in 2002, and the rate of usage has been steadily climbing since the mid-1990s, although these figures are suspect since many heroin users such as the homeless are not counted in the household survey. A substantial proportion of the increase is attributable to young people whose rate of usage has increased 400 percent in the last seven years (DHHS 2003).

There is a substantial portion of the population that is abusing psychoactive prescription drugs. Approximately 2.6 percent of the population or 6.2 million people reportedly are current users of psychoactive drugs for non-medical purposes. The most commonly abused prescription drugs are pain relievers, followed in order of use by tranquilizers, stimulants, and sedatives. As an example, OxyContin, a synthetic narcotic and a relatively new drug, has about 2 million abusers, which is similar to the number of cocaine users in the United States (DHHS 2003). Psychoactive drugs are diverted from pharmacies and medical providers, manufactured in clandestine labs, and smuggled into the United States from foreign countries.

As noted above, drug use is interlaced with a variety of problems. The relationship between drugs and crime is of most importance and drives a substantial proportion of the concerns with drug abuse. Thus, it is cogent to examine drug use in the criminal population. However, before examining these statistics, it is important to note that there is considerable debate on the degree to which drugs cause crime. Although drug use is attributable to some crime, many experts agree that the drug problem commingles with the crime problem and that criminals reside in a culture that is conducive to drug use. These experts argue that it is not a clear-cut causal relationship (McBride & McCoy 2003; Faupel et al. 2004).

To this end, three models explaining the crime–drug relationship have evolved (Goode 2005). First, the enslavement model posits that individuals become addicted to drugs as a result of some life situation or happenstance. They become trapped in their addiction and must resort to crime to support their drug needs. Proponents of the enslavement model see legalization of drugs as a viable method of reducing drug-related crimes. Second, the predisposition model states that criminals are deviants or anti-social people who have a predisposition to commit crime and take drugs, and reside in a culture where drugs are accepted and plentiful. Drugs and crime become an accepted part of life. Finally, the intensification model basically states that drug usage intensifies criminal behavior. This is supported by the fact that when addicts desist from drug usage, the number of crimes they commit declines precipitously (Ball et al. 1983). Inciardi (1992) sees drug use as intensifying an already existing criminal career.

A significant proportion of those arrested regardless of crime are abusing drugs. The Arrestee Drug Abuse Monitoring Program (ADAM) examines drug use rates in 39 large and medium-sized cities in the United States. Essentially, jail inmates are interviewed about their drug use and asked to provide a urine sample, which is analyzed to determine if drugs are present and the kinds of drugs inmates were taking at the time of their arrest. Screening concentrates on illegal drugs and a limited number of prescription drugs: cocaine, opiates, marijuana, methamphetamine, PCP, barbiturates, benzodiazepines, methadone, and propoxyphene. ADAM is an important program in that it provides access to drug use information about the criminal population, which assists in the development of more effective criminal justice policies.

In terms of male arrestees, the median percentage of arrestees testing positive for one of the above nine drugs in 2003 was 67, and the median percentage for females was 68. The 2002 National Survey on Drug Use and Health reported that 11.6 percent of the population aged 12 or older had used an illicit drug in the past month. Although ADAM and the National Survey use different methodologies, the differences between arrestees and the population are striking and demonstrate that drug usage among the criminal population is significantly higher. The median use rate for female arrestees across cities was one percentage point above the male rate. Females used crack cocaine, cocaine, and heroin at a higher rate, while males used marijuana and methamphetamine at a higher rate (Zhang 2004). The difference in usage rates between males and females may be the result of sample characteristics or police discretion when deciding to make an arrest as opposed to actual use rates. The police may apply laws more strictly to the males. Regardless, the data show that drug usage and abuse is high among all arrestees with some differences across cities.

The ADAM statistics reveal that for the most part, cocaine and marijuana primarily are being used by those arrested. PCP appears in the drug testing fairly infrequently, and methamphetamine and heroin use, although widespread, seem to be regionalized with some locations having moderate numbers of users, while other locations have minimal numbers of users who are arrested.

If drug usage statistics were examined in detail for a period of several years, it would reveal that there is an ebb and flow of drug problems. Drugs of choice, to some extent, vary by region of the country, age of the population, and city. Historically, society and government have not recognized that there are multiple drug problems, and for the most part have developed prevention, suppression, and treatment programs that may be applicable to one part of the country or one type of drug, but have less utility for other parts of the country and other drugs. The drug problems must be fully understood in terms of patterns of usage, and more effective programs must be fashioned that address specific populations and types of drugs. This can only be accomplished by monitoring drug usage patterns and researching programs at the micro level. An understanding of what works and the conditions that facilitate success must be understood. Only then can effective responses to the drug problems be implemented.

SEE ALSO: Addiction and Dependency; Alcohol and Crime; Drugs, Drug Abuse, and Drug Policy; Drugs and the Law; Drugs/Substance Use in Sport

REFERENCES AND SUGGESTED READINGS

Abdinsky, H. (2004) *Drugs: An Introduction*, 5th edn. Wadsworth, Belmont, CA.

Ball, J. C., Shaffer, J. W., & Nurco, D. N. (1983) The Day-to-Day Criminality of Heroin Addicts in Baltimore: A Study in the Continuity of Offense Rates. *Drug and Alcohol Dependence* 12: 119–42.

Cooper, J. R., Czechowicz, D., & Molinari, S. (1993) *Impact of Prescription Drug Diversion Control Systems on Medical Practice and Patient Care*. National Institute of Drug Abuse, Rockville, MD.

Department of Health and Human Services (DHHS) (2003) *Results from the 2002 National Survey on Drug Use and Health: National Findings*. Department of Health and Human Services, Washington, DC.

Faupel, C., Horowitz, A., & Weaver, G. (2004) *The Sociology of American Drug Use*. McGraw-Hill, New York.

Goode, E. (2005) *Drugs in American Society*, 6th edn. McGraw-Hill, New York.

Inciardi, J. A. (1992) *The War on Drugs II: The Continuing Epic of Heroin, Cocaine, Crack, AIDS, and Public Policy*. Mayfield, Mountain View, CA.

Lyman, M. & Potter, G. (2003) *Drugs in Society: Causes, Concepts, and Control*, 4th edn. Anderson, Cincinnati.

McBride, D. & McCoy, C. (2003) The Drugs–Crime Relationship: An Analytical Framework. In: Gaines, L. K. & Kraska, P. (Eds.), *Drugs, Crime, and Justice*. Waveland, Prospect Heights, IL, pp. 100–19.

National Institute on Drug Abuse (NIDA) (2004) Nida.nih.gov/ResearchReports/Prescription/prescriptions.

Zhang, Z. (2004) *Drug and Alcohol Use and Related Matters Among Arrestees – 2003*. Office of Justice Programs, Washington, DC.

drugs, drug abuse, and drug policy

Emma Wincup

The term "drug" has been both broadly and narrowly defined. At its simplest, it is reserved for substances which are prohibited under criminal law. Deploying this definition, the range of substances classified as drugs varies across time and across jurisdictions. However, typically, it refers to substances such as heroin, cocaine, ecstasy, and amphetamines. At the other extreme, more inclusive definitions of the term have been adopted. In addition to outlawed substances, in these instances, drugs can refer to alcohol and tobacco, plus substances such as solvents, prescribed medication, and over-the-counter remedies used illicitly. When developing policies, countries are most likely to utilize a narrow definition and focus attention on illegal drugs.

The terms "drug abuse" and "misuse" are frequently used in policy documents to describe the most harmful forms of drug use which warrant attention. However, there is an emerging consensus that these terms should be avoided because they are highly subjective and judgmental descriptions of patterns of drug use. Instead, the term "problem drug use" is preferred, which typically describes patterns of use which create social, psychological, physical, or legal problems for an individual drug user. Although many problem drug users will be classified as emotionally or physical dependent on drugs, this is not inevitably the case. Instead, their drug use can be regarded as problematic because they engage in high-risk behaviors (e.g., injecting drugs or consuming large quantities in one session). It is important to note that unambiguous distinctions between patterns of drug use are difficult to draw, not least because at one level all drug use can be viewed as problematic due to its potentially negative implications for an individual's health and well-being.

Problem drug use has been defined as a law and order, social, medical, and public health problem. Defined as a law and order problem, policy attention is likely to be focused on strategies to reduce the supply of drugs through tackling drug markets or to decrease the demand for drugs through attempts to break the link between drugs and crime. This link is often viewed simplistically as a causal one, with drug users committing crime to finance their drug use. Consequently, policies such as coercive drug treatment are advocated to break the link.

Problem drug use has also been understood as a social problem. A challenge for sociologists is to explore why problem drug use has been defined in this way and who has done the defining. The policy implications which flow from understanding problem drug use as a social problem are not readily apparent. On the one hand, it could lead to a policy agenda which tries to overcome the social exclusion experienced by problem drug users by understanding the social-structural factors related to problem drug use. However, on the other hand, it could lead to policies based on the premise that problem drug use is the result of the personal characteristics of individuals who experience it, further marginalizing them from society.

Approaching problem drug use as a medical problem involves equating it with a disease. The development of a medical model for understanding problem drug use was influential in moving understanding away from moral failure. Policies which flow from conceptualizing problem drug use in this way emphasize particular forms of treatment, and have been criticized for failing to appreciate the social causes and consequences of problem drug use.

Perceiving problem drug use as a public health problem stems from a concern about its effects on health and well-being for individuals and the communities they live in. For example, community members may be exposed to used drug paraphernalia. Consequently, advocates of this approach suggest the need to pursue a harm-reduction strategy, which includes practices such as operating needle-exchange schemes and prescribed substitute medication.

Different conceptualizations of the type problem drug use presents have influenced, at different times, the policy approach adopted by individual countries. For example, during the 1980s and most of the 1990s, the UK adopted a public health approach to drug use. This was a response to the realization that unsafe injecting practices could transmit HIV. As the new millennium drew near, a criminal justice approach to drug policy was adopted: problem drug use and offending became increasingly interlinked. This can be perceived as an example of policy transference, with the UK following – in part – policies adopted in the US. On both sides of the Atlantic critics have suggested that pursuing a law and order approach to tackling drug use amounts to a war on drug use and a war on drug users. Contemporary drug policy in the UK, as in other countries, is best described as based upon a range of different conceptualizations of the type of problem drug use poses, which results in a wide range of policies being adopted. These policies are implemented by a varied group of organizations (e.g., criminal justice, health care, and social work agencies). In reality, this may mean that drug users are exposed to seemingly contradictory policies; for instance, policies which have the effect of criminalizing growing numbers of drug users can be pursued alongside policies which increase opportunities for drug users to give up drug use or to use drugs in a less harmful manner.

SEE ALSO: Addiction and Dependency; Deviance, Crime and; Drug Use; Drugs and the Law; Social Problems, Concept and Perspectives

REFERENCES AND SUGGESTED READINGS

Barton, A. (2003) *Illicit Drugs: Use and Control*. Routledge, London.
Blackman, S. (2004) *Chilling Out: The Cultural Politics of Substance, Consumption, Youth and Drug Policy*. Open University Press, Buckingham.
Natarajan, M. & Hough, M. (Eds.) (2000) *Illegal Drug Markets: From Research to Prevention*. Criminal Justice Press, New York; Willan Publishing, Cullompton.
South, N. (1999) *Drugs: Cultures, Controls and Everyday Life*. Sage, London.
Wincup, E. (2005) Drugs, Alcohol and Crime. In: Hale, C., Hayward, K., Wahidin, A., & Wincup, E. (Eds.), *Criminology*. Oxford University Press, Oxford, pp. 203–22.

drugs and the law

Brian K. Payne

At the broadest level, law can be defined as a written policy designed to control human behavior. Drug laws, then, are written policies designed to control drug-using behaviors. The aggressive response to drug-using behaviors, however, is a relatively modern phenomenon in the United States. A series of early American drug laws precipitated current efforts to control drug-related behaviors. These laws included the Pure Food and Drug Act of 1906, the Harrison Narcotics Tax Act of 1914, and the Marijuana Tax Act of 1937. In fact, between the early 1900s and 1969, hundreds of federal drug laws were passed in the United States.

Perhaps the most influential piece of drug legislation framing the current response to drug-using behaviors, the Comprehensive Drug Abuse Prevention and Control Act of 1970 repealed all prior federal drug laws and placed all drug laws under this broad, encompassing law (Payne & Gainey 2005). One of the significant aspects of this law was that it created a mechanism by which drugs could be categorized into various "schedules" based on the drug's medical utility and harm. Schedule I drugs (e.g., heroin, methaqualone, LSD, marijuana, and hashish) are considered to have no medical use and a high potential for abuse. Schedule II drugs (demerol, methadone, cocaine, PCP, and morphine) are those that do have currently accepted medical uses but also have high potential for abuse. Schedule III drugs (opium, vicodan, Tylenol with codeine, and some other amphetamines and barbiturates) have an accepted medical use and a medium potential for abuse. Schedule IV and V drugs have medical uses and a low potential for abuse. These schedules are significant, not just for a classification scheme, but because of the fact that criminal penalties parallel the drug's schedule. Offenses involving Schedule I drugs would warrant the stiffest penalty, followed by Schedule II, III, IV, and V drugs respectively.

The Comprehensive Drug Abuse Prevention and Control Act of 1970 also included a civil asset forfeiture clause which allowed for seizure of drugs and items used in the drug trade. It was expanded in 1986 with the "Substitute Assets Law," which said the government could take the suspect's property if the drug assets are no longer available (Blumenson & Nilsen 1998).

Asset forfeiture is justified on punitive, deterrent, and economic grounds. Problems that have arisen with these policies include the use of the asset forfeiture as revenue, changing priorities in the drug war, goal displacement, and systemic failure (Payne & Gainey 2005). In terms of asset forfeiture's revenue-generating phenomenon, there is reason to believe that some police departments have come to rely on asset forfeitures as a form of revenue needed for the department to survive at the most basic levels. In fact, a survey of 1,400 local law enforcement agencies found that the department depended on a significant amount of civil asset forfeiture funds "as a necessary budgetary supplement" (Worrall 2001: 171). With regard to the changing priorities of the drug war, it is believed that rather than taking efforts to control and prevent crime, police may select cases which can generate the largest profit with little regard for the social benefit of the case (Miller & Silva 1994). On a related point, goal displacement occurs inasmuch as "revenue generation becomes a sub-goal of the criminal justice response to illicit drug activity" (Payne & Gainey 2005: 128). Finally, systemic failure occurs when asset forfeiture policies keep the justice system from attaining its goals (Vecchi & Sigler 2001a, b).

Though drug laws vary from the federal to the state level and across the states, today, at least five types of drug laws exist (US Department of Justice 1993). First, *possession laws* are those drug laws that stipulate it is illegal for individuals to possess certain types of substances. *Trafficking laws* are those drug laws which aim to control the movement and distribution of drugs. The difference between possession and trafficking laws usually has to do with the amount of drugs possessed. If an individual possesses a large amount, it could be regarded as a trafficking offense, regardless of whether that individual intends to distribute or sell the drugs. Penalties attached to trafficking offenses are much more severe than those attached to possession offenses.

Use laws are those drug laws that stipulate that individuals cannot use certain substances.

For example, if an individual tests positive for marijuana use after being pulled over for a traffic violation, he can be arrested and prosecuted for using the drug even if he does not possess it. In contrast, *misuse laws* are those laws which regulate the amount of a particular substance individuals are permitted to use. Driving while intoxicated laws are an example. Finally, *paraphernalia laws* are those laws which regulate the possession and sale of items that can be used to promote the use or distribution of controlled substances.

Penalties attached to drug offenses have received a great deal of scrutiny and criticism. In particular, some argue that the drug laws assigning penalties for cocaine and crack cocaine are racist and unfair. Individuals convicted of cocaine possession tend to be more affluent while those convicted of crack possession tend to be poorer. The effects of the two drugs are believed to be similar, but the penalties for crack offenses are much more severe than the penalties for cocaine offenses.

SEE ALSO: Addiction and Dependency; Alcohol and Crime; Drug Use; Drugs, Drug Abuse, and Drug Policy; Law, Sociology of

REFERENCES AND SUGGESTED READINGS

Blumenson, E. & Nilsen, E. (1998) Policing for Profit: The Drug War's Hidden Economic Agenda. *University of Chicago Law Review* 65: 35–115.

Blumenthal, R. N., Kral, A. H., Erringer, E. A., & Edlin, B. R. (1999) Drug Paraphernalia Laws and Injection-Related Infectious Disease Risk Among Drug Injectors. *Journal of Drug Issues* 29(1): 1–17.

Katz, J. (2003) White House Tries to Ban the Bong. *Rolling Stone*, July 24, pp. 54–5.

Miller, J. M. & Silva, L. H. (1994) Drug Enforcement's Double-Edged Sword. *Justice Quarterly* 11: 313–35.

Payne, B. K. & Gainey, R. (2005) *Drugs and Policing: A Scientific Perspective*. Charles C. Thomas, Springfield, IL.

US Department of Justice (1993) *Drugs, Crime, and the Justice System*. US Government Printing Office, Washington, DC.

Vecchi, G. M. & Sigler, R. T. (2001a) *Assets Forfeiture: A Study of Policy and Its Practice*. Carolina Academic Press, Durham, NC.

Vecchi, G. M. & Sigler, R. T. (2001b) Economic Factors in Drug Law Enforcement Decisions. *Policing: An International Journal of Police Strategies and Management* 24: 310–29.

Worrall, J. C. (2001) Addicted to Drug Asset Forfeiture. *Journal of Criminal Justice* 29: 171–87.

drugs/substance use in sport

Ian Ritchie

In the *Commission of Inquiry into the Use of Drugs and Banned Practices Intended to Increase Athletic Performance* (Dubin 1990), commissioned by the Canadian government in the aftermath of the infamous Ben Johnson drug scandal at the 1988 Seoul Summer Olympic Games, Chief Justice Charles Dubin stated that the problem of drug/substance use represented the single greatest moral crisis in high-performance sport today. His statement was prescient in that there is probably no other issue that is seen by either the general public or authorities in major sport organizations to be a greater threat to the integrity of international sport than the use of banned drugs/substances. Certainly no other issue warrants the same commitment of resources and bureaucratic effort, especially since the creation of the World Anti-Doping Agency in 1999, which now oversees anti-doping efforts worldwide. The problem of drug use in sport also presents for sociologists and those in related academic disciplines in sports studies an opportunity to study the deviant subculture of drug use, the social and political dynamics of modern sport, and even more generally to explore the sociology of deviant behavior and the social construction of "normal" and "pathological" categories in a major sphere of social life.

An intriguing aspect of the use of banned substances and methods in sport is the fact that, according to historical evidence, it was only at a relatively recent moment in history – the International Olympic Committee formally banned drugs in the Olympic Games in 1967 – that certain substances and methods have been defined as unethical or deviant. Athletes have used a variety of performance-enhancing substances during many time periods and in diverse cultural contexts, including the ancient Greeks who had few qualms about the use of performance enhancers in the ancient Olympic Games. So referring to incidences as "cheating" in sport's now-distant past is more a reflection of transposing contemporary sensibilities onto history than it is the reality of those practices and morals. During multiday, ultra-marathon cycling races and the late nineteenth-century pedestrianism craze, for example, there were few attempts by athletes or trainers to hide the use of various performance-enhancing concoctions, except to keep the composition of the mixtures undisclosed to competitors.

Given its recent construction as a "deviant" or "unethical" practice, then, the use of banned substances and methods, and the various organizational efforts to create and enforce "anti-doping" policies, provide an opportunity to study first-hand the creation of deviant behavior and a deviant category, and more general issues of power and control over the ongoing construction of what is considered normal versus pathological behavior in sport.

Four streams of thought and research have emerged in sociology and related disciplines in sports studies to consider this important social problem. First, in the philosophy of sport, debates regarding the ethical arguments that underlie the prohibition of drugs have been ongoing, especially since the early 1980s at the height of Olympic Cold War sport when the organized and systematic use of drugs in various national high-performance sports systems became impossible to ignore. More specifically, three main arguments, which have been most commonly used to warrant the prohibition of banned substances in official policy statements, have been debated: that drugs are harmful to athletes; that drugs corrupt the ideal of the "fair playing field" in sport; and finally, that drugs corrupt the central ideals, ethos, or "spirit" of sport. While debates regarding these fundamental issues are ongoing, and while the philosophical arguments have become more sophisticated over time, the justifications themselves continue to be plagued by often obvious contradictions of performance-enhancing techniques, technology, science, and the like that

are permitted but still contradict the central arguments used in support of anti-doping prohibitions.

The second stream of research falls within policy studies, which considers the efficacy of procedures to detect and deter athletes; the power, structure, and legitimacy of organizations that attempt to control drug use; and, more recently, the rights of athletes and their involvement – or lack thereof – in the policy creation and implementation process. Most policy analysis has concentrated on three important organizations: the International Olympic Committee, the various International Sport Federations that oversee policies for separate sports within the Olympic Movement, and the World Anti-Doping Agency.

Third, studies in the sociology of deviance and deviant behavior consider the issue from the perspective of the creation of deviant subcultures in which substances are both latently and manifestly encouraged, and more generally from the perspective of the general social construction of deviance, including issues of organizational power that have come to play in defining certain substances as deviant or unethical.

Finally, critical historical accounts have attempted to understand the specific social and political circumstances out of which the widespread use of performance-enhancing substances and methods – banned or otherwise – emerged. Here efforts have concentrated on the post-World War II era, and specifically the development of bureaucratically organized national high-performance sports systems in the Olympic Movement, because it was in this context that the scientifically, technologically, and medically assisted pursuit of the linear record became the sine qua non of international competitive sport. The most obvious example was the former German Democratic Republic, which for approximately three decades maintained a state-run system of "supplementary materials." However, performance enhancers became integrated components of the high-performance sports systems of many East and West bloc countries during the Cold War era, and these practices continue today.

The latter two disciplinary streams are the most important for sociologists and their attempts to understand the drug/substance use issue. In terms of critical historical accounts, a seminal text is John Hoberman's *Mortal Engines* (1992). Hoberman traces the birth of performance enhancement in sport back to the original development of relationships formed between biomedical scientists and athletes in the late nineteenth century. Interestingly, however, scientists had little interest in helping athletes boost performances; the real interest was merely studying athletes – because of the physical extremes to which they pushed their bodies in training and competition – to discern biophysiological "truths" about the human body as a whole. Only later in the 1920s and 1930s did the idea begin to emerge that athletes' bodies might have unlimited physical potential. From that point on, biomedical scientists were joined by a cadre of other self-proclaimed experts who attempted to use virtually any means possible to enhance athletes' abilities to train, compete, and push the body to ostensibly endless limits. This trend only accelerated during the Olympic Cold War years as national sports systems vied for gold medals and national ideological aggrandizement. Hoberman convincingly demonstrates that the push toward the use of increasingly sophisticated scientific and technological means of enhancement developed into a mania of sorts in the last half of the twentieth century, during which time drug use became only the more visible symptom of this uninhibited obsession. Hoberman cautions, then, that we need to think carefully about the ultimate purpose of this obsession, because while science and technology have almost limitless possibilities, the human body does not.

With respect to understanding substance use from the perspective of the sociology of deviant behavior, a landmark study is Robert Hughes and Jay Coakley's "Positive Deviance Among Athletes" (1991). Adding to Robert Merton's classic typology of modes of individual adaptation to cultural goals and institutional means, the authors maintain that in the right environment athletes "overconform" to a "sport ethic" – a set of value orientations that guide the decisions and actions of serious athletes. The ethic's criteria – unwritten but nevertheless extremely pervasive in athletes' lives – include making sacrifices, taking physical risks, and refusing to accept limits in the pursuit of performance potentials and goals. With respect to drug use, the implication of the model

developed by Hughes and Coakley is that the constellation of criteria that determine the sport ethic constitute for serious athletes a very different line of demarcation between what is normal versus pathological than what the general public or, for that matter, many sports authorities might consider it to be. The sport ethic – and not just drug use per se – will, the authors claim, have to be taken into account before the "moral crisis" of drug use can be resolved.

These studies reflect two major streams of inquiry that are crucial in developing a more complete understanding of the drug/substance use issue. First, a better understanding of the historical development of modern high-performance sport as a whole is necessary. While Hoberman's work has brought attention to the important role the development of biomedicine played in the general emphasis on performance enhancement, surprisingly little is known about the specific social and political environments out of which the use of drugs has emerged. Today, while the decision taken by an individual athlete-agent to use a banned substance may appear to be an isolated and perhaps voluntary one, in reality that decision takes place within the context of a large, complex set of historically created and socially situated actions and relationships. The use of performance enhancers reflects, at minimum: the general historical forces and relations that have comprised the real world of high-performance sport as it has developed in the twentieth century, especially since World War II and during the Olympic Cold War years; the particular set of political circumstances that motivated nation-states to develop sophisticated and well-funded sports systems in the pursuit of the linear record and gold medals, utilizing virtually any available scientific and technological means necessary, including drug supplementation; and the general emphasis on and triumph of instrumental rationality in modern life, which affected high-performance sport as much as, if not more than, any other sphere of social life.

Second, there is a glaring lacuna in the sociological literature in that very little is understood about the real lived experiences of high-performance athletes, their training and working conditions, and the processes through which their athletic identities are created. To a much greater degree sociologists have studied the socialization processes that lead boys and girls into sport and physical activity, and to a lesser but nevertheless still significant degree the social and psychological process of serious athletes retiring or disengaging from sport and the athlete identity. However, there is little understanding of the experience of becoming a competitive, national- or world-class athlete and the processes through which methods of performance enhancement – banned or otherwise – become part of an athlete's identity and his or her everyday, lived experience.

These two macro and micro streams of analysis are crucial when trying to explain the moral crises in high-performance sport to which the Canadian *Commission of Inquiry* referred. The existence of the World Anti-Doping Agency reflects the legitimacy of efforts to rid sport of drug and substance use but it also attests to the fact that the problem persists unabated. Like all similar elements of social life defined as deviant and regarded as major social problems, the issue of substance use in sport will continue to play an important role in the development of provocative streams of sociological thought and research, especially as the use of drugs and other performance technologies in sport intensifies on a global scale.

SEE ALSO: Deviance; Deviance, Sport and; Drug Use; Drugs, Drug Abuse, and Drug Policy; Drugs and the Law; Health and Sport; Olympics; Socialization and Sport; Sport as Work

REFERENCES AND SUGGESTED READINGS

Beamish, R. & Ritchie, I. (2004) From Chivalrous "Brothers-in-Arms" to the Eligible Athlete: Changed Principles and the IOC's Banned Substance List. *International Review for the Sociology of Sport* 39(4): 355–71.

Dubin, C. L. (1990) *Commission of Inquiry into the Use of Drugs and Banned Practices Intended to Increase Athletic Performance.* Canadian Government Publishing Center, Ottawa.

Hoberman, J. M. (1992) *Mortal Engines: The Science of Performance and the Dehumanization of Sport.* Free Press, New York.

Houlihan, B. (1999) *Dying to Win: Doping in Sport and the Development of Anti-Doping Policy.* Council of Europe, Strasbourg.

Hughes, R. & Coakley, J. (1991) Positive Deviance Among Athletes: The Implications of Overconformity to the Sport Ethic. *Sociology of Sport Journal* 8(4): 307–25.

Miah, A. (2004) *Genetically Modified Athletes: Biomedical Ethics, Gene Doping, and Sport.* Routledge, London and New York.

Waddington, I. (2000) *Sport, Health, and Drugs: A Critical Sociological Perspective.* E&FN Spon, London and New York.

Wilson, W. & Derse, E. (Eds.) (2001) *Doping in Elite Sport: The Politics of Drugs in the Olympic Movement.* Human Kinetics, Champaign, IL.

Yesalis, C. E. & Bahrke, M. S. (2002) History of Doping in Sport. *International Sports Studies* 24 (1): 42–76.

Du Bois: "Talented Tenth"

Rutledge M. Dennis

At crucial moments in a people's history, the question "What is to be done?" is raised. Alongside this question, additional questions will follow, such as "Who will do it, when, and how?" When one explores such works as Plato's *Republic*, Machiavelli's *The Prince*, Comte's *Course in Positive Philosophy*, and Marx's *Communist Manifesto*, one is deeply aware of the sense of crisis expressed by the writers and the urgency with which they raised the questions posed above. One must therefore understand the responses to group or national crises and the urgency of responses to such crises before fully understanding W. E. B. Du Bois's own urgent response to the national crisis of race, and to the many ways in which the crisis was more pronounced and devastating to blacks.

Du Bois first proposed a highly visible role for the educated segment of the black population in an article entitled "The Talented Tenth" (1903), and throughout his long life, at least until the 1950s, his life and the organizational and institutional networks he constructed both amplified and represented the importance of the role of the educated. But what was successful in practice was, however, not quite as successful when it came to justifying the theory. In fact, Du Bois's theory was attacked from two main quarters. First, Booker T. Washington criticized the usefulness of those who had devoted much of their life to book learning, and he doubted their proficiency in dealing with real people and their problems. Secondly, the very idea of an elite stratum, even one devoted to a good cause, did not sit well with many. Indeed, the elite theme was one closely associated with white supremacy, white privilege, and black exclusion. But a careful scrutiny of Du Bois's logic surrounding an educated elite would lead one to disavow and refute both criticisms.

The justification for such a stratum was deeply rooted in the economic, cultural, and political realities of the United States, especially the South, during the last quarter of the nineteenth century. Du Bois urgently wanted to jump-start and accelerate racial and social change within black communities as well as open the larger society to black participation in all realms, especially the political. In this sense, the educated cadre had a dual mission, one of which would be addressing internal black matters such as education, health, and economics; the other, that of addressing the resistance to freedom, democracy, and justice which permeated white society. What is often missing from the criticisms leveled against the concept was the heightened sense of dedication, sacrifice, and special mission of this stratum that was at the core of Du Bois's rationale for such an elite. The "Luke theorem" could be presented as a justification for expecting much from this educated stratum. The theorem found in Luke 12:48 asserts that: "For unto whomever much is given, of him shall be much required: and to whom men have committed much, of him they will ask the more." Du Bois would certainly have disavowed any grounding of his idea in scripture given his general agnostic views, but the theorem clearly states the terms in the manner in which du Bois often stated why the educated stratum had an obligation to assist the black community: with its talent, skills, and opportunities, this stratum, Du Bois believed, comprised the natural leadership of black America.

Du Bois embedded his talented tenth concept in an array of organizational and institutional structures. This point becomes obvious in any analysis of the organizations Du Bois assisted in founding: the Negro Academy, the Niagara Movement, the National Association for the Advancement of Colored People (NAACP), the various Pan-African Conferences and Assemblies, and the Atlanta University Studies. In addition, there were the journals and periodicals: *Crisis, Phylon, Moon,* and *Horizon.* Du Bois viewed these organizations and periodicals as essentially tools to be used in propagandizing the population, blacks and whites. For blacks, the tools represented vehicles for presenting a more accurate and objective view of themselves, their successes and failures, but also their hopes and aspirations for new and rewarding racial and social advancements. For whites, Du Bois wanted to dislodge racial stereotypes and feelings and to present a picture of the New Negro, a term made popular by the anthology edited by Alain Locke (1969 [1925]).

The idea of a viable and unique educated cadre would decline in importance in the 1950s, partially due to Du Bois's disappointment at the lack of support for him among educated blacks when he was arrested and charged with treason during the McCarthy era, and perhaps partly due to a slow movement by Du Bois into the international communist movement. He formally joined the party in 1961, but even before doing so, he ceased to view black Americans as a possible beacon of strength and devotion to the cause of their own liberty, believing instead that freedom from the worst vestiges of segregation and terror only enabled blacks to follow whites down a path of worshipping money and success rather than a devotion to struggles for their liberation. But this view coincided with an increasing emphasis on the class factor in contemporary life.

A review of Du Bois's concept of a talented tenth does not suggest that he wanted this cadre to lord over blacks, as Washington and others suggested. Rather, his rationale was a simple recognition that there were individuals with skills, talents, and interests who were willing to place their economic, educational, and cultural assets where they might be more useful to an entire population for its collective benefit; that there were those whose leadership skills would serve, from Du Bois's perspective, as the natural bridge between the black and white worlds. What Du Bois wanted, above all, was a fighting cadre, one which would confront people and issues and fight the good fight for blacks, just as he had been doing himself.

Du Bois would agree with the assertion that the talented tenth is alive today, though many who comprise this group would refrain from using the term. They are organized into many professional, educational, political, social, and cultural groups. The Congressional Black Caucus would constitute such a group, as would groups such as the Association of Black Sociologists, associations of political scientists, psychologists, historians, anthropologists, and the various Black Studies Associations, and literally hundreds of other professional organizations and associations. Included in this group would also be the numerous black fraternities and sororities, as well as other interest groups. When one reads the goals and objectives of these organizations and associations, it is clear that the shadow of Du Bois lurks over them, because they all speak of a need to address and redress issues in black life. Black Americans were not unique in having one of their great scholars and leaders enunciate a theory of leadership to address pressing social issues. What was unique was the timing of such a leadership strategy and its emergence in an evolving American democracy during the last quarter of the nineteenth century when the nation, especially its black population, was in great emotional, political, social, economic, and cultural disarray. What was also unique was the enunciation of such a scheme in a society in which blacks were hated by many, greatly disliked by others, and largely ignored by still others. Du Bois's concept of black leadership continues to be a viable and necessary feature of the American reality as long as race and the black presence continue to be a bone, as de Tocqueville so clearly stated it, in the throat of white America.

SEE ALSO: Double Consciousness; Du Bois, W. E. B.; Marginality; Race

REFERENCES AND SUGGESTED READINGS

Dennis, R. M. (1977) Du Bois and the Role of the Educated Elite. *Journal of Negro Education* 46: 388–402.

Dennis, R. M. (1996) *W. E. B. Du Bois: The Scholar as Activist*. JAI Press, Greenwich, CT.

Du Bois, W. E. B. (1903) The Talented Tenth. In: Washington, B. T. et al., *The Negro Problem*. James Pott, New York.

Locke, A. (1969 [1925]) *The New Negro*. Atheneum, New York.

Du Bois, W. E. B. (1868–1963)

Rutledge M. Dennis

W. E. B. Du Bois was a sociologist and historian, born in Great Barrington, Massachusetts. Though he wanted to attend Harvard after high school, the lack of funds and the advice of a few of his teachers dissuaded him, so, instead, he attended Fisk, where he received his BA in 1888. He received a second BA from Harvard University in 1890, from where he was also awarded an MA (1891) and a PhD (1895) with the dissertation "The Suppression of the African Slave Trade to the United States of America, 1638–1870." Between 1892 and 1894 Du Bois was a graduate student at the University of Berlin, made possible by a combination gift/ loan from the Slater Fund. This experience would have enduring consequences on both his personality and his scholarship, though, as he stated in his classic *Souls of Black Folk* (1903), his experiences at both Fisk and Harvard had already shaped some of his views on race, class, and philosophy.

Du Bois's sociological significance rests on three major themes: (1) his role as one of the early sociology pioneers; (2) his role as a sociologist of race; and (3) his role as a scholar-activist. As one of the early modern pioneers, along with Durkheim, Weber, and Simmel, Du Bois viewed the connection between theory and research as inextricably linked to the alleviation of social problems and as contributors to overall societal reform. This was important to Du Bois because so little data had been collected in areas in which scholars allegedly knew so much. For his first major social research project Du Bois used some of the methodologies culled from Charles Booth's famous London study. Indeed, Du Bois was the first American scholar to use sociological methods – questionnaires, interviews, and participant observation, use of city directories, and church and civic organizational records – to study the social structure and behavioral characteristics of a minority group within a larger majority and dominant class and amid a racially exclusive urban setting. This study provided much insight into the significance of the black church as a religious and social center in black life. The result was the classic urban-community study, *The Philadelphia Negro* (1899). Earlier, he conducted a study of a small Virginia town, *Farmville Negro* (1897). These two studies, one of the North, the other of the South, permitted Du Bois to delve into comparative analyses between the black North and the black South, some of which are seen in *The Souls of Black Folk* and in a series of articles (which were in fact sociological essays) written for Northern newspapers and later collected by others and published as *The Black North* (1901). The research–reform dialectic can also be seen in Du Bois's editorship of the Atlanta University Studies which sought, via research, to study almost every facet of black life and culture in the US, and to use the results to push for societal reform, especially along racial and class lines. But his youthful faith in science, knowledge, and truth as obviating factors in prejudice and discrimination would be greatly shaken by the realization that knowing the truth would not offset the great economic, political, and sociocultural advantages groups derived from oppressing other groups.

Even as Du Bois fought mightily to believe that science and objectivity would make a difference in matters of race, class, and social justice, his scholarly and sociopolitical activities illustrated that he would be the Great Dialectician, whose mind, interests, and concerns might reflect shifting intellectual modes and themes. So, even as theme (1), science and research, was in operation, as a good dialectician he was already into theme (2) with its focus on a sociology of race. For example, his paper "The Conservation of Races" (1897) was a justification for maintaining certain racial/cultural values, even as blacks sought greater entry into the larger society. Today, such a claim is understandable under the rubric of social and cultural pluralism. This article and a later one, "The Study of the Negro Problem"

(1898), but especially *The Souls of Black Folk*, would make race analysis, its shape, depth, and contours, as important for many as Marx's class analysis had been and continues to be. It is here as a sociologist of race that later generations of scholars and students would find sociological richness in concepts such as the talented tenth, double consciousness, the color line, the veil, racial solidarity, and masking.

Du Bois's prescient assertion in *Souls* that "the problem of the twentieth century is the problem of the color-line" was a bold prediction for what was in store for the western world, but also presaged a lifetime struggle for himself, as he vowed to lend a hand in the destruction of that color line. The very title, *The Souls of Black Folk*, would be an exploratory search and revelation as Du Bois would lay bare, for whites to see, the heart and soul of a people. What was also patently visible was the heart and soul of the young scholar Du Bois, for even before C. Wright Mills asserted his version of a sociological imagination, Du Bois, in *Souls* (p. 87), had inserted himself personally into a larger national and international sociology and history. He was to define himself through his race, and conversely he wanted to define his race through his exemplary bearing, behavior, and sense of self-worth: "I sit with Shakespeare and he winches not ... I summon Aristotle and Aurelius and what soul I will ... So, wed with truth, I dwell above the Veil." It was clear in *Souls* that Du Bois would not only be a part of the great history he foresaw for the twentieth century, but would also make and shape that future history. This was no clearer than in his great debate with and attack on the preeminent black leader of the early twentieth century, Booker T. Washington. The intellectual skirmishes, flank attacks, and the subtle and not-so-subtle innuendoes from both men and their respective camps reflected the belief of each that he had the key to the black present and future. Neither succeeded. That is why the profound issues in the Du Bois–Washington debate – the importance of industrial vs. higher education, the priority of economics vs. politics and civil rights, and the style and type of leadership needed for black America – continue to resonate today, often with the same vigor and emotion as they did during the height of the debate.

The more one researches the life of Du Bois, the more it becomes abundantly clear that neither his life nor his intellectual and scholarly activities can be neatly compartmentalized, and his ideas are found in so many intellectual niches and corners. So profound were his scholarly output and the causes for which he fought that one could objectively view his era as the Age of Du Bois, and it is in theme (3), the scholar-activist, that this is best expressed (Dennis 1996, 1997). With the increasing loss of faith in science Du Bois began to define himself as a scholar-activist – he uses the term "propagandist" – and would become, as the chief "propagandist for the race," the scholar as organizer: organizer of four Pan-African Congresses; founder and general secretary of the Niagara Movement; one of the founders of the NAACP; founder and editor of *The Moon*; founder and editor of *The Horizon*; founder and editor of *The Crisis*; founder and editor of *Phylon*. And during this same period he writes sociologically significant books, books reflecting his markedly leftward political shift: *John Brown* (1909), *Black Reconstruction* (1935), *Dusk of Dawn* (1940), and *The World and Africa* (1947). *In Battle for Peace* (1952) was written after he had been indicted, placed on trial, and acquitted for being an unregistered foreign agent of the Soviet Union, as a result of his leadership in various peace movements and organizations. Given his pronounced political preferences and pronouncements throughout the 1940s and 1950s, it was not surprising to many when in 1961 Du Bois joined the Communist Party of the United States. In a masterful stroke marking him as a true dialectician, Du Bois, that same year, accepted an invitation from President Nkrumah to go to Ghana to complete his Encyclopedia Africana Project, a project which would be a version of the Encyclopedia of the Negro, which Du Bois initiated in 1909. In 1963 he renounced his American citizenship and became a citizen of Ghana. He died on August 27, 1963 on the eve of the historic March On Washington. Four autobiographical works (Du Bois 1903, 1920, 1940, 1968) aptly document Du Bois the scholar, the intellectual, the academician, the social activist, the organizer-propagandist, and the international political spokesman. Each volume also provides more than a glimpse of Du Bois the sociologist.

Du Bois is a man of many parts, and these parts are significant to many laypersons and scholars in a variety of disciplines. Since the 1960s – when he was largely the "forgotten sociologist" – we have entered an era in which there is increased attention on Du Bois the sociologist, who historically tended to be overshadowed by Du Bois the activist. A brief perusal of today's introductory texts and books on theory illustrates the strides many have made in fighting to ensure Du Bois's rightful place in the sociological pantheon among the other great pioneers.

SEE ALSO: Accommodation; Color Line; Double Consciousness; Du Bois: "Talented Tenth"; Pluralism, American; Race and Ethnic Consciousness; Separatism

REFERENCES AND SUGGESTED READINGS

Dennis, R. M. (1975) The Sociology of W. E. B. Du Bois. Dissertation, Washington State University.

Dennis, R. M. (1996) *W. E. B. Du Bois: The Scholar as Activist*. JAI Press, Greenwich, CT.

Dennis, R. M. (1997) *The Black Intellectuals*. JAI Press, Greenwich, CT.

Du Bois, W. E. B. (1896) *The Suppression of the African Slave Trade to the United States, 1638–1870*. Longmans, Green, New York.

Du Bois, W. E. B. (1897) The Conservation of Races. American Negro Academy, *Occasional Papers* 2.

Du Bois, W. E. B. (1898) The Study of the Negro Problem. *Annals of the American Academy of Political and Social Science* 11 (January): 1–23.

Du Bois, W. E. B. (1898) The Negroes of Farmville: A Social Study. *Bulletin of the United States Department of Labor* 3: 1–38.

Du Bois, W. E. B. (1899) *The Philadelphia Negro: A Social Study*. University of Pennsylvania Press, Philadelphia.

Du Bois, W. E. B. (1901) *The Black North in 1901: A Social Study*. Arno Press, New York.

Du Bois, W. E. B. (1903) *The Souls of Black Folk: Essays and Sketches*. A. C. McClurg, Chicago.

Du Bois, W. E. B. (1909) *John Brown*. George Jacobs, Philadelphia.

Du Bois, W. E. B. (1920) *Darkwater: Voices from Within the Veil*. A. Jenkins, Washington, DC.

Du Bois, W. E. B. (1940) *Dusk of Dawn: An Essay Toward an Autobiography of a Race Concept*. Harcourt, Brace, New York.

Du Bois, W. E. B. (1947) *The World and Africa.* Viking Press, New York.

Du Bois, W. E. B. (1952) *In Battle for Peace.* Masses and Mainstream, New York.

Du Bois, W. E. B. (1968) *The Autobiography of W. E. B. Du Bois.* International Publishers, New York.

dual-earner couples

Pamela Aronson and Sara Gold

Dual-earner couples are romantically involved (either married or unmarried) and each contribute to the financial support of their household through their work outside the home. The presence of dual-earner couples has increased over the last 40 years, as there has been a shift away from the traditional male breadwinner and female homemaker family type. The breadwinner-homemaker model waned in prevalence as women entered the workforce in large numbers, especially after the 1950s. For example, in 1976, 31 percent of women with infants under 1 year old worked outside the home; by 2002, 54.6 percent did so (US Census Bureau 2002). These figures are significantly higher for women with school-aged children and women who are not parents. The influx of women into the workplace occurred for a number of reasons, including more equal access to education and occupations, greater demand for workers in the service sector of the economy, and social changes brought on by the women's movement. As a result, an increasing number of women provide significant financial support to their families (Gornick & Meyers 2003).

Families with lower incomes have historically been more likely than those with middle or higher incomes to rely on the earnings of two workers. Today, however, advantaged women (such as middle-class, white, married women) are increasingly likely to contribute to their family incomes. Dual-earner couples are more common in part because of the declining value of men's wages. Women's earnings have been extremely important in helping families maintain their standard of living, especially for working-class and lower-middle-class couples (Bianchi & Spain 1996). Although women's wages have risen over time, women still earn substantially less than men for nearly all occupations (US Census Bureau 2000).

Dual-earner couples are diverse in their family situations and experiences. They can be married with children, married without children, cohabitating heterosexual couples, or cohabiting same-sex couples. The experiences associated with having two workers in the household also vary depending on one's stage of life. For example, dual-earner couples with young children face different rewards and challenges in balancing work and family than "empty nest" couples who are looking toward retirement (Moen 2003). Despite this diversity in experience, dual-earner couples often encounter particular benefits, strains, and tensions as they integrate and balance two careers with a romantic relationship and home life.

Dual-earner couples often make decisions about when and whether to have children with the concerns of balancing two careers and a family in mind. Dual-earner couples are increasingly delaying having children until their career paths are established. In 1960, 60 percent of women aged 20 to 24 and three-quarters of women aged 25 to 29 had become parents (White 1999). Forty years later, the percentage of women with children in these age groups had declined to 33 and 55 percent, respectively (US Census Bureau 2002). In addition to delaying children, some dual-earner couples choose not to have children.

Dual-earner couples frequently must decide whose career will receive a higher priority. Decisions that advance one member of the couple's career may, at the same time, put the other's career on hold. In the past, priority was almost always given to the husband's career. Presently, though this approach remains a common strategy, these couples are less likely to place a higher priority on the husband's career and are more likely to take a variety of factors beyond gender into consideration.

Dual-earner couples must redefine what their breadwinner/homemaker counterparts have already classified as measures of success. Traditionally, a breadwinner husband is successful when he financially supports his family and a homemaker wife is successful when she emotionally supports her family and takes care of their home. Dual earning affords both members of a couple opportunities to feel successful by fulfilling both home and work responsibilities. Moen et al. (2003) report that feelings of success are not dependent on a tradeoff or balancing act between the two realms of home and work, but on a sense of living a well-rounded life. The benefits of the dual-earning situation include financial stability, the potential for greater gender equality, and positive mental health.

To meet their personal and professional needs, dual-earner couples rely on a number of strategies to structure their work and home lives, such as carefully negotiating schedules or number of work hours. Those with children are more likely to have a large discrepancy in the number of hours that each parent works, whereas couples without children typically have similar work hour arrangements. Mothers are still much more likely than fathers to scale back or rearrange their work hours in order to take care of children. This gender difference reveals that dual-earner couples' choices are often "neo-traditional" in character (Moen & Sweet 2003). Many of these families with children work different shifts – such as weekends or nights – in order to minimize the amount of necessary childcare. One study, for example, found that one-third of dual-earner couples with preschool-aged children worked such a "split shift" (Presser 1999).

The absence of a full-time homemaker makes it necessary for these families to employ a variety of strategies to achieve a well-managed household, as they must fit the responsibilities of running a household into their often limited time at home. The total amount of time spent doing housework in America has been declining, especially among employed wives. Many families hire outside help to fill this time gap. Although some dual-earner couples strive for an egalitarian division of labor, others do not. As a result, women are more likely to take on the "second shift" responsibilities at home (Hochschild 1989). That is, despite labor force participation, women are more likely to take on a managerial role in the home and perform about twice as much of the housework as men. The "time bind" that results from combining long work hours with home responsibilities can be a source of stress for many families. As work offers greater

external rewards than home, many families report feeling more successful and relaxed at work, while time-pressed at home (Hochschild 2000).

Dual-earner couples often experience what is known as "spillover:" "the transfer of mood, affect, and behavior between work and home" (Roehling et al. 2003: 101). Spillover can be both positive and negative. For example, positive work-to-family spillover occurs when feelings of success at work lead to a relaxed attitude at home. Conversely, when stress at work causes a parent to lose patience with a child at home, negative work-to-family spillover may be to blame. An example of positive family-to-work spillover occurs when workers are more productive on their jobs as a result of experiencing a satisfying family life. An example of negative family-to-work spillover includes family intrusions on work time. Workplaces that are supportive of employees' home commitments and that offer higher levels of worker autonomy tend to result in less negative spillover. The opposite is true of jobs with lower levels of support or flexibility. For dual-earner couples, negative spillover can have a significant impact, as both partners are negotiating similar work and family commitments. Negative spillover tends to be less of a problem for those couples who work similar, and fewer (less than 45), hours per week (Roehling et al. 2003).

The benefits, strains, and tensions of the dual-earning situation are commonly thought of as personal matters. This perception persists even though there is a widening gap between workers' needs and governmental and workplace policies. For example, the Family and Medical Leave Act of 1993 guarantees many workers up to 12 weeks of unpaid leave to care for an immediate family member during a time of serious illness. While this policy is helpful for many workers, not all employees are covered under the law and its unpaid nature makes it difficult for many workers to take leave from their jobs. Workplace policies, the most common of which is flextime, do not adequately recognize the demands facing dual-earner couples. For example, employers often expect workers to place all home-life responsibilities on their spouses. Issues pertaining to childcare, health care benefits, and the number of hours that employees must work to be considered "full-time" are all ripe for new policy innovation to support the most common working arrangement among American families. Whether policymakers will push for more changes to bring work-life policies in line with home-life realities remains to be seen.

SEE ALSO: Divisions of Household Labor; Gender, Work, and Family; Life Course and Family; Marital Power/Resource Theory; Stratification, Gender and; Stress and Work; Women, Economy and; Work, Sociology of

REFERENCES AND SUGGESTED READINGS

Bianchi, S. M. & Spain, D. (1996) Women, Work, and Family in America. *Population Bulletin* 51: 3.

Gornick, J. C. & Meyers, M. K. (2003) *Families That Work: Policies for Reconciling Parenthood and Employment*. Russell Sage Foundation, New York.

Hochschild, A. (with A. Machung) (1989) *The Second Shift*. Viking, New York.

Hochschild, A. (2000). *The Time Bind: When Work Becomes Home and Home Becomes Work*. Henry Holt, New York.

Moen, P. (2003) Epilogue: Toward a Policy Agenda. In: Moen, P. (Ed.), *It's About Time: Couples and Careers*. Cornell University Press, Ithaca, NY, pp. 334–7.

Moen, P. & Sweet, S. (2003) Time Clocks: Work-Hour Strategies. In: Moen, P. (Ed.), *It's About Time: Couples and Careers*. Cornell University Press, Ithaca, NY, pp. 17–34.

Moen, P., Waismel-Manor, R., & Sweet, S. (2003) Success. In: Moen, P. (Ed.), *It's About Time: Couples and Careers*. Cornell University Press, Ithaca, NY, pp. 133–52.

Presser, H. B. (1999) Toward a 24 Hour Economy. *Science* 284: 177–9.

Roehling, P. V., Moen, P., & Blatt, R. (2003) Spillover. In: Moen, P. (Ed.), *It's About Time: Couples and Careers*. Cornell University Press, Ithaca, NY, pp. 101–21.

US Census Bureau (2000) Occupations: 2000. Online. www.census.gov/prod/2003pubs/c2kbr-25.pdf.

US Census Bureau (2002) Fertility of American Women: June 2002. Online. www.census.gov/prod/2003pubs/p20–548.pdf.

White, L. (1999) Sure, I'd Like to Get Married . . . Someday. In: Booth, A., Crouter, A. C., & Shanahan, M. J. (Eds.), *Transitions to Adulthood in a Changing Economy: No Work, No Family, No Future?* Praeger, Westport, pp. 56–65.

dual labor markets

Tony Elger

The concept of labor market dualism was first developed by institutionalist economists critical of conventional analyses of the labor market (Peck 1996). They argued that different categories of workers faced contrasting management policies, as white male workers were preferentially recruited to jobs offering training, pay gains, promotion, and job security. This meant access to organizational job ladders which constituted "internal labor markets" governed primarily by organizational rules. Meanwhile, women and minority ethnic groups generally had access to insecure, low-paid jobs without internal training and promotion prospects, and were confined to the external labor market constituted by such jobs. This analysis contested neoclassical economic models of the allocation of individual workers across a spectrum of jobs according to individual skills and preferences, and emphasized the ways in which organizational structures and management decisions generated a division between primary and secondary labor markets which operated according to different logics.

Dual labor market theorists nevertheless differed in their analyses of the organizational logic of dualism. Some linked it to the contrast between large oligopolistic employers and small competitive enterprises. Since large employers themselves differentiated between primary and secondary workforces, however, others argued that managers constructed primary labor markets to retain relatively skilled workers, especially after investing resources in firm-specific training. Finally, radical commentators suggested dualism was often the result of management tactics of divide and rule, rather than technical calculations about protecting investment in training.

These analyses were primarily designed to explain the *persistence* of labor market dualism, but recent organizational restructuring has involved a reduction in stable routes of career progression and a growth in less secure forms of employment (Grimshaw et al. 2001). Meanwhile, areas of skills shortage, combined with equal opportunities policies, have opened *some* doors for qualified but hitherto excluded groups. One dual labor market analysis which addressed change rather than stability was the "flexible firm" model, which contrasted core "insiders" providing functional flexibility with peripheral "outsiders" characterized by numerical flexibility (Kalleberg 2003). The core experienced horizontal movements within teams or across tasks more than vertical advancement, while the periphery included part-time, temporary, and subcontract work. However, this model was more a prescription than an analysis, recommending that employers and the state codify and develop their employment practices in this way. It was criticized for (1) imputing a coherent strategic orientation to management, when such policies are often ad hoc, reactive and constrained; (2) conflating distinctive forms of numerical flexibility, such as part-time, casual, and consultancy work, with quite different labor market implications for those involved; and (3) ignoring substantial sector differences (Pollert 1988).

Debates from the 1980s have prompted the development of more complex analyses of labor market *segmentation* by institutionalist economists and economic sociologists (Rubery & Wilkinson 1994; Peck 1996). Descriptively this has involved identifying multiple labor market segments rather than a simple dualism. Distinctions have been made between professional and managerial segments involving vertical progression through moves within and between employers; semi-professional and craft segments involving predominantly horizontal moves between relatively secure positions with different employers; white-collar and manual segments involving modest internal job ladders within specific organizations; relatively secure non-career jobs often associated with part-time work; and persistently insecure forms of employment. Such segments are not seen as entirely stable, but rather as modified and remade. They involve shifting clusters of opportunities and insecurities, sometimes linked to changing sources of labor supply, rather than a uniform movement towards flux and insecurity.

Such segmentation analyses have been underpinned by discussions of both the social organization of the demand for labor and the social organization of the supply of labor (Peck 1996). While management decisions are pivotal on the demand side, changing family and household relations are central to the supply side, while state policies help to structure both. The elaboration of this conceptual framework has provided leverage in the analysis of differences in the social organization and regulation of labor markets over time and between different states, as they embedded in distinctive social institutions of capitalism.

SEE ALSO: Capitalism, Social Institutions of; Ethnic and Racial Division of Labor; Ethnicity; Households; Labor/Labor Power; Labor Markets; Stratification, Gender and

REFERENCES AND SUGGESTED READINGS

Grimshaw, D. et al. (2001) Organizations and the Transformation of the Internal Labor Market in the UK. *Work, Employment and Society* 15(1): 25–54.

Kalleberg, A. (2003) Flexible Firms and Labor Market Segmentation: Effects of Workplace Restructuring on Jobs and Workers. *Work and Occupations* 30(2): 154–75.

Peck, J. (1996) *Work-Place: The Social Regulation of Labor Markets*. Guilford Press, New York.

Pollert, A. (1988) The "Flexible Firm": Fixation or Fact. *Work, Employment and Society* 2(3): 281–316.

Rubery, J. & Wilkinson, F. (Eds.) (1994) *Employer Strategy and the Labor Market*. Oxford University Press, Oxford.

Durkheim, Émile (1858–1917)

Anne Warfield Rawls

Émile Durkheim, often referred to as the founder of sociology, was born April 15, 1858 in Épinal, France. Appointed to the first professorship of sociology in the world, he worked tirelessly over three decades as a lecturer and writer to establish sociology as a distinct discipline with its own unique theoretical and methodological foundation. After an illustrious career, first in Bordeaux and then after 1902 in Paris at the Sorbonne, Durkheim died in

November 1917, still a relatively young man, never having recovered from grief after most of the young sociologists he had trained, including his own son André, were killed in World War I.

Durkheim's basic argument was that the human rational being is fundamentally a creation of social relations. His related arguments against all forms of individualism, and for a distinct sociological object and method, stand at the heart of sociology as a discipline. Motivated from the beginning by a recognition that the organization, rationality, and morality of modern societies are different from traditional belief-based social forms in fundamental ways, he argued that these differences pose serious challenges to contemporary society. He credited Rousseau and Montesquieu with inspiring his emphasis on the social origin of the individual, an emphasis he holds in common with other classical social thinkers (e.g., Comte, Marx, Weber, and Mead). The individual as a social production, and the centrality of social phenomena in all aspects of human experience, are ideas that distinguish sociology from other disciplines' approaches to social order, social action, modernity, economic exchange, mutual intelligibility, and justice.

Durkheim's arguments have played a central role in the development of almost every aspect of sociology since its inception. His position was popularized as functionalism by Talcott Parsons in the late 1930s, and as a focus on symbolic systems by Lucien Lévy-Bruhl and Claude Lévi-Strauss from the 1920s to the 1960s. Postmodernism and poststructuralism, which developed in the 1960s and remained popular through the turn of the century, are both reactions to the way these two earlier conflicting interpretations of Durkheim's arguments developed over time.

Durkheim's innovative use of statistics in *Suicide*, and his articulation of a sociological method of measuring what he called "social facts" in *The Rules of the Sociological Method*, remain a foundation for sociological methodology even today. His arguments with regard to the social origin of ideas inspired the development of the sociology of knowledge and, more recently, cultural sociology. His arguments regarding universes of discourse have also been taken up by the sociology of science

where they rival those of Wittgenstein in their importance with regard to various sociologies of practice.

Durkheim's emphasis on practices, first articulated in *The Division of Labor in Society* (1893), then elaborated in *The Elementary Forms of the Religious Life* (1912), stands as one of the most modern approaches to social order of its time and continues to pose challenges to the sociological understanding of modernity. In that work, what would later emerge in the arguments of Wittgenstein and others as problems with the conception of meaning and rules took shape as Durkheim sketched out the problem of meaning in a modern context of differentiated multicultural exchange. He formulated a distinction between two forms of society, one modern and based on differentiated labor, the other traditional and based on shared beliefs. The contrast between the two, he argued, involved a contrast between rules that self-regulate and rules that depend on external beliefs and sanctions for their efficacy. Only the former, he argued, could sustain order and meaning in a modern context. The latter belonged strictly to traditional social forms. The way Durkheim used different types of law to illustrate his argument about the new form of rules inspired sociological studies of crime and law.

Durkheim argued that a confusion about the difference between traditional and modern social forms and a tendency to try to apply traditional forms of law/rule to modern societies were responsible for many social problems. Arguably, the tendency of Durkheim's interpreters to confuse the two social types has had a detrimental effect on the field's development. His emphasis on the distinctiveness of the modern is an essential part of the sociological legacy.

Durkheim's position was modern in crucial ways. For instance, whereas Freud's *Totem and Taboo* (1913) reflected the prejudices of the times by likening the primitive mind to the mentally ill, Durkheim's *The Elementary Forms of the Religious Life*, published a year earlier, insisted that aboriginal social forms and their corresponding beliefs were as rational as their modern counterparts. This was a surprisingly modern stand against the explicit and politically accepted ethnocentrism of Durkheim's time. He regarded *reason* as a social product, rendering nonsensical distinctions such as mentally inferior or superior, and infusing his sociology with a fundamental egalitarianism – a new moral philosophy grounded in social facts, and a new sociological epistemology with universal applicability.

Students of Durkheim's who survived the war – the most famous of whom was his nephew, Marcel Mauss – contributed to anthropology rather than to sociology. Because of Durkheim's early death, the long and influential careers of Mauss and others of these students constitute Durkheim's main influence in France. In *The Gift*, Mauss introduced the idea of gifts as reciprocal and symbolic exchanges that create networks of mutual obligation, an idea that challenged the established contrast between "pure" gift and economic exchange. Like Durkheim, Mauss disputed the prevailing individualism of an economic approach to exchange, imbuing it with a thoroughly social character.

For many years Durkheim's popularization in sociology was left to Parsons, resulting in interpretations of Durkheim that were consistent with Parsons's own structural functionalism. It was only with the increasing unpopularity of structural functionalism in the 1960s and 1970s that sociologists began to look for alternative interpretations of Durkheim's work. Thus, there was a revival of Durkheim studies at the end of the century.

Feminists sometimes argue that Durkheim's work ignored women, or adopted an insensitive stance toward them. He certainly did not theorize about women in any depth, but very few men were aware of women's issues at all in the 1890s. Even so, it is significant that Durkheim not only argued for the rational status of aboriginal people, but also had some awareness of the position of women. For instance, in *Suicide* he noted that there seemed to be a fourth form of suicide which he called "fatalistic," particularly prevalent among women. While noting that he lacked sufficient evidence, he suggested that marriage, while beneficial to men, may have a negative effect on women. Durkheim also noted in *The Division of Labor* that studies of aboriginal people suggest women were once as strong as men and that the development of society, and the positions women hold in modern societies, have made women weaker. Given the turn of the century tendency to view women as innately gentle and weak, Durkheim's opinion in this regard is noteworthy.

PERSONAL HISTORY

Durkheim married Louise Dreyfus in 1887, the year he first accepted teaching duties at Bordeaux. Her family was from Alsace and her father owned a business in Paris. Not much has been written about Louise, but by all accounts theirs was a very happy marriage in which she acted as a companion in work, as well as household manager. Lukes (1973: 99ff.) quotes from a letter written by Mauss that Louise "never left his side, and that, being well educated, she even collaborated with him in his work; she copied manuscripts, corrected proofs and shared in the administrative and editorial work of the *Année sociologique*."

There were two children from this marriage: André-Armand and Marie. André studied with Durkheim at the Sorbonne and had just completed his aggregation when the war broke out. He was sent to the Bulgarian front late in 1915 (Lukes 1973: 555). Marie's husband also was drafted by the army, as were five of Durkheim's nephews. Of the 342 students at the École Normale Supérieure called up for service, 293 went to the front and 104 were killed (Lukes 1973: 548), and many more would suffer crippling physical and emotional wounds.

For Durkheim, the loss of his son André was particularly acute for they had been close intellectual companions. Durkheim wrote in his son's obituary that "for a long time I was his sole teacher and I always remained closely associated with his studies. Very early he showed a marked interest in the researches to which I have devoted myself and the moment was near when he was about to become a companion in my work. The intellectual intimacy between us was thus as complete as possible" (1917: 201).

Sociology was a family enterprise for the Durkheims. As in the marriages of other major figures at the time, notably that of Marianne Weber (a scholar in her own right who compiled the posthumous papers of her husband Max), Louise shared significantly in Durkheim's intellectual labors. Not only his son André, but also various nephews and their friends studied sociology with Durkheim. André in particular seems to have been present for the lectures on pragmatism (Durkheim 1960 [1913–14]). Long hours spent with students and extended family, lecturing, editing, and discussing, would have made sociology a congenial focus of family relations. Thus, the personal losses of the war for Durkheim also devastated French sociology precisely because it had been such a collaborative effort among close friends and family.

The damage to French sociology caused by World War I was compounded when the Nazis invaded Paris in World War II. Durkheim's daughter Marie, who had inherited his papers, was forced to flee and the entire archive of his papers and notes, kept carefully in a separate room, was destroyed by the Nazis (Mestrovic 1988).

Like other classical social theorists, often referred to disparagingly as "Dead White Men," Durkheim was not a member of the ruling elite in France, holding instead the marginal status of a Jewish minority. Born on the border between France and Germany and descended from a long line of rabbis, Durkheim experienced anti-Semitism and his social situation was always fragile. The idea of "whiteness" and of "white men" as a dominant social group is a peculiarly American idea. In Europe, distinctions on the basis of class, religion, and ethnicity always rivaled those of race in importance.

Durkheim would have carried his Jewish origins with him always and would never have enjoyed the privileged status of a white male in America. Shortly after the death of his son in the spring of 1915, while overcome with grief, Durkheim was subjected to several serious public incidents of anti-Semitism. His French residency was challenged and defended in the Senate, the dispute finding its way into the papers. On January 19, 1916 in the *Libre Parole*, Durkheim was called "a Boche with a false nose" and accused of working for the Germans (Lukes 1973: 557). Given the battle he was waging to regain focus after the death of his son, these incidents would have weighed heavily on Durkheim and likely contributed to the stroke he suffered later that year.

Durkheim's argument in *Division of Labor* that justice is required by the self-regulating practices of modern states, and that modern social forms that do not achieve justice are abnormal and cannot persist over time, is illustrated in a letter he wrote about the war on September 15, 1914: "Never had the ideal to which we are all attached shown its strength more clearly ... Prussia and Austria are unnatural aggregates, established and maintained by force, and they have not been able gradually to replace force and compulsory subjection by voluntary support. An empire so constructed cannot last. The geography of Europe will be remade on a rational and moral basis" (Lukes 1973: 547–8). In the midst of the war, Durkheim found confidence in his own argument that modernity required a new form of moral solidarity. Germany might rail against the new egalitarian and democratic forms of society and resist by force, and many of Durkheim's students and family members might be killed, but in the end it could not work. The cost in terms of the war would be great, but the outcome always was certain.

MAJOR SUBSTANTIVE CONTRIBUTIONS

According to Durkheim, the transformation of the individual biological being into a social being cannot be explained by either individual biology or psychology. Biological capacities exist, but they require redirection and reformation by social processes. Durkheim argued that dualism, a popular philosophical argument referring to the distinction between mind and body, really represented the distinction between the pre-social animal being and the social human being. The former, he says, is not a rational being. There is no innate human reason or personality. Reason is a result of social processes. In fact, he argued that particular social processes and forms of association, or social bonding, are required to create and maintain social individuals. There are no social individuals except in the context of particular social configurations. Consequently, any position that begins with the individual, such as psychology, economics, or philosophy, and tries to explain social phenomena on the basis of aggregations of individual actions will miss exactly what is important about society.

Durkheim elaborated these ideas in four major works, *The Division of Labor in Society* (1893), *The Rules of the Sociological Method*

(1895), *Suicide* (1897), and *The Elementary Forms of the Religious Life* (1912). Each was designed to illustrate a different point. In addition, Durkheim wrote a second thesis on Montesquieu, countless articles for *l'Année sociologique* (which he also edited), and gave lectures on pragmatism, socialism, moral education, and Rousseau. Taken together, these substantively different sociological studies make up a unified, empirically based theoretical view.

It was Durkheim's position that social processes create entirely new dimensions of persons and associations between persons, creating social configurations in ways that add up to more than the sum of the individual parts. He explored the differences between two social forms, which he associated with traditional and modern society in *The Division of Labor*. There Durkheim explained the need of social beings for particular sorts of social bonding, which could only be maintained by fulfilling certain basic *functional requirements*. Social entities have a coherence in their own right that makes demands on participants. For this reason, Durkheim argued that it is necessary to focus on the effects of social processes on individuals, not the other way round, and that a new discipline was needed. The concrete nature of these social processes manifests in institutions and practices that can be studied empirically. Durkheim called these *social facts*. He outlined the new discipline of sociology and its methodology in *Rules* and referred to sociology as the study of social facts.

Social facts have a coherence that does not result simply from an aggregation of individual parts, and cannot be studied by a focus on the parts. The study *Suicide* was designed to demonstrate that even this most personal of acts could be explained on the basis of the ways in which persons were associated with one another and bonded together socially. What appear as individual feelings, thoughts, and values, he argued, are the products of social participation.

In *Elementary Forms*, Durkheim lays out an argument connecting social forms to individuals. The social experience of the sacred is the moment at which social connections are born and also gives rise to the individual social being. Reason is a result of this process. Symbols also first acquire shared meaning through totemism and its enacted rituals. Durkheim employed his analysis of totemic rites in formulating a challenge for all individualist approaches.

THE DIVISION OF LABOR: FUNCTIONALISM, PRACTICES, AND JUSTICE

Durkheim's brand of functionalism was first elaborated in *The Division of Labor*. It addresses equilibrating processes in two very different kinds of large systems. In the first of these, *mechanical solidarity*, equilibrium is created and sustained through shared beliefs. In the second, *organic solidarity*, self-regulating rules provide for stable and coherent social contexts through shared practices. Because shared beliefs require the authority of a common and enforced morality, equilibrium based on shared beliefs can only succeed if beliefs and values can be controlled by force and constraint. This social form results in a conventional morality that varies from social group to social group and requires a repressive form of law. When the equilibrium of societies is based on shared practices, however, different beliefs and values can be accommodated, and laws guaranteeing the autonomy of these contexts and their contracts emerge. Participation in self-regulating practices requires trust, reciprocity, equal access, and other qualities only possible in a system based on freedom, equality, and justice. Durkheim's functionalism proposed that justice becomes a requirement as reciprocity in self-regulating practices replaces the external constraints of traditional social forms.

Durkheim illustrated this functional argument in two ways. First, throughout the body of the text he contrasts the way legal sanctions developed and are applied in traditional and modern social forms. Modern contractual economic exchange, he says, requires a legal support that protects contracts and the autonomy of self-regulating practices, whereas traditional belief-based systems of ritual reciprocity require a legal system that protects and enforces the harmony of shared beliefs that sustain it. Durkheim's assessment of the relationship between law and society remains important and was the foundation for the development of both criminology and legal studies in sociology.

Durkheim's second way of illustrating the difference between traditional belief-based and modern practice-based social forms consisted of contrasting professional groups based on self-regulating practice – particularly scientific practice – with religious ritual and belief. Both produce solidarity and make intelligibility possible, but in very different ways. Only the self-regulating practices of professional groups, he argued, are compatible with differentiated labor, science, and truth.

While functionalism is often associated with political conservatism, in Durkheim's analysis it is only conservative with regard to traditional social forms. In a modern practice-based system, Durkheim's functional argument supports a strong egalitarianism. It is his position that even the practice of inheritance, which most scholars consider to be an integral part of a modern property-based system, is a holdover from earlier collective social forms, and as such threatens the necessary equality. "Every form of superiority has repercussions on the way in which contracts are arrived at," he says (1984 [1893]: 319). "If therefore it does not depend upon the person of individuals and their services to society, it invalidates the moral conditions of the exchange … In other words, there can be no rich and poor at birth without there being unjust contracts."

One source of confusion is that Durkheim's functionalism consists of two corresponding sorts of arguments. The first way of thinking about functionalism involves Durkheim's use of examples drawn from the human body. The brain needs the heart to pump blood to it. But, the heart also needs the brain to signal the muscle to contract. There is a functional interdependence between the two. This form of functionalism tends to be associated with a conservative relativism: things may be bad for individuals, but nothing can be changed without damaging the whole society.

Durkheim's functionalism could also be described as an *if/then* statement, however. *If* the brain depends on oxygen, *then* in order to stay alive it needs to get oxygen. Many of Durkheim's arguments are of this form. *If* a social form depends on shared belief, *then* in order to sustain it shared beliefs must be maintained. *If* a modern social form depends on shared practices and not on shared beliefs, *then* that which

shared practices require becomes necessary. This latter form of functional argument is not subject to the usual criticisms. It also overcomes the contingency usually associated with social phenomena, allowing for a degree of philosophical necessity with regard to practice-based societies.

In the context of modern differentiated societies, Durkhem's functionalism does not emphasize either conflict or consensus. He argued that modern practices require freedom, equality, and justice. Therefore, in a modern context the functional prerequisites of practices are, not coincidentally, the same thing individuals strive for. Conflict occurs only in abnormal forms where freedom, justice, and equality have not been achieved. Furthermore, shared beliefs, which place contingent moralities before individual good, are no longer necessary in a society based on justice, and the coercion they require to produce consensus is problematic because it interferes with the development and maintenance of self-regulating practices.

RULES AND *SUICIDE*: METHODS, SOCIAL FACTS

In his classic study *Suicide*, Durkheim introduced the sociological use of statistics, demonstrating that different suicide rates could be explained on the basis of differential patterns of social connectedness when they could not be explained on the basis of individual psychology. For instance, individual characteristics do not explain why older men commit more suicide, but their unmarried – unconnected – status does. In addition to introducing the use of statistics, Durkheim also used various qualitative and archival methods, particularly in his research on law and religion. Durkheim's method, whether statistical or qualitative, focused on the character of forms of association and on the consequences of those associations for the health of the social individual and/or group. By contrast, statistics in contemporary sociology are generally used to measure relationships between the demographic character of individual actions and various institutional constraints (values, goals, sanctions). This has been the predominant sociological method since the 1940s and is often equated with "macro" sociological concerns. It is, however, a later interpretation of Durkheim's method, influenced by structuralism and not entirely consistent with his own approach.

Durkheim used statistics as indicators of social facts. For Durkheim, social facts in a modern differentiated society consist of forms and patterns of association, not beliefs and values. What matters are the ways in which members of various groups are associated with one another, not their orientation toward valued courses of action, which had been important in earlier social forms. Where statistics such as suicide rates provide indicators of these associations, they may be of use to sociologists.

Durkheim's approach did not correlate individual characteristics with value-oriented behavior, however. He used statistics to indicate the strength and character of various forms of association. For instance, if the forms of association in a group were very weak, then people in the group could be expected to have a greater number of moral and psychological problems. If the forms of association in a group were too strong, then people could be expected to sacrifice themselves for the group whenever necessary. The tricky part is specifying the ideal forms of association. Durkheim argued that this varies across societies. *The Division of Labor* worked out the difference between two forms of social solidarity whose forms of association were entirely different, and *Suicide* demonstrated that the conditions under which ties to the group would be too weak or too strong also differ. Suicide in traditional and modern societies would therefore have to be understood in entirely different terms – for Durkheim, more proof that suicide was a function of social relations.

This approach differs from that of many contemporary sociologists who use statistics to measure and predict the behavior of individuals as effected by their orientations toward social goals, values, and sanctions. The focus on individuals and their relationship to social factors runs counter to the method Durkheim proposed: demonstrating the impact of social facts, assessing solidarity mechanisms, and measuring the group-level effects of beliefs and values.

Furthermore, the popular characterization of Durkheim as a quantitative macro sociologist implies a disinterest in qualitative approaches. In fact, *The Division of Labor* is based largely on

an analysis of historical changes in the law, and *Elementary Forms* both adopts and advocates a qualitative approach. In the latter, Durkheim argued repeatedly that if order cannot be found in a single case, then it cannot be established however many cases are examined.

It was Durkheim's position in *Rules* that sociologists should focus on the social facts of recurrent institutional and orderly social forms. He treated social order as a central topic for sociology and argued that methods should treat the social as primary, avoid individualism, and be broadly scientific (i.e., consist of practices recognizable to other scientists). He did not argue for methodological hegemony and in Durkheim's work the character of particular social facts, and not some a priori prescription, seems to have determined the methods he used.

ELEMENTARY FORMS: DUALISM, EPISTEMOLOGY, UNIVERSES OF DISCOURSE

In *Elementary Forms*, Durkheim argued that it is through participation in religious practices that social beings acquire the basic forms of human reason: space, time, classification, force, causality, and totality. He argued that the concept of classification has logical primacy. The first emotional experience of the distinction between sacred and profane gives birth to this category and makes possible the enactment of the rituals that create the other categories.

In his conclusion Durkheim outlined the view that all concepts, or *collective representations* as he calls them, have a social origin. Concepts adhere in universes of discourse and a proper understanding of reason, language, and mutual intelligibility would require a study of the way various words/concepts have meanings in the context of the social forms of association in which they are used.

The argument that religion developed to serve functions that were primarily social, rather than society developing to serve religious functions, would have been very unpopular in 1912 and remains so today. To the religious, the meaning of religion has nothing to do with sustaining social orders. Durkheim does not deny that religious beliefs may be true. But for him their "truth" lies in their capacity to motivate ritual practices. Beliefs alone do not explain the development of organized religions. Frequently they serve to coerce and constrain individual faith so as to support traditional social forms.

External constraint is part of the social control function of religion in traditional societies. In modern societies, however, this function is no longer required and religious diversity becomes possible. Thus, religion does not fulfill exactly the same functions in modern and traditional societies. Rituals create and sustain shared practices in both, but the need for homogeneity differs. So, while religion still fulfills epistemological functions, it is no longer connected with social orders in the same way.

For Durkheim the essential first human moment came with the creation of the first distinction between sacred and profane, and because of the importance of this moment it permeates the argument of *Elementary Forms*. In his view, it is essential that social connections and symbolic meanings are established through ritual practices. Only in this way can individual social actors be created in the first place. Without engagement in ritual practices humans are only animals, he says, and can only think like animals.

In giving the social primacy over the biological or individual rational being, Durkheim was also taking a position on the equality of all persons. He regarded *reason* as the *function* of social forms and all successful societies must produce it. Differences in the apparent reasoning powers of people, therefore, were not due to differences in innate intelligence, but rather to the different needs of the societies in which people lived and the varying ways in which reasoning was socially structured.

Durkheim's position was remarkable given the pervasiveness of the belief in racial and gender inequality, not only in his day but extending into the present. One early American critic dismissed Durkheim's sociology for proposing the allegedly absurd view that if "Negroes or Eskimos" were to live in the same society with whites they would become their equals. Not until the late 1960s would the developing public awareness of human equality begin to catch up with Durkheim's position. We can only imagine how large a price sociology paid for the inability of popular opinion to appreciate Durkheim's position in this regard at the time. According to Durkheim, popular opinion with regard to racial and gender inequality was simply wrong. It was only in their social forms, and the ways in which persons were transformed by participation in those social forms, that human beings differed. Thus, Durkheim gave sociology a distinctively democratic and egalitarian foundation.

MAJOR INTERPRETATIONS, INFLUENCES, AND CONTROVERSIES

There have been five major streams of interpretation of Durkheim's work. From the 1930s onward Talcott Parsons, who incorporated Durkheim into structural functionalism, became the primary interpreter of Durkheim's work in English. As a consequence, a positivist and functional interpretation of Durkheim became prevalent in the United States. In France, by contrast, his work was taken up by anthropologists, the best known being Lévy-Bruhl and Lévi-Strauss, who elaborated his argument regarding the relationship between the development of concepts, ideas, and societies, developing symbolic anthropology on this foundation. Each of these two early interpretations distorted the original work by capturing only parts of it. The movements that emerged against structural functionalism and symbolic anthropology – poststructuralism and postmodernism – thus also have certain shared roots.

In the wake of these intellectual revolutions, there was a revival of interest in Durkheim in both the humanities and social sciences. In the US the "cultural" side of Durkheim that had been eliminated by structural functionalism began to come to the fore and was elaborated by Jeffrey Alexander in particular. There was also an effort, beginning with and inspired by Randall Collins, to draw out the connections between Durkheim and contemporary interactionism, notably the work of Erving Goffman and later Harold Garfinkel. This interpretation also made its way into the sociology of science where it found affinities with the arguments of Ludwig Wittgenstein. Among Marxists there have been a number of persuasive articles emphasizing the radical political character of Durkheim's work (e.g., Sirianni; Parkin) that challenge the Parsonsian view of Durkheim as a conservative.

In the wake of this renewed interest, some of Durkheim's work has been retranslated and republished. Durkheim's "Sens Lectures," previously unavailable in English, were published in 2004.

While at the Sorbonne, Durkheim studied philosophy and wrote a dissertation on Montesquieu before completing his final thesis on the division of labor. Montesquieu and Rousseau were important for Durkheim because both treated social forms and processes as prerequisites for the social person. He studied with neo-Kantians like Renouvier, studied for a year in Berlin, and was caught up in the interest in the work of William James that swept through Paris at the turn of the century. It is clear from Durkheim's 1913–14 lectures that he saw pragmatism as another individualistic argument, and thus sharpened his own vision of a science of social facts against the philosophy of James.

When Durkheim arrived at the Sorbonne, sociology was associated with the work of Auguste Comte (1798–1857), Saint-Simon (1760–1825), and Herbert Spencer (1820–1903). Spencer's was an evolutionist sociology that soon fell out of favor. Comte and Saint-Simon, on the other hand, influenced such disparate thinkers as John Stuart Mill (1806–73) and Karl Marx (1818–83). It was Comte's position that as the shared beliefs and values of an earlier age diminish through the effects of progress they need to be replaced. Comte proposed a general philosophy as a more enlightened and scientific ideology that could serve the purpose. Early on Durkheim associated this position with socialism, and was critical because of the central role accorded to beliefs and ideology.

It was Durkheim's position that modernity produces new social forms, bound together not by ideology but by forms of association and self-regulating practices. Social solidarity was a product not of shared beliefs but of the diversity of interdependent positions in the division of labor. Where social solidarities formerly depended on shared beliefs enforced by strong sanctions, new forms of association produced a form of self-regulation requiring no external sanction. Durkheim argued that in modern society the state needed to support, rather than sanction and impede, self-regulating practices.

Durkheim's first example of self-regulation in *The Division of Labor* was scientific laboratory practice. When he published the second edition in 1902, he added a preface on professional groups that offered a more extensive example of how social solidarity in modern differentiated social forms is based on many different sets of shared self-regulating practices rather than on shared beliefs.

Because he studied with Renouvier and wrote about the dualism of human nature, many scholars have associated Durkheim with Kant. Certainly Durkheim was well versed in Kant's arguments and mentions him frequently in his writings, but he was generally critical. There are also many references in Durkheim's work to Hume and James, with whose arguments he also was well versed but critical.

At the time Durkheim began his studies there were no sociologists per se. Although Comte is sometimes called the first sociologist, Durkheim was the first to officially hold that title. His training would have consisted primarily of courses in philosophy, political economy, psychology, and anthropology, disciplines which treat social phenomena as the secondary, or aggregated, result of individual action. From the first it was Durkheim's objective to replace these perspectives with a new, more scientific way of working that replaced the inherent individualism of the other disciplines with a study of social forms and processes as primary phenomena. In *The Division of Labor*, he introduced this argument and the original introduction presented sociology as a new form of moral philosophy. The same theme of replacing philosophy with sociology can be seen clearly in his last work, *Elementary Forms*. Durkheim was trying to deliver firm imperatives about justice on the basis of social argumentation – to remove the contingencies from the social.

Because philosophers consider anything social to be contingent, Durkheim's efforts to establish a moral philosophy on social facts are generally interpreted as relativistic. Furthermore, because of the emphasis he placed on the universal and positive character of his findings, he is often taken by philosophers to have contradicted himself. This was true for the earliest of his American critics (Elmer Ghelke;

Charles Schaub) and consistently has been reflected in his reception among philosophers.

What Durkheim argued is that a universal sense of justice can be established on the basis of the social facts of self-regulating practices in modern societies. He does not accept the assumption that anything social is contingent. One of the points of Durkheim's functionalism is that if a social form needs a particular thing in order to survive, then its survival implies that it must have achieved that thing. These are statements of necessity, not contingency, and in his view are not teleological.

One of the more important issues confusing the reception of Durkheim's work is his rejection of philosophical individualism and his argument that the social comes before the individual. Durkheim's position is that those elements of reason that distinguish persons from animals, particularly moral reasoning, are not inborn. His position, which he attributes to Rousseau, is that only in society is there a need for moral reasoning and therefore only as participants in social processes do people develop this capacity.

This was a complete shift in thinking away from individualism. One of the many difficulties the argument has faced is that it continues to be appraised by people who take an individualist position, believing the social is therefore contingent, then applying individualistic criteria in its evaluation. This leads to labeling Durkheim falsely as an idealist, positivist, subjectivist, objectivist, rationalist, and so on. It has also often led to the view that there are two Durkheims – or that he has contradicted himself. But, the rational individual simply does not exist for Durkheim. In this he is in agreement with other classic sociological thinkers like Marx and Mead, and with more contemporary thinkers like Goffman and Garfinkel.

RELEVANCE TO THE HISTORY OF CONTEMPORARY SOCIOLOGY

Durkheim created a blueprint for the discipline of sociology that defined it in entirely new terms. Understanding social theory, and engaging in the practice of sociology without contradiction, entails giving up philosophical

positions like individualism from which the sociological object, as Durkheim defined it, is rendered absurd.

As sociology has struggled over the decades to define itself against philosophical individualism and to establish the social at its center point, Durkheim has always been the inspiration. Structural functionalism, cultural anthropology, cultural sociology, postmodernism, poststructuralism, sociological studies of science, sociology of knowledge, and legal studies were all inspired by Durkheim's arguments, some negatively and some positively. The work of Garfinkel, Goffman, symbolic interaction, and social constructivism is similarly indebted. Durkheim's arguments with regard to social character of the individual self, the importance of concrete forms of association between people, and the special characteristics of self-regulating practices in modern social contexts are an important foundation of these contemporary arguments.

The true importance of sociology as Durkheim envisioned it was not to play handmaiden to philosophy and to submit empirical studies for philosophical appraisal and evaluation. He envisioned a sociology that evaluated social facts on their own terms. He rejected the idea that social facts were contingent and wanted to establish that certain social forms and processes were necessary or, put another way, that certain social needs must be fulfilled in order for society to go on. Once this is established, those necessities become the non-contingent social facts against which arguments can be anchored.

Durkheim would have objected to the idea of theory as a perspective of dead white men or anyone else. It was his idea to deconstruct the individualism that comprised the Enlightenment perspective, and he did so from a position that was both scientific and marginal. If we cannot see what we take for granted, then we need incongruities to crack open the surface of the taken for granted so that we can see beneath. It is science, the practices of observation and analysis of what incongruities make available to us, that makes this a worthwhile exercise for sociology.

Durkheim would have resisted allowing individualistic perspectives or disciplines to judge the validity of sociological arguments. He also would have disagreed with the currently popular position (Coleman) that the problem with sociology is that it does not focus enough on individuals and on individual reason. Other disciplines would regard sociology more favorably if it did so, but the whole point of sociology from the beginning has been to challenge them in this regard. Sociology begins with the premise that individualism is wrong. To argue that it could become more popular by adopting an individualist view is to argue that sociology should surrender that which defines it as a unique and viable discipline. There would be no sociology if the individualism of philosophy, economics, and psychology were accepted. Only if the social is primary does sociology have a reason to exist as a discipline in the first place. On this foundation, Durkheim hoped to ground a sociological understanding of the requirements for justice in modern society.

SEE ALSO: Anomie; Anthropology, Cultural and Social: Early History; Collective Consciousness; Comte, Auguste; Criminology; Durkheim, Émile and Social Change; Ethnomethodology; Goffman, Erving; Individualism; James, William; Knowledge, Sociology of; Marx, Karl; Mead, George Herbert; Parsons, Talcott; Postmodernism; Poststructuralism; Pragmatism; Religion, Sociology of; Scientific Knowledge, Sociology of; Social Justice, Theories of; Solidarity, Mechanical and Organic; Statistics; Structural Functionalism; Weber, Max

REFERENCES AND SUGGESTED READINGS

Alexander, J. C. (Ed.) (1988) *Durkheimian Sociology: Cultural Studies*. Cambridge University Press, Cambridge.

Bloor, D. (1976) *Knowledge and Social Imagery*. Routledge & Kegan Paul, London.

Coleman, J. (1990) *Foundations of Social Theory*. Harvard University Press, Cambridge, MA.

Collins, R. (2004) *Interaction Ritual Chains*. Princeton University Press, Princeton.

Coser, L. (1984) Introduction. In: Durkheim, É., *The Division of Labor in Society*. Free Press, New York.

Dennes, W. R. (1924) The Methods and Presuppositions of Group Psychology. *University of California Publications in Philosophy* 6(1): 1–182.

Douglas, M. (1966) *Purity and Danger: An Analysis of Concepts of Pollution and Taboo*. Praeger, New York.

Durkheim, É. (1915 [1912]) *The Elementary Forms of the Religious Life*. Free Press, New York.

Durkheim, É. (1917) Notice sur André-Armand Durkheim. *L'Annuaire de l'Association des anciens élèves de l'École Normale Supérieure*, pp. 201–5.

Durkheim, É. (1951 [1897]) *Suicide*. Free Press, Glencoe, IL.

Durkheim, É. (1960 [1913–14]) *Pragmatism and Sociology*. University of Michigan, Ann Arbor.

Durkheim, É. (1982 [1895]) *The Rules of the Sociological Method*. Free Press, New York.

Durkheim, É. (1984 [1893]) *The Division of Labor in Society*. Free Press, New York.

Durkheim, É. (2004 [1883–4]) *Durkheim's Philosophy Lectures: Notes from the Lycée de Sens Course, 1883–1884*. Ed. N. Gross, R. A. Jones, & A. Lalande. Cambridge University Press, Cambridge.

Garfinkel, H. (1967) *Studies in Ethnomethodology*. Prentice-Hall, Englewood Cliffs, NJ.

Ghelke, C. E. (1915) Émile Durkheim's Contribution to Social Theory. *Columbia University Studies in Economics, History, and Public Law* 7–187. 1 (VCIII).

Giddens, A. (1971) *Capitalism and Modern Social Theory*. Cambridge University Press, Cambridge.

Goffman, E. (1959) *The Presentation of Self in Everyday Life*. Doubleday Anchor, New York.

Jones, R. A. (1986) *Émile Durkheim: An Introduction to Four Major Works*. Sage, Beverly Hills.

LaCapra, D. (1972) *Émile Durkheim: Sociologist and Philosopher*. Cornell University Press, Ithaca, NY.

Lévi-Strauss, C. (1963 [1958]) *Structural Anthropology*. Basic Books, New York.

Lévy-Bruhl, L. (1966 [1910]) *How Natives Think*. Washington Square Press, New York.

Lukes, S. (1973) *Émile Durkheim, His Life and Work: A Historical and Critical Study*. Stanford University Press, Stanford.

Lukes, S. (1982) Introduction. In: Durkheim, É., *The Rules of the Sociological Method*. Free Press, New York.

Mauss, M. (1990 [1925]) *The Gift*. W. W. Norton, New York.

Mestrovic, S. (1988) *Émile Durkheim and the Reform of Sociology*. Rowman & Littlefield, Lanham, MD.

Parkin, F. (1992) *Durkheim*. Oxford University Press, Oxford.

Parsons, T. (1937) *The Structure of Social Action*. Free Press, New York.

Poggi, G. (2000) *Durkheim*. Oxford University Press, Oxford.

Rawls, A. W. (2004) *Epistemology and Practice: Durkheim's The Elementary Forms of the Religious Life*. Cambridge University Press, Cambridge.

Schmaus, W. (2004) *Rethinking Durkheim and his Tradition*. Cambridge University Press, Cambridge.

Sirianni, C. (1981) Justice and the Division of Labor: A Reconsideration of Durkheim's *Division of Labor in Society*. *Theory and Society*: 449–70.

Wittgenstein, L. (1945) *Philosophical Investigations*. Blackwell, Oxford.

Durkheim, Émile and social change

Edward A. Tiryakian

One may look in vain in Durkheim's oeuvre for an explicit discussion of social change, to be found neither in his major texts nor as a rubric in the 12 *Année Sociologique* volumes published in his lifetime. *Social change* does not figure in Durkheim's major divisions of sociology. Yet, like the Scarlet Pimpernel, it is here, it is there, it is everywhere. No consideration of Durkheim can be considered complete without taking into account his immanent social realism: societal systems structurally change from within, ultimately from qualitative and quantitative changes in social interaction (a presupposition widely shared with Marx and Weber, albeit for different primary factors). This seeming paradox can be best understood if one takes into account that the nineteenth century which provided the context for Durkheim was the modern period's crucible of enormous economic, political, cultural, and technological transformations of the social order, with Durkheim's predecessors and contemporaries all seeking to ascertain the major features, causes, and outcomes of the transformation. If Durkheim did not write explicitly about social change, he and his immediate followers (the "Durkheimians," who will be briefly mentioned here) were indeed very cognizant and attentive to addressing social change. This was at least partially recognized long ago by Robert Bellah in a seminal article (1960) pointing to the significance of history in Durkheim's epistemological and substantive thought.

Ultimately, following the general dictum of Durkheim that to explain social facts one must seek recourse to social processes, to account for social change one needs to consider changes in the thickness or density of social interaction in time and space (i.e., in the frequency and extent of social interaction). This paramount focus is to be found in at least three major works, where social change takes on different manifestations.

As Lukes noted in his landmark intellectual biography (1977: 167), Durkheim proposed in his doctoral dissertation *The Division of Labor in Society* a misunderstood theory of social change invoking a morphological key variable: an increase in the "moral" or "dynamic density" of society. The division of labor and its concomitant "organic solidarity" are advanced by demographic factors of population increase in urban areas and by technological factors of increased means of communication and transportation. This perspective has been at the core of much of the initial modernization theory of the 1950s and 1960s stressing structural differentiation as change internal to social systems. As such, Durkheim's theory of societal change as structural differentiation is not altogether novel, since elements of it are to be found in Spencer. However, Durkheim proposed not only the mechanisms of change but also the problematic of the (normative) integration of societal systems in the wake of structural differentiation. This of course involves the question of *anomie* in the modern social order, which is treated in a separate entry.

Much of the treatment of long-term social change in Durkheim as well as other social scientists of the nineteenth and early twentieth centuries rests on the evolutionary paradigm. An understanding of the contemporary present forms of society and their interrelationships was viewed in the optic of biological evolution, by tracing the development of origins from simpler to more complex forms of social organization: the more complex, the more organized a social species, the more advanced it is in the evolutionary ladder. While Durkheim analyzed social change in such evolutionary terms (Durkheim 1978 [1899–1900]: 154), he rejected a linear view of the succession of societies (and of institutions), and even more of social Darwinism, which lent itself to colonialism and imperialism in justifying the rule of "advanced" societies over those seen to be more "primitive."

Durkheim's deployment of an evolutionary perspective, utilizing historical data, is evidenced in his various analyses of long-term institutional change. Among these may be mentioned his study of (1) the evolution of penal institutions, formulated in terms of laws of quantitative and qualitative changes in punishment (1978 [1899–1900]); (2) the evolution of individualism in its interrelation with the evolution of the state and political society (1957); and (3) the evolution of the institution closest to Durkheim's heart, higher education (1977 [1938]). The last named represents his most elaborate tracing of the development of an institution critical to modernity, written at a time when France in a period of turmoil and uncertainty was grappling with the course to take in educational reforms (p. 7).

Durkheim maintained in positivist fashion that secondary education needed a sound theoretical foundation based upon knowledge of how educational theory and its applications developed over time. The strengths and weaknesses of these theories in different epochs should be uncovered so as to inform policymakers and public opinion and connect proposed legislation and decrees with reality. We need not detail the evolutionary historical path Durkheim drew in going back to the origins of modern education to Rome as the initial starting point of modern higher education, and then following it forward at various stages. It is a richly textured organizational analysis of the emergent university system, seeking to cull what features in an evolutionary perspective appear to have lasting merit and hence deserving to be part of the contemporary educational system, and which do not and should be discarded (p. 160).

Durkheim's rejection of linear progress in evolutionary change is manifest in his redressing of the negative image of the Middle Ages (as an era of coarseness, harsh discipline, and little educational merit of the Scholastics); instead, he argued, this was a dynamic setting for educational development, bringing forth virtually from scratch "the most powerful and comprehensive academic organism which history has ever known" (p. 160). On the other hand, later educational systems had shortcomings: the Renaissance, with its overwhelming stress on classical education and self-centeredness, or the later Renaissance, with Jesuits in charge who made discipline and control more important than students exploring and discovering on their own.

Durkheim's study of the evolution of education, and in particular of the university system, is still of twofold merit, besides an important congruence between Durkheim and his great contemporary educator, John Dewey, with whom he shared the view that educational reforms should promote and facilitate the development and creativity of the student. First, because *The Evolution of Educational Thought* documents that at different periods of modernity, the university and secondary education have felt the need to reinvent themselves. Durkheim's study presents here comparative materials that may provide a perspective for the twenty-first century, where higher education is subject to new challenges (multiculturalism, new fiscal constraints, and so on). Second, because it lays to rest the criticism that the functionalist mode of analyzing complex modern social institutions does not address the question of social change.

There is a third sort of social change in Durkheim's work, one which has as its focus short-term, intensive transformation of the social whole. Some elements of the analysis in *The Elementary Forms of Religious Life* (1995 [1912]) are surprisingly similar to the analysis of long-term structural differentiation in Durkheim's first period, yet the accent is on what may be termed "dedifferentiation" rather than "differentiation." In common with *The Division of Labor*, written 20 years earlier, Durkheim posits that increased interaction and the density of actors interacting, in a concentrated time and place, underlie changes in social consciousness. Brought about by religious rituals in the case of the Australian aborigines or by extraordinary events as in the case of the all-night meeting of the French National Assembly in August 1789, or by similar "effervescent social milieux" in our own times from Managua and Tehran in 1979 to Eastern Europe in November 1989 (Tiryakian 1995), what is at stake is the renovation of collective solidarity at a critical moment. Durkheim sees such extraordinary moments of interactive intensity unparalleled in ordinary quotidian life. They are moments of destructuration or dedifferentiation, moments of collective enthusiasm, attended by a collapse of hierarchical status distinction and even, on occasion, of antinomian behavior. While Durkheim drew his theory of the genesis of the sacred in the extraordinary interaction setting involving the whole social group, he also pointed out that social life oscillates between two poles: colorful, festive periods of "hyperexcitement" and periods of "secular activity" of "utter colorlessness" (Durkheim 1995 [1912]: 221). Short-term intensive change gives way to "normalcy." In modern society, the contrast, as Durkheim noted, is more muted, although the need for periodic assemblies and reaffirmation of collective sentiments remains.

Various of Durkheim's collaborators dealt with social change, some with traditional and some with modern society. As an instance of the former, Mauss and Beuchat, in advance of *The Elementary Forms*, published a monograph on the social life of the Eskimo in two major seasonal cycles, winter and summer (Mauss & Beuchat 1979 [1904–5]). A study in social morphology, it analyzed variations in social organization and density of interaction. In the summer, the group is disbanded and the cultural life that integrates Eskimo society is at a minimum, as individual families are on their own. In the winter, they come together and cultural life is thick with the renovation of "a genuine community of ideas and material interests" (p. 76). Quantitative changes in interaction produce qualitative changes of increased group solidarity and consciousness, sometimes even leading to sexual license. Finding similar seasonal patterns in other North American native settings, Mauss and Beuchat proposed a general law: social life goes through cycles (phases) of increased and decreased intensity, of activity and rest, of dispersion and concentration, at the individual and collective levels (p. 79). Essentially, changes in the cultural life of a group correlate with changes in the form of a group.

François Simiand, a collaborator of the *Année Sociologique* who, with Maurice Halbwachs, was in charge of the major rubric "Economic Sociology," also developed a long-term, cyclical view of change, one applied to economic cycles (Simiand 1932). After extensive historical studies of the movements of prices, wages, economic production, and other indices of economic life, Simiand proposed that there are fluctuations with two major cycles: a cycle of general expansion – the major A-cycle – and one of contraction – the major B-cycle. Writing in a period of global economic crisis, Simiand analyzed it as the early phase of a B-cycle and criticized patchwork economic solutions that failed to realize the complex set of factors that make up economic life, including as a critical variable the social psychological reality of confidence or trust in economic conditions (1932: 113). The reality of economic progress, economic development, Simiand argued, is A + B, and mistaken are those theories or models of society that ignore fluctuations and believe they can organize a static economy. There is no general panacea for economic ills, but various options are present that require a knowledge of previous economic conditions in periods of transition from A to B or B to A.

Simiand's two phases have been utilized in world-systems theory, which has developed cycles complementing long-term (secular) growth of global capitalism. However, more attention has been paid to a Russian contemporary of Simiand, Nikolai Kondratieff, whose theories of alternating "long waves" of expansion and contraction did not fit in the Soviet model of a planned economy. A comparative assessment of Simiand and Kondratieff would provide an important chapter in the history of political economy.

SEE ALSO: Anomie; Dependency and World-Systems Theories; Dewey, John; Division of Labor; Durkheim, Émile; Kondratieff Cycles; Solidarity, Mechanical and Organic; Spencer, Herbert

REFERENCES AND SUGGESTED READINGS

Bellah, R. N. (1960) Durkheim and History. *American Sociological Review* 24(4): 447–61.

Durkheim, É. (1957) *Professional Ethics and Civic Morals*. Routledge & Kegan Paul, London.

Durkheim, É. (1977 [1938]) *The Evolution of Educational Thought: Lectures on the Formation and Development of Secondary Education in France*. Trans. P. Collins. Routledge & Kegan Paul, London.

Durkheim, É. (1978 [1899–1900]) Two Laws of Penal Evolution. In: Traugott, M. (Ed.), *Émile Durkheim on Institutional Analysis*. University of Chicago Press, Chicago, pp. 153–80.

Durkheim, É. (1995 [1912]) *The Elementary Forms of Religious Life*. Trans. K. E. Fields. Free Press, New York.

Lukes, S. (1977) *Émile Durkheim, His Life and Work: A Historical and Critical Study*. Penguin, New York.

Mauss, M. & Beuchat, H. (1979 [1904–5]) *Seasonal Variations of the Eskimo: A Study in Social Morphology*. Trans. J. Fox. Routledge & Kegan Paul, London.

Simiand, F. (1932) *Les Fluctuations économiques à longue période et la crise mondiale*. Félix Alcan, Paris.

Tiryakian, E. A. (1995) Collective Effervescence, Social Change, and Charisma: Durkheim, Weber, and 1989. *International Sociology* 10 (September): 269–81.

Traugott, M. (Ed.) (1978) *Émile Durkheim on Institutional Analysis*. University of Chicago Press, Chicago.

dyad/triad

Dan E. Miller

The smallest and most elementary social unit, a dyad is a social group composed of two members while a triad is a social group composed of three members. The study of dyads and triads is significant in two respects. First, dyads and triads form the most basic elements of sociological analysis. That is, most structural conditions and social processes can be found in dyadic and triadic interaction. Second, the analysis of dyads and triads clearly demonstrates the poverty of strict psychological reductionism, and calls into question the validity of methodological individualism. These issues and others were first addressed by Georg Simmel (1950) in his pioneering work on pure social forms.

A dyad differs from other quantitative social groupings in that each member interacts with only one other. Thus, in order to maintain the group both participants must construct reciprocal interaction with a high level of involvement with each other. Subsequently, a dyad is more fragile and precarious than other social units. If one person leaves or if one's attention is diverted elsewhere, the dyad dissolves. Because dyads are characterized by reciprocal interaction and relatively equal involvement, they tend to become egalitarian over time. This egalitarian element is enhanced by the tendency for each member to relate to the other as an individual and not in terms of a categorical identity. In addition, the intensity and necessary constancy of interaction create the conditions in which intimacy can develop between the dyad's members. A dyad's intimacy is dependent on the exclusivity of shared knowledge and experience, on the fact that whatever is shared is shared only by the two and stays within the dyad. In such circumstances the dyad's members may become devoted to each other, a quality found in close friendships and romantic love.

Three distinct types of dyads can be identified. In *pure dyads* both members are free of other obligations and responsibilities. Each is responsible only to the other for the maintenance of the relationship. The world external to the dyad, including the passage of time, tends to evaporate in pure dyadic interaction. With *representative dyads* one or both members have allegiances to other social units. How they act and respond to the other is, in part, based on their identities as representatives of the larger social units. For example, sales managers from two companies meeting over lunch to discuss a possible business arrangement constitute dyadic interaction, but their interaction differs significantly from the pure form of two lovers having lunch, lost in each other's company. Dyads (and triads for that matter) need not be made up of individuals. *Supra-individual dyads* are comprised of larger social units such as families, organizations, tribes, or societies. That is, larger social networks take on dyadic qualities when they communicate with each other. In this way we can understand how two businesses compete, two governments cooperate, and political party coalitions form.

It is common in the opening phase of dyadic interaction for new participants to engage in reciprocal self-disclosure in order to get to know each other. This shared knowledge is instrumental in the formation of a bond between the two, opening up the arrangement to further possibilities. The two members may form a cooperative social unit in order to accomplish a common goal, or the two may disagree with each other, argue, and develop a conflict relationship or a rivalry. The participants may enter into polite conversation, or they may decide to play a game with each other.

On the other hand, participation in dyadic interaction may be disagreeable for one or both parties. This disagreeableness often is accompanied by a sense of being stuck with no easy way to escape. Ironically, in pure dyads, leaving is relatively easy in that only one other person stands in the way. The knowledge of impending freedom from the constraints of dyadic interaction can be liberating. These qualities are not evident in representative dyads whose members are constrained to keep the dyad intact at least until practical matters are accomplished.

In its most elementary form a dyad comes into being when one member enters another's perceptual space. Interdependence develops when each becomes aware of the other's presence, attention, and responsiveness. Once copresence has been established, both members of the dyad take into account the anticipated response of the other as they construct and regulate their own behavior (Goffman 1963). Two people sitting on adjacent park benches notice each other, quickly establish eye contact, and return to their previous activities. Each is accessible to the other. In order to minimize the potentialities of sensory accessibility both must act in a way that will communicate that, while they are aware of each other's presence, neither person is available for more focused interaction. Identifying each other as non-threatening strangers the dyad most likely will settle into a minimal degree of interrelatedness, one of civil inattention. In this situation each accommodates the other by not interfering, while maintaining a degree of attention with minimal responsiveness. The two, constrained by their interrelatedness, inhibit untoward and potentially embarrassing behaviors.

When two people who know each other establish copresence, they may join together to become a couple. Being a couple is a more complex and focused form of dyadic interaction than mere copresence (Goffman 1971). People who constitute a couple maintain ecological proximity allowing easy access to each other, including the intimate element of touch, while at the same time restricting availability to outsiders. Unlike a copresent dyad, couples are more attentive and responsive to each other. Their interactions can range from minimal

involvement, as when they are reading together in a library, to walking together down a street or to being highly involved in conversation with each other.

Moving from situations of copresence and couples to cooperative social action requires an increasingly focused and complex form of interaction. In order to construct cooperative social interaction the following elements of interrelatedness must be established and maintained by the members of the dyad. Both must attend to the other, acknowledge that attention, and become mutually responsive to each other's behavior. On this foundation members must establish congruent situated identities and agree on the shared focus of their interaction. Finally, the dyad must designate a social objective (a desired future state) if the purpose of the cooperative interaction is to accomplish some goal (Hintz & Miller 1995). A couple sitting in a coffee shop discussing an upcoming vacation must establish and maintain the aforementioned elements of interaction if they are to successfully complete their vacation plans. If any of the dimensions of interaction are not established or maintained, then the interaction will cease, in which case the dyad will dissolve or the couple must repair the structure before they can continue.

When a third member joins a dyad, forming a triad, not only do the interpersonal dynamics of the dyad change, but also a new array of possible social relationships emerges. The addition of a third member creates a supra-individual quality to the group. That is, if one member leaves, the group continues. Other members can be recruited and socialized with little interference in the group's activities. When a third person enters a dyad's copresence the dyad's behavior becomes public. The special character of the dyad is lost. Intimacy is compromised. A couple with a new child loses much of the intimate reciprocity that previously dominated their relationship. The new parents must focus a great deal of their attention and actions toward the needs of the child. No matter how civilly inattentive the third party behaves, the dyad has acquired an audience that at once inhibits certain actions and alters others. The members of the dyad take the presence of the third into account as they construct their actions. If the third party is a stranger and merely copresent, then an element of surveillance or voyeurism emerges. If the third party is known to the other two he may be invited to join, or he may be treated as an unwanted intruder who is not only excluded but also alienated from the dyad and the interaction.

In his brilliant essay "Quantitative Aspects of the Group," Georg Simmel (1950) describes three forms of interaction that emerge with the formation of a triad – *divide et impera* (divide and rule), *tertius gaudens* (the third who enjoys), and the impartial mediator. Divide and rule is a form in which a third party engenders conflict between a solidary dyad, thus dividing them and then gaining advantage over them. A well-known example in the social sciences and in crime dramas is the prisoner's dilemma. In a prisoner's dilemma (Axelrod 1990) two suspects to a crime are arrested, brought to the police station, placed in separate interrogation rooms, and questioned by a detective. After a time the detective informs each suspect that the other is beginning to talk and that the suspect's punishment will be much lighter if he confesses. The dilemma is whether to talk or not. Both suspects will go free if neither talks, but talking means a shorter sentence. Faced with this dilemma most suspects cooperate with the detectives and confess. By employing the strategy of divide and rule, the detective was able to gain the necessary advantage.

In *tertius gaudens* triadic interaction the third member turns a disagreement (or competition) between the other two to his or her advantage. Unlike divide and rule, in *tertius gaudens* the other two are not a solidary unit. For example, a gasoline price war between two rival oil companies is advantageous to the consumer, who enjoys a break in high gasoline prices. Similarly, a child of a divorcing couple may enjoy the attention and gifts received from parents competing for the child's affection. In another situation two job candidates competing for the same position in a tight job market allow the employer to offer a lower salary and a smaller benefits package.

The third triadic form described by Simmel is that of the impartial mediator whose interaction with the other two is intended to bring them together to settle their differences. Marriage counselors exemplify the impartial mediator with the married couple and the counselor entering into cooperative interaction. However, the impartiality of a mediator is not always a certainty. It is not uncommon for a marriage counselor or a therapist to unwittingly align with one party in a dispute, thus altering the relationship and further dividing the dyad. A variation on the role of impartial mediator is that of the arbitrator. Whereas the impartial mediator brings people together to help them settle differences through cooperative interaction, the arbitrator in an authoritarian role decides how the dispute will be settled. When contract negotiations between labor and management break down with little chance of reaching an agreement, an arbitrator may be brought in to settle the dispute in a fair and just manner. In a more elementary situation, a father may intervene in an argument between his two children over who controls the television by turning it off and instructing the children to not turn it on.

Coalitions are formed when two parties join together for the purpose of gaining advantage over a third party (Caplow 1969). Coalition formation in triads is about control – majority control. The tendency for coalitions to form in triads constitutes a social fact and, thus, is not reducible to the characteristics of the individuals who form them. In a revolutionary coalition a control hierarchy is overthrown when the member with the least power joins with the party with the second degree of power to wrest control from the most powerful party. With a conservative coalition the power hierarchy is maintained. A more prosaic form of coalition interaction arises when two people (a majority) formally or informally demand conformity on the part of the third person under the threat (or fear) of exclusion.

A coalition is unstable if the two parties who control the third have relatively equal power. In such situations the one with the least power can exert considerable influence by the known possibility that the low-power party may join with one of the coalition members to gain control over the deposed other. For example, a small political party may gain numerous concessions by joining with one or the other more powerful parties. More interesting is the situation in which the majority parties modify their own policies in order to mollify the minority party who, each fears, may form a coalition with the rival majority party.

Triads forming one-to-two situations are commonplace. In one-to-two triads differentiation is established identifying the "one" as distinct from the others – as a leader or representative. The "one" defines and acts toward the others as a unit – as an audience, as students, as followers, or as captives. In one-to-two situations responsibility for the actions within the triad falls to the "one." A public speaker commands the attention of the audience, a tutor controls the focus of attention and behavior of her two pupils, and a tyrant controls his subjects. One-to-two triads are asymmetrical, ranging from the modest asymmetry of a one-on-audience situation to the increasingly asymmetrical arrangements found in authority relations, followings, and tyrannies.

The study of dyads and triads is relevant in many areas within the social sciences, including: bargaining and negotiation studies; counseling and psychotherapy; courtship, marriage, and family; conversation analysis; leadership; obedience and compliance research; and politics.

SEE ALSO: Group Processes; Interaction; Interpersonal Relationships; Simmel, Georg

REFERENCES AND SUGGESTED READINGS

Axelrod, R. (1990) *The Evolution of Cooperation*. Penguin, New York.

Caplow, T. (1969) *Two Against One: Coalitions in Triads*. Prentice-Hall, Englewood Cliffs, NJ.

Gamson, W. A. (1961) A Theory of Coalition Formation. *American Sociological Review* 26: 565–73.

Goffman, E. (1963) *Behavior in Public Places: Notes on the Social Organization of Gatherings*. Free Press, New York.

Goffman, E. (1971) *Relations in Public: Microstudies of the Public Order*. Basic Books, New York.

Hintz, R. A. & Miller, D. E. (1995) Openings Revisited: The Foundations of Social Interaction. *Symbolic Interaction* 18: 355–69.

Mead, G. H. (1934) *Mind, Self, and Society*. University of Chicago Press, Chicago.

Simmel, G. (1950) *The Sociology of Georg Simmel*. Trans. and Ed. K. Wolff. Free Press, New York.

early childhood

Harriett Romo

Early childhood includes infancy, preschool, and the early years of formal schooling. Sociologists are interested in early childhood for a number of reasons. The children in a society will continue the social organizations, values, and mores of that society. Moreover, the ways a society cares for and socializes its children tell much about the structure and nature of that society.

Ariès (1962) documented the ways childhood has been viewed over time and how those views have changed over different centuries in western society. He studied depictions of children in medieval art and other historical documents to show that the concept of childhood as we recognize it today did not exist in those times. Instead, children were dressed and treated as little adults. Then thirteenth-century artists portrayed children as sweet, innocent angels quite different from adults. Perceptions shifted again when sixteenth- and eighteenth-century moralists argued that childhood was a period of immaturity when children must be trained and disciplined in preparation for adulthood. Ariès claimed that modern society has focused on social problems of children, such as abuse and neglect, and separated children from the adult world. Although Ariès's work has been criticized for his generalizations, his analysis provided convincing evidence that children and childhood are perceived differently in different time periods.

Sociologists are also interested in childhood because child socialization and childrearing practices differ across cultures (Ochs & Schieffelin 1986). Childhood socialization involves children acquiring language skills, forming the core of personality, and learning the central norms and values of the adults of their society. The parent–child relationship has been studied extensively, especially the interactions between the mother and the child. Attention has also been given to how others in society, including fathers, extended family, siblings, peers, and other significant adults, influence the growing child. Corsaro and others (Corsaro & Miller 1992; Corsaro 1997) have argued that the socialization of children is a collective process that occurs in the public as well as a private realm. They emphasize the importance of language and cultural routines in children's socialization. As children participate in cultural routines, they acquire social skills and knowledge and also creatively contribute to the production of culture through their interactions with adults and other children.

Concerns about the separation of children from the world of family and adults appeared in much of the sociological research on families and children during the 1970s as more parents and other adults worked longer hours, and families struggled to find appropriate care for their children. Issues of quality and adequacy of childcare became crucial for mothers who pursued careers opened up as a result of the women's movement.

As very young children had greater contact with institutions outside the family, more attention was paid to their social, moral, and educational development outside the family. Preschool in many societies has become a common solution to the problem of how to care for, socialize, and educate children between infancy and the start of formal schooling. In the US, early childhood education has been a response to the changing patterns of men's and women's work, high divorce rates, and the needs of single-parent families (Tobin et al. 1989). Researchers in the twentieth century emphasized that children are shaped by their own personal histories and experiences, and they are also actors in the shaping of their experiences and of their environment and culture (Corsaro 1997). For example, children socialize their parents into how parents should behave. Infants demand attention by crying and initiate contacts with adults in interactions. In social learning, children observe the behavior of others, repeat behavior that is rewarded, and avoid behavior that is punished. Children organize and interpret experiences for themselves and make judgments about behaviors. The work of Corsaro has suggested that sociologists can learn much about the daily lives and mores of adults in a society by observing and analyzing the behaviors of children and what they say.

As children spend greater amounts of time in educational institutions, sociologists have focused on the socialization and stratification that occur in schools and classrooms. Peer and media influences on children, the social problems of children, and the effects of changes in family composition on early childhood have also been topics of research. Contemporary research in psychology and education has suggested that infants and toddlers have many more cognitive capacities than previously realized, and a multitude of new research has been generated on infant brain development, cognition, the importance of play in children's lives, peer and family relationships, and emergent literacy.

The research focused on children's educational development has meant a greater awareness of the serious gaps in achievement between children from different socioeconomic, racial and ethnic, and linguistic backgrounds. As more and more US children attend preschool programs, a growing gap exists between children who arrive at formal schooling with extensive preschool experience and those who have not had access to early formal learning. Early childhood represents a critical opportunity for children to develop language and emergent literacy skills that constitute the foundation for more sophisticated literacy skills (Tabors & Snow 2002). Increasingly, children arrive at the first grade of schooling knowing how to write their names, count and recognize numbers, and recite the alphabet. Skills formerly taught in early kindergarten programs are now

taught in preschool programs for 3- and 4-year-olds, giving children who have access to such programs an advantage in learning formal school skills.

Immigrant children are the fastest growing sector of the US population. Roughly one in six children in the US today lives in an immigrant-headed household. The effect of immigration and the experiences of second-generation US-born children are topics of increasing research interest. A number of distinguished scholars have argued that immigration is structured by forms of transnationalism, suggesting that families and children often live in more than one nation-state simultaneously. Children may be born in the US but schooled in their native community, or vice versa. Immigrant children may be raised by relatives in the native community while their parents work in the US and then join their parents in the US when they reach school age. Large numbers of immigrant children find themselves increasingly segregated from white, English-speaking children (Portes & Rumbaut 2001). Some immigrant children do quite well in US schools, surpassing native-born children in performance on standardized tests and attitudes toward education. Other immigrant groups tend to achieve below their native-born peers. Successful adaptations among immigrant children may relate to cultural values or patterns of economic and social capital. Immigrant parents often struggle to maintain social control of their children as their offspring enter the formal US school system. Recent research suggests that length of residence in the US may be associated with declining health, school achievement, and aspirations. Many parents find it difficult to encourage their children to maintain their home language or their cultural values as they interact with others outside their home and family. Segregation or exposure to American society, English language skills, place of birth, age upon arrival, length of residence in the US, and the social and economic resources of their family influence the adaptation of immigrant children. Outcomes of adaptation are also influenced by where the immigrants settle, the type of childcare or school they attend, and the group of peers with whom they associate. Children with poorly educated parents often find themselves growing up in underprivileged neighborhoods, poor schools, and a generally disruptive social environment.

There has been much emphasis on the impact of poverty on children. Families from racial and ethnic groups are disproportionately represented among the poor in the United States. Duncan and Brooks-Gunn (1997) compiled research on the effects on children of growing up poor. They emphasized key transitions or turning points in child development that might alter behaviors or contexts for children and may be affected by income poverty. Nutrition in the prenatal and early infancy period can affect birth weight and later outcomes in school achievement and behavior. Infants from poor families are less likely to have immunizations or early health care and often receive childcare of lesser quality than that provided for families of different income levels. Persistent poverty has very negative effects on all children's achievement scores and verbal abilities.

A number of social policies and programs have aimed at interventions to assist children during this key period of early childhood. Fruitful strategies have been to improve the school readiness and cognitive ability of young children. Head Start is a preschool program for low-income 3- and 4-year-olds and Early Head Start reaches mothers, infants, and toddlers. Other effective strategies include helping parents read more to their children and teaching parents about effective parenting and stimulating learning activities they can do with their children.

SEE ALSO: Child Abuse; Childcare; Childhood; Consumer Culture, Children's; Differential Treatment of Children by Sex; Divorce; Family Structure and Child Outcomes; Parental Involvement; Socialization

REFERENCES AND SUGGESTED READINGS

Ariès, P. (1962) *Centuries of Childhood*. Vintage, New York.

Corsaro, W. A. (1997) *The Sociology of Childhood*. Pine Forge Press, Thousand Oaks, CA.

Corsaro, W. A. & Miller, P. J. (Eds.) (1992) *Interpretive Approaches to Children's Socialization*. Special edition of *New Directions for Child Development* 58 (Winter).

Duncan, G. J. & Brooks-Gunn, J. (Eds.) (1997) *Consequences of Growing Up Poor*. Russell Sage Foundation, New York.

Ochs, E. & Schieffelin, B. (Eds.) (1986) *Language Socialization Across Cultures*. Cambridge University Press, Cambridge.

Portes, A. & Rumbaut, R. G. (2001) *Legacies: The Story of the Immigrant Second Generation*. University of California Press, Berkeley; Russell Sage Foundation, New York.

Tabors, P. O. & Snow, C. E. (2002) Young Bilingual Children and Early Literacy Development. In: Neuman, S. B. & Dickinson, D. K. (Eds.), *Handbook of Early Literacy Research*. Guilford Press, New York, pp. 159–78.

Tobin, J. J., Wu, D. Y. H., & Davidson, D. H. (1989) *Preschool in Three Cultures: Japan, China, and the United States*. Yale University Press, New Haven.

earner–carer model

Joya Misra

The earner–carer model is a fundamentally gender egalitarian welfare state approach, which assumes that men and women equally engage in both caregiving and paid employment (Gornick & Meyers 2003). Welfare state structures always rest on gendered assumptions about men's and women's roles in the family and workplace. Through social policies, such gender ideologies reflect but also reinforce supposed roles of men and women as citizens, workers, and carers.

The dominant vision of the western welfare state during the twentieth century was the "male breadwinner–female caregiver" or "family wage" model (Sainsbury 1999). According to this model, families were presumed to be composed of a man working outside the home, a woman providing care within the home, and children. In order for this model to operate effectively, men needed to earn a wage large enough to support all of the members of this family. The welfare state would only intervene to replace the male breadwinner's wage in case of unemployment, disability, sickness, or old age, or occasionally to support women's caretaking within the home (Fraser 1994). However, by the late twentieth century, it became increasingly clear that the male breadwinner model, which had never been accurate for most working-class and poor families, was no longer tenable for even middle-class families – both because few jobs pay enough to support an entire family, and because most women are now also labor market participants (Crompton 1999). Scholars suggest three main models to replace the family wage model: the universal breadwinner model, the caregiver parity model, and the earner–carer model.

The "universal breadwinner" model posits a society in which both men and women are equally invested in labor market participation. Rosemary Crompton (1999) refers to this model as the "dual earner/state carer" or "dual earner/marketized carer" model. In such a model, the welfare state should work to eliminate differences between men and women by engaging women in the paid labor force. Such a model requires workplace reforms aimed at equalizing women's opportunities, state or market provision of childcare, eldercare, and other care services, and the development of high-quality full-time positions that carry full social insurance benefits for women workers. This model would require either state or market provision of care, so that women are free to pursue paid employment (Fraser 1994).

The "caregiver parity" model posits a society in which women are valued and rewarded for providing care. In such a model, the welfare state should recognize gender difference and value care (Sainsbury 1999). Rather than encouraging women to pursue employment patterns that mimic men's, a caregiver parity strategy would make the difference between men's and women's employment patterns cost-less to women, by supporting the time and effort women spend on care. Such a model would require the state to provide generous caregiver allowances in order to support informal carework, as well as workplace reforms such as parental leaves and flextime that make it easier for women to pursue care and paid employment. Rather than shifting care to the market and state, such a model emphasizes the family as the primary site for the provision of care (Fraser 1994).

The "earner–carer" model rejects both of these strategies to suggest a new vision, in which men and women both must balance informal carework and labor force participation. In this model, feminists pursue a strategy that encourages men's lives to more closely resemble women's lives, and requires social institutions to adjust to meet the needs of men and women who do not specialize in either formal work or informal care, but instead are involved in both formal work and informal care. Such a model would require all jobs to assume workers who are both earners and carers, with shorter workweeks, and employment-enabling services. Unlike the universal breadwinner strategy that privileges state and market provision of care, the earner–carer model assumes that care will take place both inside and outside of households. Unlike the caregiver parity model, the earner–carer model attempts to break down gendered norms of care and employment (Fraser 1994; Crompton 1999; Gornick & Meyers 2003). However, this model remains difficult to institute effectively. As Anne Lise Ellingsaeter (1999) and Diane Sainsbury (1999) suggest, despite efforts to institute a more flexible combination of employment and care in Norway and Sweden respectively, gendered models remain. However, as Sainsbury (1999: 196) notes, "The lack of far-reaching change . . . should not blind us to the merits of policy construction which integrates market work and care work in the home and simultaneously grants equal entitlement to men and women."

SEE ALSO: Carework; Citizenship; Gender Ideology and Gender Role Ideology; Gender, Work, and Family; Inequality/Stratification, Gender; International Gender Division of Labor; Maternalism; Social Policy, Welfare State

REFERENCES AND SUGGESTED READINGS

Crompton, R. (Ed.) (1999) *Restructuring Gender Relations and Employment: The Decline of the Male Breadwinner*. Oxford University Press, New York.
Ellingsaeter, A. L. (1999) Dual Breadwinners Between State and Market. In: Crompton, R. (Ed.), *Restructuring Gender Relations and Employment: The*

Decline of the Male Breadwinner. Oxford University Press, New York, pp. 40–59.

Fraser, N. (1994) After the Family Wage: Gender Equity and the Welfare State. *Political Theory* 22 (4): 591–618.

Gornick, J. C. & Meyers, M. K. (2003) *Families That Work: Policies for Reconciling Parenthood and Employment*. Russell Sage, New York.

Sainsbury, D. (1994) Women's and Men's Social Rights: Gendering Dimensions of Welfare States. In: Sainsbury, D., *Gendering Welfare States*. Sage, London, pp. 150–69.

Sainsbury, D. (1999) *Gender, Equality, and Welfare States*. Cambridge, New York.

ecofeminism

Noël Sturgeon

Ecofeminism refers to theories and political practices that make connections between feminisms and environmentalisms. Basically, ecofeminists claim that the oppression, inequality, and exploitation of certain groups (people of color, women, poor people, LGBT people, third world people, animals) are theoretically and structurally related to the degradation and overexploitation of the environment. Ecofeminism involves a double intervention: the claim that feminist issues need to be part of environmentalist agendas and analyses; and the claim that environmental issues need to be part of feminist agendas and analyses. Outside of this basic insight, there is little agreement over the specific character or mechanism of the connection between social inequalities and environmental problems.

Both an activist and an academic phenomenon, ecofeminisms can be found in most parts of the world and in many disciplines, especially women's studies, philosophy, literary criticism, religious studies, history, sociology, geography, cultural studies, and ethnic studies. Several major areas of theoretical and political conflict and disagreement exist. One of the major areas of conflict is how to conceptualize the "woman/nature" connection. Are women the majority of grassroots environmental activists because the gender division of labor puts them in charge of domestic responsibilities such as familial health,

food purity, community viability, and – especially in the global South – access to potable water, availability of fuel, and small-scale agricultural sustainability? Or are women concerned about the environment because they are associated ideologically with nature, the body, and animals – especially in western cultures? These aspects, however, are not necessarily opposed, but can be conceptualized from constructivist or essentialist positions. Still, one of the major internal and external critiques of ecofeminism has been of the apparent biological essentialism of some (especially early) ecofeminist arguments that women have a special role to play in environmentalism (Sturgeon 1997).

The set of interconnected ideas called ecofeminism (that nature and women are similarly exploited by the patriarchal system's disregard for life, health, and equality; that access to clean water, air, and food is part of a broader feminist concept of human rights) has served as an inspiration for many activists since the late 1970s. Different versions of ecofeminism have been articulated over time by activists in the anti-nuclear, anti-militarist, anti-colonialist, and anti-corporate globalization movements, as well as in environmental movements involving species extinction, wilderness preservation, animal liberation, environmental justice, sustainable agriculture, and anti-GMO foods. Ecofeminism cannot be manageably characterized as one social movement, but appears more or less simultaneously in a number of political arenas in the late 1970s and the early 1980s, especially in the context of feminist anti-nuclear activism in the US (Starhawk 1982), England, Australia, and the South Pacific. The label, often attributed to François D'Eaubonne, a French activist and writer who used the term in 1974, is more likely a neologism produced by feminist activists from a number of different environmental movements (King 1990). Questions of racism in white feminism, and ethnocentrism in northern/western hegemonic feminism, were also contentious issues for ecofeminist politics.

In the international context, beginning at the 1980 World Women's Conference in Nairobi, many feminist activists from the global South insisted that environmental issues such as deforestation, desertification, and water purity were central parts of women's struggle against poverty and colonialism. They argued for more materialist analyses of the relation between environmental and women's issues than was common in western ecofeminist activism, which in the 1980s had a strong spiritualist and ideological strand (Agarwal 1992). The label "ecofeminism" was criticized (in both political and academic interventions) as standing in for universalistic, essentialist conceptualizations of the "woman/nature connection" that did not account for unequal power and privilege in the distribution of exposure to environmental problems. The development of this critique accompanied the growing interest in environmentalist feminism in the NGO and UN political arenas, sometimes going under the name "gender and development" (Braidotti et al. 1994). NGOs such as DAWN, WEDO, WEED, and the Committee on Women, Population, and the Environment, as well as movements such as the Green Belt movement in Kenya (headed by Wangari Maathai, awarded a 2004 Nobel Peace Prize for her work) and the Chipko movement in India, constituted a loose set of affiliations that brought environmental issues to the attention of international feminist organizers, and vice versa (Sturgeon 1997).

Ecofeminist arguments have had a noticeable effect on both environmental and gender policy (Buckingham 2004). At the 1992 UN Conference on Environment and Development in Rio, the final document, Agenda 21, contained a chapter on women's stake in environmental issues; and in 1995, at the UN Conference for Women in Beijing, the environment was prominent in the list of women's concerns. Ecofeminism is not just a western movement: for instance, the activism and writing of Indian ecofeminist Vandana Shiva has raised the profile of new issues, such as corporate ownership of genetic materials, as both feminist and environmental concerns within a global political economy, despite what some feminist critics of Shiva see as her essentialist and ahistorical vision of women subsistence farmers. Since the 1970s, the journal *Women and Environments International*, located in Toronto, has published accounts of different environmental feminist activist efforts around the world.

In the academy, a burst of ecofeminist publications has made it difficult to keep pace, especially given that the literature spans so many disciplines. As indicated above, the label "ecofeminism" itself is now controversial, so much contemporary scholarship tends to use the terms environmental feminism, ecological feminism, or feminist environmentalism, or other more specific emendations of the label such as ecowomanism, environmental justice ecofeminism, or materialist ecofeminism. Early writing that was important to the first theorizations of the field, such as Sherry Ortner's anthropological article "Is Female to Male as Nature is to Culture?" (1974), Annette Kolodny's historical and literary *The Lay of the Land* (1975), Susan Griffin's literary *Woman and Nature* (1978), and Carolyn Merchant's historical *The Death of Nature* (1980), demonstrated the disciplinary variety present at the outset, as well as the theoretical problems of establishing connections between feminism and environmentalism. *The Death of Nature* was not just an inspiration for ecofeminists, but also an important foundation for feminist science studies, which has had an interestingly intertwined but sometimes antagonistic relationship with ecofeminism. All four of these works demonstrate the power of an analysis that simultaneously addresses the means by which sexism and environmental overexploitation are reproduced and maintained, but they also demonstrate some of the dangers of such an analysis. The temptation to lump all women together without cultural, racial, class, and historical distinctions leads to universalisms that are politically and theoretically problematic. Merchant's later work, *Ecological Revolutions* (1989), *Earthcare* (1996), and *Reinventing Eden* (2004), constitutes a detailed historical environmental feminist treatment that carefully accounts for race and class differences, ranging from the European conquest of the US to the present.

Early ecofeminist scholarship located the twin problems of the oppression of women and the exploitation of the environment in a western dualism that separated and unequally valued men/women, culture/nature, reason/emotion, mind/body, white/black, and human/animal. Ecofeminist philosophers Karen Warren (2000) and Val Plumwood (1994) have separately developed a detailed critique of this dualist framework and implicated it in a number of structures of domination, not just those affecting women and nature, but also in racism, colonialism, and speciesism. Other ecofeminist theorists such as Greta Gaard (1997) and Catriona Sandilands (1999) have examined the ways in which heterosexism is also upheld by dualist structures of domination as well as other problematic concepts of nature. Carol Adams (1990), among others, has written extensively on the relation between the exploitation of animals and sexist/heterosexist ideologies. Vandana Shiva (*Staying Alive*, 1988), Maria Mies (*Patriarchy and Accumulation*, 1986; Mies & Shiva 1993), and Mary Mellors (*Breaking the Boundaries*, 1992) have written about the dangers of capitalist and colonialist economies for both women and the environment. Joni Seager (*Earth Follies*, 1993) has argued that the patriarchal structures of corporations, governments, and militaries are implicated in these institutions being the three major causes of environmental problems.

As a corrective to the narratives and practices of domination identified by this wide-ranging scholarship, Warren (2000) and Merchant (2004) have offered the idea of a partnership ethic, a way of understanding nature not as other, or as resource, but as active agent in a process of co-construction of reality with human beings. These ideas are close to those of Donna Haraway (*The Companion Species Manifesto*, 2003; *The Haraway Reader*, 2004), who has allied herself with a thoroughly non-essentialist version of ecofeminism in several places (Sandilands 1999), though she never uses the language of partnership with nature, but rather the notion of "naturecultures" as a way to shake up notions of binary difference and to see nature as composed of multiple, interdependent actors. Chris Cuomo (1998) has written about another way of conceptualizing a more positive social and environmental ethics, using the complex and promising concept of "flourishing" as a guidepost to constructing social and environmental relationships that are just, flexible, and sustainable.

Sociological work on the relationship between feminism and environmental issues has analyzed particular movements, explored overlap between feminist and environmental values, and surveyed ecofeminist theoretical arguments (Norgaard 1996). Overviews of environmental movements sometimes include ecofeminism as a variant (Merchant, *Radical Ecology*, 1992) but ecofeminism is often ignored or excluded by social movement historians or theorists, despite, or perhaps because of, ecofeminism's widespread manifestations in a number of different environmental political contexts (Sturgeon 1997). Robert Gottlieb (*Forcing the Spring*, 1993) and Dorceta Taylor (1996) have both done interesting and useful work in challenging standard environmental histories that emphasize wilderness preservation and white male founders such as John Muir. Instead, Gottlieb and Taylor have emphasized working-class (occupational health), female (progressivism and social welfare), and African American (urban reform and civil rights) movements as historical antecedents to the common concerns of feminist environmentalists and environmental justice advocates.

Environmental justice and ecofeminism movements have similar foci, operating from slightly different but related frameworks, with ecofeminism stressing gender, and environmental justice stressing race. Both positions, however, end with emphasizing the interconnections of race, class, gender, and class inequality with environmental issues. The exploration of the relationship between ecofeminism and environmental racism, however, is a fraught discussion, given that the label ecofeminism has been associated early in its existence with white feminists not necessarily allied with the issues of race and class important to environmental justice activists (Kirk 1997). Yet, there is a set of historical, political, and theoretical interrelations here worth exploring, given the large number of women who have been activists in grassroots environmental justice organizations, and some of the struggles they have had with sexism in these organizations (Di Chiro 1992). Laura Pulido (*Environmentalism and Environmental Justice*, 1996) and Devon Peña (*Chicano Culture*, 1997) also recognize the importance of gender as well as race and culture in constructing and analyzing environmental justice movements. A recent attempt to bridge the divide between environmental feminisms and environmental justice is the collection edited by Rachel Stein, *Environmental Justice: Gender, Sexuality and Activism* (2004).

The future of activist ecofeminism might very well lie in directions that will cause the label to disappear entirely. Ironically, as the label becomes less used, the cornerstone of ecofeminism, the interconnections of the issues of social inequality and environment, is an analysis widely accepted by the global justice movement, and scholarly approaches which deploy environmentalist and feminist analyses together are becoming more critical as tools in understanding a broad array of social and cultural phenomena. Joni Seager (2003: 950) identifies four areas in which "the best of the recent feminist environmentalist scholarship engages with and extends transnational, postcolonial, and poststructuralist deconstructions and challenges." These four areas, according to Seager, are the work being done by feminist environmentalist scholars on animal rights, public health, global political economy, and population issues. More and more environmental feminist work includes the ecofeminist critique of dualist structures, but also looks more generally at the use of ideas of nature and the natural as tools of legitimation in a global political economy (Sturgeon, *The Politics of the Natural*, 2006). This expanded theoretical agenda provides a broader scope on the world's present problems, in which the interrelated issues of growing inequality and planetary environmental crises are central.

SEE ALSO: Environment, Sociology of; Environmental Movements; Essentialism and Constructionism; Ethic of Care; Feminism and Science, Feminist Epistemology; Feminism; Feminism, First, Second, and Third Waves; Gender, Development and; Gender, Social Movements and; Strategic Essentialism

REFERENCES AND SUGGESTED READINGS

Adams, C. (1990) *The Sexual Politics of Meat: A Feminist-Vegetarian Critical Theory*. Continuum Press, New York.

Agarwal, B. (1992) The Gender and Environment Debate: Lessons from India. *Feminist Studies* 18(1): 119–58.

Braidotti, R. et al. (1994) *Women, the Environment, and Sustainable Development: Towards a Theoretical Synthesis*. Zed Books, London.

Buckingham, S. (2004) Ecofeminism in the 21st Century. *Geographical Journal* 170(2): 146–54.

Cuomo, C. (1998) *Feminism and Ecological Communities: An Ethic of Flourishing*. Routledge, London.

Di Chiro, G. (1992) Defining Environmental Justice: Women's Voices and Grassroots Politics. *Socialist Review* 22(4): 93–130.

Gaard, G. (1997) Towards a Queer Ecofeminism. *Hypatia* 12(1).

Griffin, S. (1978) *Woman and Nature*. Harper & Row, New York.

King, Y. (1990) *What is Ecofeminism?* Ecofeminist Resources, New York.

Kirk, G. (1997) Ecofeminism and Environmental Justice: Bridges Across Gender, Race, and Class. *Frontiers* 18(2): 2–20.

Merchant, C. (2004) *Reinventing Eden: The Fate of Nature in Western Culture*. Routledge, London.

Mies, M. & Shiva, V. (1993) *Ecofeminism*. Zed Books, London.

Norgaard, K. (1996) Explorations of Nature and Culture: Ecological Feminism and the Enrichment of Human Ecology. *Advances in Human Ecology* 5.

Plumwood, V. (1994) *Feminism and the Mastery of Nature*. Routledge, London.

Sandilands, C. (1999) *The Good-Natured Feminist: Ecofeminism and the Quest for Democracy*. University of Minnesota Press, Minneapolis.

Seager, J. (2003) Rachel Carson Died of Breast Cancer: The Coming of Age of Feminist Environmentalism. *SIGNS* 28,3 (Spring): 945–72.

Starhawk (1982) *Dreaming the Dark: Magic, Sex, and Politics*. Beacon Press, Boston.

Sturgeon, N. (1997) *Ecofeminist Natures: Race, Gender, Feminist Theory, and Political Action*. Routledge, London.

Taylor, D. E. (1996) American Environmentalism: The Role of Race, Class, and Gender, 1820–1995. *Race, Gender and Class* 5(1): 16–62.

Warren, K. J. (2000) *Ecofeminist Philosophy*. Rowman & Littlefield, Lanham, MD.

ecological models of urban form: concentric zone model, the sector model, and the multiple nuclei model

Kent Schwirian

Ecological models of urban form describe and explain the spatial patterns taken by the distribution of people, buildings, and activities across a city's terrain. This orderly set of spatial arrangements is known as the city's land use pattern or spatial form. Through the years ecological researchers have identified three major models of the geometry of city form: concentric zone, sector, and multiple nuclei. While the three models are conceptually distinct, in the actual development of most cities various elements from the three models become uniquely combined into a spatial pattern that gives each city its own individual spatial geometry. Each of the three models was developed to explain urban morphology in industrial cities of the twentieth century. The concentric zone model was presented by Ernest Burgess in 1925. The sector (Hoyt 1939) and multiple nuclei (Harris & Ullman 1945) models were presented later as alternatives to the concentric zone model. Through time the three have become intellectually linked and widely considered as "the classic models of urban land use." They are "classic" in the sense that the three models have stood the test of time and have proven to be catalysts of research on cities in both developed and developing societies.

The three models share common assumptions: (1) that the city is growing in population and expanding in economic activities; (2) a relatively free land market that is responsive to the economic principles of supply and demand with little in the way of government regulation; (3) an economic base that is mainly a mix of industrial-commercial activities; (4) private ownership of property; (5) specialization in land use; (6) a transportation system that is fairly rapid and efficient, and generally available in terms of cost to the majority of the population; and (7) freedom of residential choice, at least for the higher socioeconomic strata. Even though sharing these assumptions, the three models predict different spatial geometries (see Figure 1).

CONCENTRIC ZONE MODEL

For the Chicago School sociologists (1914–45), Chicago was the prototypical growing industrial city. What was true for Chicago, they argued, was true for most others. Chicago was both their window on city life and their laboratory for community study. The concentric zone model described Chicago, they argued, and, in essence, described other cities as well.

The concentric zone model, attributed to Ernest Burgess, posits a city undergoing rapid population and economic growth. As different population groups, industrial enterprises, and organizations come to the city, an enormous land market competition develops for highly prized locations. The groups with the most available resources (e.g., business and industry, the upper class) are able to obtain the locations they desire while those with fewer resources (e.g., impoverished immigrant groups) have to make do elsewhere. In 1929 Robert Park called the city, through the operation of its land market, a "great sifting and sorting mechanism . . . so that every individual finds, eventually, either the place where he can, or the place where he must live" (Park 1952: 79).

Central location is valued most highly since the old industrial city had but one vital downtown center. Central location minimizes transportation costs to all other locations in the city. Consequently, land values at the city's center soar and can only be afforded by the most resource-laden groups – typically, business and industry. The *central business district* (CBD) forms the organizing node of the city and is identified as Zone 1 of the model. It includes banks and other financial institutions, corporate offices and headquarters, large department stores and specialized retailers, museums, hotels and night clubs, bars and restaurants, theaters and other entertainment venues, and government administrative offices.

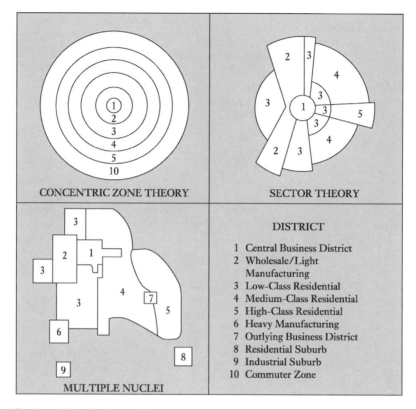

CONCENTRIC ZONE THEORY

SECTOR THEORY

MULTIPLE NUCLEI

DISTRICT

 1 Central Business District
 2 Wholesale/Light
    Manufacturing
 3 Low-Class Residential
 4 Medium-Class Residential
 5 High-Class Residential
 6 Heavy Manufacturing
 7 Outlying Business District
 8 Residential Suburb
 9 Industrial Suburb
10 Commuter Zone

Figure 1   Classic models of urban spatial geometry.

Zone 2, the *zone in transition*, is located around the CBD on all sides. It is in the process of shifting from residential to industrial-commercial land uses as the growing CBD spills its various activities into it. It is an area of intense land speculation and profit-taking by property owners. The area's increasing blight and deterioration drive out the middle- and working-class residents. Their leaving makes the zone an available place of residence for those groups that cannot obtain housing elsewhere – the segregated racial and ethnic minorities, the socially stigmatized, the downwardly mobile, and those seeking impersonality, anonymity, and seclusion. Slums, prostitution, crime, mental and physical illness, and the drug war flourish in the zone in transition. It is a socially distressed area inhabited by socially distressed individuals.

Just beyond the zone in transition is found Zone 3, the *zone of workingmen's homes*. It is a

blue-collar neighborhood inhabited by stable families where "respectability" is a driving ethos. The housing is neat and tidy and the residents are alert and "on guard" against incursions of minorities from the zone in transition. Residential invasions of the poor and ethnic minorities are usually met with resistance. Blockbusting realtors operate in the zone to open housing opportunities for those minority group members moving up socioeconomically and out spatially. Once a "tipping point" has been reached and inmigrating minorities flood the zone, the working-class residents flee further out, typically into the adjacent Zone 4, the *zone of better residences*, which houses the middle class. In turn, the middle class moves further out in response to the perceived downgrading of its neighborhoods by the newcomers. It relocates to the next adjacent zone, the *commuters' zone*, which at one time housed the city's upper crust. Later Burgess identified two additional zones in the metropolis – the agricultural districts and the metropolitan hinterland (Burgess 1930).

The shifting of people and activities from one zone to another according to this model resembles the pattern that is observed when a pebble is tossed into a lake. The concentric ripples it creates follow and run into each other in their outward rush. The turnover rate of urban neighborhoods from one population type or activity type to another is governed by several factors. First is the rate of growth in people and activities that demand housing or buildings. Second is the rate of construction of dwellings, industrial buildings, and commercial confines. Third is the investment decisions made by developers, financial institutions, and political regimes. If construction lags behind population and economic growth, stagnation and the piling up of people and activities take place. Demand for developed land increases and the prices for developed parcels escalate. If construction exceeds population and economic growth, vacancy rates rise and land prices decline, but new opportunities are created that may serve to attract future growth. Or, in the extreme, with high vacancies and little growth, a collapse of the local development economy may take place which sends the city into economic depression.

SECTOR MODEL

On the basis of studying 142 American cities, Homer Hoyt (1939) argued that, contrary to the concentric zone model, the city's urban geometry is better described by a sector pattern of land development. The distributions of rents and the city's socioeconomic status groups are organized in homogeneous, pie-shaped wedges or sectors that run from the city's CBD to the periphery. The characteristic land use, activity mix, and population composition for any sector are different from those sectors adjacent to it. The implication is that if one were to drive from the CBD to the periphery while remaining in the same sector, one would remain in generally the same type of land use, resident population composition, and activity mix. The concentric zone model provides the driver with a much different view of the city. As one travels

from the CBD to the periphery, regardless of direction, one passes through the same gradation of an ever-increasing status composition of neighborhoods.

The sector model is based on an axial conception of the city. It incorporates Richard Hurd's (1924 [1903]) idea that growth and development first take place along main transportation routes from the city's center to the hinterland; these include rail lines, highways, and navigable bodies of water. At some point, it becomes cheaper in travel time and money to develop the open land between the axes than to continue the outward push along the axes. As the area between the axes becomes filled, another cycle begins with development shifting to the axes again and pushing out along them into the undeveloped hinterland.

In a city with a sector spatial geometry, sectors of industry, warehousing, and poor-quality land tend to be surrounded by sectors of low-income and working-class residents. Middle-class housing sectors tend to buffer those of upper status from the sectors of low income, industry, and noxious activities. The high-status populations command the most desirable sites in the city. The high-rent sectors tend to occupy high ground that is free from risk of floods and deluxe apartment areas tend to be established near the business centers in old established residential areas. Low-rent areas and the areas occupied by the poor and marginalized race and ethnic groups tend to be located on the opposite side of the city from the high-income sector.

The location and movement of the sectors occupied by the wealthy and upper socioeconomic groups have a major impact on the location of the other sectors. Hoyt's model argues that high-rent residential growth tends to proceed from its given point of origin along established lines of travel or toward another existing nucleus or trade area. The high-rent sectors tend to spread along lake, bay, river, and ocean ports where the waterfronts are non-industrial. High-rent residential districts tend to grow toward open country, away from "dead-end" sectors that prevent expansion by natural or artificial barriers, and toward the homes of the community leaders. The growth of high-rent neighborhoods continues in the same direction for a long time. Real estate developers may bend the direction of high-grade residential growth, but they cannot negate or reverse the effects of the general principles embodied in the model.

MULTIPLE NUCLEI MODEL

Unlike the other models, the multiple nuclei model of Chauncy Harris and Edward Ullman (1945) does not view the city as being organized around the CBD. Rather, it postulates that there are a number of different growth nuclei, each of which exerts influences on the distribution of people, activities, and land uses. Each nucleus specializes in markedly different activities, ranging from retailing through manufacturing, education and health services to residential. Nuclei vary in size. Some are large, such as the industrial sites; other are small, such as a strip shopping center. Thus, the city's spatial geometry is much like a patchwork quilt of differing nuclei that are not organized around a single center. The CBD is but one of several functionally important nuclei.

The multiple nuclei model uses four basic principles to explain both the emergence of separate nuclei and the change in them through time. (1) Certain activities require specialized facilities located in only one or a few sections of the metropolis, as seen in the case of manufacturing plants requiring large blocks of undeveloped land located near rail lines. (2) Certain like activities profit from adjacent congregation, as seen in the clustering of retail establishments into malls and shopping centers. (3) Certain unlike activities are antagonistic or detrimental to each other, as seen in the case of manufacturing plants and upper-class residential developments. (4) Certain activities are unable to afford the costs of the most desirable locations, as seen in the case of low-income residential areas and high land with a much sought-after view.

The number and mix of nuclei in a city vary greatly. Larger cities have more nuclei than do smaller places, and they tend to be more specialized in the larger community. For example, a small city may have a retailing nucleus, but in a larger city the separate retail activities may spin out into their own nucleus, as seen in the "diamond" district in New York City. Some

nuclei have existed from the origins of the city, as seen in the CBD; others developed as the city grew, such as ethnic enclaves established by arriving immigrant groups, and through urban redevelopment as one land use supplants another, as in the case of an arena project being built on the site of a former prison.

MODELS IN COMBINATION

In examining the comparative utility of the three models, researchers have found that in many cities socioeconomic status tends to vary by both sector and distance. That is, some sectors tend to contain a larger percentage of the affluent than do others, and there is a general tendency for the socioeconomic standing of neighborhoods to increase with distance from the CBD. Studies have also shown that housing types and values often vary by sector. Regardless of the extent to which a city's spatial geometry approximates concentric zones or sectors, overlaying the whole pattern tends to be numerous nuclei devoted to such things as educational campuses, medical complexes, race and ethnic group ghettoes and enclaves, industrial plants, parks, and historic districts.

In applying the models to other societies, researchers have identified elements of the three models in the geometry of spatial structure of their cities. A main difference between the geometry of cities in developed and developing societies is that in the developing societies, socioeconomic status tends to be inversely related to distance from the core, while in cities in developed societies, status tends to have a direct relationship with distance. Some have suggested that as cities in developing societies increasingly become part of the global network, they experience economic, social, and political changes and those changes are manifest in the transition of their spatial geometries to a pattern consistent with the patterns of cities in developed societies (Schwirian 1983).

Increasingly, researchers have argued that the spatial geometry of post-industrial cities such as Los Angeles does not conform to the classic models. Their origin lies not in the industrial centralization of the twentieth century as assumed by the classic models, but, rather, in the decentralized and dispersed multicentric metropolitan region of the postmodern age (Dear 2001).

SEE ALSO: Blockbusting; Built Environment; Central Business District; Chicago School; City Planning/Urban Design; Ethnic Enclaves; Exurbia; New Urbanism; Park, Robert E. and Burgess, Ernest W.; Restrictive Covenants; Suburbs; Urban Ecology; Urban Renewal and Redevelopment

REFERENCES AND SUGGESTED READINGS

Burgess, E. W. (1925) The Growth of the City. In: Park, R. E., Burgess, E. W., & McKenzie, R. W., *The City*. University of Chicago Press, Chicago.

Burgess, E. W. (1930) The New Community and its Future. *Annals of the American Academy of Political and Social Science* 149: 161, 162.

Dear, M. J. (Ed.) (2001) *From Chicago to LA: Making Sense of Urban Theory*. Sage, Thousand Oaks, CA.

Harris, C. D. & Ullman, E. L. (1945). The Nature of Cities. *Annals of the American Academy of Political and Social Science* 242: 7–17.

Hawley, A. (1950) *Human Ecology*. Ronald Press, New York.

Hoyt, H. (1939) *The Structure and Growth of Residential Neighborhoods in American Cities*. Government Printing Office, Washington, DC.

Hurd, R. M. (1924 [1903]) *Principles of City Land Values*. Record and Guide, New York.

Park, R. E. (1952) *Human Communities*. Free Press, Glencoe, IL.

Schwirian, K. P. (1983) Urban Spatial Arrangements as Reflections of Social Reality. In: Pipkin, J. S., LaGory, M. L., & Blau, J. R. (Eds.), *Remaking the City: Social Science Perspectives on Urban Design*. State University of New York Press, Albany.

ecological problems

Peter Preisendörfer and Andreas Diekmann

Although human beings have overused natural resources and local environments throughout history, today's ecological problems such as the greenhouse effect, the reduction of biodiversity, overfishing of the oceans, or shortages of clean drinking water are relatively recent phenomena. They started with the period of industrialization in the first half of the nineteenth century, and had their real takeoff after World War II. Serious warnings about impending global ecological disasters were first issued in the 1960s by scientists like Rachel Carson (1962), Paul Ehrlich (1968), Garrett Hardin (1968), and Dennis Meadows et al. (1972).

Given Durkheim's view that sociology should concentrate on social facts and their social origins, sociologists were long reluctant to deal with the environmental challenge and to incorporate it into their discipline. Although the Chicago School in sociology pioneered urban "ecological" studies in the first half of the twentieth century, it took a relatively long time before a specialty called environmental sociology was established. Today, an environmental sociology devoted to describing, explaining, and contributing to the solution of ecological problems is an institutionalized subsection of sociology. It has its own textbooks and review articles (e.g., Berger 1994), and is part of the teaching program at many universities. There are at least three major areas of research in which environmental sociologists are active: theories of the emergence of ecological problems, environmental attitudes and behavior of the general public, and environmental behavior of corporate actors (business firms, environmental movement organizations, and the state). Other research topics deal with the social diffusion of environmentally friendly technologies, the perception of ecological risks, and the social distribution of ecologically harmful emissions ("environmental justice").

THEORIES OF THE EMERGENCE OF ECOLOGICAL PROBLEMS

Overwhelming majorities of people answer in surveys that they want to live in a sound and healthy environment – one without noise, air pollution, toxic waste, traffic jams, and the like. However, such unpleasant collective effects occur, and the question is why. Theories of ecological problems developed in answer to this question fit neatly into the four general paradigms of sociological theory: functionalism/system theory, conflict theory/the political economy perspective, rational choice theory, and interactionist/constructivist approaches.

Approaches developed in the tradition of functionalism/system theory locate the reasons for ecological problems in the complexities of systems, both ecosystems and social systems. Systems usually consist of many elements and the relations among them, which may be understood to a better or worse extent. Changes in one or a few system elements can have far-reaching and unexpected consequences. The discernment of such contingencies is hampered by the existence of feedback processes, interactive linkages, positive and negative loops, and the fact that, while some changes have short-term consequences, others have only long-term consequences. Caught in simple "cause-and-effect" thinking, human beings have difficulty perceiving and predicting the dynamic system effects of their actions, so they endanger and destroy the equilibrium of well-adapted and finely tuned ecosystems. The most prominent examples of such a system theoretic approach to environmental problems are the "limits of growth" scenarios from the Club of Rome and its members (e.g., Meadows et al. 1992). One of sociological system theory's core ideas is that modern societies are characterized by functional differentiation, i.e., that they consist of a set of relatively autonomous subsystems (political, economic, and legal subsystems, and so on). All these subsystems have their own "codes" and their own logic, and maintain efficiency at the cost of a certain amount of one-sidedness. The problem of environmental protection affects several different societal subsystems, which is seen as an impediment to a reasonable solution of this problem in functionally differentiated societies (e.g., Luhmann 1986).

The conflict theory/political economy perspective, which has its historical basis in Marxist theory, blames mainly the logic of the capitalist and/or neoliberal economic system for the environmental crisis. In a neoliberal world, successful businesses and prosperous economies require permanent growth, which involves new products and innovations, short product cycles, and a rapid process of creative destruction. The built-in dynamics of industrial production (the industrial metabolism) relies not only on the exploitation of workers and human resources, but to an even greater extent on that of natural resources. The profit-seeking exploitation of resources is not confined to the industrialized countries, but has instead expanded to the whole world during a process of mainly economic globalization. Proponents of the political economy perspective of ecological problems are authors in the tradition of the neo-Marxist world-system theory, prominent anti-globalization activists, and scientific writers like Allan Schnaiberg who have often focused on the "treadmills of production and consumption" in western countries (e.g., Schnaiberg & Gould 1994).

The first contribution of rational choice theory to the explanation of ecological problems is the elementary assumption that, if environmental behavior is not optimal, something must be wrong with the incentive structure. People might not act in an environmentally responsible way because environmentally responsible behavior would cost them something they value, for instance, because prices of ecoproducts are too high or because driving a speedy (but fuel-inefficient) car enhances social status. Rational choice theorists insist that environmental behavior cannot be well understood if it is conceptualized as altruistic behavior, but only if it is seen as subjectively rational, self-interested behavior. One of the important reasons why incentives to pro-environmental behavior are often distorted stems from the fact that many environmental goods and services are public goods. A defining element of such goods is that no one can be excluded from their use, which induces people both to overuse these goods and to withhold their own contribution to their production (the problem of free-riding). Market prices are often poor signals of the real value not only of such public goods, but also of the value of private goods, because they do not include the true costs of negative externalities (e.g., the water pollution caused by the production of these goods). In other words, rational choice theory states that ecological problems often have the structure of a social dilemma such as a "commons dilemma" or a "prisoner's dilemma." In a social dilemma, the rational individual strategy is non-cooperation, i.e., in this case pursuing one's own interests at the expense of the environment. For a public good, individual and collective rationality diverge, lowering cooperation among actors.

A solution to a social dilemma is establishing enforcing institutions to help change the incentive structure so that cooperative behavior will be in the self-interest of individual actors. A well-known study reflecting this line of reasoning is Elinor Ostrom (1990).

Proponents of interactionist/constructivist approaches emphasize that environmental problems – like all other societal problems – are socially defined and culturally patterned. The social construction of the environmental crisis can be demonstrated by looking at historical differences in the definition of the problem and by cross-national comparisons of problem-solving preferences. Given this focus, constructivist theorists are interested primarily in the social and political processes through which ecological problems are placed and kept on the problem agenda. Groups with vested interests in environmental issues and the presence or absence of pro-environmental movements play a crucial role in the modern construction of the environmental crisis, as does the focus of the mass media. Douglas and Wildavsky (1982) are the authors of a classic study on social and cultural influences on the definition of environmental problems (and especially on the perception of risk).

Another analytical tool is provided not by those four theoretical approaches but by a useful conceptual scheme, the IPAT formula suggested by Ehrlich and Ehrlich (1991). According to this "accounting scheme," ecological impact (I) is the product of the population (P), the pro capita consumption level (affluence A), and technology (T). As an example, consider the impact of carbon dioxide emissions from private cars. Impact measured in tons per year results from the population P times the average number of miles a person drives per year (A) times the average CO_2 emission per mile (T). There are two main ways to reduce environmental impact: less consumption (the "sufficiency strategy") or better technology (the "efficiency strategy"). Programs aimed at uncoupling economic growth and energy consumption or "factor-x programs" (those intended to enable affluence with lower overall energy input) follow the latter strategy (Weizsäcker et al. 1998). Economic and sociological theories such as modernization theory or social diffusion theory try to explain how social and economic conditions affect lifestyles, the consumption level, and the development of more environmentally efficient technologies.

ENVIRONMENTAL ATTITUDES AND BEHAVIOR IN THE GENERAL PUBLIC

Moved to action by alarming scientific studies, in the 1960s a growing part of the general public began to develop an attitude summarized by the term "environmental concern." This concern was first observed in the US, but it spread to other countries in a rapid social diffusion process. Today, we can speak of a global or worldwide environmental concern (Dunlap et al. 1993). Judging by the results of surveys in different western countries, environmental concern increased to a peak around 1990, but has since decreased or at least stagnated. Those who retain an attitude of environmental concern are more likely to be young, female, highly educated, have a higher income, and hold a progressive/liberal political worldview. Comparing different countries, a higher GNP is associated with more widespread environmental awareness. The positive correlation between income/GNP and environmental concern has often been interpreted as an indication that the quality of the environment is a luxury good, important primarily to the rich.

There are two main expectations in focusing on environmental concern in attempting to resolve ecological problems. First, that it can put pressure on the political system to take action in favor of the environment. Second, that it can directly affect citizens' environmentally relevant behaviors. The first mechanism has some intrinsic appeal, but is difficult to validate. The second, that environmental attitudes strongly influence environmental behavior, has been proven shaky because the relation between environmental concern and behavior reported in numerous studies is of only modest strength. Although there has been some lamentation about the discrepancy between environmental attitudes and behavior, this discrepancy is typically observed in attitude–behavior research in general. The disconnect between environmental attitudes and behavior has roots similar to inconsistencies in other areas of study. Environmental attitudes are simply one of many factors influencing environmental behavior.

Empirical studies on the behavorial effects of environmental attitudes are regularly confronted with the problem of measuring and conceptualizing "environmental behavior." If we define it only as behavior that affects the natural environment, most behavior belongs to the category. It is therefore necessary to rank different kinds of behavior according to their impact on the environment. Concentrating on those behaviors with the largest impact leads to "indicators of sustainable household consumption" (Lorek & Spangenberg 2001). These indicators can be used to provide the public with recommendations on how to improve their environmental performance. Mobility/transport (the use of cars, airplanes, public transportation), housing (size of one's home, the presence of a heating system or air conditioning), and nutrition (local ecofood, the consumption of meat) are the three areas in which individual behavior has the strongest environmental consequences. Common wisdom about and public attention to what constitutes environmentally relevant behavior tend to diverge from these scientifically established facts.

Starting from the premise that ecological problems are (also) caused by maladaptive individual behavior, much research focuses on the question of which factors determine this behavior and how environmentally harmful behavior can be changed. There are two opposing schools of thought on that issue: attitudinal approaches and structural approaches. Whereas psychology tends to give priority to influencing attitudes (through moral suasion, value change, environmental education, and so on), sociology and economics have a clear preference for structural settings (convenient access to preferred alternatives, legal restrictions, financial rewards for desirable behavior, and the like). These two views may be reconciled through the hypothesis that environmental attitudes are important when stakes and/or inconvenience of a certain behavior are low (low-cost condition), but lose their influence in favor of structural circumstances when stakes and/or inconvenience is high (high-cost condition). Diekmann and Preisendörfer (2003), along with others, have presented findings supporting this low-cost hypothesis.

ENVIRONMENTAL BEHAVIOR OF CORPORATE ACTORS

Modern societies consist not only of individual actors, but also of corporate actors. The interests and behaviors of these corporate actors are as important for the quality of the environment as those of individual citizens. The activities of business firms and corporations have tremendous effects on the state of the environment, both direct and indirect. They use natural resources as inputs in their production process, they decide which types of goods and services they produce and how they produce them, they have the capacity to influence the consumers and to direct their wishes and their demand for certain products, and often they use the environment as "waste sink." Given all these forms of potential impact, it is important to monitor and to explain firms' environmentally relevant activities. Empirical studies by environmental sociologists investigate which industries cause the most serious environmental damage, under what conditions firms are motivated to improve their ecological performance, which instruments or strategies they use to do so, and what barriers prevent a successful implementation of technological devices developed to reduce negative environmental impacts (e.g., Schot & Fischer 1993). Empirical evidence demonstrates that most pro-environment policies pursued by firms and industries are forced upon them by governmental regulation (ecological push incentives, as opposed to ecological pull incentives). Even though there are some dedicated entrepreneurs deeply motivated by environmental considerations, the typical firm engages in voluntary environmental action only if there is (the expectation of) a positive financial payoff. Economically successful businesses have been observed to invest more in pro-environmental behavior than less successful firms. Most studies on the causal order of this relation between firm performance and pro-environmental activity indicate that good performance induces firms to engage in pro-environmental action, and not vice versa (or at least to a lesser extent).

Corporate actors directly fighting for an improvement of environmental conditions (those such as Greenpeace, the WWF, or Robin Wood) have grown out of the so-called environmental movement that began at the end of the 1960s in many countries. These environmental organizations have traditionally varied in the radicality of their strategies (and continue to do so), follow somewhat differing ideologies, and concentrate on different kinds of ecological problems. Sociologists have established a separate line of inquiry called social movement research, which is also dedicated to the environmental movement and to environmental NGOs. This research now has its own theoretical approaches (resource mobilization, political process, and framing theories), and it has a core set of substantive research questions (e.g., Rucht 1991; Giugni 1998). These include the social profile of movement entrepreneurs, the individual decision to join a movement or the organizations involved (even though they are engaged in producing a public good, namely, better environmental quality), causes of cross-national variation in the strength of environmentalism, the mobilization strategies adopted by different groups, and the temporal processes of the institutionalization of a social movement. As is the case with environmental concern in the general public, the environmental movement seems to be on the decline in many parts of the world.

One reason for the shrinking importance of the environmental movement in rich countries is that many claims and proposals originally articulated by environmental activists and organizations have found acceptance in the conventional political system and are now part of the programs and platforms of mainstream political parties, governmental agencies, community councils, and so forth. This means that corporate actors in the political arena have become the dominant players in the field of ecological problems. On the national level, governments have founded their own ministries for the environment, enacted numerous environmental laws, and initiated many other policies aimed at the protection of natural resources. Despite disagreement over strategies and measures of success, most governments today declare "sustainable development" to be the guiding principle behind their environmental policies. Of course, in many countries there is still a large gap between official environmental goals and the actual state of the environment. Ecological problems are also an object of regular negotiation among countries. Whereas these processes

have been relatively successful in the case of stopping the depletion of the ozone layer, progress is very slow in the case of the reduction of carbon dioxide emissions, preserving biodiversity, providing clean water in developing countries, stopping deforestation, averting soil degradation, and preventing the depletion of resources like ocean fish.

On a global scale, a large proportion of the world's population is excluded from living in an intact and healthy environment, and in some rapidly growing economies such as China the state of the environment will deteriorate in coming years. Within a given country, the poorer population is usually the group exposed to higher environmental and health risks such as noise, pollution, and toxic substances. Since the 1980s the "environmental justice movement" has addressed the social problem of an unequal distribution of the environmental impact among members of different social classes or income categories. A large amount of empirical research, particularly in the health sciences and to a lesser degree in sociology, demonstrates the existence of a "social gradient," i.e., a negative correlation between socioeconomic status and various environmental risks (Evans & Kantrowitz 2002; O'Neill et al. 2003). There is also evidence that environmental risks have a larger detrimental impact on health among the poor than among wealthier people.

According to the well-known Brundtland Report (Brundtland 1987) which elaborated and disseminated the idea of sustainable development on the international stage, such a development can and should guarantee that future generations will have a chance to fulfill their basic human needs in a sound and healthy environment. Two decades after the release of this report, it is safe to say more remains to be done in order to narrow the gap between sustainability goals and the actual condition of the environment.

SEE ALSO: Conflict Theory; (Constructive) Technology Assessment; Decision-Making; Ecology and Economy; Environment, Sociology of the; Environment and Urbanization; Environmental Movements; Framing and Social Movements; Functionalism/Neofunctionalism; Interaction; New Social Movement

Theory; Political Process Theory; Rational Choice Theories; Resource Mobilization Theory; Risk, Risk Society, Risk Behavior, and Social Problems; Social Movements; Social Problems, Concept and Perspectives; Social Problems, Politics of

REFERENCES AND SUGGESTED READINGS

Berger, J. (1994) The Economy and the Environment. In: Smelser, N. J. & Swedberg, R. (Eds.). *The Handbook of Economic Sociology*. Princeton University Press, Princeton, pp. 766–97.

Brundtland, G. H. (1987) *World Commission on Environment and Development: Our Common Future*. Oxford University Press, Oxford.

Carson, R. (1962) *Silent Spring*. Houghton Mifflin, Boston.

Diekmann, A. & Preisendörfer, P. (2003) Green and Greenback: The Behavioral Effects of Environmental Attitudes in Low-Cost and High-Cost Situations. *Rationality and Society* 15: 441–72.

Douglas, M. & Wildavsky, A. (1982) *Risk and Culture: An Essay on the Selection of Technological and Environmental Dangers*. University of California Press, Berkeley.

Dunlap, R. E., Gallup, G. H., & Gallup, A. M. (1993) Of Global Concern: Results of the Health of the Planet Survey. *Environment* 35: 33–9.

Ehrlich, P. R. (1968) *The Population Bomb*. Sierra Club/Ballantine, New York.

Ehrlich, P. R. & Ehrlich, A. H. (1991) *Healing the Planet*. Addison-Wesley, Reading, MA.

Evans, G. W. & Kantrowitz, E. (2002) Socioeconomic Status and Health: The Potential Role of Environmental Risk Exposure. *Annual Review of Public Health* 23: 303–31.

Giugni, M. G. (1998) Was it Worth the Effort? The Outcomes and Consequences of Social Movements. *Annual Review of Sociology* 98: 371–93.

Hardin, G. (1968) The Tragedy of the Commons. *Science* 162: 1243–8.

Lorek, S. & Spangenberg, J. H. (2001) Indicators for Environmentally Sustainable Household Consumption. *International Journal of Sustainable Development* 4(1): 101–20.

Luhmann, N. (1986) *Ökologische Kommunikation (Ecological Communication)*. Westdeutscher Verlag, Opladen.

Meadows, D. H., Meadows, D. L., Zahn, E., & Milling, P. (1972) *The Limits to Growth*. Universe Books, New York.

Meadows, D. H., Meadows, D. L., & Randers, J. (1992) *Beyond the Limits*. Chelsea Green, Post Mills.

O'Neill, M. S. et al. (2003) Health, Wealth, and Air Pollution: Advancing Theory and Methods. *Environmental Health Perspectives* 111: 1861–70.

Ostrom, E. (1990) *Governing the Commons: The Evolution of Institutions for Collective Action*. Cambridge University Press, Cambridge.

Rucht, D. (Ed.) (1991) *Research on Social Movements*. Campus, Frankfurt.

Schnaiberg, A. & Gould, K. A. (1994) *Environment and Society: The Enduring Conflict*. St. Martin's Press, New York.

Schot, J. & Fischer, K. (Eds.) (1993) *Environmental Strategies for Industry: International Perspectives on Research Needs and Policy Implications*. Island Press, Washington, DC.

Weizsäcker, E. von, Lovins, A. M., & Lovins, L. H. (1998) *Factor Four: Doubling Wealth – Halving Resource Use*. Earthscan, London.

ecological view of history

Harumi Befu

An ecological view of history has to do with how history is accounted for in relation to the ecological conditions in which civilization is situated. The Japanese have developed a unique approach to the understanding of this issue. The idea that ecology has an impact on culture and history and the philosophical underpinning of the particular Japanese approach have their history in the pre-World War II era. A short review of the genealogy of this concept is called for.

The distinctly Japanese ecological approach is closely associated with the Kyoto School of thought. This school encompasses philosophy, history, civilization, evolution, and other fields. The best-known scholar of this school is arguably Kitarô Nishida (1870–1945), a philosopher who amalgamated western philosophy, notably that of Henri Bergson and the neo-Kantians, with Zen philosophy and developed his own unique philosophy, the representative work being *Inquiry into the Good* (1990). One important element of his philosophy is his concept of self, which sees the self and its environs – other beings, nature, and the universe – as an integrated whole, rejecting the dichotomy between self and its environs – an approach accepted in western philosophy.

This conception of oneness of self and the universe was inherited by Tetsurô Watsuji (1889–1960), a major figure in ecological history. Watsuji is probably the first in modern Japan to systematize the interrelationship between environment and culture. His work was first published in *Fudo* (1935) and later translated into English (1961, 1988). Having studied in Germany, Watsuji was heavily influenced by German philosophy, in particular that of Herder and Hegel. It is important, in terms of the sociology of knowledge, that he was moved to construct his theory in direct response to the western theory of the relationship between nature and humans. Watsuji reviews the genealogy of scholarship on the human–nature relationship in western intellectual history from Hippocrates on. He homes in on Herder's conceptualization of the human–nature relationship in terms of *Geist* (spirit). Watsuji sees Hegel as the inheritor of Herder's theory, which places western civilization as the latest and crowning achievement in human history. Watsuji, however, unsurprisingly takes exception to Hegel's claim of Europeans as "the chosen people." Thus Watsuji's ecological theory was developed in reaction to the western supremacist bias he saw in Herder and Hegel.

Watsuji also rejects the basic stance of western philosophy where humans and nature are distinguished and pitted against each other. Watsuji additionally rejects scientific causality and determinism, where environment determines human action, culture, and civilization. In this conception of *fudo*, environment and humans are not separate entities defined by a causal relationship between them, as Berque (1996) explicates. Watsuji instead develops the idea of oneness of humans and nature (Befu 1997). This fusion is expressed in the very term *fudo*, the title of his major work. To Watsuji, *fudo* refers to humans and their environment as one, not to be analytically separated into various conventional components such as the individual, social groups, natural environment, and so on. Berque (1990) has coined the term "*médiance*" to refer to Watsuji's concept of *fudo*.

Watsuji develops a tripartite ecological classification of (1) monsoon type, (2) desert type, and (3) pasture (German *Wiese*) type. The first "monsoon" type is represented in Asia, East and South. Its salient meteorological characteristic is humidity, which according to him is expressed in just about every aspect of human life. The Middle East represents the second type, climatically characterized by aridity as the major metaphor for its civilization and as a way of life. The third "pasture" type is represented by Europe, which combines the humidity of the monsoon type and the aridity of the desert type. In this classification, Africa is curiously missing, except for North Africa, which might be classified in the desert type. Likewise missing in his classification is the western hemisphere.

Watsuji's main focus is on the first type, especially as it affects Japan. Japan's uniqueness within the monsoon region arises from the fact that although impacted by the monsoon in the summer, it is also subjected to a severe winter climate originating in Siberia, traversing the Japan Sea, and ultimately enveloping the whole island chain of Japan. It is manifested, according to Watsuji, most directly in human character and the pattern of subsistence economy in Japan, which is based on rice cultivation. This in turn affects village organization and the family system as well as the aesthetics of a people. Ultimately, as he develops his ideas in subsequent publications, this ecological argument is expanded to the levels of the national polity (*kokutai*) of Japan and to its imperial system.

His argument persuaded generations of Japanese scholars all through the war period and into the post-war era, setting the stage for legions of younger scholars to select themes from his theory and develop their own. For example, rural sociologists like A. Tamaki (1978) and H. Tsukuba (1969) cite Watsuji in discussing village structure and peasant personality. Even business management specialists such as K. Odaka (1981), an erstwhile dean of industrial sociology (now glossed as "management science"), and M. Tsuda (1977) explained the reputed Japanese management style by deriving it ultimately from the rice-growing rural community structure. Nippon Steel Corporation, in its handbook for employees destined for foreign posts, also derives the Japanese management style from the rice-growing rural community structure.

Another giant in the intellectual genealogy of the Kyoto School is biologist Kinji Imanishi, who developed his own unique, explicitly anti-Darwinian theory of biological evolution. A key concept in his theory is *specia*, in which a species and the social organization it constitutes are treated as a unitary, indivisible unit of evolution (Imanishi 2002). Here again one sees a rejection of opposition and dichotomy between an object and its environment in diachronic development.

The last in this genealogy of intellectual giants in the ecological view of history is Tadao Umesao, one of Imanishi's direct intellectual descendants and the acknowledged doyen of the anthropological profession in Japan. His views were made well known initially through his 1957 work, which has been revised and updated several times. The latest version has been translated into English, with a new chapter added (Umesao 2003). Umesao shares his intellectual stance with his predecessors in the Kyoto School. He too starts by rejecting western thinking. His treatise on ecological history was in fact triggered by Arnold Toynbee's theory of civilization, and is an explicit rejection of it.

Umesao does not acknowledge his debt to Watsuji. But Umesao's ecological theory does show some critical similarities to Watsuji's. For instance, Umesao, like Watsuji, divides the Eurasian continent into three sections. He acknowledges the arid middle zone, which he calls *Chūyō*, or "mediant." Moreover, Umesao also more or less ignores Sub-Saharan Africa and the western hemisphere. But similarities end here. Rather than seeing the eastern and the western portions of the Eurasian continent as being different, as Watsuji does, Umesao collapses the two regions into one type.

Also, rather than working out just three archetypes, as Watsuji does, Umesao fine-tunes the variable civilizational characteristics of regions bordering the central "mediant" and the two zones lying east and west of it through contingent historical interactions between them. He sees the middle region, the mediant, as one in which historical ravages of one war after another, one conquest after another, in its hostile arid environment, have created a situation inimical to civilizational development. In the zones at the eastern and western extremes of the Eurasian continent, on the other hand, the relative geographical protection made for an environment in which civilization could modernize. In both regions, civilizations developed in a similar fashion, both going through the feudal age and industrialization with relative ease.

When Umesao's theory first appeared in 1957, it immediately received wide acclaim in the intellectual community. Since its publication, this work has impacted generations of Japanese and has now become a classic. It was selected as the fourth most important book, pre- or post-war, fiction or non-fiction, for its intellectual influence on modern Japanese history by a jury of 58 leading Japanese intellectuals in all fields, including politics, the arts, literature, and business.

As early as 1957, like his intellectual predecessors, Umesao rejected the hegemonic status claimed by the West vis-à-vis Japan, a position which is increasingly acknowledged by Asian as well as western scholars in the past few decades. One thing that characterizes all these efforts at understanding the nature of human ecology is that Japanese theorists are all reacting against the West's hegemonic claim of knowledge and proposing alternative views. In these alternative views, humans are conceptualized as an integral, and even indivisible, part of the universe and nature, rather than being pitted against them. In opposition to western metaphysics, Japanese intellectuals are staking out a claim that historical and evolutionary changes take place through integrated transformation of the whole, rather than by one segment causing change in another.

SEE ALSO: Civilizations; Culture, the State and; Ecological Problems; Ecology; Ecology and Economy; Empire; Environment, Sociology of the; Environment and Urbanization; Micro–Macro Links

REFERENCES AND SUGGESTED READINGS

Befu, H. (1997) Watsuji Tetsuro's Ecological Approach: Its Philosophical Foundation. In: Asquith, P. J. & Kalland, A. (Eds.), *Japanese Images of Nature*. Curzon, Surrey, pp. 106–20.

Berque, A. (1990) *Médiance: de milieux en paysages*. Reclus, Paris.

Berque, A. (1996) *Chikyū to Sonzai no Tetsugaku* (*The Philosophy of the Earth and Existence*). Chikuma Shobō, Tokyo.

Imanishi, K. (2002) *A Japanese View of Nature: The World of Living Things*. Routledge, London.

Nishida, K. (1990) *Inquiry into the Good* (*Zen no Kenkyū*). Yale University Press, New Haven.

Odaka, K. (1981) *Sangyō Shakaigaku Kōgi* (*Lectures in Industrial Sociology*). Iwanami Shoten, Tokyo.

Tamaki, A. (1978) *Inasaku Bunka to Nihonjin* (*Rice-Growing Culture and the Japanese*). Gendai Hyōronsha, Tokyo.

Tsuda, M. (1977) *Nihon-teki Keiei no Ronri* (*The Logic of the Japanese-Style Management*). Chuō Kōronsha, Tokyo.

Tsukuba, H. (1969) *Beishoku Nikushoku no Bunmei* (*Rice-Eating and Meat-Eating Civilization*). Nippon Hōsō Shuppan Kyōkai, Tokyo.

Umesao, T. (2003) *An Ecological View of History: Japanese Civilization in the World Context* (*Bunmei no Seitaishi-kan*). TransPacific Press, Melbourne.

Watsuji, T. (1935) *Fudo*. Iwanami Shoten, Tokyo.

Watsuji, T. (1961) *A Climate: A Philosophical Study*. Government Printing Bureau, Tokyo.

Watsuji, T. (1988) *Climate and Culture*. Greenwood Press, New York.

ecology

Marc M. Sanford

Ecology generally refers to the scientific study of an organism or community of organisms and their relationship to each other as well as to the environment. The ecological framework is used in biological sciences, social sciences, botany, zoological sciences, and other research areas and is applied to myriad subareas including human ecology, cultural ecology, organizational ecology, plant ecology, population ecology, spatial ecology, and more. Early writings on ecology were influenced by the works of Malthus and Darwin. This can be seen in ecology's use of natural selection and the presence of other competing species in the race for survival.

The concept was developed by famous phytogeographers such as Humboldt and Grisebach in the first half of the nineteenth century. However, many acknowledge that the term's modern meaning became fixed in a publication by Häckel in 1865, in which he coined the term "oekologie" and defined it as the relation of an animal to its organic and inorganic environment. Despite the widespread credit given to Häckel for coining the term, there are sufficient claims that the term ecology was in use at the same time by at least seven other biological researchers. One researcher on the topic credits the very first use of the term to Henry David Thoreau in 1858.

Many early studies in botany and biology employed the term "plant geography" and ecology. Early writings on plant ecology looked at vegetation in different climates and discussed how each type was determined by climatic and edaphic factors. Botanists, biologists, and zoologists in the late nineteenth century were interested in the interdependent nature of life, or the "web of life" that intertwines all living creatures. They were interested in recording the mutual adaptations of one species as it depended on another for its survival. Later research on the subject matter of animal ecology, at least through the mid-twentieth century, focused on the individual organism, the population of organisms, and the community.

Social scientists borrowed the ecological framework directly from the biological and plant sciences. Ecology's quantitative approach influenced both the conceptual approach to the human community and the methodological one. The term "human ecology" was used in the social sciences by Charles C. Adams in 1913. However, ecology as a social scientific approach received systematic formulation around 1915 from Robert Park. The classical human ecologists writing in the 1920s and 1930s applied to the interrelations of human beings a type of analysis previously applied to the interrelations of plants and animals. The human ecologists claimed that although the conditions that affect and control the movement and numbers of populations are more complex in human societies than in plant and animal communities, they exhibited extraordinary similarities.

Robert Park (1936), Ernest Burgess (1925), and Roderick McKenzie (1929) applied biotic principles of competition, differentiation, and invasion/succession to ethnic groups, class groups, and other subcultures in the city of Chicago. Competition operates in the form of communities vying for land and housing. The highest land values are found in the central shopping district and central banking area. From these points land values decline and determine the locations of other social institutions and businesses. As the city expands, the pressures of businesses and social institutions steadily increase at the center. This pressure is then diffused to every other part of the city and acts to sort businesses and population groups. Differentiation occurs through population groups settling in areas that do not match official administrative boundaries. These areas became known as "natural areas." Throughout the ecological process, generally, we expect increased functional differentiation or specialization of populations and communities. Invasion and succession occurs when population groups move into areas where they were not present beforehand.

Custom, tradition, and culture also occupy a central role in human ecology. Robert Park hypothesized that the individual is both incorporated and subordinated to the local community and local social order. This community and social order is comprised of ecological, economic, political, and moral components. The move away from the biotic was further emphasized by Roderick McKenzie. McKenzie claimed that "human ecology is the study of the spatial and temporal relations of human beings as affected by the selective, distributive, and accommodative forces of the environment." Although McKenzie continued to speak of invasion and succession, he tied the ecological approach to specific divisions of space and developed a typology of city functions: the primary service community, the commercial community, the industrial town, and the community which lacks a specific economic base. The human ecology perspective focuses on the form and functions of populations, communities, and cities and carried a great amount of weight until the early 1960s.

Another application of ecology in the social sciences is organizational ecology. Organizational ecology emerged from economic and general systems theory and places a distinct emphasis on selection mechanisms. Organizational ecology generally focuses on the environmental and organizational determinants of the formation of the firm, including organizational life cycle transitions and the competitive and demographic structures of industry. Organizational ecology considers the implications of changes in the firm's environment that are a result of organizational actions. Organization theory often focuses on firm-level demographic processes, including entry, exit, and reorganization.

Within organizational ecology organizational structures are affected by the social conditions at the time of their creation. An organization's structure and organizational goals are historically shaped. Both a firm's organization and historical conditions influence its organizing activities in various social environments and entrepreneurship. Organizational ecology also speaks to whether firms should specialize or generalize depending on the uncertainty of the business and economic environment. In uncertain environments, organizations should become more generalist in their orientation in order to survive.

Criticisms of the ecological approach within the social sciences include whether change can originate from within the socio-ecological system and whether communities and environments can be analyzed as truly being closed systems. Furthermore, recent use of the ecological framework in the social sciences is scarcely influenced by the original biological analogy. Despite the wide variation in the use of the term "ecology," the term for sociologists often becomes a synonym for "spatial" and loses much of the systematic interplay between environment and community.

SEE ALSO: Ecological Models of Urban Form: Concentric Zone Model, the Sector Model, and the Multiple Nuclei Model; Ecological Problems; Ecology and Economy; Environment, Sociology of the; Environment and Urbanization; Invasion-Succession; Organization Theory; Urban Ecology

REFERENCES AND SUGGESTED READINGS

Burgess, E. W. (1925a) The Growth of the City: An Introduction to a Research Project. In: Park, R. E., Burgess, E. W., & McKenzie, R. D. (Eds.), *The City*. University of Chicago Press, Chicago, pp. 47–62.

Burgess, E. W. (1925b) *The Urban Community*. University of Chicago Press, Chicago.

Hoiberg, E. O. & Cloyd, J. S. (1971) Definition and Measurement of Continuous Variation in Ecological Analysis. *American Sociological Review* 36, 1 (February): 65–74.

Michaels, J. W. (1974) On the Relation Between Human Ecology and Behavioral Social Psychology. *Social Forces* 52, 3 (March): 313–21.

Park, R. E. (1936) Human Ecology. *American Journal of Sociology* 42, 1 (July): 1–15.

Park, R. E. & Burgess, E. W. (1967) *The City*. University of Chicago Press, Chicago.

Park, T. (1946) Some Observations on the History and Scope of Population Ecology. *Ecological Monographs* 16, 4 (October): 313–20.

Tansley, A. G. (1947) The Early History of Modern Plant Ecology in Britain. *Journal of Ecology* 35, 1/2 (December): 130–7.

Wholey, D. R. & Brittain, J. W. (1986) Organizational Ecology: Findings and Implications. *Academy of Management Review* 11(3): 513–33.

Zorbaugh, H. W. (1929) *The God Coast and the Slum*. University of Chicago Press, Chicago.

ecology and economy

David John Frank

For sociologists, the consideration of ecology – and thus ecology's role in the economy – is relatively new to the agenda. In a semantic sense, this is necessarily the case. The word "ecology" and its apparatus of meaning only recently entered the vocabulary. But sociology's ecological turn is much more than the result of semantic invention. It embodies a profound shift in the institutionalized model of nature itself (Frank 1997).

From roughly the mid-nineteenth through the mid-twentieth centuries, what we now call "ecology" barely existed in the social imagination. Nature appeared in the public realm mostly in the narrowly rationalized form of resources – particular material goods, with status external and subordinate to human society. For instance, in the guise of natural resources, trees materialized as timber and cows took form as livestock. The ecology–economy relationship was uncomplicated accordingly. The ecological system served both as store of natural inputs – raw materials to economic production – and sink for outputted wastes (Berger 1994). In utilizing this system, humans exercised their rightful dominion over earth.

Especially in the West, this resource model of nature grew deeply institutionalized – i.e., taken for granted in culture and organization. Most importantly, perhaps, the resource model helped fuel the twin expansions of industrialism and capitalism, both of which required the exploitation of natural goods on historically unprecedented scales. Even at the world level during this period, natural resource views gained precedence over the alternatives, expressed for instance in the 1911 International Fur Seal Convention, which set conservation measures aimed at maintaining the commercial exploitation of North Pacific fur seals.

By and large in this era, sociologists took the terms of discourse at face value. This means that to the limited extent they noticed at all, sociologists interpreted ecology's role in the economy in straightforward resource terms (Buttel 2002). Certainly, sociologists recognized that societies differed in relative shares of nature's bounty and varied by advances in the means of utilization. But seldom did sociologists challenge the central imagery itself, in which ecology referred to natural resources, meaning basic economic provisions.

During the latter twentieth century, much of this changed. To a striking and extraordinary extent, scientists extended and intensified nature's rationalization well beyond the resource frame. What had formerly been defined in terms of inputs and outputs acquired a host of new meanings, which rendered nature as ultimately valuable and functional to human society. Scientists reconceived nature as an interconnected ecological "environment" – a planetary life-support system. In this resource-to-ecology shift, for example, trees transcended the meaning of timber and came to appear as oxygen producers, greenhouse gas sinks, species habitats (endangered and otherwise), and themselves essential nodes in the web of life.

Of course this broad redefinition of nature hardly meant that resource imageries disappeared. On the contrary, scientists participated in the invention of technologies that opened vast new natural territories to utilization. Still with the rapid profusion of the environment's life-sustaining properties, the warehouse imagery of nature quickly lost dominant standing.

Within the new paradigm, the old one-way road from ecology to economy got widened, bringing new focus to the reverse economy-to-ecology relationship. Most strikingly, there appeared widespread public concern over the ways economic systems damaged ecological systems, thereby threatening not only material goods but also earth's life-bearing capacities (Berger 1994).

The emergent ecological model of nature gained institutionalization most rapidly in the West, where scientific authority stood tallest. There it catalyzed, for example, changes in the longstanding conservation movement, participants in which began to pose economic activity as the antagonist of environmental vitality. And even at the world level, the new imageries acquired legitimacy, as exemplified by the 1972 founding of the United Nations Environment Program, around the mission "to provide leadership and encourage partnership in caring for the environment."

As they had previously, sociologists operated within the set parameters of discourse. Most importantly, sociologists offered analyses of the logics and mechanisms whereby different economic configurations caused more or less ecological damage (e.g., Schnaiberg & Gould 1994). Capitalism in particular came under scrutiny. Researchers showed, for instance, ways the profit motive and private ownership combined to exacerbate ecological ills. For the private owner, maximized profit meant maximized exploitation, extracting nature's commodity values without regard to environmental consequences, as exemplified by the clear-cut forest. Likewise for the private owner, maximized profit implied minimized amelioration, privileging the least costly means of exploitation, even when those means wreaked the greatest ecosystem havoc, as illustrated by the strip mine. Furthermore for the private owner, maximized profit rewarded the disposal of "wastes" into the commons, polluting those aspects of nature (notably air and water) shared by the public at large, as in the case of smokestack industries. In virtually all such sociological analyses, the revised ecological definition of nature took priority over the old resource one.

Of course changing conceptions of "nature" continue apace, spurring ongoing reconsideration of the ecology–economy linkages. Along with society at large, sociologists now increasingly notice that economic activity need not be antithetical to ecological well-being. Indeed, some sociologists have recently called attention to the environmental benefits of economic activity, which may cause birth rates to decline and environmental values to rise (Inglehart 1990). As the new ideas take hold, such concepts as sustainable development – promising the union of robust economies with healthy ecologies – seem less like pipe dreams than previously. A new ecology–economy partnership may be forging in the public eye.

In some quarters, of course, nature continues to be seen through the resource lens – in simple input–output terms. In other quarters, meanwhile, any economic rise still indicates certain ecological fall. Both views increasingly, however, seem simplistic and divisive (as seen, for example, in conflicts between wealthy northern and poor southern countries at recent environmental conferences [Shiva 2000]). In the contemporary world, the aspiration to economic betterment seems unwavering and universal. And in the same world, environmental protection is becoming ever more rule-like. The satisfaction of both ends will require ingenuity and compromise. In this middle ground, the sociological study of ecology and economy may be most promising.

SEE ALSO: Consumption, Green/Sustainable; Ecological Problems; Economic Development; Environment and Urbanization; Environmental Movements; Nature; Population and the Environment; Science, Social Construction of

REFERENCES AND SUGGESTED READINGS

Berger, J. (1994) The Economy and the Environment. In: Smelser, N. J. & Swedberg, R. (Eds.), *The Handbook of Economic Sociology*. Princeton University Press, Princeton.

Buttel, F. H. (2002). Environmental Sociology and the Sociology of Natural Resources: Institutional Histories and Personal Legacies. *Society and Natural Resources* 15(3): 205–11.

Frank, D. J. (1997) Science, Nature, and the Globalization of the Environment, 1870–1990. *Social Forces* 76 (December): 409–35.

Inglehart, R. (1990) *Culture Shift in Advanced Industrial Society*. Princeton University Press, Princeton.

Schnaiberg, A. & Gould, K. A. (1994) *Environment and Society: The Enduring Conflict*. St. Martin's Press, New York.

Shiva, V. (2000) Ecological Balance in an Era of Globalization. In: Wapner, P. & Ruiz, L. E. J. (Eds.), *Principled World Politics: The Challenge of Normative International Relations*. Rowman & Littlefield, Lanham, MD.

economic determinism

J. I. (Hans) Bakker

The concept of economic determinism refers to monocausal determinism by material, economic factors. The idea is often associated with Karl Marx's "historical materialism," but it is not clear that Marx himself was a strict economic determinist, or even a materialist (Gouldner 1980; Simmel 1990 [1900]; Landry 2000). The Romantic strain in the work of the early Marx did not disappear entirely, which is evident in terms of his view of species being and the teleology of communism. Some commentators differentiate between economic determinism and dialectical materialism, where dialectical materialism allows for more flexibility and may even include a feedback mechanism. Rigid versions of economic determinism are often associated with Marxist-Leninism and Stalinism. In Marxist parlance, the forces of production determine the relations of production in any mode of production. Sometimes that statement is modified to include the disclaimer that such economic determinism is only true in the final analysis. But precisely what "in the final analysis" means is rarely specified exactly. Closely related is the concept of economic reductionism (Robertson & White 2005: 355–7), where emphasis is placed on the idea that the economy is closely intertwined with all forms of the culture of consumerism. Thus, for example, advertising images can be viewed as ideological constructs that are the product of economic forces working on decision-makers in corporations. Concern with capitalist globalization has

been premised in part on the theory that economic globalization is determinative of all aspects of civil society, not just consumption. Studies of the origins of the "capitalist world system" have moved the classical Marxist argument about economic determinism from relations of production within nation-states to a global arena that involves the interaction among societies. Wallerstein (1974, 1980, 1989) "emphasized the causal significance of economic-material factors, relegating other aspects of epiphenomenal status" (Robertson & White 2005: 357). There are also counterarguments which stress "civilizational" or "cultural" factors as determinative (e.g., Huntington 1996). Weber's 1904–6 thesis (2002: 125) concerning the Protestant ethic is often misinterpreted as a one-sided idealist argument, but he explicitly points out that it is not his intention to replace a one-sided economic determinism with an equally misleading, one-sided idealist (ideological-cultural) determinism. There are few sociological writers who take a strictly economic determinist view, but there is a strong movement to go beyond the labor theory of value and classical and neoclassical economics models and to recognize the importance of multivariant and reciprocal social factors within economic institutions.

SEE ALSO: Althusser, Louis; Base and Superstructure; Dependency and World-Systems Theories; Dialectical Materialism; Globalization; Gramsci, Antonio; Marx, Karl; Weber, Max

REFERENCES AND SUGGESTED READINGS

Gouldner, A. W. (1980) *The Two Marxisms: Contradictions and Anomalies in the Development of Theory*. Oxford University Press, New York.

Huntington, S. P. (1996) *The Clash of Civilizations and the Remaking of World Order*. Simon & Schuster, New York.

Landry, L. Y. (2000) *Marx and the Postmodernist Debates*. Praeger, Westport, CT.

Robertson, R. & White, K. E. (2005) Globalization: Sociology and Cross-Disciplinarity. In: Calhoun, C., Rojek, C., & Turner, B. (Eds.), *The Sage Handbook of Sociology*. Sage, London, pp. 345–66.

Simmel, G. (1990 [1900]) *The Philosophy of Money*. Routledge, London.

Wallerstein, I. (1974, 1980, 1989) *The Modern World System*, 3 vols. Cambridge University Press, New York.

Weber, M. (2002 [1904]) *The Protestant Ethic and the Spirit of Capitalism*. Trans. S. Kalberg. Roxbury, Los Angeles.

economic development

Thomas D. Beamish and Nicole Woolsey Biggart

Economic development studies are concerned with how societies have, could, and should pursue improvement in the quality and quantity of life for their inhabitants. Since the decades following World War II when development studies began and were implemented as policies, there has been neither consensus on how to pursue the goal of economic and social improvement nor unqualified improvement in the quality of life for most of the world's population. Nonetheless, the politically and socially important pursuit of economic development continues and involves academics, nation-states, regional and international organizations, non-governmental organizations, and philanthropic foundations.

Development scholarship arose out of the major social, political, and economic changes that accompanied the end of World War II and the restructuring of the global geopolitical map. As a consequence of the war, there was both a felt need to reconstruct the destroyed economies of Europe and Japan, and to supply financial assistance to the newly freed colonial possessions of losing states. Early efforts focused on the construction of critical industrial goods and state-owned infrastructures, and the overall modernization of political and economic institutions. Rebuilding activities were based on assumptions of social and economic "convergence": a belief that all societies progress in a stepwise fashion from traditional social orders toward increasingly modern social and economic systems as manifest by western industrial states.

The most stubborn development problem to defy eradication is the unequal relationship that remains between developed and underdeveloped regions. Events such as the fall of the Soviet Union and the dissolution of the tripartite breakdown of global nation-states – first world, communist world, and third world or neutral countries – brought a new set of social and geopolitical issues that theories of the post-World War II modernist tradition, as well as those critical of modernist assumptions, could not adequately address. Continuing economic hardship in Asia, Latin America, and Russia called into question the economic strategies of global development organizations such as the World Bank and the International Monetary Fund. Standardized protocols for development did not stimulate the expected convergence of the underdeveloped and developed economies and rarely sustained development in undeveloped regions.

Proposed economic treatments for laggard economies tended to reflect a common belief that all economies are fundamentally the same and operate on a universal set of economic principles that when violated lead to suboptimal outcomes. Economic policies were premised on the assumption of a neoclassical market ideal where firms are dispersed and contracts assured by a regulatory state. Deviations from this ideal are assumed to need restructuring to better approximate the ideal market model, the basis for Anglo-American economies.

Critics argue that economic differences are not necessarily imperfections of an ideal market economy. Rather than assume that all economies are the same and destined to converge as they modernize, critical development scholars cite important differences on which economic competitiveness can be built. These differences – the result of history, social traditions, and institutionalized political structures – allow nations to organize themselves politically, culturally, and economically in ways that are culturally meaningful and that enable them to successfully leverage their capabilities and social predispositions in the economy. For example, research has shown that French, German, Japanese, British, and American firms (among others) excel at different things in the global economy because of their different social structures and endowments.

During the early period, economic development theories were largely based on the belief that all societies developed through a set of stages that ultimately would lead to a modern nation-state and industrial economy. This evolutionist approach urged political and social reforms that would develop "primitive" or "backward" societies into modern economic systems like those in the West. This approach is rooted in western cultural beliefs about progress. It encouraged individualism and western-style institutional structures, such as constitutional democracies, even in places based on radically different social arrangements such as lineage structures and group-based economic institutions. New institutions and practices were taught by development specialists who worked with governments and educational ministries in developing countries, and were reinforced by economic incentives that tied loans and funding packages to reforms.

By the mid-1960s ideas about evolutionary progress and convergence toward a single model had been formalized in scholarly research and development policy such as modernization theory. Modernization theory (Rostow 1969) reflected three geopolitical trends that characterized this period: (1) the rise of the US as a superpower and with it Anglo-American style capitalism; (2) the simultaneous rise of the Soviet Union and its influence over Eastern Europe, China, and North Korea; and (3) the disintegration of the European colonial empires in Asia, Africa, and Latin America. The threat of communist expansion produced generous funding and attention to development research. Social science theorizing that supported western industrial practice and the expansion of capitalist social and economic forms played a key role in producing a body of thought to counter the influence of socialist development schemes.

By the 1970s, another state-centric view of development emerged to counter the modernist view. An outcome of the turbulent experiences of Central and South America, Asia, and Africa as states there attempted to mimic first-world economies and states, scholars such as Frank (1969) noted that developing countries, far from improving their economic circumstances, continued to be both dependent on and increasingly impoverished because of their relationship with western industrial states. Called dependency theory, these theorists pointed out

that the underdeveloped world reflected colonial pasts that had not been substantially changed despite decades of development attempts to alter institutions and practices through economic loans and subsidies. According to dependency theorists, direct political domination under pre-World War II colonialism had merely been exchanged for post-World War II economic dependence on former colonizers. Third-world states were dependent on first-world states for economic opportunities, financing and development loans, new technology and training, and access to first-world markets, all of which retarded the third world from developing.

By the early 1980s, however, it became increasingly evident that state-centric ideas, whether of the modernization or dependency schools, could not entirely capture the whole of development outcomes for the rich and especially the poorer parts of the world. Attention by Wallerstein (1980) and others to global exchange structures painted a picture of a capitalist world economic system where economic outcomes are not determined by the actions of any one state. All states are part of a networked capitalist system and the prospects of any one state are influenced by its place in that system and its relation to other states.

During the 1980s and continuing into the 1990s, a resurgence in economic theorizing had an especially strong influence over global development institutions, especially lending institutions and donor countries. The World Bank and International Monetary Fund promoted neoclassical economic precepts, including laissez-faire trade policies such as low tariffs, few import controls, no export subsidies, and free labor markets through loan conditions and repayment terms. Taken together as a neoliberal policy agenda, these practices are known as the Washington Consensus and include the willingness of a developing nation to conform to fiscal discipline, lower taxes, a competitive exchange rate, liberalized foreign direct investment policies, privatization, property rights, and deregulation. These conditions have been a prerequisite for developing nations receiving funds from global development bodies.

Critics of the Washington Consensus point out that these policies and programs create an environment favorable to transnational firms wanting to do business in developing countries, and do not place the social and economic needs of those countries first.

In the late 1970s and 1980s, with the rise and economic success of the "East Asian Tigers" – Japan, Taiwan, Hong Kong, and Singapore – state-centric scholarship resurged as the "developmental state" approach, a belief that development outcomes could be explained in part on the role of states as active participants in the economy. According to this theory, the success of these East Asian states reflected key interventions by quasi-authoritarian states. The economic principle that state intervention retards capitalist development was not validated by the empirical record of the industrializing East. The developmental states argument stands in marked contrast to the laissez-faire, "hands off" state model advocated by traditional economics, but it also complicates ideas of earlier dependency, modernization, and world systems theories that do not consider individual state actions as central to development outcomes.

Finally, resurgence in the 1990s of institutional analysis also affected development studies. For example, Biggart and Guillén (1999) identify three important premises that neo-institutionalism brings to development: (1) that institutional arenas, such as developing societies, are internally coherent and based on organizing logics that inform action and meaning; (2) that economic and managerial practices and actions not consistent with the institutional logics of a society, even if they are in the abstract "technically superior" or more "efficient," will not be readily recognized or incorporated; (3) that organizing logics are not merely constraints on development as traditionally conceived, but provide the basis for successful economic activity because they represent social and culturally based repositories of distinctive capabilities and competencies. This scholarship points out that in pursuing uniform policies and single-minded development strategies that ignore the unique experience of each society, developing countries lose the possibility of building on the existing strengths of any "institutional endowments" they may have developed over time. Ignoring the import of the social, historical, and cultural

basis of a society, according to institutionalists, is tantamount to ignoring what specialized capabilities and talents that society brings to development, and the legacy on which any customized development plan might be premised.

Economic growth typically has been measured in terms of an increase in the size of a nation's material output. Gross domestic product, which supplanted the use of gross national product in the 1990s, is the most frequently used index of both the size and health of a domestic economy. Calculating a nation's GDP involves adding domestic consumption rates with investment, government purchases, and net exports. Increasingly, consumption has become the largest component in this measure.

While GDP details gains of economic significance, according to development scholars critical of this metric, it masks declines in the quality of life experienced by a good portion of the world's population, instead mostly capturing gains for elite countries and specifically the elites within those countries. Critics have devised a number of more inclusive measures of "well-being," such as Osberg and Sharpe's (2002) Index of Economic Well-Being (IEWB), Redefining Progress's Genuine Progress Indicator (GPI) (Cobb et al. 1995), and the United Nations Development Program's Human Development Index (HDI) (UNDP 2001), among a growing list of such efforts (Hagerty et al. 2001). In addition to the traditional economic indicators of growth, "Quality of Life Indexes" typically try to move toward a fuller representation of both economic and non-economic well-being and include measures of "social health" such as education rates, income distribution, and national health. In some instances, indexes go so far as to include crime rates, measures of social benefits and safety nets, and rates of pollution, resource depletion, and long-term environmental damage. Advocates contend that these metrics better assess the overall health of a nation, not just the state of its material economy.

These measures also provide a very different picture of development trends than does GDP. Using social, economic, and environmental indicators, GPI shows there has been an overall decline in quality of life in the US since World War II and Osberg and Sharpe (2002), using the IEWB (a more conservative model), found that gains were also much flatter than those represented by US GDP. Ultimately, such quality of life measures have sensitized development scholars to the reality that social and environmental deterioration can accompany robust economic growth. This has been almost entirely missed by traditional development policies and policymakers, which have been dominated by assumptions of social and economic convergence, and traditional economic measures of growth as proxies for social health and environmental well-being.

In the early twenty-first century development studies have been concerned with forces opposed to western ideas of progress and economic success. Ethnic awareness and the resilience of cultural identity in many parts of the world have created strong local opposition to policies that favor western institutions, programs, and culture, and to regimes that favor western alliances. At the extreme, religious fundamentalism has spurred the development of anti-western terrorist organizations. At the minimum, there is skepticism that economic riches are available to all countries, or that one standard of quality of life need be universally applied. Environmental movements are increasingly powerful actors in development debates, arguing that unbridled consumption, of the sort at the foundation of modern industrial economies, is economically and socially unsustainable.

SEE ALSO: Dependency and World-Systems Theories; Developmental State; Economic Sociology: Economy, Culture and; Economy (Sociological Approach); Neoclassical Economic Perspective; Global Economy; Modernization

REFERENCES AND SUGGESTED READINGS

Biggart, N. W. & Guillén, M. F. (1999) Developing Difference: Social Organization and the Rise of the Auto Industries of South Korea, Taiwan, Spain, and Argentina. *American Sociological Review* 64: 722–47.

Cobb, J. B., Halstead, T., & Rowe, J. (1995) *The Genuine Process Indicator: Summary Data and Methodology*. Redefining Progress, San Francisco.

Frank, A. G. (1969) *Latin America: Underdevelopment or Revolution*. Monthly Review Press, New York.

Hagerty, M. R. et al. (2001) Quality of Life Indexes for National Policy: Review and Agenda for Research. *Social Indicators Research* 55: 1–96.

Osberg, L. & Sharpe, A. (2002) An Index of Economic Well Being for Selected OECD Countries. *Review of Income and Wealth* 48.

Rostow, W. W. (1969) *The Stages of Economic Growth*. Cambridge University Press, Cambridge.

United Nations Development Program (2001) *Human Development Report, 2001*. Oxford University Press, New York.

Wallerstein, I. (1980) *The Modern World-System II: Mercantilism and the Consolidation of the European World-Economy, 1600–1750*. Academic Press, New York.

economic geography

Jürgen Essletzbichler

According to Lee (2000), economic geography is "the geography (or, rather, geographies) of people's struggle to make a living." Economic geography is concerned with spatial variation in the organization of production, distribution, and consumption of commodities and the influence of externalities, place-specific institutions (on various spatial scales), and cultural practices on economic activity. As in other disciplines, the research foci of economic geography shifted as a result of exogenous changes and as a consequence of internal discourse, cooperation, and rivalries among members of the discipline. And although the discipline has never been homogenous and progressing towards some "preordained epistemological mission" (Scott 2000), it is possible to trace out a set of paradigm shifts that have occurred in the discipline over time (Livingstone 1992; Barnes 1996, 2001; Martin 1999; Scott 2000).

Geography's origin as an academic discipline was tied to the needs of colonialism in the nineteenth century, the exploration and exploitation of new territory and, in the case of economic geography, the mapping of resources and transportation routes. The first disciplinary crisis resulted from the apparent end of colonial and polar exploration and the closure of continental frontiers that seemed to leave geography without a purpose. Two world wars provided ample work for geographers, however. Until the end of World War II, economic geography adopted idiographic methods of investigation and was concerned with regional description and synthesis. Theoretical and methodological changes that occurred in other disciplines – such as a move towards logical positivism in the social sciences and a shift to general equilibrium modeling in economics and to rational choice theory in sociology – had, at first, little or no impact on the direction of the discipline.

At the end of World War II the discipline was once more confronted with a serious identity crisis. Although a number of the disciplinary rank and file defended the idiographic approach, theoretical and methodological changes outside geography, practical problems posed by the needs of a fast-expanding economy, and the rise of young, ambitious faculty eager to apply their quantitative skills to address those problems triggered the "quantitative revolution" and ushered in a new phase in economic geography, best described as spatial analysis and/or regional science paradigm (Johnston & Sidaway 2004). This new generation of quantitative economic geographers was strongly influenced by the old German location theorists and regional scientists who aimed to incorporate distance as a major variable in neoclassical economics and demanded that "geography as a whole must become an analytical, law-finding discipline conjoined with quantitative methodologies" (Scott 2000). While regional science reached its peak in the late 1960s in the US and diffused to the UK in the mid-1960s, it was unable to penetrate French or German geography. By the end of the 1960s, the external circumstances shifted again. The slowdown of the economy, rising rates of unemployment and inflation, and the gradual abandonment of the Keynesian welfare state combined with political and social upheaval to pose new problems and opportunities that required new theoretical and methodological approaches.

Regional science and the underlying equilibrium models had little to say about social and spatial inequality, the rise and persistence of poverty, job loss, deindustrialization, and regional decline. On the contrary, the methodological individualism underpinning its models and claims to objective truth delivered by quantitative methods were considered increasingly as smoke-screens to hide structural inequalities produced through capitalist accumulation. As a result, the applications of Marxist approaches to explain the evolution of the capitalist space-economy started to dominate research in economic geography in the 1970s and early 1980s. While the immanent crisis of the 1970s necessitated the engagement with the destructive aspects of capitalism, in particular the causes and implications of the decline of old industrial regions, the early 1980s witnessed the emergence of new, formerly "backward" regional production systems in Italy, Southern Germany, and California that were inhabited by different kinds of industries, characterized by different labor processes and forms of industrial organization, and appeared to be strongly embedded in particular cultural and institutional practices.

Economic geography in the 1980s then turned to examine and explain the economic, organizational, cultural, social, and political characteristics of these new industrial spaces. Different research groups emphasizing Marshallian industrial districts, vertical disintegration and local linkages, flexible specialization, or innovation-driven regional growth, emerged. This research was in part influenced by French Regulation Theory used to tie region-specific changes to broader economic and sociopolitical shifts. It became obvious that national and regional variation of economies could not be explained through economic principles alone, but that differences in governance systems, conventions, culture, and institutions had to be introduced to account for existing variation. The success of this research area may be attributed to the importance attributed to "place" as explanation of economic success. Rather than treating place as a container where socioeconomic processes unfold, social interaction between agents embedded in a common, region-specific institutional environment was said to result in emergent properties at the level of the region that would not emerge from interaction of actors in networks that span over long distances. The work on regional economies constituted probably the last identifiable core research area of economic geography.

While the region provided a focus for economic geography, it also meant a branching out and fragmentation of the discipline. Recognizing the importance of "non-economic factors" such as culture and institutions, meant a move away from economics (orthodox or Marxist) and alignment with other disciplines such as anthropology, cultural studies, management, sociology, or evolutionary and institutional economics. For Barnes (2001), this fragmentation also signified a more fundamental move from "epistemological" to "hermeneutic" theorizing, a move away from foundationalism to theorizing as social practice, a "cultural turn" in economic geography.

Economic geography has arrived, once again it seems, at a critical juncture to decide its future disciplinary trajectories. However, contrary to earlier periods where the lack of a core research area triggered an identity crisis, the present absence of a well-identified core has resulted in a flourishing of theoretically and methodologically diverse approaches addressing a variety of research questions that would not have been classified as economic geographic only 15 years ago. Instead of a single core, a number of theoretical avenues pursued by economic geographers can be identified.

Regional science has been resurrected and rebuilt on "solid" microfoundations in the form of the "new geographical economics," modeling equilibrium landscapes and urban hierarchies (Martin 1999). The main addition is the incorporation of increasing returns at the regional level allowing for multiple equilibria and unequal development.

Political economic approaches continue to emphasize the operation of structural forces that enable and constrain economic actors, but have become more sensitive to space/time contingencies that influence the crystallization of these processes in unpredictable ways. The bodies of research produced in this mold include work on the scalar reconfiguration of governance systems, the relationship between nature and society, work on neoliberalism and the new imperialism, the dynamics of regional growth and decline, labor geographies, political ecology, and gender studies.

The work on regional worlds has evolved into a series of research areas, including work on global city regions as motors of the globalization process; the analysis of culture, conventions, and untraded interdependencies to promote or obstruct regional development; and research on clusters, regional innovation systems, and learning regions. This work borrows heavily from economic sociology (in particular, Mark Granovetter) and reaches back to Polanyi's work on tacit knowledge.

A relatively new research area in economic geography borrows from evolutionary and institutional economics to understand the relationship between variety of individual behavior, firms, sectors, and institutions in a region on the one hand and the aggregate pace and direction of regional growth on the other; path-dependent regional development; and the emergence and evolution of industry-regions. The inclusion of cultural practices is not restricted to analysis of the commodity-producing sectors, but penetrates work on consumption and retailing, the financial sector, and cultural products.

Economic geography is not confined to market-transactions, but is increasingly interested in alternative forms of exchange, household economies and, more generally, the reproductive sphere.

Work on the body bridges the productive and reproductive sphere and is linked to a variety of issues ranging from consumption to prostitution and performance.

Diversity in research topics also fuels a variety of theoretical approaches ranging from positivism on the one end to non-representational theory on the other. While inspiration is still drawn from Descartes, Popper, and Marx, much of the recent work in economic geography is influenced by Foucault, Derrida, Deleuze, and Latour. Not surprisingly, this diversity in theoretical frameworks is also reflected in the methodological approaches employed by economic geographers who conduct secondary data analysis, interviews and focus groups, textual and visual analysis, and experiment with creative writing and visualization to capture complex and dynamic problems. The majority of practitioners interpret this development as a sign of a viable and active discipline that builds bridges with other disciplines where necessary and appropriate and understand it as the way forward in a world of increasing complexity, where disciplinary boundaries start to wither away. On the other hand, the dissolution of a core identity and the diversity of subjects covered might result in a widening gap among members of the discipline, each group trapped in its theoretical, methodological, and linguistic worlds that they share with colleagues outside the discipline, but that prevent them from communicating with other economic geographers. Economic geography has become hard to define and the discipline is likely to maintain its diversity of research questions, theoretical frameworks, and methodologies in the near future. But if the history of economic geography has taught us anything, it is the inherent unpredictability of the future disciplinary trajectory entailed in a dynamic, fast-changing environment.

SEE ALSO: Culture, Economy and; Economic Sociology: Neoclassical Economic Perspective; Hermeneutics; Institutionalism; Paradigms; Political Economy; Positivism; Rational Choice Theory (and Economic Sociology)

REFERENCES AND SUGGESTED READINGS

Barnes, T. J. (1996) *Logics of Dislocation: Models, Metaphors, and Meanings of Economic Space*. Guilford Press, New York.

Barnes, T. J. (2001) Retheorizing Economic Geography: From the Quantitative Revolution to the "Cultural Turn." *Annals of the Association of American Geographers* 91: 546–65.

Barnes, T. J., Peck, J., Sheppard, E. S., & Tickell, A. (Eds.) (2004) *Reading Economic Geography*. Blackwell, Oxford.

Clark, G. L., Gertler, M., & Feldman, M. (Eds.) (2000) *The Oxford Handbook of Economic Geography*. Oxford University Press, Oxford.

Johnston, R. J. & Sidaway, J. (2004) *Geography and Geographers: Anglo-American Human Geography since 1945*, 6th edn. Hodder Arnold, London.

Lee, R. (2000). Economic Geography. In: Johnston, R. J., Gregory, D., Pratt, G., & Watts, M. (Eds.), *The Dictionary of Human Geography*, 4th edn. Blackwell, Oxford, pp. 195–9.

Lee, R. & Wills, J. (Eds.) (1997) *Geographies of Economies*. Arnold, London.

Livingstone, D. N. (1992). *The Geographical Tradition: Episodes in the History of a Contested Enterprise*. Blackwell, Oxford.

Martin, R. (1999) The New "Geographical Turn" in Economics: Some Critical Reflections. *Cambridge Journal of Economics* 23: 65–91.

Scott, A. J. (2000) Economic Geography: The Great Half-Century. *Cambridge Journal of Economics* 24: 483–504.

Sheppard, E. S. & Barnes, T. J. (Eds.) (2000) *A Companion to Economic Geography*. Blackwell, Oxford.

economic sociology: classical political economic perspectives

Milan Zafirovski

Classical political economy broadly understood is the stage and branch of economics during the period from the late eighteenth century to the second half of the nineteenth century. In a narrower specification (by Schumpeter) it encompasses the "publications of the leading English authors from 1776 to 1848," specifically from Adam Smith's *Wealth of Nations* to J. S. Mill's *Principles of Political Economy*. In addition to Smith – usually considered the "father" of (classical) political economy – and Mill as its codifier, its other prominent representatives include David Ricardo, Thomas Malthus, Jean-Baptiste Say, and William Senior, as well as Karl Marx (described as a "dissident") and John Cairnes (deemed the "last" classical economist). Following Smith's implied definition, its representatives typically define classical political economy as the study of the production, distribution, exchange, and consumption of wealth.

In general, classical political economy can be divided into two broad branches: pure economics or the theory of a market economy (catallactics), and social economics or economic sociology. For example, Smith's political economy is sometimes described as a blend of market theory (catallaxy) and economic sociology or sociological economics, as are its versions in Say, Mill, and Marx. Presumably, the theory of a market economy is primary and foundational within classical political economy and of more interest to pure economists, and social economics secondary and supplementary, but more interesting for economic sociologists.

Classical political economy involves a number of versions and elements of social economics or economic sociology understood as an analysis of the societal setting of economic life, frequently intertwined with those of pure economics or market theory. The archetypical instance is what some economists identify as the "economic sociology of Adam Smith" (Schumpeter 1949), concentrating on the institutional-social structure of the economy, or Smithian "sociological economics" (Reisman 1987) that, interlaced with his market theory, attributes comprehensiveness to his political economy and makes him a broad "sociological economist" (Reisman 1998). Moreover, others state that "precisely" on the account of this comprehensiveness, specifically his "concentration on structural-institutional change, Smith deservedly won acclaim as the father of Political Economy" (Buchanan 1975: 171).

Another version of economic sociology or social economics within classical political economy is provided by Say, Smith's continental (French) follower. Say can probably be credited with inventing the concept of "social economy" (Swedberg 1998), as acknowledged and adopted by Mill later. Further, Say proposes social economy as a more appropriate conception and designation than political economy for economics on the grounds that this is a science involving observations on the "nature and functions of the different parts of the social body," specifically the "economies of societies." Notably, Say implies that social economy treats economic laws as special instances of the "general laws" or "general facts" of society (i.e., of sociological uniformities) as the domain of sociology (the "science of politics and morals").

Mill furnishes still another version of economic sociology within classical political economy. For instance, Schumpeter estimates that about a third of Mill's magnum opus *Principles of Political Economy* contains elements of economic sociology – a remarkably high proportion by the standards of contemporary economics – which are mixed with the two-thirds of market theory. The influence of Comte's sociology on Mill is mostly responsible (along with that of

Say's social economy) for the presence of such elements. Moreover, reportedly Mill, "when he came to write his *Principles*, abandoned his ambition to work out a purely abstract theory and adopted a broader view of the scope and method of political economy under the [sociological] influence of Comte" (Bladen 1941: 18). In general, Mill proposes a "science of social economy" defined as a study of the "laws of society," "laws of human nature in the social state," "conduct or condition of man in society," or "natural history of society," thus as essentially equivalent to Comte's sociology. Further, Mill considers political economy, understood as the study of "acquiring and consuming wealth," an "important division" or "branch" of the science of social economy, apparently influenced by Comte's consideration of economics as part of sociology.

Economic sociology within classical political economy centers on, generally, the "social framework of the economic course of events" (Schumpeter 1949: 61), particularly the impact of society on the economy, and comprises a number of elements. For example, the "division of labor, the origin of private property, increasing control over nature, economic freedom, and legal security – these are the most important elements constituting the economic sociology of Adam Smith" (Schumpeter 1949: 60). A particularly important element of Smith's and other economic sociology in classical political economy is recognizing the impact of institutional arrangements, as an integral part of the social framework of economic life, on the latter. This impact includes institutional-political influences on economic welfare, for example. Thus, Smith observes that there are many social institutions (and laws) tending to enhance the "public welfare," noting in particular that those of civil government may tend either to "promote or to disturb the happiness both of the individual and of the society." Similarly, so does Say, remarking that the state often provides a "powerful stimulus" to individuals' economic activities (e.g., through "well-planned public works") and so their well-being. The economic impact of social institutions also involves institutional influences on wealth distribution, as Senior suggests in observing that the latter is affected by the "peculiar institutions of particular Countries," such as slavery, legal monopolies, and poor laws. Developing and reinforcing this observation, Mill states that wealth distribution "is a matter of human institution only" in the sense of being dependent on the "laws and customs of society." Notably, he adds that the institutional rules which determine wealth distribution "are what the opinions and feelings of the ruling portion of the community make them," thus echoing Smith and even anticipating Marx. In particular, following Smith and Ricardo, Mill describes private property as the "primary and fundamental" institution which underpins the "economic arrangements of society."

In addition, Smith and Mill suggest that the institutional or political regulation of prices and markets is a salient instance of the influence of social institutions on the economy. For instance, Smith notices that particular policy regulations can hold the market prices of many commodities for a long time a "good deal" above their "natural" value (i.e., labor cost). He finds another example in the prohibition of interest (as the "price" of money) in medieval Europe and "Mahometan nations" on extra-economic, especially moral-religious grounds. Mill especially emphasizes the effects of traditions on markets, prices, and wages, observing that in early society "all transactions and engagements" are under the "influence of fixed customs."

Another prominent element of economic sociology in classical political economy is identifying and examining the role of social classes in and as part of the societal setting of the economy. This includes in particular what Schumpeter (1954) identifies as the "connection between the social rank of a class and its function" (and rewards) in the economy. Thus, Smith observes the existence of "different ranks and conditions of men in society," specifying that "three great, original, and constituent orders of every civilized society" are landowners ("those who live by rent"), laborers ("those who live by wages"), and capitalists ("those who live by profit"). Notably, he admonishes that no capitalist society can be "flourishing and happy" if laborers – the "far greater part" of its members – are "poor and miserable." In particular, he deplores the "rich and powerful" ("men of rank and fortune") for merely selecting from the "heap what is most precious and

agreeable," lamenting that their "sole end" is gratifying their "own vain and insatiable desires" from the labors of those they employ. Also, Smith says that "whenever the legislature attempts to regulate the difference between masters and their workmen, its counselors are always the masters," thus anticipating Mill's "ruling portion of the community" and even Marx's ruling class.

Elaborating on Smith's ideas, Ricardo (considered the most able classical economist) posits that wealth is distributed among "three classes of the community" (landowners, capitalists, and workers) in the form of rents, profits, and wages as respective class rewards. Further, Ricardo implies that social classes have a central economic role by arguing that discovering the laws governing wealth distribution is the "main problem" of political economy.

Building on but also going beyond Smith, Ricardo, and Mill, Marx's ideas about the role of social classes in the economy, notably capitalism, are so numerous, manifold, and controversial, as well as (un)popular, that they require a separate treatment. At this point, suffice it to mention that Marx treats the totality of class (or property) relations as the "economic structure of society – the real foundation, on which legal and political superstructures arise and to which definite forms of social consciousness correspond."

Still another important element of economic sociology in classical political economy pertains to the social conditions or requisites of production, consumption, and related activities. An instance is the effect of the (societal and technical) division of labor, another element of the social framework of the economy, on economic productivity, as analyzed and celebrated since Smith. Smith famously contends that the "greatest improvements" in productivity result from the elaborate division of labor and that in civilized society individuals are "at all times in the need of cooperation and assistance of great multitudes." Another instance involves the impact of overall social conditions on economic laws, including those of production and distribution. This is what Cairnes suggests in viewing the laws of production and distribution of wealth as the effect of the "combined operation" of political-social conditions (along with the "principles of human nature" and the "physical laws of the external world"). So does he, alternatively, by acknowledging that the production and distribution of wealth have their causes in the social-political (and physical) "laws and events" of the "external world" (alongside the "principles of human nature"). An additional instance of the above element of economic sociology is treating the process of production as a specific social condition or relation involving individuals and groups (classes). This is particularly characteristic for Marx, who treats material production as (also) a "social relationship" between its participants, specifically, workers and property owners. Thus, he states that producers establish "definite social and political relations," which indicates the "connection" of social-political structures with productive processes in the sense that a certain "mode of production" connects to a "certain mode of cooperation or social stage" (as a productive force). Notably, Marx treats economic capital as a "social relation of production" (i.e., a sum of "social magnitudes" like exchange values), more precisely a "bourgeois relation of production, a relation of production of bourgeois society."

Still another case of the social conditions of production and consumption concerns the sociocultural origins, multiplicity, and development of economic (and other) preferences and wants, as Mill, Cairnes, and Marx suggest. Thus, Mill posits the social multiplicity of preferences in stating that many economic activities actually ensue from "a plurality of motives," not only the "mere desire of wealth" (though he concedes that political economy usually makes "entire abstraction of every other human passion or motive"). So does Cairnes, who even goes further by suggesting not only this multiplicity of motives, but also the social formation and development of material wants and tastes. He does so by observing that the "desires, passions and propensities" influencing actors in their pursuit of wealth are "almost infinite" and, notably, "may be developed in the progress of society," citing the role of customs in "modifying human conduct" in this pursuit. Marx suggests that preferences are subject to societal formation and historical evolution, stating that human tastes or wants (and pleasures) have their origins in society, which gives them a social (and so relative) character.

Lastly, some other explicit or implicit elements of economic sociology within classical political economy may include the long-run interaction between population and the economy (Malthus), institutional and other non-market restrictions on market competition, including free trade (Smith, Mill, Cairnes), the economic implications of "moral sentiments" like sympathy, justice, and benevolence (Smith pre-1776), and so on.

SEE ALSO: Economic Sociology: Neoclassical Economic Perspective; Malthus, Thomas Robert; Markets; Marx, Karl; Marxism and Sociology; Mill, John Stuart; Political Economy; Population and Economy; Schumpeter, Joseph A.; Smith, Adam

REFERENCES AND SUGGESTED READINGS

Bladen, V. W. (1941) Mill to Marshall: The Conversion of the Economists. *Journal of Economic History* 1 (Supplement 1): 17–29.

Buchanan, J. (1975) *The Limits of Liberty*. University of Chicago Press, Chicago.

Reisman, D. (1987) *Adam Smith's Sociological Economics*. Macmillan, London.

Reisman, D. (1998) Adam Smith on Market and State. *Journal of Institutional and Theoretical Economics* 154: 357–84.

Schumpeter, J. (1949) *The Theory of Economic Development*. Harvard University Press, Cambridge, MA.

Schumpeter, J. (1954) *History of Economic Analysis*. Oxford University Press, New York.

Swedberg, R. (1998) *Max Weber and the Idea of Economic Sociology*. Princeton University Press, Princeton.

economic sociology: neoclassical economic perspective

Milan Zafirovski

Neoclassical economics is the stage and branch of economic science since the 1870s through the 1930s and beyond. It was mostly the product or sequel of what economists (Schumpeter

1954) call the Copernican marginalist revolution in economic theory during the 1870–90s. Specifically, the crux of marginalism was a marginal-utility theory of exchange value and its extensions (e.g., marginal-productivity principle of income distribution) in reaction and contrast to the labor-cost conception in classical political economy. The founders or pioneers of marginalism are commonly considered to be William Jevons (England), Carl Menger (Austria), and Leon Walras (Switzerland/France), who almost simultaneously in 1871–4 "discovered" marginal-utility value theory as a putative revolutionary alternative to its labor-based versions in Smith, Ricardo, Mill, Marx, and others. (For instance, Jevons specifically attacked Ricardo and Mill's theories, prompting neoclassical economists like Alfred Marshall to rise in their partial defense.) The term neoclassical economics was invented by Thorstein Veblen (Groenewegen 1995), a heterodox institutional economist, in the early 1900s to indicate that marginalism (e.g., marginal-utility theory) was, in virtue of utilitarianism and hedonism, essentially continuous with and so "scarcely distinguishable" from classical political economy (which apparently overlooks the opposition of the marginalist revolution to Ricardo et al.'s labor theories of value). In this sense, the terms marginalism and neoclassical economics become interchangeable, though the first term is probably more accurate and precise for describing this stage and type of economic theory. Moreover, historians of economics such as Schumpeter (1954: 919) object that "there is no more sense in calling the Jevons-Menger-Walras theory neoclassic than there would be in calling the Einstein theory neo-Newtonian." This suggests that neoclassical economics is essentially marginalism (with partial exceptions like Marshall), but not conversely: the marginalist revolution is not newly, but counter-classical (that is what makes it presumably "Copernican").

In addition to Jevons, Menger, and Walras, some other prominent representatives of marginalist or neoclassical economics include Philip Wicksteed, Eugen Böhm-Bawerk, Friedrich von Wieser, Knut Wicksell, Francis Edgeworth, Vilfredo Pareto, Marshall (in part), Irving Fisher, and John B. Clark. Although narrower in analysis and more formal (mathematical) in

method than classical political economy, neoclassical economics also comprises two general branches: pure economic theory premised on the principle of marginal utility and social economics or economic sociology. For instance, Jevons proposes incorporating what he (perhaps for the first time in social science) terms economic sociology into the divisions of economics, alongside pure (marginal-utility) theory. So does Walras, who seeks to integrate what *à la* Say he calls social economy with "pure" political economy. If pure (marginal-utility) market theory is a primary and defining division of neoclassical economics and in the focus of most economists, economic sociology is a secondary and supplementary one, yet more appealing to sociologists as well as to social economists.

Some pertinent formulations or anticipations of economic sociology within neoclassical economics include the following. A remarkable (and perhaps surprising) moment is that an ostensibly pure marginalist economist, Jevons, probably invented the term economic sociology (Swedberg 1998), though under the likely influence of Comte (filtered through Spencer and Mill). Notably, within marginalism and beyond, Jevons provides the first explicit proposal for economic sociology as an integral branch of (neoclassical) economics. Moreover, he proposes that "it is only by subdivision, by recognizing a branch of Economic Sociology ... that we can rescue our [economic] science from its confused state." Jevons implicitly defines economic sociology as the "Science of the Evolution of Social Relations" in relation to the economy (apparently adopting a Spencer-type definition of sociology in general). Jevons's early follower, Wicksteed, carries this proposal even further by suggesting, under the acknowledged sociological influence of Comte, that economics "must be the handmaid" of sociology, which implies an idea of economic sociology. So does the project of Edgeworth (also Jevons's follower) for what he calls mathematical sociology (or "mathematical psychics"). Moreover, he states that marginal-utility theory ("Calculus of Variations" in utility) is the "most sublime branch" of sociological analysis, invoking Comte's view of economics as the branch "most applicable to Sociology."

Walras's counterpart to Jevonian economic sociology is social economy, a concept he probably adopted from Say and Mill. Walras specifically defines social economy as the "theory of the distribution of social wealth" in contrast to "pure" political economy defined as the "theory of price determination under the hypothetical regime of absolutely free competition." Moreover, Walras goes a step further than Jevons in implementing the proposal for economic sociology by writing a book on social economy in a deliberate attempt at its integration with pure (and applied) economics. Closely following Walras, Wicksell adopts the idea of social economy defined as an "investigation of the issue how economic laws and practical precepts would be properly applied for getting the most possible social gain, and what changes in existing economic and legal structure of society are necessary for this end." Like Walras, he seeks to integrate social economy thus understood with pure or theoretical (and applied) economics within economic science as a whole. So does Clark, who considers what he calls social economic dynamics as a proxy for dynamic economic sociology, economics' "third division" to be integrated with its other "natural divisions." Notably, he establishes these divisions of economics on the basis of "sociological evolution." Also, Walras's successor, Pareto, implies an idea and approach of economic sociology by suggesting that economists "have to consider not just the economic phenomenon taken by itself, but also the whole social situation, of which the economic situation is only a phase." Pareto therefore implicitly conceives economic sociology in terms of a consideration of the "whole social situation" of the economy as its integral part.

Still another proposal for economic sociology within marginalism is implicit in Wieser's project of social economics, mostly prompted and influenced by Weber. Wieser (a sociologist-turned marginalist economist) implicitly defines economic sociology as an analysis of the "social relations of the economy" or the "sociological problems of economic theory" (which reveals Weber's influence). He suggests that economists should describe and explain economic processes with "sociological phenomena," citing exchange-value as one of those "sociological fields" which makes possible "more rapid and certain progress" in analyzing the economy than do others. Also, Marshall's neoclassical

economics implies some ideas or intimations of economic sociology. For instance, Schumpeter (1941) comments that, reminiscent of Mill, Marshall's *Principles of Economics* contain ("behind, beyond and all around the kernel" of pure market theory) an "economic sociology of nineteenth-century English capitalism which rests on historical bases of impressive extent and solidity." Other economists also notice that, like Smith, Marshall produces "sociological insights" and displays a "sociologist's awareness that approbation and self-approbation are relevant even in the economic marketplace" (Reisman 1990: 264).

Like that of Smith and other classical economists, Jevons et al.'s economic sociology identifies and examines the social character and context of the economy (Schumpeter 1949: 61). First, some neoclassical economists acknowledge that the economy represents a social category by virtue of existing and functioning within society. This is what Walras does by observing that economic relations, including market transactions, necessarily take place in society. So does (more strongly) Pareto, who argues that the "states" of the economy are "particular cases of the general states of the sociological system," described as "much more complicated"; he considers, consequently, economics as an "integral" part of sociology in which "complications are greater still and by far." Moreover, he adds that in many situations economic problems are "subordinate" to the sociological; for example, material interests and rational actions to sentiments ("residues") and non-rational conduct. Also, Menger describes the (national) economy as the "social form" of economic activity or simply a social economy, and economic processes as instances of "concrete social phenomena." His follower Wieser provides an instance in this respect by observing that every actor interprets the (marginalist) economic principle of attaining the highest total utility at the lowest cost "in the light of his social environment."

Walras and Menger and Wieser imply what Wicksteed states explicitly: the reason the economy is a social phenomenon is that it "compels the individual to relate himself to others," which makes economic laws the "laws of human conduct" – so psychosocial rather than physical ones. Marshall presents a case of such relations in which market actors can create "particular" markets involving "some people or groups of people" in "somewhat close touch" with each other, such that "mutual knowledge and trust" lead to favoring these insiders at the expense of strangers, thus perhaps anticipating the social embeddedness conception of modern economic sociology. Similarly, Clark observes that the "socialization" of the economy leads to social differentiation by arranging producers (and consumers) into differentiated and unequal social groups and subgroups. Also, he essentially treats economic change or dynamics as a particular dimension of "sociological evolution," as do later neoclassical economists like Schumpeter, who places economic development within a "theory of cultural evolution" on apparent Durkhiemian grounds that the "social process is really one indivisible whole."

Second, neoclassical economists recognize the impact of society, including politics and culture, on economic life. Thus, Clark acknowledges that many economic phenomena (e.g., "hired labor" or "loaned capital") are dependent on "social organization." In particular, Walras, while advocating the laissez-faire doctrine, admits that an economy cannot properly operate without "interference" from some political and other authority. Further, Wicksteed observes that, due to political and other interference, the market "never has been left to itself," even suggesting that it "never must be," which provides an empirical rationale to his proposal for making economics the "handmaid" of sociology. Wicksteed thereby adopts and generalizes Jevons's observation that in many cases market transactions "must be settled upon other than strictly economical grounds" (e.g., bargaining power), as well as that the future supply and demand in markets often hinge on the "political considerations of the moment." In addition, some neoclassical economists register the impact of cultural phenomena, like traditions or customs, on economic agents and behaviors. Specifically, evoking and developing Mill's views on the economic impact of rigid traditions in early society, Marshall emphasizes what he describes as the cumulative inhibiting effects of customs on the "methods of production and the character of producers."

SEE ALSO: Economic Sociology: Classical Political Economic Perspectives; Jevons, William; Markets; Mill, John Stuart; Pareto, Vilfredo; Schumpeter, Joseph A.; Smith, Adam; Veblen, Thorstein; Weber, Max

REFERENCES AND SUGGESTED READINGS

Groenewegen, P. (1995) *A Soaring Eagle*. Edward Elgar, Aldershot.
Reisman, D. (1990) *Alfred Marshall's Mission*. St. Martin's Press, New York.
Schumpeter, J. (1941) Alfred Marshall's Principles: A Semi-Centennial Appraisal. *American Economic Review* 31: 236–48.
Schumpeter, J. (1949) *The Theory of Economic Development*. Harvard University Press, Cambridge, MA.
Schumpeter, J. (1954) *History of Economic Analysis*. Oxford University Press, New York.
Schumpeter, J. (1965) *Imperialism: Social Classes*. World Publishing, Cleveland.
Swedberg, R. (1998) *Max Weber and the Idea of Economic Sociology*. Princeton University Press, Princeton.

economy, culture and

Marion Fourcade-Gourinchas

In traditional academic discourse, "culture" and "economy" have long been regarded as separate analytical spheres: on the one hand, the realm of shared cognitions, norms, and symbols, studied by anthropologists; on the other, the realm of self-interest, where economists reign supreme. Though the two disciplines overlap occasionally (in economic anthropology mainly), radical differences in the conceptual and methodological routes each field followed during the twentieth century have prevented any sort of meaningful interaction.

By contrast, the interaction between culture and the economy has always been a central component of sociological analysis. All the founding fathers of sociology were, one way or another, interested in the relationship between people's economic conditions and their moral universe. In his famous presentation in the *Preface to a Contribution to the Critique of Political Economy*, for instance, Marx described "forms of social consciousness" essentially as an epiphenomenon of material relations. Later interpretations, however, have suggested that even for Marx and Engels the relationships between "material base" and "superstructure" were far from deterministic. The "western" Marxist traditions that developed in Europe after World War I proposed a somewhat more sophisticated analysis that emphasized the integration of culture into the apparatus of domination – either because the hegemony exerted by bourgeois culture induces the masses into implicitly consenting to their own economic oppression (Gramsci 1971), or because the incorporation of culture into the commercial nexus of capitalism leads to uniformity of spirit and behavior and the absence of critical thinking (Adorno & Horkheimer 2002). Still, in these formulations, culture remains wedded to its material origins in capitalist relations of production.

Partly reacting against what they perceived to be a one-sided understanding of the relationships between base and superstructure in Marxist writings, Weber and Durkheim both sought to demonstrate the greater autonomy of the cultural realm, albeit in quite different ways. Both insisted that people's behavior is always infused with a meaning that is not reducible to their material positions. Weber, more than anyone else, demonstrated the influence of preexisting ideas and, in particular, religious worldviews on the economic conduct of individuals. For instance, even though their actions may look rational from the outside, the behavior of early Protestant capitalists was quite illogical from the inside: anxiety about salvation, rather than self-interest, motivated them to accumulate (Weber 2002). In other words, their search for profit was not based on instrumental rationality, but it made *psychological* sense given the religious (cultural) universe in which they lived. In fact, Weber considered that all religions condition individual attitudes toward the world and therefore influence involvement in practical affairs – but they, of course, all do it differently, so that the "economic

ethics" of individuals varies substantially across social contexts.

It is Durkheim, however, who best articulated the *collective* basis of our meaning-making orientation: groups of individuals share certain understandings that they come to take for granted in their routine dealings with each other. Hence how people behave, including in economic settings, is not a priori reducible to a set of predetermined individual preferences and the interests they support. Rather, most of people's actions are motivated by habit and routine; and preferences, as well as the institutions they support, are informed by cultural norms (Meyer & Rowan 1977). In each society, then, culture and institutions act in tandem to shape individual consciousness and thereby representations of what is understood to be "rational." This is what DiMaggio (1994) calls the "constitutive effect" of culture. Because these mental maps are widely shared, they have much greater efficacy than others that would be out of place, or misunderstood, in the same context.

THE CULTURAL SHAPING OF ECONOMIC INSTITUTIONS

As a system of representations that exists separately and independently of individuals, culture may shape economic behavior in many different ways. It may be more or less institutionalized. Corporate cultures, for instance, are often highly formalized, even bureaucratized, but the rules that underlie bazaar interactions, though obviously codified, remain very informal (Geertz 2001). Second, the effect of culture may be more or less profound: Meyer and Rowan (1977), for instance, have famously suggested that many organizational rules are adopted in a purely ceremonial way but have little impact on actual practice – a claim that has been notably supported by research on educational institutions and hospitals. On the other hand, substantial evidence has come out of cross-national studies of a deep patterning, not only of economic values and norms (Hofstede 1980), but also of economic institutions and organizations (e.g., Dore 1973; Hamilton &

Woolsey-Biggart 1988). The critical question, then, is whether the two are related, and how.

NATIONAL CULTURES AND THE ECONOMY

One possible answer has been provided by Dobbin's (1994) suggestion of the existence of an elective affinity between economic and political culture (see also Beckert 2004). In his comparative analysis of the development of the railway sector in the nineteenth century, Dobbin shows that public officials in three countries sought to achieve economic growth in very different ways, and were influenced in doing so by their cultural perceptions about the nature and sources of the political order in their own nation. In the United States, they strove primarily to protect community self-determination; in France, they oriented themselves toward centralized planning by the state in an effort to avoid logistical chaos; and in the United Kingdom, they were mainly concerned with protecting the individual sovereignty of firms. Ultimately, then, the economy of each country ended up "reflecting" the polity it originated from.

Some sociologists, however, would argue that there is no such inherent consistency to national cultures. Biernacki (1995), for instance, finds that the process of their formation is eminently fragile, almost serendipitous. In his comparative study of textile mills at the onset of the industrialization process, he finds that the concept of "labor" had a substantially different meaning in Britain and Germany, but that these differences originated in on-the-ground practices by workers and employers rather than in some preexisting mental categories. These practical conceptions, derived from the material context of industrialization in each country, tended then to crystallize into full-fledged meaning-making systems, which became eventually codified in writing – by political economists and other intellectuals. Through this process they acquired a great cultural depth, and ended up shaping a whole set of outcomes in the development pathways of the two countries – such as the wage calculation system, disciplinary techniques

within factories, forms of workers' collective action, and even industrial architecture. Yet even then, the systems remained vulnerable to a change in practices (which eventually took place in the early twentieth century).

THE EMERGENCE OF CULTURE WITHIN THE ECONOMY

Biernacki's study illustrates particularly well the fact that we should think about the role of culture primarily through its inscription in *practices*. Economic settings, therefore, do not simply display, or reflect, preexisting cultural understandings, but should be regarded as places where distinctive local cultures are formed and carried out. There are two main ways in which this point has been articulated in the sociological literature. The first emphasizes the social meanings people produce (whether voluntarily or involuntarily) through their use of economic settings and economic objects, and is best illustrated by consumption studies. The second suggests that some form of social order – i.e., regulating norms and practices – emerges out of the interpersonal interactions that take place within economic settings, particularly formal organizations and markets.

Consumption

The first set of questions goes back to Veblen's and Simmel's analyses of consumption, and was most noticeably extended by Bourdieu (1984). The fundamental idea here is that consumption is not about individual parameters (preferences, income) but is profoundly *relational*. Consumption practices are the site of a competitive struggle whereby individuals seek to position themselves vis-à-vis other individuals in the social space. For Veblen (1994 [1899]), it is essentially about vertical hierarchy – leisurely elites seek to demarcate themselves from those below them by wasting money and time on perfectly useless purchases and activities. For Bourdieu, the structure of the social "space" is more complex: education and socialization into high culture (or not) play as much a part as money in determining taste and, beyond, consumption practices. What structures consumption practices (as all forms of action), then, is what Bourdieu calls "habitus" – a system of dispositions that is formed through the individual's trajectory in the social space (understood, again, in a relational manner vis-à-vis other individuals).

The study of consumption practices thus provides an extraordinarily rich terrain for analyzing how people relate to one another, both structurally and cognitively. In a creative variation on this theme, Zelizer (1994) has shown that these relational meanings are not only expressed through *what* people purchase, but often in *how* they pay for it – cash, gift certificates, checks, food stamps. People, in fact, constantly personalize, differentiate, and earmark money in ways that can be understood as metaphors about social relations and identity. (Whether the *how*, like the *what*, is also subject to the logic of habitus remains to be studied systematically.)

Organizations

The second question – the cultural universe produced within and by economic institutions – has also given rise to a diverse and extremely rich literature. We may illustrate this point with three examples: antitrust law; financial markets; and the McDonald's corporation. Fligstein (1992), most prominently, has studied the way in which the legal environment shapes the formation of distinctive economic cultures. Corporate managers, he argues, act on the basis of "conceptions of control" – shared understandings about how a particular market works. These conceptions evolve in close connection with changes in the legal regulation of corporate competition, which tip the balance of power toward management groups with certain organizational cultures at the expense of others. In the course of the twentieth century, for instance, the American corporation was a contested and historically evolving cultural terrain, where conceptions of control shifted from production to sales and marketing, and finally finance and shareholder value. In this case, organizational culture fundamentally emerges out of a combination of institutional forces and power struggles.

Of course, such tacit understandings and patterned practices may emerge in a more decentralized way, out of interpersonal interactions in corporations, factories, workshops, and markets, including the most "rational" ones. Sociologists, for instance, have revealed the existence of all kinds of rituals, beliefs, customs, and informal control structures that regulate social life in the financial markets – the very heart, supposedly, of instrumental action. In fact, the economic potential of culture has not been lost on corporations, many of which try actively to "engineer" predictable behaviors and commitments on the part of their employees through the use of quasi-religious rituals and the enforcement of strict codes regulating social interactions.

The organizational innovations introduced by the McDonald's corporation are probably among the most potent examples of the cultural effects of corporate logics. As Ritzer (2004) has shown, they had a dramatic effect on human experience and social organization well beyond the boundaries of the firm of origin – helping spread the values and practices of efficiency, calculability, predictability, and control to various organizations and social institutions (education, medicine, or the criminal justice system), both in the United States and abroad. The sheer success of this model is thus a precious reminder that instrumental rationality – as Weber worried – is also a very powerful "culture" in and of itself.

THE ECONOMY AS THE CULTURE OF MODERNITY?

The example of McDonald's suggests a broader point, then: the constitution of economic categories themselves is through and through a social process. Consequently, what gets incorporated (or not) into the sphere of the marketplace reveals much about how we understand ourselves, about our "culture." As Polanyi (2001 [1944]) argued long ago, the hallmark of post-eighteenth-century modernity was the emergence of a distinctive social order dominated by market relations. Following nineteenth-century critics (among them Marx,

Weber, and Simmel), Polanyi articulated the dehumanizing effect of modern capitalism and calculative rationality on personality and human relations, whereby individuals come to be seen as commodities and means to an end rather than as ends in themselves.

Empirically, however, there is quite a bit of debate about whether such effects really exist: recent economic experiments in small-scale societies, for instance, have suggested that market integration is *positively* correlated with human cooperation (Henrich et al. 2004), thereby vindicating earlier commentaries about the civilizing (Hirschman 1977) and socially integrating effects of commerce. It is also unclear whether the penetration of markets has been as universal and far-reaching as some skeptics believe. Modernity certainly does not mean that everything has been engulfed into the sphere of the marketplace: for instance, the study of the conditions under which boundary "objects" such as children, death, organs, or art are subject to economic exchange has revealed a quite varied landscape. Hence, as sources of economic benefit, children were *removed* from labor markets around the turn of the twentieth century in the United States (and countries that continue to authorize such practices today face grave political and economic pressures). On the other hand, as sources of emotional and social benefit, they were commodified in ways that were not foreseen in the nineteenth century, mainly through the adoption, insurance, and consumption markets (Zelizer 1985).

The intellectual challenge, then, is twofold: to specify the distinctive nature of the moral order capitalism relies upon, and to understand how it is produced. Perhaps this challenge is nowhere as obvious as in the current emergence of a new and eclectic vocabulary that seeks to overcome the conceptual divide between culture and economy, and focuses instead on the always inextricably moral dimensions of economic discourses and practices (Amin & Thrift 2004). Particularly noticeable is the work on logics of moral justification, which identifies the recent appearance of the discursive figure of "connectivity" as a new regime of justification conceived in and for the post-industrial capitalist economy (Boltanski & Chiapello 2005). Dezalay and Garth (2002) explore another exciting avenue in their analysis of the mutually reinforcing, profoundly entangled, discourses of economic and political individualism – e.g., human rights and the market – and their worldwide diffusion under US hegemony. Finally, Callon (1998) and others have investigated the *performative* nature of the knowledge forms that sustain the development of capitalism, mainly economics and accounting. They have shown that through their language, techniques, and representations, these disciplines produce a world of "calculative agencies" and create a host of new institutions in which these agencies may exercise their calculative power – thereby formatting, little by little, our cultural selves onto the model fiction of *homo economicus*. This outburst of work seems to signal that sociology is finally ready for a real engagement with economics that will demystify it as a cultural form, as the discursive rationalization and active formatting, by capitalism, of itself and for itself – not merely the science of how the economy "works."

SEE ALSO: Civilization and Economy; Consumption; Culture; Globalization; Globalization, Culture and; McDonaldization; Moral Economy

REFERENCES AND SUGGESTED READINGS

Adorno, T. & Horkheimer, M. (2002) *Dialectic of Enlightenment*. Stanford University Press, Stanford.
Amin, A. & Thrift, N. (Eds.) (2004) *The Cultural Economy Reader*. Blackwell, Oxford.
Beckert, J. (2004) *Unverdientes Vermögen. Soziologie des Erbrechts*. Campus Verlag, Frankfurt am Main.
Biernacki, R. (1995) *The Fabrication of Labor: Germany and Britain, 1640–1914*. University of California Press, Berkeley.
Boltanski, L. & Chiapello, E. (2005) *The New Spirit of Capitalism*. Verso, London.
Bourdieu, P. (1984) *Distinction*. Harvard University Press, Cambridge, MA.
Callon, M. (1998) The Embeddedness of Economic Markets in Economics. In: Callon, M. (Ed.), *The Laws of the Markets*. Blackwell, Oxford.
Dezalay, Y. & Garth, B. G. (2002) *The Internationalization of Palace Wars: Lawyers, Economists, and*

the Contest to Transform Latin American States. University of Chicago Press, Chicago.

DiMaggio, P. (1994) Culture and Economy. In: Smelser, N. & Swedberg, R. (Eds.), *The Handbook of Economic Sociology*. Princeton University Press, Princeton, pp. 27–57.

Dobbin, F. (1994) *Forging Industrial Policy*. Cambridge University Press, Cambridge.

Dore, R. (1973) *British Factory, Japanese Factory: The Origins of National Diversity in Industrial Relations*. Allen & Unwin, London.

Fligstein, N. (1992) *The Transformation of Corporate Control*. Harvard University Press, Cambridge, MA.

Geertz, C. (2001) The Bazaar Economy: Information and Search in Peasant Marketing. In: Granovetter, M. & Swedberg, R. (Eds.), *The Sociology of Economic Life*, 2nd edn. Westview Press, Boulder, CO.

Gramsci, A. (1971) *Selections From the Prison Notebooks*. Ed. and Trans. Q. Hoare & G. Nowell Smith. Lawrence & Wishart, London.

Hamilton, G. & Woolsey-Biggart, N. (1988) Market, Culture, and Authority: A Comparative Analysis of Management and Organization in the Far East. *American Journal of Sociology* 94: 52–94.

Henrich, J. et al. (2004) *Foundations of Human Sociality: Economic Experiments and Ethnographic Evidence from Fifteen Small-Scale Societies*. Oxford University Press, Oxford.

Hirschman, A. (1977) *The Passions and the Interests*. Princeton University Press, Princeton.

Hofstede, G. (1980) *Culture's Consequences: International Differences in Work-Related Values*. Sage, Newbury Park, CA.

Meyer, J. & Rowan, B. (1977) Institutionalized Organizations: Formal Structure as Myth and Ceremony. *American Journal of Sociology* 83(2): 340–63.

Polanyi, K. (2001 [1944]) *The Great Transformation*. Beacon Press, Boston.

Ritzer, G. (2004) *The McDonaldization of Society: Revised New Century Edition*. Pine Forge Press, Thousand Oaks, CA.

Smith, C. (1990) *Auctions: The Social Construction of Value*, rpt. edn. University of California Press, Berkeley.

Veblen, T. (1994 [1899]) *The Theory of the Leisure Class*. Penguin, New York.

Weber, M. (2002) *The Protestant Ethic and the Spirit of Capitalism*. Routledge, New York.

Zelizer, V. (1985) *Pricing the Priceless Child*. Princeton University Press, Princeton.

Zelizer, V. (1994) *The Social Meaning of Money*. Princeton University Press, Princeton.

economy, networks and

Gordon Walker

The intersection of economic and social behavior has long been an interest of sociologists. Since Simmel's (1955) seminal work on affiliation, it has become clear that the extent, kind, and structure of relations in a society have a potentially crucial impact on how well it functions, and by implication how much wealth it creates. Two current research programs are outlined here, small worlds and interfirm networks, which are related broadly to market creation and robustness. Both of these research programs capture core aspects of Granovetter's (1985) concept of embeddedness and suggest new directions for examining the sociological roots of economic behavior.

An economy runs on its volume of transactions, both between businesses and between businesses and consumers. An increase in transactions is generally considered a sign of economic health; a drop in volume a sign of weakness. One of the most important mechanisms that stimulates transaction volume is the fabric of institutional and social relationships that connects potential transaction partners with each other. Such a network, extending broadly across the economic, demographic, and class strata of a society, is essential for the creation and distribution of wealth through market forces. The more constrained the range of network ties, the greater the limitation placed on economic growth and ultimately on the viability of the economy. To understand the probity of this assertion, one need only consider the severe long-term problems faced by command societies or the huge short-term loss caused by the national shutdown in the United States after September 11, 2003.

Perhaps the best-developed model of an extensive network is the small world. Milgram's (1967) early experiments showed that individuals in a referral chain can use simple social markers to home in on a targeted person, even across wide geographical distances. The average chain in his study was composed of six people, connected in sequence, hence the title of John Guare's play *Six Degrees of Separation*. But if we are all tied to each other through just a few ties, how is it that we are surrounded mostly by people whom we know and who frequently know each other?

Watts and his colleagues (Watts 1999) have developed a variety of models of small world structure that answer this question. Their basic model has two salient components consistent with intuition. The first component is high local clustering (my friends are also friends of each other), and the second is a low global path length (it only takes a few steps to get from my position to someone on the other side of the network). Many networks with important economic implications have been found with such a structure, including the Internet, interlocking boards of directors, and interlocking groups of corporate owners (see Kogut & Walker 2001).

Where do small worlds come from? What determines them? The classic answer to this question is the following. At first, a population of potential transactors is segmented into discrete groups, like cavemen clustered in isolated tribes. Then, one or a few members of each tribe strike out on their own and make contact with other groups, establishing relationships, even as the tribes themselves remain highly internally related. Interestingly, Watts (1999) finds that just a few of these intergroup connections are sufficient to tie the network together, consistent with Milgram's results, and preserve the inbred relationships of the tribes. Although this story of global network development is appealing, it has problems.

The first concerns why isolated tribes connect with each other. A reasonable intuition is that they are looking for things they don't have. That is, without the promise of gain, there is no economic motivation to leave home. So trade across the network, not just with neighbors, implies a search for value enhancement. Unfortunately, the distribution of information in the network has to be just so in order for a broad search process to be efficient; and as this distribution departs from the optimum, search becomes highly inefficient very quickly. In most networks, then, search alone will not be a feasible explanation of small world development.

What other mechanisms might lead to the emergence of a small world? There are two possibilities. One is that relationships are formed randomly, since chance encounters can surface opportunities. However, Watts and his colleagues have shown that randomly generated ties ultimately destroy local clustering, which violates the small world model where strong neighborhood relations endure. Moreover, casual observation suggests that not all contacts among individuals or firms are random; the fact that those that are make a strong impression proves that they are exceptional. A second possibility is that relationships between tribes emerge as their members meet in one or more secondary social or economic institutions, such as schools, professional associations, social clubs, governing boards, and places of work. These groups constitute a sociologically distinct dimension from the local clusters, since in the tribes-first model clustering occurs before the network is integrated. Thus, networks become integrated as small worlds when social institutions develop or are made available to link up isolated tribes.

An important characteristic of small world properties of networks constructed through common memberships in institutions is that these networks can be highly dependent on the size distribution of the groups that individuals belong to. Larger groups obviously provide more individuals with exposure to each other. In fact, for some networks, both the degree of clustering in local neighborhoods and the number of ties to span the overall population have been shown to be completely dependent on group sizes.

Therefore, in order to understand the formation of a small world, one needs to attend more closely to the opportunity structures that bring individuals together. Without a sufficient set of opportunities for gathering individuals with differing backgrounds, the network is fragmented, search is frustrated, and the volume of transactions remains small. Where these institutions originate depends on the network being integrated. However, it seems unlikely that an isolated set of tribes would be able to establish ties with each other through common membership in institutions that they themselves would have to develop. A more likely possibility is that institutions enter the tribes' domain from the outside, suggesting that small world development cascades across networks from the more to the less developed, bringing with it greater integration and the potential for an increased transaction frequency and economic growth.

Another problem with the caves-first model is that not all networks start off as fragmented. That is, some networks are integrated first and develop local clusters second. The US venture capital syndication network, for example, was highly integrated nationally very early in the history of the industry. The network only slowly developed an identifiable structure of clusters, based on the common geographical location of the firms in cities or regions, such as New York, Boston, Northern California, Dallas, Minneapolis, and Chicago. What stimulated the rise of such a local focus is not known, but some possibilities are that: common preferences arose within a region to invest in local startup firms as the volume of opportunities increased; regional specialization in local startup industries increased (Silicon Valley – semiconductors; Boston and San Diego – biotechnology), leading to venture capital firm specialization and co-venturing; and venture capitalists became more mobile across firms within the same city or region. All of these represent opportunities for expanding local search and hence for the development of regional syndication clusters. Such a pattern indicates that economic motivations may spur the development of clusters just as they may influence building ties between them.

To understand a small world, then, one needs to identify and analyze the relevant social and economic trends and structures that infuse it. These create and shape the opportunities individuals and firms have to form relationships and therefore for network development overall. In this regard, it would not be inappropriate to explain the emergence of regional production clusters, which have attracted so much study over the last 30 years, as a crescive combining of geographically bounded technological, social, and demographic factors that together enable a local interfirm network with small world properties. Focusing on relationships alone is insufficient to understand how the small world develops to facilitate economic behavior. These ties need to be motivated and sustained by substantive opportunities and venues for interaction.

In addition to the effect of small worlds on the volume of transactions throughout an economy, other kinds of network structure have important economic consequences by affecting behavior within industries (see Burt 1980). We have evidence of network influence on five areas of economic activity: technological innovation, financial performance, investment behavior such as venture syndication and acquisitions, entry into an industry, and further development of the network itself. These cases vary in the types of network structure and linkages among firms that constitute the network. Some of these structures can be embedded within the small world, but they differ in their consequences, depending on the industry in which they occur. Interestingly, we observe interfirm alliances in almost all sectors, including extractive industries, financial services such as investment banking and venture capital, high technology, discrete manufacturing, and large-scale processing industries. So industry networks in general are pervasive and important for the overall economy.

A frequently stated assumption about an interfirm network is that it is a complex pathway for the flow of information, and within the network the position of the firm determines the information available to it (see Podolny 2001). A common additional assumption is that the information a firm receives from partners that are related to each other in a cluster is to some extent redundant, since these partners are likely to share it in their relationships with each other. Thus, the more information a firm receives through its alliances with organizations that are not related to each other, the broader the firm's exposure to market and technological trends and opportunities. A broader exposure in turn leads to a higher rate of innovation (Ahuja 2000) and, in moderation, to higher rates of firm survival (Uzzi 1996). In some cases, greater exposure to information may also increase firm performance.

Redundant information can also provide an economic benefit. Tight clustering among firms through their alliances can lead to technological spillovers, which increases the rate of innovation. Alternatively, clustering can impose normative constraints on behavior (Coleman 1988), which induces firms to cooperate and raises the likelihood of future partnering (see Ingram & Roberts 2000). Thus, the most effective structure for a firm's alliance network seems to be partners that are closely connected to each other but not tied to the same firms outside the local neighborhood.

Occupying a central position in a network of alliances (Gulati & Gargiulo 1999) also provides more information, with a variety of possible economic consequences for firms. In the semiconductor industry, central firms experience stronger firm growth; and centrally positioned banks tend to diversify more extensively. Further, venture capital firms that are central in the industry's network of syndications are more likely to invest in startups that are geographically distant. Finally, because they are closer to more potential partners, central firms are more likely to enter into more alliances. This broad range of centrality benefits shows clearly how network position affects firm behavior and through it the distribution of assets in the overall economy.

Just like firms, an industry-wide network may be more or less centralized, and higher centralization indicates that one or a few firms dominate the industry through their alliances, possibly because their technologies have become standard. In fact, by reflecting the competition for standards dominance, the trend in industry centralization affects the pattern of entry by suppliers to the competing firms. It has been observed that potential suppliers tend to enter the industry when its level of centralization is rising, indicating that some firms are winning the standards competition and therefore that they are safer as long-term partners. When standards competition is fierce and industry centralization is falling, it is less clear who the eventual winners will be; so suppliers, in the interest of not choosing a failing customer, hold off and do not enter. In technology-based industries, the signaling role of network structure can thus have an effect on the structure of adjacent markets and therefore indirectly on the economy.

Local interpersonal and interfirm networks provide the normative context for exchange. But they also influence the economy through extensive, global structures, such as the small world, that facilitate the efficiency and increase the volume of transactions. The creation and persistence of these global networks, often through societal institutions, therefore expand

economic behavior. Moreover, in a developed economy, networks of alliances within industries influence many important economic variables, including the rate of innovation, firm performance, and investment behavior. These may have an indirect, but ultimately powerful, effect on the growth and overall robustness of a nation's economy.

SEE ALSO: Capitalism, Social Institutions of; Economy (Sociological Approach); Exchange Network Theory; Management Networks; Networks; Organizations; Organizations and the Theory of the Firm; Political Economy; Social Network Analysis; Social Network Theory; Weak Ties (Strength of)

REFERENCES AND SUGGESTED READINGS

Ahuja, G. (2000) Collaboration Networks, Structural Holes, and Innovation: A Longitudinal Study. *Administrative Science Quarterly* 45: 425–55.

Burt, R. (1980) Autonomy in a Social Topology. *American Journal of Sociology* 85: 892–925.

Coleman, J. (1988) Social Capital in the Creation of Human Capital. *American Journal of Sociology* 94: S105–S120.

Granovetter, M. (1985) Economic Action and Social Structure: The Problem of Embeddedness. *American Journal of Sociology* 91(3): 481–510.

Gulati, R. & Gargiulo, M. (1999) Where Do Interorganizational Networks Come From? *American Journal of Sociology* 40: 1439–93.

Ingram, P. & Roberts, P. (2000) Friendships Among Competitors in the Sydney Hotel Industry. *American Journal of Sociology* 106: 387–423.

Kogut, B. & Walker, G. (2001) The Small World of Germany and the Durability of National Networks. *American Sociological Review* 66: 317–35.

Milgram, S. (1967) The Small World Problem. *Psychology Today* 2: 60–7.

Podolny, J. (2001) Networks as the Pipes and Prisms of the Market. *American Journal of Sociology* 107: 33–60.

Simmel, G. (1955) *Conflict and the Web of Affiliation.* Free Press, Glencoe, IL.

Uzzi, B. (1996) The Sources and Consequences of Embeddedness for the Economic Performance of Organizations: The Network Effect. *American Sociological Review* 61: 674–98.

Watts, D. (1999) Networks, Dynamics, and the Small-World Phenomenon. *American Journal of Sociology* 105: 493–527.

economy, religion and

Rachel M. McCleary

The modern study of religion and economics begins with Adam Smith's *An Inquiry into the Nature and Causes of the Wealth of Nations* (1776). Smith applied his economic analysis to several aspects of religion that researchers since developed with quantitative research. Smith's fundamental contribution to the study of religion was that religious beliefs and activities are rational choices. As in commercial activity, people respond to religious costs and benefits in a predictable, observable manner. People choose a religion and the degree to which they participate and believe (if at all).

In the 1970s, the rational choice approach to religion, or the economics of religion, reinvigorated social science investigation of religion (Young 1997). The first formal model of religious participation was developed by Corry Azzi and Ronald Ehrenberg (1975). Laurence Iannaccone's (1998) literature survey of economics attributes to Azzi and Ehrenberg the framework that served as the basis for future research on religion. Using Gallup survey data, Azzi and Ehrenberg found that the opportunity cost of time influences religious behavior. Within a given household, women whose wages are typically lower will spend more time in religious activity. Likewise, individuals whose real wages increase over time can be expected to participate less in religious activities. Education, just as wages, plays an important role in participation in religious activities. Edward Glaeser and Bruce Sacerdote found that the level of education of believers influences their choice of religion. The payoff for higher-educated people is social capital in the form of networking rather than stronger religious beliefs. Benito Arruñada found that more education increases the costs of participating in the institution of confession. Individuals with higher education tend to engage in moral "self-policing," relying less on priests for such enforcement.

The family and its dynamics, a popular subject of anthropology, sociology, and psychology, are currently undergoing reinterpretation by rational choice theorists. Evelyn Lehrer (1999), using data from the National Survey of Families and Households, looks at how religious upbringing influences the number of years of schooling a person attains. She also explores how a woman's religious preference influences her choice of marriage or cohabitation. Maristella Botticini and Aloysius Siow (2003) reexamine the dowry institution and seek to explain parental choices in using different forms of intergenerational transfers.

Religious extremism, both in non-violent and violent forms, is explained according to rational choice theory for similar reasons. Iannaccone's cost-benefit analysis of strict religions led to the development of a theoretical model of the evolution of organized religion. Taking Ernst Troeltsch's (1931) sect–denomination distinction, Iannaccone applied a cost-induced commitment to organized religion. He argued that denominations and extremist sects can be construed as distinct modes or "clubs" of religious organization based on consumer (believer) preferences. Using the club model of religion, Iannaccone sought to explain the success of strict religions (cults, sects). Using a cost-benefit analysis, Iannaccone argued that people choose to undergo stigma and self-sacrifice and engage in unconventional behavior to eliminate free-riders, thereby increasing the commitment of believers and benefits to members. Iannaccone's economic analysis provided a rational explanation for behavior that other professions categorized as brainwashing or a form of pathological behavior.

Eli Berman (2000, 2003) applied the club model to Israeli Ultra-Orthodox Jews, as well as to Hamas, the Taliban, and the Jewish underground militias. Berman found in the case of the Israeli Ultra-Orthodox community that the benefits of remaining in the group outweighed the costs of sacrifice and stigma. For the Taliban, the sacrifices demanded by the group, seemingly gratuitous acts of violence, destroyed outside options and, thereby, increased group loyalty.

Scholars who investigate the demand side of religion tend to favor the view that religious preferences change over time for both the individual and social groups. Sociologists Roger Finke and Rodney Stark (1992) maintain that individual preferences remain constant. Finke and Stark contend that the supply of religious goods changes over time, not the demand for them. Analyzing membership data beginning in the American colonial period, Finke and Stark argue that religions begin small, supplying the religious goods that consumers want. As the religion grows and more members join, the religion accommodates the variety of membership demands by becoming less strict until it loses its religious relevance and declines.

However, religious strictness can reach an optimal level, after which it becomes detrimental to a religion. Extreme religions deter people from joining. A common example is the Shaker movement that practiced celibacy. Because of its inability to attract new members, it became obsolete. Religious strictness is not the only reason a religion declines. Adam Smith argued that state subsidies to organized religion create a dependency upon a regular and enforceable income. State-subsidized religion tends to change in two ways. It devolves, losing those aspects of religious devotion that are relevant to people practicing their faith and the authority of its doctrine. Second, it tends to become a religion for elites, and to the degree that the clergy itself becomes an elite group in society, of elites. By contrast, those religious groups that depend solely on voluntary contributions must continually address the religious needs of their congregants to stay in existence.

Smith extended his analysis to the evolution of organized religion. Observing the nonconformist religious groups – "upstarts" – Smith noted that the spiritual, imaginative, and emotional bases of the new religious movements successfully challenge state-sanctioned religion. As a reaction to popular criticism of its elitist ways, state religion resorts to coercion, repression, and even violence to maintain its financial, political, and social arrangement in society. Religion, Smith concluded, is more vibrant where there is a disassociation between church and state. The absence of state religion allows for competition, thereby creating an environment for a plurality of religious faiths in society (Smith 1791 [1776]). By showing no preference for one religion over others, but rather permitting any and all religions to flourish, the state encourages an open market in which religious groups engage in rational discussion.

This competitive but non-coercive environment supports an atmosphere of "good temper and moderation." Where there is a state monopoly on religion or an oligopoly among religions, one will find zealousness and the imposition of ideas on the public. Where there is an open market for religion and freedom of speech, one will find moderation and reason.

Correcting Adam Smith's argument, it has been contended that the relaxing of state regulation on religion unleashes competitive forces in the economic marketplace but not necessarily competition among religious faiths (Jeremy 1988). The focus of this variant argument lies with the legal recognition in England during the Industrial Revolution of nonconformist religious groups – the upstarts. These groups challenged the dominant religion – in some cases state religion – with different views of the linkages between salvation and economic activity. Although these nonconformist religious groups did not necessarily increase in membership to challenge the dominant position of the state religion or mainstream faiths, they contributed to and altered economic activity. Thus, state inclusion of nonconformist religious groups can have a positive effect on the economic productivity of society without seriously challenging state religion. This variant view is compatible with what Smith said the effect of religious pluralism would be: the continual subdividing of sects into numerous ones and small units so that a single religion does not dominate (Smith 1791 [1776]).

Economic historians have applied economic analysis to religious institutions. For example, Robert Ekelund, Robert Hebert, and Robert Tollison treat a religious organization as an economic firm to explain the rent-seeking practices of the medieval church. More recently, they assess the competitive entry of Protestants into the medieval religion market (Ekelund et al. 2002). They analyze the Roman Catholic Church's response in the form of the Catholic Reformation. Timur Kuran (2004) investigates the effects of Islamic legal institutions on economic growth and the distribution of goods. Kuran finds the institutions that generated evolutionary bottlenecks include the Islamic law of inheritance, which inhibited capital accumulation; the absence in Islamic law of the concept of a corporation and the consequent weaknesses of civil society; and the *waqf* – the religious endowment of property for specific, usually philanthropic, purposes to the exclusion of all other uses – which locked vast resources into unproductive organizations for the delivery of social services. All of these obstacles to economic development were largely overcome through radical reforms initiated in the nineteenth century. Nevertheless, traditional Islamic law remains an impediment to economic growth.

A recent application of economic analysis to religion and religious beliefs is the cross-country quantitative analysis of Robert Barro and Rachel McCleary (2003). Using international survey data on religiosity for a broad panel of countries, they investigate the effects of church attendance and religious beliefs on economic growth. They find that religious beliefs are more important for economic activity than religious participation. Rene Stulz and Rohan Williamson, using data on financial markets of various countries, find that a country's principal religious preference is relevant for predicting creditor rights. The improvement of data collected on various religions as well as aspects of religious preferences and institutions will continue to spur research on religion, particularly from an international perspective. The more important data sets used are described below.

The World Values Survey (WVS), directed by Ronald Inglehart at the Inter-University Consortium for Political and Social Research (ICPSR), offers four waves of surveys (1981–4; 1990–3; 1995–7; 1999–2001), now covering over 50 countries. Each survey includes a series of questions on religious beliefs, activities, commitments, and values, as well as a variety of economic, political, and social variables. For discussions and uses of these data, see Inglehart and Baker (2000).

Another useful data set is the International Social Survey Program (ISSP), which is a cross-national collaboration of surveys (including the General Social Survey or GSS for the United States). The 1991 and 1998 waves are dedicated to religion, the latter for 30 countries. As with the WVS, the ISSP includes an array of other variables. For discussions and uses of the ISSP data, see International Social Survey Program 2002 (available at www.issp.org/data.htm).

Gallup International has collected cross-national survey data on religion for many years. The Gallup Millennium Survey has useful indicators on church attendance and religious beliefs for over 50 countries in 1999; see Gallup International Millennium Survey 2002 (available at www.gallup-international.com/survey15.htm). Currently, these data are not easily accessible to researchers, although negotiations with Gallup International are underway.

Jonathan Fox and Shmuel Sandler (2004) are assembling a religion and state database (RAS) in which they classify the relation between religion and state into four broad groupings: separation of religion and state, discrimination against minority religions, restrictions on majority religions, and religious legislation. They examine religion and state separation between 1990 and 2002 in 152 states with populations of over 1 million.

The American Religion Data Archive (ARDA), under the leadership of Roger Finke at Penn State University, will prove beneficial. The ARDA (available at www.thearda.com) is widely used as a source of data on religion for the United States and Canada. It provides additional software enhancements for selected ecological files. For the most heavily used files, such as Church and Church Membership Surveys, the site offers "Mapping" and "Report" options. Here state or national maps on church membership totals or rates can be constructed for any denomination in the data file. Users can also get a profile of religious denominations for any state, county, or metropolitan area selected.

SEE ALSO: Attitudes and Behavior; Buddhism; Capital: Economic, Cultural, and Social; Catholicism; Hinduism; Political Economy; Protestantism; Religion; Religion, Sociology of; Smith, Adam

REFERENCES AND SUGGESTED READINGS

Azzi, C. & Ehrenberg, R. (1975) Household Allocation of Time and Church Attendance. *Journal of Political Economy* 83, 1 (February): 27–56.

Barro, R. & McCleary, R. (2003) Religion and Economic Growth. *American Sociological Review* 68 (October): 760–81.

Berman, E. (2000) Sect, Subsidy, and Sacrifice: An Economist's View of Ultra-Orthodox Jews. *Quarterly Journal of Economics* 115 (August): 905–53.

Berman, E. (2003) Hamas, Taliban, and the Jewish Underground: An Economist's View of Radical Religious Militias. National Bureau of Economic Research Paper, September.

Botticini, M. & Siow, A. (2003) Why Dowries? *American Economic Review* 93, 4 (September): 1385–98.

Ekelund, R., Hebert, R., & Tollison, R. (2002) An Economic Analysis of the Protestant Reformation. *Journal of Political Economy* 110(3): 646–71.

Finke, R. & Stark, R. (1992) *The Churching of America, 1776–1990: Winners and Losers in Our Religious Economy*. Rutgers University Press, New Brunswick, NJ.

Fox, J. & Sandler, S. (2004) World Separation of Religion and State in the Twenty-First Century. Paper presented at the International Studies Association Conference in Montreal, Canada, March.

Iannaccone, L. (1998) Introduction to the Economics of Religion. *Journal of Economic Literature* 36 (September): 1465–96.

Inglehart, R. & Baker, W. (2000) Modernization, Cultural Change, and the Persistence of Traditional Values. *American Sociological Review* 65: 19–51.

Jeremy, D. (Ed.) (1988) *Business and Religion in Britain*. Gower, Aldershot.

Kuran, T. (2001) The Provision of Public Goods under Islamic Law: Origins, Impact, and Limitations of the *Waqf* System. *Law and Society Review* 35, 4 (December): 841–97.

Kuran, T. (2004) The Economic Ascent of the Middle East's Religious Minorities: The Role of Islamic Legal Pluralism. *Journal of Legal Studies* 33 (June): 475–515.

Lehrer, E. (1999) Religion as a Determinant of Educational Attainment: An Economic Perspective. *Social Science Research* 28: 358–79.

Smith, A. (1791 [1776]) *An Inquiry into the Nature and Causes of the Wealth of Nations*, 6th edn., Strahan, London, Book V, Article III.

Troeltsch, E. (1931) *The Social Teaching of the Christian Churches*, Vols. 1 and 2. Foreword by J. L. Adams. Westminster/John Knox Press, Louisville, KY.

Young, L. A. (Ed.) (1997) *Rational Choice Theory and Religion: Summary and Assessment*. Routledge, New York.

economy (sociological approach)

Thomas J. Fararo

The general problem of how to conceptualize and explain the relations of the economy to wider contexts of human behavior has been one of the main themes of major theorists in the sociological tradition. In the classical phase of the tradition, Marx, Weber, and Durkheim each treated the problem. In the writings of Marx, what has been called the base–superstructure model rests upon the concept of a mode of production that includes social relations of production and forces of production, corresponding approximately to economy and technology, respectively. Social classes consist of persons who occupy the same position in the social relations of production, such as lord and serf in the feudal mode of production and capitalist and wage laborer in the capitalist mode of production. The dominant class employs its power advantage to shape a superstructure consisting of non-economic institutions along with a dominant ideology reflecting the interests of the ruling class. This model is associated with a theory of social change, as in *The Communist Manifesto*, in which Marx and Engels analyze the historical dynamics of the rise and fall of capitalism in terms of revolutionary change involving conflicts among aristocrats, who represent the declining feudal mode of production, and the bourgeoisie, who in ushering in the capitalist mode of production are also giving birth to their own "gravediggers," the class of wage laborers.

One implication of this analysis is that cultural phenomena are reflections of economic and political interests, whether in support of the status quo or antagonistic to it. In the writings of Weber, however, we find cultural orientations playing not just a reflective role relative to the economy. In *The Protestant Ethic and the Spirit of Capitalism* (1904), unintended consequences of religious ideas arising out of the Protestant Reformation are hypothesized to have been an important factor in the rise of modern rational capitalism in the West.

Calvinists were motivated by their religious ideas to seek economic success in the world and yet to maintain an ascetic lifestyle, a combination quite favorable to the formation of a bourgeois class. Eventually, however, as some of the religious spokesmen of the time feared, the religious element of the ethic was undermined by its very success in stimulating material gain. The result is the culture of modern rational capitalism, which no longer has or needs a religious meaning. In this and other studies, Weber set out a wide-ranging sociology of the economy that included, in particular, complex and historically variable relationships between culture and economy. For Weber, the emergence of modern rational capitalism is only one instance of a wider historical process in which other institutional forms of rational social organization developed, especially bureaucracy. Indeed, he emphasizes that the modern capitalist enterprise, no less than the modern state, is a bureaucratic structure within which all action is organized in terms of norms of efficiency.

Durkheim made another type of theoretical contribution pertaining to economy and society. In one of his major works, *The Division of Labor in Society* (1893), he produced a new type of analysis of the division of labor. More than a century earlier, Adam Smith, in his treatise *The Wealth of Nations* (1776), had demonstrated the economic function of the division of labor in terms of gains in productivity. By contrast, Durkheim traces out its *social* function in the sense of social integration. He argues that simpler societies with little division of labor are held together mainly by the similarity of sentiments and ideas of their members, while complex societies with an extensive division of labor are held together by an organic form of solidarity, i.e., by the effects of the extensive interdependence of the differentiated members. Thus, in a somewhat oversimplified statement, we can say that just as Weber's study illuminated the relation between the economy and its cultural environment, Durkheim's study illuminated the relation between the economy and what the later social theorist Talcott Parsons called "the societal community," a system of social relationships among individuals and groups.

The approach that Parsons took was to place the economy in its larger setting of human action and society in such a way as to delineate its various environments and how they constrained and enabled economic action. This approach is grounded in an action frame of reference and in a methodology of functional analysis. Any system of action has four functional problems: adaptation to its environment (A), definition and attainment of its goals (G), the integration of action elements (I), and the maintenance of meanings that are presupposed in the various actions (L). This AGIL scheme is applied recursively starting from the most general level of human action in which there is a non-action (biophysical) environment. Behavioral systems, personality systems, social systems, and cultural systems respectively arise as solutions to the AGIL problems at this general action level. In particular, a social system has a structure that consists of institutionalized normative culture, e.g., the definition of rights and obligations.

From this analytical standpoint, the biophysical environment of the action system as a whole includes the living bodies of the members of the social system and the nature of the habitat in which they are collectively embedded. Thus the social system's adaptation problem – which we may denote IA – is one of gaining some degree of institutionalized control of these environmental states. For instance, human bodies have their own functional imperatives, such as adequate food, water, and shelter. The habitat may enable but also constrain how these needs can be satisfied. Thus, provision of these primary needs in the given biophysical environment and of other needs of personalities that arise in and through action processes within a cultural tradition constitutes a functional imperative of the social system to which its economy is the ongoing institutional solution, perhaps quite inadequate from a normative point of view in the sense that what prevails may be a condition of widespread hunger and/or alienation.

As a subsystem of the social system, the structure of the economy is defined in terms of differentiated institutionalized normative culture in the sense of socially sanctioned rights pertaining to ownership, contract, employment, and the like. The actions of the members of the social system also may be analyzed, not only in terms of how the social system "solves" its adaptation (IA) problem but also in terms of how it produces some solution to its political (IG) problem, its social integrative (II) problem, and what Parsons later called its "fiduciary" (IL) problem of maintaining social value commitments.

Parsons and Smelser in their volume *Economy and Society* (1956) treat each of these problems and solutions in terms of their system model, so that a social system includes an economy, but also three other functional subsystems, namely a polity, a social community, and a fiduciary system, respectively, which form the *social* environment of the economy. Its wider *action* environment consists of behavioral, personality, and cultural systems. Parsons and Smelser also attempt to delineate the nature of intra-economic processes in terms of the AGIL scheme as applied to the economy as a system with its own four functional problems, e.g., adaptation of its social environment with its political, social integrative, and fiduciary features. Concretely, these features may include, for instance, a weak or strong state, a weak or strong legal tradition, and an educational system that provides more or less appropriate skills and motivation for participation in productive activities. That these variable features profoundly constrain and/or enable productive economic activity is illustrated by the contemporary difficulties of establishing a market economy in a social environment in which there is an unstable polity, little by way of enforceable laws protecting private property, and an educational system that discourages individual initiative.

Functional analysis has certain conceptual implications. Parsons and Smelser (1956: 14) note, for instance, that "the whole society is in one sense part of the economy, in that all of its units, individual and collective, *participate in* the economy. ... But no concrete unit participates *only* in the economy. Hence, no concrete unit is '*purely* economic.'" This is best illustrated by reference to collective units. Schools (fiduciary specialists) participate in the economy as purchasers of needed facilities, services, and supplies. In a capitalist system, firms (economic specialists) participate in the fiduciary system that reproduces capitalist values simply by hiring workers, making profits, distributing dividends, and the like, all of which contribute to retention of value orientations supportive of

capitalism. As Weber noted, modern capitalism no longer requires religion for the reproduction of the culture of capitalism. It should be noted, however, that financial scandals involving corporations are dysfunctional in terms of the fiduciary function, undermining faith in the virtues of capitalism.

Many of the interactions in a differentiated social system are functionally specialized exchanges of various sorts and, in the aggregate, produce market or market-like phenomena. For instance, the labor market connects the economy to the fiduciary system in that the latter produces actors who can take positions in some context of production that enables them to enact the corresponding roles in relation to others. At the micro level, two people may engage in an exchange process, one of whom is in a representative role for a firm while the other may be connected to a household as one of its employed members and whose income performs a significant function in the context of that social subsystem of the system under analysis. At the macro level, this is but one exchange among numerous others that together form what Parsons and Smelser call an "interchange system," which connects the economy and the fiduciary system.

Since the Parsons–Smelser model is abstractly general, it can have applications at various levels. As one example, consider the social system of the world, "world society." Its polity is a fractured one, consisting of numerous sovereign states with competing claims and incessant outbursts of violent conflicts. Its social integration is proceeding rapidly, however, via the impact of increasingly faster and more efficient modes of communication as well as the formation of collectivities that transcend nation-state boundaries. In this context, there is the world economy with its increasing globalization of production and consumption as well as numerous markets still enclosed within more local sectors of the world society. This world society is embedded in a world system of human action that includes cultural systems such as value systems, religions, ideologies, and sciences. World fiduciary processes in the form of education, for instance, reproduce particularistic values associated with national or other identities but also, although not uniformly, other more universalistic values that are incompletely realized in world institutions such as the United Nations. Globalization, in large part driven by economic actions, is a historical process that has increasingly come under analysis by sociologists as they interpret the world economy as embedded in a larger system of action that includes world culture, world polity, and so on.

Although the model proposed by Parsons and Smelser is of considerable value in addressing the question of how the economy relates to its environments, issues relating to lack of clarity and rigor in the formulation of the model have limited its usefulness to other analysts of economy and society. Perhaps for this reason, the tradition of economic sociology went into a kind of hibernation for about two decades before being revived in the mid-1980s. At about that time, a number of research programs that involve both theory and empirical investigations were initiated. Taken together, these programs have been called "the new economic sociology" by Granovetter (1985) in an influential article that stimulated the rebirth of the field.

The key theme of this new economic sociology is the analysis of economic phenomena in terms of social structure and culture, treating economic action as embedded in a wider context of social and cultural relationships. Although the formulation is similar to that of Parsons and Smelser, the newly reborn field emphasizes the empirical application of more recent sociological ideas such as social network and social capital and also intersects cultural sociology, another major field of sociological investigation. Very importantly, the field now includes a relatively large number of empirical investigators in contrast to the small number of earlier analysts. Hence a summary statement of the state of sociological research on economy and society is difficult to make in a very fluid and rapidly growing field. Swedberg (2003) sets out a rare effort in this direction and also has co-edited a handbook (Smelser & Swedberg 2003). Chapters in the latter point to the way in which recent work has added rich empirical detail to the relationships between the economy and its social environments, for instance political and educational institutions.

A brief indication of the sort of theory and research characteristic of the new economic

sociology can be communicated by reference to investigations that emphasize social structural elements, especially those relating to the concepts of social network and social capital.

A social network is a population of actors – individual or collective – that are in some mode of connection with one another which mediates the form and content of their interaction. Actors may be dependent upon certain others for resources or they may trust certain others, among other types of connections. For instance, in application to an economy, one theory pertains to the argument that there are advantages to actors in certain positions within networks. A network may consist of a series of largely disconnected components except for certain relations that connect actors in distinct components. Such a network has "structural holes" – sectors with many absent relations. Actors whose relations form a bridge between otherwise disconnected components have certain competitive advantages in terms of information and control. It has been shown that they "enjoy higher rates of return on their investments because they know about, have a hand in, and exercise control over, more rewarding opportunities" (Burt 1992: 46). In another example of a social structural approach to economic phenomena, Baker (1984) analyzes stock options trading on the floor of a major securities exchange in the US, showing how price volatility is a function of network variables.

The economic concept of capital includes physical and financial resources employed in productive activities. Economists have extended this concept in referring to educational training as "human capital," consisting of resources in the form of learned skills and the like. Sociologists have made use of a still further extension of the concept in analyzing the benefits of "social capital," whereby social relationships function as resources that actors can employ to attain their ends. Like much else in social life, this particular form of capital is a byproduct of social relations formed for other reasons. For instance, among members of a certain occupation, a social club may be formed in order for the members to enjoy convivial activities, but at a later time, when some of the members become unemployed, the club may function as an informal employment service (Coleman 1990).

The extended concept of capital also plays a major role in the field theory of Pierre Bourdieu (1986), whose studies intersect economic and cultural sociology. A field may be defined as a competitive social space of positions characterized in terms of the total volume and relative composition of various forms of capital. While economic theory postulates consumers who make rational choices based on given preferences or tastes, field theory provides a conceptual basis for representing the heterogeneous social structural basis for such tastes, treating them as modes by which actors make distinctions (e.g., in the clothing or cars that they can afford to purchase) which in turn serve to distinguish them from other actors. In a somewhat similar mode in terms of investigating meanings and functions of economic phenomena from a wider perspective, Zelizer (1994) has emphasized that the social meaning of money extends beyond its function as a medium of exchange in the economy.

Comparing the new economic sociology to "the old" in the sense of the systems model of Parsons and Smelser, a major contrast is that Parsons and Smelser aimed to integrate sociological theory and economic theory by embedding economic concepts and mechanisms within a unified framework consisting of the general theory of action and an accompanying methodology of functional analysis. For instance, they attempt to "find a place" within the AGIL scheme for the factors of production set out by economic theorists. Labor, for instance, is a value commitment to work – with a variable cultural work ethic, following up Weber's ideas in this regard – that is acquired in the fiduciary system (in this instance in households) and enters the economy through an interchange process rooted in exchange processes regulated by an institution which, in market societies, is the employment contract. In a similar mode, but not always clearly or convincingly, it is argued that through interchange processes, capital enters the economy from the polity and organizing (entrepreneurial) activity enters it from the social integrative system. The fourth factor of production, traditionally "land" in economics, is somewhat vaguely treated in terms of facilities that are "givens" for the shorter-term economic processes. Similarly, the various types of markets and other processes

(e.g., investment) treated in economic theory are "located" in terms of the AGIL scheme.

By contrast, the new economic sociology largely disavows any attempted integration of theory of the two disciplines and, in fact, the research often is initiated in a polemical mode as opposing some assumptions made in economic theory. However, in both its old and its new form, the sociology of the economy is characterized by the application of sociological concepts and theories to analyze economic phenomena. In some instances, the concepts relate closely to some traditional economic concept such as capital. In other instances, the concepts have no linkage to traditional economic ideas. This is especially true of network concepts such as structural holes and bridges. In either case, the sociological analysis – whether in older forms or the new forms – tends to differ from economic analysis. The reason for this is that sociology, as a discipline, is concerned above all with patterns of social relations arising out of and shaping social interaction. It is this shared perspective that sociologists have employed in the analysis of the economy in relation to society.

SEE ALSO: Bourdieu, Pierre; Capitalism, Social Institutions of; Culture, Economy and; Durkheim, Émile; Ecology and Economy; Economic Development; Economic Geography; Economy, Culture and; Economy, Networks and; Economy, Religion and; Education and Economy; Emotions and Economy; Engels, Friedrich; Ideology, Economy and; Marx, Karl; Parsons, Talcott; Smith, Adam; Social Network Theory; Weber, Max

REFERENCES AND SUGGESTED READINGS

Baker, W. (1984) The Social Structure of a National Securities Market. *American Journal of Sociology* 89(4): 775–811.

Bourdieu, P. (1984) *Distinction: A Social Critique of the Judgment of Taste.* Harvard University Press, Cambridge, MA.

Burt, R. S. (1992) *Structural Holes: The Social Structure of Competition.* Harvard University Press, Cambridge, MA.

Coleman, J. S. (1990) *Foundations of Social Theory.* Harvard University Press, Cambridge, MA.

Granovetter, M. (1985) Economic Action and Social Structure: The Problem of Embeddedness. *American Journal of Sociology* 91: 481–510.

Parsons, T. & Smelser, N. J. (1956) *Economy and Society*. Free Press, New York.

Smelser, N. & Swedberg, R. (Eds.) (2003) *Handbook of Economic Sociology*, 2nd edn. Russell Sage Foundation and Princeton University Press, Princeton.

Swedberg, R. (2003) *Principles of Economic Sociology*. Princeton University Press, Princeton.

Zelizer, V. (1994) *The Social Meaning of Money*. Basic Books, New York.

education

Anna Strassmann Mueller

Changes in developed economies and societies stemming from the Industrial Revolution have shifted responsibilities for the education of young people from the family and community to schools. Schools are now a major institution, educating the vast majority of children and youth in the developed world and functioning as a primary engine of change in developing countries. Although education brings about changes in society as a whole as well as in individuals, schools are also influenced by larger social forces. Sociological theories address these central roles that schools play in society from differing perspectives.

The functionalist paradigm emphasizes the role that education plays for society. Émile Durkheim, one of the founders of sociology, was among the first educational researchers to focus on the function schools serve for the larger society. Durkheim (1961) argued that the main goal of education was to socialize individuals so that they share values with the larger society. Ensuring that all students received the same moral education allowed for a more integrated society with less social conflict about wrong behaviors or attitudes. A second important functionalist perspective on education developed in economics through research on human capital (Schultz 1961). The human capital perspective describes education as a set of investments that increase individuals' knowledge and skills, which in turn improves national labor productivity and economic growth. Education then becomes an important tool for societies to increase the efficiency and size of their economy.

While the functionalist perspective emphasizes the role of education for society as a whole, the conflict paradigm focuses on divisions within society that education maintains or reinforces. Max Weber (2000) was one of the first to argue that education serves dual and potentially conflicting functions for society. First, schools can be an equalizing institution where individuals, regardless of their social status, can gain access to high-status jobs through their own talent and hard work. Second, schools can reinforce existing status hierarchies by limiting opportunities to individuals from high-status backgrounds. In other words, Weber recognized schools' potential to either facilitate or block social mobility. Weber's incorporation of the notion of social status into the function of schools in society was extremely influential in shaping sociological research on education. Randall Collins (1979), Samuel Bowles, Herbert Gintis, and others furthered Weber's ideas on status attainment by arguing that schools socialize individuals to accept their place in an unjust, capitalist society. This work shifted the emphasis found in human capital theory away from schools as providers of skills and training to schools as providers of hollow credentials that are rewarded in the labor market. Critically, these credentials do not represent higher levels of skills, but simply serve as status markers that employers use to sort workers into low- and high-prestige occupations.

Both historically and when comparing countries today, the structure of a country's educational system is closely linked to its economic and political history. Developed countries are generally characterized by a history of relatively steady economic growth, a stable political system, and freedom from the devastation of war. This common context enables developed countries to form a cohesive formal schooling system that serves all children until at least the age of 15 or 16. In recent decades, developed nations have incorporated the ideals of equality of educational opportunity and providing opportunities to children from disadvantaged backgrounds into their goals for educational policy.

Though all developed nations provide universal education and many are motivated by similar ideals, the structure of schooling can vary drastically from developed country to developed country (for an overview, see Brint 1998). In Japan, France, and Sweden, the school system is run by a central governmental ministry of education that ensures standardized curricula and funding. Other countries, such as Germany, Canada, and the US, are more decentralized and allow local or regional governments to maintain control over public education. Additionally, the school systems in these nations vary in how they structure opportunities to learn and earn credentials. In his classic article, Ralph Turner (1960) contrasted the English and US school systems, characterizing the former as a "sponsored" system, in which talent is identified in the early years and nurtured in a stratified system. The US system, on the other hand, is a "contest" system, consisting of a series of contests in which all students compete on a level playing field. Though "sponsored" and "contest" systems are "ideal types," most developed nations' school systems reflect aspects of sponsored or contest systems.

In the developing world, many countries have been independent from colonizing powers for approximately only 50 years and do not have the same history of political stability, economic security, and times of peace that privilege developed countries. These instabilities (along with problems related to poverty) affect the ability of developing countries to provide and prioritize universal education. In many developing countries, the school system is inherited in large part from former colonizers and is heavily shaped by the policies of the World Bank. The World Bank promotes a model of schooling that emphasizes primary schools, private spending, balances equity and efficiency, and discourages vocational education. Though the structure and experience World Bank policies provide can improve schooling priorities in developing nations, they sometimes do not recognize that factors unique to a particular country may require modifications. A central question concerning the role of education in developing nations concerns how important education systems are to economic growth. Much of the research on education in developing nations examines this question and generally finds that having a disciplined and educated labor force is a positive and important step in economic development.

Though commonalities in the structure of schooling exist across countries in the developed and developing world, each country is generally unique in the development of its particular educational system. Systems of education not only reflect national values and attitudes, they also play a major role in shaping national culture and social status hierarchy. In the US, the idea of public schooling – or the common school – developed in the early nineteenth century as a response to political and economic shifts in American society (see Parkerson & Parkerson 2001 for a history). Prior to common schooling, the majority of Americans were educated by their families, and only children from wealthier families could afford formal schooling. As the US moved away from a barter-and-trade economy toward markets where goods were exchanged for cash, white Protestant Americans from the middle and working classes recognized that the fragmented and informal system of schooling was no longer adequate preparation for their children to be competitive in the market-driven economy. This realization led these Americans to demand that a quality primary education be made available to their children. The ideal of equality emphasized during the American Revolution meant that there was already growing political support among the Protestant political elite for the idea of public education for white children.

The end result of these forces was the development of the common school. Common schools had two main goals: first, to provide knowledge and skills necessary to being an active member of economic and social life; and second, to create Americans who value the same things – namely, patriotism, achievement, competition, and Protestant moral and religious values. Significantly, these goals were important both to individuals trying to make it in the new economic and social order and to the success of solidifying the young United States into a coherent nation. Religious diversity was not tolerated in the nascent nation, and Catholic immigrants were often seen as threats to the dominant Protestant way of life. Therefore, though common schools were open to all white

Americans, the emphasis on Protestant values (which went hand in hand with anti-Catholic attitudes) alienated many Catholics. This religious tension eventually led Catholics to pursue alternative schooling and resulted in the development of Catholic private schools.

Though common schools provided more equitable access to education than the previous informal system, these schools still reflected the values of the ruling elite – white Anglo-Saxon Protestants – in US society. In addition to appreciating Protestant values over those of other religions, educating white boys was generally seen as more important than educating white girls as white boys were more likely to benefit from their education upon entry into the formal labor market. Furthermore, African Americans, freed or enslaved, were almost categorically excluded from common schools in the early 1800s as the flawed "ideal of equality" applied only to white Americans.

Despite the development of the common school, elite white Protestant Americans were able to maintain educational superiority by opting out of the common school system. The elite private and boarding school system began before the American Revolution and flourished during the nineteenth century (at the same time that the common school system was expanding). Though the growing public education system diminished the percentage of secondary students in private schools, private schools maintained an exclusivity that appealed to elite parents eager to pass on status and advantage to their children. In *Preparing for Power: America's Elite Boarding Schools* (1985), authors Cookson and Persell explore the admissions process and the demographic characteristics of "the chosen ones," America's most privileged students. Historically, these elite schools tended to have a homogeneous student body in terms of family background, religion, and race, and admission was based not on openly stated academic requirements but on a complicated balance of merit, family wealth, social standing, and an individual's ability to fit the school's ideal. Thus, the presentation of self as a person of status – someone with ambition, confidence, and poise – was just as important as academic capacities to gaining access to America's most elite secondary education. Though these private schools continue to promote an

elite social class identity, currently they also face pressure to diversify the racial composition of their student bodies.

While elite private schools have historically allowed privileged Americans to opt out of public schooling, religious schools have offered an important private alternative to non-elite, and sometimes marginalized, Americans throughout the history of the US. Catholic schools were a part of Colonial America and are among some of the oldest educational institutions in the US. In contrast to elite private schools, religious schools had a moral purpose of teaching religious beliefs and producing religious leaders. Beginning in the 1800s, Catholic schools provided an alternative to the public school where children read the Protestant version of the Bible. Today, Catholic schools serve a more diverse student population in terms of race, social class, and religious beliefs. Catholic schools today are known for providing good opportunities to learn and prepare for college (Bryk et al. 1993). Critics suggest that Catholic schools select more promising students, an option not available to public schools.

Though research on elite and Catholic private schools suggests that access to a private versus public education affects students' academic opportunities, inequalities between schools within the public sector have long plagued the American educational system, with serious implications for children with no choice other than public schooling. As mentioned previously, the common school system generally excluded African American children until after the end of the Civil War and Reconstruction. Though the end of slavery meant that the common school system finally included African American children, they were generally educated in separate facilities (see Orfield & Eaton 1996 for a history). By 1896, the idea of "separate but equal" schools was officially sanctioned by the Supreme Court through its decision in *Plessy* v. *Ferguson*. Racially segregated schools became the norm across the US, though whether this segregation was by law or by practice varied by state and region. Equitable distribution of resources between racially segregated schools never existed; white schools received substantially more financial and academic support. "Separate but equal" schools were eventually declared inherently unequal in the Supreme Court decision *Brown* v. *Board of Education of Topeka* (1954), and schools were ordered to desegregate "with all deliberate speed."

Though *Brown* is perhaps one of the most widely celebrated Supreme Court decisions, schools in the US have failed to reflect the ideals of desegregation and educational equality put forth in the ruling. Early research in sociology of education recognized that stratification in educational attainment was related to students' family background, such as race or ethnicity, rather than simply differences in achievement test scores (e.g., Coleman et al. 1966). These differences were social and had to do with the schools' social context rather than factors that could be affected by redistribution of funding levels alone. Since the Coleman Report (1966) and its political consequences of busing that shocked the nation, educational researchers and policymakers have struggled to know how to provide equality of educational opportunity within a context of socioeconomic inequality.

Beginning around 1980, sociologists of education turned their attention to stratification systems at work *within* schools. Secondary schools tend to group students in courses or "tracks" (such as academic, general, or vocational), and through these groupings schools can either reinforce or disrupt the relationship between family background and attainment. Typically, the high school curriculum is organized into sequences of courses in which subject knowledge gained from one course prepares a student for the next course. Mobility between sequences is restricted and forms the foundation of a stratification system for adolescents. Furthermore, schools tend to provide more resources, such as higher-quality instruction, to students in higher-level courses, which can have serious consequences for low-ability students (Hallinan 1994). The result is that students' course-taking patterns follow a trajectory or sequence of courses over the years of high school in which mobility between course sequences is unusual. This is especially true in mathematics, where mobility into the elite college preparatory classes is nearly impossible after the sequence has begun. Students' placement in these sequences explains much of why family background is linked to students' attainment and is strongly related to a variety of

outcomes that indicate students' basic life chances.

Research on stratification within schools further confirmed the results of Coleman's earlier analysis on equity in education – schools are more effective at educating students from privileged family backgrounds. Because schools have been idealized as a great equalizing force, understanding why family background is linked strongly to education became the next important goal of sociology of education.

Annette Lareau (1987), building on Pierre Bourdieu's (1973) idea of cultural capital, offered one explanation of how parents transmit advantages to their children when she found that parents interacted with teachers and schools very differently depending on their social class backgrounds. In addition to conditioning how parents interact with the school, parents' cultural capital also influences how they socialize their children. Lareau describes middle-class parents' childrearing strategies as "concerted cultivation" or active fostering of children's growth through adult-organized activities (e.g., soccer, music lessons) and through encouraging critical and original thinking. Working-class and poor parents, on the other hand, support their children's "natural growth" by providing the conditions necessary for their child's development, but leaving structure of leisure activities to the children. These different styles have implications for students' abilities to take advantage of opportunities in schools.

Coleman's concept of social capital articulated another way that families transmit advantages to their children. In parenting, social capital refers to "the norms, the social networks, and the relationships between adults and children that are of value for the child's growing up" and can exist within families and communities (Coleman 1987: 334). Social capital within families taps how close parents and children are and how closely parents are able to monitor their child's development. For example, Coleman (1988) found that a higher percentage of children from single-parent families (who have less social capital in the home) drop out during high school than children from intact families. Social capital in communities is also important, as Coleman et al. (1982) demonstrated: students in Catholic high schools were less likely to drop out compared to their peers in other private and public schools, not because of school-related differences (such as quality curriculum), but rather because of the close-knit adult relationships surrounding Catholic schools. The cohesive Catholic community allowed adults to better transmit norms about staying in school to teenagers.

Though the principal manifest function of schools is undoubtedly to provide opportunities for learning, schools also serve as the primary location for social interaction with peers and for the development of adolescent cultures. Since Durkheim first emphasized schools as a socializing institution, sociologists have investigated how schools' adolescent cultures affect adolescents' priorities, goals, and behaviors. James Coleman's *The Adolescent Society* (1961) recognized the importance of "adolescent culture" in schools to the decisions, both academic and social, that adolescents make. Coleman stated that adolescents turn to each other for social rewards, not to adult communities; therefore, understanding the value systems of adolescent society is key to understanding what motivates students. Importantly, for some adolescents, the goals of formal schooling – achievement, engagement – are reflected in the adolescent culture; however, when students rebel against the formal goals of schooling, it can reinforce preexisting inequalities based on family background.

Fordham and Ogbu (1986) have examined how adolescents' oppositional culture to schooling develops and how it explains in part the links between family background and students' achievement. Given the history of racism in the US, Fordham and Ogbu argue that doing well in school has come to represent "acting white" to African American youth in an urban school. This may lead many African American students who are academically able to perform significantly below their capabilities. It also creates a tension for African American students who want to succeed academically; not only do they have to cope with the challenge of coursework, but they also have to deal with the burden of appearing to act white. More recently, this perspective has been challenged by researchers who argue that African American students actually hold educational values in high esteem and do not reject academic success.

Much of the sociological research on education has focused on equity – with good reason. Education has serious implications for adolescents' future lives. Individuals' academic credentials affect the jobs they are able to get and the incomes they earn. Individuals with a college degree earn higher wages than those with a high school degree who earn more than high school dropouts (Arum & Hout 2000). Educational attainment also has serious implications for health throughout the life course. More highly educated individuals experience better health (including self-perceived health, morbidity, and mortality) than people with less education (Ross & Mirowsky 1999). Education also shapes the social relationships that individuals form. People tend to marry others with similar amounts of education. Taken together, these findings indicate that education plays a powerful role in individuals' lives. Though we don't fully understand *how* education affects these diverse aspects of the human experience, it is clear that education is an important social institution.

SEE ALSO: *Brown* v. *Board of Education*; Colleges and Universities; Community College; Cultural Capital in Schools; Dropping Out of School; Educational Attainment; Educational Inequality; Globalization, Education and; Opportunities for Learning; School Segregation, Desegregation; Schools, Common; Schools, Public; Schools, Religious; Social Capital and Education; Status Attainment; Tracking

REFERENCES AND SUGGESTED READINGS

Arum, R. & Hout, M. (2000) The Early Returns: The Transition From School to Work in the United States. In: Arum, R. & Beattie, I. R. (Eds.), *The Structure of Schooling: Readings in the Sociology of Education*. McGraw-Hill, New York, pp. 423–34.

Bourdieu, P. (1973) Cultural Reproduction and Social Reproduction. In: *Knowledge, Education, and Cultural Change*. Tavistock, London.

Bowles, S. & Gintis, H. (1976) *Schooling in Capitalist America: Educational Reform and the Contradictions of Economic Life*. Basic Books, New York.

Brint, S. (1998) *Schools and Societies*. Pine Forge Press, Thousand Oaks, CA.

Bryk, A. S., Lee, V. E., & Holland, P. B. (1993) *Catholic Schools and the Common Good.* Harvard University Press, Cambridge, MA.

Coleman, J. S. (1961) *The Adolescent Society: The Social Life of Teenagers and Its Impact on Education.* Free Press, New York.

Coleman, J. S. (1987) Families and Schools. *Educational Researcher* 16(6): 32–8.

Coleman, J. S. (1988) Social Capital in the Creation of Human Capital. *American Journal of Sociology* 94 (Supplement): S95–S120.

Coleman, J. S., Campbell, E. Q., Hobson, C. J., McPartland, J., Mood, A. M., Weinfall, F. D., & York, R. L. (1966) *Equality of Educational Opportunity.* Department of Health, Education, and Welfare, Washington, DC.

Coleman, J. S., Hoffer, T., & Kilgore, S. (1982) Cognitive Outcomes in Public and Private Schools. *Sociology of Education* 55(2/3): 65–76.

Collins, R. (1979) *The Credential Society: A Historical Sociology of Education and Stratification.* Academic Press, New York.

Cookson, P. W. & Persell, C. H. (1985) *Preparing for Power: America's Elite Boarding Schools.* Basic Books, New York.

Durkheim, É. (1961) *Moral Education: A Study in the Theory and Application of Sociology of Education.* Trans. E. K. Wilson & H. Schnurer. Free Press, New York.

Fordham, S. & Ogbu, J. U. (1986) Black Students' School Success: Coping With the Burden of "Acting White." *Urban Review* 18(3): 176–206.

Hallinan, M. T. (1994) Tracking: From Theory to Practice. *Sociology of Education* 67(2): 79–84.

Lareau, A. (1987) Social Class Differences in Family–School Relationships: The Importance of Cultural Capital. *Sociology of Education* 60: 73–85.

Orfield, G. & Eaton, S. E. (1996) *Dismantling Desegregation: The Quiet Reversal of Brown v. Board of Education.* New Press, New York.

Parkerson, D. H. & Parkerson, J. A. (2001) *Transitions in American Education: A Social History of Teaching.* RoutledgeFalmer, New York.

Ross, C. E. & Mirowsky, J. (1999) Refining the Association Between Education and Health: The Effects of Quantity, Credential, and Selectivity. *Demography* 36(4): 445–60.

Schultz, T. W. (1961) Investment in Human Capital. *American Economic Review* 51(1): 1–17.

Turner, R. H. (1960) Sponsored and Contest Mobility and the School System. *American Sociological Review* 25: 855–67.

Weber, M. (2000) The "Rationalization" of Education and Training. In: Arum, R. & Beattie, I. R. (Eds.), *The Structure of Schooling: Readings in the Sociology of Education.* McGraw-Hill, New York, pp. 16–19.

education, adult

David B. Bills

Perhaps because so much adult education takes place outside the boundaries of formal educational institutions, sociologists have devoted less scholarly attention to adult education than they have to most other kinds of schooling. There is little agreement on the boundaries of adult education and no clear consensus on a definition that specifies what is included and excluded. Even the terminology pertaining to adult education is inconsistent and shifting, as the range of terms used to refer to this broad and diverse category of education has included continuing, adult, further, recurrent, popular, second-chance, educational extension, and lifelong learning (Kett 1994). One could add even more recent additions to this list of terms.

But while any definition of adult education is inevitably somewhat arbitrary, a few common features emerge. Perhaps the salient feature of adult education is that it is non-compulsory or voluntary. Adult education typically involves educational reentry after one has left formal schooling to pursue work or family activities. It does not traditionally include full-time enrollment in postsecondary degree or diploma programs although it often includes part-time enrollment in such programs (Kim et al. 2004: v). Some analysts consider vocational education, worker training, and other clear forms of "human capital investment" as components of adult education, while others prefer to focus on education for leisure, self-improvement, and personal development. Kett (1994) argued that adult education has more to do with its function of providing additional learning for those who have left the educational system than it does with age.

There is nothing in the United States that could be characterized as an "adult education system." The vast panorama of adult education programs and offerings in the US is an utterly non-coordinated and decentralized "non-system," ranging in quality from atrocious to excellent and in cost from free to prohibitive for most would-be participants. The many professional associations and accreditation agencies with an interest in adult education are at best loosely confederated and organized.

Because of the diversity of adult education, definitional uncertainties about its boundaries, and the lack of any national database on adult education, it is impossible to offer any definitive statistical portrait of its distribution. Still, a few kinds of adult education are especially prevalent. One of the most common is a huge infrastructure of providers of instruction to prepare high school non-completers to take the General Educational Development, or GED, examination. The GED has been used for decades in the US to signify the equivalence of a high school degree. In the year 2000, about 860,000 people took the GED exam, with about 60 percent successfully passing it.

While statistics are less reliable, even larger numbers of people have participated in various kinds of adult literacy programs. These vary greatly in length, intensity, and pedagogical sophistication. Adult literacy programs are deeply rooted in American history, resurging particularly during waves of heavy immigration. While often presented as a means to alleviate educational and economic inequality, their actual impact on this, despite their other virtues, has been modest (Raudenbush & Kasim 1998).

A great deal of adult education is offered in response to the demand for instruction in avocational interests, hobbies, and personal growth. Unlike most compulsory education, much adult education is better characterized as consumption than as investment. That is, the goals of K–12 schooling are routinely stated in terms of the development of desired changes in young people's repertoires, preparing them to effectively assume adult roles as citizens, workers, and community members. In contrast, a large share of adult education is "consumed" for its own sake, for the personal satisfaction and edification that it offers. Sociological models of adult education that adopt the economic perspective of "education as investment" are often of limited value in explaining people's decisions to invest time and money in adult education from which they expect no economic returns.

Individuals pursue adult education from a wide variety of providers. Many providers are located in traditional educational institutions, from K–12 settings to community colleges to four-year colleges and universities. Other adult learning is situated in community organizations, business and industry, church groups, and libraries. Increasingly, vendors are providing adult education through various distance-learning technologies, notably the World Wide Web and other asynchronous forms of instructional delivery.

Sociologists have had limited engagement with the mainstream adult education field and rarely draw on even the recognized classics of the adult education literature. Much of the adult education literature is quite normative, being rooted more in social movements of self-improvement than in a systematic understanding of the sociology of adult education. Statistically and methodologically sound analyses and evaluations of virtually any aspect of adult education – participation, effectiveness, outcomes – are extremely rare.

The uncertainty about definitional boundaries creates a host of measurement and other methodological problems in the study of adult education. Even the inclusive definition offered by the National Center for Education Statistics (see Kim et al. 2004) is restricted to adult education activities in which an instructor is present. A wide variety of self-paced, non-certified, non-formal learning activities that would clearly fall into any accepted categorization of learning (e.g., reading professional journals in one's field, or watching the History Channel) are often systematically excluded from consideration.

Adult education is a critical part of one of the most enduring social movements in American history, that of self-betterment. Since the earliest days of the republic, adult Americans have pursued educational opportunities through such diverse venues as Chautauqua institutes, voluntary associations, libraries, reading groups, correspondence study, elder hostels, and church organizations (Kett 1994). The pursuit of adult education figures prominently in the American myth of the "self-made man."

More recently, such impulses toward self-improvement have given way to a more economically motivated agenda of "Lifelong Learning" or "the Learning Society." The rhetoric of Lifelong Learning is not as deeply institutionalized in the US as in many other postindustrial nations, some of which have elevated the model of the Learning Society to the top of the economic development agenda. Advocates of the Learning Society believe that globalization and rapid technological change are increasingly rendering one's current stock of education obsolete. They add that policies to promote ongoing learning throughout the life course are needed to compete in the global marketplace. Even in the United States with its traditions of adult education for self-betterment, most proposals to reform adult education eventually appeal to economic logic. Despite the cautions of many observers that the provision of skills is not sufficient in itself to meet the demands of changing markets (Crouch 1997), the engine driving adult education is changing quite inexorably from self-improvement to social mobility.

There is no single data series that can document trends in adult education over more than a few years. Under any definition, however, participation in adult education has grown substantially over the past 30 years. Using the rather expansive definition adopted by the National Center for Education Statistics (NCES), in 2001 about 46 percent of American adults (about 92 million people) participated in some form of adult education. This was up from 40 percent in 1995. The most common form of adult education was work-related, but personal development education was also very popular. In fact, fee-based personal development education attracts more students to many community colleges than does tuition-based coursework in degree programs. Less common but still very significant forms of adult education were English as a Second Language (ESL), basic skills education, vocational and technical degree programs, and apprenticeships.

Collectively, adult education adds a great deal to the nation's overall stock of formal schooling. Jacobs and Stoner-Eby (1998) estimated that about 7 percent of the total educational attainment of recent American cohorts is the result of reentry education.

Individuals have very different opportunities to participate in adult education. For the most part, access to adult education is influenced by many of the same factors that influence access to other valued educational and socioeconomic outcomes. Whites participate at higher rates than African Americans and Hispanics. Women participate at higher rates than do men, and have done so at least since the late 1970s. There is evidence, however, that the sorts of job training in which women participate tend to yield lower economic returns than the job training provided to men. There is little variation in participation rates for adults aged 16–50 (about 54 percent), but rates of participation in adult education drop sharply for those aged 51–65 (41 percent) and over age 65 (22 percent). More highly educated individuals are far more likely to participate in adult education than are those with less schooling (a finding that holds in many nations). Those in more privileged occupational and employment positions have greater likelihoods of participating in adult education than do those in less advantaged work situations, and those with higher household incomes are similarly advantaged (Kim et al. 2004).

Because much adult education is not based in formal school settings, the decision to pursue adult education is not strictly the same as the decision to return to school. Particularly for women, the ability to return to school hinges on a variety of marital and family factors, such as responsibilities for childcare and the amount of emotional and financial support received from one's partner. Most often, analysts focus on the "barriers" that stand between people and their ability to participate in adult education. There is as yet no widely accepted conceptual framework for understanding these barriers.

The growth in adult education is closely related to some important long-term demographic trends. Foremost among these is the increasingly "disorderly" life course lived by many Americans. By "disorderly," demographers direct attention to the dissolution of the normative life course of linear and predictable sequences from one social role to another and its replacement with a life course regime in which people hold educational, employment, and family roles out of their traditional sequence and in many cases simultaneously. Thus, individuals are increasingly likely to structure their lives in ways that facilitate occasional or even frequent episodes of educational reentry.

Moreover, the aging of the population, in particular those born during the 1946–64 baby boom in the United States, is resulting in a large "supply side" of potential participants in the adult education market. There are many more people in the typical "adult education" ages than ever before. Even though baby boomers evidently do not return to school at higher rates than earlier cohorts did, their sheer numbers have put enormous upward pressure on adult education. On the demand side, many American colleges and universities, to say nothing of community colleges, have expanded their adult education course offerings while redoubling their efforts to make education accessible to adults with work and family commitments. The adult education market is particularly open to adult education aspirants because of the relatively easy access to virtually any form of adult education in the US. Of course, as baby boomers are coming to be replaced by the much smaller 1965–82 birth cohort of "baby busters," the supply of potential adult learners available to colleges and universities will shrink quite precipitously. As Jacobs and Stoner-Eby (1998) observed, in the near future the college population of the US will return to its traditional demographic composition of young adults.

SEE ALSO: Aging, Demography of; Aging and the Life Course, Theories of; Community College; Educational Attainment; Educational Inequality; Educational and Occupational Attainment; Life Course and Family; Life Course Perspective; Socialization, Adult; Transition from School to Work

REFERENCES AND SUGGESTED READINGS

Crouch, C. (1997) Skills-Based Full Employment: The Latest Philosopher's Stone. *British Journal of Industrial Relations* 35: 367–91.

Jacobs, J. A. & Stoner-Eby, S. (1998) Adult Enrollment and Educational Attainment. *Annals, AAPSS* 559 (September): 91–108.

Kett, J. F. (1994) *The Pursuit of Knowledge Under Difficulties: From Self-Improvement to Adult Education in America, 1750–1990.* Stanford University Press, Stanford.

Kim, K., Hagedorn, M., Williamson, J., & Chapman, C. (2004) *Participation in Adult Education and Lifelong Learning: 2000–01.* NCES 2004–050. US Department of Education, National Center for Education Statistics. US Government Printing Office, Washington, DC.

Raudenbush, S. W. & Kasim, R. (1998) Adult Literacy and Economic Inequality: Findings from the National Adult Literacy Survey. *Harvard Educational Review* 68: 33–79.

education and economy

Richard K. Caputo

The relation between education and economy is interdependent and reciprocal. Education is a form of human capital, an intangible form of accumulated capital stock, which includes level and dispersion of education as well as those of applied and basic research. It has many measurable forms, including years of aggregate schooling, rates of enrollment, public education expenditures, and levels, types, and use of on-the-job training programs. Economic activity is understood as economic growth, usually measured as changes in the size or rate of gross or per capita gross domestic output, and determinant of how much improvement will occur in a society's standard of living. Unlike business cycles, which reflect short-term (<10 years) aggregate fluctuations in output, incomes, and employment, economic growth is a long-term concept, depending on past investments in physical capital like industrial plants and machinery, human capital, and the pace of technological innovation.

The major dimensions of education and economy include the causal directions and the levels of analysis for effects. The effects of education on economic growth are to be distinguished from effects of the economy on educational expansion. Microscopic research analyzes the effects of education on individual characteristics such as wages and occupational status. Macroscopic research focuses on the effects of education on aggregate output and productivity for national economies. Five theories guide related research: class reproduction, human capital, functional, institutional, and stratification. In addition, contemporary growth models are more likely to rely on total factor production, addressing the efficiency with which factors of production are used and reflecting a broad range of economic and socio-cultural influences, rather than growth accounting, which is limited to a narrower range of economic factors of production.

Early reliance on human capital theory in economics and functional theory in sociology posited that education increased the productivity of national economies through increasing the productivity of individuals. Human capital and aggregate productivity studies assumed that more highly educated workers were more productive on the job, arguing that wages were the measure of worker productivity. It was questionable, however, whether wages should be used as a measure of marginal productivity, since this assumed a perfectly competitive labor market in equilibrium.

In regard to effects of the economy on education, earlier empirical studies challenged the functional theory view that as economies industrialize and jobs require greater literacy and technical skills, education expands in response. Secular mass schooling often preceded demand for high-level industrial jobs in industrial and undeveloped countries. Early industrialization was also found to retard educational development. Early pressures to develop formal schooling were typically from political, religious, or cultural elites and focused on training state bureaucrats, military leaders, and religious cohorts, not on developing economic skills.

Class reproduction, human capital, functional, institutional, and stratification theories on the whole present clear though different images of education and the economy. The empirical evidence through the mid-1990s blurred lines separating them, many variables used were proxies for difficult-to-measure attributes, and the quality of data varied across studies.

Bleaney and Nishiyama (2002) examined three competing models of economic growth. All three study models had 26 explanatory measures in common, including the log of initial per capita GDP. No one model dominated the others, implying that an encompassing model with explanatory variables from all three fit the data better than any of the original models or any pair of them. In the final encompassing model passing a battery of tests for adequacy, human capital (that is, male schooling),

institutions, specialization in primary products, and terms of trade changes were all determinants of growth between 1965 and 1990.

Although inconsistencies across studies and complexities about relationships remain, contemporary research benefits from cross-country, cross-sectional panel data with a focus on the question, "Under what conditions does education contribute to economic growth and vice versa?" Barro (2001) has shown that economic growth is positively related to the starting level of average years of school attainment of adult males at the secondary and higher levels and has no relationship to primary education. Judson (1998) has shown that allocation matters: higher investment in universal primary education plays a positive role in economic growth, especially in poorer countries.

Kalaitzidakis et al. (2001) show a nonlinear relationship between education, measured as mean years of schooling, and economic growth, measured as per capita GDP growth between 1960 and 1990. They also report no relationship between education and economic growth *for high income/capital countries*, due in part to contrasting effects of male (positive) and female (negative) education.

Krueger and Kumar (2004) contend that higher rates of publicly subsidized investments in vocational education was one possible factor contributing to increased economic growth in Europe vis-à-vis that of the US in the 1960s and 1970s. As the rate of technological progress increased throughout the 1980s and 1990s, such subsidies contributed to the slower rate of economic growth than that of the US.

Bils and Klenow (2000) show that schooling accounted for less than one-third of per capita GDP growth and that schooling responded to the anticipated rate of growth from income-accompanying increases in GDP. They also note the importance of institutional factors such as better enforcement of property rights and greater openness in inducing faster GDP growth and higher school enrollments.

Galor and Tsiddson (2002) show that the evolutionary pattern of human capital distribution, income distribution, and economic growth were determined simultaneously by the interplay between a local home environment externality and a global technological externality. When the home environment externality was the dominating factor, the distribution of human capital and the wage differential between skilled and unskilled labor became polarized. Inequality enabled members of more highly educated segments of society to overcome forces of a low, stable, steady-state equilibrium and to increase investment in human capital. As such investment increases and "trickles down" to the less-educated segments of society via technological progress in production, the return to skill improves, and investment in human capital becomes more beneficial to members of all segments of society.

Finally, correcting for the conceptual unsuitability of many indicators of institutional quality, both political and social, Glaeser et al. (2004) show that human capital investment between 1960 and 2000 was a robust predictor of economic growth independently of institutional development and that institutional improvement follows economic growth. Equally important, findings of this cross-national study indicated that the key human capital externality was not technological, but political: courts and legislators replaced guns. These institutional improvements in turn brought about greater security of property and economic growth.

SEE ALSO: Economic Development; Economic Sociology: Neoclassical Economic Perspective; Educational Attainment; Educational Inequality; Educational and Occupational Attainment; Institutionalism; Rational Choice Theory (and Economic Sociology)

REFERENCES AND SUGGESTED READINGS

Barro, R. J. (2001) Human Capital and Growth. *American Economic Review* 91(2): 12–17.
Bils, M. & Klenow, P. J. (2000) Does Schooling Cause Growth? *American Economic Review* 90: 1160–83.
Bleaney, M. & Nishiyama, A. (2002) Explaining Growth: A Contest Between Models. *Journal of Economic Growth* 7: 43–56.
Galor, O. & Tsiddson, D. (2002) The Distribution of Human Capital and Economic Growth. *Journal of Economic Growth* 2: 93–124.
Gemmell, N. (1998) Reviewing the New Growth Literature. *New Political Economy* 3(1): 129–34.
Glaeser, E. L., La Porta, R., & Lopez-De-Silanez, F. (2004) Do Institutions Cause Growth? *Journal of Economic Growth* 9: 271–303.
Judson, R. (1998) Economic Growth and Investment in Education: How Allocation Matters. *Journal of Economic Growth* 3: 337–59.
Kalaitzidakis, P., Mamuneas, T., Savvides, A., & Stengos, T. (2001) Measures of Human Capital and Nonlinearities in Economic Growth. *Journal of Economic Growth* 6: 229–54.
Krueger, A. B. & Lindahl, M. (2001) Education for Growth: Why and for Whom? *Journal of Economic Literature* 39: 1101–36.
Krueger, D. & Kumar, K. B. (2004) US–Europe Differences in Technology-Driven Growth: Quantifying the Role of Education. *Journal of Monetary Economics* 51(1): 161–90.
Piazza-Georgi, B. (2002) The Role of Human and Social Capital in Growth: Extending Our Understanding. *Cambridge Journal of Economics* 26: 461–79.
Rubinson, R. & Browne, I. (1994) Education and the Economy. In: Smelser, N. J. & Swedberg, R. (Eds.), *The Handbook of Economic Sociology*. Princeton University Press, Princeton; Russell Sage Foundation, New York, pp. 581–99.
Schreyer, P. & Pilat, D. (2001) Measuring Productivity. *OECD Economic Studies* 33(2): 127–70.

educational attainment

David B. Bills

Educational attainment refers to the highest level of formal education completed by the members of a population. Because national systems of education differ greatly from one another, the measurement of educational attainment is typically restricted to education completed in the country where the education was received (Siegel & Swanson 2004: 220), although researchers have developed various metrics to translate levels of completed schooling across countries (Kerckhoff & Dylan 1999). Educational attainment is sometimes recorded as the number of years of schooling that individuals have completed, but is more often measured as the highest grade or highest level completed. The distinction between years of schooling and highest level completed is particularly important in highly schooled and highly economically developed societies in which primary and secondary schooling are virtually universal. Moreover, in highly economically developed societies distinctions at the upper levels of the educational distribution are of more social consequence than are distinctions expressed simply in years of schooling.

Educational attainment is a measure of the *stock* of education in a population (Duncan 1968). It is useful to distinguish educational attainment from various measures of the *flow* of education through a population. The most common measures of flow are school enrollment and educational progression. Educational attainment also differs from educational achievement, which pertains to various kinds of cognitive and analytic skills acquired in school, and literacy, a more judgmental measure of the distribution through a population of proficiency in reading and writing.

A difficulty in measuring educational attainment is that there is no fixed age at which individuals permanently sever their participation in formal schooling. The inclusion of individuals who have not yet completed their education in the calculation of the educational attainment of a population systematically underestimates the overall level of educational attainment. Because of this, the measurement of educational attainment must specify a lower age boundary in order to include only those who are most likely to have completed their education. Age 25 is a quite standard cut-off for this purpose, but even this definition can become problematic as increasing shares of the population continue their education later in the life course and as educational re-entry becomes more common.

The US Census Bureau began to measure educational attainment in the 1940 census by asking about the highest grade of schooling that the respondent had attended and completed. It maintained that practice through the 1980 census. Because this conceptualization of educational attainment failed to provide data on the degrees earned by respondents to the census (in particular, post-secondary degrees), in 1990 the Bureau began to ask about the highest level of education completed. This change from years of education to levels of education had important implications for charting historical trends in the educational attainment of the population. Specifically, it is no longer possible to use census data to calculate the mean and the median number of years of completed schooling in the population. Demographers generally regard this as an acceptable tradeoff for the greater precision and timeliness afforded by the new measurement procedure (Kominski & Siegel 1993).

The US Census Bureau publishes an annual report on the educational attainment of the population using data collected in the Current Population Survey. This administration of the CPS was once known as the Annual Demographic Survey, or more commonly the March Supplement. It is now entitled the Annual Social and Economic Supplement (ASEC).

The educational attainment of the American population has risen steadily since the mid-nineteenth century. This upward trend was especially rapid in the twentieth century. The US attained virtually universal primary education before the end of the 1800s, near universal secondary education a half century later, and mass higher education not long after that (Walters 2000). The story is not simply one of uninterrupted growth in educational attainment. The trend line has shown some fluctuations, not all sociodemographic groups have participated equally in the growth of attainments, and there are recently signs of decelerating or even reversed growth. Still, the enormous growth of the educational attainment of the American population has been of unquestioned social, cultural, and political-economic significance (Goldin 1998).

The US has historically been a world leader in the mass provision of opportunities for educational attainment, but the growth of educational attainment has been a worldwide phenomenon. This growth has often been rapid and dramatic. An important series of publications by Meyer and his colleagues have characterized the global expansion of formal education as "the world educational revolution" (Meyer et al. 1977).

Analysts of social stratification have regularly regarded educational attainment as pivotal to modern systems of social stratification. As conceptualized in Blau and Duncan's classic *The American Occupational Structure* (1967), opportunities for educational attainment are unequally allocated across several fundamental socioeconomic dimensions. Varying levels and types of educational attainment are in turn crucial in allocating people into unequally rewarded positions in socioeconomic hierarchies.

Key to this simple model of social stratification is the distinction between ascription and achievement. Ascription (or ascribed status) refers to individual and aggregate-level characteristics over which the individual has no control. Many of these have been hypothesized and empirically demonstrated to influence educational attainment. These include such factors as race, socioeconomic background, and sex. In contrast, achievement (or achieved status) includes those factors that are more under the control of the individual, such as effort, motivation, or ambition. These too have been shown to have significant impacts on educational attainment.

In the US, the relative importance of different ascribed characteristics has changed over time. For many years, girls and women received significantly less educational attainment than did boys and men. More recently, however, American females are receiving higher levels of educational attainment than are males at all but the very highest levels of the educational system. In many cases, such as many professional post-secondary programs leading to remunerative careers, even these barriers are beginning to fall. The transformation of female educational disadvantage into female advantage is evident in many other countries as well.

The gap in educational attainment between white Americans and African Americans, which was once extremely large, has narrowed significantly. On some measures of educational attainment African Americans have even reached relative equality with the white population. Adducing many of the same social and historical factors that contributed to the decline in the educational gap between males and females, Gamoran (2001) anticipates that the racial gap in educational attainment too will continue to decline. At the same time, some Asian American groups have among the highest levels of educational attainment in the nation, while the gap in educational attainment between many Hispanic and Latino populations and the majority population has narrowed more slowly.

On the other hand, the role of socioeconomic status or class (including such indicators as parental education levels, neighborhood poverty, parental occupational status, and family income) as a determinant of educational attainment has shown little sign of weakening over time and considerable evidence of persistence. The ability of researchers to understand the critical role of socioeconomic background as a determinant of educational attainment was greatly enhanced with the introduction and elaboration of the influential "transition model" of school continuation decisions developed by Mare (1980, 1995). This model drew attention to the continuing importance of social class at transitions from one level of the educational system to another, processes that were often overlooked under earlier linear conceptualizations of the determinants of educational attainment.

Not all of the factors that have been demonstrated to lead to variations in educational attainment are straightforward measures of ascription or achievement. Many researchers have assessed the role of cultural capital and social capital as important determinants of educational attainment (Coleman 1988). Cultural capital refers to culturally valued resources and dispositions that are held disproportionately by the more highly educated. Cultural capital need not reflect job skills or productive capacity in any significant way, but can nonetheless lead to enhanced life chances because of its association with the culture of privileged and elite classes. By social capital, analysts draw attention to how the placement of individuals in supportive social networks can provide educational advantages beyond those offered by an individual's own skills and talents.

While educational attainment is itself an unequally distributed and scarce social good, in a similar way the possession of educational credentials is a principal means by which status, prestige, and other aspects of life chances are distributed in modern societies. Higher levels of educational attainment are statistically associated with all manner of positive social outcomes. Relative to less educated individuals, more highly educated people have greater access to high-paying and prestigious work with which they are more satisfied. They are generally in better health and display more healthy behaviors. Further, more educated people exhibit higher levels of community and civic participation. These findings should be interpreted with care. In part, the benefits of educational attainment are due to the socializing effects of education itself, in part they are due to the greater access to economic resources facilitated by educational attainment, and in part they arise from selection effects into advanced levels of education.

These generalizations about the salutary benefits of educational attainment are true at the aggregate levels of states, regions, and nations, as well as the individual level (Buchmann & Hannum 2001). In comparison with less educated nations, more educated nations are more economically prosperous, healthier, and politically open. Once again, questions of cause and effect need to be carefully considered.

SEE ALSO: Education, Adult; Educational Inequality; Educational and Occupational Attainment; Meritocracy; School Transitions; Status Attainment

REFERENCES AND SUGGESTED READINGS

Blau, P. & Duncan, O. D. (1967) *The American Occupational Structure*. Wiley, New York.

Buchmann, C. & Hannum, E. (2001) Education and Stratification in Developing Countries: A Review of Theories and Research. *Annual Review of Sociology* 27: 77–102.

Coleman, J. S. (1988) Social Capital in the Creation of Human Capital. *American Journal of Sociology* 94: S95–120.

Duncan, B. (1968) Trends in Output and Distribution of Schooling. In: Sheldon, E. B. & Moore, W. E. (Eds.), *Indicators of Social Change: Concepts and Measurement*. Russell Sage Foundation, New York, pp. 601–72.

Gamoran, A. (2001) American Schooling and Educational Inequality: A Forecast for the 21st Century. *Sociology of Education* extra issue: 135–53.

Goldin, C. (1998) America's Graduation from High School: The Evolution and Spread of Secondary Schooling in the Twentieth Century. *Journal of Economic History* 58: 345–74.

Kerckhoff, A. C. & Dylan, M. (1999) Problems with International Measures of Education. *Journal of Socioeconomics* 28: 759–75.

Kominski, R. & Siegel, P. M. (1993) Measuring Education in the Current Population Survey. *Monthly Labor Review* 116(9): 34–8.

Mare, R. D. (1980) Social Background and School Continuation Decisions. *Journal of the American Statistical Association* 75: 295–305.

Mare, R. D. (1995) Changes in Educational Attainment and School Enrollment. In: Farley, R. (Ed.), *The State of the Union: America in the 1990s*. Vol. 1: *Economic Trends*. Russell Sage, New York, pp. 155–213.

Meyer, J. W., Ramirez, F. O., Rubinson, R., & Boli-Bennett, J. (1977) The World Educational Revolution, 1950–1970. *Sociology of Education* 50: 242–58.

Siegel, J. S. & Swanson, D. A. (2004) *The Methods and Materials of Demography*, 2nd edn. Elsevier, Amsterdam.

Walters, P. B. (2000) The Limits of Growth: Social Expansion and School Reform in Historical Perspective. In: Hallinan, M. T. (Ed.), *Handbook of the Sociology of Education*. Kluwer, New York, pp. 241–61.

educational inequality

Yossi Shavit

In their classic study of stratification in the US, Blau and Duncan (1967) found that the effect of education on occupational attainment increased over time. They interpreted this to mean that America was becoming increasingly meritocratic. A meritocratic social system is one in which the attainment of desirable social rewards, such as good jobs, is determined by effort and ability rather than by inherited privilege. It is often assumed that the attainment of educational credentials requires both effort and ability and that education represents merit. However, educational attainment is also determined by social origin. An equally valid interpretation of Blau and Duncan's finding is that the intergenerational transmission of social privilege is increasingly mediated by education. The extent to which this is so is determined by the relative magnitude of two factors: the effects of social origin on educational attainment and the effect of education on occupational and economic attainments. Searching for a social system that is both meritocratic and egalitarian, researchers try to understand why there is a strong association between social origin and educational attainment and how to weaken it. This entry reviews the main determinants of educational attainment and of educational inequality between social strata and between men and women. Sociologists attribute educational inequalities between strata to processes at work in families and the educational system.

FAMILY FACTORS

Ability, Encouragement, and Aspirations

The Wisconsin model is arguably the single most influential model of social stratification (Sewell et al. 1975). The model posits a chain of relationships between variables that affect educational and occupational attainment and begins by showing that there are substantial differences between social strata in students' scholastic ability. Next, it shows that both students' social origin and their ability affect their grades in school. The three groups of variables determine how much encouragement students receive from significant others (teachers, peers, and parents) regarding their future educational and occupational aspirations. Aspirations, in turn, affect students' ultimate educational and occupational attainments. However, the model explains only about 30 percent of the variance in educational attainment. This means that it explains a large part of the difference between people in educational attainment but also that most of the variance between them is due to other factors, such as luck, cultural differences between families, school differences, and more. The Wisconsin model has been replicated in many other countries.

Cultural Capital

Bourdieu (Bourdieu et al. 1977) has argued that school curricula reflect the codes and values of the dominant culture in society. He defined cultural capital as familiarity with these codes and values. The dominant culture is the culture of the privileged social strata. Children raised in these strata internalize the values of the dominant culture effortlessly and enjoy an advantage in the educational attainment process. In this way, the intergenerational transmission of cultural codes facilitates the reproduction of educational and social inequality between generations. These claims are cited often in studies of educational inequality, but empirical data show that they overstate the extent to which cultural capital actually reproduces social inequality. Cultural capital is often measured by familiarity with highbrow cultural codes (the names of composers or painters) or by the frequency of participation in highbrow activities (visits to museums or classical concerts). Bourdieu's model expects to find rather strong correlations between these measures and school performance, but studies typically find weak ones. Recently, scholars like De Graaf et al. (2000) found that the main component of cultural capital that affects educational achievement is not the students' familiarity with highbrow culture or participation in it, but rather their exposure to books and reading at home. Children raised in affluent homes and whose parents are educated are more likely to benefit from the availability of books in the home and to do well in school. These findings are consistent with a large body of research showing that the home reading environment is important to the early acquisition of scholastic aptitude and reading and writing skills.

Family Size and Cohesion

There is a substantial body of research on the US and other developed countries showing that sibship (the number of one's brothers and sisters) is inversely related to children's cognitive ability and educational achievement. The resource dilution hypothesis suggests that children raised in small families benefit from a larger share, on average, of the families' resources, including parental attention which, in turn, enhances their cognitive development and educational attainment. The negative effect of family size is stronger when siblings are closely spaced because they draw on family resources simultaneously. The negative effects are weak when some siblings are old enough to contribute to the resource pool and can help in the development and education of younger ones (for a detailed exposition of this idea, see Zajonc & Markus 1975).

Studies on non-western and some religious communities do not find a uniform negative effect of sibship size on achievements. For example, for Muslims living in Israel, students attending Catholic schools in the US, and

Orthodox American Jews the negative effect of sibship size on educational achievement is weak or even reversed. In these subpopulations, nuclear families are embedded in extended families or supportive communities whose assistance and resources mitigate the dilution effects of large sibships. Thus, whereas family size can be a liability in the educational attainment process, the social cohesion of extended families and communities is an important asset.

Social Capital in Families

Sociologists often refer to social cohesion of this kind as social capital, defined as the characteristics of one's social network (family, friends, etc.) that can facilitate the attainment of a goal (Coleman 1988). An important aspect of a family's social capital is family structure, namely whether or not both parents are present while the child is growing up. The educational achievements of children raised in two-parent families are substantially higher than those of children raised in one-parent families (McLanahan & Sandefur 1994). Research identifies three main reasons for this: first, single-parent families, especially those headed by mothers, are economically disadvantaged; second, children raised by single parents receive less attention and guidance, on average, than those raised by two parents; and third, single-parent families maintain a weaker social bond with the community and lack the social capital upon which other families can draw when in need.

Financial Resources

Children's educational attainment is also affected by their family's income because high-income families can afford the direct and opportunity costs of education. The effects of family income on cognitive development and educational attainment are larger in the early ages (0–5) than in adolescence. Moreover, family income in childhood has a stronger effect on educational attainment at the secondary level than does contemporaneous family income (Duncan et al. 1998). This suggests that the effect of family income on educational attainment is mediated by developmental processes rather than simply the ability to afford the costs of schooling. As Duncan and associates point out, preschool ability sets the stage for subsequent educational achievements, and children raised in poverty are less likely to develop the cognitive skills necessary for educational success.

And yet a recent study suggests that most research tends to underestimate the magnitude of the effect of financial resources on children's educational attainment. Conley (2001) compared the effects of current family income to the effect of the family's total wealth (including savings and home ownership) and found that the latter has a much stronger effect on American adolescents' likelihood to obtain a college education. Evidently, wealthy families can draw on their savings to pay for college expenses.

SYSTEMIC FACTORS

Most of the explained variance in students' educational achievements is due to individual and family characteristics of the kind discussed above. However, some variance is also explained by characteristics of the schools that students attend. Students benefit from attending small schools and from having a small student–teacher ratio in the classroom, as well as from attending schools that are attended by peers of privileged social origin. Two additional institutional characteristics of schools affect variance in educational achievement: curriculum organization and tracking, and the expansion of the educational system.

Organization of the Curriculum and Tracking

Fields of knowledge and school subjects are stratified by prestige. Although the hierarchy of subjects varies between societies, academic and scientific subjects usually enjoy higher prestige than utilitarian or nonscientific ones. Prestigious subjects are considered more difficult and deemed more suitable for able students who are likely to come from privileged families. The utilitarian and nonscientific subjects are offered to weaker students who often come from lower socioeconomic strata (Ayalon 1994). In most countries, success in prestigious subjects at the secondary school level is a prerequisite for admission to selective colleges or universities. Therefore, curricular hierarchies play a role in the intergenerational reproduction of inequality of educational opportunity.

Most educational systems place students into distinct curricular tracks or streams. The most common distinction is between the academic tracks that teach the prestigious subjects and prepare students for higher education, and tracks that prepare them for immediate entry into the labor force. Track placement is determined largely by the students' prior achievements. But because student achievements are correlated with their socioeconomic origins, students from less privileged strata are more likely to attend non-academic tracks; track placement, in turn, affects their subsequent educational attainment. Not surprisingly, academic track students are more likely to attend higher education and obtain lucrative jobs in the labor market. Thus, tracking transmits inequality between generations (Shavit 1990).

Expansion of Education

In recent decades, educational systems in most countries have expanded dramatically. In the 1950s and 1960s only about a third of children living in economically advanced countries completed upper secondary schools. This proportion has since increased sharply and now approaches 90 percent. Tertiary education in these countries expanded as well. In the 1960s higher education was attended by less than 20 percent of the relevant age group; by the 1990s attendance rate reached about 50 percent. Many policymakers believe that the expansion of education can reduce educational inequalities because expansion draws in adolescents of less privileged origin, raises their educational attainment, and reduces inequality between their education and that of the middle and upper classes. Scholars of social stratification are less optimistic. In the early 1980s, Mare (1981) developed a sophisticated model for analyzing educational stratification. The model views the educational attainment process as a sequence of transition points at which students and their families decide whether to continue to the next level or drop out. Their decisions are determined by variables representing the student

and family characteristics discussed above. Inequality of educational opportunity is measured as the effect of these variables on the odds of making the various transitions. The odds may decline at some transition points and increase or remain stable at others. Mare studied change in the stratification of education in the US during the first seven decades of the twentieth century. Although this was a period of dramatic educational expansion in America, the effects of social origin did not decline and even increased slightly. Replications of Mare's study in many countries, both industrialized and developing, produced similar results (Shavit & Blossfeld 1993). Several studies found exceptions to this pattern, but especially at lower educational levels where attendance rates of the privileged strata are approaching 100 percent. Any further expansion at these levels can only draw on the lower strata, among which attendance is not yet universal, and reduce inequality between strata in attendance rates.

Gender Gap in Education

Historically, when the rates of labor-force participation by women were low, families preferred to invest resources in the education of their sons, which was viewed as an investment that would yield substantial income gains, rather than that of their daughters. Daughters were expected to function primarily in the private sphere: marry, bear children, and perform housework, activities not deemed to require an education above the very basic levels. The ensuing gender gap in education persisted for generations. Recently, this has changed dramatically. Women's educational levels have caught up and, in some countries, surpassed those of men (Bradley 2000). The equalization of gender differences in educational attainment is due to a pervasive change in the role of women in modern society. First, since the 1970s, there has been a global effort to promote norms of gender equality. Several international organizations, such as the United Nations, the World Health Organization, the World Bank, and the OECD, actively promote the status of women. Gender equality in education was identified as the primary mechanism by which women's status could be improved. Second, the expansion of the public sector and the welfare state created demand for workers in service-providing occupations. Third, the expanded provision of these services by the state played a double role: it relieved wives and mothers from some of their housework, and created jobs for them in the labor market. As a consequence, the labor-force participation rates of women increased sharply.

While gender differences in access to higher education were eliminated and even reversed, differences between men and women in the type of institution and in fields of study remain. Women are still more likely than men to attend lower-tier institutions such as two-year or less prestigious colleges and are less likely to study the exact sciences and engineering. But these differences are also declining.

SEE ALSO: Capital: Economic, Cultural, and Social; Cultural Capital in Schools; Dropping Out of School; Educational Attainment; Educational and Occupational Attainment; Meritocracy; Opportunities for Learning; School Transitions; Schooling and Economic Success; Stratification and Inequality, Theories of; Tracking; Transition from School to Work

REFERENCES AND SUGGESTED READINGS

Ayalon, H. (1994) Monopolizing Knowledge? The Ethnic Composition and Curriculum in Israeli High Schools. *Sociology of Education* 67: 264–78.
Blau, P. M. & Duncan, O. D. (1967) *The American Occupational Structure*. Wiley, New York.
Boudon, R. (1974) *Education, Opportunity, and Social Inequality: Changing Prospects in Western Society*. Wiley, New York.
Bourdieu, P., Passeron, J.-C., & Nice, R. (1977) *Reproduction in Education, Society and Culture*. Sage, London.
Bradley, K. (2000) The Incorporation of Women in Higher Education: Paradoxical Outcomes? *Sociology of Education* 73: 1–18.
Coleman, J. S. (1988) Social Capital in the Creation of Human Capital. *American Journal of Sociology* 94: S95–S120.
Conley, D. (2001) Capital for College: Parental Assets and Postsecondary Schooling. *Sociology of Education* 74: 59–72.
De Graaf, N. D, De Graaf, P. M., & Kraaykamp, G. (2000) Parental Cultural Capital and Educational Attainment in the Netherlands: A Refinement of the Cultural Capital Perspective. *Sociology of Education* 73: 92–111.
Duncan, G. J., Yeung, W. J., Brooks-Gunn, J., & Smith, J. R. (1998) How Much Does Childhood Poverty Affect the Life Chances of Children? *American Sociological Review* 63: 406–23.
Erikson, R. & Jonsson, J. O. (Eds.) (1996) *Can Education Be Equalized? The Swedish Case in Comparative Perspective*. Westview Press, Boulder.
Jencks, C. et al. (1972) *Inequality: A Reassessment of the Effect of Family and Schooling in America*. Basic Books, New York.
McLanahan, S. & Sandefur, G. (1994) *Growing Up with a Single Parent: What Hurts, What Helps*. Harvard University Press, Cambridge, MA.
Mare, R. (1981) Stability in Educational Stratification. *American Sociological Review* 46: 72–87.
Sewell, W. H., Hauser, R. M., & Alwin, D. F. (1975) *Education, Occupation and Earnings: Achievement in the Early Career*. Academic Press, New York.
Shavit, Y. (1990) Segregation, Tracking, and the Educational Attainment of Minorities: Arabs and Oriental Jews in Israel. *American Sociological Review* 55: 115–26.
Shavit, Y. & Blossfeld, H.-P. (1993) *Persistent Inequality: Changing Educational Attainment in Thirteen Countries*. Westview Press, Boulder.
Zajonc, R. B. & Markus, G. B. (1975) Birth Order and Intellectual Development. *Psychological Review* 82: 74–88.

educational and occupational attainment

Juanita M. Firestone and Richard J. Harris

Both educational and occupational attainments are important (and related) aspects of prestige differences in the United States as well as throughout the more developed and developing countries. Prestige is used as a measure of social status and therefore is a part of the broader social stratification system. Social status is viewed as a subjective concept, based on individuals' perceptions about lifestyles. Most of us are aware of differences in lifestyles based on styles of clothing, types (and numbers) of automobiles, value and location of housing, and so on. The point is that differences in occupation and education combine to produce differences in income, which then allow individuals and families to live a certain lifestyle. We then attach differences in social value to the different lifestyles; some are awarded high standing in society, while others are deemed to have little or no value. These judgments are played out within the contexts of gender, race/ethnicity, and class, and have been remarkably constant over time (at least since 1947 in the US) and across a wide variety of countries.

OCCUPATIONAL PRESTIGE

Most individuals place a lot of emphasis on a person's occupation when assessing prestige. For example, we make systematic judgments about a person's lifestyle based on whether we know they are a blue-collar or a white-collar worker. Sociologists often use prestige scores to rank occupations, which hypothetically could fall along a continuum from a low score of zero to a high score of 100. However, results for research generating occupational prestige scores indicate they rarely drop below 20 or above 80. Prestige scores, which are based on averages of individual scores, remain fairly stable over long periods of time and across different subgroups in the population. The lowest-ranked occupations tend to be manual laborers (e.g., janitor, housepainter, garbage collector, housecleaner) or basic sales (supermarket cashier, furniture sales clerk, shoe/clothing sales clerk) or office (file clerk, telephone solicitor) positions. Medium-prestige jobs include skilled manual (electrician, plumber, mechanic) or office (secretary, bookkeeper, bank teller, postal clerk) jobs. The highest-prestige jobs are professional (judge, physician, professor, lawyer, registered nurse) or managerial (hospital administrator, general manager, accountant), which are typically ranked by level of expertise or responsibility. Importantly, there is a lot of within-group variation as well, thus the prestige of neurosurgeons is much higher than that of general practitioners, although both fall in the highest-prestige range. Interestingly, while specific types of occupations may vary, especially in developing countries (e.g., from a high score for chief of state to a low score for gatherer), the standard occupational prestige scale is extremely highly correlated with prestige hierarchies of other countries, indicating similar prestige rankings cross-nationally.

Gender and Occupational Prestige

In recent decades women's entry into the paid labor force has accelerated, especially among those with young children and babies. One important characteristic has been associated with the entry of larger percentages of women in the labor market – occupational segregation. Women have been segregated into a relatively small number of occupations, which are associated with stereotypes about feminine skills (e. g., secretaries, cashiers, hairdressers, nurses, elementary and kindergarten teachers). On the one hand, women's increasing labor force experience along with the decline in blue-collar employment is creating a slow decline in occupational segregation. On the other hand, even when employed in higher-prestige occupations, most women are concentrated in three fields: nursing, teaching, and social work. Thus, women's occupational profiles remain different from men's, and the average prestige scores for women's jobs within categories are lower than those for men. This is especially true in the technical/sales and skilled blue-collar jobs. At the professional/executive level, the prestige scores are virtually identical, though there are still substantial differences in earnings.

These general patterns are consistent across different countries in spite of differences in the types of jobs available in developing compared to more developed countries. Cross-culturally, stereotypes related to differences in job-related skills between men and women remain strong. For example, students in various countries (both developing and more developed) identify managerial skills in stereotypical masculine terms. Furthermore, differences in career advancement of men and women are affected by the fact that differences in levels of career ambition vary according to national values. In many developing countries, career aspirations for women are optional at best and resisted strongly at worst. In the latter case, women are prevented by custom or policy from attaining the requisite skills to work in high-prestige occupations.

Race and Occupational Prestige

Changes in race relations in the United States, along with anti-discrimination legislation and equal opportunity and affirmative action programs, created dramatic changes in the occupational distribution of blacks over the years. For example, based on looking at the 10 highest- and lowest-ranked occupations in 1940, almost 80 percent of black workers were concentrated in the four lowest-ranked categories, but by 1980 about 70 percent of black workers were in the upper six categories. In spite of these dramatic changes, blacks are still underrepresented at the top of the occupational hierarchy and overrepresented at the bottom, especially among service workers, which remained in 2000 the largest single black occupational category, as it had been in 1940. Recent occupational shifts (fewer blue-collar jobs, growth of white-collar jobs) have had a negative impact on black workers, thus in relative terms many young blacks have lost ground compared to whites because of higher unemployment and underemployment rates.

In the world context, racial differences in occupational prestige are often associated with the extent to which members of different races or ethnicities are perceived as outsiders with alien values. Thus "guest workers" or immigrants of different races and who exhibit other differences in cultural values (e.g., language, dress, religion) may be relegated to lower-prestige jobs or to specific types of occupations (diamond cutters, sailors, traders). In both cases, members of races considered outside the typical citizenry are segregated occupationally based on stereotypes about their race; however, the latter groups are more likely to become integrated into a larger society.

Ethnicity and Occupational Prestige

Because of high birth rates and immigration rates, Hispanics as a group (including various subgroups, e.g., Mexican, Cuban, South/Central American, Puerto Rican) have become the largest minority group in the United States. As a result, Hispanics will become an increasing share of the future labor market. While the various subgroups of Hispanics have different labor force characteristics (education level, experience, skills), one issue that may impact their position in the occupational hierarchy is English proficiency. This may be particularly true for recent immigrants, who may become underemployed or unemployed if they do not have the English proficiency to get and hold a professional or managerial position. The changes in the US occupational structure which positively impacted African Americans have had similar impacts on Hispanics. Thus, the percentage of Hispanics in higher-prestige jobs has increased since 1980, although the largest percentage of Mexican-origin workers are still concentrated among operators, fabricators, laborers, and lower-level sales clerks. On average, the prestige of Hispanics in the US remains lower than that of white, non-Hispanic workers.

As with different racial groups, intercultural encounters within countries can produce situations where individuals are stereotyped as incapable of working in higher-prestige jobs. While it may be possible to learn superficial aspects of a different culture within a short period of time, it may be more difficult to absorb underlying values, especially if they are radically different from one's own culture. Thus, even foreigners who attempt to fit in to a new culture may be viewed with suspicion. One way of controlling suspicious individuals can be to limit their ability to climb the occupational ladder and achieve greater economic success.

EDUCATIONAL ATTAINMENT

The average education level of Americans is increasing, so that most adults in the US have a high school degree, and between 25 percent and 75 percent of individuals attend a college or university, depending on the economic background of their families. Thus, 25 percent even of individuals from lower socioeconomic circumstances attend at least a community college. In a general sense, everyone seems to understand that staying in school until you complete a degree pays off economically. With some exceptions, people with higher levels of education tend to have higher-status jobs and earn more income. Sociological research indicates that education does pay a dividend for all categories of workers. However, the less educated, those with fewer or outdated skills, and those with less experience may be losing ground with respect to wages. Research demonstrates considerable variation in wages within education levels (e.g., those with a high school degree, BA degree, or higher level degree) based on group memberships (e.g., gender, race, ethnicity). As with respect to occupational attainment, women and race/ethnic minorities tend to be on the lower end of statuses and wages within those groupings.

While a college education has a positive impact on individuals' prestige and earnings, access to college remains unequal based on the socioeconomic background of students. Graduation rates also vary based on group membership of students. In 2000, more than half of 18- to 24-year-olds from families in the top income quartile completed college degrees, but only 1 percent of those from families in the bottom half of the income distribution completed degrees. The black–white difference in completing a college degree is smaller than in the past, but remains large.

Comparing educational attainment across different countries is a difficult task because of the heterogeneity of educational systems, particularly vocational and non-academic training across various countries. Some researchers argue that it may not yet be possible to compare quantity of education (e.g., years, levels) across nations, but rather some system measuring quality of education would be preferable. One such process suggests assessing the differences in earnings or employment of educated workers that are attributable to the individuals' schooling. To accomplish this, a labor-income-based measure is created by weighting different segments of the workforce by the ratio of earnings at different levels of education. An alternative approach uses estimated rates of return to education rather than duration of schooling as weights in creating a comparative measure. The variations in available estimates for different countries highlight how such comparative measures can be sensitive to political assumptions about the social benefits of education, opportunity costs of missed wages, and other cultural values.

Gender and Educational Attainment

In recent decades the educational attainment of men and women has narrowed considerably. While the gap in college degrees between men and women has narrowed, the types of degrees earned vary by the sex of the individual. Men tend to earn degrees in fields associated with higher statuses and higher wages. In addition, educational attainment yields greater economic returns to males than to females. A part of this disparity is due to the occupational segregation discussed earlier. In the past, another part was due to women's intermittent labor force participation, when they were likely to move in and out of the labor force for family reasons (pregnancy, young children, husband's job moved elsewhere). Increasingly, maintaining a middle- or upper-middle-class standard of living requires two incomes, and women's labor force participation is becoming more continuous over time.

In spite of a decreasing gap in male–female educational attainment, the gender gap in earnings remains larger than the race/ethnic gap. Some argue that at least a portion of the remaining gap among women of different race or ethnic groups results from minority women's greater likelihood of becoming single-parent householders, being out of the labor force, living in low-income neighborhoods, and facing various forms of discrimination. The gap between educational attainment of minority and white women leads to the continuing problem of double jeopardy. In sociology, double jeopardy refers to the compounding effects of being in two different minority groups (e.g., black and female or Hispanic and female).

Historically, Hispanic women have had significantly lower levels of education than non-Hispanic women and lower than all groups of men. Early explanations of this difference focused on an idealized model of motherhood supposedly common among Hispanics that supported a patriarchal system that devalued female educational attainment in favor of becoming a wife and mother. Recent data suggest that increases in female-headed households and marginal economic circumstances among many Hispanic groups have led to increasing awareness of the need to complete more years of education. As with other groups of women, research indicates that Hispanic women do not receive the same returns for increasing levels of education. Language difficulties would likely compound these negative impacts.

Race and Educational Attainment

Sociological studies indicate that the economic penalty of race has declined since the 1960s — occupational mobility has increased, as has movement toward wage parity. These differences vary a lot based on the age of the individual. For example, among younger workers with college degrees, race disparities in occupational status and earnings have decreased considerably. A college degree moves black wages closer to parity with whites, although black incomes do not attain equality with whites. As noted earlier, however, access to education and completion rates for college degrees fluctuate across racial groups. Thus, to the extent that many blacks remain segregated from whites in inner cities and income-disadvantaged areas, their access to the same educational and occupational opportunities as whites is limited.

Ethnicity and Educational Attainment

Past research has focused on differences in the ways Hispanics invest in higher education. Because of lower income and high poverty levels, many Hispanics attend community colleges or trade schools rather than attending universities or four-year colleges. Because they often are also employed to support family needs, the opportunity costs associated with attending a university can be higher. Additionally, the increase in tuition costs and the lack of access to financial aid have impacted those from lower-income families dramatically. In combination, these mean that Hispanics are more likely to delay a college education, drop out of college, or attend a community college, all of which can have a negative impact on educational and, as a result, occupational status.

CURRENT STATE OF RESEARCH

Changes in modern society have created opportunities for well-educated professionals,

technicians, and managers. Alternatively, there have been important losses of well-paid blue-collar jobs because of the decline in manufacturing. Increases in the occupational service sector are associated with a polarization of the occupational status structure. On the one hand, opportunities for higher-status jobs such as hospital administrators, medical technicians, accountants, hotel managers, and computer specialists have increased. On the other hand, there has been a commensurate increase in low-status jobs such as fast food workers, janitors, and hospital orderlies. In addition, the distribution of individuals within occupational classifications is unequal, with women and race and ethnic minorities to a greater extent located in the lower-status positions within classifications.

Along with this process, access to the college education needed to enter the high-status occupations remains unequal. For example, the percentage of students enrolling in universities is much lower for race/ethnic minority groups and for individuals from the lowest income levels. Even among those who attend college, the background characteristics of students vary based on sex and race/ethnicity, and impact the type of degree attained. Thus, white males tend to receive degrees associated with higher-status jobs (engineering, medical research), while women receive degrees associated with pink-collar positions (human services, social work, elementary teaching) and race/ethnic minorities receive degrees associated with lower occupational status (general manager, office manager).

Cross-nationally, changes include stronger focus on educating the populations of more developed countries. In the transition from rural to urban existence, education plays an increasing role for access to occupational positions. One interesting aspect of this process links directly both to the occupational structure of developing countries and to the occupational structure of more developed countries like the US. Outsourcing may mean an even stronger focus on education and professional skills in more developed countries, which could help stem the tide of highly educated and or skilled natives seeking to immigrate to places that pay better wages. Labeled by many as the "brain drain," selective out-migration has depleted the ranks of better-educated individuals, especially in countries like India and Taiwan that are in the process of becoming highly developed. Less developed countries still lag behind or may link education to sex, so that only boys are provided educational opportunities, or education may be linked to upholding traditional cultural values rather than creating an educated populace (e.g., Middle Eastern countries).

CONCLUSION

The occupational structures of the US and the more developed countries in the world have changed from one in which most workers were employed in predominantly goods-producing jobs to one in which most are employed in service sector jobs. This change has produced a considerable amount of polarization with respect to occupational prestige, because it creates a demand both for professional jobs where high educational credentials are expected and for those that can be filled by individuals with limited educational credentials.

Educational status has increased along with this change in the occupational structure, although the changes have been non-linear. The greatest gains in status in the US have gone to those with post-high school degrees, especially those from prestigious institutions. Thus the absolute worth of some educational credentials may be devalued, creating a situation where individuals are underemployed given their educational attainment. For example, some argue that in the US at least, a bachelor's degree has the same value in today's labor market that a high school degree had ten years ago. Similarly, a master's degree today has the same value today as a bachelor's degree had ten years ago. In more developed countries, the greatest gains in status are associated with the skills that are utilized by multinational firms for outsourcing.

Changes in occupational and educational attainment are further impacted by gender, race/ethnicity, and class. Women, race/ethnic minorities, and those from lower income groups are more likely to be undereducated, have degrees from less prominent institutions, be employed in lower-prestige occupations, or be underemployed relative to their educational credentials, contributing to increasing stratification within American society. In less developed countries, minority group status, whether based on religion, sex, race, or ethnicity, still has the largest impacts on educational and occupational attainment.

SEE ALSO: Class; Education, Adult; Education and Economy; Educational Attainment; Educational Inequality; Ethnic and Racial Division of Labor; Income Inequality and Income Mobility; Lifestyle; Occupational Mobility; Occupational Segregation; Outsourcing; Status Attainment; Stratification, Gender and; Stratification, Race/Ethnicity and; Women, Economy and

REFERENCES AND SUGGESTED READINGS

Barro, R. J. & Lee, J. W. (1996) International Measures of Schooling Years and Schooling Quality. *American Economic Review* 86(2): 218–23.

Blau, P. & Duncan, O. D. (1967) *The American Occupational Structure*. Wiley, New York.

Featherman, D. L. & Hauser, R. M. (1978) *Opportunity and Change*. Academic Press, New York.

Jencks, C. & Peterson, P. (1991) *The Urban Underclass*. Brookings Institute, Washington, DC.

McCall, L. (2001) *Complex Inequality: Gender, Class, and Race in the New Economy*. Routledge, New York.

Trieman, D. J. (1977) *Occupational Prestige in Comparative Perspective*. Academic Press, New York.

Veblen, T. (1934) *The Theory of the Leisure Class*. Modern Library, New York.

Weber, M. (1946) *From Max Weber: Essays in Sociology*. Ed. H. H. Gerth & C. Wright Mills. Oxford University Press, New York.

Wilson, W. J. (1987) *The Truly Disadvantaged: The Inner City, the Underclass, and Public Policy*. University of Chicago Press, Chicago.

effect sizes

Bruce Thompson

Sociologists historically have emphasized statistical significance testing as the *sine qua non* of empirical research. Statistical significance tests yield a $p_{\text{CALCULATED}}$ value that estimates "the probability (0 to 1.0) of the sample statistics, given the sample size, and assuming the sample was derived from a population in which the null hypothesis (H_0) is exactly true" (Thompson 1996).

Effect sizes, on the other hand, are indices of practical significance that may be used either in place of, or as a complement to, statistical significance tests (Kirk 1996; Thompson 2006). Effect sizes quantify the extent to which sample results diverge from the expectations specified within the null hypothesis. Thus, if sample results exactly correspond to the null hypothesis (e.g., for the null hypothesis that the medians of three groups are equal, and the sample medians of the three groups are all 12.5), the effect size is zero. Effect sizes deviate further from zero as the sample results diverge increasingly from the null hypothesis (Thompson 2006a).

Across disciplines as diverse as economics, education, psychology, and the wildlife sciences, the frequency of published criticisms of this reliance has grown exponentially over the last few decades (Anderson et al. 2000). Indeed, some of these critics have argued that statistical significance tests should be banned from journals. As an example of the tenor of some of these views, Schmidt and Hunter (1997) can be cited as arguing that "statistical significance testing retards the growth of scientific knowledge; it never makes a positive contribution." Similarly, Rozeboom (1997) suggests that "null-hypothesis significance testing is surely the most bone-headedly misguided procedure ever institutionalized in the rote training of science students . . . It is a sociology-of-science wonderment that this statistical practice has remained so unresponsive to criticism."

During this same period, advocacy for the use of effect sizes as the basis for result interpretation has grown steadily. The 1994 *Publication Manual* of the American Psychological Association, used by more than 1,000 journals, first mentioned effect sizes and "encouraged" their use. The 2001 fifth edition of the *Manual* went further and described the failure to report effect sizes as a "defect." Because these admonitions are easily lost within the book-length *Manual*, the editors of 24 journals have made effect size reporting an explicit manuscript requirement. Included are the flagship journals of two associations that are both received by more than 50,000 members. Indeed, as

Fidler (2002) recently observed: "Of the major American associations, only all the journals of the American Educational Research Association have remained silent on all these issues."

There are dozens of different effect size statistics (Kirk 1996). Common examples are Cohen's *d*, Glass's delta, η^2, ω^2, R^2, adjusted R^2.

Some effect sizes are in a standardized score metric (e.g., Cohen's *d*, Glass's delta). Other effect sizes are in a squared, variance-accounted-for metric (e.g., η^2, R^2).

Some effect sizes are *not* corrected for the estimated influences of sampling error (e.g., η^2, R^2). On the other hand, for some effect sizes adjustments are made for estimated sampling error influences (e.g., ω^2, adjusted R^2). These types of estimates will differ less as (1) sample size is larger, (2) the number of measured variables is smaller, and (3) the true population effect size is larger. Effects are also attenuated by poor score reliability.

Because there are so many effect sizes, with more constantly under development, authors should be expected to note explicitly which effect size is being reported (Vacha-Haase & Thompson 2004). Such reporting also facilitates the use of conversion formulas with which effect sizes can be converted into alternative effects (Thompson 2006b).

The correct use of effect sizes is not as widely understood as might be hoped (Thompson 2002). Many researchers tend to rely on Cohen's benchmarks for "small," "medium," and "large" effects as regards result typicality. However, as Thompson (2001) noted, "if people interpreted effect sizes [using fixed benchmarks] with the same rigidity that α [i.e., the probability of a Type I error] = .05 has been used in statistical testing, we would merely be being stupid in another metric." At least in relatively established areas of research, "there is no wisdom whatsoever in attempting to associate regions of the effect-size metric with descriptive adjectives such as 'small,' 'moderate,' 'large,' and the like" (Glass et al. 1981).

Instead, effect sizes should be interpreted by *explicit*, *direct* comparisons of effects with those reported in the related prior literature. These comparisons, unlike statistical significance tests, inform judgments regarding result replicability.

SEE ALSO: Hypotheses; Reliability; Statistical Significance Testing

REFERENCES AND SUGGESTED READINGS

Anderson, D. R., Burnham, K. P., & Thompson, W. (2000) Null Hypothesis Testing: Problems, Prevalence, and an Alternative. *Journal of Wildlife Management* 64: 912–23.

Fidler, F. (2002) The Fifth Edition of the APA *Publication Manual*: Why Its Statistics Recommendations Are So Controversial. *Educational and Psychological Measurement* 62: 749–70.

Glass, G. V, McGaw, B., & Smith, M. L. (1981) *Meta-Analysis in Social Research*. Sage, Beverly Hills.

Kirk, R. E. (1996) Practical Significance: A Concept Whose Time Has Come. *Educational and Psychological Measurement* 56: 746–59.

Rozeboom, W. W. (1997) Good Science is Abductive, Not Hypothetico-Deductive. In: Harlow, L. L., Mulaik, S. A., & Steiger, J. H. (Eds.), *What If There Were No Significance Tests?* Erlbaum, Mahwah, NJ, pp. 335–92.

Schmidt, F. L. & Hunter, J. E. (1997) Eight Common But False Objections to the Discontinuation of Significance Testing in the Analysis of Research Data. In: Harlow, L. L., Mulaik, S. A., & Steiger, J. H. (Eds.), *What If There Were No Significance Tests?* Erlbaum, Mahwah, NJ, pp. 37–64.

Thompson, B. (1996) AERA Editorial Policies Regarding Statistical Significance Testing: Three Suggested Reforms. *Educational Researcher* 25(2): 26–30.

Thompson, B. (2001) Significance, Effect Sizes, Stepwise Methods, and Other Issues: Strong Arguments Move the Field. *Journal of Experimental Education* 70: 80–93.

Thompson, B. (2002) What Future Quantitative Social Science Research Could Look Like: Confidence Intervals for Effect Sizes. *Educational Researcher* 31(3): 24–31.

Thompson, B. (2006a) *Foundations of Behavioral Statistics: An Insight-Based Approach*. Guilford Press, New York.

Thompson, B. (2006b) Research Synthesis: Effect Sizes. In: Green, J., Camilli, G., & Elmore, P. B. (Eds.), *Complementary Methods for Research in Education*. American Educational Research Association, Washington, DC.

Vacha-Haase, T. & Thompson, B. (2004) How to Estimate and Interpret Various Effect Sizes. *Journal of Counseling Psychology* 51: 473–81.

elder abuse

Chris Phillipson

Recognition of abuse as a feature of older people's lives has been present in research and social policy for at least three decades. Mistreatment of elderly people has, however, had a much longer history. At worst, it has taken the form of outright persecution of those who, lacking resources of any kind, were thrown upon the mercy of their fellow citizens. At another level, mistreatment has been expressed through intergenerational tensions, for example during periods of economic recession as families struggle with the pressures arising from meeting the care needs of older as well as younger generations (Stearns 1986). At the same time, the meanings attached to, and the concerns expressed about, mistreatment of the old have varied from generation to generation. It is only very recently (in historical terms) that attempts have been made to translate a generalized concern about the suffering of the old into a more precisely defined concept of abuse. This transition has not been without difficulty, with complex issues raised about distinctions regarding the experience of abuse among different age groups, between various types of abuse, and the reasons for abusive behavior.

In the UK, the first discussions about elder abuse occurred in the mid-1970s, although no systematic research on the topic was completed until the early 1990s. Thereafter, there was a significant growth of interest, with research reviews and surveys (Ogg & Bennett 1992), the development of pressure groups (notably Action on Elder Abuse), and guidelines designed to protect vulnerable adults (e.g., Department of Health 2002).

Among researchers and practitioners there has been extensive debate about the precise nature of abuse and neglect, with a range of definitions circulating in the literature. Following the work of Wolf and Pillemer (1989), the main elements of elder abuse are generally agreed to comprise:

- *Physical abuse:* the infliction of physical harm or injury, including physical coercion, sexual molestation, and physical restraint.

- *Psychological abuse:* the infliction of mental anguish.
- *Financial abuse:* the illegal or improper exploitation and/or use of funds and resources.
- *Active neglect:* the refusal or failure to undertake a caregiving obligation (*including* a conscious and intentional attempt to inflict physical or emotional distress).
- *Passive neglect:* the refusal or failure to fulfill a caretaking obligation (*excluding* a conscious and intentional attempt to inflict physical or emotional distress).

Glendenning (1997) concluded from his review that a number of uncertainties still surrounded definitions of elder abuse. These he identified as (1) the relationship between domestic and institutional abuse; (2) the issue of whether elder abuse can be clearly differentiated from the abuse of other adults; and (3) the relationship between neglect and other forms of abuse.

A limited number of studies have been carried out attempting to provide estimates of the prevalence (total number of cases) and incidence (new cases) of abuse and neglect. The first major prevalence study was the Boston study of Pillemer and Finkelhor (1988), which involved interviews with 2,000 older people and focused on three types of maltreatment: physical abuse, verbal aggression, and neglect. The study found that slightly more than 3 percent of the population aged 65 plus had been mistreated: 20 cases per 1,000 were physically mistreated; 11 per 1,000 were psychologically abused; and 4 per 1,000 were neglected. The authors estimate that if a national survey produced similar results, such numbers would represent almost 1 million people in the US.

A UK survey with a nationally representative sample conducted in 1992 by Ogg and Bennett (1992) reported on results from interviews with almost 600 people aged 65 and over, as well as 1,366 adult members of households in regular contact with a person of pensionable age. The study focused on older people's experience of physical, verbal, and financial abuse with family members and relatives. Approximately 5 percent of older people (60 plus) had experienced psychological (verbal) abuse, and 2 percent

reported physical or financial forms of abuse. Adults in contact with elderly people were asked whether they had recently found themselves "shouting at, insulting or speaking roughly to them or pushing, slapping, shoving or being rough with them in any other way." Responses indicated verbal abuse of older people running at 9 percent, but a lower rate of physical abuse (less than 1 percent).

The most detailed survey to date has been the American National Elder Abuse Incidence Study (NEIS) conducted in 1994–8, which focused on abuse and neglect of older people 60 years and over living in non-institutionalized settings. The objective of the study was to collect reports of a random sample of cases of abuse and neglect occurring within a specified time period that could be weighted to represent annual estimates of *incidence* for the nation as a whole (Thomas 2000). Findings identified 450,000 older people experiencing abuse and/or neglect in domestic settings; taking account of self-neglect increased the figure to 551,000. Of these, women were abused at a higher rate than men; the very elderly (80 plus) stood out as the most vulnerable age group; and perpetrators were most likely to be adult children and spouses.

In general, studies have found that risk of abuse appears to be higher for those older people living with someone and who have problems linked to mental or physical incapacity. Perpetrators are invariably presented as experiencing stress and/or social isolation. An under-researched area concerns abuse and neglect of older people in residential care homes. McCreadie and Tinker (2003) cite research in 57 residential and nursing homes in the US which found that 10 percent of staff admitted to at least one act of physical abuse in the preceding year, with excessive restraint as the most frequently recorded form. Staff reported a very much higher rate of verbal abuse in comparison to physical abuse.

Attempts to define and map the extent of elder abuse indicate that it should not be viewed as a single, monolithic phenomenon, but that it takes a variety of forms in different settings and in different kinds of relationships. Victims and perpetrators exhibit a variety of characteristics depending on the nature of the abuse. From a sociological perspective, elder abuse must be located across a number of levels, including familial, institutional, and societal. Research has tended to focus on the first of these, drawing on models of family violence. But institutional settings such as residential homes are also important and may generate different types of abuse and neglect. Finally, it is important to acknowledge the extent to which abusive situations are themselves socially created, through poverty, inadequate community care, and agism within society. Informal care and family care in particular may be affected by inequality in later life. The tendency has been to focus on the influence of "family pathology" in creating certain types of abuse. But highlighting the role of individual families ignores wider issues about the labels attached to older people and the resources available to them to resist mistreatment. Attention to these broader issues is vital for a proper understanding of the range of factors influencing abuse and neglect in old age.

SEE ALSO: Aging and Social Support; Elder Care; Family Conflict; Gerontology; Gerontology: Key Thinkers

REFERENCES AND SUGGESTED READINGS

Biggs, S., Phillipson, C., & Kingston, P. (1995) *Elder Abuse in Perspective*. Open University Press, Buckingham.
Department of Health (2002) *No Secrets*. Department of Health, London.
Glendenning, F. (1997) What is Elder Abuse and Neglect? In: Decalmer, P. & Glendenning, F. (Eds.), *The Mistreatment of Elderly People*, 2nd edn. Sage, London.
McCreadie, C. & Tinker, A. (2003) Elder Abuse. In: Tallis, R. C. & Fillit, H. M. (Eds.), *Brocklehurst's Textbook of Geriatric Medicine and Gerontology*, 6th edn. Churchill Livingstone, Edinburgh.
Ogg, J. & Bennett, G. (1992) Elder Abuse in Britain. *British Medical Journal* 305: 998–9.
Pillemer, K. & Finkelhor, D. (1988) The Prevalence of Elder Abuse: A Random Sample Survey. *Gerontologist* 28(1): 51–7.
Stearns, P. (1986) Old Age Family Conflict: The Perspective of the Past. In: Pillemer, K. & Wolf, R. (Eds.), *Elder Abuse*. Auburn House, Dover.
Thomas, C. (2000) The First National Study of Elder Abuse and Neglect: Contrasts with Results from Other Studies. *Journal of Elder Abuse and Neglect* 12(1): 1–14.
Wolf, R. & Pillemer, K. (1989) *Helping Elderly Victims*. Columbia University Press, New York.

elder care

Norah Keating

Elder care is assistance provided to a senior because of that senior's chronic health problem or disability. Tasks include household work, indoor and outdoor home maintenance, banking and financial management, personal care, and care management (Keating et al. 1999). The term has been part of the gerontology lexicon for many years. Its origins lie in the description of the tasks provided by formal or paid caregivers (i.e., nurses or home support workers) to seniors with chronic illnesses such as dementia. More recently, the term has also been used to describe family members and friends who care for frail older adults. In contrast to formal caregivers, their care is called informal. Tasks done by these formal and informal caregivers are not unique and may be provided to younger adults as well. While adults over age 65 are considered seniors, in contemporary discussion elder care denotes assistance to those who are very old. In developed countries, onset of age-related chronic illnesses is prevalent after age 75 and most people in residential (nursing home) settings are over age 80.

Formal and informal caregivers to frail seniors differ in a number of ways. Formal caregivers have an agency–client relationship based on an agreement to provide services, most often for pay. The services they provide in community settings are discrete, based on the mandate of the organization and time limited. In residential settings services are provided to support the health and daily living needs of frail older adults; in these settings employees are more likely to provide a variety of tasks. In contrast, family members and friends provide care because of the personal history that exists between giver and recipient – one that is based on kinship, other affective ties, or a longstanding relationship. These caregivers spend most time on household tasks and personal care that help keep seniors at home. If the senior is placed in residential care, their tasks shift toward care management, which includes monitoring and managing formal care and visiting (Keefe & Fancey 2000).

Kinship ties make family members more obliged to help; spouses and adult children are the most common family caregivers, though more distant kin such as nieces, nephews, and grandchildren also assist. About 20 percent of informal caregivers are friends and neighbors who are most likely to provide tasks other than personal care or to give high levels of assistance in the absence of kin (Wenger 1997).

Providing care to increasing proportions of frail seniors is one of the challenges of a worldwide trend toward population aging. A contemporary approach to this challenge is reducing the amount of residential and formal care and shifting toward an emphasis on community-based care with high levels of family-friend involvement (Ward-Griffin & Marshall 2003). This approach has been called sending care home. Care in the community is seen as more responsive to the needs of frail seniors because it is provided in familiar settings by people who know them best. Yet community care has costs to informal caregivers who provide the majority of this care and whose work is likely to be unpaid, invisible to others, and who may receive little respite from their caregiving duties. Countries are engaged in debates about the ideal mix of public/family-friend elder care services and have found different solutions. For example, Scandinavian countries have higher levels of publicly funded elder care services than do countries in Southern Europe. In community settings in Canada, informal caregivers provide substantially more assistance to frail seniors than formal caregivers, often caring for more than 2 years with multiple caregiving responsibilities for seniors and others. Almost one quarter of frail seniors receive no care from either formal or informal sources.

The terms elder care, care giving, and informal care are controversial. Elder care is viewed as a useful concept in fostering recognition of the support needed by frail older adults and raising awareness of the activities and commitments of their caregivers. Yet elder care also has been criticized as having connotations of decline, disease, and illness which have become associated with aging (Sims-Gould 2005). Though this is not always understood, elder care is meant to denote a response to frailty in old age, not to old age itself. The term caregiving is broader in scope and is useful in distinguishing everyday exchanges of support from tasks provided in response to a chronic health problem. Caring families who are concerned about their older family members are not the same as caregiving families who do things for their older relative because of that person's chronic health problem and in order to help the person maintain their independence. Yet the word caregiving is criticized because it seems unidirectional, placing frail seniors as passive recipients of tasks rather than as members of social groups which evolve, have complex interactions and provide to, as well as receive from, others in the group (Guberman & Maheu 1999). The term informal caregiver was created to provide a clear contrast to those whose caring work was designated as formal. Because of the intensity and duration of care, the term family/friend care increasingly is used as an alternative to informal, which can denote involvement that is casual, intermittent, or periodic.

New directions in understanding elder care are addressing some of these controversies. These include considering how groups of family members and friends organize to provide care and focusing on caregiving as a career rather than a static situation.

Current knowledge of elder care is based primarily on studies of dyads of individual family-friend caregivers and care recipients. The term primary caregiver comes from this tradition. A single caregiver, normally a family member, is identified as the main provider of services to the frail senior. This approach, while convenient, has led to a view that elder care is the domain of women and close kin.

Researchers have begun to analyze how groups of people with social or kin ties to older adults organize themselves to provide care.

Networks differ on a number of dimensions, including network size, age and employment status composition, and proximity to the frail senior, as well as proportions of kin and friends and women and men (Litwin & Landau 2000). Men are just as likely to be part of elder care networks as women, but they do different tasks such as home maintenance, while women are most likely to do household work and personal care. Some networks have substantial proportions of friends and distant kin, as well as close kin such as adult children. Half of frail seniors with family-friend care networks receive formal care as well.

Increasingly, elder care is seen as an evolution of previous patterns of family interaction. Viewing caregiving as part of family solidarity and interaction over time shows how elder care emerges from families' history of relationships with one another. It provides a dynamic view of how caregiving changes in response to health or other transitions (Martin-Matthews 2000) and of which family members and friends can sustain support as it evolves into more intensive elder care. This information is important in intervening to support family-friend caregivers. Families with a history of difficult relationships may not do well in the intense task and intimacy requirements of elder care. Their relatives may be better served by receipt of care from formal services.

Elder care research is moving toward more qualitative studies to create deeper understandings of the experiences of caregivers and of the frail seniors for whom they care. Understanding their experiences is providing better conceptualizations of how social networks evolve into care networks and which frail seniors are likely to be without care. Further methodological development will help move elder care research from dyads to networks so that the sharing of care can be better understood. Rural researchers have begun to examine how communities might differ in creating supportive environments for older adults with chronic illness. This research also needs to include a time dimension to track changes in supportiveness of communities over the lifetime of adults who live there. Analyses of the interactions of family-friend, formal, and community networks

are needed to have a more complete view of the contexts and sources of elder care.

SEE ALSO: Age Prejudice and Discrimination; Aging, Demography of; Aging and Social Support; Elder Abuse; Gender, Aging and; Intergenerational Relationships and Exchanges; Later-Life Marriage; Longevity, Social Aspects (the Oldest Old)

REFERENCES AND SUGGESTED READINGS

Guberman, N. & Maheu, P. (1999) Aging and Care Giving in Ethnocultural Families. In: Neysmith, S. (Ed.), *Critical Issues for Future Social Work Practice with Aging Persons*. Columbia University Press, New York, pp. 143–54.

Keating, N., Otfinowski, P., Wenger, C., Fast, J., & Derksen, L. (2003) Understanding the Caring Capacity of Informal Networks of Frail Seniors: A Case for Care Networks. *Ageing and Society* 23: 115–17.

Keating, N., Fast, J., Frederick, K., & Perrier, C. (1999) *Eldercare in Canada: Context, Content and Consequences*. Statistics Canada, Ottawa.

Keefe, J. & Fancey, P. (2000) The Care Continues: Responsibility for Elderly Relatives Before and After Admission to a Long-Term Care Facility. *Family Relations* 49: 235–44.

Litwin, H. & Landau, R. (2000) Social Network Type and Social Support among the Old-Old. *Journal of Aging Studies* 14: 213–28.

Martin-Matthews, A. (2000) International Care Giving: How Apocalyptic and Dominant Demographies Frame the Questions and Shape the Answers. In: Gee, E. & Gutman, G. (Eds.), *Overselling Population Aging*. Oxford University Press, Oxford.

Sims-Gould, J. (2005) Family Care Giving: Examining Meanings in Academic Gerontological Research. Paper presented to the symposium Interdisciplinary Perspectives on the Costs and Contributions of Care, Trent University, Peterborough, Canada.

Ward-Griffin, C. & Marshall, V. (2003) Reconceptualizing the Relationship between "Public" and "Private" Eldercare. *Journal of Aging Studies* 17: 189–208.

Wenger, C. (1997) Social Networks and the Prediction of Elderly People at Risk. *Aging and Mental Health* 1: 311–20.

elective affinity

J. I. (Hans) Bakker

The term elective affinity is currently associated with Weber's thesis concerning modern capitalism. A key aspect concerns the linkage, attraction, or inner "affinity" between "the Protestant Ethic/Protestant sects" and the "spirit" of modern capitalism. The idea of an affinity could be indicated by any two factors seeming to go together – to be "connected." Weber argues that there is an "inner affinity" (*innere Verwandtschaft*) between several things, especially between (1) a this-worldly asceticism of sects (e.g., Quakers, Mennonites) and (2) the underlying "spirit" (*Geist*) of modern capitalism. Rather than hedonism, among Protestants there is an ascetic outlook, an estrangement from joy, as indicated by Benjamin Franklin's maxims.

The modifier "elective" is a vestige from Albertus Magnus, Scholasticism, Galileo, and the Latin of chemists like T. O. Bergman: *attractio electiva simplex* or *affinitas electiva*. The German term *Verwandtschaft* alone means "affinity," but the classical Latin phrase "elective affinity" had an impact on Goethe (Adler 1990). The term Elective Affinity (*Wahlverwandtschaft*) became a title for one of Goethe's romantic novels about marriage and "chemical" erotic attraction. Weber greatly admired Goethe and accepted an epistemology that stresses complexity rather than reductionism in the study of social action. Weber does not presuppose the same ontology as Goethe, but he used Goethe's word knowing his readers would understand the implicit referent. However, it gets lost in translation.

Many thinkers have been critical of Weber's thesis. Some critics have assumed that Weber's argument is a temporal, *causal* argument concerning the effects of an ethos on a material mode of production. Cohen (2002 29, 79–89) provides a thorough statement of the elective affinity argument in terms of "degree of similarity" and "rational effects," but concludes critically that "Weber's method of elective affinities can do nothing to sort out the causal ordering." The lack of possibility of a temporal causal argument is already emphasized in Weber's 1905 statement (Weber 2002a), published at the same time as his famous methodological essay on "Objectivity." Weber was attempting to avoid positivistic causal argumentation of the sort characteristic of dialectical materialism. He was not attempting to replace a one-sided materialist argument with an equally misleading one-sided idealist argument. Since statistics had not yet been invented there was no universally agreed term to represent the notion of an "association" or "co-relationship" between two factors or variables.

SEE ALSO: Dialectical Materialism; Weber, Max

REFERENCES AND SUGGESTED READINGS

Adler, J. (1990) Goethe's Use of Chemical Theory in his Novel, *Elective Affinities*. In: Cunningham, A. & Jardine, N. (Eds.), *Romanticism and the Sciences*. Cambridge University Press, Cambridge, pp. 263–79.

Cohen, J. (2002) *Protestantism and Capitalism: The Mechanisms of Influence*. De Gruyter, New York.

Goethe, J. W. (1809) *Elective Affinities*. In: *Goethe: The Collected Works*, Vol. 11. Trans. V. Lange & J. Ryan. Princeton University Press, Princeton.

Howe, R. (1978) Max Weber's Elective Affinities: Sociology within the Bounds of Pure Reason. *American Journal of Sociology* 84: 366–85.

Weber, M. (1930 [1920]) *The Protestant Ethic and the Spirit of Capitalism*. Trans. T. Parsons. Scribner's, New York.

Weber, M. (2002a [1905]) *The Protestant Ethic and the Spirit of Capitalism – the Version of 1905, Together with Weber's Rebuttals of Fischer and Rachfahl and Other Essays on Protestantism and Society*. Penguin, New York.

Weber, M. (2002b [1920]) *The Protestant Ethics and the Spirit of Capitalism*. Trans. S. Kalberg. Roxbury Publishing, Los Angeles.

elementary theory

Pamela Emanuelson

Consistent with the classical theories of Marx, Weber, and Simmel, elementary theory is a multilevel theory of interaction in social relations. For example, elementary theory (hereafter ET) predicts power exercise, who benefits in social relations such as exchange, coercion, and conflict. ET's actor-level assumptions are (1) that actors pursue valued states called interests within social relations and (2) that an actor's interests can be inferred from the social relations and structures in which activity occurs. On a structural level, ET embeds social relations in social structures, which consist of two or more connected social relations. Social structures are in turn characterized by rules and restrictions, including but not limited to rules delimiting the maximum and minimum number of exchanges at a position and rules mandating the sequence of social interaction across a structure. ET makes predictions in light of the interrelations among relational and structural conditions and actor's interests.

Willer and Anderson (1981) demonstrated that ET predicts action in a diversity of social structures ranging from legal systems to political networks to several distinct community systems. Through an interactive process involving the relaxation of scope conditions, the discovery and conceptualization of new structural conditions, theory integration, and experimental testing, ET expanded beyond its original formulation in 1981 to predict action in increasingly complex structures. Major contributions made to the growth and development of ET include the discovery of new structural conditions (Patton & Willer 1990; Szmatka & Willer 1995; Corra & Willer 2002), the conceptualization of distinct network types (Markovsky et al. 1993; Lovaglia et al. 1995), and bridging between ET and status characteristics theory (Willer et al. 1997; Thye 2000). Recent growth in ET addresses the phenomenon of power-at-a-distance (Willer 2003; Emanuelson & Willer 2003) and the effects of coalition formation on power exercise (Borch & Willer 2006). ET continues to grow with the goal of achieving a fully general theory of human behavior in relations and structures. To date, ET applies a modeling procedure, two principles, two laws, and seven structural conditions to predict action in relations embedded in structures.

MODELING PROCEDURE

ET uses network models to conceptualize relations in social structures. For instance, letters

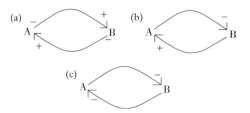

Figure 1 Exchange relations.

such as A and B represent social actors. Paired signed arcs connecting social actors representing sanctions form social relations. The positive and negative signs at each end of the arcs represent the effect of transmitting or receiving. Signs at the receiving end of a sanction differentiate positive and negative sanctions. For instance, in Figure 1(a), the receipt of a positive sanction from A increases B's preference state but transmitting that positive sanction is costly and decreases A's preference state. Pairing negative and positive sanctions results in the three basic social relations, exchange (Fig. 1a), coercion (Fig. 1b), and conflict (Fig. 1c).

PRINCIPLES AND LAWS

Principle 1 defines ET's actor model. It asserts that *all social actors act to maximize their expected preference state alteration*. For instance, employees seek to maximize wages while employers seek to minimize wages. The first law is a payoff function. For employee *j*, Law 1 states that the payoff to *j* equals the value per unit times the quantity of money received plus the value per unit times the quantity of labor expended. Although Principle 1 accounts for employers' and employees' interests, determining the wage agreed upon requires a principle that applies to mixed-motive relations.

In mixed-motive relations both actors (1) prefer agreement to disagreement and (2) seek to increase their preference state at the other's expense. In the above example, when the payoffs to employer and employee are both positive, both benefit from continuing the relation, and the wage changes that increase the employers' benefit decrease the employees' benefit and conversely.

In this and other mixed-motive relations, ET applies Law 2, resistance. An actor's resistance is the ratio of an actor's interests. The numerator represents the interest in receiving the best possible payoff while the denominator represents the interest in avoiding disagreement.

Assume that an employer breaks even when paying $16/hour of work and assume further that dollar bills are not divisible. Then the maximum for an hour of work is $15. If j, the employee, does not reach an agreement with the employer, j receives nothing. The employee's resistance takes into consideration the $15 maximum benefit and the $0 payoff at confrontation. The employer k's resistance for both of his/her relations is determined in a like manner.

Principle 2 sets the resistance of two actors equal to each other. More specifically, Principle 2 states that *agreements occur at the point of equiresistance for undifferentiated actors in a full information system*.

STRUCTURAL CONDITIONS

ET asserts that structural conditions affect relations embedded in social structures. The theory (1) identifies seven structural conditions and (2) offers point predictions for the conditions' effects on outcomes in exchange relations. For exclusion, the strongest, most widely studied, and tested structural condition, three distinct network types have been identified: strong, equal, and weak power. The three are discussed below. Other structural conditions are four connection types, null, inclusion, inclusion-null, and inclusion-exclusion, and two variants, hierarchy/mobility (a variant of exclusion) and ordering (a variant of inclusion).

A typology identifying the number of an actor's connections and the maximum and minimum number of relations in which an actor can benefit generates types of connection. For the employer example, N_k is the number of potential employees k can reach, M_k is the maximum number of employee relations in which k can benefit, and Q_k is the minimum number of those relations in which k must reach agreement to benefit from any one.

An actor is exclusively connected if $N > M$. For example, imagine that employer k can reach j_1, j_2, and j_3 all of whom need employment. Employer k, however, needs and wants only one new employee. Since $N_k = 3$ and $M_k = 1$, two potential employees will necessarily be excluded and the relations are exclusively connected at k. When the js have no alternative employment, the structure is strong power. Networks containing exclusive connection can also be weak or equal power.

Strong power networks are networks with one or more high power positions that are never excluded and two or more low power positions at least one of which is always excluded. Low power positions are connected only to high power positions. In strong power networks, high power positions gain maximally at the expense of low power positions. In the above example, the js compete to be hired by k until the one j is hired to work for $1/hour while k profits maximally at $15.

Equal power networks are networks in which all positions are identically connected. It follows that either no position is excluded or all face an equal probability of exclusion. Since positions are identical, none has a structural advantage over any other and payoffs are equal to all.

Weak power networks include all networks in which power is produced by exclusion that are not equal or strong. In weak power networks, positions have different likelihoods of being included in an exchange relation. An actor's likelihood of being included is calculated under the assumption that actors seek exchange equally with all other connected actors. As network size increases, the difficulty of calculating likelihood values increases; however, an applet program for calculating likelihood values is available on the faculty web page of David Willer at the University of South Carolina.

The resistance-likelihood assumption asserts that the actor's evaluations of best possible payoff and confrontation payoff vary with the likelihood of being included (Lovaglia et al. 1995). When V is the total value in the relation, the confrontation payoff ranges between 0 and V/2 and the best possible payoff ranges between V/2 and V.

Compound networks are composed of "subnetworks," at least one of which is strong power: they break between the high power position(s) and position(s) which are never excluded. All breaks occur at suboptimal relations, but not all suboptimal relations are breaks. A relation is suboptimal when exchange in it reduces the number of exchanges that can occur in the network. To predict the distribution of benefit, the first step is to find and remove breaks. Once they are found, the resulting subnetworks are solved individually.

Hierarchy/mobility is not a connection type: it is a variant of exclusion. Hierarchy/mobility occurs when each step up in a bureaucratic organization decreases the number of offices, increases the salary and perquisites associated with each office, and promotion is competitive. Hierarchy/mobility's competitive mobility centralizes power to the top. Applying hierarchy/mobility, the effects of discriminatory practices on organizations are apparent. For instance, if an organization discriminates against promoting women, no woman will have an interest in competing. Therefore, the power of upper offices over those women decreases and may also decrease over men because of reduced competition.

An actor is inclusively connected if more than one exchange is necessary to benefit: $Q > 1$. For example, if employer k needs both j_1 for specialized task $s1$, and j_2 for specialized task $s2$ to benefit, k is inclusively connected. Actor k's minimum number of exchanges is $Q_k = 2 > 1$. Inclusive connection increases the costs of confrontation for the inclusively connected actor, thereby decreasing that actor's power.

In inclusively connected networks, power differences increase sequentially. Assume that k exchanges with j_1 and j_2 in that order. The consequence of disagreement in the first exchange is that k and j receive nothing. Hence, the k–j_1 exchange is at equipower. In the k–j_2 exchange, k will lose the investment made in the first exchange if agreement between k and j_2 is not reached. In contrast, j_2 has invested in nothing and has a confrontation payoff of zero. k is less powerful than j. When $Q > 2$, across exchanges, the inclusively connected actor's investments increase, as does the potential cost of not completing the next necessary exchange. Consequently, the last position to exchange with the inclusively connected position is the most powerful.

Ordering is not a connection type: it is a variant of inclusion. An actor connected by ordering must complete $Q > 1$ exchanges *in a specified sequence*. For example, ordering advantages gatekeepers. A gatekeeper controls access to valued goods that he or she does not own. For example, suppose that employer k has a secretary that determines which js k interviews. If the secretary is dishonest, he or she can demand fees for admittance to the valued interview. The power exercised by the secretary varies with the value of the interview to the interviewees.

By definition, an actor disadvantaged by ordering must complete exchanges in sequence; however, the incidence of power effects in the sequence is the reverse of the incidence found for inclusive connection. For ordering, the largest effect is in the first relation and decreases across exchanges until, in the last exchange, the power is equal. In the above example, the secretary is in the first relation and is powerful because he or she can block j's valued outcomes.

Whereas for exclusive connection N_k the number of k's relations is greater than M_k, the largest number of exchanges from which k can benefit, for null connection $N_k = M_k$. Therefore, when k is null connected to all js, k can complete all k's exchange relations and benefits from each. Actors have identical estimations of maximum possible payoff and payoff at confrontation. All actors and exchanges are equal.

Inclusion-null and inclusion-exclusion are each a single connection type which mixes qualities of two other types. For inclusion-null $N = M > Q > 1$ but for inclusion-exclusion $N > M \geq Q > 1$. Imagine that employer k needs at least two ($Q_k = 2$) of three ($N_k = 3$) js to complete a project. If k hires all three js ($M_k = 3$), the project will be completed faster. Since $N_k = M_k = 3$ and $Q_k = 2 > 1$, k is inclusive-null connected. Because k need not necessarily include all three js, any inclusive advantage is eliminated and the three exchanges are equal power.

Now imagine that k needs at least three ($Q_k = 3$) of four ($N_k = 4$) js to complete the project, and k can hire a maximum of only three js ($M_k = 3$). Since $N_k = 4 > M_k = 3$ and $Q_k = 3 > 1$, k is inclusive-exclusive connected. Because k must necessarily exclude one j, any inclusive advantage is eliminated and k benefits maximally in each exchange.

COERCIVE STRUCTURES

Positions in coercive relations are distinct; one is the coercee and the other the coercer. The coercee is under threat of receiving the negative sanction while the coercer can transmit the negative sanction or receive positive(s) from the coercee. The coercer's power is based on the effect on the coercee of the negative sanction; the larger that effect, the larger the flow of positives at agreement. Resistance predicts that flow in applications is not unlike its applications to exchange.

The asymmetry in the coercive relation produces power differently for coercee central and coercer central structures. For example, imagine that coercee *j* has an option of three coercers, *k*s. The *j* must choose a coercer, but once chosen, *j* cannot be coerced by any other *k*s. The *k*s will bid against each other until *j* pays the minimum possible for protection. In this coercee central structure, exclusion produces power like it does in exchange. Now imagine that *k* is connected to three *j*s. The *j*s are told that the *j* that does the least work will receive a negative sanction. In fact, this is a strong coercive structure in which the *j*s compete to not be the least productive and *k* benefits maximally.

DIFFERENTIATED ACTORS IN EXCHANGE

Status value theory bridges between ET and status characteristics theory, a theory of status and influence, to make predictions in exchanges that include actors differentiated by status. Status value theory assumes that resources of high-status actors are valued more highly than resources of low-status actors. As a consequence, high-status actors gain favorable outcomes. A recent advance in ET combines values quantifying status effects into resistance equations to make point predictions for exchange outcomes in networks with status-differentiated actors.

Current research seeks to link legitimacy theory to ET. The goal is to determine whether legitimacy of coalitions in exchange networks affects actors' willingness to join. Coalitions are organizations of individuals that act as a single actor. Previous research has shown that coalitions substantially improve payoffs to low power actors. At issue in research now being conducted is whether legitimacy stabilizes coalitions by resolving first- and second-order free-riding and thus countervails power.

THE EFFECT OF RESOURCE MOVEMENT ON EXCHANGE

ET offers predictions for networks where resources move only between adjacent positions (discrete networks), and networks where resources move across a network (flow networks). The structures discussed above were all discrete networks. Nevertheless, the structural conditions discussed above also apply to flow networks. In a flow network, *k* sells X to *j* and *j* sells the X bought from *k* to *h*. Since only *k* starts out with X, and *k* is not connected to *h*, for *h* to receive X the sequence of exchange is determined: first *k–j* and then *j–h*. Therefore, ordering affects power in the first relation. Since $Q_j = 2$, *j* is disadvantaged by inclusion in the *j–h* relation. Whereas all flow networks contain ordering in first exchange and inclusion in the second, exclusion can mask their effects. For instance, if *j* was connected to two *k*s and *j* could buy X from only one, exclusion would mask the effect of ordering and *j* would pay the minimum price for X.

Predictions for flow networks take into consideration the structural conditions of exclusion, inclusion, and ordering, and the effect of sequence in reducing value available for negotiation in exchange relations across a flow network. As the resource X moves across the network, the total value of exchanges in the network is the difference between X's initial and final value. In each exchange relation, some of that value is appropriated. For example, let *h* value X at $16 and let resources be highly divisible. Suppose *j* pays *k* $8 for X. Now the value available for negotiation has reduced from $16 in the first exchange to $8 in the second. Thus, the most *j* can make selling X to *h* is $8 or the most *h* can profit is $8.

CONCLUSION

ET is still growing. Initially, its applications were largely limited to micro-level structures.

Now, research on coalitions and flow networks is applicable to complex meso and macro structures such as bureaucratic organizations and interorganizational networks. Furthermore, most work in ET uses experimentation with the aim of building strong theory. The rigorously tested and scope expansive theory is now useful for applications outside the laboratory. Lastly, much of the recent growth in ET has focused on networks of exchange relations. ET would benefit from new research aimed at examining coercive and conflict networks.

SEE ALSO: Exchange Network Theory; Experimental Methods; Legitimacy; Mathematical Sociology; Power-Dependence Theory; Power, Theories of; Rational Choice Theories; Social Exchange Theory

REFERENCES AND SUGGESTED READINGS

Borch, C. & Willer, D. (2006) Power, Embedded Games, and Coalition Formation. *Journal of Mathematical Sociology*.

Corra, M. & Willer, D. (2002) The Gatekeeper. *Sociological Theory* 20: 180–205.

Emanuelson, P. (2005) Improving the Precision and Parsimony of Network Exchange Theory: A Comparison of Three Network Exchange Models. *Current Research in Social Psychology* 10: 149–65.

Emanuelson, P. & Willer, D. (2003) The Middleman. Presented at the Annual Meeting of the American Sociological Association, Atlanta.

Girard, D. & Borch, C. (2003) Optimal Seek Simplified. *Current Research in Social Psychology* 8: 225–41.

Lovaglia, M. J., Skvoretz, J., Willer, D., & Markovsky, B. (1995) Negotiated Outcomes in Social Exchange Networks. *Social Forces* 74: 123–55.

Markovsky, B. (1992) Network Exchange Outcomes: Limits of Predictability. *Social Networks* 14: 267–86.

Markovsky, B., Skvoretz, J., Willer, D., Lovaglia, M. J., & Erger, J. (1993) The Seeds of Weak Power: An Extension of Network Exchange Theory. *American Sociological Review* 58: 197–209.

Patton, T. & Willer, D. (1990) Connection and Power in Centralized Exchange Networks. *Journal of Mathematical Sociology* 16: 31–49.

Szmatka, J. & Willer, D. (1995) Exclusion, Inclusion, and Compound Connection in Exchange Networks. *Social Psychology Quarterly* 58: 123–32.

Thye, S. R. (2000) A Status Value Theory of Power in Exchange Relations. *American Sociological Review* 65: 407–32.

Thye, S. R., Willer, D., & Markovsky, B. (2005) From Status to Power: A New Model at the Intersection of Two Theories. *Social Forces*.

Willer, D. (1999) *Network Exchange Theory*. Praeger, Westport, CT.

Willer, D. (2003) Power-at-a-Distance. *Social Forces* 81: 1295–334.

Willer, D. & Anderson, B. (Eds.) (1981) *Networks, Exchange, and Coercion*. Elsevier/Greenwood, New York.

Willer, D. & Skvoretz, J. (1997a) Network Connection and Exchange Ratios: Theory, Predictions, and Experimental Tests. In: Markovsky, B., Lovaglia, M. J., & Troyer, L. (Eds.), *Advances in Group Process*, Vol. 14. JAI Press, Greenwich, pp. 199–234.

Willer, D. & Skvoretz, J. (1997b) Games and Structures. *Rationality and Society* 9: 5–35.

Willer, D. & Szmatka, J. (1993) Cross-National Experimental Investigations of Elementary Theory: Implications for the Generality of the Theory and the Autonomy of Social Structure. In: Lawler, E. J., Markovsky, B., Heimer, K., & O'Brien, J. (Eds.), *Advances in Group Processes*, Vol. 10. JAI Press, Greenwich, pp. 37–81.

Willer, D., Markovsky, B., & Patton, T. (1989) Power Structures: Derivations and Applications of Elementary Theory. In: Berger, J., Zelditch, M., Jr., & Anderson, B. (Eds.), *Sociological Theories in Progress: New Formulations*. Sage, Newbury Park, CA, pp. 313–53.

Willer, D., Lovaglia, M. J., & Markovsky, B. (1997) Power and Influence: A Theoretic Bridge. *Social Forces* 76: 571–603.

Elias, Norbert (1897–1990)

George Ritzer and J. Michael Ryan

Norbert Elias was born in Breslau, Germany in 1897. He was the son of a small manufacturer and was brought up in comfortable surroundings. After serving in the German Army during World War I, Elias returned home to study medicine and philosophy at the University of Breslau. It was his study of medicine that gave him a sense of the interconnections among the various parts of the human body that would be so important to shaping his understanding of human interconnections – what he would term figurations. Elias received his PhD in 1924 and then went to Heidelberg, where he become very actively involved in sociology circles, most notably one headed by Marianne Weber. He also became friend and assistant to Karl Mannheim. This relationship led Elias to follow Mannheim as his official assistant to the University of Frankfurt in 1930.

After Hitler came to power in early 1933, Elias and many other Jewish scholars (including Mannheim) left Germany, first for Paris and later for London. Elias's most famous book, *The Civilizing Process*, was published in German in 1939. Unfortunately, there was no market in Germany for a book authored by a Jew and it also received little attention in other parts of the world. During the war and for nearly a decade after it ended Elias could not obtain secure employment and remained a marginal figure in British academic circles. In 1954, however, Elias began his career (at the age of 57) at the University of Leicester. He remained unpopular, however, among both faculty and students and during his time there none of his books were ever translated into English. However, during the 1950s and 1960s on the Continent, particularly in the Netherlands and Germany, Elias's work began to be discovered. It was during the 1970s that Elias's work began to receive both academic and public attention in Europe. This recognition is still growing today throughout the world. Elias died at the age of 93, living just long enough to bask in the early years of the much-delayed recognition of his work.

FIGURATION

Elias proposed the concept of figuration as an alternative to thinking of the "individual" and "society" as different or antagonistic (Elias 1978). Figurations are not static, but instead are social processes. In fact, during the latter part of his career, Elias chose the label *process sociology* to describe his work (Mennell 1992: 252). Figurations involve the "interweaving" of people. They describe the relationships between people rather than describing a type

of structure which is external to or coercive over people. In other words, individuals are viewed as open and their relationships with one another compose figurations. Figurations are in a state of constant flux because of the changing nature of power, which is central to their understanding. They develop in largely unforeseeable ways.

The idea of a figuration is a broad one in that it can be used to apply to the micro and the macro, and to every social phenomenon in between. This image is best represented by Elias's notion of "chains of interdependence," which constitute the real focus of his work.

CIVILIZATION

In addition to figurations and chains of interdependence, Elias's work is largely concerned with the "sociogenesis" of civilization, especially in the Occident (Bogner et al. 1992). In particular, Elias (1997) is interested in what he perceives to be the gradual changes that have occurred in the behavioral and psychological makeup of those living in the West. In his study of the history of manners, for example, Elias is concerned with the historical transformation of a wide array of rather mundane behaviors which have culminated in what we would now call civilized behavior. Some of the behaviors which most interest Elias include what embarrasses us, our increasing sensitivity, how we have grown increasingly observant of others, and our sharpened understanding of others.

Elias uses books (and other sources) on manners written between the thirteenth and nineteenth centuries to get at these changes. He concludes that our threshold of embarrassment has gradually advanced. For example, what people did at the dinner table in the thirteenth century – passing gas, for one – would cause great embarrassment to one in the nineteenth century (and twenty-first century as well). Thus, that which is considered distasteful is over time increasingly likely to be "removed behind the scenes of social life" (Elias 1994a: 99). In another example, one thirteenth-century poem warns, "A number of people gnaw on a bone and then put it back in the dish – this is a serious offense" and another volume states: "It is not decent to poke your fingers in to your ears or eyes, as some people do, or to pick your nose while eating" (pp. 68, 71). The implication is that such behaviors were typical at that time and did not cause those who engaged in them much embarrassment. These texts provide admonitions against such behavior in an effort to "civilize" people. As time goes by, the knowledge that these things are not appropriate spreads throughout society and there is no longer a need to remind people that such behavior is inappropriate. Thus, a late sixteenth-century document says: "Nothing is more improper than to lick your fingers, to touch the meats and put them into your mouth with your hand, to stir sauce with your fingers, or to dip bread into it with your fork and then suck it" (p. 79). Of course, there are some things (e.g., picking one's nose) that are deemed more improper than others (e.g., licking one's fingers), but by this time civilization has already progressed to the point where it is widely recognized that such behaviors are uncivilized. With certain behaviors safely behind the scenes, society then moves on to find other, less egregious behaviors that it defines as uncivilized.

POWER AND CIVILIZATION

In *Power and Civility* (1994b) Elias is concerned with changes in social constraint that are associated with the rise of self-restraint, the real key to the civilizing process. The most important of these social constraints is the macrostructural phenomena of the lengthening of interdependency chains. This also contributes to the corresponding need for individuals to moderate their emotions by developing the "habit of connecting events in terms of chains of cause and effect" (p. 236). Thus, the ever-increasing differentiation of social functions plays a central role in the process of civilization. In addition and in conjunction with this differentiation is the importance of "a total reorganization of the social fabric" (p. 231). This is how Elias describes the historical process of the emergence of increasingly stable central organs of society that monopolize the means of physical force and taxation. Central to this development is the emergence of a king with absolute status, as well as of a court society. Elias is especially interested in the case of France during the

reign of Louis XIV, although he points out that the courts of Europe all came to be closely linked. What Elias calls a "royal mechanism" is operating here in that kings are able to emerge in a specific figuration where competing functional groups are ambivalent (they are characterized by both mutual dependency as well as mutual hostility) and power is evenly distributed between them, thus prohibiting either a decisive conflict or a decisive compromise. As Elias puts it, "Not by chance, not whenever a strong ruling personality is born, but when a specific social structure provides the opportunity, does the central organ attain that optimal power which usually finds expression in strong autocracy" (p. 174). In other words, a king emerges only when the appropriate figuration is in place.

The king and his court were of particular importance to Elias because it was here that changes took place that would eventually affect the rest of society. The court noble was forced to be increasingly sensitive to others while simultaneously curbing his own emotions because, unlike the warrior, his dependency chains were relatively long. The noble was further restrained in that it was the king alone who was gaining increasing control over the means of violence. This monopoly of violence, in turn, is strongly related to the king's ability to hold a monopoly over taxation, since it is taxes that allow the king to pay for the control of the means of violence (p. 208). The noble is further disadvantaged in that while taxes increase the king's income, they reduce the nobility's, further enhancing the power of the king (Elias 1983: 155). The nobles play an important role in the civilizing process because they carry the changes from the court to the rest of society. Further, changes in the West are eventually spread to other parts of the world. Thus, the rise of the king and his court and the shift in importance from warrior to courtier represent a key "spurt" in the civilizing process. This idea of a spurt is how Elias deals with social change – it is not an even, unilinear process, but rather one that stops, starts, and goes back and forth.

Despite the importance of the king, the nobles, and the court, the ultimate cause of the most decisive changes is related to the changes in the entire figuration of the time. In other words, the real importance of change is found in the changing relationships between groups, as well as those between individuals in those groups. Further, this figuration ends up constraining both the king and the nobility, as there is a gradual movement toward a state. It is the private monopoly of the means of violence and of taxation (by the king) that sets the ground for a public monopoly of those same resources (by the state). The rise of the controlling agencies in society is linked to the rise of the controlling agencies within the individual. These two processes work in tandem to wield unprecedented power over individuals' ability to act on their emotions. That is not to say that individuals before this time were completely unrestrained and emotionally flamboyant, but rather that self-control and moderation became increasingly important in constraining people's emotional lives. Elias recognizes that this increasing control is not entirely good. While life has become safer (fewer people act out violently), it has also grown less enjoyable. Unable to express their emotions directly, people turn to alternative outlets such as dreams and books to express themselves. Further, external struggles become increasingly internalized as (to use Freud's terms) battles between the id and the superego. Thus, a reduction in violence is accompanied by an increase in boredom and restlessness.

Longer dependency chains are thus ultimately associated with greater control of emotions and a simultaneous increasing sensitivity to others. This causes people's judgments about one another to become more finely nuanced and they are better able to control both themselves and others. With a reduction in the fear of violence and death, people turn their concerns to more subtle threats. This increasing sensitivity is a key contributor to the civilizing process and its continuation.

Another important aspect of the civilizing process is the socialization of the young to develop appropriate self-restraint. This increase in self-restraint, however, is also accompanied by problems, as "the civilizing of the human young is never a process entirely without pain; it always leaves scars" (Elias 1994b: 244).

SEE ALSO: Civilizations; Civilizing Process; Figurational Sociology and the Sociology of Sport; Micro–Macro Links

REFERENCES AND SUGGESTED READINGS

Bogner, A., Baker, A., & Kilminster, R. (1992) The Theory of the Civilizing Process: An Idiographic Theory of Modernization. *Theory, Culture, and Society* 9: 23–52.
Elias, N. (1978) *What is Sociology?* Columbia University Press, New York.
Elias, N. (1983 [1969]) *The Court Society*. Pantheon, New York.
Elias, N. (1994a [1939]) *The Civilizing Process*. Blackwell, Oxford.
Elias, N. (1994b [1939]) *The Civilizing Process*, Part 2: *Power and Civility*. Pantheon, New York.
Elias, N. (1997) Towards a Theory of Social Processes. *British Journal of Sociology* 48: 355–83.
Mennell, S. (1992) *Norbert Elias: An Introduction*. Blackwell, Oxford.

elite culture

Adrian Franklin

Elite culture can be defined as those "high" cultural forms and institutions that were exclusive to, and a distinguishing characteristic of, modern social elites. It is a term that particularly references the cultural tastes of the established aristocracy, the commercial bourgeoisie, educated bureaucrats and political power brokers, and the professions in the eighteenth, nineteenth, and twentieth centuries. Over most of this period such groups dominated those who consumed and supported such cultural styles as opera, symphony orchestras, ballet and dance companies, the decorative arts, fine art, museums and galleries, and the literary end of live theater. While these forms all thrive in contemporary times, it is no longer clear that elite culture can be distinguished from popular culture in the way it was before the mid-twentieth century (Blau 1986, 1989). While sociologists still identify the power and significance of social elites and their relatively closed cultural domains, their exclusive grip on elite culture has relaxed while at the same time they have become more *omnivorous* in their taste and now consume widely and freely from all styles, from the lowbrow to the highbrow. At the same time, new styles that blur elite and popular cultural forms emerged from around the 1960s: the Beatles, for example, combined African American rhythm and blues with British working-class "brass band," with western elite orchestral and strings, *and*, in places, with traditional Indian music. In turn, their audience base spanned the entire social spectrum. Artists such as Andy Warhol and Damian Hurst produced other such blurring or fusions and are credited with popularizing modern art.

According to Raymond Williams (1981: 97), the word *elite* does not emerge until the mid-eighteenth century but was more commonly in use around the early nineteenth century. It was used to express social distinction by rank and Williams argues that its emergence can be attributed to a crisis over leadership. As he says: "there had been a breakdown in old ways of distinguishing those best fitted to govern or exercise influence by rank or heredity, and a failure to find new ways of distinguishing such persons by formal ... election." Secondly, in response to socialist arguments about rules by class and class political conflict generally, it was widely argued that elites were more effective than classes (for example, by the Italian sociologists Pareto and Mosca). It is no accident therefore that this elitism, and the elite culture it produced, soon drew a cultural drawbridge up to distinguish itself from and cut out the "others." This is evident in Kant's "principle of pure taste," which identified absolute aesthetic value and valorized refinement, the attainment of virtuosity, and educated reflection over the popular, easygoing, immediate, simple, or traditional. But as Bourdieu argued, pure taste and its aesthetics were based on a *refusal* of the vulgar, simple, primitive, or popular and therefore constituted a *social* device or techniques of distinction. In the nineteenth century particularly, and long into the twentieth century, considerable energy was put into the creation of "high" cultural institutional development. At the same time, those low cultural forms which had hitherto been part of mainstream everyday culture were undermined and devalued as shallow and vulgar.

In the second half of the twentieth century, the possession of education (or what Bourdieu calls *cultural capital*) which distinguished the social elite became more commonplace through mass secondary education and the expansion of the universities. Hitherto the social elite had been a relatively closed and circumscribed social group, sharing not only culture in common but also background, schooling, social networks, and experience. However, from the 1960s many from non-elite backgrounds were being recruited into elite positions and making it in the culture industries and professions. It was this generation that reclaimed the cultural value and aesthetic depth of popular culture and placed it on an equal footing with elite culture. Meanwhile radio, television, and other media alongside new electronic technologies made elite culture more available to a wider audience and popular culture more popular with the elites. From the 1970s onwards, while it is still possible to identify elite culture, it has become more entwined in a broadening of popular, indeed globalized culture (DiMaggio 1997) and has now been identified in a new class formation, what Florida (2002) calls the *creative class*.

This is reflected in sociological surveys of consumer taste. Peterson and Kern (1996) looked at musical taste in the United States and found that highbrow consumers (those who mainly like opera and classical music) are increasingly consuming middlebrow (say, musicals) and "lowbrow" (country music, rock and pop). However, as with Bourdieu's pathbreaking book *Distinction*, a study of cultural taste in France, it is still possible to detect broad patterns of taste based on different combinations of cultural and economic capital and the habituses in which they combine. In Australia, another survey modeled on Bourdieu's (Bennett et al. 1999) found the cultural elite still cultivated a taste for highbrow cultural forms. So, while two-thirds of those with minimal education could identify only two classical composers from a list of ten music works, almost half of those with higher degrees knew eight or more. In broad terms, Bourdieu's distinction thesis was found to be true for Australia. However, an important caveat was that "the entire configuration of relations in our sample appears to have been skewed towards cultural forms which in Bourdieu's terms are 'popular,' devalued, or of diminished aesthetic value. Moreover, class judgments of taste seldom display a logic that is separate from the confounding effects of age and gender."

SEE ALSO: Bourdieu, Pierre; Cultural Capital; Culture; Culture Industries; Distinction; Elites; Globalization, Culture and; Highbrow/Lowbrow; Mass Culture and Mass Society; Media; Media and Consumer Culture; Music; Popular Culture; Television; Williams, Raymond

REFERENCES AND SUGGESTED READINGS

Bennett, T., Emmison, M., & Frow, J. (1999) *Accounting for Taste: Australian Everyday Cultures.* Cambridge University Press, Melbourne.

Blau, J. R. (1986) The Elite Arts, More or Less de Rigueur: A Comparative Analysis of Metropolitan Culture. *Social Forces* 64(4): 875–905.

Blau, J. R. (1989) *The Shape of Culture.* Cambridge University Press, Cambridge.

Blau, J. R., Blau, P. M., & Golden, R. M. (1985) Social Inequality and the Arts. *American Journal of Sociology* 91(2): 309–31.

Bourdieu, P. (1984) *Distinction: A Social Critique of the Judgment of Taste.* Harvard University Press, Cambridge, MA.

DiMaggio, P. (1997) *The Sociology of Culture.* Cambridge University Press, Cambridge.

Florida, R. (2002) *The Rise of the Creative Class: And How It's Transforming Work, Leisure, Community, and Everyday Life.* Basic Books, New York.

Peterson, R. A. & Kern, R. M. (1996) Changing Highbrow Taste: From Snob to Omnivore. *American Sociological Review* 61(5): 900–7.

Williams, R. (1981) *Keywords.* Fontana, London.

elites

Jaap Dronkers and Huibert Schijf

"History is a graveyard of aristocracies." With this phrase the Italian Vilfredo Pareto, who introduced the word elite in social sciences, formulated his idea of the decline and fall of elites, especially the political elite. For both him and Gaetono Mosca, the second founding father, the key concept was the circulation of elites (Bottomore 1993: 35). Many of these early writings on elites have a moral trademark. This can be seen in Machiavelli's *The Prince* (1513), where he gives a somewhat cynical but insightful analysis of the behavior of a ruler, but also provided instructions on how to act.

Theoreticians like Pareto and Mosca, but also the German Robert Michels (who formulated the famous "iron law of oligarchy" based on the inevitability of minority rule within the German Social Democratic Party), hold strong opinions on how elites should act and how their positions can be justified. The rightful behavior of elites is still, of course, fiercely debated in the public arena, but less so in modern social research on elites.

Today, the word elites is used in a very wide sense, for instance by speaking of a "sport elite." Nevertheless, in modern studies, elites are usually defined as the incumbents of top positions in both the public and private sector, like members of parliament or boards of executives. The focus is on the individual characteristics of these incumbents, the extent to which they are interconnected with each other, or the chance that people with certain characteristics are able to obtain such an elite position. However, the problem of sampling is transferred from individuals with high qualities to institutions (their influence in society is sometimes debated).

Information on elites (after all, public figures who draw much attention from the media) is easy to collect. Biographical summaries abound, both for the public and private sector, but publications like *Who's Who* are always a collection of persons where the criteria of inclusion of people, the rich and famous, very much depend on the bias of the editors and the information does not always have the quality required for thorough social research. However, many printed sources exist and are useful in situations where specialized surveys or interviews are difficult and certainly expensive (Moyser & Wagstaffe 1987; Bürklin et al. 1997).

By emphasizing the circulation of elites, Pareto and Mosca tend to underestimate the potential of elites to adapt to changing circumstances. Today, questions about openness or closeness of certain institutions and the chance that a particular person with certain characteristics will occupy an elite position are at the top of the agenda for sociological elite studies. Such investigations can be incorporated into the wider field of social stratification and mobility. Thus, the French sociologist Pierre Bourdieu emphasizes the process of *reproduction* of elites through scholarly and cultural capital and spends much time in describing the French elite schools, les *Grandes Écoles*. A large study conducted by Bürklin et al. (1997) on members of the German elites in several public and private sectors tried to answer the question of whether elites from East Germany have been integrated into the local and national elites from West Germany.

Studies on elites can be summarized by means of two dichotomies. The first is directed to questions on *horizontal* and *vertical* integration. A classical study on horizontal integration of the American elite is C. Wright Mills's *The Power Elite* (1956). Mills wanted to show that the governmental, military, and business elites – all male, white, and Christian – are highly interconnected. The term *pantouflage* is used in France to describe the quite common shift of the French governing elites from the public to private sector and vice versa. In societies with cleavages along religious lines elites from each group are sometimes able to cooperate at the national level. On the borderline between studies of corporate networks based on linkages between corporations, created through multiple functions of some members of the boards of executives, and elite studies, is work by Windolf (2002). Vertical integration deals with the question how representative are incumbents with respect to the population as a whole. Usually, they are not representative and elites prefer contacts among their own kind than with people 'below'. Much debate on the trust of citizens in democratic institutions can be seen in the light of a steady decline of vertical integration.

The second dichotomy is between an *individualistic* and a *structural* approach. The first emphasizes the characteristics of individual persons, while the latter focuses on the links between these individuals and larger structures ranging from family connections to common membership in an institution, past or present. Many studies within the individualistic approach focus on parliamentary representatives (Best & Cotta 2000), other political figures, or civil servants (Page & Wright 1999). Families can be seen as a separate research unit, where both approaches are incorporated. Harbor barons or industrial families sometimes show a great ability to stay in top positions, creating an almost dynastic continuity. In contrast to the accepted open and meritocratic character of modern societies, research shows that the ability to obtain an elite position in the Dutch nobility, an elite based on birth, has hardly declined during the twentieth century, although nobility is often seen as a relic from the past in Dutch public opinion (Schijf et al. 2004).

Very much in the tradition of research on social mobility, the German sociologist Hartman (2002) looked at the social background of engineers, lawyers, and economists who finished their high school education in 1955, 1965, 1975, and 1985. He then examined who was able to reach an elite position later in life. His conclusion is that the openness of the German educational system has increased, but that this is not true for the chance of obtaining an elite position, which still depends on an appropriate high social background. This use of longitudinal data seems to be promising for elite research in the future, because this research focus on the chances of obtaining such an elite position for a large group of persons and therefore highlights the openness or closedness of a society as a whole.

During the twentieth century many members of local elites became members of national elites. Today, one can see rapid development of a global economy, increasing popularity of international business schools, and the availability of large-scale international communication. Nevertheless, although rather scare, research shows (e.g., Hartman 1999) that so far there are few indications of the rise of an international business elite. In the boards of executives in countries like France, Germany, Great Britain, and the US, the overwhelmingly majority of members of these boards have the same nationality as the countries where these corporations are located. The only exceptions are foreign subsidiaries. Many executives had educational careers in their country of birth. This might change in the future, but it is very likely that top managers will follow a mainly local career instead of a global one. With the development of the European Union and its institutions, there might be an international bureaucratic elite in the making, but that is still not certain.

Other research topics on elites are less developed. For instance, little knowledge is available about the lifestyle of the elites or the neighborhoods they live in. The study by Pinçon and

Pinçon-Charlot (1989) on elite quarters in Paris offers an inspiring example of such research. The present research on elites also shows much emphasis on formal characteristics of incumbents. Far less information is available on how elites operate in (in)formal settings, or how the horizontal connections really work.

Evidence of much modern research shows that countries where no dramatic changes have taken place show a remarkable stability in their elites. Of course, the circulation of political elites often happens due to regular elections as part of the democratic process, but other groups or families turn out to be able to maintain elite positions over several generations by adapting to new circumstances.

SEE ALSO: Bourdieu, Pierre; Elite Culture; Michels, Robert; Mills, C. Wright; Pareto, Vilfredo; Power Elite

REFERENCES AND SUGGESTED READINGS

Best, H. & Cotta, M. (Eds.) (2000) *Parliamentary Representatives in Europe, 1848–2000: Legislative Recruitment and Careers in Eleven European Countries.* Oxford University Press, Oxford.

Bottomore, T. (1993) *Elites and Society.* Routledge, London.

Bürklin, W. et al. (1997) *Eliten in Deutschland.* Leske & Budrich, Opladen.

Hartmann, M. (1999) Auf dem Weg zur transnationalen Bourgeoisie. *Leviathan* 27: 113–41.

Hartmann, M. (2002) *Der Mythos von den Leistungseliten. Spitzenkarrieren und soziale Herkunft in Wirtschaft. Politik, Justiz und Wissenschaft.* Campus, Frankfurt.

Moyser, G. & Wagstaffe, M. (Eds.) (1987) *Research Methods for Elites Studies.* Allen & Unwin, London.

Page, E. C. & Wright, V. (Eds.) (1999) *Bureaucratic Elites in Western European States: A Comparative Analysis of Top Officials.* Oxford University Press, Oxford.

Pinçon, M. & Pinçon-Charlot, M. (1989) *Dans les beaux quartiers.* Éditions du Seuil, Paris.

Schijf, H., Dronkers, J., & van den Broeke-George, J. (2004) Recruitment of Members of Dutch Noble and High-Bourgeois Families to Elite Positions in the 20th Century. *Social Science Information* 43(3): 435–77.

Windolf, P. (2002) *Corporate Networks in Europe and the United States.* Oxford University Press, Oxford.

Ellis, Havelock (1859–1939)

Jeffrey Weeks

Havelock Ellis, editor, critic, essayist, and pioneer sexologist, was born on February 2, 1859 in Croydon, Surrey. His father was a sea captain and rarely at home, so Ellis's mother was the dominant influence in his early life. She was an ardent evangelical Christian who had experienced a conversion at the age of 17, but Ellis early on slipped away from the more rigid aspects of her faith. He was provided with a basic education in private schools in south London, but his main education derived from wide reading. The crucial formative influence was his stay in Australia for four years from the age of 16.

Here, in the outback, in almost total isolation, he began to experience conflicts in his awakening sexual life and in his spiritual outlook. Born in the year of the first publication of Charles Darwin's *On the Origin of Species*, Ellis was a child of a new scientific optimism, unattracted to a religious world outlook which he saw as dying, but repelled by the absorption of science into a chilly utilitarianism. It was in this state of mind that he reread a book by James Hinton, a writer on political, social, religious, and sexual matters, entitled *Life in Nature* (1862). The book sparked a spiritual transformation. In particular, for the young Ellis, the belief that sexual freedom could bring in a new age of happiness helped direct him towards the scientific study of sex. To prepare him for this, he resolved to train as a doctor, and returned to London in April 1879 ready to face his new life.

His actual work as a doctor was spasmodic. During his training and in the years that followed his real preoccupation was with his literary and scientific studies. The London of the 1880s was a focus of intense intellectual and political ferment, and Ellis immersed himself in this new culture. Through his involvement in various progressive groupings he met many of the radical luminaries of the time. He began editing and writing, publishing essays on religion, philosophy, travel, and politics. However, Ellis was never a political activist. Even as a well-known writer in later life, giving his formal support to campaigns for sex reform, eugenics, abortion, and voluntary euthanasia, he was extremely reluctant to become involved in public controversy. It was in private involvements, through a vast daily correspondence, and by his voluminous writings that he exercised his influence. Even in his publications, his manner was often indirect, preferring, as he put it, to express the shocking things in a quiet, matter-of-course way, sugar-coating the pill. Yet both his private life and his public writings had the potentiality to shock his contemporaries.

It was in these early years of incessant intellectual activity that Ellis began the two most important emotional involvements of his early life. The first was with the South African feminist author Olive Schreiner, already famous for her novel *The Story of an African Farm* (1883) when they met early in 1884. It is not clear whether their relationship was conventionally consummated. Ellis himself appears not to have been strongly drawn to heterosexual intercourse, and had a lifelong interest in urolagnia, a delight in seeing women urinate. The sexual ardor, certainly on Schreiner's part, appears to have soon cooled, though the emotional intensity remained. It survived Schreiner's return to South Africa in 1889, continuing until her death via an almost daily correspondence and occasional meetings.

Ellis's relationship with the woman who was to become his wife, Edith Mary Oldham Lees, began the year after Schreiner's departure, and was strengthened by a common interest in the work of Hinton. She too was a passionate woman, who, despite an intense mutual involvement with Ellis (he was to devote almost half of his autobiography to their relationship), pursued an independent life as a lecturer and writer. By Victorian standards the partnership was highly unconventional. Edith's emotional and sexual passions were primarily lesbian, and both she and Ellis were to have a series of close emotional involvements with other women, certainly sexual in Edith's case, more ambiguously erotic in Ellis's case.

By the early 1890s Ellis was ready to embark on what he regarded as his crowning achievement, *Studies in the Psychology of Sex* (1897–1910, with a seventh, supplementary,

volume in 1928). The series began with *Sexual Inversion*, the first serious study of homosexuality published in Britain. It was conceived as a collaboration with the poet and critic John Addington Symonds, himself homosexual, and anxious to promote a more tolerant climate towards homosexuality. He completed the book after Symonds's death in 1893, the first printing appearing in German, then in English in 1897 under their joint names. Ellis now became embroiled in an unfortunate series of events. First of all, Ellis was forced by Symonds's family to withdraw his co-author's name from the book. The aftermath of the trials of Oscar Wilde was not the best time to publish a major text on homosexuality that might sully another aesthete's reputation. Then Ellis found himself caught in the web of a dubious publisher, and a subsequent trial of the secretary of the sexually progressive Legitimation League, George Bedborough, for selling the book. In the 1898 trial, which did not directly involve Ellis, the book was labeled a "certain lewd, wicked, bawdy, scandalous libel" and subsequently withdrawn from sale. Ellis was confirmed in his caution about getting involved in public controversy. More crucially, he determined thereafter that the *Studies* should be published in the US; no complete edition has ever appeared in Britain.

Despite this unfortunate beginning, the *Studies* were to prove enormously influential. The first volume set the tone. By collating all the available evidence, historical, anthropological, social, and scientific, the aim was to demonstrate that homosexuality (or inversion, his preferred term) was not a product of peculiar national vices or periods of social decay, but a common and recurrent part of human sexuality, a quirk of nature, a congenital anomaly. In line with what was then considered advanced thinking, his conviction of the biological origins of human behavior was to color much of his thought. First, he sought to establish the natural basis of human sexuality in all its forms; nothing that was based in nature could be seen as inherently wrong. But secondly, he attempted to reconcile these variations to what he regarded as the supreme biological origin and function of sex, the man wooing a woman for the purpose of reproduction. Though an advanced advocate of a woman's right to sexual fulfillment, his view of an essential female passivity in sexual matters subsequently attracted sharp criticism, particularly as it appeared to subordinate female sexuality to male. His biological determinism was to lead him to give support throughout his life to eugenics, the planned breeding of the best, and to differentiate him from his great contemporary, Sigmund Freud. Yet despite his biological preoccupations, Ellis was no empirical scientist. His method was that of the naturalist, collecting facts from a vast variety of sources and presenting them in an ordered, but essentially descriptive fashion. As a result, he never established a scientific school. But for his progressive contemporaries he seemed a prophet of a more humane attitude to sex. Through the *Studies*, probably more read about than read, he became internationally famous as a sexologist, and a magnet for other would-be reformers.

On completing the sixth volume of the *Studies* Ellis wrote: "The work that I was born to do is done." In fact, many years of productive writing, and growing fame, lay ahead. He continued writing on sexual matters, including a textbook, *The Psychology of Sex* (1933). His various other interests were reflected in a number of collections of essays; and the publication of *The Dance of Life* (1923) for the first time made him a bestselling author. From the 1920s he also contributed short articles to American newspapers and journals, which did little for his intellectual reputation, but contributed significantly to his finances.

Edith Lees had died in 1916, after some years of growing ill health. In the last months she had secured a legal separation from Ellis, but her death left him emotionally bereft. His emotional life was not, however, over. From 1918 he shared his life with an acquaintance of Edith's, Françoise Lafitte-Cyon, also known as Delisle (1886–1974), separated wife of a Russian journalist, and mother of two boys. As with Edith, for many years, Ellis retained his own home, and each of them continued to cultivate strong relationships outside their partnership. But in the last years they lived together. These final years were shadowed by ill health, as well as continuing poverty. He died on July 8, 1939.

Havelock Ellis has been described as one of the great "modernizers" of sex. Certainly, he was to become an inspiration to many liberal reformers of the 1950s and 1960s. In retrospect, however, perhaps his major contribution was not as a scientist or theorist, or even great reformer, but as an outstanding example of a pioneer in writing about sex and sexuality in a calm and dispassionate way. He put sexuality into words that helped shape the erotic climate of the twentieth century.

SEE ALSO: Femininities/Masculinities; Freud, Sigmund; Sexuality Research: History

REFERENCES AND SUGGESTED READINGS

Ellis, H. (1940) *My Life*. Heinemann, London.
Grosskurth, P. (1980) *Havelock Ellis: A Biography*. Allen Lane, London.
Weeks, J. (2000) Havelock Ellis and the Politics of Sex Reform. In: *Making Sexual History*. Polity Press, Cambridge.
Weeks, J. (2004) Ellis, (Henry) Havelock (1859–1939). In: *The Oxford Dictionary of National Biography*. Oxford University Press, Oxford.

emergent norm theory

Mikaila Mariel Lemonik Arthur

Emergent norm theory hypothesizes that non-traditional behavior (such as that associated with collective action) develops in crowds as a result of the emergence of new behavioral norms in response to a precipitating crisis. For proponents of emergent norm theory, collective action includes all types of social behavior in which the conventional norms stop functioning as guides to social action, and instead people collectively overturn or go beyond the normal institutional practices and frameworks of society (Turner & Killian 1987) and therefore new conventions must form as part of the collective action. The basic suppositions of emergent norm theory are that collective action is rational, that collective action is a response to a precipitating event, and that new norms of behavior appropriate to the collective action situation emerge through group processes without prior coordination and planning.

First proposed by Turner and Killian in 1972, emergent norm theory has grown out of two main traditions. The LeBonian tradition of thinking of crowds as normless entities and collective action as irrational behavior led Turner and Killian to think about how norms are instituted in crowds. Second, symbolic interactionism and small group analysis contributed a model of norms as developing through interaction.

Emergent norm theory suggests that crowds come together because a crisis occurs that forces people to abandon prior conceptions of appropriate behavior and to find new ways of acting. When a crowd forms, there is no particular norm governing crowd behavior and no leader exists. But the crowd focuses in on those who act in a distinctive manner, and this distinction is taken on as the new norm for crowd behavior. As this new norm begins to be institutionalized within the crowd, pressures for conformity and against deviance within the crowd develop, and discontent is silenced. This silencing of alternative views contributes to the illusion of unanimity within the crowd.

The norms that develop within crowds are not strict rules for behavior. Rather, they are more like overarching frameworks for behavior that set limits on what is appropriate (Turner & Killian 1987: 9–11). These norms develop through either emergent or preexisting social relationships. Turner and Killian suggest that anything which facilitates communication among crowd participants facilitates the emergence of norms, and they call this process "milling." In addition, though the emergent norm theory perspective does, as noted above, contest the notion that crowd behavior is particularly irrational, it suggests that many crowd participants are suggestible and that this suggestibility contributes to the spread of emergent norms.

There are two main avenues of criticism that have faced emergent norm theory. The first, proposed by Reicher (1987), suggests that when crowds come together, they bring norms with them. Therefore, new norms do not have to emerge. These norms are different depending on the group making up the crowd – for instance, an urban mob will exhibit different norms than a group of suburban teenagers at a rock concert. These differences reflect the different ways that crowds behave, but are norms nonetheless.

The second line of criticism suggests all social behavior results in the renegotiation of social norms, and second, that the creativity in norm creation and behavior that has come to be seen as "norm emergence" emerges not from interaction but rather through long-term rational planning processes or through reliance on small changes to established repertoires. Couch (1968), while writing before the development of emergent norm theory, is often cited to support this criticism. An additional area of criticism suggested by some researchers is that there are significant methodological difficulties in tracing the emergence of a norm in a crowd setting.

While emergent norm theory was originally applied to a variety of forms of collective behavior, it is most commonly relied on to help understand the behavior of large groups, or crowds. In particular, emergent norm theory has gained a strong foothold in disaster research, as it is used to understand the behavior of groups who experience a precipitating crisis (a disaster) and then are forced to find new ways to respond that will help to ensure the safety and survival of as many people as possible. Tierney (2002), for instance, has used emergent norm theory to help understand the civilian-initiated evacuation of the World Trade Center on September 11, 2001. Other researchers, such as Johnson (1987), have suggested that emergent norm theory can explain not just orderly civilian-initiated evacuation but also the aggressive and selfish behavior sometimes seen in mass panics. Johnson believes that in certain situations, the breakdown of social order leads to these types of behavior as rational responses to the new social circumstances.

SEE ALSO: Collective Action; Crowd Behavior; Disasters; Norms; Riots; Social Movements, Networks and; Symbolic Interaction

REFERENCES AND SUGGESTED READINGS

Aguirre, B. E., Wenger, D. E., & Vigo, G. (1998) A Test of the Emergent Norm Theory of Collective Behavior. *Sociological Forum* 13(2): 301–20.

Couch, C. J. (1968) Collective Behavior: An Examination of Some Stereotypes. *Social Problems* 15: 310–22.

Dynes, R. R. & Tierney, K. J. (1994) *Disasters, Collective Behavior, and Social Organization.* University of Delaware Press, Newark.

Johnson, N. R. (1987) Panic and the Breakdown of Social Order: Popular Myth, Social Theory, Empirical Evidence. *Sociological Focus* 20(3): 171–83.

Reicher, S. D. (1987) Crowd Behavior as Social Action. In: Turner, J. C., Hogg, M. A., Oakes, P. J., Reicher, S. D., & Wetherell, M. S. (Eds.), *Rediscovering the Social Group: A Self-Categorization Theory.* Blackwell, Oxford.

Tierney, K. J. (2002) Strength of a City: Disaster Research on the World Trade Center Attack. In: Social Science Resource Council, *After September 11: Perspectives in the Social Sciences.* Online. www.ssrc.org/sept11/.

Turner, R. H. & Killian, L. M. (1987) *Collective Behavior,* 3rd edn. Prentice-Hall, Englewood Cliffs, NJ.

Emerson, Richard M. (1925–82)

Karen S. Cook

Richard Marc Emerson, a primary architect of social exchange theory and power-dependence theory, received his PhD from the University of Minnesota in 1955 where his primary advisors were Don Martindale (sociological theory) and Stanley Schachter (psychology). He attended graduate school after serving during World War II in the elite 10th Army Mountain Division upon completing college at the University of Utah, where he majored in sociology and minored in philosophy. His first academic appointment was at the University of Cincinnati. He joined the faculty in 1955 and received tenure in 1957. While at Cincinnati he wrote a number of important papers and participated in research projects related to family relations (as a senior research associate in psychiatry) and in leadership training, a popular field of study post-World War II. He was recruited to the Department of Sociology at the University of Washington in 1965, where he served on the faculty until his premature death in 1982 at the peak of his academic career.

Richard Emerson is best known for his work on social power. In the early 1960s he published two highly significant papers, "Power–Dependence Relations" (1962) and "Power–Dependence Relations: Two Experiments" (1964), that changed the way social scientists subsequently viewed social power. Both are now citation classics. The 1962 article is one of only 30 that have received over 500 citations since being published in the *American Sociological Review*. The primary significance of this work is that it changed the way power was typically defined in sociology and political science. In Emerson's theoretical framework, power is viewed as a function of a social relation rather than as an attribute of a particular person, group, or collectivity. This conceptualization is the basis of what is known as *power-dependence theory*. The key insight in this formulation was that power was determined by the dependence of one party on another for resources or services of value. Dependence is a function of: (1) the *value* of that service or resource and (2) its *availability* from alternative sources. Emerson later used this conception of power in his analysis of social exchange relations. Thus the power of actor A over actor B in a two-party exchange relation specified as $Ax:By$ (where A and B are actors and x and y are resources of value) increases as a function of the value of y to A and decreases proportional to the degree of availability of y to A from other sources. The more dependent B is on A, the more power A has over B in the $Ax:By$ exchange relation. The postulate that power is based on dependence is the central proposition in Emerson's theoretical formulation: $Pab = Dba$.

Emerson developed his exchange theory in two papers written in 1967 and circulated widely in unpublished form before they finally appeared in 1972. In these papers he laid out a micro-foundation for social exchange (Part I) based on behavioral psychology similar to the basis of the exchange formulation developed in 1961 by George Homans. In Part II Emerson developed a theory of social exchange networks building upon his dyadic exchange formulation.

The extension of exchange theory from dyads to networks laid the foundation for much of the subsequent theoretical and empirical development of exchange theory in sociology in the three decades after the publication of these seminal papers. An important feature of this work was its focus on network positional determinants of power.

Networks, according to Emerson, were sets of connected exchange relations. They could be simple or complex networks that represented actors linked by ties of exchange. The nature of the exchange connections depended upon whether or not the exchange relations involved cooperative social exchange (positive connections) or competitive access to alternative resources (negative connections). If exchange in one network relation enhanced exchange in another, the two exchange relations were positively connected at a node (actor). If exchange in one network relation reduced the likelihood of exchange in another relation, the two relations were defined as negatively connected (or as alternative exchange relations). More complex variants of the nature of connections and the determinants of positional power were subsequently developed by Markovsky et al. (1988), Willer, and their collaborators who developed not only an alternative method of representing network connections, but also different methods for calculating the locus of power in a network (e.g., using the graph theoretic index of power or *GPI* and its modifications). Experimental research supports the idea that the link between power and centrality in a network is dependent upon the nature of the exchange connections involved, among other factors (Cook & Emerson 1978; Cook et al. 1983; Yamagishi et al. 1988).

To analyze change in networks, Emerson proposed that power-balancing mechanisms often came into play to alter the distribution of power in a network of exchange relations. For example, coalitions could form among power-disadvantaged actors in a network and such collective action could result in a redistribution of power if the disadvantaged actors could act collectively to alter the terms of trade to their advantage. Emerson referred to this form of structural change as network consolidation. A different form of change involved network extension. In this case power-disadvantaged actors could seek alternative exchange partners to reduce their dependence upon a particular powerful actor by gaining access to resources from others. These were two of the main forms of structural change posed by Emerson as potentially "power-balancing" forces within exchange networks. Two other mechanisms of "power-balancing" focused on changes within the dyadic exchange relation, not the network. These mechanisms included "status-giving" or an effort to enhance the value of the resources offered to the one in power in the exchange relation, and "withdrawal," which entailed terminating the relationship, a more drastic means of reducing dependence.

While the focus of much of the work on social exchange has been on the determinants of power in dyadic exchange relations and in exchange networks, other features of social exchange relations have also been examined, including social cohesion, relational satisfaction, fairness or distributive justice, commitment between exchange partners, especially under uncertainty, and trust. Even though some of these topics were included in Emerson's original theoretical formulation, they were not empirically investigated very extensively in the laboratory until after his death, with the exception of the study of commitment, which was included in an early experimental study by Cook and Emerson (1978; see also Cook & Emerson 1984). Linda Molm and Edward Lawler are two of the investigators in the past decade who have studied relational cohesion, trust, and commitment experimentally. Lawler's focus has been on affect and relational commitment. Molm has focused on comparing different forms of exchange, such as negotiated and reciprocal exchange, and their differences not only in terms of the use of power, but also in the levels of cohesion, relationship satisfaction, and trust that develop between the partners.

Emerson's fieldwork on power and authority relations in Pakistan is less well known than his theoretical work on exchange and his collaborative laboratory studies of exchange networks with Cook, Yamagishi, and others. He published several papers before his death on the effects of the British system of authority and rule on the small villages and principalities of Pakistan and India. These articles relied more on historical data and observations that Emerson collected while in the field in Pakistan and India, where he spent time on several sabbaticals as well as on various mountaineering expeditions. In fact, some of his laboratory studies of power were representations of his interest in the factors that resulted in the centralization or decentralization of power in various village structures. Although he is best known in the current era for his laboratory work on exchange theory and power in exchange networks in collaboration with his colleagues at the University of Washington, he is also known there for his love of mountains and his interest in the anthropology of the remote mountain villages he often visited during his career as a sociologist.

Apart from his love of academia, Emerson had considered becoming a sculptor before entering graduate school and was an excellent photographer. He was also a serious mountaineer, having grown up surrounded by snow-capped mountains in Utah. While in the Northwest he climbed mountains for much of his life and was a member of the first expedition on Mount Everest to make a successful ascent up the West Ridge (in 1963). The National Science Foundation funded his involvement in the expedition as part of a research project that he had initiated on reactions to performance feedback under conditions of high stress. The mountain climbers were required to keep diaries during the ascent to record their reactions to various performance feedback studies that Emerson was conducting during the climb. Just before his assassination, President Kennedy decorated Richard Emerson with the Hubbard Medal on behalf of the National Geographic Society for this research. Two of Emerson's climbing partners on this adventure suffered serious injury from frostbite and one of the porters died on the climb. During his life Emerson returned a number of times to the mountains of Pakistan, often with a new research idea in mind.

SEE ALSO: Blau, Peter; Collective Action; Elementary Theory; Homans, George; Networks; Power-Dependence Theory; Power, Theories of; Social Network Theory

REFERENCES AND SUGGESTED READINGS

Cook, K. S. & Emerson, R. M. (1978) Power, Equity, and Commitment in Exchange Networks. *American Sociological Review* 43: 721–39.

Cook, K. S. & Emerson, R. M. (1984) Exchange Networks and the Analysis of Complex Organizations. *Research in the Sociology of Organizations* 3: 1–30.

Cook, K. S., Emerson, R. M., Gillmore, M. R., & Yamagishi, T. (1983) The Distribution of Power in Exchange Networks: Theory and Experimental Results. *American Journal of Sociology* 89: 275–305.

Emerson, R. M. (1962) Power–Dependence Relations. *American Sociological Review* 27: 31–41.

Emerson, R. M. (1964) Power–Dependence Relations: Two Experiments. *Sociometry* 27: 282–98.

Emerson, R. M. (1972a) Exchange Theory, Part I: A Psychological Basis for Social Exchange. In: Berger, J., Zelditch, M., Jr., & Anderson, B. (Eds.), *Sociological Theories in Progress*, Vol. 2. Houghton Mifflin, Boston, pp. 38–57.

Emerson, R. M. (1972b) Exchange Theory, Part II: Exchange Relations and Network Structures. In: Berger, J., Zelditch, M., Jr., & Anderson, B. (Eds.), *Sociological Theories in Progress*, Vol. 2. Houghton Mifflin, Boston, pp. 58–87.

Emerson, R. M. (1976) Social Exchange Theory. *Annual Review of Sociology* 2: 335–62.

Emerson, R. M. (1981) Social Exchange Theory. In: Rosenberg, M. & Turner, R. (Eds.), *Social Psychology: Sociological Perspectives*. Basic Books, New York, pp. 30–65.

Emerson, R. M. (1987) Toward a Theory of Value in Social Exchange. In: Cook, K. S. (Ed.), *Social Exchange Theory*. Sage, Newbury Park, CA, pp. 11–58.

Lawler, E. J. & Yoon, J. (1996) Commitment in Exchange Relations: A Test of a Theory of Relational Cohesion. *American Sociological Review* 61: 89–108.

Lawler, E. J. & Yoon, J. (1998) Network Structure and Emotion in Exchange Relations. *American Sociological Review* 63: 871–94.

Markovsky, B., Willer, D., & Patton, T. (1988) Power Relations in Exchange Networks. *American Sociological Review* 53: 220–36.

Molm, L. D. & Cook, K. S. (1995) Social Exchange and Exchange Networks. In: Cook, K. S., Fine, G. A., & House, J. S. (Eds.), *Sociological Perspectives on Social Psychology*. Allyn & Bacon, Boston, pp. 209–35.

Molm, L., Takahashi, N., & Peterson, G. (2000) Risk and Trust in Social Exchange: An Experimental

Test of a Classical Proposition. *American Journal of Sociology* 105: 1396–1427.

Yamagishi, T. & Cook, K. S. (1993) Generalized Exchange and Social Dilemmas. *Social Psychology Quarterly* 56: 235–48.

Yamagishi, T., Cook, K. S., & Watabe, M. (1998) Uncertainty, Trust and Commitment Formation in the United States and Japan. *American Journal of Sociology* 104: 165–94.

Yamagishi, T., Gillmore, M. R., & Cook, K. S. (1988) Network Connections and the Distribution of Power in Exchange Networks. *American Journal of Sociology* 93: 833–51.

emic/etic

Michael Agar

"Emic" and "etic" have become shorthand terms, especially in anthropology, for an "insider" versus an "outsider" view of a particular social world. For example, an outsider view of an economic exchange might hold that the seller's goal was to maximize profit. An insider view from people actually involved in the exchange might show that profit was only one of many concerns. Kinship ties, a long relationship history, previous social favors, earlier non-cash trades, a desire to curry favor – such social threads in a relationship might result in an exchange that, to an outsider, would look "irrational," while to an insider it would make perfect sense.

The distinction between emic and etic, insider and outsider, originated in the linguistics of the 1950s, most famously in the work of Kenneth Pike (1967). Linguists of that era were primarily concerned with learning and describing unwritten languages in field settings. As part of this larger task, they had to master the phonology, or sound system. As a means to this end, they created a notational system that allowed them to describe all possible sounds that the human organism can produce. This notational system was called phonetics, and that term later became abbreviated to etic.

Phonetics offered a classification of sounds that humans could produce, given the physiological possibilities of the articulatory system. Training tapes, much like a foreign language course, taught the budding linguist how to hear sounds that his own language had trained him not to hear. For example, if one raises the tongue so that the two sides touch the alveolar ridges while allowing air to pass through the middle, one is producing what a phonetician would call a "lateral fricative." While the sound is unfamiliar to most English speakers, it is critical for a speaker of Navajo.

The fact that a lateral fricative would sound strange to an English speaker is why the concept of "phonemic" was invented. The speakers of a particular language, like English or Navajo, will not perceive all the sounds described by phonetics. Instead, they will hear only a subset. As they acquire language as children, speakers learn to hear some sounds and ignore others. The sounds that speakers of a particular language hear as significant, the units of sound that make a difference for them, are the "phonemes" of that language. "Phonemic," as we will see, was shortened to "emic."

Here is an example. In English, say the word "pin" and the word "spin" with a hand held in front of the mouth. After the "p" in "pin" a puff of air will be felt on the hand. After the "p" in "spin" little or no air will be felt. A linguist doing phonetics would say the first "p" is aspirated while the second "p" is not. This difference makes no difference to a native speaker of English. One could say "pin" without aspiration or "spin" with it, and though it might sound unusual, the different pronunciations would still be heard as the same words. Aspiration, in English, is not phonemic. In other languages, such as Hindi, it is. "Pin" with aspiration and "pin" without it would signal two different words.

Here is another example. In Kannarese, a language of South India, a "d" can be alveolar or retroflex. Say "d" with the tip of the tongue along the alveolar ridge just behind the teeth. Now say "d" with the tongue rolled back, the tip tapping the back of the ridge as it moves forward to articulate the "d" sound. That is retroflex. In Kannarese, there are two words that an English speaker would spell "nadi" and hear as the same. One – with the alveolar "d" – means "river." The other, with the retroflex "d," means – loosely translated – an impolite "get out of here."

The field linguist began by first writing things down using phonetic notation. Then, using methodologies that are beyond the scope of this entry to describe, the linguist would analyze the phonetic transcription of the language to determine which differences made a difference for native speakers and which did not. The linguist would then develop a phonemic notation to symbolize those differences.

What about the phonetic variations? To return to the earlier English example, a linguist would note that aspiration after a "p," or any other "stop," is *not* phonemic for English speakers. Instead, the linguist would posit a rule that aspiration occurs after a stop that begins a word which is then followed immediately by a vowel, a word like "pin." This kind of phonemic rule lets the linguist use the single symbol "p" for both aspirated and unaspirated versions. The rule works for other stops in English as well, sounds like "b," "t," "d," "k," and "g." Now, instead of writing a full phonetic transcription, the linguist can shift to a less cumbersome phonemic transcription that reflects the psychological significance of sounds to local speakers.

Now consider the earlier example from South India, the alveolar and the retroflex "d." Since these two "d's" do make a difference to speakers of Kannarese, a linguist has to represent that difference in the phonemic transcript. He can't just use the single symbol "d." Fortunately, the original phonetic notation with which the linguist began his work provides a way to write this difference down, usually with a dot under the "d" for the alveolar version and a wedge under the "d" for the retroflex.

In the 1960s, anthropology borrowed and shortened the linguist's distinction between phonetic and phonemic and began talking about "etic" and "emic." But the abbreviated concepts were applied to ethnography as a whole, not just to language. Just as in the case of phonetics, an etic approach meant an ethnographer described and explained events with a language external to the social world in which those events occurred. And like phonetics, the etic language of description might be rooted in human biology, as in Edward T. Hall's studies of "proxemics," his shorthand term for the use of social space (Hall 1959). Measures of physical distance or bodily motion served as the etic framework. Other etic approaches drew on "outsider" languages from social theory, exemplified by Marvin Harris's writings of the time (for a recent version of his arguments for etic ethnography which began in the 1960s, see Harris 1998). He advocated an etic framework grounded in his commitment to neo-Marxian theory.

Halls's proxemics, as the name suggests, was also emic, since his ultimate goal was to describe how different groups had different interpretations of social space. For example, one group might expect two people to stand closer than another group would during an informal conversation between strangers. Where such emic differences existed, a person from the former group would read the other as "cold," while a person from the second group would read the first person as "pushy."

The concept of emic ethnography flourished with the growth of cognitive anthropology (D'Andrade 1995), an approach that concerned itself with what was then called psychological reality. Their "phonetics" were assumed universals of human cognition, for example, taxonomy. Their "phonemics" were the way particular taxonomies of plants and animals were filled in by different peoples living in different parts of the world. Many other kinds of emic studies were done as well, involving local concepts and their organization, to reveal the variety of ways that people organized their experience, their emic, using their universal human capacity to do so, the etic.

Unfortunately, because of acrimonious debates between "materialist" or etic and "symbolic" or emic approaches to anthropology during the era, "etic" and "emic" turned into labels for competing kinds of ethnographic descriptions. This was a fundamental error, since neither the original linguistic concepts nor their development in cognitive anthropology had defined an "either/or" use of the terms. The shift to etic/emic as a partition of the ethnographic space rather than a process by which it was explored introduced distortion into the use of the terms that continues to this day. The question should not be, does one do emic or etic ethnography? The question should be, how does one tack back and forth between human universals and the particular shape that a social world takes at the time an ethnographer encounters it?

The emic/etic distinction appeared about half a century ago. With the many changes in the world and in our theories about it since then, the emic/etic distinction looks more complicated than it used to. It is worth considering a few examples here to foreshadow the future of the concepts, as well as to reflect on their past.

Phonetic/phonemic endows the linguist with the privileged position in language description. She is the one who defines the universals that limit what the local differences might be. She controls the methods that will make that determination, and she declares what the phonemic is and when it is done. With work in sociolinguistics that began with Labov in the 1960s (Labov 1966), we learned that sound differences that were not "phonemic" according to the old 1950s approach in fact signaled important social meanings that convey a speaker's and listener's sense of identity and situation. Phonetic was more important than the original distinction allowed.

This problem of authority becomes even more striking when phonetic/phonemic in linguistics shifts to etic/emic in ethnography. What is the etic for humanity in general and who decides? What is the universal set of beliefs, values, or rules for behavior that cover all possible configurations that are human across regions and through history? And on what grounds would a researcher claim to know what they are whereas the subjects of his research could not? Recent anthropological debate centers on just this bias in an academic field that traditionally considered itself "culture free." Those who privilege themselves to define the etic, one could argue, are just another kind of emic.

Say an encounter between an outsider and an insider is an encounter between two kinds of emic, not between an etic and an emic. In this formulation, the encounter is cast in a more egalitarian light. Two different meaning systems, two different emics, try to make sense out of each other, rather than an outsider with prior knowledge of universal human universals figuring out the locally relevant system that draws on that universal scheme. But what about the etic? Don't universals play a necessary role in bridging local differences? They have to, or else no bridge would be possible. In our poststructural, postcolonial era, though, we see that the etic has also become more complicated. There are no clear lines between "insider" and "outsider" in today's world. In our transnational times we can expect that any two people who share a local social world will to some extent have different interpretations of that same world. The fact that they share activities will not imply a perfectly overlapping emic perspective. On the other hand, any two people from anywhere in the world will to some extent share interpretations of some phenomena, as soon as they meet, without any prior contact. They will partially overlap in emics, even though they have never had anything to do with each other directly.

With all these complications, what are we to make of the emic/etic distinction in contemporary research? It still has value as a general alert, a caution that what X says about what Y is doing or thinking probably doesn't correspond to what Y would say, certainly not perfectly, sometimes off by several orders of magnitude. This fairly simple – and usually accurate – principle is worth contemplating for its breadth of application, its explanatory power, and its call for uses of the distinction in public policy. It is also worth contemplating why this simple principle is so seldom attended to.

A second enduring use of the emic/etic distinction returns us to its linguistic roots in the 1950s. One useful definition of ethnography is making sense out of human differences in terms of human similarities. Recall the early use of the phonetic/phonemic distinction as a tool to help a field linguist achieve exactly that goal. Phonetics laid out the human territory; phonemics described its particular shape among a particular group at a particular point in time.

Any ethnography is a mix of human universals and local histories. Without the universals, comprehension across differences would not be possible. Without the local histories, the universals would mislead when it came to understanding a different world. Here, etic and emic signal a still-undeveloped strain of social research, one that celebrates the richness of particular human moments while at the same time integrating the various universal theories of the human situation that they bring to life. Long ago, Robert Redfield, engaged in a post-World War II review of anthropology sponsored by the Social Science Research Council, said that good ethnography was like good literature. It gave a "glimpse of the eternal in the ephemeral" (Redfield 1948). Etic and emic are ways, in ethnographic jargon, to continue the spirit of the wise writing of that ancestor. Etic and emic are both part of any human understanding, not distinct varieties of it.

SEE ALSO: Analytic Induction; Culture; Ethnography; Interviewing, Structured, Unstructured, and Postmodern; Observation, Participant and Non-Participant

REFERENCES AND SUGGESTED READINGS

D'Andrade, R. G. (1995) *The Development of Cognitive Anthropology*. Cambridge University Press, Cambridge.

Hall, E. T. (1959) *The Silent Language*. Doubleday, Garden City, NY.

Harris, M. (1998) *Theories of Culture in Postmodern Times*. Alta Mira Press, Walnut Creek, CA.

Labov, W. (1966) *The Social Stratification of English in New York City*. Center for Applied Linguistics, Washington, DC.

Pike, K. L. (1967) *Language in Relation to a Unified Theory of Human Behavior*. Mouton, The Hague.

Redfield, R. (1948) The Art of Social Science. *American Journal of Sociology* 54: 181–90.

emotion: cultural aspects

Jack Barbalet

The relationship between emotions and culture has been discussed ever since there was interest in what it means to be human, and since then that relationship has been contrastingly characterized as either inimical or reconcilable. Culture can be understood as the defining values, meanings, and thoughts of a local, national, or supranational community. When emotions are conceived in terms of psychological feelings and physical sensations, then they appear inimical to culture. This is because such a perspective suggests the involuntary nature and disorganizing consequence of emotions. The opposition between cognition as reason and emotion, implicit in this representation, is classically defended in Plato's critique of dramatic poetry in the *Republic*, for instance. Plato's supposition that emotion is pleasure or pain dissociated from thought or knowledge was corrected, however, by Aristotle's more comprehensive appreciation of emotion as not merely physical but also cognitive, in which culture and emotions are reconciled.

In his treatment of anger, for instance, in *Rhetoric*, Aristotle agrees that emotion has a biological component, the physical sensation of pain, and also a complex cognitive component, including perception of an undeserved slight, and an intention, desire for revenge. Thus Aristotle distinguishes between emotions in terms of both the different physical sensations associated with them and their different cognitive or cultural elements: hatred and anger are different not just in their physical sensations, but also in the way in which each emotion conceives its object, as when Aristotle says that anger has an individual as its object whereas hatred applies to classes such as thieves or informers. Similarly, fear and shame are distinguished not just physically but cognitively, as expectation respectively of imminent harm or disgrace. There is something else, then, that should be noticed in this account, even though Aristotle does not make it explicit; namely, that imagination is important in the experience of emotion. Thus culture is unavoidable in emotion through a number of routes. The situation that provokes an emotion, as opposed to the physical or biological structure that supports it, is broadly cultural, and so is the intention it promotes; finally, thought itself or imagination may lead to emotional experience.

The different conceptions of the relation between emotion and culture found in Plato and Aristotle stand as models for all subsequent statements. Relevant changes in accounts of emotions since classical Athens have included improvement in understanding the physical structures and processes underlying emotions, but also a difficulty in maintaining the methodological reach of Aristotle's approach to the cultural dimensions of emotions. In the Middle Ages, for instance, because the only emotional commitment approved by the Church was love of Christ, emotions were seen as ardent, vehement, and overpowering, as passions, a term unavoidably also associated with Christ's suffering. Any emotion apart from Christian devotion was thus regarded as subversive of religious faith and correspondingly condemned as irrational. By the sixteenth and seventeenth centuries, probably through the emergent significance of market exchanges and diplomacy in which it was necessary to form a view of the intentions of others, an operational interest in emotions loosened from theological prejudice and emphasizing their expressive and rhetorical significance became the subject of numerous publications in France, Spain, and England. This trend was consummated in the eighteenth-century discussion of moral sentiments, in which "moral" meant not merely ethical but especially social and cultural analysis, and "sentiments" implied the cognitive, even intellectual, content of emotions and feelings. From the nineteenth century, however, treatment of emotion focused on its physical basis at the expense of its ideational components, a development encouraged by enormous strides in anatomical, physiological, and neurological sciences. This trend was reinforced by subsequent psychological experimentation that treated only those emotions amenable to laboratory investigation – visceral, reactive, and of short duration – and thus reinforced the partial and limited idea that emotions disrupted thought and were therefore inimical to culture.

By the 1980s the cultural dimensions of emotions were again given their due. In some quarters this meant a focus on the cognitive elements of emotion to the exclusion of anything else. This arose through a number of factors but was legitimated intellectually by broad recognition of the significance of what psychologists call the cognitive appraisal process, namely, that the type and intensity of an emotion elicited by an event depend on the subject's interpretation and evaluation of perception of its circumstance and environment. Psychologists recognized that this process is extremely complex involving both inordinately rapid and automatic central nervous system processes as well as more controlled and conscious activities, sociologically described as "interpretation and definition of the situation." The neurological revolution in emotions research came from focus on the first aspect of

this process and the constructionist theory of emotions from the second.

The majority of sociologists and anthropologists and large numbers of psychologists and philosophers who have written on emotions over the last 25 years believe that emotions are constructed by cultural factors. The constructionist position holds that emotional experiences depend on cultural cues and interpretations, and therefore that linguistic practices, values, norms, and currents of belief constitute the substance of experience of emotions (McCarthy 1994). Biological and even social structural factors are irrelevant for this approach. A corollary of constructionism is that persons can voluntarily determine the emotions they experience, that the cultural construction of emotions entails emotions management. The constructionist approach has enlivened discussion of emotions and drawn attention to the ways in which emotions are differentially experienced across societal divisions and through historical time. The object of any emotion will be influenced by prevailing meanings and values, as will the way emotions are expressed; thus what is feared and how people show fear, indeed how they may experience fear, will necessarily vary from culture to culture. The strength of this perspective is demonstrated by the fact that emotions attract cultural labels or names. In this way emotions become integrated into the broader conceptual repertoire of a culture and prevailing implicit cultural values and beliefs are infused into the meaning of named emotions (Russell 1991). Thus the notorious difficulty of translating emotion words from one language to another.

But by treating emotions exclusively as strategic evaluations derived from local meaning systems, the constructionist approach is arguably itself captive of cultural preferences. It is important to remember that emotions that escape cultural tagging are not thereby without individual and social consequence. Indeed, there is much evidence that socially important emotions are experienced below the threshold of conscious awareness and cannot be fully accounted for in only cultural terms (Scheff 1990). If culture shapes or constructs emotions, what is it that is shaped or constructed?

In a neglected but important discussion, Agnes Heller (1979) argues that cultural adaptation of innate emotions involves elaboration of cognitive-situational feelings that regulate them. These affective interpretations of emotions achieve their regulatory capacity by virtue of being secondary modifications of physically based affects or emotions, such as fear, that are provoked by events and expressive of them. Thus it is necessary to describe the cause of fear, for instance, in physical (endocrino-neurological) or social structural (insufficiency of power) terms, while the object of fear – what persons are afraid of – must largely be defined culturally. From this perspective the cognitive dimensions of emotions are not treated at the expense of their physical and social structural elements, but together with them. The real significance of this position, found in writers such as Norbert Elias (2000) and Émile Durkheim, is that it permits exploration of an aspect of the relationship between emotions and culture ignored by the constructionist approach, namely, the contribution emotions make to cultural experiences and components.

In *The Division of Labor in Society* (1893), Durkheim includes emotions within the category of collective conscience, the latter standing for a determinative cultural formation. In *The Elementary Forms of Religious Life* (1912), his treatment of cultural institutions refers to the sustaining importance of emotional effervescence. Ritual settings, argues Durkheim, provide a framework within which emotional experiences are formed, and the affective dimensions of the emotions and their directing energy give life to cultural practices and institutions. In particular, attention to common cultural objects, coordination of actions and symbolic gestures, and diffusion of orientation and practice through a society are all achieved as a result of emotional focus and contagion. Unlike constructionist arguments, Durkheim's discussion regards emotions as irreducible foundational forces of cognitive and cultural phenomena.

There are a number of ways in which emotions support and shape culture. Randall Collins (1990: 27), for instance, has suggestively claimed that values "are cognitions infused with emotion." This is an insightful corrective to the position found in sociology through the influence of Max Weber's approach, for instance, namely, that values and cognitions

operate through exclusion of emotions. Indeed, Adam Smith's pioneering cultural sociology, *The Theory of Moral Sentiments* (1759), shows how self-judgment and judgment of the conduct of others are based in emotional appraisals, and how such emotions interact with what he calls custom and fashion. More recently and from a quite different perspective, Jonathan Turner (2000) demonstrates that emotions underlie not only attunement of interpersonal responses and social sanctioning, but also moral coding and the evaluations of social resources. On a more macrosociological level, it is useful to consider the composition of broad cultural temper in terms of underlying emotional patterns. Suggestive statements of the relevant processes are in papers by Joseph Bensman and Arthur Vidich (1962), and Joseph de Rivera (1992).

In their discussion of the differential impact, both positive and negative, on opportunities for income through movements in the business cycle, Bensman and Vidich indicate the sources of emotionally informed outlooks of distinct economically defined groups that impact on the broader societal culture, as when descending real income gives rise to status defensiveness and resentment of others. In a similar fashion, Rivera shows how political developments impact on the cultural ambience of whole societies through what he calls emotional climates. These studies point to the economic and political sources of the aggregation of collective emotional patterns from individual-level emotions arising out of structured situations. The emotional climates that are identified in this process function as both orienting patterns of culture, which influence individual appraisals, and collective outcomes of individual emotional experiences.

The role of emotions in the construction of culture points not only to the composition of emotion but also significantly to its function. Emotions alert individuals to changes in and elements of their environment that are of concern to them, provide focus to situations in which these things are integral, and facilitate appropriate strategies to normalize these situations. That is, emotions both define the situations of persons and indicate what their interests are or intentions might be within them. It is a short step from this statement of the function of emotion to one concerning the emotional contribution to culture. It was mentioned above that cultural regulation of emotion occurs through elaboration of cognitive-situational feelings. It is likely that this process can be understood as emotional reaction to emotional experience, and that much cultural variation can be understood in this way. Jealousy, for example, is a widespread if not universal emotion. But in "traditional" or "Mediterranean" societies people are proud of their jealousy, whereas in "modern" or "western" societies people may be ashamed of it. Even the apparent absence of certain emotions from particular cultures can be explained in this way, as with Simmel's "blasé feeling," the emotional antidote to self-regarding emotions under conditions of metropolitan life.

This discussion encourages reconsideration of the process of cultural appraisal or definition of the situation, which constructionists typically explain through application of "feeling rules." But artifacts such as feeling rules, following Bourdieu, might better be understood as outcomes rather than determinants of practices. That insult of Untouchables leads to acquiescence rather than anger may be explained through cognitive appraisal implicit in Hindu religious belief, in which gratitude results from receiving caste deserts. But such cultural explanations fail to account for the sustained coercion by higher-caste persons in maintaining Untouchable subservience, or the mass conversions of Untouchables to Islam or Christianity when opportunity permits. Alternatively, constraints of social inferiority provide a sufficient structural antecedent precondition to account for Untouchable emotional experience of apathy and hopelessness, emotions that contribute to Untouchable culture. In this account, social structural relations elicit emotional reactions that then contribute to cultural experience (Kemper 1978; Barbalet 1998).

Not all social relations generative of emotional experience are current or past; they may also be imagined. Imagined relations are central to future-oriented emotions, such as fear, anxiety, and hope, but also vicarious emotions in which persons at some level and in some manner imagine themselves to be others. This latter form is especially important for an understanding of cultural experiences led by entertainment and advertising industries that pervade, indeed dominate, the present (Illouz 2003). As the rapid communication and electronic projection of images stimulating vicarious emotions are characteristic of modern commercial culture, so the significance of emotions for the support of cultural experience is to that degree reinforced.

SEE ALSO: Affect Control Theory; Emotion: Social Psychological Aspects; Emotion Work; Emotions and Economy; Emotions and Social Movements

REFERENCES AND SUGGESTED READINGS

Barbalet, J. M. (1998) *Emotion, Social Theory, and Social Structure*. Cambridge University Press, Cambridge.

Bensman, J. & Vidich, A. (1962) Business Cycles, Class, and Personality. *Psychoanalysis and the Psychoanalytic Review* 49: 30–52.

Collins, R. (1990) Stratification, Emotional Energy, and the Transient Emotions. In: Kemper, T. (Ed.), *Research Agendas in the Sociology of Emotions*. SUNY Press, Albany, pp. 27–57.

Elias, N. (2000) *The Civilizing Process*. Blackwell, Oxford.

Heller, A. (1979) *A Theory of Feeling*. Van Gorcum, Assen.

Illouz, E. (2003) *Oprah Winfrey and the Glamor of Misery*. Columbia University Press, New York.

Kemper, T. D. (1978) *A Social Interactional Theory of Emotions*. Wiley, New York.

McCarthy, E. D. (1994) The Social Construction of Emotions: New Directions from Cultural Theory. In: Wentworth, W. M. & Ryan, J. (Eds.), *Social Perspective on Emotion*, Vol. 2. JAI Press, Greenwich, CT, pp. 267–80.

Rivera, J. de (1992) Emotional Climate: Social Structure and Emotional Dynamics. In: Strongman, K. T. (Ed.), *International Review of Studies on Emotion*, Vol. 2. Wiley, New York, pp. 197–218.

Russell, J. A. (1991) Culture and the Categorization of Emotions. *Psychological Bulletin* 110(3): 426–50.

Scheff, T. J. (1990) *Microsociology: Discourse, Emotion, and Social Structure*. Chicago University Press, Chicago.

Turner, J. (2000) *On the Origins of Human Emotions*. Stanford University Press, Stanford.

emotion: social psychological aspects

Leslie Wasson

People may perceive emotion as residing in the individual and composing some portion of personal subjective experience. However, certain common patterns of emotional experience exist. We have shared social definitions of emotions, which are generally recognized and which can be evoked or referenced in socially appropriate situations. These emotion norms then become incorporated into the definition of the situation. While psychology and psychiatry have investigated emotions as internal to the individual, sociology has only recently contributed a social, interactionist analysis of emotion, or affect, to scholarly discourse.

The sociological approach to the study of emotion rests on a two-stage theory of emotion. The first stage is an internal state of biological arousal, and the second is a reflexive process using situational cues to interpret or identify which emotion is an appropriate response in that situation (Rosenberg 1990). There may also be a process of negotiation with others as to the emotional definition of the situation.

One of the most fundamental issues in the sociology of emotions is the tension between universality and variability in the experience and expression of emotions, particularly the emotions of shame or embarrassment, since these are so evocative of sympathy or empathy from situated others. Data from cross-cultural research imply that the type of community or social structure is a determining factor in the variability of emotional experience and expression. Yet, when we behold expressions of certain emotions from other societies, such as the grief of the Iranians at the death of Ayatollah Khomeini, we have little difficulty recognizing the emotions they represent (Flaherty 1991). Universality, then, may be found in the subjective experience and expression of these emotions, and variability is found in the situations in which these emotions are negotiated as appropriate responses.

The sociology of emotions claims adherents from two different theoretical orientations: positivists and constructionists. Extreme positivists would assert that there are affective roles which are coercive or deterministic in their effect on people's behavior and emotions, and that these emotions are somehow "hardwired," or biologically inherent in the human species. From this standpoint, the individual would presumably feel only those emotions that were appropriate to the operative role. While not denying the existence and influence of affective roles and conventions, the constructionist paradigm states that these affective roles are manipulated and negotiated situationally by the individual through interaction with other participants. Under the constructionist paradigm, an individual might or might not feel appropriately in a given situation, but may in fact be giving a sufficiently convincing portrayal of the emotional conventions for the interaction to proceed as negotiated (Goffman 1959). These two positions define the extremes of a theoretical continuum. Presumably, many sociologists would employ some combination of the two positions, such as the social psychological approach discussed below, which focuses on structural influences on individual experiences of emotion.

In keeping with this distinction between determinism and constructionism, the sociology of emotions literature demonstrates many other analytical and theoretical differences common to much of sociology as a whole. The most important theoretical or analytical differences are as follows: cognition vs. emotion, structure vs. interaction, biology vs. socialization or political economy (e.g., gender), the social control of emotions vs. emotional forms of social control, and physiology vs. phenomenology (Kemper 1990). Similarly, the chief methodological debates center on questions of quantitative vs. qualitative methods of analysis, and prediction vs. description. Although there are significant areas of overlap, one convenient way to characterize the field of sociology of emotions is to examine it in terms of symbolic interactionist approaches and social psychological approaches.

Traditional sociological examinations of the self (Mead (1962 [1934]); Goffman 1959) have generally left open the question of emotion. Emotion has often been mentioned in passing, relegated to the discipline of psychology, or carefully skirted in treatises on motivation or motive. Social psychological research on emotions had until recently focused extensively on the use and recognition of physiological cues connected to emotional states, primarily under experimental conditions.

There are some notable exceptions, however. In 1962, Schachter and Singer undertook an experiment to test the source of emotional definitions of the situation. Their participants were injected with substances that stimulated states of physiological arousal for which there were no affective cues in the situation. Subjects were then provided with cognitive cues toward one or another emotion. After controlling for the influences of the experimental setting, Schachter and Singer concluded that, although physiological arousal is necessary to emotion, it is not sufficient. Cognitive or, in symbolic interactionist terms, situational cues or definitions indicated the appropriate emotion label for the participants.

Affective arousal can be ambiguous, but so can situations. Certainly, something is happening physiologically that we are interpreting as the presence or occurrence of emotion. However, the same physiological sensations may be defined as any one (or more) of a variety of emotions, or, in some cases, as symptoms of illness. Affective roles do exist and are passed along through socialization. However, the implementation of all or part of these affective roles is subject to a good deal of interpretation and negotiation. While the affective convention is the unquestioned default for many situations, the endless variation of human interactions (and their sometimes unanticipated consequences) creates environments in which improvisation may be the most successful interaction strategy for the individual.

Gross and Stone (1964) wrote a pioneering article on the emotion of embarrassment, in which they proposed a theoretical justification for the treatment of embarrassment (and, by association, emotions in general) as a social phenomenon. Gross and Stone contributed two key ideas to the study of embarrassment. First, they commented on the social nature of embarrassment, and pointed out that certain situations are more prone to the effects of embarrassment than others (i.e., situations requiring "continuous and coordinated role performance" [1964:

116]). Second, they pointed out that certain situated identities are more precarious than others, and are therefore more prone to embarrassment, such as the identity of adolescents. Early work by Goffman (1959) also indicated that emotions could be described as forms of situated interaction.

Research in the sociology of emotions has, to some extent, left out the feeling actor, whether as researcher or as participant. It may leave unexamined the tension between reflecting and feeling described by Mills and Kleinman (1988). Mills and Kleinman suggest that reflexivity (or cognition) and emotionality are not two ends of the same continuum, but rather two entirely different processes. This approach suggests one possible resolution of the cognition versus emotion debate.

Randall Collins (1990) argues that emotions are the third element of a core theory of society, along with structure and cognition. Emotions, for Collins, make up a "moral order" in society, without which social solidarity would not be possible. Emotions then become a medium of exchange, in which emotional energy is the coin. Collins's model is unusual in that he portrays the positive emotions as being of high emotional energy, and the negative emotions are perceived as low emotional energy. Emotional interaction is a manifestation of structural needs in this model, and, in a sense, the needs of this market structure predict individuals' emotional states.

Hochschild (1979) proposes a conceptualization of emotion which resembles that of Collins (1990), but which provides greater autonomy for the subjective individual. Her model links structure and interaction via ideology to explain ways in which structure influences or limits emotion. She proposes a gender strategy of emotion management (as well as a class or ethnic strategy) to explain differences in expressivity between men and women. Hochschild contends that the public ideology of emotion (the situational emotion norm) becomes the private (or at least the appearance of the private) experience. Gordon (1990) provides a treatment of structural effects on emotion resembling that of Hochschild (1979). However, his mechanism for the influence of structure and culture on emotional states is language rather than ideology. His "open system" model has four components: bodily sensations, expressive gestures and actions, a social situation or relationship, and emotional culture.

Kemper (1990) provides a more interactionally based, if also more deterministic, picture of emotions in social relations by calling for a systematic codification of situational conditions that predict emotions. Kemper compares these systematic rules to the laws of motion or physics. However, his formulation cannot account for the deviance phenomena or for the frequent occurrence of mixed emotions and ambivalence.

Theories of socialization have postulated the existence of learned patterns of emotional experience (Schott 1979). Through internalization of emotion norms in early socialization, individuals learn what emotions are appropriate to types of situations, and are therefore equipped to manage situated emotional identities. At minimum, an examination of emotional socialization and the uses of emotions in social control provides some idea of the contents of the emotional and interactional resources carried by individuals from one encounter to another. At about age 1 year 6 months, a child shows tenderness or affection toward significant others. However, it is not until the age of 5 or 6 that the child recognizes the selfhood of themselves and others. This development of the "looking-glass self" (Cooley 1902) allows the growing social actor to experience sympathy or empathy, which Shott considers a prerequisite for the adoption of the "role-taking" emotions of pride, shame, or envy.

A figurative or virtual audience, which Mead (1962 [1934]) might have identified as the "generalized other," serves an internal regulative function similar to that provided by the literal social audience. Feeling rules and the consequent emotion work are the media through which the self learns to control his or her own behavior and feelings. This conforms to Schott's (1979) assertion that emotional social control becomes articulated in adult society as emotional self-control. This is not the social control of emotions, but rather the attribution of an emotional social control from within the individual.

The development of a sociology of emotions has led to the formulation of several conceptual models and middle-range theories. In the intellectual dialogue surrounding the formulation of these constructs, theoretical, epistemological, and methodological issues have arisen. Theoretical issues in the sociology of emotions include the familiar debate between positivists and constructionists, and structural or cultural versus interactional causal arguments. Epistemological questions regarding the relative functions of cognition versus emotion are still being debated, and questions of objective emotional symbols versus subjective emotion and introspection have been posed by emotions researchers.

Contemporary research on emotions in the symbolic interactionist tradition is alive and well. A sample of recent publications might include: Lois (2001) on emotions in a volunteer search and rescue group, Lundgren (2004) on social feedback and self-appraisals, and Sharpe (2005) on the emotional labor exercised by adventure guides.

Sociologists who posit a predictive, interactionally based model for emotion, called affect control theory, include David Heise and Lynn Smith-Lovin (Smith-Lovin & Heise 1988). An essential component of affect control theory is the belief that there are set patterns of emotional response that are situationally specific, and therefore predictable. Affect control theorists program a computer to model human affective responses based on situational inputs. If the researcher enters the proper contextual elements, supposedly the computer can predict the affective state of participants in the situation. This is a fairly structural model of emotionality. Affect control theory is concerned with prediction rather than description, and with objective emotional responses to situational contexts rather than the subjective experience of particular emotions.

Some researchers in the social psychology of emotion utilize quantitative or structural methods and models to measure the correlations between particular emotions and situational conditions or social arrangements (Robinson et al. 2004). Their research findings have implications at the micro level for the transformation of emotions in social group or organizational contexts, and at the macro level for the recognition of the influence of larger social characteristics and institutions on emotion.

Other examples of contemporary researchers using a social psychological framework might include Lawler (2001) on using an affect theory to explain social exchange, or Van Kleef et al. (2004) on the interpersonal effects of emotions in negotiations.

FUTURE DIRECTIONS

Some research on socialization supports the assertion that emotion rules and conventions are learned by novice social actors as part of the socializing process. Through interaction with caregivers, and later with peers, "the child gradually constructs a conception of the whole emotion with its components" (Gordon 1990: 159). Emotional socialization reflects the social position of the individual in the social structure as well as the prevailing emotional culture norms. However, less empirical research has been forthcoming on the mechanics of acquiring emotion norms or feeling rules.

Research on emotions is beginning to occur in disciplines besides sociology. In history, for example, one might read Strange (2002) on death, grief, and mourning among the working class at the turn of the twentieth century. In philosophy one might read Nichols (2002) on the role of emotion in cultural evolution, or in the theory literature Reed (2004) on emotions in revolutions.

Empirical research that explores the relationships among emotions, identities, socialization, and social control is needed to ground theoretical constructions about emotional social control. Research should explore not only the specific mechanisms through which emotional social control is exercised, but also the conditions under which these control efforts vary. This intersection of self and society, in which the internal characteristics of the individual come to replicate and reinforce the external structures of society, is an essential connection between micro- and macrosociology.

SEE ALSO: Affect Control Theory; Cooley, Charles Horton; Emotion: Cultural Aspects; Emotion Work; Identity: Social Psychological Aspects; Mead, George Herbert; Psychological Social Psychology; Symbolic Interaction

REFERENCES AND SUGGESTED READINGS

Collins, R. (1990) Stratification, Emotional Energy, and the Transient Emotions. In: Kemper, T. (Ed.), *Research Agendas in the Sociology of Emotions*. SUNY Press, Albany, pp. 27–57.

Cooley, C. H. (1902) *Human Nature and the Social Order*. Scribner, New York.

Flaherty, M. G. (1991) The Derivation of Emotional Experience From the Social Construction of Reality. *Studies in Symbolic Interaction* (Summer).

Goffman, E. (1959) *The Presentation of Self in Everyday Life*. Doubleday, Garden City, NY.

Gordon, S. L. (1990) Social Structural Effects on Emotions. In: Kemper, T. (Ed.), *Research Agendas in the Sociology of Emotions*. SUNY Press, Albany, pp. 145–79.

Gross, E. & Stone, G. P. (1964) Embarrassment and the Analysis of Role Requirements. *American Journal of Sociology* 70 (July): 1–15.

Hochschild, A. R. (1979) Emotion Work, Feeling Rules, and Social Structure. *American Journal of Sociology* 85: 551–75.

Kemper, T. D. (Ed.) (1990) "Introduction" and "Social Relations and Emotions: A Structural Approach." In: Kemper, T. (Ed.), *Research Agendas in the Sociology of Emotions*. SUNY Press, Albany, pp. 3–23, 207–37.

Lawler, E. J. (2001) Affect Theory of Social Exchange. *American Journal of Sociology* 107(2): 321–53.

Lois, J. (2001) Managing Emotions, Intimacy, and Relationships in a Volunteer Search and Rescue Group. *Journal of Contemporary Ethnography* 30 (2): 131–80.

Lundgren, D. C. (2004) Social Feedback and Self-Appraisals: Current Status of the Mead–Cooley Hypothesis. *Symbolic Interaction* 27(2): 267–87.

Mead, G. H. (1962 [1934]) *Mind, Self, and Society*. University of Chicago Press, Chicago.

Mills, T. & Kleinman, S. (1988) Emotions, Reflexivity, and Action: An Interactionist Analysis. *Social Forces* 66: 1009–27.

Nichols, S. (2002) On the Genealogy of Norms: A Case for the Role of Emotion in Cultural Evolution. *Philosophy of Science* 69(2): 234–56.

Reed, J. (2004) Emotions in Context: Revolutionary Accelerators, Hope, Moral Outrage, and Other Emotions in the Making of Nicaragua's Revolution. *Theory and Society* 33(6): 653–703.

Robinson, D. T., Rogalin, C. L., & Smith-Lovin, L. (2004) Physiological Measures of Theoretical Concepts: Some Ideas for Linking Deflection and Emotion to Physical Responses during Interaction. *Advances in Group Processes* 21: 77–115.

Rosenberg, M. (1990) Reflexivity and Emotions. *Social Psychology Quarterly* 53: 3–12.

Schachter, S. & Singer, J. (1962) Cognitive, Social, and Physiological Determinants of Emotional State. *Psychological Review* 69: 379–99.

Schott, S. (1979) Emotion and Social Life: A Symbolic Interactionist Analysis. *American Journal of Sociology* 84(6).

Sharpe, E. K. (2005) Going Above and Beyond: The Emotional Labor of Adventure Guides. *Journal of Leisure Research* 37 (Winter): 29–51.

Smith-Lovin, L. & Heise, D. (1988) *Analyzing Social Interaction: Advances in Affect Control Theory.* Gordon & Breach, New York.

Strange, J.-M. (2002) "She Cried Very Little": Death, Grief, and Mourning in Working-Class Culture, ca. 1889–1914. *Social History* 27(2): 143–62.

Van Kleef, G. A., De Dreu, C. K. W., & Manstead, A. S. R. (2004) The Interpersonal Effects of Emotions in Negotiations: A Motivated Information Processing Approach. *Journal of Personality and Social Psychology* 87(4): 510–29.

emotion work

Jackie Eller and Renata Alexandre

INTELLECTUAL AND SOCIAL CONTEXT

Emotion, hence emotion work, has been considered in the work of many early sociologists, such as Durkheim, Simmel, and Weber (see Barbalet 2002; Turner 2006), but it was not until Hochschild's work in the 1970s and 1980s that a sociology of emotions was taken seriously. Although today's researchers do not always agree with Hochschild on a precise definition of emotions, or how best to study them, there is general agreement that emotions are socially defined, made meaningful within socio-historical situations, and critical to any analysis of social interaction.

Drawing on the symbolic interactionist perspective and the rich heritage of Mills and Goffman, Hochschild (2003) states that an emotion has a signal function that communicates information telling us where we stand in relation to the situation, to social expectations, to ourselves, and to other actors. Furthermore, emotions are managed (emotion work) through situationally and culturally relevant feeling rules so that ideally each encounter with others receives its expected and appropriate amount of feeling. Emotion work, according to Hochschild, is the management of one's emotions in private contexts, in contrast to emotional labor which is the management of feeling in public contexts. Context gives meaning to the *exchange value* of emotional labor (managing self and others' emotions as an aspect of one's labor power; commercialization of feeling in the marketplace) and the *use value* of emotion work, but both refer to the evocation, transformation, or suppression of one's feeling through surface and deep acting. Surface acting is purposeful management of behavioral expression so that one appears to feel the emotion called for in a given situation. Deep acting, on the other hand, refers to one's efforts to construct the genuine emotion that underlies the expected behavioral expression.

Of particular interest in Hochschild's examinations of emotion work and emotional labor have been gendered expectations within organizations and the costs of emotional inauthenticity, noting that women have historically shouldered the burden of emotion work in the household and in the workforce, specifically within the service industry. Her work helped to make visible this invisible labor done inordinately by women, as well as to stimulate studies of emotional labor of Wal-Mart greeters, midwives, paralegals, and academics, among others.

CHANGES OVER TIME

A great deal of research on emotions has been conducted over the past 30 years clearly indicating their significance in understanding social interaction and organizations. Research has also reiterated the importance of status, specifically gender, on emotional expectations and management. The major change though, has been in the agreement that emotion management (the more likely used synonymous term for emotion work) occurs within many work and work-unrelated contexts beyond the household and service industry and that it is a complex process of managing self and others (e.g., Thoits 1996). Somewhat in contrast to Hochschild's work, the study of the sociology of emotion in the last couple of decades also tends to interpret cultural norms as being less influential on human behavior and attaches more authority to human agency with regard to emotion work.

CURRENT AND FUTURE EMPHASES

Drawing on such approaches as affect control theory, which "posits that sentiments about role identities, behaviors, settings, and individual attributes and emotions interrelate through three dimensions of affect" (Lively & Heise 2004: 1110), social constructionism, power and structural theories, and the deviance literature in addition to Hochschild's theory, current research on emotion work can be organized into four general, often overlapping, categories: (1) a particular identity, emotion (e.g., guilt, shame, remorse, anger, jealousy, envy, ambivalence, or anxiety) and its management in given situations (e.g., in the context of being ill or in response to the illness of others, as an aspect of terrorism, tragedy, or personal failure); (2) gender, emotions and emotion management, particularly within the context of feminist analyses (on gender and emotion, see Simon & Nath 2004); (3) emotion management within widely varying organizations (e.g., prisons, legal profession, among paramedics and firefighters, medical arenas, academia, service organizations, and commercial leisure) and social movement activism (e.g., women's rights, environment, animal rights, among hate groups, and in recruitment efforts); and (4) negative and deviant emotions (emotions or emotional expressions perceived as threatening to social order either for their connection to criminal behaviors or their inappropriateness to the social context). The management of remorse, for example, has been examined in the context of trials and jury deliberations.

As emotion work is first and foremost an interactive process, the majority of research is qualitative in nature, including participant observation, ethnographic, narrative, in-depth interviewing, or focus groups. However, there is a significant body of research based in affect control theory which draws on mathematical models to predict emotions called forth in particular situations and hence an examination of the likelihood and extent of emotion work (Heise 2002; Smith-Lovin 1995). In fact, Lively and Heise (2004) use survey data to analyze the integration of emotion management and affect control theories which has led to broader micro- and macrosociological understandings of emotion in social interaction.

An interesting business application of social science emotions research is found in the workplace. Businesses/employers understand that they can gain in sales, repeat customers, and workplace relations by facilitating effective emotion management among employees. In fact, this ability to effectively monitor, understand, use, and change one's own and others' emotional expressions is commonly referred to as one's emotion intelligence.

In his "Lifetime Achievement Award Acceptance Statement" (Emotions Section of the American Sociological Association) (2003), Kemper envisioned that the future study of emotions and emotion work would reflect the pervasiveness of emotions in social life, examining them in all institutional sectors of society and in large and small groups. His vision is apparently becoming a reality.

SEE ALSO: Affect Control Theory; Disneyization; Emotion: Cultural Aspects; Emotion: Social Psychological Aspects; Emotions and Economy; Emotions and Social Movements

REFERENCES AND SUGGESTED READINGS

Barbalet, J. (Ed.) (2002) *Emotions and Sociology.* Blackwell/ Sociological Review, Oxford.

Heise, D. R. (2002) Understanding Social Interaction with Affect Control Theory. In: Berger, J. & Zelditch, M., Jr. (Eds.), *New Directions in Sociological Theory: Growth of Contemporary Theories.* Rowman & Littlefield, New York.

Hochschild, A. R. (2003) *The Managed Heart: Commercialization of Human Feeling.* University of California Press, Berkeley.

Lively, K. J. & Heise, D. R. (2004) *American Journal of Sociology* 109(5): 1109–37.

Simon, R. W. & Nath, L. E. (2004) Gender and Emotion in the United States: Do Men and Women Differ in Self-Reports of Feelings and Expressive

Behavior? *American Journal of Sociology* 109(5): 1137–77.

Smith-Lovin, L. (1995) The Sociology of Affect and Emotion. In: Cook, K., Fine, G. A., & House, J. S. (Eds.), *Sociological Perspectives on Social Psychology*. Allyn & Bacon, Boston, pp. 118–48.

Thoits, P. (1996) Managing the Emotions of Others. *Symbolic Interaction* 19(2): 85–109.

Turner, J. H. (2006) Sociological Theories of Human Emotions. *Annual Review of Sociology* 32.

emotions and economy

Jocelyn Pixley

Emotions and economy, according to orthodoxy, are as far apart as passions from rationality. Some classical sociologists removed emotion categories from modernity; for others, emotions are significant (Durkheim and Simmel), uniform "residues," sentiments (Pareto), or ambiguously traditional (Weber). Economics, with honorable exceptions (like Adam Smith), associates emotions with irrationality. Economy is the home of instrumental rational action. This distinction is completely inconsistent with uncertainty.

Social action oriented to future economic provision or gain must be launched by emotions, often below cognitive awareness. Dull compulsion may involve low levels of emotional energy, whereas emotions are heightened by choices which depend – tenuously – on future outcomes of relationships. Rationality and, preferably, reason can play a role in decisions, but only by accepting the future as inaccessible. In practice, this is hard to do (Pixley 2004). Uncertainties – possibly greatest in monetary economies – are here not trivial but "matter": there may be vulnerabilities to losses, broken promises, or threatening prospects of a damaged reputation from mistakes or default. In face of perceived and unperceived, unimaginable futures, a range of emotions is involved in this largely internal process (i.e., endogenous, not just exogenous, as neoclassical theory concedes, at least). Specific anticipatory emotions disregard, play down, or help suppress the future's unknowability, and so provoke decisions and action. Gullibility, distrust, trust,

caution, and fear are the main emotions in forming expectations. Such practices are colloquially called consulting gut feelings, soothsaying, intuition, or, more grandly, prognostications.

With the later outcomes or unexpected events come equally uncontrollable emotions, immediately and then retrospectively cast. All are just as diverse and unpredictable. Expected outcomes may lead to smugness, *entscheidungsdfreudig* (joy in decision-making), arrogance, or vice versa: grim confirmation, even despair. Unexpected outcomes give shock and anger, or relief, whereas the unintended events (a backfire) may provoke shame or *schadenfreude*.

Emotion categories are theoretically included in economy by a number of contemporary sociologists (e.g., Collins, Kemper, and Barbalet) and economists (e.g., Heilbroner, Hirschman, and potentially Minsky), but excluded from both ends of the ideological spectrum (Pixley 1999). Orthodox economic theories of "markets," even of "firms," assume rational actors can make predictions, while Soviet theories of command economies assumed that planning overcomes uncertainty. In practice, command economies removed choice and devolved anxiety, fear, or fatalism onto workers and, basically, whole populations. But "in theory," trust and trepidation play no role in decisions: in neoclassical theory, failures occur mainly from *the intrusion of emotions* – as would a "virus" or psychological "disability" – and their complete irrationality. Few sociologists have any faith in probability theory or fervent conviction in planning. In fact, both types of positivism deny choice and the unknowability of the future. Yet sociologists are not usually well versed in Keynesian notions of expectations, or how these "govern" economic action. In the Keynesian view, because decision-makers do not know the future, they act on "imagination and hope" (Shackle 1972).

Typical emotions are diverse, then, and depend on the prevailing economic and cultural arrangements (Luhmann). Emotions also vary by status, class, other social positions (resentment, humiliation), and further vary by phases in the business cycle (Barbalet; Collins). Orthodox economics, however, reduces human motivation to a universal and *timeless* emotion, namely, greed, cast at the macro-level of an aggregate of individuals. Its watered-down version – "interest" – is said to be rational, not emotional like greed or avarice. "Interest" comprises orthodoxy's hope for theoretically predictable models. But events are not predictable, *nor is greed* (Pixley 2002): outcomes of its pursuit are unknowable and even identifying what future interests "will be" is fraught. In contrast to economics, sociological perspectives include a whole range of likely emotions induced by various factors. Individuals, in aggregate, sharing a common social experience (rural labor for survival, or modern unemployment) may share similar emotions. Luhmann distinguishes premodern emotions – of faith in, or resignation to, fortune and fate – from modern, strategic emotions of trust for gain. Other sociologists focus on group emotions arising out of interactions between members. Durkheimian ideas about the emotional power of ritual processes which foster collective symbols, and the way effervescence in group life can spread contagiously, have been taken up by economic historians. Contagions, "manias," or panics may cause an emotional "climate" – a depression, irrational exuberance, or animal spirits. Unsurprisingly, this is seen as invariably dysfunctional. In contrast, emotion research shows that impersonal organizations *require and elicit specific emotions*, some cognitively managed and others below the threshold of awareness.

When the term "economy" is reduced to a machine-like entity or sole aim like "maximizing utility or profits under scarcity" – "constrained maximization" – or action directed to "means of survival," it is difficult to identify relevant emotions. Aristotle's distinction between householding – *oikonomia* – and *chrematistics* is useful to make comparisons and to direct research on emotions to the various ways of "studying up" and "studying down." Expectations in the first, *oikonomia*, may entail emotions of caution, prudence, and trepidation, because householding is long-term management for increasing value and conserving resources for the members of the household and their future generations. The second, *chrematistics* – manipulation of property and wealth for short-term returns to the owner – presupposes a continual future orientation with all its anticipatory emotions like distrust and hope.

Modern households have "expectations" somewhere between these cautious and relentless future-gazing poles. Engaged in both market and non-market economic activities, households are only marginal economic decision-makers in either householding or manipulative terms (*oikonomia* or *chrematistics*), being so dependent on broader social relations. Households form expectations that depend on crucial decisions in corporate and bureaucratic domains, and must cope with intended, unintended, and unexpected consequences of decisions imposed top-down.

Constant short-term manipulation of wealth *or* cautious long-term conservation are both beyond the effective capacity of modern households in aggregate. It is true that a rise or fall in consumption patterns, in "climates" of depression, confidence, or exuberance, can easily effect great change, but modern households are positioned by the money economy. Thus Simmel sees cynicism and the blasé attitude not only as typical emotional and defensive responses to the market, but also as the emotional sources for modern rationality. Even so, present and future orientations provoke different levels of emotional intensity. The unknowable future can be "unbearable" at the economic peak, but plays a reduced role in domestic and much paid labor (i.e., *oikonomia*), with their focus on immediate tasks and skills. Service sector, creative, professional, productive, and unpaid caring tasks are absorbing and present oriented, often with low-level economic emotions: pride in a job well done (or self-blame) and generally vague confidence in large-scale organizations (like banks) or anxiety about future life chances of family members.

Confidence is a matter of lack of choice: if misfortune occurs (e.g., from a corporate collapse), blame is cast elsewhere at the actors making decisions to trust the unknowable future. If paid labor requires cut-throat competition, trust and fearlessness may be required from above: this often induces recklessness and necessary scapegoats after the fallout. These are corporate policy issues. Emotions also vary according to historical memory of economic events across all economic *and* political spheres, and how the household sector is positioned by states, corporations, and markets (short-term manipulation) and social movements' impact on states (long-term conservation policies "from below").

In democratic welfare states where many households are mutual or social property owners, through state pensions, public housing and health, anxiety may be reduced by the "freedom from fear" of joblessness or homelessness. Under privatized arrangements, households are positioned – indirectly – as individually "responsible" property owners through banks, real estate markets, and investment fund firms. Individuals may be enthusiastic speculators from a contagion of optimism fostered by the investment firms dealing in stock and property markets. Others may experience anger, cynicism, or fear when let down by their confidence or loyalty in banks and corporations. Lack of confidence in economic institutions varies among countries. The principle of "buyer beware" implies a distrust that is ineffectual for lone individuals if consumer regulations are weak. Confidence in the safety of products for sale may hold under more regulated regimes (usually brought about by social movement protest).

These emotions connected with economy may seem starkly different from Weber's line that affective-emotional action is opposed to goal-directed rational action. Yet Weber's analysis of passionately held values to guide rational action, the modern loss of brotherliness, and his famous attribution of extreme anxiety to Puritans facing the uncertainty of everlasting damnation all suggest his ambivalence toward emotions. Whether the rise of capitalism depended, unintendedly, on an anticipatory emotion focused on predestination, today, corporate and financial attempts to control the future are routine.

Modern large-scale organizations are highly future oriented and relentlessly engaged in short-term decisions (the "iron cage"). The more competitive the situation, the more actors tend to rely on trust and distrust. Inside the mighty investment firms, emotions and their physiological symptoms – sweaty palms, rapid pulse – are fairly well documented. Fearlessness and arrogance are standard operating procedures to cope with daily uncertainty and to avoid the future abyss altogether (the latter point also argued by the late Robert Heilbroner). Traders who learn fear are often sacked because it takes time to unlearn fear. This intensity of the preoccupation with the future

is emotion generating. It is extremely hard to *accept* the inaccessible future if one is constantly dealing in it. This may explain the attractions of orthodox rational choice and rational expectations – in providing business with a sense of certainty – owing to their theoretical inability to conceptualize present and future. Likewise, futurists (from Toffler to Bell) offer their comforting technological determinism, and so too, at worst, do financial "gurus." Yet temptations to gain and use "insider" knowledge are ubiquitous. It is the illegal recourse to a "sure thing" (and "unfair" in breaking stock exchange, or horse-racing, rules of spreading "risk") which emphasizes the unknowability of the future. Also, why insure if the future is "certain"? Herein lies the ambiguity between prudence, speculation, and gambling: life insurance started with gambling on "lives," but needed legislation so as not to "hasten deaths."

The business and financial world is preoccupied by the future – indeed, "overwhelmed by numbers" – with endless forecasts and inquiries into the "state" of individuals' current feelings (business and consumer confidence surveys). However, economists conduct little research on the emotions essential to future gazing. In contrast, contemporary sociology has developed an impressive literature on trust and risk. This includes warnings about collapsing the future into the present, on the unavoidable and often highly rational emotions like trust, the institutions of impersonal trust, and the reflexivity of risk society. But the focus tends to be on risk, not the "radical uncertainty" argued by Keynesians (money being radically uncertain).

Economists mostly see emotions as irrational sources of error (and, save for "interest," unpredictable), whatever their disputes about uncertainty. Pareto lies somewhere midway between marginalist economics and sociology. His conservative conclusions about emotions dictating all social action are partially behind today's elitist assumptions about the "masses" or "mom and dad investors" suffering from irrational exuberance or panics. In this view, emotions apparently do not afflict rational or "smart" financiers. Pareto is more ambivalent. Rational actions *mainly* arise from "interest," whereas non-rational or "non-logical" actions originate in sentiments or "residues" which are ideologically justified in "derivations," most notably or coldly by elites. Although these extra-rational or irrational elements of human nature lead to "errors," there are positive aspects to non-logical rituals. In Pareto's view, relatively changeless sentiments are best manipulated by "elites" (Meisel 1965; Finer 1966).

Although Pareto qualifies the economic view of rationality, his conservatism influenced managerial theories (Burnham) about rational decision-making being an exclusive "property" of elites. But the modern economy faces *radical uncertainty* with frequent outcomes – quite frankly – of gross corporate errors. The future cannot be controlled by unknowable future "interests" or calculated by probabilistic risk. Risk is the only future for neoclassical approaches, rational choice theory, and behaviorists (apart from external "shocks" or allegedly neutral "technical change"). Neoclassical economics argues predictions are possible, and denounces emotion per se as an irrational interference at the level of its microeconomic models. Behavioral economists take another line on risk, and use emotions as another *deus ex machina* to explain unexpected events, such as "irrational exuberance" and crashes. For behaviorists, "people" fail because they lack mathematical skills or forget basic skills – in fact, often blinded by their models of a risk-free future. This makes them all "overconfident," leading to mistakes in calculating probability, not because no one knows the future.

The distinction between risk and uncertainty was set out clearly by Frank Knight (see Pixley 2004: 35). Risk must comprise a set of known chances to be measurable. Anything that is unmeasurable is a true uncertainty: this was taken up by Keynes and Hayek, later by Minsky. Keynesians, institutionalists, and chaos theorists insist on radical uncertainty, not a future of mere risk. The weather is "only moderately uncertain" compared to the unpredictability of finance (Keynes 1937: 24). Probability can only be assessed "objectively" by comparing invariant factors, such as two dice and a table. Subjective probability is about imagining completely incompatible and unknowable futures which cannot be weighed or compared: extrapolation is frequently pointless.

Economic and financial forecasting is usually published with a ceteris paribus escape clause; however, "other things" rarely remain equal because forecasting is about past, recorded trends of discrete factors, not endlessly surprising "new" endogenous events, nor policy changes, external events, and their unimaginable combinations. Forecasts tend to "cluster" due to forecasters' competitive fear of being alone and wrong. These are reputation issues which matter inordinately in economic action, yet reputations are always retrospective: a reputation is built on lack of contrary evidence, whereas a potential default or mistake can only be imagined.

In addition, during the last 30 years, money has been treated as a commodity capable of infinite trading, but money involves claims and credits, a social relation itself (Ingham 2004). This commodification of promises and privatization of social or mutual security into "securities" has heightened the emotions of distrust and gullibility. Such a climate of oscillating emotions – anxiety, hope, anger, and fear – is due to the excessive impact of financial trading and demands for shareholder value on the "non-financial" sector (itself heavily trading in securities and debt these days). It explains, more starkly, how cynicism and the blasé attitude are recreated once trust is broken.

A major unresolved research issue in emotions and economy is the extent to which trust is *only* an emotion or is completely strategic: this is a huge debate (e.g., Cook; Swedberg). Another is about how to characterize impersonal, interorganizational relations as emotional. Emotions create physiological symptoms in individuals. Faceless organizations cannot be said to "feel" any more than they "think" or have a "conscience." One debate is over how emotions are institutionalized in specific organizations. A more controversial dispute is how interorganizational relationships are emotionally structured. For example, the organizations in the business of impersonal trust, like credit-rating agencies and accountancy firms, are required to *access the future*. They are paid to predict what amount of capital will be needed in the future or how creditworthy a firm or country will be. All other sectors rely on these predictions and some collapse when inevitable failures occur. Reputations for trustworthiness are lost, credibility disappears under claims and counterclaims about which organization is to blame. Huge global banks were "bedazzled" by the arrogance of long-term capital management in 1998, said the chair of the US Federal Reserve, a disaster which apparently brought the entire financial "system" to near collapse (until its bailout). Methodologically, it is difficult to account for endogenous emotions like "bedazzlement" among "organizations," if they can only be "felt" by the office-bearers of those entities: competition plays a part, but also the virtuosity of *entscheidungsdfreudig*, as Neil Smelser alluded to, in passing, years ago.

This question of credibility is not tautological (i.e., credibility means "believability") if one includes social processes of attribution (Mieg 2001). Meso-level struggles over attributions are continuous, as evident in lawsuits and public relations campaigns. Private and public institutional reputations can be subject to impression management for only so long. The point at which such "confidence games" start to resemble "con games" is unpredictable, but these processes ("rituals" even?) are ubiquitous, as evident in the way that struggles over attributions of success, failure, and blame are reported daily in the business news.

Many post-war Keynesian policymakers hoped to *reduce emotions* from economy with demand management and global control over money. They hoped to provide stability by trying to give certainty to the convention that the future will validate present decisions. For sociological emotions research, emotions are not irrational, needless intrusions into economy, nor extraneous and dysfunctional interferences with economic action. In this conception emotions are unavoidable, although cautious emotions (required SOPs) would provide more stability than corporate demands for fearlessness. Past data – rational calculations, extrapolated under the convention that the past continues into the future – combine with retrospective emotions about outcomes of previous decisions (and outcomes of attribution struggles). These retrospective feelings and extrapolations create an imagined future, while a projected hope, trust, or distrust motivates decisions and *moves* a boardroom to act today: after the event, these emotions can rapidly turn into their contraries: shame, anger, disappointment, or relief; smugness for "prescience" and foolish arrogance.

Contemporary debates on emotions and economy have been revived by renewed sociological analysis of emotions in general: one future direction that needs developing is research on emotions at "global" interorganizational levels. Another is the problem of trust in face of the unbearable future.

SEE ALSO: Attribution Theory; Durkheim, Émile; Economic Sociology: Neoclassical Economic Perspective; Emotion: Cultural Aspects; Emotion, Social Psychological Aspects; Emotion Work; Emotions and Social Movements; Luhmann, Niklas; Positivism; Rational Choice Theory (and Economic Sociology); Risk, Risk Society, Risk Behavior, and Social Problems; Simmel, Georg; Smith, Adam; Weber, Max

REFERENCES AND SUGGESTED READINGS

Barbalet, J. M. (1998) *Emotion, Social Theory, and Social Structure*. Cambridge University Press, Cambridge.

Collins, R. (1975) *Conflict Sociology*. Academic Press, New York.

Collins, R. (1990) Stratification, Emotional Energy, and the Transient Emotions. In: Kemper, T. (Ed.), *Research Agendas in the Sociology of Emotions*. SUNY Press, Albany, pp. 27–57.

Cook, K. S. (Ed.) (2001) *Trust in Society*. Russell Sage Foundation, New York.

Finer, S. E. (1966) *Vilfredo Pareto: Sociological Writings*. Pall Mall Press, London.

Ingham, G. (2004) *The Nature of Money*. Polity Press, Cambridge.

Kemper, T. D. (1978) *A Social Interactional Theory of Emotions*. Wiley, New York.

Keynes, J. M. (1937) The General Theory of Employment. *Quarterly Journal of Economics* 51 (February): 209–33.

Luhmann, N. (1988) Familiarity, Confidence, Trust. In: Gambetta, G. (Ed.), *Trust: Making and Breaking Cooperative Relations*. Blackwell, Oxford.

Meisel, J. H. (Ed.) (1965) *Pareto and Mosca*. Prentice-Hall, Englewood Cliffs, NJ.

Mieg, H. A. (2001) *The Social Psychology of Expertise*. Lawrence Erlbaum, Mahwah, NJ.

Pixley, J. F. (1999) Beyond Twin Deficits: Emotions of the Future in the Organizations of Money. *American Journal of Economics and Sociology* 58(4): 1091–118.

Pixley, J. F. (2002) Emotions and Economics. In: Barbalet, J. (Ed.), *Emotions and Sociology*. Blackwell, Oxford.

Pixley, J. F. (2004) *Emotions in Finance: Distrust and Uncertainty in Global Markets*. Cambridge University Press, Cambridge.

Shackle, G. L. S. (1972) *Epistemics and Economics*. Cambridge University Press, Cambridge.

Shilling, C. (2002) The Two Traditions in the Sociology of Emotions. In: Barbalet, J. (Ed.), *Emotions and Sociology*. Blackwell, Oxford.

Social Research (2004) *The Worldly Philosophers at Fifty*. Special issue on Robert Heilbroner, 71(2).

Swedberg, R. (2003) *Principles of Economic Sociology*. Princeton University Press, Princeton.

emotions and social movements

Guobin Yang

Emotions are spontaneous, self-induced, or externally produced self-feelings. Examples include positive feelings of love, loyalty, pride, joy, and enthusiasm and negative feelings of hatred, sympathy, fear, anger, sorrow, sadness, jealousy, shame, and dejection. Emotions are both embodied and take symbolic forms. A sense of anger or joy has tell-tale somatic signs; often, it finds symbolic expression in voice, gestures, words, and tones, not to mention literary and artistic forms.

Emotions have a distinct social character. They often occur in social situations and arise out of social interactions. A society has its emotion culture, which sets social rules and norms for the appropriate kinds of emotions on specific occasions and for the legitimate ways of publicly expressing emotions. The emotion culture of a society embodies and expresses the values of that society. If a feeling of indignation is directed at an act of injustice, it is because society condemns injustices. Emotion culture therefore resembles a habitus, an embodied cultural and social milieu that shapes feeling and action. Practical action activates emotion culture and is guided by it.

Emotions condition and accompany collective action and social movements. Their absence or presence, as well as the types and intensity of emotions present, underpin every phase of a social movement from emergence to decline. Preexisting social networks of friends and neighbors are crucial for mobilization – they are networks of trust and loyalty. Events of social injustice may provoke moral shocks, indignation, and anger and thus move citizens to action. Once initial mobilization starts, the emotional dynamics of collective action become complex and fluid. Both movement activists and their opponents perform emotion work in order to shape the outcomes of the movement. Activists strive to build emotional solidarity and a sense of collective identity. Opponents typically attempt to sow fear as a deterrent to collective action. When this happens, movement participants mobilize "encouragement mechanisms" (Goodwin & Pfaff 2001) such as communal gatherings to manage fear.

These "encouragement mechanisms" are among many possible practices used by movement activists to reduce negative emotions and create positive emotional energy. Activists' emotion work varies depending on whether it is directed at themselves, at the public, or at opponents. The most common practice is rituals. Rituals encompass a wide range of patterned and ceremonial activities such as anniversary celebrations and public parades. As Émile Durkheim long ago understood, rituals create emotional effervescence and revitalize the ritual group. In social movements, rituals are used to build internal solidarity, to move the bystanders and the general public, and to shame opponents. In repressive political environments, activists may appropriate official rituals for mobilization purposes.

Rituals have symbolic components – singing, dancing, and the like. Yet not all symbolic forms are ritualistic. The symbolic expression of emotions in collective action is analytically a distinct practice. To build pride and enthusiasm among participants, to win sympathy from the public, and to arouse anger at the opponents, movement activists tell stories, sing songs, play music, compose poems, chant slogans, and dress up in colorful costumes. These symbolic expressions can be serious or playful. A spirit of play is a familiar part of social movements. Jokes, humor, and parody can undermine the seriousness of power in forceful ways.

Emotions not only influence various phases of a movement, they are also the very stakes of struggle. Structures of power and inequality shape what emotions are appropriate to what social groups. For example, in bureaucratic institutions, anger is the privilege of the superiors, not the subordinates. The dominant emotion culture in contemporary society is emotion management. As Arlie Russell Hochschild (1983) shows, this culture forces individuals to manage how they feel – to stir up or suppress a feeling as the occasion requires. Such management serves instrumental-rational purposes at the expense of emotional fulfillment. Emotion management is thus a culture of instrumental control over emotions. It has a built-in mechanism against collective action. To free collective action of this cultural constraint, social movements, at least in their more radical moments, operate outside, not within, the dominant emotional codes. They seek to subvert existing feeling rules and mobilize counteremotions. In this way, emotions become the stakes of struggle.

Emotions long took a back seat in modern sociology. They were either ignored or conceptualized as the opposite of rational and purposive action. This was so even in the study of collective action and social movements. Before the 1960s, emotions were used to explain away crowd behavior. The standard theory was that crowd behavior was irrational and pathological, and so were the emotions that drove it. In the 1970s, many students of social movements rejected this line of thinking and its associated categories. They abandoned the concept of crowd behavior and talked instead about collective action and social movements. A resource mobilization theory based on rational actor assumptions was developed. Studies exemplary of this new thinking postulate that individuals' inclination to join social movements depends on the material and organizational resources available to them. Emotions disappear from this picture.

These two theoretical orientations were shaped by the social conditions in which they were born. In post-World War II Europe and the United States, material prosperity, a cozy family life, and law and order were the concerns of the day. Thus when sociologists rejected crowd behavior on the basis of its irrationality and pathology, they were responding to the moods of the times. The new thinking that rejected theories of crowd behavior and gave rise

to resource mobilization models of social movements similarly reflected the social conditions. The tumultuous days of student protests had just gone by. The new generation of intellectuals had first-hand experiences in the protest activities. Not surprisingly, these scholars affirmed social movements as rational, democratic political struggles. In their endeavor to rationalize social movements, however, they went to another extreme and dropped emotions from their theoretical models.

Emotions reentered the study of social movements in the late 1980s. By then, cultural analysis and the sociology of emotions had gained influence. These new intellectual trends reflected renewed attention to the centrality of meaning and human agency in sociological explanation. Among others, the works of Norman Denzin, Randall Collins, Theodore Kemper, and Arlie Hochschild significantly advanced the understanding of the social nature of emotions, opening the way for a new wave of sociological studies of emotions and movements. Since then, many articles have appeared. *Passionate Politics* (2001), a volume of articles based on a conference held in 1999, marked the first major collective endeavor made by sociologists to bring emotions back to the study of social movements. In 2002, the international journal *Mobilization* published a special issue on emotions and social movements. Another edited volume, *Emotions and Social Movements*, was published in 2005.

While the growing literature on emotions and movements is diverse in theoretical and methodological approaches, there are two distinct trends. First, there are many efforts to bring emotional dynamics into the explanation of all aspects of collective action and social movements. Emotions are considered to affect recruitment processes, movement emergence, the internal dynamics of a movement, as well as movement demise. The most exciting current research on this topic is in this area. Second, there is an attempt to incorporate emotions into existing categories of social movement theory, including organization, identity, framing, repertoires, and political opportunity structures. There is a growing understanding, for example, that studies of collective identity prioritize the cognitive dimension of identity at the expense of its emotional dimension.

These two lines of research have greatly enriched the understanding of collective action and social movements. But many challenges remain for students of emotions and movements (Polletta & Amenta 2001). One is methodological. One reason for the neglect of emotions in the study of social movements and sociology more broadly has to do with the fact that emotions, despite somatic signs, are not directly observable. The texture of emotional events consists of fleeting and ephemeral details such as gestures, voices, and smiles, yet these details do not often leave concrete records. Of course, many movements have left behind narratives of various kinds, and so far these have provided a main source of data analysis. But these narratives cannot fully capture the fluid dynamics of emotions. A possible corrective is to rely more on ethnography and visual sociology.

Secondly, in attempting to incorporate emotions into the study of social movements, many analysts tacitly or explicitly treat emotions in an instrumental manner. As Craig Calhoun (2001) cautions, some scholars have simply considered emotions as just another thing for movement organizers to manage or another resource to use against the opponents. In effect, then, emotions are turned into another kind of rational preference. Such an approach falls into the same trap as theories devoid of emotional components. This tendency is rooted in the dichotomizing of mind/body and reason/emotion that fundamentally structures modern western thinking. "Putting emotions in their place," as Calhoun puts it, is to study emotions in such a way as to transcend, not reproduce, this pervasive dualism.

To meet this challenge, one research agenda is to conduct more studies of collective action and social movements in non-western societies. As anthropologists (Lutz 1988) have shown, these societies have different emotion cultures. Emotions may thus have very different meanings and expressions. Do interests have the same kind of influence on collective action as in modern western societies? Is it possible to separate emotions from interests? How do emotions structure social action in such cultures? Exploring these questions will help to uncover ways of transcending the reason/emotion dualism still prevalent in current research. Another

research agenda is to study how social movements are not only suffused with emotions, but also aim to transform emotion cultures. Are there influential movements that target or change emotion cultures? What are their characteristics? How do they compare with other movements in their trajectories? Addressing these questions will contribute to the understanding of both the constraints of the dominant culture of instrumental rationality in contemporary society and the possibilities of emotional emancipation.

SEE ALSO: Collective Action; Collective Identity; Culture, Social Movements and; Emotion: Cultural Aspects; Emotion Work; Emotions and Economy; Resource Mobilization Theory; Ritual; Social Movements

REFERENCES AND SUGGESTED READINGS

Calhoun, C. (2001) Putting Emotions in Their Place. In: Goodwin, J., Jasper, J. M., & Polletta, F. (Eds.), *Passionate Politics*. University of Chicago Press, Chicago, pp. 45–57.

Denzin, N. K. (1984) *On Understanding Emotion*. Jossey-Bass, San Francisco.

Flam, H. (1990) Emotional "Man." 1: The Emotional "Man" and the Problem of Collective Action. *International Sociology* 5(1): 39–56.

Flam, H. & King, D. (Eds.) (2005) *Emotions and Social Movements*. Routledge, London.

Goodwin, J. (1997) The Libidinal Constitution of a High-Risk Social Movement: Affectual Ties and Solidarity in the Huk Rebellion, 1946 to 1954. *American Sociological Review* 62: 53–69.

Goodwin, J. & Pfaff, S. (2001) Emotion Work in High-Risk Social Movements: Managing Fear in the US and East German Civil Rights Movements. In: Goodwin, J., Jasper, J. M., & Polletta, F. (Eds.), *Passionate Politics*. University of Chicago Press, Chicago, pp. 282–302.

Goodwin, J., Jasper, J. M., & Polletta, F. (2000) The Return of the Repressed: The Fall and Rise of Emotions in Social Movement Theory. *Mobilization* 5(1): 65–84.

Goodwin, J., Jasper, J. M., & Polletta, F. (Eds.) (2001) *Passionate Politics*. University of Chicago Press, Chicago.

Hochschild, A. R. (1983) *The Managed Heart: The Commercialization of Human Feeling*. University of California Press, Berkeley.

Jasper, J. (1998) The Emotions of Protest: Reactive and Affective Emotions In and Around Social Movements. *Sociological Forum* 13: 397–424.

Kemper, T. D. (1978) *A Social Interactional Theory of Emotions*. Wiley, New York.

Lutz, C. A. (1988) *Unnatural Emotions: Everyday Sentiments on a Micronesian Atoll and Their Challenge to Western Theory*. University of Chicago Press, Chicago.

Polletta, F. & Amenta, E. (2001) Second That Emotion? Lessons from Once-Novel Concepts in Social Movement Research. In: Goodwin, J., Jasper, J. M., & Polletta, F. (Eds.), *Passionate Politics*. University of Chicago Press, Chicago, pp. 303–16.

Taylor, V. (1995) Watching for Vibes: Bringing Emotions into the Study of Feminist Organizations. In: Ferree, M. M. & Martin, P. Y. (Eds.), *Feminist Organizations: Harvest of the New Women's Movement*. Temple University Press, Philadelphia, pp. 223–33.

Yang, G. (2000) Achieving Emotions in Collective Action: Emotional Processes and Movement Mobilization in the 1989 Chinese Student Movement. *Sociological Quarterly* 41(4): 593–614.

empire

Lloyd Cox

In its broadest transhistorical sense empire refers to a large-scale, multi-ethnic political unit (usually with a state at its core) that directly or indirectly rules over, and therefore encompasses, smaller political units that were previously independent. Hence, empire always involves relations of domination and subordination between core and peripheral areas and their populations, which are most often established by conquest and maintained, in the last instance, by the exercise or threat of force. Nevertheless, empire may fall short of direct colonial rule and instead be implemented through informal mechanisms of political control based on indigenous elites and indirect methods of cultural domination and economic exploitation. These formal and informal practices of empire, and the ideologies that justify them, constitute *imperialism*. Both terms have their etymological roots in the Latin *imperium*.

In ancient Rome, the meaning of *imperium* was originally restricted to the authority of Roman magistrates to act in the name of Rome and its citizens, at home (*imperium domi*) and abroad (*imperium militiae*). With the territorial expansion of Roman rule around the time of Julius Caesar and Augustus, the term came to connote authority abstracted from any particular bearer of that authority; the distinction between *imperium domi* and *militiae* progressively collapsed; and the term took on an explicitly territorial dimension. Rome and the territories over which it ruled were now considered to form a single *Imperium Romanum* (Armitage 1998: xv–xvi). This *imperium* was in principle limitless, embodying a universalist ethos that distinguishes it from modern empires premised on the particularist and territorially circumscribed claims of national states. It also defined itself as coterminous with "civilization," labeling all those outside its parameters as barbarians and therefore legitimate targets of conquest – a Manichean distinction borrowed from the Greeks, but one that is overtly or covertly a feature of all empires.

The existence of empire in antiquity was not, of course, limited to the Romans. The ancient Egyptians, Assyrians, Babylonians, and Greeks all built significant empires, as did the Macedonians, Persians, Incas, and Chinese. In fact, the unification of the latter under the Ch'in and Han dynasties in the two centuries BCE eventually realized an imperial dominion that rivaled if not exceeded that of Rome, both in terms of geographical extent and technological dynamism. The ocean-going exploits of the Chinese eunuch Admiral Cheng-Ho in the early 1400s even held out the possibility of a Chinese alternative to European modernity and global expansion, albeit one that was, for reasons that were bound up with China's domestic political economy, ultimately not realized.

If for the moment we leave aside the empires of Christian Europe, the other great premodern empire is represented by the expansion of Islam out of the Arabian peninsular from the seventh century CE, followed by its various off-shoots in the second millennium (principally the Mogul and Ottoman empires). During the course of this thousand year expansion, what had initially been an empire was politically fragmented. From the early centuries of the second millennium it is therefore more appropriate to speak of Islam as a *civilization* encompassing several empires, rather than as an empire in its own right. What lent it a degree of coherence was the written Arabic language and the capacity of shared Islamic religious values to impose a pattern of family resemblance on the institutions of otherwise diverse localities. By the end of the eighteenth century, Islam and its last great imperial vestige – the Ottoman Empire – was coming under increased pressure from European imperial powers, which had begun their inexorable global expansion from the late fifteenth century.

EUROPEAN EMPIRES OLD AND NEW

The establishment of modern European empires can be roughly divided into three periods. The first runs from the late fifteenth to the middle of the seventeenth century, and is marked by Portuguese and Spanish expansion and then decline. The Iberian invasion of the Americas was sealed with the ideological and legal imprimatur of the Roman Catholic Church, which legitimized the invasion in terms of the salvation of the Godless. The subjugation of the indigenous populations, and their forced induction into slavery and other forms of coerced labor, laid the foundation for the massive export of silver and gold bullion back to Europe from the 1530s. This not only helped to maintain the power of Iberian and Austrian monarchs, under the auspices of the Habsburg Empire and Holy Roman Emperor, it also oiled the wheels of European commerce and contributed resources to future maritime exploration, conquest, war, and empire-building. It also, however, elicited multiple challenges to Spanish/Habsburg power, instantiating the historical tendency for empires to beget resistance to their further expansion.

The second period runs from approximately the middle of the seventeenth to the middle of the nineteenth century, and was initiated by successful challenges to Spanish/Habsburg hegemony by Holland, Britain, and France, and by their own establishment of maritime empires. Along with the expansion of the African slave trade, this period of European empire-building is marked out by two key attributes that distinguish it from the previous

imperial periods. On the one hand, a new conception of sovereignty was institutionalized in Western and Northern Europe, which recast the relationship between political power, territory, and property. In this new conception, sovereignty was idealized as the absolute and indivisible condition of states, whose rule was uniformly exercised over a clearly defined, bordered territory into which other states could not legitimately intervene. Political space became increasingly nationalized and decoupled from church and dynasty, which prefigured the formation of empires conceived in national terms. On the other hand, this was the period in which the great national trading companies (the French India Company, the Dutch and English East India Companies, and many more) and the associated doctrine of mercantilism became key factors in the extension of European imperial dominance across much of the world. These companies secured special trading rights and military protection in return for the revenues and territorial influence that they extended to their respective states, which was expressed in accelerating commercial and military rivalries. In many ways, the national trading companies represented the thin end of the colonialist's wedge, as they were often the forerunners to direct colonial rule.

The third and final period of European Empire begins in the second half of the nineteenth century and is not concluded until widespread decolonization in the decades following World War II. The decades between 1870 and 1914 represent the zenith of European imperialism, with the vast majority of the planet's surface being ruled directly or indirectly by Europeans or their descendents. This period was characterized by several widely acknowledged defining features. First, colonial annexation became the rule rather than the exception, though it was exercised rather differently depending on the colonial power. British rule, for example, was typically more indirect (frequently deploying modified indigenous structures of power to secure its dominance) than say French rule, which was more centralized and assimilationist. Second, the imperialism of this period was coupled with a virulent nationalism that embodied the pseudo-scientific language of racial superiority. The hierarchy-engendering realities of European empires required an explanation and legitimization, for which theories of racial superiority and survival of the fittest were perfectly suited. The coincidence of political, military, and economic inequalities with differences of phenotype offered a seemingly self-evident reason and justification for the continued domination of non-whites by whites. Third, it was a period of intensifying militarism and inter-imperialist rivalries between the great powers. The acquisition of colonial territories both contributed to and was a gauge of a state's status as a great power. This helps explain why European states were so keen to acquire colonial territories, even in some circumstances where the economic benefits of doing so were marginal or even negative. Finally, the last decades of the nineteenth century were ones where the character of capitalism underwent important changes, which many contemporaries of the period argued had profound implications for the trajectory of empires and imperialism.

THEORIES OF EMPIRE AND IMPERIALISM

In the *Communist Manifesto* (1847) Marx and Engels had famously provided a thumbnail sketch of the globalizing logic of capitalism. It is principally the needs of a constantly expanding market for its products which, they suggest, "chases the bourgeoisie over the whole surface of the globe," with cheap commodities being "the heavy artillery with which it batters down all of the Chinese walls." They were ambivalent in their normative judgments about this process, with early articles on India and China arguing for the historically progressive role of capitalism imposed from the outside (notwithstanding the brutal means by which this was accomplished), while articles on Ireland suggested that colonial rule could just as likely retard as promote economic development. Such ambivalence was mirrored in the views of later liberal and socialist commentators, as capitalism matured beyond its free-market, competitive forms that were the backdrop to Marx's theorizing.

The most important early twentieth-century liberal analysis of empire and imperialism is that of John Hobson (1938). His argument is basically that monopoly capitalism, unlike its competitive predecessor, entails a tendency to over-savings and therefore under-consumption. Depressed domestic demand in turn depresses opportunities for profitable investment at home, which drives capital export and overseas investment. These investments, plus possibilities for future investment, must be protected from the predatory capitalists of other national states. This creates economic and political pressures for the formal annexation of colonies and thus intensified imperialist rivalries and militarism. He was adamant that a small group of financiers were the main culprits driving government policy in this imperialistic direction.

In subsequent critiques of Hobson and those who followed his lead, it has been pointed out that his "financiers" were not nearly as homogeneous in their interests as he assumed, and nor were they the exclusive or even main beneficiaries of imperialism. Moreover, the alleged link between under-consumption and capital export is tenuous. As many commentators have suggested, capital may be exported not because opportunities for profitable investment do not exist at home, but because the rate of return on investment is simply greater abroad. And nor do such investments depend upon colonial annexations. The US and Argentina, for instance, were key destinations for British investment in the late nineteenth century, while many of its colonial possessions proved to be of little value in terms of investment or trade.

Despite the weaknesses, Hobson had a significant influence on early twentieth-century debates on empire, not least those within the socialist movement. Traces of Hobson's ideas can be found in the substantial treatises on imperialism by Luxemburg, Hilferding, and Bukharin, as well as in the more synoptic work by Lenin. While the former works are more weighty in their intellectual contributions, it is Lenin's *Imperialism* that has had the most enduring historical legacy, as it was canonized by orthodox Marxists, becoming the standard against which other theories and praxis were piously judged.

Lenin defined imperialism as the "highest" stage of capitalism, characterized by five main features: (1) the concentration and centralization of capital into great monopolistic trusts and cartels; (2) the progressive merging of banking and industrial capital into "finance capital"; (3) the centrality of capital export as opposed to commodity export; (4) the emergence of international capitalist monopolies that share the world among themselves; (5) the completion of the territorial division of the planet among the capitalist powers. Like Hobson, Lenin placed particular emphasis on the third of these features, with capital export being necessitated because capitalism becomes "overripe" in some advanced countries, with a "superabundance" of capital outstripping opportunities for profitable investment at home. The competitive quest for spheres of profitable investment in the capitalist periphery would, he argued, ultimately lead to militarism and war.

Lenin's *Imperialism*, and implicitly all of those theories largely based on it, has been criticized on empirical and theoretical grounds. Empirically, the merging of industrial and banking capital has not proven to be the inexorable trend that Lenin expected, and nor has capital export been mainly from more to less economically developed parts of the world. In Lenin's time, and even more so today, the predominant trend has been for the bulk of foreign direct investment to occur within and between the advanced capitalist states – those that are, in Lenin's terms, overripe and exhibiting a superabundance of capital. Theoretically, Lenin has also been taken to task for failing to specify adequately the causal relationship between his five key characteristics of imperialism, and between them and the broader tendency he identifies toward militarism and war. In addition, his work has been criticized for defining imperialism as a *stage* of capitalism. This unduly narrows the compass of the term imperialism. A strict application of Lenin's criteria would place many clear-cut examples of empire outside of his definition, including the Soviet, Nazi, and Japanese empires established between the wars.

In the quarter century following World War II, the almost universal process of decolonization marked the denouement of formal European empires. It did not, however, engender the expected fruits of modernity in many of the new states or end foreign involvement in their politics and economies. On the contrary, political independence frequently concealed continued economic and political subjugation which, from the 1960s, inspired new generations of radical theories focused on "neo-imperialism" or "neocolonialism" – basically the idea that postcolonial societies, while formally independent, were in substance still politically and economically dominated by a few wealthy imperialist states and multinational corporations based in those states.

André Gunder Frank's theory of the "development of underdevelopment," Arghiri' Emmanuel and Samir Amin's analysis of unequal exchange, and Immanuel Wallerstein's world-systems theory were hugely influential in this new generation of thinking about imperialism. Following the theoretical leads of radical theorists Paul Baran and Paul Sweezy, and in Wallerstein's case that of the *Annales* school of French historiography, these theories shared the view that a lack of development in the "third world" was not an original condition, but one that was the product of the 500-year expansion of European powers and the capitalist world market. Simplified greatly, the argument was that this history had divided the world into mutually conditioning metropolitan/core or satellite/peripheral areas, with the former systematically retarding development in the latter by expropriating its economic surplus and imposing relations of dependency through unequal terms of trade. Such positions have been criticized for homogenizing diversity with all-embracing labels such as core and periphery (and, for Wallerstein, semiperiphery), and for failing to account for dramatic economic advances in peripheral states such as South Korea, Taiwan, Mexico, and Brazil. They have also been disparaged for their economism and disregard of culture.

Intellectual currents that emerged in the 1980s sought to remedy this neglect of culture. Edward Said's *Orientalism* (1978) prompted a plethora of new studies emphasizing how discursive practices constitute the colonized "other" in ways that help to reproduce relations of domination. While not ignoring economic subordination, Said's primary focus was on Orientalism as "a political vision of reality whose structure promoted a binary opposition between the familiar (Europe, the West, 'us') and the strange (the Orient, the east, 'them')." Through a close textual analysis of novels, travelogues, colonial records, and other cultural artifacts, Said demonstrates how European self-image is itself a construction of Orientalism, essentially derived from the counterposing of a rational, progressive, and civilized "us" to an irrational, inert, and barbaric "them." Such insights had been anticipated by an earlier generation of intellectuals and activists in the colonized world, such as Frantz Fanon and Aimé Césaire, who had drawn attention to colonialism's objectifying, dehumanizing, and stereotyping of the colonized subject. Where Said went beyond them was in his treatment of the mutually constitutive relations between knowledge and power, and in his use of literary materials to illustrate and substantiate these relations.

Said's Orientalism thesis, and the numerous contributions that follow his lead, often brought under the label of postcolonial studies, has generated much controversy, and not just from those whom Said would label as Orientalists. Many have pointed out that Said presents Orientalism's binary oppositions as relatively static categories, which underplay the extent to which they have been a site of continual contestation and change. Others have taken Said to task for homogenizing the West, and thereby falling into the very ways of thinking that he is seeking to challenge. Finally, Said, and postcolonial theorists more generally, has been criticized for over-inflating the importance of literature and discourse, at the expense of the material and institutional factors upon which all empires stand or fall.

In the 1990s, discussion of empire and imperialism was overshadowed by the new conceptual innovations centered on globalization, globalism, and globality. Much of this literature questioned the contemporary applicability of concepts such as imperialism, arguing that the maturation of multilateral institutions, international law, and global cultural flows rendered them anachronistic. A recurring motif is the erosion of state capacities in the face of accelerated cross-border flows of information, capital, and people, which is said to decenter political power on the world stage. In this view, empire is a phenomenon of the past, not of the present or future.

More recently, however, new theories of empire have proliferated, largely in response to the foreign policy stance adopted by the US since the events of September 11, 2001. This has re-raised debate about the nature of empires and the factors contributing to their decline, such as imperial over-stretch. A major contribution is Hardt and Negri's *Empire* (2000), which has enjoyed widespread popularity and publicity. Its main thesis is that sovereignty has been rescaled upwards from the national to the global level, thereby constituting empire as a deterritorialized global entity. In this view, empire is transnational rather than American. Many subsequent analyses have rejected this deterritorialized, non-national vision of empire, instead arguing that the global projection of US power and its readiness to undertake unilateral and preemptive military action is evidence of the existence of, or aspirations to acquire, an empire (Mann 2003; Johnson 2004). Others agree that the US is an empire, but argue that it is a liberal empire that may well be beneficial for those populations that are subject to US rule (Ferguson 2004). The continued US occupation of Iraq, and its military involvement in many other regions of the world, promises to sustain this renewed interest in empire and imperialism, whatever our normative judgments about its costs and benefits might be.

SEE ALSO: Colonialism (Neocolonialism); Decolonization; Global Politics; Nation-State and Nationalism; Orientalism; Socialism; Sovereignty; War

REFERENCES AND SUGGESTED READINGS

Armitage, D. (Ed.) (1998) *Theories of Empire 1450–1800*. Ashgate, Aldershot.

Ferguson, N. (2004) *Colossus: The Rise and Fall of the American Empire*. Penguin, London.

Hardt, M. & Negri, A. (2000) *Empire*. Harvard University Press, Cambridge, MA.

Hobson, J. A. (1938 [1902]) *Imperialism: A Study*, 3rd edn. George Allen & Unwin, London.

Johnson, C. (2004) *The Sorrows of Empire: Militarism, Secrecy, and the End of the Republic*. Verso, London.

Kennedy, P. (1988) *The Rise and Fall of Great Powers: Economic Change and Military Conflict from 1500 to 2000*. Fontana, London.

Lenin, V. I. (1950 [1917]) *Imperialism, the Highest Stage of Capitalism*. In: *Selected Works*, Vol. 1. Foreign Languages Publishing House, Moscow.

Mann, M. (2003) *Incoherent Empire*. Verso, London.

Russell-Wood, A. J. R. (Ed.) (2000) *Government and Governance of European Empires, 1450–1800*. Ashgate, Aldershot.

Said, E. (1978) *Orientalism*. Penguin, London.

Wallerstein, I. (1974) *The Modern World System I: Capitalist Agriculture and the Origins of the European World-Economy in the Sixteenth Century*. Academic Press, New York.

Wallerstein, I. (1980) *The Modern World System II: Mercantilsim and the Consolidation of the European World Economy, 1600–1750*. Academic Press, New York.

empiricism

Charles McCormick

The term empiricism refers to both a philosophical approach toward understanding the world and the principles and methods that ground modern scientific practices. The philosophy of empiricism, which was first stated by Aristotle and other classical philosophers, came to fruition in the writings of Enlightenment-era scholars including David Hume and John Locke. A key philosophical question at the time was whether knowledge should be generated based on experience, as the empiricists argued, or on a combination of intellect and intuition, as proposed by rationalists such as René Descartes. An increased acceptance of the empirical approach to understanding the world fostered the growth both of modern science and the Industrial Revolution.

Empiricist philosophy has become codified as modern principles of scientific inquiry which include the formulation of verifiable hypotheses that are tested through unbiased and repeatable experiments. While physical sciences allow for precise measurement of phenomena of interest, this is more difficult in the social sciences for several reasons, including the "observer effect," where people who are aware they are under scientific observation may change their behaviors to conform with or thwart researcher expectations, and the fact that the effects of social pressures cannot be measured directly. The founders of sociology, including Émile Durkheim and Max Weber, helped create an empirical approach to studying society when they addressed these issues.

Durkheim helped found the scientific approach to the study of society with his publication *Rules of Sociological Method* in 1895, which explains that sociology rests on the observation and measurement of the effects of social forces on people through measurable phenomena such as crime and suicide rates. The hermeneutic approach to sociology provides an alternative approach toward understanding the effects of society on human behavior, by using methods such as interviews, textual analysis, and self-observation to understand social phenomena. Max Weber is considered a foundational researcher in this approach primarily as a result of his study *The Protestant Ethic*, which argued that the Protestant belief system provided a strong foundation for the growth of capitalism.

The scientific approach to sociology popularized by Durkheim and the hermeneutic approach roughly correspond to the modern quantitative and qualitative approaches to sociology. Within each of these camps there is a further division over the role that social theory should play in driving social research.

Researchers who support the deductive or "theory-driven" approach argue that studies should focus on testing existing social theories, while supporters of the inductive or "data-driven" approach argue that researchers should approach social phenomena with few preconceived notions and then allow their theories and research questions to evolve over the course of their research.

Perhaps the best way to understand the difference between the inductive and deductive approaches is to consider two very different studies that attempted to explain the causes of minor crimes.

In *Fixing Broken Windows: Restoring Order and Reducing Crime in Our Communities* (1998), criminologists George Kelling and Katherine Coles used the deductive approach to test the "broken windows" theory of crime. Kelling and Coles gathered evidence on the enforcement of minor crimes such as aggressive panhandling and found that lack of enforcement of these crimes sends a sign to criminals that additional crimes will be tolerated, in turn suggesting that police and community groups should focus much of their attention on prevention and rapid punishment for minor or "nuisance" crimes, rather than on higher-profile detective work, and on "community building," which helps convince the landlord of a property, for example, that a broken window is worth fixing. In accord with the deductive approach, Kelling and Coles's research was tested and refined in a large-scale longitudinal study in Chicago which found that collective efficacy, or "social cohesion among neighbors and their willingness to intervene on behalf of the common good," is at least as important as the enforcement of minor crimes emphasized in most municipal reforms in preventing crime.

The inductive approach to researching crime was taken by sociologist Jack Katz in his book *Seductions of Crime* (1990). Katz approached the problem of crime with few preconceived notions about whether poverty, a lack of education, or other factors drive crime and his inductive approach yielded surprising and controversial results. After talking with shoplifters and analyzing detailed narratives of situations that precipitated murders and other crimes, Katz finds that the immediate emotions associated with committing the criminal act are a fundamental driver behind many crimes. In the case of murder, Katz explains that murder rarely provides economic benefits to perpetrators and that murders are generally committed by otherwise sane individuals. The primary driver of most murders, Katz argues, is the murderer's feeling of righteous indignation which is used to justify his act as in defense of "the Good." For example, when an individual repeatedly refused to move a car that was blocking another man's driveway, even at gunpoint, the property owner shot and killed him. As in this case, Katz found that murderers are often attempting to defend moral goods that most people support, such as property rights or self-respect, but using unjustifiable means to do so. Similarly, he found that minor crimes such as shoplifting are driven by "sneaky thrills" as much as by economic need, again providing evidence that the "criminal mind" is driven by normal human emotions rather than by psychological pathology or cold-blooded economic calculations.

Both inductive and deductive studies are important building blocks of the social sciences. Inductive approaches often generate theories which can be tested with deductive methods, and deductive theories can form a framework for inductive studies. For example, researchers have used more formal methods to test whether the "seductions of crime" are major drivers behind crime (Phillips & Smith 2004), and researchers have used broken windows theory as a starting point for an inductive study of *how* and *why* minor crimes act as a signal that more and more serious crimes will be tolerated (Sampson & Raudenbush 2004). This integration of inductive and deductive approaches is important because it helps to resolve some of the limitations of social science that only emphasize one approach.

SEE ALSO: Methods; Quantitative Methods

REFERENCES AND SUGGESTED READINGS

Coles, K. & Kelling, G. (1998) *Fixing Broken Windows: Restoring Order and Reducing Crime in Our Communities*. Free Press, New York.
Durkheim, É. (1982 [1895]) *Rules of Sociological Method*. Free Press, New York.
Katz, J. (1990) *Seductions of Crime: Moral and Sensual Attractions in Doing Evil*. Basic Books, New York.
Phillips, T. & Smith, P. (2004) Emotional and Behavioural Responses to Everyday Incivility: Challenging the Fear/Avoidance Paradigm. *Journal of Sociology* 40–4: 378–90.
Sampson, R. & Raudenbush, S. (2004) Seeing Disorder: Neighborhood Stigma and the Social Construction of "Broken Windows." *Social Psychology Quarterly* 67–4: 319–42.
Weber, M. (2001 [1905]) *The Protestant Ethic and the Spirit of Capitalism*. Routledge, New York.

employment status changes

Richard Layte

The three decades that followed the end of World War II are often referred to by social scientists as the "Golden Age of Capitalism" in Europe and North America. This period of relative peace was marked by rising living standards and high levels of employment within societies where the "traditional" family structure still held sway. In this environment, individual employment status changes were fairly few – into a job or career following education and retirement sometime around age 60, with women moving out into full-time motherhood at the birth of their first child. This "Golden Age" began to unravel in the 1970s as widespread changes in attitudes changed behaviors and high oil prices increased inflation and constrained growth. By the early 1980s, the labor markets of western industrial nations were very different from earlier decades, with high levels of structural unemployment and an increasing "feminization" of the labor force as women sought to combine marriage and childbirth with a job or career. In this new environment, simple models of a homogeneous "life cycle" were replaced by more complex and dynamic understandings based on the "life course," where uncertainty and instability were the norm and individuals experienced multiple employment status changes across their life.

This interest in the role of structural change was accompanied by a growing awareness among social scientists that there were winners and losers in this more fluid environment, and that social class processes and educational qualifications were essential for understanding the problems some individuals had in entering the labor market initially and avoiding unemployment once in the labor force. Social behavior occurs within a context, however, and this was increasingly recognized as European integration and particularly European Commission funding for comparative research focused attention on the role that varying educational systems, labor market institutions, and legal regulation had on the pattern of employment status change. The role which labor market structure, education, and social class processes and institutional context play in the increasingly complex patterns of employment status change is discussed below. The focus is on the processes associated with entry into the labor market and the role of flexible working practices in increasing employment status volatility across the life course.

The transition from education to work is one of the central changes in a person's life

and research suggests that its impact can last a lifetime (Korpi et al. 2003). The transition from education to work has changed considerably across most countries in the last three decades. Unemployment among young people increased sharply in the 1980s, with the consequence that young people stayed in education longer and gained higher-level qualifications. The transition itself also became more protracted, with young people taking longer to make the transition and more likely to experience spells of unemployment, particularly those with lower educational qualifications, from manual social classes, or from ethnic minorities. From a microsociological or microeconomic perspective, the transition into the labor market is a "matching process" within which young people balance their present and future returns with continued education and training and employers attempt to recruit those individuals who are most productive and least costly to train. This matching process will be reflected in the stratification of outcomes for individuals. Higher levels of education, skills, and productivity will be of vital importance, but these are also structured by the social class background of the individual, their sex, and their ethnicity (Shavit & Müller 1998). However, this micro-level understanding also needs to be placed within the structural context of the prevailing economic environment and the impact of differential education and labor market systems. In some countries (notably the US, Ireland, and Southern Europe), the education system is oriented toward providing general qualifications with little concern for the relevance of these qualifications for employers. In this sense, qualifications are general "signals" of the individuals' possible productivity. Other countries (Germany, Austria) have extensive vocational training systems featuring large-scale apprenticeship schemes, with training in the workplace as well as in the classroom. The latter have been shown to provide a much smoother entry for young people into the labor market, which avoids spells of unemployment and entrapment in poorly paid insecure work. Poor outcomes for young people have also been associated with "rigid" labor market regulation in terms of the employment protection for those already in the labor force (Bernardi et al. 2000). Changing economic structures in industrialized countries after the mid-1970s led to increasing levels of unemployment and worklife turbulence for those in employment, with redundancy reaching far into the previously stable middle classes, although unemployment was still more concentrated among the manual classes and unskilled. Across Europe, many states responded to higher levels of unemployment with deregulation, or "reregulation," of the labor market to allow greater use of "fixed-term" or short-term contracts and part-time working in an attempt to stimulate employment. This led to a surge in these types of contracts across many countries and to a substantial growth in the numbers of women working (Gallie et al. 1998). The question for researchers was whether fixed-term contracts and part-time hours were a "bridge" to better employment, or rather a "trap" locking people into jobs with poor prospects, conditions, and security. Research (Layte et al. 2000) has shown that previous unemployment spells are a major determinant of future unemployment and of downward occupational mobility, but research on the impact of fixed-term contracts is mixed. Although research suggests that fixed-term contracts are more likely to lead to unemployment, they can also act as a stepping stone to a more permanent contract, although evidence for both is mixed. Part-time work has also been shown to be complex in its impact, with employment conditions and prospects dependent more on the type of job and contract rather than on the number of hours worked per se (Gallie et al. 1998). In conclusion, it is clear that the last three decades have seen an increase in volatility in employment status changes, with an increased risk of unemployment both for those entering the labor market and for those already working. However, these risks are not evenly spread and sociological research has detailed the influence of individual and social characteristics such as social class and the role of national educational and labor market systems.

SEE ALSO: Educational and Occupational Attainment; Life Course Perspective; Unemployment; Unemployment as a Social Problem; Women, Economy and

REFERENCES AND SUGGESTED READINGS

Bernardi, F., Layte, R., Schizzerotto, A., & Jacobs, S. (2000) Who Exits Unemployment? Institutional Features, Individual Characteristics, and Chances of Getting a Job. A Comparison of Britain and Italy. In: Gallie, D. & Paugam, S. (Eds.), *Welfare Regimes and the Experience of Unemployment*. Oxford University Press, Oxford.

Gallie, D., White, M., Cheng, Y., & Tomlinson, M. (1998) *Restructuring the Employment Relationship*. Oxford University Press, Oxford.

Korpi, T., de Graaf, P., & Layte, R. (2003) Vocational Training and Career Employment Precariousness in Great Britain, the Netherlands, and Sweden. *Acta Sociologica* 46(1): 17–30.

Layte, R., Levin, H., Hendrickx, J., & Bison, I. (2000) Unemployment and Cumulative Disadvantage. In: Gallie, D. & Paugam, S. (Eds.), *Welfare Regimes and the Experience of Unemployment*. Oxford University Press, Oxford.

Shavit, Y. & Müller, W. (1998) *From School to Work*. Oxford University Press, Oxford.

en

Hirochika Nakamaki

En is originally a Buddhist concept for indicating causal relations, but it is also a term that is used regularly in Japanese social life. It has also proved to be a very convenient term in academic analysis. In Buddhist terms, *en* is used as a common idiom to refer to an individual's destiny from a previous reincarnation. *En*, however, refers to an indirect causal relationship rather than a direct causal relationship. In Buddhist usage, the concept of *kechi-en* refers to relations with a particular Bodhisattva (Enlightenment-Being). In Esoteric Buddhism, the *kechi-en kanjou* is a rite based on *kechi-en*. Here, in a secret ritual, the disciple throws flowers onto the top of a Mandala, and establishes a relation or tie with the Bodhisattva hit by them. *En* days are specially designated days said to have a special connection with the Bodhisattvas. Kannon day is the 18th day of the month, Jizou is the 24th, and Fudou is the 28th. On these days, a visit to a temple is said to be a particularly pious act that brings substantial rewards.

The concept of *en* became separated from stricter Buddhist usage, and came to be used as a term to refer to general social and personal relations. *En-gumi*, to make a connection, is a common term to indicate marriage, and *en-dooi*, a "distancing of relations," refers to a state where a potential marriage is considered impossible. Good *en* refers to a happy married life, and one particular form of bad *en* is "rotten relations" between a husband and wife, where one cannot separate even if one tries, what is recently termed co-dependency. To have *en* indicates a positive prospect for the construction of human relations, whereas to lack *en* implies a resignation, a lack of probability for the building of a successful relationship. These are all commonly heard expressions in daily life.

En came to be used as a new term in academic analysis, and is found in use in the media and general society. *Chi-en* and *ketsu-en* are good examples. In the former, the term indicates local social relations, the latter refers to relations of kith and kin. Also, compound terms that utilize the word *en*, such as "kin groups" and "residential groups" or "local society," are connected to references to society and group. The terms "local relations" and "kinship relations" refer to exceptionally restrictive social relations, what Chizuko Ueno has referred to as "non-optional relations," or ascriptive relations. Examples of such kin-*en* (*ketsu-en*) have continued since the times of hunting, fishing, and gathering societies. It is thought that local-*en* (*chi-en*) have become stronger since agriculture developed. In sociology and social anthropology, there is a huge body of knowledge about kin relations such as family, and consanguineous and affinal kinship relations. Moreover, within the East Asian civilizations sharing the Chinese writing style, there is a special quality in the application of the term *en* to newer types of human relations. To give two examples, the corporate or company relations of Japan (*sha-en*), and the academic relations (*hagyeon*) of the Republic of Korea.

When Europe entered the modern era, ties of locality and kinship came to be replaced by new forms of social relations, and concepts such as *gesellschaft* and association were provided by scholars. In Japan, on the other hand, the cultural anthropologist Toshinao Yoneyama proposed the concept of "associational ties" (*kessha-en* or *sha-en*) in the early 1960s. He reworked the concept of "association" (*sha-en*) to provide a more inclusive meaning than that then being used by journalists (*kaisha-en* or corporate association), in order to emphasize the function by which companies were associated with each other in corporate social networks. It was worked out specifically as a relational concept, an equilateral accompaniment to associations based on kin and locality, and also intended to emphasize the remarkable increase in the importance of these relations that accompanied industrialization and urbanization. As a background note to this work, during the post-war period, one in which continuously high levels of socioeconomic growth were achieved, social groups based on company/corporate association came to stand in equal importance to associations of kinship and locality. The very concept of corporate associations (*sha-en*) is itself a product of that period, the background of which was the substantial levels of corporate development that occurred. Naturally, the roots of corporate associations can be found in the various forms of ascriptive and associative units of sociopolitical organization dating from the Edo period (1600–1868). Another primary factor contributing to the development of corporate association is the fact that, compared to China and Korea, Japan has always had a relatively weak principle of paternal succession. As pointed out by the anthropologist Tadao Umesao, the origins of corporate association as a social unit are to be located first and foremost in the Japanese household, characterized by a strong paternal authority (*ie*). It was that particularly Japanese legal fiction known as the parent–child (*oya-ko*) relationship that led the way from the household unit to the modern form of corporate association. The latter, born in this manner, is without a doubt the most important development in social relations in modern Japanese society. Yoneyama has emphasized that the so-called License/Qualifications Society (*shikaku-shakai*) is the result of these developments.

Technically speaking, since corporate associations are voluntary forms in terms of association and withdrawal, the term itself refers to a second-order social unit. Nonetheless, looking at the typical form of associations found in Japanese corporations until the bursting of the bubble economy in the early 1990s, the difficulty of resigning from a company once employed was such that these forms must be seen as having a highly restrictive quality. In this connection, the sociologist Chizuko Ueno has proposed the concept of optional associations, or associations of choice (*sentaku-en*) as a residual category to kin, locality, and company associations. Born as an effort to better conceptualize new forms of human relations in urbanizing societies, such forms are free in association and withdrawal, and so lacking in the restrictive qualities of other forms. Examples of such social groups include the audiences at concerts, and so-called "e-friends," persons whose social networks are mediated by electronic media such as the Internet. Further examples include hobby associations such as poetry or bird-watching circles. Ueno has paid particular attention to urban women, especially socially isolated housewives. In opposition to the ways in which their husbands were immersed in their corporate social networks, these women found it necessary to construct a whole new variety of social groups based on voluntary association, such as those centered on their childrens' education, their hobbies, and so on. Teruko Yoshitake has also christened such forms as "women's associations" (*jo-en*). In fact, there is even such a women's group based on the joint ownership of grave plots. These optional associations, however, have little restrictive power, and so tend to be unstable in nature. Nonetheless, as Ueno has pointed out, as we face a rapidly aging society, we have reached a period where such optional forms of association are increasingly in demand, to replace associations of kinship, locality, and corporation.

In Japan there have been a number of terms coined using the root term *en* to define different forms of association, besides company associations, optional associations, and women's associations. Yasuyuki Kurita and Tadashi Inoue have defined "information associations" (*jouhou-en*), and Teruhiko Mochizuki has defined "value associations" (*chi-en*) and "knowledge associations" (*chi-en*). At the same time, the historian Yoshihiko Amino has discovered material regarding the use of the term association (*en*) in medieval documents. He has reinterpreted the term *mu-en* (literally, no relations), a term seeming to imply a lack of social associations or relations. He argues that this term does not in fact refer to a lack of social relations, but rather to the social situation of people removed from restrictive social relations based on fixed residence, as implied in the term *u-en*, that is, "to have" social relations. Moreover, Amino has pointed out that the *mu-en* form of association is itself seen as the associational basis of urban social relations.

The term *en* has proven so useful for expressing particular forms of social association that it has even appeared in texts translated into Japanese. As an example, Francis Hsu's term "kin-tract" has been translated into Japanese as "*en*-tract." Furthermore, based on Hsu's term, Tsuneo Ayabe has provided a definition of club associations as a contractual type of association (*yaku-en*).

In this current era, characterized by social trends such as global population flows, nomadic lifestyles, aging societies, and so-called "gender-free" marriages, we are seeing the attenuation of the restrictive nature of older forms of association based in kinship, locality, and company associations. At the same time, we are groping for new kinds of association that will entrust social bonds in the future. One phenomenon spurring on such developments is the spread of information technologies. A major focus of attention in coming years will certainly be the "virtual-*en*" found in IT networks.

SEE ALSO: Buddhism; *Chonaikai*; *Ie*; Kinship; *Nihonjinron*; Organization Theory; *Seken*

REFERENCES AND SUGGESTED READINGS

Inoue, T. (1987) Shaen no ningen kankei. In: Kurita, Y. (Ed.), *Nihonjin no ningen kankei*. Domesu Shuppan, Tokyo.

Ueno, C. (1987) Eraberu en, erabenai en. In: Kurita, Y. (Ed.), *Nihonjin no ningen kankei*. Domesu Shuppan, Tokyo.

Yoneyama, T. (2003) Shaen to no en. In: Nakamaki, H. & Sedgwick, M. (Eds.), *Nihon no soshiki: Shaen bunka to informal katsudo*. Toho Shuppan, Osaka.

encoding/decoding

James Procter

The terms encoding and decoding are keywords within a theory of communication first developed by Stuart Hall (1973). This paper challenges the established, empirical theories of mass communications research, which assume media messages are relatively transparent and stable. Hall uses the terms encoding and decoding to demonstrate that the media message is neither transparent nor dependent on the competence of individual receivers/viewers, but is in fact *systematically* distorted by the entire communication process.

In particular, Hall argues there is a lack of fit between the two sides in the communicative exchange between the moment of "encoding," when the message is translated into the aural-visual signs of televisual discourse, and the moment of "decoding," when the viewer translates the encoded message. Hall notes that the visual nature of televisual discourse means we tend to overlook the mediated nature of media imagery, which appears to be a transparent reflection rather than a systematic construction of the world around us. Hall's sense that televisual discourse creates a communicative boundary that distorts media messages is informed by structuralist theory. Just as structuralism argues that language and sign systems do not reflect, but structure and construct, the real, so Hall argues that the visual discourse of television translates reality into two-dimensional planes, and therefore is not to be confused with the referent it signifies. As he famously put it: "The dog in the film can bark but it cannot bite!"

Hall goes on to employ the structuralist distinction between denotation (a sign's literal meanings) and connotation (a sign's associated meanings) in order to pursue the competing meanings generated by the same media message. If at the denotative level there is a general agreement about the meaning of a sign – "the photo-image of a sweater *is* (denotes) an object worn" – at the connotative level, meaning is contingent and can change depending on the context in which it appears and is read. Within the discourse of the fashion industry, Hall

suggests, the sweater may connote *haute couture* tyle of dress." However, located within the discourses of contemporary (1970s) romance, it may connote "long autumn walk in the woods" (Hall 1973: 12–13). It is at the level of connotation that the sign acquires its ideological significance, a significance that is capable of changing depending upon the context in which it is used. Hall is particularly interested in the "polysemic values" of the televisual sign within this context. An apparently innocent item such as a sweater acquires different, potentially conflicting meanings and ideological values depending on the context in which it is encoded and decoded.

Hall's account ultimately differs from an orthodox structuralist reading in that it is not simply interested in language and discourse as a closed, formal or ahistorical system, but with the "social relations" of the communicative process at any given moment. Adopting Marx's theory of commodity production, Hall likens encoding to "production" and decoding to "consumption." When an item is depicted on the news, it does not appear as a raw unreconstructed event; it is discursively produced, or encoded in terms of what Hall calls the "institutional structures of broadcasting." These might include such things as conducting interviews with authority figures, specialists, and eyewitnesses, researching news archives, obtaining relevant photographs and film clips, and so on. While these institutional processes help to secure or determine meaning in significant ways, creating what Hall calls "dominant" or "preferred" meanings, there is no intrinsic meaning embedded within televisual discourse. For the encoded message to generate meaning it must first be decoded by the viewer. It is only at this moment that the television message acquires "social use or political effectivity."

Hall regards decoding as the most significant and the most overlooked aspect of the communication process. Where mass communications theory suggested the viewer plays a passive role in the construction of meaning, Hall regards audiences as active consumers. If audiences were once regarded as an undifferentiated "mass," Hall is keen to distinguish between different positions taken up by audiences. In order to do this he develops three hypothetical categories first posited by Frank Parkin in *Class Inequality and Social Order* (1971): the dominant-hegemonic position, the negotiated position, and the oppositional position.

Viewers that decode a particular media message in terms of the preferred meanings of the dominant social order might be said to occupy the dominant-hegemonic position. For example, a viewer watches a report on the "War on Terror" led by President George Bush following 9/11 and concurs that, yes indeed, something must be done to stop global terrorism. The negotiated position refers to viewers who adopt a more contradictory response to the media message, and whose acceptance of the preferred or dominant meaning is conditional. For example, a viewer watches the same report on the "War on Terror," accepts the need for action, but questions the treatment of prisoners at Guantanamo Bay on humanitarian grounds. The oppositional position refers to that of the viewer who recognizes but rejects the dominant meanings of the media message. For example, a viewer who watches the "War on Terror" report, but reads it in oppositional terms as a war to secure US hegemony. As Hall views it, these three positions are not static or discrete, but constitute an overlapping continuum across which viewers move. Nor are these positions individual, personal, and self-conscious responses to particular media messages. Rather, they refer to ideological and therefore largely unconscious positions taken up by certain social groups, communities, and constituencies relating to class, gender, ethnicity, and so on.

Hall's paper became particularly influential in the 1980s and early 1990s, when it prompted fresh research within cultural studies into the neglected issue of audiences. One of the most influential research projects to develop Hall's encoding/decoding model was conducted by David Morley in *The "Nationwide" Audience* (1980). *Nationwide* was a popular early evening light news program broadcast by the BBC until 1983. Morley applied the three hypothetical positions associated with dominant, negotiated, and oppositional readings to actual audience responses to *Nationwide*. Morley, who grouped his audiences in terms of occupation, class, and so on, found that reading positions did reflect the ideological values of these different social

groups to an extent, but concluded that these positions were in no way reducible to social categories such as class.

SEE ALSO: Audiences; Birmingham School; Hegemony and the Media; Semiotics; Television

REFERENCES AND SUGGESTED READINGS

Hall, S. (1973) Encoding and Decoding in the Media Discourse. *CCCS Stencilled Paper* 7: 1–20.

Hall, S. (1980) Encoding/Decoding. In: *Culture, Media, Language*. Hutchinson, London, pp. 128–38.

Hall, S. (1993) Reflections Upon the Encoding/Decoding Model: An Interview with Stuart Hall. In: Cruz, J. & Lewis, J. (Eds.), *Reading, Listening: Audiences and Cultural Reception*. Westview Press, Boulder.

Hall, S., Connell, I., & Curti, L. (1981) The "Unity" of Current Affairs Television. In: Bennett, T. (Ed.), *Popular Television and Film*. Open University, London.

Hall, S., Hobson, D., Lowe, A., & Willis, P. (1980) *Culture, Media, Language: Working Papers in Cultural Studies*. Hutchinson, London.

Morley, D. & Chen, K. (Eds.) (1996) *Stuart Hall: Critical Dialogues in Cultural Studies*. Routledge, London.

Wren-Lewis, J. (1983) The Encoding/Decoding Model: Criticisms and Redevelopments for Research on Decoding. *Media, Culture and Society* 5: 179–97.

endogamy

Nazli Kibria

"Endogamy" refers to in-group marriage, or a pattern of marriage in which the partners have a shared group affiliation. Its conceptual counterpoint is exogamy, or a pattern of marriage in which the partners are different in their group affiliation. For scholars of race and ethnic relations, the significance of endogamy stems from its relationship to group boundaries and the processes by which they are maintained, transgressed, and negotiated. Indeed, endogamy is generally understood to be among the most important social mechanisms in the formation and re-formation of racial and ethnic groups.

Endogamy is increasingly recognized to be a complex and emergent social process. Underlying this recognition are theoretical developments in the study of ethnic identity, which is increasingly seen as multiple and fluid rather than singular and stable in character. This conceptualization also suggests that definitions of endogamy will also shift, depending on what particular aspect of identity is under consideration as well as the historical circumstances and meanings that surround it. As, for example, in the case of a marriage in which the partners are different in their ethnic affiliation but similar in their religion, a marriage that is endogamous in one respect may not be so along another dimension. Furthermore, there is a sense in which marriage itself, regardless of whether it initially involves persons who are similar or different in a particular way, may work to create endogamy or at least make exogamy invisible. As highlighted by situations in which one spouse undergoes conversion into the religious affiliation of the other spouse, marriage may result in the incorporation of the "outsider" into the group in question.

Even with these considerations, it would be fair to say that endogamy, defined as a marriage pattern that preserves the primary group distinctions prevalent within a society, has been and continues to be a widespread norm. In premodern societies, endogamy was largely ensured by prevalent structural conditions, in particular the limited degree of social and geographical mobility available to and experienced by most persons. In addition, marriages were understood not as matters of individual negotiations of romantic love but as practical contracts that were closely intertwined with the authority and interests of the larger kin group (Giddens 1992). These conditions too were encouraging of in-group marriage in the sense that in pre-industrial societies the endogamy of members was generally advantageous to the kin group, allowing it to consolidate and to expand its local networks and resources.

In late modern societies, endogamy continues to be the norm, particularly with respect to the boundaries of social class and race. This is certainly the case in the contemporary United States. In some parts of America, interracial marriage remained illegal until the 1960s. Today, however, it is maintained not by laws but by other dynamics, most importantly perhaps by the presence and power of informally segregated social networks in the organization of people's lives. Writing of the contemporary US, Whyte (1990) observes that "dating and mating" almost invariably take place within rather than across race- and class-based networks. However, while racial endogamy continues to be the norm in the US, it is also the case that it has declined over time. In 1960, 99.6 percent of all marriages were racially endogamous, in comparison to 94.6 percent in 2000. As noted by Nagel (2003), rates of racial exogamy are highest among Native Americans (67 percent), followed by Asians (26.3 percent), Hispanics (26.1 percent), blacks (10.9 percent), and whites (6.1 percent).

The rise in racial exogamy has generated a growing body of literature on its implications, particularly for the "mixed-race" children who emerge from these unions. Scholars writing about interracial marriages in the 1930s and 1940s were overwhelmingly pessimistic about the fate of the children, emphasizing their identity confusion and lack of acceptance by others (Song 2003). Much of the contemporary literature has a very different tone, emphasizing the positive aspects of a mixed heritage. Instead of choosing the affiliation of one parent over another, "mixed-race" persons are increasingly inclined to acknowledge and to maintain their diverse heritage, thereby challenging the singular conception of racial identity that has been prevalent in the US (Root 1992). This is so even among those who have one black parent, and who thus face the deeply rooted US "one drop rule" whereby any black ancestry results in one's automatic assignment by others to the category of black. It was in part due to the efforts of "mixed-race" persons that the US Census underwent an important policy shift in 2000. Respondents are now allowed to check off as many race affiliations as they wish instead of being limited to a single one.

SEE ALSO: Biracialism; Color Line; Interracial Unions; Marriage; One Drop Rule; Passing

REFERENCES AND SUGGESTED READINGS

Giddens, A. (1992) *The Transformation of Intimacy*. Stanford University Press, Stanford.

Nagel, J. (2003) *Race, Ethnicity, and Sexuality*. Oxford University Press, Oxford.

Root, M. (1992) *Racially Mixed People in America*. Sage, Thousand Oaks, CA.

Song, M. (2003) *Choosing Ethnic Identity*. Polity Press, Cambridge.

Whyte, M. K. (1990) *Dating, Mating, and Marriage*. Aldine de Gruyter, New York.

endogenous development

Kosaku Yoshino

Endogenous development was presented as an alternative perspective on development that reconsidered modernization theory, which had until the 1960s been the dominant analytical paradigm of social change, especially in American sociology. From the late 1960s throughout the 1970s, criticisms were directed against modernization theory on the grounds that modernization was a West-centric model and that as such it would not necessarily lead to industrial growth and fair distribution of social benefits in non-western settings.

The notion of "endogenous development" originates in two sources. One is a report entitled "What Now: Another Development," produced by the Dag Hammarskjöld Foundation. It was presented to the Seventh Special Session of the United Nations General Assembly in 1975. The Assembly met in the midst of a deep crisis in development and international economic relations, with problems being brought to the fore in areas such as food, energy, population, the environment, and economic and monetary matters. The central elements of this alternative mode of development, according to the report, are that it is (1) "geared to the satisfaction of needs, beginning with the eradication of poverty"; (2) "endogenous and self-reliant, that is, relying on the strength of

the societies which undertake it"; and (3) "in harmony with the environment." It was proposed that an endogenous and self-reliant development stems "from the inner core of each society," relies on "the creativity of the men and women who constitute" a human group, becomes "richer through exchange between them and with other groups," and entails "the autonomous definition of development styles and of life styles." Thus, the notion of endogenous development is not narrowly that of economic development per se, but deals also with cultural and social development (Dag Hammarskjöld Foundation 1975).

The other original contribution came from a Japanese sociologist, Kazuko Tsurumi. She first used the term "endogenous development" in 1976. As someone who studied under the supervision of Marion Levy, Jr. and as a long-time student of the indigenous scholarship of Kunio Yanagita, a founding father of Japan's folklore studies, Tsurumi was in a good position to critically examine western theories of social change and modernization in light of non-western experiences. In an attempt to construct an alternative model of development to modernization, she emphasized the value of "endogeneity" of development on the following grounds.

First, modernization theory as formulated in Europe and culminated in the United States in the 1960s identified early developers such as England, the US, and France as endogenous developers who pioneered the model of modern society. By contrast, latecomers to modernization such as Japan, China, and other Asian, African, and Latin American countries are exogenous developers or model receivers. Endogenous refers to something internal that is generated from within a system, as opposed to exogenous, which means something generated from outside. The early developers created models of modernization out of their own traditions, whereas all latecomers borrow models from the early developers. This, of course, causes tensions between exogenous models of technology, science, and social organization and the indigenous patterns of technology, social structure, and values.

Second, from the point of view of the non-western world, Tsurumi emphasized the development of the non-material life. Through "spiritual awakening" and "intellectual creativity," people can become active agents of social change. This theme was explored at the United Nations University's Asian Regional Symposium on "Intellectual Creativity in Endogenous Culture" at Kyoto in 1978 (Abdel-Malek & Pandeya 1981). In offering some concrete examples of such development, Tsurumi drew attention to the revival of the idea of symbiosis of nature and people in the movement to regenerate the pollution-devastated area of Minamata in Japan, the conscious use of traditional social structure to avoid or mitigate the more negative aspects of industrialization and urbanization in the Jiangsu Province of China, and the Buddhism-based self-help movement in Thailand and Sri Lanka.

Tsurumi summarizes the essential elements of endogenous development as follows. The goal of endogenous development, first and foremost, is for all humans and their groups to meet basic needs in food, clothing, shelter, and medical care as well as to create conditions in which individuals can fully utilize their potentialities. This goal is common to all human beings, but paths to it follow diverse processes of social change. To achieve this goal, individuals and groups in each region must autonomously create social visions and ways forward to the goal by adapting to their own ecological systems and basing development programs on their own cultural heritage and traditions. With this as a starting point, foreign knowledge, technology, and institutions can be more effectively and harmoniously adopted to aid the development process. She argues that "the expansion of endogenous development on a global scale would mean the achievement of multilinear development. We can then exchange models with one another regardless of whether the models are those of early comers or latecomers" (Tsurumi 1989).

Modernization theory was constructed using a society (a nation-state) as the basic unit. In turn, dependency theory, formulated as a critical response to modernization theory, focused on relations between center and periphery. As such, dependency theory, too, presupposes a nation-state and its subsystems as its basic units of analysis. By contrast, the theory of endogenous development identifies a region as its analytical unit. Here, region is not the same as a subsystem of a nation-state but an entity that quite often crosses boundaries between nation-states. In formulating the concept of region, Tsurumi relies on Tamanoi (1979), who defines "regionalism" as "a pursuit of administrative autonomy and economic self-reliance as well as cultural independence by the residents of a region, who hold a sense of attachment to their regional community on the basis of its climatic and ecological characteristics."

The notion of endogenous development began to be employed extensively in the late 1970s by organizations, including the United Nations and UNESCO, as well as by individual researchers in various countries and regions. It was an attempt to explore an alternative route to development in a world faced with dangerous and seemingly intractable global problems, such as disruption of ecosystems, poverty, and famine.

SEE ALSO: Dependency and World-Systems Theories; Development: Political Economy; Developmental State; Modernization

REFERENCES AND SUGGESTED READINGS

Abdel-Malek, A. & Pandeya, A. N. (Eds.) (1981) *Intellectual Creativity in Endogenous Culture.* Asian Regional Symposium, Kyoto, Japan, November 1978. United Nations University, Tokyo.

Dag Hammarskjöld Foundation (1975) *What Now: Another Development.* The 1975 Dag Hammarskjöld Report on Development and International Cooperation. Prepared for the Seventh Special Session of the United Nations General Assembly, New York, September 1–12.

Tamanoi, Y. (1979) *Chiiki-shugi no Shiso (The Idea of Regionalism).* Nosangyoson Bunka Kyokai, Tokyo.

Tsurumi, K. (1979). *Aspects of Endogenous Development in Modern Japan.* Research Papers, Series A-36. Institute of International Relations, Sophia University, Tokyo.

Tsurumi, K. (1989). Naihatsu-teki Hatten Ron no Keifu [A Genealogy of the Theory of Endogenous Development]. In: Tsurumi, K. & Nishikawa, J. (Eds.), *Naihatsu-teki Hatten Ron (The Theory of Endogenous Development).* University of Tokyo Press, Tokyo.

Engels, Friedrich (1820–95)

Clifford L. Staples

Without Karl Marx, of course, few people today would know the name of Friedrich Engels; but without Engels we might have heard much less from Karl Marx.

Engels was born into a wealthy, devout, Protestant family in the industrial town of Barmen (now Wuppertal) in the Rhineland region of what is now Germany. The industrialist father wished his eldest son to follow in his footsteps, and so in 1838, before he could even finish high school, Engels was sent to clerk for a business in Bremen. But his lack of higher education did not prevent Engels from tackling difficult philosophical issues. In Bremen, free from the fundamentalism of his Pietist parents and teachers, he became a voracious reader of literature, philosophy, history, and science. Critically, neither his privileged family background nor his own eventual success as a capitalist prevented him from devoting his life to destroying capitalism. He also had a natural talent with languages – a skill he would put to good use in his later years as an international political figure and organizer.

It didn't take much to be a political radical under the Prussian monarchy in the 1830s, and so Engels published his early anti-Pietist and democratic views under the pen name of Friedrich Oswald. He was soon drawn, however, to the more intellectually challenging work of the "Young Hegelians," a cluster of Hegel's followers. In 1841, at the age of 21, Engels moved to Berlin and volunteered for the military. Doing so allowed him to satisfy his required military service while attending university lectures, writing articles and pamphlets, and meeting with the Young Hegelians. While Engels would retain a keen interest in military science and strategy throughout his life, he seems to have had plenty of energy, as well, for books and bars and in causing as much trouble for the authorities as possible.

The Young Hegelians wanted to apply Hegel's philosophy of dialectical change, development, and progress to church, state, and society: a radical turnabout that was most unwelcome by the establishment. But there were disagreements among the young radicals and many of them, while expressing anti-establishment views, remained committed to Hegel's idealism – an idealism that others (Ludwig Feuerbach, Karl Marx, and Friedrich Engels among them) found untenable.

While Engels was in Berlin, Ludwig Feuerbach published *The Essence of Christianity*, a book that, for some, pointed the way out of the confines of the Hegelian system and urged a reconsideration of materialism. And while Engels as well as Marx would reject the somewhat crude materialism of Feuerbach, Engels some years later described Feuerbach's view as an "intermediate link between Hegelian philosophy and our own conception."

In 1842, after completing his military service, Engels traveled to Cologne, where he met with Karl Marx and Moses Hess, both of whom were editors at the *Rheinische Zeitung*, hich Engels had written. Hess saw England as the country most likely to produce his hoped-for communist revolution. As it happened, Engels's father had significant financial interests in a large textile factory in Manchester, and so Engels, now a communist himself, went for two years to Manchester to work in the factory as a clerk. In addition to directly observing conditions in the factory, he also met trade unionists, socialists, and other radicals, and based on fieldwork in the neighborhoods of Manchester, wrote articles about social and economic conditions for Marx's *Deutsch-Franzosische Jahrbucher*. He also began a critical study of the works of English political economists. In 1845 he would publish a book entitled *The Condition of the Working-Class in England, 1844* based on his fieldwork in Manchester, and his work on the English political economists would point Marx toward the material for *Capital*.

On his way home to Barmen, Engels made a brief stop in Paris and again met with Marx. As Engels later wrote: "When I visited Marx in Paris in the summer of 1844 we found ourselves in complete agreement on questions of theory and our collaboration began at that time." In the next two years Engels would marry Mary Burns – a working-class Irish woman – with whom he would live until her death in 1867 (after which he lived with her sister), and he and Marx would collaborate on several manuscripts, including *The Holy Family* and *The German Ideology* in which they would make some attempt to flesh out their philosophical and political positions and distinguish themselves from a number of rivals. This writing – or theory – was done, of course, in the interest of furthering the radical political practice to which both were committed. And it was out of this collaboration, and at the request of the London-based League of the Just, that perhaps the world's most famous political pamphlet, *The Communist Manifesto*, was written.

In 1848 the rebellions in France spread to Germany, and Marx and Engels quickly took up the fight against the Prussian monarchy by moving to Cologne and taking over editorship of the *Neue Rheinische Zeitung* newspaper. But afraid of the growing strength of the workers, the German bourgeoisie sided with the aristocracy and moved to crush the workers. Marx was soon deported, but Engels took an active part in the uprising, serving as an aid to a commander fighting against the Prussians. As defeat neared, Engels escaped to Switzerland, and from there made his way to London.

With the defeat of the 1848 rebellion, Marx and Engels concluded that the near-term prospects for revolution were unlikely and so turned their attention to scholarly and organizing work that they hoped would prove useful when the revolutionary moment reappeared. Marx began his work on political economy in the British Library while Engels once again took up the position of clerk, and eventually partner, in his father's Manchester factory. For the next 20 years Engels lived and worked in Manchester, providing both for himself and for the Marx family living in London.

While Marx worked on *Contribution to the Critique of Political Economy*, published in 1859, and the first volume of *Capital*, in 1867, Engels would clerk by day and by night keep up an almost daily correspondence with Marx, ghost write many of the articles that Marx had agreed to write for the *New York Daily Tribune*, and continue with his own wide-ranging studies in natural sciences, history, and military science. A man of boundless energy and optimism, Engels also managed to find time for a lively social life.

In 1870 Engels sold his share of the Manchester factory, moved to London, and joined Marx on the General Council of the International Workingmen's Association – the First International – which had been founded in 1864. Now retired, he took over the burden of the organization's correspondence, freeing Marx for his more scholarly work.

Of particular concern to Engels and Marx at this time was the emergence of the German Social Democratic Party in 1875, a move they supported, though not unconditionally, as Marx wrote in the *Critique of the Gotha Program*. For his part, Engels wrote a series of articles defending Marx and himself against the attacks from within the Social Democratic Party by the followers of Eugen Duhring. Later, these articles were collected together into a book known as the *Anti-Duhring*, selected chapters of which were then excerpted and published in a widely read pamphlet entitled *Socialism: Utopian and Scientific*. In 1981 the German Social Democratic Party dropped the Gotha program and adopted a Marxist program largely because of the influence of the *Anti-Duhring*.

After Marx's death in 1883 Engels devoted the rest of his life to Marx and Marxism, largely at the expense of his own work. Although he did manage to publish *The Origins of the Family, Private Property, and the State* in 1884, his *Dialectics of Nature* was published in 1925, long after his death. His first priority was to see to it that the remaining volumes of *Capital* were published – no simple task given the disorganized state in which Marx left his papers. Volume 2 was published in 1885 and Volume 3 appeared in 1894. His second priority was leading the international socialist movement, which he did by continuing his worldwide correspondence, writing articles for and advising the leaders of the Second International, and meeting with visiting intellectuals and revolutionaries, such as Georgi Plekhanov, one of Russia's first Marxists. Engels also managed to visit the US for two months in 1888, and in 1893 addressed the final session of the Congress of the Second International in Zurich. Vigorous until the end, Engels died of throat cancer in 1895.

Much of what Engels had to say to sociologists is learned via the study of his more famous collaborator, Karl Marx. But, as is evident from the multiple ways in which Engels supported Marx during, and even after, Marx's life, without Engels Marx might never have become the legendary figure we know today. This is why we continue to recognize Engels's contribution to Marxist sociology.

But Engels is and should continue to be appreciated on his own. As capitalism spreads to all corners of the globe, the conditions of the English working class in 1844 are today being reproduced in the conditions of the Chinese, Mexican, and Malaysian working classes. Thus, Engels's *The Conditions of the English Working Class in England, 1844* could continue to be studied and analyzed by fieldworkers as one approach to critical ethnography. Beginning in the 1970s, feminist anthropologists and sociologists read Engels's *The Origin of the Family, Private Property, and the State* as they sought to understand women's subordination and oppression across cultures and over time. To this date, Engels's book is often included on lists of key works in feminist theory, though of course his claim that women were the first oppressed class continues to be critiqued and debated. Finally, many sociologists have come to believe that the discipline should be more attentive to and focused on the needs of the public rather than the needs of elites, and it is difficult to think of anyone who might better fit the description of a "public sociologist" than Friedrich Engels. We should, therefore, continue to study his life as well as his work – with and without Karl Marx.

SEE ALSO: Communism; Feminist Anthropology; Marx, Karl; Materialism; Socialism; Theory

REFERENCES AND SUGGESTED READINGS

Henderson, W. O. (1976) *Friedrich Engels: Young Revolutionary*. Frank Cass, London.
Marx, K. & Engels, F. (1975–2005) *Collected Works*, 50 vols. Lawrence & Wishart, London.
Nimtz, A. H., Jr., (2000) *Marx and Engels: Their Contribution to the Democratic Breakthrough*. State University of New York Press, Albany.
Riazanov, D. (1927) *Karl Marx and Friedrich Engels*. International Publishers, New York.

Sayers, J., Evans, M., & Redclift, N. (1987) *Engels Revisited: New Feminist Essays*. Tavistock, New York.
Symonds, P. (1995) *Frederick Engels: 1820–1895*. World Socialists Website. Online. www.wsws.org/history/1995/aug1995/engels.shtml.

enterprise

Alberto Martinelli

The sociological analysis of the enterprise focuses on the relationships between enterprises and their social environment (Martinelli & Smelser 1990), with specific regard to two major topics: the study of organizational models and social systems of production and the study of the context of entrepreneurship.

Since the 1970s the productive model based on mass production and Fordist/Taylorist work organization in the large corporation have undergone crisis and transformation. As a consequence, a new economic sociology has arisen, which centers on the origins and developments of new organizational models of production based on flexibility. These changes at the micro-level of the enterprise's organization were accompanied with parallel changes at the macro-level of the relationships between state and market, as Fordism in the work place was often related to a government's Keynesian policies.

The Fordist/Taylorist model was the dominant model of enterprise organization in the twentieth century and reached its peak in the two decades after World War II. Its key distinctive elements were mass production, vertical integration, the use of a low-skilled labor force, and the fragmented organization of working tasks. This model of enterprise organization had been analyzed in the earliest studies of economic sociology (like those of Sombart and Weber), but it became the main object of sociological industrial research in the course of the twentieth century, although the timing and speed of its diffusion varied in the different capitalist countries. Typical examples of this kind of research are the work of Kerr et al. (1960) on the organization of

American enterprises, the studies of the French school of *Sociologie du travail* on the consequences of technological change, and Dore's (1973) comparative research on British and Japanese enterprises.

In the last decades of the twentieth century the internal structure of the enterprise organization underwent major changes, first of all in the decline of mass standardized production in favor of flexible specialization, customized production, and diversified quality mass production. The main factors accounting for this change – a true "second industrial divide" (Piore & Sabel 1984) – were the growing demand for more diversified and higher-quality products by better informed and more demanding consumers in the mass markets of developed countries; and the spread of the new information and communication technologies that allow just-in-time production and better quality controls. These changes fostered a diversification of productive models and a reframing of the firm's relationships with the social context. In the light of these changes a new economic sociology has developed, which focuses on the analysis of "social systems of production." These systems include the internal structure of the enterprise, industrial relations, training systems, relationships with competitors, suppliers, and distributors, the structure of capital markets, the nature of state interventions, and the conception of social justice (Hollingsworth & Boyer 1997). Analyses of these systems explore the links between the various institutional forms of the enterprise and its social environment using concepts like social networks, trust, social capital, cultural values, and norms.

In the new phase of industrial organization we witness multiple and diversified productive models affecting both large and small enterprises. The most interesting organizational developments studied by sociologists concern the large enterprises as networks and industrial districts. The need to reduce the separation between the design and the making of products – which was typical of Fordism – meant that large enterprises changed both the internal organization of labor in the direction of just-in-time production and greater cooperation with workers, and the external networks of cooperation with specialized suppliers all along the supply chain. As far as small firms are concerned, sociological research has focused on industrial districts, which grow where either one or both the following contextual factors are present: traditions of good craftsmanship and strong community ties (as in areas of northern and central Italy) and first-quality higher education and research institutions (as in areas like Silicon Valley, Boston Route 128, Baden-Wurtemberg, and the Fukuoka region). Critical elements in the success of industrial districts are such intangible assets as trust and capacity to cooperate, which are in turn rooted in strong local identities.

Enterprise as networks and districts of small and medium-size firms are not, however, the only forms taken by flexible specialization. The other side of flexibility is the informal economy or, more specifically, the hidden economy. The informal economy includes, besides the production of illegal goods and services with illegal means (criminal economy), and the production of goods and service for self-consumption without the intermediation of money (family or communitarian economy), the production of legal goods and services by illegal means (hidden economy). The hidden economy develops wherever greater flexibility and competitiveness are sought by violating fiscal and labor laws and disregarding standards of both environmental sustainability and social responsibility. The enterprises of the hidden economy are influenced by their cultural and institutional context: areas of the hidden economy are, for instance, well entrenched in immigrant communities of major American and European cities. Actually, all the new flexible forms of productive organization are more embedded in their social contexts than those predominant in the Taylorist/Fordist phase.

The other major sociological contribution to the study of the enterprise is the analysis of the context of entrepreneurship. Sociologists have contributed significantly to the study of entrepreneurship, critically integrating economic theory. Most economists, with notable exceptions like Schumpeter and Kirzner, seem to think that entrepreneurial activities will emerge more or less spontaneously, whenever economic conditions are favorable, as an instance of rational profit maximization. Context is either ignored or taken into account, disregarding its social and cultural complexity and the variety of different historical settings, and there is no appreciation of the interaction between actor and context.

Most sociologists consider entrepreneurship as a much more problematic phenomenon, deeply embedded in societies and cultures; they focus on the influence of, and the mutual interplay among, non-economic factors such as cultural norms and beliefs, class and ethnic relations and collective action, state intervention and control, organizational structures, bounded solidarity and trust, deviant behavior and marginality status, social approval of economic activity, business ethics, and motivations for achievement. A key concept in the sociological analysis of entrepreneurship is that of double embeddedness (Kloosterman et al. 1999), which highlights the two major ways in which the context of entrepreneurship can be analyzed: first, as the politico-institutional environment of market capitalism, such as types of markets (of factors of production and of goods and services), and types of laws (fiscal, labor, anti-trust) and institutions of governance; second, as the social and cultural background of entrepreneurs, such as cultural attitudes favoring technological innovation and risk-taking and networks of social relations and social capital.

The study of the institutional context of entrepreneurship is a longstanding tradition of research, from the Harvard Center for Entrepreneurial History to recent studies on institutional coordinating mixes and on the varieties of capitalism. Entrepreneurship is basically defined by technological innovation in a competitive market. However, both technology and competition require an extensive social organization. Successful entrepreneurs are those who succeed in establishing stable relationships with their internal and external stakeholders (i.e., persons or groups who claim rights or interests in a corporation and its activities, past, present, or future – not only shareholders but also workers, suppliers, customers, and local communities). The ability to establish these relationships is itself dependent on the production of stable societal institutions such as governments and laws. Contrary to the view that firms are efficient wealth producers while

governments are intrusive and inefficient, the sociological analysis of entrepreneurship shows that the establishment of a stable and reliable legal and political environment through government legislation and policies (patents, antimonopolistic laws, consumers' protection laws, public spending to sustain aggregate demand, support for exporting firms, etc.) is required for entrepreneurial activities to develop and endure.

There is no single appropriate institutional environment for entrepreneurial development that can pretend to universal validity. Different varieties of capitalism exist and evolve through time, as do different modes of corporate control (Fligstein 1990). But the institutional context of entrepreneurship is not limited to the interplay between markets, firms, and governments. Studies on the institutional varieties of capitalism have shown how more complex institutional mixes of markets, states, hierarchical organizations, communities, clans and networks, and associations coordinate and regulate business activities (Crouch & Streeck 1997). Each of these coordinating mechanisms has its own logic – its own organizational structure, its own rules of exchange, its own procedures for enforcing compliance both individually and collectively; each can be evaluated in terms of efficiency, effectiveness in delivering private and collective goods, and capability to meet the claims and expectations of various stakeholders of the firm.

This richness of institutional contexts has not diminished because of globalization. Contrary to a widespread belief, globalization does not induce homogenization toward a single model, but stimulates a variety of institutional responses, which are rooted in the specific cultural codes and social relations of different countries and regions.

Sociological research on entrepreneurship has also focused on the other side of double embeddedness: the social and cultural background of entrepreneurs. The question of the contextual conditions which produce entrepreneurs has been traditionally addressed in terms of deviance and marginality. Acting in a hostile social milieu, where prevailing attitudes are against innovation, and being excluded from political power, marginal entrepreneurs concentrate on business, but, being outside the dominant value system, they are subjected to lesser sanctions for their deviant behavior. More recent works on ethnic communities (Portes 1995) and women show that factors like racism, sexism, and credentialism render people "outsiders" through processes of exclusionary closure; such outsiders often form "feeder groups" from which new entrepreneurs emerge.

Weber's comparative analysis of religious ethics and economic action in the origin of capitalism provides the basis for studies stressing cultural context variables. Neo-Weberian research focuses on the degree to which the forces of rationalization responsible for dislodging individuals from their embeddedness in nature, religion, and tradition continue to shape economic growth and social modernization (Berger 1991). Economic growth develops from the bottom up, not from the top down: ordinary individuals, competing with each other to achieve a variety of goals – including economic profit and self-advancement – in their everyday activities, practices, habits, and ideas, create the basis for other distinctly modern institutions to emerge that may mediate between them and distant, large-scale structures of society.

The most convincing contributions to the study of the context of entrepreneurship are those integrating various approaches and selecting the most appropriate mix for the analysis of specific empirical questions and historical realities, as in the case of research on ethnic entrepreneurship (Waldinger et al. 1990). All these studies work out models which try to combine a plurality of variables in order to understand the relation between the entrepreneur and the context in which he or she is embedded: social networks, selective migration trends, settlement patterns, structure of markets, access to ownership, residential patterns, group culture and aspiration levels, immigration, and labor market policies.

SEE ALSO: Capitalism; Immigration; Institutionalism; Management Theory; Markets; Modernization; Organization Theory; Post-Industrial Society; Social Embeddedness of Economic Action; State and Economy

REFERENCES AND SUGGESTED READINGS

Berger, B. (Ed.) (1991) *The Culture of Entrepreneurship*. ICS Press, San Francisco.

Crouch, C. & Streeck, W. (Eds.) (1997) *Modern Capitalism or Modern Capitalisms?* Sage, London.

Dore, R. (1973) *British Factory, Japanese Factory: The Origins of Diversity in Industrial Relations*. University of California Press, Berkeley.

Fligstein, N. (1990) *The Transformation of Corporate Control*. Harvard University Press, Cambridge, MA.

Hollingsworth, J. R. & Boyer, R. (Eds.) (1997) *Contemporary Capitalism: The Embeddedness of Institutions*. Cambridge University Press, Cambridge.

Kerr, C., Dunlop, J. T., Harbison, F., & Meyers, C. A. (1960) *Industrialism and Industrial Man*. Harvard University Press, Cambridge, MA.

Kloosterman, R., van der Leun, J. P., & Rath, J. (1999) Mixed Embeddedness, Migrant Entrepreneurs and Informal Economic Activities. *International Journal of Urban and Regional Research* 14(5): 659–76.

Martinelli, A. & Smelser, N. J. (Eds.) (1990) *Economy and Society: Overviews in Economic Sociology*. Sage, London.

Piore, M. & Sabel, C. (1984) *The Second Industrial Divide*. Basic Books, New York.

Portes, A. (Ed.) (1995) *The Economic Sociology of Immigration: Essays on Networks, Ethnicity and Entrepreneurship*. Russell Sage Foundation, New York.

Waldinger, R. (1990) *Ethnic Entrepreneurship: Immigrant Business in Industrial Societies*. Sage, Newbury Park, CA.

enterprise unions

Ross Mouer

The enterprise union (*kigyobetsu kumiai*) has been the dominant form of union organization in post-war Japan. When the interest in Japan's economic prowess suddenly surfaced in the 1970s, the *kigyobetsu kumiai* was singled out as one of the three features constituting the Japanese model of industrial relations. Possibly the least understood of the three, the enterprise union was often confused with the company union and an approach to employee relations whereby the union is coopted by management to foster and to maintain a compliant labor force subservient to the needs of management (Galenson & Odaka 1976). The Japanese have a term (with a negative connotation) for this kind of unionism – the *goyo kumiai*, literally, a union at his majesty's (i.e., management's) service. The debate on the nature of the enterprise union in Japan brought to the general discussion of unions a more subtle delineation between different types of union organization (e.g., as in Kawanishi 1992).

Kigyobetsu kumiai refers to a form of union organization which restricts union membership to regular employees at a given enterprise. "Regular employees" are those employed on a permanent long-term basis. In larger firms these employees have access to career paths within the firm's internal labor market(s). Two or more enterprise unions may exist at the same enterprise. Generally, "the enterprise" is a designated place of business, and each firm, company, or corporation may have multiple places of business. Accordingly, a manufacturing firm with five factories might have one (or more) independent enterprise union at each factory. It is common for ideologically aligned unions at different enterprises operated by the same firm to join together in a firm-wide federation (known as a *kigyoren*). Such a federation may recast itself as an enterprise union with the union organization at each enterprise (e.g., factory) having branch status (as a *shibu*). Enterprise unions may affiliate with an industrial federation either directly or through a firm-level federation. It should be noted that several forms of union organization exist in Japan at the enterprise level.

The labor movement in post-war Japan has been characterized by ideological fissures, with a good proportion of firms in the 1960s embracing the branch of a left-wing, politically active industrial union (known within the firm as a "number one union") and an economically oriented conservative enterprise union (known as a "number two union") (see Fujita 1968). Number one unions were in many cases affiliated with a left-wing national center known as "Sohyo" (General Council of Trade Unions of Japan) via an industrial federation or directly as a branch of an industrial union; the number two unions were affiliated with a national peak organization known as "Domei" (Japanese Confederation of Labor) through their industrial federation (see Fig. 1).

In many firms the antagonistic competition between these two types of enterprise unions produced an interesting dynamic in many firms and, more generally, within the economy as a whole. Sohyo (founded as a national center in 1949), its industrial unions (and federations), and the number one unions tended to focus more on workers' rights, social justice, and other issues related to the autonomy of workers on the shop floor. Domei (founded as a national center in 1964), its industrial federations, and the number two unions tended to focus more on ways to cooperate with management to improve productivity and, ultimately, the remuneration which could be paid to employees. Although each approach had its own rationale, during Japan's first four post-war decades many workers entertained a dual consciousness which was open to both emphases. Management at many firms responded by adopting a middle-of-the-road approach which combined, for example, the egalitarian demands for an age-based wage system with elements that rewarded performance and other characteristics more tightly linked to improving efficiency. However, the merger of the two major national centers at the end of the 1980s to form Rengo (Japan Union Confederation) diminished the significance of this form of "latent functional specialization" which resulted from the way Japanese workers organized themselves.

The pros and cons of the *kigyobetsu kumiai* were vigorously debated during the 1970s and 1980s, owing in part to the relevance attached to it as part of the Japanese model (e.g., Shirai 1983). Among the positives, various observers have pointed to the ability of the enterprise union to understand the financial realities of a particular firm and the various individuated needs of its employees within the context of a dynamic labor market. To the extent that those needs revolved around employment security and higher incomes, the union was seen to be in a superior position when it came to tailoring an overall package of demands which would be predicated on the firm's economic health as the basis for achieving the long-term employment security and income-related goals of its

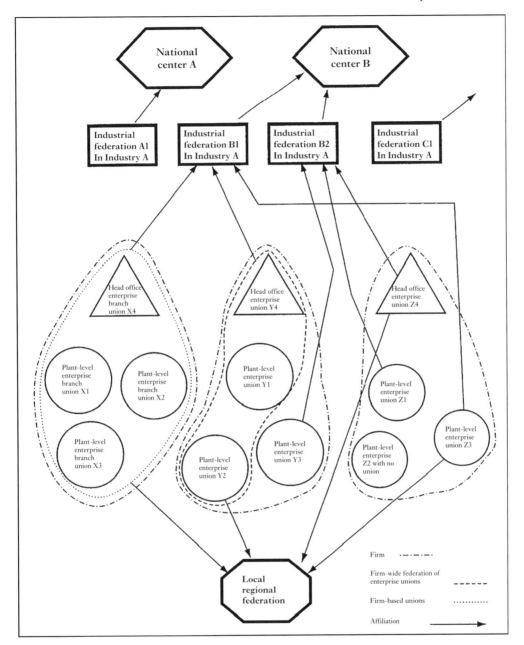

Figure 1 Enterprise unions.

members. It was argued that leaders of the enterprise union were as "insiders" better positioned than "outsiders" from an industrial union (1) to obtain relevant information from management in their firms and (2) to understand the decision-making/negotiation strategy of their own firm. This in turn would result in a greater likelihood that concessions would be won. In return for a conciliatory approach, it was argued, a firm would later reimburse its labor force as the economy continued to expand. Some would see in this arrangement a tradeoff between wage restraint and the maintenance of the other two components of the model mentioned above – especially the guarantees of long-term employment.

There was in this approach, however, a feeling among some critics that firms were "buying off" union leaders and their membership. Critics of the *kigyobetsu kumiai* have maintained that too much closeness between labor and management resulted in labor and management postponing many of the hard decisions that needed to be made to establish sustainable rates of change in the enterprise. Recognizing the ability of union leaders to discipline the labor force in a responsible manner, some critics have focused on how enterprise unions have functioned like adjunct personnel departments facilitating management programs that intensified workloads or even implemented redundancy packages and other measures designed to rationalize further the way firms are run. Performing this kind of personnel management function for management, such critics would argue, many enterprise unions ended up sacrificing the interests of their members. The enterprise union has also been criticized for keeping union assets and resources in a disaggregated state, and for relying on locally generated leadership which is often more committed to resuming roles on the firm's management team than to training as professional leaders for the union movement. In this regard, the tendency for effective union leaders to be promoted back onto the management team has been noted.

These concerns have focused attention on the ability of enterprise unions to negotiate successfully with management to achieve long-term and short-term outcomes in the interests of their members. Another set of concerns has revolved around the elitest characteristics of the enterprise union as an organization reserved for the privileged regular (male) employees in Japan's largest firms. Here critics have noted the tendency of the enterprise union to ingrain among its members a fairly strong consciousness that they are the aristocracy of labor. Over time, it has been argued, members of many enterprise unions came to believe that their own interests were well served by tiered subcontracting, an arrangement from which they benefited when the working conditions for

employees doing the same work in smaller subcontracting firms were inferior to their own. In this sense, then, the enterprise union has been predicated on the assumption that fairly extensive internal labor markets would ensure the future well-being of union members, and has been extremely effective in representing the interests of the workers it represents. From this perspective, however, the most lasting criticism might be that enterprise unions have tended not to be concerned with non-members – those casually employed by the firm, those who are no longer employed by the firm (as a result of voluntary and involuntary separation), and those in the firm's tiered pyramid of subcontractors. It is not surprising, therefore, that the enterprise union has been prevalent mostly in Japan's large firms.

A final debate concerns to what extent enterprise unionism accounts for the decline in the unionization rate in Japan from about 35 percent in 1975 to just over 20 percent in 2000. However, declining rates seem to be rather universal, and aspects of this phenomenon have been noted overseas (e.g., concerning globalization and changing industrial structures). Already in the 1990s moves were made to form new types of special interest unions (e.g., for women employees or for line supervisors – *kacho* – or for part-time workers) or more general unions (which could embrace unemployed workers). The immediate challenge in Japan will be for the union movement to somehow embrace both the non-regular employee and the 60 percent of the labor force still employed in Japan's smaller firms that employ fewer than 100 persons. For the enterprise union, the organization of those in the first group may be possible in large firms, but efforts of such unions are likely to run against the diseconomies of (small) scale when it comes to doing so in Japan's smaller establishments. However, as the first group becomes more diverse, there, too, the difficulties faced by the enterprise unions in trying to differentiate their appeal may be insurmountable.

For some time the enterprise union has been seen as the most uniquely Japanese component of the Japanese industrial relations model (the other two components being long-term employment and seniority wages). Its prevalence was explained largely in cultural terms.

However, as an appreciation of how it functions in structural terms, the merits of enterprise bargaining have been recognized abroad to the extent that it was introduced (without the enterprise union) to Australia in the late 1980s and early 1990s to remove the complexity which comes from management (and union negotiators) having to deal with a large number of industrial unions, and the complex array of industrial awards that often resulted from having multiple unions involved across an array of jurisdictions.

SEE ALSO: Japanese-Style Management; *Nenko Chingin*; *Shushin Koyo*; Unions

REFERENCES AND SUGGESTED READINGS

Fujita, W. (1968 [1955]) *Daini kumiai* (*The Second Union*), new edn. Nihon Hyoronsha, Tokyo.
Galenson, W. & Odaka, K. (1976) The Japanese Labor Market. In: Patrick, H. & Rosovsky, H. (Eds.), *Asia's New Giant*. Brookings Institute, Washington, DC, pp. 587–671.
Kawanishi, H. (1992) *Enterprise Unionism in Japan*. Trans. R. Mouer. Kegan Paul International, London.
Mouer, R. & Kawanishi, H. (2005) *A Sociology of Work in Japan*. Cambridge University Press, Cambridge, ch. 9.
Shirai, T. (1983) A Theory of Enterprise Unionism. In: Shirai, T. (Ed.), *Contemporary Industrial Relations in Japan*. University of Wisconsin Press, Madison, pp. 117–43.

environment, sociology of the

Riley E. Dunlap

Environmental problems attract sociological attention because they are fundamentally social problems: they result from human social behavior, they are viewed as problematic because of their impact on humans (as well as other species), and their solution requires societal effort. It is therefore not surprising that sociologists

have shown growing interest in environmental issues in recent decades and that environmental sociology has become a recognized field. Yet, sustained sociological investigation of environmental problems did not come easily.

To establish a new discipline, the founders of sociology emphasized its unique focus on the explanation of social behavior by *social* as opposed to biological and physical phenomena. The Durkheimian emphasis on explaining social phenomena only in terms of "social facts" created an anti-reductionism taboo that delegitimated use of biological and geographical factors in sociological analyses. It was important for sociology to move beyond, for example, explanations of racial and cultural differences in terms of genetics and climate, respectively. In the process, however, sociology adopted an implicit sociocultural determinism that provided infertile ground for sociological analyses of environmental problems. In mainstream sociology, "the environment" came to refer to the social context of the entity (group, community, institution, etc.) being examined, and the physical environment was seen as little more than the stage on which social behavior was enacted (Dunlap & Catton 1979).

Consequently, when environmental issues burst upon the scene in the 1970s in North America and shortly thereafter in Europe and the rest of the world, sociologists were not among the vanguard studying them. And when sociologists did focus on environmental issues, they typically analyzed the social processes involved in "constructing" environmental conditions as problems. There were numerous studies of the roles played by environmental activists, the media, scientists, and policymakers (including Green parties) in placing environmental problems onto the public agenda, as well as of the public's perceptions of such problems. Sophisticated models of the social construction of environmental problems gradually evolved (Hannigan 1995).

The onset of energy shortages and widespread discussion of the "limits to growth" in the 1970s led a few sociologists to question the popular notion that modern societies had overcome resource constraints (Catton 1980). Likewise, continuous discoveries of serious pollution (from local toxic contamination to acid rain) and increasing incidences of resource degradation (from strip-mining to deforestation) led others to accept the reality of environmental deterioration and to investigate its social causes and consequences (Schnaiberg 1980). This generated an interest in societal–environmental relations (and at least an implicit rejection of anti-reductionism), which some sociologists saw as representing the arrival of an "environmental sociology" (Dunlap & Catton 1979).

The constructivist and realist approaches to the sociological investigation of environmental problems have both continued to evolve. Although an intensive debate occurred between their proponents over the past decade, both traditions remain strong, with the realist camp predominating in North America and the constructivist being strong in Europe.

Sociological work on environmental issues continues to reflect the inherent social dimensions of environmental problems, encompassing investigations of the causes of environmental problems, the societal impacts of such problems, and strategies and prospects for ameliorating these problems. These realist-oriented approaches are complemented by constructivist analyses not only of how conditions come to be defined as problems, but also of controversies over the causes and impacts as well as the very existence of environmental problems.

CONSTRUCTIVIST AND REALIST APPROACHES

Building upon such basic observations as levels of airborne particulates being ignored in one era and/or locale but seen as "pollution" later on or in other places, a rich body of sociological literature clarifies how various environmental conditions become defined as "problems"; the frequently contested nature of such problems; and the implications of competing interpretations of the sources, impacts, and solutions of the problems. Originally relying heavily on perspectives from social problems and the sociology of science (Yearley 1991), over time such analyses have drawn on social movement theory, discourse analysis, cultural sociology, and postmodern theorizing.

Numerous studies of claims, claims-makers, and claims-making activities have yielded valuable insights into the social processes necessary for gaining widespread acceptance of conditions – ranging from local toxic wastes to global environmental change – as "problematic." Originally the emphasis was on environmental activists as key claims-makers, but the importance of scientists has drawn increasing attention. The vital role of the media both in publicizing and in interpreting claims has also received attention. Such analyses have demonstrated that environmental problems do not simply emerge from objective conditions, but that their recognition is contingent upon issue entrepreneurs being successful in overcoming a series of barriers and gaining widespread societal acceptance of their definition of the situation (Hannigan 1995).

Besides clarifying how various conditions come to be accepted as environmental problems, constructivist analyses have shed light on the importance of how the problems are defined. For example, the notion of "*global* environmental change" conveys an image of global contributions to climate change, deforestation, and biodiversity loss, and thus shared responsibility for dealing with them – thereby masking crucial differences between the contributions and capabilities of rich and poor nations.

Early environmental problems like air and water pollution were readily perceptible, but newer problems such as toxic wastes, ozone depletion, and climate change depend on scientific measurements and interpretation for their discovery, analysis, and possible amelioration. The resulting heavy dependence of environmental advocates on scientists has received scrutiny from sociologists. Analysts such as Yearley (2005) have emphasized that the environmental movement's heavy reliance on science is a mixed blessing for several reasons: (1) demands for scientific proof can be used to stall action, particularly by unsympathetic politicians; (2) the probabilistic and tentative nature of scientific evidence falls short of the definitive answers laypeople and policymakers seek; and (3) reliance on scientific claims makes environmentalists vulnerable to counterclaims issued by "skeptic scientists" supported by industry.

Attention to discourse has allowed other analysts to provide insight into the importance of how environmental problems and policies are "framed" by different interests. In addition to the above-noted implications of framing macro-level issues such as climate change and loss of biodiversity as "global" problems, sociologists have noted how dominant conceptions of sustainable development fostered by powerful institutions such as the World Bank reflect a "green neoliberal" ideology that serves the interests of wealthy nations and western capital (Goldman 2005). On the other hand, attention has also been given to how an "environmental justice" frame has been created to represent the interests of minority and working-class communities exposed to disproportionate levels of environmental hazards, illustrating that the underprivileged can also benefit from strategic framing.

Constructivist work demonstrates that environmental problems do not simply emerge from changes in objective conditions, that scientific evidence is seldom sufficient for establishing conditions as problematic, and that the framing of problems is consequential. These are major insights, and represent a quintessential sociological contribution that, for example, helps environmental activists and scientists understand why their claims frequently fail to produce the desired effect while still allowing constructivists to avoid charges of environmental reductionism or determinism.

In the 1990s some constructivists followed postmodern fads and "deconstructed" not only environmental problems and controversies, but also "the environment" (or, more typically, "nature") itself. Proclamations that "there is no singular 'nature' as such, only a diversity of contested natures" (Macnaghten & Urry 1998: 1) were not uncommon. This provoked a reaction from environmental sociologists of a realist bent, who argued that while one can deconstruct the concept of nature, an obvious human (and culturally bound) construction, this hardly challenges the existence of the global ecosystem and by implication various manifestations of ecosystem change construed as "problems."

Representatives of the realist camp such as Ted Benton, Peter Dickens, Raymond Murphy, and Riley Dunlap argued that a strong constructivist approach that ignores the likely validity of competing environmental claims slips into relativism, has the potential of undermining environmental scientists and playing into the hands of their opponents, precludes meaningful examination of societal–environmental relations seen as fundamental to environmental sociology, and at least implicitly resurrects the disciplinary tradition of treating the biophysical environment as insignificant (Benton 2001).

In response, many constructivists replied that they were not denying the "reality" of environmental problems, as their postmodern rhetoric sometimes suggested, but were simply problematizing environmental claims and knowledge. In eschewing relativism in favor of "mild" or "contextual" constructivism, most constructivists have moved toward common ground with their realist colleagues. The latter, in turn, have moved toward a "critical realist" perspective that, although firmly grounded on acceptance of a reality independent of human understanding, recognizes that scientific (and other) knowledge is imperfect and evolving (Carolan 2005). The result is that the "realist–constructivist wars" of the 1990s are subsiding and the sociology of environmental issues (increasingly grounded in ontological realism and epistemological relativism) is a more intellectually vital area as a result of housing both approaches.

While seldom problematizing environmental knowledge, environmental sociologists in the realist camp often go to pains to examine the validity of measures of environmental problems such as deforestation (Rudel & Roper 1997). The defining feature of their work is use of empirical indicators of environmental conditions – from local air pollution to national CO_2 emissions – in their analyses. Such work is often quantitative, and bears on each of the three aspects of environmental problems noted above – their causes, social impacts, and potential solutions.

CAUSES OF ENVIRONMENTAL DEGRADATION

A central focus of environmental sociology, particularly in the US, has been to explain why environmental degradation seems endemic to modern industrial societies, and thereby provide sociological insight into the causes of environmental problems. Early work often critiqued natural scientists' monocausal explanations, emphasizing factors such as population growth, technological developments, or overconsumption. Frequently coming from a neo-Marxist or political economy perspective, sociologists called attention to the roles of capitalism and its supporting governmental structure ("the state") in creating environmental degradation.

Arguably the most influential analysis was offered by Schnaiberg (1980), who provided a cogent critique of Paul Ehrlich's emphasis on population growth, Barry Commoner's emphasis on technological developments, and the widespread emphasis on materialistic consumers as the key sources of environmental degradation. Schnaiberg's "treadmill of production" model offered a sophisticated alternative that stresses the inherent need of market-based firms to grow, the accompanying pressure to replace costly labor with advanced technologies, and the inevitable increase in resource use and pollution that results. He further clarified how a powerful coalition of capital, state, and labor develops in support of continued growth, making it difficult if not impossible for environmental advocates to halt the resulting "treadmill."

A number of other environmental sociologists working from a Marxist tradition, most notably Ted Benton and Peter Dickens in the UK and James O'Connor and John Bellamy Foster in the US, have offered alternative insights into why capitalism produces environmental degradation, but the treadmill argument has thus far garnered more attention.

Despite the appeal of Schnaiberg's treadmill model, it has proven difficult to test empirically on a macro level, and has been used primarily to explain the lack of success of local recycling programs and environmental campaigns. In an era of economic globalization, the treadmill model needs to be integrated with global-level perspectives such as world-systems theory in order to provide the theoretical leverage necessary for adequately examining the relationship between the globalization of capital and environmental degradation. In addition, recent sociological attention to the importance of consumption raises questions about Schnaiberg's dismissal of consumers' contributions to

environmental degradation (Yearley 2005). And finally, proponents of "ecological modernization" have challenged the fundamental premise that capitalism inevitably produces environmental degradation.

Ironically, given the dismissal by Schnaiberg and many other sociologists of the perspectives of Ehrlich and Commoner, a recent alternative to the treadmill draws explicitly from the "IPAT equation" (holding that environmental impact is a function of population, technology, and affluence) that evolved from debates between the two ecologists. Rooted in the human ecology tradition espoused by some early environmental sociologists (Benton 2001: 5–6), the "STIRPAT" (or "Stochastic Impacts by Regression on Population, Affluence, and Technology") model developed by Dietz, Rosa, and York offers a way of testing the relative impacts of various driving forces on environmental degradation (York et al. 2003). Early results, which will no doubt provoke further studies, suggest that population is more important than most sociologists believe, resurrecting the neo-Malthusian perspective of Catton (1980).

In between the neo-Marxist and human ecology perspectives lie a host of efforts to explain the sources of environmental degradation, exemplified by Rudel and Roper's (1997) sophisticated analyses of the origins of tropical deforestation. The past decade has witnessed a flood of empirical, comparative studies – often taking the nation-state as their unit of analysis – that investigate the relationship between a range of factors (demographic, technological, economic, political, etc.) and various indicators of environmental degradation ranging from deforestation to CO_2 emissions to ecological footprints (e.g., York et al. 2003).

IMPACTS OF ENVIRONMENTAL DEGRADATION AND RESOURCE SHORTAGES

Sociologists have devoted less attention to the social impacts of environmental degradation, perhaps due to lingering fears of environmental determinism. The earliest focused not on environmental degradation but on the impacts of the 1970s energy shortages. While diverse impacts, from regional migration to purchasing behavior, were investigated, equity impacts were the primary focus. Studies documented that both the shortages and policies for dealing with them (e.g., higher prices and taxes) tended to be regressive, with lower socioeconomic strata bearing a disproportionate cost.

Inequities have been a persistent concern in environmental sociology and attention next shifted to the distribution of environmental hazards such as air pollution and waste sites. A consistent finding from US studies is that lower socioeconomic strata are disproportionately exposed to environmental hazards, and the same is true for racial/ethnic minorities. While there has been debate over the relative importance of income and race in generating inequitable exposure, many analysts argue that the evidence suggests a pattern of "environmental racism" (Brulle & Pellow 2006).

The environmental justice theme is increasingly extended to the international level, as numerous studies find that the lower strata (and sometimes ethnic minorities) in poor nations also suffer disproportionately from environmental degradation. More generally, sociologists have documented unequal ecological exchanges among nations, with rich countries importing poor country's natural resources at bargain prices while shipping their own wastes (sometimes directly, but often by relocating dirty industries) to those same countries. These findings of consistent inequalities in exposure to the burdens of environmental degradation are at odds with Beck's model of the "risk society," which posits that exposure is becoming a universally shared experience.

Studies of communities that have been subjected to toxic contamination or other serious environmental hazards are also common, and often bridge the realist–constructivist divide. While some document the debilitating community impacts stemming from obvious contamination, many focus on the controversies that arise when allegations of contamination are countered by denials. Communities subjected to a "technological disaster" such as toxic contamination tend to experience severe conflict between parties holding competing views of its seriousness. This results in a "corrosive" community that stands in stark contrast to the "therapeutic" community that typically develops in response to a "natural disaster" such as an earthquake, hurricane, or flood (Freudenburg 1997).

SOLUTIONS TO ENVIRONMENTAL POLICIES

Sociological contributions to environmental protection policies have largely occurred via policy evaluations. Sociologists commonly question the efficacy of information campaigns to stimulate pro-environmental behaviors among consumers, emphasizing, for example, that providing community-wide collection of recyclables along with garbage collection is more effective than encouraging people to use recycling centers. In a similar vein, research has highlighted the degree to which energy consumption is embedded in sociotechnical systems over which consumers have little control, and that promoting energy-efficient construction standards may be more effective than appealing for household conservation. Studies highlighting the structural constraints on consumer behavior have enabled sociologists to offer valuable input into assessments of environmental policies (Dietz & Stern 2002).

Some environmental sociologists in Northern Europe have engaged more fully with environmental policy by attempting to explain what they see as a pattern of significant progress in environmental protection in their nations. Reversing the field's traditional focus on explaining environmental degradation, proponents of "ecological modernization" argue that a core task of environmental sociology is to explain environmental progress (Buttel 2003). Their evolving theoretical efforts have emphasized the importance of technological innovations, new patterns of cooperation between industry and government, and the gradual growth of an "ecological rationality" that offsets the traditional dominance of economic criteria in decision-making. More generally, advocates of ecological modernization have argued that economic growth and environmental protection are compatible, and that capitalism can lead to environmental improvement rather than degradation (Mol & Sonnenfeld 2000).

Ecological modernization has encountered heavy criticism, particularly from American

environment, sociology of the

scholars who have questioned the adequacy of its standard methodology (case studies of particular industries or governmental entities), its focus on institutional change rather than improvements in environmental quality, and its generalizability beyond Northern Europe. Most fundamentally, trends toward ecological modernization such as improvements in the eco-efficiency of industries have not been adequate to offset economic and population growth, with the result that the "ecological footprint" of most nations and certainly the entire world continues to grow at an unsustainable rate.

Although ecological modernization has been found deficient by a growing number of critics, and certainly lacks face validity given downward trends in most indicators of global ecological health, it may offer insights into how and why particular industries and governmental entities (such as US corporations and communities that voluntarily develop CO_2 emission reduction programs) become more environmentally responsible.

Debates such as those between constructivists and realists, neo-Marxians and neo-Malthusians, and proponents of ecological modernization and their critics reflect the intellectual vitality of environmental sociology, and resolution of these debates via empirical tests and theoretical syntheses promises to move the field forward. Add in the fact that strong environmental sociology organizations exist in many nations, as well as within the International Sociological Association, and that the subject matter of the field (environmental problems) shows no sign of disappearing, and it seems safe to assume that sociological study of environmental issues has a promising future.

SEE ALSO: Built Environment; Ecofeminism; Ecological Problems; Ecology; Environment and Urbanization; Environmental Criminology; Environmental Movements; Life Environmentalism; Population and the Environment

REFERENCES AND SUGGESTED READINGS

Benton, T. (2001) Environmental Sociology: Controversy and Continuity. *Sosiologisk Tidsskrift* 9: 5–48.

Brulle, R. J. & Pellow, D. N. (2006) Environmental Justice: Human Health and Environmental Inequalities. *Annual Review of Public Health* 27.

Buttel, F. H. (1987) New Directions in Environmental Sociology. *Annual Review of Sociology* 13: 465–88.

Buttel, F. H. (2003) Environmental Sociology and the Explanation of Environmental Reform. *Organization and Environment* 16: 306–44.

Carolan, M. S. (2005) Realism Without Reductionism: Toward an Ecologically Embedded Sociology. *Human Ecology Review* 12: 1–20.

Catton, W. R., Jr. (1980) *Overshoot: The Ecological Basis of Revolutionary Change.* University of Illinois Press, Urbana.

Dietz, T. & Stern, P. C. (Eds.) (2002) *New Tools for Environmental Policy.* National Academies Press, Washington, DC.

Dunlap, R. E. & Catton, W. R., Jr. (1979). Environmental Sociology. *Annual Review of Sociology* 5: 243–73.

Dunlap, R. E. & Michelson, W. (Eds.) (2002) *Handbook of Environmental Sociology.* Greenwood Press, Westport, CT.

Freudenburg, W. R. (1997) Contamination, Corrosion and the Social Order: An Overview. *Current Sociology* 45: 41–57.

Goldman, M. (2005) *Imperial Nature: The World Bank and Struggles for Social Justice in the Age of Globalization.* Yale University Press, New Haven.

Hannigan, J. A. (1995) *Environmental Sociology: A Social Constructionist Perspective.* Routledge, London.

Macnaghten, P. & Urry, J. (1998) *Contested Natures.* Sage, London.

Mol, A. P. J. & Sonnenfeld, D. A. (2000) *Ecological Modernization Around the World: Perspectives and Critical Debates.* Frank Cass, London.

Redclift, M. & Woodgate, G. (Eds.) (1997) *The International Handbook of Environmental Sociology.* Edward Elgar, Cheltenham.

Rudel, T. K. & Roper, J. (1997) The Paths to Rain Forest Destruction: Crossnational Patterns of Tropical Deforestation, 1975–90. *World Development* 25: 53–65.

Schnaiberg, A. (1980) *The Environment: From Surplus to Scarcity.* Oxford University Press, New York.

Yearley, S. (1991) *The Green Case.* HarperCollins, London.

Yearley, S. (2005) The Sociology of the Environment and Nature. In: Calhoun, C., Rojek, R., & Turner, B. (Eds.), *The SAGE Handbook of Sociology.* Sage, Thousand Oaks, CA, pp. 314–26.

York, R., Rosa, E. A., & Dietz, T. (2003) Footprints on the Earth: The Environmental Consequences of Modernity. *American Sociological Review* 68: 279–300.

environment and urbanization

Richard York and Eugene A. Rosa

The rapid urbanization of the world's population (accompanied by the rise of megacities) and the profound growth in the scale of impacts on the natural environment were two dominant trends of the twentieth century. Today over 3 billion people, nearly one-half the human population, live in urban areas (United Nations 2004). Humans have altered the composition of the atmosphere, contributing to global climate change, have changed land cover over a large proportion of the earth's surface, and have contributed to a dramatic rise in the rate of species extinction.

All signs point to a continuance of these trends in the twenty-first century. More than half the world's population will live in urban areas before 2010 and nearly two-thirds will be urban residents by 2030 (United Nations 2004). It appears that environmental impacts will likely follow a similar pattern of growth. The parallelism of these trends points to the importance of assessing the connection between urbanization and environmental degradation. The causes and consequences of urbanization are highly complex as they are embedded in other global processes, such as modernization, population growth, trade liberalization, migration, and the expansion of global capitalism. Global environmental change is similarly embedded in a complex of transformative processes.

Nevertheless, urbanization plays a dominant role in the mounting global pressures on ecosystems. It is largely responsible for greenhouse gas accumulations, upper atmospheric ozone depletion, land degradation, and the destruction of coastal zones. There are broad reciprocal dynamics between urbanization and environmental change and the consequences for ecosystems and human capital.

ENVIRONMENTAL DEGRADATION AS A DRIVER OF URBANIZATION

Natural increase accounts for 60 percent of urban growth while migration, particularly rural–urban migration, accounts for the remaining – substantial – 40 percent (United Nations 2004). There is a reciprocal, reinforcing dynamic between migration from rural to urban areas and environmental degradation. The rapid rise in global urbanization accounts for one side of the environmental degradation dynamic. Around the world, human concentrations pressure nature's capital and services primarily in rural areas with natural resources, contributing to the degradation of rural environments (deforestation, soil erosion, and desertification) and undermining the livelihoods of many people, particularly the rural poor in developing countries. This rural degradation has often served to limit the ability of rural peoples to maintain their way of life and, therefore, has served as a major push factor in rural-to-urban migration. Indeed, Shandra et al. (2003) found substantial empirical support that rural environmental degradation is a major driving force behind urbanization in developing countries. There is little doubt that part of the reason for rural environmental degradation can be traced to the activities of rural populations themselves – such as forest clearing for subsistence agriculture. But, increasingly, rural environmental degradation is driven in large part by non-local forces. Hence, urbanization drives environmental degradation in rural areas, which, in turn, drives rural–urban migration, resulting in further urbanization and further degradation.

URBANIZATION AS A DRIVER OF ENVIRONMENTAL DEGRADATION

Urbanization introduces direct internal and external environmental impacts. For example, cities account for 80 percent of all CO_2 emissions and 75 percent of industrial wood use (Hinrichsen et al. 2001). The immediate and direct environmental consequences of urban development, such as congestion, concentrated pollution, and paved-over natural habitats, are obvious to everyone, particularly to the urban population itself. Temperatures tend to be higher in city centers than in surrounding areas and nighttime cooling is less, due to the large heat-trapping structures and treeless concrete jungles of cities. These concrete jungles affect "heat retention, runoff, and pollution, resulting in urban heat islands" (Karl & Trenberth 2003: 1720) that impact public health. Furthermore, the environmental consequences of urbanization stretch well beyond their urban point source, contributing to regional and even global pollution. The pollution problems of urbanization are orders of magnitude larger for megacities (generally defined as those with populations over 10 million, like Mexico City), of which there are now 17 according to the United Nations.

Urbanization is responsible not only for direct impacts, but also for diffuse ones. However, the consequences of urbanization for the environment are complex. On the one hand, all else being equal (e.g., total population, economic production, level of industrialization), urban populations have a lower impact on the environment than rural populations because concentration in urban areas allows for more efficient use of space and transportation. For example, per capita energy use for climate control (heating and cooling) is typically much lower in urban areas due to the preponderance of multifamily housing with their common walls, floors, and ceilings (Darmstadter et al. 1977). On the other hand, despite these direct internal benefits, the most important environmental consequence of urbanization is the effect it has on the structure of regional, national, and global economies, production systems, and political structures.

Historically, economic, cultural, social, and military power has concentrated in cities, which have controlled social systems over large areas. In fact, over the past five millennia the world-system has been dominated by a handful of cities exerting dramatic influence over global production (Chew 2001). As noted above, the environmental consequences of urbanization, therefore, are not restricted to the immediate environs of the city. In fact, the most severe impacts of urbanization may be felt at great distances from cities themselves, where resources are extracted for consumption in urban areas. For example, Chew (2001) documents the environmental consequences, such as deforestation, driven by the demand of ancient cities for natural resources. A more recent example documents how the growth of Chicago in the nineteenth century was in large part responsible

for the rapacious extraction of natural resources from the American West (Cronon 1991). Cities require massive quantities of resources for their construction and maintenance, and, therefore, shape land areas much larger than themselves to provide for their material appetites. For example, the highly urbanized Netherlands consumes resources from a total surface area equivalent to 15 times larger than itself (McMichael 2000: 1122).

Urbanization leads to changes in the culture and lifestyle of the population, including expanding the consumption of resource-intensive goods – with clear consequences for the global environment. For example, urbanization, at least in the modern world, generally increases the per capita consumption of meat, which is particularly resource intensive to produce. The modern city is also intimately associated with the rise of the automobile. For example, Riley (2002) argues that urbanization may lead to the acquisition of cars not only by urban residents (due to their affluence and car-friendly urban infrastructure), but also by rural residents seeking access to urban amenities. Private car ownership, which is increasing at a spectacular rate, totals more than 750 million vehicles worldwide (McMichael 2000).

Urbanization impacts lifestyle and human capital in indirect ways, too. It increases the demand for centrally generated commercial energy (as opposed to the individual use of traditional fuels, such as biomass), resulting in the accelerated combustion of fossil fuels in power plants. An unavoidable consequence of fossil fuel burning in power plants and in transportation is the production of greenhouse gases, such as CO_2, and a whole host of air pollutants such as particulate matter, ozone, carbon monoxide, sulfur dioxide, and nitrogen oxides. Virtually all of these pollutants have adverse effects on public health, a key component of human capital, and the World Health Organization (WHO 2002) estimates that worldwide air pollution is responsible for 3 million deaths annually.

The most serious consequence of urbanization for the natural environment may be the changes it introduces in the quality of human interaction with nature. Building upon a foundation laid by Marx, Foster (2000) argues that urbanization, in large part driven by capitalism, generates a "metabolic rift" between town and country – between changing forms of social organization and the environment. The primary factor generating such a rift is the separation of people from the land when they become concentrated in urban centers.

The separation of people from the land leads to two reinforcing dislocations. First, organic matter (e.g., agricultural and human waste) that can provide nutrients to biological systems (a potential ecological benefit) is separated from where it can be recycled into the rural soil and becomes concentrated in urban areas. Second, due to the separation between the sites of agricultural production (rural areas) and the sites of consumption (urban areas), a potential ecological benefit (nutrient-rich organic matter) is transformed into an ecological cost (a waste problem). Instead of fertilizing the soil, as it would if it were not concentrated in urban areas, this "waste" must be disposed of, which leads to second-order demands on resources and attendant ecological disruptions, due to, for example, the energy and land needed for sewage treatment plants and landfills.

Note that the metabolic rift thesis does not necessarily suggest that urban residents have a higher per capita impact on the environment than rural residents. Rather, it argues that the process of urbanization affects the structure of national production and consumption systems, resulting in an upward spiral of environmental degradation. In a sense, the urbanization process can "urbanize" the countryside too, so that rural residents may in fact adopt lifestyles similar to urban residents (e.g., rural residents may consume non-local products and landfill "waste" that could be recycled into the soil).

Counter to the claims that urbanization leads to a metabolic rift, some scholars of modernism argue that urbanization, by contributing to the development of the structures of modernity, serves to *reduce* environmental degradation (Ehrhardt-Martinez 1998). This body of work comes out of either the "ecological modernization" perspective in sociology or the "environmental Kuznets curve" perspective in economics. Ecological modernization theorists argue that the structures of modernity contribute to the development of ecologically rational institutions, policies, and technologies that help to curtail environmental degradation

(Ehrhardt-Martinez 1998). Likewise, environmental Kuznets curve (named after economist Simon Kuznets) theorists propose an inverted U-shaped relationship between economic development and environmental degradation, where environmental impacts increase in the early stages of development, but level off and then decline as societies modernize (Grossman & Krueger 1995).

Although the work of Ehrhardt-Martinez (1998) has demonstrated that national deforestation tends to follow a Kuznets curve relative to urbanization, other work (York et al. 2003b) suggests that this finding, considering the full effect of urbanization, and modernization more generally, on the environment, is spurious. Since, particularly in the contemporary era of globalization, the resources a nation consumes do not necessarily come from within its own borders, environmental degradation in a particular nation may not be tied to the consumption of that nation, but, rather, to the consumption of other nations linked to global markets. Cross-national research on the "ecological footprint," a measure of the amount of land area needed to support the resource consumption and waste emissions of nations that takes into account imports and exports, suggests that urbanization, as well as other indicators of modernization, tend to increase, not decrease, pressure on the environment (York et al. 2003b). Furthermore, urbanization also tends to drive up national CO_2 and methane emissions, the principal greenhouse gases (York et al. 2003a). In fact, urbanization appears to have a greater effect on methane emissions than does economic growth (York et al. 2003a). Taken together, these results suggest that continuing urbanization represents a serious threat to the environment and new patterns of urbanization may exacerbate that threat even further. For example, the growing suburban sprawl taking place in many developed countries, particularly the United States, represents a severe threat to the environment, since it devours land and is strongly associated with motorization.

Of course, not all types of urban development are the same, and the hope for the twenty-first century is that the worst effects of urbanization can be avoided or mitigated. The current challenge around the globe, then, is threefold. First, it appears important that "overurbanization" be curtailed. This will require a greater understanding of the factors that drive urbanization in the first place, and the identification of socially acceptable options for limiting unnecessary urban development. Second, less environmentally destructive forms of urban development need to be devised since it is clear that, for the foreseeable future, many urban areas around the world will experience rapid growth. Third, empowering those in rural areas by addressing social, political, and economic inequalities around the world may help curtail the unsustainable exploitation of the rural periphery by the urban core.

SEE ALSO: Ecological Problems; Political Economy; Population and Development; Population and the Environment; Urban Ecology; Urban Political Economy; Urban–Rural Population Movements; Urbanization

REFERENCES AND SUGGESTED READINGS

Chew, S. C. (2001) *World Ecological Degradation: Accumulation, Urbanization, and Deforestation 3000 BC–AD 2000.* Rowman & Littlefield, New York.

Cronon, W. (1991) *Nature's Metropolis: Chicago and the Great West.* W. W. Norton, New York.

Darmstadter, J., Dunkerley, J., & Alterman, J. (1977) *How Industrial Societies Use Energy: A Comparative Analysis.* Johns Hopkins University Press, Baltimore.

Ehrhardt-Martinez, K. (1998) Social Determinants of Deforestation in Developing Countries: A Cross-National Study. *Social Forces* 77(2): 567–86.

Foster, J. B. (2000) *Marx's Ecology: Materialism and Nature.* Monthly Review Press, New York.

Grossman, G. & Krueger, A. (1995) Economic Growth and the Environment. *Quarterly Journal of Economics* 110: 353–77.

Hinrichsen, D., Blackburn, R., & Robey, B. (2001) *Cities Will Determine the Living Standards for Mankind.* Report of the Johns Hopkins Bloomberg School of Public Health. Online. www.jhuccp.org/pr/urbanpre.stm.

Karl, T. R. & Trenberth, K. E. (2003) Modern Global Climate Change. *Science* 302: 1719–23.

McMichael, A. J. (2000) The Urban Environment and Health in a World of Increasing Globalization: Issues for Developing Countries. *Bulletin of the World Health Organization* 78: 1117–23.

Riley, K. (2002) Motor Vehicles in China: The Impact of Demographic and Economic Changes. *Population and Environment* 23(5): 479–94.

Shandra, J. M., London, B., & Williamson, J. B. (2003) Environmental Degradation, Environmental Sustainability, and Overurbanization in the Developing World: A Quantitative, Cross-National Analysis. *Sociological Perspectives* 46(3): 309–29.

United Nations (2004) *World Urbanization Prospects, the 2003 Revision.* United Nations, Population Division, New York.

World Health Organization (WHO) (2002) Air Pollution Fatalities Now Exceed Traffic Fatalities by 3 to 1. Press Release. WHO, Rome.

York, R., Rosa, E. A., & Dietz, T. (2003a) A Rift in Modernity? Assessing the Anthropogenic Sources of Global Climate Change with the STIRPAT Model. *International Journal of Sociology and Social Policy* 23(10): 31–51.

York, R., Rosa, E. A., & Dietz, T. (2003b) Footprints on the Earth: The Environmental Consequences of Modernity. *American Sociological Review* 68(2): 279–300.

environmental criminology

Jacqueline L. Schneider

Environmental criminology is a generic phrase that encompasses a number of different approaches aimed at reducing the occurrence of criminal events by examining the physicality in which the crimes occur. Rooted in human and social ecology, environmental criminology studies crime, criminality, and victimization as they relate to place, space, and their interaction (Bottoms & Wiles 2002). Specifically, environmental criminology explores how criminal opportunities are generated given the nature of the existing setting (see Felson & Clarke 1998). The aim is to identify ways to manipulate attributes of space in order to reduce opportunities to commit crime at various points in time.

Crime has four determinants: law, offenders, targets, and places (Brantingham & Brantingham 1991). Classical criminology addresses legal aspects of criminal activity, while the positivists have traditionally focused on offenders.

The pioneering work of Jacobs (1961) and Newman (1972) brought targets and places into focus, thus redressing the balance between the four determinants. It is the emphasis on targets and place that sets environmental criminology apart from other more traditional criminological schools of thought such as classical criminology and positivism. For example, rather than seeking to understand why offenders commit crime, preventive measures are designed after analyzing the ways in which the environment generates crime opportunities. In other words, crime can be designed out of an area once patterns of crime events are identified. The behavior of the offender in terms of where and how crime is committed becomes more important to the environmental criminologist than the motivation behind the behavior.

According to the Brantinghams (1991), locations, characteristics of locations, and movement paths that allow the intersection of victims and offenders, along with the perceptions of crime locations, fall under the auspices of environmental criminology. According to Cohen and Felson (1979), patterns of interaction and activities of daily life are not random; rather, patterns of interaction across time and place are routine, thus bringing routine activity theory to light. Since the organization of our routine activities pertaining to time and space is predictable, explanations of crime patterns can be identified and preventive measures designed. Eck and Weisburd (1995) expand our understanding of crime events by combining rational choice theory (Cornish & Clarke 1987) with routine activity theory in order to explain the distribution of crime events.

Several themes run through the environmental criminological philosophy: (1) activities are routine; (2) location is chosen by a structured search and decision-making process by participants; (3) crime generators and attractors exist; and (4) measurement issues pertaining to spatial reliability need exploring (see Bottoms & Wiles 2002). Target and place are studied at three basic levels: macro is the highest level of spatial aggregation and focuses on the distribution between countries, states, or cities; the intermediate or meso level of analysis examines subarea distributions of targets, offenders, populations, and routine activities; and

micro-level analysis studies specific crime sites, focusing on building types, landscaping, lighting, or other physical interventions.

Environmental criminology, while underutilized, has slowly gained in prominence since the 1970s. Crime mapping, a tool used by environmental criminologists, has raised the profile of crime pattern analysis and has helped identify areas where crime is occurring. This technology, however, has also become useful in predicting where crime events are most likely to occur (see Bower et al. 2004; Ratcliffe 2004).

SEE ALSO: Crime; Criminology; Criminology: Research Methods; Rational Choice Theory: A Crime-Related Perspective; Routine Activity Theory

REFERENCES AND SUGGESTED READINGS

Bottoms, A. E. & Wiles, P. (2002) Environmental Criminology. In: Maguire, M., Morgan, R., & Reiner, R. (Eds.), *The Oxford Handbook of Criminology*. Oxford University Press, Oxford, pp. 620–56.

Bower, K. J., Johnson, S. D., & Pease, K. (2004) Prospective Hotspotting: The Future of Crime Mapping? *British Journal of Criminology* 44: 641–58.

Brantingham, P. J. & Brantingham, P. L. (Eds.) (1991) *Environmental Criminology*. Waveland Press, Prospect Heights, IL.

Cohen, L. E. & Felson, M. (1979) Social Change and Crime Rate Trends: A Routine Activity Approach. *American Sociological Review* 44: 588–608.

Cornish, D. & Clarke, R. V. (1987) Understanding Crime Displacement: An Application of Rational Choice Theory. *Criminology* 25: 933–47.

Eck, J. E. & Weisburd, D. (Eds.) (1995) *Crime and Place*. Criminal Justice Press, Monsey, NY.

Felson, M. & Clarke, R. V. G. (1998) *Opportunity Makes the Thief*. Police Research Series, Paper 98. HMSO, London.

Jacobs, J. (1961) *Death and Life of Great American Cities*. Random House, New York.

Newman, O. (1972) *Defensible Space: Crime Prevention Through Urban Design*. Macmillan, New York.

Ratcliffe, J. H. (2004) The Hotspot Matrix: A Framework for the Spatio-Temporal Targeting of Crime Reduction. *Police Practice and Research* 5: 5–23.

environmental movements

Christopher Rootes

Environmental movements are networks of informal interactions that may include, as well as individuals and groups who have no organizational affiliation, organizations of varying degrees of formality (including even political parties, especially Green parties) that are engaged in collective action motivated by shared identity or concern about environmental issues. Such networks are generally loose and uninstitutionalized, but their forms of action and their degree of integration vary. However, environmental movements are not identical to organizations or episodes of protest. It is only when organizations (and other, usually less formally organized actors) are networked and engaged in collective action, whether or not it involves protest, that an environmental movement exists (Diani 1995: 5; Rootes 2004a).

Such linkages are not always readily visible. Where environmental movements are well established, the balance of their actions is likely to have shifted from highly visible protest to less visible lobbying and even "constructive engagement" with governments and corporations. Just as the collective action of the movement may become less visible, so too, where environmentalism has become most entrenched, there are many "subterranean" linkages among groups and organizations, and the full range of movement activities is less and less adequately represented in mass media.

The methodological implications of this are that no one strategy is likely to yield anything approaching a complete picture. Although studies of protest events (Rootes 2003) may represent the most visible face of the movement and escape the constraints of organizational studies that necessarily omit the less organized part of the movement, they are unlikely to give an adequate account of the less public – or simply less publicized – activities of the movement, including a great deal that happens locally and beyond the focus of mass media. Careful ethnographies of both national organizations and local campaigns are thus a necessary complement to event-based studies.

FORMATION OF THE MODERN ENVIRONMENTAL MOVEMENT

Although concern about the environment has a long history, modern environmental movements date from the late 1960s. The increasingly obvious effects of accelerating industrialization and exploitation of natural resources provided growing audiences for the alarums of conservationists and preservationists. It was, however, the radical critique of capitalist industrialism and representative democracy associated with the New Left and the counter-culture that created the public space for the development of new social movements, as well as furnishing their tactical repertoire. Especially in the US, environmentalism benefited from being a relatively consensual issue in a period of intense political polarization, but concern about the environment soon gave rise to new and more radical environmental movement organizations (EMOs) that embraced nonviolent direct action, and rapidly spread to Western Europe. Thus, Friends of the Earth (FoE) and Greenpeace arose in response to the apparent timidity of conservationist EMOs such as the Sierra Club. The internationalism of these EMOs, as well as their skilfull exploitation of mass media to put pressure on governments and corporate decision-makers, struck a chord, and these were the fastest growing EMOs during the 1980s.

Their rise encouraged innovation in the tactics, and especially the agenda, of older conservation organizations, and by the end of the 1980s networking among older and newer organizations and joint campaigns were increasingly common. Indeed, the history of environmentalism on both sides of the Atlantic has been one of successive waves of critique, innovation, and incorporation, and radical ecologist groupings and the environmental justice movement (EJM) have in turn grown out of dissatisfaction with increasingly institutionalized reform environmentalism.

Many organizations formed in earlier waves of environmental concern have, to varying degrees, adapted to accommodate subsequent concerns and developments in ecological consciousness. In the US, despite observers' doubts that established, "wilderness obsessed" EMOs are capable of accommodating the concerns of the EJM, especially since 2000, the Sierra Club and Greenpeace have taken the environmental justice agenda seriously. In Western Europe the environmental justice frame has been increasingly adopted, especially by FoE, while established EMOs such as the World Wide Fund for Nature (WWF) and the national bird protection societies have developed a more inclusive ecological perspective and have broadened the range of their campaigns to include issues of habitat and the welfare of human populations (Rootes 2005). The rhetoric of conflict and critique may give a misleading impression of divisions within environmental movements whose existence can be demonstrated by the persistence, despite such differences, of network links of varying degrees of strength and intensity (Dalton 1994).

VALUES AND SOCIAL BASES OF ENVIRONMENTAL ACTIVISM

The rise of values and attitudes favorable to environmentalism is frequently explained in terms of "post-materialism" (Inglehart 1977). According to this thesis, post-material values prioritizing aesthetic, intellectual, and self-actualization needs are gradually supplanting materialist values that place a higher priority on economic and security needs, chiefly because new, younger generations raised in relative affluence and security are replacing older generations who had, during their formative years, more often experienced economic privation and the insecurities of war. The rise of environmentalism was counted among the consequences of this "culture shift," but post-materialism may not be as good a predictor of environmentalism as has been supposed because it embraces both post-materialist aesthetic and principled concerns with environmental protection *and* essentially materialist concerns with safety and security. Even global environmental concern, often portrayed as unproblematically post-materialist, might be represented as a materialist concern.

Post-materialism is relatively weakly correlated with support for environmentalism because concerns for the environment are held both by highly educated "post-materialist" ecologists, who are not so much fearful for their own security as concerned about global environmental problems whose effects are relatively remote, as well as people, usually less well educated, who are more exercised by fear of the threats that pollution poses to their own immediate material security. Post-materialism is a better predictor of environmental *activism* than of environmental concern because activism, unlike concern, is highly correlated with higher education, which is itself an antecedent of most forms of political activism.

Most research on the social backgrounds of environmental activists and the members of national EMOs has concluded that they are disproportionately highly educated and employed in the teaching, creative, welfare, or caring professions and, especially, the offspring of the highly educated (Rootes 1995). As a result, environmentalism has sometimes been interpreted as the self-interested politics of a "new class" of traffickers in culture and symbols, opposed or indifferent to the interests of those whose labor involves the manipulation of material things. However, environmental activists are not exclusively drawn from such backgrounds, and approval of EMOs and environmental activism, as well as pro-environment attitudes, are widespread among most segments of society.

Grassroots environmental movements involve a broader cross-section of society than do the major national EMOs, in part because locally unwanted land uses are more often imposed upon the poor. Women play more prominent roles in grassroots mobilizations than in national EMOs, reflecting women's greater attachment to and confidence in acting in the local community than in the wider public sphere, and the fact that the barriers to entry to the local political sphere are lower than in national politics. Grassroots environmental activism is thus an important means of social learning about environmental issues, a school for participation generally, an entry point for new activists and new issues, a source of revitalization of the environmental movement, and a means by which it may be made more socially representative.

VALUES AND FORMS OF ACTION

Theorists have distinguished among conservationism, environmentalism, and ecologism, but it is unusual for such clear philosophical distinctions to be precisely mirrored in divisions among movement organizations, their members and supporters. Organizational formalizations of ideological division are more likely in the formal political sphere, where membership tends to be exclusive, than in the movement milieu, where organizations are more fluid, overlapping memberships are common, and where the flexibility of the network structure is better able to accommodate differences without their becoming overtly conflictual.

The discursive frames adopted by environmentalists have consequences for the ways in which they campaign and the forms of organization they adopt (Brulle 2000). Yet, as Dalton (1994) discovered, whether European EMOs had been originally committed to conservationism or ecologism made surprisingly little difference to their choices of strategies, tactics, and styles of action. The apparent convergence within the broad environmental movement sector was not simply a matter of the progressive institutionalization and incorporation of more radical organizations such as FoE and Greenpeace; just as FoE and Greenpeace learned the etiquette necessary to smooth dealings with the powerful, so traditional conservationist organizations became less conflict-averse in their tactics and more skilled in the use of mass media. Although EMOs' values do influence their strategy and tactics, greater effects are attributable to "political opportunity structures" – the pattern of opportunities and constraints inherent in the structures of the national political systems within which those organizations operate.

Even where they embrace direct action, environmental movements are almost wholly nonviolent, but movement cultures do not exist in a social and political vacuum. Violent environmental protests in Italy and Spain were carry-overs from other, wider political ructions – in Italy, the tail end of the political violence of the 1970s and 1980s, and in Spain, the temporary association of militant Basque nationalism with environmentalist struggles. Similarly, confrontational environmental protest in Britain in the 1990s rode the wave of more general confrontational protest that rose with the campaign against the poll tax (Rootes 2003). National political cultures explain less than political conjunctures.

INSTITUTIONALIZATION AND ITS DISCONTENTS

Conventionally, it has generally been assumed that "success" for a social movement means its institutionalization, usually as a political party. However, Eyerman and Jamison (1991) argue that a movement exists only in the relatively brief liminal period when a new, autonomous public space is created. Thus, from their perspective, the identity of the environmental movement dissolves as its organization fragments and its "movement intellectuals" become established in universities, industrial organizations, law and journalism, professionalized campaigning organizations such as Greenpeace, and political parties, including Green parties. For Eyerman and Jamison, movements are by definition transient, and the institutionalization of the environmental movement is a contradiction in terms.

Recent history suggests that environmental movements may have squared the circle. Whether measured by size, income, degree of formality of organizations, number and professionalization of employees, or frequency and kind of interaction with established institutional actors, EMOs in most industrialized countries have, since the late 1980s, become relatively institutionalized. Yet such institutionalization has not simply entailed the deradicalization of the movement or a loss of shared identity.

Some have worried that institutionalization has turned EMOs into "protest businesses" (Jordan & Maloney 1997) or a "public interest lobby" (Diani & Donati 1999) increasingly incapable of mobilizing supporters for action. Yet, in Germany, a substantially institutionalized movement coexisted in the 1990s with the revival of highly confrontational, at times violent, anti-nuclear protest, and established EMOs gave assistance to local anti-nuclear groups (Rucht & Roose 2003). In Britain, during the 1990s, EMOs grew in numbers and size as well as access and influence, but reported environmental protest also increased and became more rather than less confrontational (Rootes 2003).

The rise of new, more radical groupings such as Earth First! can be traced in part to dissatisfaction with the apparent timidity of more established EMOs, but shared identity among environmental campaigners survived even as their tactical repertoires varied. Even the radical "disorganizations" most committed to direct action were connected by networks of advice and support to more established organizations. The sense of identity among the constituent parts of the British environmental movement did not dissolve as a result of the institutionalization of its more established organizations and the reactions against it, but instead grew as groups came to practice a division of labors and to realize the advantages of cooperation.

The European experience shows that it is possible for an environmental movement to retain many of the characteristics of an emergent movement while taking advantage of the opportunities presented by institutionalization, and that institutionalization is no barrier to the mobilization of protest. While some writers have referred to the "self-limiting radicalism" of Green parties, it is the "self-limiting institutionalization" of environmental movements that is the more striking and that has more profound implications for sociological theory. Their survival and their resistance to the deradicalizing effects of institutionalization has distinguished environmental movements from the other "new social movements." Because pressing environmental problems are part of the chronic condition of an industrialized world, western environmental movements, although by no means universally anti-capitalist, are recurrently influenced by the critical analyses of their radically anti-capitalist constituents, as campaigns against genetically modified organisms and neoliberal globalization have shown.

BEYOND THE NATIONAL

The character of environmental movements varies from one country to another according to material differences in their environments. Thus, in the US, Canada, Australasia, and the Nordic countries, wilderness issues have often been more salient than pollution issues. In Western Europe, where the physical environment is more obviously a human product, the concern to protect landscapes is more readily combined with concerns about the consequences of environmental degradation for people.

In the most recently industrialized parts of Southern Europe and in the countries of Central and Eastern Europe ravaged by rapid industrialization under communism, environmental concern is more often a matter of personal complaint than of global environmental consciousness. As a result, despite occasionally intense local campaigns, EMOs are relatively weak. Environmental movements were credited with a major role in the popular mobilizations against communist regimes, but their subsequent weakness suggests that green was often protective camouflage for anti-regime activists who subsequently turned to mainstream political roles, or that the political and economic urgencies of post-transition states have sidelined environmental concerns.

Especially in the less industrialized countries of the global South, environmental issues are bound up with struggles surrounding the distribution of social, economic, and political power and resources, and mobilizations rarely take the form of environmental movements. The lack of safeguards for democratic political activity or possibilities of judicial redress of grievances, and the underdevelopment of civil society, present severe impediments, and success for their campaigns often depends upon the support of Northern environmental or human rights organizations.

It is not, however, only in the global South that environmental struggles bundle claims for environmental protection with demands for social and economic justice, and often for substantive democracy as well. Thus, in Britain, EMOs have increasingly been prominent participants in a variety of humanitarian and anti-war campaigns. In the US, environmental demands have, especially in and since the 1990s, been conjoined with the critique of class and especially racial inequalities. Distrustful of the alleged elitism of established EMOs, the environmental justice movement took the form of a loose network of local campaign groups (Schlosberg 1999).

A preference for deliberately informal networks rather than formal organization is characteristic of recent waves of environmental activism on both sides of the Atlantic, but the relationship of local environmental protests to environmental movements is problematic. Most local protests are NIMBY in origin and, although some undergo a convincing transformation into universalist campaigns that reach out to and link up with others and with the environmental movement generally, others remain particularistic and do not centrally involve even the local branches of established EMOs. Only exceptionally do local campaign groups grow into more general EMOs, but they may nevertheless serve as sources of innovation and renewal within national environmental movements, by "discovering" new environmental issues, initiating new generations of activists, and devising new tactics.

National and local political cultures and material differences affect the forms, development, and outcomes of environmental movements, as do differences among political opportunity structures. National EMOs are dependent for their resources and legitimacy upon national publics, and their dynamics and trajectories are shaped by locally and nationally idiosyncratic events and institutions. Consequently, the concertation of transnational environmental activism is difficult. Even within the best developed supranational polity – the European Union – EMOs remain primarily national in their networks, collective action repertoires, and thematic concerns, despite the EU's importance as the principal locus of environmental policymaking (Rootes 2004b).

The absence of a developed global polity presents even greater obstacles to the formation of a global environmental movement. Although international agreements and agencies encourage the development of transnational environmental NGOs, the latter are not mass participatory organizations and, outside the North, rarely have deep roots in civil society. The consequent lack of democratic accountability is unlikely to be merely temporary. However, if the prospects for an effective and genuinely democratic global environmental movement appear limited today, better and cheaper means of communication promise to erode distance just as increasing access to higher education gives more people the skills and resources necessary to operate transnationally. The example of Earth Action International, and the increasingly effective internationalization of FoE International, may be straws in the wind.

Since the 1980s the study of environmental movements has increasingly moved beyond local and national case studies (which have nevertheless proliferated) and toward systematic comparative studies. Since the mid-1990s these have come increasingly to revolve around the issues raised by the prospect of a transnational movement addressing global environmental issues. It is here that the practical challenges and the need for sociological work are greatest.

SEE ALSO: Direct Action; Ecofeminism; Ecological Problems; Global Justice as a Social Movement; Globalization and Global Justice; Political Opportunities; Social Movements; Social Movements, Networks and; Social Movements, Non-Violent; Social Movements, Political Consequences of; Transnational Movements

REFERENCES AND SUGGESTED READINGS

Brulle, R. (2000) *Agency, Democracy and Nature: The US Environmental Movement from a Critical Theory Perspective*. MIT Press, Cambridge, MA.

Dalton, R. J. (1994) *The Green Rainbow: Environmental Groups in Western Europe*. Yale University Press, New Haven.

Diani, M. (1995) *Green Networks: A Structural Analysis of the Italian Environmental Movement*. Edinburgh University Press, Edinburgh.

Diani, M. & Donati, P. (1999) Organizational Change in Western European Environmental Groups: A Framework for Analysis. In: Rootes, C. (Ed.), *Environmental Movements: Local, National and Global*. Frank Cass, London, pp. 13–34.

Eyerman, R. & Jamison, A. (1991) *Social Movements: A Cognitive Approach*. Polity Press, Cambridge.

Inglehart, R. (1977) *Silent Revolution*. Princeton University Press, Princeton.

Jordan, G. & Maloney, W. (1997) *The Protest Business? Mobilizing Campaign Groups*. Manchester University Press, Manchester.

Mertig, A. G., Dunlap, R. E., & Morrison, D. E. (2002) The Environmental Movement in the United States. In: Dunlap, R. E. & Michelson, W. (Eds.), *Handbook of Environmental Sociology*. Greenwood Press, Westport, pp. 448–81.

Pakulski, J. & Crook, S. (Eds.) (1998) *Ebbing of the Green Tide? Environmentalism, Public Opinion and the Media in Australia*. School of Sociology and Social Work, University of Tasmania, Hobart.

Rootes, C. (1995) A New Class? The Higher Educated and the New Politics. In: Maheu, L. (Ed.), *Social Movements and Social Classes: The Future of Collective Action*. Sage, London, pp. 220–35.

Rootes, C. (Ed.) (1999) *Environmental Movements: Local, National and Global*. Frank Cass, London.

Rootes, C. (Ed.) (2003) *Environmental Protest in Western Europe*. Oxford University Press, Oxford.

Rootes, C. (2004a) Environmental Movements. In: Snow, D. A., Soule, S. A., & Kriesi, H. (Eds.), *The Blackwell Companion to Social Movements*. Blackwell, Oxford, pp. 608–40.

Rootes, C. (2004b) Is There a European Environmental Movement? In: Barry, J., Baxter, B., & Dunphy, R. (Eds.), *Europe, Globalization, Sustainable Development*. Routledge, New York, pp. 47–72.

Rootes, C. (2005) A Limited Transnationalization? The British Environmental Movement. In: della Porta, D. & Tarrow, S. (Eds.), *Transnational Protest and Global Activism*. Rowman & Littlefield, Lanham, MD, pp. 21–43.

Rucht, D. & Roose, J. (2003) Germany. In: Rootes, C. (Ed.), *Environmental Protest in Western Europe*. Oxford University Press, Oxford, pp. 80–108.

Schlosberg, D. (1999) Networks and Mobile Arrangements: Organizational Innovation in the US Environmental Justice Movement. In: Rootes, C. (Ed.), *Environmental Movements: Local, National and Global*. Frank Cass, London, pp. 122–48.

Seel, B., Paterson, M., & Doherty, B. (Eds.) (2000) *Direct Action in British Environmentalism*. Routledge, New York.

Taylor, B. (Ed.) (1995) *Ecological Resistance Movements: The Global Emergence of Radical and Popular Environmentalism*. State University of New York Press, Albany.

Wapner, P. (1996) *Environmental Activism and World Civic Politics*. State University of New York Press, Albany.

epidemiology

Hung-En Sung

Epidemiology is the study of the distribution of disease as well as its determinants and consequences in human populations (Bhopal 2002). It uses statistical methods to answer questions on how much disease there is, what specific factors put individuals at risk, and how severe disease outcomes are in patient populations, in order to inform public health policymaking. The term disease encompasses not only physical or mental illnesses but also behavioral patterns with negative health consequences, such as substance abuse or violence.

The measurement of disease occurrence begins with the estimation of incidence and prevalence. Disease incidence is the number of new cases in a population within a specific period of time. First-ever incidence picks up only first-ever onsets; in contrast, episode incidence records all onsets of disease events, including those of recurrent episodes. Cumulative incidence expresses the risk of contracting a disease as the proportion of the population who would experience the onset over a specific time period.

Prevalence is the number of people in a population with a specific disease. Point prevalence counts all diseased individuals at a point in time, whereas period prevalence records those with the disease during a stated time period. Cumulative prevalence includes all those with the disease during their lives or between two specific time points. The nature of the disease itself determines the appropriate choice of measure. For example, for single-episode conditions with a clearly defined onset such as chickenpox, first-ever and cumulative incidence rates are most useful, but for recurrent conditions with ill-defined onsets such as allergy, period and cumulative prevalence rates are most often analyzed.

Population epidemiology attempts to unravel causal mechanisms of disease with a view to prevention. Since most diseases are determined by multiple genetic and environmental factors, exposures to single risk factors are usually neither sufficient nor necessary causes of a disease. Consequently, efforts are devoted to quantify the level of increased risk when exposed to a particular risk factor. Risk is normally measured as either a ratio of the prevalence of disease in two populations or the ratio of the odds of exposure to a particular risk factor between two groups. Clinical epidemiology, in turn, aims at the identification of disease outcomes with the goal of controlling the damage done to patients.

The successful application of epidemiological methods to the study of social maladies (e.g., divorce, homicide, drug addiction, etc.) and the emergence of social epidemiology using sociological constructs (e.g., social inequalities, racial discrimination, sexism, residential segregation, etc.) in the analysis of disease herald an even closer collaboration between epidemiologists and sociologists in the coming years (Berkman & Kawachi 2000).

SEE ALSO: Disease, Social Causation; Gender, Health, and Mortality; Health and Social Class; Health Risk Behavior; Race/Ethnicity, Health, and Mortality; Social Epidemiology

REFERENCES AND SUGGESTED READINGS

Berkman, L. F. & Kawachi, I. (Eds.) (2000) *Social Epidemiology*. Oxford University Press, New York.
Bhopal, R. S. (2002) *Concepts of Epidemiology: An Integrated Introduction to the Ideas, Theories, Principles, and Methods of Epidemiology*. Oxford University Press, New York.

epistemology

Thomas A. Schwandt

The Greek words for knowledge and explanation are *episteme* and *logos*, respectively. Epistemology is the study of the nature (theory) of knowledge and justification. Epistemology is the kind of philosophy (or the primary role assigned to philosophy) valued in the scientific view of the world. In such a world, significant emphasis is placed on providing evidence for our claims to know, and philosophy has the task

of examining the logic and methods involved in questions of *how* we know and what gives knowledge the property of being valid. The phrase "after epistemology" or "overcoming epistemology" often heard in philosophical circles is, in part, a reaction to restricting philosophy to epistemological concerns, to matters of "knowing about knowing." The tradition of Continental philosophy (hermeneutics, existentialism, critical theory, phenomenology, etc.) that inspires much thinking in the social sciences today, expands the concern with knowing to "knowing about being and doing." In other words its concerns are not strictly epistemological, but also metaphysical and aesthetic.

Debates between the two great classical modern philosophies of rationalism and empiricism that developed in the seventeenth and eighteenth centuries form the backdrop for understanding the emergence of social science methodologies. Empiricist epistemology (Locke, Hume, Berkeley) argued that knowledge is derived from sense experience; genuine, legitimate knowledge consists of beliefs that can be justified by observation. Rationalist epistemology (Descartes, Spinoza) held that reason is the sure path to knowledge. Rationalists may claim that sense experiences are an effect of external causes; that a priori ideas (concepts, theories, etc.) provide a structure for making sense of experience; and/or that reason provides a kind of certainty that the senses cannot provide. Kant's philosophy is recognized for (among other things) its grand synthesis and reconciliation of the key insights of these two theories of knowledge.

Empiricism as an epistemology continues to occupy a central place in thinking about methodology, particularly in Anglo-American traditions. It is one of the cornerstones of the naturalistic interpretation of the social sciences – the view that the explanatory and predictive methods of the natural sciences, as well as the aim of developing a theory of the way the natural world works, ought to be extended to the social (human or moral) sciences. Empiricism today in the social sciences most often appears within a mix of ideas drawn from positivism, logical positivism, behaviorism, representationalism, meaning realism, and operationalism, such that it is probably more proper to speak of empiricist epistemology as an orientation or disposition toward investigation of social (and behavioral) phenomena. Key components of this disposition include placing primary emphasis on a set of epistemic (cognitive) virtues thought to comprise scientific rationality (e.g., objectivity, value-neutrality, critical reliance on method), objectifying that which one studies (i.e., treating it as an object that stands independent of the inquirer), distinguishing meaning from significance (meaning inheres in texts and social action and is discoverable; grasping that meaning is not to be confused with judging its significance for any person at any particular place and time); and deep skepticism of the scientific status of interpretation and understanding. What is widely recognized as the "interpretive turn" in the social sciences arises from, in part, a strong critique of this nexus of beliefs within which the epistemology of empiricism occupies a central place.

Rationalist and empiricist epistemologies are foundationalist; that is, they hold that any claim labeled as "knowledge" must rest on a secure (i.e., permanent, indisputable) foundation. The rationalist locates this foundation in reason; the empiricist, in sense experience. While acknowledging that reason and experience are important in understanding the nature of knowledge, much contemporary epistemology is nonfoundationalist – it rejects the view that knowledge must be erected on an absolutely secure foundation. Nonfoundationalists argue there simply are no such things as secure foundations; hence, our knowledge is always conjectural and subject to revision. This distinction between foundationalist and nonfoundationalist epistemologies is one way of marking the difference between philosophies of positivism and postpositivism. The former believe in the possibility (and necessity) of unassailable ground for any claim to knowledge; the latter abandon this idea. However, postpositivism does not discard the idea that knowledge is built up from (relatively) neutral observations of the "way things are." It simply acknowledges that, at any given time, our understanding of the way things are might be mistaken. Postpositivists are thus fallibilists with respect to knowledge – the presumption is that current knowledge is correct given the best available procedures, evidence, and arguments, yet current understandings can be revised in light of new criticism or evidence. In Popperian and other critical rationalist postpositivist philosophies, empirical data continue to serve as a very important basis or underpinning of knowledge, but evidence (empirical data) is never considered to be forever beyond dispute, and subsequently knowledge claims based on data should never be considered beyond the possibility of revision.

Some postpositivist epistemologies significantly depart from empiricist thinking in this regard while accepting the general idea of fallible knowledge. Philosophical hermeneutics, critical theory, pragmatism, and some versions of feminist epistemology argue that knowledge is never something created out of neutral empirical data; rather, it is actively constructed – hence, knowledge claims are always interpretations that are culturally and historically contingent, reflective of certain interests, and infused with moral and political values. Of course, efforts to know always have at their disposal something to work with (i.e., material events, actions, texts, people, and so on). But what we make of the meanings of what is to be known is always constructed in some significant way. These epistemologies reject the notion that a subject (inquirer) can remain disengaged from the object of understanding, as well as the idea that a subject's knowledge is a straightforward representation of "what is out there." Distinctions among these constructionist epistemologies relate, in part, to how they interpret the consequences of the fact that all knowledge is constructed in and out of interaction between human beings and their world.

Some constructionist epistemologies endorse a pragmatic and practical rationality and look to dialogue, argumentation, and practical reason in an Aristotelian sense as the ways in which knowledge is created in social practices. They accept that knowledge is by definition uncertain and that the best we can do is make a stand on the basis of (admittedly fallible) human judgment that requires the use of both reason and evidence. We make this stand in light of contingent, practical circumstances. In other words there is no ultimate test for what constitutes adequate and legitimate knowledge independent of the demands of a given situation. We are always deciding what is appropriate and effective action and knowledge given the moral-practical situation in which we find ourselves.

So, for example, one could never give an unconditional and unqualified answer to the question, "What would it mean to intervene effectively in this situation?" absent a full grasp of the situation in question. This response abandons epistemology with a capital "E" – the search for the foundations or essences of knowledge – but retains the idea of epistemology with a lowercase "e" – reflection of various kinds about what it means to know in given circumstances. Operating in this way, these constructionist epistemologies are relatively continuous with the Enlightenment belief in the emancipatory power of reason.

Other constructionist epistemologies are, at the very least, a good deal less hopeful about the power of reason (and dialogue, argument, etc.) and, at worst, seek to rupture the connection with this Enlightenment notion. These epistemologies promote radical skepticism or epistemological nihilism. They hold that plural constructions of meaning, diverse perspectives, the absence of certainty and foundations, shifting identities of subjects, and the like all add up to either a radical undecidability of all claims to know, or that what constitutes knowledge is inextricably connected to analytics of interest/power. These epistemologies (if they can be called this) are dedicated to demonstrating dissensus and disruption in supposed understanding, and constantly aiming to unsettle any claim to know.

SEE ALSO: Feminism and Science, Feminist Epistemology; Knowledge; Knowledge, Sociology of; Objectivity; Postpositivism; Pragmatism

REFERENCES AND SUGGESTED READINGS

Bohman, J. (1991) *New Philosophy of Social Science: Problems of Indeterminacy*. MIT Press, Cambridge, MA.

Grayling, A. C. (1996) Epistemology. In: Bunnin, N. & Tsui-James, E. P. (Eds.), *The Blackwell Companion to Philosophy*. Blackwell, Oxford, pp. 38–63.

Haack, S. (1998) *Manifesto of a Passionate Moderate*. University of Chicago Press, Chicago.

Hiley, D. R., Bohman, J. F., & Shusterman, R. (Eds.) (1991) *The Interpretive Turn*. Cornell University Press, Ithaca, NY.

Hollis, M. (1996) Philosophy of Social Science. In: Bunnin, N. & Tsui-James, E. P. (Eds.), *The Blackwell Companion to Philosophy*. Blackwell, Oxford, pp. 358–87.

Taylor, C. (1995) Overcoming Epistemology. In: *Philosophical Arguments*. Harvard University Press, Cambridge, MA.

Turner, S. P. & Roth, P. A. (2003) *The Blackwell Guide to the Philosophy of the Social Sciences*. Blackwell, Oxford.

essentialism and constructionism

Ken Plummer

The debate over constructionism and essentialism is a longstanding philosophical argument, from Plato and Aristotle to contemporary debates over deconstruction in literary theory. Broadly and simply, essentialism suggests that qualities are inherent in objects of study, with little reference to contexts, ambiguities, and relativities. It is a "belief in the real, true essence of things" (Fuss 1989: xi). By contrast, constructionism (and its allied concept deconstruction, as put forward by Derrida) suggests qualities are always bound up with historically produced, contextually bound meanings or discourses. They are always open to change and never fixed. Many terms are allied antinomies such as absolutism and relativism, realism and interpretivism, and holism and methodological individualism. Other terms, such as humanism, can be used by either camp.

These ideas came to be applied to the field of sexuality during the late 1960s and 1970s and for two decades it was the primary debate in the newer groups studying sexuality. Drawing initially from the work of symbolic interactionists (Blumer's *Symbolic Interactionism*, 1969; Gagnon and Simon's *Sexual Conduct*, 1973), the highly influential work of Peter Berger and Thomas Luckmann's *The Social Construction of Reality* (1967), of feminism, and of the later Foucault (in *The History of Sexuality: Volume 1*, 1977), the core idea emerged that human sexuality was socially constructed. This meant that, for example, homosexuality was also socially constructed: it had a history, and was produced in different ways at different times. There was no uniform type of homosexual; it was a multiple experience that was constantly open to change. By contrast, essentialists clung to the idea that sexuality was a fixed and powerful biological drive and that the homosexual was a clear kind of being (often defined by biology). Conflicts over these positions became widespread, culminating in two international conferences in Amsterdam – one headed by the essentialists, the other by the constructionists (Van Nierkerk & Van Der Meer 1989).

Essentialist theories of sexual identities suggest that an inner sense of self unfolds through biological or psychic processes, and the task is to uncover the "true" meaning of who one is sexually. A classic reading of Freud would suggest that although one is born of "polymorphous perversity" and potential bisexuality, that is channeled into a relatively stable and repressed sexual and gender identity through the resolution of the Oedipal complex. Through inner struggles with feelings towards the mother and father, children assemble a (largely unconscious) libidinal structure which helps to define then as male and female, homosexual and heterosexual.

Constructionist theories of sexual identities are concerned with locating oneself within a framework of sexual categorizations. Most commonly, identities are seen as heterosexual, homosexual, bisexual. But there are many others, such as sado-masochistic, sex worker, pedophiliac, or person with AIDS (PWA). Such terms, once invented, can be seen to characterize a person. But many of these are new; they are historically produced. Thus, Ned Katz in *The Invention of Heterosexuality* (1995) suggests that the idea of the heterosexual was not invented until the late nineteenth century, and that indeed the identity of homosexual was invented prior to this. This was also a period of clear sexual polarization – identities of being sexual were divided into a clear binary system that did not exist before (as Thomas Laqueur suggests in his *Making Sex*, 1990).

VARIATIONS AND PUZZLES

Several problems have been identified with this debate. The first suggests that the debate tends to erect a false dualism or binary tension, in which each term actually comes to depend on the other. Without essentialism, constructionism would not make sense (Fuss 1989). Secondly, it is suggested that the debate is frequently drawn too starkly and sharply and that there are in fact "different degrees of social construction," ranging from those who more modestly suggest historical and cultural variability of meanings to those who suggest "there is no essential . . . sexual impulse" (Vance 1989). Thirdly, it has been suggested that ideas of constructionism when taken in their simplest form create ways of thinking that are almost commonplace. And finally, the political implications of the debates are unclear. Constructionists can be radical and conservative; and so can essentialists. Spivak (1984–5) suggest that strategic essentialism champions essentialism even if it is not fully believed in because it is needed in the fighting of conflicts, intellectual arguments, and political battles. It can be a useful shorthand.

This debate has been one of the most prominent in sexual theory in the latter part of the twentieth century and has at least had the virtue of making researchers more aware of the shifting social meanings of sex and the sexual cultures that are linked to them.

SEE ALSO: Constructionism; Foucault, Michel; Homosexuality; Lesbianism; Symbolic Interaction; Womanism

REFERENCES AND SUGGESTED READINGS

Fuss, D. (1989) *Essentially Speaking*. Routledge, London.

Greenberg, D. (1988) *The Construction of Homosexuality*. University of Chicago Press, Chicago.

Van Nierkerk, K. & Van Der Meer, T. (Eds.) (1989) *Homosexuality? Which Homosexuality?* An Dekker, Amsterdam.

Vance, C. S. (1989) Social Construction Theory: Problemss in the History of Sexuality. In: Van Nierkerk, K. & Van Der Meer, T. (Eds.) (1989) *Homosexuality? Which Homosexuality?* An Dekker, Amsterdam, pp. 13–34.

Velody, I. & Williams, R. (1998) *The Politics of Constructionism*. Sage, London.

Spivak, G. C. (1984–5) Criticism, Feminism and the Institution. *Thesis Eleven* 10–11: 175–87.

ethic of care

Joya Misra

During the 1980s, a number of feminist scholars developed the concept of an ethic of care, which posited an approach to morality focused around caring. This approach drew upon many earlier currents of thought, which argued women's morality centers around nurturing/mothering, cooperation, and maintaining relationships. Sara Ruddick (1980, 1989) espoused an ethics focused around "maternal thinking" (attentive love and trust), which she argued could be used to transform private relations of love and caring into public discussions of peace. Nel Noddings (1984) similarly suggested that an ethic of caring could help create moral people, criticizing dominant ethical approaches as problematically placing "principles above persons." These works valorize the assumed ethical values of "women," and have been criticized for their essentialist tendencies.

During the same period, Carol Gilligan (1977, 1982), in her groundbreaking research on moral development, coined the term "ethic of care," which she compared to an "ethic of justice" to describe two modes of gendered moral reasoning. Gilligan argued that while an ethic of justice primarily reflects fairness and abstract, individual rights, an ethic of care centers around specific contextual circumstances and responsibility in relationships (Lister 1997). According to Gilligan, men are more likely to draw upon an ethic of justice, while women express both ethics, in part because women are more likely to view themselves as connected to others relationally. Gilligan's work has been tremendously influential. However, it has also been roundly criticized for an implied gender essentialism, though Gilligan herself rejects any notion of absolute gender differences (Larrabee 1993; Tronto 1993). Scholars such as Linda Nicholson and Carol

Stack also effectively critique Gilligan's lack of focus on historical context and the potential differences in moral reasoning among women, by class, race/ethnicity, age, and so on. (Larrabee 1993). Yet, Patricia Hill Collins (1990), while critical of Gilligan's formulation, draws from the ideology of an ethic of care in discussing black feminist approaches, linking caring to political activism.

For more recent theorists, an ethic of care must be separated from essentialist notions of "women's morality," which places women on the outside of political and cultural institutions, and excludes many women from its definition. In doing so, recent scholarship emphasizes the importance of bringing the ethic of care into the public sphere, or politicizing care (Larrabee 1993; McLaughlin 1997). Joan Tronto (1993) argues for shifting from a "feminine" to a feminist care ethic by placing care within its political context, and in doing so, recognizing how care is central to existing structures of inequality and power in society. An ethic of care requires attentiveness to the need for care, taking responsibility for care, providing competent care, and responsiveness from the care receiver. The central moral question for an ethic of care then revolves around how we can best meet our care responsibilities, taking account of the needs of both caregivers and care receivers (Tronto 1993). Yet, in order to improve the status of care and caregivers and the quality of care, we must understand care as a political idea, and recognize how social, political, and cultural institutions shape care and could be reformulated to support care more effectively. Tronto (1993) suggests that an ethic of care requires dedication to both valuing care and reshaping institutions to reflect the importance of care. An ethic of care is then not simply an abstract principle, but an ethic that forces us to consider inequalities inherent at both local and global levels.

Recent scholarship emphasizes the importance of viewing the ethic of care as related to and interdependent with an ethic of justice based on rights. For these scholars, an ethic of care is a necessary but not sufficient element to create a moral and just society. As Ruth Lister (1997: 115) argues, both an ethic of care and an ethic of justice are enriched in combination; indeed, an ethic of care without an ethic of justice could "perpetuate the exploitative gendering of care relationships." These works also emphasize the importance of placing an ethic of caring within its political context, and recognizing its potential role in activism and social change.

SEE ALSO: Black Feminist Thought; Caregiving; Carework; Elder Care; Gender Ideology and Gender Role Ideology; Maternalism; Socialization, Gender

REFERENCES AND SUGGESTED READINGS

Collins, P. H. (1990) *Black Feminist Thought: Knowledge, Consciousness, and the Politics of Empowerment.* Routledge, New York.

Gilligan, C. (1977) In a Different Voice: Women's Conceptions of Self and of Morality. *Harvard Educational Review* 47(4): 481–517.

Gilligan, C. (1982) *In a Different Voice: Psychological Theory and Women's Development.* Harvard University Press, Cambridge, MA.

Larrabee, M. J. (Ed.) (1993) *An Ethic of Care: Feminist and Interdisciplinary Perspectives.* Routledge, New York.

Lister, R. (1997) *Citizenship: Feminist Perspectives.* New York University Press, New York.

McLaughlin, J. (1997) An Ethic of Care: A Valuable Political Tool? *Politics* 17(1): 17–23.

Noddings, N. (1984) *Caring: A Feminine Approach to Ethics and Moral Education.* University of California, Berkeley.

Ruddick, S. (1980) Maternal Thinking. *Feminist Studies* 6(2): 342–67.

Ruddick, S. (1989) *Maternal Thinking: Toward a Politics of Peace.* Beacon Press, Boston.

Tronto, J. C. (1993) *Moral Boundaries: A Political Argument for an Ethic of Care.* Routledge, New York.

ethics, business

Martin Kornberger and Carl Rhodes

The concept of ethics has a long history in western philosophy. Usually, ethics is understood as reflecting on and recommending concepts of right and wrong behavior. Following this definition, business ethics is the reflection on the ethical behavior of business organizations.

Much discussion of business ethics focuses on the ethical consequences of the pursuit of economic interests by business. On the one hand, some argue "good ethics is good business," suggesting that the pursuit of economic interests within lawgiven restrictions will automatically lead to ethical behavior. On the other hand, more critical ethicists argue the pursuit of economic self-interest by firms is fundamentally opposed to ethical conduct. In their perspective, financial profit and moral principles cannot be aligned. Such considerations engender considerable debate both within organizations and in the public sphere more generally. The practical implications of this in contemporary times is that organizations are more and more under pressure to rethink the ethical consequences of their behavior and readjust their actions accordingly (for a business example, see Royal Dutch/Shell Group 1998).

The young but rapidly growing body of academic literature reflects the importance of business ethics. Although ethics have their antecedents both in ancient philosophy and religion, business ethics is an emerging discipline. Further, while a consideration of the ethics of business can be traced to the seminal work of Adam Smith (1863), the explicit development of business ethics as a field of research and study is much more recent. The first *Journal of Business Ethics* was founded in 1981, quickly followed by others such as *Business and Professional Ethics Journal, Journal of Business and Professional Ethics*, and *Business Ethics Quarterly*. The breadth of research areas within business ethics includes ethics and trust, ethics, management and leadership, ethics and organizational reward systems, ethics and organizational culture, ethics and empowerment, ethics and organizational power, interpersonal relationships and ethics, corporate social responsibility, corporate sustainability, ethics and financial investment, and ethical decision-making.

NORMATIVE AND DESCRIPTIVE ETHICS

For some, business ethics is conceived of as a *normative* ethics in that it seeks to establish means of judging whether business practices are right or wrong. This can be done both to assist managers in dealing with moral dilemmas and to enable past actions to be judged as to their ethicality. Business ethics is also an applied ethics because it seeks to use such normative models in order to investigate the ethicality of the nature and consequences of particular events or practices in business. In this normative approach, business ethics in practice is generally understood as being related to the rules and/or cultural norms that govern, or should govern, organizational conduct. In organizations this commonly means that managing ethics is done through formalized codes of conduct that should govern everyday actions and decisions. Indeed, it is reported that 78 percent of the US top 1000 companies have a code of conducts (Nijhof et al. 2003). This approach is also used in theories of business ethics which develop normative models for passing ethical judgment on business practices (Gatewood & Carroll 1991) or propose the development of ethical rules for organizations (Beyer & Nino 1999).

The study of business ethics has also been pursued as a *descriptive* exercise because it uses scientific analysis to describe the actual behavior of organizations and their members. This descriptive approach would not seek normative guidelines that ought to be applied in practice, but rather monitor and describe what actually happens. The key question in both approaches is whether ethics are *relative* to history and tradition (e.g., given that bribery might be an established part of one country's business culture, it would be considered unethical in other countries) or whether is a set of *absolute* norms that are valid any time, anywhere in the world (e.g., men and women should be treated equally regardless of religious belief). These differentiators are contested in the face of key issues in business ethics such as corruption, manipulative advertising, whistle blowing, the environmental impact of business, customer rights, workplace harassment, and equal opportunities for women and minorities. Business ethics is also concerned with the ethical treatment of employees, echoing longstanding concern over the possibilities of worker exploitation in the capitalist labor process. Conversely, there have also been controversies over rising levels of

remuneration for chief executives and other top-level managers.

RELATIONSHIP BETWEEN ETHICS AND BUSINESS

A key issue that has been addressed and debated within business ethics is the possible relationship between ethicality and business activity in general. One approach suggests that ethics and business can and should be aligned in order to create competitive advantage (Raiborn & Payne 1996). The core argument is that ethics does not contradict the driving forces behind business organization and that there is no conflict of interest between profits and principles. As an example, Francis and Armstrong (2003) argue an ethically informed risk management strategy increases commercial outcomes, prevents fraud, and lifts corporate reputation. This reflects a more general position that an organization's ethical commitment is aligned with its self-interest. Such a perspective dates back to Adam Smith's argument that maximizing personal advantage will lead through the mechanism of self-interested actors competing in the market to a maximum of collectively beneficial outcomes. In sum, this suggests that "good ethics is good business" and that profits and principles are mutually inclusive. Another example of this is the practice of "strategic philanthropy" (Porter & Kramer 2002), where organizations choose to make charitable and philanthropic donations in order to strengthen their competitive position by, for example, developing the business environment in the markets where they operate or enhancing their public image. Similarly, it has been argued that an increased focus on ethics by organizations can lead to an increase in organizational commitment and hence productivity (Cullen et al. 2003). According to this approach, good management will be by definition both a harbinger of profits and ethical outcomes.

More critical approaches to business ethics question the convenience of the arguments outlined above and are skeptical about the possibility of profit-seeking organizations being ethical. This approach criticizes the core assumptions that provide the cornerstones of classic management and organization theory by suggesting that moral principles are of higher priority than profits (Quinn and Jones 1995). Here, ethics are seen as confronting business rationality because each abides by different and contradictory values. At an extreme, this approach asks whether business ethics is possible in a (capitalist) system driven by the pursuit of profits (Jones 2003). This suggests that the reason for labeling strategic behavior as ethical, or for developing ethical rules, is seen as calculative by nature and thus ethically dubious. Further, even when ethical rules are developed, this may be done not with a concern for the ethicality of organizational action, but rather for external consumption (Kjonstad & Willmott 1995) by shareholders, customers, governments, and other stakeholders. The argument is that the very idea of business ethics is an oxymoron.

ORGANIZATIONAL AND INDIVIDUAL RESPONSIBILITY

Another key issue for understanding business ethics is a consideration of the relationship between the ethical responsibility of individuals and that of the organization as a whole. For some, ethics resides very much with the individual human being (manager or employee) who has to defend ethical values and make ethical choices, often in spite of their organization. This also suggests that unethical organizational behavior results from the individual actions of "bad apples" who are either amoral or guided by immoral principles. Such an individualization of ethics suggests that it is particular people who are ultimately responsible for ethical behavior and that the organizational requirement is for an "empowering ethics" which supports moral learning and development instead of restricting ethics through codes (Konjstad & Willmott 1995). Business ethics thus emerges when people are "morally assertive" and use their personal ethics to mediate corporate priorities (Watson 2003). In short, this suggests that ethics is a moral task of managers who are personally "in charge" of ethics. In relation to ethical rule systems in organizations, such a view has been used to argue that because rules reduce individual margins of freedom they provide a form of discipline that can prevent people from acting ethically in order to transform organizations (Ibarra-Colada 2002: 178). In this scenario, the organization (and its rules) is a powerful, restricting machine, against or within which the ethical individual can/should act ethically. From this perspective, an organization is an ethically questionable entity whose ethicality can only be tempered by individuals who act in relation to the rules that constitute organizations through behavior guided by a personal ethics (ten Bos 1997).

In contrast, others have argued that organizational systems can provide the basis for ethics in a way that transcends individual action alone. Such an approach can be traced to Weber's seminal work on bureaucracy in the early twentieth century. In contemporary times this has emerged from a critique of changes to organizations that have seen them move away from bureaucratic forms of organizing. This suggests that organizational changes favoring flexibility, enterprise, and short-termism wither away trust, loyalty, and mutual commitment in organizations (Sennett 1998). Thus, organizations can and should be organized such that they pursue a communal ethics. This opposes an individualistic ethics which stresses autonomy, moral responsibility, and freedom towards one of mutual obligation and respect for standards. From this perspective, it is argued that it is precisely formal organization that makes ethics possible by training managers in technical expertise, and through a clearly defined hierarchy that describes everybody's responsibility, duty, and rights, through the understanding of the office as "vocation," detached from personal privileges, passions, and emotions (du Guy 2000).

Given the growing impact of business organizations on the lives of individuals, global politics, and the environment, a consideration of business ethics is critical to responsible forms of business. As corporate disasters such as Enron, the rise of NGOs such as Greenpeace, and the success of "ethical" businesses such as the Body Shop show, business ethics will be one of the key future challenges for businesses. Thus, managing ethics will be just as important as managing finance, production, or distribution.

SEE ALSO: Culture, Organizations and; Ethics, Fieldwork; Ethics, Research; Norms; Values

REFERENCES AND SUGGESTED READINGS

Beyer, J. M. & Nino, D. (1999) Ethics and Cultures in International Business. *Journal of Management Inquiry* 8(3): 287–98.

Cullen, J., Parboteeah, K., & Victor, B. (2003) The Effects of Ethical Climates on Organizational Commitment: A Two-Study Analysis. *Journal of Business Ethics* 46: 127–41.

du Guy, P. (2000) *In Praise of Bureaucracy: Weber, Organization, Ethics*. Sage, London.

Francis, R. & Armstrong, A. (2003) Ethics as a Risk Management Strategy: The Australian Experience. *Journal of Business Ethics* 45: 375–85.

Gatewood, R. D. & Carroll, A. B. (1991) Assessment of Ethical Performance of Organization Members. *Academy of Management Review* 16: 667–91.

Ibarra-Colada, E. (2002) Organizational Paradoxes and Business Ethics: In Search of New Modes of Existence. In: Clegg, S. (Ed.), *Management and Organization Paradoxes*. John Benjamins, Amsterdam, pp. 165–84.

Jones, C. (2003) As If Business Ethics Were Possible, "Within Such Limits." *Organization* 10: 223–48.

Kjonstad, B. & Willmott, H. (1995) Business Ethics: Restrictive or Empowering? *Journal of Business Ethics* 14: 445–64.

Nijhof, A., Cludts, S., Fisscher, O., & Laan, A. (2003) Measuring the Implementation of Codes of Conduct: An Assessment Method Based on a Process Approach of the Responsible Organization. *Journal of Business Ethics* 45: 65–78.

Porter, M. & Kramer, M. (2002) The Competitive Advantage of Corporate Philanthropy. *Harvard Business Review* (December): 37–68.

Quinn, D. P. & Jones, T. M. (1995) An Agent Morality View of Business Policy. *Academy of Management Review* 20: 22–43.

Raiborn, C. & Payne, D. (1996) TQM: Just What the Ethicist Ordered. *Journal of Business Ethics* 15: 963–72.

Royal Dutch/Shell Group (1998) *Profits and Principles: Does There Have To Be A Choice?* AIA, London.

Sennett, R. (1998) *The Corrosion of Character: The Personal Consequences of Work in the New Capitalism*. W. W. Norton, New York.

Smith, A. (1863) *The Wealth of Nations: An Inquiry Into the Nature and Causes of the Wealth of Nations*. Black, Edinburgh.

ten Bos, R. (1997) Business Ethics and Bauman Ethics. *Organization Studies* 18: 997–1014.

Watson, T. J. (2003) Ethical Choice in Managerial Work: The Scope for Moral Choices in an Ethically Irrational World. *Human Relations* 56: 167–85.

ethics, fieldwork

Jane Zeni

Ethics in social sciences fieldwork draws on the perspectives of philosophy, law, and psychology to guide decision-making by researchers and policymakers. Ethics can be defined as "the study of right and wrong; of the moral choices people make and the way in which they seek to justify them" (Thompson 1999: 1). Consciously or otherwise, field researchers make ethical decisions whenever they gather, interpret, or present their data. There is a growing consensus that ethical practice in fieldwork cannot simply be guided by the rules that govern biomedical or psychological research in laboratory settings.

These rules are based on the Nuremberg Code (1949), which established the principle of "informed consent," and the Declaration of Helsinki (1964), which mandated the protection of human participants in biomedical research. Institutional Review Board (IRB) and Research Ethics Committee (REC) reviews have their roots in such notorious abuses as the experiments by Nazi physicians on concentration camp prisoners. In the United States, the Tuskegee syphilis study recruited indigent black men for research they believed would include treatment; instead, researchers documented their illness and eventual deaths for 40 years, even after the discovery of penicillin offered a cure.

Since 1974, all research conducted in US colleges and universities that receive federal funding must be approved by an IRB; in Australia and increasingly in the UK, the REC plays a similar role. This process has now been adapted by many schools and public agencies. The protection of human participants has expanded to research across the social sciences, in qualitative as well as experimental modes. An IRB review typically starts with a set of yes/no questions:

- Is this research designed to study normal educational practices conducted in an established educational setting?
- Does the research use survey procedures, interviews, educational tests, or observation of public behavior? (Subquestions ask if participants will remain anonymous, and if not, whether they will be at risk.)
- Does the research involve collection or study of existing data, documents, or other records? (Anonymity is encouraged except in public records.)

The prospective researcher next explains the purpose and methods of the study and attaches the consent documents to show that research participants will be clearly informed before they agree to participate. Research using data from vulnerable and underage participants must undergo a more extensive review.

An IRB also mandates training in research ethics. Many US universities have adopted a free web-based course from the National Institutes of Health (NIH) that guides novice researchers through the principles underlying ethical review with a set of cases and dilemmas (www.nihtraining.com/crtpub_508/index. html). While these reforms are significant, the ethical reviews pose problems for qualitative researchers in the social sciences.

As the use of NIH training suggests, the model is quantitative experimental and survey research. Cases are drawn from biomedical and psychological studies. If "research ethics" in qualitative fieldwork is identified with IRB/REC principles, some important risks may be misconstrued. Two such principles – "informed consent" and "anonymity" – can illustrate the dilemma.

Informed consent has been considered the core of ethical review. However, at the start of most qualitative studies even the researcher cannot fully predict the course of the inquiry. Trying to cover all possibilities, the researcher may prepare a document in legal language that is meaningless or frightening to the uninitiated. One solution is to negotiate informed consent in stages. A teacher might launch a classroom study with a newsletter asking parents for a simple consent to participate. During the months of data gathering and interpretation, the teacher-researcher would communicate openly with participants. Later, if the work will be published, certain parents would be asked for explicit consent to share their child's data (Clayton Research Review Team 2001). People need to know the kind of text or presentation, the audience(s) who will have access, and the context in which their words, names, or pseudonyms will appear.

Anonymity to protect the privacy of research participants is generally recommended for research in all genres. However, anonymity may offer little protection in fieldwork involving literate and knowing participants. For example, if a sociologist conducts a small-scale qualitative study of dating practices among university students, the published report may lead to lively speculation on campus. Similarly, if a vivid case study appears under a teacher-author's name, the students may be recognized from the lunch room to the school board. Any social researcher should realize that publication may touch the "subjects" of a study – whether or not they are named.

Ethical dangers in fieldwork usually arise, not in the methods or process of research, but in its later dissemination. The findings may place individuals at risk of professional embarrassment, personal reprisals, or loss of reputation. On the other hand, participants who have worked collaboratively with the author may want credit for their intellectual contributions rather than anonymity. Choosing the most ethical approach to informed consent, anonymity, or intellectual property rights requires thinking through the local situation as well as the global principles of the ethical review.

Ethical guidelines specific to field researchers doing qualitative studies have been developed inductively through analysis of a growing body of cases. A useful way to organize this body of material is to examine the researcher and the researched – how each is constructed, their roles in the study, and the relationships between them. Studies can be arranged on a continuum from traditional "outsider" (researcher enters the field as a stranger) to complete "insider" (researcher has an established role – educator, social worker, community organizer – within the field being studied). Moving along the continuum will foreground certain ethical issues while resolving others.

At one end of the continuum are "outsider" studies in which a scholar, typically from a university or research institution, examines a community that is both unfamiliar and distinct from the communities where the scholar normally resides. If the researcher maintains the outsider stance, revealing little of his or her own subjectivity, then the ethical decisions and dangers seem clear-cut: present the facts, avoid bias, do no harm. Smith (1990) describes three notorious cases from the 1960s and the 1970s in which social researchers assumed roles that gave them access to observe gay sex, terrorist plots, and apocalyptic religion. Today's IRBs, however, forbid deception in field studies unless the researcher has evidence of proportionate benefits and a plan for honest and prompt debriefing.

Since the 1980s, discussions of ethics in fieldwork have increasingly advocated knowing interaction between the researcher and the researched. According to the principles of "participant observation," rooted in the social sciences rather than in medicine (Glaser & Strauss 1967; McCall & Simmons 1969), a researcher enters the field from somewhere outside, but strives to understand the perspective of the insider. The researcher is ethically obliged to present his or her role and purpose to participants; the researcher is also obliged to represent the participants respectfully in published findings.

Recent scholars are moving further along the continuum, away from the ideal of the neutral observer. The anthropologist constructs an authorial "signature," a sense of "being there" (Geertz 1988) to become for the reader a trustworthy narrator of this story. This increasing self-representation in fieldwork has generated two ethical arguments. According to one, the author should "bracket" whatever personal experience or bias might distort the picture; according to the other, the author should claim that insider position as the source of credibility. The former view, associated with phenomenology, has been criticized for an underlying postpositivism (Guba 1990: 20–3). The latter, called standpoint theory, is associated with feminism and critical social theory. Standpoint

theorists propose that researchers who resemble the participants in race, class, gender, ethnicity, sexual orientation, disability, or other dimensions of culture are best positioned to understand their experience. Researchers from marginalized groups are "outsiders-within," having access to the perspectives of the majority culture as well (Banks 1998; Collins 1998). Critics, however, warn that standpoint theory makes the self, and one's own roles and communities, the only legitimate field of study.

Researchers from a dominant culture are also exploring these issues. They hope to offer trustworthy insights by analyzing their own lenses as well as the experiences of the Other. By shedding the mask of cultural invisibility, perhaps any researcher can gain a double perspective that minimizes distortions (Kirsch 1999). "Covenantal ethics" (Smith 1990) aptly names such relationships of mutual respect and caring.

If traditional scholarly "outsiders" represent one end of a continuum, then the opposite end is represented by researchers who are themselves "insiders," full participants with roles to play that did not originate with the study. This is the action research stance (also called "practitioner research" or "teacher research" in the field of education). An action researcher does not struggle with the challenges of entering the field, and the risk of deception is small. Yet new ethical questions emerge. Mitchell (2004) warns of the tension between the researcher role and the teacher role, and the risk that students will be exploited. Maclean and Mohr (1999), however, argue that the professional role and commitment to students, coworkers, and community members must always take priority over the data; they define ethics among colleagues as "respect for each other's professionalism" (p. 129).

Practitioners doing action research or collaborative studies should especially beware of relying on the traditional approaches to informed consent and anonymity. Reputations can be at risk if the findings include "bad news." Should a researcher protect certain participants by composite portraits rather than traditional interviews? Should some fieldnotes remain unpublished if the point can be supported by data that will not embarrass participants? Such ethical questions can be answered only at the level of specific studies in specific field settings.

One new field setting is not a physical place, and it disrupts such categories as "being there," "interviewing," and "participant observation." Social research in electronic communities is burgeoning, along with new ethical dilemmas for researchers. Privacy is difficult to protect when numerous, perhaps unknown "others" participate in a listserv or blog. Consent forms present new challenges, and electronic signatures may or may not be accepted by an IRB. Following an action research model, a researcher might send an electronic newsletter explaining the study, inviting questions, and promising to omit any data from people who opt out. Later, if there is to be a publication quoting certain participants, a paper consent letter would be sent by regular mail. Mann and Stewart (2000) suggest that since the "online world" lacks the network of laws and traditions that regulate most social behavior, it gains an aura of transgression.

Field researchers must accept that no perspective can be free of ethical dilemmas. Instead, a research dialogue should bring together insiders and outsiders. Such approaches include "constructivist inquiry" (Denzin & Lincoln 2000) or the "deliberative democratic view" (House & Howe 1999). The ethical mandate is inclusion, representing the perspectives of multiple others as well as the self. As Fred Erickson quipped, "Neither the insider nor the outsider is gifted with immaculate perception" (in Cochran-Smith & Lytle 1993: ix).

Turning from the researcher to the researched, Sharon Lee (2001) proposes a parallel continuum: subject, informant, participant, collaborator. The traditional term, "human subjects," falls at one end, isolating the researched from any contamination by the researcher, and stripping the context where the research happens. Currently, the preferred federal language is "human participants," implying some level of involvement rather than passive consent. Going further, van den Berg (2001) refers to the "inhabitants of the research," suggesting context as well as collaborative relationships. Reflecting on this continuum, Eikeland (2006) rejects the "condescending ethics" of protecting research subjects, arguing that the standard for fieldwork is the "community of inquirers and interpreters."

Nevertheless, respect for participants calls for the acknowledgment that most research communities have a fixed time period and predictable end. Seeing an interviewer as a friend and sharing personal life stories is an abuse of trust if that "friend" will disappear to write up a case study (Kirsch 1999: 30). The "therapeutic assumption" or the "educative assumption" may lead participants to see a doctor's main goal as healing and a teacher's main goal as student learning. They may consent to a study whose goal is to benefit, not themselves, but some wider population in the future.

Fieldwork usually takes place amid asymmetrical power relations. Most researchers "study down" (portraying the experiences of people with less social or institutional power, from families in poverty to college students) rather than "study up" (portraying the experiences of corporate executives or elites). Ethical field studies must treat a participant holding less power with the respect that participants holding more power would demand. Issues of ownership and intellectual property rights are now being discussed in English departments, where composition studies include samples of student writing, and in social sciences, where oral histories are recorded (Anderson 1998).

Collaborative research introduces another set of power issues. When a university professor or doctoral candidate engages in research with a community leader, teacher, or others in the field, the research may benefit one party disproportionately; university careers require publication, while the others do not. One party may also incur more risk than another; in the classic Smith and Geoffrey study (1968), the professor used his real name and the teacher, "Geoffrey," chose a pseudonym.

The "voice" of the report is rarely discussed as an ethical decision. While scholarly dialect can facilitate conversations among researchers, it can also exclude others from those conversations. A fieldworker should report at least some findings in language comprehensible to the stakeholders. To convey the variety of perspectives, some researchers create multigenre and multivoiced texts that honor the participants' right to co-interpretation (or counterinterpretation). For example, van den Berg (2001) redefines "accountability" as the researcher's

ethical and political responsibility to people in
the research scene. Participants are invited to
review a draft, and their responses may be
woven into the final report or appended as an
alternative view. Gloria Ladson-Billings (1994),
in her ethnographic portraits of urban teachers,
also portrays herself in three voices: as scholar,
as teacher, and as child recalling her own school
experiences. Such texts call attention to themselves as constructions. Some readers find them
powerful and convincing, literary as well as
scholarly; others may question how the portrait
was shaped by the writer.

As these examples suggest, an ethical review
of fieldwork should be more (not less) complex
than what is typically recommended for laboratory experiments. Instead of yes/no questions,
the researcher can adopt an inquiry stance,
returning to examine ethical issues at several
points in the process. Mason (1996: 29) suggests "a practical approach to ethics which
involves asking yourself difficult questions –
and pushing yourself hard to answer them."

To supplement the ethical review questions
cited above, field researchers have proposed
alternative lists (Sunstein 1996; Zeni 1998,
2001; Bishop 1999):

- What question am I exploring? Why?
- To whom am I professionally accountable?
- Which participants do I have some power
  over? Which have some power over me?
- Whose views of reality am I representing?
- Am I trying to interpret the experience of
  those who differ from me in culture (race,
  gender, class, etc.)?
- How have I prepared myself to understand
  the "other"?
- Is this my story, my informants' story, or a
  story that fits someone else's theory?
- What would happen if I shifted point of
  view to tell this story?
- Should my report include the voices of
  others, especially when their views differ
  from mine?

Such "difficult questions" can move ethical
decisions beyond the legalistic into the personal, the relational, the covenantal. Dialogue
among insiders and outsiders can help to nur-
ture an ethical practice of fieldwork.

SEE ALSO: Action Research; Ethics, Research;
Ethnography; Feminist Methodology; Feminist
Standpoint Theory; Institutional Review Boards
and Sociological Research; Naturalistic Inquiry;
Observation, Participant and Non-Participant;
Postpositivism; Trustworthiness

REFERENCES AND SUGGESTED READINGS

Anderson, P. V. (1998) Simple Gifts: Ethical Issues
in the Conduct of Person-Based Composition
Research. *College Composition and Communication*
49(1): 63–89.
Banks, J. (1998) The Lives and Values of Research-
ers: Implications for Educating Citizens in a
Multicultural Society. *Educational Researcher* 27
(7): 4–17.
Bishop, W. (1999) *Writing Ethnographic Research.*
Utah State University Press, Salt Lake City.
Clayton (Missouri) Research Review Team (2001)
"Who Owns the Story?" Ethical Issues in the
Conduct of Practitioner Research. In: Zeni, J.
(Ed.), *Ethical Issues in Practitioner Research.* Tea-
chers College Press, New York, pp. 45–54.
Cochran-Smith, M. & Lytle, S. (1993) *Inside/Out-
side: Teacher Research and Knowledge.* Teachers
College Press, New York.
Collins, P. H. (1998) *Fighting Words: Black Women
and the Search for Justice.* University of Minnesota
Press, Minneapolis.
Denzin, N. K. & Lincoln, Y. (2000) *Handbook of
Qualitative Research,* 2nd edn. Sage, Thousand
Oaks, CA.
Eikeland, O. (2006) Condescending Ethics and
Action Research: Extended Review Essay. *Action
Research* 4(1).
Geertz, C. (1988) *Works and Lives: The Anthropologist
as Author.* Stanford University Press, Stanford.
Glaser, B. & Strauss, A. (1967) *Discovery of Grounded
Theory.* Aldine, Chicago.
Guba, E. (Ed.) (1990) *The Paradigm Dialog.* Sage,
Thousand Oaks, CA.
House, E. & Howe, K. (1999) *Values in Evaluation
and Social Research.* Sage, Thousand Oaks, CA.
Kirsch, G. (1999) *Ethical Dilemmas in Feminist
Research: The Politics of Location, Interpretation,
and Publication.* SUNY Press, Albany, NY.
Ladson-Billings, G. (1994) *The Dreamkeepers: Suc-
cessful Teachers of African American Children.*
Jossey-Bass, San Francisco.
Lee, S. S. (2001) "A Root Out of a Dry Ground":
Resolving the Researcher/Researched Dilemma.
In: Zeni, J. (Ed.), *Ethical Issues in Practitioner*

Research. Teachers College Press, New York, pp. 61–71.

McCall, G. & Simmons, J. L. (1969) *Issues in Participant Observation: A Text and Reader*. Addison-Wesley, Reading, MA.

Maclean, M. & Mohr, M. (1999) *Teacher-Researchers at Work*. National Writing Project, Berkeley.

Mann, C. & Stewart, F. (2000) *Internet Communication and Qualitative Research: A Handbook for Researching Online*. Sage, Thousand Oaks, CA.

Mason, J. (1996) *Qualitative Researching*. Sage, Thousand Oaks, CA.

Mitchell, I. J. (2004) Identifying Ethical Issues in Self-Study Proposals. In: Loughran, J. J., Hamilton, M. L., LaBosky, V. K., & Russell, T. L. (Eds.), *International Handbook of Self Study of Teaching and Teacher Education Practices*. Kluwer, Dordrecht.

Pritchard, I. (2002) Travelers and Trolls: Practitioner Research and Institutional Review Boards. *Educational Researcher* 31(3): 3–13.

Smith, L. (1990) Ethics, Field Studies, and the Paradigm Crisis. In: Guba, E. (Ed.), *The Paradigm Dialog*. Sage, Thousand Oaks, CA, pp. 139–57.

Smith, L. & Geoffrey, W. (1968) *Complexities of an Urban Classroom*. Holt, Rinehart, & Winston, New York.

Sunstein, B. (1996) Culture on the Page: Experience, Rhetoric, and Aesthetics in Ethnographic Writing. In: Mortenson, P. & Kirsch, G. (Eds.), *Ethics and Representation in Qualitative Studies of Literacy*. National Council of Teachers of English, Urbana, IL, pp. 177–202.

Thompson, M. (1999) *Ethical Theory*. Hodder & Stoughton, London.

van den Berg, O. (2001) The Ethics of Accountability in Action Research. In: Zeni, J. (Ed.), *Ethical Issues in Practitioner Research*. Teachers College Press, New York, pp. 83–91.

Zeni, J. (1998) A Guide to Ethical Issues in Action Research. *Educational Action Research* 6(1): 9–19.

Zeni, J. (Ed.) (2001) *Ethical Issues in Practitioner Research*. Teachers College Press, New York.

ethics, research

J. I. (Hans) Bakker

It has always been important to recognize the rights of research subjects as individuals and as members of various kinds of groups or collectivities. Ethnic minorities and racial groups, for example, should not be treated any differently. They should be given the same respect as any other subgroup. That has not always been the case in the past. That was brought home particularly as a result of atrocities during World War II. "Ethics review ... emerged from the aftermath of the horrors of the Second World War, when Nazi-sponsored medical experiments furthered macabre social aims" (Hoonaard 2002: 3). The Nuremberg Code was an important step. The UN's Universal Declaration of Human Rights is another. However, beyond the more obvious concern with extreme violations, the precise philosophical articulation of ethics can vary according to whether the ethicist holds to some kind of theologically based or secular perspective.

There has been very little consideration of the context in which discussions of ethics occurs; societal "frames" and sets of such frames are often unstated assumptions which do not have conceptual or operational definitions outside of very specific times and places (Scheff 2005). Generally, humanist, neo-Kantian, pragmatist, or other secular ethical systems are most common (Canti 2004). The principle of the separation of church and state makes it difficult to adopt religiously based notions of the sacredness of the individual, but Kant's secular version, emphasizing respect for individual human dignity and autonomy, results in a similar awareness of the importance of not violating human dignity. While the philosophical questions concerning ethics are not frequently asked, there nevertheless are implied ethical standards that can be traced to ancient Greek and Enlightenment ethical viewpoints. For example, the ethics proposed by Descartes are quite different from Aristotelian ethics (Kahn 2005), but much current thinking goes back to Aquinas and Aristotle rather than Cartesian Enlightenment themes. Yet such issues are rarely discussed. A commonsense version of respect for human dignity and civil liberties is usually in the forefront. The general notion of utility is also frequently mentioned, with beneficence outweighing any possible harm. Mention of Aristotle's non-utilitarian notions of justice and equity (Smith 2001) would be considered out of place. The concept of ethics that is applied is not universal, but specific to a "modern" historical and societal context. That became apparent in the case of a sociological study of casual sex in public places (Humphries 1970). In the US, practical interpretations have been largely based on a form of pragmatist philosophy that does not attempt to interfere with research that could be considered reasonable, but also does not try to impose too many rules. Denzin and Lincoln (2003) take a somewhat critical view of some of the assumptions underpinning current notions of "interpretation" and their well-known book has had a significant impact among qualitative researchers. Denzin (2003: 486–9) projects greater interest in research guided by "postpositivist, constructivist, critical theory, and poststructural sensibilities." Ethical guidelines which operate now do not directly confront such postmodern approaches at a philosophical level, hence "ethics" is mostly regarded from a strictly "modernist" perspective.

While there has not been much discussion concerning philosophical underpinnings, there has been great concern expressed with regard to practical application. It is clear to all that there should be some ethical guidelines. Nevertheless, many researchers have felt inhibited by specific aspects of the protocols. The question of written versus verbal consent is deemed to be of great practical importance by many researchers. It may be difficult, for example, to obtain candid opinions from individuals or members of communities if the researcher has first to obtain written consent. Similarly, certain forms of experimental research may be considered too likely to interfere with respect for privacy or respect for autonomy. Institutional concerns are not necessarily deeply rooted in philosophical ethics. Instead, there is a desire to conform to the letter of the law. It is common practice to have a lawyer on an ethics board since the legal implications of violation of ethics are frequently a cause for concern among administrators. The importance of research ethics in the social sciences has been emphasized a great deal more as a result of legislation in the US which has created Investigative Review Boards (IRBs) that are ultimately the responsibility of the Office for Human Research Protection (OHRP). US federal guidelines for the protection of human "subjects" or participants have been interpreted in different ways by various actors (Levine 2001). According to the "Common Rule" (Section 46.101

[b]), certain categories of research may be exempt, but individual researchers are not free to exempt themselves. Key components which members of an IRB committee may consider for IRB approval involve (1) informed (written) consent, (2) confidentiality, (3) anonymity, (4) permission to drop out of the study at any time, (5) feedback to research participants, and (6) further steps in the approval process should the research be varied in any way. The data must be stored in a secure environment and is supposed to be destroyed after the study has been completed. Complete anonymity is often difficult to accomplish. Any deviation from any of those principles may result in lack of approval. Permission must be secured in writing. However, it is not always possible to secure informed consent in written form. Hence, for fieldwork in a developing country, a researcher may be granted permission to obtain only verbal consent, as per Section 46.117(c) of the regulations (AAA 2004). Information collected in everyday situations cannot be used retrospectively, since ethical approval was not obtained in advance. Then, too, there may be studies which require some degree of ruse. Obviously, it is not possible to obtain written informed consent from research participants who are not actually being informed about the true intent of the study. In psychological research, however, it is frequently necessary to keep the actual goal secret in order to obtain spontaneous responses. When interviewing mentally challenged individuals it is not always clear what guidelines should prevail (Flynn 1986).

Discussions of practical aspects of the IRB-REB model in the US and Canada have led to critiques of managerial aspects of the status quo and those practical concerns have in turn led to a rekindled interest in some of the broader methodological questions. The IRB model has been criticized for being basically a "biomedical" approach to research (WMA 2002), sometimes involving physically invasive procedures and frequently based on the application of a strict version of the "hypothetico-deductive method" as the key part of the scientific method (Nagel 1961). That deductive approach has not been easy to translate into ethnographic fieldwork and other forms of qualitative sociological research. Many qualitative researchers take a "grounded theory" approach and do not begin their research with hypotheses drawn from the existing literature. Hence, it is difficult to decide in advance what research instruments will be used. At the same time, "there is no logical reason to believe that qualitative analyses cannot be used to test deductive theory" (Lucas 2003).

Recent approaches which stress the way in which different models of science lead to different kinds of considerations concerning "values and objectivity" (Lacey 2005) are frequently left out of consideration. For example, a phenomenological approach to sociology (Barber 2004) can involve "ethnomethodological" research (Garfinkel 1972). In attempting to study nuances of expectations in everyday situations it would be deeply disturbing to announce ahead of time what is happening. The study of a "breach" in normal expectations requires that participants not be informed before the fact. Moreover, the research may not even be inductive. It may be exploratory research which involves a certain amount of guesswork, or "abduction." Such studies might at one time have been dealt with in an expedited manner by one or two individuals, but they now often require approval by a full committee. In reaching a decision the members of the committee may not all be equally well informed about all relevant questions pertaining to the theory being investigated, since they cannot all have expert knowledge on all social science theories. There may be a bias for or against experimental research as opposed to research in naturally occurring settings.

Certain categories of research do not require ethical approval from IRBs. For example, survey questionnaires which are distributed by an organization for the purposes of administrative change are not considered true research requiring ethical approval. Moreover, certain aspects of research are not subject to IRB approval. For example, the IRB is not concerned with the methodological approach of the research and does not offer advice concerning research design, use of statistical tests, and other such details of implementation. The primary concern is with research participants. Indeed, the move away from using the word "subjects" is probably indicative of the greater awareness of the importance of ethics, an awareness prompted by certain extreme cases of abuse.

Instances where research participants were administered drugs such as LSD without their knowledge or consent and earlier cases where subjects were given sexually transmitted diseases (Jones 1993) are grievous examples. Of course, much social science research is relatively harmless, or would appear to be so on the surface (Hoonaard 2002). An undergraduate or graduate research project involving a survey questionnaire does not necessarily constitute a great risk to participants. Nevertheless, all research has to be vetted by IRBs in the US. In Canada a similar approach is maintained by Research Ethics Boards (REBs), with similar concerns. The REBs were established in accord with a statement issued by the three major funding councils. The so-called "Tri-Council Policy Statement" of September 17, 1998 has had a major impact on the regulation of funded research proposals in Canada. The type of research being conducted can influence the way in which ethical guidelines are interpreted. The normative framework can also be influenced by the source of funding. Generally, there is less concern with ethical considerations in non-funded, social science student research that is not invasive and more attention paid to detail in heavily funded biomedical research that is heavily invasive (e.g., administration of drugs or carrying out of surgical procedures). Similarly, minors and "incompetent" adults may be regarded as having greater risk even if the research is perceived as being balanced by significant long-term benefits.

Confidentiality involves the data only being used for the explicit purposes for which permission had been granted and further consent prior to disclosure to third parties. Recontacting participants in order to obtain consent for secondary use of data requires further IRB (REB) approval. Whenever a human being is vulnerable it is highly likely that ethical approval should not be granted, especially if it is clear that their compromised position makes such persons manipulable. It can be argued that the principle of distributive justice requires that the burdens and benefits of all forms of research should be distributed among all sectors of the population.

Aunger (2004) argues forcefully that in ethnographic research a high degree of reflexivity is necessary. For example, informants may learn new information between one interview and the next. His comments can be applied to the ways in which all applications of research ethics procedures may sometimes disturb the way in which a subject is presented and understood. It is not just a matter of the skill level of the researcher; it is a systemic problem related to research design. The most extreme criticism comes from some postmodern ethnographers who deny the "objectification" that goes with "essentialist" notions of the self and therefore conclude that certain ethical guidelines do not easily fit in with their nuanced objectives (Angrosino & Mays de Pérez 2003; Taylor 2003). A pragmatic balance between methodological and practical concerns continues to be an elusive goal and the enormous variety of types of research undertaken make straightforward generalizations highly problematic and sometimes contested.

SEE ALSO: Ethics, Fieldwork; Ethnography; Institutional Review Boards and Sociological Research; Pragmatism

REFERENCES AND SUGGESTED READINGS

American Anthropological Association (2004) Statement on Ethnography and IRBs. *Code of Ethics*. AAA, Arlington, VA.

Angrosino, M. V. & Mays de Pérez, K. A. (2003) Rethinking Observation: From Method to Context. In: Denzin, N. K. & Lincoln, Y. S. (Eds.), *Collecting and Interpreting Qualitative Materials*, 2nd edn. Sage, Thousand Oaks, CA, pp. 107–54.

Aunger, R. (2004) *Reflexive Ethnographic Science*. Alta Mira Press, Walnut Creek, CA.

Barber, M. D. (2004) *The Participating Citizen: A Biography of Alfred Schütz*. State University of New York Press, Albany.

Canti, F. et al. (2004) *Tutorial in Research Ethics*. Québec Ministère de la Santé et des Services Sociaux, Montreal.

Denzin, N. K. (2003) The Practices and Politics of Interpretation. In: Denzin, N. K. & Lincoln, Y. S. (Eds.), *Collecting and Interpreting Qualitative Materials*, 2nd edn. Sage, Thousand Oaks, CA, pp. 458–98.

Denzin, N. K. & Lincoln, Y. S. (Eds.) (2003) *Collecting and Interpreting Qualitative Materials*, 2nd edn. Sage, Thousand Oaks, CA.

Flynn, M. (1986) Adults Who Are Mentally Handicapped as Consumers: Issues and Guidelines for Interviewing. *Journal of Mental Deficiency Research* 30: 369–77.

Garfinkel, H. (1972) Studies in the Routine Grounds of Everyday Activities. In: Sudnow, D. (Ed.), *Studies in Social Interaction*. Free Press, New York, pp. 1–30.

Hoonaard, W. C. van den (2002) *Walking the Tightrope: Ethical Issues for Qualitative Researchers*. University of Toronto Press, Toronto.

Humphries, L. (1970) *Tearoom Trade: Impersonal Sex in Public Places*. Aldine, Chicago.

Jones, J. H. (1993) *Bad Blood: The Tuskegee Syphilis Experiment*, 2nd edn. Free Press, New York.

Kahn, C. H. (2005) Aristotle versus Descartes on the Concept of the Mental. In: Salles, R. (Ed.), *Metaphysics, Soul, and Ethics in Ancient Thought*. Clarendon Press, Oxford, pp. 193–208.

Lacey, H. (2005) *Values and Objectivity in Science*. Rowman & Littlefield, Lanham, MD.

Levine, F. J. (2001) Weighing In on Protecting Human Research Participants: Let Our Voices Be Heard. *ASA Footnotes* 29(1): 2.

Lucas, J. W. (2003) Theory-Testing, Generalization, and the Problem of External Validity. *Sociological Theory* 21(3): 236–53.

Nagel, E. (1961) *The Structure of Science*. Harcourt Brace, New York.

Office for Human Research Protections (OHRP) (2005) *Federal Policy for the Protection of Human Subjects ("the Common Rule")*. US Government, Washington, DC.

Scheff, T. (2005) The Structure of Context: Deciphering *Frame Analysis*. *Sociological Theory* 23(4): 368–85.

Smith, T. W. (2001) *Revaluing Ethics: Aristotle's Dialectical Pedagogy*. State University of New York Press, Albany.

Taylor, B. C. (2003) Postmodernism, Ethnography, and Communications Studies. In: Clair, R. P. (Ed.), *Expressions of Ethnography: Novel Approaches to Qualitative Methods*. State University of New York Press, Albany, pp. 65–75.

World Medical Association (WMA) (2002 [1964]) *Ethical Principles for Medical Research Involving Human Subjects*. WMA, Washington, DC.

ethnic cleansing

Dusko Sekulic

The term ethnic cleansing refers to various policies of forcibly removing people of another ethnic group. At the more general level it can be understood as the expulsion of any "undesirable" population from a given territory not only due to its ethnicity but also as a result of its religion, or for political, ideological, or strategic considerations, or a combination of these characteristics.

The term entered the international vocabulary in connection with the Yugoslav wars. It comes from the Serbian/Croatian phrase *etnicko ciscenje*, whose literal translation is ethnic cleaning. In the Yugoslav media it started to be used in the early 1980s in relation to the alleged Kosovar Albanian policy of creating ethnically homogeneous territory in Kosovo by the expulsion of the Serbian population. The term itself was probably taken from the vocabulary of the former JNA (Yugoslav People's Army), which spoke of cleansing the territory (*ciscenje terena*) of enemies to take control of a conquered area. In the wars of Yugoslav succession, ethnic cleansing was a strategy used widely by all sides, starting with the expulsion of Croats from the areas in Croatia inhabited by Serbs. The main goal of these actions was to alter the demographic structure of the territory by getting rid of the unwanted ethnic groups.

The origin and the extended usage of the term ethnic cleansing in the public discourse of the 1990s could create the impression that it describes a historically new phenomenon. In reality it was only an invention of a new term to describe an age-old practice. It was carried out widely with or without significant coercion or as part of murderous genocidal campaigns. Ethnic cleansing could be used as a component of state policies, sometimes even based on international treaties, or as a consequence of spontaneous outbursts motivated by prejudice, hatred, and/or revenge. It was employed by empires, small communities, dictatorial and democratic regimes, and in all historical periods. Mann (1999) puts ethnic cleansing on a continuum together with assimilation and genocide. The targeted population for cleansing could be a religious minority, an ethnic group, or simply political-ideological opponents. The political and historical context of cleansing can also be strategic, with the goal of removing the population that presents a potential threat.

Historical evidence reveals numerous examples of the practice. Some historical accounts indicate, for example, that Assyrian rulers made a state policy of forced resettlement of their conquered lands and the replacement of the population by settlers from another region (Bell-Fialkoff 1999). In the Middle Ages cleansing was mainly applied against religious minorities. Anthony Marx (2003) argues that religious intolerance – specifically, the exclusion of religious minorities from the nascent state – provided the glue that bonded the remaining population together.

The rise of modern nationalism and the nation-state created a new framework for such cleansing activities. It is inherent in the modern project of nationalism that "We the people" generates a sense of the alien "other." And because the sovereignty of the modern nation-state is territorial, the "other" may be physically excluded from the territory of the people.

There are endless examples of cleansing, exchanges, or exoduses of populations accompanying the creation of modern nation-states. Exchanges of populations between Greece, Bulgaria, and Turkey were sanctioned by international treaties (the 1913 Convention of Adrianople and the peace treaty between Bulgaria and Turkey). The partition of India, the creation of the state of Israel, the division of Cyprus, and the successor states of the former Yugoslavia are just a few examples.

One of the biggest ethnic cleansings, culminating in extermination, was the Nazi campaign against the Jews. The Holocaust combined elements of deportation, expulsion, population transfer, massacre, and genocide. Some other examples of very similar practices in modern times are the holocaust of Armenians and the massacres of Tutsis by Hutus known as the Rwandan genocide.

Stalin's regime cleansed ethnic groups because of strategic considerations and also perceived internal political enemies on a grandiose scale. The expulsion of Poles from Belorussia and the Ukraine (1932–6) to Kazakhstan, the deportations of Poles, Lithuanians, Latvians, and Estonians from areas occupied by the Soviet Union in the 1930s, the mass deportations and exile of the Chechens, Ingush, Volga Germans, Balkars, Kalmyks, and Crimean Tatars in 1943–4, all fall into the first category.

The second type of cleansing was directed toward different types of class enemies – kulaks, alleged enemy spies, and collaborators. In Asia, the Chinese and Cambodian communists accepted bloodlines as a way of identifying class enemies. The Khmer Rouge took this approach a step further into something that Mann (1999) calls "classicide" as an analogy to genocide. It killed about half the number of Cambodians with a bourgeois background.

In analyzing the transformation of empires into nation-states, Brubaker (1995) states that the occurrence of migrations and different forms of ethnic cleansing depended on the extent to which disintegration was accompanied by war or other types of violence, on the established nature of the potential target for cleansing, on the anticipated and actual policies of the successor states toward the minorities, on the availability and quality of resettlement opportunities, and on "voice" as an alternative to "exit." There is nothing preordained about its occurrence. It happens under conditions that can be understood, explained, and predicted.

SEE ALSO: Assimilation; Ethnic Groups; Ethnicity; Genocide; Holocaust; Nationalism; Pogroms; Prejudice; Race; Race (Racism)

REFERENCES AND SUGGESTED READINGS

Ahmed, S. A. (1995) "Ethnic Cleansing": A Metaphor For Our Time? *Ethnic and Racial Studies* 18 (1): 1–25.
Bell-Fialkoff, A. (1999) *Ethnic Cleansing*. Palgrave, Macmillan and St. Martin's Griffin, New York.
Brubaker, R. (1995) Aftermaths of Empire and the Unmixing of Peoples: Historical and Comparative Perspectives. *Ethnic and Racial Studies* 18(2): 189–218.
Carmichael, C. (2002) *Ethnic Cleansing in the Balkans: Nationalism and the Destruction of Tradition*. Routledge, New York.
Mann, M. (1999) The Dark Side of Democracy: The Modern Tradition of Ethnic and Political Cleansing. *New Left Review* 235 (May/June): 18–45.
Marx, W. A. (2003) *Faith in the Nation: Exclusionary Origins of Nationalism*. Oxford University Press, New York.
Naimark, N. M. (2001) *Fires of Hatred: Ethnic Cleansing in Twentieth-Century Europe*. Harvard University Press, Cambridge, MA.

ethnic enclaves

Jan Lin

The ethnic enclave is a subeconomy that offers protected access to labor and markets, informal sources of credit, and business information for immigrant businesses and workers. Ethnic enclaves offer entrepreneurial opportunities and earnings for immigrant owners and managers through the exploitation of immigrant labor in poor working conditions. They are phenomena that advance our understanding of the changing experience of immigration and social mobility in America. The enclaves of Asian and Latino immigrants emerging since the 1960s are comparable to the enclaves of Jewish and Italian immigrants at the turn of the twentieth century. They present a route for economic and social mobility by promoting positive returns on human capital for immigrants in the labor market. During the decades of immigrant restriction, ethnic enclaves were shunned in the US as economic and spatial barriers to the successful assimilation and upward mobility of immigrants to American life. Since the 1960s, however, ethnic enclaves have been increasingly seen as agents for economic and social mobility. Ethnic enclaves are proliferating in both the cities and suburbs of contemporary immigration gateway cities such as New York, Miami, Houston, and Los Angeles. They constitute and convey the process of globalization as nodes of trade and transaction in flows of ethnic labor, capital, commodities, and cultural products across trading regions. There are costs as well as benefits that come with the insertion of ethnic enclaves into the complex social dynamics of contemporary global cities.

Pathbreaking research in the early 1980s on the concept of the enclave economy initially focused on the contrast between the Cuban enclave and the black economy of Miami (Wilson & Portes 1980; Wilson & Martin 1982). This research methodology utilized input–output multiplier matrices. The Cuban-owned firms of the Miami area were found to comprise a dynamic subeconomy of construction, manufacturing, retail and wholesale trade, and banking firms that recirculated and multiplied income through interindustry and consumption linkages. The economy of black neighborhoods, by contrast, was impoverished and capital-scarce, with income constantly leaking out of the community through branch manufacturing plants and chain stores owned by whites and large corporations. The enclave economy was conceptualized as an alternate subeconomy from the segmented mainstream economy, which was split into an upper tier of jobs with good mobility ladders, and a lower tier of dead-end jobs in which minorities and the economic underclass predominated. Investment capital was commonly raised in ethnic enclaves through devices such as kinship networks and rotating credit associations. These ethnic enclaves offered a protected sector for immigrants newly arrived without English language skills, good education, or official papers.

The study of the enclave economy was extended to a number of Latin American and Asian enclaves and comparisons made with earlier European immigrants (Portes & Manning 1986). In her research on New York's Chinese enclave, Min Zhou (1992) drew a distinction between an "export sector" that derived earnings from outside the enclave, and a "protected sector" that derived from earnings from sales to co-ethnics. The dynamism of the ethnic enclave economy is based in large part upon the multiplier effect, by which export earnings are spent and recirculated among co-ethnic enterprises throughout the remainder of the protected sector. For example, garment manufacturing can be viewed as an export sector that multiplies enclave income through forward and backward linkages with co-ethnic suppliers and buyers, as well as consumption linkages with other co-ethnic enterprises such as restaurants and markets. On the other hand, ethnic restaurants and other retail businesses comprise characteristics of both an export and protected sector. The concept of an "export sector" is clearer in theory than in practice, comment John Logan et al. (1994). They concluded that ethnic enclave economies are best typified by co-ethnicity of owners and workers, spatial concentration, and sectoral specialization. Evidence of sectoral specialization can be found in measuring overconcentration of ethnic enterprises or labor in particular industries as compared with the general population. A greater degree of sectoral specialization indicates a more successful ethnic enclave.

A segment of the research utilized a "returns on human capital" research methodology, which determined that positive returns accrued to employers at the expense of workers. This research found that ethnic enterprises undertook a kind of ethnic self-exploitation by which immigrant employers profited from their ability to exploit co-ethnic workers in a "sweatshop" sector under poor working conditions and poor labor rights. There was some debate regarding whether the enclave should be defined by place of work, place of residence, or industry sector (Sanders & Nee 1987). "Sweatshop" is a label for an enterprise that exploits workers with poor wages and benefits, bad working conditions, and low occupational security. Some researchers found evidence of significant gender differences in labor market outcomes. Positive returns for men were to some degree derived from negative returns to women as subordinate workers (Zhou & Logan 1989). The surplus value generated through ethnic solidarity in the enclave economy was derived effectively through worker exploitation by socioeconomic class and gender. The disparity in short-run benefits is followed by positive aggregate benefits in the long run.

Contemporary Asian and Latin American immigrants have succeeded the European immigrants of the turn of the twentieth century, in the urban industrial districts and residential neighborhoods of many US cities. Their appearance has helped revive many commercial, warehousing, and manufacturing districts that had been declining since the 1950s, as a result of suburbanization, the outmovement of industry, and the "runaway shop" to the developing world. The new ethnic enclaves are not just an illustration of immigrant succession, they are an outgrowth of neoliberal economic and free trade policies since the 1960s, which promoted the mobility of labor and capital between the US and its trading partners. The Hart-Cellar Immigration Act of 1965 removed restrictive quotas and restrictions on immigrant flows, as well as introducing banking deregulation to encourage capital outflow and inflow, and policies oriented to encouraging the import and export of goods (Sassen 1988). The new gateways of globalization include cities such as New York, Washington, DC, Miami, Atlanta, Houston, Los Angeles, and San Francisco. The growth of ethnic enclaves in the Frostbelt as well as the Sunbelt leads us to a revision of our understanding of post-industrial urban transition, through which the dynamism of globalization and immigration can be seen as superseding the decline associated with deindustrialization.

Ethnic enclaves are not just a factor in the insertion of immigrants into the American economy. They are nodes in the flow of immigrant labor, capital, and culture between the US and the emerging economies and trading regions of Asia, Latin America, and the Caribbean. The sweatshops of the immigrant garment industry are connected with trends of global sourcing in manufacturing. The banks of the ethnic enclave are crucial institutions in mediating transnational capital flows, whether they are inflows such as investments for overseas investors or outflows such as remittances for immigrant labor. New Asian and Latino immigrants have succeeded the earlier generation of Italian and Jewish immigrants in the traditional central city "urban village," but many enclaves are appearing in suburban locations, with ethnic signage proliferating in strip-malls and commercial arterials. The ethnic suburb, or "ethnoburb," has become a common feature of life in some American cities. The ethnoburb is a symbol not only of immigrant success, but also of intergroup conflict in the global city.

The insertion of ethnic enclaves into the social and economic dynamics of the post-industrial cities has been in some areas a vociferously conflicted and contested process. In some cases such as the Cuban enclave of Miami and the Chinese enclave of Monterey Park, California, in the 1980s, the proliferation of ethnic businesses and signage led to the growth of nativist and xenophobic reactionary local social movements, and support for English-only language ordinances. In Monterey Park, the link between the ethnic enclave and rapid commercial development also sparked a growth control movement among local homeowners and politicians (Horton et al. 1987; Li 1999). Some immigrant entrepreneurs focus on certain occupational niches as economic and social "middleman minority" between dominant white

groups and poor minorities. Chinese, Korean, and Indian immigrants commonly operate small business groceries, liquor stores, and motels. They fulfill a function undesired by white elites. They act as a social buffer between the dominant and oppressed groups of a society, and in situations of crisis may bear the brunt of underclass anger, as seen in the black/Korean violence that followed the Rodney King disturbances of 1992 in Los Angeles (Min 1996).

For most of US history until the 1960s, ethnic identity and customs were generally suppressed in cities through projects of urban settlement and social reform work that sought to assimilate immigrants to the English language and American values. Chicago was the seminal expression of the modern industrial city in the early twentieth century, the paradigm of the "human ecology" school of urban sociology. The ethnic ghetto was stigmatized as a place of vice, crime, moral corruption, and public health hazards. This was a time of immigrant restriction and Americanization campaigns. Chicago School sociologists such as Robert Park codified the view that immigrant colonies such as the Jewish "ghetto," Little Italy, and Greek Town, which occupied the "zone in transition" surrounding the central business district, would eventually dissipate with the eventual upward mobility of working-class immigrants into the suburbs and their cultural assimilation into the middle class. Douglas Massey (1985) later articulated this phenomenon as the "spatial assimilation" thesis. Upward social mobility into better jobs and social status was linked with spatial mobility into better homes and neighborhoods. Ethnic enclaves were seen to create social immobility and spatial entrapment.

The human ecology school held the prevailing view of the social reformers in the early twentieth century that ethnic enclaves were dysfunctional slums that harbored social pathologies and blight (Ward 1989). During this period of urban growth, city managers and the federal government actively began bulldozing ethnic enclaves under slum clearance policies of the interwar period and urban renewal in the post-war period, to make room for expressway arterials, middle-class housing, expansion of the central business district, and government buildings. Chinatowns, Little Italies, and Mexican neighborhoods were viewed as obstacles to modernization and cultural assimilation. Herbert Gans, in the seminal study *The Urban Villagers* (1962), decried the officials and policymakers who designated the Italian American West End neighborhood as a slum and led to its demolition to make way for middle-class housing. In Los Angeles during the same period, a celebrated Mexican American community was razed to make way for the construction of Dodger Stadium. Since the 1960s, however, city managers and planners have increasingly come to see ethnic enclaves as tools rather than as obstacles to growth. The preservation of ethnic places and neighborhoods is of growing utility in efforts to promote globalization in metropolitan economies through the construction of world trade centers, convention centers, and urban tourism.

The growing emergence and persistence of ethnic enclaves has changed the meaning of ethnicity and American identity. Ethnicity in contemporary America is becoming less of an ascribed experience that preserves ancestral traditions, and more of an achieved experience where these traditions may be created and enacted for outside consumers as much as co-ethnic participants. Ethnic enclaves are increasingly producing for the export sector of American consumers as well as the protected sector of immigrant consumers. At the turn of the last century, when ethnic minorities were suppressed by doctrines of manifest destiny and assimilation, the sustaining of ethnic foodways and folkways protected bonds of communal social capital and spiritual meaning. In the current era of the multicultural and global city, ethnicity is increasingly tolerated, celebrated, and transacted. Ethnicity has been activated and affirmed by consumers of such culinary trends as Japanese sushi, Chinese dim sum, and Spanish tapas. Ethnicity has also been appropriated and branded by transnational fast food franchises such as Taco Bell. As ethnicity becomes increasingly transacted in the era of global consumer capitalism, the original intention, authenticity, and ownership of local ethnic culture can come under threat.

In the current era of economic and cultural change, ethnic enclaves constitute and convey global processes in US immigration gateway cities. Opportunities have arisen for ethnic entrepreneurs to profit from a growing American interest in consuming and experiencing ethnic foods, music, theater, arts, fashion, museums, and festivals. The Civil Rights Movement also resulted in legal and political protections for racial and ethnic minorities, dampening the power of assimilation rhetoric and promoting the sustaining of ethnic cultural heritage and a politics of cultural pluralism. Trends of economic globalization have led to widespread outsourcing of manufacturing employment to offshore locations, stimulating growth of post-industrial activities onshore in a range of industries involving the production of culture for consumption. The cultural endowments of urban regions, like the mineral or agricultural resources of their hinterlands, have become important components in their repertoire of economic activities. The competition among cities for prosperity in the global economy has promoted strategies of urban "branding" for entertainment and tourism, to help boost cities suffering economic decline. The "branding" process is promoted through corporate trademarking of office buildings, sports stadiums, concerts, and festivals. Urban redevelopment in the new "symbolic economy" involves the use of devices such as museums, theaters, restaurants, and local cultural districts (Zukin 1995). The growth of the ethnic cultural economy involves the mobilizing of the "creative capital" of a new talented and credentialed class of workers including artists, curators, designers, and chefs, who are qualified in the production and distribution of creative goods. The creative economy has an innovative edge in the area of high technology and a cosmopolitan edge since it prospers in areas of cultural diversity and tolerance (Florida 2002). In the new creative economy of cities, economic innovation links with a pattern of urbanity that draws talented individuals and traders from the hinterlands and other trading regions to create value in products based on taste, fashionability, and design.

A host of social conflicts and contradictions affecting ethnic producers of culture as well as white consumers accompany these trends. Many ethnic enterprises such as restaurants provide opportunities for a "front region" staff of owners, gourmet chefs, and waiters while exploiting a "back region" staff of dishwashers and kitchen assistants (Zukin 1995). Immigrant restaurants may exploit the back region staff with poor wages and working conditions. For the manual workers in the back region of the restaurant, the enclave economy offers certain economic opportunities, but their chances for upward social mobility are as limited as for those who toil in the low-wage service sector in such enterprises as cleaning, security, and fast food restaurants. The best advantages of the ethnic restaurant sector accrue to the front region staff, whose profitability depends upon their ability to effectively mobilize their ethnic creative capital.

The marketing of ethnicity carries a host of positive as well as pernicious implications. The consumption experience of "eating the Other" is problematic insofar as it permits white Americans to assume a positive association with the culture of subaltern racial/ethnic minorities while camouflaging ongoing social inequality and white privilege. The growth of an ethnic "creative class" is a stimulus to urban redevelopment through a cultural affairs strategy that promotes the gentrification of inner-city neighborhoods and the displacement of low-income residents. Issues of cultural authenticity and ownership come to the fore as ethnic neighborhoods are preserved and marketed like theme parks in American cities. As it becomes increasingly acceptable for ethnic foods and cultures to be consumed and transacted, some forms may become aesthetically incorporated into the repertoire of tastes and "cultural capital" associated with the elite social classes in America. Increasing the aesthetic appeal of a cuisine increases its chances for marketability. Some ethnic groups, such as Puerto Ricans, have faced more challenges than groups such as Cubans or Japanese immigrants in successfully creating and defining a market for their cultural products. The production and consumption of ethnicity is a growing factor in the larger dynamics of American social inequality and stratification.

SEE ALSO: Assimilation; Ecological Models of Urban Form: Concentric Zone Model, the Sector Model, and the Multiple Nuclei Model; Ethnic/Informal Economy; Ethnic Groups; Ethnicity; Global/World Cities; Globalization, Culture and; Immigration; Migration and the Labor Force; Mobility, Horizontal and Vertical

REFERENCES AND SUGGESTED READINGS

Florida, R. (2002) *The Rise of the Creative Class.* Basic Books, New York.

Horton, J. et al. (1987) *The Politics of Diversity: Immigration, Resistance, and Change in Monterey Park.* Temple University Press, Philadelphia.

Li, W. (1999) Building Ethnoburbia: The Emergence and Manifestation of the Chinese Ethnoburb in Los Angeles' San Gabriel Valley. *Journal of Asian American Studies* 2(1): 1–28.

Logan, J. R., Alba, R. D., & McNulty, T. L. (1994) Ethnic Economies in Metropolitan Regions: Miami and Beyond. *Social Forces* 72(3): 691–724.

Massey, D. (1985) Ethnic Residential Segregation: A Theoretical and Empirical Review. *Sociology and Social Research* 69: 315–50.

Min, P. G. (1996) *Caught in the Middle: Korean Communities in New York and Los Angeles.* University of California Press, Berkeley.

Portes, A. & Manning, R. D. (1986) The Immigrant Enclave: Theory and Empirical Examples. In: Olzak, S. & Nagel, J. (Eds.), *Competitive Ethnic Relations.* Academic Press, New York, pp. 47–68.

Sanders, J. M. & Nee, V. (1987) The Limits of Ethnic Solidarity in the Ethnic Enclave. *American Sociological Review* 52, 6 (December): 745–67.

Sassen, S. (1988) *The Mobility of Labor and Capital.* Cambridge University Press, New York.

Ward, D. (1989) *Poverty, Ethnicity, and the American City: 1840–1925.* Cambridge University Press, Cambridge.

Wilson, K. L. & Martin, W. A. (1982) Ethnic Enclaves: A Comparison of the Cuban and Black Economies in Miami. *American Journal of Sociology* 88(1): 135–60.

Wilson, K. L. & Portes, A. (1980) Immigrant Enclaves: An Analysis of the Labor Market Experiences of Cubans in Miami. *American Journal of Sociology* 86, 2 (September): 295–319.

Zhou, M. (1992) *Chinatown: The Socioeconomic Potential of an Urban Enclave.* Temple University Press, Philadelphia.

Zhou, M. & Logan, J. R. (1989) Returns on Human Capital in Ethnic Enclaves: New York's Chinatown. *American Sociological Review* 54 (October): 809–20.

Zukin, S. (1995) *The Cultures of Cities.* Blackwell, Cambridge, MA.

ethnic groups

John Stone and Bhumika Piya

Ethnic groups are fundamental units of social organization which consist of members who define themselves, or are defined, by a sense of common historical origins that may also include religious beliefs, a similar language, or a shared culture. Their continuity over time as distinct groups is achieved through the intergenerational transmission of culture, traditions, and institutions. Ethnic groups can be distinguished from kinship groups in as much as ties of kin arise largely from biological inheritance. The term is derived from the Greek word *ethnos*, which can be translated as a people or a nation. The sociologist Max Weber provided one of the most important modern definitions of ethnic groups as "human groups (other than kinship groups) which cherish a belief in their common origins of such a kind that it provides the basis for the creation of a community."

There are two competing perspectives on ethnic groups: objectivist and subjectivist. Objectivists, taking an etic stance, assert that ethnic groups are inherently distinct social and cultural entities that possess boundaries which delineate their interaction and socialization with others. Subjectivists, on the other hand, embrace an emic perspective and regard ethnic groups as self-categorizations that determine their social behavior within and outside the group. Subjectivists like Frederik Barth argued that ethnic groups should be defined on the basis of self-identification or categorical ascription. Such a standpoint has led to the creation of legislation such as an Australian government policy in the early 1970s which classified Aboriginal people on the basis of self-identification by an individual and acceptance by an Aboriginal community. Conversely, the objectivists have adopted the idea that ethnic groups are characterized by cultural and historical traits that have been passed down from generation to generation rather than on pure self-conception. Despite the lack of consensus while defining ethnic groups, it is safe to assume that such groups are distinct entities with boundaries, be they real or constructed. The boundaries of ethnic groups often overlap with similar or related categories such as "races" or nations. There is a consensus among scholars that "race" is a socially defined category that has no biological significance, despite lingering popular beliefs that still regard "races" as biological groups made up of a people with a distinct genetic heritage. There is no scientific evidence to support these notions. However, one could regard race as a variant of ethnic group, for racial groups are perceived to be physiologically different by outsiders, if not by the group members themselves.

The term nation implies a self-conscious ethnic group mobilized with the goal of creating or preserving a political unit in which it is the predominant or exclusive political force. According to Weber, nations are politically mobilized ethnic communities in which members and their leaders try to create a special political structure in the form of an independent state. Ethnic groups may also embrace solidarity and group enclosure in order to achieve advantages over other groups. Such enclosure tactics could take several forms, such as endogamous marriage, which is marriage within a social group, or business practices such as the dominance of Jews in the Antwerp diamond-cutting industry.

In those societies that have been influenced by large-scale immigration – like the United States, Canada, Australia, New Zealand, and Argentina – the importance of ethnic groups can be seen as a central feature of their social, economic, and political life. However, it is useful to note that immigrants having the same region of origin are often categorized under generic ethnic groups despite the absence of cohesion and common culture. Systematic research on American ethnic groups can be traced to the sociologists of the Chicago School during the 1920s, led by W. I. Thomas and Robert Ezra Park, who were concerned with the processes of ethnic group assimilation into the dominant white Anglo-Saxon Protestant (WASP) mainstream. Park's *race relations cycle*, which outlined a sequence of stages consisting of "contact, competition, accommodation, and assimilation," implied that successive immigrant groups would be gradually absorbed into a relatively homogeneous US society. The underlying assumption of ethnic group theory was that these long-term trends would result in the disappearance of separate ethnic communities as they merged into a wider American melting pot.

This model implying a straight-line progression gave way to more pluralistic conceptions of ethnicity in the US, in which various dimensions of assimilation were identified by sociologists like Milton Gordon, who wrote the classic work on the subject. In *Assimilation in American Life* (1964), Gordon distinguished between cultural assimilation (*acculturation*) and structural assimilation, the former signifying the adoption of the language, values, and ideals of the dominant society, while the latter reflected the incorporation of ethnic groups into the institutions of mainstream society. While cultural assimilation did not necessarily result in an ethnic group's inclusion within the principal institutions of society, structural assimilation invariably meant that assimilation on all other dimensions – from personal identification to intermarriage – had already taken place.

Scholarly concern with ethnic groups and ethnic conflict became increasingly salient in the second half of the twentieth century. Inadequate assumptions about the nature of modernization and modernity have been demonstrated by the pattern of social change under capitalism, socialism, and in the developing world. Expectations that modernity might lead to a smooth transition from *gemeinschaft* to *gesellschaft*, accompanied by the gradual dissolution of ethnic group affiliations, were no longer plausible. Some social scientists argued that there was a primordial basis to ethnic group attachments, while others explained the apparent persistence of ethnicity as a criterion of group closure in more instrumental terms, as a political resource to be mobilized in appropriate situations which may be activated by power or guided by cultural factors. Not only has ethnicity failed to recede in industrial and post-industrial societies, but also ethnic divisions have continued to stand in the way of movements to promote democracy and economic growth in large sectors of the non-industrial or industrializing world. The failure of the political regimes in the communist bloc unleashed an upsurge in ethnic and national identity, some of which filled the void created by the demise of Marxism, while other elements of the same development, notably in the former Yugoslavia, turned into bloody ethnonational conflicts and ethnic cleansing (Sekulic 2003).

The increasing visibility of ethnic diversity due to postcolonial migration and globalization has engendered remarkable responses, ranging from expulsion or persecution of ethnic groups to their integration and assimilation into dominant cultures. The extermination of Jews and Gypsies during World War II under the Nazi regime is a classic example of the persecution of people to dispose of "undesired" ethnic groups; hence, it is claimed, deterring potential ethnic discord. The expulsion of ethnic groups can take the form of a forced exodus as well. Forced eviction of more than 100,000 of the Lhotshampas ethnic groups from Bhutan, starting from 1989 and still continuing under the "Driglam Namzha" decree, is another example of ethnic cleansing. The royal decree, declaring the recent "one country, one people" policy, seeks to homogenize the Bhutan population by imposing the indigenous Buddhist culture of the majority Drukpa, including their language, dress code, and customs, on the rest of the people (Hutt 2003). In contrast to the aforementioned policies, the majority of contemporary responses have been toward assimilation or acculturation and pluralism.

The example of more or less voluntary assimilation is seen in the US, where ethnic groups, including immigrants and natives, have embraced the mainstream American culture. This is advantageous to ethnic minorities in terms of upward mobility in the economic and political spheres of the society. An archetypal pluralistic society is Switzerland, which has separate cantons for different ethnic groups. Ethnic groups remain socially and politically differentiated, and enjoy a certain degree of autonomy within the democratic federation. Besides assimilation and pluralism, a new trend of embracing pan-ethnic identity is emerging. Ethnic groups form a conglomerate and join together under larger umbrella groups. Such practice is common among South Asians and Latinos in America.

The escalating incidence of interethnic conflicts has incited heated debate amongst policymakers and scholars as to how the state should respond to ethnic divisions. Some scholars such as Jürgen Habermas assert that all people should be treated equally, regardless of their ethnic backgrounds or national origin. Hence, they are entitled to equal legal and political rights as autonomous individual subjects. Others, like Will Kymlicka, have criticized the notion of autonomous individual subjects as being impractical. Kymlicka advocates the recognition of ethnic group membership and a pluralistic approach in policymaking to accommodate the distinctive needs of ethnic groups. Some also stress the point that ethnic conflicts are not really "ethnic" but mainly political or economic.

At the end of the millennium, the focus of research on ethnic groups was shifting away from studies of specific groups toward the broad processes of ethnogenesis, the construction and perpetuation of ethnic boundaries, the meaning of ethnic identity, the impact of globalization (Berger & Huntington 2002), and the importance of transnationalism (Levitt & Waters 2002). While traditional patterns of international migration continue to play an important role in the generation of ethnic diversity, they have been modified and changed by political and economic factors in complex and unpredictable ways. In the United States, large numbers of Mexican migrants, both legal and undocumented, have contributed to the growth of the Latino population into the largest single minority group (Bean & Stevens 2003). In Germany, the central economic component of the European Union, the relations with immigrants and ethnic minority groups will be a crucial element in determining the progress and stability of the emerging political structure, no matter whether it becomes a superstate or remains a loose federation (Alba et al. 2003).

SEE ALSO: Acculturation; Assimilation; Boundaries (Racial/Ethnic); Conflict (Racial/Ethnic); Ethnic Cleansing; Ethnicity; Ethnonationalism

REFERENCES AND SUGGESTED READINGS

Alba, R., Schmidt, P., & Wasmer, M. (2003) *Germans or Foreigners? Attitudes Toward Ethnic Minorities in Post-Reunification Germany*. Palgrave Macmillan, New York.

Bean, F. & Stevens, G. (2003) *America's Newcomers and the Dynamics of Diversity*. Russell Sage Foundation, New York.

Berger, P. & Huntington, S. (Eds.) (2002) *Many Globalizations: Cultural Diversity in the Contemporary World*. Oxford University Press, New York.

Gordon, M. (1964) *Assimilation in American Life: The Role of Race, Religion, and National Origins*. Oxford University Press, New York.

Hutt, M. (2003) *Unbecoming Citizens: Culture, Nationhood, and the Flight of Refugees from Bhutan*. Oxford University Press, Oxford.

Levitt, P. & Waters, M. (Eds.) (2002) *The Changing Face of Home: The Transnational Lives of the Second Generation*. Russell Sage Foundation, New York.

Sekulic, D. (2003) The Creation and Dissolution of the Multi-National State: The Case of Yugoslavia. In: Stone, J. & Dennis, R. (Eds.), *Race and Ethnicity: Comparative and Theoretical Approaches*. Blackwell, Malden, MA.

Weber, M. (1978 [1922]) *Economy and Society: An Outline of Interpretive Sociology*. Ed. G. Roth & C. Wittich. University of California Press, Berkeley.

ethnic/informal economy

Jimy M. Sanders

Ethnic/informal economies are inconsistently defined by scholars. This slows progress in explicating the social underpinnings of ethnic/informal economies and in understanding how these economic systems affect the socioeconomic well-being of members of various ethnic groups. Fortunately, there is a common theme to the definitions one finds in the literature. All variants convey a sense of economic action embedded in solidaristic, co-ethnic social relations. Economic behavior is influenced by informal rules and practices that govern the normative behavior of group members. Beyond this common theme, however, widely differing definitions involving self-employment, employment niches among those who are not self-employed, and geographical clustering have been applied. Light and Gold (2000) suggest three definitions as a way to reduce this chaotic state of affairs. The first is the combination of business owners, unpaid family labor, and paid co-ethnic employees (ethnic ownership economy). The second includes the first, but adds the requirement of spatial clustering (enclave economy). The third points to occupational and industrial employment niches (not business ownership) where the overrepresentation of an ethnic group enables its members to benefit from the advantages of informal control (ethnic-controlled economy).

An informative literature has emerged despite the lack of consistency in defining ethnic/informal economies. Researchers concentrate on how foreign-born groups establish and maintain economic niches that are usually accentuated by a profusion of small businesses. The field examines how limited acculturation and structural assimilation in the immigrant generation gives rise to collective action that promotes enterprising economic action. A substantial body of research documents how immigrant minorities draw on social ties in order to facilitate the development of informal economic relations. Family ties and ethnic group membership typically provide the social underpinnings of these economic relations.

The ability to draw on social connections in order to gain access to resources that are useful for economic action is an example of what scholars refer to as social capital. The literature describes many ways in which immigrants make use of family- and ethnic-based interpersonal connections in gaining access to resources such as business-related information and financial credit. Understanding these practices, which are often steeped in informal institutionalized arrangements, is essential for understanding the origins and maintenance of ethnic/informal economies.

Bonacich and Modell's (1980) study of three generations of Japanese Americans reveals how hostility from the dominant group can generate a defensive reaction from minority groups. In the case of the Japanese on the US West Coast, this encouraged ethnic solidarity and strengthened social boundaries that were reinforced by a shared sense of ethnic identity. This strong sense of community, in turn, gave rise to cooperation and collective action that generated and distributed group resources that facilitated the rise and expansion of the Japanese ethnic economy. This economic system was the basis of Japanese upward mobility prior to World War II. Scholars show how ethnic businesses fill niches created by the demand for goods and services in an ethnic community. These markets are partially closed to out-group businesses due to cultural and ecological barriers. Research also considers the role of informal credit and savings associations in helping prospective entrepreneurs acquire startup capital and in expanding the availability of credit to those who already own a business. Such economic activities, embedded in social relations, necessitate a sense of interdependence among in-group members that engenders trust and solidarity, and allows for sanctions to be imposed on those who violate the trust of others (Portes & Sensenbrenner 1993).

Interest in ethnic/informal economies is part of a larger scholarly interest in economic segmentation. This view conceives of the labor market as divided into a primary market where opportunities for advancement are prevalent and a low-wage secondary market with little opportunity for advancement. In the wake of growing international migration in the 1960s and 1970s, scholars concerned themselves with the range of economic options encountered by immigrants. Concluding that these opportunities were limited, researchers began to explore how the economic advancement of immigrant minority groups might be generated in a context of labor market segmentation and ethnic-based strategies of economic action.

Thus far, a large share of this research has been produced in the United States. This is not surprising given the importance of immigration in the history of the country's development, the large number of scholars at American universities who are engaged in research, and that the country has once again become the host society for large numbers of international migrants. But the United States is not alone in opening its doors to immigration. Research into ethnic/informal economies is also conducted in immigrant-receiving societies such as Canada, Australia, and in several European nations. Earlier immigration to South America also receives a good deal of attention. Numerous studies from various societies are reviewed in Aldrich and Waldinger (1990). This excellent review considers how characteristics of an ethnic group and the structural opportunities (or lack thereof) they encounter jointly influence the emergence of ethnic strategies that facilitate the rise and maintenance of an ethnic/informal economy. The review includes several historical and contemporary examples of the importance of both structural opportunity (e.g., elite sponsorship of middleman minorities in Southeast Asia, Africa, the Ottoman Empire, and tsarist Russia) and group characteristics (e.g., the rise of the Chinese-Vietnamese informal economy in Paris). Inasmuch as some relatively rich Asian nations are making use of guest workers from poorer Asian nations, we will probably see more research from this part of the world in the future – to the extent that these workers establish ethnic/informal economies.

Studies of how ethnic strategies develop and support ethnic/informal economies often consider the importance of ethnic-based social networks. Focusing on the role of social networks in generating economic opportunities, Portes and colleagues (e.g., Portes & Bach 1985) conducted an important study on an emerging Cuban economy in Miami. Ethnic solidarity facilitated the vertical and horizontal integration of a burgeoning business community. But an unclear picture emerged as to the economic implications of participating in the Cuban economy. Some of the research finds that working with fellow Cubans or other minorities negatively affects earnings and working under a Cuban boss has no effect on earnings. By contrast, other publications report that participation in the Cuban economy gives rise to advantages in occupational prestige, and occupational prestige positively associates with earnings. The importance of this latter finding is that it appears to counter the ecological hypothesis of assimilation theory, which contends that continued spatial segregation in terms of the labor market and residential patterns limits the upward mobility of ethnic groups.

An engaging debate arose over the question of whether the ecological hypothesis of assimilation theory was indeed inconsistent with the experiences of Cubans in Miami. The first exchange was initiated by the criticism that failure to distinguish between self-employed Cubans and their employees accounts for the apparent disconfirmation of the ecological hypothesis. Sanders and Nee (1987) appear to

show that the positive association between participating in the Cuban economy and occupational prestige is largely due to the occupational prestige of business owners rather than that of their employees. Hence, business owners financially benefit from participating in the densely co-ethnic regional economy, but their employees tend not to experience such a benefit. This pattern implies the Cuban experience is similar to that of earlier immigrant groups. The debate was rejoined by Jensen and Portes (1992) and Sanders and Nee (1992). An earnings advantage is confirmed for Cuban business owners, but no comparable advantage is found for Cuban employees. Indeed, for men, a negative main effect obtains for employment in the Cuban economy. The bottom line is that ethnic/informal economies, like other market-driven systems, not only generate wealth, they also generate inequality.

The field was beginning to concentrate less on any supposed earnings advantage that ethnic/informal economies provide to employees and more on how shared ethnicity facilitates internal forms of social organization and institutional behavior that increase employees' chances of becoming self-employed. Bailey and Waldinger (1991), for example, show how informal ethnic networks in New York City's Chinese garment industry provide information to employers that helps them recoup the cost of training employees. These networks also provide employees with inside information that increases their chances of becoming self-employed. Several subsequent studies have documented that informal training systems operate in various ethnic economies. But these systems, by facilitating greater self-employment within an ethnic group, can drive up the cost of co-ethnic labor and therefore immigrant entrepreneurs often draw from out-group minorities to fill their labor needs.

As the literature converged on the importance of ethnic/informal economies as an engine to increase self-employment, and thereby improve opportunities for upward mobility, some scholars were questioning the evidence that ethnic small business owners experience an earnings advantage. A key part of this critique is that the economic benefit to ethnic self-employment may be largely due to business owners practicing self-exploitation by working

70 or 80 hours per week. Others recognize the long hours of work required of ethnic entrepreneurs, but the literature generally regards this to be one of the costs of economic success through self-employment. Portes and Zhou (1996) examine the argument that ethnic self-employment fails to produce an earnings advantage. They find a substantial advantage to self-employment, but this advantage is concentrated among unusually successful entrepreneurs as opposed to being spread throughout the business community.

Toward the close of the twentieth century, scholars continued to refine their understanding of the social bases of ethnic entrepreneurship. Sanders and Nee (1996), for example, demonstrate that the family plays a key role in ethnic enterprise, much as it had with earlier immigrant groups. The family is a strategic resource in ethnic entrepreneurship because the social ties it embodies tend to be the most intense and trust-evoking of all interpersonal relationships. This literature shows that, by focusing on the ethnic group as a resource for collective economic action, many scholars have overlooked the role of the smaller, more tightly integrated social institution of the family.

What has the literature taught us about the social bases of ethnic/informal economies? Researchers have revealed a number of informal mechanisms based on social relations that facilitate economic action. The most important outcomes of these mechanisms are the dissemination of employment and business-related information, and providing access to informal financial institutions. Normative use of these resources and the repayment of debts are encouraged by enforcing trustful behavior under the threat of sanctions. Informal social bases of economic action tend to emerge among groups as members try to overcome limited economic options due to language barriers, poor human capital, or non-fungible foreign-earned human capital. And immigrant groups often face discrimination and prejudice. A tendency for group members to react to these problems by looking within their group for practical and emotional support encourages ethnic solidarity, which in turn encourages informal group practices that provide access to resources. Internally generated resources contribute to the growth of self-employment and

this leads to increased opportunities for getting ahead. But there are winners and losers in the ethnic community. People seeking to better their lives and that of their family are involved in the rough and tumble environment of market economics. Even a modicum of success in small business usually requires outperforming some competitors and matching the performance of others. This is a daunting task because ethnic/informal economies tend to be hotbeds of competition between small businesses.

SEE ALSO: Economy, Networks and; Ethnic Enclaves; Ethnic and Racial Divison of Labor; Immigrant Families; Immigration; Social Embeddedness of Economic Action; Transnationalism

REFERENCES AND SUGGESTED READINGS

Aldrich, H. & Waldinger, R. (1990) Ethnicity and Entrepreneurship. *Annual Review of Sociology* 16: 111–35.

Bailey, T. & Waldinger, R. (1991) Primary, Secondary, and Enclave Labor Markets: A Training Systems Approach. *American Sociological Review* 56: 432–45.

Bonacich, E. & Modell, J. (1980) *The Economic Basis of Ethnic Solidarity: Small Business in the Japanese-American Community*. University of California Press, Berkeley.

Jensen, L. & Portes, A. (1992) The Enclave and the Entrants: Patterns of Ethnic Enterprise in Miami Before and After Mariel. *American Sociological Review* 57: 411–14.

Light, I. & Gold, S. (2000) *Ethnic Economics*. Academic Press, San Diego.

Portes, A. & Bach, R. (1985) *Latin Journey: Cuban and Mexican Immigrants in the United States*. University of California Press, Berkeley.

Portes, A. & Sensenbrenner, J. (1993) Embeddedness and Immigration: Notes on the Social Determinants of Economic Action. *American Journal of Sociology* 98: 1320–50.

Portes, A. & Zhou, M. (1996) Self-Employment and the Earnings of Immigrants. *American Sociological Review* 61: 219–30.

Sanders, J. & Nee, V. (1987) Limits of Ethnic Solidarity in the Enclave Economy. *American Sociological Review* 52: 745–73.

Sanders, J. & Nee, V. (1992) Problems in Resolving the Enclave Economy Debate. *American Sociological Review* 57: 415–18.

Sanders, J. & Nee, V. (1996) Immigrant Self-Employment: The Family as Social Capital and the Value of Human Capital. *American Sociological Review* 61: 231–49.

ethnic and racial division of labor

Michael Lichter

An ethnic or racial division of labor exists in a society in which ethnic or racial groups have distinctive concentrations or specializations in particular lines of work. Ethnic/racial divisions of labor may arise through relatively benign labor market sorting processes, or they may be the result of systematic acts of bigotry and discrimination, often with state sanction. Regardless of how they arise, ethnic/racial divisions of labor can be observed and traced over time, and they can have measurable effects on social and political dynamics within societies.

Ethnic/racial divisions of labor have a long history. For example, in Athens of classical antiquity, landowners and other free citizens were almost exclusively Athenian, but the slaves who performed the bulk of the society's work were typically (but not universally) ethnic outsiders, as were the *metic* and *xenoi* artisans and merchants who dominated many areas of trade. More recently, European colonial powers created ethnic divisions of labor across the globe, installing themselves as a ruling class and frequently selecting a specific ethnic group within a colonized territory to fill privileged positions in colonial administration or trade. Apartheid in South Africa and slavery and Jim Crow in the American South are two examples of legal systems in former colonies that enforced racial divisions of labor, reserving desirable positions for whites while largely restricting subordinated groups to menial occupations. Ethnic divisions of labor in many countries are among the most persistent legacies of European colonialism.

Social theorists have developed a number of explanations for the creation and maintenance of ethnic divisions of labor. Neo-Marxists have alternated between two seemingly contradictory positions. The first position, which dates back to Marx, holds that capitalists are the architects of ethnic/racial divisions of labor, offering privileged positions to some groups of workers while assigning the most onerous tasks to others. The capitalists' goal is to foster conflict and competition within the working class, keeping it divided and weak. So-called radical theories of labor market segmentation mostly adopt this position. The second position, espoused most forcefully by Bonacich in the early 1970s, does not hold capitalists responsible for anything beyond creating a context that forces workers to compete with each other in order to survive. In Bonacich's scheme, when relatively privileged workers face a threat from ethnically or racially distinct others, they use ethnic solidarity, labor organization, and other social and political resources at their disposal to insulate themselves from competition. When they are unable to completely exclude the other group from the labor market, they are often able to create an ethnically/racially split labor market, reserving the best positions for themselves. The split labor market persists as long as ethnic/racial others remain a threat.

Development in these macro-level neo-Marxist theories has virtually stalled since the late 1980s. Most recent work has focused at lower levels of abstraction – the metropolitan area, the industry, or even the individual firm. Ecological approaches to the ethnic/racial division of labor, for example, typically concern metropolitan labor markets. These approaches treat local labor markets as metaphorical ecologies, with ethnic/racial groups pictured as metaphorical species struggling to find and expand their "niches." In his study of native blacks and white immigrants at the dawn of the twentieth century, Lieberson (1980) proposes a "model of occupational composition" that frames the ethnic/racial division of labor as the outcome of a struggle for group position within a fixed hierarchy of occupational positions. For a particular group, the outcome of this struggle is determined by the overall group composition of the metropolitan area, group members' "objective" qualifications, group members' occupational preferences, the desirability of particular occupations, and, perhaps most importantly, the ethnic/racial preferences of employers and potential co-workers and customers. This approach helps account for collective upward mobility among ethnic groups, although it does little to explain the extra efforts made by immigrant whites to exclude blacks.

While Lieberson focused on earlier immigrant waves, mass movements to the US and Europe since the mid-1960s have sparked considerable interest in understanding how ethnic divisions of labor are formed and transformed over time. In the 1980s and early 1990s, the phenomenal growth of immigrant enterprises and the role of these businesses in providing co-ethnic workers with employment niches attracted much attention. Portes and his colleagues developed the notion of the ethnic enclave economy, a separate economy semi-detached from the mainstream economy in which ethnic entrepreneurs both exploit co-ethnic workers and provide new business opportunities for them. Among immigrant groups that bring entrepreneurial expertise and a modicum of capital, opportunities for small business play a major role in shaping the group's place in the overall ethnic/racial division of labor.

Views on the consequences of ethnic/racial divisions of labor vary. Few disagree about the destructive consequences of coercive systems like apartheid and Jim Crow. Contemporary immigration scholars who study the entry of comparatively small groups of newcomers into larger ethnic/racial divisions of labor, however, tend to view these divisions of labor as inevitable. They also often see the consequences as very favorable to the new immigrants. Some, however, point out that not all immigrants locate favorable niches and that, furthermore, immigrants may be squeezing native minorities out of opportunities.

Neo-Marxists tend to view ethnic divisions of labor as wholly undesirable because they are based on discrimination, leave some groups disproportionately impoverished, and undermine class unity. Hechter's influential work on the "cultural division of labor" provided clarification on this last point. Hechter distinguishes two major dimensions to the ethnic or racial division of labor: the degree of between-group hierarchy and the degree of group specialization or distinctiveness. To the extent that an ethnic or racial group is concentrated at one level in the occupational hierarchy, whether at the top, bottom, or middle, it will share interests with other groups at the same hierarchical level and tend toward class politics. On the other hand, to the extent that a group specializes in particular lines of work, and thus has high levels of within-group interaction and interdependence, the greater is the salience of ethnic politics.

Three areas promise to be most fruitful in the future study of racial/ethnic divisions of labor. First, studies of the "new second generation," the children of the post-1965 immigrants to the US, should expose the extent to which specifically ethnic and racial factors still structure the opportunities available to natives. Second, feminist scholars, particularly those studying immigration, have been making progress in gendering our understandings of ethnic/racial divisions of labor, and this progress is likely to continue. Third, as global integration grows more important, so does attention to its effects on national ethnic/racial divisions of labor. Continuing research on, for example, how the new "transnational" migrants fit into ethnic/racial divisions of labor will be invaluable.

SEE ALSO: Affirmative Action (Race and Ethnic Quotas); Apartheid and Nelson Mandela; Discrimination; Immigration; Middleman Minorities; Racial Hierarchy; Transnationalism

REFERENCES AND SUGGESTED READINGS

Bonacich, E. (1972) A Theory of Ethnic Antagonism: The Split Labor Market. *American Sociological Review* 37: 547–59.

Hechter, M. (1978) Group Formation and the Cultural Division of Labor. *American Journal of Sociology* 84: 293–318.

Lieberson, S. (1980) *A Piece of the Pie: Blacks and White Immigrants Since 1880*. University of California Press, Berkeley.

Model, S. (1993) The Ethnic Niche and the Structure of Opportunity: Immigrants and Minorities in New York City. In: Katz, M. (Ed.), *The "Underclass" Debate: Views from History*. Princeton University Press, Princeton.

Nakano Glenn, E. (1991) Cleaning Up/Kept Down: A Historical Perspective on Racial Inequality in "Women's Work." *Stanford Law Review* 43: 1333–56.

Omi, M. & Winant, H. (1986) *Racial Formation in the United States: From the 1960s to the 1980s.* Routledge & Kegan Paul, New York.

Portes, A. & Jensen, L. (1989) The Enclave and the Entrants. *American Sociological Review* 54: 929–49.

Waldinger, R. (1996) Who Makes the Beds? Who Washes the Dishes? Black/Immigrant Competition Reassessed. In: Duleep, H. O. & Wunnava, P. V. (Eds.), *Immigrants and Immigration Policy: Individual Skills, Family Ties, and Group Identities.* JAI Press, Greenwich, CT, pp. 265–88.

Wilson, W. J. (1978) *The Declining Significance of Race.* University of Chicago Press, Chicago.

ethnic, racial, and nationalist movements

Susan Olzak

Political expressions of ethnicity and nationalism range broadly, from small-scale or sporadic protests that may be relatively peaceful (as in civil rights marches), to sustained campaigns of violence against authorities or others (such as ethnic cleansing). Though often analyzed separately, ethnic, racial, and nationalist (E/R/N) movements voice strikingly similar demands for sovereignty and invoke rights of self-determination. The major E/R/N movement categories are distinguished by claims, goals, tactics, and organizational forms. Once these definitions are established, some key explanations of the emergence, persistence, transformation, and decline of these social movements are outlined.

Social movements generate collective action advocating fundamental changes in the political or economic arrangements in a society. Social movements typically involve sustained activity over time and place (whereas collective action may be fleeting). Most scholars also find that adherents of a social movement tend to support a coherent set of values that define its core identity. Boundary perspectives further explore how race and ethnic groups use ethnic markers to demarcate membership with reference to core features of group identity (Barth 1969).

The defining feature of ethnic and racial social movements (E/R) is that, in such movements, claims are made based upon a particular identity or boundary, defined by the presence of racial or ethnic markers. These markers typically include skin pigmentation, ancestry, language, and history of discrimination, conquest, or other shared experience. For simplicity (and to avoid invoking unscientific assumptions about the genetic basis of race), many researchers prefer the more generic label of *ethnicity* over race.

Ethnic mobilization can be defined apart from ethnic solidarity. Solidarity is characterized as the conscious identification (and loyalty) with a particular race or ethnic population, measured by attitudes, institutional involvement (or organizational participation), and monitoring capacity. Mobilization is the capacity to harness resources (including solidarity, organizations, and material resources) in an effort to reach some collective goal.

Nationalist movements generally express claims over the legitimate right to govern a specific geographical area (Hechter 2000). The pursuit of sovereignty rights typically also provokes conflict (and perhaps also warfare) with existing regimes. Such conflict can remain quiescent for long periods of time, erupting suddenly into full-blown armed guerrilla warfare, or civil war, depending on regime strength, outside support, primary export commodities, internal mobilization of resources, and reaction by state authorities to nationalist movements (Fearon and Laitin 2003, 2005).

It is important to note that nationalist movements do not always depend upon a shared race or ethnic identity. Instead, they may rest upon a group's geographical concentration, political jurisdiction and leadership, and/or legacy claims to legitimate authority. Alternatively, nationalist movements may claim sovereign rights by invoking other types of identities, based upon religious identities, as in the case of nationalistic Islamic movements. Other forms of nationalist movements make claims that they had been forcefully removed and dispersed from their ancestral homeland, as in the case of some diaspora movements. Members of nationalist movements may share a territory that lies under another jurisdiction (e.g., Québécois nationalism), or they may invoke a national identity spread across multiple regions (e.g., Kurdish nationalism). A final type involves state-building movements in which a single identity is being forged from many different, smaller ethnic or regional identities within an existing territory (e.g., pan-Indian identity in the US) (Nagel 1996).

By sharpening the differences between ethnicity and nationalism, empirical studies of these movements gain precision and focus. While race and ethnicity are designated by reference to cultural markers, phenotype, outward expressions of loyalty, celebration, or self-identification, nationalism is a social movement making a territorial claim. According to Hechter (2000), the distinguishing features of nationalist movements include the presence of claims for self-determination and authority over a specified territory and the fact that these demands are not now satisfied. Gellner (1983) adds that nationalism is "primarily a political principle" in which a governing unit should not cut across nor exclude members who share a common cultural boundary.

Brubaker (1996: 6–12) categorizes nationalism as one of three types of collective action mobilized by national minorities, nationalizing states, and external national homelands. This tripartite definition has the advantage of treating the outcomes of nationalist movements as contingent upon the behavior of a nationalizing group in contest with an existing regime, empire, colonial power, or host nation. Put differently, ethnicity becomes transformed into nationalism when it makes specific historical claims and attempts to administer the group as a political community.

Social movement perspectives add the insight that movements can be further distinguished by their relative duration, target, tactics, violence, and audience. These distinctions yield six broad categories: (1) regional or national minority movements that demand sovereignty over a particular territory; (2) civil rights protests that demand expansion of a group's civil and economic rights or demand an end to discrimination; (3) antagonist movements directed against specific ethnic targets, including collective attacks ranging from genocide, ethnic cleansing, and mob violence, to symbolic threats; (4) state-strengthening nationalism, which attempts to unify diverse cultures

(state-building nationalism) or merge politically divided territories into one state (unification nationalism); (5) separatist or secession movements, claiming rights of withdrawal from formal state authority; and (6) genocide or ethnic cleansing, which is an extreme form of violent social movement against a target population.

While these definitions clarify some important distinctions, the application of these terms often becomes tricky when conducting research on E/R/N movements because race and ethnic boundaries are porous, dynamic, and flexible. From different political vantage points and at different times, the same movement may be seen as engaging in senseless violence or as a nationalist liberation movement. Moreover, movements commonly adapt to changing political environments, espousing new goals and engaging in new tactics. Such changes may engender fears that the movement has been coopted and that its authenticity has become compromised. While these transformative qualities of social movements undoubtedly create problems for researchers, there is a hidden advantage as well. Taking these shifts into account might reveal new information about how group identity becomes transformed into social movements.

CORE RESEARCH QUESTIONS

Questions about the origins, persistence, and success of movements drive research efforts in this area. First, how does ethnic, racial, religious, territorial, or national identity become transformed into active social movements? This question underscores the importance of maintaining a distinction between cultural expressions of identity (e.g., ethnic self-help organizations, immigrant festivals, head scarves) from social movements that express claims for expanded rights to some set of authorities, or violence directed against specific groups. Accordingly, scholars ask under what conditions will specific boundaries (e.g., language vs. skin pigmentation) come to be *politically* activated (Barth 1969; Olzak 1992). By posing the issue of mobilization as a question, researchers can analyze the dynamics of ethnic mobilization (or nationalism) based upon ethnicity without assuming it.

Scholars have analyzed the transformation of identity into collective action in terms of the diffusion of protest (Beissinger 2002), event-history analyses of rates of ethnic conflict among groups (Olzak 1992), and ethnic nationalism from a comparative/historical perspective (Brubaker 1996). Such studies highlight the instrumental importance of resources and organizational infrastructure support. The evidence further suggests that favorable changes in economic, legal, and political opportunities facilitate (or hinder) ethnic movements (McAdam 1982).

Second, what factors explain the emergence and persistence of E/R/N movements? Until recently, social scientists focused mainly on the internal characteristics of states to explain E/R/N movements. Thus, poverty, rough terrain, imposition of direct rule, warlord corruption, or some other structural feature of the political system or economy triggers have been identified as factors raising levels of ethnic conflict (Fearon & Laitin 1999, 2003). Others have drawn attention to the advantages of viewing social movements as a function of global and transnational mechanisms that transform local organizations into global movements of violence and claims-making activity (Olzak 2006).

A third question asks whether ethnic movements are truly novel, or whether they are simply political movements that once, earlier in history, adopted other forms. Without undertaking a long historical analysis, answering this question is difficult. However, it seems plausible that social movements are now more likely to be couched in distinctly ethnic terms, as a function of self-determination norms and UN declarations on minority rights. Some scholars claim that E/R/N movements are distinct from other bases of political contests (such as regional or religious social movements) because they employ distinctly *modern* claims (Gellner 1983; Smith 1991). However, this characteristic does not imply that such movements espouse modern values or contemporary themes. Indeed, many nationalist movements (e.g., Islamic nationalist movements) have invoked themes demanding a return to the past. Instead, for most scholars, evidence that these movements are modern rests on the idea that there is a shared identity of a "people" with boundaries beyond a parochial village or town (Anderson 1991).

A fourth orienting question concerns the shift in the scope of activity: What are the mechanisms that cause social movements to expand their scope from local concerns to encompass national goals? Brubaker (1996) describes "nationness" as an institutional process that begins to crystallize with state expansion. Similarly, Anderson (1991) posits a causal relationship between the development of ethnic movements that coincided with state-building and the spread of literacy; such models suggest a causal link between state-building and ethnic mobilization. Yet recent research suggests that the density of international connections among states may be reducing the number of nationally based movements, as transnational movements now mobilize across state administrative units in reaction to global processes (Olzak 2006).

Another set of issues raises questions about the nature of the relationship between ethnic conflict and internal civil war. For instance, they ask, under what conditions does ethnic conflict promote civil war? Alternatively, others are concerned with the duration of conflict, asking whether the presence of ethnic conflict prolongs the duration of civil wars. Several innovative lines of research have suggested that there is a strong link between ethnic cleavages and violence, in which group differences mobilize and sustain the capacity for groups to incite civil wars. For instance, Sambanis (2001) finds that civil wars based upon ethnic and/or religious identities are more likely to erupt in countries with high levels of ethnic heterogeneity and low levels of political democracy. In contrast, in nonethnic (or revolutionary) civil wars, economic and development indicators (especially energy consumption) have more influence than do measures of ethnic heterogeneity and indicators of democracy.

Scholars have also explored a reverse causal argument. In this view, economic (or political) instability *results from* prior conflict, or economic decline follows the public's anticipation of civil unrest. In an attempt to sort out the causal ordering of economic effects on ethnic wars, current empirical evidence supports the notion that economic decline raises rates of internal civil war, rather than the reverse, but that political instability and state strength may be endogenous to the process of ethnic and nationalist mobilization (Olzak 2004).

Ethnic diversity also prolongs the duration of civil wars. Fearon and Laitin (2003) find that the duration of violent civil conflict increases when there are a small number of large ethnic groups, when there are conflicts over land use, and when rebels have access to external (or contraband) resources. Not surprisingly, the evidence shows that ethnic wars and civil wars are causally and temporally related.

LEADING THEORETICAL PERSPECTIVES

Perspectives offering explanations of the emergence, growth, and decay of E/R/N social movements emphasize one or more processes of changing economic, political, or social conditions. Each tradition has generated a number of important empirical studies, which are linked by common theoretical concepts and mechanisms.

Periods of nation-building apparently play a central role in determining the nature of the identity of an imagined "nation." Thus, one explanation for the fact that ethnic movements take on different forms is related to the events surrounding a country's national origin. The literature on nation-building has suggested that ethnic movements are most likely to turn violent early in (more or less legitimate) administrative-unit stages of nation-building, when contested claims of power and legitimacy remain unresolved (Hechter 2000). In this view, nations were "birth marked" by the nature of conflicts – religious, territorial, ethnic, or otherwise – that prevailed during a particular historical period.

The legacy of colonialism provides a number of instructive lessons for understanding the emergence and timing of nationalist movements. Territorial boundaries drawn during periods of colonialist rule (especially in Africa and the Middle East) provide examples of how ethnic cleavages can turn into violent rebellions against attempts to subdue indigenous populations. During nation-building and state-formation, outcomes depend upon complicated negotiations between opponents, nation-builders, and external participants. Reactive anti-colonialist movements can become transformed into nationalist movements when regimes become perceived as illegitimate and artificial, when repression recedes, and when allies infuse new resources into nationalist movements.

Ethnic movements are fundamentally embedded in (often contradictory) legends and myths about various group identities and actions that have shaped their histories. Language, religion, immigration, and migration histories all play a role in building the defining characteristics of a region. However, periods of nation-building apparently play a central role in determining the nature of identity of an imagined "nation." Thus, one explanation for the fact that ethnic movements take on different forms is related to the events surrounding a country's national origin. The literature on state-formation has suggested that ethnic movements are most likely to turn violent during the early (and less legitimate) stages of nation-building, when contested claims of power and legitimacy remain unresolved.

During periods of instability within states or colonial empires, the content of ethnic claims (especially territorial rights) often brings them into confrontation with regimes that have not completely won the hearts and minds of the inhabitants of the contested territory. Outcomes depend upon complicated negotiations between opponents, nation-builders, and often-external participants, who may favor one or the other side. Although some theorists once assumed that the process of nation-building could be analyzed as an evolutionary set of stages, such assumptions seem naïve today. Evidently the process of creating a legitimate nation with an accepted system of authority and leaders is better conceptualized as a dynamic set of negotiated meanings (Brubaker 1996). National identities and ethnic communities are constantly being reconstructed and boundary lines redrawn. Social construction theories of race/ethnic social movements have helped clarify Anderson's (1991) claim that nations are "imagined communities," whose organizational form serves obvious political purposes and ends, but may have little factual basis.

Anderson's work has provided a useful starting place for understanding why nationalist and ethnic movements aim to reconcile the lack of correspondence between state boundaries and national identity. Smith (1991), Hechter (2000), and many others have emphasized the fact that few (if any) nation-states are homogeneous entities; not only do states sometimes encompass many nations (as in the notion of multiculturalism), but also many nations exist without a state. If a "nation" is demarcated by a self-identified boundary, then one nation may be dispersed across multiple state boundaries (as in the concept of a Kurdish nation), which may ultimately acquire its own state (Brass 1991). This implies that, even if they are only temporarily successful, ethnic movements can undermine the legitimacy of a state attempting to unify under assumptions of ethnic homogeneity.

During the mid-1970s an important tradition emerged suggesting that the combination of economic deprivation and cultural subordination produces enduring cleavages facilitating ethnic political mobilization. Internal colonialism theory suggests that a combination of uneven industrialization and cultural differences among regions in core nations causes ethnic grievances to become the basis of enduring political contention (Hechter 1975). This tradition has also been applied to local markets that are based upon an ethnic stratification system. Within internal colonies, this theory suggests that a *cultural division of labor* often emerges, in which dominant ethnic populations monopolize administrative and supervisory occupations (and rewards), while subordinate ethnic populations are relegated to lower-status occupations (often in extractive industries). As a consequence, ethnic and labor market cleavages triumph over other types of possible loyalties.

Competition theories of race/ethnic movements emerged during the early 1980s to counter these claims (Olzak & Nagel 1986). These perspectives suggested that economic changes and political opportunities that favor disadvantaged groups can intensify competition among groups, which in turn activates ethnic boundaries and provokes ethnic mobilization. According to competition theory, declining inequality among regions (or groups) promotes competitive conflict among groups. This is because declining inequality and intergroup contact release forces of competitive exclusion and conflict (Barth 1969). In this view, E/R social movements result from conditions of *niche overlap* (rather than from niche segregation, as in internal colonialism theory). For example, competition theorists

argue that ethnic conflict rises when ethnic groups within nations come to compete in the *same* labor markets and increase their access to similar sets of political, economic, and social resources (Bonacich 1972; Olzak 1992).

A key variant of competition theory is split labor market theory, which holds that ethnic antagonism peaks when two or more ethnically or racially differentiated groups command different wage prices within the same labor market niche (Bonacich 1972). This theory has been supported by evidence on Chinese laborers, the US labor movement, contemporary South Africa, analyses of post-industrial racial conflict in the US, analyses of race and ethnic conflict in cities in the nineteenth-century US, and the former republics of the Ukraine, Latvia, Estonia, and Lithuania (Beissinger 2002).

Rational choice theorists state that modern ethnic movements occur with regularity because ethnic groups lower monitoring costs and increase benefits attached to ethnic mobilization, allowing ethnic groups to overcome the free-rider problems attached to other types of mobilization efforts (Hechter 2000). Because ethnic groups are able to form dense social networks easily, costs of monitoring commitment are minimized, which fosters ethnic mobilization. Building on rational choice models, Fearon and Laitin (1996) have linked the strategic aspects of ethnic identity to violence, as elites build on existing ethnic loyalties (see also Petersen 2002). Such loyalties can prove fatal to group members. Moreover, the presence of genocidal norms (defined as a threat of sanctions to in-group members who decline participation in ethnic mayhem) increases the scale of ethnic violence. These authors offer an explanation for one persistent and counterintuitive finding in the literature: despite a history of intergroup cooperation, tolerance, intermarriage, and trust among different groups interacting within a region, the intensity of ethnic killing and violence may remain high due to the presence of genocidal norms.

Similarly, theorists have extended prisoner's dilemma models to consider the implications of game theory for ethnic mobilization, including outbreak of ethnic war (Fearon & Laitin 1996). While armed ethnic rebellions tend to last longer than nonethnic ones (Fearon 2004), a variety of ethnic and cultural characteristics have few systematic effects on the onset or duration of civil wars in general (Fearon & Laitin 2003).

Applying game-theory models to four specific ethnic movements, Laitin (1995) compares violence in the Basque country and Catalonia in Spain and post-Soviet Georgia to ethnic mobilization in the Ukraine. Laitin finds that three factors predict the outbreak of violence (holding a number of cultural and historical factors constant): (1) rural social structure, which facilitates group monitoring and expedites militant commando operations; (2) tipping game mechanisms that explain the conditions under which costs to joining nationalist campaigns (and recruitment of soldiers to nationalist armies) are reduced; and (3) sustaining mechanisms, which rely on several random shocks which trigger a culture of violence that becomes culturally embedded in regional and collective memories.

Political perspectives emphasize the role of shifts in political constraints and opportunity structures that influence the trajectory of E/R social movements. These theories emphasize institutional arrangements, court rulings and reforms, and regional concentration of ethnic populations as viable political instruments leading to mobilization. Two studies from India illustrate these points. Chandra (2004) argues that political systems based on ethnic patronage systems can inadvertently provide the foundation for permanent hostilities. Alternatively, Varshney (2002) finds that when business, civic, and voluntary associations integrate and/or cross-cut ethnic lines, confrontations are significantly less likely to erupt.

In cross-national studies of the influence of political structures, Gurr (1993) and Gurr and Moore (1997) emphasize the centrifugal force of ethnic political parties, which maintain ethnic loyalties through institutional arrangements and patronage based on ethnic loyalties. Such forces produce fierce loyalties when language, religion, or some other marker also distinguishes a population that is geographically concentrated (Fearon & Laitin 2003). Other scholars have argued that while ethnic regional concentrations are important, they do not necessarily lead to ethnic violence. Instead, these scholars emphasize proximate causes or triggering mechanisms, such as political changes in authority, collapse of colonial authorities or empires, or transition to market economies or democracies.

Social movement perspectives suggest that shifts in political opportunities (either positive or negative) drive the rates of protest activity and insurgency. Political shifts in regimes or power arrangements that offer new opportunities for formerly disadvantaged ethnic minorities within the newly democratizing states can encourage mobilization. So the decline of authoritarian regimes seemingly coincides with the resurgence of E/R/N movements, because the retreat of strong repressive authorities leaves a power vacuum. As the former military and administrative structures recede, local-level elites mobilize ethnic loyalties and take advantage of this vacuum.

Evidence from civil wars in Bosnia and Kosovo provides another example of how regime instability shapes opportunities for E/R/N movements. At the same time, policies that involve ethnic resettlement programs often concentrate ethnic populations and create new networks that provide new recruits for mobilizing ethnic violence, as examples from the West Bank in Israel, or the Kurds in Germany, suggest. Thus, transitions to democracy may mobilize ethnic movements by offering new political advantages to ethnic groups that were more easily submerged in repressive regimes.

States often respond to challenges from nationalist movements by alternating between strategies of repression and concession (Hechter 2000). For example, the evidence suggests that states shift from strategies of repression to accommodation, depending on both the virulence of dissident protest behavior and state capacity to repress these challenges. However, others have suggested the intriguing hypothesis that it is the vacillation of states itself that incites nationalist violence, signaling a weakness in the state's internal capacity to act (for reviews, see Olzak 2004).

The potential for ethnic separatism also influences the intensity of collective violence in a country and this effect is stronger in states with weakened political institutions. The evidence finds that the potential for ethnic separatism increases political violence overall, but that this relationship holds only in countries with relatively low levels of political institutionalization (defined by the presence of binding rules on political participation) (Sambanis 2001).

The imposition of external political authority on ethnic minorities compared to imposition of structures of indirect authority has important consequences for ethnic and nationalist movements. Hechter (2000) has argued that the seeds of nationalist movements are embedded in specific political structural arrangements in which colonialist or federated authority cedes formal authority to local leaders. Under such conditions, local elites are delegated political power and authority by centralized authorities, yet the power of local elites is fundamentally based upon regional identities and loyalties. When central authority is weakened or challenged (by external events such as war, famine, or economic crises), or when central authority is withdrawn (as in the case of the Soviet Union), local elites can mobilize on the basis of regional/ethnic identity. According to this argument, the imposition of direct rule at this point can encourage both state-building nationalism (due to its centralizing authority and integration processes) and peripheral nationalism, cultural politics, or regional subnational movements within states.

Brubaker (1996) reflects these themes in his work on "new nationalisms" in Western Europe. Instead of arguing that the erosion of Soviet power and authority allowed ethnic tensions to surface and diffuse across former Soviet territories, Brubaker argues that the federated system of regional and ethnically defined republics in the Soviet Union created the structural basis for the ultimate disintegration of these republics. Wilkinson (2004) finds empirical support for this argument, reporting that states in India with a high degree of institutionalization of ethnic parties produce significantly higher rates of ethnic violence and hostility.

Recent theoretical analyses emphasize both the cultural and cognitive components of social movements, suggesting that group identity is both an important mobilizing strategy and a consequence of mobilization. In particular, movements invoke one or more cultural themes of nationalism, rights of self-determination, expansion of human rights, and basic rights of sovereignty (Smith 1991; Brubaker & Laitin 1998; Brubaker 2004). In this view, a socially constructed ethnic identity is not a given, but it

may be the *result* of prior collective action. This perspective allows researchers to study how social mechanisms of contact, conflict, borrowing, and other forms of interaction might influence the emergence of new ethnic or racial categories. Over time, as ethnic conflicts recur along the same cleavage lines, identities (and revenge tactics) fall along recognizable race and ethnic categories. As group violence and revenge escalates on either side to a conflict, small-scale or individual skirmishes became redefined as collective events requiring a response. In analyzing forces escalating group conflict, social movement scholars tend to underscore the emergent properties of both identities and conflict.

Although useful for case studies of social movements that did happen, one drawback of a purely constructionist perspective is that it becomes difficult for researchers to determine the causal ordering of emergent group identity and ethnic mobilization. In studying the impact of ethnic identity on ethnic social movements, Smith (1984) provided a (as yet untested) framework that might unravel the causal steps implied by this process. Smith lists the conditions under which ethnic identity is likely to become activated. These include intervals (1) during prolonged periods of conflict and warfare, when group identities are under siege or are threatened by others (including third parties to the conflict, as in the Cold War), (2) during periods of secularization or cultural change, in which a technologically superior or economically dominant culture threatens a more traditional culture, and (3) during periods of intense commercialization, which integrate a society into a broader system of economic exchange dominated by more advanced technologies or more powerful adversaries.

Economic and political crises that once affected only local areas now have repercussions in vastly different and formerly unconnected regions and states. Since the advent of modern media, civil wars, terrorist acts, and acts by ethnic social movements have produced reactions across national borders. Transnational social movements (TSMs) are social movements that span multiple national borders, target forces of global integration, or are social movements that concern global-level issues (e.g., global environmental concerns). Taking an international perspective helps clarify how economic interdependence within states has reinvigorated ethnic politics. Regional associations such as the EU, OPEC, NATO, and other supranational organizations promote interstate migration and decrease reliance of regions within states on the military and economic power of the nation-state (Olzak & Nagel 1986). Multistate organizations also provide an audience for insurgent groups demanding new sovereignty rights (Koopmans & Statham 2000). In this view, an increasingly dense network of international economic relations, exemplified by multinational corporations, growing trade and foreign investment, and supranational economic associations, will continue to produce more large-scale ethnic movements.

A global strategy offers arguments about forces of globalization that produce inequality, competition, and mobilization. Olzak (2006) holds that integration of a world economic and political system has encouraged ethnic fragmentation within states. It does so by increasing the access of formerly disadvantaged groups to political resources, creating new political opportunities for mobilizing, and increasing levels of economic inequality in peripheral countries, which increases the potential for competition and conflict among groups within these states. Competition among groups escalates the number of demands for amelioration of injustice or ethnic inequalities. Moreover, the process of integration of the world's states has varying effects on different sectors of the world system.

As the world's states have become more directly linked through communication and media channels, information about inequality and claims for redress of this inequality have increased sharply. Thus, the global forces of integration tend to crystallize and empower local-level cleavages, increasing solidarity and heightening the capacity to mobilize movements challenging state authority. Together, the dual trends of increasing political access and decreasing ethnic economic disparity shape ethnic protest.

This perspective suggests that individual states will become less powerful in negotiations when confronting non-state actors and/or transnational movements than in the past. As state economies and politics become more integrated, international associations and events occurring outside state boundaries will become

increasingly salient. It seems likely that as integration of the world's states (politically, diplomatically, and economically) proceeds, ethnic groups within states will become less constrained by their own state authorities. The growing predominance of an integrated set of states ironically decreases the ability of any one state to dominate its internal borders. Highly integrated nation-states cannot simply repress, jail, or torture the ethnic challengers without risking international condemnation, sanctions, and boycotts. Furthermore, neighboring countries may directly or indirectly finance campaigns of instability, using political refugees or exiles as mercenary soldiers. There is growing evidence on transnational environmental and human rights movements that supports these contentions (Olzak 2006).

Diffusion of ideologies, resources, and personnel accelerates these trends. Ethnic social movements occurring in neighboring countries have powerful diffusion properties, destabilizing or threatening nearby regimes. Sambanis (2001) argues that elite factions (or warlords) offering military and financial support from neighboring countries have played crucial roles in prolonging ethnic wars in Africa and Central Asia in recent years. Although it is difficult to study (because many of the transactions are clandestine and sources of data are unreliable), corruption feeds upon an increased flow of arms, mercenaries, and illegal drugs. It is likely that networks of local warlords also fuel ethnic wars (without state or international sanctions) in neighboring countries (Fearon & Laitin 2003; Fearon 2004).

Global perspectives suggest another way that an ideology supporting human rights has accelerated the spread and acceptance of an ideology supporting ethnic rights. In this view, as the worldwide human rights movement gained momentum, claims for national sovereignty, group rights, and freedom became intertwined. Recent analyses of the diffusion of world culture and ideology have shifted the emphasis of world-systems theory to consider the ideological implications of the integration of the world system (for reviews, see Olzak 2006). In this view, the diffusion of human rights organizations and intergovernmental associations (including social movement organizations) has motivated social movements to increase demands for expansion of group rights in states that declared independence since 1945.

Global approaches suggest that, as nation-states became linked in networks of military and economic associations, national political boundaries weaken and political regimes become vulnerable to international and external challenges. The same forces that encouraged the diffusion of nationalism as an ideology also affect ethnic movements within and between state boundaries.

Several lines of research on ethnic conflict support these contentions. Thus, one (perhaps unanticipated) consequence of the integration of the European monetary system is that ethnic tensions have risen rather dramatically (for examples, see Koopmans & Statham 2000). Furthermore, as political and economic barriers have declined, labor (and capital) flow move more freely across states. However, one potential consequence of increasing flows of foreign workers across borders has been that new right-wing parties across Western Europe have mobilized sentiment against foreign workers. To the extent that the integration of the European Union has restructured local politics within European countries, the opportunity has arisen for ethnic politics on both sides of the immigration question. As a consequence, anti-foreigner sentiment, nationalist political parties, and attacks on foreigners also appear to be rising in most Western European countries, especially in Germany, France, the Netherlands, and England (Koopmans & Olzak 2004).

Military interdependence constitutes an obvious way that international relations affect conflicts within countries. Although such strategies are not new, superpowers arm and train ethnic and subnational groups in order to stabilize or in some cases destabilize regimes. The cases of recent rebellions financed and supported by transnational forces (on both sides of the struggles) in civil wars in Afghanistan, Nicaragua, Vietnam, Iraq, and many other settings illustrate this point. If arguments suggesting a link between international networks and E/R/N movements are correct, then an increase in transnational processes could potentially weaken the viability of the nation-state as a main organizing strategy for territorial authority and control.

A final international trend in social movements deserves attention. This is reactive movements that span national borders, making vague claims about identities that are contrary to existing modernization or development efforts by dominant countries, ideologies, or ethnicities. In the contemporary era, some of these movements have been characterized as loosely connected by anti-modernist claims that have a basis in religious fundamentalism. These movements share a concern with symbols of identity politics (and with symbols that seem ethnic – such as the wearing of head scarves), but they diverge from most E/R/N movements because they rarely express specific claims to territorial rights and instead voice demands for ethnic/religious purity. Whether or not such movements will continue to gain momentum remains an open question.

EVALUATION OF VARIOUS PERSPECTIVES

Many scholars analyze different types of E/R/N movements separately, by historical period, regional groupings, and by specific goals or tactics. While it has become popular for scholars to claim that E/R/N movements are produced by a constellation of historically contingent factors, this strategy has hampered our ability to develop powerful explanations that identify some general mechanisms of social change. Yet other social scientists have demonstrated that there are substantial theoretical payoffs attached to analyzing the similarities across E/R/N movements. By paying attention to the commonalities among forms of ethnic and nationalist movements, we stand to gain more leverage over questions about how protest escalates and diffuses, or how spontaneous protests become transformed into sustained (or violent) social movements that challenge existing authority structures.

Approaches that seek to emphasize the continuities and discontinuities among social movements and their emergent forms allow cumulative and testable theories to be constructed and evaluated. In contrast, if multiple types of ethnic mobilization (from civil rights movements to ethnic civil wars) are analyzed separately by country, time period, and movement goals, it becomes impossible to know when to stop creating new categories and crafting unique explanations to cover each new occurrence of a nationalist event or ethnic campaign. Truly comparative work that seeks to build theories that can be falsified empirically holds far more promise than does a strategy that views each movement as a unique and separate category. In the context of complex dynamics of transnational social movements, activists and organizations engage in activity that engages and activates ethnic identity within nations. Such reactive movements can have reverberations to kindred or disaporic groups beyond a single nation. Understanding the commonalities among these forms in the context of a global system seems especially relevant.

Assessing the relative importance of various causal factors explaining ethnic movements over time is also hampered by the fact that ethnic and racial boundaries (and labels) often change over time. Answers to questions about the nature and trajectory of ethnic movements lie in conducting careful empirical analyses and comparisons of different kinds of events – ethnic, civil rights, national, religious, civil wars, and autonomy social movements of various kinds that share some (but not all) root causes.

Recent trends have taken these dynamics into account by emphasizing the emergence of a more densely connected global system. The globalization of social movements has led current research on ethnic and national movements away from a sole emphasis on internal features of states and toward the international context of collective actions. Clearly, the internationalization of the world economy and political integration of organizational, diplomatic, and trade linkages have prompted us to reconsider previous assumptions that rest on stable characteristics of states. Research reviewed here depicts social movements that have produced strikingly similar social movements that share similar forms, goals, tactics, and ideologies. Thus, theories that focus solely on the internal bases of discontent now seem shortsighted. A resulting network of economic and political ties cuts across the state system. As a consequence, ethnic mobilization at the global level provides fertile ground for new types of movements based upon national, ethnic, and other cultural identities.

Applying lessons from colonialism and imperialist regimes to new forms of nationalism may allow us to better understand sources of fundamentalist nationalism, terrorist networks, and international networks of social movement recruitment and training. Such movements are both local and international in scope, and, because of this flexibility, they are able to shift direction quickly, often without warning. By turning to explanations firmly based on theories of international connections and processes, we may be able to understand the emergence of this new form of nationalism.

SEE ALSO: Collective Identity; Nation-State; Nationalism; Protest, Diffusion of; Race; Race and Ethnic Consciousness; Race and Ethnic Politics; Race (Racism); Social Movements; Transnational Movements

REFERENCES AND SUGGESTED READINGS

Anderson, B. (1991) *Imagined Communities*, 2nd edn. Verso, London.

Barth, F. (1969) *Ethnic Groups and Boundaries*. Sage, Los Angeles.

Beissinger, M. (2002) *Nationalist Mobilization and the Collapse of the Soviet State*. Cambridge University Press, Cambridge.

Bonacich, E. (1972) A Theory of Ethnic Antagonism. *American Sociological Review* 37: 547–59.

Brass, P. R. (1991) *Ethnicity and Nationalism: Theory and Comparison*. Sage, Newbury Park, CA.

Brubaker, R. (1996) *Nationalism Reframed: Nationhood and the National Question in the New Europe*. Cambridge University Press, Cambridge.

Brubaker, R. (2004) *Ethnicity Without Groups*. Harvard University Press, Cambridge, MA.

Brubaker, R. & Laitin, D. D. (1998) Ethnic and Nationalist Violence. *Annual Review of Sociology* 24: 423–52.

Chandra, K. (2004) *Why Ethnic Parties Succeed*. Cambridge University Press, Cambridge.

Fearon, J. (2004) Why Do Some Civil Wars Last So Much Longer Than Others? *Journal of Peace Research* 41: 275–302.

Fearon, J. & Laitin, D. D. (1996) Explaining Interethnic Cooperation. *American Political Science Review* 90: 715–35.

Fearon, J. & Laitin, D. D. (1999) Weak States, Rough Terrain, and Large-Scale Ethnic Violence Since 1945. Paper presented at the annual meetings of the American Political Science Association, Atlanta.

Fearon, J. & Laitin, D. D. (2003) Ethnicity, Insurgency, and War. *American Political Science Review* 97: 75–90.

Fearon, J. & Laitin, D. D. (2005) Primary Commodity Exports and Civil War. *Journal of Conflict Resolution* 49: 483–507.

Gellner, E. (1983) *Nations and Nationalism.* Cornell University Press, Ithaca, NY.

Gurr, T. R. (1993) *Minorities at Risk.* Institute of Peace, Washington, DC.

Gurr, T. R. & Moore, W. H. (1997) Ethnopolitical Rebellion. *American Journal of Political Science* 41: 1079–103.

Hechter, M. (1975) *Internal Colonialism.* University of California Press, Berkeley.

Hechter, M. (2000) *Containing Nationalism.* Oxford University Press, New York.

Horowitz, D. L. (2001) *The Deadly Ethnic Riot.* University of California Press, Berkeley.

Koopmans, R. & Olzak, S. (2004) Discursive Opportunities and the Evolution of Right-Wing Violence in Germany. *American Journal of Sociology* 110: 198–230.

Koopmans, R. & Statham, P. (2000) *Challenging Immigration and Ethnic Relations Politics.* Oxford University Press, Oxford.

Laitin, D. D. (1995) National Revivals and Violence. *Archives European Sociologie* 36: 3–43.

McAdam, D. (1982) *Political Process and the Development of Black Insurgency.* University of Chicago Press, Chicago.

Nagel, J. (1996) *American Indian Ethnic Renewal: Red Power and the Resurgence of Identity.* Oxford University Press, New York.

Olzak, S. (1992) *The Dynamics of Ethnic Competition and Conflict.* Stanford University Press, Stanford.

Olzak, S. (2004) Ethnic and Nationalist Social Movements. In: Snow, D., Soule, S., & Kriesi, H. (Eds.), *The Blackwell Companion to Social Movements.* Oxford University Press, Oxford, pp. 666–93.

Olzak, S. (2006) *The Global Dynamics of Race and Ethnic Mobilization.* Stanford University Press, Stanford.

Olzak, S. & Nagel, J. (Eds.) (1986) *Competitive Ethnic Relations.* Academic Press, Orlando.

Petersen, R. (2002) *Understanding Ethnic Violence.* Cambridge University Press, Cambridge.

Sambanis, N. (2001) Do Ethnic and Nonethnic Civil Wars Have the Same Causes? *Journal of Conflict Resolution* 45: 259–82.

Smith, A. (1984) National Identity and Myths of Ethnic Descent. *Research in Social Movements, Conflict and Change* 7: 95–130.

Smith, A. (1991) *The Ethnic Origin of Nations.* Blackwell, Oxford.

Varshney, A. (2002) *Ethnic Conflict and Civic Life: Hindus and Muslims in India.* Yale University Press, New Haven.

Wilkinson, R. (2004) *Electoral Competition and Ethnic Violence in India.* Cambridge University Press, Cambridge.

ethnicity

Richard Jenkins

The ancient Greek word *ethnos*, the root of "ethnicity," referred to people living and acting together in a manner that we might apply to a "people" or a "nation": a collectivity with a "way of life" – some manners and mores, practices and purposes – in common, whose members share something in terms of "culture." Thus the anthropologist Frederick Barth (1969) defined ethnicity as "the social organization of culture difference." Ethnicity is not only a relatively abstract collective phenomenon, however: it also matters to individuals. To quote another anthropologist, Clifford Geertz, ethnicity is "personal identity collectively ratified and publicly expressed" (1973: 268).

After kinship, ethnicity is perhaps the most ubiquitous way of classifying and organizing humans into collectivities. It requires shared perceptions that certain people are similar to each other and different from others. Ethnic inclusivity and exclusivity build on the cultural differences and similarities that people regard as significant to generate boundaries and dramatize them. How the nuanced complexities of culture are organized into ethnicity is, however, neither obvious nor straightforward. People may appear to differ enormously in terms of culture and yet be able to identify themselves as ethnic fellows: think, for example, about the diversity that is subsumed within Jewishness. Nor does apparent cultural similarity preclude strong ethnic differentiation. Viewed by an anthropologist from Mars, Danes and Norwegians, for example, might look very similar, or even the same; they, however, do not see things this way.

This suggests that our understanding of ethnicity cannot simply depend upon a crude model of discrete and different cultures seen "in the round." Some cultural themes offer more scope for ethnic identification than others: language, notions of shared descent, historical narratives, locality and co-residence, and religion have all proved to be particularly potent ethnic markers. Even so, a common language, for example, or shared religious beliefs and practices do not necessarily do the trick in themselves. Nor do shared space and place: living together may be a potent source of common identification, but space and place can also divide people. They may be a resource for which to compete and the interaction that is necessary for a sense of difference to emerge takes up space: it needs a terrain. Lines are drawn in the sand, and borders and boundaries come to delineate arbitrary group territories.

This further suggests that ethnicity is not a matter of definable degrees or obvious kinds of cultural similarity or difference. There is no checklist with which to determine whether or not members of Group A are *really* ethnically different to members of Group B, or whether Group C is an ethnic group or some other kind of collectivity. Enumerating cultural traits or characteristics is not a useful way to understand or identify ethnic differences. Human beings are distinguished by their voices, and the baseline is always whether a group is seen by its members to be different.

Self-definition is not *all* that matters, however. It is also necessary that a group be categorized as distinctive by others (Jenkins 1997: 51–73). This means that power – whose definition counts in any given situation – is always a lurking presence. There can be no such thing as unilateral ethnicity. Ethnicity always involves ethnic *relations*: connections and contacts between people who are seen to be different, as well as between those who are seen to be the same. A sense of ethnicity can only arise in the context of relationships and interaction with others: without difference there is no similarity. Defining *us* implies – if nothing stronger – an image of *them*. It is difficult to imagine a meaningful identification, ethnic or whatever, that is not at least recognized by others. It is not enough to assert, "I am an X," or "We are Xs," for either of these things to become so.

To say this, however, begs a question: what counts as "being an X" in the contemporary

world? Looking at the range of relationships of similarity and difference that might be said to involve "culture" reveals a broad spectrum of possibilities. Neighborhood and locality are among the more immediate. Local senses of belonging that we call "community" – built on an "us" and a "them," apparently shared understandings, and ways of doing things in common – are well documented (Cohen 1985). Kinship ties may also be invoked as criteria of membership. More abstract regional identities, such as the North–South distinctions that still play so well in England and the United States, are also clearly related. From here it is but a step to the nation (Anderson 1983). While the boundaries of community and region are policed by the informal powers of individuals and groups to accept or reject identity claims, national identity is a formal package that includes citizenship, a passport, political rights and duties within and without the national borders, and so on. This is a domain of formal power and authority. Even here, however, everyday practices such as language, taste in food, and perhaps religion may come into the picture: ways of life are still significant.

Descent and kinship may also be important in understandings of the nation (as in the German model of the national identity, defined in terms of "blood" rather than "soil"; Bauman 1992). This requires us also to look at "race," the belief in distinctive populations sharing common ancestors in the remote past, human stocks with their own characteristics. From this point of view, Germans are different from Poles, for example: they are not the same "kind" of people. And although "racial" categories may draw upon the visible features of bodies to assert the "naturalness" of particular similarities and differences, let us remember that "race" is culturally defined, not natural.

The words "ethnic" or "ethnicity" do not appear in the two paragraphs above. Yet in terms of the definition of ethnicity offered earlier, much of the similarity and difference that has been referred to looks something like ethnicity. This suggests some questions. Where does ethnicity end and communal identity, or local identity, or regional identity, or national identity, begin? What is the relationship between community and locality, or locality and region? And what are the differences between all of these things? Where does "race" fit in with them? Are community, locality, region, nation, and "race" even the same kind of thing? The answer is no, and yes. No, in that they appear to be about different things, each evoking its own combinations of criteria of similarity and difference. No, in that some of these criteria are more flexible than others. Locality or citizenship, for example, are easier to change than descent-based criteria such as family or "race." No, in that some of these identities are more likely than others to find expression through ideologies, such as nationalism and racism, which describe the world as it is believed to be and as it should be. But yes, in that the criteria of similarity and difference in each case are cultural. Yes, in that they all contribute to the social organization of a broad and distinctive genre of collective identification, which is not reducible to either kinship or social class, to pick only the most obvious comparisons. And yes, in that they all offer the potential for political organization.

Instead of searching for ever more precise definitions, a better approach might suggest that communal, local, regional, national, and "racial" identities are locally and historically specific variations on a generic principle of collective identification, ethnicity. Each says something about "the social organization of culture difference" and "the cultural organization of social difference." They are culturally imagined and socially consequential, a way of phrasing the matter which recognizes that distinctions between "the cultural" and "the social" may not be particularly helpful. These communal, local, regional, national, and "racial" identities also offer the possibility of "collectively ratified personal identity." They may make a considerable personal difference to individuals, both in their sense of self and in their judgment and treatment of others.

This broad understanding of ethnicity acknowledges that ethnic identification is a contextually variable and relative process. That ethnicity may be negotiable, flexible, and variable in its significance from one situation to another is among the most important lessons of the specialist social science literature (Cornell 1996). Which also means that, depending on cultural context and social situation, ethnicity may *not* be negotiable. There may not be much

of a choice. And when ethnicity matters to people, it has the capacity to *really* matter, to move them to action and awaken powerful emotions.

That ethnicity can be a source of powerful affect and meaning is at the heart of a long-standing debate between "primordialists," who believe that ethnic attachments are immutable and irresistible, and "constructionists," who argue that they are a matter of strategy and negotiation; between what Marcus Banks (1996: 186–7) has evocatively described as models of "ethnicity in the heart" and "ethnicity in the head." There are several things to bear in mind about this debate. First, the degree to which ethnicity and its variants matter, and to whom, differs demonstrably from epoch to epoch and place to place. There is no consistency with respect to the strength of ethnic attachments, although that humans form ethnic attachments seems to be fairly universal. Nor do we need to resort to notions of essence and nature to explain why, when ethnicity matters to people, it can matter so much: the nature and content of primary socialization, the power of symbols, the implacability of some local histories, and the often considerable consequences of identification are probably sufficient to account for this. What matters is not whether ethnicity is a primordial personal and cultural essence, into which we are born and about which we can do nothing, but that many people fervently believe this to be so and behave accordingly.

Recently, questions have been asked about whether concepts such as ethnicity and identity actually explain behavior (Martin 1995; Brubaker & Cooper 2000). Does ethnicity shape what people do? Does it, in fact, *matter*? This is partly a response to ambitious postmodern claims about "identity politics," "hybridity," and the like. The argument is that words such as "identity" and "ethnicity" have been bandied about so much that they have become analytically meaningless. While it is easy to sympathize with this view, it is an argument for rehabilitating these concepts, not abandoning them.

The debate is also about the relationship between ethnicity and interests (Goldstein & Rayner 1994): is talking about ethnicity an analytical and political smokescreen to obscure the fact that people are, as they have always done, simply pursuing their material interests? We are back here with Barth's original account of ethnicity as an emergent property of transactions and negotiations. Now, as then, we have to ask whether it is possible easily to disentangle identification from interests. For example, who I am, whether that is defined individually or collectively, will influence how I define what is in my interests and what is against them. From another direction, how other people identify me has some bearing on what they perceive my – and, indeed, often *their* – interests to be. What's more, my pursuit of particular interests may cause me to be identified in particular ways by myself and by others. Finally, how I identify others may have influences on which interests I pursue.

Interests and ethnicity are entwined in each other, not opposing principles of motivation: where ethnic identification is locally salient, one cannot be understood without the other. Locally – and ethnicity is always a local matter – primary socialization, the affective power of symbols, obstinate history, and the consequences of being identified in a particular way by others conspire to ensure that where it matters, ethnicity really matters. Ethnic attachments do not determine the choices that people make, but they cannot be ignored either.

SEE ALSO: Boundaries (Racial/Ethnic); Collective Identity; Ethnic Groups; Ethnocentricism; Identity Politics/Relational Politics; Identity Theory; Imagined Communities; Nationalism; Race; Race and Ethnic Consciousness; Race (Racism)

REFERENCES AND SUGGESTED READINGS

Anderson, B. (1983) *Imagined Communities: Reflections on the Origins and Spread of Nationalism*. Verso, London.
Banks, M. (1996) *Anthropological Constructions of Ethnicity: An Introductory Guide*. Routledge, London.
Barth, F. (1969) Introduction. In: Barth, F. (Ed.), *Ethnic Groups and Boundaries: The Social Organization of Culture Difference*. Universitetsforlaget, Oslo.
Bauman, Z. (1992) Soil, Blood and Identity. *Sociological Review* 40: 675–701.
Brubaker, R. & Cooper, F. (2000) Beyond Identity. *Theory and Society* 29: 1–47.
Cohen, A. P. (1985) *The Symbolic Construction of Communities*. Tavistock, London.
Cornell, S. (1996) The Variable Ties That Bind: Content and Circumstances in Ethnic Processes. *Ethnic and Racial Studies* 19: 265–89.
Geertz, C. (1973) *The Interpretation of Culture*. Basic Books, New York.
Goldstein, J. & Rayner, J. (1994) The Politics of Identity in Late Modern Society. *Theory and Society* 23: 367–84.
Jenkins, R. (1997) *Rethinking Ethnicity: Arguments and Explorations*. Sage, London.
Martin, D. C. (1995) The Choices of Identity. *Social Identities* 1: 5–20.

ethnocentrism

Stephen E. Brown

Ethnocentrism is a belief that the norms, values, ideology, customs, and traditions of one's own culture or subculture are superior to those characterizing other cultural settings. The term was coined by William Graham Sumner in his *Folkways* (1906) and has long served as a cornerstone in the social analysis of culture. While ethnocentrism arguably is a universal phenomenon that facilitates cohesion and continuity at all levels of social organization, it provides the rationalization for attack on other cultures or subcultures in its more extreme forms. It may, for example, motivate criminalization of practices within subcultures or be used to justify going to war with other nation-states. Ethnocentrism is intricately tied to definitions of deviance wherein the deviant is seen as not only different, but also as morally inferior or even evil. Members of the in-group stereotype those in the out-group as ignorant, bad, or even subhuman and these characterizations provide the basis for culture conflict.

Ethnocentrism falls on a continuum along which the more ethnocentric tend to hold to more absolutist or objectivist moral positions. That is, as ethnocentrism grows stronger, there is more acceptance of the notion that there is a single proper way to behave at all times and places. Conversely, cultural and moral relativism is associated with lesser degrees of ethnocentrism. The relativist views social reaction as playing an important role in defining norms and deviance. From such an interactionist perspective people absorb the values and norms of their own culture through a process of enculturation. Cultural values are transmitted down through generations as a result of learning experiences within any cultural setting. Acknowledging such culturally specific learning processes serves to undermine harsher judgments of cultural disparities.

While ethnocentrism in its various degrees is considered a universal cultural phenomenon, a rare, but intriguing phenomenon is inverse ethnocentrism, wherein an individual holds a reverse cultural bias. The more usual derogatory stereotyping of other cultures is replaced by a tendency to see characteristics of other cultural milieus as inherently superior to those of one's own culture. Obviously, persons holding such views tend to be at odds with their own cultural environment and are likely defined by others as eccentrics, traitors, or other deviant identities. Another variation of this is the critique that the relativist is not firmly committed to any moral standards or is tolerant of moral abuses occurring in other cultural settings. The classic argument offered to bolster this concern is that complete relativity would withhold condemnation of atrocities such as genocide. Cultural relativism, however, is central to sociological and anthropological analysis, but does not mean that the sociologist cannot apply any moral criteria to the examination of cultures. It only means that one should not blindly apply the values and standards of one culture to another. Practices within a culture should be analyzed within their own cultural context and moral judgment held in abeyance until their meaning is identified.

Sensitivity to ethnocentrism is vital to understanding social relations because it constitutes blinded bias. Thus, ethnocentrism is at the heart of prejudice and discrimination toward out-groups. Understanding the dynamics of ethnocentrism is thereby central to analyzing human conflict.

SEE ALSO: Acculturation; Assimilation; Deviance, Absolutist Definitions of; Diversity; Ethnic Groups; Ethnicity; Ethnonationalism; Eurocentrism; Homophobia; Multiculturalism; Race; Race (Racism)

REFERENCES AND SUGGESTED READINGS

Curra, J. (2000) *The Relativity of Deviance*. Sage, Thousand Oaks, CA.

Reynolds, V., Falger, V. S. E., & Vine, I. (Eds.) (1987) *The Sociobiology of Ethnocentrism: Evolutionary Dimensions of Xenophobia, Discrimination, Racism and Nationalism*. University of Georgia Press, Athens.

Sumner, W. G. (1906) *Folkways: A Study of the Sociological Importance of Usages, Manners, Customs, Mores, and Morals*. Ginn, Boston.

ethnography

Martyn Hammersley

Literally, ethnography means writing about people, or writing an account of the way of life of a particular people. In early anthropology, what was aimed at was a descriptive account that captured a distinctive culture. Initially, ethnography was contrasted with ethnology, which was concerned with the historical and comparative analysis of cultures based on ethnographic accounts, the latter often being produced by travelers and missionaries. Over time, the term ethnology has fallen out of favor, and ethnography has come to refer to a combination of theoretical interpretation of cultures and firsthand investigation carried out by anthropologists themselves. Moreover, the term has a double meaning, referring both to a form of research and to the product of that research: ethnography as a practice produces ethnographies. And, recently, a distinction has sometimes been drawn between doing ethnography and using ethnographic methods. This has been employed by some anthropologists in an attempt to mark off their own practice from what passes for ethnographic work within sociology and other areas (Wolcott 1999).

For most anthropologists in the past, ethnography required living with a group of people for an extended period, for a year or several years, in order to document their distinctive way of life and the beliefs and values integral to it. However, the term is used in a much looser way within sociology today, to refer to studies that rely on participant observation and/or in-depth, relatively unstructured interviews. As a result, there is considerable overlap in meaning with other concepts, these also often being ambiguous or having fuzzy boundaries, such as "qualitative research," "fieldwork," "interpretive method," and "case study." There is also no firm distinction between ethnography and the study of individual life histories, as the example of "autoethnography" shows, this term referring to an individual researcher's study of his or her own life and context.

In practical terms, as a method, ethnography usually involves most of the following features:

- People's actions and accounts are studied primarily in everyday contexts rather than under conditions created by the researcher, such as in experiments or highly structured interview situations. In other words, research takes place "in the field."
- Data are gathered from a range of sources, including documentary evidence, but participant observation and/or relatively informal conversations are usually the main ones.
- Data collection is "unstructured" in the sense that it does not involve following through a fixed and detailed research design set up at the beginning. Nor are the categories that will be used for interpreting what people say or do built into the data collection process itself via prestructuring of observation, interviews, or documentary analysis.
- The focus is usually on a small number of cases, perhaps a single setting or group of people, typically small scale, with these being studied in depth.
- The analysis of the data involves interpretation of the meanings and functions of human actions and how these are implicated in local and wider contexts. What are produced, for the most part, are verbal descriptions, explanations, and theories; quantification and statistical analysis play a subordinate role at most.

As a set of methods, ethnography is not far removed from the means that we all use in everyday life to make sense of our surroundings. However, it involves a more deliberate and systematic approach and, also, a distinctive mentality. This can perhaps best be summarized as seeking to make the strange familiar, in the sense of finding intelligibility and rationality within it, and making the familiar strange, by suspending those background assumptions that immediately give apparent sense to what we experience (Hammersley & Atkinson 1995).

Over the course of its development, ethnography has been influenced by a range of methodological and theoretical movements. Early on, within anthropology, it was shaped by German ideas about the distinctive character of history and the human sciences, by folk psychology, and by positivism. Subsequently, in the form of the case-study approach of the Chicago School, it was also influenced by philosophical pragmatism, while in more recent times Marxism, phenomenology, hermeneutics, structuralism, and poststructuralism have all played an important role.

While these influences have led to a diversification in approach, ethnography still tends to be characterized by a number of distinctive methodological ideas about the nature of the social world and how it can be understood. As we shall see, these ideas overlap in their implications, but also conflict in some respects. To one degree or another, ethnographers tend to make the following assumptions about the nature of the social world:

- Human behavior is not an automatic product of either internal or external stimuli. Responses to the world are constructed and reconstructed over time and across space in ways that reflect the biographies and sociocultural locations of actors, and how they interpret the situations they face.
- There are diverse cultures that can inform human behavior, and these operate not just between societies or local communities but also within them; and perhaps even within individual actors.
- Human social life is not structured in terms of fixed, law-like patterns, but displays emergent processes of various kinds that involve a high degree of contingency.

In recent times, there has been significant dispute over the character of the phenomena that ethnographers study. We can formulate this as a tension between naturalism and constructionism. The first takes the task of ethnography to be documenting stable cultures, patterns of social interaction, institutions, and so on, as they exist in the world independently of the researcher. By contrast, constructionism is concerned with the interactional or discursive processes whereby cultures, institutions, etc. are continuously and contingently produced and sustained. In line with this, constructionists do not use informants' accounts as a source of information about the world, or even about informants' own experience, but rather study them as exemplifying discursive practices, narrative strategies, or distinctive voices. Moreover, in its more radical forms constructionism treats the social phenomena studied by ethnographers as effectively constituted in and through the research process itself, and especially through the process of writing (Clifford & Marcus 1986).

These assumptions about the nature of the social world are closely linked with ideas about how we can understand it. And here too significant tensions come to the surface. One of these is between a focus on the details of what happens in particular contexts on particular occasions, and a concern to locate what has been studied within the context of some larger whole, or even to use it to show what is happening within that larger whole. Over the past few decades there has been a trend towards more micro-focused ethnographies, perhaps stimulated by the availability of highly portable audio and video-recording equipment which generate large amounts of data, and also by the rise of discourse analysis. By contrast, in the past, under the influence of functionalism and Marxism, there was emphasis on locating what is studied in a wider context, where the unit of analysis was usually taken to be a particular community or society. More recently there have been calls for ethnographies to take account of global social forces. Parallel to this have been criticisms of much ethnography for being preoccupied with describing and explaining what happens in relatively short time periods, thereby neglecting longer-term trends. One response to this has been to advocate longitudinal ethnographies, for example following the development of a group of people's lives over several years and focusing on the patterns of change experienced. Also relevant here are attempts to link ethnographic with historical work.

A second tension is between seeking to study cases in all their uniqueness or being concerned with producing generalizations or engaging in comparative analysis to build theories. Ethnographers vary considerably in their position on this spectrum, but most seek to satisfy all these demands in one way or another. The concept of thick description represents one sort of trade-off, where theories are relatively low level and are means for understanding what is going on in particular cases. Towards the other end of the spectrum are grounded theorizing and analytic induction, where the product of ethnographic work is some kind of general theory, albeit instantiated in detailed analysis of particular cases.

A third issue concerns whether the primary task is seen as explicating the perspectives, or cultural orientations, of the people being studied, or as explaining why they see the world and act in the ways that they do, and the consequences of this. The first approach emphasizes the role of careful description, of understanding what people say and do in its own terms; whereas the second often produces accounts that raise questions about the validity of people's beliefs about themselves and their world. This may involve explaining why people believe what they believe and do what they do in terms of causal factors whose existence or significance they do not acknowledge or even explicitly deny. Indeed, there may be a hermeneutics of suspicion in operation which assumes that what people say hides as much as it reveals. There is variation here in the extent to which an aim is to challenge official appearances, or the fronts people display, in order to find out what they really believe or what really goes on; or whether social life is viewed as inevitably a matter of performative fronts, with the task of analysis being to study the processes or strategies by which people bring off particular performances on particular occasions.

Even for those ethnographers who place emphasis on understanding insider perspectives, there are questions about how far it is ever possible or necessary for ethnographers to understand participants' perspectives "from the inside." It has been suggested that this involves reducing the Other to the Same, forcing what is different into terms that are familiar. At the same time, ethnography has also sometimes been accused of "othering," of rendering other societies exotic and alien, a criticism that parallels Said's discussion of "orientalism" (Said 1978). Closely related are criticisms of the totalizing orientation of much older ethnography, where cultures are described as if they were objects in the world, and as if membership of a culture determined everything of importance about any individual person.

In its early forms, ethnography involved a concern to capture the beliefs and actions of the people being studied in such a way as to minimize the effects of the research process. As a result, ethnography was usually distanced from concerns with practical improvement, and therefore adopted a non-judgmental or appreciative orientation (Matza 1969). However, in the mid-twentieth century there developed forms of applied anthropology that treated ethnography as a basis for interventions designed to improve the lives of the people being studied. And, later, some ethnographers adopted Marxist or "critical" perspectives in which the phenomena studied were to be located within a political perspective generating evaluations and recommendations for social change. The influence of feminism and anti-racism reinforced this tendency, while that of poststructuralism and postmodernism challenged reliance on political positions involving metanarratives in favor of subordinating ethnographic work to local struggles, with one of its tasks being seen as liberating those repressed forms of knowledge to be found on the margins of conventional society.

Closely associated with these developments have been pressures to do ethnographic work *with* people rather than *on* them, in the manner of various participatory forms of inquiry. In some cases this built on a commitment to advocacy by anthropologists and on the notion of indigenous ethnography, while within sociology it derived from feminist and other approaches to research ethics which challenged what was seen as the hierarchical relationship between

researcher and researched. However, there is a tension here not only with older approaches to ethnography but also between subordinating research to participants' orientations and using it as a means of raising their consciousness, in the form of a "critical" orientation designed to generate desirable social change.

There has also been increasing pressure to recognize the extent to which and ways in which all research, including ethnography, plays a political role in the world. To some degree this began long ago with criticism of how anthropological ethnography was implicated in western imperialism. In more recent times the concern with the politics of ethnography has become much broader, reflecting the influence of new social movements of various kinds. On the part of some commentators what is at stake is not simply how research might be distorted by its social context, or even the consequences that it could have, but rather how the whole enterprise of research is political through and through, in the sense that it cannot but involve reliance on value assumptions, and that these cannot but reflect the identity, commitments, and social location of the researcher as a person. This runs against earlier forms of ethnography where research was treated as concerned simply with producing objective scientific knowledge about diverse cultures, an orientation that is now regarded by many, though not all, ethnographers as simply an ideological disguise for political interests that serve the status quo.

As indicated earlier, ethnography refers not just to a process of inquiry but also to a particular type of product: to the written account generated by ethnographic research. Prior to the early 1980s the task of "writing up" ethnographies was given relatively little attention in the methodological literature. Most of the focus was on problems surrounding data collecting and analysis. However, in the last three decades there has been considerable interest in this topic, not just from a practical point of view but also in terms of analyzing how ethnographic accounts represent or effectively constitute the social contexts and people investigated. Epistemological, political, and ethical concerns are intermingled in what has come to be seen as a "crisis of representation."

Developments in technology have also had an important impact on ethnographic work over the past few decades. In particular, the availability of easily portable audio and video-recorders has meant that fieldnotes have come to play a subordinate role in much ethnographic work, and as noted earlier it may have encouraged an increasingly micro-focus concerned with the details of what is said and done on particular occasions. Furthermore, video-recording has built on earlier developments in visual ethnography that employed photographs and film. The development of microcomputers and of software for processing qualitative data is another important area of development, one where there is disagreement about whether the technology serves or distorts ethnographic practice. What seems clear, though, is that digitization of data and the increased capacity of computers to handle multimedia material will open up considerable opportunities for ethnographers, as well as no doubt also raising new problems, or old problems in novel forms. Closely related here is the development of the Internet and the opportunities that this provides, not just as a source of information but as a collection of virtual sites that can be studied by ethnographers (Hine 2000).

Finally, it is worth mentioning a significant feature of the changing environments in which ethnographers seek to carry out their work. Both anthropologists and sociologists have encountered increasing barriers in gaining access to settings in many societies. These stem from a variety of factors, among which are increasing governmental control, commercialization, and forms of regulation within both privately owned and publicly funded organizations. Another important external factor is increasing ethical regulation, notably in the field of health, but also more widely for research sponsored within universities. The ethical codes on which this is based often assume a model of research that is at odds with both the theory and practice of ethnography.

SEE ALSO: Autoethnography; Chicago School; Constructionism; Culture; Ethics, Fieldwork; Ethics, Research; Interviewing, Structured, Unstructured, and Postmodern; Observation, Participant and Non-Participant; Performance Ethnography

REFERENCES AND SUGGESTED READINGS

Clifford, J. & Marcus, G. (Eds.) (1986) *Writing Culture: The Poetics and Politics of Ethnography*. University of California Press, Berkeley.
Hammersley, M. & Atkinson, P. (1995) *Ethnography: Principles in Practice*. Routledge, London.
Hine, C. (2000) *Virtual Ethnography*. Sage, London.
Matza, D. (1969) *Becoming Deviant*. Prentice-Hall, Englewood Cliffs, NJ.
Said, E. (1978) *Orientalism*. Pantheon, New York.
Wolcott, H. F. (1999) *Ethnography: A Way of Seeing*. Alta Mira Press, Walnut Creek, CA.

ethnomethodology

Douglas W. Maynard and Teddy Kardash

Ethnomethodology is an area in sociology originating in the work of Harold Garfinkel. It represents an effort to study the methods in and through which members concertedly produce and assemble the features of everyday life in any actual, concrete, and not hypothetical or theoretically depicted setting. Ethnomethodology's proposal – one that is incommensurate with respect to other sociological theory (Garfinkel 1988) – is that there is a self-generating order in concrete activities, an order whose scientific appreciation depends upon neither prior description, nor empirical generalization, nor formal specification of variable elements and their analytic relations. Moreover, raw experience – the booming buzz of William James – is anything but chaotic, for the concrete activities of which it is composed are coeval with an intelligible organization that actors already provide and that is therefore available for scientific analysis. Members of society achieve this intelligible organization through actual, coordinated, concerted, procedural behaviors or *methods* and *practices*.

Garfinkel was a student in Harvard's Department of Social Relations where he went to study with Talcott Parsons, although Garfinkel's developing concerns with the empirical detail of ordinary life and activity came to be at odds with Parsons's emphasis on conceptual formulation and theoretical generalization. While at Harvard, Garfinkel deepened his knowledge of phenomenology – an interest that had been sparked at the University of North Carolina where he had completed a master's degree – by meeting with Alfred Schütz and Aron Gurwitsch, who were both European "philosophers in exile" at the New School for Social Research. There is a strong influence of phenomenology on ethnomethodology, but Garfinkel deemphasized perceptual knowledge as a mental process or activity in favor of a concern with embodied activity and the practical production of social facts as that production resides in lived experience, whether that experience involves rhythmic clapping, responding to a "summoning" phone, traveling in a freeway traffic wave, standing in a service line, or any other ordinary matter.

After finishing his degree at Harvard and a short stint at Ohio State University, Garfinkel moved to Kansas where Harvard classmate Fred Strodtbeck invited him to help with a project on jury decision-making. While working on how jurors, in their deliberations, struggle with issues of evidence, demonstration, relevance, facts versus opinion, and other "methodological" matters, Garfinkel turned to the Yale cross-cultural area files and came upon terms such as ethnobotany, ethnophysiology, ethnophysics, and others. It was then he realized that *methodology* was something jurors were producing as a prominent and serious feature of their deliberations. Hence, Garfinkel coined "ethnomethodology" (see Garfinkel 1974) to refer to the study of how members of the jury engage in practices whereby they could decide indigenous problems of adequate accountability, description, and evidence in relation to the deliberative outcomes they produced.

In the fall of 1954 Garfinkel joined the faculty at UCLA. While there, he trained several generations of students and produced his most well-known work, *Studies in Ethnomethodology* (Garfinkel 1967). To obtain access to members' methods in a variety of settings, Garfinkel introduced his famous "breaching experiments," which reversed the usual sociological preoccupation with factors that contribute to social stability. Breaching involves asking what can be done to make for trouble

in everyday events, and demonstrates that troublesome events are themselves revelatory of the ordinary practices whereby stability is achieved.

A tic-tac-toe exercise, for example, involves the experimenter inviting a participant to play. After the participant starts the game by placing an "X" in a square formed by the tic-tac-toe matrix, the experimenter puts an "O" on a line of the game matrix rather than in a square. The trouble thereby created brings members' methods to the fore as sources of order. These methods are manifest in the restorative or reparative efforts of participants. When a participant protests to the experimenter, "Is this a joke?" it shows that an ordinary game is to be engaged seriously and by respecting common-sense practices for placing Os and Xs. The practices of common sense are employed not by following rules of the game but by behaving in ways that are retrospectively consistent with those rules. In other words, behavior is to be accountable to rules and this means engaging in concrete and embodied practices that are orderly in their own right and are not explained or provided for in the rules that these practices make visible.

However, Garfinkel also went beyond experimental breaches to examine more naturally occurring disruptions to everyday life. In his influential *Studies* chapter on Agnes, a male-to-female transsexual, he set the agenda and tone for many subsequent investigations into the accomplishment of "gender." Garfinkel's extensive interviews and observations concerning Agnes provide access to something that is utterly routine in everyday life: the achievement of one's visible and objective status as a man or woman, boy or girl. Because Agnes did not experience her gender visibility as routine or taken for granted, Garfinkel was able to document how members regularly employ tacit means for securing and guaranteeing the rights and obligations attendant upon being seen as a normal, natural, adult female. Agnes was a "practical methodologist" and artfully displayed what is required of anyone who claims to be a bona fide woman.

Garfinkel notes that he initially attempted to use a game metaphor in order to comprehend the various occasions in which Agnes had to "pass" or come across as the normal female person. But he realized that Agnes's passing eluded attempts to reduce it to playing a game by the rules. There are, he argued, various "structural incongruities" between playing a game and sexual passing. Unlike a game, to pass as a member of a particular gender has no "time outs," no exits from the work of passing, and only limited capacity for planning one's strategies for passing because of the ubiquity of unanticipated happenings. Agnes could not be a strategic actor in the way that sociologist Erving Goffman portrays the matter, because she could never know in advance exactly what would be required of her for displaying herself as the natural female in any given interaction. She was learning what it took to be a woman even as she acted as if she were non-problematically a woman in the first place.

In 1959, while on sabbatical from UCLA, Garfinkel met Harvey Sacks, who was pursuing his law degree at Yale but would eventually move to the department of sociology at Berkeley for graduate work. Sacks remained in touch with Garfinkel, who brought him to Los Angeles in 1963. Sacks's lectures and thinking formed the beginning of what would become the field of conversation analysis. Mutual influences between Garfinkel and Sacks are of considerable interest. Their collaborative endeavors are partially embodied in a joint publication, "On Formal Structures of Practical Actions" (Garfinkel & Sacks 1970), where they argue that sociological reasoning has often aimed to distinguish between "indexical" expressions, whose sense derives from their relation to aspects of the immediate context in which they are used, and objective expressions, whose sense is purportedly context free. Garfinkel and Sacks argue that the quest for objective expressions is endless, because such expressions always depend upon an orderliness that necessarily ties them to the situation of their use. Accordingly, Garfinkel and Sacks recommend a policy of "ethnomethodological indifference," whereby investigators abstain from judging the status of objective expressions in terms of their adequacy, value, or consequentiality. Instead, the orderliness of any and all human expressions – the practical means by which those expressions attain their sense – is to be brought under study. The orderliness that

Sacks and collaborators in conversation analysis began to pursue was the sequential organization of everyday talk and interaction, although there is also a stream of conversation analytic work on "membership categories" as devices that are deployed for purposes of making interactional sense.

Meanwhile, Garfinkel's own interests developed in the direction of scientific and work practice, and his contributions have been taken up in sociological studies of technology and science. In the 1980s, Garfinkel and his students turned to the examination of technical competencies in mathematics and the natural sciences, including astronomy (Garfinkel et al. 1981) and other domains. These studies probe the details of "shop work and shop talk" that form the tangible fabric of scientific practice. There is always "something more" to methodological practice than can be provided in highly detailed instructions, formalized guidelines, or accounts of inquiry. The "something more" includes routine practices at the workbench in laboratories and other settings of work. Indeed, lately Garfinkel (2002) has become preoccupied with what he calls the "shop floor problem," having to do with how generic descriptions of work settings, which attempt to specify the constituents of practice within those settings, confront "details in structures" or coherences in embodied practices that cannot be anticipated by, and utterly defy, the generic descriptions.

In his recent book, Garfinkel (2002) makes more explicit the central claim of ethnomethodology – namely, that it is in the business of working out Durkheim's aphorism, "the objective reality of social facts is sociology's fundamental phenomenon." Rather than claiming that order can only be revealed by aggregating across large sets of data and replacing the concrete, observable detail of "immortal ordinary society" with concepts, ethnomethodology claims that there is a plenitude of order that is lost to the formal analytic theorizing as it exists in the field of sociology and elsewhere in the human sciences. Indeed, ethnomethodology "respecifies" Durkheim's aphorism in a way that formal analytic techniques do not and in fact cannot. Garfinkel is careful here to emphasize that ethnomethodology is not proposing itself as an alternative to formal analysis as if it were possible to escape from the search for objective expressions by engaging in a more interpretive endeavor. Rather, ethnomethodology proposes *alternates* that are not only coeval but also autochthonous, i.e., grounded practices that spring up and exist alongside formal analytic inquiries. The ethnomethodological alternate is, however, asymmetrical to formal analytic theorizing, meaning that ethnomethodology – but not formal analysis – makes it possible to investigate how members of any grouping achieve, as practical, concerted behaviors, the sense of formal truth and objectivity as this sense is necessarily embedded in their everyday casual and work lives.

SEE ALSO: Conversation Analysis; Information Technology; Language; Phenomenology; Sacks, Harvey; Schütz, Alfred; Science and Culture; Social Psychology; Theory

REFERENCES AND SUGGESTED READINGS

Garfinkel, H. (1967) *Studies in Ethnomethodology*. Prentice-Hall, Englewood Cliffs, NJ.

Garfinkel, H. (1974) On the Origins of the Term "Ethnomethodology." In: Turner, R. (Ed.), *Ethnomethodology*. Penguin, Harmondsworth, pp. 15–18.

Garfinkel, H. (1988) Evidence for Locally Produced, Naturally Accountable Phenomena of Order, Logic, Reason, Meaning, Method, etc. in and as of the Essential Quiddity of Immortal Ordinary Society (I of IV): An Announcement of Studies. *Sociological Theory* 6: 103–9.

Garfinkel, H. (2002) *Ethnomethodology's Program: Working Out Durkheim's Aphorism*. Rowman & Littlefield, Lanham, MD.

Garfinkel, H. & Sacks, H. (1970) On Formal Structures of Practical Actions. In: McKinney, J. D. & Tiryakian, E. A. (Eds.), *Theoretical Sociology*. Appleton Century Crofts, New York, pp. 337–66.

Garfinkel, H., Lynch, M., & Livingston, E. (1981) The Work of a Discovering Science Construed with Materials from the Optically Discovered Pulsar. *Philosophy of the Social Sciences* 11: 131–58.

Heath, C. & Luff, P. (2000) *Technology in Action*. Cambridge University Press, Cambridge.

Heritage, J. (1984) *Garfinkel and Ethnomethodology*. Polity Press, Cambridge.

Livingston, E. (1987) *Making Sense of Ethnomethodology*. Routledge, London.

Lynch, M. (1993) *Scientific Practice and Ordinary Action: Ethnomethodology and Social Studies of Science*. Cambridge University Press, Cambridge.

Maynard, D. W. & Clayman, S. E. (1991) The Diversity of Ethnomethodology. *Annual Review of Sociology* 17: 385–418.

ethnonationalism

Walker Connor

Ethnonationalism (variant: *ethnic nationalism*) connotes identity with and loyalty to a nation in the sense of a human grouping predicated upon a myth of common ancestry. Seldom will the myth find support in scientific evidence. DNA analyses of the patrilineally bequeathed Y chromosome attest that nations tend to be neither genetically homogeneous nor hermetical, and analyses of the matrilineally bequeathed mitochrondrial DNA customarily attest to still greater heterogeneity and transnational genetic sharing. However, the popularly held conviction that one's nation is ethnically pure and distinct is intuitive rather than rational in its wellsprings and, as such, is capable of defying scientific and historic evidence to the contrary.

Ethnonationalism is often contrasted with a so-called *civic nationalism*, by which is meant identity with and loyalty to the state. (Until quite recently the latter was conventionally referred to as *patriotism*.) The practice of referring to civic consciousness and civic loyalty as a form of nationalism has spawned great confusion in the literature. Rather than representing variations of the same phenomenon, the two loyalties are of two different orders of things (ethnic versus civic), and while in the case of a people clearly dominant within a state (such as the ethnically Turkish or Castilian peoples) the two loyalties may reinforce each other, in the case of ethnonational minorities (such as the Kurds of Turkey or the Basques of Spain) the two identities may clash. World political history since the Napoleonic Wars has been increasingly a tale of tension between the two loyalties, each possessing its own irrefragable and exclusive claim to political legitimacy.

The concept of political legitimacy inherent in ethnonationalism rests upon the tendency of people living within their homeland to resent and resist rule by those perceived as aliens. Evolutionary biologists classify xenophobia as a universal which has been detected on the part of all societies studied thus far (Brown 1991). Buttressing this finding of universality are the histories of multi-ethnic empires – both ancient and modern – which are sprinkled with ethnically inspired insurrections. The modern state system has proven even more vulnerable. In the 130-year period separating the Napoleonic Wars from the end of World War II, all but three of Europe's states had either lost extensive territory and population because of ethnonational movements or were themselves the product of such a movement. Ethnonationalism's challenge to the multinational state continued to accelerate during the late twentieth century, culminating in the dissolution of the Soviet Union and Yugoslavia.

During the course of its development, the equating of alien rule with illegitimate rule came to be called *national self-determination*, a phrase probably coined by Karl Marx and subsequently frequently employed by the First and Second Internationals. Two points are worth noting. (1) The phrase only gave name to a force present throughout history; it did not create it. Marx was no proponent of national self-determination, but he had come to recognize its influence and the wisdom of appearing to ally with it as a means of fostering the proletarian revolution. (2) Although national self-determination is often described as a principle or a doctrine, the impulse underlying it is far more universal and deeply felt than either term conveys.

National self-determination holds that any group of people, simply because it considers itself to be a separate nation (in the pristine sense of a people who believe themselves to be ancestrally related), has an inalienable right to determine its political affiliations, including, *if it so desires*, the right to its own state. *If it so desires* is a key consideration. The essence of self-determination is choice, not result. The Soviet Union on the eve of its decomposition offers a number of illustrations of ethnonational groups opting for separation: a poll conducted in October 1990, for example, indicated that

91 percent of the Baltic nations (Estonians, Letts, and Lithuanians) and 92 percent of all Georgians favored secession. Similarly, in September 1999, 78.5 percent of those East Timorese who risked death to vote, voted for independence from Indonesia. On the other hand, in the overwhelming number of cases for which there are attitudinal polling data, a majority – usually a substantial majority – of homeland-dwelling people are prepared to settle for something less than independence. However, the attitudinal data also show that a substantial majority of each of these same homeland-dwelling people do desire alterations in their state's power structure, alterations which would result in greater autonomy. The minimal changes that will satisfy the ethnonational aspirations of those individuals desiring greater autonomy can vary across a broad spectrum from homeland primacy in policymaking over matters involving education and language to everything short of full independence. But when aspirations for greater autonomy are denied, the appeal of separate statehood strengthens.

The willingness of nationally conscious homeland-dwelling people to remain within a state in which they are a minority if they are granted sufficient autonomy should not be viewed as a renunciation of their right of self-determination. Autonomy has the potential for satisfying the principal aspirations of the group. Devolution – the decentralization of political decision-making – has the potential for elevating a national group to the status of master in their own homeland. As reflected in their chief slogan – *Maître Chez Nous* – the Québécois feel that within the homeland of Québec they must have ultimate power of decision-making over those matters most affecting ethnonational sensibilities and nation maintenance. Such power within the homeland may be quite enough to appease the self-determination impulse. Ethnonational aspirations, by their very nature, are driven more by the dream of *freedom from* – freedom from domination by outsiders – than by *freedom to* – freedom to conduct relations with states. Ethnocracy need not presume political independence, but it must minimally presume *meaningful* autonomy.

Growing acknowledgment by the central governments that the national self-determination impulse can perhaps be accommodated within a sufficiently decentralized multinational structure is becoming increasingly manifest. Whereas the tendency prior to the very late twentieth century was toward the ever greater concentration of decision-making power in the center, evidence of a possible countertrend is now present. Belgium, Canada, Italy, Spain, and the United Kingdom are examples of well-established states with a tradition of centralized control that have transferred significant powers from the center to ethnic homelands in order to assuage ethnonational resentments. But while perhaps portentous, such cases are still exceptional. The central authorities of most multi-homeland states have tended to perceive any significant increase in autonomy as tantamount to, or an important step toward, secession. As a result, the challenge of ethnonationalism to the territorial integrity of states continues to spread.

SEE ALSO: Ethnic Groups; Ethnicity; Nation-State; Nation-State and Nationalism; Nationalism; Race and Ethnic Politics; Self-Determination

REFERENCES AND SUGGESTED READINGS

Brown, D. (1991) *Human Universals*. Temple University Press, Philadelphia.
Conversi, D. (Ed.) (2002) *Ethnonationalism in the Contemporary World*. Routledge, London.
Hayes, C. (1926) *Essays on Nationalism*. Macmillan, New York.
Poliakov, L. (1974) *The Aryan Myth*. Basic Books, New York.
Ranum, O. (Ed.) (1975) *National Consciousness, History, and Political Culture in Early Modern Europe*. Johns Hopkins University Press, Baltimore.

eugenics

Gabriele Abels

The term eugenics is derived from the Greek *eugenes* ("good in birth" or "noble in heredity"). Eugenics refers to a set of ideas and activities aiming to improve the quality of the human race by deliberate selection of parents and their offspring. In contrast to Social Darwinism, which applies categories of evolutionary biology (survival of the fittest) to the social world, the key feature of eugenics is *deliberate* selection of the "genetically fit" and corresponding active policies. Eugenics relies on two strategies: (1) manipulation of heredity or breeding practices in order to produce "genetically superior" or "fit" people ("positive" eugenics), and (2) extermination of those considered "genetically inferior" ("negative" eugenics).

The history of eugenics goes back to ancient Greece (Kevles 1985). For example, Plato proposed the idea of "breeding better people" and government control over human reproduction. Sir Francis Galton (1822–1911), an English anthropologist and cousin of Charles Darwin, founded modern eugenics and coined the term in 1883. He defined eugenics as "the science which deals with all influences that improve the inborn qualities of a race; also with those that develop them to the utmost advantage." According to him, the social status of Britain's ruling class was determined by inherited leadership qualities. He advocated improving the human race in the manner of plant and animal breeding.

Eugenics is based, firstly, on the development of genetics as a scientific discipline in the late nineteenth century and, secondly, on new concepts of social planning and rational management. The social context is the development of industrial society, which went along with urbanization, the growth of a poor "working class," and also the rise of the labor movement and socialist political parties. Eugenic "science" was considered by its proponents to be the application of human genetic knowledge to social problems such as pauperism, alcoholism, criminality, violence, prostitution, mental illness, etc. Such problems were thought to have biological roots based in people's defective genetic make-up and biological "solutions" were proposed. Thus, the early concept of eugenics had a strong class and racial bias.

In the early twentieth century eugenics became a social movement first in Great Britain and then in the US, as well as in many other (European) Protestant countries. The First International Congress of Eugenics was held in London in 1912. In the 1920s and 1930s eugenics became part of popular culture. Eugenic societies organized public information campaigns using eugenic exhibits, educational movies, "fitter family contests," etc. and eugenics was widely taught in schools and at universities. Influential biologists such as Hermann J. Muller, Aldous Huxley, and Charles B. Davenport advocated eugenics.

Concurrently, eugenics entered public policy and found support from across the political spectrum, ranging from conservatives (e.g., Rockefeller Foundation) to progressives (e.g., Civil Rights activist W. E. B. Du Bois and feminist and founder of Planned Parenthood, Margaret Sanger) and leftists (e.g., social democratic parties and the social author H. G. Wells). While there was agreement on some eugenic principles (e.g., biological foundation of social problems), there was, however, disagreement about policies, means, and political aims (e.g., the role of coercion; social change). Many countries introduced eugenically motivated sterilization laws or laws requiring premarital screening for genetic or mental illnesses. The first such law was adopted in 1896 in Connecticut, USA; it prohibited the marriage of "feeble-minded" persons and was later enforced by compulsory sterilization. Similar laws to sterilize not only the mentally ill, but also epileptics or criminals were adopted up to 1917 in 15 US states. After World War I, eugenic sterilization laws were also introduced in many European countries. Some were still in effect into the 1970s (e.g., Sweden and Canada), while in the US compulsory sterilizations came to an end in the 1960s. In general, European eugenicists were preoccupied with class issues, while the focus of eugenic policies in the US was on racial and ethnic minorities. For example, the Racial Integrity Act and also the 1924 US Immigration Act were informed by eugenic ideas.

The largest and most radical eugenic movement was German Fascism. In the 1920s the Nazi concept of "racial hygiene" was associated with eugenics (Weingart et al. 1988). Immediately after Hitler's rise to power in 1933, the Law for the Prevention of Defective Progeny was adopted and put into force. Until 1945 about 360,000 compulsory sterilizations were conducted. In addition, tens of thousands of people belonging to minority groups considered "not worth living" (*lebensunwert*) – such as Romanies and Sinti, disabled and mentally retarded persons, and homosexuals – were killed in a policy called euthanasia or mercy-killing. By referring to eugenic arguments, the Nazi "selection and eradication" program claimed to have a scientific basis – a reasoning later used by the Nazi defendants in the Nuremberg trials. This program of the extermination of minority groups can be regarded as an ideological and practical bridge to the genocide against the Jewish population, the Holocaust. In addition to coercive "negative" eugenics, the Nazis also implemented policies of – coercive as well as voluntary – "positive" eugenics aiming at the breeding of "Aryans." Examples are the introduction of rewards for "Aryan" mothers with large numbers of children (*Mutterkreuz*), a program for impregnating "racially pure" single women by SS officers (*Lebensborn*), and the prohibition of abortion for "Aryan" women.

Eugenic policies were justified on grounds of societal or state interests: those deemed "genetically unfit" were stigmatized as an *economic* and *moral* burden. The Nazis also referred to genetic damage to the healthy *Volkskörper* (the nation's body). Eugenics became discredited after World War II, firstly on political grounds because it was associated with Nazi politics; and secondly, scientists started to question the scientific foundation of the "old" eugenics. However, some "reform eugenicists" (Kevles 1985) such as Muller, Huxley, and J. B. S. Haldane proposed developing sound scientific human genetics free of any racial and class bias; many eugenicists became highly respected scientists in related disciplines. With new discoveries (e.g., the double helix structure in 1953) and the rise of molecular biology, human genetics was slowly "freed" from its eugenic heritage. Yet some scholars argue that there are not only continuities among the promoters of eugenics and human genetics as a scientific discipline, but also ideological continuities. A prominent example is the 1962 CIBA Symposium "Man and his Future." Twenty-seven well-known geneticists and molecular biologists (e.g., Huxley, Haldane, Muller, Joshua Lederberg) met in London to discuss their visions for human genetic manipulation and enhancement.

Historically, eugenics has been part of an oppressive and discriminatory ideology; it was defended on societal interests and often mandated by the state. Critics believe that this is part of the very nature of eugenics. However, since the 1980s a public debate has begun on whether or not there has been a rise of a "new" eugenics and how to assess the development normatively. There is agreement that the justification of eugenic policies has changed over time. Modern eugenics is based on the notion of individual rights instead of societal interests; it is not the state that decides on selection criteria, but individuals themselves. State neutrality distinguishes the old from a "new" or "liberal" eugenics. It is freed of its classist bias, yet not totally of its racist or ethnic bias (cf. the "bell curve" debate).

This debate developed against the background of technological progress in the field of human genetics and genetic engineering. A major application of human genetics is prenatal diagnosis, which identifies the genetic status of the unborn. If the embryo or fetus has a genetic or biological "defect," the only alternatives usually available are carrying it to term or aborting. Sometimes abortion laws allow for (late-term) abortions based on embryopathic or eugenic reasons (i.e., the fetus is diagnosed as potentially disabled). This practice is criticized especially by anti-abortion activists and also by (some fractions of) the disability rights movement as a threat to their "right to life." A recent additional technology is preimplantation genetic diagnosis (PGD) on the early *in vitro* embryo. In case of a "defect," the embryo is not used in the follow-up IVF procedure, but discarded. PGD allows for the selection of embryos not only for therapeutic, but also for eugenic reasons. With the advent of "reprogenetics" (i.e., the linking of genetic engineering with new reproductive technologies), "designer babies" via genetic manipulation or even human enhancement via germ line engineering, exchanging genes, or adding new ones, now seem possible. Once again, eugenics and genetic manipulation have reappeared in popular culture; in particular, the genre of science fiction has taken up genetic engineering.

Two arguments have been raised against human genetic engineering: firstly on technological grounds (i.e., the techniques are not (yet) safe), and secondly on the basis of ethics. While the first of these may be overcome in time, the second one is a matter of principle. Philosophers and bioethicists have begun to debate the ethics of eugenics and human genetic engineering. Some distinguished scientists involved in the Human Genome Project, for example, have announced their support for voluntary eugenics. Proponents of eugenic practices that rely on genetic manipulation are labeled liberal eugenicists. Fletcher (1974) laid the groundwork for liberal eugenics; he proposed active family planning via deliberate genetic control instead of the natural "reproductive roulette." Since the 1990s, proponents of liberal eugenics (e.g., Agar 2004) argue in favor of individual choices: parents should have the right to choose if they want to enhance the genetic traits of their offspring as part of their parental authority (e.g., by choosing egg and sperm or direct manipulation), at least as long as the eugenic freedom of parents does not collide with the personal freedom of children. They criticize the distinction between genetic and social (i.e., educational) modification (e.g., dietary improvement, use of non-medical drugs, or cultivating the child's talents) as incoherent, and they speak out against a remoralizing of human nature. A further voice promoting human selection and enhancement is the transhumanism movement (e.g., Hughes 2004), a philosophy that is in favor of improving the human condition by the use of science and technology such as genetic engineering.

Some utilitarian bioethicists are proponents of extending selection practices to newborns, thereby linking eugenics to euthanasia. The most prominent examples are the Australian philosophers Peter Singer and Helga Kuhse, who argue for the euthanasia of severely mentally retarded newborns (infanticide) by excluding them from medical treatment. They argue that those newborns lack substantial qualities of personhood such as self-awareness. "Letting them die" would on the whole maximize happiness for the parents.

Anti-eugenicists and critics of liberal eugenics (e.g., Jonas 1985; Fukuyama 2002; Habermas 2003) are overall in favor of therapeutic options of biomedical technologies, but oppose any form of enhancement. Furthermore, they argue that the therapeutic/eugenic distinction is not clear-cut. They fear that allowing new technological options for genetic engineering opens a "backdoor to eugenics" (Duster 1990) or inevitably leads to a slippery slope of unethical measures. They also criticize the economic approach to procreative behavior. The new eugenics is "privatized" and takes the "free-market" route: "old eugenics meets the new consumerism" (Michael J. Sandel). Therefore, many critics argue in favor of absolute moral limits. They also argue against an instrumental and utilitarian perspective on human life, which is more ubiquitous in Anglo-American bioethics. Their key argument, usually based on Kant's post-metaphysical categorical imperative, is that genetic manipulation, enhancement, and human cloning are a violation of human dignity and rights, and, as some claim, also of human nature. Habermas, for example, opines that all enhancements, even if they are favorable ones such as musical talent or athletic prowess, can violate children's right to choose their own lives, thereby constituting an encroachment upon their autonomy.

Many countries have started the legal regulation of genetic engineering and its application to humans; profiting from medical progress while avoiding eugenics is a prominent theme. Also, international (e.g., UN) and European (e.g., Council of Europe) regulation has only just begun. The "old" eugenics is well researched. The future development of eugenics and its normative assessment depend on the dynamic interlinkage between technological and social change. Therefore, research on modern eugenics has to link social studies of science and technology to normative bioethical debates.

SEE ALSO: Abortion as a Social Problem; Disability as a Social Problem; Euthanasia; Family Planning, Abortion, and Reproductive Health; Fascism; Genetic Engineering as a Social Problem; Human Genome and the Science of Life; Marriage, Sex, and Childbirth; New Reproductive Technologies

REFERENCES AND SUGGESTED READINGS

Agar, N. (2004) *Liberal Eugenics: In Defence of Human Enhancement*. Blackwell, Oxford.

Duster, T. (1990) *Backdoor to Eugenics*. Routledge, New York.

Fletcher, J. (1974) *The Ethics of Genetic Control: Ending Reproductive Roulette*. Doubleday & Company, New York.

Fukuyama, F. (2002) *Our Posthuman Future: Consequences of the Biotechnology Revolution*. Picador, New York.

Habermas, J. (2003) *The Future of Human Nature*. Polity Press, Cambridge.

Hughes, J. (2004) *Citizen Cyborg: Why Democratic Societies Must Respond to the Redesigned Human of the Future*. Westview Press, Cambridge, MA.

Jonas, H. (1985) *Technik, Medizin und Eugenik*. Suhrkamp, Frankfurt am Main.

Kevles, D. J. (1985) *In the Name of Eugenics: Genetics and the Use of Human Heredity*. Alfred A. Knopf, New York.

Weingart, P., Kroll, J., & Bayertz, K. (1988) *Rasse, Blut und Gene: Geschichte der Eugenik und Rassenhygiene in Deutschland*. Suhrkamp, Frankfurt am Main.

Eurocentrism

Syed Farid Alatas

Eurocentrism is a particular case of the more general phenomenon of ethnocentrism. Ethnocentrism refers to the regard of one's own ethnic group or society as superior to others. Other groups are assessed and judged in terms of the categories and standards of evaluation of one's own group. Eurocentrism, therefore, is defined as a thought style in which the assessment and evaluation of non-European societies is couched in terms of the cultural assumptions and biases of Europeans and, by extension, the West. Eurocentrism is a modern phenomenon and cannot be dissociated from the political, economic, and cultural domination of Europe and, later, the United States. It may be more accurate to refer to the phenomenon under consideration as Euroamericocentrism. Eurocentrism is an important dimension of the ideology of modern capitalism (Amin 1989) and is manifested in both the daily life of lay people and the professional lives and thought of sociologists and other social scientists. Furthermore, although Eurocentrism originates in Europe, as a thought style it is not confined to Europeans or those in the West.

Eurocentrism in sociology is defined as the assessment and evaluation of European and other societies from a decidedly European (read also American) point of view. The European point of view is founded on concepts derived from European philosophical traditions and popular discourse which were gradually applied to the empirical study of history, economy, and society, giving rise to the various social science disciplines including sociology. The empirical field of investigation is selected according to European criteria of relevance. Constructions of history and society are based on European-derived categories and concepts, as well as ideal and material interests. Generally, the point of view of the Other is not presented (Tibawi 1963: 191, 196; Tibawi 1979: 5, 13, 16–17).

There was concern with the phenomenon of Eurocentrism before the term itself came into usage in the nineteenth century among thinkers living in colonial societies. The Muslim thinker and reformer Sayyid Jamal al-Din al-Afghani (1838/9–1897) debated against western constructions of Islam and was conscious of the need to appropriate relevant western ideas without blindly imitating the West. Among the earliest of thinkers to critique Eurocentric perspectives was the Filipino José Rizal (1861–96), who attempted revisions of Filipino history from a Filipino point of view via his annotation of Antonio de Morga's history of the Philippines (Morga 1962 [1890]). The first sociologist to critique the dominance of Eurocentric constructions was probably the Indian Benoy Kumar Sarkar (1887–1949), who wrote against the prevailing Indology of his time, noting its one-sided emphasis on the idealistic, mystical, and metaphysical aspects of Hinduism (Sarkar 1985 [1937]). One of the first among the Dutch in particular, and Europeans in general, to raise the problem of Eurocentrism in the social sciences was Jacob Cornelis van Leur (1937, 1940). He was critical of Eurocentric tendencies in Dutch scholarship on the Netherlands Indies and is well known for his critique of perspectives arrived at from "the deck of the ship, the ramparts of the fortress, the high gallery of the trading house" (1955: 261). For example, he questioned the appropriateness of the eighteenth century as a category in the history of the Netherlands Indies, as it was a category borrowed from western history (1940).

Van Leur, nevertheless, was himself Eurocentric in several of his pronouncements and remarks. Joseph Needham wrote on the basic fallacy of Europocentrism, namely, the view of the universality of European culture (Needham 1969 [1955]: 13–14). In 1956, Syed Hussein Alatas from Malaysia referred to the "wholesale importation of ideas from the Western world to eastern societies" without due consideration of their sociohistorical context as a fundamental problem of colonialism.

The traits of Eurocentrism as manifested in sociology and other social sciences include (1) the subject–object dichotomy; (2) the fore-grounding of Europeans; (3) the view of Europeans as originators; (4) the imposition of European categories and concepts; and (5) the view of the objective superiority of European civilization.

The subject–object dichotomy: Europeans are the knowing subjects while non-Europeans remain as unheard objects whose standpoints are conveyed only through the agency of Europeans. Non-Europeans are passive, non-participating, non-active, non-autonomous, and non-sovereign (Abdel-Malek 1963: 107–8). Non-Europeans are like Flaubert's Egyptian courtesan who never represented herself. Rather, it was Flaubert who spoke for her (Said 1979: 6). This "omniscience" resulted in problematic constructions of non-European or "Oriental" history and society. These constructions had come under attack at three levels – they do not fit empirical reality; they overabstract, resulting in the erasure of empirical variety; and they are founded on European prejudices (Wallerstein 1996: 8).

Europeans in the foreground: Europeans are foregrounded, resulting in the distortion of the role of non-Europeans. For example, modernity is seen as a specifically European creation and encounters with non-Europeans are not viewed to have brought about significant changes relevant to the emergence of European modernity.

Europeans as originators: Europeans are generally seen as originators of modern civilization where in fact there should be the consideration of its multicultural origins. In texts, Muslim philosophers are often seen as having simply transmitted Greek thought to the European world of the Renaissance. Alfred Weber, the younger brother of Max Weber and author of a history of philosophy, notes that the Arabs were "apt pupils of the Greeks, Persians, and Hindoos in science. Their philosophy ... is more learned than original, and consists mainly of exegesis, particulary of the exegesis of Aristotle's system" (Weber 1925: 164n).

The imposition of European categories and concepts: Tibawi brought attention to the "persistence in studying Islam and the Arabs through the application of Western European categories" (1979: 37). To the extent that the process of modernization in Europe was universal and replicable elsewhere, so too were the social sciences that explained modernization. Non-European societies are regarded as worthy objects of analysis but rarely as sources of concepts and ideas.

Belief in the objective superiority of European civilization: Modern civilization as modernity is a European creation and is due to European superiority whether this is viewed in biological, cultural, or sociological terms.

While the Eurocentric nature of sociology and other social sciences has been noted, efforts to address the problem in the teaching of sociology and in research has not been forthcoming. In the teaching of both the history of sociological theory and sociological theory itself, the five traits of Eurocentrism are present.

In most sociological theory textbooks or works on the history of social thought and theory, Europeans are the knowing subjects, that is, the social theorists and social thinkers. To the extent that non-Europeans figure in these accounts, they are objects of the observations and analyses of the European theorists, such as the Indians and Algerians in Marx's writings or Turks, Chinese, and Jews in Weber's works. They do not appear as sources of sociological concepts and ideas. In works on the history of social thought, the focus is on European thinkers at the expense of thematizing intercivilizational encounters that possibly influenced social theory in Europe. For example, Maus does not refer to any non-European in his chapter on the antecedents of sociology (Maus 1962 [1956]: ch. 1). This absence can also be seen in teaching. The *Resource Book for Teaching Sociological Theory* published by the American Sociological Association contains a number of course descriptions for sociological theory. The range of classical theorists whose works are taught are Montesquieu, Vico, Comte, Spencer, Marx, Weber, Durkheim, Simmel, Tönnies, Sombart, Mannheim, Pareto, Sumner, Ward, Small, Wollstonecraft, and several others. No non-European thinkers are included.

European (and by extension, western) sociologists continue to be foregrounded in works on the history of the discipline, although there are exceptions. Becker and Barnes in their *Social Thought from Lore to Science*, first published in 1938, devote many pages to the social thought of Ibn Khaldun. While non-western sources of sociology have been acknowledged by some in the West in a few early works, they are not discussed in mainstream theory textbooks and other works.

Europeans, therefore, tend to be seen as the sole originators of sociology. There were a host of other thinkers in India, China, Japan, and Southeast Asia during the nineteenth and early twentieth centuries who would qualify as modern social thinkers but who are only briefly mentioned in the early histories of sociology (e.g., Maus, Becker & Barnes) or totally ignored in more recent works. Not all European thinkers, however, ignored their non-European counterparts. For example, Becker and Barnes discuss the influence of Ibn Khaldun on Gumplowicz (1928 [1899]) and Oppenheimer (1922–35), a theme that was never taken up in later accounts of the history of social thought. The generations after Gumplowicz, Oppenheimer, and Becker and Barnes have erased non-European thinkers from the history books.

Connected with the above is the dominance of European concepts and categories in sociology at the expense of non-European ones. This dominance also translates into research. In the study of religion, for example, the bulk of concepts originate from Christianity. Concepts in the philosophical and sociological study of religion such as church, sect, denomination, and even religion itself are not devoid of Christian connotations and do influence the social scientific reconstruction of non-Christian religions. The field of the sociology of religion has yet to enrich itself by developing concepts and categories derived from other "religions" such as Islam, Hinduism, Judaism, and so on. Underlying this is an assumption of the greater suitability of categories and concepts developed in the social sciences in Europe and North America.

There is a danger that the critique of Eurocentrism in sociology may lead to nativism, that is, the trend of going native among western and local scholars alike, in which the native's point of view is elevated to the status of the criterion by which descriptions and analyses are to be judged. This involves an intolerant stance with regard to western knowledge. Nativism is founded on an essentialist approach. For example, there is a tradition in Japanese sociology that is defined by *nihonjinron* (theories of Japanese people), which are informed by essentialized views on Japanese society, with the stress on cultural homogeneity and historical continuity. This remains squarely in the tradition of western scholarship on Japan with the difference that the knowing subjects are Japanese. Hence the term auto-Orientalism as discussed by Lie (1996: 5). The challenge, therefore, is to correct the Eurocentric bias in sociology.

A more universalistic approach to the teaching of sociology as well as research in sociology would have to raise the question of whether it is possible to identify examples of sociological theorizing and concept formation outside the western/European cultural milieu. This would in turn imply radical changes in sociology theory curricula (Alatas & Sinha 2001). This does not require that western sociological content be removed from the sociology syllabi. Rather, more and more sociologists are recognizing the need to look to additional sources of concept formation and theory building from outside the usual corpus of knowledge that is confined to one civilization.

SEE ALSO: Captive Mind; Colonialism (Neocolonialism); Ethnocentrism; Hidden Curriculum; Multiculturalism; *Nihonjinron*; Orientalism; Race; Race (Racism); Rizal, José; Scientific Racism; Third World and Postcolonial Feminisms/Subaltern

REFERENCES AND SUGGESTED READINGS

Abdel-Malek, A. (1963) Orientalism in Crisis. *Diogenes* 44: 103–40.

Alatas, S. F. & Sinha, V. (2001) Teaching Classical Sociological Theory in Singapore: The Context of Eurocentrism. *Teaching Sociology* 29(3): 316–31.

Alatas, S. H. (1956) Some Fundamental Problems of Colonialism. *Eastern World* (November).

Amin, S. (1989) *Eurocentrism*. Zed, London.

Gumplowicz, L. (1928 [1899]) *Soziologische Essays: Soziologie und Politik*. Universitats-Verlag Wagner, Innsbruck.

Lie, J. (1996) Sociology of Contemporary Japan. *Current Sociology* 44(1): 1–95.

Maus, H. (1962 [1956]) *A Short History of Sociology*. Philosophical Library, New York.

Morga, A. de (1962 [1890]) *Historical Events of the Philippine Islands by Dr. Antonio de Morga, Published in Mexico in 1609, recently brought to light and annotated by José Rizal, preceded by a prologue by Dr. Ferdinand Blumentritt*. Writings of José Rizal Volume 6. National Historical Institute, Manila.

Needham, J. (1969 [1955]) The Dialogue of East and West. In: Needham, J., *Within the Four Seas: The Dialogue of East and West*. George Allen & Unwin, London. Adapted from the Presidential Address to the Britain–China Friendship Association, 1955.

Oppenheimer, F. (1922–35) *System der Soziologie*. Jena.

Said, E. (1979) *Orientalism*. Vintage, New York.

Sarkar, B. K. (1985 [1937]) *The Positive Background of Hindu Sociology*. Motilal Banarsidass, Delhi.

Tibawi, A. L. (1963) English-Speaking Orientalists. *Muslim World* 53: 185–204, 298–313.

Tibawi, A. L. (1979) Second Critique of English-Speaking Orientalists and Their Approach to Islam and the Arabs. *Islamic Quarterly* 23(1): 3–54.

Van Leur, J. C. (1937) Enkele aanteekeningen met betrekking tot de beoefening der Indische geschiedenis (Some Notes Concerning the Study of the History of the Indies). *Koloniale Studiën* 21: 651–66.

Van Leur, J. C. (1940) Eenige aanteekeningen betreffende de mogelijkheid der 18ᵉ eeuw als categorie in de Indische geschiedschrijving (Some Notes on the Possibility of the 18th Century as a Category in the Writing of the History of the Indies). *Tijdschrift voor Indische Taal-, Land- en Volkenkunde uitgegeven door het (Koninklijk) Bataviaasch Genootschap van Kunsten en Wetenschappen* 80: 544–67.

Van Leur, J. C. (1955) *Indonesian Trade and Society: Essays in Asian Social and Economic History*. W. van Hoeve, The Hague.

Wallerstein, I. (1996) Eurocentrism and its Avatars: The Dilemmas of Social Science. Paper read at the KSA–ISA Joint East Asian Regional Colloquium on "The Future of Sociology in East Asia," organized by the Korea Sociological Association, November 22–3.

Weber, A. (1925) *History of Philosophy*. Trans. F. Thilly. Scribner, New York.

euthanasia

Clifton D. Bryant

The dictionary defines euthanasia as an "act or method of causing death painlessly so as to end suffering: advocated by some as a way to deal with victims of incurable diseases." This is something of an over-simplification, however. The practice of euthanasia has long been a contentious issue and a matter of disputatious debate. Some have termed euthanasia "mercy killing" (Vernon 1970: 310), but others have reported that some critics have labeled it as murder (Sanders 1969; Charmaz 1980: 112).

While euthanasia has generally taken place within a medical context, historically, euthanasia, as a humanitarian act, has also occurred within other contexts, such as war. There are historical accounts (from all wars) of soldiers encountering badly wounded fellow soldiers or wounded enemy soldiers. If their wounds were severe and it appeared they would not survive and they could not be transported to a medical facility, the soldiers sometimes killed the wounded individual out of compassion, administering the "coup de grace" – in effect, putting the wounded man out of his misery (Leming & Dickinson 2002: 283). Euthanasia most frequently, however, has occurred within a medical context, and this term has come to be associated with terminal illness and the medical setting. The discomfort of terminal illness is not the only motivating factor in euthanasia. Grossly deformed infants have sometimes been euthanized (or it was intended that they be euthanized until a court intervened) (Vernon 1970: 310; Charmaz 1980:113; DeSpelder & Srickland 2002: 203–4).

There are two distinctly different modes of operationalizing euthanasia: *positive* euthanasia and *negative* euthanasia (Charmaz 1980:112). Positive euthanasia refers to the practice of deliberately ending the life of a patient through active means (e.g., giving the patient an overdose of sedatives, knowing that this will kill the individual). This practice is sometimes euphemistically termed "snowing." Negative euthanasia describes the practice of discontinuing interventive treatment, or withholding some life-sustaining "drugs, medical devices, or procedures" (Despelder & Srickland 1999: 200). Charmaz (1980: 113) describes positive euthanasia as an act of *commission* and negative euthanasia as an act of *omission*. DeSpelder and Srickland (1999: 200) indicate that "this distinction is sometimes characterized as the difference between 'killing' and 'letting die.'" Some writers (e.g., Leming & Dickinson 2002: 290, 294) apply the terms *passive* euthanasia (rather than negative) when treatment and drugs are withdrawn or withheld, and *active* euthanasia (rather than positive euthanasia) when "the individual is helped to die."

Another dimension of euthanasia is the matter of who makes the decision concerning the termination of the life of an individual. Most writers bifurcate euthanasia into *voluntary* euthanasia, where a competent individual requests and gives informed consent to withhold treatment, and *informal* euthanasia, where the decision to terminate an individual's life is made by others. One set of writers (Corr et al. 2003), however, suggest that there are three variations of decision-making in euthanasia. They also articulate the definitions of the variations somewhat differently. As they conceptualize the paradigm, *voluntary* euthanasia refers to the instance of an individual asking for and/or assenting to their death. Where the individual is unable to make such a decision (such as a person who is unconscious or in a coma, or, perhaps, an infant) and "a second person somehow intentionally contributes to the death of this sort of person, it is *nonvoluntary* euthanasia." They further assert that where a person wishes to be kept alive but someone else elects to terminate the individual's life, the process should be correctly labeled *involuntary* euthanasia (more like homicide than like a "good death").

Euthanasia, whether active or passive, voluntary or involuntary, or nonvoluntary, is socially (and legally) controversial. Assertive and persuasive arguments concerning euthanasia have been advanced by both proponents and opponents. According to Charmaz (1980: 112) there are "three interrelated ethical questions constituent to the controversy." First, should individuals have the right to *elect* and *control* death? Second, at what *point* might an individual legitimately exert these rights? Third, whose *interests* are going to be given priority, those of the individual or those of the society?

Euthanasia (and also sterilization) has sometimes been carried out with the presumed best interest of the society as rationale. This is essentially an operationalization of "the utilitarian doctrine of the greatest good for the greatest number" (Charmaz 1980: 114). Opponents often cite examples of the programs of euthanasia such as those where individuals considered to be "unproductive," "defective," and "mentally unfit," such as handicapped and retarded persons, Gypsies, Jews, and homosexuals, were systematically euthanized (exterminated) at concentration camps like Auschwitz for the so-called benefit of society (Leming & Dickinson 2002: 300). This is known as the "slippery-slope-to-Auschwitz" argument (Potter 1993; Wilkinson 1995).

"Altruistic" euthanasia has not only occurred in Nazi Germany. Some years ago a famous American novel, *Not As a Stranger* (Thompson 1954), chronicled the experiences of a young idealistic physician who had just begun to practice medicine in a small town in the upper Midwest in the 1930s. The young physician learned, to his horror, that the administrator of the local county hospital was systematically having long-term elderly senile patients placed in beds in a cold room with open windows at the rear of the hospital during the winter. Predictably, the elderly patients contracted pneumonia and died. This freed up additional bed space for younger sick patients coming in for treatment. This initiative was viewed by the hospital administrator as a necessary effort for the good of the community. While the account is fictional, there is little doubt that this and other similar instances of systematic euthanasia have been carried out in real life for the presumed "good of society."

Arguments for and against euthanasia were advanced many decades ago and have proved to be quite durable. Charmaz (1980: 114), for example, articulated four potent arguments in favor of voluntary euthanasia. These include:

1 Individuals have the right to choose their deaths.
2 This right is underscored by the fact that technological medicine obscures the moral dimensions of the dilemma and usurps choice.
3 Individuals may decide that suffering is of a magnitude to warrant release through death.
4 Individuals may specify that they do not wish dying to be prolonged when irreversible damage results in the loss of human attributes.

Charmaz also detailed the arguments against euthanasia. These include the belief that euthanasia is immoral on religious grounds; that it is incompatible with the belief in the sanctity of human life; that the state of knowledge (errors in tests and diagnosis, sudden new medical breakthroughs) may radically alter the circumstances; and that there is no way of knowing what patients would want once they are unable to communicate.

More recent arguments in favor of intentionally ending a human life have been summarized by Corr et al. (2003: 495–6), who articulate three such arguments, including prevention of suffering, enhancement of liberty, and quality of life. They also point to arguments against intentionally ending a human life, including a commitment to the preservation of life, the slippery slope argument, and additional arguments ("Medicine is at best an uncertain science; medicine moves quickly and … new therapies and new cures are discovered at unknown moments; … assisted suicide and euthanasia … may detract from the role of the physician as healer and preserver of life").

The main thesis of voluntary passive euthanasia is that in the case of terminally ill patients, they may desire that no *extraordinary* methods be used to prolong life. There is great ambiguity in the term *extraordinary*, however. Corr et al. (2003: 493) have provided several criteria for a refined definition of these terms. They indicate that *ordinary* means of treatment are those that have outcomes that are predictable and well known, offer no unusual risk, suffering, or burden for either the person being treated or others, and are effective. *Extraordinary* means of treatment, on the other hand, fail to meet one or more of these criteria. Such means of treatment have sometimes been referred to as "heroic measures," suggesting that interventive initiatives of this variety tend to constitute treatment efforts "above and beyond" what might be normally expected within conventional medical protocol.

Much of the controversy surrounding euthanasia rests on the issue of the priority of two disparate perspectives or values. These two ideological value postures are the *sanctity-of-life view* and the *quality-of-life view*. The former invokes the notion that "all 'natural' life has intrinsic meaning and should be appreciated as a divine gift" (Leming & Dickinson 2002: 284). In the instance of the latter, these writers assert "the quality of life orientation holds that when life no longer has quality or meaning, death is preferable to life." Both views have obvious merit, but the question of primacy is both philosophically weighty and obviously disputatious.

Passive (or negative) euthanasia, generally speaking, is legal in the US. Active euthanasia, by and large, is not legal, although there is some degree of social toleration for this procedure. Such toleration might include such examples as a physician actively bringing about the death of a terminally ill patient, with the knowledge and tacit assent of nurses and medical staff, who do not report such an act to law-enforcement officials. Another example might be an instance of jury nullification, whereby an individual who killed a terminally ill spouse or parent is not convicted, contrary to law and the facts, by a jury who viewed the murder as a mercy killing (Sanders 1969; Vernon 1970: 310).

While active euthanasia is illegal, there are nevertheless organizations that support that mode of death. The Hemlock Society advocates active euthanasia for persons who have terminal illnesses and who are experiencing unrelieved pain, or who are facing a "life devoid of meaning and purpose" (Leming & Dickinson 2002: 299). The Hemlock Society makes a distinction between suicide, self-deliverance, and mercy killing. According to Leming and Dickinson, the Hemlock Society describes suicide as a socially condemned stigmatized act, "religiously selfish," and an "overreaction of a disturbed mind," and self-deliverance as "a positive action taken to provide a permanent solution to long-term pain and suffering for the individual and her or his significant others faced with a terminal condition." Mercy killing is essentially homicide, although temporary insanity and compassion may be invoked as defenses.

Generally speaking, most religious faiths, including Christianity, Judaism, Hinduism, Islam, and Buddhism, condemn active euthanasia as morally unacceptable (Walker 2003).

Euthanasia as a controversial concept overlaps with several other controversial issues. These include abortion, which has been classified by many as involuntary (or nonvoluntary) active euthanasia. Another overlapping issue is suicide, which can be technically viewed as self-directed voluntary, active euthanasia. This would seem to be especially the case if the suicide is conceptualized as self-deliverance as articulated by the Hemlock Society. Similarly, assisted suicide and particularly physician-assisted suicide would be tantamount to voluntary active euthanasia. Arguments pro and con are essentially the same for all of these processes.

The enactment of legislation recognizing the legal legitimacy of "living wills" in all 50 US states and the District of Columbia has effectively institutionalized passive euthanasia. Active euthanasia, while currently illegal in almost all states, may well undergo a legal metamorphosis in the US in the decades ahead. In 1994 Oregon passed the Death with Dignity Act, which allowed physician-assisted suicide. Physicians can legally prescribe lethal medication for patients who request it, who have requested hastened death three times, who are 18 years of age, and who have a life expectancy of 6 months or less. There are additional requirements. This legislation effectively legalizes active euthanasia. Oregon renewed the act by referendum in 1997 (Walker 2003). Undoubtedly, other states will follow suit. In 2001 the Netherlands passed a law that decriminalized active, voluntary euthanasia.

With an aging population in the US and in many other countries of the world, euthanasia will assume more and more relevancy with time. Passive euthanasia is legal and widely practiced and active euthanasia is obviously moving more in the direction of social acceptance. Euthanasia would seem to be an idea whose time has arrived.

SEE ALSO: Abortion as a Social Problem; Death and Dying; Suicide

REFERENCES AND SUGGESTED READINGS

Charmaz, K. (1980) *The Social Realities of Death.* Addison-Wesley, Reading, MA.

Corr, C., Nabe, C. M., & Corr, D. M. (2003) *Death and Dying, Life and Living.* Wadsworth, Belmont, CA.

DeSpelder, L. A. & Strickland, A. L. (1999) *The Last Dance: Encountering Death and Dying.* Mayfield Publishing, Mountain View, CA.

DeSpelder, L. A. & Strickland, A. L. (2002) *The Last Dance: Encountering Death and Dying*, 6th edn. McGraw Hill, Boston.

Leming, M. R. & Dickinson, G. E. (2002) *Understanding Dying, Death and Bereavement.* Harcourt College Publishers, Fort Worth.

Potter, A. C. (1993) Will the "Right to Die" Become a License to Kill? *Journal of Legislation* 19(1): 31–62.

Sanders, J. (1969) Euthanasia: None Dare Call It Murder. *Journal of Criminal Law, Criminology, and Police Science* 60(3): 351–9.

Thompson, M. (1954) *Not as a Stranger.* Scribner, New York.

Vernon, G. M. (1970) *Sociology of Death: An Analysis of Death-Related Behavior.* Ronald Press, New York.

Walker, G. C. (2003) Medical Euthanasia. In: Bryant, C. D. (Ed.-in-Chief), *Handbook of Death and Dying.* Sage, Thousand Oaks, CA, pp. 405–23.

Wilkinson, B. W. (1995) The "Right to Die" by Russell Ogden: A Commentary. *Canadian Public Policy* 21(4): 449–55.

evaluation

James R. Sanders

Evaluation is a systematic process of determining the merit or worth of some entity, which is commonly referred to as the evaluand (Scriven 1967, 1991). Evaluation, like research, is a form of disciplined inquiry (Cronbach & Suppes 1969). As such, emphasis is placed on public examinations of arguments and inquiry methods, on discussion of limitations and margins of error in conclusions, and on adherence to generally accepted standards of practice, which include impartial, detailed, and unambiguous methods of inquiry. The systematic processes of evaluation and research can be compared on several dimensions. This conception of evaluation contrasted to research began with discussions of the emerging methodology of evaluation in the late 1960s, as described by Worthen and Sanders (1973).

The goal of evaluation is to determine value (merit, worth) of an evaluand, while the goal of research is to develop generalizable knowledge. The roles of evaluation include use for product, performance, and program improvement, as well as use for guiding choices among decision alternatives. The roles of research include building a body of knowledge on which theories and product development can draw. The motivation of evaluators toward what to study is primarily external, whereby evaluators provide services to others. The motivation of researchers in choosing what to study is primarily internal, whereby curiosity and a desire to extend existing knowledge are prime stimuli for research. Related to motivation of the inquirer is autonomy of the inquiry. Evaluators mostly serve clients and are accountable to them. Researchers often establish their own problems and direction of inquiry.

Investigative techniques used by evaluators must be diverse so that a broad range of questions that comprise the conception of value of an evaluand can be addressed. Researchers will often pursue a small number of important questions that require few investigative techniques. Evaluators are methodological generalists, while researchers tend to be methodological specialists. The disciplinary base and, consequently, the breadth of training of evaluators is necessarily broad in order to enable them to seek answers to a broad range of questions. The disciplinary base of researchers is usually found in mastery of a single field of study. Psychologists conduct psychological research, sociologists focus on sociological problems, and so on. And researchers tend to use the methodologies of their home disciplines.

Standards for judging the adequacy of evaluations include utility, feasibility, propriety, and accuracy (Joint Committee 1981, 1988, 1994, 2003), while research is judged on internal and external validity of the inquiry, as well as its contribution to the existing knowledge base (Campbell & Stanley 1963; Cook & Campbell, 1979). The salience of the value question in evaluation is high, while judging the value of an object of study does not dominate research.

These distinctions are useful for making the point that research and evaluation are different in important ways, even though there are areas of overlap. In the real world of inquiry, moreover, many of these distinctions blur, as complex projects may have multiple roles, goals, and motives, where both research and evaluation are needed.

METHODOLOGY OF EVALUATION

Discussions of a methodology of evaluation grew in the late 1960s when it became evident that traditional research methodologies could not address the needs of evaluators who were being asked to evaluate existing and newly funded social, educational, economic, engineering, health, and technological programs, products, and performances. A seminal work that established a foundation for the theory and practice of modern evaluation methodology was published in 1967 by Michael Scriven. In this work, Scriven distinguished between the roles of formative and summative evaluation, and the implications of this distinction for evaluation methodology. Formative evaluation was defined as feedback during the developmental stages of an evaluand that serves to improve it. It is kept internal to the group engaged in development. Summative evaluation was defined as information about a finished evaluand that is used to make decisions such as continuation, termination, adoption, and funding level.

A distinction must be made between formative/summative roles of evaluation and process/product questions about an evaluand. Confusion often appears when formative and process evaluation are seen as synonymous, and summative and product evaluation are seen as synonymous. They are not. Perhaps the best way to illustrate these distinctions is through the following matrix:

	Formative	*Summative*
Process	Evaluation of means to some ends as a way of improving the means.	Evaluation of alternative means to some ends in order to select the best means.
Product	Evaluation of the ends accomplished by an evaluand under development as a way to identify where changes may be needed.	Evaluation of the acceptability of ends of competing evaluands in order to identify the evaluand with the best ends.

Formative process and formative product evaluations are aimed at improving means and ends, respectively, during developmental stages. Summative process and summative product evaluations are aimed at selecting the best means and ends from among competing alternatives.

EVALUATION APPROACHES

Depending on such factors as the training background and experience, the philosophical orientation, and methodological preferences of the evaluator, and the stated needs for evaluation, evaluators have developed different evaluation approaches, sometimes called models for evaluation. Stufflebeam (2001) has identified 22 different approaches. Among the most popular are those that are:

- *Goal based:* The focus is on achievement of desired ends as a basis for judging an evaluand.
- *Program theory based:* The focus is on the logical relationships and adequacy of program inputs, activities, and outcomes as a basis for judging programs.
- *Decision based:* The focus is on addressing the administrative decisions faced by managers in organizations. Planning, designing, budgeting, monitoring, and accountability decisions are all important sources of evaluation questions.
- *Consumer based:* The focus is on product decisions faced by consumers.
- *Expert based:* The focus is on standards and criteria identified by credible and qualified experts in the specific field of the evaluand.

- *Participant based:* The focus is on issues and concerns identified by stakeholders in the evaluand. Stakeholders are defined as those who are affected by the evaluand and those who affect the evaluand in some way (such as staff and funders).

EVALUATION DESIGN

The design of evaluation studies begins with the questions that are to be addressed in the evaluation. Some designs are narrow in scope because they seek to address one or a small number of questions. Others are very broad in scope because they seek to address many, often complex and diverse, questions related to the value of the evaluand. Some evaluators see their role as having the responsibility of determining the questions to be addressed. Others see the questions being generated by a negotiation process between evaluator and client (the funder of the evaluation), while still others see the questions being determined by stakeholders of the evaluation.

Evaluators typically begin designing an evaluation by identifying potentially important value questions. This is called the *divergent* phase of the design (Cronbach 1982). Once questions are listed, the evaluator determines for each question (1) the information needed to answer the question, (2) the source(s) of this information, (3) the tasks or steps required to generate answers, (4) who will perform each task, and (5) the cost of completing each task. A draft budget, time schedule, and staffing plan can then be prepared so that the *feasibility* of the design can be seen. If the design needs to be reduced in scope, as is usually the case, the evaluator begins the *convergent* phase of the design, during which some questions are eliminated. The questions that are dropped constitute in part the *limitations* of the evaluation.

Most evaluators agree that it is impossible and imprudent to identify the final set of evaluative questions at the beginning of the study. Evaluators learn as they become engaged in the evaluation, and consequently the evaluation design evolves. The distinction between *preordinate* evaluation designs (where all questions are determined beforehand) and *responsive* or emergent evaluation designs (where questions emerge as

learning about the evaluand takes place) is described by Stake (2004).

EVALUATION TECHNIQUES AND PROCEDURES

Stufflebeam (1969) defined five processes involved in evaluation: design, data collection, data analysis, reporting, and management of the evaluation. Design was covered in the preceding section. The remaining four processes will be discussed next.

Data collection involves the gathering of information needed to answer the questions posed for the evaluation. These data may be quantitative (numerical) or qualitative (nonnumerical). Quantitative techniques and procedures have been well developed by researchers in the social and physical sciences. They include such methods as testing and psychometrics, surveys, physical measurements, cost analysis and econometrics, sociometrics, and scaling. Qualitative techniques and procedures have also been well developed by researchers, particularly in the social sciences. They include such methods as ethnographies, case studies, and observation, including participant observation, focus groups, document analysis, narrative interviews, unobtrusive measures, and photography.

In addition to the data collection techniques and procedures that have been developed by researchers there are data collection methods that have been developed by evaluators to serve the unique demands of evaluation. These methods include needs assessment, advocate team studies, logic models and program theory, values analysis and validation, goal-free evaluation, and cluster evaluation.

Data analysis involves the reduction and summarization of data so that evaluative meaning can be derived for the complex combination of data generated by most evaluation studies. Descriptive and inferential statistics, graphs, tables, and charts are most often used to analyze quantitative data collected during an evaluation. Searching for key incidents, patterns, and categories is a common method of qualitative data analysis. Analytic induction in qualitative data analysis involves several steps, including (1) exploring qualitative data and forming impressions, (2) identifying themes, (3) focusing for further observation and documentation, often using working hypotheses, (4) verification and support of tentative conclusions, and (5) assimilation into the broader context of what is known about the evaluand.

Data analysis in evaluation also involves a valuing process whereby conclusions based on evidence are combined with values to arrive at evaluative interpretations. It is this aspect of data analysis that sets evaluation apart from other forms of disciplined inquiry.

The reporting process of evaluation can take many forms, ranging from daily updates and discussions to compilations of written final reports. The utility of evaluation is highly dependent on the reporting and communications process (Fitzpatrick et al. 2004: ch. 16). Characteristics of effective evaluation reporting include accuracy, timeliness, frequency, balance, fairness, clarity, level of detail, communication style, and providing an opportunity to intended users for reviewing draft reports.

Evaluation management begins at the design stage of the evaluation process and continues through helping users of the evaluation to move from evaluative conclusions to application and action. Coordinators of evaluations must ensure that adequate time, funds, expertise, and communications are present. They must supervise and direct evaluation operations so that the results of the evaluation are as accurate and valid as the limitations of the evaluation study allow. Delivering a product that is on time, within budget, and meets professional standards and principles (Joint Committee 1994; American Evaluation Association 1995) depends on sound evaluation management.

METAEVALUATION

All evaluations inevitably have some degree of uncertainty and bias, as do any other scientific undertakings. For this reason the professional evaluator will typically plan for a metaevaluation, or evaluation of the evaluation. Internal review can be a continuous part of the evaluation process, whereby qualified colleagues can provide formative feedback to the evaluator beginning with the evaluation design, and continuing through the evaluation process and final communications with the client. External

reviews can be arranged with independent qualified consultants who may prepare reports and recommendations at discrete points in the evaluation process, such as when the design is submitted, when reports are delivered, and when the evaluation has been completed. These outside reviewers most often report to the client with an opportunity for the evaluator to respond. The metaevaluation process is intended to strengthen the evaluation and to increase the certainty that may be placed on evaluative findings.

SEE ALSO: Effect Sizes; Grounded Theory; Organizational Learning; Performance Measurement; Quantitative Methods; Validity, Qualitative; Validity, Quantitative; Values

REFERENCES AND SUGGESTED READINGS

American Evaluation Association (1995) Guiding Principles for Evaluators. In: Shadish, W., Newmann, D., Scheirer, M., & Wye, C. (Eds.), *New Directions for Program Evaluation, No. 66*. Jossey-Bass, San Francisco, pp. 19–26.

Campbell, D. & Stanley, J. (1963) Experimental and Quasi-Experimental Design for Research on Teaching. In: Gage, N. (Ed.), *Handbook of Research on Teaching*. Rand McNally, Chicago, pp. 171–246.

Cook, T. & Campbell, D. (1979) *Quasi-Experimental: Design and Analysis Issues for Field Settings*. Rand McNally, Chicago.

Cronbach, L. (1982) *Designing Evaluations of Educational and Social Programs*. Jossey-Bass, San Francisco.

Cronbach, L. & Suppes, P. (1969) Research for Tomorrow's Schools: Disciplined Inquiry for Education. Macmillan, New York.

Fitzpatrick, J., Sanders, J., & Worthen, B. (2004) *Program Evaluation*. Allyn & Bacon, Pearson, Boston.

Joint Committee on Standards for Educational Evaluation (1981) *Standards for Evaluations of Educational Programs, Projects, and Materials*; (1988) *The Personal Evaluation Standards*; (1994) *The Program Evaluation Standards*; (2003) *The Student Evaluation Standards*. Corwin Sage, Thousand Oaks, CA.

Scriven, M. (1967) The Methodology of Evaluation. In: Stake, R. (Ed.), *Curriculum Evaluation*. Rand McNally, Chicago, pp. 39–83.

Scriven, M. (1991) *Evaluation Thesaurus*, 4th edn. Sage, Thousand Oaks, CA.

Stake, R. (2004) *Standards-Based and Responsive Evaluation*. Sage, Thousand Oaks, CA.

Stufflebeam, D. (1969) Evaluation as Enlightenment for Decision-Making. In: Beatty, W. (Ed.), *Improving Educational Assessment and an Inventory of Measures of Affective Behavior*. Association for Supervision and Curriculum Development, Washington, DC, pp. 41–73.

Stufflebeam, D. (2001) Evaluation Models. In: *New Directions for Evaluation, No. 89*. Jossey-Bass, San Francisco.

Worthen, B. & Sanders, J. (1973) *Educational Evaluation: Theory and Practice*. Wadsworth, Belmont, CA.

everyday life

Martha Easton

Everyday life, in the field of sociology, has been positioned as a condition, a social space, a political goal, and a methodological analytic. Its meaning has shifted with time, and its potential consequences have shifted with its meaning. One thing that has not changed has been the home of the concept, under the wing of the conflict school of theory. But while everyday life started its move into theory as a negative extension of Marx's idea of alienation, it has evolved into a celebrated realm for modern-day feminist sociology.

Henri Lefebvre, one of the most important French Marxist sociologists of the mid-century, first wrote of everyday life as a mind-numbing, alienating set of social conditions. His book *Critique of Everyday Life* was published in 1947. In it he linked what he called "everydayness" to Marx's theory of alienation. According to Lefebvre, everydayness was a modern-day extension of the grip of alienation, part of the consequence of the rise of a modern form of capitalism. Lefebvre argued that capitalism had gotten so powerful that it had grown beyond organizing our productive and social relations in society; it also actually sucked the meaning out of everyday life. Alienation, the feeling of exhaustion, stress, and poverty consequential from the act of being forced to sell one's labor, was experienced more painfully under modern capitalism precisely because the experiences of everyday life outside of work had been invaded by capitalism. Without the

genuine meaning and connection that had once taken place in everyday life outside of work, modern workers turned to consumption to fill the gap. The lifestyle of consumption grew stronger and stronger under modern capitalism, and everyday life was marked by the purchase of commodities, which furthered the cycle of alienation.

Lefebvre's view of everyday life as a kind of negative alienating condition shaped by the structural influences of capitalism was a powerful position in social theory during the mid-twentieth century. But by the 1960s, a different view of everyday life began to emerge in social theory.

Everyday life got a new set of meanings along with the reemergence of arguments about the public sphere and the private sphere. As the concept of the public sphere began to be increasingly defined as the world of work, politics, and the service of citizenship, the private sphere began to be seen as the space of everything else, or the space of everyday life. This loaded the idea of everyday life with the content of all that was seen as somehow being personal and private: love, family, sex, relationships, housework, emotions, and so on.

It was in this context that feminist sociologists retrieved the idea of everyday life, and reinterpreted it as a social space that primarily contained that which was seen as belonging to women. The public sphere was the world of men, while the private sphere (and everyday life) was the realm of women. Feminist sociologists argued that the world of women and the social relations of everyday life should be celebrated and valued. Some also argued that the line between the public and private sphere should be obliterated, allowing women into the public realm and, more important, removing value judgments from the assessment of the realms in which people pursue social interaction. In other words, the obligations of everyday life – like helping a child with homework – are just as important as the work of the public realm – like participating in the work of a political party.

The women's movement politicized the idea of everyday life. Home, and the private world, were sites for battle over the work and role of women. The "personal is political" was a key theme for analysis and activism, and everyday life became a battleground.

By the 1970s, feminist sociologists such as Dorothy E. Smith had added an important new dimension to the concept of everyday life. They argued that the social reproduction of inequality could be seen in the normal interactions of everyday life. This analytical insight helped reshape the focus for feminist research. As a topic of analysis, the social relationships of everyday life became increasingly important. New empirical research during this time period began to focus on topics that had formerly been seen as banal, or unimportant, or too "everyday." Topics such as domestic violence, housework, mental illness, and childrearing emerged as critical – and controversial – areas for research. Everyday life was not just what was left over from the important work of the public realm, but was in itself a set of social relations that created and reproduced social inequalities. The experiences of everyday life were important pieces of knowledge about our social world, and everyday life became a key focus of empirical study.

In addition, everyday life anchors an important feminist methodological tradition. The practice of institutional ethnography depends on a close analysis of the ways in which normal people experience and know their own everyday lives. Dorothy E. Smith first articulated the importance of this method in 1983, growing out of her previous work on the knowledges of women's everyday experiences in the private sphere. This method looks at the institutions that organize the experiences of everyday life, and works backwards from individual experience to make visible the power behind the relations of ruling. Smith takes as an example her experiences as a single mother dealing with the school her children attended. As she worked with the school to help one of her children who had a problem with reading, she began to see that the problem was that she was a single mother. Helping a child learn to read was not seen as work, and yet the school was highly dependent on the work of mothers in socializing their own children. The institution of education rested on unrecognized class and gender assumptions: that essential child socialization would be done by women who had no other jobs (i.e., were middle class). Children raised by families that did not conform to middle-class gender and social standards were constituted by their everyday behavior as abnormal or problemed. By reading backward from the experiences of everyday life, institutional ethnography can explicate the power relations behind important social institutions.

Everyday life is an important part of social theory. It is a condition, a political focus, and a set of experiences. Historically, the idea of everyday life was associated with Marxist ideas of alienation. Currently, the concept of everyday life is strongly associated with feminist sociology, and is an important focus of the feminist work.

SEE ALSO: Alienation; Feminism; Feminism and Science, Feminist Epistemology; Feminist Methodology; Lefebvre, Henri; Personal is Political; Public and Private

REFERENCES AND SUGGESTED READINGS

Lefebvre, H. (1992 [1947]) *Critique of Everyday Life.* Verso, New York.
Smith, D. E. (1987) *The Everyday World as Problematic: A Feminist Sociology.* Northeastern University Press, Boston.

evolution

Amanda Rees

The concept of evolution has a vexed and often misunderstood history as far as the social sciences are concerned, and one that has consistently been mired not just in intellectual and scientific debates, but also in political and economic confrontations and conflicts, ranging from the eugenic policies practiced by many western nations at the beginning of the twentieth century, to the execution and exile of Soviet biologists unwilling to toe the Lysenkoist party line in the 1950s, to the decision of the Kansas Board of Education in 1999 to delete the teaching of evolution from the state's science curriculum. There are a number of reasons why this concept – which at its simplest can be defined as the way things (people, societies, ideas, environments) change over time – has been bogged down in so many confusions and conflagrations, most of which can be found in the particular contexts and purposes in which evolutionary ideas are and have been expressed.

At present, the idea of evolution is most commonly associated with Charles Darwin's (1859) theory of evolution through natural selection. This is based on four key assumptions: that more individuals are born than can possibly survive; that each of these individuals differs in some distinctive way; that these differences will mean that some of these individuals will be better able to survive in particular environmental circumstances than others; that those better able to survive will leave more offspring than those less well adapted to their environment. In other words, to use the phrase coined by an early Darwin enthusiast, Herbert Spencer, evolution is a process based on the "survival of the fittest." Clearly, this account of how populations evolve or change over time is based on an entirely contingent match or "fit" between individual characteristics and current environmental context: if the demands placed on the individual by the environment change, then so will the nature of the characteristics that promote survival. Dinosaurs were enormously well "fitted" to the environment that existed prior to the atmospheric upheavals known to have taken place at the K/T boundary, but it was the small, rat-like mammals that were to prosper in the millennia that followed that ecological catastrophe.

Nonetheless, one of the key reasons for the confusion surrounding the concept of evolution in social and political theory and thinking has been the persistent ambiguity attached to the term "fittest." In the classic sense, it refers to the "fit" between individual and environment; however, it was in both the nineteenth and twentieth centuries also used to refer to the ideal of progress. Evolution could be taken to mean "evolving toward" ever more complex or ever more intelligent organisms or individuals, progressing toward the attainment of ever-higher levels of biological, social, and psychological being. Consequently, for the social sciences, it became associated with particularly hierarchical conceptions of the political and cultural world, both within and between particular societies and communities. It was used as, and was taken to be a justification for, the dominance of men over women, of white people over black, of Christians over Jews, of Europeans and North Americans over the peoples of Africa, Asia, and South America. As a result, and for these good historical reasons, a distaste for explanations of society and social interactions based on explicitly biological evolutionary theory developed among the social sciences and the humanities, an unease which first became unequivocal in the aftermath of World War II, and then was exacerbated during the 1970s with the publication of E. O. Wilson's *Sociobiology* (1975) and the UNESCO declaration on race and racial prejudice (1978). Social theorizing based on biological principles was declared anathema, and the extent of the opposition to the intrusion of biology into sociology can perhaps be judged from the famous incident where Wilson, speaking at an American Association for the Advancement of Science meeting in 1978, was drenched with water by a group of activists who had stormed the stage chanting "Racist Wilson, you can't hide, we charge you with genocide" (Segerstrale 2000).

Yet the story of evolution is far more complex and complicated than this. The concept itself was not the sole product of the biological sciences, but was a key element in the work of many nineteenth- and twentieth-century social theorists. Even within the biological sciences, the word "evolution" was and is not restricted to Darwinian natural selection, but can be taken to mean many different aspects of the way in which populations change over time. The use of the concept for political purposes was not restricted to fascist, or even conservative, social thinkers, but can also be tied to the development of socialist and Marxist philosophy. Ironically, bastions of conservatism, particularly in the United States, have explicitly rejected evolution and evolutionary thinking, condemning it as the source of moral laxity, the emergence of the permissive society, and the breakdown of social and community spirit. Finally, and perhaps most interestingly, the latter half of the twentieth century has also seen the emergence of a perspective that uses evolutionary principles to put forward an explicitly feminist agenda. Evolution as a word, as a concept, and as a rule is slippery at best, and predictably unpredictable at worst.

It is clear that many different scientific interpretations of "evolution" have existed, different interpretations that have both been firmly based within particular cultural contexts and had social and political consequences. So, for example, the development of the concept of evolution in the eighteenth and nineteenth centuries was tied to the development of geology and natural history, and based on the emergent cultural acceptance that the myth of creation outlined in Genesis did not explain or even necessarily accord with the conclusions that natural philosophers were reaching with regard to the age of the earth or the existence of fossilized creatures unknown and unrecognizable to modern eyes. This period saw an increased willingness to seek out and to create accounts of the world that did not involve the work of intangible or preternatural forces, but instead could be shown to depend on the interaction of material and utterly apprehendable rules of nature. The most famous alternative to Darwin's theory emerged in the early years of the nineteenth century – the work of the chevalier de Lamarck. Writing many years prior to the publication of Darwin's theory, Lamarck focused on what has come to be called the "inheritance of acquired characteristics." This is the presumption that parents can pass to their offspring those characteristics that they have physically achieved in their lifetimes. So, for example, giraffes acquired their extraordinarily long necks because each generation of giraffes stretched their necks as far as they could to eat the leaves on tall trees, passing this on to the next generation who in turn stretched their necks a little further. Alternatively, to give a human example, this interpretation of evolution would mean that a blacksmith's son would be blessed with significantly stronger muscles than the son of a clerk. This was the version of evolution that was to be taken up by Trofim Lysenko in the USSR during the 1950s, as a much more acceptable kind of evolutionary thinking than that based on the cutthroat individualistic competition of Darwin's natural selection. Lamarck preceded Darwin, but even after the publication of *The Origin of Species*, scientific debates continued on the nature of evolution and the mechanisms through which it proceeded. By the end of the nineteenth century and the beginning of the twentieth, Darwinism had been abandoned by most biologists. Evolution as a concept, and understood to refer to "change through time," remained unquestioned, but the principles of natural selection had been rejected – not least because they were unable to explain exactly how new species could emerge. Lamarck's views seemed much more useful here, and other perspectives such as orthogenesis (evolution toward fixed goals) flourished. It was not until the fusion of Darwinian natural selection with Mendelian principles of inheritance in the 1930s and 1940s that the place of Darwin in the history of evolution was assured.

However, the nineteenth century had also seen the adoption of evolutionary principles by many social philosophers. In contrast to the conception of society commonly held before the Enlightenment – that "mankind" was in the process of steadily declining from the achievements of antiquity – the eighteenth and nineteenth centuries had seen a steady growth in the confidence of European societies, aided by the material achievements of the Industrial Revolution, the intellectual accomplishments of the Scientific Revolution, and the political and military consequences of the developing European imperial project. Anthropologists were quick to make use of evolutionary and hierarchical ideas to explain the different levels of technological and political development achieved by the different societies that were increasingly coming under, not just the European gaze, but also European political and economic control. Writers such as Lewis Henry Morgan and Edward B. Tylor argued that all cultures were in the process of evolving from the simple to the complex, and that each encountered society could be placed correctly on the hierarchy of progress. European societies, naturally enough, occupied the highest steps, but other societies were in the process of evolving toward such heady pinnacles – they had simply not progressed up the ladder of progress from savagery to civilization as far as they might. This perspective was to become one of the key justifications of imperialism and colonialism, as administrators and politicians spoke of their "civilizing mission," the "burden" placed on the "white man" to provide the example, and the education that would enable these communities to accelerate their social evolution.

Several of the founding fathers of sociology were also eager to adopt the notion of development through time, not so much to explain the relationships between different societies as a means of making sense of the nature of the social developments that were occurring within European societies. The idea of progressive evolution was at the heart of Auguste Comte's positivist philosophy, with the assertion that human understanding of the world was naturally constituted so as to pass through three stages – the theological, the metaphysical, and the scientific – each constituting a more complex and more accurate comprehension of mundane reality. As people proceeded through these stages, so society itself would evolve toward a higher state, and part of the reason for his desire to establish a scientific sociology was his belief that the existence of such a science would aid humanity in its progress toward the most superior kind of society. Similar approaches to the notion of social evolution can be found in the work of Émile Durkheim and Karl Marx. Durkheim cast his account of society in terms of the consequences of the shift from mechanical solidarity to organic solidarity; from simple solidarity based on shared understanding of the nature of a largely agricultural community to a complex interdependence based on the increasing complexity of the division of labor in an increasingly industrial society. Again, we see evolution presented as the movement from the simple to the complex, heavily overladen with the assumption that by these means, social progress is achieved. Similarly, Marx and Engels drew on the notions of change over time not just to develop their materialist account of the immediate and antique past, but also to project into the future their understanding of the nature and apparatus of social change and progressive evolution toward a more perfect form of society. Inherent in all of these approaches to the study of human cultures is the idea that there are universal laws that govern the development of all forms of society – and that these laws can be best apprehended through the principles of evolution and progress. It was this notion of "universal laws" of human development that was to come under such sustained critique over the course of the twentieth century.

Perhaps the most famous nineteenth-century social evolutionist, however, was Herbert Spencer. It was he who coined the phrase "survival of the fittest," with all the ambiguity which that entails, and it was he who did most to introduce the philosophy known as "social Darwinism" to a wider public. However, he was not a Darwinist in the sense that he accepted natural selection as the principal means through which evolution operated. Instead, Spencer chose to stress the influence of external forces on the organism or society, and additionally, maintained a strong Lamarckian perspective. Moreover, for him, "social progress" meant the progression toward a society in which individuals experienced ever more freedom, leading him to oppose the introduction of governmental programs intended to alleviate the suffering of the poor and needy. Spencer had accepted the Malthusian argument concerning the role of population pressure, and considered this to be both the means through which the unfit were eliminated and the dynamo behind economic development: increasing population meant a constant drive to improve technological capacity in order to prevent people's needs entirely outstripping scarce resources. However, the logical result of the application of social Darwinism would be the adoption of an extreme form of *laissez-faire* capitalism, with the state restricted from any interference. The market alone would determine success or failure, and individuals must be left to sink or swim according to their capacities. This attitude toward cutthroat economic competition, combined with the increasing popularity among the middle classes of the eugenic theories first put forward by Darwin's cousin, Francis Galton, meant that by the turn of the twentieth century, evolutionary theories and concepts were not just being used to justify the class system as a reflection of natural reality, but were in some cases being used in an attempt to manipulate the composition and interrelationships between social classes in order to create a more perfect and progressive society.

The particular nature of that society, however, depended on one's political philosophy. There was nothing about the concept of evolution that marked it as the natural ally or particular property of one party or another. Having read *The Origin of Species*, Marx is said to have been so impressed with its account of the competitive basis of individual survival that he offered to dedicate part of *Das Kapital* to

Darwin. This story has been shown to be a myth, but it is one that reflects the close correspondence that many authors have felt exists between a description of the biological struggle for the "survival of the fittest" and the ruthless competition characteristic of the late Victorian capitalist society that Marx analyzed. Similarly, Lysenko's adoption of a Lamarckian conception of evolution was endorsed by the Soviet authorities because it eliminated the random competition characteristic of Darwinian evolution, and emphasized the potential for the development of a self-improving society. But the link between Darwinism and capitalism is not unproblematic, nor is it necessarily the result of controversy between the natural sciences and social sciences: the most vicious evolutionary debates of the twentieth century have been conducted not between biologists and social scientists, but within biology itself, as "Marxist biologists" have battled "sociobiologists" for the ultimate prize of inheriting Darwin's biological legacy.

This debate began in 1975, with the publication of E. O. Wilson's magisterial *Sociobiology: The New Synthesis*. For 26 chapters, Wilson, an entomologist based at Harvard University, provided a state-of-the-art review of what was then known about how and why animals behaved in the way in which they did. The book was a synthesis of the revolutionary new thinking about the ways in which selection and adaptation could work on a population, and introduced the word "sociobiology" to the wider public. Essentially, "sociobiology" was a project intended to explain the rules that both encouraged and made it possible for animals to live in social groups, showing how Darwinian natural selection could be supplemented by theories of kin selection and inclusive fitness (or the idea that an animal's "fitness" is measured not only by his or her own reproductive success but also by the success of close genetic relatives) to elucidate the basis on which altruism, for example, might evolve. After all, if the business of an animal is to concentrate on maximizing the genetic contribution to the next generation – that is, have as many offspring as possible – then why should any animal be willing to share resources or to refrain from reproduction? The answer was to be found in the closeness of the relationship between the altruist and the recipient and in the adoption

of a perspective that considered the reproduction of the gene to be more significant than the reproduction of the individual, a position now associated most publicly with the work of Oxford biologist Richard Dawkins. J. B. S. Haldane encapsulated this calculative, genetic perspective when he joked, in response to the question of whether he would lay down his life to save that of his brother, "No, but I would for two brothers, or for eight cousins." Since one shares half of one's genes with one's brother, and one-eighth with a cousin, Haldane was specifying the conditions under which it would make sociobiological sense to risk one's life. This perspective on the evolutionary basis of social behavior was uncontroversial (and has remained largely so) when applied to animals. However, in Wilson's twenty-seventh chapter, he extrapolated these rules of animal behavior and applied them to human beings. And the result was explosively dramatic.

Wilson's final chapter was, in practice, the first sustained attempt to analyze the impact that human biological evolution might have had on the development of human culture and society since World War II had ended. Opposition to Wilson's speculative attempt to extend his account of animal society to human society was immediate, intense, and passionate. However, what was interesting was that this hostility initially arose not from the social sciences – who had, by the 1970s, reached a consensus that biology was irrelevant as an explanatory factor in dealing with human society – but from other biologists. In fact, and ironically, the core of the opposition to Wilson's sociobiology was to be found in the office beneath his own at Harvard's Museum of Comparative Zoology – the office belonging to Richard Lewontin, another Harvard biologist, but one who was at that point committed to the development of a holistic, Marxist biology that would work toward the attainment of greater human freedom and equality. Lewontin was a key figure in the establishment of the Sociobiology Study Group, which along with the Boston-based organization Science for the People wrote a letter to the *New York Review of Books*, which condemned sociobiology on two fronts: first, the absence of adequate scientific evidence in its support, and second, the restrictive and anti-democratic political philosophy that they felt underpinned the theory. When the letter was published in November 1975, it compared Wilson's account of human sociobiology to the eugenic sterilization laws introduced in the years before World War II by the United States, and to the gas chambers of Nazi Germany. Wilson's final chapter may not, as he maintains, have been an attempt to demonstrate that aggression, war, and xenophobia were inevitable and natural aspects of human society, but it certainly provoked violence and intemperate language on both sides of the debate, including the public and physical assault on Wilson himself – a rare event in modern scientific debate, but one which demonstrated the depth of the passions that had been provoked by the suggestion that human culture and society might have their basis in biological evolution.

Biological opponents of sociobiology, such as Lewontin and his late Harvard colleague Steven Jay Gould, adopted a holistic rather than a reductionist account of how evolutionary processes might work, opposing the adoption of an overwhelmingly genetic perspective and attacking what they considered to be the adaptationist assumption. They criticized the presumption that most, if not all, of an organism's features must be "adaptive" – that is, must have some kind of biological purpose – as the modern version of the older assumption that evolution must in some sense be progressive, and emphasized the difficulty of identifying individual genes, much less specifying what they might prove to be genes "for." They stressed the need to consider gene and environment in interaction, drawing much more strongly from the themes and methods of natural history rather than the experimental tradition in biology. Rather than attempting to isolate genes in the laboratory, they chose to use particular historical and observational examples to demonstrate the way in which, for example, the particular genetic heritage of an individual (their "genotype") is limited in its physical expression (the "phenotype") by the nature of the environment in which the individual finds itself. In one of their most famous examples, they pointed to the fact that while genetics determines how tall an individual could potentially grow, it is the environment that determines the extent to which that potential will be realized. Individuals with the capacity to grow to 6 feet 2 inches will not reach that scale in the absence of adequate childhood nutrition – and in fact, may turn out to be shorter than individuals with a smaller genetic capacity but a better nurturing environment. If the ultimate cause of a clearly measurable and unarguable factor like height can be so difficult to define, then they emphasized that it must be even more important to consider the environmental (social, cultural, economic) context when examining such politically charged and difficult to define notions as "aggression," "intelligence," and the differences between the sexes.

By the early 1990s, the sociobiological dust had largely settled, but the role of evolution in explaining human society and culture had by no means been settled. At least three different sets of linked debates were now taking place in academic discussions of evolution. In the first place, while sociobiology per se had for the most part disappeared, in its place had emerged two different disciplines. One, behavioral ecology, applied a sociobiological perspective to animal behavior. The other, evolutionary psychology, worked from the premise that the human mind, like the human brain, was the product of evolution, and that if one wished to explain how the mind worked, the place to start was from the evolutionary perspective. In the second place, what has become known as the "Science Wars" had broken out between groups of scientists and social scientists. Ironically enough, at least part of the impetus for these "wars" had been the attempts by some sociologists and historians to study and to explain science and scientists; just as the social scientists had been affronted by the presumption that natural science could explain the complexities of human social behavior, so natural scientists were perturbed by the premise that scientific activities might have social or cultural explanations. Thirdly and finally, another new discipline had emerged, in the United States at least – that of "scientific creationism," the idea that it was possible to provide a scientific explanation of the events in the biblical story of Genesis – or at least, that it was possible scientifically to disprove the theory of evolution.

Evolutionary psychology, along with associated disciplines like memetics and gene–culture coevolution, sought to take the sociobiological project a few steps further, basing their approach on the idea that it was both possible and useful to identify specific mechanisms within the human brain that were the product of evolution, in the sense that they could be shown to impact on the presumed reproductive success of a given individual. While the term evolutionary psychology had been coined in the 1970s, it was not until the publication of Leda Cosmides and John Tooby's book *The Adaptive Mind* (1992) that the term came to be widely used, and in 1995, the "Darwin@LSE" research group was established at the London School of Economics, with the intent of raising the public profile of Darwinism both within the social sciences and with regard to a more general audience. At the heart of evolutionary psychology was the premise that there existed within the human mind "evolved psychological mechanisms," which are universal to the human species, but may be expressed in one sex rather than another, or at particular points in the life cycle of the individual. These psychological mechanisms were largely identified by reference to what evolutionary psychologists call the "environment of evolutionary adaptedness" (EEA) – or the hypothesized, hunter-gatherer-type societies in which humanity evolved, and which were therefore the environments in which, unlike industrial urban capitalism, humanity is biologically adapted for success. Thus, for example, one controversial explanation for the apparent fact that men prefer younger, slimmer women, and women prefer older, richer men, could be that in the EEA female fertility could be directly linked to youth and the pattern of bodily fat deposits, or the hip to waist to breast ratio (hence, "slimness"). Men would therefore prefer to mate with those females whose physique seemed to offer the best chance of reproduction, while those females who restricted their reproductive activity to males with adequate resources (wealth) to take care not only of them, but also of any children that might result, would reap larger benefits in terms of their contribution to the next generation.

This perspective has attracted much criticism from social scientists. Like sociobiology, the basic premise of evolutionary psychology was that universals of human nature existed, but the question remained of whether such universals can be proven to have a biological

or psychological existence, or whether they are the product of the dominance of certain cultural stereotypes – were they the result of socialization rather than evolution? Similarly, many critics have pointed out that paleoanthropology can realistically be certain about very few of the characteristics thought to be associated with the posited "environment of evolutionary adaptedness," making many evolutionary psychology hypotheses seem speculative at best, and at worst attempts to naturalize the political and sexual inequalities of western industrial capitalism. Similar critiques were made of the other novel disciplines that emerged in the 1990s with the intent to apply evolutionary insights in order to explain human culture and society. Memetics, for example, sought to treat culture in the same way that biologists dealt with the body, searching for the "memes" that formed the basis of cultural interaction in the same way that "genes" were the basis of sexual reproduction – but defining "memes" was shown to be problematic at best, since examples of memes provided by memeticists tended to range from advertising jingles to western Christianity.

However, the 1990s also saw the emergence of what has become known as the Science Wars, and the debate surrounding the place of evolution in cultural and public life soon became caught up in the wider struggles over the relationships that existed, or were thought to exist, between science and society. In 1994, Paul Gross and Norman Levitt, a biologist and a mathematician, published a book called *Higher Superstition*, which sought to expose and to denounce what they considered to be the insidious attacks on science and rationality that were being made by feminists, multiculturalists, environmentalists, and sociologists. They argued that the programs for understanding the social context of science that had been in the process of development since the publication of Kuhn's *Structure of Scientific Revolutions* (1962) were not in fact intended to study science at all, but to subvert and to denounce it by demonstrating that science was "merely" a cultural construction. Exacerbated by Alan Sokal's "spoof" article in the journal *Social Text*, the Science Wars blazed for most of the latter half of the decade, and at their heart was the question of whether scientific knowledge was a true representation of natural reality or the product of social constructionism. Since many of the debates surrounding the role and impact of evolution on the understanding of human social life tend to turn on a similar pivot, it is understandable that they came to be partly subsumed within the bigger picture. However, it was unfortunate, since it led to a situation in which battle lines became drawn even more deeply than might otherwise have been the case. As in the example of sociobiology, this also divided biologists. Many biologists were unhappy with a situation in which what they considered to be speculative and tentative claims about the evolutionary basis of human society were being treated as hard fact and presented to the public as such. In response, they found themselves lumped by their colleagues with unspecified hardline feminist multiculturalists, were accused by these colleagues of being unwilling to accept the existence of "facts," and were, for example, invited to "test" the law of gravity by jumping out of an upper-story window.

In some senses, particularly in the American case, there were genuine grounds to fear that science, and especially evolution, was indeed under attack. The potential for conflict between the revealed truth of the Christian religion and the developing scientific worldview had existed since geological and paleontological research had indicated as far back as the eighteenth century that the earth might be far older than the Bible suggested, and the relationship between science and religion in the West had been seriously damaged by the publication of Darwin's theory of evolution. However, in most cases and countries the debate was resolved in science's favor, even though it took the pope until 1996 to recognize that evolution was more than a hypothesis. Science and scripture could largely live in peace, since the one concerned itself with *how* things happened, the other with *why* these things occurred. The prominent exception to this separate spheres argument could have been found in the Bible Belt of the American Midwest. Opposition to the teaching of Darwinism and evolution had grown more fervent after the end of World War I, culminating in the state of Tennessee's Butler Act of 1925, which forbade the teaching of evolution in public schools. This Act directly led to the Scopes trial of 1925, in which Christian fundamentalism won the battle but eventually lost the war; John T. Scopes was

found guilty of teaching evolution and fined, but the coverage of the trial made creationists, as they were shortly to become known, into a laughing-stock. However, by the late 1970s, fundamentalism was on the rise in the United States once more, and with increased numbers, self-confidence, and a new theoretical twist focusing overwhelmingly on the notion of "intelligent design," creationists began to set in train a number of legal challenges to the teaching of evolution.

By 1980, a number of institutes such as the Institute for Creation Research and the Center for Scientific Creation had been established and the pattern of the modern-day battle between science and religion had been set. A key difference between the present-day debates and those characteristic of the past has been the role played by "science," and incidentally, by the sociology of science. Emphatically, modern opponents of evolution have done their best to don the robes of science. The names "scientific creationism" and "creation science" themselves indicate the extent to which creationists have attempted to adopt the language, rhetoric, and at least ostensibly, the methodology and philosophy of science to justify their position in the public sphere, presenting themselves as more "scientific" than their opponents. So, for example, creationists have tried to demonstrate that the theory of evolution is not falsifiable in the Popperian sense, and therefore cannot be scientific. They have adopted Kuhn's account of paradigm change as a justification for the existence of two incompatible but equally scientific accounts of life on earth – that given according to the theory of evolution by natural selection, and that provided in Genesis. They have seized on evolutionary debates such as those surrounding punctured equilibrium (the idea that major biological change might occur suddenly and swiftly, rather than steadily and gradually) as evidence that the evolutionary consensus was falling apart, requiring more and more special pleading to be allowed to stand as science. A number of legal challenges to the teaching of evolution in schools were made in the closing years of the twentieth century, and more have occurred in the new millennium. In early 2005, the Kansas State Board of Education again held hearings on the topic of the scientific status of evolution and concluded that it was indisputably in doubt. Opponents of evolution have, in some cases successfully, managed to portray evolution publicly as a theory in crisis, and to accuse scientists of fraudulently seeking to hide this in planning school textbooks. Ironically, the theory that was initially criticized by social scientists for naturalizing and therefore legitimizing the social and political inequalities of capitalist society is itself now the target of ultra-conservatism in the United States.

At the same time, another strand of evolutionary theorizing has developed over the course of the twentieth century, a position that has become known as feminist sociobiology. Initially, one of the major criticisms of sociobiological thought had been that it portrayed men and women as fundamentally and naturally different types of beings with separate spheres and interests, which therefore accounted for the fact that most societies are patriarchal to a greater or lesser degree, that there is inequality between the sexes, and that woman's ultimate concern was with her children. This depiction of the woman's place as firmly situated within the home had been one of the key reasons for the intense and furious feminist opposition to sociobiology when it emerged in the late 1970s – and the emergence of such a perspective at the point when the equal rights movement was gaining ground on both sides of the Atlantic was not treated by activists as a coincidence. However, during the late 1980s and the 1990s, an increasing number of scientists and social scientists have been willing to put themselves forward as "feminist sociobiologists." The intent of writers such as Sarah Hrdy, an anthropologist from UC Davis, Barbara Smuts (a primatologist at the University of Michigan), and Patricia Gowaty (a biologist from the University of Georgia) has been to address the initial feminist critique of sociobiological thinking and to seek to use insights from evolutionary theory to understand the nature of gender relations in the twenty-first century as a first step to learning how to change them. They have revolutionized the way in which biology has studied and portrayed reproduction in humans and other animals, most famously by challenging the association between the feminine and the passive, demonstrating the active role that female animals take in making reproductive decisions. Overall, this new take on understanding the nature of evolution represents an active attempt by some scientists to combine their feminist politics with their scientific practice, identifying and avoiding both the naturalistic (that what *is* is what *ought* to be) and the moralistic (that what *should not* be *is not*) fallacies, in order to develop new perspectives on both sexual politics and evolution as well as the reconsideration and the reordering of the relationship between evolutionary theory and human societies in the new millennium.

SEE ALSO: Comte, Auguste; Durkheim, Émile; Falsification; Fundamentalism; Gay Gene; Kuhn, Thomas and Scientific Paradigms; Malthus, Thomas Robert; Marx, Karl; Neoconservatism; Science and Religion; Science, Social Construction of; Scientific Knowledge, Sociology of; Society and Biology; Spencer, Herbert

REFERENCES AND SUGGESTED READINGS

Adas, M. (1990) *Machines as the Measure of Man: Science, Technology, and Ideologies of Western Dominance*. Cornell University Press, Ithaca, NY.

Bowler, P. (2003) *Evolution: The History of an Idea*. University of California Press, Berkeley.

Dawkins, R. (1976) *The Selfish Gene*. Oxford University Press, Oxford.

Gould, S. J. (1984) *The Mismeasure of Man*. Penguin, London.

Gowaty, P. (Ed.) (1996) *Feminism and Evolutionary Biology: Boundaries, Intersections, and Frontiers*. Kluwer, London.

Hrdy, S. (1999) *Mother Nature: A History of Mothers, Infants, and Natural Selection*. Pantheon, New York.

Laland, K. & Brown, G. (2002) *Sense and Non-Sense: Evolutionary Perspectives on Human Behaviour*. Oxford University Press, Oxford.

Lewontin, R. (2003) *The Triple Helix: Gene, Organism, and Environment*. Harvard University Press, Cambridge, MA.

Numbers, R. (1998) *Darwinism Comes to America*. Harvard University Press, Cambridge, MA.

Rees, A. (2000) Higamous, Hogamous, Woman Monogamous. *Feminist Theory* 1.

Rose, H. & Rose, S. (Eds.) (2000) *Alas, Poor Darwin: Arguments Against Evolutionary Psychology*. Jonathan Cape, London.

Rose, S., Lewontin, R., & Kamin, L. (Eds.) (1984) *Not in Our Genes: Biology, Ideology, and Human Nature*. Penguin, London.

Ross, A. (Ed.) (1996) *Science Wars*. Duke University Press, London.

Ruse, M. (2001) *Mystery of Mysteries: Is Evolution a Social Construction?* Harvard University Press, Cambridge, MA.

Segerstrale, U. (2000) *Defenders of the Truth: The Battle for Science in the Sociobiology Debates and Beyond*. Oxford University Press, Oxford.

Wright, R. (1995) *The Moral Animal: The New Science of Evolutionary Psychology*. Pantheon, New York.

exchange network theory

Henry A. Walker

Exchange network theories focus on the processes through which network structures affect power distributions, power exercise, and benefits gained in exchange. Sociologists use the term exchange network theory to describe several theories, models, and research programs. The field grew out of research in social exchange theory – an orienting strategy that traces its roots to Aristotle and other philosophers of classical antiquity. George C. Homans's *Social Behavior* (1961, 1974), John Thibaut and Harold H. Kelley's *The Social Psychology of Groups* (1959), Richard M. Emerson's paper on "Power–Dependence Relations" (1962), and other contemporaneous works are responsible for reinvigorating exchange research in the late 1950s and early 1960s.

Modern exchange theories focused initially on dyadic relations. Homans (1961) discussed triads, but exchange network research awaited theoretical statements from Emerson (1972), James S. Coleman (1973), and David Willer and Bo Anderson (1981). Their theories directed the attention of exchange analysts to the unique properties of triads and larger networks.

Emerson (1972) extended the dyadic power-dependence theory to networks and devised the standard definition of a network as a system of two or more connected exchange relations. Two relations are connected if exchange in one affects exchange in the other. For example,

the system A-B-C is a three-actor network built by connecting two dyads, A-B and B-C, at B. Power-dependence researchers were also responsible for the innovative use of resource-pool relations rather than exchange relations in experiments. Positions in resource-pool relations do not exchange valued resources. Instead, they bargain for shares of a resource pool but gain nothing if they fail to reach agreement. Although they are not true exchange relations, the payoff matrices for resource-pool negotiations mirror those in exchange situations.

Coleman's theory, *The Mathematics of Collective Action* (1973), was the first to create systematic procedures that locate power in network structures, describe power use and resource flows, and predict payoffs at equilibrium, i.e., the amounts at which exchanges stabilize in the long run. Willer and Anderson began work on elementary theory in the mid-1970s and presented it in *Networks, Exchange, and Coercion* (1981). Elementary theory presented models that make clear the distinctions between social exchange, economic exchange, conflict, and coercive relations. The late 1980s and early 1990s brought new developments. Elementary theory spawned network exchange theory (Markovsky et al. 1988; Willer 2000), Friedkin (1992) developed the expected value model, and Bienenstock and Bonacich (1992) applied game theory to network structures.

Exchange network theories differ in their assumptions about the processes that link structure to power. They also have different scope limitations, including the numbers and types of network connections to which their analyses apply. Finally, they use different procedures to locate power and to predict power use and payoff structures.

NETWORK CONNECTIONS

The distribution of power in exchange networks varies with the types of connections within them. Power-dependence theory uses two characteristics of network relations – symmetry and valence – to devise a typology of connection types. Consider an A-B-C network. It is connected *unilaterally* if AB exchange affects BC exchange but BC exchange does not affect AB exchange. It is *bilaterally* connected if

AB exchange affects BC exchange *and* BC exchange affects AB exchange. The network is *positively* connected if exchange in one relation increases the likelihood of exchange in the other. Finally, it is *negatively* connected if exchange in one relation reduces or precludes the possibility of exchange in the second. Four connection types are possible: unilateral positive, unilateral negative, bilateral positive, and bilateral negative.

Network exchange theory uses alternative classifications that have the advantage of compatibility with standard logical operators (e.g., *conjunction* and *disjunction*). The classification takes into account N, the number of positions connected to a position i; M, the maximum number of relations from which i can benefit; and Q, the minimum number of relations within which i must exchange before it can gain any benefit. Given two or more relations connected at i, the five connection types are defined as follows:

inclusive connection : $Ni = Mi = Qi > 1$

exclusive connection : $Ni > Mi \geq Qi = 1$

null connection : $Ni = Mi > Qi = 1$

inclusive-exclusive connection : $Ni > Mi \geq Qi > 1$

exclusive-null connection : $Ni = Mi > Qi > 1$

For example, the A-B-C network is inclusively connected at B if B can benefit from exchanges with A *and* C, and B must exchange with both before gaining any benefit ($N=2=M=2=Q=2>1$). The network is exclusively connected if B can benefit from exchange with either A *or* C (but not both), and *must* exchange with one in order to gain any benefit ($2>1\geq1$), and similarly for the remaining connection types. Dyads are a special connection type for which $N_i=M_i=Q_i=1$; they are *singularly* connected.

PROCEDURES FOR LOCATING POWER

Power, as structural potential, affects the benefits that positions gain in exchange. Early network research on ideas drawn from other theoretical perspectives (e.g., field theory)

identified a positive relationship between a position's centrality and its capacity to influence other positions. Bavelas's (1950) studies of communication networks are classic examples. Bavelas's work was followed by important advances in the mathematical theory of graphs, theories of structural and cognitive balance, and in other field-theoretic conceptions like French's (1956) theory of power. Students of power and influence used that research to infer that positional centrality is an important determinant of power and influence.

Power-dependence researchers explored the possibility that centrality had important effects on power distributions. Their experiments showed that centrality is not a reliable indicator of power in exchange networks (Cook & Emerson 1978). Moreover, the failure of network centrality as a criterion for locating power led theorists to develop alternative methods for locating power in exchange networks.

Coleman introduced a theory-based procedure that can be applied to any number of actors who hold varying quantities of any number of valued resources. The procedure uses two matrices to characterize network structures. The first is an N (number of positions) × R (number of resources) interest matrix (X) that describes the proportion of each position's interest in every resource. The second is a R × N control matrix (C) that describes the proportion of each resource controlled by every position. Matrix operations are used to estimate a final control matrix (C*). Coleman's theory predicts that equilibrium is reached when the resources of a position, j, committed to control an event, $i(r_j x_{ji})$, are equal to the value of full control of the event times the proportion of the event j controls at equilibrium ($v_i c^*_{ij}$). That is, equilibrium is achieved when $v_i c^*_{ij} = r_j x_{ji}$ is true for all positions in the network. A very limited number of experiments and simulations have tested Coleman's ideas but the experimental networks include several types of network connections.

Power-dependence theorists initially devised procedures that used the graph-theoretic concept of *vulnerability* to measure a position's dependence. One measure, reduction in maximum flow (RMF), indexes the degree to which a network is disrupted by removal of a position. A revised procedure, CRMF, is based on removal of a line, but both measures proved inadequate for analyzing a variety of networks. Current power-dependence procedures measure B's dependence on A as the amount of resources that B can gain from exchanges with A minus the resources B can gain from alternative exchange partners (e.g., C in the A-B-C network). The theory claims that B will exchange with A (or C) over successive exchanges until they reach the point at which the partners are equally dependent on one another. With few exceptions, power-dependence procedures have been applied to negatively connected networks.

The first elementary theory experiments had participants exchange resources, but researchers using network exchange theory typically use the resource-pool paradigm. Network exchange researchers initially used a graph-theoretic power index (GPI) – a weighted function of the non-intersecting lines in a network's graph – to predict the distribution of power. Today, network exchange theorists use elementary theory's law of resistance to predict the distribution of power. The law of resistance holds that exchanges occur at the point at which partners are equally resistant to a proposed exchange. Analysts use an "iterative seek" procedure in which actors are presumed to negotiate exchanges in decreasing order of benefits. They negotiate exchanges in high-benefit relations before turning to relations from which they can expect to gain lower maximum benefits. The law of resistance is highly general and the method has been applied to networks with several connection types, although most studies have examined exclusively connected networks.

Researchers using the expected value model use a five-step process to calculate payoffs in exchange networks. First, identify the network structure. Next, identify *every* possible exchange. At the third stage, use empirical findings or theory to identify or calculate the probable frequency of occurrence for each exchange. The fourth stage requires calculating the amount of resources that can be acquired by each position in the network. Finally, calculate the expected values of payoffs and use them to infer power distributions. Researchers in this tradition were the first to apply their procedures to a variety of networks in which relations have unequally valued resource pools (Bonacich & Friedkin 1998).

Bienenstock and Bonacich's (1992) application of game theory to exchange networks is based on the core solution for cooperative games. The approach is organized around the characteristic function, *v*. For every subset of positions in a network, *v*(S) is the total payoff members can gain no matter what other positions do. The core solution is the set of all payoffs that satisfies individual, coalition, and group rationality. Individual rationality exists when no position in a coalition will accept a payoff less than it could gain on its own. Coalition rationality exists if no set of actors will accept total benefits that are less than they could earn in a coalition and that is true of every coalition in the network. Finally, group rationality exists when a grand coalition of all members maximizes its total reward. Game theory implies that networks for which there is a core will have stable outcomes. Those without a core will have unstable outcomes because some positions can improve their payoffs by joining a coalition. The core solution has been applied to exclusively connected networks, but the method can be applied to a range of situations including many that fall outside the scope of exchange network theories.

FUTURE RESEARCH

Exchange network theories have substantially advanced sociological understanding of network power processes, but the limited range of settings to which they have been applied tempers their success. Exchange networks are dynamic. They change as ties are broken, as new and different ties with different network connections are added, and as resources gain or lose value in cycles of plenitude and scarcity. Studies of dynamic systems will probably require settings in which actors with many valued resources make real exchanges. Revised theories will take into account and integrate understandings of other processes – like status and legitimacy – that affect network behavior. These are daunting challenges and much difficult work lies ahead.

SEE ALSO: Blau, Peter; Coleman, James; Collective Action; Elementary Theory; Emerson, Richard M.; Game Theory; Homans, George;

Power-Dependence Theory; Power, Theories of; Social Exchange Theory; Social Network Theory

REFERENCES AND SUGGESTED READINGS

Bavelas, A. (1950) Communications Patterns in Task-Oriented Groups. *Journal of the Acoustical Society of America* 22: 725–30.

Bienenstock, E. J. & Bonacich, P. (1992) The Core as a Solution to Exclusionary Networks. *Social Networks* 14: 231–43.

Bonacich, P. & Friedkin, N. (1998) Unequally Valued Exchange Relations. *Social Psychology Quarterly* 61: 160–71.

Cook, K. S. & Emerson, R. M. (1978) Power, Equity, and Commitment in Exchange Networks. *American Sociological Review* 43: 721–39.

Emerson, R. M. (1972) Exchange Theory, Part II: Exchange Relations and Network Structures. In: Berger, J., Zelditch, M., Jr., & Anderson, B. (Eds.), *Sociological Theories in Progress*, Vol. 2. Houghton Mifflin, Boston, pp. 58–87.

French, J. R. P., Jr. (1956) A Formal Theory of Social Power. *Psychological Review* 63: 181–94.

Friedkin, N. (1992) An Expected Value Model of Social Power: Predictions for Selected Exchange Networks. *Social Networks* 14: 213–29.

Markovsky, B., Willer, D., & Patton, T. (1988) Power Relations in Exchange Networks. *American Sociological Review* 53: 220–36.

Willer, D. (2000) *Network Exchange Theory*. Praeger, Westport, CT.

exchange-value

Rob Beamish

Exchange-value – the most misunderstood concept in Marx's analysis of the commodity – is best grasped by moving from the immediate to the complex. Useful things found in nature or procured without exchange and used for private consumption (directly or in the creation of something else for private use) have a qualitatively distinct, concrete, natural form. Their utility is what matters; they have no relevant social substance even if they are produced through labor. They are not exchanged; they do not contain value.

Useful things intended for exchange are procured or produced by social labor. Exchangeable commodities have a visible, concrete, useful form and an invisible social substance of quantitatively comparable units of congealed, socially necessary, simple, abstract, labor time. This invisible substance is value; the commodities' "plain, homely, natural form" is the physical repository of their value (Marx 1976: 138).

To be exchanged, the abstract value congealed within each commodity must achieve a particular form of expression. That form only arises in the social relations of exchange; it is, therefore, a social form. As the formal expression of value arising through exchange, Marx termed it the commodity's exchange-value.

It is often thought that value and exchange-value are interchangeable concepts; they are not. Commodities' value – the socially necessary, simple, abstract labor time congealed within them – only exists abstractly. One cannot directly see, touch, taste, smell, or hear value; immediately its reality is invisible. Value becomes manifest only in exchange – exchange-value is the manifest expression of value.

Commodities' values first became manifest in simple exchange. The congealed value of 20 yards of linen first became manifest in the "the equivalent form of value" – an equivalent form that could be seen, touched, etc. (one coat, for example). The coat became the visibly manifest, equivalent form of value for the linen – it is the manifest exchange-value of the linen. The equivalent form is a particular instance of exchange-value; it arose in the social process of exchange and because it became manifest in exchange, it was, and remains, a social form. Use-value is the concrete form of the commodity, exchange-value its visible, social form, while value remains abstract and not directly visible.

As exchange expanded, the particular social form of value changed (as did the name of each particular form). The "expanded, relative form of value" represented exchange where a number of commodities manifested each other's value (e.g., 1 coat = 10 lb. of tea = 1 ton of iron = 20 yards of linen). The "general form of value" arose as one commodity began habitually to represent the abstract value of others (e.g., the value of 1 coat, 10 lb. of tea, 1 ton of iron was expressed in the form of 20 yards of linen). As one commodity habitually became the general form – most often a precious metal – the "money form of value" arose. A sum of money became the mature, social expression of exchange-value.

SEE ALSO: Labor/Labor Power; Marx, Karl; Money; Use-Value; Value

REFERENCES AND SUGGESTED READINGS

Marx, K. (1976) *Capital*, Vol. 1. Trans. B. Fowkes. Penguin, London.

exercise and fitness

Joseph G. Grzywacz

Exercise, physical activity, and fitness are distinct but interrelated concepts (Caspersen et al. 1985). Physical activity is any bodily movement produced by skeletal muscle, while exercise is planned and repeated physical activity that is structured into individuals' lives with the purpose of maintaining or improving some attribute of either health or skill (i.e., fitness). Exercise, therefore, is a subset of physical activity that is characterized by being patterned and purposeful, and fitness is a consequence of exercise. Exercise and fitness are of major interest because they are implicated in premature death, a wide variety of disease states, and quality of life (US Department of Health and Human Services [USDHHS] 1996).

Sociological inquiry around exercise and fitness expanded and changed during the past 25 years. In the early to mid-1980s a small number of studies were catalogued in sociological abstracts delineating social status predictors of exercise and between-group differences in beliefs about exercise. In the late 1980s to early 1990s research activity doubled. During this time researchers documented how different social processes such as victimization and job stress were associated with exercise among adults, and papers began describing exercise as a form of consumption. Research doubled again in the mid- to late 1990s, with research

continuing to illustrate differences in exercise patterns *between* different groups (e.g., class), as well as examinations of exercise *within* specific contexts (e.g., rural) and social groups (e.g., age and gender groups). Body image research and papers examining the role of exercise in the social expression of self also established a foothold during this period. Research doubled again from the late 1990s to the present. New strands of research in this period included comprehensive models examining determinants of exercise from multiple levels, the role of exercise (and other health behaviors) in health trends over time and health disparities between groups, and essays examining the political agenda underlying the promotion of exercise.

This broad summary of the literature illustrates three major points about sociological research around exercise and fitness. First, exercise has only recently become an explicit area of sociological research. Second, there has been exponential growth in exercise research beginning in the mid-1990s. This growth coincided with ongoing initiatives to promote exercise as well as ongoing evaluations documenting limited success toward those goals (McGinnis & Lee 1995). Finally, the majority of research is characterized predominantly as "sociology for exercise" or the application of sociological concepts and tools for understanding variation in exercise so as to better refine or develop techniques for promoting exercise and fitness (Thorogood 1992).

There are several issues and areas for additional sociological analysis that would contribute to advancing middle-range theorizing about exercise and fitness. Two lines of future inquiry that are particularly important are outlined below. The first advocates more sociological analyses that expose the inherent values and assumptions underlying the meaning of exercise and the widespread promotion of exercise (i.e., sociology of exercise). The second line of advocated inquiry involves continued application of sociological concepts and tools to enhance understanding of exercise (i.e., sociology for exercise).

Critical analysis of the interests and values underlying exercise is needed. Consider two individuals: the first person walks 3 miles each day for diabetes control whereas the second person walks 3 miles each day to work.

By definition (Caspersen et al. 1985), the first person is "exercising" while the second person is not; yet, the physiological (and presumably the health-related) consequences of each person's structured and repeated activity are similar. (Recent public health recommendations have shifted from physical activity with the explicit goal of health maintenance or improvement to simply regular sustained physical activity [USDHHS 1996]; nonetheless, discourse around exercise continues to prioritize leisure-time physical activities that benefit cardiorespiratory health.) This example raises important questions, such as: "Whose interests are being served by widespread attempts to promote exercise?"; "Which values are being prioritized through advocacy and surveillance of exercise?"; and "What are the social consequences of defining exercise in terms of health intentions?" (Thorogood 1992).

A related area for critical analysis is an examination of the alternative approaches to health promotion that remain underdeveloped while social attention is directed toward exercise. Without question, exercise contributes to a variety of salutary outcomes; however, these same outcomes are frequently equally influenced by other factors. For example, results from the Alameda County study indicated that the nine-year mortality risk for both women and men attributed to health behaviors (including physical activity) was comparable in magnitude to the mortality risk attributed to social integration (Berkman & Breslow 1983). Why is there widespread effort to increase the number of people who exercise, but no widespread effort to increase the number of people who volunteer in their communities or participate in civic organizations? Likewise, a focus on exercise and what are typically considered individual lifestyle "choices" diverts discourse from other strong determinants of poor health such as social inequalities and poverty. To what extent does public attention toward exercise distract from other viable targets for improving population health? Answers to questions such as these will expose the values and interests underlying a focus on promotion of exercise, and they would offer important insight for building comprehensive theories of exercise.

A second line of future inquiry involves more dynamic and multifaceted applications of sociological concepts and tools for understanding exercise. Additional analyses in three areas appear particularly fruitful for theory building. First, additional analyses addressing the structure versus agency debate is essential for explaining trends in exercise over time, and for guiding attempts to increase rates of exercise. Kerry McGannon and Michael Mauws (2002) exemplify how sociological tools can be combined to explain how social and temporal contexts constrain exercise while they are simultaneously being created and recreated through individual activity and social discourse. Next, more research is needed that links exercise to social processes at multiple levels in the social ecology. Scholars have speculated exercise and other health-promoting behaviors have been undermined by macrostructural changes such as modernization and deindustrialization (e.g., Kumanyika et al. 2002). However, very little empirical support exists corroborating these claims, nor is there documentation of the mechanisms through which these changes might occur. Finally, more research examining the complex influence of multiple social structures and processes on exercise is needed. Catherine Ross's (2000) analysis of neighborhood crime, neighborhood poverty, individual poverty, and fear of victimization illustrates the relevance of multifaceted models of exercise, and it exemplifies the convergence of sociological methods of sampling, measurement, and analysis that allows for this type of research.

Sociological analyses around exercise and fitness have accelerated over the past 10 years; yet, sociology has much more to offer for building theory that adequately explains exercise. Two lines of future inquiry for advancing exercise theory have been advocated. The first involves critical analysis of exercise. The goal of this sociology of exercise is to more clearly expose the interests, values, and assumptions underlying exercise and the widespread promotion of exercise in the population. The second line of advocated research involves the continued study of exercise using sociological concepts and tools. The goal of this sociology for exercise is to move toward a more dynamic and multifaceted understanding of exercise. Results from each line of inquiry alone are insufficient, but together they provide the building material for useful theories of exercise.

SEE ALSO: Health Behavior; Health Lifestyles; Health Risk Behavior; Health and Sport

REFERENCES AND SUGGESTED READINGS

Berkman, L. F. & Breslow, L. (1983) *Health and Ways of Living: The Alameda County Study*. Oxford University Press, New York.

Caspersen, C. J., Powell, K. E., & Christenson, G. M. (1985) Physical Activity, Exercise, and Physical Fitness: Definitions and Distinctions for Health-Related Research. *Public Health Reports* 100: 126–31.

Kumanyika, S., Jeffery, R. W., Morabia, A., Ritenbaugh, C., & Antipatis, V. J. (2002) Obesity Prevention: The Case for Action. *International Journal of Obesity and Related Metabolic Disorders* 26: 425–36.

McGannon, K. R. & Mauws, M. K. (2002) Exploring the Exercise Adherence Problem: An Integration of Ethnomethodological and Poststructuralist Perspectives. *Sociology of Sport Journal* 19: 67–89.

McGinnis, J. M. & Lee, P. R. (1995) Healthy People 2000 at Mid Decade. *JAMA* 273: 1123–9.

Ross, C. E. (2000) Walking, Exercising, and Smoking: Does Neighborhood Matter? *Social Science and Medicine* 51: 265–74.

Thorogood, N. (1992) What is the Relevance of Sociology for Health Promotion? In: Bunton, R. & Macdonald, G. (Eds.), *Health Promotion: Disciplines and Diversity*. Routledge, New York, pp. 42–65.

US Department of Health and Human Services (USDHHS) (1996) *Physical Activity and Health: A Report of the Surgeon General*. Department of Health and Human Services, Centers for Disease Control and Prevention, National Center for Chronic Disease Prevention and Health Promotion, Atlanta, GA.

exhibitionism

Brendan Gough

Sexual exhibitionism is often regarded as "deviant," both in commonsense discourse where (male) "flashers" are categorized as "perverts," and in psychiatric discourse where terms denoting pathology (such as antisocial and obsessive compulsive) are applied. In the *Diagnostic and Statistical Manual of Mental Disorders-IV* (DSM-IV, American Psychiatric Association, 1994), exhibitionism is considered a paraphilia in which sexual fantasies and behaviors involve exposing one's genitals to a stranger. Diagnosis of exhibitionism is dependent on sexual fantasies and/or sexual behavior eliciting clinically significant distress or impairment in social, occupational, or other important areas of functioning.

The vast majority of literature on sexual exhibitionism can be located in a psychomedical context and is based on the assessment and treatment of men who have been incarcerated for criminal and/or disturbing behaviors. Despite this body of work, there is little consensus as to the defining characteristics of this population. While some researchers portray this group as shy, inhibited, and non-assertive, others point to low self-esteem, difficulty expressing anger, and poor self-control. In addition, some research reports an association between men who exhibit and later violent sex offenses, such as rape and pedophilia.

The virtual omission of women from the literature on sexual exhibitionism is significant since the practice of exhibitionism by women is now more prevalent than ever. In early work on women exhibitionists, gender differences were highlighted. The implicit assumption is that women's exhibitionism is somehow less real or less serious compared to that of men. For example, it has been claimed that a woman could not become erotically aroused by exposing her genitalia – unlike a man. It was thought that women are driven to exhibit themselves to gain attention and to prevent feelings of worthlessness. This emphatic disavowal of sexual desire for women who exhibit can be linked to wider cultural discourses which constrain the expression of an independent, assertive female sexuality – what has been termed the "missing discourse of desire." Indeed, feminists have long criticized the role of medicine and psychology in reinforcing traditional gender relations through pathologizing "gender-inappropriate" behavior. In particular, the unitary conceptualization of paraphilia within psychiatry does not account for variations in practice, context, and reception of sexual exhibitionism.

However, more recent work with non-clinical samples of women exhibitionists and

strippers points to the liberating and transgres-
sive potential of exposing one's body to others,
including Internet exhibitionism, part of a burgeoning industry in interactive sex entertainment. For example, interviews with women
exhibitionists highlight themes of personal fulfillment and control, peer group support, and a
sense of responsibility concerning when and
where to exhibit. Sociological and feminist
debate, however, considers the social construction of women's exhibitionism in social contexts where patriarchal ideals and practices
prevail. For example, while sexual exhibitionism might be regarded as emancipatory on an
individual level, critical analysis may implicate
this practice within the conventional male gaze
on female "objects." It is clear that further
theoretical and empirical work is needed to
interrogate the place and meaning of women's
exhibitionism in different contexts. In addition,
research is required on male exhibitionists
which is not constrained by psychiatric constructions of dangerous and deranged "flashers" so
that the complexity and variability of this phenomenon are examined. Future work should thus
explore exhibitionism with diverse samples differentiated by gender, age, social class, sexual
orientation, and ethnicity.

SEE ALSO: Sex and Gender; Sexual Deviance;
Sexual Practices; Sexualities and Consumption

REFERENCES AND SUGGESTED
READINGS

Hugh-Jones, S., Gough, B., & Littlewood, A. (2005)
  Sexual Exhibitionism Can Be Good For You: A
  Critique of Psycho-Medical Discourse from the
  Perspectives of Women who Exhibit. *Sexualities*
  8(3): 259–81.
Kibby, M. & Costello, B. (2001) Between the Image
  and the Act: Interactive Sex Entertainment on the
  Internet. *Sexualities* 4(3): 353–69.
Murphy, W. D. (1997) Exhibitionism: Psychopathol-
  ogy and Theory. In: Laws, R. D. (Ed.), *Sexual
  Deviance: Theory, Assessment, and Treatment.*
  Guilford Press, New York.
Oerton, S. & Phoenix, J. (2001) Sex/Bodywork: Dis-
  courses and Practices. *Sexualities* 4(4): 387–412.
Stewart, F. J. (1999) Feminities in Flux? Young
  Women, Heterosexuality, and (Safe) Sex. *Sexuali-
  ties* 2(3): 275–90.

existential sociology

Joseph A. Kotarba

Existential sociology emerged in the late 1970s
as the most recent version of everyday life
sociology. Writers in this perspective have
attempted to integrate symbolic interactionism's powerful concepts of the self and the
situation, phenomenological sociology's emphasis on the social construction of reality, and
ethnomethodology's telling critique of conventional sociological theory and methods, with an
innovative argument for the centrality of embodiment and feelings to human agency. Thus,
*existential sociology can be defined descriptively as
the study of human experience-in-the-world (or
existence) in all its forms.* A key feature of
experience-in-the-(contemporary) world is
change. Existential sociologists expect, if not
assume, change to be a constant feature of
people's lives, their sense of self, their experience of the social world, the other people that
populate the social world, and the culture that
provides meaning for life. Everyday life is more
than merely situational and problematic, a
point on which all the varieties of everyday life
sociology generally agree. Everyday life is *dramatic* – in an aesthetic sense – and experienced
as such. In contrast to Erving Goffman's dra-
maturgical model of social life, the drama that
existential sociologists see in everyday life does
not follow anyone else's script. The actor is
simultaneously writer, producer, and actor on
a stage not necessarily of his or her choosing,
but one that cannot simply be exited without
confrontation with the producer/director (e.g.,
agents of social control).

At a more general and intellectual level, existential sociology can be seen as part of the
broad intellectual trend that can be traced back
to the Copernican revolution that supplanted
the Aristotelian belief in an inalterable and immutable universe. Since then, modern thought
has progressed from the search for absolute
and eternal ideas to a reconceptualization of
reality as change, flux, complexity, and uncertainty. Robert Baumer (1977: 20) has referred
to this historical trend as the movement from
"being to becoming," that is, to "a mode of
thinking that contemplates everything – nature,

man, society, history, God himself – *sub specie temporis*, as not merely changing but as forever evolving into something new and different." The notion of *becoming* is central to both existential philosophy and existential sociology.

Existential sociology reflects the renaissance occurring in existential thinking with, for example, renewed interest in the work of Friedrich Nietzsche, which served as a precursor to existentialism through its illumination of the dark and non-rational side of humanity. Historical events also occasion a reconsideration of existentialist thought. The revitalization of intellectual life in the recently democratized central and eastern European societies has freed writers there to explore pro-individualistic and anti-collectivist paradigms such as existentialism. For example, Leszek Dziegel's *Paradise in a Concrete Cage* (1988) is a first-person account, written by this well-known Polish ethnographer, of the strategies developed by intellectuals in post-World War II Poland to maintain a semblance of individuality and intellectual legitimacy within that gray and depressing Stalinist era.

EXISTENTIAL (SOCIAL) THOUGHT

Existentialism gained its greatest popularity and acceptance in the years after World War II, at first in Europe, and then several years later in America. The writings of French philosopher and writer Jean-Paul Sartre, as well as the novels and essays of Albert Camus, are among the most important reasons for existentialism's initial popularity and acceptance (Craib 1976). The formal literature of the existentialist tradition is known by its emphasis on these central themes: the nature of the individual; the central role of the passions and emotions in human life; the nature and responsibilities of human freedom; and the non-rational aspects of life. Diverse existentialisms have arisen to address these questions, and all express a certain attitude of rebellion. It is a rebellion against the received and inherited "wisdom" of one's culture, against what most people think, against what most intellectuals consider true, against the herd mentality and its popular culture, against conformity. From

this, it is not surprising that existentialists have aligned themselves with the full range of human values and opinions, including fundamentalist Christianity, anti-Christianity, atheism, humanism, communism, anti-communism, socialism, anti-socialism, left-wing politics, right-wing politics, anti-politics, pro-democracy, anti-democracy, and so on. Even on some of the fundamental intellectual or philosophical issues, existential thought runs the full gamut: Sartre says that individuals have absolute freedom, whereas for Nietzsche, freedom is a philosophical myth.

Existentialist ideas began influencing the social sciences more than four decades ago. In 1962, Edward Tiryakian published *Sociologism and Existentialism*, an influential work of sociological theory, which sought to resolve two very different ways of thinking about human social life and existence. The first is "sociologism," a term commonly associated with the seminal sociological scholarship of Émile Durkheim. The idea behind sociologism is very simple to grasp: individuals don't matter very much. Social reality is a reality *sui generis*, or in and of itself, to use Durkheim's phrase. The larger social structures of society are seen as superseding and transcending the lives and meanings of individuals, and are not dependent on individuals in any meaningful way. The second perspective is that of "existentialism," and this view tends to place a much greater emphasis on individuals, their choices, their responsibilities, their passions, their decisions, their cowardice, their virtues, and so on. Tiryakian proposed to bring these two seemingly incompatible perspectives together in a manner that would retain the integrity of each. In 1967, Peter Berger and Thomas Luckmann published *The Social Construction of Reality*, which, like Tiryakian's work, sought to bring together two prevalent social science views about life. Berger and Luckmann used the terms *man in society* and *society in man* to draw a similar analytical contrast (see also Manning 1973).

In 1977, Jack Douglas and John Johnson edited a collection of essays titled *Existential Sociology*, in which the authors engaged structuralists and other cultural determinists, stressing the relative freedom of individuals, and the partial independence of individuals from their social and cultural contexts. They emphasized that social and cultural realities are not determined, but rather are socially constructed, meaning that the agency, choice, will, intention, and interpretation of actual individuals were decisive for the determination of meaning. That early work additionally stressed the relative independence and dominance of feelings and emotions over thoughts and cognition, and in addition their relative independence and dominance over values.

FEELINGS AND EMOTIONS

Emotions and emotionality underlie all human experience and social life, shaping all subjectivity, intersubjectivity, everyday interaction, social exchange, social bonds, and social divisions. Emotions are not only inevitable, and not only forces destructive to the social order. Emotions are also essential for forming and perpetuating human societies.

As Candace Clark (2002) notes, since the scientific community made the conceptual and linguistic shift from the *passions* to *emotions* 300 years ago, most of the disciplines in the social and natural sciences – including sociology – proceeded to ignore emotions and emotionality. In short, for most of western history, common wisdom has presumed that emotion and reason are separate and contradictory, and the bias has been against emotions and in favor of cognition. In the midst of this overrationalized view of life, Jack Douglas strongly reminded other sociologists to take seriously the notion of *brute being*, the core of feeling and perception that is our innermost selves, our beings. He argued that we must recognize the crucial role that passions play in social life.

The study of feelings and emotions in existential sociology stresses the importance of seeing how people experience affect in concrete situations when they are attempting to define and master immediate problems and issues. Put differently, existential sociology argued early for the ethnographic study of feelings and emotions. Every culture and subculture includes its own emotion labels, definitions, feeling rules, roles, values, "knowledge," and "social logics" pertaining to emotions and emotionality. Together, these make up what Clark refers to as *emotional culture*. The taken-for-granted

"knowledge" and "social logics" concerning when emotions occur, how emotions affect the individual, and what happens when emotions are expressed or displayed to others are also extremely variable. Emotional culture in western societies includes such capitalistic phenomena as the greeting card industry, which instructs us in the proper feeling rules toward mothers, fathers, friends, birthday boys and girls, the bereaved, benefactors, the sick, recovering addicts, valentines, and marriage partners through which authentic sentiments are reduced to small pieces of paper – with accompanying envelopes to facilitate delivery.

THE EXISTENTIAL SELF

In 1984, Joseph Kotarba and Andrea Fontana edited a collection of essays titled *The Existential Self in Society*. The book was an effort not only to refine the existential sociology perspective, but also to respond to a movement within sociology toward renewed interest in humanistic and interpretive concepts of the self as opposed to positivistic and measurable concepts. The concept of the existential self is concerned with the experience of individuality – through the perspective of the subject – as it unfolds, adapts, and copes in concrete, everyday life situations. Since existential sociology is designed to monitor closely the tone of and trends in contemporary life, attention is given to the many people in all walks of life who are dissatisfied with both their own sense of who they are and society's demands of who they should be. Furthermore, new social forms, whether they are entirely innovative or simply reconstructions of existing social forms, are reflections of new and innovative ways in which members of our society are coming to think and feel about themselves. The conceptual relationship between innovative social forms and changes in the self is complex. But it is clear that many members of our society are actively seeking new ways of fulfilling and expressing themselves.

The following working definition of the existential self is intended to display the relative fluidity of the modern self and to account for the internal as well as external manifestations of the process of making sense of one's being.

The existential self refers to an individual's unique experience of being within the context of contemporary social conditions, an experience most notably marked by an incessant sense of becoming and an active participation in social change. The following is a brief discussion of the major features of the existential self.

The existential self is embodied. Being-within-the-world means that feelings and primordial perception precede rationality and symbol use and, in fact, activate them. Joseph Kotarba's (1983) research on chronic pain clearly illustrates the limitations on the rational/scientific/medical strategies for making sense of and mastering bodily afflictions. Most people in western societies, regardless of social class, trust modern medicine to alleviate pain. Yet, when pain fails to go away or respond to modern medicine, the person is likely to abandon unquestioned faith in modern medicine in favor of whatever alternative healing modalities promise help (e.g., chiropractic, faith healing, holistic health care). The primary definition of being sick comes from the person's body. Even the social definition, "it's all in your head" (or more professionally, "psychosomatic disease") that refers *directly* to the self, is disregarded. The wellness movement is another example of the ways people in late capitalistic American society attempt to perfect the self by perfecting the body in terms not only of health but also of appearance (Kotarba & Bentley 1988).

The existential self is becoming. Jean-Paul Sartre, in his philosophical and literary writings, argued dramatically that we are condemned to be free, condemned to choose continually who we are, because existence in itself is empty and meaningless. The phenomenologist Maurice Merleau-Ponty takes a more moderate view, and one more conducive to the sociological project, by insisting that our becoming must be grounded in the real, social world if we have any intention of being effective in coping with the given world. The individual is encouraged by the brute reality of life to acquire some distinctive *style* of self-actualization. Freedom, therefore, is viable only to the degree that it allows us to *control* the goals of our endeavors and to utilize them for our own personal growth. Put differently, existentialism presents an image of the self-to-society relationship that is quite apropos to today's world: the image of the self *confronting* society. We constantly attempt to shape and manipulate society – that is, society as we experience it – in order to have it as a meaning resource for fulfilling our most basic needs and desires. Existential sociology examines the various social activities in which people engage to preclude or escape meaninglessness including, for example, religion, spirituality, recreational drugs, music, dance, art, sex, athletics, self-actualization, and intellectual endeavors.

The existential self evolves continuously throughout the life course. Joseph Kotarba (2003) has described the way rock 'n' roll music informs the becoming of self among middle-aged people in our society. Rock 'n' roll can affect adults' sense of self in many ways: as continuing rock 'n' roll fans, as parents of rock 'n' roll fans, as adults who construct lifestyles and work styles incorporating rock 'n' roll, as citizens contending with the political and ethical issues surrounding rock 'n' roll, and simply as people who, over the course of their lives, have come to use rock 'n' roll music and culture as a source of meaning for their joys and their sorrows.

The existential self occasions social change. The sociological literature on social change commonly places the self in the position of dependent variable. From the existential perspective, the self is seen as an active agent in the process of social change. The intention is not to swing the pendulum of causality in the opposite direction, by asserting the preeminence of the Meadean "I" over the "me," but only to view the process of social change *reflexively*. By focusing on the self, we can arrive at the following tentative model of social change. The individual perceives an uncertainty or change occurring in the segments of the social world that impinge on his or her existence. This uncertainty, whether it is "real" or imagined, can occur at the level of technology, attitudes, values, rules, or any other realm of social life. What is crucial is that the individual views these changes as *critically relevant* to maintaining a coherent and satisfying self. This relevance can take two forms. The individual may decide that uncertainty in social conditions leaves existing modes of self-actualization obsolete. Or the individual may perceive new possibilities for self-actualization emanating from changing social conditions. In either case, the individual will seek new means for self-actualization, usually in the form of new social roles. This search is likely to be a *collective* endeavor, for the individual will either actively cooperate with others who are experiencing similar concerns for self and are therefore instituting new social forms, or he or she will passively share in new social forms created by others. The process is then perpetuated when these new social forms provide still other individuals with a new basis for perceiving uncertain social conditions. The recently evolved role of the ex-nun and the emergence of the primitive house church are examples of the ways people respond to uncertainty occurring in organized religion (Kotarba & Fontana 1984).

THE POSTMODERN TURN IN EXISTENTIAL SOCIOLOGY

In 2002, Joseph Kotarba and John Johnson edited *Postmodern Existential Sociology*, a collection of essays examining similarities between the two perspectives, such as distaste for the master narratives of the Enlightenment and an appreciation for rich and metaphoric writing. Furthermore, the advent of postmodern thinking in sociology over the past 15 years or so provides some useful strategies for the continuing evolution of existential sociology.

An important similarity between postmodernism and existential sociology is the heavy emphasis both place on understanding the mass media. Postmodernism sees the mass media as virtually synonymous with culture in late capitalistic society. In existential sociology, the mass media are becoming one of the most compelling audiences to the self, supplanting religion, the community, and even the family to some extent (Altheide 2002). While it is clear that the mass media significantly shape politics, from an existential perspective politics and power reside in the same everyday life world as personal feelings and perceptions. Existential sociology views macro phenomena like politics and power as practical processes and tasks that are conducted and accomplished by real people in concrete situations. Following the existential notion of agency, politics becomes an organized method for people to manage personal feelings,

perceptions, and objectives. The techno/rave scene in popular music, for example, illustrates the way young people have given up on the politics of their (baby boomer) parents by disregarding the political values of the 1960s (e.g., revolt against tradition, commitment to changing the world) in favor of *existential strategies* (Hitzler & Pfadenhauer 2002) by which youth struggle dramatically for individuality through obstinate aesthetic tendencies, private preferences, or simply conspicuous patterns of consumption.

One of the most fruitful points of compatibility between the existential sociology project and postmodernism is in the area of research methods. Both perspectives agree that there is no inherent hierarchy of methods in terms of power or truthfulness. Research is inherently political/organizational and practical, and it is designed and conducted for practical reasons (e.g., journal editorial policies and contract obligations to funding agencies). Both perspectives also agree that the composition and style of research reports and the dissemination of research findings are personal to the writer. Finally, both perspectives argue that the researcher has an extremely wide range of presentation styles to choose from, many of which can be borrowed from the humanities as well as the social sciences. Innovative methods include video ethnography, such as Kotarba's (2003) portrayal of the impact of popular music on everyday family interaction, and the short story, such as Fontana's (2001) vivid autobiographical description of working as a pit crew member while studying racing at the Bonneville Speed Week.

Finally, existential sociology is critical of certain features of postmodern social thought. In addition to their tendency to rely on armchair theorizing instead of direct observation of the everyday life world, some postmodern sociologists discard one of the most important concepts in everyday life sociology: the subject. The term "subject" refers to the object/actor we study in sociology. As Stanford Lyman (1997) notes, in everyday life sociology, including existential sociology, the subject is a real person of flesh who navigates through life encountering situations and making the best decisions possible, not merely a *narrative* or story created by mass-mediated culture.

SEE ALSO: Emotion: Social Psychological Aspects; Ethnomethodology; Everyday Life; Phenomenology; Self; Symbolic Interaction

REFERENCES AND SUGGESTED READINGS

Altheide, D. (2002) *Creating Fear*. Aldine, New York.

Baumer, R. (1977) *Modern European Thought*. Cambridge University Press, New York.

Clark, C. (2002) Taming the "Brute Being": Sociology Reckons with Emotionality. In: Kotarba, J. A. & Johnson, J. M. (Eds.), *Postmodern Existential Sociology*. Alta Mira, Walnut Creek, CA, pp. 155–82.

Craib, I. (1976) *Existentialism and Sociology: A Study of Jean-Paul Sartre*. Cambridge University Press, New York.

Douglas, J. D. (1971) *American Social Order*. Free Press, New York.

Douglas, J. D., Adler, P. A., Adler, P., Fontana, A., Freeman, C. R., & Kotarba, J. A. (1980) *Introduction to the Sociologies of Everyday Life*. Boston, Allyn & Bacon.

Fontana, A. (2001) Salt Fever: An Ethnographic Narrative in Four Sections. *Studies in Symbolic Interaction* 24: 147–63.

Hitzler, R. & Pfadenhauer, M. (2002) Existential Strategies. In: Kotarba, J. A. & Johnson, J. M. (Eds.), *Postmodern Existential Sociology*. Alta Mira, Walnut Creek, CA, pp. 87–101.

Johnson, J. M. (1975) *Doing Field Research*. Free Press, New York.

Kotarba, J. A. (1979) Existential Sociology. In: McNall, S. G. (Ed.), *Theoretical Perspectives in Sociology*. St. Martin's Press, New York, pp. 348–68.

Kotarba, J. A. (1983) *The Chronic Pain Experience*. Sage, Beverly Hills, CA.

Kotarba, J. A. (2003) *Our Parents' Music*. A video ethnography presented at the session on Visual Sociology at the annual meetings of the American Sociological Association, Atlanta, Georgia, August.

Kotarba, J. A. & Bentley, P. (1988) Workplace Wellness Participation and the Becoming of Self. *Social Science and Medicine* 26: 551–8.

Kotarba, J. A. & Fontana, A. (Eds.) (1984) *The Existential Self in Society*. University of Chicago Press, Chicago.

Kotarba, J. A. & Johnson, J. M. (Eds.) (2002) *Postmodern Existential Sociology*. Alta Mira, Walnut Creek, CA.

Lyman, S. (1997) *Postmodernism and a Sociology of the Absurd*. Arkansas University Press, Fayetteville.

Manning, P. (1973) Existential Sociology. *Sociological Quarterly* 14: 200–25.

expectation states theory

David G. Wagner and Joseph Berger

Expectation states theory is a set of closely related theories concerned with various processes by which social interactants or *actors* draw information from their social and cultural environment and organize that information into expectation states that determine their interaction with others. Together with research testing these theories and other research applying them to problems in everyday interaction (such as interracial interaction in schools), expectation states theory constitutes a *theoretical research program*.

POWER AND PRESTIGE THEORY

The earliest work in the expectation states program concerns the process by which actors come to develop differentiated performance expectations even in groups where there are no significant social or cultural differences among the group members. Extensive research by Bales and his colleagues (see, e.g., Bales et al. 1951) revealed that inequalities in the initiation of activity, in the receipt of activity, and on ratings of best ideas and group guidance regularly emerged in such groups. Moreover, these inequalities were highly stable and, with the possible exception of sociometric rankings, tended to be intercorrelated. Berger (1958) and Berger and Conner (1969) conceptualized these inequalities in their power and prestige theory as components of an *observable power and prestige order* (OPPO) consisting of four intercorrelated behaviors: (1) chances to perform (action-opportunities); (2) problem-solving attempts (performance outputs); (3) communicated evaluations of problem-solving attempts (rewards); and (4) changes of opinion when confronted with disagreement (influence). They argued that actors communicate their evaluations of one another's contributions in the normal course of interaction, eventually leading members to anticipate differences in their future performances, and thus to develop differentiated expectation states for these actors. Once these states emerged, they determined the group's OPPO. While OPPO behaviors are functions of the underlying expectations, they also operate to maintain these expectations. Consequently, the power and prestige order of the group tends to be stable. An important consequence of a generalized version of this theory (Berger & Conner 1974) is that inequalities in any of the OPPO components can determine an actor's position in the OPPO.

STATUS CHARACTERISTICS THEORY

While the power and prestige theory deals with groups in which actors initially are similar in terms of status, status characteristics theory is concerned with groups in which actors initially differ on such status distinctions as gender, race, or occupational positions. Extensive research already existed in the 1950s and 1960s that showed that such status distinctions consistently determine the distribution of power and prestige positions in task groups, whether or not the distinction is related to the group's task. The initial status characteristics theory (Berger et al. 1966, 1972) was formulated to provide a theoretical explanation for this important relation. Subsequently, this theory was elaborated and formalized (Berger et al. 1977).

Berger et al. (1977) explain the powerful effect of such statuses as gender or race on the basis of the activation in the group of cultural beliefs about these status distinctions. A coherent set of such beliefs defines a *diffuse status characteristic* (D). A characteristic (say gender) is a D for members of a given group at a given time if and only if they (1) differentially evaluate two or more states of D (e.g., men are in general more highly valued than women), (2) stereotypically relate these states to evaluated states of other characteristics (e.g., men are more mechanically skilled than women), and (3) stereotypically relate these states to similarly evaluated generalized expectation states (e.g., men are more capable at tasks in general than women).

Beliefs about D become *salient* in a group if D is relevant to the group's task (e.g., the task is believed to favor males or females) or if D is a basis of discrimination in the group (as in a mixed-gender group). If salient and not initially relevant, D will normally become relevant to the group's task by a *burden of proof* process, unless its relevance is challenged or it is dissociated from the task. By virtue of this process, status advantages tend to be generalized from situation to situation. If new actors enter the group, a *sequencing* process takes place. Status information relating to the new actor is processed by the original actors through the salience and burden of proof processes and adjoined to their previously processed information as long as the original actors remain in the situation.

If multiple status characteristics become relevant to the group's task, actors will combine the information in these characteristics in forming performance expectations for themselves and the others. This *combining process* takes into account whether the status information creates expectations for success or failure at the task, and the weight of that information, that is, how relevant it is to the group task. Finally, by the *basic expectation* assumption, once actors have formed expectations for self and others, their power and prestige behaviors are determined by these expectations.

Status characteristics theory is abstract and general and has been used to describe status processes involving a variety of status distinctions including gender, race, ethnic identities, educational attainment, occupational position, sexual orientation, physical attractiveness, and the status structures of work teams. In addition, the theory's arguments and consequences have been supported by extensive empirical studies (e.g., Wagner & Berger 2002).

GROWTH OF THE PROGRAM

Over the years the expectation states program has grown in different ways. Formulations have been constructed that represent theoretical *elaborations* of the core status characteristics theory described above. One such extension is the reward expectations theory that describes how reward expectations are formed in status situations, and how reward allocations generate performance expectations. Other formulations have been constructed that represent *integrations* of different theories in the program. This is the case with the behavior-status theory that

Table 1   Expectation states theory[a]

Theory	Phenomenon of concern
Power and prestige	Emergence and maintenance of differentiated OPPOs in status-undifferentiated groups
Status characteristics and expectation states	Formation of expectation states based on socially established status characteristics; maintenance of OPPOs in status-differentiated groups
Distributive justice	Reward expectations and justice norms arising from the relation of reward expectations to actual reward allocations
Sources of evaluation	Formation of expectations and their effects on behavior based on evaluations of actors with legitimated rights to evaluate others
Evolution of status expectations	Evolution of status expectations as actors move through different task situations with different others
Status cues	Role of verbal and non-verbal cues in attributions of performance capacities and status categories; their dependence on actors' established status positions
Reward expectations	Interrelation of status, task, and reward expectations and the inequalities created by these interrelations
Behavior-status	Integrates research from the power and prestige and the status characteristics branches
Evaluations-expectations	Integrates research from status characteristics and source theory branches
Legitimation	Legitimation and delegitimation of OPPOs
Sentiments and status	Interrelation of affect and sentiment processes with status and expectation state processes
Multiple standards	How multiple standards maintain prevailing status distinctions
Status construction	How institutionalized status characteristics are socially constructed and diffused through society

[a]OPPO stands for "observable power and prestige order."

integrates concepts and principles of the power and prestige theory with those of status characteristics theory. Finally, there are formulations that represent *proliferations*. These theories tackle new substantive problems while building on the concepts and principles already established within the program, as with Foschi's theory of multiple standards. Table 1 presents a summary of the major current branches of the program.

An examination of two of these branches will illustrate how the concerns of the program have expanded and deepened. The first of these branches extends the core status characteristics theory to deal with the legitimation of power and prestige orders. The second focuses on an important new problem within the program concerned with the creation of status characteristics.

STATUS LEGITIMATION THEORY

Ridgeway and Berger (1986, 1988) have constructed an extension of the core status characteristics theory that describes the conditions and processes under which the power and prestige order in a group becomes legitimated. First, they argue that the cultural framework within which the group operates incorporates consensual beliefs about how high- and low-valued status positions are generally allocated to individuals, based on their status characteristics, capacities, and achievements. One such belief, for example, is that men occupy more highly valued status positions than women in contemporary American society. The theory describes the conditions under which such beliefs become salient to the members of a given task-oriented group.

Actors use these consensual beliefs to form expectations regarding who will occupy which status positions in their immediate group. In turn, these expectations determine differences in the generalized deferential behaviors – the respect, honor, and displays of social importance that actors accord to different members of the group. Assume, for example, that the generalized deferential behaviors accorded to a high-status member of the group are validated by the behaviors of others in the group. Then, the greater the number of others validating the original deferential behaviors, the greater the probability that the power and prestige order involving that high-status member becomes a legitimated order. Behavior is *validated* if others engage in similar behavior, or at least engage in no behavior that contradicts the original behavior.

With legitimation, expectations become *normative* and there is a presumption that group members will collectively support them. The high-status actor, for example, has the right to initiate problem-solving behaviors for the group and to expect others to be receptive to such behaviors. At the same time, others have the right to expect more valued contributions from that actor than from the low-status actor. In addition, high-status actors come to have rights to exercise controlling behaviors, such as dominating behaviors, over the actions of others. Berger et al. (1998) extended this theory to explain how a legitimated power and prestige order can become delegitimated. This formalization shows, among other things, how the number of status distinctions in a group, the consistency of these status distinctions, and their relevance to the group's task each affect the likelihood that a power and prestige order becomes legitimated.

The legitimation theory explains why low-status group members meet resistance when they engage in task behaviors that are "above their rank." It also explains the resistance that women and other minorities generally face when they employ directive behaviors while in task leadership positions. The theory argues that, because of their low external status, when such individuals become task leaders they are more likely to be working from a non-legitimate OPPO, and therefore controlling and directive

behaviors are less likely to have collective support in the group.

The legitimation theory, like other theories in this program, is multilevel. Action in a group is conceived of as occurring with a pre-given cultural framework. A particular process begins with the activation of status categories or cultural beliefs from that framework. But for a structure to emerge (say, a power and prestige order) or for it to be transformed (say, from a non-legitimated order to a legitimated order) requires the contingent behaviors of the members of the group, whose expectations and validating behaviors are involved in creating the local realities within which the group operates.

STATUS CONSTRUCTION THEORY

Cecilia Ridgeway (1991, 1997) has theorized about the construction of institutionalized status characteristics. She argues that such characteristics are most likely to emerge out of what she calls *double dissimilar situations*. Imagine a population in which individuals are discriminated in terms of a characteristic, call it N, whose states partition the population so that there are two types of people, N(a) and N(b). Further imagine that there are differences in this population in the resources (rewards) possessed by individuals so that there are individuals who are resource rich and those who are resource poor. These resources or rewards may be either tangible (like honorary titles and corner offices) or intangible (like friendship or social acceptance).

Now consider an interaction situation involving N(a) and N(b) type individuals such that, say, the N(a)s are rich and the N(b)s are poor. Because of the resource difference in the group, Ridgeway argues, a power and prestige structure will emerge where those in higher positions tend to be the resource rich and those in lower positions are resource poor. On the basis of this inequality in behavior, individuals are likely to develop beliefs in the abilities of the N(a) and N(b) individuals that correspond to their different positions in the OPPO. In general, if particular states of N are consistently associated with high and low resources, and if they occur frequently enough, eventually individuals come to attribute differences in individual abilities to their respective states of N. A new status characteristic will thereby emerge. Finally, for such an evolving characteristic to become part of actors' cultural framework, it must be diffused through a social population.

CONCLUSION

Expectation states theory is a cumulative program. Current theories say more than what was said in earlier theories, and current empirical research upon which these theories rest is more extensive than that of an earlier stage. Further, investigation of expectation states processes has spread beyond the United States, now including research in Israel, Germany, Australia, Canada, Holland, and Turkey. At the same time, researchers are tackling new theoretical and applied problems while working with the concepts and principles within the program. (For a more detailed review of much of this work, see Wagner & Berger 2002). Thus, although it clearly has grown (see Table 1), expectation states theory is still a program in progress.

SEE ALSO: Legitimacy; Mathematical Sociology; Micro–Macro Links; Social Influence; Status Construction Theory; Theoretical Research Programs; Theory Construction

REFERENCES AND SUGGESTED READINGS

Bales, R. F., Strodtbeck, F. L., Mills, T. M., & Roseborough, M. E. (1951) Channels of Communication in Small Groups. *American Sociological Review* 16: 461–8.

Berger, J. (1958) Relations Between Performance, Rewards, and Action-Opportunities in Small Groups. PhD Dissertation, Harvard University, Cambridge, MA.

Berger, J. & Conner, T. L. (1969) Performance Expectations and Behavior in Small Groups. *Acta Sociologica* 12: 186–98.

Berger, J. & Conner, T. L. (1974) A Generalization of the Theory of Status Characteristics and Expectation States. In: Berger, J., Conner, T. L., & Fisek, M. H. (Eds.), *Expectation States Theory: A Theoretical Research Program*. Winthrop, Cambridge, MA, pp. 163–205.

Berger, J., Cohen, B. P., & Zelditch, M., Jr. (1966) Status Characteristics and Expectation States. In: Berger, J., Zelditch, M., Jr., & Anderson, B. (Eds.), *Sociological Theories in Progress*, Vol. 1. Houghton Mifflin, Boston, pp. 29–46.

Berger, J., Cohen, B. P., & Zelditch, M., Jr. (1972) Status Characteristics and Expectation States. *American Sociological Review* 37: 241–55.

Berger, J., Fisek, M. H., Norman, R. Z., & Zelditch, M., Jr. (1977) *Status Characteristics and Social Interaction: An Expectation States Approach*. Elsevier, New York.

Berger, J., Ridgeway, C. L., Fisek, M. H., & Norman, R. Z. (1998) The Legitimation and Delegitimation of Power and Prestige Orders. *American Sociological Review* 63: 379–405.

Ridgeway, C. L. (1991) The Social Construction of Status Value: Gender and Other Nominal Characteristics. *Social Forces* 70: 367–86.

Ridgeway, C. L. (1997) Where Do Status-Value Beliefs Come From? New Developments. In: Szmatka, J., Skvoretz, J., & Berger, J. (Eds.), *Status, Networks, and Structure: Theory Development in Group Processes*. Stanford University Press, Stanford, pp. 137–58.

Ridgeway, C. L. & Berger, J. (1986) Expectations, Legitimation, and Dominance Behavior in Task Groups. *American Sociological Review* 51: 603–17.

Ridgeway, C. L. & Berger, J. (1988) The Legitimation of Power and Prestige Orders in Task Groups. In: Webster, M., Jr. & Foschi, M. (Eds.), *Status Generalization: New Theory and Research*. Stanford University Press, Stanford, pp. 207–31.

Wagner, D. G. & Berger, J. (2002) Expectation States Theory: An Evolving Research Program. In: Berger, J. & Zelditch, M., Jr. (Eds.), *New Directions in Contemporary Sociological Theory*. Rowman & Littlefield, Lanham, MD, pp. 41–76.

expectations and aspirations

Stephen L. Morgan

Expectations and aspirations, within sociological research on education and social inequality, are stable prefigurative orientations composed of specific beliefs about one's future trajectory through the educational system and one's ultimate class or status position. As adolescents age, these expectations and aspirations are presumed to condition current behavior and, in the process, become self-fulfilling prophecies.

Expectations are sometimes distinguished from aspirations in theory, with the former stipulated to refer to realistic appraisals rather than idealistic goals. Nonetheless, almost all empirical research has utilized the same straightforward operationalization for both concepts. Educational expectations and aspirations are usually answers that adolescents give to questions such as: "Do you plan to go to college?" and "As things stand now, how far in school do you think you will get?" Occupational expectations and aspirations are responses to questions such as: "What type of job do you plan or expect to have at age 30?" These survey questions elicit future plans which are generally quite optimistic, thereby qualifying as sufficiently idealistic for the analytic and explanatory purposes of those who wish to have a measure of aspirations.

Measurement of expectations such as these began with the work of educational psychologists employed by the Educational Testing Service in the early 1950s. Since then, sociologists have dominated their study. The 1953 article entitled "Educational and Occupational Aspirations of Common Man Boys," written by Joseph A. Kahl, is perhaps the most influential early piece, as it was completed as a research report for the Mobility Project led by Talcott Parsons just as structural functionalism was in its ascendancy. The central question of Kahl's study was: "What influences the aspirations of the boys in the lower middle levels of the status range whose environment gives them a wide choice?" (Kahl 1953: 189). In order to show that "these boys must make a conscious and pointed decision at some stage of their careers," he reported the results of in-depth interviews with 24 boys of middling social origins, only half of whom expected to go to college. His goal was then to "explore the decision-making of such boys," whose beliefs about the future were not predetermined either by expectations grounded in their class origins or by their cognitive abilities. And, out of this effort, he sought a reasonable causal account of how beliefs about

the future are shaped by one's social context and then compel future behavior.

Kahl identified parental pressure as the most crucial determinant. Corresponding roughly to two types of students, he saw two types of parents: those who sought to raise "getting by" children and those who sought to raise "getting ahead" children. Many of the factors that determined whether parents adopted the getting ahead rearing strategy were idiosyncratic, and yet there were some systematic differences, relating primarily to parents' own experiences with the labor market. The extent to which parents saw college as having a genuine payoff for occupational attainment, based on their own experiences in the workplace, was crucial.

Expectations and aspirations then became the central mediating variables in status attainment research, especially following the publication of what became known as the Wisconsin model of status attainment, which was based on early analyses of the Wisconsin Longitudinal Survey (a random sample of all high school seniors in the state of Wisconsin in 1957). The full model was first fully specified in two influential articles published in the *American Sociological Review* (Sewell et al. 1969, 1970) that reported results from both the original 1957 data and the follow-up 1964 data on the educational and early occupational careers of young men. Beyond Kahl's focus on exploring the formation of college plans, these articles aimed to explain the entire process of educational and occupational attainment.

According to the original 1969 Wisconsin model, the joint effects of a high school student's family background and mental ability on his eventual educational and occupational attainments can be completely explained by the expectations that others hold of him. In particular, significant others – parents, teachers, and peers – define expectations that students then internalize as educational and occupational aspirations. Because the underlying theory assumes that students are compelled to follow their own aspirations, the model is powerfully simple and implies that significant others can increase a student's educational and occupational attainment merely by increasing their own expectations of him.

Regarding the specific processes of aspiration formation, the principal social psychological theorist, Archibald Haller, maintained that aspirations are formed in three ways: imitation, self-reflection, and adoption. Once formed, Haller (1982: 5–6) wrote that aspirations are embedded in "approximately consistent and mutually reinforcing cognitions" which then "have an inertia of their own and are expressed in corresponding behavior." Thus, students' educational and occupational aspirations become stable abstract motivational orientations (see Spenner & Featherman 1978), and the measured Wisconsin model variables – college plans and expected future occupation – are merely realistic indicators of these latent status aspirations.

Although the theory underneath the original Wisconsin model was bold, its creators were well aware of its many limitations. Almost immediately upon publication, they began to qualify its basic mechanisms, and in the process they weakened its most parsimonious theoretical claims by allowing for the addition of supplemental direct effects of socioeconomic status on all endogenous variables. The addition of paths not predicted by the original socialization theory presented problems for the powerful claims of the 1969 article. In particular, the claim that significant others could raise students' educational and occupational attainments by simply imposing higher expectations on them began to seem less credible. Instead, the revised models of the 1970s and 1980s suggested that significant others and educational institutions have direct effects on the educational and occupational attainment process. If so, then it had to be conceded that structural constraints (and perceptions of them) could play an important role in models of educational and occupational attainment.

These revisions were, in part, a response to research critical of the Wisconsin model and its supposed origins in structural-functionalist sociology. Critics argued that structural constraints embedded in the opportunity structure of society should be at the center of all models of educational attainment, and hence that concepts such as aspirations and expectations offer little or no explanatory power. Most famously, Pierre Bourdieu dismissed the work of sociologists who assert that associations between aspirations/expectations and attainments are causal. Rather, for Bourdieu, the unequal opportunity structures of society "determine aspirations by determining the extent to which they can be satisfied" (Bourdieu 1973: 83). And, as such, aspirations and expectations have no autonomous explanatory power, as they are nothing other than alternative indicators of attainment.

Critiques such as these helped to bring an end to the brief dominance of status attainment theory in the study of social inequality. The cutting edge of research in the sociology of education then shifted toward studies of institutional and demographic effects on educational achievement and attainment, as researchers generally sought to avoid debates over whether social psychological models unnecessarily blame the victims of a constrained opportunity structure. Even so, variables measuring expectations continued to be deployed as standard covariates in the sociology of education for the analysis of a variety of outcomes (for a review, see Morgan 2005: ch. 2).

In the most recent research, however, new models of educational attainment are now attempting to account for the beliefs that determine educational attainment. Some researchers have begun to focus on changes in post-industrial society and how these are reflected in the processes by which adolescents plan for their futures. Others, seeking to integrate sociological and economic approaches, have attempted to build models of educational achievement and attainment that are sensitive to the exogenous impact of shifts in costs and benefits but that also give substantial scope to independent belief formation processes that can overwhelm narrow expected utility calculations. By and large, this new work has the potential to help determine how structural dynamics should be incorporated into models of educational attainment, as structure that is imposed from the outside as the rigid constraints maintained by institutions or via individual responses to perceived structural constraints.

SEE ALSO: Bourdieu, Pierre; Educational and Occupational Attainment; Parental Involvement in Education; Parsons, Talcott; Significant Others; Status Attainment; Structural Functional Theory; Teachers

REFERENCES AND SUGGESTED READINGS

Bourdieu, P. (1973) Cultural Reproduction and Social Reproduction. In: Brown, R. K. (Ed.), *Knowledge, Education, and Cultural Change: Papers in the Sociology of Education*. Tavistock, London, pp. 71–112.

Haller, A. O. (1982) Reflections on the Social Psychology of Status Attainment. In: Hauser, R. M., Mechanic, D., Haller, A. O., & Hauser, T. S. (Eds.), *Social Structure and Behavior: Essays in Honor of William Hamilton Sewell*. Academic Press, New York.

Kahl, J. (1953) Educational and Occupational Aspirations of Common Man Boys. *Harvard Educational Review* 23: 186–203.

Morgan, S. L. (2005) *On the Edge of Commitment: Educational Attainment and Race in the United States*. Stanford University Press, Palo Alto.

Sewell, W. H., Haller, A. O., & Portes, A. (1969) The Educational and Early Occupational Attainment Process. *American Sociological Review* 34: 82–92.

Sewell, W. H., Haller, A. O., & Ohlendorf, G. W. (1970) The Educational and Early Occupational Status Attainment Process: Replication and Revision. *American Sociological Review* 35: 1014–24.

Spenner, K. I. & Featherman, D. L. (1978) Achievement Ambitions. *Annual Review of Sociology* 4: 373–420.

experiment

Javier Lezaun

Experiments play a central role in most theories of science as the key mechanism through which theories and hypotheses are corroborated or refuted. Most especially in the work of Karl Popper, the acceptability of a theory – the extent to which it can be conceivably characterized as "scientific" – is determined by its falsifiability, that is, by whether it can be put to the test in an experiment. Experimentation is thus the foremost *trial of strength* for knowledge claims, and the sociology of science has investigated the particular social practices on which this validating function rests.

Despite its centrality to most analytical accounts of the scientific enterprise, experimentation, as a social practice in its own right, has remained largely unexamined by philosophers of science, partly because their emphasis tended to be on theory and theoreticians. Also, it was often assumed – rather than proved – that experiments were fundamentally logical process reducible to a series of analytical steps, and thus capable of determining unambiguously the validity of a knowledge claim if conducted according to formal instructions.

In the 1980s the sociology of science began to take a closer look at how knowledge is put to the test under experimental conditions. This investigation was influenced by the groundbreaking historical work of Kuhn (1962), and received much of its inspiration from innovative reinterpretations of the history of science. A sociologically informed history of science and a historically grounded sociology of science have since walked hand in hand.

One of the most influential treatments of experimentation in the sociology of scientific knowledge (SSK) was offered by Collins (1985). Collins's main target was the idea of replication: that success or failure in repeating of an experiment could provide unambiguous and definitive proof of the validity of a knowledge claim. The notion of replication can appear deceptively straightforward in most empiricist philosophies – a matter of simply repeating an experiment under slightly different conditions to prove or disprove a previous result. Yet Collins showed that the practice of replication cannot be reduced to a set of formal rules. A judgment of sameness or difference is always required, and such a judgment is irreducibly social. If, for instance, Experiment B fails to reproduce the result of Experiment A, the experimenters must still decide whether this is because Experiment A was faulty or wrong, or rather because Experiment B was dissimilar from A in key aspects and thus failed to truly replicate and therefore disprove it. According to Collins, any effort to formulate a set of definitive rules about this decision, the attempt to turn what is a matter of socially embedded judgment into a series of formalized, logical steps, would lead to an "experimenter's regress." The meaning of a particular experiment is thus a matter to be determined by a community of expert practitioners making a socially contingent judgment, a judgment that is dependent on, among other things, the distribution of tacit skills and instruments among experimenters. This notion of a regress, or an incapacity to reduce the social practices and processes of experimentation to a set of formal instructions, was developed as the "testers' regress" by MacKenzie (1989, 1990) in his sociological studies of technological communities and missile accuracy.

A similar concern with the role of material context and technical instruments, skills and tacit knowledge, the social organization of scientific groups, and the enculturation of its practitioners characterizes the work of Galison (1987) on the history of twentieth-century experimental physics. Galison focused on the decision to end an experiment and declare an experimental inquiry completed. His study drew attention to the extent to which experimentation had become, at least in the field of physics, a distinct epistemological tradition and a social practice in its own right, shaped by the particular social and material conditions under which it was conducted (for a continuation of this research program, see Galison 1997).

Another strand of historical research helped shed light on the social uses of experiments and on the role of experimental practices in the production of public demonstrations of truth. The book of Shapin and Schaffer (1985) was groundbreaking in its analysis of the context in which experimentation emerged as a particularly forceful and persuasive form of demonstration in early modern England, and in its parallel treatment of experimentation as an instrument of knowledge production and as a disputed component in the political philosophies of the time. Shapin and Schaffer contrast the opposing philosophies of Boyle and Hobbes, which reflected diametrically different views of the epistemological value of public experiments, as well as of the proper ordering of a political community. Central to Boyle's ultimately victorious emphasis on observable experiments as the key machinery for the production of "matters of fact" was, Shapin and Schaffer argue, a logic of witnessing, by which the public testimony of those watching the proceedings (or, eventually, of those reading the experimental report) was fundamental to the legitimacy of the trial and the trustworthiness of its results. Science and experimentation were an essentially public form of knowledge-making, to be conducted and displayed, literally or

virtually, before the eyes of reliable audiences. The rise of scientific experimentation in England, Shapin and Schaffer argued, went hand in hand with forms of political experimentation that also granted public witnessing a central role in political affairs. In further articles, these authors explored in more detail the role of the particular sites where experiments are conducted (Shapin 1988) and the function of the experimental apparatus in the production of conviction (Schaffer 1989).

The public nature of experiments, the degree to which audiences and their influence are central to the logic of experimentation, has become a central theme in the sociology of science (Gieryn & Figert 1990). It is contestable whether, as Collins (1988) has argued, the sociology of science should still try to draw a distinction between proper experiments, in which the result is up for grabs and an element of surprise cannot be ruled out, and mere "displays of virtuosity" or "demonstrations," in which previous rehearsals reduce to a minimum the possibility of upsets, revelations, or failures, and whose purpose is simply to illustrate a principle to an audience.

Finally, the sociological and historical interest in the experimental production of knowledge in the natural sciences has more recently been extended to experimentation in the social sciences, particularly economics (Guala 2005; Muniesa & Callon 2006) and psychology (Dehue 2001; Brannigan 2004).

SEE ALSO: Experimental Design; Experimental Methods; Falsification; Induction and Observation in Science; Materiality and Scientific Practice; Science; Scientific Knowledge, Sociology of

REFERENCES AND SUGGESTED READINGS

Brannigan, A. (2004) *The Rise and Fall of Social Psychology: The Use and Misuse of the Experimental Method*. Aldine de Gruyter, New York.

Collins, H. (1985) *Changing Order: Replication and Induction in Scientific Practice*. University of Chicago Press, Chicago.

Collins, H. (1988) Public Experiments and Displays of Virtuosity: The Core-Set Revisited. *Social Studies of Science* 18: 725–48.

Dehue, T. (2001) Comparing Random Groups: The History of Experimentation in Psychology. In: Smelser, N. J. & Baltes, P. B. (Eds.), *International Encyclopedia of the Social and Behavioral Sciences*. Elsevier Science, Oxford.

Galison, P. (1987) *How Experiments End*. University of Chicago Press, Chicago.

Galison, P. (1997) *Image and Logic: A Material Culture of Microphysics*. University of Chicago Press, Chicago.

Gieryn, T. & Figert, A. (1990) Ingredients for a Theory of Science in Society: O-Rings, Ice Water, C-Clamp, Richard Feynman and the Press. In: Cozzens, S. & Gieryn, T. (Eds.), *Theories of Science in Society*. Indiana University Press, Bloomington, pp. 67–97.

Guala, F. (2005) *The Methodology of Experimental Economics*. Cambridge University Press, Cambridge.

Kuhn, T. (1962) *The Structure of Scientific Revolutions*. University of Chicago Press, Chicago.

MacKenzie, D. (1989) From Kwajalein to Armageddon? Testing and the Social Construction of Missile Accuracy. In: Gooding, D., Pinch, T., & Schaffer, S. (Eds.), *The Uses of Experiment: Studies in the Natural Sciences*. Cambridge University Press, Cambridge.

MacKenzie, D. (1990) *Inventing Accuracy: A Historical Sociology of Nuclear Missile Guidance*. MIT Press, Cambridge, MA.

Muniesa, F. & Callon, M. (2006) Economic Experiments and the Construction of Markets. In: MacKenzie, D., Muniesa, F., & Siu, L. (Eds.), *Performing Economics*. Princeton University Press, Princeton.

Schaffer, S. (1989) Glass Works: Newton's Prisms and the Uses of Experiment. In: Gooding, D., Pinch, T., & Schaffer, S. (Eds.), *The Uses of Experiment: Studies in the Natural Sciences*. Cambridge University Press, Cambridge.

Shapin, S. (1988) The House of Experimentation in Seventeenth-Century England. *Isis* 79: 373–404.

Shapin, S. & Schaffer, S. (1985) *Leviathan and the Air-Pump: Hobbes, Boyle, and the Experimental Life*. Princeton University Press, Princeton.

experimental design

Roger E. Kirk

Experimentation involves the deliberate manipulation of one or more independent variables followed by the systematic observation of the effects of the manipulation on one or more dependent variables. The emphasis on experimentation in the sixteenth and seventeenth centuries as a way of establishing causal relationships marked the emergence of modern science from its roots in natural philosophy (Hacking 1983). According to the nineteenth-century philosopher John Stuart Mill, a causal relationship exists if (a) the cause preceded the effect, (b) the cause was related to the effect, and (c) we can find no other plausible alternative explanation for the effect. Carefully designed and executed experiments continue to be one of science's most powerful methods for discovering causal relationships. An *experimental design* is a plan for assigning experimental units to treatment levels and the statistical analysis associated with the plan (Kirk 1995: 1). The design of an experiment involves a number of interrelated activities:

1 Formulation of statistical hypotheses that are germane to the scientific hypothesis. A *statistical hypothesis* is a statement about (a) one or more parameters of a population or (b) the functional form of a population. Statistical hypotheses are rarely identical to scientific hypotheses – they are testable formulations of scientific hypotheses.

2 Determination of the treatment levels (independent variable) to be manipulated, the measurement (dependent variable) to be recorded, and the extraneous conditions (nuisance variables) that must be controlled.

3 Specification of the number of experimental units required and the population from which they will be sampled.

4 Specification of the randomization procedure for assigning the experimental units to the treatment levels.

5 Determination of the statistical analysis that will be performed (Kirk 1995: 1–2).

In short, an experimental design identifies the independent, dependent, and nuisance variables and indicates the way in which the randomization and statistical aspects of an experiment are to be carried out.

The seminal ideas for experimental design as it is practiced today can be traced to Ronald A. Fisher, a statistician who worked at a small agricultural research station 25 miles north of

London. The publication of Fisher's *Statistical Methods for Research Workers* in 1925 and *The Design of Experiments* in 1935 gradually led to the acceptance of three key principles of experimental design: randomization, replication, and local control or blocking. Fisher's idea that experimental units should be randomly assigned to treatment levels initially met with disdain. Prior to Fisher, most researchers used systematic schemes, not subject to the laws of chance, to assign experimental units. According to Fisher, random assignment has three important benefits. First, it helps to distribute the idiosyncratic characteristics of experimental units over the treatment levels so that they do not selectively bias the outcome of the experiment. Second, random assignment permits the researcher to compute an unbiased estimate of *error effects* – those effects not attributable to the manipulation of the independent variable. Third, random assignment helps to ensure that the error effects are statistically independent. Through random assignment, a researcher creates two or more groups of experimental units that at the time of assignment are probabilistically similar on the average.

Sometimes, for practical or ethical reasons, random assignment cannot be used. It is necessary, for example, to use preexisting or naturally occurring experimental units when the research question involves the effects of a particular illness. In such cases, a *quasi-experiment* that is similar to an experiment except for random assignment can be used. Unfortunately, the interpretation of the results of quasi-experiments is always ambiguous. In the absence of random assignment, it is difficult to rule out all variables other than the independent variable as explanations for an observed result. In general, the difficulty of unambiguously interpreting the outcome of research varies inversely with the degree of control that a researcher is able to exercise over randomization.

Fisher popularized two other principles of good experimentation: replication and local control or blocking. *Replication* is the observation of two or more experimental units under the same conditions. According to Fisher, replication enables a researcher to estimate error effects and obtain a more precise estimate of treatment effects. *Blocking*, on the other hand, is an experimental procedure for isolating

variation attributable to a nuisance variable. As the name suggests, *nuisance variables* are undesired sources of variation that can affect the dependent variable. Three experimental approaches are used to deal with nuisance variables:

1 Hold the variable constant.
2 Assign experimental units randomly to the treatment levels so that known and unsuspected sources of variation among the units are distributed over the entire experiment and do not affect just one or a limited number of treatment levels.
3 Include the nuisance variable as one of the factors in the experiment.

The third experimental approach uses local control or blocking. The procedure, which is illustrated later, isolates variation attributable to the nuisance variable so that it does not appear in estimates of treatment and error effects.

A statistical approach also can be used to deal with nuisance variables. The approach, which is called *analysis of covariance*, combines regression analysis with analysis of variance. The procedure involves measuring one or more concomitant variables in addition to the dependent variable. The *concomitant variable* represents a source of variation that has not been controlled in the experiment and one that is believed to affect the dependent variable. Through analysis of covariance, the dependent variable is adjusted to remove the effects of the uncontrolled source of variation. The potential advantages are (a) reduction in error variance and, hence, increased power and (b) reduction in bias caused by differences among experimental units where those differences are not attributable to the manipulation of the independent variable. Researchers often combine analysis of covariance with one or more experimental approaches in an effort to control more nuisance variables. The three principles that Fisher vigorously championed – randomization, replication, and local control – remain the foundation of good experimental design. Next, the layout and randomization for several simple experimental designs are described.

One of the simplest experimental designs is the randomization and analysis plan that is used with a *t* statistic for independent samples.

Consider an experiment to compare the effectiveness of two ways of presenting nutritional information – newspapers denoted by a_1 and TV denoted by a_2 – in getting obese teenage boys to follow more nutritious diets. The dependent variable is a measure of improvement in each boy's diet one month after the presentation. Assume that 30 boys are available to participate in the experiment. The researcher assigns $n = 15$ boys to each of the $p = 2$ presentations so that each of the $(np)!/ (n!)^p = 155,117,520$ possible assignments has the same probability. This is accomplished by numbering the boys from 1 to 30 and drawing numbers from a random numbers table. The boys corresponding to the first 15 numbers drawn between 1 and 30 are assigned to treatment level a_1; the remaining 15 boys are assigned to a_2. The layout for this experiment is shown in Figure 1.

The t independent-samples design involves randomly assigning experimental units to two levels of a treatment. A completely randomized analysis of variance design extends this strategy to any number of treatment levels. Again, consider the media experiment and suppose the researcher wants to evaluate the effectiveness of three media – newspaper, TV, and the Internet. Assume that 45 obese teenage boys are available to participate in the experiment. The boys are randomly assigned to the three media with the restriction that 15 boys are assigned to each. The layout and randomization procedures for the experiment are the same as those for the t independent-samples design in figure 1, except that the completely randomized design has an additional treatment level, a_3.

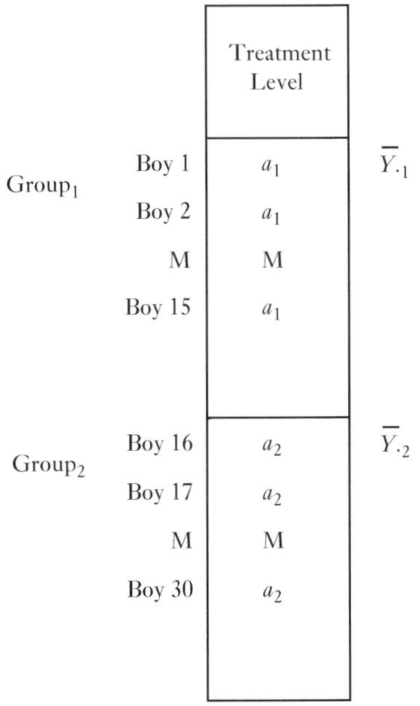

The two experiments just described use independent samples. Samples are independent if a researcher randomly assigns experimental units to p groups or randomly samples units from p populations. In both experiments, the nuisance variable of gender was held constant: only boys were used. Other nuisance variables such as initial obesity and age were probabilistically controlled by random assignment. Differences in improvement of the diets of the boys who received the same treatment level provide an estimate of error effects. Error effects reflect the idiosyncratic characteristics of the experimental units – those characteristics that differ from one unit to another – and any other variables that have not been controlled. Designs that are described next permit a researcher to use local control or blocking to isolate and remove some sources of variation that contribute to error effects.

One design for isolating a nuisance variable is the randomization and analysis plan used with a t statistic for dependent samples. As the name suggests, the design uses dependent samples. Dependent samples can be obtained by any of the following procedures:

1 Observe the experimental units under each treatment level.
2 Form sets (blocks) of experimental units that are similar with respect to a variable that is correlated with the dependent variable.
3 If the experimental units are people, obtain sets of identical twins in which case the units have similar genetic characteristics.

Figure 1 Layout for a t independent-samples design. Thirty boys are randomly assigned to two levels of a treatment with the restriction that 15 boys are assigned to each level. The mean diet improvement for the boys in treatment levels a_1 and a_2 is denoted by $\bar{Y}_{.1}$ and $\bar{Y}_{.2}$, respectively.

4   If the experimental units are people, obtain units who are matched by mutual selection (e.g., husband and wife pairs or business partners).

Let us reconsider the media experiment. It is reasonable to assume that responsiveness to nutritional information is related to the amount by which a boy is overweight. The design of the experiment can be improved by isolating this nuisance variable. Suppose that instead of randomly assigning 30 boys to the treatment levels, the researcher formed pairs of boys so that prior to administering a treatment level the boys in each pair are overweight by about the same amount. The boys in each pair constitute a block of matched units. A simple way to form the blocks is to rank the boys from least to most overweight. The boys ranked 1 and 2 are assigned to block one, those ranked 3 and 4 are assigned to block two, and so on. In this example, 15 blocks of dependent samples can be formed from the 30 boys. After all the blocks have been formed, the two boys in each block are randomly assigned to the two media presentations. Clearly, the randomization plan for the t dependent-samples design is more complex than that for a t independent-samples design. However, the added complexity is usually accompanied by greater power to reject

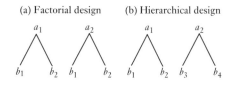

Figure 3   Comparison of designs with crossed and nested treatments. In (a), treatments A and B are crossed because each level of treatment B appears once and only once with each level of treatment A and vice versa. In (b), treatment B is nested in treatment A because b_1 and b_2 appear only with a_1 while b_3 and b_4 appear only with a_2.

a false null hypothesis. The increased power results from isolating the nuisance variable – amount by which the boys are overweight – so that it does not appear in the estimate of the error effects. The layout for this experiment is shown in Figure 2.

The layout and randomization procedures for the t statistic for dependent samples design can be extended to a design with any number of treatment levels. The design is called a *randomized block analysis of variance design*. It has $p \geq 2$ treatment levels and n blocks of dependent units. When the design has two treatment levels, the layout and randomization procedures are identical to those for the t dependent-samples design shown in Figure 2.

Often, researchers want simultaneously to test hypotheses for two or more treatments each having two or more levels. This can be accomplished by using either a factorial design or a hierarchical design. As shown in Figure 3, a factorial design uses crossed treatments in which each level of, say, treatment B appears once and only once with each level of treatment A and vice versa. In a hierarchical design, each level of treatment B appears with only one level of treatment A. A hierarchical design has at least one nested treatment; the remaining treatments are either nested or crossed. For a discussion of these and other experimental designs, the reader is referred to the books on experimental design in the References and Suggested Readings.

	Treatment Level	Treatment Level
Block$_1$	a_1	a_2
Block$_2$	a_1	a_2
Block$_3$	a_1	a_2
M	M	M
Block$_{15}$	a_1	a_2
	$\overline{Y}_{\cdot 1}$	$\overline{Y}_{\cdot 2}$

Figure 2   Layout for a t dependent-samples design. Each block contains two boys who are overweight by about the same amount. The two boys in a block are randomly assigned to the treatment levels. The mean diet improvement for the boys in treatment levels a_1 and a_2 is denoted by $\overline{Y}_{\cdot 1}$ and $\overline{Y}_{\cdot 2}$, respectively.

SEE ALSO: Experiment; Experimental Methods; Hypotheses; Random Sample; Scientific Knowledge, Sociology of; Statistical Significance Testing; Variables, Dependent; Variables, Independent

REFERENCES AND SUGGESTED READINGS

Fisher, R. A. (1925) *Statistical Methods for Research Workers*. Oliver & Boyd, Edinburgh.

Fisher, R. A. (1935) *The Design of Experiments*. Oliver & Boyd, Edinburgh.

Hacking, I. (1983) *Representing and Intervening: Introductory Topics in the Philosophy of Natural Science*. Cambridge University Press, Cambridge.

Harris, R. J. (1994) *ANOVA: An Analysis of Variance Primer*. F. E. Peacock, Itasca, IL.

Keppel, G. (1991) *Design and Analysis: A Researcher's Handbook*, 3rd edn. Prentice-Hall, Upper Saddle River, NJ.

Kirk, R. E. (1995) *Experimental Design: Procedures for the Behavioral Sciences*, 3rd edn. Brooks/Cole, Pacific Grove, CA.

Maxwell, S. E. & Delaney, H. D. (2004) *Designing Experiments and Analyzing Data: A Model Comparison Perspective*, 2nd edn. Lawrence Erlbaum, Mahwah, NJ.

Shadish, W. R., Cook, T. D., & Campbell, D. T. (2002) *Experimental and Quasi-Experimental Designs for Generalized Causal Inference*. Houghton Mifflin, Boston.

Winer, B. J., Brown, D. R., & Michels, K. M. (1991) *Statistical Principles in Experimental Design*, 3rd edn. McGraw-Hill, New York.

experimental methods

Henry A. Walker and David Willer

An experiment is a research method for which the investigator plans, builds, or otherwise controls the conditions under which phenomena are observed and measured. Experiments are the investigative method of choice in the physical sciences, and increasingly in economics, but they are used less frequently in sociology. Experimental sociologists are disproportionately located in the research subfields of (small) group processes and social psychology.

There are two interdependent reasons why sociologists rarely use experiments. First, very few sociology training programs include courses or course materials that focus on the experiment as an investigative technique. As a result, researchers unfamiliar with experiments turn to commonly used research techniques to study problems even if they are better studied experimentally. In turn, low demand for information about experimental methods contributes to the scarcity of systematic training. Second, limited information about experimental methods combines with unresolved debates within sociology to reduce further the numbers of sociologists willing to design experimental investigations. Unresolved issues include (1) the possibilities and uses of abstract explanatory theory in sociology, (2) the unique character of social phenomena, (3) the suitability of physical science techniques for sociological research, and (4) the artificiality of experiments.

Many sociologists and some non-sociologists associate experimental research with theoretical explanation. They assume that experiments only test abstract theories and point to research in physics, chemistry, and other physical sciences as the standard. Abstract explanatory theories are presumed to be in short supply, if they exist at all, in sociology. In the most optimistic view, theoretical development in sociology is stalled by the unique character of social phenomena.

Those who presume that the uniqueness of social phenomena precludes application of experimental methods to them can hold any or all of several positions. Some take the position that sociological phenomena are temporally bound – much like events studied by historians. This position is often used to buttress a related idea – that social phenomena are inconstant – and it reinforces the (false) assumption held by many that science only explains immutable phenomena. In this view, temporal specificity and inconstant phenomena make social behaviors and processes unfit candidates for theoretical analysis and experimental tests of theory. Finally, some sociologists point to the artificiality of experimental situations as an objection to experimentation in sociology. They claim that experiments use artificially contrived settings and, in the worst case, studies of artificial situations are uninformative. In the best case scenario, experimentation can make only limited contributions to sociological knowledge.

Experimental sociologists recognize that each experimental study is only one stage in a complex, multistage research process. The process begins when a researcher identifies constructs, conditions, or factors that are thought to be important for understanding the phenomenon of interest. For some experiments, researchers devise hypotheses – concrete statements about relationships between variables or operational measures – and identify *initial conditions*. Initial conditions are concrete empirical conditions that create a framework for the experiment. In many instances, the initial conditions persist for the life of an experiment, ending only at its conclusion. Experimental researchers also identify or develop *measures* to track changes in variables and to record *intermediate* and *final conditions*. Experimental data include measurements taken before, during, and at the end of an experiment. Taken as a whole, an experiment begins when a researcher creates or establishes the initial conditions. It continues with measurements of the processes under study and ends with observation, analysis, and interpretation of outcomes.

OBJECTIVES OF EXPERIMENTS

At the conceptual level, there are two and only two kinds of experiments. One class of experiments is designed to explore or discover phenomena and the other is designed to test theories. All experiments bring evidence to bear on hypotheses but only *theory-driven experiments* test hypotheses drawn from theories or theoretical models. Exploratory experiments investigate purely speculative or pre-theoretical hypotheses. Experimenters who design exploratory experiments create conditions in order to learn (or discover) what happens when a particular factor is present or absent in varying degrees. Researchers hope to uncover phenomena or relationships between phenomena. The conditions they create do not follow from the application of contrasting theoretical models. Instead, their designs follow the logic of Mill's (1919 [1875]) canons or of statistical tests. Most exploratory experiments have clearly defined *experimental* and *control* conditions. A typical control condition measures outcomes when a variable under study is absent (i.e., its value is set at zero). Results from control conditions are compared with results drawn from other experimental conditions for which the value of the variable under study is non-zero.

Many medical experiments are methods of discovery. A research team administers a new drug or treatment to a group of patients and observes changes in their conditions. Observations taken on participants in the experimental conditions are compared with participants in the control condition who do not receive the treatment. Control participants are often given placebos in medical experiments. Since placebos do not affect the phenomena under observation, the "experimental" variable under study is set at zero. Researchers use placebos to hold constant the effects of social psychological processes that might be triggered by the participant's awareness that she is being treated and observed.

Experiments designed to test theory investigate contrasting models that explain relations between theoretical constructs. Said somewhat differently, theory-driven experiments observe relations between variables that measure key theoretical constructs in theories and models. As such, it is arbitrary to classify the conditions they study as either experimental or control conditions. For example, in his pioneering test of status characteristics theory, Moore created a condition in which female participants believed they had high education status compared with their partners. Moore compared results from that condition with a second condition in which female participants believed they had low education status relative to their partners. Actually, neither treatment condition is a control condition. Moore's objective was to determine whether variations in status affected behavior consistent with hypotheses drawn from the theory's basic arguments.

Exploratory and theory-testing experiments have different roles in science and it is inappropriate to characterize either type of experiment as "better." A researcher's choice of design depends on the question under investigation and the state of theory development in her field of endeavor. Researchers exploring questions that ask for systematic description or historical/empirical explanations will build method-of-discovery experiments. Researchers who have a well-developed theory in hand will use the theory to design experimental tests of theory.

UNITS OF ANALYSIS

Participants in many sociological experiments are drawn from available pools of university students. The use of college students leads many non-experimentalists to conclude that experimental researchers only study individual phenomena. The perception is accurate, but only for a select group of experiments. Experiments that investigate social psychological phenomena often focus on individuals. For example, many classic studies in the literature on equity and justice processes (Hegtvedt & Markovsky 1995) measure individual responses to situations that produce varying degrees of injustice. Data are collected on individuals and the individual is the proper unit of analysis.

By way of contrast, other studies conducted by sociologists who study group processes and social psychology collect data from individuals but relations and social structures are the proper units of analysis. Moore's study of status-organizing processes involved participants who had either high or low status relative to their (simulated) partners. Observations were taken on individual participants but the data are informative of the processes that create power, prestige, and influence hierarchies in collectively oriented task groups. Neither the theory under test nor researchers in the status characteristics theory tradition are concerned primarily with the behavior of individuals.

Exchange network theory brings individuals into situations that require them to negotiate resource distributions under a variety of structural conditions. All exchange network theories make predictions for exchange outcomes – outcomes that vary with the structural conditions of exchange. The focus of such research is not on individuals' behaviors during negotiations but on how contrasting kinds of social structures affect the exchanges they make. Here, the exchange relation as it is embedded in a structure is the proper unit of analysis.

EXPERIMENTAL SITUATIONS

Researcher control is the hallmark of experimental investigations. However, sociological experiments are conducted in a variety of situations (or sites) and the degree to which researchers can exercise control varies substantially across research sites. We describe natural, field, survey, and laboratory experiments in order of increasing experimenter control.

Natural Experiments

As the term implies, natural experiments occur in settings free of artificial contrivances. At times, researchers are able to take advantage of naturally occurring events to study important social phenomena. Natural experiments are distinguished from other forms of experimentation by the *absence* of experimenter control of key events. Natural experiments can either test existing theory or uncover phenomena that require theoretical explanation. The Nixon administration's implementation of a draft lottery during the Vietnam War is an example of an event that permitted natural experimentation.

The draft lottery organized men's eligibility for the military draft by randomly selecting days of the year. Men whose birth dates were selected early in the lottery were very likely to be drafted. Those whose birth dates came later (e.g., number 340) could anticipate being bypassed by the draft. As such, the lottery created "natural" experimental groups, for example, (1) men with low numbers who would almost certainly be asked to report for the draft, (2) men who had a high probability of being asked to report, and so on. Researchers have found that those with low draft numbers had higher long-term, non-military mortality rates than those with high numbers (Hearst et al. 1986). In an unpublished study, Walker found that draft-eligible male students with very low lottery numbers (1–50) expressed more positive attitudes toward the Vietnam War than students with high or very high numbers. The finding was explained by applying cognitive dissonance theory to the findings.

Field Experiments

Field experiments, like natural experiments, are conducted in naturally occurring situations. However, field experimenters exercise some degree of control over participants, events, and key theoretical or practical factors. Social psychological research on bystander intervention is an example of field experimentation. Piliavin et al. (1969) chose particular subway cars but they could not select the passengers who became their experimental "participants." Their sample is properly described as an an accidental or convenience sample. However, characteristics of the "victims" in need of assistance were under strict experimental control.

Piliavin et al.'s research can be contrasted with the Robbers Cave experiments conducted by Muzafer Sherif and his colleagues (Sherif et al. 1961). Sherif et al. exercised substantially greater control over conditions in their studies. The researchers exercised some control over (1) the process used to select youthful participants, (2) key elements of the site at Robbers Cave State Park in Oklahoma, (3) the assignment of boys to two groups (e.g., putting friends in separate groups), and (4) events that were presumed to affect relationships between the two groups.

Survey Experiments

Survey experiments combine all the advantages of experiments with many desirable characteristics of survey research. Survey researchers can conduct studies with large samples, control the selection of participants, and randomly assign participants to treatments. The result can be a powerful tool for discovering important social relationships or for testing sociological theory. Small-scale surveys may use face-to-face interviewing or survey administration of survey instruments. However, many contemporary surveys use computer-assisted interviewing (CAI) and they can be conducted by telephone or through Internet connections.

Experiments using the vignette technique pioneered by Rossi (1979) are increasingly common in sociological social psychology. Participants in contrasting experimental treatments respond to situations described by vignettes embedded in survey instruments. Jasso and Webster's recent research studying gender of evaluators, gender of putative employees, and assessments of just (fair) wages is an outstanding example of this experimental form. Other social psychologists control important features of the situations under which participants respond to survey items. For example, Krysan and Couper varied the presence of interviewers (whether in the room or on a video screen) and interviewers' race. Their experiment studied the responses that black and white participants gave to surveys that contained items designed to measure attitudes toward race or ethnic groups and issues important to race relations. Among their important findings, Krysan and Couper discovered that "subtle" items designed to expose hidden or covert race prejudice were the most sensitive to race of interviewer and presence effects. Their findings are inconsistent with the rationales that previous researchers had advanced for incorporating subtle items in survey research on politically and personally sensitive topics.

Laboratory Experiments

Laboratory experiments offer the greatest opportunities for experimental control. Laboratory scientists can select participants and control the conditions under which participants are studied. The ability to select participants can be very important when an experiment is testing a scope-delimited theory. As an example, we can use Moore's selection of women from a particular community college for his study of status-organizing processes. Since all were women and students at the same institution, Moore could tell participants that their simulated partners were also women who differed from them on a single characteristic – the school the partner attended. The high degree of control was important because one scope restriction on the theory under test required group members to differ on one (and only one) characteristic.

Experimenter control is also crucial in the Krysan and Couper study described above. Krysan and Couper's surveys were administered in a laboratory. Under laboratory conditions, the researchers could standardize the actions of virtual and live interviewers. Participants in the virtual interview treatment saw the interviewer on a split-screen monitor as they read survey instructions. Participants in the live interview treatment read survey instructions on the same computer screens but interviewer images were not projected on their screens. The high degree of control that is exercised in laboratory experiments permits more accurate and useful tests of hypotheses drawn from theory.

THE FUTURE OF EXPERIMENTATION IN SOCIOLOGY

Experimental research in sociology appears to have a bright future. First, social scientists in other disciplines are increasingly aware of the utility of experimental research as a technique for testing theory. Experiments were very rare in economics and political science as recently as the 1960s. Today, experimental economics is a burgeoning field and experimentalists in economics, political science, and sociology are using the Internet to conduct experiments in virtual laboratories (Willer et al. 1999). It remains to be seen whether the spread of experimental techniques to other social and behavioral sciences will increase their visibility in all fields and create greater demand for sociologists trained in experimental methods.

SEE ALSO: Experiment; Experimental Design; Group Processes; Methods; Social Psychology; Survey Research

REFERENCES AND SUGGESTED READINGS

Hearst, N., Newman, T. B., & Hulley, S. B. (1986) Delayed Effects of the Military Draft on Mortality: A Randomized Natural Experiment. *New England Journal of Medicine* 314: 620–4.

Hegtvedt, K. A. & Markovsky, B. (1995) Justice and Injustice. In: Cook, K. S., Fine, G. A., & House, J. S. (Eds.), *Sociological Perspectives on Social Psychology*. Allyn & Bacon, Boston, pp. 257–80.

Mill, J. S. (1919 [1875]) *A System of Logic*, 8th edn. Longmans, Green, London.

Piliavin, I. M., Rodin, J., & Piliavin, J. A. (1969) Good Samaritanism: An Underground Phenomenon? *Journal of Personality and Social Psychology* 13: 289–99.

Rossi, P. H. (1979) Vignette Analysis: Uncovering the Normative Structure of Complex Judgements. In: Merton, R. K., Coleman, J. S., & Rossi, P. H. (Eds.), *Qualitative and Quantitative Research: Papers in Honor of Paul Lazarsfeld*. Free Press, New York, pp. 176–86.

Sherif, M., Harvey, O. J., White, B. J., Hood, W. R., & Sherif, C. W. (1961) *Intergroup Conflict and Cooperation: The Robbers Cave Experiment*. University Book Exchange, Norman, OK.

Willer, D., Rutstrom, L., Karr, L., Corra, M., & Girard, D. (1999) A Web–Lab to Enhance Social Science Infrastructure: Experiments, Simulations, and Archiving. *Journal of Knowledge Management* 3: 276–87.

expertise, "scientification," and the authority of science

Stephen Turner

The problem of the role of experts in society may seem to be a topic marginal to the main concerns of sociology, but it is in fact deeply rooted in the sociological project itself. Sociologists and social thinkers have long been concerned with the problem of the role of knowledge in society. Certain Enlightenment thinkers, notably Turgot and Condorcet, believed that social progress depended on the advance of knowledge and the wider dispersion of knowledge in society. But Condorcet especially recognized that this idea had complex political implications. On the one hand, it required science, which for him included social science, to be supported by the state, yet retain independence or self-governance in order to advance without political interference. On the other hand, he recognized that social advance required that the most enlightened be the rulers, and that this conflicted with the ideas of democracy and equality.

Condorcet's solution to this problem was education. But he also recognized that even the educated citizen would never be the equal of the scientist. Thus, his conception of the role of the expert in politics depended on the hope that a more educated citizenry would defer politically to the most enlightened, thus bringing about *de facto* expert rule through democratic means. Saint-Simon extended this reasoning, but it was made into a sociological system by Comte, and, in the course of doing so, Comte created the term sociology.

Comte's central idea was the law of three stages, which held that every science goes through the successive stages of theological, metaphysical, and positive. He argued that sociology was to be the last science to reach the positive stage, and that this law itself was the first and most fundamental positive law of sociology. Comte also believed that consensus was a central requirement for order and orderly progress in society and looked to science to provide the intellectual basis for this consensus.

Comte regarded freedom of opinion as inappropriate to an age of knowledge. If the facts of a social life could be reduced to science, the principles of this science should be the basis of state action rather than the misguided views of citizens, who, if they disagreed with the principles, were merely ignorant and needed education rather than the right to voice their ignorance. Expertise thus would correct the anarchy of opinion of liberal discussion. The authority of science was to be the basis of state authority. This posed the problem of education, to which Comte had an authoritarian solution: the lessons of sociology should be inculcated in the masses through the same kind of techniques that the Catholic church in the past had used so effectively to inculcate religious dogma.

His critics, such as John Stuart Mill, saw in this a kind of authoritarianism, but acknowledged the logic of his position. Later thinkers such as Karl Pearson defended similar views about the necessary role of experts. These ideas in turn influenced such movements as Fabianism in Britain, technocracy in the US, and the social relations of science movement of the 1930s, whose ideas were a precursor to the modern sociology of science. The social relations of science movement was dominated by communists, and communism itself may be understood as a form of expert rule in which experts direct social life "scientifically" (through planning) on behalf of the people rather than as their instructed representatives.

In the 1940s and 1950s the sociology of science concerned itself with the related problem of the authority of science. Robert Merton was particularly concerned with conflicts between science and democracy. In some of his later writings he discussed what he called the ambivalence of ordinary citizens to science and expertise. Later sociologists of science, influenced by social constructionism in the study of the generation of scientific facts, turned their attention to expertise as well. They identified specific mechanisms, such as "boundary objects," through which scientific or expert claims were constructed into a form of "fact" that was usable by the public, and considered issues about the construction of the appearance of expert knowledge and the kind of citizenship education that might be required in the face of a politics in which expert claims played a large role. Some influential research in this tradition concentrated on failures of expertise and the problem of integrating relevant lay knowledge with expert opinion, one of the sources of failure in the application of expert knowledge in concrete situations.

Other research focused on the social and organizational roles of experts, the place of expert knowledge in the law, judges' construction of expert knowledge, and the implicit conception of science which is assumed in legal decision-making about scientific questions. This literature deals with such issues as the gap between the law's treatment of scientific results and scientists' view of them.

Another body of research-related strategies came from the professionalization literature in American sociology in the mid-twentieth century and focused on the professionalization of domains of practice and the consequent transformation of these domains into subjects governed by expert knowledge. An important example of this is the medicalization of issues (e.g., behavioral issues) which had previously been regarded as matters that could appropriately be dealt with by lay knowledge. Many forms of social behavior, such as child abuse and alcoholism, were transformed in this way. Subsequently, a social constructionist literature grew up discussing the process by which these transformations occurred.

These discussions had the effect of questioning the concept of expert knowledge itself, and pointing to the difficulties of judging expertise. Experts may have specialized knowledge, but they are not universal experts. They often do not have the local knowledge necessary to apply this knowledge correctly, and are often unaware of the limitations of their own knowledge. Lay people also may have specialized forms of knowledge that need to be integrated into decision-making in order for knowledge to be effectively used. Thus, there is a problem of aggregating or bringing expert knowledge and other forms of knowledge together. Similar issues arise when experts from different fields must cooperate in decision-making. Experts in one field become lay people when faced with expertise in another field, and must make non-expert judgments about the validity, relevance, and significance of the expert claims made by other experts.

The issues raised by Condorcet about the conflict between expert knowledge and democracy are still relevant today. They point to a fundamental conflict between a participatory model of democracy and the undeniable fact that many of the issues that face modern states are understandable only by experts. The newer literature on expertise points to the fact that expert knowledge, and the "facts" which citizens accept as matters of expertise and act on, are the product of complex processes of social construction, and thus of a kind of politics.

SEE ALSO: Controversy Studies; Merton, Robert K.; Science and Public Participation: The Democratization of Science; Scientific Literacy and Public Understandings of Science; Speaking Truth to Power: Science and Policy; Scientific Literacy and Public Understanding of Science

REFERENCES AND SUGGESTED READINGS

Condorcet, Marquis de (1976 [1793]) Fragment on the New Atlantis, or Combined Efforts of the Human Species for the Advancement of Science. In: Baker, K. M. (Ed.), *Condorcet: Selected Writings*. Bobbs-Merrill, Indianapolis, pp. 283–300.

Hacking, I. (1999) Kind-Making: The Case of Child Abuse. In: *The Social Construction of What?* Harvard University Press, Cambridge, MA, pp. 125–62.

Selinger, E. & Crease, R. P. (Eds.) (2006) *The Philosophy of Expertise*. Columbia University Press, New York.

Wynne, B. (1996) May the Sheep Safely Graze? A Reflexive View of the Expert–Lay Knowledge Divide. In: Lash, S. et al. (Eds.), *Risk, Environment, Modernity: Towards a New Ecology*. Sage, London, pp. 27–43.

exploitation

Andrew Kliman

Exploitation occurs when someone or something (e.g., a material resource, an opportunity) is used or taken advantage of. Social scientists are chiefly concerned with the exploitation of people and classes, who are generally considered exploited if they are required, by force or by circumstances, to contribute more to some process than they receive in return. Crucially important to Marxian thought, the concept of exploitation is also employed in neoclassical economics and related sociological work. Yet the concept is controversial among sociologists; many eschew it entirely.

Karl Marx held that working people are exploited if some of the labor they perform is surplus labor, labor for which they receive no equivalent. The extraction of surplus labor is most transparent in the *corvée* system, in which serfs worked part of the time for themselves on one plot of land, and for the lord, on another plot of land, during their remaining working time. This division of working time is not so transparent in other cases, but Marx regarded it as a feature of all class-divided societies. Workers in all such societies, he argued, are compelled to perform surplus labor because they lack access to land and other means of production. To survive, the workers must work for other people or companies. The latter can require the performance of surplus labor because they have exclusive ownership or control of the means of production.

Marx employed this theory in three main ways. First, he defined classes and identified divergent class interests and antagonisms in terms of surplus-labor extraction. Exploited working classes perform surplus labor; exploiting non-working classes live off of it. The former have an interest in ending this exploitation; the latter have an interest in perpetuating it. Class antagonisms and struggles arise as a result of: (1) these contrary interests; (2) efforts by one side or the other to lessen or augment the amount of surplus labor performed; (3) domination, oppression, and violence employed in order to perpetuate and augment this exploitation; and (4) social conditions associated with it, such as alienation, poverty, and inequality.

Secondly, Marx distinguished among different class-divided societies in terms of their different "forms," or systems, of surplus-labor extraction. He argued that a society's other economic and political relationships are based upon and correspond to its specific form of surplus labor.

Finally, and most controversially, he utilized the theory in order to explain the existence and magnitude of surplus value, or profit, under capitalism. Marx argued that surplus labor is the exclusive source of surplus value and its subcomponents (profits of industrial firms, rent, interest, etc.). Although capitalists seemingly pay for workers' labor, and thus workers seemingly receive as wages a sum of value equal to the value that their labor adds to the product, Marx (1990) argued that capitalists actually purchase workers' *labor power*, or capacity to work. The amount of labor they subsequently perform is therefore not determined by the wage contract. Consequently, surplus value arises when, and to the extent that, workers are made to work longer than the amount of time during which their labor adds an amount of new value equal to their money wages.

The magnitude and rate of surplus value, or rate of exploitation, thus depend upon struggles over the length and intensity of work, as well as wages. Marx argued that, owing to the dynamics of the business cycle and the replacement of workers by machines, wages cannot rise to levels that would seriously threaten the generation of surplus value.

Many Marxist and non-Marxist authors maintain that the production of surplus value cannot rightly be deemed exploitative unless an ethical argument is provided. That workers are required to perform surplus labor is insufficient. Marx, on the other hand, held that the exploitation of workers is fair and lawful, violating none of their rights. From the perspective of present-day society, there is nothing to criticize. It admits of criticism only from the perspective of a future classless society.

Marx's profit theory seems to contradict the fact that industries which extract the same amounts of surplus labor obtain quite different amounts of profit. Although he acknowledged this fact, Marx (1991) argued that if some industries obtain more profit than they generate by means of surplus-labor extraction, others must obtain less, and the gains and losses exactly offset one another in the aggregate. It is thus at the level of the aggregate economy that surplus labor is the exclusive source of profit.

Critics have persistently claimed, however, that Marx's demonstration of this proposition has been proven internally inconsistent. The alleged inconsistency has profoundly affected the trajectory of subsequent profit theory and class analysis. It is the principal reason given for rejection of the exploitation theory of profit. Theorists seeking to preserve some elements of that theory, but to jettison Marx's theories of value and surplus value, also invoke the alleged inconsistency as their principal justification. This latter category includes economists who have advanced revised versions of the exploitation theory of profit, Marxist sociologists who seek to ground class analysis in a revised account of surplus-labor extraction (e.g., Wright 2000), and a non-Marxist sociologist who proposed a different concept of exploitation as the basis for class analysis (Sørensen 2000).

Key to the attempted reformulations of the exploitation theory of profit is the fundamental Marxian theorem (FMT). The FMT has widely been held to have rigorously proved, without the use of Marx's value concepts, that surplus labor is necessary and sufficient for the existence of profit. Thus, even though he was supposedly wrong to claim that aggregate profit and surplus value are equal, the FMT has seemed to confirm Marx's conclusion that surplus labor is the exclusive source of profit.

The FMT was also at the basis of Roemer's (1988) effort to root class differences and surplus-labor extraction in initial differences in wealth. In his rational choice model, initial differences in wealth lead, with rare exceptions, to strictly corresponding differences in class and exploitation status. Moreover, the initial distribution of wealth is the sole determinant of the class and exploitation hierarchies. Whether poor people become proletarians, or independent producers exploited in credit markets, makes no difference. These results significantly influenced the thinking of many economists, sociologists, and philosophers. Prior to Roemer's work, many Marxists had simply assumed that labor markets and capitalist control of the labor process were important determinants of the degree of exploitation.

Yet recent counterexamples may have demonstrated that the FMT actually fails to prove that surplus labor is either necessary or sufficient for profit. If these counterexamples are valid, they show that the theorem applies only to very special cases – static equilibrium and an economy in which all physical surpluses of all goods are always positive. (If, on a given day, the steel industry produces less steel than the auto, construction, and other industries use up, then the physical surplus of steel is negative.) Given even a slight relaxation of these special case restrictions, profit can be negative when surplus labor is extracted and positive without surplus labor having been extracted, according to the FMT's definitions (Kliman 2001).

This does not mean that profit theory and class analysis rooted in surplus-labor extraction have necessarily come to an end. During the past quarter-century, a new school of Marx interpretation claims to have refuted the alleged proofs of internal inconsistency in his value theory. It maintains that the apparent inconsistencies, including the one discussed above, are simply the byproducts of a particular mathematical formalization of his theory, since the inconsistencies disappear under this school's alternative interpretation (see, e.g., Freeman & Carchedi 1996). If these findings are correct, they do not prove that Marx's profit theory is empirically correct, but they do remove the standard justification for dismissing his theory as logically unsound.

Unequal exchange theory, pioneered by Emmanuel (1972), is often understood as a theory of exploitation. However, Emmanuel himself did not refer to unequal exchange as exploitative; he sought to supplement, not replace, Marxian exploitation theory. He argued that less developed countries (LDCs) receive relatively low earnings, and developed countries (DCs) receive relatively high earnings, for their exports. The distortion of export earnings serves to retard economic growth in the LDCs while stimulating it in the DCs. Unequal exchange theory is thus closely associated with dependency theory, especially with the notion that underdevelopment is an active process, not a static condition.

The source of unequal exchange, proponents of the theory argue, is the confluence of unequal international wage rates and the tendency of rates of profit to equalize. Wages and thus costs of production are high in the DCs and low in the LDCs. If rates of profit are equal, prices will likewise be high in the DCs and low in the LDCs.

The reason why exchange at these prices is deemed unequal is that the earnings of LDCs are low, and the earnings of DCs are high, in relation to the amounts of labor that workers in these countries perform. Yet since this inequality is mainly the result of LDCs' relatively low *productivity*, other authors deny that a distinct theory of unequal *exchange* is needed in order to account for it. For instance, some hold that Marx's value theory already accounts for it: low-productivity producers create less value ("social value") per labor-hour than high-productivity producers.

In contrast to Marx's theory, neoclassical economics implies that exploitation of capitalists by workers (through, for instance, the formation of unions) is as likely as the exploitation of workers by capitalists. All people who provide productive inputs (labor, machinery, etc.) are considered exploited if they are paid less, or exploiters if they are paid more, than what neoclassical theory regards as the input's contribution to production: the value of its marginal product. The marginal product is the extra physical output that results from the employment of an extra unit of the input; the value of this extra output is the hypothetical price it would command if the economy were perfectly competitive and in equilibrium. Exploitation would therefore be absent in a perfectly competitive equilibrium, but the conditions needed for perfect competition – perfect information and the inability of any seller or buyer to set prices – cannot be satisfied in the real world.

Another key difference is that, while Marx assessed workers' contributions to production in terms of the amount of labor they perform, neoclassical theory assesses an input's contribution to production in terms of the extra physical output it yields. This procedure is frequently criticized as conceptually dubious. Critics argue that physical output is the result of many inputs operating in concert, and that it is frequently impossible, even in principle, to ascribe distinct contributions to each. If, for instance, every delivery requires a driver and a truck, then the marginal product of an extra driver or extra truck (given no increase in the other input) is zero, so there is no way of determining whether the trucking firm exploits its drivers or vice versa.

The recent work of Sørensen (2000) seeks to make the neoclassical concept of exploitation the basis for sociological class analysis. He argues that those who can exact what neoclassical economists call "rent" – payments for their inputs that exceed the minimum amount needed to make the inputs available – constitute exploiting classes. Not only are they better off, and others worse off, than if there were no rent, but the very purpose of rent-seeking behavior (e.g., lobbying the government for protection from competition) is to enhance one's well-being at the expense of others. As an adaptation and application of neoclassical exploitation theory, Sørensen's work shares its main features and possible shortcomings.

The various theories of exploitation are controversial partly because of their political and ideological implications, and partly because assessment of whether individuals and groups are exploited gives rise to significant conceptual problems. Although some key controversies – particularly those surrounding Marx's theory, the FMT, and neoclassical exploitation theory – can seem to be purely technical controversies over measurement, they are, at a deeper level, controversies over these difficult conceptual problems.

SEE ALSO: Bourgeoisie and Proletariat; Capitalism; Dependency and World-Systems Theories; Distributive Justice; Economic Sociology: Neoclassical Economic Perspective; Labor/Labor Power; Labor Process; Marx, Karl; Marxism and Sociology

REFERENCES AND SUGGESTED READINGS

Emmanuel, A. (1972) *Unequal Exchange: A Study of the Imperialism of Trade.* Monthly Review Press, New York.

Freeman, A. & Carchedi, G. (Eds.) (1996) *Marx and Non-Equilibrium Economics.* Edward Elgar, Cheltenham.

Kliman, A. (2001) Simultaneous Valuation vs. the Exploitation Theory of Profit. *Capital and Class* 73: 97–112.

Marx, K. (1990, 1991) *Capital: A Critique of Political Economy*, Vols. 1 and 3. Penguin, London.

Roemer, J. (1988) *Free to Lose: An Introduction to Marxist Economic Philosophy.* Radius, London.

Sørensen, A. B. (2000) Toward a Sounder Basis for Class Analysis. *American Journal of Sociology* 105 (6): 1523–58.

Wright, E. O. (2000) Class, Exploitation, and Economic Rents: Reflections on Sørensen's "Sounder Basis." *American Journal of Sociology* 105(6): 1559–71.

extracurricular activities

Anna Strassmann Mueller

Extracurricular activities such as band, debate, or soccer are optional activities offered by the school that complement the academic curriculum and enhance the school's sense of community. These activities provide settings within schools for adolescents to develop facets of their personalities that contribute to their emerging independence and their eventual assumption of adult roles. Extracurriculars offer opportunities for leadership, travel, skill development, and social engagement and integration in the school. There is growing evidence that adolescents who are involved in extracurricular activities are generally happier and healthier than their uninvolved peers. In particular, research suggests that extracurricular participation positively influences adolescents' psychosocial development, problem and risk behaviors, relationship formation, and, perhaps most importantly, their academic achievement.

Since James Coleman's classic study *The Adolescent Society*, researchers have recognized that schools serve as the primary location for adolescent social development. In schools, adolescents meet friends, internalize values, and develop interests and talents. Often, extracurricular activities play a major role in these processes. Because adolescents choose to engage in extracurricular activities, these activities can become important defining experiences for their budding sense of identity. In fact, there are close ties between adolescent participation in particular activities such as sports or debate and self-reported identity, as, for example, a "jock" or a "brain" (Barber et al. 2001). These self-reported identities then shape other aspects of adolescents' lives, such as drinking and marijuana use, or college matriculation and graduation. Additionally, extracurricular activities may provide a forum for the development of adolescent gender identity. Athletic extracurricular activities for males and cheerleading for females may contribute to the development of traditional gender roles because of the emphasis on competition found in sports as opposed to the emphasis on appearance found in cheerleading (Eder et al. 1995). Though girls are significantly less likely to participate in team sports, those who do may experience a nontraditional gender socialization that includes skills that may help them succeed in domains of life outside of sports.

The status hierarchy of extracurricular activities within the school can also shape how extracurricular involvement impacts students' lives. In some schools there is substantial overlap between the schools' learning objectives and officially sponsored extracurricular activities. In these schools, extracurricular activities become another way for schools to promote their academic goals. Another common emphasis in schools is on athletic competitions such as football: athletes in these schools may find that their athletic identity is central to their sense of self. If the school sponsors events such as pep rallies that increase the visibility of athletes, being an athlete may also come with more social status and increased popularity with peers (Eder et al. 1995). Though extracurriculars can reinforce or create adolescent status hierarchies, they can also provide adolescents safe alternative contexts in which they can explore identities that do not match the popular norms of the school. For example, nerds may take refuge in extracurriculars that allow them to be themselves and not worry about adhering to popular student norms (Kinney 1993). Thus, extracurricular activities serve an important social function for the school. They diversify the school experience for adolescents and allow students to feel integrated and connected to the school. They also provide a physical and social location in the school where school policies and priorities can shape the adolescent culture.

Because keeping students engaged and enrolled in school is an important policy issue, the role of extracurriculars as a tool for improving students' achievement has been considered seriously in the academic literature. This body of literature has demonstrated that extracurricular activities have an important impact on adolescents' academic achievement. Even after controlling for socioeconomic status and family background, adolescents involved in extracurricular activities do better in school and have more positive attitudes toward their education. Students who are extracurricularly involved have higher grades, attend school and complete their homework more regularly, and are more likely to select college-preparatory coursework. They also feel more confident in their academic work and both plan and realize higher educational goals (like attending college) more than students who are not involved in extracurriculars. In low-class and middle-class schools, where less than half the students go on to 4-year colleges, identifying as an athlete is particularly strongly associated with higher grades and higher educational aspirations. Though it is possible that in this body of research better students are more likely to participate in extracurricular activities (rather than the extracurricular activities improving the students who participate), similar results have been obtained in longitudinal studies controlling for relevant behaviors prior to participation. This implies that extracurricular activities to some extent do improve the academic achievement of participants. In addition to improving the achievement, being involved in extracurriculars can be crucial for students who are seriously struggling in school, as it can dramatically reduce their likelihood of actually dropping out.

In addition to better integrating students into schools, extracurricular involvement can improve students' experiences during the sometimes difficult adolescent years. Students who participate in the extracurriculum tend to make better life decisions particularly with regard to high-risk behaviors. They take fewer risks sexually and are less likely to engage in delinquent or problem behaviors. Generally, students involved in extracurriculars are less likely to drink, smoke, or use drugs, although some research has shown that students who participate in team sports (such as football) consume more alcohol. Perhaps even more importantly, adolescents who participate in extracurricular activities tend to exhibit better mental health as indicated by higher self-esteem and healthier self-concept. They also tend to report greater self-efficacy and more control over their lives, an important developmental step toward a healthy adulthood. Furthermore, involved adolescents generally experience higher levels of life satisfaction than their peers who do not participate. These positive influences do not necessarily end during adolescence. Extracurricular involvement can shape adolescents' adult lives, producing more conscientious citizens in early adulthood. For example, extracurricular participation has been linked to greater civic involvement, such as voting and volunteering.

While much research has focused on how participation in extracurriculars improves adolescents' developmental and academic trajectories, participation in these events also provides an invaluable opportunity for adolescents to form social relationships with adults. During a period of adolescent development that involves large gains in independence from parents and families, extracurricular activities offer an institutionally structured opportunity to engage in extra-familial relationships. These activities provide opportunities for adolescents to connect with adults who can guide them on their academic paths and serve as advocates if necessary, helping to maximize the school's ability to meet students' needs. Research has shown that adolescents involved in school-based extracurricular activities do tend to seek out educational and occupational advice more frequently and from a wider range of adults than their uninvolved peers. These sources of engagement with encouraging adults outside of the household are particularly important for at-risk adolescents, who generally lack access to such social support. In addition, extracurricular activities can strengthen the social ties between students, parents, and the school. When parents and school personnel know one another (thus increasing the social capital available to adolescents within the school), the school can

more effectively realize its developmental and academic goals for students.

Just as extracurricular activities structure relationships between students and adults, they can shape who adolescents are exposed to within the school context. In particular, extracurricular activities provide a potentially unique opportunity within the school structure for exposure to students from different backgrounds. Unlike classes which tend to draw students with similar academic histories (and thus from more homogeneous family backgrounds), extracurricular activities draw anyone with talent or interest. This opportunity, the influence of institutional support, and the equal contribution and contact of a group of individuals combine to position extracurricular activities as a conduit by which to promote positive race and ethnic relations. However, this potential is limited by race and gender differentials in individuals' likeliness to participate in extracurriculars and how participation affects students' academic and personal trajectories. Further, how integrated extracurricular activities are may vary by school, and in some schools opportunities to participate may be extended to only a small number of students.

Because extracurricular activities appear to have a resoundingly positive role in adolescent life, these inequalities in participation are of concern, as they imply that involvement works better for some adolescents than for others. Although across race and ethnic groups, girls' participation in sports is increasing, their rates still lag behind those of boys. The reverse is true of non-athletic activities and school and community service activities: girls participate in much higher percentages than boys (American Association of University Women 1999). Girls are underrepresented in activities that encourage exercise, which has important implications for health, while boys are underrepresented in non-athletic activities, which can play an important role in their academic achievement. In addition to being stratified by gender, participation rates differ based on socioeconomic background: students from families with higher socioeconomic status are more likely to participate in extracurriculars, particularly sports, academic clubs, and music. School size and school sector (public or private) also influence the rates and effects of participation.

Though the majority of research on extra-curricular activities is based on the experiences of US adolescents, there is some research that suggests leisure and extracurricular activities are important cross-nationally (Verma & Larson 2003). Internationally, these activities seem to serve a similar developmental purpose: they provide adolescents with opportunities to gain skills, to integrate into social groups, and to develop personal interests and talents. Though there are some commonalities in participation across countries (the popularity of sports is almost universal), the national context does shape the role of participation in adolescent life. For example, in Japan where achievement and competition are important elements of the national culture, extracurricular activities are viewed as an additional way for students to cultivate discipline and become well rounded. Because of this motivation, participation tends to add stress to Japanese adolescents' lives and is linked to negative emotional states. This is contrary to findings from the US and Europe and points to the importance of international research on extracurricular activities and adolescent development.

Academic achievement and engagement, health and risk behaviors, and formation and maintenance of social relationships have been linked to high school extracurricular activities. Students spend many intense hours in extracurricular settings during their adolescent years, rendering these contexts crucial to understanding how adolescent society operates in schools and how experiences in extracurriculars influence adolescent identity and behavior. Though these generally positive forces have been widely explored in the literature, there is still much that researchers do not know. For example, extracurricular participation may not be stable over the high school years. Students may experience a trajectory of extracurriculars; they may focus on drama one year and basketball the next. How do these trajectories affect the developing adolescent? Continuing to explore adolescents' dynamic experiences in extracurriculars over the course of the middle and high school years should be an important goal of future research. An improved understanding of participation in extracurricular activities will enable policy-makers to more effectively harness the school

as a powerful force in shaping adolescent culture and outcomes.

SEE ALSO: Dropping Out of School; Educational Attainment; Expectations and Aspirations; Parental Involvement in Education; School Climate; Social Capital and Education; Sport, College

REFERENCES AND SUGGESTED READINGS

American Association of University Women (1999) *Gender Gaps: Where Schools Still Fail Our Children*. Marlowe, New York.

Barber, B. L., Eccles, J. S., & Stone, M. R. (2001) Whatever Happened to the Jock, the Brain, and the Princess? Young Adult Pathways Linked to Adolescent Activity Involvement and Social Identity. *Journal of Adolescent Research* 16(5): 429–55.

Coleman, J. (1961) *The Adolescent Society*. Free Press, New York.

Eccles, J. S., Barber, B. L., Stone, M., & Hunt, J. (2003) Extracurricular Activities and Adolescent Development. *Journal of Social Issues* 59(4): 865–89.

Eder, D., Evans, C. C., & Parker, S. (1995) *School Talk: Gender and Adolescent Culture*. Rutgers University Press, New Brunswick, NJ.

Kinney, D. A. (1993) From Nerds to Normals: The Recovery of Identity Among Adolescents From Middle School to High School. *Sociology of Education* 66(1): 21–40.

Verma, S. & Larson, R. (Eds.) (2003) Special Issue: Examining Adolescent Leisure Time Across Cultures: Developmental Opportunities and Risks. *New Directions for Child and Adolescent Development* 99.

exurbia

Jeff Crump

Exurbia is a form of residential development that straddles an often ill-defined zone between densely packed suburbs and rural and small town locations. Although its boundaries are usually indistinct, exurban development begins somewhere beyond the sprawling suburbs and lies outside easy commuting distance to the central city. At its far reaches, exurbia does not so much end as it blends into the surrounding agricultural countryside. Residents of exurbia occupy an uneasy middle ground between the perceived ills of the city and adjoining suburbs and rural places where it is believed that people live in harmony with the bucolic rural landscape (Marx 1964).

At the core of the debate over exurbanization is the question of whether exurbia represents a "clean break" in prevailing patterns of suburban development or if it is simply another form of suburban sprawl (Nelson & Sanchez 1999). Proponents of the "clean break" hypothesis argue that exurbia represents a new settlement form populated by a distinctive group of residents who seek out particularly rural environments. The residential choices of exurbanites are driven by an anti-urban bias which leads them to seek out idealized rural and small town locations (Nelson 1992).

Here, the argument is that exurbia and exurbanites are somehow unique and their choice to live in exurbia is reflective of a different set of values than those of people who choose to live in suburbs (Nelson & Dueker 1990). Exurban residents are said to base their residential location decision on a calculus that places an overriding value on the perceived environmental amenities offered by a rural location. Rural environments, open space, privacy, and the pursuit of "hobby farming" (e.g., raising a few head of cattle or a 5-acre vineyard) are characteristics that set exurbanites apart (Crump 2003).

Not everyone accepts the argument that exurban development is distinctive. By contrast, those arguing against the uniqueness of exurbs argue that exurban development is simply another form of suburbia. For example, Nelson, who at one time argued for the distinctiveness of exurbia, recently found that exurbanites are no different than those who seek solace in more traditional suburbs (Nelson 1992; Nelson & Sanchez 1999).

Much of the writing on exurbia is found in the popular literature. For example, the terms exurban and exurbanite were first popularized in 1955 with the publication of *Exurbanites* by the journalist A. C. Spectorsky (1955). According to Spectorsky, exurbanites are a unique group seeking relief from the "rat race" of Manhattan. The exurban émigrés transformed many formerly rural enclaves such as Westport, Connecticut.

Anti-urbanism is often cited as the main motivating factor for exurban migration. Marx (1964) argued that Americans have a prevailing anti-urban bias which leads them to idealize rural life and seek out rural environments in which to live. In addition to anti-urbanism, improved transportation and communication were crucial to the development of exurbia. Increasing affluence, when coupled with advances in transportation and communication, has also allowed people to express their residential preferences more easily. In this process, a new kind of city is being created which defies traditional definitions over what is and is not urban.

Interest in exurbanization reached a peak during the 1970s and 1980s. In the 1980s the increased research on exurban growth was largely stimulated by significant rural population gains. Termed the "rural renaissance," rural population growth represented a reversal of long-term patterns of rural depopulation in the US. However, although there was little doubt that rural areas were growing, the question was why. Several surveys of rural residents identified two major factors. First, anti-urbanism was leading people to seek out exurban locations. Second, industrial growth in rural areas was also expanding the employment options available in rural locations.

Exurban expansion has led to the spread of residential development across wide swaths of formerly rural landscapes (Davis et al. 1994). The ever-growing exurban landscape is the result of innumerable local planning decisions that result in a sprawling, patchwork quilt of development. Controlling exurban development is difficult as developers resist growth limitations and seek jurisdictions that present the easiest path toward profitable development. They leapfrog places that seek to control growth, thereby increasing the cost of service provision.

Although academic interest in exurbanization has waned in recent years, newer studies find that the continued decentralization of employment is an important factor in exurban growth (Nelson 1992). Certainly, numerous employment nodes have grown on the edge of US cities and provide employment options for exurbanites. Termed "edge cities" by the journalist Joel Garreau (1991), satellite business and retail centers now characterize the freeway interchanges that mark the beginning of exurbia in the 1990s.

Hayden (2003) develops a three-way classification of exurban development. According to Hayden, the three emblematic landscapes of exurbia are reluctant suburbs, hot towns, and Valhallas. Reluctant suburbs are rural towns that often find themselves overwhelmed by population growth. Hot towns are well-off locations that attract telecommuters, sometimes termed "lone eagles." Certainly, telecommuting has grown apace with the advent of high-speed Internet service and allows exurban residents to avoid long and tiring commutes. Yet, even though the proponents of telecommuting celebrate the end of the conventional commute, critics argue that telecommuting destroys the boundary between home and work (Hayden 2003). Many telecommuters, especially women, find themselves on call 24/7. For them, telecommuting means balancing household chores with job demands. Lastly, there are the exurban Valhallas. These exclusive communities are located in environmentally attractive areas. However, access to nature's bounty is restricted to high-income residents who can afford to purchase homes within the confines of high-security gated "communities."

Interest in exurbia continues, particularly in the popular media. Here, exurban residential development is often linked with the growth of edge city employment and retail centers. Some observers go so far as to claim that exurbia is now the trendsetting political landscape for America (Brooks 2004). Interestingly, that's the same claim made by Spectorsky in 1955.

SEE ALSO: Built Environment; City Planning/Urban Design; Multinucleated Metropolitan Region; New Urbanism; Suburbs; Urban Policy; Urban Space

REFERENCES AND SUGGESTED READINGS

Brooks, D. (2004) *On Paradise Drive.* Simon & Schuster, New York.

Crump, J. R. (2003) Finding a Place in the Country: Residential Preferences and Exurban Development in Sonoma County, California. *Environment and Behavior* 35: 187–202.

Davis, J. S., Nelson, A. C., & Dueker, K. J. (1994) The New 'Burbs and Their Implications for Planning Policy. *Journal of the American Planning Association* 60: 45–59.

Garreau, J. (1991) *Edge Cities: Life on the New Frontier.* Doubleday, New York.

Hayden, D. (2003) *Building Suburbia.* Pantheon Books, New York.

Marx, L. (1964) *The Machine in the Garden.* Oxford University Press, New York.

Nelson, A. C. (1992) Characterizing Exurbia. *Journal of Planning Literature* 6: 350–68.

Nelson, A. C. & Dueker, K. J. (1990) The Exurbanization of America and Its Planning Policy Implications. *Journal of Planning Education and Research* 9: 91–100.

Nelson, A. C. & Sanchez, T. W. (1999) Debunking the Exurban Myth: A Comparison of Suburban Households. *Housing Policy Debate* 10: 689–709.

Spectorsky, A. C. (1955) *The Exurbanites.* J. B. Lippincott, New York.